MYSTERIUM LIBERATIONIS

MYSTERIUM LIBERATIONIS

Fundamental Concepts of Liberation Theology

Edited by
IGNACIO ELLACURÍA, S.J.
and
JON SOBRINO, S.J.

ORBIS BOOKS
Maryknoll, New York 10545

CollinsDove
A Division of HarperCollins*Publishers*

English translation copyright © 1993 by Orbis Books
Published in the United States of America by Orbis Books, Maryknoll, NY 10545
Published in Australia by Collins Dove, A Division of HarperCollins*Publishers* (Australia) Pty Ltd, 22-24 Joseph Street, North Blackburn, Victoria 3130
The English edition has been abridged and adapted from the original Spanish edition, published as *Mysterium Liberationis: Conceptos Fundamentales de la Teología de la Liberación* 2 vols., © 1990 by Editorial Trotta, S.A., Ferraz 55, 28008 Madrid, Spain.

The present edition has been translated with the assistance of the Department of Books and Libraries of the Spanish Ministry of Culture.

The following essays have been omitted from this edition: Juan Luis Segundo, "Libertad y liberación"; Pedro Trigo, "Creación y mundo material"; Antônio Moser, "Sexualidad"; José María Castillo, "Sacerdocio, episcopado, papado"; Alberto Parra, "Ministerios laicales"; Diego Irarrazaval, "Religión popular"; Paulo Suess, "Inculturación"; Franz Damen, "Sectas"; Carlos Palacio, "Vida Religiosa"; R. Aguirre and F. J. Vitoria Cormenzana, "Justicia"; J. B. Libânio and F. Taborda, "Ideología"; Juan Hernández Pico, "Revolución, violencia, y paz."

The translation of "Utopia and Prophecy" by Ignacio Ellacuría was originally published in *Towards a Society That Serves Its People*, eds. John Hassett and Hugh Lacey (Washington, D.C.: Georgetown University Press, 1991). It is reprinted with permission of Georgetown University Press.

Library of Congress Cataloging-in-Publication Data

Mysterium liberationis. English. Selections.
    Mysterium liberationis : fundamental concepts of liberation
theology / edited by Ignacio Ellacuria and Jon Sobrino.
       p.   cm.
    "English edition abridged and adapted from the original Spanish."
    Includes bibliographical references and index.
    ISBN 0-88344-917-X
    1. Liberation theology. 2. Catholic Church—Latin America—
Doctrines. I. Ellacuria, Ignacio. II. Sobrino, Jon. III. Title.
BT83.57.M942513   1993
230'.046—dc   93-32064
                                      CIP

The National Library of Australia Cataloguing-in-Publication Data

[Mysterium liberationis. English. Selections]. Mysterium
liberationis : fundamental concepts of liberation theology.
    Bibliography. Includes index.
    ISBN 1 86371 313 1.
    1. Liberation theology. I. Ellacuria, Ignacio. II. Sobrino, Jon.
    III. Title: Mysterium liberationis. English. Selections.
230.046

Contents

Part II
Systematic Contents of the Theology of Liberation

Preface

This preface was to have been written by Ignacio Ellacuría and myself. But, as we know, Ignacio Ellacuría is no longer among us. On November 16, 1989, he was murdered, along with five of his fellow Jesuits—Juan Ramón Moreno, Amando López, Segundo Montes, Ignacio Martín-Baró, Joaquín López y López—their cook, Julia Elba, and her daughter Celina, in the residence of Archbishop Romero Center at Central American University José Simeón Cañas. It becomes my task, then, to write this introduction, in my name and his, in the name of the living and in the name of the Salvadoran martyrs, with Ignacio's martyr's blood still fresh. It will not be the usual kind of introduction, and the reader will understand if its tone is very personal.

First of all I should like to say that these martyrdoms, and all the many others in Latin America, make an introduction to this book very largely unnecessary. If we reflect why the Jesuits, and the two simple women who symbolize the entire Salvadoran and Latin American people, were killed, we shall also understand how they lived—what their faith, hope, and commitment were. And this is precisely what this book is about—life and death, sin and grace, God and the poor, Jesus and his body in history. In this book all of these realities are conceptualized and theologized, but without these realities this book could not have been written. After all, it is on the basis of these realities—central to our reflection here—that the theology of liberation presented in this book is done.

Life and death in Latin America will not replace theological reflection; but without the former, the latter cannot grow as Latin American liberation theology or indeed be correctly understood. Therefore readers will surely permit me to suggest and urge that they keep the Latin American martyrs, and the Paschal reality they express, very much in mind when reading or reflecting on the essays in this book. This Paschal reality—its dark side murder, and its light side martyrdom, the cross of death, and the resurrection of life—is the authentic *Sitz im Leben*—as well as the *Sitz im Tode*, let us add, although this is customarily ignored in other theologies—of liberation theology. It is the most radical hermeneutic locus of an understanding of these pages. And so I invite readers to read them as the gospels are read—as Easter accounts, at once challenge and good news.

With this as our basic perspective, let us now say a few brief words about the goal and content of this book, as well as about the difficulties through which it has passed in its development and about its ultimate meaning.

The goal of this book is to offer a systematized presentation of the core and nucleus of the theology of liberation. We, the authors, think that this theology continues to be necessary and beneficial for the liberation of the poor and for the Christian cultivation of the reality of Latin America. It might be thought that a systematization of this theology might mean its death, as sometimes occurs with systematization. But we do not think that this is the case with this book. Its every page is steeped in the original intuition that gave life to the theology of liberation. Systematization here is viewed as a kind of exponential "factoring." It "squares" or "cubes" a faith-reflection on reality by providing an opportunity and challenge for greater theoretical rigor, for serious dialogue among the theologians of Latin America and other climes, for a raising of consciousnesses with respect to this theology, both in its achievements and in its limitations, as well as its agenda for tomorrow. All of these are things Ignacio Ellacuría regarded as so important; it was in view of them that he began to conceive and dream of the present work.

In our selection of the contents we have opted to present a few basic theological concepts that express the essence of the Christian faith and of liberation theology. We could not have included all of the concepts encountered in the systematic treatises. There are lacunae, then, and the systematization we offer is, up to a point, fragmentary rather than exhaustive. Still, we think the book offers abundant material in the direction of a synthesis, which will always be provisional, of the theology of liberation.

We have arranged our content in two large blocks. The first block — historical and methodological aspects — sketches the historical development and the basic presuppositions of the task of this theology. The second block — systematic content — treats the basic themes of all theology from the perspective of liberation theology: the relationship between transcendence and concrete history, between the divine reality itself and creation, between the reality of the church, on the one hand, and anthropological and social reality on the other.

It has not been an easy matter, any more than with any work of joint authorship, to achieve a perfect correlation among the various articles. Readers will find a variety of styles and focuses indicating the freedom with which each author has worked. Nor has it been possible to avoid a certain amount of repetition — especially in an emphasis on the reality of the poor, the point of departure for the theology being done here. As an aid to further research on certain topics, as well as to a study of others that do not figure among the titles of our articles, an index and bibliography are provided at the end of the book.

Let us also say a word about the process by which this book has been put together, since that will afford something of an illustration of the concrete conditions under which liberation theology is produced. First of all, it has been anything but easy to coordinate, from El Salvador, a country at war, the work of so many collaborators — although by way of compensation we have had the dedication and love that they have all put into this work, even though they are pressured by so many other tasks. And when the book was almost finished, the murder of Ignacio Ellacuría and Juan Ramón Moreno cut off in midstream the articles they had been preparing. Ignacio Ellacuría had been assigned the articles entitled "Salvation History," "Church of the Poor," and "Conflict in the Church." Juan Ramón Moreno had been writing an article on "Justice." Neither of them had been able to finish with their pens and their words the essays they have now written in their blood. But lest there be further delay in the publication of this collective work, we have decided to include certain essays these two theologians had already written, since they fit into this work perfectly. And so we publish Ignacio Ellacuría's "Historicity of Salvation," "Utopia and Prophecy," "Church of the Poor," and "The Crucified People." And we publish Juan Ramón Moreno's "Evangelization in the Contemporary World."

The ultimate meaning of this book lies in its attempt to show forth, once more, through theology, the concrete reality of the Latin American peoples and the entire Third World—that widest of concrete realities—in order to demonstrate what manner of faith, hope, and love best respond to this reality, and in order to show what Christian theology best represents that faith, that hope, and that love as a way of responding and corresponding today to the God of Jesus Christ.

Far from being on the wane, we think the fundamental intuition of the theology of liberation is more relevant than ever before. Liberation theology has put its finger on the sore point of the reality of the Latin American continent. It is this sore point—which continues to fester and to be inflamed—that the theology of liberation seeks to cleanse. That is why liberation theology understands itself as "the theory of a concrete ecclesial praxis" (Ellacuría)— or an *intellectus amoris, misericordiae, justitiae*, as we have reformulated it.

But the reality of the Latin American continent is also shot through with hope, creativity, commitment, and martyrdom, and it is that reality, as well, that seeks to have the floor in the theology of liberation. It is from the suffering and creativity, the dedication and love, the martyrdom and hope of these crucified peoples, that liberation theology wishes to derive its life, so that it might give a voice to the voiceless, to combat lies and injustice, and to foster truth and community.

This theology is no passing fancy. Neither, unfortunately, is its correlative, oppression. On the contrary, oppression is on the rise. Thus the theology of liberation continues to be quite necessary. After all, Christian faith must respond today with credibility—and through its theology, with rationality—to the oldest and most current of problems: "How to tell the poor of this world that God loves them" (Gustavo Gutiérrez).

Therefore, too, this book could be very useful in celebrating—as God would have it celebrated—the important date of 1992. Just what is being celebrated on this date is a matter of contention. What seems to us to be indisputable, however, is that it is only from a point of departure in a commitment to the liberation of the Latin American peoples that this date can be celebrated in a Christian manner. From this outlook the past can be analyzed in terms of its element of terribly serious sin, as well as in its element of grace; but especially, this perspective will enable us to analyze what needs to be done in order that the future may be unambiguously one of grace, and not of sin.

By way of concluding this introduction, I should like to thank, in my own name, and posthumously in that of Ignacio Ellacuría as well, all of our brother and sister theologians who have collaborated on this book. We thank them all for their patience and understanding in the face of the vicissitudes through which the publication of this book has come, and we thank them all for the effort, devotion, and love that has made this book possible.

I should like especially to mention Javier Jiménez Limón, author of the article "Suffering, Death, Cross, and Martyrdom," who died suddenly on February 27, 1990. With his death the poor of Latin America lost a great defender and scholarship lost a great theologian.

March, 1990
On the tenth anniversary
of the martyrdom of Archbishop Romero

Jon Sobrino, S.J.
Ignacio Ellacuría, S.J. (d. Nov. 16, 1989)
Central American University José Simeón Cañas, San Salvador

— Translated by Robert R. Barr

Preface to the English Edition

Already more than three years have passed since the original publication of the Spanish edition of this work, and in this time various things have transpired which make it appropriate to add some brief words to the original preface. There is no doubt that many people continue to find the theology of liberation highly relevant, seeing on the horizon no other mode of doing theology that so effectively addresses the fundamental problems of our time: poverty, marginalization, injustice, destruction—in short, the concerns of the human family. But at the same time, and for a number of reasons, many people have accepted the opinion that the time for a theology of liberation has passed. It is this opinion that we would like to address in the form of a brief *apologia pro teologia liberationis*, which is an expression of something much more important, an *apologia pro pauperibus*.

Among the supposed reasons for doubting the continued relevance of the theology of liberation, three are commonly cited. Some say that this theology has become repetitive without adding anything special to the themes which occupy people today, such as ecology, women, indigenous peoples, and so forth. Others say that the theology of liberation has revealed its impotence before the spectacular rise of fundamentalist "sects" in Latin America, and that in fact it has indirectly contributed to their rise. Finally, there are those who say that after the recent collapse of organized socialism the theology of liberation has lost any economic or political horizon. In any case, all these forms of criticism add up to the same conclusion—that the theology of liberation has seen its day.

These objections are made in both good faith and bad, with sincere concern or with ill-concealed joy, and they may even reflect a partial truth. But none of them reflects the complete truth nor, above all, the most fundamental truth.

As far as the first objection goes, it is true that the theology of liberation must incorporate new themes and must confront new forms of oppression, but it is also true that the oppression occasioned by unjust poverty remains in force and indeed continues its steady advance. And it remains true, above all, that the most original and fruitful features of the theology of liberation, more than any concrete thematic content, remain its mode of understanding the business of theology as a theoretical reflection on praxis, or *intellectus amoris*, the identification of the world's poor as a *locus theologicus*, and the ultimate goal of this project, which is to "remove the crucified peoples from their cross." All of this remains supremely important and supremely relevant up to the present day, because, among other things, we see no other theology which seriously occupies itself with poverty and injustice, liberation and justice, hope and utopia. And if these things are of no concern to theology, then one may ask what it means to believe in God, at least in the God of Jesus, and how one may distinguish this supposed faith from a disguised, if not a sordid, egocentrism. And one can ask if a theology which ignores these themes is not, strictly speaking, an unreal theology. The charge holds in a quantitative sense, since such a theology fails to touch the reality of the majority of humanity, who live amidst conditions of frightful poverty and injustice. And it holds as well in a qualitative sense, since such a theology not only fails to do anything to transform reality, but it declines even to be affected by its most flagrant feature: the slow or violent death of the poor.

Regarding the second objection, it is true that certain fundamentalist sects are proliferating rapidly in Latin America, although this is not the case among the groups which have been most influenced by the theology of liberation — that is, the basic ecclesial communities. It would be a serious error to assign primary responsibility to the theology of liberation for this proliferation; indeed, it is necessary to recall that this theology tries to offer a *popular* ecclesial alternative to the sects. What happens is that this theology offers theoretical direction to a popular ecclesial movement that still requires institutional support if it is to become a reality (as happened in El Salvador during the time of Monseñor Romero, when it was the base communities and not the sects which proliferated). United with an effectively popular ecclesial leadership, the theology of liberation reveals its capacity to exert a widescale influence.

Finally, and this is what is most important to emphasize, historic socialism had no part in the origin of the theology of liberation, nor was it essential in its development, even though it proved helpful (as is evidently the case even in some encyclicals of John Paul II) in the critique of capitalism and in nourishing certain utopian horizons. The origin, impulse, and direction of the theology of liberation did not come from socialism, but from the experience of God in the poor of this world, an experience at once of grace and challenge. Thus, as long as this experience exists, there can and will be a place for the theology of liberation. By the same token, as long as conditions of oppression continue there will be and must a theology of liberation.

For us, there is no doubt that the theology of liberation remains a possibility and a necessity. In similar language, the language of the option for the poor, our point is echoed in the words of Dom Pedro Casaldáliga, expressed with his characteristic vigor: "Today the option for the poor is more timely than ever. There are two reasons: There are more of them, both in Latin America, and in all the Third World; and they are ever-poorer."

With our gaze fastened on these poor and oppressed of the world, in their ever-increasing numbers, we offer this volume to the English-speaking reader, with the request that you also keep before your eyes these poor of the world, the better to enhance your reading.

JON SOBRINO, S.J.
San Salvador
September 1993

— *Translated by Robert Ellsberg*

Abbreviations

EN   Exhortation *Evangelii nuntiandi* (Pope Paul VI), 1975.

GS   *Gaudium et spes* (Vatican II). Pastoral Constitution on the Church in the Modern World.

LC   *Libertatis conscientia* (Congregation for the Doctrine of the Faith). Instruction on Christian Freedom and Liberation, 1986.

LE   Encyclical *Laborem exercens* (Pope John Paul II), 1981.

LG   *Lumen Gentium* (Vatican II). Dogmatic Constitution on the Church.

LN   *Libertatis nuntius* (Congregation for the Doctrine of the Faith). Instruction on Certain Aspects of the Theology of Liberation, 1984.

Medellín   Second General Conference of the Latin American Bishops' Conference, 1968.

MM   Encyclical *Mater et magistra* (Pope John XXIII), 1963.

OA   Apostolic Letter *Octogesima adveniens* (Pope Paul VI), 1971.

Puebla   Third General Conference of the Latin American Bishops' Conference, 1979.

QA   Encyclical *Quadragesimo anno* (Pope Pius XI), 1931.

RN   Encyclical *Rerum novarum* (Pope Leo XIII), 1891.

PART I

HISTORY, METHODOLOGY, AND DISTINCTIVE FEATURES OF THE THEOLOGY OF LIBERATION

History of the Theology of Liberation

ROBERTO OLIVEROS

Twenty-five years ago the Second Vatican Council was getting under way. How quickly the time slips away! We seem still to feel the excitement of anticipation that throbbed in the heart of Pope John XXIII. But how many trails have been blazed and traversed in these few years!

At the same time, we are approaching the year 1992, in which shall be commemorated the encounter of Europe and America. In Latin America the huge challenge of the "new evangelization," Pope John Paul II's challenge in Bogota in 1986, is becoming more and more acute. The new evangelization is certainly making its way among us in a deeply meaningful fashion, as we see in the base-level ecclesial communities of Latin America, which are "now . . . one of the causes for joy and hope in the Church" (Puebla Final Document, no. 96).

But the practice of this "new evangelization in Latin America" means we must review our experiences in the light of faith, thereby allowing them to become deeper experiences and furnishing them with new impulse for the life of the Christian and the church. And the practice of the new evangelization of our world, a world rejuvenated in Vatican II, is accompanied and fostered, especially in Latin America, by the theology of liberation.

When we speak of theology in Latin America, we must speak of the theology of liberation. Here, for the first time in the history of our subcontinent, a theology is appearing that belongs to us—a theological reflection incarnate in the situation of the persons and peoples of America. Current Latin American reality, subjected to an in-depth reflection in the light of faith by the theology of liberation, has furnished theologians with a reorientation and has rejuvenated the task of Christianity and of the church in our lands.

What is the theology of liberation? What is its origin? How has it grown? What are its central contributions? Why does it stir such controversy? It is these and other similar questions that I shall attempt to elucidate and answer here. In order to facilitate the exposition, I shall concentrate on six points: the foundational experience of liberation theology; its method; its historical development, including the central features of its rereading of the great theological themes; criticisms and challenges; principal contributions; and the conclusions of the theology of liberation.

3

I. LIBERATION THEOLOGY: ITS FOUNDATIONAL EXPERIENCE

What is liberation theology's foundational experience? What are the facts attending its appearance among us?

A condition of its emergence was the Second Vatican Council and its call for, and implementation of, an openness to the world in which the church is to act as a sacrament of salvation. Vatican II pulled down many of the objective and subjective walls that removed us from and deformed reality.[1]

As we turn to the world of the Latin American popular masses and open our eyes to see those masses, we find ourselves face to face with the results of centuries of institutionalized injustice. Millions upon millions of persons are subjected to an inhuman, demeaning poverty. We run up against this unjust poverty with every step we take, and the collision deeply shakes the hearts of Christians of good will. This experience has enabled us to bridge the gap of the ages and feel in our own skins the plight of Moses confronted with the situation of his Israelite brothers and sisters in Egypt: this situation of slavery could not be the will of God! Moses' faith in the God of Israel enabled him to understand his mission.

Just so, the brutal fact of the slavery and poverty of the Latin American masses has been decisive in our reflection upon reality in the light of the God of Jesus Christ. Now we grasp our mission, and we are driven. In order to proclaim and live the Good News of the Reign of God, we must acquire a new consciousness of the being and task of the church.

What seminal experience and intuition has given rise to the theology of liberation? Purely and simply, the daily experience of the unjust poverty in which millions of our fellow Latin Americans are obliged to live. In and from this experience emerges the shattering word of the God of Moses and of Jesus: this situation is not the will of that God.

In this basic foundational experience, we may discern three important elements: the poor, the guise of Christian charity today, and conversion.

1. The Poor and Their Poverty

The decade of the 1970s was the scene of an ongoing debate over the identity of the poor in the gospels. What is evangelical poverty?[2] Medellín had pointed a prophetic finger at the injustice in which entire peoples live:

> The Latin American episcopate cannot remain indifferent to the tremendous social injustices that exist in Latin America. These injustices keep the majority of our peoples in woeful poverty, which in most cases goes so far as to be inhuman misery.
>
> A muted cry wells up from millions of our people, begging their pastors to provide them with a liberation that they cannot get from anywhere.[3]

That observation has opened the hearts of many to the cause of the poor. It has also fostered the enrichment of the faith from the perspective of the oppressed of the earth. But it has stirred reactions of mistrust as well, and even rejection. Indeed, the climate of confusion and obscurity that has been generated once again threatens to conceal the facts of the matter.

Toward the end of the 1970s it was still possible to hear that the poor were in their situation because they were indolent and vice-ridden. Or that persons who were materially rich were very poor in spiritual values. Utterances like these, in their generalization of evil and their failure to distinguish cause and effect, had the tendency, at the least, to encourage the observer's acquiescence in the face of tremendous social injustices.

And yet the experience of the centuries-old suffering of peasants, natives, and blacks, which in the past has seemed mute has taken new forms in the Latin American slums and rural districts. Its cry has become more clear and shrill by the day (Puebla Final Document, no. 89) and continues to provide an impulse to the reflection of liberation theology. The Third General Conference of the Latin American Episcopate, held at Puebla, in Mexico, assiduously drew up a description of who the poor are and forthrightly declared that the occasion of their situation is not casual, but causal:

> So we brand the situation of inhuman poverty in which millions of Latin Americans live as the most devastating and humiliating kind of scourge. And this situation finds expression in such things as a high rate of infant mortality, lack of adequate housing, health problems, starvation wages, unemployment and underemployment, malnutrition, job uncertainty, compulsory mass migrations, etc.
>
> Analyzing this situation more deeply, we discover that this poverty is not a passing phase. Instead it is the product of economic, social, and political situations and structures, although there are also other causes for the state of misery. (Puebla Final Document, nos. 29-30)

This situation, that of the great masses of our peoples, is due in large part to the social system under which we suffer (cf. Puebla Final Document, nos. 92, 311-13), not the will of God. This foundational experience, which is now in the process of redirecting and constructing a society of brothers and sisters, was adopted in the Puebla Conference and expressed with prophetic clarity:

> Viewing it in the light of faith, we see the growing gap between rich and poor as a scandal and a contradiction to Christian existence. The luxury of a few becomes an insult to the wretched poverty of the vast masses. This is contrary to the plan of the Creator and to the honor that is due him. In this anxiety and sorrow the Church sees a situation of social sinfulness, all the more serious because it exists in countries that call themselves Catholic. (Puebla Final Document, no. 28)[4]

A few lines further on the bishops assert that in the faces of children, the poor, the natives, marginalized *campesinos*, the elderly, and so on, we must recognize the suffering traits of Christ (Puebla Final Document, nos. 31-39).

The concrete, shocking experience of the suffering of the poor opens us to the experience of the One who is present in them: the Lord Jesus (Matt. 25:31-46).

To speak of God is to "do theology." In the foundational experience of the theology of liberation, it has been rediscovered that to speak of the poor is to speak of Christ, "Yahweh's poor one." But to speak today of the poor is to speak of the exploited third-world human being. To speak of the poor is to speak of the Latin American masses. Within Christ's solidarity with the impoverished of the earth is concealed the mystery of the human being. Christ is encountered and revealed in the least ones—whom the eyes of the worldly overlook and forget (Matt. 11:25-27).

The central theme of our lives, and of all spirituality—which is how to meet God, where it is that God is loved and known—leads straight to the heart of the gospel: loving God and neighbor. But this topic acquires a radical reality when we look into the face of someone poor. What does it mean to love God and neighbor in Latin America today?

2. Loving God and Neighbor in Latin America Today

It is easy to understand and explain why this second central element in the founding experience of the theology of liberation has had such an impact on Latin American Christian awareness.

> Everyone who loves is begotten of God
> and has knowledge of God.
> The man without love has known nothing of God,
> for God is love. (1 John 4:7-8)

Now, if we turn our back on the great impoverished majorities, how are we going to love them? At most they will receive certain charitable donations in the form of paternalism.

Opening our eyes and heart to the poor has permitted us to discover their situation realistically and to experience being evangelized by them. The parable of the rich man and Lazarus has become clear. The wealthy man had closed himself up in his things and had forgotten his brother (Luke 16:19-31, Gen. 4:9). He never swerved from his own beaten path, never trod the path of the needy, and did not know God. The same central message appears in the parable of the Samaritan, which begins with the question of the central commandment (Luke 10:25-37). Our neighbor is not primarily our near relatives, our circle of friends: "Our neighbor is not the one whom I find in my path, but rather the one in whose path I place myself—the one whom I approach and actively seek."[5]

The Lord Jesus and the Pharisees knew the Decalogue and the prescriptions of the Torah. They *knew* that the first and greatest commandment is love for God and neighbor. In fact, they both preached it, proclaiming it as the very cornerstone of their teaching. Why, then, this awful confrontation between such "pious" persons, if indeed both parties agreed on the essentials of the message?

The question comes down to the experience of and the content assigned to "neighbor" and consequently "brotherly love." The Pharisees claimed to love God and neighbor — and they crucified Jesus.

In Latin America today scripture is reread in liberation theology from the viewpoint of the poor — from the viewpoint of the exploited class with which Christ joined in solidarity. Hence the question: What demands does love for our neighbor involve today? This is not simply one of the topics addressed in the theology of liberation; it is its heart and soul. Here is the lifeblood of the experience, original intuition, and very existence of the Christian groups engaged in the praxis of liberation. Loving God and neighbor means turning from the beaten path, entering the pathways of the oppressed, those struck down by injustice, and making a commitment to their cause.

To be sure, behavior of this kind frequently involves a risk to one's very life — as Jesus, the Good Shepherd, said it would.[6] But it is *becoming* sisters and brothers among the poor, and not just *knowing* that we are sisters and brothers and thus being content with words, that leads us to do our building upon a rock (Matt. 7:21-27). A commitment to the poor enables us to avoid reducing love for our neighbor to love for "souls," along with every other other kind of distorting spiritualization. The same must be said of reducing love for neighbor to mean only love for our own family or the closed group around us. Love for our neighbor who is poor opens us to universality, to the recognition that we are all children of the same Father.

The universality of love for neighbor acquires the weight of truth when it adopts as its primary concern a love for those brothers and sisters of ours whom the world scorns and vilifies: the indigenous peoples, the illiterate, the marginalized, blacks, and others. "If you love those who love you, what merit is there in that? Do not tax collectors do as much?" (Matt. 5:46). The sense and meaning of this element of the foundational experience of the theology of liberation was also adopted and expressed by the regional synod of Puebla, which was attentive to the voice of the Spirit, who cries out from among a people of the poor:

> The love of God, which is the root of our dignity, necessarily becomes loving communion with other human beings and fraternal participation. For us today it must become first and foremost a labor of justice on behalf of the oppressed (Luke 4:18), an effort of liberation for those who are most in need of it. The fact is that "one who has no love for the brother he has seen cannot love the God he has not seen" (1 John 4:20). . . . Confronted with the realities that are part of our lives today, we must learn from the Gospel that in Latin America we cannot truly love our fellow human beings, and hence God, unless we commit ourselves on the personal level, and in many cases on the structural level as well, to serving and promoting the most dispossessed and downtrodden human groups and social classes, with all the consequences that will entail on the plane of temporal realities. (Puebla Final Document, no. 327)

Christ lived love efficaciously, both as prophet and as the crucified One. To love as Christ loved still implies taking up his cross and following him. The

Lord did not conceal the fact that following him entails, sadly, that parents and children break off contact with one another, that friends betray friends, and that disciples deliver up their teachers. Today's mission to create a society of sisters and brothers—to love in history—has a political dimension; this mission must be performed in a charity that, like Jesus' charity, subverts the social disorder and institutionalized injustice.

Evangelical love leads to oneness:

> That all may be one
> as you, Father, are in me, and I in you. (John 17:21)

But the unity of human beings is achieved only by transcending the contradictions in which we find ourselves concretely situated. One must overcome the darkness that cancels the iight:

> To his own he came,
> yet his own did not accept him. (John 1:11)

Today the loving blood of God is spilled once more—the blood shed by the oppressed in the struggle they wage with their oppressors that they may cease to be oppressors, blood shed not in hatred, but with a sense of mission. The hot blood of Christ, who is love, steeps the theology of liberation. The human warmth of love, including its affective traits, is revived when we live among the poor and for their cause.

Jesus' "new style" of loving God and neighbor took the mentality of his time by surprise. And we are still surprised today by his style of loving and constructing unity from amid the poor, just as we are surprised at the consequences of that style. What a contradiction! To love, to make an effort to build a society of brothers and sisters, brings persecution and death.

> No slave is greater than his master.
> They will harry you
> as they harried me. (John 15:20)

But this struggle and suffering is accompanied by the certainty of triumph:

> Take courage!
> I have overcome the world. (John 16:33)

3. The Poor and Christian Conversion

In our history, communion with our neighbor passes necessarily by way of the option for the poor. Our love of neighbor becomes reality when we love the impoverished of the earth. The word *conversion,* etymologically, denotes a "turning to." Christian conversion is a turning to the poor, a harmonizing of our heart with theirs, a weeping with their suffering, a rejoicing in their joys.

The thrust of the Spirit does not end with the discovery of the battered victim lying in the ditch. It drives us, to make a commitment to that victim, to enter actively upon his or her pathway, to make a commitment to his or her liberation. This element of the foundational experience has led us to an in-depth understanding of *metanoia*, the Christian conversion to which we are all called.

To be converted to Christ means becoming a brother or sister of the poor. When the wealthy young person who had been so well-trained and was so observant of the commandments asked Jesus what he had to do to win eternal life, he received a clear and loving response from the Teacher, for he had won his affection with his sincerity: "Go and sell what you have and give to the poor. . . . After that, come and follow me" (Mark 10:21). But the youth was caught by surprise. This answer had not been taught him by his teachers. They had taught him, and he had complied with, the moral norms of not stealing, respecting his neighbor's wife, not becoming intoxicated, and so forth. But to become poor with the poor in order to live a communion of brothers and sisters had never entered his head. The same had happened with Nicodemus.

The Lord announced: "This is the time of fulfillment. The reign of God is at hand! Reform your lives and believe in the gospel!" (Mark 1:15). This implied a very concrete commitment: Sell your goods, become a brother or sister to the poor, and you shall have treasure in the Reign of Heaven. In its experience of walking with the impoverished of our urban slums or rural zones, liberation theology has been enlightened as to the core of Christian conversion and has accepted it. We have understood, in all its breadth, what is meant by evangelical poverty.

We are all called to make the option for the poor and to live evangelical poverty. The division between rich and poor is sinful; it is not according to the will of God. It must be denounced and defeated. Jesus and his disciples offered a model for life; they proclaimed it as a beatitude: "This model of the poor life is one that the Gospel requires of all those who believe in Christ; so we can call it 'evangelical poverty' (Matt. 6:19-34)" (Puebla Final Document, no. 1148). Religious are called to live this poverty radically. But it is the legacy of the whole people of God as well. Without the sharing of goods, a society of sisters and brothers is caught in a quagmire of empty desires. Those who share their goods enter the Reign of Heaven (Matt. 25:31-46). Evangelical poverty is not asceticism. Evangelical poverty, which involves love for the neighbor that we see, is the rock on which a communion of sisters and brothers is built. It is no vain utopia. It is not something beyond the realm of possibility. "The Church rejoices to see many of its children, particularly the more modest members of the middle class, living this Christian poverty in concrete terms" (Puebla Final Document, no. 1151).

This sharing of goods frees the heart to live a mission:

> . . . to proclaim liberty to captives,
> Recovery of sight to the blind
>   and release to prisoners,
> To announce a year of favor from the Lord. (Luke 4:18-19)

To be converted is to be delivered from any bonds that might prevent us from building and living in communion from the midst of the least ones.

When the apostles recounted to Jesus how the simple folk were receiving the message of the Reign—the message that we are all brothers and sisters, children of the same Father—his heart filled with joy, and he blessed his Father for having revealed this and for its being received by the simple and the lowly (Matt. 11:25-27). Our bishops, too, frequently share an understanding of the call and invitation to conversion and communion in the option for the poor and their liberation:

> With renewed hope in the vivifying power of the Spirit, we are going to take up once again the position of the Second General Conference of the Latin American episcopate in Medellín, which adopted a clear and prophetic option expressing preference for, and solidarity with, the poor. We do this despite the distortions and interpretations of some, who vitiate the spirit of Medellín, and despite the disregard and even hostility of others. We affirm the need for conversion on the part of the whole Church to a preferential option for the poor, an option aimed at their integral liberation. (Puebla Final Document, no. 1134)[7]

This renewed hope in the power of the Spirit does not discount a worsening situation of injustice: "The vast majority of our fellow humans continue to live in a situation of poverty and even wretchedness that has grown more acute" (Puebla Final Document, no. 1135). This only provides a greater impulse for a prophetic solidarity with our impoverished brothers and sisters—necessarily entailing an ongoing conversion to the Servant of Yahweh:

> Service to [the poor] really calls for constant conversion and purification among all Christians. That must be done if we are to achieve fuller identification each day with the poor Christ and our own poor. (Puebla Final Document, no. 1140)

Thus, evangelical conversion is not a matter of empty sentimentality. Neither is it the simple observance of the Ten Commandments. Rather, it consists in actually becoming brother or sister to the poor, and from this starting point living a life of universal communion. This experience, which is that of so many Christians committed to the poor and to their liberation, constitutes the third element in the basic foundational experience from which Latin American theological reflection springs.

II. LIBERATION PRAXIS AND THEOLOGICAL METHOD

At Vatican II itself, in the introduction to *Gaudium et Spes*, we can catch a glimpse of a theology in its beginnings—a theology that would subject the living word of the reality of our peoples to a critical reflection in the light of faith. It was a rich intuition, and it came just before close of the Council. That intuition was to grow deeper and find its methodological expression in Latin American theology.

Before Vatican II theological learning seemed reserved for those preparing for the ministerial priesthood, together with only a few other persons. Theological content and method polarized in and reduced almost exclusively to a seminary theology, had powerfully influenced our manner of regarding and understanding our faith.

1. Rational Knowledge and Academic Theological Method

St. Anselm's "faith seeking understanding" found an artisan of great genius in Thomas Aquinas. The scientific tools of Thomas's time were philosophical. Here was his greatness and his limitation. He was a revolutionary theologian in his time.

Bernard Lonergan, in his study of theological method, presents us with an analysis of how, with the conquest of knowledge by way of the contribution of the natural and human sciences, philosophy both lost and gained in its position as theology's route to understanding. It lost its monopoly on reason, along with its right to interfere in the domain of the sciences. It gained in being duly situated as an epistemology (theory of knowledge) and ontology (theory of being).[8]

But the theology that, after Trent, came under the slow but inexorable influence of the ecclesiastical magisterium was gradually reduced to an auxiliary discipline of that magisterium. Its function became simply to set forth and explain defined truths and to denounce and dismantle false teachings.[9] The reduction of theology as rational knowledge to a purely scholarly theology constituted a serious impoverishment.

We are not suggesting that it is of no value for the theological enterprise to make an academic effort to delve more deeply into the meaning of our faith. This is necessary and good. But what of the perspective and context of this reflection? To claim that theological reflection ought to be practiced on some "neutral ground" is tantamount to placing it in the service of the great economic and political powers of the laissez-faire capitalistic system. Theological reflection is a matter of objectivity and intentionality. It must be at the service of the liberative activity of the poor in their efforts to construct a society of sisters and brothers.

2. Optatam Totius and Theological Method at Vatican II

The reduction of theology and its method to the presentation of defined truths and the refutation of errors, like the reduction of the theological ministry to its academic context, were transcended and enriched by Vatican II.

In underscoring the fact that the church is the people of God in history and that we are all called to holiness by the Spirit that we have received in baptism and confirmation, the Council enabled us to recover the sense of a people who are the vehicles of the gospel—people who can and should communicate the salvific message that they have received—an evangelizing people, who have as one of their functions the doing of theology.

"The study of sacred scripture must be as the soul of all theology" (*Optatam Totius*, no. 16). In this short sentence the Council epitomizes its recovery of the Bible for the theological undertaking. The Bible, as the norm that is not subordinated to any other norm, is to be the permanent criterion of the pilgrimage of the church. The theological enterprise is enriched. No longer is it reduced to the repetition of truths. Now it investigates and illuminates the life of the church by allowing the light of sacred scripture to shine upon it. This task is further extended under the light of the Fathers of the Church of East and West.

The study of dogmas is thus enriched, contextualized, and balanced. The method furnished by Vatican II to the theological undertaking recovers the sense of history—the sense of the process of a people whose vocation is to be a sacrament of salvation, and who have as their instrument and special light, holy scripture.

But what is the Christian outlook when it comes to doing theology? What are the basic Christian commitments? Vatican II did not formally render these matters explicit. Rather, it stood at the door, beckoning (*Gaudium et Spes*, no. 4).

3. Theology as Critical Reflection on the Praxis of Liberation

The value of the human, of history, of our cultures, of our material world, was recovered by the Council in its statement that "by His incarnation the Son of God has united Himself in some fashion with every man" (*Gaudium et Spes*, no. 22). The Council presently reemphasizes the same doctrine: "Christ died for all men, and . . . the ultimate vocation of man is in fact one, and divine." Gone is the Manichaeism that regarded the material and the spiritual, or from another perspective, the natural and supernatural, as two distinct realities, sometimes even mutually opposed, in which the temporal and the natural have no salvific weight and therefore no Christian value.

In restoring to theology the fact of the incarnation of the Word and its consequences for all that is human, Rahner's declaration, "christology is the end and the beginning of anthropology" expresses the entire scope of that incarnation.[10] There is no material distinction between profane and sacred history. There is only one history and vocation: the divine.

But in our Latin American reality the scandalous breach between rich and poor has driven us to discover the suffering face of Christ in the poor and thus correctly to situate our theological perspective. Theology does not have the first word. Theology is the second word. The first word belongs to the life of the people, whose faith operates through charity. Among these people, Christ is revealed in a special way in the poor. Thus Pope John Paul II, in his encounter with the marginalized poor of Guadalajara, cried: "The pope loves you because you are God's favorites" (Puebla Final Document, no. 1143).[11] Theological reflection must be attentive to the situation of the poor, take up their yearnings and aspirations as its own, plumb the depths of these in the light of faith and then hand them back to the people. This process reflects the reason we experience the theological undertaking as the second word. The function and service of theology as critical reflection on the human and ecclesial event recapitulates the meaning and contribution of the Latin American theological method.[12] This theological reflection, as second word, is carried on from a point of departure in the poor and with a view to their liberation.

St. Anselm's "faith seeking understanding" is comprehensible only in the light of Christ's own life journey: he was born, he lived, and he died for the liberation of the poor and the subsequent building of the Reign of brothers and sisters.

> Everyone who loves is begotten of God
> and has knowledge of God.
> The man without love has known nothing of God. (1 John 4:7-8)

Pascal says the same thing in different words: "The heart has its reasons that reason knows not of." An atheist can hold a dissertation on Christ with a great deal of scientific social knowledge, but he or she will not be a Christian and biblical theologian. Theologians are believers. Hence their reflection arises and takes form from compassion for the crucified poor and a passion for the Good News of Jesus Christ.

The full revelation of God in history occurred in Jesus Christ. It was manifested in the poor. That context became the privileged locus for the knowledge and experience of the God of Jesus. Thus the privileged theological locus is constituted by the poor and the cause of their liberation. The question of the basic perspective and commitment required for the doing of theology receives in the theology of liberation and its method this clear response: the poor and their cause. The climate, the context, and the perspective for theologizing after the fashion of Christ are the poor. In their life the Spirit comes to the highest expression; the poor are the first word, inviting us to fidelity. The theological wealth and openness of the Council have found new impulse in their application in Latin America. In conformity with the dynamics of the Council, theological method in liberation theology was radically enriched with:
- The poor as the *locus theologicus* par excellence of the manifestation of God.
- The perspective of the poor and of their liberation as the viewpoint from which events are read and history reread.
- The service of theology as second word—as critical reflection on human and ecclesial activity.

With this wealth—with these new eyes—biblical knowledge, tradition, dogma and magisterium, service and ministry, and theological systematizations past and present are scrutinized and revamped. The contributions and need of the exegete, and of academic theological work, are evaluated, enriched, and correctly situated. No longer is theology confined to the universities, to books. Academic theology is necessary, but the people are also theologians. They too express the voice of God. The people "do theology" in their hymns, their prayers, the reflections expressed in their own language.

The conciliar theological method and its hermeneutic key are enriched and resituated when the poor and their cause are established as privileged theological locus and all of the various basic theological themes taken up from their perspective. Their rereading of the Bible is particularly important; "the poor teach us how to reread sacred scripture."[13] In a commitment to the poor, and in the dynamism of biblical history, liberation theology takes advantage of the material and the language of the human sciences, with special attention to the social. These sciences offer valuable approaches to and explanations of today's social phenomena.

The validity of this effort in church life, and the need for the same, are identified by the Puebla synod:

> We fully recognize the efforts undertaken by many Latin American Christians to explore the particularly conflict-ridden situations of our peoples in terms of the faith and to shed the light of God's Word on them. We encourage all Christians to continue to provide this evangelizing service and to consider the criteria for reflection and investigation. (Puebla Final Document, no. 470)[14]

The Latin American theological method, rooted in the experiences of so many church communities who live their faith as liberation praxis, situates the theologian within the historical and ecclesial reality of today; it places theology at its service as second word. The theology of liberation did not spring into being full-fledged. It has had to grow and consolidate, as does any process.

III. GESTATION, GENESIS, GROWTH, AND CONSOLIDATION OF A REFLECTION

In the following material we shall discuss the important periods of the process of formation of the theology of liberation. Four such periods stand out very clearly: gestation, genesis, growth, and consolidation.

1. Gestation (1962–68): Historical Milestone of the Regional Synod of Medellín

The open veins of Latin America were the matrix of the development of the theory of dependency, which focused on showing the deep causes of the impoverishment of our popular masses. According to this theory, that unjust situation could be overcome only by way of a breach with the prevailing capitalist system. These studies made a profound impression in intellectual and university circles. Our situation of exploitation was not casual, but causal.[15]

John XXIII inaugurated the Second Vatican Council in 1962 in order to bring the church and its mission "up to date." During the Council the Latin American episcopates were nicknamed the "church of silence"—so spare was their active participation in the Council. The problems of the European groups dominated the Council. But the Council opened doors and windows for regional and local churches to ask themselves how to evangelize from a point of departure in their own situations.

Up until the time of Vatican II, theologians in Latin America had made very few contributions to the scientific thinking of the universal church. The strength and wealth of the missionary impulse among our peoples stood in stark contrast with our scanty theological production. However, the opportunity that the Council offered Latin American bishops, along with a few theologians, to meet together in an ecclesial climate of openness, quest, and theological creativity enabled some of them to meet and to begin to do new theological reflection in the light of faith, and from the midst of the originality of our situation and culture.[16]

Paul VI gladly approved the proposal of Cardinal Larrain, spokesperson for the Latin American episcopate, that a Second General Conference of the Latin American Episcopate convene in 1968 at Medellín, Colombia. The years 1966–68 were years of a veritable explosion of meetings, declarations, and documents at both the national and the regional levels. They were produced at the hands of various Christian groups at various strata of the people of God. At the root of this phenomenon was the fact that once eyes and windows were opened to the surrounding reality, that reality penetrated the church with all its vitality.

The series of problems that surfaced in these documents shows the influence of Christians already committed to social changes. The fact of the exploitation of the popular masses is inescapable in the outlying urban slums, as among the *campesinos* engulfed in misery and destitution. These experiences and social studies on the reasons for this situation of dependence came to be more and more widely known; they shook the Christian conscience of many a good shepherd. A new church awareness began to grow, recognizing a *new way of living the faith* on the part of those who were committed to the poor and their liberation.[17]

The regional synod of Medellín is a milestone in the recent history of the Latin American church. It snaps the century in two like a dry twig. Instead of a church dependent on Europe for its theological reflection and pastoral praxis, the Latin American church began to develop its own themes.

The variety of matters treated at Medellín were not allowed to obfuscate these realities and central themes. The various meetings that had been held in preparation for the Conference allowed our peoples to make their voices heard and bring their situation to expression.[18] Thus, the central themes at Medellín were the poor and justice; love for our brothers and sisters, and peace in a situation of institutionalized violence; and the oneness of history and the political dimension of faith.

The sensitivity of our shepherds brought the painful reality of the impoverished masses to the awareness of the bishops assembled at Medellín, and they passed the following judgment on this situation.

Many studies have been done on the situation of the person of Latin America. All of them describe the destitution that marginalizes great human groups. This misery, as a collective fact, is an injustice that cries to heaven.[19]

But, as shepherds, they lucidly observed that progress could not consist simply in knowing and denouncing that injustice. The most important thing would be to work to apply a remedy: "The poverty of countless people calls for justice, solidarity, witness, commitment, and extra effort to carry out fully the salvific mission entrusted to [the church] by Christ."[20]

The theme of love for our oppressed sisters and brothers, which means struggling for justice and peace, is a key notion in the theology of Medellín. How is Christian love to be lived in this situation? Which tasks should have priority? How are we to be builders of peace?

If "development is the new name for peace," then the underdevelopment of Latin America (with distinctive traits in each country) is an unjust situation promoting tensions that conspire against peace.[21]

Further on the bishops indicated that where there were social inequalities, there was a rejection of the peace of the Lord, and consequently of that Lord himself. In the face of such inequalities they issued a call for comprehensive, daring transformations:

It is clear that in many parts of Latin America we find a situation of injustice that can be called institutionalized violence. . . . This situation, which violates fundamental rights, calls for "bold innovations that will work profound changes" (*Populorum Progressio*, no. 32).[22]

These reflections on the part of the bishops could seem incursions into forbidden territory: the world of the social, of the political. Their approach to the subjects of the oneness of history and the theology of the Incarnation underlying that doctrine was based on Vatican II's rich integration of doctrine with pastoral practice. Human progress is growth in Christ. The pastoral task is that of "passing from less human to more human forms of life" (*Populorum Progressio*). Human growth is itself divinization. Our divinization occurs in growth, in human progress. This raises the challenge of the relation between the Reign of God and human emancipation.[23]

Latin American reality, the challenges to pastoral theology arising out of that reality, and the manner of approaching these challenges in reflection upon faith, were delineated in the postconciliar years and given shape at the prophetic regional synod of Medellín.

2. Genesis (1969–71): "Theology of Liberation"

The institutions, draft proposals, articles, symposia, Medellín orientations, investigations, and subsequent in-depth studies finally came to crystallization in Gustavo Gutiérrez's *A Theology of Liberation*.[24] The theological effort of the 1970s found form and direction in this book. It clearly and penetratingly expressed the central theme of the theological challenge in Latin America. "To speak about a theology of liberation is to seek an answer to the following question: what relation is there between salvation and the historical process of human liberation?"[25]

Gutiérrez approaches his subject with the theological method we have described above, which is delineated and developed in this study. He opens perspectives for a rethinking and resituation of the grand themes of theology.

Gutiérrez's book is a landmark, a quantum leap in Latin American theology. It draws the line between the before and the after. To call it a landmark, however, is not to say that Gutiérrez has either finished the work to be done or worked without roots in the past. It is a matter of a process. But his book sketched out the broad strokes for the development of a theology of liberation. The framework of the house is not the entire edifice; yet it is *this* house that will be constructed on the basis of that framework. In Gutiérrez's study, Latin American theological thought at last achieved a life of its own.

It is important to note that neither theologians nor pastors have remained indifferent to the theology of liberation as expressed by Gustavo Gutiérrez, or to the commitments that are consistent with this theology. Dozens of important books have now appeared along the same lines, while dozens of others have criticized the new reflection. What Latin American theological writing has ever stimulated so much theology? This is what we mean by calling Gutiérrez's book a landmark in Latin American ecclesial thought. The work is essential for understanding and judging what is meant by *liberation theology* and thus for differentiating it from other theological reflection.

In addition to what has already been said, certain other elements have proved influential for the development of later theology.

a) **Theological method.** The classic concerns of theology have been studied and resituated. They are now enriched with the additional function of theology as critic of human and ecclesial activity. Advantage has been taken of the advances and language of the social sciences.

b) **Development of the basic concepts of the theology of liberation.** Concepts like the poor and poverty, liberation, utopia, and salvation are expounded and explained in such a way, on their various levels and from various viewpoints, as to avoid confusion and encourage an improved practice.

c) **Reorientation of the great themes of Christian existence from the praxis of liberation.** The recovery of the Lord's special manifestation in the poor, and the theological reflection consequent on this recovery, have regained a lost wealth and provided a correct view of the encounter with and discipleship of Christ. Likewise analyzed are faith and its political dimension (the responsibility of faith in a situation of injustice and institutionalized violence), the church community and its mission to build a society of equals, and the experience, in this task, of eschatology.

d) **Spirituality and spiritual theology.** In presenting the theological operation in a way that links it vitally and organically to human and ecclesial life, emphasis is laid on the fact that all authentic theology is spiritual theology. The latter is not a topic or question on a list of many subjects. The reflection of faith must be, and be translated into, Christian wisdom.

e) **Temporality of the theology of liberation.** It is no small merit of Gustavo Gutiérrez to have insisted that this theological reflection, like any other, has historical significance only for such time as those problems, needs, and characteristics that have occasioned its appearance prevail in society and the church. Liberation theology is only one theology in salvation history.

The moment of genesis signified by the name "theology of liberation" has decisively nourished and energized the theological enterprise in Latin America. It has taken up and relaunched the spirit and dynamics of the Council and of Medellín.

3. Growth (1972–79): Fears and Hopes – the Puebla Synod

The prophetic ferment at work at the Council and at Medellín was a saving leaven for many Latin American Christians. These persons began to bend their efforts to implement the "radical, daring changes" to which the bishops had invited them. Precious apostolic experiences opened up. Paths and routes were traveled that had been covered over with the dusts of time.

This prophetic fervor promptly collided with the reaction of the dominant system. Christians and non-Christians engaged in liberation suffered heavy blows. Pinochet's coup in Chile provided the guidelines, and "National Security" regimes spread across the whole subcontinent. These dictatorial, corrupt governments were propped up by "petrodollars," which had to be circulated in order to achieve the transnationalization of the economy and commerce. What is more, powerful sectors of the ecclesiastical hierarchies turned away from the Council and Medellín. At the same time, under the pretext of applying the brakes to the advance of "international Communism," many priests and religious, as well as some bishops, were not only branded as suspect by reason of their commitment to the poor, but were viciously attacked or removed from their local churches or congregations.[26]

The liberation of the oppressed added heavy burdens to an already intolerable load (cf. Exod. 5:6-23). Nevertheless, despite all the difficulties and persecutions, the new seed of the church in the spirit of Vatican II and Medellín, was beginning to peep through a fertile soil, as indicated clearly by the growth of the base ecclesial communities between 1968 and 1979. The reflection of faith accompanying this social and ecclesial process also grew and was purified in its trials.

We shall look at this growth process under three aspects: the significant moments of this pre-Puebla stage, the theological aspects of Christian progress being made, and the historic landmark of the bishops' conference at Puebla.

1. Significant Events of 1972–79

Five events may be considered the most important to have occurred during the period under consideration. They catalyzed the in-depth assimilation of key elements already present in outline in *A Theology of Liberation*, especially with respect to certain themes emerging from the praxis of liberation itself. These same events also provided a point of departure or incentive for an in-depth approach to a number of other questions.

1. *The El Escorial meeting* (July 8–15, 1972) featured an exchange between Latin American theologians and some of their European counterparts, especially Spaniards, concerning the direction and method of the respective theo-

logical thought of the two contingents. It resulted in a valuable mutual enrichment.[27]

2. *The Mexico City meeting* (August 11–15, 1975) focused on theological method. There had been no attempt to present the method of liberation theology exclusively, but the latter was acknowledged as the richest when it came to assimilating the inspiration of Vatican II, as well as the method most appropriate to the situation and needs of our Latin American church.[28]

3. *The Detroit meeting* (August 18–24, 1975) is of singular importance because of the way in which it was prepared and conducted. Various base groups in the United States spent a year preparing their contributions to the gathering, and the meeting was a key factor in these groups' commitment to their Christian brothers and sisters struggling for liberation. It likewise provided a forum for Latin American and certain North American theologians to become acquainted. Finally, it was a step toward coming to know and being able to collaborate with fellow-Christians of other denominations.[29]

4. *The Dar-es-Salaam meeting* (August 5–12, 1976) was an opportunity for the best theologians of Asia, Africa, and Latin America to meet and share their thinking. Sprung from peoples marked by colonialism and oppression, these theologians founded the Ecumenical Association of Third World Theologians (EATWOT), whose meetings and fertile toil have taken us another step along the path of church awareness and praxis in the struggle for the integral liberation of our peoples.[30]

5. Convocation and Preparation for *the Puebla Conference* (1977–78). Toward the end of 1976, preparation began for another general meeting of the Latin American episcopate. Its declared purpose was to study and evaluate the ecclesial process begun at Medellín. The summoning of this conference stimulated intense theological work. Indeed, it was an effective stimulus for the purification, broadening, and deepening of the service of the theology of liberation. The studies and contributions of the local and national churches called for reflection on the being and task of these churches.

To the original group of liberation theologians—Segundo Galilea, Juan Luis Segundo, Hugo Assmann, José Míguez Bonino, Gustavo Gutiérrez, and so on—the decade of the 1970s added Leonardo and Clodovis Boff, Raúl Vidales, Ronaldo Muñoz, Jon Sobrino, Pablo Richard, Enrique Dussel, Ignacio Ellacuría, and others. This corps of theologians, along with their collaborators, advanced the discussion of various theological topics.

2. Important Advances in Liberation Theology (1972–78)

Seven themes are salient in the theological advances of this period. No precise chronological order can be assigned to them, since they were not the object of a precise program. Rather, these themes simply emerged from the situation and "felt needs" of the various church communities. While some of these themes are interconnected, they are presented approximately as they were developed.

1. *The interlocutor* of the theology of liberation: In the El Escorial meeting, Gustavo Gutiérrez offered a positive appraisal of the efforts of modern Euro-

pean theology, which had come to fruition at the Council, in its attempts to respond to the challenges of the *nonbeliever*. But in Latin America, he observed, unbelief is minimal; by contrast, misery and poverty are maximal. Hence the Latin American theology of liberation takes as its interlocutor not the nonbeliever, but the multitudes whose situation is that of *nonperson*. The question in Latin America is not how to speak of God in a "secularized world that has come of age," but how to proclaim God as a Father in a context of dehumanization and injustice.[31] A determination and explanation of this theological interlocutor helped to situate correctly the advances and the criticisms of emerging Latin American thought.

2. *The Bible*, reread and reflected upon from the viewpoint of the poor: While various theologians engaged in this practice and reflection,[32] it was Carlos Mesters who crowned much of their work and succeeded in molding a method.[33] The Council's invitation and impulse regarding the use of scripture now became reality in thousands upon thousands of Christians and communities who took advantage of Mesters's methodological elements. A key point in biblical hermeneutics is life and solidarity with the poor. From this communion springs a "community hearing" of biblical passages, and the community's intuitions and reflections are gathered together in writing and "minutes." This material, along with that of other exegetes, brings out the deeper meaning of the texts. This meaning is then systematized and distributed in popular booklets. Mesters and a handful of others sowed the seeds of this praxis throughout the decade of the 1970s.

3. *The history of the church*, reread from the underside of history: Here Enrique Dussel's *A History of the Church in Latin America* (1974) is of particular importance.[34] His was the first attempt to reorientate a reading of church history from the praxis of liberation. This focus marks the distance between Dussel's reading and traditional readings. Dussel used Fessard's analytical instrument and paradigm, with its three basic relationships: sibling-sibling (political justice), man-woman (erotic, sexual, familial), and parent-offspring (pedagogical). These are the elements of the ethico-mythical nucleus, which gives meaning to the life of peoples. With Spanish colonialism that nucleus was oppressed in the natives—the Christendom stage. In the second stage (1808–1930), that of "modern states," Dussel pointed out, the oppressed switched masters but continued in their dependency, now a dependency on political ideologies and structures springing from the French Revolution. The third stage, which began in 1930, is that of the subcontinent's awakening and incipient liberation. This attempt at a rereading was destined to help enlighten and refocus the toil of many who were engaged in the work of church history.[35]

4. The *power of the poor for justice* in the unfolding of history: Gustavo Gutiérrez's book *The Power of the Poor in History*[36] showed that the poor not only constitute the privileged locus of God's self-manifestation, but are also the primary bearers of the good news of liberation. The poor evangelize us, in that they constitute the historical subject of the Reign of God. From a point of departure in the poor, history can be changed; a communion of sisters and brothers can become reality. The poor have the power of the Spirit of the

Servant of Yahweh. While the powerful offer us their own historical view, the reading of the Spirit of God, who operates from among the lowly and simple, is very different.

5. *Christology* in a Latin American approach: To plumb the praxis of liberation is to penetrate the historical praxis of Christ. Christology, the heart of any Christian theology, logically came first in the development of the theology of liberation. In the period under consideration the studies of Leonardo Boff and Jon Sobrino are doubtless the finest fruit of an abundant production in this area. Boff's work emphasizes and justifies the qualification of Jesus Christ as Liberator, a title highly regarded by Christians committed to the people. Furthermore, it offers a solid biblical presentation of Christ from a Latin American perspective.[37] Jon Sobrino's christological study represents a qualitative advance in theological reflection on Christ. It profoundly criticizes christological points of departure that are not founded in the Jesus of history. And it focuses on and rereads from the perspective of the poor the central aspects of the historical event of Jesus Christ. It may not be too audacious to assert that this study was the finest piece of liberation theology to appear in the decade of the 1970s.[38]

6. *Spirituality and theological method*: A spirituality and an evangelization that do not lead to a change of heart and mind are a sham. A theology that does not show why there should be change or why theology adopts the orientation that it adopts is like a burned-out light bulb. Bishop Proaño of Ecuador has helped us arrive at this insight.[39] He shows us that evangelization must be consciousness-raising and politicizing. He writes: "For the Christian, to contemplate is to transform the true Christian faith into a faith that produces works, not discourses (Matt. 7:21-22, etc.)."[40] A contemplation and spirituality not rooted in the liberative mission of Christ are inauthentic. The same holds for the production of theology. The Latin American theological method arises from and is nourished by the spirituality of the incarnate, liberative Word. Juan Luis Segundo has written a magnificent work on theology and correct hermeneutics.[41] Likewise, Pablo Richard, in dialogue with European theology, has emphasized that the Latin American theological method takes its point of departure in the situation of oppression and liberation. Unlike European progressivist theologies, then, it is centered not on the opposition between abstract and concrete, but on that between domination and liberation; not on deduction versus induction, but on interpretation vis-à-vis transformation.[42]

7. *Church and liberation*: Base communities have offered fertile soil for the rejuvenation of the church in the spirit of Medellín. Here is the matrix for a growing reflection on the characteristics, the identifying signs or "notes" of the church. Among the moments of collation and systematization of many experiences and reflections in this direction have been the national meetings of the base ecclesial communities. Here the Brazilian church has distinguished itself in a special way. The first national meeting of the base ecclesial communities of Brazil was held in the city of Vitoria. There the process of church and theology reached a new level. The Brazilian meetings are held every three years, and each meeting supplies additional thrust to the penetration of the people

by the church and its liberative mission. The other national churches of our subcontinent are undergoing a similar process, in various ways, in step with the situations of each of our various peoples.

The elaboration and development of these themes has followed an outline determined by the particular characteristics of the Latin American theology of liberation. As this reflection with its specific traits has grown, it has distinguished itself from other kinds of reflections. Its values have lighted up the path of the church, and at the same time it has experienced the need for greater efforts to respond to the urgent cry of those who suffer in poverty. Likewise, certain fears and criticisms have appeared with the cooling of the first fervor of the Puebla Bishops' Conference.

3. A Step Forward: Historic Milestone of the Regional Synod of Puebla (February 1979)

The journey undertaken by local churches and Christian groups with their original, independent accent, in the spirit of the Council, aroused both fears and hopes. The climate was one of a veritable explosion of experiments and reflections, not only in the church, but in a goodly part of society as well. What positions would the Puebla meeting take? What would it say of the mission of the church on the subcontinent? What position would it take vis-à-vis Medellín? What judgment would it make on the inspiring, and now feared, theology of liberation?

Over the course of the year 1977, a committee appointed by the Latin American Bishops' Conference (CELAM) prepared a working document for the conference to be held at Puebla, operating from an ideology alien to the people and hence to any considerations of their genuine advantage. But this working document was rejected by most of the national episcopates, and it was sent back to the committee to be redrawn. This time its negative tone was softened somewhat, but this time too, lest its contents become too well publicized and especially lest it be criticized, it emerged from committee barely in time to be received before the beginning of the Puebla Conference. It was sent to the bishops with the approval of John Paul I, who had succeeded Paul VI in August 1978. John Paul I announced that he would travel to Puebla, and a few days before his death the working document had already been sent to the bishops. Now the conference was postponed from October 1978 to January and February 1979. The tone and goals set by the working document were diluted. As far as the actual conference was concerned—we can see this in the documents—the working draft operated as a cipher; that is, it neither helped nor hindered the work of the conference.

It is striking in how many different ways little church groups sought to make their voices heard by the bishops. The time before the conference was filled with meetings, the sending of delegations, and announcements in periodicals. Particularly enlightening was the preparatory document drawn up by the Congress of Latin American Religious (CCAR). As for the bishops, they took advice from many different quarters. But the common, deepest element was the prayer of the people of God that the Lord might send the Divine Spirit upon Puebla.

Pope John Paul II, in his first journey, was impressed by the warm, affectionate welcome accorded him by the people of Mexico. He opened the Synod personally, and in March 1979 approved its Final Document. The latter responds to the principal anxieties of those moments. It was the product of the broad, sincere prayer of millions of Catholics, and of the efforts of all who in any way took part in the work of the conference. The main focus of the call and orientations of the Puebla Conference responds to the central questions, which are none other than those raised by the theology of liberation, and thus constitute a critical evaluation of the latter. We can synthesize this central focus under four heads:

1. *Analysis of reality, pastoral overview, and discernment:* The issue of the analysis of reality during the decade of the seventies was a burning one. In some very conservative milieus this sort of analysis was confused with atheism. To undertake a scientific analysis of social, economic, and political reality was tantamount to attacking the church. Part One of the document, however, entitled "Pastoral Overview," not only approves the analysis of reality at the economic, political, and ideological level, but it actually utilizes this tool. The only question now is how to use a tool well. The bishops use it from the perspective of pastors: emphasis is on the pastoral view, in contradistinction to a sociological view, and so forth. Pastors without a view of reality could scarcely render judgment on that reality, or discern good from evil there. The key methodological toolbox of liberation theology thus comes to be turned to advantage and approved at Puebla (Puebla Final Document, nos. 28-30).

2. *Mission of the church: a liberative evangelization*: Faced with the social sin identified in Part One, in Part Two the bishops encourage a liberative evangelization after the example of Christ, whose prolongation is the church. "It is urgently necessary," Puebla says, "for the Church to be the school that educates human beings who will be capable of making history" (Puebla Final Document, no. 274). This call and need were becoming all the more urgent, because the situation of institutionalized injustice had worsened among most of our peoples. As the bishops emphasize: "We pastors in Latin America have the most serious reasons for pressing for liberative evangelization" (Puebla Final Document, no. 487). Thus the document adopts and assimilates the heart and soul of the theology of liberation: the Lord's call to liberation. To liberate, to do justice is the authentic way of loving God and one's brothers and sisters (Puebla Final Document, no. 327).

3. *Liberation and the reconfiguration of the church and society*: "Each tree is known by its yield" (Luke 6:44). "This is how all will know you for my disciples: your love for one another" (John 13:35). When sisters and brothers live in unity and share their goods, with special attention to the poor and helpless, this is a sign of the presence of the Lord. The pastors gathered in Puebla raised their voice to declare that a liberative evangelization was in operation in the base church communities, "so that now they are one of the causes for joy and hope in the Church" (Puebla Final Document, no. 96). Medellín not only raised our consciousness, but it provided us with an effective impulse to live as brothers and sisters, reflected concretely in the communities. True renewal begins at

home, regardless of what happens in the church. "If it's dark indoors, a candle in the street is a flash of blinding light," as the popular saying has it. From a starting point in a renewal in the church communities themselves, and in them especially, the Latin American church has thrown itself into its mission of cooperating in the liberation of our peoples and in the construction of the new, pluralistic society (Puebla Final Document, no. 1206). The document indicates that the communities "have become centers of evangelization and moving forces for liberation and development" (Puebla Final Document, no. 96). The church offers its hands and heart to all those involved in the construction of a just society, a society in which human rights are respected (Puebla Final Document, nos. 1206-93). Human and church groups, which provide theological reflection with its richest material, have the endorsement and encouragement of the Synod of Latin American Bishops.

4. *A liberative evangelization and the option for the poor*: The manner, the style, the strategy can be none other than that left us by Jesus, who was born, who lived, and who evangelized in poverty and in solidarity with the poor (Puebla Final Document, no. 190). This reality has been recovered in all its vigor and challenge in the theology of liberation. Recently the bishops have been supporting in their magisterium the option for the poor as proclaimed by Medellín (Puebla Final Document, no. 1134). Indeed, on the strength of this option the church wishes to be called the "church of the poor." The path of evangelization is the path of a communion of solidarity with the poor and their historical project. This orientation frames the option for justice emphasized by the bishops and presented by them as a Christian task: to be the builders of a new society. From this outlook of the option for the poor and their justice emerges the prophetic option for youth, as option for the future, as rejection of the sinful present, as an active, transforming attitude in the face of reality. "Youth is not simply an age-group. It is also an attitude toward life in a stage that is not definitive but transitional" (Puebla Final Document, no. 1167). Thus, the preferential option for the poor is seen not as something romantic or "mystical," but as entailing the quest for justice with a youthful, hopeful heart.

As is the church's way in its councils and synods, various points were aired. But these points—vocations, ministries, education, health, and so on—were reorientated from the core perspective, the nucleus, of each of these two synods. Certainly the Puebla Conference responded to the serious questions posed. Clearly and repeatedly it endorsed Medellín and that earlier meeting's prophetic stance. It emphasized that the mission of the church today is in the practice of liberation in the spirit of Jesus. It adopted, profited by, and further encouraged the service of the theology of liberation.

4. Consolidation (1979–87): Toward Maturation amidst Conflicts

The work of the liberation theologians at Puebla was followed by the work of facilitating the reading and dissemination of its message. This task filled a goodly part of the year 1979. It was very important that the people who had prayed and reflected upon their pilgrimage should know and comment on the contributions of the bishops. It was like a breath of springtime for many of the base ecclesial communities to receive the Puebla documents. Now there was room for a living faith and hope in the practice of liberation. The labor to which we have referred precluded the possibility of ignorance or deformation of the Puebla document in certain sectors of the people of God.

But the consolidation achieved during these years was to be a bone of contention as well, since it would generate an overall tone similar to that of the atmosphere before Puebla—one of suspicion, mistrust, and attack. In the midst of conflicts, liberation theology was to continue accentuating its proper traits and would come to occupy a primary place in the theology of the 1980s.

The wealth of Latin American theological reflection would continue to depend on the great evangelizing wealth of the various local churches and so many base ecclesial communities, a sign of the hope that one day a different reality would be present instead of the exploitation suffered by the majority of our peoples. In July 1979 the dictatorship of the Somozas and of the United States was overthrown in Nicaragua. The liberation process was remarkable for the presence of priests and other Christians, which was and would continue to be a sign of contradiction. This popular, challenging process, along with the pastors who further it, has received its model in Oscar Arnulfo Romero, bishop and martyr. Since his death on March 24, 1980, not only the Salvadoran people, but the Latin American people have recognized him as their exemplary pastor. His life, his commitment, his word call us to account and feed the fires of evangelization. In Archbishop Romero the spirit and orientations of Medellín and Puebla have found a Christian human being open to being taught by the Lord. On different levels and at different rates many church processes have adopted this same spirit. This spirit of pilgrimage, this ecclesial vitality, from which so many martyrs spring, says something about the source of the strength to be found in liberation theology.

Historically, in the decade of the eighties the breach between rich and poor grew wider. The great debts contracted in the 1970s to the benefit of large-scale world financial capital and channeled by corrupt governments, usually "National Security" governments, became a burden too heavy for our peoples to bear. The purposeful rise in interest rates (from 4% or 5% to 23% by the beginning of the decade) meant an endless bloodletting, which translated into less bread, more illness, and premature death in various forms. To these must be added the depletion of the supplies of the raw materials used for Latin American products. At the same time there was a resurgence of formal democracies, impotent and inoperative in practice. In some countries democracy achieved a certain level of dignity, as in Argentina. But in others it continued to generate misery, as in Honduras and El Salvador. The worsening of social conditions in Latin America is so difficult to hide that even persons who had kept their distance from social processes became involved in them, side by side with their peoples.

We now focus on two matters of consequence for liberation theology during these years. The first is the matter of the documents of the Sacred Congregation for the Doctrine of the Faith. The second is the question of the significance of the development of a theological *"summa"* in a perspective of liberation.

1. "Liberation theology is not only expedient, but useful, and necessary" (John Paul II)

A liberative evangelization received new impulse at Puebla, which encouraged it to continue along the settled lines of its theological reflection. But once again, the increase in the number of liberation theologians and their publications sparked doubts and attacks. The Congregation for the Doctrine of the Faith, under Cardinal Ratzinger, received and compiled complaints against liberation theology's principal works and thinkers, concentrating mainly on Gustavo Gutiérrez and Leonardo Boff. Then an attempt was made to have the Peruvian bishops censure Gustavo Gutiérrez; in fact, the Peruvian bishops were asked to condemn him on the occasion of their *ad limina* visit to the Vatican. But the plan failed and was remanded to the Vatican for further study. The case is not closed, and attempts continue to be made to interfere with the courses, the center of reflection, and the publishing of the celebrated theologian.

The pressure and attacks on liberation theology stirred strong solidarity, not only in the Third World, but among the best European theologians. Scholars like Congar, Chenu, González Faus, Metz, Rahner, Schillebeeckx, and others, declared their solidarity with this way of doing theology. Various European centers and universities have now bestowed honorary degrees on liberation theologians in support and recognition of their work in and for the church.

Nevertheless, the Sacred Congregation for the Doctrine of the Faith thought it fitting to establish a "dialogue" with (i.e., pass judgment upon) the best-known theologian of the Brazilian Bishops' Conference, Leonardo Boff, and enjoined a period of silence on him.[43] Boff obediently submitted, but the Brazilian bishops were disturbed by the procedure, as they had not been consulted in this matter of the censuring of one of their official theologians.

Boff was silenced one month after—and in the context of—the publication by the Sacred Congregation for the Doctrine of the Faith of the "Instruction on Certain Aspects of the Theology of Liberation" on August 6, 1984. That document stated: "The mighty, all but irresistible, aspiration of peoples for *liberation* constitutes one of the principal *signs of the times* that the Church must discern and interpret in the light of the gospel."[44] But it is thereupon observed that this wholesome aspiration, willed by the Creator, can be ideologized and manipulated. Hence a discernment is required, since the orientations of the Third General Conference of the Latin American Episcopate at Puebla are deemed insufficient for the purpose. Even more seriously, the "Instruction" repeatedly insisted that Latin American theology was based on Marxist analysis; that it manipulated biblical texts and reduced them to the political dimension; that it evacuated the content of the magisterium of the church, and confused Christian liberation with an exclusively temporal progress; and that all of this was owing to its reduction of Jesus Christ to a purely earthly dimension. One need only glance at works like Jon Sobrino's *Christology at the Crossroads*, Gustavo Gutiérrez's more recent *We Drink from Our Own Wells*, or Leonardo Boff's *The Maternal Face of God* in order to grasp the unfounded character of such assertions. If we observe the witness of their lives and their functions in the church communities in which they work, we can only be astonished at such statements in the "Instruction."[45]

Theological work, too, shares in the Paschal reality: glory comes by way of the cross, and one's memory does not have to reach back very far to recall the suffering of so many of the theologians who prepared Vatican II, like de Lubac or Daniélou, or the passion and cross of the *nouvelle théologie*, Teilhard de Chardin, and so on. These conflicts do not prevent the pilgrimage; but they surely render it laborious and unnecessarily conflict-ridden.

The "obedient silence" required of Leonardo Boff and the publication of the "Instruction" moved a goodly part of the Brazilian episcopate to seek more effective routes for bringing their voices to the pope and the Vatican. They persuaded John Paul II to meet for three days with a commission representing them on the occasion of their *ad limina* visit in March 1986. At the same time, John Paul II asked that Boff's censure be lifted. A few days later, on March 22, the Congregation for the Doctrine of the Faith published a new "Instruction on Christian Freedom and Liberation." This document is somewhat more positive and makes timorous advances.

The process culminated in a letter addressed by John Paul II to the bishops of Brazil based on the three-days' meeting, in which the pope and the bishops had engaged in an in-depth exchange of viewpoints regarding pastoral and theological work. In April 1986 Cardinal Gantin delivered John Paul's letter to the Brazilian episcopate. The letter stated, "Liberation theology is not only expedient, but useful, and necessary."[46] Furthermore, the pope entrusted to that body of bishops the urgent task of disseminating this theology and watching over its purity, thereby creating a new ecclesial framework for the development of the theology of liberation.

2. A Theological Summa in a Liberation Perspective (1985–88)

The dissemination of the Puebla documents was accompanied by the advance and in-depth investigation of the great themes of the theological task. I shall limit myself to a brief outline of the thematics of this project, and citation of some of the most important publications.

1. *Bible*: Carlos Mesters's inspiration reaches to every corner of Latin America. His outstanding publication is *Defenseless Flower: A New Reading of the Bible*.[47] Exegetical work continues apace, while the people receive Bible courses in their own language and are thereby enabled to recover that book as their own. The contributions of Xavier Saravia along these lines also deserve special mention.[48]

2. *Christology*: One of the most promising young theologians, Hugo Echegaray, died shortly after Puebla, but he left an important piece of writing, *The Practice of Jesus*, in which he brings the Latin American theological method to maturity.[49] Jon Sobrino, with *Jesus in Latin America*, continues to explore the subject.[50]

3. *Mariology*: Among the various contributions of this period, Leonardo Boff's *The Maternal Face of God* stands out, expanding on the dynamics of *Jesus Christ Liberator*.[51]

4. *Ecclesiology*: These are the years of the first syntheses, especially that of Jon Sobrino, *The True Church and the Poor*, based on the gripping story and witness of Archbishop Romero.[52] Here Sobrino also begins the work of discovering a more authentic and profound pneumatology based on the history of the church from the perspective of the poor. A fine comparative study comes from the pen of Alvaro Quiroz: *Eclesiología en la teología de la liberación*.[53]

5. *Anthropology and eschatology*: Even before Puebla, José Comblin had been working in these areas of theology. From the viewpoint of historical discernment and the political dimension of faith, the writings of J. B. Libânio stand out.[54]

6. *Spirituality*: As in ecclesiology, very important advances have taken place in this area as well, such as the publications of CLAR, along with its services of support and training. Likewise, the inspiring writings of Gustavo Gutiérrez, such as *We Drink from Our Own Wells* and his commentary on the Book of Job, lay the foundations for the spiritual journey of Christians committed to liberation.[55]

7. *Church history*: The organization of a number of church historians into CEHILA, under the presidency of Enrique Dussel, has contributed to a recovery of church history from the viewpoint of a commitment to liberation. The level of effectiveness of these groups differs from country to country, but the degree of organization already attained, the advance in methodology, and the rereading of history, for example in Brazil, promise a rich harvest for the near future.

8. *Other areas*: The studies of Diego Irarrazaval and others on popular piety are helpful in evaluating and reading the theology of the people. Also, Antonio Moser has been working on a moral theology based on liberation.[56]

Liberation theologians have long desired to gather together a great part of the work already done in the theology of liberation and to make advances in areas not yet sufficiently dealt with. Toward the middle of 1985 plans were laid to publish a collection of works in liberation theology in which the best authors and most important themes would be represented. The project was approved by more than 150 bishops; the collection would bear the title *Theology and Liberation*. The first volumes in this series have appeared, though pressures and conflicts occasioned by this new collection have slowed its progress.[57] The theological unity that has been achieved through this project, and the value of the theological contributions themselves, demonstrate the gradual consolidation of the theology of liberation.

CONCLUSION

Twenty-five years after the Council and the emergence of an adult Latin American church we can only be impressed by the distance traversed. A great deal is lacking, but the journey is well under way. From a minimal participation in Vatican Council II, from being called the church of silence, in the space of barely twenty-five years the pilgrimage of the Latin American local churches, base ecclesial communities, and theological reflection have become an inspiration, a hope, and the promise of a bright future for the universal church. The contrast is genuinely impressive.

Before the emergence of a Latin American theology arising out of and responding to the needs of our people (even apart from its universal projection), theology on our subcontinent was all but nonexistent. At the present moment, besides the enriching, inspiring contributions on various theological themes, a consolidation of Latin America's own reflection is being achieved with the publication of the fifty-two projected volumes of the *Theology and Liberation* series.

Since its inception liberation theology has been the object of suspicions and fears, albeit in a variety of tones. If we recall the pre–Vatican II theological mentality—how theological learning was imparted and what kind of texts were used to impart it—we readily understand why a harsh judgment might be handed down on this new reflection, often from life situations so different from those of the masses of our people. The conflicts have not ceased. They have helped, to an extent, purify our reflection, as these twenty-five years have shown. But also, to an extent, they hold back progress and make our work more burdensome. Finally, our little history of twenty-five years since the Council demonstrates that the pilgrimage of the poor, and their liberation, is fostered by the Spirit; the various conflicts that have arisen have occasioned growth and maturation.

Historical responsibility impels us. Christian love thrusts us forward to care for and nourish communities that are hopeful and joyful and to maintain the faith reflection that accompanies and serves them. It is still painful to recall that the church was able to destroy creative missionary work (in China, Japan, Paraguay, India, and so on) in the past, in the eighteenth century. Ecclesial responsibility and, especially, love for the poor and their cause of liberation, invite us to continue working, not only to avoid a repetition of the occurrences of the eighteenth century, but to provide an impulse for the Latin American liberative processes and their theological reflection and to ensure that the poor may have and communicate life in abundance. It is early spring in our church; in early spring you can still have a frost.

In Latin America the people are at work. They are praying that, five centuries after its arrival in these lands, the gospel of Jesus not be reduced to an empty memory, not be expressed in empty bureaucratic celebrations. A new effort is needed, and a new stage of life for that gospel. In Bogotá, in 1986 Pope John Paul II issued a call for wholehearted support of the "new evangelization" of which our subcontinent has such need. The synods of Medellín and Puebla drew the blueprint. We need only live up to that blueprint, that it may become the flesh and blood of the people, like the Lord Jesus. May we be able to say, "And the church became a people"—a church that, like Jesus, will understand its mission "to bring glad tidings to the poor, . . . to announce a year of favor from the Lord" (Luke 4:18-19).

— Translated by Robert R. Barr

NOTES

1. In the conciliar acts of *Gaudium et Spes* any dichotomy between the natural and the supernatural is explicitly corrected. The key is a proper understanding of the Incarnation. All reality is called to liberation (Rom. 8:18-25).

2. The working document of the Puebla synod, in its two stages, stands as the symbol of the debate of these years.

3. Medellín, "Document on Poverty," nos. 1, 2. The original term *option for the poor* receives at Puebla the qualification "preferential," lest any reductionism seem to be countenanced vis-à-vis salvation — as if salvation might be the exclusive possession of one sector or class. But when this meaning is misrepresented, and "preferential" is understood in the sense of an indifference to which perspective is used, that of the rich or that of the poor, then the option for the poor is stripped of its meaning. It is the salvific strategy of Jesus to save everyone *from the perspective of the poor, not of the rich.*

4. The commitment to the poor and their liberation is becoming the task that unites, ecumenically, mainline Protestants and Catholics in Latin America, especially in Brazil.

5. Gustavo Gutiérrez, *A Theology of Liberation: History, Politics, and Salvation*, trans. Caridad Inda and John Eagleson (Maryknoll, N.Y.: Orbis Books, 1973; revised edition, 1988), p. 113.

6. In Latin America, Archbishop Oscar Arnulfo Romero has become a model of the Good Shepherd. Shortly before his death Archbishop Romero left a testimonial of his free sacrifice of his life for the sake of all his people.

7. The matter of the preferential option for the poor came in for a great deal of debate during the synod, but finally it passed by a clear majority.

8. Bernard Lonergan, *Method in Theology* (London, 1972), pp. 85-99.

9. José Comblin, *Historia da teologia catolica* (São Paulo, Brazil, 1969).

10. Karl Rahner, *Escritos de teología*, vol. 4 (Madrid, 1965), p. 153.

11. These words, addressed to the outcasts of the suburbs of Guadalajara, were a mighty encouragement to the base community groups present at the pope's speech.

12. This focus is basically that of Gutiérrez in his *A Theology of Liberation*. It was very important at that time to "liberate" theology from a purely academic hermeneutics and situate it in life.

13. Carlos Mesters and his vast output deserve special mention here for his methodological clarity and exegetical rigor.

14. There was animated discussion in committee as to whether to cite the theology of liberation by name. It did not seem opportune to do so, but this is the obvious reference of the text.

15. Among many studies on this subject, see A. G. Frank, *Latin America: Underdevelopment or Revolution* (New York, 1969); F. Cardoso and E. Faletto, *Dependency and Development in Latin America* (Berkeley, 1979).

16. The documents of these original meetings, such as the one held in Petrópolis, Brazil, can be found in the archives of the Centro Bartolomé de las Casas, Lima, Peru.

17. Ronaldo Muñoz, *Nueva conciencia de la Iglesia en América Latina* (Salamanca, 1974).

18. For some commentaries on the meetings held in preparation for Medellín, see Roberto Oliveros, *Liberación y teología* (Lima, 1977), which offers a detailed study of the genesis of liberation theology up to the year 1977.

19. Medellín, "Document on Justice," no. 1. A few years before Medellín the Jesuit provincials of Latin America, stated: "Most of the people on this continent find themselves in a state of poverty, the injustice of which cries to heaven for

vengeance" (*Between Honesty and Hope: Documents from and about the Church in Latin America*, trans. John Drury, Maryknoll Documentation Series [Maryknoll, N.Y.: Maryknoll Publications, 1970], doc. 19, "The Jesuits in Latin America, no. 2, p. 144; citing *Populorum Progressio*, no. 30).

20. Medellín, "Document on Poverty," no. 7.

21. Ibid., no. 1.

22. Ibid., no. 16.

23. Cf. Gustavo Gutiérrez's address at Chimbote, "Hacia una teología de la liberación" (Montevideo, 1969). English translation appears in Alfred Hennelly, ed., *Liberation Theology: A Documentary History* (Maryknoll, N.Y.: Orbis Books, 1990), pp. 62-76.

24. Gutiérrez, *A Theology of Liberation*. Citations are from the revised anniversary edition of 1988.

25. Ibid., p. 29.

26. We need only recall here the case of Bishop Angelelli in Argentina. [This outspoken and prophetic bishop was killed in a suspicious auto accident in 1976 — Eds.] Recently, the judge presiding over the investigation stated that the bishop's death had been premeditated: it had been no accident. Notice was duly taken in newspapers throughout Argentina.

27. Cf. *Fe cristiana y cambio social en América latina* (Salamanca, 1973).

28. Cf. *Liberación y cautiverio* (Mexico City, 1976).

29. Cf. *Theology in the Americas*, ed. Sergio Torres and John Eagleson (Maryknoll, N.Y.: Orbis Books, 1976).

30. See *The Emergent Gospel,* ed. Sergio Torres and Virginia Fabella (Maryknoll, N.Y.: Orbis Books, 1978). EATWOT has held a series of triennial international conferences. The first one was followed by meetings in São Paulo, Brazil (1980), India (1983), and most recently, Mexico City (1986). See respectively, *The Challenge of Basic Christian Communities,* Sergio Torres and John Eagleson (Orbis Books, 1981); *The Irruption of the Third World,* ed. Virginia Fabella and Sergio Torres (Orbis Books, 1983); *Third World Theologies,* ed. K. C. Abraham (Orbis Books, 1990).

31. Gustavo Gutiérrez, *The Power of the Poor in History* (Maryknoll, N.Y.: Orbis Books, 1983) pp. 36-74.

32. Ernesto Cardenal's book on his experience of reading the gospel with the poor of Solentiname is very widely known, for example: *The Gospel of Solentiname* 4 vols. (Maryknoll, N.Y.: Orbis Books, 1976-1982).

33. Cf. Carlos Mesters, *Defenseless Flower: A New Reading of the Bible* (Maryknoll, N.Y.: Orbis Books, 1989).

34. Enrique D. Dussel, *History of the Church in Latin America* (Grand Rapids, Mich.: Eerdmans, 1981; originally published Buenos Aires, 1974).

35. We see this in the formation and work of the historians of CEHILA, the Commission for the Study of the History of the Church in Latin America.

36. Gustavo Gutiérrez, *The Power of the Poor in History* (Maryknoll, N.Y.: Orbis Books, 1983).

37. Leonardo Boff, *Jesus Christ Liberator: A Critical Christology for Our Time*, trans. Patrick Hughes (Maryknoll, N.Y.: Orbis Books, 1978).

38. Jon Sobrino, *Christology at the Crossroads: A Latin American Approach*, trans. John Drury (Maryknoll, N.Y.: Orbis Books, 1978). For an examination of this study see Oliveros, *Liberación y teología*, pp. 416-39.

39. L. Proaño, *Concientización, evangelización, política* (Salamanca, 1974).

40. Ibid., pp. 216-17.

41. Juan Luis Segundo, *Liberation of Theology*, trans. John Drury (Maryknoll, N.Y.: Orbis Books, 1976).

42. Pablo Richard, "Teología de la liberación: un aporte crítico a la teología europea," *Páginas* 3 (1976).

43. An account of this episode may be found in Harvey Cox, *The Silencing of Leonardo Boff* (Oak Park, Ill.: Meyer-Stone Books, 1988).

44. "Instruction on Certain Aspects of the Theology of Liberation," no. 1; see Hennelly, ed., *Liberation Theology,* pp. 393-414.

45. It seems to me that our Lord's observation about seeing the mote in the eye of another is applicable here. The percentage of "unbelievers" among the population of Latin America is extremely small, while in Europe it is considerable. On occasion, as in the case of the worker-priest movement in France, the church in Europe has failed to provide its movements with adequate pastoral support. This failure to learn from experience is puzzling. See Hennelly, *Liberation Theology,* pp. 448-506.

46. There are those who argue that the reference here is to a "sound" theology of liberation. But what is a "sound" theology of liberation? Current liberation theology, developed in Latin America, that of Boff, Gutiérrez, Sobrino, and so on, is surely open to criticism, but there is no other theology of liberation.

47. Mesters's *Defenseless Flower* (Maryknoll, N.Y.: Orbis Books, 1989) was originally published in Brazil in 1983.

48. Worthy of special note among Saravia's works: *El poplado de la Biblia* (Mexico City, 1986), and *El Apocalipsis* (Mexico City, 1987).

49. Echegaray, *The Practice of Jesus* (Maryknoll, N.Y.: Orbis Books, 1984).

50. Sobrino, *Jesus in Latin America* (Maryknoll, N.Y.: Orbis Books, 1987).

51. Boff, *The Maternal Face of God* (San Francisco: Harper & Row, 1988).

52. Sobrino, *The True Church and the Poor* (Maryknoll, N.Y.: Orbis Books, 1984).

53. Alvaro Quiroz, *Eclesiología en la teología de la liberación* (Salamanca, 1983).

54. J. B. Libânio, *Spiritual Discernment and Politics* (Maryknoll, N.Y.: Orbis Books, 1982).

55. Gutiérrez, *We Drink from Our Own Wells* (Maryknoll, N.Y.: Orbis Books, 1984); *On Job: God-Talk and the Suffering of the Innocent* (Maryknoll, N.Y.: Orbis Books, 1987). This dimension of theology, like spiritual theology, was present in the work of the liberation theologians from the outset, as is manifest in the spiritual experience from which that reflection springs.

56. Eds.: See Antonio Moser and Bernardino Leers, *Moral Theology: Dead Ends and Alternatives* (Maryknoll, N.Y.: Orbis Books, 1990).

57. Eds.: At the time of publication, a dozen volumes from this series have appeared in English translation, published jointly by Orbis Books (U.S.A.) and Burns & Oates (U.K.).

2

Reception of the Theology of Liberation

JUAN JOSÉ TAMAYO

Latin American liberation theology constitutes an unprecedented phenomenon in the recent story of Christian thought. For the first time in history, a theological creation of the Third World has acquired relevancy and meaning in Europe and the First World. Indeed, it has produced an unexpected impact here, and has stirred the most widely varied reactions. On one side, the new theology has profoundly penetrated not a few slumbering Christian consciences. Thus, it has contributed to a revitalization of important movements of church renewal—among them, in a very special way, the base communities. It has seeped into the hoary lecture halls of the seminaries and theological schools, and is leaving its imprint on the most prestigious and creative theologians of our continent. On the other side, it has been the object of harsh condemnations—to be sure, recently nuanced—on the part of the most authorative Vatican offices, as well as at the hands of a certain sector of academic theology.

The theology of liberation comes forward as a theological discourse not structured mimetically on the European model, but developed on the basis of Latin American reality itself—with a number of identifying marks of its own, and with an original methodology—and seeks to respond, on the basis of the faith as interpreted in a liberation "key," to the political, socioeconomic, cultural, and religious challenges of Latin America. The following testimonial by Uruguayan theologian Juan Luis Segundo, one of the most important initiators of the theology of liberation, will confirm what we have just declared.

Our intent here is to reflect on the condition of alienation attaching to theology as we have found it on the Latin American continent. As is evident, a human reality endowed with characteristics of its own ought not to be without its theology—that is, an application of the Christian message to actual reality . . . Latin American theology does not, any more than does the European, do this by virtue of its "application" in Latin America of the theology done in Europe, in the fashion that a branch office might be limited to addressing some narrower concrete problem than that addressed by the main office. Theology here will not be more authentic for leaving to European theologians a concern for studying grace, or the Trinity.[1]

From the outset, liberation theology has been conscious of its regional or particular character in terms of the sociocultural context in which it has sprung to life; but at no moment has it ever renounced its will to universality. "Contextuality" and universality are two of the identifying notes of liberation theology. The two are related not in contradiction, but dialectical correlation.

The theology of liberation is developed neither in the dark recesses of the monastic libraries of yore, nor in academic centers of knowledge and culture, nor in the classic loci of the concentration of theological knowledge and church power. Rather, it is generated in the framework of the liberation processes, and concrete, "historical" liberation movements, of Latin America: hence its sociopolitical dimension, which is consubstantial to it but does not exhaust it. It is generated in the broad spaces of "not knowing" and "not having": hence its prophetic and denunciatory nature. It is generated on the periphery of the world: hence its frequently alleged "marginality" and "partiality."

This does not mean, however, that it renounces what has traditionally defined theology—the giving of an account of one's faith and hope. It only means that the theology of liberation moves in the ambit not of pure reason, but of practical reason. The be-all and end-all of liberation theology is to give an account (*razón*) of faith in the God of the poor, and of the hope that proclaims a future of greater justice for the oppressed masses. Or, in the felicitous expression of Salvadoran theologian Ignacio Ellacuría, this theology seeks "to give reasons (*razones*) for the reason (*razón*) of a believing people."

Until somewhat recently, and even today among not a few school theologians, the only theology seen to be worthy of the name has been the one cultivated in academe—the theology developed by professional theologians in theological schools or seminaries in the service of the church institution and the magisterium. Today, as German theologian Johannes B. Metz keenly observes, alongside this way of doing theology, another one of no less importance makes its appearance. Nor may this new theology, Metz goes on, be characterized simply as an example of grassroots theology in the manner of black or feminist theology. Rather, this new theology strives for an adequate harmony between methodological effort and prophetic will.[2]

I. EUROPEAN PROGRESSIVE THEOLOGY IN THE EYES OF THE THEOLOGY OF LIBERATION

1. Rejection or Indifference?

Latin American liberation theologians are rather frequently accused of a sense of contempt or rejection of, or at least of indifference toward, European theology of a progressive mold. In his foreword to *Concilium*, no. 96, devoted in its entirety to the theology of liberation and containing the contributions of a goodly number of its creators, French theologian Claude Geffré maintained:

> But what surprises us the most is that Latin American theologians reject (in more radical a fashion than that of the neointegralism currently springing

up in the United States and in certain European countries) the various "progressive" theologies of the Western world, whether these be "theologies of secularization" or "political theologies."[3]

A year later, at the Congress of Latin American Theology held in Mexico City, Jon Sobrino addressed this evaluation of Geffré's, conceding the raw fact of a certain "indifference" on the part of Latin American theologians for European theology, but identifying the precise nuance of this relative indifference. The latter, in Sobrino's judgment, must be understood as stemming not from an ignorance of European theology, nor from a contempt for it or sense of superiority, nor from a disdain of the undeniable achievements of European theology. Rather, this "indifference" is owing simply to the absence of a harmony of interest between the theological knowledge of one side and that of the other. Sobrino then remarked, correctly enough, that as long as European theology understands itself from a point of departure in the geopolitical center of the world, it will find it impossible to "grasp affliction and torment," and, however unconsciously, play into the hands of Western capitalist society.

However, it is to be observed that a considerable number of Latin American liberation theologians have been trained in European universities, where they have received the wherewithal to achieve a better articulation of their theological reflection. They make use of tools of the European theological tradition themselves, especially those of the "progressive" tradition. They explicitly acknowledge the conceptual wealth and important attainments of that theology, focusing on, among others: its advances in exegetical research; its self-deliverance from dogmatism and abstract orthodoxy; its concern to bestow meaning on a faith which seemed to be without such meaning; its rediscovery of the sociopolitical mediations of faith, and a consequent effort to overcome attitudes of privatization in Christianity; its recovery of the perilous, subversive memory of the Judeo-Christian tradition, which sets a process of social transformation under way; and so on.

2. Differentiating Elements and Moment of Breach

Liberation theologians do not reject across the board the theologies developed in the center. They do, however, take a certain distance from them, adopt a critical attitude toward them, and, with a view to reasserting their own originality and specificity, emphasize the moment of breach or rupture with them:

— On one hand, a *political breach*, as Gustavo Gutiérrez emphasizes, a breach defined by the tension of political conflict prevailing between their respective representatives.

— On the other, an *epistemological breach* with the old ways of knowing, which are helpless to take account of the specific problems of the Third World.

The moment of breach, holds Giulio Girardi, derives from the centrality ascribed by the theology of liberation, to social conflict, and from the centrality it ascribes to the praxis of liberation. Let us examine this in greater detail.

A. A first differentiating element regards the respective interests, and method of approaching reality, of each of the two theologies. Jon Sobrino has brought this out with keenness and precision.[4] For Sobrino, European theology approaches reality through the mediations of thought (culture, philosophy, theology), and tends to reconcile misery with theological thought rather than deliver reality from its misery. European theology has its ties with the First Enlightenment (Kant), and its interest centers on freeing reason from authoritarianism and dogmatism or in other words, the deliverance of an enslaved subjectivity.

By contrast, the theology of liberation seeks to respond to the challenge of the Second Enlightenment (Marx). In the eyes of this theology, the liberating function of knowledge becomes concretized in the transformation of reality, and thereby recovers the threatened meaning of faith. In the mind of the liberation theologians, knowledge possesses no sheerly interpretative character. "It is never praxically or value-neutral. It always has, implicitly or explicitly, a praxic and ethical character" (Sobrino).

B. A second point of differentiation and breach regards the interlocutors, social subjects, challenges, and questions, of the two theologies respectively. This aspect of the question has been developed by Gustavo Gutiérrez, who observes that the primary addressee of progressive European theology is the unbelieving, atheistic, or skeptical bourgeois individual—the modern spirit and the liberal, laissez-faire ideology whose subject is the bourgeois class. Here, the challenge to theology is lodged by a criticism of religion on the part of secularization and atheism.[5] The tension is between theism and atheism, faith and unbelief, and appears most markedly in the case of official European theology.

The questions to which European theology seeks to respond are the same as those that had already been posed by Dietrich Bonhoeffer in his *Letters from Prison*: How is God to be rendered believable in the midst of unbelief?

But the theology that has been developed as a response to these questions — which in Europe are inescapable and very important—frequently fails to take into account, Gutiérrez believes, "that persons are the new dominant subjects in humanity, and that this fact has given rise to a by-product, namely nonpersons—today's poor."[6] Gutiérrez asks whether a critique should be made of this theology that it "fails to look at more than one side of history. For, on the other side, which we call the underside of history, we have the creation of new forms of oppression." While it is true that human oppression did not begin with modernity, it is equally true that the modern human beings who question the faith, the persons to whom European theology seeks to respond, "belong to social groups, cultures, and countries that have been creating new forms of domination."[7]

The primary addressees of liberation theology are, instead, Latin America's oppressed masses, "history's absent and anonymous," the "scourged Christs of the Indies," the exploited classes, the despised cultures, the outcast races. And the questions to which it would offer response are of another order than those of modern theology. How is God to be proclaimed as Parent of all and generator of brotherhood and sisterhood, in an inhuman, inhumane, and unjust world devoid of solidarity? How may one speak of God to the victims of the modern history of freedom? How may one speak of God from the other face, from the "lining," from the "underside" of history? How is that gospel to be announced that is a proclamation of life, in a situation that wears the seal of death? How to be Christians in a poor and impoverished world and not rebel against a misery that "cries to heaven"? These and many other questions remain to be posed.

The challenge of the theology of liberation, consequently, is not atheism, but idolatry — the implicit worship of that assembly of idols that sow death everywhere, and that call for human sacrifices on the altar of the maintenance of an order that favors only a few.

C. A third difference has its roots in the understanding maintained by European progressive theology and the Latin American theology of liberation, respectively, of the relationship between Christian hope and historical reality. It is Juan Luis Segundo, especially, who has called attention to this difference.[8] Segundo observes that, from a point of departure in the "eschatological proviso," European theology relativizes intrahistorical utopias, at the same time relegating them all to the same plane as if they were all equidistant from the Reign of God. In liberation theology, not all historical projects are seen to be at the same distance from the Reign of God. Thus liberation theology establishes a hierarchization of those projects: to the extent that any given projects achieve a higher proportion of justice, community, equality, freedom, and reconciliation among persons and peoples, those projects will be found to be nearer the Reign of God than those whose activity mounts an opposition to the values cited. In fact, Segundo posits a relationship of causality, however ephemeral and fragile, between historical liberation projects and the Reign of God.

D. Fourth, the theology of liberation finds European theologies in default when it comes to acknowledging the importance of a liberation praxis in the construction of the Reign of God. This, insists Sobrino, is a lacuna to be filled: the Reign of God calls for a practice calculated to lead to partial realizations of that Reign, through concrete historical mediations. After all, even though, being a utopia, the Reign of God cannot receive "adequate" (exhaustive) realization in the course of finite time, nevertheless it can and does stand as the "principle of historical realities, practices, attitudes, and values."[9] Thus, fidelity to the Reign comports an effort to "render [that reign] real, to be drawn ever and again by that fullness, and to be moved ever and again to its realization. The realization of the Reign of God is the ultimate goal of the theology of liberation; hence this theology's function as the ideological moment of an ecclesial, historical praxis" (Ellacuría).[10]

E. Fifth: liberation theology lodges with European theology a criticism of the intrasystematic captivity in which the latter is caught, being a theology constituted in a system of concepts — developed by way of interpretations of interpretations, as Leonardo Boff observes.[11] This criticism extends to its high degree of abstraction, which interferes with its ability to call the mechanisms of domination by name. It is likewise, and on the same basis, a criticism of the ultimate value accorded to Enlightenment consciousness.

F. Liberation theology's critique of progressive European theology focuses in a special manner on Moltmann's theology of hope, and on Metz's political theology.

First of all, it criticizes the difficulty encountered by these two theologies when it comes to proposing, beyond the prevailing project of the system and short of the eschatological horizon, a historical project of political, economic, cultural, and gender liberation.[12] In the judgment of Enrique Dussel, Moltmann's theology of hope operates only as a professional ethic of reaction, not as a movement calculated to subvert the system across the board.

Particularly mordant in his criticism of the theology of hope is Brazilian theologian Rubém Alves, according to whom Moltmann's "future" is already predetermined. It is an object, when it should be a horizon. The future Moltmann anticipates as already present has no capacity to reject the present, to call it on the carpet in its constitutive elements. In the theology of hope, Alves sees a tendency to docetism, since instead of incarnation being the generator of the future, it is the transcendent future that renders the human being aware of its incarnation.[13]

The theology of liberation shows Metz that his prophetic criticism is caught in a framework of the ambit of the national, so that it fails to notice the international injustice provoked by the First World, and that his deprivatizing system affects only internal elements of the system, not the system as such, or its roots.

G. But, while acknowledging the existence of differences, and of a moment of breach between liberation theology and progressive European theology, the former does not see the fundamental problem in a simple contraposition between the two. The line between oppression and liberation, as Pablo Richard indicates, is not drawn between continents, but between oppressors and oppressed, as well as between interior psychological "parts" of each one of us. It will be in order to recall that in Latin America, as well, a theology is being developed that is bound up with the centers of power and is dependent on Europe; and that in Europe a theology is being developed that is sensitive to, and bound up with, the Third World and the "peripheries," the world of the outcast.

The root of the main contradiction in the current theological confrontation lies in the dialectic between oppression and liberation. This explains why liberation theologians struggle so determinedly to avoid not only a certain chauvinism, but a kind of general European guilt complex, as well.

3. Dialogue and Communication

In conclusion, we may say that liberation theology's critical attitude toward progressive European theology, and its emphasis on the moment of breach with that theology, does not mean that it closes itself off from dialogue with it. On the contrary, lines of communication are growing ever broader and better established. In the various meetings of the Ecumenical Association of Third World Theologians, a hand is always extended to the theologians of Europe, and the calls for a dialogue between the theology of the periphery and that of the center are constant. There are certain cautions to be observed, however, as Enrique Dussel indicates:

The dialogues of the periphery have manifested the differences between Africa, Asia, and Latin America, as well as between the center and the periphery. They have also pointed to potential bridges to an understanding of each other's position, and thereby to an attainment of methods and categories (paradigms) capable of opening themselves to a future world theology—a new analogical totality to be built in the twenty-first century on the basis of the particularisms that have been declared and developed (among these, the particularisms of Europe and the United States).[14]

For the dialogue to be possible and fruitful, North Atlantic theologies must cease to function as cultural forms of domination over the Third World; and on the other hand, both theologies must acknowledge themselves to be particular responses to particular situations, inasmuch as it is only from a point of departure in particularisms that that future universal theology can be constructed for which Dussel steps forward as advocate.

II. THEOLOGY OF LIBERATION IN THE EYES OF EUROPEAN THEOLOGY

The theology of liberation has aroused a broad echo throughout Europe, although reactions have been very dissimilar and contradictory. Numerous monographic issues of practically all periodicals devoted to Christian thought, symposiums, congresses, theology courses, and pastoral encounters have all made the new theology an object of their study. Liberation theology has served as a source of inspiration for the theological reflection, life, and emancipating praxis of the base communities, as well as of the prophetical Christian movements that have arisen in the church since Vatican II.

A goodly proportion of the cultivators of liberation theology have been honored by various Catholic universities and schools of theology with honorary doctorates—which, besides being an honor bestowed on their recipients, means academic recognition of their theological enterprise. Theologians beyond all suspicion of playing to "Third-World-ism," such as Rahner, Schillebeeckx, Chenu, Duquoc, Alfaro, Metz, and Moltmann, have performed the not always very comfortable role of defenders of that theology.

But European theologians' reactions are very far from being unanimous, and range from suspicion, threat, and condemnation to the most enthusiastic support.

Let us review some of these reactions, ranging them on the basis of their varying degrees of affinity.

1. Indifference and Condemnation

With the first diffusion of the theology of liberation in Europe, in the early 1970s, not a few European theological sectors, those having close ties to official and academic theology, adopted an attitude of indifference mixed with an undisguised superiority complex: this new theology could really have nothing to contribute to the theological debate. Just as Jesus' contemporaries wondered, skeptically, whether anything good could come out of Nazareth, these theologians wondered how Latin America, a culturally and theologically underdeveloped continent, could possibly make any contribution to European theology. After all, Europe was the cradle of thought, of the scientific revolutions, of well-wrought theology, of the historico-critical methods, and so many other achievements. Their arrogance went beyond all bounds. They regarded liberation theology as a fad. Not a great deal of attention need be paid to it, since it was a transitory, rather insubstantial product.

Those who reacted in this fashion thereby laid bare the roots of a theological and ecclesial Eurocentrism. Their attitude connoted a great insensitivity toward the series of problems prevailing between North and South, between poor countries and rich countries, between developed peoples and underdeveloped peoples, the church of the First World and the church of the Third World. These theologians likewise demonstrated an indefensible refusal of solidarity with the most disadvantaged, and a disdain for Vatican II's invitation to engage in theological reflection on the basis of the identifying marks of each people. Their theological narrowness was out in the open now. To the mind of these theological sectors — and this was the basic problem — the questions posed by the theology of liberation had nothing to do with theology.

A variant on the stance upon which we are commenting is that of those who refuse to ascribe to liberation the status of theology, reducing it to a mere sociological theory of Latin American society, or considering its cultivators minor theologians. Such is the case with the former Secretary of the Spanish Bishops conference, Fernando Sebastián, who has gone so far as to say that liberation theologians are not theologians in the strict sense because they fail to concern themselves with grand theological themes like that of the Holy Trinity.

In the aftermath of the Vatican's negative judgment on the theology of liberation, some of the sectors to which we are referring, at first merely indifferent, have adopted a belligerent attitude. They have approached liberation theology in terms of a distorted, prejudice-ridden reading of that theology that seems to them to authorize an attack on it more out of visceral feeling than by way of solid argumentation.

They see in liberation theology a grave, potentially lethal threat to the Christian faith, inasmuch as, in their judgment, the faith is placed in the service of a revolutionary politics and a Marxist ideology. It is along these lines, we must recognize, that we have the "Instruction on Certain Aspects of the Theology of Liberation," published by the Sacred Congregation of the Doctrine of the Faith, which accuses the theology of liberation of:

—Having recourse to a hermeneutics dominated by rationalism;

—Having uncritically adopted elements of the Marxist ideology, which is ruinous for the faith;

—Making an exclusively political reading of the Bible;

—Understanding the Latin American popular church as a class church;

—Reducing the Christian faith to a purely earthly project — evacuating it of its transcendent dimension.

The European sectors that move along the horizon of the Roman document have made common cause with the most combatively antiliberationist Latin American sectors, represented by Cardinal López Trujillo, who asserts that, through the theology of liberation, Marxism has infiltrated the very heart of the church, and the class struggle has replaced the word of God.[15] This posture is reaffirmed in the so-called Declaration of the Andes, where it is said that, in certain theologies of liberation, the meaning of a liberation praxis is plainly an offshoot of Marxism, and comes to constitute a fundamental risk for the faith of the people of God.[16] In the meeting from which that declaration emerged, European theologians (including Spaniards) joined their Latin American counterparts.

In Spain, the sectors radically opposed to liberation theology are organized around the University of Navarre and the Seminary of Toledo, under the tutelage of the Primate of Spain, Cardinal Marcelo González.

While acknowledging a certain distance between them from the positions just cited, we must also refer to the successive pronouncements of the former Secretary of the Spanish Bishops Conference, Fernando Sebastián. In all respect for the moral attitude of Latin American theologians in favoring the liberation of the poor, Sebastián has enunciated disqualifications more in the spirit of Cardinal Ratzinger than of other European bishops and theologians, who, while critical, maintain a posture of dialogue and openness. This is how Sebastián expressed himself in an "Open Letter to Ignacio Ellacuría, S.J.":

> What many of us in the church think is that the theological development of the commitment to the poor being made by some Latin American theologians does not seem to us to be adequate, but rather, inadequate, mistaken, and dangerous.[17]

A suspicion colored with more nuances appears in the Declaration of the International Theological Commission, "Human Promotion and Christian Salvation" (1977), which calls attention to a supposed ambivalence in the use of the social sciences in theological work, and manifests its dismay at the utilization of Marxism in theological reflection. In the more recent Roman documents— the "Instruction on Christian Freedom, and Liberation" (March 22, 1986), and John Paul II's letter to the Bishops of Brazil, "Orientations for the Ecclesial Life and for the Task of Evangelization" (April 9, 1986) — one discerns a more comprehensive, less condemnatory, attitude toward the theology of liberation.

But the sectors to which we have now referred, while exercising more than a little influence on European theology and on the European church as a whole, and which are therefore not to be ignored, nonetheless fail to exhaust the gamut of positions taken by European theologians vis-à-vis the theology of liberation.

2. Openness and Dialogue

Accordingly, we shall now address the positions of theologians who maintain a different attitude — a more open, more dialogal, and less impervious attitude, such as that adopted by so-called progressive theology. Its position regarding the theology of liberation may be summarized in the following terms.

—It acknowledges, in general lines, the theological authenticity of liberation theology.

—It attaches a positive value to, and to a considerable extent adopts, the great intuitions of that theology (the option for the poor, the centrality of a liberation praxis, and so on), to the point that these exercise a notable influence on the intellectual endeavors of not a few theologians.

—It shows itself open to the challenges thrown out by liberation theology to the church and theologies of the First World.

—It manifests a decided will to dialogue, claiming to see undeniable contributions, as well as limitations, in the theology of liberation.

Testimonials of Support and Solidarity

Everyone is aware—and we have taken note of it above—of the explicit support expressed by prestigious European theologians for liberation theology and its cultivators, especially in the face of attacks from Rome. Rahner pronounced in favor of the orthodoxy of the theology of liberation in a letter addressed to the Archbishop of Lima, Cardinal Landázuri, in which he observed that "the voice of the poor ought to be heard in theology in the context of the Latin American Church," and that "a theology that ought to be in the service of concrete evangelization may never prescind from the cultural and social context of evangelization, in order that the latter be effective in the situation in which the addressee lives."[18] He likewise declared to the Archbishop of Lima his conviction of the great importance of the social sciences in theology.

In a testimonial of warm solidarity, French theologian M.-D. Chenu, recently deceased, says he regards Gustavo Gutiérrez as one of the theologians who have most enlightened him and been his best companions along his theological journey, which has led him to discover historical praxis as part of the "understanding of the faith" (intellectus fidei).[19]

Christian Duquoc denies any basis for the accusations of temporal messianism and "Marxifilation" lodged against the theology of liberation, and decries attempts to saddle that theology with succumbing anew to Christendom's everlasting temptation: that of reducing Christianity to a political utopia, the agent of a perfect society.[20]

Edward Schillebeeckx acknowledges that liberation theology is a young theology, and that it therefore may manifest certain "childhood diseases here or there." But in the very next line he calls attention to the enormous harvest of results it has reaped in such a short time. In fact, "it is studied all over the world. Even its weak points are examined. What theologian has never made a mistake?"[21]

Juan Alfaro considers liberation theology to be eminently self-authenticating, and does not think it has any need to present its credentials to other theologies. He stresses the authenticity of its commitment to the poor and its emergence from the people. "As long as this occurs, the theology of liberation will be a living theology."[22]

Nor are these pronouncements simple rhetorical declarations—shall we say, by way of "moral support." Underlying them and other, similar utterances that we could cite, what strikes the investigator is the remarkable influence that liberation theology is exerting on the very orientation of European theology. Let us see this more concretely in two theologians belonging to two different Christian confessions: the Protestant Moltmann and the Catholic Metz. Both are paradigmatic examples of the new European sensitivity to problems of the Third World, with a corresponding availability to penetration by the theology of liberation. In both of these theologians, quite a significant evolution has occurred in these respects.

Jürgen Moltmann: From Condemnation to Defense of the Theology of Liberation

In an open letter to Argentinian theologian José Míguez Bonino, dating from 1975 and striking a broad echo in European and Latin American theological circles, Moltmann reacted with severity to the criticisms leveled against his own theology by the theology of liberation. In this letter, he labeled liberation theology "theological provincialism," and issued a criticism, across the board, of its use of Marxism. That theology, he said then, contains more of the sociological theories of Western socialists than it does of the story of the life of the Latin American people.[23] Rather than detailed, precise analyses of the situation of the people, what Moltmann saw in these theologians' works were "declamations of seminary Marxism as *Weltanschauung*." The process of liberation postulated for Latin America by Gustavo Gutiérrez in his *A Theology of Liberation* seemed to Moltmann to have been simply lifted wholesale from the European history of liberty.

Ten years later, Moltmann hands down a very different judgment on the theology of liberation than the one he enunciated in that letter. Avoiding all ambiguity, he declares for its authenticity. Here is his testimony, which he expresses in terms by whose eloquence I personally am touched.

> The theologians of liberation have sunk their roots in the base communities, which are a promising sign of reform of the church and society, and which inject life in a way that has something of the miraculous about it in a rather apathetic, centralistic church. And that is where the theology of liberation now has its organizational relationship. Different from Marxism? I should say so! Today, then, I can state that liberation theology is a solid, sound theology, and I drop, part and parcel, the complexities I formulated in that letter of mine. I know that many objections exist against the theology of liberation, especially with regard to the popular church. However, I believe that the experience being lived under the name of popular church is a new experience of the Holy Spirit—a new experience of Pentecost. Here is the community of the faithful that seeks to be subject of its own history.[24]

Moltmann's new viewpoint coincides with that of Metz, as we shall see below. The evolution of the theologian of hope begins to be perceived in his *The Crucified God*, where Sobrino is happy to be able to discern liberation theology's positive influence. Here Moltmann takes up once more the questions of the "negative dialectic" and "critical theory" of Adorno and Horkheimer, together with the viewpoints of classic dialectical theology and existential philosophy, and develops, from a point of departure in those interlocutors, a *theologia crucis* calculated to transcend theism and atheism, rediscovering the subversive and liberating strength of the cross, and blazing the new trail along which the historical theologies of the death of Christ will travel. "Without a perception of the pain of the negative," declares Moltmann, "Christian hope cannot be realistic, or function in a liberating manner."[25]

We see a closer affinity for the theology of liberation is seen in Moltmann's *The Church, in the Power of the Spirit*, where he captures perfectly the open, pluridimensional character of the concept of liberation as employed by Latin American theologians. He tells us:

[The concept of liberation as employed by Latin American theologians], erected on a foundation of the suppression of an exploitation based on the dominion of some classes over others, and proceeding by way of the political elimination of oppression and dictatorship, and the removal of racism, [extends] all the way to liberation from the slavery of sin, [which is a liberation] experienced in faith, and to eschatological liberation from the power of death.[26]

For Moltmann, the option for liberation means taking sides with the lowly and oppressed, at the same time as supposing the conquest of a free, human, and humane future for them. He believes that he finds both of these aspects in the theology of liberation. Hence it is, in Moltmann's judgment, that the new theology is "capable of overcoming the particularistic mentality that divides and dominates humanity, as well as the narrow, fanatical mentality that surfaces in any conflict situation."[27]

Moltmann acknowledges that European political theology and Latin American liberation theology, while being developed in different contexts, are engaged in a common struggle: the battle "for life against death, for liberation against oppression."

Johannes B. Metz: The System's Victims as Locus Theologicus

In the thought of Catholic theologian Johannes B. Metz, as well, a considerable evolution has occurred since his transcendental anthropological orientation of the 1970s under the influence of his mentor Rahner. This process may be traced from his early endeavors as a political theologian who underscored the public, critical, and practical character of faith, and now in his latest works, where he delineates a paradigm of prophetic Christianity conceived as transcending bourgeois religion, restoring to the sufferers of history, the "losers," the victims of the systems, their status as protagonists of that history, and doing justice to the dead.

Metz, declares J. Ramos Regidor, is the "European Catholic theologian who has best succeeded in expressing the challenge of the [local and regional] churches of the poor to the churches of the rich countries."[28] Thus, I doubt that it is still possible today to address to his theology the same criticisms as were leveled by certain Latin American theologians in the early 1970s. Far from hardening his position in the face of the onslaught, he has accepted these criticisms with great intellectual honesty, and has come to the realization that the Christians of his country have to live with the suspicion that they are oppressors.

As has no other European theologian, and in step with liberation theology, Metz has implemented a penetrating criticism of modern reason, and called attention to the limitations of the processes of the Enlightenment — processes which, in his judgment, threaten theology with a twin reduction: that of privatization, which eviscerates messianic religion of its consubstantial dimension of public criticism; and that of rationalism, which walks hand in hand with too radical a renunciation of myths and symbols, by reason of the cognoscitive overload of the abstract world of the modern sciences.[29] One of the central tasks Metz assigns theology in the face of this twofold reduction is that of unmasking the idea of a completely secularized, rationalized society as a piece of simple "rationality" and show it for what it is: a genuine myth, generated by a nondialectical absolutization of the Enlightenment.

Metz believes that the local and regional churches of the poor, the base communities, and Latin American liberation theology constitute a powerful aid for the defeat of the double reduction we have just indicated, inasmuch as, in these churches, communities, and theology, a new relationship is being forged between grace and liberation, between experience of redemption and experience of liberation. The new relationship, "naturally, is not exempt from conflicts" between religion and society, between mysticism and politics. The reason is that it is a new way of dovetailing things that tend to present themselves to us as compartmentalized: theory and praxis, logic and mysticism, spirit and resistance, prayer and politics.[30]

The base communities, and the liberation theology that has made its commitment to them, work a considerable upheaval in the traditional way of understanding authority in theology. The authority with which they are invested comes to them from the voiceless authority of those who suffer, through whom is heard the voice of the Spirit and of the holiness of a political mystique. Liberation theologians can appeal to the authority of a helpless Jesus, a wisdom born of discipleship, and the consensus of a goodly number of bishops who have immersed their own lives in the life of the poor.[31] Theology, Metz insists, "shares in this authority to the extent that it shares in the praxis and the construction of this base church community."[32]

This "new way of doing theology," and the new concept of authority in the theological task, involve a change of the locus and position, subject or agent, and even object or topic of traditional theology, and thereby dictate a revision of the subjects or agents, loci, contexts, and interests of theology.

Metz continues to regard professional academic theology, which he represents, as valid and necessary. To it he ascribes the following functions, among others:

—That of integrating the church's new experiences, and the new praxis, with the comprehensive memory of the church, lest these experiences and this praxis remain merely transitory and ephemeral, and thereby risk disintegration;

—That of bringing these experiences into confrontation with the "faith reserves" of the church, that they may benefit from the support of tradition;

—That of taking care that the ecclesial "base" not fall into the conceptual isolation typical of a sect.

But the base communities, together with the theology of liberation, show academic theology the modesty of its position, and its need for a productive self-limitation. In other words, academic theology is still necessary, but now, as a subsidiary, instead of as the only way of doing theology.[33]

Metz considers it necessary to take the step from a culturally monocentric church—the church and theology that prevailed during the centuries of a hegemony of Hellenism and European culture—to a church and theology of genuine world dimensions: that is, to a culturally polycentric church and theology.[34] Thus the hegemony of European theology over the theologies of the poor countries would evanesce, and a mutual inspiration and reciprocal assimilation would prevail among the various particular theologies.

This new perspective occasions a "Copernican revolution" in our understanding of the church, and entails the defeat of the imperialism exercised by the churches of Europe and the United States over those of the Third World:

> The Catholic Church no longer "has" simple "branches" in the countries that lie far from Europe and North America. . . . It does not simply "have" a church of the Third World, but rather, empirically speaking, the latter "is" a church of the Third World, whose historical origin is Western European.[35]

Metz advocates a "second Reformation" as an indispensable requirement if Christianity is to continue to assert its proper historical identity in this step or passage from bourgeois society to the postbourgeois world. But he thinks that this Reform would come not from Wittenberg, or from Rome, or from the Christian Europe of the West, or at the hands of great reformers like those of the past. It will come rather from a Christianity of liberation such as Christianity is experienced and formulated by the churches of the poor, in the base communities—which, from within the base stratum of society and the church, strive to combine their religious praxis and their social praxis, and which, in the communion of their Eucharistic community, welcome conflict. Thus, Christians would cease to be an object of social and ecclesial aid and become the active subjects of their own religious and political history.[36]

The Catholicism of our wealthy lands stands at a great historical crossroads—that of accepting, or rejecting, this reforming mission of the poor churches and integrating it into the universal church—that of welcoming, or spurning, this new manner of understanding and experiencing freedom, and of renouncing, or lodging, the objection that this mission is but a particular manifestation on the part of the churches of the Third World.

Just as the theology of liberation takes the poor, and a preferential option for the poor, as its theological and epistemological locus par excellence, so Metz, for his part, proposes to "regard the scenario of history with the victims' eyes," and has resolved never to do theology with his back to the sufferings of the poor and oppressed of the world.[37] The affinities are manifest.

3. Lacunae in the Theology of Liberation

There are not lacking, however, among progressive European theologians, those who, while in ideological and vital harmony with liberation theology and its liberation hermeneutic, have called attention to what they regard as important lacunae in Latin American theologians' discourse. Let us examine some of these desiderata.[38]

A. Liberation theology justifies its discourse about God with an appeal to the liberation praxis maintained by believers. As Gustavo Gutiérrez puts it, God is approached not by complicated philosophical proofs or abstract lines of reasoning, but "by contemplating and practicing God." In the same perspective, Jon Sobrino asserts: "The God of liberation is made known in the praxis of liberation, the good and merciful God in the praxis of goodness and mercy, the hidden, crucified God in steadfastness in persecution and in martyrdom, and the God who implements utopia in the praxis of hope." Well and good.

But such formulations scarcely so much as scratch the surface of the debate stirred by the atheistic negation. Modernity's criticism of the discourse upon God, or, more concretely, the criticism of religion on the part of the so-called "masters of suspicion," emerges unscathed. True, certain texts of the liberation theologians make passing reference to that criticism, but without any suggestion that it might be relevant for liberation theology. After all, it "has no bearing" on this theology. However, as we are about to see, it surely has.

Precisely by failing squarely to confront this challenge, liberation theology's discourse upon God has been characterized — unfairly, in my judgment — as fundamentalistic.

Here we seem to have one of the causes — nor perhaps the least of them — of the difficulties that surface for a critical dialogue between the theology of liberation and Enlightenment and post-Enlightenment "reason." When such a dialogue is initiated, it usually focuses on social and political presuppositions, rather than on religious elements, where the problem becomes especially relevant for theology.

B. Some European theologians have charged liberation theology with an impoverished epistemology. The theology of liberation, in the judgment of A. Fierro, "sticks on the level of Christian awareness, functioning as a mere amplifier, and rarely reaching a strictly theological range of reflection."[39]

These same theologians refer to the use, on the part of a considerable number of cultivators of liberation theology, of a naive and precritical biblical foundation, which seems to neglect scientific exegesis.

There are authors who radicalize this same criticism, relegating the theology of liberation to the status of a proclamatory and testimonial discourse. These writers refuse to consider liberation theology as a proper theology, regarding it as lacking the minimal exercise of criticism that would be required in order to have a rigorous theology.[40]

C. The theology of liberation assigns priority to Christianity's messianic force, and lays out the biblical traditions and experiences that are most subversive and destabilizing of the established order, such as the exodus, the preaching of the prophets, Jesus' liberation message and practice, and so on. So far, no objections. On the contrary, thanks to the theology of liberation, a biblical current sidetracked and stifled for long centuries recovers its historical operationality.

But the theology of liberation seems to take it "as a given that messianism and the affirmation of God coincide." In other words, it simply begs a unity between liberation praxis and discourse upon God. However, that congruence and that unity not only are not self-evident, but have been explicitly questioned by modernity and rejected. Bloch, for example, regards messianism as the core of Jewish and Christian religion, and admits that, as this core has been handed down to us, it must be dealt with. But it implies, for Bloch, not the affirmation, but rather the negation of God. Bloch presents God as a "utopianly hypostatized ideal of the forgotten human being."[41] According to Bloch, atheism constitutes the authentic presupposition of the religious utopia: "Without atheism there is no place for messianism." The atheism he postulates is not an atheism that limits itself to simple negation, but one that assumes the legacy of religion in its messianic substance.

Under this assault, it will be of no avail simply to assert the coincidence, the congruency, suggested above. That congruency will have to be demonstrated.[42] Along these same lines, liberation theology is asked to clarify a question that so far remains obscure: that of the relationship between the biblical promises and the movement of our history—that is, the question of how to translate biblical messianism, and its force for transgressing the prevailing order, into a historical praxis of liberation without falling into naive political messianisms. The question must be addressed in terms of the originality of Jesus' messianism—as is done, in my judgment, in fine style by Christian Duquoc.[43]

D. European theologians also perceive in the theology of liberation an ambiguity with reference to its own social and political implications. For example, it does not seem clear whether liberation theology adopts, albeit with all the correctives necessary for the case of Latin America, the democratic system as the ideal form of coexistence in freedom, or whether it inclines rather toward certain forms of revolutionary populism, whose fundamental element is the spontaneous mobilization of the people, even in the absence of any clear notion of the end result.

4. European Theology of Liberation?

Finally, we must make mention of those European theologians who inquire into the possibilities and viability of a theology of liberation in the First World— and more specifically, in Europe itself. These theologians begin with an acknowledgment of the complexity of the problem, and prefer to speak of the "possibility" of a liberation theology for our lands, without venturing to give a categorical response.

They are not unaware that Latin American and European theology are situated in very different contexts, as Clodovis Boff has also recently emphasized. Boff cites a threefold difference: historical, social, and religious. They likewise regard as inadequate the mimetic transposition of the Latin American theology of liberation to our First World. But are the conditions at hand for the actual development of a European liberation theology?

A. For liberation theologians, theology is a "second act," and this in a twofold sense. In the first place, theological discourse appears after one has already had the experience of faith lived as practice within the historical processes of liberation. Theology is a "reflex" act, a form of contemplation. In the second place, theology is not the most important thing. More important than theology is the evangelization of the poor and the liberation of the oppressed. Theology appears on the scene as ancillary to that evangelization and liberation, and therefore as something secondary. And the liberation aimed at "is in itself a social, historical, lay, and autonomous process, endowed with its own rationality."[44]

On this basis, a first condition for the possibility of a theology of liberation in the First World would be the actual existence of liberation processes driving toward the transformation of current structures, and the significant, relevant presence of Christians in these processes. Not that these processes need simply march in perfect step with those of Latin America, of course.

B. As Girardi has so appositely emphasized, the theology of liberation takes its point of departure in two presuppositions, respectively methodological and historical. Its methodological presupposition is that reflection on the religious and Christian phenomenon ought to be entertained in the light of the dialectic prevailing between domination and liberation. Its historical presupposition is that, in this context, Jesus comes forward as an alternative to the society of his time.[45]

On this basis, it will be in order to inquire whether the dialectic of domination and liberation is indeed at work in the First World; then whether that dialectic is central enough to constitute a call to take sides; and finally, what the principal manifestations of this dialectic are. One thing seems plain enough: in the First World, situations of oppression are characterized by a great complexity, so that a bipolarization as neatly defined as that operative in the Third World will not be easy to establish. Among the factors that render the verification of this bipolarization difficult, Girardi cites the following.

The diversity and fragmentation of problems, needs, and conflicts; the difficulty of determining a historical subject that can be denominated "the poor"; the growing importance, in modern society, of the middle classes, and the difficulty of fitting them into categories of the conflict between oppressors and oppressed; a crisp diversification of the popular classes, especially of the working class, which precludes their categorization as group protagonists of a common historical project; the absence of a revolutionary project worthy of credibility even among the parties of the left, which deprives the option for the poor of concrete political content.[46]

C. Indeed, the response of certain European theologians whose positions are progressive to the questions indicated here is to proclaim the need, in Europe, of developing a "prophetic political theology"[47] endowed with certain peculiar traits:

—This prophetic political theology "would take the challenge of liberation theology altogether seriously, and reflect upon God and the First World under the sign of the preferential option for the poor."[48]

—While renouncing neither the European history of liberty nor the Enlightenment, it would thereupon take cognizance of the dialectic of the Enlightenment, as well. That is, it would be equal to the challenges thrown down by Enlightenment and post-Enlightenment reason, and be able to respond to them with lucidity and a spirit of criticism. While accepting the Enlightenment's unquestionable achievements, it would discover, as well, its limitations and reductionisms.[49]

—It would keep its sights trained on the praxis of liberation, and remain free of the abstraction in which European theology is so frequently caught.[50]

III. RECEPTION OF THE THEOLOGY OF LIBERATION IN CHRISTIAN RENEWAL MOVEMENTS

How has liberation theology been received in the various sectors of the European church? Here it will be in order carefully to distinguish, as we did when examining the reception on the part of the theologians, various reactions.

There are sectors that, in an emotional way, and without the application of any rigorous argumentation, accuse the theology of liberation of a politicization of Christianity, of Marxism, of communism, and generally employing "buzzwords" of this kind. Evil lurks everywhere, and behind any expression of faith in terms of liberation nothing is seen but anti-Christian, laicist conspiracies that bid fair to undermine the foundations of "the faith." The complainants are the same persons who resist the concept of an inculturation of the faith along the lines set forth by Vatican II. They have a Eurocentric conception of the church, and still dream of the restoration of a colonial church in Latin America. Their principal concern is for orthodoxy, and for the preservation of a model of the church that would consist of a Christendom in alliance with the dominant classes.[51]

Some church movements have appropriated the language of liberation theology without adopting the content of that language in all of its historical density and theological depth. They have emptied the language of liberation theology of its eschatologico-revolutionary thrust, and given it a spiritualistic tinge. These movements are incapable of grasping the socioanalytic categories employed by the theology of liberation and the historical mediations of liberation. Liberation remains stuck in the personal, interior sphere, and does not impinge on society. Historical praxis is practically left out of account. Christian solidarity and sharing are reduced to a communion in faith bereft of any translation into visible activities and deeds of support for the countries of the Third World.

At the opposite extreme, there have been Christian groups in Europe which have made the theology of liberation their gospel, receiving it in a fundamentalistic spirit, and ignoring the contextual differences between European and Latin American reality. These groups have limited themselves to importing a crassly simplified version of the themes, the series of problems, and the experiences of liberation theology, without any reflection of their own, expecting to be able validly to apply these themes, approaches to problems, and experiences here and now "as is." Among the risks run in this focus are two: that of ignoring European reality, and that of renouncing the task of fashioning a liberation response to that reality in terms of faith. We must say in all fairness that this mimetic, uncreative reception of the theology of liberation on the part of European Christians occurs only in very isolated cases, and may be dismissed as irrelevant.

Where the theology of liberation has doubtless found a mightier echo has been in the Christian renewal movements of Europe launched in the spirit of Vatican II. These range from the specialized apostolic movements of Catholic Action, and organizations like Justice and Peace, to Christians for Socialism, and the base communities, across a broad spectrum of church groups committed to the struggle for a more just, more egalitarian society of brothers and sisters. They have all offered, in their different accents, a serene, warm, vital, and unfanatical welcome to the theology of liberation. The movements to which we are referring read liberation theology from a point of departure in the reality that they themselves are experiencing, but with their gaze fixed on the reality of Latin America. Actually, their rereading of Latin American liberation theology has for its goal a discovery of the meaning of that theology for European society and churches, and at the same time, of the contribution that this society and these churches can make to the transformation of Latin American reality.

I believe that the theology of liberation has fertilized the base church movements, serving as an inducement to them to undertake their community experience of faith; as a help in their reformulation of the Christian message; and as a challenge in their commitment to the poor.

I should like to single out here, for particular consideration, the role played by the theology of liberation in the European base communities. And I shall begin by saying that one of the most favorable effects of the encounter of these communities with liberation theology has been that of the manifold forms of solidarity maintained by these groups with the struggles of the Third World. The theology of liberation has instilled in our base communities a deep sensitivity to the situation of domination/dependency experienced by Latin America. This continent feels a very close kinship with the one across the seas. We might say that it feels as if it were the next patient in line, waiting to be healed. Nor does that sensitivity abide on the plane of feeling alone. It is being translated operationally, in multiple forms—in some cases, through the creation of committees of solidarity and support; in others, through the foundation of centers for study and for information on Latin American problems; in others, through a participation, on one's own ground, in social, political, and cultural initiatives; in still others, through pastoral work in various local churches of Latin America.

In order to be creative, and mutually challenging, solidarity with the struggles of the Third World ought to have, as Ramos Regidor indicates, the following characteristics. It should be based on a critical awareness of the situations of a distant reality. It should influence the political exterior of Europe, with the object of having a critical impact on the logic of the contraposition between the blocs.[52]

Another of the results of contact between European base communities and the theology of liberation has been an affirmation of church communion. Let us see why. From their birth, our base communities have had an antihierarchical tone. That is, they have a strong propensity to fall into overly critical attitudes and behaviors vis-à-vis the church hierarchy, from the bishops to the pope. This is understandable, of course, given the initial reaction of hierarchical organs, and the subsequent harassment to which they have been subjected by the same, along with the low prophetical temperature of the official church.

The theology of liberation tends instead to accentuate the element of communion with the hierarchy, although without renouncing criticism of the hierarchy. It customarily does positive readings of episcopal, curial, and papal documents, even when these are admonitory in its regard and fraught with overtones of condemnation. We all know of Leonardo Boff's acceptance of the temporary silence imposed on him by the Vatican, and the justification he gave for his attitude of reverence for the condemnatory measure: "I would rather journey with the church, than walk alone with my theology."

This stance has left its imprint on the European base communities. Without renouncing the intraecclesial critique — an intrinsic component of faith, a constant in the history of Christianity, and a necessary moment in the construction of a prophetic church — they make an effort to build bridges of dialogue with the hierarchy, and to emphasize the bonds of communion, albeit it of a communion in dialectical tension.

The welcome extended to liberation theology on the part of the base communities has redounded to the benefit of the latter in terms of an articulation of interrelationships binding communities, theologians, and theology. Theology is accustomed to be regarded in European church circles as the exclusive task of professional theologians. Theology and base communities present themselves as two independent quantities. The life of the communities goes one way, and theology and theologians go another. Everything in its place. The gap between the theologians and the base communities is notorious. Very few are the professionals in theology who show themselves sensitive to the community movement, and still fewer are the ones who live their faith in the very bosom of the communities. This situation has given rise to an anti-theological current among the Christian base groups — understandably enough, given the elitist manner in which professional theologians have understood theology.

In this state of affairs, the new way of doing theology in Latin America has contributed to a consciousness-raising with respect to the irreplaceable role the communities are playing in the theological enterprise. As Clodovis Boff asserts, the epistemic subject of theology is the community.[53] Reflection on faith is not something entrusted to theologians alone. It is a demand made on all Christians, who are all called to give an account of their faith. The base communities are not simply receivers or addressees of a theology done by professionals. They also reflect on their faith, in terms of the living experience of believing as community. That reflection enriches the faith. Before all else, theology is a collective, community reflection carried out along various channels: liturgical celebrations, encounters for purposes of reflection, group projects, community readings of the Bible, collective declarations, and so on.

This manner of understanding the theological task is in continuity with the Christianity of the earliest decades. As we have had it demonstrated by "form history" and "redaction history," the primitive Christian communities shared actively and creatively in the early theological development of the faith, and their labors were reflected in the redaction of the gospels.

In their discovery of their role as active subjects of Christian reflection, the base communities have no intention of supplanting, belittling, or denying the role that falls to professional theologians in this reflection. They are merely resituating the specific function of professional theologians within the community, where the latter are called to live their faith together with the rest of believers. The task of the professional theologians is to "help the community to think its faith with seriousness—that is, in a critical, articulate manner."[54]

In the same spirit as the theology of liberation, our base communities are beginning to understand theology in its twofold dimension: as "collective practice" and as "organic practice."

Finally, let us turn our attention to one final element of the topic of the reception of liberation theology in Europe: the Latin American proposition concerning the option for the poor, which has penetrated very deep into our communities. Solidarity with the poor used to be regarded, in our communities, as a question of ethics, and the practice of that solidarity presented itself as a moral exigency flowing from the social ethic of the gospel. The turnabout produced on this point under the influence of the theology of liberation is familiar to all. The option for the poor has ceased to function as a mere slogan for action. Its place is no longer merely the field of ethics or pastoral theory. It constitutes the hermeneutic and epistemological locus of faith and theology. Before all else, the option for the poor is a theological and christological truth: it is rooted in the mystery of God, a God who has wrought a self-manifestation historically in someone poor (Jesus of Nazareth), and who thereby assumes the social condition of a poor person, and a God who is just, and therefore partial to the poor. An indissoluble, rock-solid unity obtains between God and the poor. Thus, between Jesus and the poor a direct and immediate relationship prevails. An understanding of God and the poor, Jesus the Christ and the poor, in separation from one another would mean watering down one of the basic and most original nuclei of Christian revelation.

From this it follows, as Jorge Pixley and Clodovis Boff declare: "Far from being incidental and adjectival for Christians, the option for the poor is central in the mission of the church, and this by reason of the fact that it is intimately bound up with the very heart of God and the center of revealed mystery."[55]

— Translated by Robert R. Barr

NOTES

1. Juan Luis Segundo, *De la sociedad a la teología* (Buenos Aires: 1970), pp. 11, 12, 15.

2. Johannes B. Metz, "Theology in the Modern Age," *Concilium*, no. 171 (1984), p. 34.

3. Claude Geffré, "A Prophetic Theology," *Concilium*, no. 96 (1974), p. 303.

4. Jon Sobrino, "Theological Understanding in European and Latin American Theology," in *The True Church and the Poor* (Maryknoll, N.Y.: Orbis Books, 1984), pp. 7-38.

5. Gustavo Gutiérrez, *The Power of the Poor in History: Selected Writings*, trans. Robert R. Barr (Maryknoll, N.Y.: Orbis Books, 1983), esp. pp. 167-221.

6. Gutiérrez, *The Truth Shall Make You Free* (Maryknoll, N.Y.: Orbis Books, 1990), p. 24.

7. Ibid.

8. Juan Luis Segundo, "Capitalism-Socialism: A Theologica Crux," *Concilium*, no. 96 (1974), pp. 105-23.

9. Sobrino, "Teología de la liberación y teología europea progresista," *Misíon Abierta* 1984/1, pp. 11-26.

10. Ibid.

11. Leonardo Boff, *Teología de la liberación y del cautiverio* (Madrid, 1978), p. 94.

12. Enrique Dussel, "Domination-Liberation: A New Approach," *Concilium*, no. 96 (1974), pp. 34-56.

13. Rubém Alves, *Cristianismo, ¿opio o liberación?* (Salamanca, 1973), pp. 95-114.

14. Dussel, "Theologies of the 'Periphery' and the 'Center': Encounter or Confrontation?" *Concilium*, no. 171 (1984), pp. 87-97.

15. See *Adista*, October 11, 12, 13, 1982.

16. See the report on this meeting in *Vida Nueva*, no. 1498, p. 35. A translation of the document appears in Alfred Hennelly, ed., *Liberation Theology: A Documentary History* (Maryknoll, N.Y.: Orbis Books, 1990), pp. 444-50.

17. The daily, *Ya*, December 22, 1985.

18. See Hennelly, *Liberation Theology*, pp. 351-52.

19. M.-D. Chenu, "La autoridad del evangelio y la teología," in various authors, *Vida y reflexión: Aportes de la teología de la liberación al pensamiento teológico actual* (Lima, 1983), p. 19.

20. Christian Duquoc, "Mesianismo y teología de la liberación," in various authors, *Vida y reflexión*, pp. 101-20.

21. Edward Schillebeeckx, "Una opción equivocada," *Misión Abierta* 1985/1, p. 102.

22. Juan Alfaro, in various authors, *Liberación y cautiverio*, p. 582.

23. Jürgen Moltmann, "An Open Letter to José Míguez Bonino" (March 29, 1975), reprinted in Hennelly, *Liberation Theology*, pp. 195-204.

24. Idem, "Dalla teologia politica all'etica politica," *Il Regno*, no. 507 (1984), pp. 205ff.

25. Idem, *The Crucified God* (London: SCM Press, 1974) p. 5.

26. Idem, *The Church in the Power of the Spirit* (London: SCM Press, 1977), p. 17.

27. Ibid.

28. J. Ramos Regidor, "Europa y las teologías de la liberación," *Iglesia Viva*, nos. 116/117 (1985), p. 177. This work by Ramos Regidor, together with his *Gesù e il risveglio degli opressi* (Milan, 1981), have been of great utility to me for a study of the relations between liberation theology and European theology.

29. Metz, "Theology in the Modern Age," p. 33.

30. Ibid., pp. 38-39.

31. Idem, "Un nuevo modo de hacer teología: Tres tesis," in various authors, *Vida y reflexión*, p. 54; see, along these same lines, *Concilium*, no. 180 (1985), devoted to "The Teaching Authority of the Believers," especially Schillebeeckx, "The Teaching Authority of All," pp. 12-22; and Sobrino, "The Doctrinal Authority of the People of God in Latin America," pp. 54-62.

32. Metz, "Nuevo modo de hacer teología," p. 53.

33. Ibid., pp. 55-56.

34. Idem, "Theology in the Modern Age," p. 37.

35. Idem, "Facing a Torn World," *Concilium*, no. 170 (1983), p. 27.

36. Idem, *Al di là della religione borghese* (Brescia, 1981), pp. 62-82.

37. Idem, "Facing the Jews: Christian Theology after Auschwitz," *Concilium*, no. 175 (1984), pp. 26-33.

38. See J. J. Sánchez, "Teología política y teología de la liberación: Un discurso crítico liberador sobre Dios," in various authors, *El Dios de la teología de la liberación* (Salamanca, 1986), pp. 118-20.

39. A. Fierro, *El evangelio beligerante* (Estella, 1975), p. 382. (*ET, The Militant Gospel* [Maryknoll, N.Y.: Orbis Books, 1977].)

40. Fierro calls Gustavo Gutiérrez' first book, *A Theology of Liberation: History, Politics and Salvation* (Maryknoll, N.Y.: Orbis Books, 1973; original Spanish version published in 1971), an excellent testimonial and profession of faith of a politically committed Christianity, and lists it in the category of rhetorical theology (Fierro, *El evangelio beligerante*, pp. 277-78); Fierro offers a similar evaluation of liberation theology in his *Presentación de la teología* (Barcelona, 1980).

41. Ernst Bloch, *El principio esperanza*, vol. 3 (Madrid, 1980); see chap. 7 of my *Cristianismo: profecía y utopía* (Estella, 1987), entitled, "Utopía y esperanza en el cristianismo según Ernst Bloch" ("Utopia and Hope in Christianity according to Ernst Bloch").

42. See Duquoc, "El Dios de Jesús y la crisis de Dios en nuestro tiempo," in various authors, *Jesucristo en la historia y en la fe* (Salamanca, 1977), p. 50. In this excellent work, Duquoc addresses the Blochian challenge and suggests various avenues for a response.

43. Idem, *Mesianismo de Jesús y discreción de Dios* (Madrid, 1986), pp. 137-38.

44. Ramos Regidor, "Europa y las teologías," p. 185.

45. G. Girardi, "Posibilidad de una teología europea de la liberación," *Misión Abierta* 1984/1, p. 157. See also idem, two other studies of closely-packed theological and cultural content: "Possibilità d'una teologia europea della liberazione," *IDOC Internationale* no. 1 (1983), pp. 30-47; "De la 'Iglesia en el mundo' a la 'Iglesia de los pobres': El Vaticano II y la teología de la liberación," in C. Floristán and Juan José Tamayo, eds., *El Vaticano II, viente años después* (Madrid, 1985), pp. 429-63.

46. Girardi, "Posibilidad de una teología," p. 153.

47. The proposal comes from German theologian N. Greinacher, in his "Liberation Theology in the 'First World'?" *Concilium*, no. 187 (1986), pp. 81-90. In this article, which seems to me to be programmatic, the author sketches some of the elements he regards as important at the moment of the development of a prophetic theology in the First World: For example, a struggle against any form of political and cultural neocolonialism; an in-depth questioning of the consumer model, which eventually destroys the culture of the individual; a battle with alienation by wealth, which is specific to the First World; a new lifestyle in the ambits of the individual, the family, the church, and society; a criticism of the capitalist economic system; the option for the poor, those of the Third World as well as those generated by the capitalistic system of the First World; the adoption of the theory of dependency, in the recognition that we, too, are oppressors; a critique of aid for development; a criticism of the structural sin presupposed in the world economic system.

48. Greinacher, "Theology of Liberation," p. 83.

49. See José Ignacio González Faus, "Los pobres: Lugar teológico," in various authors, *El secuestro de la verdad* (Santander, 1986), pp. 103-59, especially III, 2: "El pobre como crítica teológica a la Ilustración" ("The Poor as Theological Critique of the Enlightenment"), pp. 143-56. The poor, declares González Faus incisively, bring out in the open three great defects of the Enlightenment—all three presented as theoretical ideals in the eighteenth century by the Enlightenment movement. They are: a progress that largely runs counter to equality; a "reason" that takes insufficient account of "fraternity"; and the sin consisting in constricting persons' liberty. Over against these shortcomings of the Enlightenment, the poor supply theology with three categories for its dialogue with the world: a progress in solidarity, a dialogical "reason," and the victims of the prevailing system as point of reference.

50. Girardi, "Posibilidad de una teología," p. 159.

51. We find an example of a "gut reaction" unwilling to apply even the most elementary rigor of argumentation to its response to the theology of liberation in Ricardo de la Cierva's two voluminous pamphlets, *Jesuitas, Iglesía y marxismo: La teología de la liberación desenmascarada* (Barcelona, 1986); and *Rebelión en la Iglesia: Jesuítas, teología de la liberación, carmelitas, marianistas y socialistas* (Barcelona, 1987).

52. Ramos Regidor, "Cristiani di sinistra, solidarità con il Terzo Mondo e crisi del marxismo," *IDOC Internationale*, nos. 2-3.

53. Clodovis Boff, "The Nature of Basic Christian Communities," *Concilium*, no. 144 (1981), pp. 53-58.

54. Ibid.

55. Jorge Pixley and Clodovis Boff, *Opción por los pobres* (Madrid, 1987), p. 131; the theological foundation of the option for the poor is set forth in chapters 6, 7, and 8 of the book. (*ET, The Bible, the Church, and the Poor* [Maryknoll, N.Y.: Orbis Books, 1989].)

3

Epistemology and Method of the Theology of Liberation

CLODOVIS BOFF

We shall address our subject under three heads: the theoretical status of the theology of liberation; the forms this theology takes; and its method.

I. THEORETICAL STATUS OF LIBERATION THEOLOGY

What is the epistemological identity of the theology of liberation? Here it is in order to observe two things. On the one hand, the visage of liberation theology has not yet acquired its complete physiognomy: it finds itself entirely in an (accelerating) developmental stage. At the same time, its outlines at least, while not yet definitive — liberation theology is still too new for that — have acquired a certain delineation.

Let us posit certain basic theses from the outset, with a view to determining, insofar as possible, the situation in which the epistemological profile of liberation theology is presently to be found. Thus, we shall attempt to resolve some of the (seeming) gaps of this theology, which have become targets of attack and even condemnation. Furthermore, we shall take into account the "Instruction on Certain Aspects of the Theology of Liberation" (*Libertatis Nuntius*) of 1984 and "Instruction on Christian Freedom and Liberation" (*Libertatis Conscientia*) of 1986, as well as the important "Message of John Paul II to the Episcopate of Brazil" of April 9, 1986.

Thesis 1: The theology of liberation is an integral theology, treating all of the positivity of faith from a particular perspective: that of the poor and their liberation.

It must be said that in theory as well as in practice, liberation theology comes forward as a *global* or comprehensive theology. It spans the entire spectrum of theological thematics. But it does not rest there. It is not content with a general, abstract view of the Christian faith. From the general it advances to the *particular*; that is, it develops the meaning of the gospel as historically liberative. To borrow a metaphor from the morphology of language, it "declines" *all* of theology in specific terms: those of liberation. Taking its point of departure in a comprehensive faith viewpoint, it develops a particular (special, but not exclusive) faith viewpoint. Furthermore, it includes in its theological thematics the themes of the oppression and liberation of the poor, for example, economic production, shared power, the land questions, democracy, the historical project, and so on.

So, while liberation theology is general, it is not abstract. And while it is particular, it is not "sectarian" partial. It is *materially* general and *formally* particular.

What, indeed, is the object of the theology of liberation? Is it faith, or is it history? It is both. It is the entire deposit of faith, inasmuch as liberation theology develops the liberative meaning of that deposit; and it is the process of oppression/liberation itself, inasmuch as it interprets that process in the light of faith.

The important thing is that liberation theology always stands in a relationship of faith vis-à-vis oppression, and this in a *dialectical* manner. Pope Paul VI spoke in *Evangelii Nuntiandi* of an "unceasing interplay of the Gospel and of man's concrete life" (no. 29). We must add, however, that the dominant pole in that dialectic must be the givenness of faith, as the Instruction *Libertatis Conscientia* asserts in systematic fashion, and as John Paul II indicates in his message to the Brazilian episcopate: "To prefer the second [dimension, the ethico-social] to the first [the soteriological] is to displace and denature authentic Christian liberation" (no. 6).

Libertatis Conscientia moves in a downward direction, that is, from faith to the reality of oppression (although the general structure of the document proceeds from below, that is, from the actual process of liberation). It recognizes that it is legitimate "to begin with a particular experience," provided that experience be reinterpreted "in the light of tradition and of the experience of the church itself," that is from a more radical, more primary viewpoint (no. 70).

This being the case, we may give two definitions of the theology of liberation. First, *liberation theology is historical, in the light of integral liberation.* Here the emphasis is on the specific character of liberation theology as distinguished from classical theology. This specific character, intrinsic to liberation theology, is on the same level as its direct object or raw material: historical, concrete liberation.

Second, *the theology of liberation is the theology of integral liberation, emphasizing historical liberation.* Here the accent is on the comprehensive nature of liberation theology; integral liberation is the general horizon of all of its reflection.

Liberation theology began by plumbing the thematics arising from historical, concrete liberation (the first definition), but eventually came to see that its task consisted in covering the entire *mysterium salutis*, while continuing to maintain its congenital proper "point," the concrete liberation of the oppressed. By way of illustration, we have the important fact that the liberation theologians of Latin America are developing an entire collection of over fifty volumes, *Theology and Liberation*, covering the whole area of thematic theology (integral theology) but preserving the perspective of the historical liberation of the Latin American continent (specific theology).

In this sense *liberation theology* can even be regarded as a provisional designation, but the theoretical task it indicates pertains to the vocation of all theology, as we shall observe below.

Thesis 2: The primary, basic viewpoint of the theology of liberation, as of any theology, is the givenness of faith; its secondary, particular viewpoint, as one theology among others, is the experience of the oppressed.

This means that while the larger horizon of liberation theology will always be the plane of salvation, its secondary horizon is the concrete, historical process of the liberation of the poor. In other words, at the ultimate root of liberation theology, whether thematically or operatively, is *objective* (positive) *faith*, the word of God, or revelation. This is what makes it theology. But this is not all. Next, structurally and dialectically connected to the perspective of objective faith, comes the perspective of the oppressed, that is, *subjective faith*. This is what makes our theology precisely a theology *of liberation*.

This same problem can be posed in terms of the point of departure of the theology of liberation. Will that point of departure be faith or praxis — God or the poor?

Here it is important to situate the question concretely. What is this point of departure, this starting point? If it were a *pre-theological* experience that framed the genesis of liberation theology, in terms of the "spiritual experience of the poor," then we would have to say that the point of departure is actually *living faith*, or, in other words, the *praxis of faith*, as a "synthetic experience." Here, de facto, elements come in not only of positive faith (viewpoint, interpretation, and so on), but of praxis, as well (compassion, solidarity, and so on). Hence the structural origin of liberation theology. And hence the origin of its "proper manner" of theologizing, as we shall see.

If we now move to the properly *theological* sphere, we can say that liberation theology's starting point is a distinct one. True, we are dealing with faith as well as with praxis, but each of the two retains its place. Faith is the *formal* starting point or the "determining hermeneutic principle" (*Libertatis Nuntius*, part 10, no. 2), and praxis is the *material* starting point, that is, the raw material. There is no contradiction here, but only an interrelationship of distinct "instances" standing in reciprocal relation and duly ordered. Only a dialectical logic permits a correct approach to these questions, which seem "aporetic" in a first approach.

Although the vocabulary of liberation theology is not always fine tuned here, its actual theological practice usually operates correctly; that is, it starts with the poor, and with Christ as the first among them. To be sure, when we theologians say we start with the poor — just as when we say we start with reality — we are actually starting further away than that: with faith. It is only methodologically that we begin with "seeing," or "reality," when in fact faith is always there as the alpha and omega of the entire process. And this is even more evident in the reflection, the liberation theology, of the people themselves, who are at once oppressed and religious.

Thesis 3: The theology of liberation represents a "new stage" in the long evolution of theological reflection, and today constitutes a historically necessary theology.

This is the position of Pope John Paul II in his 1986 "Message to the Episcopate of Brazil" (no. 5). Thus, liberation theology is far from being a theology that happens to be in style — a purely conjunctural theology. Rather, it is an *epochal theology* — as the question of the liberation of the oppressed is epochal. The problems treated are authentically structural and historical.

But the theology of liberation is more than this. Inasmuch as liberation theology has discovered the "continent that is history" (always from a point of departure in the outcast), it has come to stay. Henceforth all theology will have to confront *faith* (and its power for liberation) with *history* (and its contradictions, or injustices). Were any theology not to do so, it would be suspect of alienation, it would be vulnerable to all manner of manipulation and could become "opium religion." It is becoming ever more difficult to understand how a theology could close its eyes to the real history of the oppressed. This would be true even in a society in which abject poverty had been eliminated. Even in such a society the theology of liberation would be valid, since the questions would remain: Who are the last ones here? Who are the victims? In this sense, liberation theology constitutes an intrinsic dimension, henceforward permanent, of any present or future theology.

Although the theology of liberation is not an *exclusive* theology, inasmuch as it defines itself strictly as a theology developing the social function of faith from the perspective of the poor, nevertheless it is *not merely one theology among others*. It is a theology which, from a point of departure in its fundamental project, challenges all theologians, precisely because it bears on a question having a relation to all other questions: the concrete question of the social emancipation of today's oppressed. Through its official documents on the theology of liberation, addressed to the whole church, Rome has made a decisive contribution to the acceptance of this theology as a universal (catholic) theology.

This fact has not gone unnoticed by the most attentive theologians of our time:

> Rarely has there been such a thing as the official acceptance of a particular theology. . . . For the last few years, [the theology of liberation] has been adopted by the church universal as its own. . . . Not even Thomism accomplished this in so short a time.[1]

> In Latin America today . . . something of great importance for the *entire* church is occurring. . . . The new phenomenon of this moment is that, in Latin America, a new Christian awareness of authentic Christianity is arising, a Christian awareness of a world of brotherhood and justice. This, to my view, is tantamount to a revolution. It will have repercussions — and is already having repercussions — in Europe. The most important contribution made by the theology of liberation has been . . . the awakening of Christian faith to responsibility for a Christian commitment to justice.[2]

> Linking the theology of liberation to the option for the poor, Hans Urs von Balthasar had this to say: "There [in Latin America] something absolutely central for Christianity is making its appearance: the option for the poor. Henceforward this may never be renounced."[3]

To be sure, what is per se universal is not this or that particular theology of liberation, but its *essential project*. In this sense, rather than being a theological movement, the theology of liberation is *all theology in movement*. What is known today as the theology of liberation is a provocation to this movement. Hence the well-known theologian Edward Schillebeeckx's response to the question posed to him in an interview, "What theologians of value do you see around you?"

> The leaders among the theologians of the West, European or American, are now the liberation theologians. We learn much from them. We are too academic. Liberation theologians oblige us to do our thinking from a point of departure in the life of the Christian community.[4]

In other words, every theologian must adopt a liberation theology. But theology must not be concerned merely with *historical* liberation. The *personal* (prepolitical) and *eschatological* (postpolitical) dimensions of the life of faith must also be developed (even in behalf of the oppressed, who are already, and who will continue to be, human persons). Even so, it must be said that, in the *comprehensive* (not necessarily the individual) process of theological production, the question of the oppressed must today constitute the *dominant perspective*, that is, not the exclusive perspective, but not just one among many, either.

Pope John Paul II has declared the theology of liberation "necessary" for the church. He has stated this repeatedly.[5] Both of the Roman "Instructions" speak in the same way: "It is impossible to forget for a single instant the situations of traumatic destitution from which this challenge to theologians springs" (*Libertatis Nuntius*, no. 1). And "A theology of freedom and liberation . . . constitutes a *demand* of our time" (*Libertatis Conscientia*, no. 98).

We are dealing, then, with an obligatory theology, not an optional one. It is not a matter of personal taste. One cannot appeal to theological pluralism. The pluralism will be found within liberation theology itself: Latin American liberation theology, European liberation theology, socialist bloc liberation theology, African, Asian, Black, feminist, Indian liberation theology, and so on.

Is a theology conceivable today that would address the great truths of faith and not thematically develop their social and political content? In the abstract, it is possible. The reason is that faith cannot be exhausted by the social and political dimension. Faith has an intrinsic and supremely *human* meaning, independent of its direct political bearing. Even when theology is done in behalf of the poor, all dimensions of faith must always be addressed: personal, social, and eschatological. Christianity is not only social *transformation*, it is individual *conversion*, and it is *resurrection* of the dead, as well. Therefore metaphysical or transcendent questions may not be suppressed in favor of (or on the pretext of) physical or immanent questions—precisely because the poor are not only poor, but men and women called to eternal communion with God.

Nevertheless, this theological reflection must remain open to a potential thematic and practical broadening in terms of historical liberation. It must remain very attentive to the question of social justice; otherwise it may be manipulated as a tool for alienation and injustice.

Furthermore, we must recall that if the great question of our era is the liberation of the oppressed, then this must also be the dominant or privileged perspective of the comprehensive theological reflection of our day. We speak here in epochal or kairological terms, not in abstract, ahistorical ones.

Thesis 4: The theology of liberation comprehensively integrates ethico-political liberation, which holds the primacy of urgency (and thereby also the methodological, and at times the pastoral, primacy), with soteriological liberation, which unequivocally maintains its primacy of value.

Obviously the axiological primacy (the primacy of value) belongs to evangelization and the soteriological dimension of liberation. Nevertheless, the primacy of historical *urgency* does not always coincide with the primacy of value. For a hungry people, the first concern will be bread, as Jesus showed when he saw the hungry crowd (Mark 6:30-44). Paul, too, says: "The spiritual was not first; first came the natural and after that the spiritual" (1 Cor. 15:46).

As the practice of work with the people shows, these two levels or orders can be combined very well without special problems. The confusion arises from the fact that frequently the "first" in the order of the hierarchy of values is confused with the "first" in the order of time; or again, when the "first" in the order of *intention* is not distinguished from the "first" in the order of *execution*.

As a matter of fact, *liberation* in liberation theology denotes first of all *social liberation*. This is *the* question of our time. And this was the question from which the theology of liberation sprang. This was the reason it arose in the Third World.

At first sight, or initially, *liberation* is liberation from physical wretchedness. However, this idea is open to what is above, open to faith, to communion with God — open to soteriological liberation. But our historical and methodological point of departure has always been the process of oppression-and-liberation of the excluded of history.

As for the magisterium of the church, it has adopted the thematic of the theology of liberation. But it has adopted it in its own way. First, it has transformed the notion of liberation into the great notion that embraces the whole mystery of salvation. Second, it starts with the soteriological dimension of liberation (liberation from sin and death), and from there moves to the social dimension (liberation from historical oppression). For its part, the theology of concrete liberation has begun with the latter, to move to the former. From the beginning liberation theology plunged *in medias res*; it began with the raw, naked reality of oppression.

In this wise, Rome *arrives* at ethico-social liberation, while Latin American liberation theology *arrives* at soteriological liberation. The semantic weight of liberation is distinct in either of the two discourses. But the two weights are not contrary. Indeed, far from being opposed, the two perspectives complement each other; in each case, the one opens out upon the other.

To enter by the door of material and historical liberation or by the door of spiritual and eternal liberation is a question of purely *methodological and pastoral* convenience, and not of theological truth. For example, in Europe it is faith that is surely without a safe footing, while in Latin America it is bread that is not guaranteed. Hence the distinct but not contradictory emphases.

What influence has Latin American liberation theology had on Rome's position, and through the latter, on the universal church? The principal historical merit of the theology of liberation has been to have introduced into the church the cry of the masses of the poor—and this from the starting point of the *particular viewpoint* of these masses—no longer in a perspective of natural law (that of mere human rights), but in one of *biblical theology*.

Indeed, what is actually in question in the debate over liberation theology is not God, Christ, or the church, but the *oppressed*—and how, beginning with them, one is situated anew in relation to God, Christ, and the church, even in the Roman documents.

In this case, why speak of liberation theology and not, more concretely, of political theology, critico-social theology, or even a theology of historical praxis?

The reason is one of evocation rather than indication—connotation rather than denotation. Liberation is an *idea* that attracts, not a *concept* that designates.

Thus, the reasons are practical rather than theoretical. Liberation has the advantage of being an idea that "speaks" to the modern human being, including, and especially, the poor. Actually, liberation is the name of the spirit of the times in which we happen to be living, as the two Roman "Instructions" declare (*Libertatis Nuntius*, part 1, no. 1; *Libertatis Conscientia*, nos. 1, 5, 17, 61). It is an idea open to manifold dimensions.

Liberation is a word extremely rich in biblical resonances (*Libertatis Nuntius*, part 3, no. 4), which accords it full citizenship in the church and in theology. Furthermore, it is a "concrete" word, while *history* or *politics* or *society* are abstract, relatively nonmotivating words. Thus, the name "theology of liberation" is more to be recommended as a "distinctive sign" and as a "lemma" than as a definite designation of a determinate theme.

Thesis 5: Vis-à-vis other theologies, present and past, the theology of liberation stands in a relation not of opposition or substitution, but of critical complementarity. Meanwhile, its radical novelty compared with these others is the encounter with the poor as historical subject.

In the first place, liberation theology is not distinguished from or opposed to the great theologies of the past, such as patristic theology or scholastic theology. On the contrary, it may be regarded as their successor or heir. As we have seen, the pope, in his "Message to the Episcopate of Brazil," states very clearly that the theology of liberation "must constitute a new stage—*intimately connected with those that have gone before*—of the theological reflection" developed throughout the course of history (no. 5; emphasis added). Later in the same document the pope returns to the same point, insisting that "this correct, necessary theology of liberation" must "develop . . . *in homogenous and not heterogeneous fashion* vis-à-vis the theology of all times" (no. 5).

The relationship between liberation theology and the great theologies of the past, then, is one of critical complementarity. Liberation theology *adopts on the level of liberation* of the poor the great intuitions of the theology of the past. Thus it brings these theologies up to date by applying them to the series of problems faced by the oppressed. The relationship between today's liberation theology and these theologies is that of a fruit to its seed. We are dealing with a harmonious development, like that of the history of dogma.

From the standpoint of the perspective of faith (pertinency) and doctrinal content, liberation theology can only be homogeneous with the great theologies of old. But there is an undeniable heterogeneity on the level of *themes, language,* and *posing of the problems* (the problematic), as well as with regard to concrete *methodology* (cultural mediations, etc.).

One must ask, for example, whether the theologies of St. Augustine, St. Thomas Aquinas, or Karl Rahner could not be regarded as forms of the theology of liberation, inasmuch as — according to the Roman documents — they treat particularly of soteriological liberation.

But it is not appropriate, in this case, to speak of theologies of soteriological liberation. The acceptance of the term *liberation* would thereby be too much, and abusively, broadened, thus entirely depriving liberation theology of its interests and specific character.

Surely there is danger of falling into generalities — but not in the direction in which the dominant semantics of liberation theology is headed, as in the Third World.

Furthermore, one must take care that liberation as the foundational concept of theology not eliminate the inescapable, traumatic question of the *material* liberation of the poor. To use the same term to designate both liberation from destitution and liberation from sin might *appear* to foster an interconnection of these distinct levels of an "integral liberation." However, such language tends to absorb material liberation into spiritual liberation (contrary to the pope's prescription in "Message to the Episcopate of Brazil," no. 6b), as well as to eliminate the discontinuities between the one and the other (faith does not immediately entail bread, nor bread faith).

In this sense, the very notion of integral liberation, in the current usage of Latin American liberation theology, has occasioned facile solutions, which, while their practical advantages are undeniable, betray a reductionistic theoretical scope.

But what would be new in current Latin American theology of liberation compared with previously existing theologies that reflect on the social and political dimension of faith, such as "political theology," the "theology of hope," and so on? Will not all of these be "liberation theologies," without distinction, regardless of whether they bear the name?

We respond as follows.

1. In current liberation theology, as done, for example, in Latin America, the *starting point is the oppressed* and not abstract topics or general ideas like "justice," "politics," "praxis," or even "liberation." Concrete liberation theology supposes a practical relation with practice, and not a merely theoretical (thematic) relation. It implies a living contact with the struggle of the poor. Today's "liberation theologian" is someone concretely committed to the cause of the oppressed. Thus it is said that the theology of liberation has always sprung from compassion with those who suffer and from a commitment to their pilgrimage of liberation.

2. From its point of departure in a concrete praxis at the side of the oppressed, liberation theology comes forward today as a new way of doing theology. It is not so much a specific method as a new theological spirit, a new manner of theologizing. This new manner is expressed in a concrete language, not an abstract one, a language charged with *pathos*, not a cold, dry one, a language that is prophetic, not doctrinaire.

3. Existing liberation theology is a theology directed upon praxis — precisely, a praxis of social transformation. Thus, it is at once critical and utopian.

For these reasons, current liberation theology must expect the opposition of all who are desirous of maintaining the status quo. Liberation theology is criticized more for political than for properly theological reasons, although the latter may justly exist.

But does liberation theology always presuppose a base or antecedent theology, such as that expressed, for example, in classical theology?

Not necessarily. What a concrete liberation theology presupposes, especially in view of its pastoral purpose, is faith. What liberation theology actually does is draw the social consequences of such and such a salvific truth, or reflect on such and such a concrete problem (hunger, popular organization, and so on) in the light of faith. It is impossible to do a theology of liberation without starting from the "deposit" of faith, whether or not theologized.

On the other hand, a liberation theology that fails to bestow a more consistent theological character upon its faith-basis runs the risk of "running out of gas" and coming to a halt. Therefore, on the level of the organic and systematic development of the theology of liberation, it is indeed essential to sink deep theological roots into the actual fundamentals of faith. Rather than speaking of a "first theology" (which would discuss the meaning *in se* of the mysteries of faith, for example of the resurrection or divinity of Jesus) and a "second theology" (which would develop the concrete impingement of the mystery in question on the social and historical field), it would be better to speak of a "first moment" and a "second moment" in a *single* theological process. Let us observe that the order of the moments here refers to the *structure* of the theological act and not to the (temporal) process of its method, which generally begins with "seeing." Between the two, an unmistakable dialectical movement obtains.

The thrust of liberation theology is toward a development of the entire deposit of faith from a point of departure in this theology's own specific sensitivity — the sensitivity that emerges from the experience of God in the poor. This is how an *integral* theology is done. Indeed, liberation theology seeks to "thematize" even the first moment of the overall theological process, the moment of the fundamental and transcendent aspect of faith: the truths concerning Christ, the Spirit, grace, and so on.

In this sense liberation theology's method incorporates the method of classical theology, but not without recasting it, in depth, from its own specific theological viewpoint: that of the oppressed. For example, a christology from Latin America utilizes all of the methodological tools of any classical christology (critical exegesis, hermeneutics of dogma, systematic reflection, and so on), but it does so in its own style.

At this point we must observe that the novelty of the theology of liberation is genuinely radical, that is, it consists in an element to be found at the very root of the theological act. This root contains something of the pre-theological: the encounter with the poor, and the shock, the rebellion, and the commitment of this encounter. The radical originality of liberation theology lies not in the topics it treats (oppression, struggle, and so on), nor in its method (the use of the social sciences or of Marxism), nor in its language (prophetic and utopian), nor in its addressees (the poor and their allies), nor even in its final cause (social transformation). The radical originality of the theology of liberation lies in the *insertion of the theologian in the real life of the poor*, understood as a collective, conflictive, and active (the poor as subject or agent) reality.

This is what is decisive in liberation theology, and what determines all else beside — its thematics, its methodology, its relationship with Marxism, its biblical reading, and so forth. All of these things are done from the starting point of the poor. As we can see, it is something in the theologian rather than in the theology. This first act of liberation theology marks the anteriority of a faith praxis over the theological theoretization of that praxis (second act).

Unquestionably, the encounter with the poor is the *indispensable* condition for doing liberation theology. But it is an *insufficient* reason. It is not enough for theologians to be committed. They must also produce the desired theology, and do so by way of a theoretical application to the theme under examination. A materially theological experience is a necessary condition for, but not a substitute for, theological *intelligence*. After all, while theology is (externally) dependent on the life of faith, yet it possesses its own (internal) autonomy where the rules of its production are concerned.

Thus, we have attempted to offer a better definition of liberation theology's epistemological profile. If that profile is not yet sufficiently clear, this is because, when all is said and done, this theology, still so new, is growing with the people on their way to liberation.

II. THREE FORMS OF LIBERATION THEOLOGY: PROFESSIONAL, PASTORAL, AND POPULAR

The term *liberation theology* calls to mind its best-known theologians, Gustavo Gutiérrez, Jon Sobrino, Pablo Richard, and so on. But the theology of liberation is far too rich and complex an ecclesial and cultural phenomenon to be limited to the output of professional theologians. It is a type of thinking that actually pervades a goodly part of the ecclesial body, especially in the Third World.

In fact, the grassroots of the church, the so-called base communities and the Bible circles, are permeated by a wholesale faith reflection that we might well describe as a theology of liberation. It is a kind of thinking that is homogeneous with a scientifically developed liberation theology. After all, this grassroots theology, too, brings Christian faith to bear on the situation of oppression; and as we shall see, it is precisely herein that the theology of liberation consists.

Finally, sandwiched in between this more elementary level and the most elevated level of liberation theology, we find an intermediate level. Here is where the reflection of our shepherds is situated: our bishops, priests, religious, and other pastoral ministers. This level is like a bridge, spanning the gap between the more elaborate theology of liberation and our Christian grassroots.

Each of these levels reflects the same thing: faith confronted with oppression. However, each of them reflects that faith in its own way, as we shall see below in more detail.

It is important to observe here that from the bases to the intermediate plane to the highest level, we find the same, continuous flow of thought in a single comprehensive theological process.

1. A Single Reflection

Liberation theology is like a tree. If you see only professional theologians, you are looking only at the branches. You are missing the trunk, which is the reflection of the pastors and other ministers, and you are certainly missing all the roots, which are beneath the surface of the soil and maintain the entire tree, trunk and branches alike. After all, this is how it is with the vital, concrete reflection, still underground and anonymous, of tens of thousands of Christian communities who live their faith and do their thinking in a "liberative key."

This theological current is intimately bound up with the people's very existence—with their faith and their struggle. It is part and parcel of their conception of Christian life. At the same time, it remains organically linked to the pastoral practice of the ministers; it is the theory behind these persons' action. Now, when liberation theology has arrived at this level of vital rooting and incarnation—when it has penetrated spirituality, liturgy, and ethics, when it has become social practice—then it has become practically indestructible.

Following is a chart of these three levels of development in the theology of liberation, together with a specification of their interrelationships.

This framework presents liberation theology as a broad, differentiated phenomenon. Liberation theology is any way of thinking the faith in the face of oppression. When we actually hear the term *liberation theology*, of course, it is almost always being used in its strict, technical sense, and it is primarily in this sense that we liberation theologians use it ourselves. But it is impossible to overlook those broad, dense, and fertile grassroots from which professional liberation theology draws its sustenance.

What unifies these three levels of a liberative theological reflection? Their unifying element is the singleness of their shared, single basic inspiration: a faith capable of transforming history, or, to put the same thing in different words, concrete history reflected in the light of faith. This means that the substance of Gustavo Gutiérrez's liberation theology is the same as that of a Christian tenant farmer of the Brazilian Northeast. The basic content is the same. The sap that runs through the branches of the tree is the same that runs through the trunk, rising from the roots of the tree in the secret recesses of the earth.

The distinction among these various types of theology is in their logic, and more concretely in their language. After all, theology can be explicitly articu-

	Professional Liberation Theology	*Pastoral Liberation Theology*	*Popular Liberation Theology*
Description	More developed and rigorous	More organic regarding praxis	More diffuse and less organized; almost spontaneous
Logic	Scientific: methodical, systematic, and dynamic	Logic of action: concrete, prophetic, impelling	Logic of life: in words, gestures, and sacraments
Method	Socioanalytic mediation, hermeneutic mediation, and practical mediation	Seeing, judging, and acting	Confrontation of gospel and life
Place	Theological institutes, seminaries	Pastoral institutes, training centers	Bible circles, base church communities, etc.
Privileged moments	Theological congresses	Church assemblies	Training courses
Agents	Professional theologians (teachers)	Pastors and pastoral ministers: lay ministers, religious sisters, etc.	Members and coordinators of the base church communities
Oral production	Conferences, lectures, advisory posts	Discussions, preaching	Commentaries, celebrations, dramatizations
Written production	Books, articles	Pastoral documents, mimeographed documents	Itineraries, maps

lated in a greater or lesser degree. Obviously, popular theology will be done in vernacular terms, with their spontaneity and color, while professional theology adopts a more conventional language, with its peculiar rigor and severity.

We readily understand what liberation theology is, then, by examining it first of all "from below," that is, by analyzing what the base communities do when they read the gospel and set it in confrontation with their lives of oppression and of longing for liberation. Professional liberation theology does nothing else—only, it expresses itself in a more sophisticated way. Pastoral theology, for its part, on the intermediate level, adopts a logic and language that draws from both.

2. An Integrated and Integrating Theology

It is important to notice that these three kinds of theological reflection do not stand in isolation, or even in mere juxtaposition. Most of the time the progression among them is an integral one. This integration appears at each level. At the level of popular liberation theology it occurs when, for example, a pastor (priest or bishop) or theologian sits among the people at a community center, reflecting with them on their struggle and pilgrimage. Integration can also occur at the level of *scientific* liberation theology, for example, when pastoral ministers and laity at the base are enrolled in systematic courses of theology. For that matter, we see it whenever we see laity taking theology courses or attending lectures that explore the faith. But the most obvious integration occurs precisely on the *intermediate* level, that of pastoral liberation theology, especially on the occasion of church assemblies. Here we see pastoral ministers (bishops, priests, sisters, and other liberated persons) posing their problems, grassroots Christians recounting their experiences, and theologians contributing their lights, evaluating the data presented and drawing conclusions. We should note that on such occasions, just as in the diocesan or episcopal assemblies, other social analysts take part as well, professional persons who now walk the path of liberation—sociologists, economists, educators, and technologists who have placed their professional competence at the service of the poor.

The theology of liberation, at least in the space of the model springing from the church, which is the space of liberation, is gradually assimilating pastors, theologians, and laity, now in concert and caught up in a common concern: that of a liberating mission. We are far from the old fragmentation here—still prevailing in a great part of the church—among a canonical, official theology produced in episcopal curias, a critical theology of protest carried on in centers of study and research, and a raw, rough-hewn theology developed on the margins of the church.

The schema presented above also demonstrates that the entire people of God reflect on their faith. All of the people, in some manner, do theology, not just the professionals. Or better, there is no such thing as faith without a minimum of theology. Why? Because faith is human and "seeks to understand," as the classical theologians used to say. Everyone who believes desires to understand something of his or her faith. And when a person thinks of faith, he or she is thereby doing theology. Thus, every Christian is to some extent a theologian, and all the more so the more this person thinks about his or her faith. The subject of the faith act is the subject or agent doing theology. After all, theology is faith thinking and thought, cultivated collectively in the context of the church. A base ecclesial community attempting to draw lessons for today from a page of the gospel is doing theology. Or better, popular theology is a thinking of faith done in a group; each person gives his or her opinion, complementing or correcting the opinions of the others, until the question is assimilated with greater clarity. Do the people not have the right to think? Are they only *ecclesia discens*, the church taught, reared, and in no wise the church teaching and educating?

3. An Oral, Symbolical, and Pastoral Theology

Popular theology is by and large an oral theology, spoken theology. The function of writing here is either that of guiding a faith dialogue or of preserving a summary of what has been discussed. But popular liberation theology is more than oral. It is a sacramental theology, as well; that is, it is carried out through gestures and symbols. For example, the people at the base are accustomed to representing capitalism in the form of a tree bearing rotten fruit and having poisonous roots. They stage dramatizations of gospel scenes in an up-to-date setting. One gospel group represented the situation of prostitutes today by displaying a placard over their heads: "Last in Society, First in the Kingdom." Another group, which was taking a course on the Book of Revelation, prepared one day's morning prayer by sketching a seven-headed dragon about to attack a wounded, standing lamb. They then invited those present to name the seven heads. Men and women arose and wrote, spelling out the words they had chosen as best they could, *multinationals, National Security, foreign debt, military dictatorship,* and even the names of cabinet ministers. Under the lamb someone wrote *Jesus Christ the Liberator.* Then a woman went up and penciled underneath *The Poor One of the poor.*

An entire religious thinking prevails here. In other words, a whole theology is present. Not that it is called theology, of course. It does not need to be. But what we see is actually an anonymous, collective theology, a theology with all the vigor of truth. It is a de facto theology, just as home medicine is real medicine.

Is it a critical theology? It surely is. It is lucid and prophetic; it is critical not in the academic sense, but in the authentic sense of taking account of causes and proposing means for their discernment. We may as well admit that it often far surpasses the so-called critiques of the academics, who can describe the monster in the minutest details, but who have never looked it in the face.

There is surely a pastoral theology in Latin America, the theology that projects the light of the saving word upon the reality of the injustices around us with a view to encouraging the activity of the church in the struggle for liberation. It is a theology of a special kind. It is in the same line and basic inspiration as the liberation theology that is known as such. Both have the same root—an evangelical faith—and pursue the same objective—the liberative practice of love.

These two kinds of theology enrich each other. Theologians accept pastoral concepts and subject them to an in-depth analysis, while pastors incorporate the most fertile viewpoints and conclusions of the professional theologians.

Pastors know how indebted they are to their theological advisers. On the occasion of Cardinal Ratzinger's "Instruction" on the theology of liberation, the bishops of Brazil (in their general assembly of April 1985) declared that, in spite of any possible "ambiguities and confusions," what was known as liberation theology "fosters evangelization" by dint of "explaining the nexus between movements for human liberation and the reality of the Reign of God" (no. 5 of the bishops' document).

The bishops are not satisfied, any more than are priests and other pastoral ministers, with simply appropriating the liberation theology of professional theologians. They do their own liberation theology in accordance with their mission. They can, of course, enrich their own reflection with specific developments in the area of scholarly liberation theology.

For the rest, the institutional church has never regarded (nor could it do so) any scholarly theology as binding for faith. It is enough for the institutional church to have the basic message of the scriptures and of the great church tradition. Nevertheless, in order to perform its mission in each historical epoch, pastors have always had recourse (nor could it have been otherwise) to the theological currents that offered them the most help. This is what is transpiring between the pastors of liberation and the theologians of liberation.

This evinces an intense spiritual harmony between professional liberation theology and the pastoral liberation theology of the third-world church. This is particularly clear in the case of the bishops who strive for liberation. Pope John Paul II addressed to the Brazilian bishops gathered in their assembly of May 1, 1984, the following challenging exhortation:

> Let the bishops of Brazil remember that they are to deliver the people from the injustices they suffer, which, I know, are grave. Let them take up their role of liberators of the people along pathways and with methods that are sure.

But a liberation bishop must ply a liberation theology. His work is not summed up in the production of theology in the centers of reflection, study, and investigation, which are usually the schools and institutes of theology in which the church forms its priests and trained laity. We must recognize that these places constitute the principal locus of development of liberation theology. But the liberation theologian is not an ivory-tower intellectual. Rather he or she is an "organic intellectual," a "theological activist," a pilgrim with the people of God and a collaborator with those persons who have a pastoral charge. They have one foot in the center of reflection and the other in the life of the community. (And the latter is their right foot.)

4. The Theologian's Concrete Activity

The liberation theologian can be found *at the grassroots*. He or she is bound up with the concrete community, vitally inserted into it. Performing a service toward theological enlightenment, he or she is yet part and parcel of the community pilgrimage. You see the theologian during an informal weekend colloquium, in a group in an urban slum, or in a country parish. He or she is in all of these places, on pilgrimage with the people, speaking, learning, listening, questioning and submitting to questions. There is no such thing as a pure theologian — a theologian who only knows theology.

As we have seen, the liberation theologian should possess in a high degree the art of connecting. He or she must connect the discourse of society, that of the world of popular significations, with the discourse of faith and the great tradition of the church. In the context of liberation, to wish to know only theology is to condemn oneself to not even knowing theology. Thus, the liberation theologian lives in a pastoral moment, a moment as analyst, a moment as interpreter, a moment as connector, and a moment as sister or brother in faith, as fellow pilgrim. He or she must be a person of the Spirit, to be able to encourage and to translate, in the reflection of faith, hope, and committed love, the demands of a gospel confronted with the signs of the times appearing in the popular milieus.

The theologian can also be found in *meetings* with the people of God. Such meetings may be spiritual retreats or diocesan meetings for drawing up or reviewing a program. They may be Bible courses, or they may be meetings on rural ministry or marginalized women. They may be debates on the challenges of black or native culture. The theologian is there primarily as an adviser. He or she hears the problems, then hears the theology done in and by the community—that first, basic reflection that is the people's theology done from a starting point in their lives. At the invitation of the assembly the theologian then seeks to reflect, to go deeper, to criticize, to re-pose the series of problems arising, always in the light of the word of revelation, of the magisterium, and of the great tradition of the church. Then we can say that: this theologian is doing theology with the people.

Finally, we find the theologian engaged in *professional work*—reading; researching; preparing talks, classes, and courses; writing articles and books. Here is the theoretical or scholarly moment. It is here, in this laboratory, that grassroots experience and the praxis of pastoral ministers are critically reconsidered, reflected upon in depth, in the light of faith, and developed in the form of concepts, that is, in rigorous scholarly fashion. The theologian emerges from this work place not only for pastoral encouragement, to advise pastoral ministers, or for some debate, but also for classes, talks, or congresses, sometimes making journeys abroad, speaking in metropolitan centers of power and production. This is a theology *from among* the people and *in the name* of the people.

The enormous number of things to do, the practical and theoretical demands of this kind of theology, often result in exhaustion or even "burnout" in a liberation theologian. The questions outstrip the capacity of the individual theologian for reflection and development. This theology, then, is fundamentally a task to be executed collectively, in organic articulation with the entire church, and through the various forms of development that we have described.

When all is said and done, the liberation theologian cannot be described otherwise than in the words placed by our Lord on the lips of his ministers: "We are useless servants. We have done no more than our duty" (Luke 17:10). No wonder that theologians, bound by ties of life and death to their family in faith, have an active share in their fate: that of persecution and martyrdom.

This last aspect will always have its shining symbol in Father Ignacio Ellacuría, theologian of El Salvador, savagely cut down with five confreres and two co-workers in the capital of his country in November of 1989. This *victor sub gladio* will henceforward be honored as a great forerunner of a liberated America and certainly as the protomartyr of liberation theology.

III. METHOD OF LIBERATION THEOLOGY

What we are about to present bears on the theology of liberation as a particular theology—as the theology that deals with the concrete liberation of the oppressed. But if we conceive of liberation theology as a single and unified theology, we shall have to say that what we shall expound here is only the distinctive mark of this theology—the "second moment" in its integral theoretical process. Thus, we shall be prescinding from the method of the "first moment," which corresponds to classical theology and which is structured on its two levels: the *auditus fidei* (positive theology) and the *cogitatio fidei* (speculative theology). Let us add that the outcome of this operation can thereupon be adopted by liberation theology in its "second moment," as a series of illuminative principles in the light of faith.

The operation of the first moment is not always performed by the theology of liberation itself. Liberation theology surely presupposes faith, but not necessarily in its theologized form. When it does itself perform the first moment, liberation theology acts, if not with a method of its own, at least in a manner of its own, critically integrating theologies already built up, transcending them creatively by exploring new dimensions, and opening them to their liberative meaning. We might dub the operation one of epistemological recasting—a dialectical effect of the return of the problematic of the second moment upon the first moment.

Let us leave aside this latter, then, to limit ourselves to what is newest and most typical in the theology of liberation, framed as that theology is by the concrete problematic and by the impingement of faith upon that problematic—its second moment.

1. The Antecedent Moment

Before we do theology we have to do liberation. The first step for theology is pre-theological: We must live the faith commitment. We must share in some way in the liberative process, be committed to the oppressed.

Without this concrete antecedent condition, liberation theology remains mere literature. Here, then, it is not enough to reflect on practice. We must first establish a living nexus with living practice. Otherwise, the poor, oppression, revolution, and a new society will be reduced to mere words that may be found in any dictionary.

Let us be perfectly clear: *At the root of the method of the theology of liberation is the nexus with concrete praxis.* It is within this major dialectic of theory (of faith) and practice (of charity) that liberation theology operates.

Truly, only the actual nexus with liberative praxis can bestow on the theologian a "new spirit," a new style or new way of doing theology. To be a theologian is not to manage methods but to be imbued with the theological spirit. But before constituting a new theological method, the theology of liberation is a new way of being a theologian. Theology is always a second act, the first being "faith, which expresses itself through love" (Gal. 5:6). Theology (not the theologian) comes afterward. First comes liberative practice.

It is of the essence, then, to have a direct knowledge of the reality of oppression/liberation through a disinterested commitment of solidarity with the poor. This pre-theological moment means a concrete conversion of life and implies a class conversion in the sense of involving actual solidarity with the poor and a commitment to their liberation.

To be sure, the concrete, proper manner in which a theologian makes a commitment to the oppressed is to produce a good theology. However, what we wish to emphasize here is that this enterprise is impossible without a *minimal contact* with the world of the oppressed. Actual physical contact is necessary if a person is to acquire a new theological sensitivity. This contact can occur in various forms and degrees, depending on persons and circumstances.

1. There are liberation theologians who maintain with the grassroots a *more or less restricted communication*, either sporadic (visits, meetings, special occasions, or the like) or regular (a weekend ministry, a position as a pastoral theologian in a community or popular movement, and so on).

2. Others *alternate* periods of theoretical work (teaching, research and development) with periods of practical work (pastoral work or theological consultation in a given diocese).

3. Others, finally, actually *join* popular milieus, living and even working together with the poor.

In all cases, however, one thing is clear. Anyone hoping to do an adequate theology of liberation has to be willing to "take a qualifying exam" in union with the poor. Only after having been a pupil with the humble will he or she be in a position to enter the school of the doctors.

2. Basic Schema of the Method

Liberation theology develops in three fundamental moments, corresponding to the three "times" of the celebrated pastoral method: seeing, judging, and acting.

Liberation theologians speak of three principal mediations: the socioanalytic mediation, the hermeneutic mediation, and the practical mediation. We use the term *mediation* because we are speaking about means or instruments of theological construction. First, let us briefly identify these three mediations and show how they are interconnected. Then we shall examine them in greater detail.

The *socioanalytic* mediation contemplates the world of the oppressed. It seeks to understand why the oppressed are oppressed. The *hermeneutic* mediation contemplates the word of God. It attempts to see what the divine plan is with regard to the poor. Finally, the *practical* mediation contemplates the aspect of activity and seeks to discover the appropriate lines of operation for overcoming oppression in conformity with God's plan.

Now let us explain these mediations in greater detail.

1. Socioanalytic Mediation

Liberation is liberation of the oppressed. Therefore liberation theology must begin by stooping down and examining the actual conditions in which the oppressed find themselves, whatever these conditions may be.

To be sure, the primary object of all theology is God. Nevertheless, before asking what oppression means in the eyes of God, the theologian must ask what

it is in itself and what its causes are. The God-event does not replace or eliminate the real-world event. "An error concerning the world," declares the great
St. Thomas Aquinas, "redounds to an error concerning God."[6]

Furthermore, if faith is to be efficacious, just as with Christian love, it must
have its eyes open to the historical reality of which it seeks to be the leaven.

Thus, to know the real world of the oppressed is a material part of the
overall theological process. It is a moment, or indispensable mediation
(although an insufficient one), for a subsequent, more in-depth understanding
of what the proper knowledge of faith is.

i) How to Understand the Phenomenon of Oppression. Confronted with the
oppressed, the theologian cannot but begin by asking: Why this oppression?
What are its roots?

The oppressed have many faces. Puebla lists them: the faces of children, of
youth, of natives, of *campesinos*, of workers, of the underemployed and unemployed, of the marginalized, of the elderly (Puebla Final Document, nos. 32-
39). Still, the characteristic visage of the third-world oppressed is that of the
socioeconomically poor. It is worn by the disinherited masses of the urban and
rural slums.

We must begin here—with this infrastructural oppression—if we wish correctly to understand all of the other forms of oppression and interrelate them
duly and acceptably. Indeed, as we shall see more clearly below, the socioeconomic form of oppression conditions in one way or another all of the others.

Beginning with this fundamental expression of oppression—socioeconomic
poverty—we ask ourselves how it is to be explained.

There are three possible alternative responses available to liberation theology: the empiricist, the functionalistic, and the dialectical. Let us briefly explain
each of them.

—The *empiricist* explanation: *Poverty is a vice.* Thus poverty is "explained"
in a simplistic, superficial way. Empiricism assigns the causality of poverty to
indolence, ignorance, or simply human malice. It fails to see the collective or
structural aspect of poverty, that the poor are entire masses, and these masses
are swelling by the day. The empirical is the vulgar conception of social destitution, and the one most widespread in society.

The logical solution in this view of the question of poverty is assistance
ranging from almsgiving to the most diversified campaigns of aid to the poor.
The poor are regarded as "unfortunates."

—The *functionalist* explanation: *Poverty is backwardness.* This is the liberal
or bourgeois interpretation of the phenomenon of social poverty. Poverty is
attributed to simple economic and social lag. With time, thanks simply to the
process of development fostered in the Third World by foreign loans and technology, "progress" must come and hunger disappear. So think the functional-
ists.

The social and political solution urged as a way out of this situation is *reform*,
understood as the gradual improvement of the prevailing system. Here the poor
appear as "objects" of an activity that descends from the top of the pyramid.

There is a positive element in this conception: it sees poverty as a *collective* phenomenon. But it fails to recognize its *conflictive* character. That is, it misses the fact that poverty "is not a passing phase. Instead it is the product of economic, social, and political structures," with the result that "the rich get richer at the expense of the poor, who get ever poorer" (Puebla Final Document, no. 30; citing Pope John Paul II's Opening Address at Puebla, III, 3).

—The *dialectical* explanation: *Poverty is oppression.* This explanation understands poverty as the fruit of the actual economic organization of society, which exploits some (workers), and excludes others (the underemployed, the unemployed, and the whole mass of the marginalized) from the system of production. As John Paul II indicates in his encyclical *Laborem Exercens,* the root of this situation is the primacy of capital over labor (chap. 3). In this historico-structural interpretation, poverty appears in all its reality, both as a collective phenomenon and as a conflictive one. The solution is an *alternative* social system. In other words, the way out of this situation is *revolution,* understood as the transformation of the bases of the economic and social system. Here the poor emerge as the "subject" or agent of the corrective.

ii) Historical Mediation and Struggle of the Oppressed. The socioanalytic interpretation just presented is appropriately complemented by a historical approach to the problem of poverty. The historical approach regards the present situation of the poor not only in itself, but as the terminus of an entire, broad process of exploitation and social marginalization. It attends to the struggles of the least "lowly" throughout the journey of history.

Indeed, the situation of the oppressed is defined not only by their oppressors, but also by the way in which the oppressed react, resisting oppression and struggling to be free. Thus, the poor are never considered in disjunction from their dimension as social co-agents—even in their subjection—of the historical process. Consequently, in order to analyze the world of the poor we must take account not only of their oppression, but also of their history and their liberative practices, however embryonic the latter may be.

iii) The Case of a Poorly Digested Marxism. When dealing with the poor and the oppressed, and seeking their liberation, how could anyone hope to avoid an encounter with Marxist groups (in the concrete struggle) and Marxist theory (on the level of reflection)? We have already seen this above, in our reference to the dialectical or historico-structural interpretation of the phenomenon of socioeconomic poverty.

As for the relationship between liberation theology and Marxist theory, let us limit ourselves here to some essential indications:

1. In the theology of liberation, Marxism is never dealt with in and for itself. It is always examined *with the poor as starting point, and for the sake of the poor.* Forthrightly adopting a position of solidarity with the lowly, the theologian interrogates Marx: What can you tell me about this situation of destitution and about the routes we may take to its defeat? Here the Marxist is subjected to the judgment of the poor and their cause, not the other way around.

2. Liberation theology, therefore, makes use of Marxism purely *instrumentally.* Marxism is not revered, as the holy gospels are. Nor is any obligation felt to give anyone an account of the use that may be made of Marxist words and

notions (whether or not they are used correctly), except to the poor, and to their faith and hope. More concretely, let us come right out and admit that liberation theology makes use of certain Marxist "methodological indications" that have proved their usefulness for understanding the world of the oppressed. Among these are the importance of economic factors; attention to the class struggle; the mystifying power of ideologies, including religious ideologies; and so on. This is what the late Jesuit General Pedro Arrupe stated in his celebrated letter of December 8, 1980, on Marxist analysis.

3. The liberation theologian, too, maintains a decidedly critical posture vis-à-vis Marxism. Marx (like any other Marxist) can doubtless be our fellow traveler (cf. Puebla Final Document, no. 544) but can never be "the" teacher. "Only one is your teacher, the Messiah" (Matt. 23:10). This being the case, for a liberation theologian Marxist materialism and atheism are not so much as a temptation. Marxism is set against the broader horizon of faith and thus radically relativized or transcended.

iv) Toward a Broadening of the Conception of "The Poor." Liberation theology is the theology of the liberation of the oppressed — the liberation of their whole person, body and soul — and all of the oppressed — the poor, the subjugated, those who suffer discrimination, and so on. We cannot attend exclusively to the purely socioeconomic aspect of oppression — the aspect of poverty itself — however basic and determining it might be. We must also look at the other levels of social oppression: racial (*blacks*), ethnic (*Indians*), and sexual (*women*).

These various types of oppression and others besides (of youth, children, the elderly, and so forth), each possess their specific nature and call for an equally specific treatment (theoretical and practical). Accordingly, an exclusively "classist" conception of the oppressed must be broadened. The oppressed are not only the socioeconomic poor; in the ranks of the oppressed we find more persons than merely those who are poor.

Here, however, it is important to observe that the socioeconomically oppressed (the poor) do not simply exist alongside the other oppressed, like the black, the Indian, or the woman (to restrict ourselves to the most significant categories of the oppressed in the Third World). No, the oppression of a class — socioeconomic poverty — is precisely the infrastructural expression of the process of oppression. The other types represent mere superstructural expressions of oppression. As such, they are profoundly conditioned by the infrastructural. A black taxi driver and a black soccer star are not the same thing. Similarly, a female domestic servant and the first lady of the land are not the same. An Indian whose land is stolen and an Indian still in possession of it are not the same.

This enables us to understand why, in a class society, the main struggles are class struggles. They set groups whose essential interests are irreconcilably at odds with one another. By contrast, the struggles of the black, the Indian, and the woman are waged between groups nonantagonistic by nature, groups whose basic interests are reconcilable in principle. While the owner (the exploiter) and the worker (the exploited) can never be definitively reconciled, black and white can be, as can Indian and "civilized," or woman and man. These oppositions are actually nonantagonistic, and take shape in our societies with and upon the basic antagonistic contradiction—the class conflict.

Conversely, we must note that oppressions of a noneconomic type aggravate preexisting socioeconomic oppression. The poor are far more grievously oppressed when, besides being poor, they are black, Indian, women, or elderly.

Beyond any doubt, for a critical understanding of the situation of the poor, or of any group of oppressed, the socioanalytic mediation is important. However, that mediation will provide only what a scientific approach can teach about oppression. It will have its limits, which are those of positive rationality. The latter captures only (and this is a great deal, to be sure) the basic, comprehensive structure of oppression. It omits all those nuances that can be perceived only in the direct experience of daily life. To be satisfied with a merely rational, scientific understanding of oppression is to fall into rationalism and thereby to omit the greater part of the reality of an oppressed people.

After all, the oppressed are *more* than what we learn about them from the social analyst—the economist, the sociologist, the anthropologist, and so on. The oppressed themselves must be heard. The poor, in their popular wisdom, actually "know" much more about poverty than does any economist. Or rather, they know it in another way, and more concretely.

For example, what is *work* for popular wisdom and for an economist? For the latter, it is a simple category or statistical calculation, while for the people *work* connotes trauma, anxiety, dignity, security, exploitation, exhaustion, life— a whole series of complex, even contradictory, perceptions. Again, what does the *land* represent for a *campesino* and for a sociologist? For the former, *land* is far more than an economic and social reality. It has a human dimension, with a profoundly affective, even mystical signification. And this is even more true, far more true, for an Indian.

Finally, when the people say "poor," they are saying dependency, weakness, helplessness, anonymity, contempt, and humiliation. In fact, the poor do not even like to call themselves poor, out of a sense of honor and dignity. It is those who are not poor who call them that. A poor woman from the poor city of Tacaimbó, in the interior of Pernambuco, hearing that she had been referred to as poor, responded: "Poor, no. Dogs are poor. We are defenseless, but we are fighting."

Hence it follows that the liberation theologian, in contact with the people, cannot be content with social analyses but needs to seize as well the rich interpretation that the poor make of their world. Thus he or she connects the socioeconomic mediation, which is necessary, with an indispensable understanding of popular wisdom—the rationality of scientific concepts with the symbolology of the ideas and images of the people.

Finally, the *Christian view* of the poor contains all this and much more. Faith sees in the poor, and in all the oppressed, precisely what the theology of liberation attempts to render explicit (and here we are already anticipating the hermeneutic mediation):

—The distorted image of God;
—A child of God become a patient, rejected servant;

—The memorial of the Nazarene, poor and persecuted;

—A sacrament of the Lord and Judge of history . . .

The concept of "the poor," without losing any of its concrete substance, is infinitely broadened by being opened to the infinite. Therefore, for the faith and mission of the church, the poor are not only persons in need and laborers; they are not only socially oppressed and historical agents. They are all of this and much more; they are vessels of an "evangelizing potential" (Puebla Final Document, no. 1147), and persons with a vocation to eternal life.

2. Hermeneutic Mediation

Once having understood the concrete situation of the oppressed, the theologian must proceed to ask: What does the word of God say about this situation? Then we find ourselves in the second moment of the process of theological construction: the specific moment by virtue of which a discourse is formally theological discourse.

It is a matter, then, of seeing the process of oppression/liberation in the light of faith. And what is the light of faith? This expression does not denote anything vague or general. The light of faith is concretely found in holy scripture. Thus, the light of faith and the light of the word of God are the same thing.

So liberation theologians go to the scriptures, carrying with them all of the problems of the suffering and hope of the oppressed. They solicit light and inspiration from the word of God. Thus they execute a new reading of the Bible: the hermeneutics of liberation.

i) The Bible of the Poor. To interrogate the totality of scripture from the viewpoint of the oppressed is to execute the hermeneutics, the specific reading, of the theology of liberation.

Let us hasten to add that this is not the only possible legitimate reading of the Bible. For us today in the Third World, however, it is the *privileged* reading. From the heart of the great biblical revelation, we extract the most enlightening and eloquent themes in the perspective of the poor: God as the Father of life and advocate of the oppressed, deliverance from the house of slavery, the prophecy of a new world, the Reign given to the poor, the church of total communion, and so on. The hermeneutics of liberation gives priority to these veins, but does not mine them exclusively. They may not be the most *important* themes (in themselves), but they are the most *appropriate* (for the poor in their situation of oppression). For the rest, it is the order of importance that determines the order of suitability.

On the other hand, the poor are more than simply poor, as we have seen. They seek life, and life "to the full" (John 10:10). Thus, the pertinent or urgent questions of the poor are interconnected with the transcendental questions: conversion, grace, resurrection.

Liberation hermeneutics actually interrogates the word of God without ideologically anticipating the divine response. As a theological hermeneutics, it is practiced in faith, or openness to the ever new and surprising revelation of God—to the unheard message that can save or condemn. The response of the word can therefore be, at any time, to call the inquiry, and even the inquirer, into question, inasmuch as it issues a call to conversion — to faith, or to a commitment of justice.

There is a hermeneutic circle, then, or "unceasing interplay" between the poor and the word of God (Paul VI, *Evangelii Nuntiandi*, no. 29). The primacy in this dialectic, however, belongs undeniably to the sovereign word of God — the primacy of value, at any rate, if not necessarily methodological priority. On the other hand, we know from the intrinsically liberative content of biblical revelation that the word of God can only sound in the ears of the poor as a message of radical comfort and liberation.

ii) **Traits of the Hermeneutics of Liberation Theology.** A reading of the Bible done from the starting point of the poor and their project of liberation is characterized by certain traits:

1. It is a hermeneutics that prioritizes the moment of *application* over that of explanation. On the other hand, it sees to it that the theology of liberation does nothing more than rediscover what has been the timeless call of any sound biblical reading (for example, in the Fathers of the Church), a call that for so long was neglected in favor of a rationalistic exegesis of intrinsic meaning. A liberative hermeneutics reads the Bible as a book of life, not as a book of curious stories. Surely it seeks the *textual* meaning there, but does so for the sake of its *life* meaning. Here the important thing is not so much to interpret the text of the scriptures as to interpret the book of life "according to the scriptures." In a word, the new/old biblical reading culminates in the experience today of the sense and meaning of yesterday. And here the second trait comes in.

2. A liberative hermeneutics seeks to discover and activate the *transforming energy* of the biblical texts. The crucial thing, after all, is to reach an interpretation that will lead to a change in persons (conversion) and history (revolution). This reading is not ideologically preconceived; biblical religion is an open, dynamic religion due to its Messianic and eschatological nature. Ernst Bloch once admitted, "It is difficult to have a revolution without the Bible."

3. A reading of the bible in terms of political theology accentuates, without reductionism, the social context of the message. It places each text in its historical context, so as to make an adequate, nonliteral translation of it in our own current historical context. For example, liberation hermeneutics emphasizes (but only emphasizes) the social context of oppression in which Jesus lived and the markedly political context of his death on the cross. It is obvious that, in this relationship, the biblical text acquires a particular importance in the context of third-world oppression, where a liberative evangelization has immediate, grave political implications, as the long list of Latin American martyrs testifies.

4. Finally, liberation hermeneutics is done *together with the poor*, incorporating on the level of the hermeneutic mediation the contribution of the popular reading of the Bible, just as it incorporates popular wisdom within the socioanalytic mediation. In this fashion the poor, or rather the church of the poor, made concrete in the base communities, appears as the privileged hermeneutical subject or agent of biblical reflection.

iii) **Preferred Books of the Bible.** Surely theology must take account of the entire Bible. Nevertheless, hermeneutic preferences are inevitable, and even necessary, as the liturgy itself and the homiletic art teach us. As for the theology of liberation, on any of its three levels (professional, pastoral, and mainly popular), the most appreciated books are indubitably:

— *Exodus*, which develops the politico-religious deed of liberation of a mass of slaves who become, by virtue of the divine covenant, a people of God.

— The books of the *Prophets*, for their intransigent defense of the liberator God, their vigorous denunciation of injustices, their championing of the lowly, and their proclamation of the Messianic world.

— The *Gospels*, obviously, for the central character of the divine person of Jesus with his message of the Reign, his liberative practice, and his death and resurrection, that absolute meaning of history.

— The *Acts of the Apostles*, for their portrayal of the ideal of a free and liberating Christian community.

— The Book of *Revelation*, for its collective, symbolic description of the immense struggle of the persecuted people of God against all the monsters of history.

In some locales other books are preferred, for example, those of the *wisdom literature*, for their recovery of the value of divine revelation in popular wisdom (proverbs, tales, and the like). In certain areas of Central America the books of the *Maccabees* nourished the faith of those immersed in a context of armed insurrection (legitimated, for that matter, by their pastors). Then, with the war at an end and the peaceful task of the reconstruction of their country under way, the communities have betaken themselves to a systematic reading of the books of *Ezra* and *Nehemiah*, because these texts portray the effort of restoration by God's people after the critical period of the Babylonian captivity.

It would be superfluous to observe here that any book of the Bible must be read in a "christological key," that is, from the high point of revelation as found in the gospels. Thus the perspective of the poor is placed within a grander perspective, that of the Lord of history, wherein it acquires all of its consistency and vigor.

iv) Recovery of the Great Christian Tradition. The theology of liberation is aware of being a new, contemporary theology of the current historical period, suited to the great masses of the poor of the Third World, both Christian and non-Christian.

Nonetheless, this theology seeks to maintain a bond of basic continuity with the living faith tradition of the Christian people. Therefore it interrogates the past in an effort to learn from it and to be enriched by it. The theology of liberation adopts toward theological tradition a double attitude:

1. An attitude of *criticism*, as it becomes aware of the limits and insufficiencies of the production of the past, the inevitable tribute, in part, to be paid to the particular age in which a theology took shape. For example, in scholastic theology (from the eleventh to the fourteenth centuries), granting its undeniable contributions to the precise, systematic development of Christian truth, we discover a no less undeniable tendency to theoreticism — to emptying the world of its historical or concrete nature (with a static view of things) — and

thus precious little sensitivity for the social question of the poor and their historical liberation. As for classic spirituality, an effort is made to transcend its ahistorical interiorism, its elitism, and its insufficient sense of the Lord's presence in the processes of liberation.

2. An attitude of *rehabilitation*, as it reincorporates forgotten, fertile theological threads that can enrich us, and even call us to account. For example, from patristic theology (the second to the ninth centuries) we can integrate its profoundly unitary conception of salvation history, its sense of the social demands of the gospel, its perception of the prophetic dimension of the church's mission, its sensitivity to the poor, and so on.

Likewise inspiring for liberation theology are the singular evangelical experiences of so many saints and prophets, of whom not a few were condemned as heretics, but whose liberative significance we clearly perceive today. Such was the case with Francis of Assisi, Savonarola, Meister Eckhart, Catherine of Siena, Bartolomé de las Casas, and, more recently, Fathers Hidalgo and Morelos, as well as Father Cícero—not to forget the precious contribution of the medieval pauperist reform movements or the evangelical demands of the great Reformers.

v) Social Teaching of the Church. In the area of the social teaching of the church, once more liberation theology maintains an open, positive attitude. It must be said, first of all, that liberation theology does not come forward as a *competitor* to the teaching of the magisterium. It could not do so even should it so wish, inasmuch as the two discourses take place on distinct levels and with distinct competencies. But whereas the social teaching of the church offers the grand orientations for Christians' social action, liberation theology seeks, on the one hand, to *integrate* these orientations into its synthesis, and on the other, to *explicate* them in creative fashion for the concrete context of the Third World.

This operation of integration and explication is founded on the dynamic, open character of the social teaching of the church (cf. Puebla Final Document, nos. 473, 539). Furthermore, in so doing liberation theology is obeying the explicit call of the magisterium itself, which, in Paul VI's *Octogesima Adveniens* (1971), declared:

> To utter a unified message and to put forward a solution which has universal validity . . . is not our ambition, nor is it our mission. It is up to the Christian communities to analyze with objectivity the situation which is proper to their own country, to shed on it the light of the Gospel's unalterable words. . . . It is up to these Christian communities . . . to discern the options and commitments which are called for in order to bring about the social, political, and economic changes seen in many cases to be urgently needed (no. 4; cf. nos. 42, 48).

Here the pope indicates precisely the three moments of the production of the theology of liberation, through which what is less concrete in the teaching of the church becomes more concrete.

Now, as we readily see, liberation theology responds to Paul VI's challenge to the social teaching of the church. That teaching, as he asserts, "does not . . . limit itself to recalling general principles. It develops through reflection applied to the changing situations of this world" (*Octogesima Adveniens*, no. 42). Thus, liberation theology takes its position squarely along the lines of the demands of the doctrine of the church. This is how liberation theology is actually regarded when it is adopted and/or developed by pastoral ministers in the form of pastoral liberation theology.

In fact, Cardinal Ratzinger himself, in his "Instruction on Certain Aspects of the Theology of Liberation," regards the social teaching of the church as a kind of pre-theology of liberation, or as a type of "pastoral theology of liberation," inasmuch as it has sought to "respond to the challenge hurled at our epoch by oppression and by hunger" (no. 1).

The conclusion of all of this can only be that there is no incompatibility in principle between the social teaching of the church and the theology of liberation. They are complementary, to the good of the whole people of God.

vi) Creative Work of Theology. Armed with the mediations they require, and with all of the material accumulated through these mediations, liberation theologians now address the construction of genuinely new syntheses of faith and the production of new theoretical significations, with a view to meeting the great challenges of today.

Liberation theologians are never mere accumulators of theological materials. They are authentic architects of theology. Thus, they arm themselves with the necessary theoretical daring and a good dose of creative fantasy, in order to be in a position to deal with the unprecedented problems they find on the oppressed continents. Extracting and creatively developing the liberative content of the faith, they attempt to realize a new codification of the Christian mystery, in order thereby to help the church fulfill its mission of liberative evangelization in history.

3. Practical Mediation

Liberation theology is anything but an inconclusive theology. It emerges from action and leads to action, and the round trip is steeped and wrapped in the atmosphere of faith from start to finish. From an analysis of the reality of the oppressed, it moves through the word of God, finally to arrive at concrete practice. Back to Action is the motto of this theology. Thus, it seeks to be a militant, committed, and liberative theology. It is a theology that leads to the public square, because the *current form* of faith today in the underworld of the disinherited is "political love," or "macro-charity." In the Third World, among the wretched of the earth, faith is *also* and *especially* political.

However, faith is not reducible to action, even liberative action. It is "ever greater," and includes moments of contemplation, and profound gratitude. The theology of liberation also leads to the temple. And from the temple it leads the believer, charged now with all of the divine and divinizing energies of that Mystery of the world that is God, once more to the public square of history.

True, liberation theology leads, as well, and today principally, to action: to action for justice, to the deed of love, to conversion, to church renewal, to the transformation of society.

The logic of the Third Moment—the practical mediation—has its own internal regime. Naturally, the degree of definition of activity depends on the theological level upon which one operates: professional, pastoral, or popular.

Thus, a professional theologian can only open grand perspectives for action. A theologian who is a pastor or pastoral minister can be somewhat more determinate as to the lines of his or her activity. And popular theologians are in a position to enter upon a plane of quite precise practical and concrete action. Obviously, at the latter two levels—the pastoral and the popular—definition of the operation can only be a collective act, carried forward by all who are caught up in the question of the case, especially by the pastoral and other ministers or "agents."

The logic of action is extremely complex. It includes many steps, such as a rational, prudential assessment of all of the circumstances of the action proposed and an anticipation of the possible consequences.

In all instances, however, the practical mediation embraces certain distinct discursive levels:

1. Level of *conjunctual analysis*: an assessment of the correlation of forces at hand, such as resistance on the part of society and the church, the capacity of the people to bear the proposals made, and so forth.

2. Level of *projects and programs*: proposals of the historically viable objectives for the short and long term. Without this step, we should only have pure utopias and sheer good intentions.

3. Level of *strategy and tactics:* definition of the concrete means for reaching the proposed objectives, that is, alliances, resources, various means, all through prudential judgments that arrive at the actual concrete level in the form of tactics.

4. *Ethical and evangelical* level: assessment of the means proposed in terms of the values and criteria of morality and faith, with priority accorded to, for example, nonviolent methods such as dialogue, moral pressure, and active resistance.

5. *Performative* level. Finally, there is even a discourse of direct operation, with its appeals and attractions to action. This level of discourse performs the function of a bridge between decision and execution.

In this third moment in the method of liberation theology, we note the presence of a cognition constructed more of practice than of theory. That is, here the process is more executive than systematic. Thus, at this point, rather than formal reason, it is the wisdom of life and the prudence of action that are at work. And here the common people, those "doctors in the school of life," often have the advantage over the "wise and prudent."

—Translated by Robert R. Barr

NOTES

1. L. Sartori, *Il Regno attualità*, May 15, 1986, p. 243.

2. Juan Alfaro, *Il Regno attualità,* July 15, 1984, pp. 323ff.

3. Hans Urs von Balthasar, *30 Giorni* (June 1984), p. 78.

4. Edward Schillebeeckx, *Il Regno attualitá*, October 15, 1984, p. 447.

5. See "Exhortation to the Representatives of the Brazilian National Bishops Conference," March 13, 1986, no. 6; "To the Brazilian Episcopate," April 9, 1986, no. 5.

6. Thomas Aquinas, *Summa Contra Gentiles*, 1. 2, c. 3.

4

Theology of Liberation and Marxism

ENRIQUE D. DUSSEL

I. EPISTEMOLOGICAL DIMENSION: FAITH AND THE SOCIAL SCIENCES

Theology, a reflection arising from praxis, has need of a series of theoretical instruments if it is to pronounce its own discourse. Having explained this first point, we still have three others to address: Which Marxism are we talking about? Why are Marxist tools used? And—the most important from a descriptive point of view—why do liberation theologians use Marxism?

1. Theology and Scientific Discourse

All theology, through the ages, has used some particular scientific discourse as a mediation for the construction of its reflection. Faith is the basic moment of theological discourse. Faith, in turn, is an aspect of *praxis—Christian* praxis. Christian activity or praxis includes the *light* in which theological thought can be regarded as Christian. That is to say, the daily praxis of existential faith is the light that shows whether activity may be seen to be the following of Jesus of Nazareth. In like manner, praxis, which includes faith as its Christian foundation, is the constituent antecedent of theology. Theology is nothing but a theoretical discourse (spiritual, sapiential and methodical, but likewise always "practical," according to Thomas Aquinas) that, from a point of departure in Christian praxis, in the light of faith, reflects, thinks, supplies with a rational foundation, the reality, the problems that saw praxis encounters on a daily basis. It belongs to theology to be a "methodical" discourse; that is, it follows the most developed rules or requirements of the most developed rationality of the epoch in which it is being practiced. In the Babylonian context of the sixth century B.C., the "Adamic myth" is a theological construction corresponding to the best of the symbolic rationality of its time (for example, vis-à-vis the myth of Gilgamesh). Jesus used the theological tools of his time (those of the rabbinical and Pharisaic schools, and so forth). From the second century of our era, with the appearance of the Greek Christian theological schools (first those of the Apostolic Fathers, then the Apologists, then Alexandrinians like Origen), Christian faith built up its theological discourse through the use of the "science" (*epistēmē*) of its time: Platonic philosophy (and theology). Platonic "categories" permitted the construction of a Christian theology through the use of tools that in the first century had been regarded as intrinsically perverse — part of a "pagan," anti-Christian culture. In the twelfth century, at a time when Aristotelianism had been *explicitly condemned*, Albertus Magnus and Thomas Aquinas used Aristotle, who provided them with a system of categories in which a theological discourse could unfold that was destined to hold sway in Catholic theology down to our very day.

In the nineteenth century, the German theologian Johan Moehler employed the instruments of the philosophy of his time to effect an in-depth renewal of a German Catholic theology that had fallen hopelessly behind a Protestant theology outfitted with the best philosophy of the Enlightenment and Hegelian thought. It was not until the twentieth century that Karl Rahner, with an existential philosophy in a Heideggerian cast, or a Johannes Baptist Metz, with the philosophy of the Frankfurt "critical school," brought theology abreast of the thinking of their time.

In other words, theology has always had to seize upon a method (traditionally almost exclusively a philosophical one) in order to construct, from praxis, from faith, a methodical, rational, scientific discourse.

2. Why Are Marxist Analytical Tools Used?

Liberation theology arises from an experience of Christian praxis — a faith praxis. Historically and concretely, theology has always been anticipated by Christian praxis and ecclesial faith — the faith and praxis of Christian groups and theologians-to-be. The concepts that a nascent Latin American theology found itself under the obligation of expounding and justifying in order to meet the needs of militant Christians were the theological reasons accounting for the meaning of the *"political* commitment" of these Christians. But why a political commitment? In order to bring about a social, economic, and political change that would permit the exploited clases (first), the poor (more theologically), and the Latin American people (last) to reach a just, humane, fulfilled life. It is the twofold demand of (1) a theological reflection on the "political commitment" (2) in order to serve the oppressed, the "poor," the people, that required this nascent theology to use other analytical, interpretative, tools from those known to previous theological tradition. Faced with the absence of an adequate theology already in existence, theologians had to seize upon the *Latin American critical social sciences* — not only "social" sciences (such as sociology, economics, and so forth), but "critical" (concerned with discovering and situating the reality of injustice) and "Latin American" (because our continent had questions "of its own" to resolve) social sciences. The decision to use these tools, then, was not an a priori dogmatic or epistemological decision. It was Christian praxis and faith, and criteria fundamentally spiritual and pastoral (the *fact* that Christians were becoming involved in politics in order to fight injustice, together with the social teaching of the church) that made adequate analytical categories necessary.

Thus it came about that an infant Latin American theology began to make use of the tools of Marxist categories (emerging historically from the Marxism of the French tradition, already being used in student and worker groups). Juan

Luis Segundo, José Comblin, Gustavo Gutiérrez, and I belonged to the generation that had studied in France or Belgium. That set of instruments—we shall see presently what it was and how it was used—made it possible for the new *theology* that began in 1968 to call itself *liberation* theology (in Rubem Alves's Princeton dissertation[1]) to reach unexpected results in the area of the analysis of historical, social, and political realities (as well as in other areas, once it had discovered its methodology, which was applicable to other levels of reflection, as would soon be the case with a theology of the liberation of women, of the oppressed races, and so on). What was occurring, if we may so speak, was an epistemological revolution in the world history of Christian theology. For the first time, the critical social sciences were being used. Political economics and sociology, which had originated only well into the nineteenth century, had never been consistently used by Christian theology. Just as modernism produced a crisis with its use of *history* in theology (from Renan to Blondel), so also liberation theology generated a crisis by adopting the *social sciences*, and among them, as their critical nucleus, Marxism. The twenty-first century will show how important liberation theology has been in its missionary function in the contemporary world, beginning at the end of our own twentieth century—in the world of the poor, in Latin America, Africa, and Asia, and very particularly, in the nations of "real socialism," where it is the only intelligible, understandable, and prophetic theology possible.

3. Which Marxism Does Liberation Theology Adopt?

What Marxism do we mean when we say that the theology of liberation makes use of Marxism? We shall return to this point below; for the moment, let us only notice that, as we might well suppose, liberation theologians adopt only a "certain kind" of Marxism, excluding other "kinds," at least implicitly, sometimes explicitly.

First of all, of the various possible Marxisms, liberation theologians unanimously reject dialectical materialism. No liberation theologian accepts the materialism expounded by Frederick Engels in his *Dialectic of Nature*, or of Lenin, Bukharin, or Stalin.[2] Marx is accepted, and adopted, as a social critic. But even Marx can be approached in two ways: by way of secondary readings (as by Yves Calvez in France); or by way of the "young" Marx (up to the *Manifesto* of 1848). In the first generation of theologians (from Juan Luis Segundo to José Comblin, Gustavo Gutiérrez, or my position at the beginning of the 1960s), the French influence was very powerful. First it was Jacques Maritain, then Emmanuel Mounier, and afterward Lebret in *Economy and Humanism*, whom we followed. Pierre Teilhard de Chardin also inspired the thought of these years. But then came Marx, by way of the Cuban revolution (1959), and we began to read, simultaneously, the young Marx and works like those of Che Guevara, Antonio Gramsci, and Lukács. That is, we read a "humanistic" Marx—as he was called at the time—clearly neither dogmatic, nor economistic, nor naively materialistic. There was, at that time, no serious direct approach to the "definitive" Marx (Marx from 1857 onward), nor, as we shall see, is there a great deal today.

Along with Antonio Gramsci, whom we have already mentioned, the first line of approach was that of the Frankfurt School. Here it was especially the North American Marcusian branch (whose influence can be seen in Rubem Alves as early as 1968), so broadly utilized elsewhere, even in theology (by Johannes Baptist Metz in Germany), that influenced us. The thought of Ernst Bloch, as well, had a comprehensive impact—especially through Jürgen Moltmann on the question of utopia and hope. And mainly, the work of Louis Althusser, pedagogically translated by Martha Harnecker in her celebrated works,[3] was to influence not only liberation theology (especially in its second generation)[4] but Latin American Marxist thought as a whole.

Obviously Fidel Castro, from 1959 onward, became required reading, especially in his position on religion. Along with numerous French thinkers, Giulio Girardi, the Italian liberation theologian, was also to have an influence by virtue of his forthright Marxist position—at first decidedly classist, but later popular, with the "people" as historical subject (agent) of liberation.

But there was a Marxism that actually left a far more indelible mark on the theology of liberation than the Marxism that we have been examining. We might call it theoretical Marxism. This is the *Latin American* sociological and economic Marxism of "dependency," from Orlando Fals Borda to Theotonio dos Santos, Faletto, Cardoso, and so on (many of whom have never actually been Marxists themselves). It is this sociology of dependency, with its criticism of functionalism and developmentalism that will occasion the epistemological breach on the part of the theology of liberation. Thus, the position of Andre Gunder Frank—with all the criticisms to which it is open—will be determinative in liberation theology before 1972. Franz Hinkelammert—as Marxist and as theologian—will perhaps be the sole representative of the "definitive" Marx. This expression emerged from a whole group at the end of the 1960s, in Santiago, that had been seriously examining *Das Kapital* (at the Centro de Estudios de la Realidad Nacional). It will be the occasion of the particularly strong presence of Marxism in a very creative current of liberation theology in the 1980s.

All of these historical interconnections are still in need of an adequate examination. Neither do we have a history of contemporary Latin American Marxism, least of all within Christian movements.[5] But what we have seen will suffice to demonstrate how simplistic a conservative criticism of liberation theology is when it accuses it of being Marxist in an ideological sense. It was precisely the theology of liberation, in all Christian responsibility, that, *long before its critics*, had the painstaking task of adopting a "certain" Marxism, one compatible with a Christian faith received from the prophets, from Jesus, and from church tradition immemorial as well as recent (and of course ecumenical currents). Anything like a Stalinist dogmatism, the economicism of the manuals, or "philosophical" Marxism is altogether foreign to liberation theology.

4. In What Way Do Liberation Theologians Adopt Marxism?

Were we to undertake to expound our subject adequately, we should need more than the space of an entire book to accomplish the task. In these brief pages, then, we shall attempt an initial sketch of the question in a few of the theologians, more by way of a limited example than as an adequate survey.

The theology of development was pre-Marxist.[6] So were the first works of Juan Luis Segundo and José Comblin.[7] On the other hand, the theology of revolution had already used Marxist instruments of analysis[8] — but not in the same fashion as liberation theology was to do. I think that, historically, the difference is in the presence or absence of the theory of dependency, which "Latin-Americanized" Marxism and gave it a historico-social dimension. Hugo Assmann was the first to furnish an adequate indication of the lack of correspondence among these theologies (of development, of revolution, Moltmann's theology of hope, Metz's political theology, and so on).[9] Let us not forget where it all started: with José Porfirio Miranda's historic *Marx and the Bible*,[10] which posed the question forthrightly and biblically. But paradoxically, what we have, of course, is a Christian looking at Marx, and not actually a Marxist interpretation of the encounter between Marx and theology.

Rubem Alves, in *A Theology of Human Hope*,[11] sets forth the problematic as it prevailed in North America in 1968. He does so in the presence of Marcuse, and from the Protestant tradition of the theology of revolution, which he here transcends for the first time. For theologian Alves, "political humanism" — that of Marcuse — overcomes mechanistic technologism,[12] and demonstrates the importance of the political element. The "humanistic messianism" of philosophical Marxism falls short of an adequate definition of the transcendency at work in the liberation movement, holds Alves. This definition must be the deed, instead, of a Christian "messianic humanism." Alves's citations of the early Marx, of Marcuse, of Alvaro Vieira Pinto,[13] of Bloch, of Paulo Freire show us the kind of Marxism then in use. There is no question of social analysis as yet.

For his own part, Hugo Assmann declares:

> Talking of liberation implies taking a new analytical stance with regard to the situation of our countries, a basically new conception of the phenomenon of under-development, and, consequently, a new point of departure from which to map out the political and economic ways out of this situation. The conclusions drawn are inevitably revolutionary, and the langauge of liberation is the language that articulates them. This relates it directly to the new analysis of under-development.[14]

Assmann's is a criticism of the "developmentalistic" language then making its appearance in certain Latin American social-science circles — not necessarily Marxist — and attempting to explain the poverty and oppression of the Latin American people. Assmann uses Marxist categories. But, once more, these are of a Gramscian and Lukácsian type (an anti-economistic critique of the ideologies), although he accepts the supra- and infrastructure paradigm. With his broad formation in this Marxist thought — and his familiarity with the German tradition, as well — he analyzes the "truth" of a discourse from a point of departure in the praxis that is its basis. However, once again criticizing traditional Marxism, he shows the revolutionary importance of the ideological struggle —

in which theology is a partner. Thus, as we have said, he was the first to succeed in establishing a clear distinction between liberation theology and the postconciliar European theologies (theology of hope, political theology, third-world theology of revolution, and so on).[15] He provided us with clear analyses of the symbolical structure as a superstructure. His discourse criticized not only Stalinist dogmatism, but even Althusser's thinking—for failing adequately to situate the question of fetishism or the relationship of theory and praxis.

Juan Luis Segundo, whose formation in sociology was more along the functionalist lines of the 1950s, also adopts Marxist categories of analysis, especially the concept of ideology.[16] He has used the social sciences from his first books onward (*Función de la Iglesia en la realidad rioplatense*, 1962), and is a matchless critic. He unveils the moments of concealment and falsification in the European or North American theologies, and even in the Roman documents, as in his critical work, *Theology and the Church: A Letter to Cardinal Ratzinger and a Warning to the Church.*[17]

Gustavo Gutiérrez begins to blaze the trail in 1964. His *A Theology of Liberation*—whose first sketches appear in 1968 with hiss critique of developmentalism—cites Gramsci in its first note,[18] where the author explains that the particular Marxism of interest to him will be an anti-economistic one, and not dialectical materialism. Gutiérrez applies a decidedly political Marxism, then, a Marxism of cultural analysis. Hence his basic thesis that theology—like philosophy in the Gramscian sense—is a "critical reflection on [Christian] praxis."[19] Like all liberation theology of the 1960s, Gutiérrez's theology starts off with a critique of the "notion of development" and posits *liberation* as the antithesis of that notion. He cites authors like Althusser, Korsch, Lukács, Mariátegui, and Sánchez Vásquez. And of course he cites Marx himself. All of this evinces the use of a critical, Latin American, and anti-economistic Marxism, a Marxism pressed into the service of a political analysis. And by way of citing Che Guevara, Gutiérrez chooses this text:

> Permit me to state, at the risk of appearing ridiculous, that the true revolutionary is guided by great sentiments of love. Every day the struggle must be waged that this love for living humanity be transformed into concrete deeds.[20]

Marxism is also found indirectly among the pertinent social sciences as an instrument for the discovery and description of the fact of the poverty of the Latin American people and the concrete projects of liberation. Gutiérrez's "Marxismo y cristianismo," unpublished, shows a prudent, profoundly theological use of Marxist categories like class struggle, revolution, and utopia.

José Míguez Bonino's *Christians and Marxists: The Mutual Challenge to Revolution*[21] is perhaps the only work to be devoted explicitly to a treatment of the bonds between Marxism and Christianity among liberation theologians—although Miranda dealt with it in *Marx and the Bible.*[22] The Argentinian theologian's familiarity with Marx is of no recent vintage, and its profundity is in evidence as early as 1969, when José Míguez Bonino asked in his critical foreword to Rubem Alves's book:

Does the renascence of humanistic Marxism not arise from the situation of the developed countries? . . . Is not our own situation very different, so that humanism will require a more elementary and "materialistic" positing that will effectively incorporate political, scientific, and technological rationality, without which liberation might become a mere dialectical game?[23]

As a theologian of "Christians for Socialism," in 1972, Pablo Richard[24] — together with Gonzalo Arroya, its founder — incorporates Marxist categories. Gramsci is his obligatory reference, especially in his book, *Death of Christendom, Birth of the Church,*[25] and he uses him systematically in defining his theoretical framework.

In Leonardo Boff, the rejection of capitalism "is oriented to a liberation in the framework of a different society."[26] Theology is constructed from two starting points: faith (biblical faith as interpreted by the magisterium and tradition) and social reality.[27] In order to rediscover this reality, and subject it to theological reflection, "recourse must be had to the human social sciences, such as anthropology, sociology, psychology, political science, economics, and social philosophy."[28] It is here that we find Boff's use of Marxism. But he explains:

[Latin American theology] makes nonservile use of the analytical tool developed by Marxist tradition (Marx and the various contributions of socialism, of Gramsci, of French academic Marxism, and others), disconnected from their philosophical presuppositions in dialectical materialism. Here Marxism is taken as science, not as philosophy.[29]

Clodovis Boff's *Theology and Praxis: Epistemological Foundations,*[30] is perhaps the most systematic theological work attempting to adopt the theoretical framework of Althusser. Boff's theoretical practice is extremely rigorous in its adoption of the French Marxism of the 1970s. It shows how a Marxist categorical framework can be used in a strictly Christian theology of the political. Now an analogous work is needed, having Marx himself as its reference. We shall return to this matter below.

For his part, Jon Sobrino indicates that many of the European theologies respond to the objections of the "first Enlightenment," that of Kant, which calls into question the relationship of faith and reason. The "second Enlightenment," that of Marx, questions the relationship between faith and historical change. Of what good is religion in historical transformations? Which will faith justify, domination or liberation?[31] It is thus that Marxism is adopted by the theology of liberation: as a theology that not only *interprets* reality, but justifies its *transformation* — even its revolutionary transformation.

Otto Maduro has taken a new approach to the question of religion in the young Marx, and in the Catholic young Engels.[32] Juan Carlos Scannone,[33] on the other hand, belongs to the wing of liberation theology that opposes Marxism — due to the particular conditions of his national situation — as does Lucio Gera.[34]

It must not be forgotten that the use of Marxism in the most profound current of spirituality and mysticism—as with Arturo Paoli[35], who had done Hegelian and Marxist studies in Italy together with an Italian Catholic Action chaplain later to be known as Paul VI, or Ernesto Cardenal in his *Santidad en la revolución*,[36] which marks the end of a de facto bottleneck when it came to recognizing the validity of revolutionary processes—reaches in the Teoponte guerrillas in Bolivia a genuinely mystical degree. (We prescind from its political suitability). Witness the case of Ne'stor Paz Zamora.[37] We could name many others.

Anticipating our conclusions, we may indicate that, as can be observed, liberation theology uses a *certain* Marxism in a *certain* way—never in such a way as to be incompatible with the foundations of the faith. Some hold a more frankly classist position; others hold a more nearly populist one. Some use only the tools of ideological criticism; others include those of social criticism, and even of a properly economic criticism (as we shall see below). Others, indeed, oppose Marxism across the board—although these find it difficult to define themselves as members of the theological movement known as the theology of liberation. Some take their inspiration in a more French current of Marxism, others in the Italian or German, and in most cases in several simultaneously. All, however, adopt the thesis of dependency propounded by the Latin American current—a thesis defined with a great deal of care, in full awareness of the criticisms to which it is open. We may assert, then, that the theology of liberation is the first theological movement to adopt Marxism—with all of the reservations that we have indicated—in the world history of Christian theology (and before its adoption by any of the other universal religions).

II. THE ACCUSATION OF MARXISM

The Christian option for the poor and oppressed, and the consequent use of the epistemological tool of the social sciences, has been interpreted by many—within and without the church—as a Marxist "manipulation" or "infiltration" of theology. This unjust accusation—unjust in its intent—is almost as old as liberation theology itself.

1. Position of the 1984 "Instruction on Certain Aspects of the Theology of Liberation"

Were we to hark back to the oldest indictment of the theology of liberation as a Marxist current, we would recall the October 1972 accusation leveled against Father Jaime Serna, as reported by Bogotá television and the dailies.[38] A headline in *El Tiempo* on November 5, 1972, read: "CELAM Accused of Marxism." This was the year the Latin American Bishops' Conference changed direction. The 1969 Rockefeller Report had spoken of a Marxist infiltration of the church.[39] The later Santa Fe (New Mexico) report became part of Reagan's 1980 campaign platform,[40] and now referred explicitly to the dangers lurking in our theology.

In 1975 R. Vekemans wrote *Teología de la liberación y Cristianos para el Socialismo*.[41] In 1978 Boaventura Kloppenburg made a similar attempt to link liberation theology with the Chilean movement Christians for Socialism.[42] Javier Lozano, in *La Iglesia del pueblo*, now argued even more one-sidedly.[43] For Vekemans, Christians for Socialism was the inspiration for the theology of liberation, and the practical upshot was a Marxist option for armed and violent struggle. For Kloppenburg, both movements, being Marxist, ultimately set up a "popular church," a new sect. For Lozano, the "popular church" was the point of departure, and liberation theology its inspiration, while the origin of that theology itself was to be found in Stalinist Marxism-Leninism.

In the 1984 "Instruction"—and we here prescind from any analysis of the theology implied in that document—we observe, beginning with Point 7, a concern with the question of Marxist analysis. The central thesis of the "Instruction," for our purposes, is as follows.

> The *thought* of Marx constitutes a *monolithic conceptualization* of the world, in which numerous data of observation and descriptive analysis are integrated into a philosophico-ideological structure that imposes on these data the meaning and relative importance ascribed to them. . . . A dissociation of the heterogeneous elements composing this epistemologically hybrid amalgam is ultimately impossible; thus, while believing we are accepting only what is presented as an analysis, we find ourselves obliged to accept the underlying ideology as well.[44]

But the "thought of Marx" himself—leaving Engels, Lenin, and Stalin aside—is philosophico-economic; and his mature, "scientific" works,[45] definitive for later tradition, bear no resemblance to the description found in the "Instruction," which declares, for example: *"Atheism* and the rejection of the *human person*, of his freedom and his rights, are at the center of the Marxist conception."[46] In our *complete* reading of the works of Marx,[47] we have seen nothing of the kind. On the contrary, Marx actually opposed the militant atheism of the Communist International. Bakunin attacked Marx for being the director of the International, which he excoriated as a "denier of atheism."[48] Indeed, Marx writes to Friedrich Bolte, on November 23, 1871, that in 1868 he had been unable to accept Bakunin's proposition of the "demand of atheism as a dogma of the members," because "the International takes no cognizance of theological divisions [*Sektionen*]."[49] On August 4, 1878, he writes to George Howell, indicating that "the *Sektion* of socialistic atheists" that Bakunin sought to impose was never accepted (neither was the YMCA) because "theological *Sektionen* are not recognized in the International."[50] Marx explicitly opposed militant atheism. The "Instruction" is obviously unaware of these facts and ignores the differences among Marx, Engels, Stalin, Gramsci, Lukács, Bloch, and so on (see "The Second 'Instruction,' 1986" below).

As for the human person, we may assert without fear of contradiction that, in Marx, this "person" (*Person* in his German) is the point of departure and continuous point of reference in the erection of his categories and in his critique. "Living work" [*lebendige Arbeit*] is the person that, when "subsumed" or "alienated" (sinned against, in Christian categories) in capital, becomes a "thing," a "tool," a mere "article of merchandise,"—the very doctrine of *Laborem Exercens*.[51]

That is, if it is evident that there are *various traditions* in Marxism, and even profound contradictions (Marx's rejection of militant atheism and Stalin's endorsement of it, the nonexistence of a dialectical materialism in Marx and its clear positing later, to indicate but two serious questions for theology),[52] the "Instruction's" entire argument is vitiated in its root. Liberation theologians *have* been able to remove from Marxism the elements that are incompatible with their faith, and have actually done so (as we have demonstrated above). The conclusion of the 1984 "Instruction," then, is a false one:

> This monolithic conception *imposes its logic*, and draws the theologies of liberation to accept *an ensemble* of positions incompatible with the Christian view of the human being.[53]

2. The Second "Instruction," 1986

The 1984 "Instruction" handed down its implied condemnation of liberation theology without having demonstrated the heterodoxy of that theology. But the desired practical result was achieved: anyone in the church looking for an excuse to shut liberation theology out of houses of formation (of seminarians, religious, or laity), universities, periodicals, and so forth, had it ready at hand. The theology of liberation was effectively prevented from reigning in the Latin American church, while it continued to grow in Africa, Asia, Europe (even in the socialist countries), and the United States. The effect was political, then.

The "Instruction on Christian Freedom and Liberation" of March 22, 1986, as we see from its title, deals primarily with the problem of freedom, especially religious freedom (hence its indirect reference to the countries of real socialism), and much less with liberation. Thus the 1986 "Instruction" opens with, "The truth sets us free," and not with texts like "I am the bread of life," or "Blessed are the poor." The theology of liberation begins with an actual, fleshly misery: hunger. The "Instruction" is concerned with truths, teachings, the struggle for freedom—which *pre*suppose that one has eaten, drunk, slept, has clothing, is in decent health, and so on, which are the criteria of the Last Judgment (Matt. 25). And so it goes so far as to say: "Under its manifold forms, . . . human misery is the manifest sign of the *congenital* weakness in which the human being is found after the first sin.[54]

And the response to this misery is "works of beneficence,"[55] or "almsgiving."[56] But at least there is no explicit repetition of the old allegations of Marxism; there are indirect accusations in the new document's frequent references to the 1984 "Instruction." Theologically, the new document's position is very similar to that of the first "Instruction."

III. PATHS NOW OPENING

Thomas Aquinas taught that theology is a science because it practices a *method*—in Thomas's case, the Aristotelian. Liberation theology's habitual use of its scientific tools is in full conformity with the tradition of earlier theologies, from the time of the Apostolic Fathers through the Fathers of the Church and the medieval Latin theologians, down to our present day. It is the *first* theology, of course, to use *Marxism* as a valid mediation—having previously set that Marxism on a level compatible with Christian faith. The Fathers of the Church used Platonism, St. Thomas used Aristotelianism, and Rahner's theology, to cite a modern example, used Heidegger. In the nineteenth century, the use of the science of history occasioned the Modernist crisis. And yet today all theology is historical: the crisis has passed. This is what will happen in the twenty-first century with Marxism. What is interesting is that it is a theology of the peripheral countries that has been the first—in virtue of the necessity imposed on it by its practical, liberative option—to attempt the use of Marxism. Thus, that theology has had to suffer criticism, misunderstanding, and even condemnation; but the road it has taken has remained open, and future generations will be able to travel it in safety, orthodoxy, and justice. Let us consider only certain present challenges, which promise a bright future.

1. Reception of Marxist Categories in the Magisterium of the Church

I should like to give only one example here, among the many I could offer, but one that will be strong enough to make it possible to understand the situation. In millions of its members, the church is now experiencing the reality of a noncapitalist world. In that world, Marxism and Marxist categories are part of daily life—what Husserl or Habermas would have called the *Lebenswelt*. In *Laborem Exercens*, the 1981 encyclical, a number of different categories are used; there is a very intelligent understanding *of Marx* in many passages *against* a naive, economistic, Stalinist Marxism. Let us see some instances of this.

The basic structure of the encyclical is that of a description of the relationships obtaining among *work*, *bread*, and *life*.[57] *Life* is the origin; human *persons* are living beings. Because they are alive, these persons consume their lives; they have *needs*. Needs call for the creative activity of work, which produces *bread* (the product par excellence in biblical thought). Then this bread, this product, consumed, *satisfies* need and restores and augments life. This is the life cycle.[58] Marx enunciates this in prototypal fashion:

> I should have objectified my *individuality* and its peculiarity in my production [read "my bread"], and should therefore have double enjoyment: during the activity, the experience of a *vital individual* expression, and in contemplating the object [the bread], the *individual* joy of knowing that my *personhood* is an objective power. My work would be the expression of free life, to the extent that it partakes of the joy of *life*.[59]

Speaking of the relationship between bread or production and consumption or satisfaction, Marx manifests a frank personalism:

> In the former [production], the producer is objectified as a *thing*. In the latter [consumption], the thing created by [the producer] becomes *person* [*personifiziert*].[60]

And this is repeated in his famous passage: "Merchandise [read "bread"] is an external object, a thing which, thanks to its properties, *satisfies human needs*."[61]

Needs, for Marx, are *human*. "Work is one of the characteristics that distinguish the human being from the rest of creatures," declares the encyclical.[62]

In conformity with Catholic social teaching, the encyclical declares that the *dignity of the human person* is the foundation of the dignity of work. On this point the agreement with Marx is even literal:

Some labors realized by the human being may have an objective *value*; . . . nevertheless, . . . they are measured by the yardstick of the *dignity of the actual subject* of the work: the person.[63]

Marx says explicitly:

Work as *absolute poverty* [*absolute Armut*] . . . exists without mediation, . . . and can only be an objectivity unseparated from the *person* [*Person*]: only an objectivity that coincides with its immediate *bodiliness* [*Leiblichkeit*].[64]

Work . . . is the nonobjectified, that is, unobjective, that is, *subjective* existence of work itself: work not as object, but as activity, . . . as living source of value.[65]

By . . . capacity for work we understand the ensemble of physical and mental faculties existing in *bodiliness*, in the *living personhood* [*lebendige Personlichkeit*] of a human being.[66]

The author of certain pages of the encyclical knows Marx's work very well. He speaks of "capacity for work" (*Arbeitsvermöge*),[67] which Marx uses in the *Grundrisse* (1857-58) and in the *Manuscripts* of 1861-63 and 1863-65, but which he replaces with "work power" (*Arbeitskraft*) in *Das Kapital* (1867), and which later Marxism therefore no longer uses. For Marx, "work *itself* has no [economic] value"; only "capacity for work" does,[68] since it is the "creative source of value"[69] because it has worth or dignity (it is an *end*) and is not a *means* (the *value* of merchandise). And for Marx, as for the encyclical, the person, the subjectivity, the dignity of work ("living work")[70] is the source of the value of all *things* — even of the *thing* called *capital*.[71]

Thus there is complete agreement that the basis of the value of "*objective work*"[72] — a properly Marxist category — is "*subjective* work"[73] — also a Marxist category: work as subject and subjectivity, from the text cited from the *Grundrisse* and many others. The encyclical (with its primacy of the human being in the *process of production*,[74] the primacy of the human being over things)[75] asserts "the principle of the priority of labor over capital,"[76] inasmuch as capital is only objectified, accumulated work.

Finally, the encyclical criticizes the isolation of persons in capitalist society, from the viewpoint of the existence or "sign of the active person amidst a community of persons,"[77] which recalls a text from the *Grundrisse*:

A free *individuality*, based on the universal development of *individuals*, subordinating their *community* [*gemeinschaftliche*] productivity . . . as social legacy constitutes the third stage. *Community* production is subordinated to *individuals* and *controlled in community fashion* by them as their own legacy. ... It is the *free* exchange *among individuals* associated on the basis of appropriation and *community control* of the means of production.[78]

For Marx, as for the encyclical, human toil ("living work," or the "subjectivity of work"), as individuality in community—that is, the human person of the worker—is the point of departure for an ethical critique. Categories like "means of production,"[79] "objective" work in the form of technology,[80] or the statement that "capital cannot be *separated* from labor, and that in no wise can labor be set over against capital,"[81] refer to categories or distinctions *strictly* of Marx himself, which the encyclical uses to criticize, and rightly so, Stalinist, dogmatic, and economistic Marxism. The encyclical, like liberation theology, makes a certain categorical use of Marx, just as St. Thomas used Aristotle.

2. Theology and Economic Criticism

Since its inception, liberation theology has used sociological and political categories, and ideological analysis. However, a *theology of economics*, in the sense of a theology of the *sacramentality* of the bread (the product) of work,[82] in social relations, as a building or destroying of the Reign of God, is a relatively recent phenomenon. Franz Hinkelammert's book, *The Ideological Weapons of Death*,[83] based on a theology of life, blazes new trails. The use of Marxism—at its proper level, the economic and philosophical—is complete, and occurs in a Christian faith that sacrifices nothing of its own tradition. Marx's criticism of fetishism is expressed in the same terms as the criticism of idolatry by the prophets and Jesus. Hinkelammert's rehabilitation of "fleshliness" (*basar* in Hebrew, *sarx* in Greek)[84] is consistent with the Christian experience:

> The enormous value placed on real life in historical materialism has a critical correlate in the Christian message. In the Christian message, the resurrection means a resurrection of human beings in their real life. ... Contrary to the way the forces of domination absolutize values, esteem for real life has always been the starting point for the ideologies of the oppressed. ... The specific element of Marxism is praxis that leads to transcendence within real life. The specifically Christian element is hope in the potentialities of praxis, going beyond what can be calculated to be humanly achievable. The connecting link between them is real material [sacramental] life as the ultimate basis for all human life.[85]

Nor is it a matter of separating Marxist philosophy which is rejected, from analysis, which is accepted. It is now a matter of a complete, integral *rereading* of Marx himself from a Christian, theological perspective. As Thomas Aquinas entered the field of "Aristotelianism" and undertook a creative task "from within" that field, so it is with this last chapter of the theology of liberation, the most recent and the most pregnant with possibilities.

For my part, my *Ethics and Community* has been an attempt at a Christian theological discourse that, while essentially biblical, is *at the same time* strictly Marxist. The concept of "community" in the Acts of the Apostles (2:42-47) and in the *Grundrisse* (and the later manuscripts, up to and including *Das Kapital*) guided my steps. Concepts (and categories) like person, social or community relation, sin and domination, alienation, work, value or "blood," product or "bread," are strictly traditional, and strictly in conformity with the "categories" constituted by Marx in the definitive period of his life (1857-80). A comparison of my *La producción teórica de Marx* and *Ethics and Community* will reveal that the epistemological hypothesis of the latter is the systematic use of Marx's categories (in the sense of the works published in *MEGA* by the Marxist Institute of East Berlin), with strict precision and a use of the biblical categories in their strict Hebrew, Greco-Christian sense. I have sought to get beyond a dualism (philosophy and Marx's analysis), but am clearly aware of the *difference* between the two discourses. Liberation theology, in the coming years, will be creatively internalized in these *missionary and prophetical* areas, to become more comprehensible in the popular world of the exploited.

CONCLUSIONS

The theology of liberation springs from, and learns in a disciplined manner from, the praxis of the Latin American people, the base Christian communities, the poor and oppressed. It justifies, first, the political commitment of militant Christians, thereupon to do the same with the entire praxis of the impoverished Latin American people. It is a critical theological discourse, then, which situates the traditional questions (sin, salvation, church, christology, sacraments, and so on) on a *concrete*, pertinent level. It does not reject the *abstract* (sin *in itself*, for example), but it situates it in *concrete* historical reality (the sin of *dependency*, for example).

It was on the basis of a need for a concrete critical theological reflection from a point of departure in the poor and oppressed that the use of the toolbox of the human sciences, especially Marxism, became necessary. The theology of liberation is the first theology in history to use these analytical instruments, and it takes them up on the strength of the demands of faith, avoiding economicism, a naive dialectical materialism, and an abstract dogmatism. Thus it can criticize as sin capital, dependency, and so forth. It fixes no political alternatives. That is not the function of theology. But it is careful not to fall into the trap of a "third way": neither capitalism nor socialism, but a Christian political solution. It does not thereby cease to be an orthodox (arising from orthopraxis), traditional (in the strong sense of the word) theology. In a missionary spirit, it enters into a dialogue with Marxism (that of Latin American political parties or movements, and even the Marxism of the countries of actual socialism, where its discourse is likewise understandable).

During certain decades, the prophetical positions of liberation theology were referred to as "the usual" by the perennial "wise." Like a Jeremiah jailed in his own Jerusalem, the theology of liberation will have to repeat the experience of criticism and persecution that the prophets had to undergo. "O Jerusalem, Jerusalem, you slay the prophets and stone those who are sent to you!" (Luke 13:34).[86]   — *Translated by Robert R. Barr*

NOTES

1. Rubem Alves, *Toward a Theology of Liberation*, published under the title of *Theology of Human Hope* (Washington, D.C., 1969).

2. See Enrique D. Dussel, *La producción teórica de Marx: Un comentario a los Grundrisse* (Mexico City, 1985), pp. 36-37.

3. For example, *Conceptos elementales del materialismo dialéctico* (Mexico City, 1974), reprinted in more than fifty editions.

4. See Clodovis Boff, *Theology and Praxis: Epistemological Foundations*, trans. Robert R. Barr (Maryknoll, N.Y.: Orbis Books, 1987).

5. See S. Silva Gotal, *Pensamiento revolucionario cristiano* (Salamanca, 1981), and Roberto Oliveros, *Liberación y teología* (Mexico, 1977).

6. F. Houtart and O. Tertano, *Hacia una teología del desarrollo* (Buenos Aires, 1967); V. Cosmao, *Signification et théologie du développement* (Paris, 1967).

7. Juan Luis Segundo, *Función de la Iglesia en la realidad rio-platense* (Montevideo, 1962); or idem, *La cristiandad, una utopia?* (Montevideo, 1964); and even idem, *Teología abierta para el laico adulto*, 5 vols. (Buenos Aires, 1968ff; Maryknoll, N.Y.: Orbis Books, 1973ff.); José Comblin, *Théologie de la paix* (Paris, 1960-63); idem, *Théologie de la révolution* (Paris, 1970-74).

8. See, for example, H. Gollwitzer, *Die reichen Christen und der arme Lazarus* (Munich, 1968); much earlier, Ernst Bloch, *Thomas Münzer* (Madrid, 1969), or Carlos Pinto de Oliveira, *Evangelho e revolução social* (São Paulo, 1962); J. Cardonnel, *L'évangile et la révolution* (Paris, 1968). Cf. R. Vekemans, *Teología de la liberación y Cristianos para el Socialismo* (Bogota, 1976), pp. 100-12.

9. Cf. Hugo Assmann, *Theology for a Nomad Church*, trans. Paul Burns (Maryknoll, N.Y.: Orbis Books, 1976), pp. 29-108.

10. José Porfirio Miranda, *Marx and the Bible: A Critique of the Philosophy of Oppression* (Maryknoll, N.Y.: Orbis Books, 1974).

11. See n. 1 above.

12. Rubem Alves somewhat conceals the meaning of these categories: "political humanism," "humanistic messianism," "messianic humanism," etc.

13. Cf. Pinto, *Consciencia e realidade nacional* (Rio de Janeiro, 1962).

14. Assmann, *Theology for a Nomad Church*, p. 130.

15. Cf. ibid., chap. 2.

16. See Segundo's extensive analysis, consisting of an entire volume at the beginning of his christology (*Faith and Ideologies* [Maryknoll, N.Y.: Orbis Books, 1984]).

17. Segundo, *Theology and the Church* (New York: Winston-Seabury, 1985).

18. Gustavo Gutiérrez, *A Theology of Liberation: History, Politics and Salvation* (Maryknoll, N.Y.: Orbis Books, 1973), p. 15, n. 1.

19. Ibid., p. 6.

20. Ibid., p. 98, n45. Gutiérrez cites Fidel Castro, pp. 98, n. 43; 120, n. 10; 123, n. 20.

21. José Míguez Bonino, *Christians and Marxists* (Grand Rapids, Mich.: Eerdmans, 1976).

22. See n. 10, above.

23. José Míguez Bonino, in the Foreword to Alves, *Religión: ¿opio o instrumento de liberación?*, pp. x-xi.

24. Pablo Richard, "Racionalidad socialista y verificación historica del cristianismo," *Cuaderno de la Realidad Nacional* 12 (1972): 144, 153. See *Origen y desarrollo del movimiento Cristianos por el Socialismo, Chile 1970-1973* (Paris, 1975).

25. Pablo Richard, *Death of Christendom and Birth of the Church* (Maryknoll, N.Y.: Orbis Books, 1987).

26. Leonardo Boff, *La fe en la perifena* (Santander, 1981) p. 125. (See *Faith on the Edge: Religion and Marginalized Existence*, trans. Robert R. Barr [San Francisco: Harper & Row, 1989]).

27. Ibid., p. 127.

28. Ibid., p. 12.

29. Ibid., pp. 75-76.

30. See n. 4, above. Originally subtitled *Teologia do politico e suas mediações*.

31. Jon Sobrino, *Liberación y cautiverio* (Mexico City, 1970), pp. 177-207.

32. See especially Otto Maduro, *Religion and Social Conflicts*, trans. Robert R. Barr (Maryknoll, N.Y.: Orbis Books, 1982).

33. Cf. Juan Carlos Scannone, *Teología de la liberación y praxis popular* (Salamanca, 1976).

34. Cf. Lucio Gera, "Aspectos eclesiológicos de la teología de la liberación," in *Liberación: diálogos en el CELAM*, CELAM, pp. 381-91; *La Iglesia debe comprometerse en lo político* (Montevideo, 1970).

35. Cf. Arturo Paoli, *Freedom to Be Free* (Maryknoll, N.Y.: Orbis Books, 1973); *Meditazione sul Vangelo di Luca* (Brescia, 1972).

36. Ernesto Cardenal, *Santidad en la revolucion* (Buenos Aires, 1971).

37. Néstor Paz, *My Life for My Friends; The Guerrilla Journal of Néstor Paz, Christian* (Maryknoll, N.Y.: Orbis Books, 1975).

38. See Dussel, *De Medellín a Puebla* (Mexico, 1979), pp. 282ff.

39. *Department of State Bulletin* (Washington, D.C.), December 8, 1969, pp. 504ff.

40. Cf. Ana María Ezcurra, *El Vaticano y la administración Reagan* (Mexico City, 1984).

41. R. Vekemans, *Teología de la liberación y Cristianos para el Socialismo* (Bogotá, 1976).

42. Boaventura Kloppenburg, *Informe sobre la Iglesia popular* (Mexico City, 1978).

43. Javier Lozano, *La Iglesia del pueblo* (Mexico City, 1983).

44. *Libertatis Nuntius*, chap 7, no. 6. We pass over the ambiguities in the formulation (because if it is a "hybrid amalgam," various conclusions, and not simply one, could be drawn) and its contradictions (in chap. 7, no. 8, we read: "Marxist thought has diversified, giving rise to various currents *differing notably* from one another").

45. *Science* is used by Marx in a strict sense: see Enrique D. Dussel, *Hacia un Marx desconocido: Un comentario a los Manuscritos del 61-63* (Mexico City, 1988), chap. 14.

46. "Instruction on Certain Aspects of the Theology of Liberation," chap. 7, no. 9.

47. The complete edition of the works of Marx, in more than one hundred volumes, is still being published. Section 2 contains all of the materials on *Das Kapital*, in four redactions. We are presently completing a commentary—after the

fashion of St. Thomas—on these "four redactions" (from 1857 to 1880), in three volumes, two of which are cited in notes 2 and 45, above.

48. Letter of Marx to Liebknecht, November 15, 1872 (*MEW*, 33: 402).

49. *MEW*, 12: 328.

50. Ibid., 19: 144.

51. *Laborem Exercens*, nos. 13-15. See Dussel, *Ethics and Community* (Maryknoll, N.Y.: Orbis Books, 1988), chaps. 11-12, 19.

52. See Dussel, *La producción teórica de Marx*, pp. 34, 36-37, 177-79.

53. "Instruction on Certain Aspects of the Theology of Liberation," chap. 8, no. 1.

54. "Instruction on Christian Freedom and Liberation," no. 68.

55. Ibid.

56. Ibid., no. 67.

57. "With his *work* man must gain his daily *bread*" (first line of the encyclical, and nos. 1, 9, etc.). On the "maintenance of life," see foreword, nos. 1, 2, 3, 8, 10, 14, 18, etc.

58. Cf. Dussel, *Filosofía de la producción*, on the "pragmatic circle" and the "poietic [productive] circle." The first "circulates" between need and consumption; the second, from need to production to product to consumption.

59. Karl Marx, *Paris Notebook* (1844): *Cuaderno de París* (1844) (Mexico City, 1974), pp. 155-56; *MEGA*, sect. 1, vol. 3 (1932), pp. 546-47.

60. Karl Marx, *Grundrisse*, Span. ed., 1: 11.

61. Karl Marx, *Das Kapital*, I, 1.

62. *Laborem Exercens*, foreword. In *Manuscript 1* of 1844, Marx clearly explains the difference between human work, which has awareness and freedom, and mere animal activity.

63. *Laborem Exercens*, no. 6

64. Marx, *Grundrisse*, Span. ed., 1: 235-36. Cf. Dussel, *Producción teórica*, chap. 7, pp. 139ff.

65. Marx, *Grundrisse*. The same text is found in *Manuscripts of 1861-1863* (*MEGA*, II, 3, p. 147; see Dussel, *Hacía un Marx desconocido*, chap. 3, sect. 1).

66. *Das Kapital* (1873), I, 4, 3 (Span. ed., p. 203; *MEGA*, II, 5, p. 120, of 1866). We shall explain this question in a work in preparation, in which we shall expound *Das Kapital* by way of a scientific commentary.

67. For example, "as capacity for work or aptitude for work" (*Laborem Exercens*, no. 5); "the capacity for work" (*Laborem Exercens*, no. 12).

68. "The only opposite to objectified work is nonobjectified work, *living work*. ... The one is value of incorporated use, the other occurs as human activity in process; the one is value, the other is *creator of value*. A given value will be exchanged for activity *creative of value*" (*Manuscripts of 1861-1863*, notebook 1: *MEGA*, II, 3, p. 30). Cf. Dussel, *Hacía un Marx desconocido*, chap. 3, sect. 1.

69. For Marx, "creation" of value is "from the nothing" of capital: "How can a greater value emerge from production than that that has entered into it, unless *something be created from nothing* [*aus Nichts*]?" (*Das Kapital*, III, chap. 1: *MEW* 25: 48).

70. See Dussel, *Hacía un Marx desconocido*, chap. 14, sect. 2. Marx writes a critique of the reified objectivity of capital from a point of departure in the *personal subjectivity* of the worker.

71. The "fetishism" is only an inversion: the *person* of the worker becomes a

thing; and the thing of capital, a person. Cf. Dussel, "El concepto de fetichismo en el pensamiento de Marx," *Cristianismo y Sociedad* 85 (1985): 7-60.

72. Marx speaks of "objectified" work, or the objective meaning of work.

73. Marx's "living work" is work as act, activity, subjectivity/subject — the individual's self, the person of the worker, poor, stripped. This is the ongoing reference of all of Marx's critical thought. His entire work is an *ethics*: "Were we *animals*, we could naturally turn our backs on the *sufferings of humanity*, and just concern ourselves with our own skins. But I should have regarded myself as rather impractical to *have died* without at least having completed the manuscript of my book *Das Kapital*" (Letter of April 30, 1867: *MEW*, 30, p. 542).

74. For Marx, the "living work" subsumed in capital is used, consumed as "work process" within capital (in the *Grundrisse*, in the *Manuscripts of 1861-63 and 1863-65*, and in *Das Kapital*).

75. *Laborem Exercens*, no. 11.

76. Ibid.

77. Ibid, foreword.

78. Marx, *Grundrisse* Span. ed., 1: 86; Germ. ed., pp. 75-77.

79. *Laborem Exercens*, nos. 12, 13, 14, etc.

80. Ibid., no. 5.

81. Ibid., no. 13. At the beginning of his *Paris Notebook* (1844), Marx notes that work cannot be "separated" from capital as if they were two autonomous "things," because the whole of capital is only objectified work. They are not two *things*. There is only one "subjectivity" (work), and capital is only this same subjectivity, *objectified*. Thus the "trinity" is transcended (the three factors, work, capital, land) that is criticized by Marx in *Das Kapital*, III (chap. 7 of the 1865 *Manuscript*, original folios 528ff., in the Amsterdam archive). For all of this see my forthcoming book on the 1863-65 *Manuscripts* (third redaction of *Das Kapital*).

82. See Enrique D. Dussel, "El pan de la celebración eucarística," *Concilium*, no. 172 (1982), pp. 236-49.

83. Franz Hinkelammert, *The Ideological Weapons of Death* (Maryknoll, N.Y.: Orbis Books, 1986; and *Crítica a la razón utópica* (San José, Costa Rica, 1984).

84. See Dussel, *Dualismo en la antropología de la cristiandad* (Buenos Aires, 1974).

85. Hinkelammert, *The Ideological Weapons of Death*, p. 41.

86. The present contribution was prepared before the events in Eastern Europe or the elections in Nicaragua: hence no reflection on these phenomena is included here.

Eds. note: For reasons of space, a section of the original chapter from the Spanish edition chronicling the history of relations between Christians and Marxists in Latin America has been omitted.

5

Liberation Theology and the Social Teaching of the Church

RICARDO ANTONCICH

A definition of the relationship between the theology of liberation and the social teaching of the church is no easy task. Witness the fact that, for certain currents within the church, a return to the social teaching of the church would be the appropriate "strategy" for defeating liberation theology by rendering it superfluous.

This interpretation regards the theology of liberation and the social teaching of the church as forces locked in combat for the same "space" in Christian reflection and commitment. On this hypothesis, the question could be asked: Why would the social teaching of the church, which came before liberation theology, have left the space empty that came to be occupied by the theology of liberation? One possible explanation might be a doctrinal, academic, ecclesiastical language alien to the world of the workers, the farm workers, the common people, despite a reference to the rights and demands of these social sectors. Other explanations, arising from Latin American reality, would point to the economic, social, and political framework of the 1970s and 1980s, which evinced Latin America's enormous dependency on centers of decision outside that continent. The church's social teaching no longer offered a concrete framework of analysis for third-world reality, although some suggestions had made their appearance in *Populorum Progressio* (cf. nos. 5-10).

On the other hand, circumstances were ripe in Latin America for the rise of liberation theology. The situation of oppression was becoming more apparent. Aspirations for liberation, in popular sectors as well as in intellectual circles, were being expressed more vigorously. Unlike what had happened in Europe, the ideal channels for expressing these struggles for social liberation (such as unions and political parties) were insufficiently well organized or else were repressed by military dictatorships based on the ideology of national security. The church, however, had been able to receive these aspirations in its base communities, in its rural and labor ministry, and in its university ministry.

Convincing as these arguments may be, we cannot accept the hypothesis of a single "space" to be monopolized by either the social teaching of the church or the theology of liberation. This would place the theology of liberation and the social teaching of the church on the same level, and ignore their differences and their distinct functions in the church.

Liberation theology cannot replace the social teaching of the church; nor vice versa. They have different tasks, and employ different, although convergent, approaches.

In the social teaching of the church, the subject or agent of the proposition of the teaching of faith is the magisterium of the church: first the pope, in the encyclicals (*Rerum Novarum, Quadragesimo Anno, Mater et Magistra, Pacem in Terris, Populorum Progressio, Laborem Exercens*) or other documents issuing from the highest authority (*Octogesima Adveniens, Libertatis Nuntius, Libertatis Conscientia*), then the documents of the magisterium of the bishops, whether published by the Council (*Gaudium et Spes*) or by other sources, such as—in the particular case of Latin America—those of the two General Conferences of the Latin American Episcopate, held at Medellín (1968) and Puebla (1979).

In the theology of liberation, the subject developing the reflection (which cannot properly be called a teaching or doctrine), is the theologian, who works within the liberation process of the Christian people, and who places his or her work at the service of this apostolic commitment of the people of God, in conformity with the orientation given by the pope (cf. *Redemptor Hominis*). Thus, the theological task is one of partnership with the traditional service rendered by the magisterium.

God's people have a right to the convergent service of their pastors and their theologians. On the other hand, the forms of the exercise of authority in doctrinal material must also be exemplary forms of Christian charity in the dialogue between pastors and theologians.

The convergence between liberation theology and the social teaching of the church can be established in terms of the Reign of God. Christian theology first hears the word of God; it pronounces its own word afterward. But God's revelation finds its plenitude in Jesus Christ, the eternal Word, the word par excellence. No theology may be anything but an ongoing, updated comprehension of the meaning of the Reign in the times at hand. Why? Because the Reign occupies the central place in Jesus' preaching. It constitutes the articulating axis of his "theoretical practice"—that is, the privileged instrument for the realization of the process of conversion from the situation of sin to the condition of the children of God. The Reign constitutes the "semantic matrix," as it were, or generative concept, that reveals the kind of relationship that is established between God and human beings. To know the Reign is to know God and the power of God in the history of human beings.

The theme of the Reign may be regarded as the articulating axis upon which one may comprehend the relationship between the human sciences and biblical research. The symbolic value of the Reign must be viewed primarily against the cultural horizon of its proclamation. But its comprehension must also be recreated in terms of the persons of today, with their language and their problems in facing the demands of the Reign.

The category of the Reign of God constitutes the junction of the theological with the sociological, inasmuch as this latter dimension is in a position to guarantee the conditions of a better *human reign*. The theological, in turn, will describe the relationship of the human reign—as human historical project—with the Reign that God wishes to establish among us.

The category of the Reign of God, as the central focus of theology, enables us to resolve the artificial antagonism between the social teaching of the church and the theology of liberation. If the Reign of God is a reign of freedom, then that Reign must be the point of reference for the theology of liberation. And if the church is the servant of this Reign, as its sacrament, then the teaching of the church must be a Christian practice of liberation.

If we start out with this convergence in the Reign of God, we can better identify the set of relationships obtaining between liberation theology and the social teaching of the church. If the theology of the Reign supposes an active role on the part of the person who collaborates with grace, and if grace embraces all of the dimensions of human life that are subject to the divine dominion, then a recourse to the social sciences is an obvious demand of human cooperation in the preparation and disposition of history to receive the gift of the Reign proclaimed and offered to us by Jesus Christ. It is here, however—on the level of the relationship with the socioanalytic mediations—that the most visible oppositions between liberation theology and the social teaching of the church have occurred, especially when liberation theology has had recourse to a science that radically questions the capitalist system.

We shall proceed, in our examination of the subject, from the more simple to the more complex. Human liberation, with the activity and grace of God, is at the heart of the gospel. The extension and scope of this soteriological phenomenon, its ethical projections, the relations of faith with political situations, methods, and solutions in which freedom is at stake, are all part of this reflection upon the fundamental fact that persons attain their freedom in Christ.

To proclaim the liberating deed of Christ, precisely in contexts of the repression of persons and of their aspirations to freedom, constitutes *liberative pastoral praxis*, which presupposes the ongoing accompaniment of a critical reflection, which we call the theology of liberation. By the nature of the social fact of oppression, and of the aspirations to freedom, it is obvious that this theology will have to strike a dialogue with the social sciences. This series of problems will be analyzed in the general relationship between the theology of liberation and the social teaching of the church. On the other hand, the problem becomes more critical at the moment in which recourse is had to Marxism as an instrument of analysis of capitalist society. It is especially at this point that the most serious animadversions of the social teaching of the church appear (for example, in *Libertatis Nuntius* [LN] and *Libertatis Conscientiae* [LC]) with respect to liberation theology and the more profound questions concerning their mutual relationship. Let us leave this core of problems for a second section, which we shall entitle, "Specific Relations."

In distinguishing these two levels of relation, we hope to be faithful to the forthright support offered by Pope John Paul II to the theology of liberation in his letter to the bishops of Brazil, and at the same time be true to the admonitions of the official church concerning Marxism.

I. GENERAL RELATION BETWEEN THE THEOLOGY OF LIBERATION
AND THE SOCIAL TEACHING OF THE CHURCH

Let us maintain the distinction between a liberative pastoral praxis and the theology of liberation. The former is a *first act* of a church that evangelizes the poor; the second is a *second act* of reflection upon this pastoral practice.

1. A Liberative Pastoral Praxis

The Second Vatican Council supplies this praxis with its frame of reference when it asserts that the church ought to be present wherever humanity experiences its joys, hopes, sorrows, and anguish. In a special way, it ought to enter into solidarity with the very poorest (*Gaudium et Spes*, no. 1). Starting with the concept of the "signs of the times" (no. 4), the Council describes certain phenomena and situations that challenge the faith and pastoral activity of the church: the hunger and wretchedness of great segments of humanity (no. 4), aspirations for transformation in the face of economic and social inequalities (no. 8), and the challenge of hungry peoples amidst the wealthy (no. 9).

In these phenomena the church recognizes a *refusal of the human calling* as issued in the plan of God. Discrimination is "contrary to God's intent." Economic and social inequalities "militate against social justice, equity, the dignity of the human person, as well as social and international peace" (no. 29). By contrast, an activity that seeks to improve conditions of human life "accords with God's will" (no. 34), and the boons of human dignity, a union of sisters and brothers, and freedom will be found once more, purified of every blemish, in the eschatological Reign of God (cf. no. 39).

The theological problem involved here is that of the meaning and value, from the perspective of the Reign of God, of those historical transformations on the economic, political, and social plane that permit a human life for all human beings, in conformity with God's design. Are social liberation and the Reign of God simply identical? Are they separate and distinct totally and absolutely? That is, is there no relationship whatever between liberation and the Reign?

One of the most critical problems in liberation theology is that of establishing the correct relationships and distinctions that must obtain between social liberation and the Reign of God. They must be distinguished. The bishops of Peru declare:

Without the distinction, grace is absorbed by nature, God by history: Christ is reduced to a mere moral teacher or social leader, the church to a human institution. Or else temporal realities come to be messianized and divinized: History, the People, the Revolution. Eschatology is diluted into the evolutionary process of history, and the Reign of God is attained only by the efforts of human beings.

But as a distinction is necessary, so also is unity. Thus, the same bishops add:

> On the other hand, unless a unity is maintained between the two dimensions, the reality of our faith is denied: creation, the Incarnation, the redemption, grace. An immanentist messianism will never lead but to the bitterest disillusionment; but to renounce all hope of bettering this world, here and now, is to deny the salvific power of the Lord. The struggle with evil in this world is a human responsibility, with the help of grace; but the definitive triumph over evil and death is the divine gift we hope for. God's alone is the power to bring history to its conclusion, as it was God alone who gave it its beginning.[1]

The theology of liberation can only be understood from the viewpoint of a liberative pastoral praxis. For this reason, *Libertatis Nuntius*, the document of the magisterium most critical of liberation theology (specifically, of the fact that it makes use of Marxism), can only be understood in the context of the Council, and of a liberative pastoral praxis.

According to *Gaudium et Spes*, a liberative pastoral praxis ought to spring up wherever there is oppression and consequent aspirations for freedom (no. 1). This is the case in Latin America. *Libertatis Nuntius*, then, understands by liberation theology a "special concern, generative of a commitment to justice, and projected upon the poor and victims of oppression" (chap. 3, no. 3). Further on, the same document describes some characteristics of that oppression (chap. 7, no. 12). Thus, one may say that "the encounter of the aspiration for liberation and the theologies of liberation is not fortuitous" (chap. 3, no. 4), and evangelization itself "has contributed to the awakening of the consciousness of the oppressed" (chap. 1, no. 4). Considered in themselves, "aspirations for liberation cannot fail to find a broad fraternal echo in the heart and spirit of Christians" (chap. 3, no. 1).

A liberative pastoral praxis is the church's response to oppression and aspirations for liberation. It must also purify these aspirations of their ambiguities (cf. LN, chap. 2, no. 2; LC, nos. 10, 13, 19). But neither must it forget the ambiguities of faith itself (LN chap. 9, no. 18; LC nos. 20, 57). This ambiguity resides not only in projects of liberation that may not be Christian, but in Christians' own project. It affects one's very manner of living the faith, which can render the believer insensitive to problems of justice and poverty (cf. LC, nos. 57, 20, 58, 60-61, 64-65).

The liberative pastoral praxis of the church must be nourished by the *word of God*. The two documents that we have been citing indicate the importance of the exodus from Egypt, since the liberating activity of Yahweh serves as the "model and reference point of all other" such activity (LC, no. 44). The situation of the poor—as persons who are marginalized, and deprived of a better life — is contrary to the covenant (no. 46). Justice is related to mercy in *Libertatis Nuntius* (chap. 4, nos. 8-9), and to love in *Libertatis Conscientia* (nos. 55-57). The theme of poverty is treated sparsely in *Libertatis Nuntius* (chap. 4, no. 9), while *Libertatis Conscientia* develops it more amply (no. 50). In the latter document, the poor are regarded as the addressees of the Good News: Jesus became poor for us and wishes to be recognized in the poor. There is a better explanation of the theological reason for this impoverishment of Christ (no. 66) and the urgency of an active commitment to liberation from the evil of poverty (no. 67). In this context, the meaning of a preferential love for the poor becomes more precise, and there is a clearer allusion to the base ecclesial communities and to the theology of liberation. The theme of liberation theology, then, is situated where the Latin American church had placed it: liberation theology is a reflection, from a starting point among the poor, from the base ecclesial communities, on their praxis of liberation.

According to *Libertatis Nuntius* and *Libertatis Conscientia*, the liberative pastoral praxis of the church, besides feeding on the message of salvation, the message of the word of God, must also be enlightened by the social teaching of the church, because this is what must constitute it a "true Christian praxis of liberation" (LC, chap. 5).

It is here that we must examine the mutual contribution — still on a general level — of the social teaching of the church and the theology of liberation.

2. Liberation Theology and a Liberative Pastoral Praxis

As is well known, liberation theologians have insisted upon the character of their theology as a *second act*. That is, liberation theology is a reflection on the life and liberative commitment that spring from faith.

> The Christian community professes a "faith which works through charity." It is — at least ought to be — real charity, action, and commitment. . . . Theology is reflection, a critical attitude. Theology *follows*; it is the second step.[2]

The critical function of theology vis-à-vis praxis begins with a concentration on the pastoral praxis of the church itself, and then extends to a critique of the church-world relationship, within the broader concept called for by the open perspectives of *Gaudium et Spes*. The object of this critique, then, will be historical praxis, the transformation of history.

> Thus, theology is understood as *actus secundus*, the first act being the praxis of liberation, first of all on the part of Christians, in a historical context of injustice and oppression. Accordingly, the social teaching of the church would not have been possible without a raised consciousness of the structural historical situation, the consequent option for the poor, and the commitment to their liberation on the part of numerous members of the Latin American people of God, made up in large part of the poor.[3]

When God's people sees itself faced with doctrinal problems (the heresies of the first centuries) or practices (the social injustices of our present moment), it anxiously seeks in its own faith the authentically evangelical responses. This search is not blind. It is guided by the Spirit (John 16:13-15), assisted by the magisterium of the church, and explained by theology.

> Theology has always had and continues to have great importance for the Church, the People of God, to be able to share creatively and fruitfully in Christ's mission as prophet. (*Redemptor Hominis*, no. 19)

Theologians, according to John Paul II in the encyclical just cited, not only must serve the magisterium, but must "place themselves at the service of the apostolic commitments of the whole of the People of God" (no. 19).

When theology seeks to assist a liberative pastoral praxis, it must enter into dialogue with the social sciences. As *second act,* or reflection, of a *first act* (a liberative pastoral praxis), theology strives (1) to enrich the understanding of the process of liberation; (2) to perceive the causes of oppression, with the help of the sciences; and (3) to help the base ecclesial communities with pastoral tools. These communities are the privileged locus of the liberative pastoral praxis, since it is in them that the encounter occurs between the oppressed poor, who aspire for liberation, and the faith-responses arising from the word of God and the social magisterium of the church. It is one and the same subject or agent, then, that asks the questions and seeks the answers. It is not a matter of the poor who are suffering, and alongside of them of a church that is responding. The base ecclesial community is the encounter point of situations of oppression and aspirations for liberation, on the one hand, with the word of God and the Christian faith, encouraged by the magisterium of the church.

1. Contribution of the Social Teaching of the Church to the Theology of Liberation

Once we admit the legitimacy of the dialogue between the social sciences and theology—a dialogue whose raison d'être is to assist the apostolic commitments of the whole of the people of God—we must ask ourselves a question. We must inquire into the criteria for a correct interdisciplinary dialogue. Such a dialogue will avoid two pernicious extremes. It will avoid distorting the proper nature of the social sciences (by "theologizing" them, that is, by withdrawing their assertions from a scientific rigor derived from the empirical basis of all science). At the same time, it will take care not to deform the proper nature of theology (by "sociologizing" it, that is, by identifying the empirical assertions springing from situations and events with a faith-reading of these same events or situations).

On the first level of the relationship between liberation theology and the social teaching of the church, we shall limit ourselves to an examination of the general principles for the discernment of sciences and ideologies, leaving the application of these principles to the particular case of Marxism for the second level of the relationship between liberation theology and the social teaching of the church.

i) **Discernment of the Sciences.** The Council was sensitive to the importance of accepting the contribution of the sciences and respecting the autonomy of their cognition. *Gaudium et Spes* defends the autonomy of science (no. 36); it encourages the dialogue with the sciences for the purpose of a better knowledge of human nature (no. 44). *Christus Dominus* exhorts bishops to use social research for pastoral praxis (no. 17). In a word, with Paul VI we must say of the social sciences that "the Church has confidence in this research also and urges Christians to play an active part in it" (*Octogesima Adveniens*, no. 40).

Now, perhaps for the first time, we have clear and definite criteria for the relation between the social sciences and theology. The problem is obviously a new one. But it is posed by the kind of reflection fostered by liberation theology in its study of the problem of social and historical praxis. *Libertatis Nuntius* indicates certain criteria. The scientific myth must be discarded (chap. 7, no. 4). The contributions of the various sciences and their perspectives are all to be confronted, with attention to the plurality of their methods and viewpoints; the sciences, in emphasizing a particular perspective, fail to attain a unified view of the problem (chap. 7, no. 5). In the dialogue between the sciences and theology, primacy must be assigned to the theological criterion of truth; the truths of the other disciplines must be judged in the light of faith and of what faith teaches concerning ultimate human destiny (chap. 7, no. 10).

ii) **Discernment of Ideologies.** The ideologies are not clearly defined in the social magisterium. *Pacem in Terris* understands them as false teachings concerning humanity's origin and end (no. 159). Their equivalency with teaching or "doctrine" is very strict (cf. PP, no. 39). Paul VI points to the discernment of ideologies as it is found in *Octogesima Adveniens* (no. 26). The legitimacy of the Christian's commitment in the area of political ideology is contingent on the possibility of separating the original ideologies from the historical movements that have sprung from them. The latter possibility was indicated, first of all, by John XXIII, in *Pacem in Terris* (no. 159), to be addressed once more by Paul VI apropos of the discernment of the socialistic and capitalistic ideologies (OA, nos. 31-35). Pope Paul VI pointed out the temptation, for those who make their option for socialism as well as for those who elect capitalism, of "forgetting" the bonds that may exist between the historical movement to which they give their adherence and the original philosophies or ideologies, to which they cannot give their adherence without contradicting their faith (cf. nos. 31, 35).

2. Contribution of the Theology of Liberation to the Social Teaching of the Church

The criteria proposed by the social magisterium must surely be kept in account by the theology of liberation in its dialogue with the social sciences. But liberation theology, in its turn, must question the heavy-handed application of the criteria of discernment proposed by Paul VI in *Octogesima Adveniens* (nos. 31-35). The importance of a discernment of the sciences and ideologies is sometimes insisted on with Marxism as if other sciences and ideologies were safe and could not distort the faith. As we shall presently observe — in the liberation theology that uses Marxism — the orientations proposed by the social teaching of the church are more universal and demanding than those demanded in concrete pastoral practice. It is a function of the theology of liberation on behalf of the social teaching of the church to contribute critically to the presentation of the social magisterium in its integrity taking into account all social and ideological realities.

Another contribution on the part of liberation theology to the social teaching of the church is its emphasis on the hermeneutical perspective. Liberation theology has sprung up on the periphery, and from a point of departure in concrete social, economic, and political situations. Thus, one contribution by this theology to the social teaching of the church is an appreciation of the importance of the *hermeneutical role* and social locus from which that same social teaching is interpreted.

After all, the social teaching of the church must not be an academic tractate, but a source of inspiration for a praxis of liberation. This objective, which the magisterium itself sets for the social teaching of the church (cf. LC, chap. 5), means that this teaching must be interpreted in such a way that its message becomes dynamic and enlightening. This being the case, we can identify four notes for the interpretation of the social teaching of the church:

1. The social teaching of the church ought to be situated in the historical context in which it has been formulated, in full cognizance of the differences or "distances," temporal as well as spatial, between the written texts and the life situations which are to be illuminated by those texts.

2. Likewise, the magisterium ought to be interpreted in terms of the law of love, which must be central to any *Christian ethics*. A convergence must prevail between obedience to the authority of the church, and the creative, responsible freedom of the children of God. To wish to impose the social magisterium as if it were a party slogan, or dogma of faith, would be an assault on the ethical nature of service to the praxis of liberation. The law of love is the supreme norm of all law in the church, because it is Jesus' sole commandment, whose contents will be clarified throughout all time.

3. The ethics to which we refer is *social ethics*; thus, it will be important to keep account of the information and contribution of the social sciences.

4. Finally, the fourth hermeneutic criterion consists in the *option for the poor*. Pope Paul VI, in *Octogesima Adveniens*, indicates very precisely that the social teaching of the church is a service to the cause of the poor (no. 42). Only by entering within this dynamic of service, expressed by the option for the poor, can we adequately understand the social teaching of the church. The contribution of liberation theology is decisive when it comes to setting in relief this fourth hermeneutic criterion.

II. SPECIFIC RELATION AMONG LIBERATION THEOLOGY, MARXISM, AND THE SOCIAL TEACHING OF THE CHURCH

In broaching the subject of the specific relationship obtaining among (1) the theology of liberation, (2) Marxism, and (3) the social teaching of the church, we address the problem of liberation theology's use of Marxist tools in its analysis of society. In general terms, we shall say that this use of methods of analysis involves some risks, which the social teaching of the church has pointed out, while at the same time it opens up some perspectives on the problem of liberation that may actually call into question the social teaching of the church.

While one must attend to the observations of the magisterium, and give them due assent, even when dogmatic truths are not at issue, on the other hand the problems objectively posed by the use of Marxism ought to be seriously addressed by the magisterium itself, inasmuch as questions to Christian faith are involved.

In a word, the encounter between liberation theology and the social teaching of the church ought to produce a significant modification in both. Liberation theology may not ignore the animadversions of the magisterium, but neither will a healthy pastoral attitude incline us to ignore the questions arising from historical situations in which Marxism has its social, intellectual, and political influence.

1. The Social Teaching of the Church Sheds Light on a Liberative Praxis and on the Theology of Liberation

The option for the poor, founded on evangelical motives and an interpretation of social conflict, must maintain the identity that springs from the faith perspective.

1. The Option for the Poor

The utilization of Marxist analytical instruments can mislead us to make concrete the meaning of *poor* exclusively in terms of an organized proletariat with a political consciousness of the class struggle.

It will be appropriate to recall, then, that the biblical concept of the poor is a broader one. It also embraces those who cannot be regarded as an historical force, whether for lack of a critical awareness, or by reason of psychological or physical limitations that would prevent effective action on their part. The option for the worker, which the magisterium itself proposes as appropriate for a "church of the poor," must not be restricted to the manual laborer or exclusively to persons of the working class who have a potential for political action. Any kind of work, in its quality as human activity with a sense of solidarity, has a value in itself, and must be defended independently of categories of work or social class (LE, intro., nos. 4a, 8c).

But while it is true that the option for the poor must be constantly "open" to the universal calling of Christian love, it is equally true that it must remain "concrete," as a demand of the same love. Thus, the pope alludes to altogether concrete situations of exploitation of labor amidst a social conflict between capital and labor (nos. 11c, 13c, 7b, 8f), and recalls that the social problem has come to be called the "labor question."

This "concreteness" can be shut up in the selfishness of a single class (no. 20d), it is true, but without it the problem to which we refer becomes obfuscated. Liberation theology, in its option for the poor, must always maintain a tension between the concrete reality of an oppressed social class and the universality of Christian love, always asserting the latter *in function of* the former.

2. The Interpretation of Social Conflict

It is upon this point that the admonitions addressed by the social teaching of the church to the theology of liberation primarily concentrate. An interpretation of social conflict in terms of class struggle, according to *Libertatis Nuntius*, comports not only the acceptance of a methodology of social analysis, but also an assumption of the postulates of a dialectical philosophy to the effect that the existence of a class struggle in history is a law of human nature.

Let us attempt to clarify this point. We shall use the expression *social conflict* instead of *class struggle* in order to respect the terminology proposed by *Libertatis Nuntius* for the problem, reserving the expression *class struggle* for the Marxist approach to the conflict on the two levels — social analysis and philosophy — that we have indicated. By contrast, the expression *social conflict* alludes to a *concrete phenomenon*, actually existing, not yet thematized by a social analysis. We insist that it is reality itself that is at issue here. Of course, this is not denied in the "Instruction," but it is interpreted in a different way.

In Part I we have established the acceptance of social analyses in the pastoral theology of the church. What is in question here is the use of a *concrete method of analysis* originating in Marxism (LN, chap. 8, no. 6). The concept of "class struggle" implies a connection, judged by *Libertatis Nuntius* to be essential and intrinsic, to the philosophy of dialectical materialism (cf. nos. 6-8).

The sociological analysis of the class struggle examines the social classes against a background of the unequal distribution of economic goods and political power. This examination establishes an antithesis: that of the powerful, rich capitalist versus the oppressed, poor laborer. In the search for an ethical justification for an option for the oppressed, the ethico-economico-political categories expressed here can be projected into an identification of moral goodness with the class of the oppressed and moral evil with the class of the oppressors. But this identification is suspect of a reduction of the ethical dimension to the status of a "by-product" of social pertinency, without the necessary confrontation of each human liberty with the moral values that realize the being of a person. A person would be good or evil because that person *belongs to a class*, and not because he or she *makes a choice* of good or evil.

This attempt at legitimation has the effect here, as it does in all collective phenomena, of bestowing a moral value on the struggles with the adversary. Now it is a struggle of the "good guys" against the "bad guys." It is a phenomenon that has been studied in depth by social psychology: human beings who would never be able to justify inhumane acts (like torture or murder) in the name of purely personal considerations, will with a clear conscience perform inhumane acts in the name of a collective notion (country, religion, race, class power). It is precisely ethics, under the light of the gospel, that inclines us to disqualify this Manichaean oversimplification of "good guys" and "bad guys," and it is here that the social teaching of the church introduces substantial modifications in conflict analysis, which liberation theology must take seriously into account.

With a view to examining the contribution of *Laborem Exercens* to an interpretation of conflict, let us recall certain theoretical presuppositions. Each human being constructs various "worlds," in accordance with his or her particular interests, for example, a religion, an artistic world, or a sports world. One and the same subject can refer itself to many worlds and use many languages proper to these respective worlds. But that subject must take care to exercise a critical vigilance in order to respect the autonomous value of each language. Actually the various worlds are integrated into the unity of the subject who experiences them. But we may speak of an objective integration, as well. We need only examine the criteria of each language and the possibility of an intercommunication among them. This is precisely the case with the "world of the social" and the "world of the ethical," which converge in an analysis of one and the same phenomenon: the social conflict.

The encyclical *Laborem Exercens* provides a good example of the integration of the sociological world, revealed in conflict analysis, and the ethical universe of values. To this purpose, John Paul II adopts two terms having a concrete meaning in the Marxist sociological world ("capital" and "labor"). Let us observe that the synchronic meaning of the terms *capital* and *labor* in the overall Marxist system is converted diachronically, and changed—used in another historical moment and another system, this time in that of Christian thought.

The possibility of a *diachronic evolution*, which would deliver the terms from their *synchronic status* within the Marxist system, responds not only to the problem of a different comprehension of these terms within the "same world" (here, that of the social sciences), but also to the problem of the integration of the two worlds, that of the sciences and that of the ethical demands deriving from Christian faith. Thanks to this diachronic evolution, there can be a Christian (in virtue of its relationship with ethics) interpretation of the conflict (which is a social phenomenon).

In this change of the semantic content of *capital* and *labor* we find the following elements:

1. Perception of the *ethical nature of the conflict*: While the scientist looks for the immediate cause-effect relationship, the believer seeks a more profound interpretation, in terms of confrontation with the absolute. Beyond the historical forms of the human conflict is an ongoing duel between justice and injustice, good and evil. Historical motives may change, technologies used in the conflict or war may change, but the ethical considerations abide. The church does not judge itself technically competent in the matter of conflict analysis (LE, no. 1), but when it speaks of economism and materialism, it goes beyond the analyses of the sciences to the values and choices of human life. If human problems were the object of scientific analysis alone, the church would have no right to deal with them in terms of faith, and the social teaching of the church would collapse, deprived of its foundation.

2. *Link between scientific analysis and the ethical*: While the ethical reduces the conflict to a confrontation between good and evil, the "historification" of that conflict must be examined by way of sociological, historical, and cultural analyses. Otherwise the ethical analysis would be inoperative, as it would be

ignorant of the circumstances in which good and evil appear in history.

3. *Reformulation of the concepts* used in science: The pope employs *capital* and *labor* as valid concepts for understanding the social conflict. However, he understands the opposition between them not in terms of class struggle, but as a value-charged, ethical antagonism. The original, purely socioeconomic and political meaning undergoes a semantic transformation, and comes to denote, in *labor,* the value of "being-in-solidarity," and in *capital,* the anti-value of "having more" as the absolute objective of human life.

The pope notably modifies the meaning of *labor* when he refuses to restrict it to the (urban industrial) working class, or to farm workers, and refers it to all labor, independent of the circumstances in which it is performed. He includes even the work of intellectuals and indicates the dangers that threaten this kind of work today, such as unemployment and exploitation.

The ethical priority of labor *over* capital, then, is not a "class option," but a "value option." *Capital* is simply incapable of receiving this priority, because of its intrinsic reference to *having*; it is endowed with moral worth only when it is at the service of *being*, and therefore only when capital is held for the good of labor. The means of production may not be possessed in opposition to labor; neither may they be possessed for the sake of possessing them, since the sole title to their possession is that they be of service to labor and thus foster the universal destination of all goods for all persons (LE, no. 14). Precisely in this context the pope does not exclude the possibility that, with a view to this universal destination, we might legitimately speak of a *socialization*.

This allusion to the socialization of the means of production could seem to imply an ideological identification of labor and its moral values with socialism — just as the allusion to capital, which is ethically regarded as negative when it exploits labor, could seem to denote the capitalist system. But this interpretation is not justified. Why? Because just as labor is not identified with a class, so neither is capital identified with a system or ideology.

It is important to keep in mind that the meaning attributed to capital as a symbol of selfish "having" can be verified not only in the Western system, which systematically exacerbates selfishness and self-interest as a dynamism of progress, but also in the socialist system, when the socialization of the means of production withdraws ownership (including social ownership) of the means of production from the workers, who are not regarded as authentic owners (collective, this time) of the means of production (cf. no. 14).

Thus, the semantic transformation at work here precludes the identification of labor with the working class or capital with the capitalist system. All work, even intellectual work, is called to be a symbol of the solidarity of the human person in quest of *being*. By contrast, capital in the Western system, even in socialism, becomes "selfish capitalism" when it is set up in opposition to labor and becomes an instrument of exploitation.

It is to be observed, however, that neither capital nor labor carry any ethical connotation in themselves, independently of the human project in which they are used. Labor can be degraded to the status of a mere tool of "selfish having," thereby losing its whole symbolical value of "being more"; while capital can be used as a tool of labor, without exploiting the latter, and thereby acquire the ethical quality of goodness, of fostering both solidarity and "being more."

4. *Ethics' capacity to challenge science*: Let us keep in mind that the use of the words *capital* and *labor* can lead to ambiguity and confusion, as if *Laborem Exercens* were encouraging the class struggle. But along with this danger, of which the pope is very well aware, there is also the possibility of a concrete, wholesome challenge; and surely in this case the latter abundantly compensates for the risk of the former. What we have is a challenge to the sciences, especially to Marxist conflict-analysis, not to reduce "capital and labor" to a mere expression of the interests of social classes in counterpoise, but to see in these words the expression of a contrariety of human values. Both ideologies, then, are invited to review their presuppositions: Capitalism ought to attenuate its stimulus to self-interest — which, when unbridled, issues in selfishness — and the right of ownership with a greater sensitivity to the social dimension of ownership and with an integral concept of the development of the person in society. In turn, socialism is called upon to transcend a narrow view of "class" in this conflict and ascribe to human labor not only the function of workers' political struggle, but the integral, humanistic sense that did not escape Marx himself. The option for labor is neither a class option nor an ideology; it is an expression of an option for human beings themselves.

5. *Intensification of the ethical commitment*: Here there can be no neutrality in the dilemma of capital or labor. All Christians wishing to be consistent with their faith option for Jesus Christ, and for the evangelical values proclaimed by him, must make their option for labor. Only then will it be possible to speak of a spirituality of labor, the theme so dear to the heart of John Paul II. It will be difficult at best to speak of a spirituality of capital, since capital is not a human *activity*, but a human *object*. Labor is an activity, and it involves human beings' *presence* to themselves. That is, it involves a human spirit, which can indeed have an encounter with the Spirit of God.

2. Liberation Theology Questions and Challenges the Social Teaching of the Church

It would be less than honest of us to omit an examination of the profound questions arising from the use of Marxism in liberation theology for the social teaching of the church itself, and of possible criticisms of the way in which the latter makes its discernment of ideologies and presents the opposition between anthropologies springing from ideologies vis-à-vis a Christian vision of the human being.

1. Marxist Criticisms of Christian Faith

Marxism is a complex phenomenon, and we must recognize the manifold currents of interpretation running within it. It is difficult, then, to find a clear category to express the problem posed to theology by Marxism.

But in addition to the specific problem of the use of Marxism in theology, there is another problem that cannot be ignored — an older, deeper one, as well as a more universal one. That is the problem of Marxism's criticisms of Christian faith.

These criticisms could be enunciated in the form of questions. When the church, with its social teaching, defends private ownership, is it likewise defending the privileges of the wealthy and the capitalist bourgeois system? When it condemns the class struggle, is it opposing the struggle of the poor for justice — offering them an "opiate," a soporific, instead? When it proclaims and worships God, does it not withdraw human beings from the construction of the world?

These questions correspond to the three levels on which *Libertatis Nuntius* has situated its animadversions: science, philosophy, and the theological projections of Marxism.

According to historical Marxism, the key to an understanding of human beings' exploitation of one another is found in private ownership of the means of production; the church identifies itself with capitalism in defending this ownership.

According to dialectical materialism, the essential conflict of history is revealed in the class struggle. In denying the class struggle as a fact and rejecting it as a method, the church prevents the oppressed from struggling for their liberation; thus it once more plays the role of legitimator of oppression, as it has done in sacralizing ownership.

While *Libertatis Nuntius* limits itself to indicating the theological deviations that can emerge from a Marxist anthropology of conflict, Marxism has long since lodged a far more radical criticism with religion itself; that is, that religion deprives human beings of the meaning of their struggle to improve history, since those human beings expect everything from a being alien from themselves. Accordingly they are "alienated," that is, they cease to "belong" to and to build their own history. An authentic humanism, according to Marxism, must be atheistic. Only thus may human beings realize themselves through the historical struggle and better the conditions of their existence.

What is at issue here is the social teaching of the church and its interpretation. The social teaching of the church can be a praxis of liberation, but only on condition that it is presented as such. Certain historical forms of its presentation have afforded a pretext for accusations — as the magisterium itself has acknowledged — that the church with its social doctrine has taken "the side of the wealthy against the proletariat" (QA, no. 44) and does nothing "except preach resignation to the poor and exhort the rich to generosity" (MM, no. 16). There have been abusive practices in which people have manipulated religion in order to protect themselves against workers' justifiable demands, as Pius XI observes (cf. QA, no. 125). Thus, it is urgent to review the way in which the social teaching of the church is enunciated. This is where liberation theology makes its contribution.

i) **Teaching on Ownership.** For a doctrinal presentation of the *private ownership of the means of production* that will take account of the criticisms of Marxism, we must return to the initial arguments brought forward by *Rerum Novarum* for the defense of this right.

Leo XIII in *Rerum Novarum* begins with a description of the changes set afoot by the industrial revolution. These include technological innovations, mutual relations between owners and workers, socio-economic differentiation, the awareness of a working-class solidarity, the relaxation of moral values — in a word, all of the elements that converge in a violent struggle between a minority, who hold the wealth, and a huge majority of the impoverished and outcast.

Leo XIII's analysis of the problem practically coincides with the positions of the socialism of his time. But he offers an alternative solution. Unlike socialism, which proposed the complete abolition of private ownership of the means of production, the church defended this ownership — arguing, however, from the right of workers to acquire private ownership of the means of production (cf. RN, nos. 1-3).

In other words, to speak precisely, the defense of ownership — in this text of *Rerum Novarum* — is not the defense of the ownership of those who have already acquired it, but of those who deserve to acquire it by means of their work, when the latter is justly remunerated. Hence, the conditions of a just wage include that the worker, after satisfying his or her vital needs, will be able to put aside savings, and by means of these savings acquire private ownership of the means of production. When the state fixes a "minimum wage" insufficient for access to ownership, the church's theoretical argument becomes inoperative, since the conditions for the exercise of this right no longer exist: a just wage permitting access to ownership of the means of production.

That theology of liberation most acutely sensitive to the questions posed by Marxism challenges the social teaching of the church to review its fundamental arguments and the understanding of ownership. A step in this direction has been taken by *Libertatis Conscientia*, which has adopted a sober, demanding attitude toward ownership. In proposing a *culture of labor*, which will demand certain "essential values," that document specifies:

It will assert the priority of labor over capital, and the universal destination of material goods. (LC, no. 84)

The right to private ownership is inconceivable without duties looking to the common good. [Private ownership] is subordinate to the higher principle of the universal destination of goods. (no. 87)

And, in an assertion charged with the highest moral force, the same document observes:

The priority of labor over capital imposes upon entrepreneurs the duty in justice of preferring the good of workers to increased profits. They have the moral obligation not to let their capital lie idle, and in their investments to regard before all else the common good. Thus it is incumbent upon them to assign priority to the consolidation or creation of new jobs for the production of genuinely useful goods. (no. 87)

An entire new style in the social teaching of the church, understood as liberation praxis, ought to arise from this viewpoint. A person's dignity ought to be assessed not in terms of what he or she possesses (by way of a defense of ownership), but in terms of the meaning and value of his or her labor. A "labor civilization" is the correct alternative to a "capital civilization," which so easily degenerates into a materialistic, consumer society indifferent to world hunger.

ii) Teaching on Conflict. Again, Marxism challenges the church from its philosophical position of dialectical materialism, in terms of which it regards the condemnation of the class struggle as a brake applied by the church to the struggle of the poor for their rights. Keeping in account, to be sure, the observations that we have seen on the part of the church regarding the interpretation of conflict, still the church must show clearly and firmly that these observations are not a brake, but an evangelical orientation of a struggle for justice. The response given by *Libertatis Conscientia* to this challenge is complemented by that of *Libertatis Nuntius*.

We may single out two aspects: the problem of violence, and the affirmation of the labor civilization in the face of resistance by the capital civilization.

Libertatis Nuntius seems to condemn all violence, indiscriminately, while *Libertatis Conscientia* recalls the traditional teaching permitting the use of violence in extreme situations (LN, chap. 11, nos. 7-8; LC, no. 79). Thus, we must read the former in light of the latter, which situates the text in tradition. On the other hand, *Libertatis Nuntius* makes the substantial contribution of a distinction between "acute social conflict" and "class struggle"; but it is *Libertatis Conscientia* that places us before the reality of conflict as a fact that must be acknowledged — although not in terms of a philosophical anthropology of conflict, but only of a simple acknowledgment of the fact. The ethical demand for solidarity with labor imposes an inescapable obligation on every human being. It dictates an option. The "labor civilization" will meet with resistance in being accepted and reduced to reality when there is a "capital civilization" invested with a totally contrary logic. Hence the inevitability of confrontation and the need for an orientation in order to experience this conflict in the spirit of the gospel.

iii) Response to the Criticism of Religion. Finally, the challenge to the alienating forms of a religion seen through atheistic eyes does not appear in *Libertatis Nuntius*, but it does in *Libertatis Conscientia*. To be sure, it would have been desirable to observe (as does *Gaudium et Spes*, nos. 19 and 21) that certain forms of atheism have arisen from alienating forms of religious experience. The best response to Marxist atheism that a Christian can make is a serious commitment to the humanization of history — a commitment that neither contradicts faith nor is alien to it, but on the contrary, is dynamized by it. After all, the commitment to justice precisely *from a point of departure in* faith is not simply a commitment to justice "along with" faith, a commitment that could have existed without it. Any breach of the bond of unity objectively prevailing between faith and justice, besides being contrary to Christian faith ("on the inside") would be a confirmation ("on the outside") of the Marxist hypothesis that religion is an alienation that prevents its followers from making historical commitments.

While the use of Marxism in theology surely entails risks, it is equally certain that it offers opportunities of examining these challenges and making a response. The praxis of liberation demonstrates that faith does not alienate us from history.

2. Interpretation of the Discernment of Ideologies

Another strong challenge that the theology of liberation must make to the social teaching of the church is in the matter of the discernment of ideologies, in terms of *Octogesima Adveniens* (nos. 31-35). The allegation of an incompatibility in the use of Marxism by a Christian is customarily based on an appeal to the text of *Octogesima Adveniens*, (nos. 32-34). But a consideration of this text in isolation from its context (OA, nos. 31-35 and the whole of OA) encumbers it with a very restrictive interpretation, which does not appear justified against a background of the totality of the Apostolic Letter.

The context of *Octogesima Adveniens* as a whole brings out the importance of a discernment to be exercised by each particular church in view of its own concrete situation. The pope has underscored the great situational diversity that makes it so difficult to propose universal, homogeneous norms. In this perspective, then, the Christian commitment must be examined in light of the various ideologies, historical movements, utopias, and sciences with which it finds itself confronted. The discernment to be exercised by each particular church surely presupposes *criteria* proposed by the papal magisterium. A criterion, however, is not a norm, but an orientation for establishing a norm.

The distinction between an ideology and a historical movement plays a basic role here. Any ideology can embrace manifold varieties of historical movements, or many different stages of these respective movements, before which it is impossible to take an absolute position.

In *Octogesima Adveniens* the pope addresses the relationship between the socialist, Marxist, and capitalist ideologies and their respective historical movements (nos. 31-35). To my understanding, the pope does not render an *actual judgment* on the question of this separation; that is, he does not declare whether or not these ideologies are de facto separated from the historical movements. Paul VI asserts that they are separable. But to assert their separability is not the same as handing down a judgment as to the de facto situation. I believe that, just as in *Octogesima Adveniens* 31 and 35 Paul VI takes no position on the question of the factual separation of the socialist or capitalist ideology from the corresponding movements, so neither in *Octogesima Adveniens* 32-34 does he pass a factual judgment on the question of their separation. He is content with presenting the opinions of the followers of Marxist currents. Number 34 is devoted to a repetition of the warnings already leveled against socialism and capitalism: although there is de facto separation, one must not *forget* the bonds between those aspects of Marxism that most resemble a historical movement (analysis, class struggle as a strategy) and others that are tantamount to an unacceptable ideology (an atheistic philosophy, a totalitarian state).

What is meant by the word "forget"? We could posit two different hypotheses: First, it might mean that all Christian commitment is forbidden, because the ideology in question is united with its historical movement. Or second, it might simply be calling attention to the bonds that a facile idealization of the historical movement tends to forget, and doing so with a view to a clearer separation of the movement from the ideology.

One of these two hypotheses must be adopted, but it has to have the same meaning in number 34 on Marxism as in number 35 on capitalism. There is no reason to interpret "forget" with the first hypothesis in the case of Marxism, and the second in the case of capitalism. Either a Christian option is ruled out in both cases, or else a mere risk is being warned against in both cases.

At all events, a pastoral warning is necessary, because experience demonstrates that certain Christians who take the route of Marxist analysis without exercising precautions, just as with some who follow the road of liberal capitalism, have ultimately adopted these respective ideologies, which are incompatible with faith, in an integral fashion. But the warning should be universal, lest a semblance of ideology be present in the very warning.

3. The Problem of the Anthropology of Conflict

From an analysis of *Libertatis Nuntius* and *Libertatis Conscientia*, we see that the objection against dialectical materialism and the projections that derive from its anthropology for christology and ecclesiology fundamentally rest neither on the *fact of violence* (which is recognized as a factual datum), nor on the *option for violence as a means* (which, in determinate circumstances, can be a legitimate moral option), but on the notion of the *intrinsic character* of violence as a necessary law of history. Ultimately, the target of the objection is a philosophical position, which demands, in the name of consistency, a logic of class struggle projected upon human history and all social reality, not excluding the church of Christ.

It will be in order to review the precise content of *human nature* in two philosophical systems, the Thomist and the Marxist. The term does not have the same content in a philosophy of substance and a philosophy of history. For the former, it is "accident" — already supposing nature; for the latter, it is constitutive of nature. In the former, there is little room for the historical; with the second, the historical is its very core. Hence, the route taken by Engels to establish the nature of the state is to analyze history, in order to see what it has actually been, and try to predict what the state will ultimately be. From this viewpoint, essence or nature has a meaning more like the one it has in science, that is, the nature of a being that operates in the same fashion on the basis of a sufficient number of empirical observations.

Christian faith, which maintains that the human being has been created by God, cannot admit that there could exist, in nature, a kind of necessary "predestination" or necessity for a class struggle. Conflict exists, there is no doubt; but according to the Christian faith that conflict is due to free choices, made by human beings themselves, choices which may surely be registered in nature itself (as the dogma of original sin asserts) but have not arisen from it. The difference is significant, inasmuch as what appears as the fruit of sin cannot be erected into an historical necessity or dynamism of human progress. In other words, a methodical, systematic option for the class struggle as an obligatory, indispensable means of the development of human history is inadmissible.

What *Libertatis Nuntius* brings out is that an anthropology (like the one, for example, arising from historical materialism) is not indifferent to the development of a christology or ecclesiology. This observation is correct, but it is also applicable to the liberal laissez-faire philosophy, which is also based on an anthropology, and therefore also impinges on ecclesiological and christological conceptions. Liberalism has a genuine philosophical postulate, an actual conviction that leads the thinking subject to believe that the dynamics of economic progress must rest on the fundamental instinct of human beings to seek primarily their own interest.

Paul VI indicates these intrinsic dimensions of the liberal philosophy in *Populorum Progressio* (no. 24). It is a matter not of isolated cases of selfishness, but of the actual conceptualization of what it is to be a human being. We could make the same reservations that we made for the case of Marxism: the liberal philosophy does not pretend to construct a metaphysical definition of human nature, but only that of an essence based on empirical observations. We could also indicate that self-interest is not intrinsically unethical; it is only that a closed selfishness may derive from it when it is not under ethical control. But it would not be just to observe these nuances without applying to the problem of conflict a consideration of how a moral sense can control and direct it. The magisterium also remarks the conflictual character of history in *Laborem Exercens*, and in doing so bestows a new, original meaning on the understanding of conflict in terms of capital and labor. The defense of the right to unionize and to strike are aspects of an acceptance of human conflict that is integrated into the social teaching of the church itself. But the theology of liberation has the function of calling attention to the unilateral nature of a teaching that can be commandeered for ideological purposes.

The mutual reference between the social teaching of the church and the theology of liberation, vitally experienced in the spirit of evangelical charity and service to the people of God, will bear rich fruit in terms of the humanization of history.

— Translated by Robert R. Barr

NOTES

1. Peruvian Bishops' Conference, *Documento sobre la teología de la liberación* (October 1984), nos. 52-53.

2. Gustavo Gutiérrez, *A Theology of Liberation: History, Politics and Salvation*, trans. Caridad Inda and John Eagleson (Maryknoll, N.Y.: Orbis Books, 1973), p. 11.

3. J. C. Scannone, "Teología de la liberación," in *Conceptos fundamentales de la teología*, ed. H. Fries (Madrid, 1979).

6

Biblical Hermeneutics

GILBERTO da SILVA GORGULHO

The problem of biblical hermeneutics in the theology of liberation can be posed in terms of two important contemporary texts.

The first begins by stating the principle of its reflection. It indicates the need for a Latin American christology and posits a solution to the hermeneutic problem as one of the indispensable conditions for the development and maturation of liberation theology. It runs as follows:

Contemporary philosophy has transported the hermeneutic problem of *texts of other times* to the treatment of current historical reality. The primordial *text* has become our reality, and within that, our praxis. The exegetes, rather tranquilly, have continued to develop various *biblical hermeneutics*. However, they frequently betray an insensitivity both to the data of the human sciences and to the urgencies of praxis. The strict interdependence between their naive political position, at times frankly reactionary, and their *hermeneutical principles* (as well as their notion of revelation) is a chapter of the history of ideology that remains to be written.[1]

The other text is a more recent one. It is an appeal from the ordinary magisterium of the church—an urgent warning not to make hermeneutics a merely subjective process that will make relative both reality and the truth of revealed faith. The text to which we refer is a document issuing from the Sacred Congregation for the Doctrine of the Faith—the "Instruction on Certain Aspects of the Theology of Liberation." It points to the danger of constructing a hermeneutics from a point of departure in the class struggle, which would make the hermeneutic process a corrosive, reductionistic ferment capable of making Christian truth relative. "In this perspective, orthodoxy as the rule of faith is replaced by the idea of orthopraxis as the criterion of truth" (Chap. X:2). And, "the new interpretation thus affects the Christian mystery as a whole and in all of its parts" (Chap. X:13).

The texts we have cited evince the complexity and scope of the problems at issue. Our intention is limited. We shall not enter into all of the problems.[2] We shall merely indicate the direction of the effort to "comprehend life as expressed in writing" (Dilthey) from the outlook of the historical praxis of liberation of the poor. Thus, we shall focus on two aspects:

1. A popular reading of the Bible poses the hermeneutic problem not academically, but experientially.

2. Hermeneutics, as the interpretation of the praxis of liberation of the poor by Jesus of Nazareth, is a discernment of the word communicated by the Spirit of life and love.

I. LIBERATION AND HERMENEUTICS

1. A Popular Reading of the Bible

The poor read the Bible in a situation of suffering and of economic and political domination.[3] No theoretical reading or quest for ideas is involved. The reading of the Bible as done by the poor is a matter of life and death, freedom and domination. The poor look into the Bible for a truth that will set them free, for light in analyzing society and its structures of violence, for the strength to maintain their resistance and their struggle for a new world of life, freedom, and solidarity. The poor believe and trust in the word of the Bible as light and strength for their liberation struggle.

Reporting what the people themselves say in the base communities about this reading of the Bible, Carlos Mesters indicates its significance and scope:[4]

1. The Bible is read not only as a history of the past, but also, and especially, as a mirror of *history occurring today* in the life of the people. Here we have once more, in a new form, what the Fathers of the Church saw in the distinction between "letter" and "spirit." What is stressed in this reading is the *currency* of God's word. God speaks today, through life as viewed in the light of the Bible.

2. The main objective of this reading is not an interpretation of the *Bible*, but of *an interpretation of life* with the *aid* of the Bible. Thus the thrust of our interpretation is different. The poor read the Bible from the standpoint of their situation of oppression. This enables them to discover the force of meaning that exegetes overlook, and even conceal with a scientific apparatus and the ideology that governs their explanation. The struggle of the poor reveals the background of the dynamism of society and of the historical process. The poor come forward as the hermeneutic key of the interpretation of life and Bible alike.

3. The poor as a people do not engage in a neutral reading. Their reading is a quest for justice, liberation, and life — a search for a way out of their situation of oppression, impoverishment, and political and cultural domination. Their reading, then, is a *committed reading, in the service of liberation*. A scientific reading claims to be "objective" and a determining condition for the validity of any other kind of reading. But the poor have demonstrated that there is no such thing as an objective reading, unless it is a reading situated within the "objective" of God's word and thereby contributing concretely to the attainment of this objective.

4. Modern exegesis is done with a new outlook. But this makes the Bible an

old book. By contrast, the poor as a people have an old view, an unarmed, fragile view (they are a "defenseless flower"), which presents the Bible as a *new book* – a vessel of strength for liberation to those who believe and who commit themselves to the liberation of the poor (Luke 4:16-21; Rom. 1:16-17). For the poor of Latin America, liberation is not a purely secular problem. First and foremost liberation denotes a reference to God. Religion is not divorced from liberation, nor liberation from religion. Quite the contrary, the liberation of the poor finds its center in religion; Christian faith is the very nucleus of liberation. The people believe that God is at hand, indeed is in their midst, in their struggle for liberation. God brings them light, strength, and direction for a new life.[5]

5. In the base communities, the poor do not approach the Bible as a source of erudition. They seek a *source of life*, of hope, and of perseverance. They seek neither a justification for their decisions, nor a plan for their liberation. At the same time, they know that the future depends more on basic options than on particular applications. They have no need of precise practical instructions; they know where to find these when they need them. The Bible teaches them self-confidence, thanks to the gifts of the Spirit and the continuous presence of Jesus among his own. The Bible reminds the poor of the great priorities of their activity: trust in God, liberation in the cross of Christ, steadfastness in persecution and martyrdom, a communion of sisters and brothers, the formation of community, and the importance of a radical commitment.

2. Text and History

This kind of reading situates the hermeneutic problem on the terrain of the experiential. But the message and content of the Bible do not vary with life circumstances. They have an objective meaning, consigned to a *text of the past*. Christian faith seeks to hear what God tells it in the *written text*. Further, the history of revelation reached its fullness in Jesus Christ. In this sense there is no longer any progress in revelation, nor any new revelation (cf. *Dei Verbum* 10). But then how are we to understand that God speaks to us today in life and in the events of that life? How does God speak, how does God engage in a self-manifestation and self-communication in the practice of the liberation of the poor? What is the objective and function of hermeneutics today – the *meaning in itself* or the *meaning for us*?

Pope Paul VI, in his address at the Twenty-First Italian Bible Week, on September 25, 1970, indicated the urgency of the hermeneutic task:

Fidelity to the word also demands, in virtue of the dynamics of the Incarnation, that the [biblical] message be presented, in its integrity, not only to the human being as such, but also to the human being of today, to whom the message is now proclaimed. Christ became the contemporary of certain human beings, speaking their language. The fidelity that is his due demands that this contemporaneity be maintained. In any interpretative process – and all the more when it is the interpretation of the word of God that is at stake — the person of the interpreter, far from being extraneous to the process, is involved in it — with his or her whole being.[6]

Pablo Richard, in a trenchant passage, indicates the route to an understanding of this hermeneutic task, and a grasp of the relationship and interaction between the meaning-*in-itself of the Bible* and the meaning-for-us of the God who comes and who acts in present history:

> In a nutshell, we may say that the material basis of evangelization is text and history — and that neither of these elements must be lacking if the faith of the church is to be able to evangelize. Text without history, or history without text, will not lead to evangelization. But we can also say something else. We can say that, although text and history are the material base of evangelization, we must subordinate the text to history, and not history to the text. It is history that illuminates the biblical text as testimony or criterion of discernment of the word of God. We must subordinate the text to history — exercise discernment upon the biblical text on the basis of our experience of God in our history.[7]

Thus, the task of hermeneutics consists in understanding the Bible as the testament that records the place and manner of the coming and the presence of God in history. In order to understand the hermeneutic function, then, one must understand what revelation is, and how the coming of God occurs in history — God's new way of existing in the life and free activity of human beings. Accordingly, it becomes necessary to penetrate the reality of the temporal mission of the divine persons, which occurs in grace. Thus, hermeneutics appears as *the discernment of the Word who comes and who communicates the Spirit of life and love in the historical practice of the liberation of the poor.*

The task of hermeneutics consists in discerning in the Bible the witness of those believers, our forebears in faith, who found in their history the God of life. This testimony is indispensable for a discernment in our history of the word of the God of Jesus Christ, who communicates the Spirit of life and love.

Accordingly, one must have a reliable criterion of discernment. That criterion is found in the historical practice of the liberation of the poor. The Bible is the testament that records and reveals the place and manner of God's coming in order to form a people. Interpretation, then, consists in the discernment of the sense of the biblical text in function of the memory the poor have of their liberation, and their memory of the promise of the coming of the Reign of God. Hermeneutics is the interpretation and discernment of life, and of the coming of the God "who is and who was and who is to come" (Rev. 1:8).

3. Function of the Memory of the Poor

The hermeneutics of liberation theology made great progress when it began to develop the potential residing in its perception of the Bible as the memory of the poor, both in the historical origin of the Bible and as the main hermeneutic key of its meaning and its historical development.

Liberation of the Poor

The memory preserved by the poor of the manner of their liberation is a prophetical and eschatological sign enabling believers to penetrate into the dynamism of history and the formation of themselves as a "people." Thereby it makes it possible to understand the objective of the history of revelation. This memory is the criterion for a perception of the new manner of the God of life — the manner in which God now exists and is communicated in historical events (cf. *Lumen Gentium*, no. 9).[8] The memory of the poor is a testimonial of the act through which the passage from the domination of death to a new life in liberty and life occurs. Liberation constitutes the social life of the people. Hence the importance of the reality of *the people* for the hermeneutics of liberation theology.

Indeed, all of the human sciences seek to define and explain this historical and sociological reality. But none of them takes the explanation all the way. In the life of the people, there is something that transcends the limitations of a purely immanent analysis governed by the criteria of anthropology, sociology, and historical criticism alone. The life of the people is a historical reality that becomes fully understandable only in terms of a gift conferred by the action of the word of the God of life, who communicates the divine Spirit of truth, justice, and solidarity. The memory the poor have of their liberation is the criterion for a comprehension of their historical social totality.

After all, *the people* are a historical subject that transcends domination and establishes egalitarian bonds of communication, union, and the full realization of life. The life of the people is a gift of God, and the history of revelation is the consolidation of this gift. The Bible shows the process of the formation of the people of God from a point of departure in the liberation of the poor. The emergence of a people of the poor creates a history that challenges and influences the history of dominations and dominators. The Bible is the testament of that history of the poor.

Hermeneutics, then, is the *discernment of the memory of the poor* as origin of the texts and the presentation of the events and structures of society. The memory of the poor demonstrates that the biblical texts are not merely the history and ideology of the court and the temple. These texts are basically the popular memorial of a prophetic resistance to the domination that destroys the life of the people. This discernment of the memory of the poor is carried out in function of scientific criteria and faith criteria (cf. Exod. 3:14-15), as Pius XII himself declared in *Divino Afflante Spiritu*.

Sociological Mediation

All of the mediations (psychological, anthropological, political, and linguistic) indicate a prism of liberation. The sociological mediation of the dynamism of the tributary and slave mode of production is a scientific commentary on the whole gamut of social relations. After all, the mode of production is the totality of social relations, in terms of work stratified on the levels of *economics, politics,* and *ideology*.

Liberation theology has insisted on the importance of this analytical mediation for an understanding of tribalism, the ambiguity of the state, and the religious community gathered around the restored temple.[9] It is the dynamism and the conflicts generated by the *tributary mode of production* that enable us to discern more precisely the sense and content of the memory of the poor. The history of the liberation of the poor is rooted in a domination and exploitation maintained through the imposition of tribute in the urban-rural relation. All domination is articulated and constructed on the basis of tribute. The latter is like a mustard seed in the system of state domination that leads to slavery and death. Biblical history is a history of continuous tension, in the land of Canaan (the exodus and the distribution of the land), in the formation and development of the monarchical state (the state and prophecy), and in the community of hamlets around the restored temple (liturgical and priestly organization versus the hope of the poor).

The sociological mediation facilitates a precise presentation of the conflict between a God who is liberator and a people who reject liberty and seek new material forms of domination. Hermeneutics, then, is a *deciphering* – a decoding of symbols, rites, and language as expressions of *social relations either of domination and exploitation or of life in a freedom characterized by equality and solidarity*. Thus, the utilization of the sociological mediation (an analysis of the production and reproduction of life in common) does not imply the choice of one reading to the exclusion of others; rather, it represents an axis upon which all other readings may be articulated.

Theological Categories

A reading of the material conditions, and of the economic and political causes, of the religious phenomenon leads to a deeper penetration of the meaning of which these realities are the vehicle and manifestation. However, a new economic and political reading does not provide a comprehensive explanation of the life of the people. We must move on to the prophetical level of "knowledge of God" in the practice of justice and solidarity. Hence the importance attributed by the hermeneutics of liberation theology to prophetical texts like Exodus 22:21-27, Hosea 6:6, Matthew 12:7, and Jeremiah 22:16. Hence also the importance of the defense of the rights of the poor as hermeneutical key of the historical social process (cf. Prov. 22:22-23, 23:11; John 19:25).

The memory of the poor is not the mere revealer of the presence of God in creation. Nor is it a vague doctrine of providence. Still less is it a representation of an image of the divinity for the purpose of solidifying and cementing state domination. It is a prophetical proclamation of the God who comes to liberate the people and grant them a life of freedom in a land that will be a fountain of life and liberty. The memory of the poor leads to a hermeneutics of liberation (Exod. 3), since it proclaims a God of life revealed and existing in a new manner in the process of the liberation of the oppressed poor. It indicates the basic theological categories to be used in the interpretation in question: Yahweh, the election of the people, the covenant, and eschatology.[10]

Thus all theological categories are intertwined, finding their full sense in the promise of the coming of the Reign of God and in the coming of the Son of Man (cf. Dan. 7; Mark 1:14-15, 8:38, 9:1).

4. Promise of the Coming of the Reign of God

The promsie of the Coming opens the historical process to its future dimension. And this active dynamism of the proximity of the Reign, or new world of life, freedom, and solidarity, is rooted in the unity of transcendence and immanence that occurs in the communication of the life and presence of God in human activity (cf. John 14:3,21). Thus, hermeneutics perceives the unity of the promise in the two Testaments — in terms of the liberation praxis of the poor and the messianic praxis of Jesus of Nazareth, who carries out his mission as Son of Man by adopting the liberation praxis of the Servant of Yahweh (cf. Matt. 10:45).

The unity of the promise determines the unity and novelty of the hermeneutic process, indicating the key texts for this kind of understanding.[11] We shall limit ourselves here to a simple schema, presented as an invitation to a more profound consideration.

PROMISE (Hebrew Scriptures)	FULFILLMENT (Christian Scriptures)
1. YAHWEH: The God of life who comes to deliver: Exod. 3	1. JESUS: Anointed with the Spirit who comes to deliver: Luke 4:16-21, Phil. 2:5-11
2. ELECTION: The people, token of a social life in justice and solidarity: Amos 3:1-2, Zeph. 3:12-14	2. THE POOR: Vessels of the novelty of Jesus' project and liberative service: Mark 10:20-29, Matt. 11
3. COVENANT: A life of community in the power of the word and of the Spirit of life: Exod. 6:2-8, Hos. 2:16-23, Jer. 31:31-34	3. NEW COVENANT: The life of the people, in the following of the Teacher, in the community of the least ones, in the spirit of the Beatitudes: Mark 7, Matt. 5-7, 18, Gal. 4-5
4. ESCHATOLOGY: Hope for the coming of Reign and resurrection: Isa. 53:61, Dan. 2, 7, 12	4. ESCHATOLOGY: Realized in the praxis of love for the poor: Matt. 25, John 14

5. Letter versus Spirit of Life

The hermeneutic problem reaches its point of greatest concentration in the interpretation of the content and sense of the mission of the Word incarnate in Jesus of Nazareth. In other words, hermeneutics is interpretation and proclamation of the gospel. But the gospel, in turn, is the testament of Jesus' liberative praxis and the proclamation of his return.

Dynamism of the Gospel

In recent years the hermeneutics of liberation theology has called attention to the importance of the gospel of Mark, and for a number of reasons. The second gospel is structured as a proclamation of the *way*, and therefore lends itself to an in-depth examination of the core of Christian praxis, which is the *following of Jesus*.[12] At the same time, this gospel facilitates a grasp of the hermeneutic task in its deeper essence: as an *interpretation of the historical praxis of Jesus and the proclamation of his coming*. The structural categories that bestow unity upon this gospel are the *basic categories of hermeneutics*.

As we know, Mark initiated the use of the narrative genre as gospel. In its profane usage, *gospel* had the connotation of imperial political propaganda. But the word also had the eschatological sense of the proclamation of the coming of the Reign of God (Neh. 2:1; Isa. 52:7ff.). Mark invokes the latter concept, in order to demonstrate that the transformation of history is in Jesus' praxis and the promise of his coming. After all, Jesus delivers from the power of Satan, communicates the Spirit, ushers in the Reign of God, and stirs the new praxis of his followers. The gospel, then, is the proclamation of the coming of Jesus, who is still at the head of his disciples as they traverse the route of history (Mark 1:1, 1:14, 8:35, 10:29, 13:10, 14:9). Narrative has the function of arousing an *act of faith in the Messiah* and the *new praxis of the following of Jesus*. This proclamation is made in the organic dynamism of five basic steps:

Novelty: The gospel is the proclamation that Jesus of Nazareth is utter novelty, at hand to liberate history. He comes to communicate the Spirit and to deliver from the power of Satan. His mission as Son and Holy One of God is the practice that delivers from the situation of oppression and disintegration evoked by the reality of the "unclean spirit," the fruit of the economic, political, and religious system that we find crystallized in the system of the temple and the law. Thus he fulfills the promises contained in the Prophets and the Law. This is the dynamism of the first unit, *Mark 1*.

Conflict: This novelty ushers in the definitive crisis. It provokes resistance and rejection on the part of the dominant groups of the old system of temple and law. This conflict shows Jesus' fundamental option, his revelation of the God of life, and his power as Son of Man. This conflict will lead Jesus to death on the cross, and it indicates the Son of Man's transcendence and condemnation of the system that condemns him to death. Thus, the gospel is gift and call, provoking decision and change, and giving its followers a new identity. This is the sense of the five controversies of *Mark 2:1-3:6*.

Discernment: The core of Mark's gospel is discernment—a comprehension and understanding of the sense of Jesus' message and practice. The object of discernment is manifested gradually, in a crescendo of totality. One must discern and comprehend the *Spirit* at work in Jesus' practice; the *project* of the *Reign of God* revealed in the parables; the *signs* manifesting his power and calling for a response to the question of who this person is; and the *significance of his Messianic practice*, which gathers together the new people of God, composed of Jews and Gentiles, in the realization of the new covenant. This is the unitary dynamism of the great ensemble of *Mark 3:7-8,26*.

New Praxis: This discernment motivates a new practice of the following of Jesus along the way of the cross. The structure of the journey is marked by three proclamations of the passion and resurrection. These three proclamations serve to mark the dynamism of the movement toward the cross, which unfolds in seven steps; at its center is the liberative praxis of the Son of Man, who is the Servant of Yahweh. This new praxis is life in the power of the Spirit. Peter's profession, his acknowledgment of Jesus as the Messiah, is the doorway and foundation of the conversion and new life to be realized in the practice of a route to the transformation of the eye, the hands, and the feet in the presence of the least ones. In this practice is liberation from the old temple system, and a new openness to the future: hope in the coming of the Son of Man, and a perspective that directs and sustains the course of history in the power of the Spirit, who is given that the disciples may be able to proclaim and attest the gospel in the time before the end. This following is realized by means of discernment and decision for newness; that is, by the passage from life according to law to the life in the Spirit that is lived in the option for the poor. This discipleship confers the identity characteristic of the followers of this path. This is the carefully structured dynamism of the ensemble, *Mark 8:27—13:36*.

Victory of Life: The passion and resurrection narratives establish the ultimate sense of this whole dynamism. Death is conquered by the life of the One who dies on the cross. Jesus conquers death, he is alive and will continue to lead his disciples along the Way. Faith in the One who was raised is a call to hope in his coming, *Mark 14:1-16:8(9-20)*.

Letter and Spirit

This dynamism of the gospel provides us with the wherewithal to situate the hermeneutic problem as it must be addressed. At last we understand why the text must be understood in function of historical praxis. The gospel consigned to the letter is the testament of the liberation praxis of Jesus of Nazareth, which in turn is the basis of the proclamation of the coming of Jesus and of the gift of the Spirit of the Reign of God in history. The gospel is the power of the word operating in the light and power of the Spirit, who comes by the mission of Jesus and continues to act in the new praxis of the disciples' following of Jesus. The gospel is not letter, but a new praxis, in the power of the Spirit.

Here we must recall St. Thomas Aquinas' theology of the new law (*ST* I-II, q. 106). In it we find the basic principles for the practice of hermeneutics in a context of the liberation of the poor: the gospel is a gift of the Spirit to those who believe in Jesus Christ, Son of God, who died and was raised, who comes to dwell in and communicate his life to those who follow him in the practice of justice and love. Hermeneutics establishes the relationship between letter and spirit, which is the principal content of the gospel. What occurs in human activity by the power of the Holy Spirit is discernment of the coming of Jesus.

Interpretation is comprehension of the *way* of Jesus of Nazareth — his salvific, liberative praxis (Mark 10:45). This praxis is at the heart of the dynamism of the praxis of the poor in their battle for the justice of the Reign of God, or the life of the people, which the God of life wills. Jesus' praxis as Servant of Yahweh (Isa. 53) is the continuation and plenitude of the liberation of the poor. Here again we must recall the explanation of St. Thomas, who posits this continuity in his assertion that the redemptive content of the act of Christ on the cross is part of the broader dynamism of the battle for justice:

It is clear that *everyone who, constituted in grace, suffers for justice*, merits salvation, as we read in Matt. 5:10: "Blest are the persecuted for justice' sake." (*ST* III, q. 48, a. 1, c.)

Jesus' act on the cross, the culmination and fullness of his historical praxis, is an act of love—of the surrender of his life in the struggle for the justice of the Reign of God. As such, it is the font of grace and liberation for all who believe in him. By this act he communicates the Spirit of life and freedom. The heart of hermeneutics is the positing of the cross as the basic *locus theologicus*. After all, the universal *locus theologicus* among us is the cross of Christ as we find it in concrete Latin American life. That is to say, this locus is the perception that life and the Spirit flow only from the cross accepted in love and in the struggle for the justice of the Reign of God. This is the reason why "the poor who die before their time" necessarily challenge us to renew our hermeneutic principles and their application to the explanation and proclamation of the word of the God of life.

Now it is clear why the gospel is, primarily, the actual infused gift of the Holy Spirit, and only secondarily a *written law*, a text. The text exists in function of history, life, and freedom—or the Holy Spirit, who is revealed and communicated in plenitude. The essence of the gospel is not in the letter. It is in the Spirit who gives life and justifies or directs a praxis in the direction of the praxis and coming of Jesus. Hence the relationship between the text and history, and hence the function of the text as a document of faith. After all, the biblical texts are

documents of faith, and precepts, for the ordering of human acts. As such, the new law does not justify. Hence the Apostle says: "The letter kills, while the spirit gives life" (2 Cor. 3:6). And Augustine explains in his book, *De Spiritu et Littera*, that by "letter" is meant *any* writing, even writing relative to moral precepts, such as those contained in the gospel. Hence, even the letter of the gospel would kill unless it were to be healed by the grace of faith. (*ST*, I-II, q. 106, a. 2)

Discernment of the Spirit

The process of interpretation proper to the theology of liberation begins with and constantly returns to the practice of the poor. A popular reading has restored the word of the gospel to the poor. It has instilled the popular struggles with the leaven of a consciousness-raising and an experience of the Spirit. It has borne fruit in the struggle and dedication of martyrs, whose lives were an interpretation in practice, to the ultimate consequences of the spirit of the Beatitudes (Matt. 5:10). The option for the poor has constituted a renewal of the life of the local and regional churches, and evangelization has been the dynamism of this renewal.

A new reflection on the spirituality of liberation has been born, a spirituality of life, of deliverance from the idols of death and the flesh, in the Pauline perspective. A spirit of solidarity with the people helps us to perceive that the kernel of this spirituality is in the wisdom that pitches its tent amidst the unity and struggles of the poor. We might say that in recent years liberation theology has become explicitly a theology of the spirit of life and freedom.[13]

Further, on the plane of hermeneutic analysis, one of the things that stands out most clearly is a progress and maturation in the use of the social mediations of analysis. A grasp of the reality of the "fetish" in the dynamism of society has marked a new beginning for reflection. Theology has the task of discerning between the fetish and the Spirit. Thus, the *actus theologicus* is an act of discernment or spritual appropriation of text and praxis alike, with a view to a deeper penetration of both the mechanisms of death and domination, and the power of the resurrection and new life of the people of God in the world.[14] Hermeneutics is a discernment of the ideological weapons of death, and a quest for the strength of the Spirit of life (cf. 1 John 4).

II. HISTORICAL PROCESS OF LIBERATION

We now enter upon a consideration of the hermeneutic thread of liberation that runs through the Hebrew Scriptures from end to end. We shall limit ourselves, of course, to establishing only certain indications of the complex problems at hand, lest our investigation become far too extensive.

1. History of Liberation: Gesta et Verba

Hermeneutics of the Hebrew scriptures is a reading of history from a starting point in the liberation of the poor. This is tantamount to saying that we seek to understand history as a process of formation of a people of solidarity and freedom. The liberation of the poor is the transition from domination to a new kind of society, a society in justice and in active solidarity as brothers and sisters. The reading with which we are dealing is a reading of the historical process from a starting point in the act of love that overcomes domination, division, conflict, sin, and death.

Accordingly, our process will be dialectical. Our reading is continual tension, and the phenomenon of the exodus is its source and guideline, from generation to generation (Exod. 3:15). Israel is a people formed by the covenant for a common task. Its members have been called to live as brothers and sisters, as equals, without dominators. Israel is a society founded on liberation from the relations of domination and on the construction of an active solidarity.

This process, meanwhile, is in a continuous tension toward the *future*. At every stage of history, the life of the people is threatened and even destroyed. The sociological stages—*tribalism*, the *tributary state*, and the restored *community*—manifest this tension. History indicates the failure of liberation: a failure in its very origins, in the land of Canaan, in the formation and consolidation of the monarchical, tributary state, and finally in the sacerdotal and Pharisaic restoration. Here is born the hope for a true life of the people as an eschatological reality. That eschatological life will come with the arrival of the Reign of God, the coming of the new human being. This will only be possible by a gift of the Spirit: the radical exodus from a life according to the law to a life in the light and power of the Spirit.

This tension occurs in the unitary dynamism of the event and the word (*gesta et verba*), in which we find the revelation of the God who comes and communicates the divine life to the people (cf. *Dei Verbum*, nos. 1-3). The objective of the interpretation of texts, in the same Spirit who has inspired them, is to grasp the meaning of this process from the starting point of the poor and the oppressed, in order to perceive the nature of God's project in history (cf. *Dei Verbum*, no. 12; *Lumen Gentium*, no. 9).

2. Gesta: *The Liberation Process*

Let us examine, in the process of the formation of the people, the analytical basis of the liberation of the dominated peoples.

The Exodus and the Land

The exodus and distribution of the land constitute the center and basis of the memory of the poor (Deut. 26:5-9). Here is the foundational experience of the life of a free people. Throughout the generations, this experience will continue to produce new effects; it will be the fundamental criterion of all hope in the future. The experience of the exodus as the source of the constitution of the people becomes even more clear in the light of the change in the explanatory view of the origins of "Israel," and of the type of society it has formed in contrast with the dominator state of Egypt and the city-states of Canaan. But here we must abandon a *culturalistic view* of the historical process (in which Israel's origins are explained as the fruit of a linear development of its semi-nomadic life, of its gradual settlement, and of the formation of an imperfect society antecedent to the formation of a centralizing monarchical state) and explain the origins of Israel (the patriarchs, the exodus, the distribution of the land) by way of a *synchronic view* of a conflictive process of social changes on the levels of economy, politics, and ideology.[15]

Israel sprang from the process of formation of a new historical subject, with an original, novel society, in which various groups of dominated and marginalized populations participated.[16] Here, by contrast with the system of domination prevailing in Egypt and in the city-states of Canaan, a liberation movement of the dominated, exploited rural populations arose and consolidated. This process culminated in the formation of a *new* kind of tribal society, based on the unification of the tribes of Israel that believed in Yahweh. Semi-nomadic tribes, dominated and marginalized "Hebrews," and especially, the group delivered from Egypt under the leadership of Moses also participated, with the latter having a decisive influence on this process of egalitarian, non-dominated social organization. The basic strength of the new amalgamation was a new religious faith, one diametrically opposed to the ideology of Egypt or the kings of Canaan, where the *gods* had been the *ideological groundwork* of the domination and exploitation of workers subjected to a city-state. The liberated tribes no longer worshiped Baal, the god of the dominating state, but Yahweh, who had been manifested as a source and bulwark of liberation and of the new social model (Exod. 3). The new people joined together and organized in the distribution of the land without the exploitation of one group by another, relying on their faith in the God of Sinai, who now became present in the struggles and the ethical and social organization of these tribes who have become that God's chosen people (Judg. 5).

The importance of the liberation of the group from Egypt (Exod. 1:11, 14:5) lies in its having had a more intimate experience of the domination of central power (Pharaoh), and in its transformation into a catalyzing, unifying ferment for other groups now undergoing a similar liberation experience.[17] The decisive element with the group from Egypt was its experience on the Sinai peninsula, where tradition places the origin of Yahweh's manifestation as the foundation of a new ethical and social awareness, expressed in the Decalogue (Exod. 20:1-17) and in the old tribal laws. This experience, transmitted to the tribes of Canaan, became the focus and ethical support of the new union and common enterprise. The interesting thing is that this ethical consciousness and its norms *do not proceed from a central power of state*; they are the manifestation of a liberating act of Yahweh, which is at the basis of the new social formation (Exod. 20:2).

The tribes of Israel regarded themselves as antithetical not only to the colonial state of Egypt, but to the Canaanite city-states, as well. Indeed, this was the rationale of their territorial requirements. Their organization and social project were based on the distribution among themselves of the land, the source of their production, without tribute having to be paid to a higher community. Here we must note the prophetical—and anti-state—implications of the description of the division of the land in Joshua 13—21: The land does not belong to the kings, but is distributed among the liberated "families." The liberation has as its goal new life in a land without domination. The battle for the land and the common distribution of its possession and its production are the basis and support of the life of a free people.

This experience of liberation, the center of faith, becomes the paradigm that will be repeated, celebrated, and transmitted from generation to generation. From here will spring the oral, liturgical, and theological narrative of the Book of Exodus, the cornerstone of the life of the people.[18]

The State and the Prophets

The prophets' criticism of the tributary Davidic and Solomonian state[19] signals the next step in the process of the liberation of the people. The state was ambiguous and idolatrous.[20] Exploitation and domination had become structural, and the social conflict acute. The state was one of imposition; it destroyed the life of equality and solidarity of the social groups. In fact, the state (in the North and in the South) had ultimately adopted a tributary economic and political regime, thus sharpening the conflict between city and countryside. A process of pauperization and domination was under way, as the protest and criticism of the prophets attest. Discernment and a call for change occur in terms of the defense of the *rights of the poor*,[21] and the rejection of structural idolatry.[22] Thereby attention is also called to the ambiguities of the state, and the Davidic dynasty is legitimated.[23] The prophets' criticism is a defense and rescue of the life of the people, in right and justice, in solidarity and in "knowing God"; Yahweh delivers the people from the idolatry of the state.

The legitimation of the Davidic royal line signals the inauguration of a theme of vigilance and positive criticism: the king is at the service of right and justice. Isaiah, prolonging the theme of God's promise and oath sworn to the Davidic dynasty (2 Sam. 7:1-14; Isa. 6:13, 9:1-7; 11:1-9), seeks to legitimate it by interpreting the function of the king as that of liberator of the poor.

But the more consistent prophetical line is one of resistance to and criticism of the state. It is in this resistance that we find the origin, strength, and social function of the most radical prophecy.[24] Plainly, the ambiguity of the monarchy was acutely perceived by the peasants from the outset, as we may gather from their criticism of the very first attempt to establish a king over the tribes (Judg. 9:15). Resistance and criticism continued in the dominated, rural milieus being plundered by the burdens of tribute and other oppressive measures adopted by the monarchical system.[25] This criticism was stimulated, articulated, and later expressed in writing in the prophetical and Levitical rural milieus. The rejection of the monarchical system on the part of the latter crystallized in the figure and struggle of Samuel; the ambiguity of the tributary state on its economic, political, and ideological level was destroying the free, egalitarian life of the people (1 Sam. 8:12-14).

The most radical prophecy, issuing from the poor, dominated milieus, is uttered as defense of the rural population and of the rights of the poor, with the imputation of an idolatry that was becoming structural (Amos; Hos.; Mic. 1−3). The state is idolatrous and the oppressor of the poor. As such, it had no future. In fact, it would be destroyed (Amos; Mic. 2−3). The future lay with the liberation and life of the people of the poor (Zeph., Jer.).

This same criticism was taken up by the Deuteronomic tradition. Once the state had been destroyed, an effort was made to demonstrate the causes of the debacle and to outline perspectives for the future. And here the Deuteronomists attest that Josiah had attempted the impossible: to structure a state that would be a synthesis of egalitarian Mosaism and the Davidism of royal authority, in which the king would simply be the brother of the people and faithfully obedient to the law of Yahweh. This initiative had been unsuccessful, and the Davidic state had gone to ruin. The Deuteronomic diagnosis saw the root of this destruction in the idolatry of a state that had sought to hold the actual place of God—and had destroyed the life of the people. The future lay with the life of the people. The people were prudent; they could discern the call to choose between life and death and had taken the path of obedience to the only absolute: Yahweh, the God of life.[26]

The Hope of the Poor

God's promise to King David was the basis of the people's hope and the criterion of their restoration in the centuries of the Babylonian and Persian domination. The prophets relied on that promise in order to project the future of a people of God who would live in freedom and solidarity. This vision of the future culminates in Second Isaiah (Isa. 40-55): God's judgment upon idolatry and domination will be manifested in the liberation of the captives of the Exile. The people will be the sign and testimonial of this God, who seeks to inaugurate what is new. But the route to the coming restoration is in the poverty of the Servant of Yahweh, who, voluntarily, as the poor one par excellence, will be the source of the justification and life of a numerous progeny.[27] Likewise during the Babylonian Exile, the Jews of Palestine, in the environs of the city of Mespha, execute the project of the people's restoration (Ps. 89, Jer. 30—31).

The process of restoration receives its orientation from Haggai and Zechariah (Zech. 1—8).[28] A time of restoration, and of a new dialectic in the face of the future, begins. One the one hand, a pragmatic spirit reigns and restores the communities of the hamlets by centering their loyalties on the temple and the high priest. Here is consolidation of sacred power, law, and worship. Here the community must find its identity and project under Persian domination. At the same time, however, a movement of resistance makes its appearance, sparked by a spirit of prophecy (freedom of the people, life in the power of the Spirit). The future is in the communities of the God-fearing poor (Isa. 61, Prov. 3, Mal. 3). Hope is reborn and directed toward the future.

After the downfall of Zerubbabel, in whom Haggai and Zechariah had placed their hopes for a restoration, once more hope wells, and a project is launched for a full restoration of the people's future. The scribes, under the influence of the community of the poor, develop the figure of the ideal David, an incorporation of the people of the poor (cf. 2 Sam. 23:1-8) and reread the ancient promises in this perspective. The psalms of the poor and the psalms of the "king" are evidence of this hope; they will be understood in a collective perspective of election of the whole people of the poor (cf. Ps. 72:2).

This hope reaches an exalted expression at the time of the conquests of Alexander the Great. The poor see their hope reborn: the future is not in a triumphant militarism, it is in the sovereignty of the poor. It is not with a Solomonic type of state, it is with the poor, in the incorporation of the community of the poor, that sign of the manifestation of the universal royalty of the God of life. Such is the hope proclaimed by the Book of Zechariah (Zech. 9—14), which can be said to be the favorite little brochure of Jesus of Nazareth and the primitive Christian communities.[29] The hope of the future is centered on the coming of the Reign of God, which will bring *resurrection* to those who struggle for justice and the freedom of the people of God (Dan. 2:12). After all, the wisdom and sovereignty of the God of life are manifested in the coming of the Son of Man (Dan. 7), who will reunite the community of saints, delivered from the bestial empires.

3. Verba: *Font of Deliverance*

In this process the presence and activity of the God of life is manifested in the power of the word. The word is manifested as *law, prophecy,* and *wisdom,* and its power for liberation is manifested from among the poor. This perspective requires us to take some cognizance of the vast, complex problems of the origin and content of the laws, the message of the prophets, and the history of the sapiential tradition.

The Law

The originality of the laws of Israel is evident even by comparison with the legislative tradition of the ancient Near East. Their originality lies in the fact that they do not proceed from the power of the state, or from a king who imposes them on his subjects, but from Yahweh, who delivers from slavery (Exod. 20:2).

In Israel, laws spring from a resistance to state power, and their purpose is the liberation of the poor. Were we to look for the groups whose history and resistance are attested by the laws, we should find the "memory of the poor" and a covert history of opposition rather than a legislation providing a foundation for domination on the part of the oppressors. The law, produced by the liberative act of resistance, manifests the will of the God of life, liberty, and egalitarian solidarity.

Understood in its motivation and function, then, the law is directed upon the constitution of a people. It is the manifestation of the *judgment of God* in terms of the defense of the rights of the poor (Exod. 22:21-27). It is the norm of *holiness*, in worship and in one's relationship with neighbor (Lev. 19:1,18). It is *manifestation of love* on the part of God, who calls and leads to life (Deut. 5:3, 30:15-20).

Prophecy

The spirit of prophecy was synthesized in the biblical presentation of history itself. History is presented as a critique of idolatry, and an ongoing call to the realization of solidarity and kinship in the life of the people. The history of kings and nations must be measured and directed by prophetical activity. In the history of the kings, the prophetic struggle and faith of Elijah appear at the center, as a light for the discernment of the historical process of the struggle for justice and for the Yahwist faith.

The kinds of prophets, as well, are measured by their origin in and dedication to the defense of the rights and life of the poor. The prophets' call to *conversion* is a quest for life, right and justice, solidarity. This is how God is "known" in the life of the people of God. The *proclamation of the future* — of the coming of the Reign of God — culminates in the hope of a sovereignty of the poor in the history of the people, indeed the history of empires (Zech. 9:9-17).

Wisdom

The originality of the biblical wisdom lies in its discernment of the basic values of the life of the worker: free toil, word, witness, the value of poverty, the value of life. Wisdom, too, begins with the defense of the poor and culminates in a discipline that ensures the life of the poor (Prov. 3). The entire sapiential tradition is seen as a quest for justice and poverty, at whose center is the living God, the liberator of the poor (Prov., Job).[30] Wisdom is identified with the law and is a discernment of the value of labor and of immortal justice (Ecclus., Eccles., Wis.).[31]

The power of the word as wisdom is the source of the life of the people. Now the people may live, by the gift of the word that communicates the Spirit of freedom and life. The wisdom of the word is the criterion for the construction of the people's solidarity, on the foundation of justice and poverty, in their prophetic dimension (Prov. 15:33, 18:12, 22:4; Zeph. 2:1-3). The wisdom of the poor is the transforming, impelling novelty of the people's itinerary of life on the road to the future.

III. JESUS AND THE PEOPLE'S FREEDOM

The core of hermeneutics is the interpretation of the reality and meaning of the person and liberative mission of Jesus of Nazareth. We shall focus our analysis of Jesus' praxis entirely on his relationship with the poor and the freedom of the people.

1. Evangelizer of the Poor

Jesus restricts his temporal mission to the confines of the ancient people of Israel. He presents himself as the eschatological messenger (Luke 4:16-21, Matt. 15:24). He comes to deliver and reconstruct the life of a people dominated and deformed by the system of the temple and the law, in a context of the power and interests of the Roman Empire.

Jesus' Mission in Israel

Jesus' mission is defined as the liberation of the poor. We must understand his gospel to the poor if we hope to understand his actions in the Jewish society of his time, a society characterized by particular economic, social, political, and religious factors. He had come to rescue the people in their identity, mission, and task.

Hence the need for an insistence on the social dimension of his praxis and message. Jesus does not seek isolated conversion alone. He seeks to re-form the life of the people, in the life of the Reign of God. This finality will be attained after the consummation of the drama of the cross, by the power of the Spirit, in terms of the resurrection and the Second Coming. Hence the relationship between the *historical Jesus* and the *Christ of faith*, manifested in and inspiring the testimony of the new, redeemed people.

Hermeneutics, then, utilizes the mediation of a sociological reading of the gospels and the other books of the Christian Scriptures.[32] The process is that of the deciphering of its categories, symbols, and images with a view to understanding the dynamism of the social life of the people in Palestine, within the characteristic mode of production in which Jesus lived, exercised his ministry, died on the cross, and manifested himself alive to the groups of disciples who had followed him and who now would proclaim his victory and coming. This reading is done in terms of the concrete social function of the *temple*, of the *poor* (including the possessed and the sinful), of the *law*, and of the hope of the coming of the *Reign of God*. Jesus redeems the life and praxis of the people (Mark 10:42-45).

The Contradiction of the Temple

The entire system of production and reproduction of the life of the people in the economic system of Palestine under Roman domination was centralized in the Jerusalem temple.

The temple was the central focus and source of the division of labor, of production and accumulation, and of the commercial and exchange system. It was the axis of the maintenance and transmission of the domination of a slave regime in Palestine, and it structured the security and identity of Judaism by maintaining the old tributary system. What is more, the temple was the center and font of the religious life of the people.

Thus, Jesus shows that this temple has been converted into the nub and core of the contradiction that is destroying the life of the people and their mission. It has become the sign and instrument of a system of domination and death. The Father's house has becomes a den of thieves.

It is understandable, then, that Jesus' words concerning the future of the temple should be one of the items of his indictment and death sentence. Indeed, Jesus' concrete praxis vis-à-vis his Father, the death system, and the redemption of the freedom of his people stands in a constant relationship with the function and meaning of the temple.

Liberation of the Poor

Jesus defines the finality of his praxis and project in terms of the poor, the afflicted, and the hungry (Luke 6:20ff., Matt. 5:1-12).[33] The poor, the suffering, the possessed, and those who sin against the law are the sign of the contradiction and destruction of the life and freedom of the people.

1. The poor, seen in a prophetical perspective, are the addressees and sign of the urgency of liberation. Their mere presence is an urgent call for change and for a radical transformation of the whole system of the temple, the law, and their mediations and institutions (Mark 2:27, 3:4).

2. Jesus was a thaumaturge of a prophetical type. His praxis in behalf of the suffering is an irrefutable historical fact. His cures are both the sign and the meaning of full life on all levels of human existence, which is a condition for the collective life of a people.

3. Jesus expelled "unclean spirits" and demons. These, as well, are a sign of the inherent contradiction of the system of death that disintegrates and destroys the life of persons. Norberf Lohfink offers a suggestive approach to the hermeneutics of the exorcisms in terms of liberation:

> René Girard has demonstrated that, in the last analysis, a society preserves its cohesion through power, and that power, precisely when it is covert, or unconscious in people's minds, is exteriorized in all manner of anxieties and needs, all kinds of schizophrenias, divisions, and [demonic] possessions that torture the individual, and through him or her, the community. Depending on the cultural context, they take the most varied forms. In Jesus' time, it was especially demons, personifications [of these anxieties and needs], who tormented individuals. This figure, too, is undone in the proximity of Jesus.

The novelty was manifested visibly, through this transformation of the evil concealed in dominant social structures altogether out of the reach of human freedom into salvation and the normality of the human being.[34]

4. Jesus' attitude toward those who were "just" according to the law, and toward sinners, evinces his praxis of liberation from sin (Mark 2:10,17). The very notion of sin enters into contradiction with that of the law. Jesus reveals this contradiction, shows the meaning of sin, and rescues sinners that they may be able to be integrated into the new life of the liberated people. The forgiveness of debts and sins is the new sign and power of the praxis of this redeemed people (Mark 7:20-23; Matt. 18:21-35).

The Service That Redeems

Jesus' praxis hews to the root of the contradiction residing in power, the law, and their mediations. Power was maintained by the Roman Empire and by the priests and scribes, who formed the parties and tendencies in Judaism (Herodians, Sadducees, Pharisees, Essenes, Zealots, and "brigandage"). Jesus was not a Zealot; he was too radical for that. His liberation praxis was not comparable with that of the parties and tendencies. He defines himself in terms of the promise and of the mission of the Servant of Yahweh and the Son of Man. His praxis redeems the contradiction of the law, rehabilitates the meaning of justice, and restores to the people their task of freedom and mission (Mark 10:45).

The context of Jesus' conflicts and finally of his death sentence is the prevailing political and religious situation (Mark 2-3, 6; Matt. 12). Jesus repudiates the contradiction of the old system, and proclaims a new covenant along prophetical lines (Matt. 7, 12:1-8, 15-16, 23).

Jesus' messianism has a new, original meaning. It goes straight to the root of the hope of the poor. It is a project of redemption of bodily life and of resurrection in the perspective of the Reign of God and everlasting life. In his project, a future of complete freedom flashes on the horizon, and the meaning of his praxis, which culminates on the cross, becomes clear.

1. Jesus is crucified by human beings who make of the law they have received from God an opaque sign and the foundation of their power, security, and domination, which is the negation of truth, justice, and love (Matt. 23:23).

2. Jesus is sacrificed by the forces of evil that hide in the shadow of this law: sin and death. But the law will lose all of its intrinsic legitimacy in Jesus' death and in the victory of the cross. The law is replaced by love for neighbor, the root of life and freedom. Law and authority become service to life, whose exigencies derive from love of neighbor. It is not that Jesus' project is reducible to the political; it is only that the new praxis of this service of redemption spurs activity and mediations calculated to make concrete the social relations and organization of life and freedom for a people being delivered from the law, sin, and death. After all, Jesus' mission and praxis are to be understood in terms of the coming of the Reign of God. This is his gospel to the poor (Mark 1:14-15).

2. Revealer of the Father

Jesus' praxis and cross are not the simple outcome of the mechanical inter-play of social forces. They are to be explained in terms of the justice of the Reign of God, and the life and love of the Father. Thus, the meaning and content of Jesus' praxis are in the revelation and communication of the God of life. The hermeneutics of the theology of liberation has therefore insisted on the importance of the Lord's Prayer (in the Lukan and Matthean version) for an understanding of Jesus' praxis and project. It likewise insists on the importance of Matthew 11 as a criterion of this novelty. Matthew 11:25-30, especially, is a key text for an understanding of the manifestation to the poor of the God of life. Jon Sobrino has called attention to this basic hermeneutic criterion:

> What we are now attempting, in analyzing the reality of God in Jesus, is only to fathom the meaning of "Jesus" and "Yahweh is salvation." It is an attempt to comprehend the mediator, Jesus of Nazareth, so as to compre-hend the mediations of God's reality. They are what lend a final meaning to the person of Jesus and, for the believer, they are the final criterion for distinguishing the true God and for recovering that God from the idolatry of death. . . .
>
> In the second meaning, Jesus should be considered a participant in the very reality of God, as his Son. This is the analysis carried out by faith. In it one grasps and accepts the basic norms set for the mediator and his mediation. In this way, the Father of Jesus, through the path of the Son and in the history begun by the Spirit, becomes God *for us*. This is not merely a matter of learning who God was to Jesus, just as one might learn who God was to Moses or Jeremiah, but rather of grasping Jesus' fundamental rela-tionship with the Father, wherein one will learn who God is, in what sense he is a God of life, how life is given, the relationship that exists between giving life and giving one's own life, and so forth.[35]

This same author broaches perspectives for an interpretation of the conflicts in which Jesus was involved, and the meaning of the cross as the basic deed of the people's liberation—their definitive liberation.[36]

3. Redemption of Love for Neighbor

The act of liberation is in the redemption of love for neighbor. The old commandment is transformed into the people's newness of life and freedom. The message and possibility of love for neighbor deliver the people from the ambiguities of the law and open the way to the praxis of a new justice (Matt. 5:43-44).[37]

The liberation in question is, first of all, liberation from the friend-enemy schema. It shatters all structures of power, security, discrimination, and domi-nation by attacking them at their individual and social roots. The measure of the freedom that is possible in a given society is the capacity of that society for love of neighbor and for forgiveness. Why? Because persons, as subjects of social relationships, define their personal and social relations by defining their friends and enemies. Liberation, then, is an ever new and active response to the question, "Who is my neighbor?"

Thus, the liberation in question is a liberation for the relation of sibling to sibling, since we are all children of the same Parent. The practice of the life of children of this Parent is the new dimension and perspective of the mission and the universalism of the task of a people redeemed in their freedom in order to love their neighbors.

This life is new life in the Spirit; it is the task of evangelization as the eschatological discourse of Mark summarizes it in the perspective of hope in the coming of the Son of Man. After all, the Spirit is the apocalyptical, eschatological Gift, who comes for the liberation and redemption of the life of a people dominated by the powers of this world. This power is made concrete in the witness of those who believe and proclaim the praxis and coming of Jesus before the final end. Evangelization in the power of the Spirit, shown in the practice of love for neighbor, establishes the meaning of the journey of a people redeemed vis-à-vis the future.[38] According to Matthew 25:15-46, which has become the symbol and core of the hermeneutics of the theology of liberation, the practice of the love of neighbor is manifested in its fullness in activity in behalf of the poor and starving:

"Lord, when did we see you hungry or thirsty or away from home or naked or ill or in prison and not attend to you in your needs?" He will answer them: "I assure you, as often as you neglected to do it to one of these least ones, you neglected to do it to me." These will go off to eternal punishment and the just to eternal life. (Matt. 25:44-46)[39]

IV. NEW PRAXIS OF FREEDOM

The people's liberation process comes to a climax in the freedom redeemed and rescued by Jesus of Nazareth. Then begins the history of the new praxis of freedom in the following of Jesus.

The basic hermeneutic principle, therefore, is the relationship between the Spirit and freedom. It is the New Covenant of the freedom of the Spirit (Gal. 5, Rom. 8:2). The new element is that in Christ, by the Spirit, we are free. The Lord is Spirit, and where the Spirit is, there is freedom (2 Cor. 3:17). Here is a proclamation that will completely transform life; it will bestow a new understanding on history and give a new orientation to human action. Thus, hermeneutics is basically the understanding of the new praxis of freedom.

This is the content of the new praxis of the primitive Christian communities and the texts they produced. Let us indicate the three horizons of interpretation most used in the theology of liberation: freedom, the option for the poor, and the struggle with imperialism.

1. Freedom and the New Human Being

St. Paul proclaimed the gospel to the Gentiles in terms of the problematic of Judaism. The novelty and core of his message are freedom: faith in Christ stirs a new freedom, and this freedom produces love, the life of the new human being.[40] Here is where we find the fundamental hermeneutic principle.

The new element, for Jews and Gentiles alike, is that freedom comes through faith in Jesus Christ. It is he who has delivered us from the law and from all slavery. Paul shows that the passage from idolatry to the service of the God of life leads to the implementation of the will of God in the freedom that inspires an existence in solidarity. Liberty produces the life of the new people (1 Thess.).

The conflict is rooted in the temptation to return to a life in the security of the law. This would mean the prolongation of the slavery of the "flesh," of "sin," and of "death," since the law does not contain within itself the intrinsic principle of liberation and life. All, Jews and Gentiles alike, are under a regime of slavery and are in need of liberation. This conflict is a challenge to live the gospel of freedom (Gal.).[41]

Freedom addresses its discernment to the various leavens and weapons of slavery, which the law conceals, and by which the law itself is transformed into an instrument of sin and death. This is the positive discernment of the covenant of liberty (Gal. 4-5) and of the basic process of the transformation of history that is the "justification" and life of the new human being, the new creation (Rom. 1 and 2 Cor.). Freedom and love proceed from the Spirit, who justifies. The just are those persons who are free to love their neighbors in the reality of the new human being, the Israel of God (Gal. 6:2,8,16).

The new praxis consists essentially in walking in a manner worthy of the gospel of Christ, the Poor One, who has delivered us. Hence the importance in the Letter to the Philippians of christology and communitarian praxis. Here it is that liberation theology constantly seeks its inspiration and its norm of reflection. Paul likewise shows that this new praxis inaugurates a genuine movement of societal liberation, a liberation of persons and changes of structures that prevent the realization of the life of the new human being (Gal. 3:28). It is in this perspective that liberation theology hermeneutics has focused the problem of Paul's position and attitude toward slavery and slaves in the Greco-Roman world. On this particular, his position in the Letter to Philemon is enlightening. He goes to the root of the problem, indicating the Christian foundation that will transform the structures of slavery.[42]

New life is in the community's praxis—in mission and witness in the world. This new praxis takes on the dimension of reconciliation, the theme that comes in for special development in Colossians and Ephesians, under the influence of Pauline thought.[43]

2. Option for the Poor

The gospels of Matthew and Luke spring from the mission of the disciples, who see the life of the people from a point of departure in the poor as the vessels of the "newness" that is to transform society and history.

Church of the Poor

Matthew posits the proclamation of the presence of Emmanuel as the well-spring of mission (Matt. 1:23, 28:16-18). The disciples, who are poor, are the prophetical depositories and vehicles of Jesus' wisdom and project. The mission is good news for the poor, calculated to create and shape the church of the least ones. It is they who are the ferment and power of the new exodus inaugurated by Jesus.

The poor are present as Matthew's gospel opens as followers of Jesus, the Poor One, and vessels of the novelty of the Spirit of the Reign of God. Life in concrete poverty is identification with the Teacher, who is poor and meek in everything about his life and mission. Here is the leaven and power of discipleship (Matt. 5-7).

The poor are at the center of Matthew's gospel. They are the prophetical criterion of deliverance from the system of the law, of liberation to the newness of the Spirit. They are the vessels of Jesus' liberating wisdom (Matt. 11-12).

They are present at the conclusion, in the eschatological discourse (Matt. 25). Praxis in behalf of the poor is the decisive criterion of history. They are the measure of the value and meaning of the new justice and of the life of the just. The correct criterion is the freedom that produces a concretely effective love of the least ones. Here is the coming and manifestation of the Judge of history.

The church of the poor, then, consists of the new people of God, subject (agent) of the newness that liberates. Jesus gathers this people, composed of Jews and Gentiles. The new subject is constituted by faith in Jesus and by following in his footsteps. This is the life of the new reality of love and pardon. Its strength is in the sovereignty of the King who is poor (Matt. 21:5), who embraces the way of the cross. This King delivers his people from the old system of the law and opens to them the perspective of the future. He reveals the meaning of a journey through history—in a faith that is hope, and in love—in the expectancy of his coming (Matt. 15:22-25).[44]

Liberation of the Poor

Luke, in his gospel and in Acts, shows that the gospel is the proclamation of the liberation of the poor. This is his central theme.[45]

Amid the *Pax Romana*, the gospel of the poor is the strength of the mission and life of the communities. The liberation of the poor is the criterion for an understanding of Jesus' mission and of the new praxis of the community.

Luke wrote before the reign of Domitian, when it was still possible to have a vision of the Empire without the ideology of imperialism and persecution. In this situation the mission must be understood as the expansion of the witness (Acts 1:8).

Nevertheless, the basic division of society into rich and poor had now penetrated the life of the communities themselves. Hence the meaning and the urgency of the content of the concept of the poor (Luke 4:16-21, 6:20-26). Poor and rich live in the same communities, under the urgency of this call whose measure is the actual praxis of Jesus, who first trod the disciples' path.

In Acts, Luke reflects on the problems that were arising. He tries to indicate a solution, in two approaches:

1. Life in *communion*. The cornerstone of Luke's description of communion is the life of the primitive community of Jerusalem. Among Christians, there is no longer anyone in need, for the rich live in communion with the poor and share their goods with them. Here is the sign and token of the Reign of Jesus in history.

2. A concrete *distribution* of goods. This distribution is made for reasons of justice (Luke 3:11-12, 12:16-21,33, 14:14, 16:19-31). In Acts, money is always associated with injustice and sin. The purpose of money is to be given to those in need. The only logion of Jesus in Acts refers to helping the poor (Acts 20:35). Wealth is the fruit of injustice and ought to serve to mold communion.[46]

In the community of the Christians a new people is born, who achieves victory over money and wealth in the prophetical perspective of the Magnificat, that crystallization of the hope of the poor.

3. Witness in the Face of Imperialism

From the time of Domitian onward, Roman imperialism wielded an ideology of domination and persecution as well as of deification of the emperor. This situation aroused a new outlook of prophetic witness and freedom as the structuring axes of the evangelical proclamation.

People of Prophets

The Book of Revelation is the favorite book of our popular communities. Here they find the encouragement they need in their struggle and a criterion for the interpretation of official persecution, that everlasting bane of the poor in our society. The communities plumb the depths of the book that is revelation, witness, and prophecy (Rev. 1:1-6), a book whose purpose is to encourage and maintain the prophetical praxis of the new people—this priestly, royal, prophetic people. The meaning of the life of the church in the persecuting Empire proceeds from the need to "prophesy again" (Rev. 10:11). It is in prophetical witness that this people finds its living liberty.

The meaning of the church in history is rooted in the witness of the gospel before the state imperialism that destroys the people's life, looming as an idol and caricature of the holy Trinity. Testimony against the state and imperial idolatry has but one weapon: the force of the gospel. A discerning judgment strips away the mask, the radical lie of the society that oppresses, to reveal its antithesis, the monarchy of Christ. Witness enters into the process of liberation—liberation from domination, and liberation to life in the heavenly Jerusalem in the communion of the Lamb who was slain.[47]

The Truth Will Set Them Free

The Gospel of John expressed the life of the communities from which it sprang. It addressed their problems from their perspective. A look at the life and struggle of these communities shows that the categories of the Fourth Gospel are anything but abstract. They reflect the concrete problems of struggle, division, and a search for solutions to these problems.[48] The context of John's gospel is the struggle being waged by Christians against the imperialism of the Empire. John goes straight to the heart of the matter: freedom. His gospel is the revelation of the truth that sets persons free.[49]

Jesus' witness is the revelation of the world of the lie and the revelation of the definitive truth. Witness arouses faith, and faith produces love. Life in love leads to the concrete realization of the witness of the Spirit, who is given that the witness of the disciples may continue to face up to a hostile world. Witness is Jesus' word uttered in God's name and running counter to the world. It is the testimonial of life as light and truth.

The truth sets persons free. It is the implementation of definitive justice. It is not based on appearances (John 7:24). It is the revelation of the structures of the world, which are shaped by the lie. It is the revelation of the life and oneness that find their origin and end in Jesus, as he rests in the bosom of the Father, and in the witness he bore in his temporal life that he might communicate the Spirit, who is the truth that sets us free.

Thus, biblical hermeneutics is the fruit of the Spirit. It is interpretation of the memory kept ever alive and active by this Spirit among the disciples, men and women who go in quest of life and freedom.

— Translated by Robert R. Barr

NOTES

1. Hugo Assmann, "Tentativa epistemológica de compreensão" (unpublished), São Paulo, 1971, pp. 67-69.

2. For a history of the hermeneutic problem, see Franz Mussner, "Geschichte der Hermeneutik von Scheiermacher bis zur Gegenwart," in *Handbuch der Dogmengeschichte* (Freiburg, 1970), pp. 3-34; J. Severino Croatto, *Exodus: A Hermeneutics of Freedom*, trans. Salvator Attanasio (Maryknoll, N.Y.: Orbis Books, 1981); idem, *Biblical Hermeneutics: Toward a Theory of Reading as the Production of Meaning*, trans. Robert R. Barr (Maryknoll, N.Y.: Orbis Books, 1987).

3. Gilberto da Silva Gorgulho, "Die Armen lesen Gottes Verheissung," *Evangelische Mission* (1985), pp. 14-26 (with a bibliography on the popular reading of the Bible).

4. See Carlos Mesters, *Defenseless Flower: A New Reading of the Bible,* trans. Francis McDonagh (Maryknoll, N.Y.: Orbis Books, 1989).

5. Cf. José Comblin, *Introdução geral ao comentário biblico* (Petrópolis, Brazil, 1985), pp. 10-11.

6. Paul VI, *L'Osservatore Romano* 42 (1970).

7. Pablo Richard, "Biblia: Memória histórica dos pobres," *Estudos Biblicos* 1 (1984), pp. 20-30.

8. Cf. "Leitura da Biblia a partir das condições reais da vida," *Estudos Biblicos* 7 (1985).

9. Ana Flora Anderson and Gilberto da Silva Gorgulho, "A leitura sociológica da Biblia," *Estudos Biblicos* 2 (1984), pp. 6-10; Gilberto da Silva Gorgulho, "Malaquias e o discernimento da justicia," *Estudos Biblicos* 14 (1987), pp. 18-31.

10. N. K. Gottwald, *The Tribes of Yahweh: A Sociology of Liberated Israel* (Maryknoll, N.Y.: Orbis Books, 1979); see part 11.

11. The texts usually regarded as key for liberation hermeneutics are those of

the Exodus, the prophets, the Servant of Yahweh, the Beatitudes, the Last Judgment, the Book of Revelation, and so on. We hope to indicate, in the course of this chapter, some hermeneutical principles that will make these texts more clear in their message of liberation of the poor.

12. I here present a summary of my "O seguimiento de Jesús," *Estudos Biblicos* 2 (1984), pp. 25-37.

13. Cf. Victorio Araya, *God of the Poor: The Mystery of God in Latin American Liberation Theology*, trans. Robert R. Barr (Maryknoll, N.Y.: Orbis Books, 1987), with a fine bibliography for the hermeneutic problem; Comblin, *The Holy Spirit and Liberation,* trans. Paul Burns (Maryknoll, N.Y.: Orbis Books, 1989).

14. Franz J. Hinkelammert, *The Ideological Weapons of Death,* trans. Philip Berryman (Maryknoll, N.Y.: Orbis Books, 1985); idem, *Democracía y totalitarismo* (San José, Costa Rica, 1987, pp. 257-73.

15. This synchronic view owes much to the analyses of N. K. Gottwald, *The Tribes of Yahweh.* Cf. Milton Schwantes, "As tribos de Javé: Uma experiência paradigmática," *Revista Eclesiástica Brasileira* 185 (1987), pp. 103-19.

16. See the articles by Milton Schwantes, Ana Flora Anderson, C. Dreher, and Sandro Galazzi in *O Exodo na memória popular* (Petrópolis, Brazil, 1988) for examples of an approach to the exodus in the hermeneutics of the theology of liberation. Cf. Pablo Richard, "El Exodo: La búsqueda de Dios en la lucha liberadora," *Cristianismo, lucha ideológica y racionalidad socialista,* (Salamanca, 1975), pp. 67-82.

17. Cf. Milton Schwantes, "Hebreus no Egito: Anotações sobre a situaçõ histórica," in *Curso de Verão* (São Paulo, 1988), pp. 61-68.

18. The reader will find an extensive analysis of all aspects of the Book of Exodus in the volume just cited, *Curso de Verão,* including a practical example of interpretation in the perspective of the theology of liberation (pp. 13-102).

19. On the hermeneutics of the prophets and the state, see Jorge Pixley, "Las utopías principales de la Biblia," in *La esperanza en el presente de América latina,* ed. Paul Vidales and Luis Rivera Pagan (San José, Costa Rica, 1983), pp. 313-30; Milton Schwantes, *Amós* (Petrópolis, Brazil, 1987); idem, "Profecía e Estado: Uma proposta para a hermeneutica profética," *Estudos Teológicos* (1982), pp. 105-45.

20. Cf. Pablo Richard, "Biblical Theology of Confrontation with Idols," in Pablo Richard et al., *The Idols of Death and the God of Life,* trans. Barbara E. Campbell and Bonnie Shepard (Maryknoll, N.Y.: Orbis Books, 1983), pp. 3-25.

21. Cf. José Porfirio Miranda, *Marx and the Bible: A Critique of the Philosophy of Oppression,* trans. John Eagleson (Maryknoll, N.Y.: Orbis Books, 1974). Miranda suggests that the core of the entire hermeneneutic task is to be found in the social and liberative sense of *mispat.*

22. Richard, "Biblical Theology of Confrontation with Idols."

23. Cf. Gilberto da Silva Gorgulho, "A promessa ao rei Davi," *Vida Pastoral* 130 (1986), pp. 9-15.

24. Cf. Milton Schwantes, "Profecia e Estado: Qual é a palavra dos profetas sobre o Estado?" *Templo e Presença* (São Paulo, 1987), pp. 26-27.

25. Cf. *Trabalhador e trablho* (Petrópolis, Brazil, 1986), an important synthesis for the sociological interpretation of the Hebrew scriptures in a perspective of the tributary regime of production.

26. Cf. Gilberto da Silva Gorgulho, "A libertação e a sabedoria," *Estudos Bíblicos* 8 (1986), pp. 12-20.

27. Cf. Carlos Mesters, *A missão do povo oprimido* (Petrópolis, Brazil, 1980), a

reading of Isaiah 40-55 in the perspective of the suffering of the poor in Latin America.

28. Cf. Milton Schwantes, *Ageu* (Petrópolis, Brazil, 1985).

29. Cf. Gilberto da Silva Gorgulho, *Zacarias: A vinda do messias pobre* (Petrópolis, Brazil, 1985), pp. 9-11, 130-31.

30. Cf. Ana Flora Anderson, *Os sábios na luta do povo* (São Paulo, 1987). Proverbs, in its current form, is structured around the God who is the *Go'el* of the poor (Prov. 23:11), and the structure of the ensemble turns upon the quest for *justice* and *poverty*, in terms of the influence of Zephaniah 2:1-3. The *Go'el* God is also the center of the theology of Job (Job 19:25ff.). Cf. Gustavo Gutiérrez, *On Job: God-Talk and the Suffering of the Innocent,* trans. Matthew J. O'Connell (Maryknoll, N.Y.: Orbis Books, 1987).

31. For an interpretation of Ecclesiastes in terms of the value of work, cf. Ana Flora Anderson and Gilberto da Silva Gorgulho, "A leitura sociológica da Biblia," pp. 63-79; R. Fitzpatrick, "A resistência da verdade," *Estudos Biblicos* 14 (1987), pp. 32-38.

32. Cf. n. 9.

33. Jacques Dupont, *Jesús: Messias dos pobres, Messias pobre* (São Paulo, 1983).

34. N. Lohfink, *Kirchen Träume* (Freiburg, 1982), pp. 120-21.

35. Jon Sobrino, "The Epiphany of the God of Life in Jesus of Nazareth," in Richard, et al., *Idols of Death,* pp. 68-69.

36. Ibid., pp. 80-91; Araya, *God of the Poor,* pp. 95-104; Ignacio Ellacuría, "Por qué muere Jesús y por qué lo matan?" in *Temas para reflexión teológica* (Managua, 1982), pp. 91-101.

37. Gilberto da Silva Gorgulho and Ana Flora Anderson, *A justiça dos pobres: Mateus* (São Paulo, 1981), pp. 52-75.

38. Gilberto da Silva Gorgulho and Ana Flora Anderson, *O evangelho e a vida: Marcos* (São Paulo, 1975), pp. 183-89.

39. Gorgulho and Anderson, *A Justiça dos pobres,* pp. 225-27.

40. José Comblin, *La libertad cristiana* (Santander, 1979). The author presents basic hermeneutic principles for an interpretation of Paul and John in a perspective of the theology of liberation.

41. Ana Flora Anderson, "O evangelho da libertade," *Estudos Bíblicos* 2 (1984), pp. 38-49.

42. José Comblin, *Epístola aos Filipenses* (Petrópolis, Brazil, 1985); idem, "A mensagem da epístola de S. Paulo a Filemon," *Estudos Bíblicos* 2 (1984), pp. 50-70.

43. José Comblin, *Teologia da reconciliação: ideología ou reforção da libertaçõ* (Petrópolis, Brazil, 1987).

44. Gorgulho and Anderson, *A justiça dos pobres,* pp. 145ff.

45. José Comblin, *Evangelizar* (Petrópolis, Brazil, 1980), pp. 49-70. For an interpretation of the Letter of James in the same ambient of rich and poor in the Christian communities, cf. J. Walker and L. Z. Konzen, "A vossa riqueza aprodreceu," *Estudos Bíblicos* 11 (1986), pp. 110-22.

46. L.I.J. Stadelmann, "Recursos audiovisuais nos Atos dos Apóstolos," *Estudos Bíblicos* 3 (1984), pp. 7ff.

47. Gilberto da Silva Gorgulho and Ana Flora Anderson, *Nao tenham medo: Apocalipse* (São Paulo, 1977); Carlos Mesters, "O apocalipse de São Joao", unpub-

lished (São Paulo, 1986); J. B. Stam, *El Apocalipsis y el imperialismo* (San José, Costa Rica, 1985).

48. Raymond E. Brown, *The Community of the Beloved Disciple* (Mahwah, N.J.: Paulist Press, 1979).

49. Ana Flora Anderson, "O evangelho da verdade que liberta," *Estudos Bíblicos* 14 (1987), pp. 51-63.

7

Theology in the Theology of Liberation

PABLO RICHARD

I. EXPERIENCE OF GOD IN LATIN AMERICA TODAY

1. Radical Experience of Death and Life

There is a radical experience today in Latin America, especially among the poor and oppressed masses: the experience of death and life. Only an open, honest mind, a mind open to reality with sincerity and hope, has the capacity for this radical experience. The experience of misery, poverty, injustice, oppression, repression, discrimination, marginalization; the experience of a premature, unjust death; and likewise the experience by the poor of the struggle for life, of hope, of awareness, and of joy — all of this is part of that radical experience of death and life in Latin America. Ideology (understood in a pejorative sense as concealment of reality and legitimation of domination) and hopelessness are what cloud the heart and mind, and preclude this lucid transparent experience of reality. Thus, we are able to understand Jesus' saying: "Blessed are the single-hearted for they shall see God" (Matt. 5:8). Only those who have pure hearts, whose hearts are free of ideology and bitterness, and who live this radical experience in a conscious option for life are able to live and understand the experience of God in our history. Our entire theological reflection was to be radically marked by this historical contrariety between death and life, which is different from the metaphysical polarity between being and nonbeing, the polarity prevailing in the dominant theology.

2. Mystery of the Presence of God In the World of the Poor

The world of the poor contains a mystery: here, God personally comes to meet us and to bestow a self-revelation. The world of the poor is now seen for what it is: the privileged locus of the presence and revelation of God. It is a mysterious reality, but one that in the light of faith can be experienced and touched. God is revealed as the life, strength, hope, gladness, and utopia of the very poorest and most oppressed. This is why the world of the poor is so disturbing. In the struggle of the poor for life, there are spiritual depths antecedent to all theological reflection, depths that surprise us, amaze us, transcend us, and fill us with joy. The liberative historical processes that we are living in Latin America today are remarkable not only for their social and political density, but also, and especially, for their spiritual and theological wealth. The experience of God in the world of the poor is the profound root of the entire spiritual, theological, ecclesial, and pastoral renewal that we are living today.

The poor express this mystery of God's presence in their midst in a form very much like what we hear in the Psalms:

> O my just God,
>   you who relieve me when I am in distress . . . (Ps. 4:2)

> The LORD is a stronghold for the oppressed,
>   a stronghold in times of distress. (Ps 9:9)

> The desire of the afflicted you hear, O LORD;
>   strengthening their hearts, you pay heed. (Ps.10:17)

> "Because they rob the afflicted, and the needy sigh,
>   now will I arise," says the LORD.
> "I will grant safety to him who longs for it." (Ps.12:6)

> For lowly people you save
>   but haughty eyes you bring low. (Ps.18:27)

> It is better to take refuge in the Lord
>   than to trust in princes. (Ps.118:9)

> For the LORD loves his people,
>   and he adorns the lowly with victory. (Ps. 149:4)

This is actually the tenor and tone of almost all of the psalms, since these poems are to a large extent the prayer in which oppressed people express their experience of God. This is also the spirituality of the poor today.

The presence and revelation of God in the world of the poor is a transcendent, novel, and radical experience; the God of life destroys death, the God of hope obliterates anguish and desperation. Our God is a transcendent God, who guarantees the oppressed the radical novelty of a full life in this world, beyond all oppression, and beyond death itself.

3. How to Name the Mystery of God and Render It Explicit

Two difficulties arise when we attempt to name God in Latin America. On one hand, God has been too much named — and usually given false or distorted names. On the other hand, the mystery of God is so radical and disconcerting in the world of the poor that any attempt to name it is almost impossible. It is so difficult to name God that many prefer silence and simply do not speak of God. Others think that it is irresponsible, even dangerous, to speak of God in a "Christian" world in which an established image of God, manipulated by the system in order to legitimate oppression, already exists. Nevertheless, it is important to try to name God, to make the experience of God explicit, in order to *mark a difference* from the false images of God, or to destroy the routine of a God who is too facile and malleable. For the poor and oppressed, it is especially important to make God explicit, because they suffer most from the manipulations of God. It is the poor, as well who acquire the greatest awareness of the tremendous contradiction between the mystery of God as revealed in their own history and the God named in routine, official fashion.

To name God is to acknowledge the presence and face of God among the most oppressed. It is a matter not of proving the existence of God, but of discerning the divine presence and revelation in the history of the liberation of the poor. In the Bible, God is always named, and acknowledged or invoked by name. Rarely is God spoken of in abstract fashion. We read, for example, "The Lord, the God of your fathers" (Deut. 1:11) and "I, the Lord, am your God, who brought you out of the land of Egypt, that place of slavery" (Deut. 5:6). Jesus called God *"Abba* (O Father)" (Mark 14:36), and so on. Today, as well, in Latin America, we say: "The God of life," "the God of the poor," "the God of Archbishop Romero," and so forth.

More difficult than proving the existence of God is proving that God is with the poor and their struggle for justice today. It is not enough to say, "I believe in God." I must specify in what God I believe. It is highly dangerous and irresponsible to speak of God in an abstract manner, without naming that God or without clearly discerning the image of God. God in the abstract has become something too routine, and there are too many, as well, who in the name of God oppress or destroy others.

4. God in Liberation Theology

Liberation theology is a critical, systematic reflection on the *experience of God* as that experience is lived, professed, and celebrated in a liberation practice. The object of liberation theology, then, as of all theology, is precisely God. The theology of liberation is not a theological reflection on liberation, but rather a reflection on God in a context of liberation. Were we to use the image of a tree, we should say that the root of liberation theology is the experience of the presence and revelation of God in the world of the poor. This experience constitutes what in Latin America is usually called a *liberation spirituality.* Liberation theology springs from this liberative spirituality and is to a large extent a spiritual theology whose center has traditionally been the experience of God.

The theology of liberation has not too much insisted on a systematic discourse on God, but is a theology that has created a space that has made it possible for God to speak personally. It is a theology that has taught us to discover the presence of God and has taught us to listen to the word of God, precisely because it has sought and listened to God just where God is and is revealed in a privileged way: in the world of the poor and oppressed. Thus, liberation theology is a theology full of the strength of God's presence, a theology that communicates God's word to us. Abstract, a-historical, and ideological theologies speak a great deal about God, but are empty of the presence and word of God. The theology of liberation is strong because it has known how to hear the word of God in the cry of the oppressed.

5. Experience of God: The Church

The experience of God's presence, word, project, and Reign is the experience of the absolute, the transcendent, the ultimate and definitive in history. The church is the institution that has enabled us to discover and celebrate this experience of God. In this sense the church is the necessary sacrament of the Reign of God in history. But in Latin America today we are daily acquiring an awareness that God is *greater* than the church—that the Reign of God is the only absolute, and that the church is relative. It is the Reign of God that gives meaning to the church. When the church is absolutized, it loses its meaning and can be transformed into an instrument of power and domination. Thus, the church must be subjected to an ongoing judgment from the viewpoint of the building of the Reign of God in history.

In historical processes, especially in its revolutionary moments, faith demands that we ask ourselves not "how the church is doing," but "how God is doing." Many church persons are excessively concerned with defending the interests and rights of the church, while forgetting to ask themselves where and how the Reign of God is being revealed in history. That Reign is revealed in the church, of course, but it is revealed beyond the church, as well, and often despite the church.

God is spoken *of* in every local church. But it may be that *God* is able to speak in very few. The church is usually a specialist in the things *of* God; but the church does not always teach us to listen to *God*. Many local churches live self-centered lives; the object of their preaching is the church, and their entire effort is expended on promoting the growth of the church. The experience of God in Latin America today thus constitutes a most profound challenge to the life of the churches. What the church fears in liberation theology is not that liberation be spoken of, but that theology be spoken of. The church is not afraid that politics will be spoken of; it fears that God and the Reign of God will be spoken of, and that out of this experience of God may come a judgment or questioning of the meaning of the entire church. Behind many of the changes in the church today, behind the commitment of many Christians to the liberation of the poor, behind an entire liberative reflection, there is almost always a novel, radical experience of God. The church has made a preferential option for the poor, but God had made one long before.

6. Experience of God: Political Responsibility

The experience of God in Latin America is not reducible to the personal or ecclesial ambit. It has direct repercussions on the public, institutional sphere of politics, whether in a negative or a positive way. It is arresting, for example, to compare two political constitutions, that of the apartheid state of South Africa and that of the revolutionary state of Nicaragua. God is mentioned in the preamble of each, but in diametrically opposite senses.

The South African Constitution says:

In humble submission to almighty God, who controls the destinies of nations and the history of peoples, who has led our ancestors from many lands and gathered them in this land which he has given them as their own, who has guided them from generation to generation, who has miraculously delivered them from the dangers that lay in wait for them . . .

The Nicaraguan Constitution says:

In the name of the Nicaraguan people, of all parties and democratic, patriotic, and revolutionary organizations of Nicaragua, of its men and women, of its laborers and campesinos, of its splendid youth, of its heroic mothers, *of its Christians, who out of their faith in God have committed themselves to and joined the struggle for the liberation of the oppressed*, of its patriotic intellectuals, of all those who with their productive labor contribute to the defense of the homeland and of those who struggle and offer their lives in the face of imperialist aggression in order to guarantee the happiness of new generations . . .

In both constitutions, the name of God is used. In the South African Constitution that name is subjected to an ideological, idolatrous usage, for the purpose of justifying racist domination. In the Nicaraguan Constitution, a historical phenomenon is cited: the universally acknowledged phenomenon of the commitment of Christians to the revolution, together with an acknowledgment of the fact that these Christians have committed themselves to the struggle for the liberation of the oppressed on the basis of their faith in God. Thus, there is no idolatrous or ideological use of God here in citing God for the legitimation of the commitment of Christians or of the revolution itself. And yet Christians' experience of God has a political repercussion on the very Constitution of the Republic.

II. THE GOD OF LIFE AND THE IDOLS OF DEATH

1. Atheism or Idolatry

In Latin America the basic confrontation of faith and belief is not with atheism but with idolatry. There are two kinds of atheism: liberal (laissez faire) bourgeois atheism and revolutionary atheism. The first is sprung from the Enlightenment. It is philosophical or humanistic atheism, created by the modern, secularized world that seeks to be delivered from the dominion of medieval christendom. This is the atheism of the world of science and technology, which was born beyond the confines of the church. This type of atheism has to some extent marked the dependent intellectual elite of Latin America, but the vast majority of the people have not been directly affected by it. What is really present and immediate to the great masses is what we call revolutionary atheism. This is the political, militant atheism of those who do battle for justice and are involved in a liberation practice. This type of atheism profoundly challenges Christian faith, but does not normally appear as an enemy of Christians. Indeed, believing and nonbelieving revolutionaries meet in a common practice, in a common historical project, and regard each other as comrades. Both revolutionary atheists and committed Christians, different though they may be in language and motivation, entertain a critical attitude toward religion. The atheistic revolutionaries speak of an ideologization of faith or of fetishism. Believers denounce the same thing as idolatry. Both do so from a common liberation practice.

What is actually opposed to Christian faith in Latin America is not atheism, then, but idolatry: both the idolatrous manipulation of the true God, and the replacement of that God with other gods created by human beings. Throughout the entire history of Latin America, the oppressors of the people have almost always declared themselves to be believers—which is tantamount to an idolatrous perversion of the name of God. The Conquistadors were all Christians, and colonization was carried out in the name of God. Likewise those responsible for slavery were Christians, supported by Christian European nations. As for the church, it endorsed slavery for centuries. Today all of the military dictators, and practically all of those responsible for economic, political, and ideological oppression, are Christian. Domination, consequently, has always been basically idolatrous, thereby involving a serious threat to the faith of a people both poor and believing. The danger to faith, then, does not come from the atheistic revolutionaries but from the idolatrous oppressors.

2. *Our Theological Undertaking Is against Idols and the Dominant Idolatry*

The basic theological task in America is not that of establishing the existence of God, but of discerning the true God from false idols. The problem is not to know *whether* God exists, but to demonstrate in *what* God we believe. Today it is no longer meaningful to declare oneself a believer; the meaningful thing is to explain *in which* God one believes. Likewise, it is meaningless to declare oneself an atheist; one must specify in *what* God one does not believe. The question of God is no longer so much whether God exists, but "how" God is, where God is, with whom God is or against whom God is, what God's project is, how God becomes present and revealed in history, why God is the God of the poor, the God of life, and so on. The basic problem is not the existence but the presence of God. It is not a matter of proving the existence of God in the abstract but of discovering in the concrete the historical presence of God in the world of the poor and oppressed. To prove the existence of God is difficult, surely; it is far more difficult and urgent today to demonstrate that God is with the poor and their liberation struggles in a special way. From an apologetical theology of the proofs for the existence of God we move to a spiritual theology of the discernment of the presence of God in our history. This discernment, this distinction, is usually made not over against revolutionary atheism, but over against the dominant idolatry.

A theological concern with the discernment between the true God and the false idols is a theological task of interest to the entire people of God. Every believer feels the need to mark the difference between the God of the poor in which he or she believes and the dominant ideology. In black theology it is customary to assert that God is black, and in the theology of women's liberation God is referred to as "she." In like manner, liberation theology speaks of the "God of the poor." God, of course, has neither color, sex, nor possessions. The point of all of these expressions is the *difference* between the experience of God had by the oppressed and the idolatrous images of God. The dominant idolatry presents us with a racist, sexist, and dominator god. Those who believe in the true God must mark the difference between their God and all the idolatrous images of God. This discernment is no theological subtlety but a problem of life or death for the believer, especially for the poor and oppressed. The struggle between the God of life and the idols of death is a genuine spiritual combat, waged in the consciousness of the believer, in the church, and in society. Liberation theology is the theological expression of this combat.

3. Forms of Idolatry Past and Present

In the Bible, two basic forms of idolatry appear: idolatry by perversion and idolatry by substitution. The first occurs in direct regard to Yahweh, when the very name or "image" of Yahweh is manipulated or perverted. The second occurs when Yahweh is replaced by other gods. In Exodus 22 we have the most typical case of idolatrous perversion with direct regard to Yahweh: the people fabricate the golden calf, moved by fear and lack of hope, in order to manipulate the transcendent, liberator God and oblige that God to return with them to the slavery of Egypt. The most abundant biblical texts, however, are those that cry out against foreign gods and false gods who seek to replace Yahweh. This anti-idolatrous critique is a basic, constant theme of the entire bible. Typical passages are Jeremiah 10:1-6, Isaiah 44:14-17, Psalm 115, Wisdom 13-15, and so on. The gospels severely criticize the idolatry of money, law, knowledge, and power. Paul identifies idolatry with lust: "No fornicator, no unclean or lustful person—in effect an idolater—has any inheritance in the kingdom of Christ and of God" (Eph. 5:5; cf. Col. 3:5). In the Book of Revelation the two great sins are blasphemy and idolatry. We could go on. The theology of liberation seeks to rehabilitate, in our day in Latin America, as forcefully as possible, the anti-idolatrous critique of the biblical tradition.

Today we have an abundant idolatrous production. There are idolaters by perversion: those who pervert the meaning of God, who manipulate God, who deform the divine image, or who use the divine name in vain. There is also idolatry by substitution: the true God is replaced by false gods. This occurs when human beings absolutize or divinize realities that they themselves create: money, capital, power, prestige, technology, institutions, or offices. We may even include idolatry of the church itself, or the text of the Bible, when they are regarded as absolutes. When a historical subject develops and identifies itself with an abstract, universal subject, that subject readily "acquires" absolute, divine, supernatural, and transcendent characteristics. Human beings are capable of creating this false spiritual dimension or idolatrous spirituality in order to impose themselves on others with greater strength and legitimacy. Idolatry is usually in the service of power, domination, and oppression. Idols are always idols of death.

4. Idolatry as the Root of Social Sin

In Latin America we speak a great deal of social sin. Surely we are correct in doing so, since there is such a sin, and we suffer tragically from it. Social sin is not an anonymous, blind, or fatal force; it consists in structures of sin created by human beings, who are responsible for it. But social sin is not the ultimate reality oppressing us, nor does it explain the entire phenomenon of the death we suffer. There is something more, something behind social sin, which gives it its power and effectiveness. That something is idolatry, which is the root of social sin.

A sinner cannot sin without limits; all sinners have bad consciences and die in their sin. There is a limit. But in social sin we observe the absence of any limits. The system oppresses and kills without limits, and with a good conscience. This is the daily experience among our peoples; oppression, repression, and death multiply without limits, and the system is not spent or destroyed in that death. Indeed, the system believes it is acting for the best. This oppression without limits and in good conscience is a mystery. There is a transcendent, spiritual power of death that gives life and a clear conscience to social sin. It is the mystery of iniquity, and we identify it with idolatry. Idolatry, then, is not neutral or harmless. It is not simply a spiritual or individual deviation, of no interest to the masses. On the contrary, idolatry is highly dangerous and criminal. It is the supernatural force of death, which continuously gives life to social sin. St. Paul says this so well:

> Our battle is not against human forces but against the principalities and powers, the rulers of this world of darkness, the evil spirits in the regions above. (Eph. 6:12)

5. Prophetical Critique and Marxist Critique of Religion

Many take scandal at the Marxist critique of religion. But the prophetical critique is much older and, in many respects, more radical and profound. The prophets, in the light of faith, criticize religion from a specific conceptualization of the intervention of God in history. Marxists criticize religion in function of an analysis of reality. They are two different types of criticism, but a prophetical, believing outlook can adopt the Marxist criticism of religion without fear, as a rational instrument of discernment between an authentic faith and an alienated religion. First, let us see the prophetical criticism and then the Marxist criticism of religion.

The distinctive element in the thought of the prophets is the notion that knowledge of God and worship of God do not occur directly but only in the practice of justice. Where there is no justice, there will be no knowledge of God, and all worship of God will be radically illegitimate. Jeremiah 22:13-16 makes a triple identification: to do justice and right, defending the cause of the poor and needy, and knowing Yahweh. These are all the same thing. Likewise in Hosea 6:6 compassion and knowledge of God are synonymous. God can be known only in the practice of justice. God is manifested only in the cry of the oppressed. The Christian scriptures continue in the same vein, and John summarizes it all very well: "Everyone who lives is begotten of God and has knowledge of God. The man without love has known nothing of God, for God is love" (1 John 4:7-8). To love and to do justice are synonymous in John (cf. 1 John 4:7, 2:29).

Likewise God detests—in the oracles of the prophets—all worship apart from justice. For example, we have Amos 5:21,24: "I hate, I spurn your feasts, I take no pleasure in your solemnities. ... Let justice surge like water, and goodness like an unfailing stream." Or Isaiah:

What care I for the number of your sacrifices? ... When you come in to visit me, who asks these things of you? ... Bring no more worthless offerings. ... Your new moons and festivals I detest. ... When you spread out your hands, I close my eyes to you; though you pray the more, I will not listen. Your hands are full of blood! ... Put away your misdeeds from before my eyes; cease doing evil; learn to do good. Make justice your aim: redress the wronged, hear the orphan's plea, defend the widow. (Isa. 1:11-16)

One of the most radical texts against religion and worship is found in Jeremiah 7. God conditions the divine presence amid the people on the practice of justice; religion is deception when it only serves as a cover to steal, kill, and oppress. Worshipers come to the temple only to seek security, that they may continue oppressing and killing in good conscience. And so Jeremiah calls the temple a "den of thieves" (Jer. 7:11)—the place where murderers and brigands find refuge and tranquility. Therefore the prophet announces the destruction of the temple. God prefers to have no temple at all, rather than have a den of thieves for a temple. Jesus will adopt the same prophetical attitude (Mark 11:15-19). All quest for God and all worship that does not go hand in hand with the practice of justice is illegitimate and idolatrous. This is the central, distinctive message of the whole Bible. This is what differentiates worship of Yahweh from all idolatrous practices.

The Marxist criticism of religion and the antireligious critique implicit in all liberation practice run along the same line as the prophetic criticism of religion. The point of departure and the inspiration is different, but what the Marxist criticism calls alienation, or fetishism, the prophetical criticism calls idolatry. We cannot develop the Marxist criticism of religion here, but we can say that

Christians in Latin America, and consequently liberation theology, accept that criticism as a challenge to Christian faith from a point of departure in the scientific analysis of society. More specifically, the Marxist criticism of religion is adopted not in terms of a rejection of all religion or all transcendent dimension, but as an instrument of discernment, utilized in critical fashion and on theological criteria, to distinguish between an authentic religion and an idolatrous or alienated religion. The Marxist critique is adopted not as a negation, but as a critical instrument of discernment among various religious expressions. Concepts like *practice, ideology,* or *alienation* are now recognized as instruments for a prophetic and theological critique of religion.

6. Idolatry as Power, and Faith in God as Spiritual Combat

The dominant system not only produces material goods, it also produces idols and idolatry. The system has the capability of producing spiritual and supernatural forces, of creating a transcendent, numinous, fantastic world. When the dominant economic, political, and cultural power succeeds in creating this spiritual dimension, then *power has more power.* A multiplication of power occurs. Idolatrized or spiritualized power is mightier than simple material, historical power. Idolatry, then, is a way of increasing power. We know from our faith that this whole spirituality is false, and an idolatrous human creation. But the dominant power, in generating this spiritual force, actually increases its power, and this multiplied, swollen power is real and tremendously effective. As the psalm says: "Their idols are silver and gold, the handiwork of men. They have mouths but speak not; they have eyes but see not; they have ears but hear not; they have noses but smell not" (Ps. 115:46). Idols in themselves are nothing, but the dominating power that produces them finds in the production of idols an effective way of increasing its power. Idolatrized power is more powerful than nonidolatrized power. Idolatry, then, is power—a power that produces more power, and a production of power without limit. It projects itself without limit toward the absolute, the infinite, the spiritual, the supernatural, the transcendent. All of this production of power occurs in a false conscience, but the power that manages to create this conscience, and impose it as the dominant conscience, genuinely increases its power. Idolatry is false, but the production of power is no illusion: it is real. Idolatrized power is more dangerous, and strikes harder and more deeply, than nonidolatrized power.

The dominant economic, political, and cultural power creates idols not only in order to increase its power, but in order to dominate persons and society spiritually. An idolatrous society is not only an economically, politically, or culturally dominated society; it is a *spiritually* dominated society, as well. Idolatry confers on domination a spiritual, supernatural, and transcendent depth. All of this power and idolatrous domination is reinforced, multiplied, and legitimated when there are churches, sects, and spiritual movements at its service. Idolatry thus becomes uncontainable and penetrates all of society. The root of idolatry is in the dominating power, but this power can convert the whole of the culture and the dominant religion into mechanisms of spiritual domination.

Idolatry is not only a theological deviation, then, or a perversion of conscience, an interior, private and neutral phenomenon. On the contrary, idolatry is a dimension of the dominating power: it is a social phenomenon, highly dangerous, affecting society and persons in their totality and in depth.

If idolatry is the spiritual force of the dominating economic, political, and cultural power; if idolatry has this personal as well as social, spiritual as well as material, dimension, then the believer's battle with idolatry has the same radicality, breadth, and depth. The anti-idolatrous struggle is not only a theological struggle or a personal struggle; it is not only a spiritual problem or one of individual conscience: it is a specific dimension of the historical practice of liberation. The believer in God is confronted with the idols of the system and the idolatry of death, in total, integral combat, on all the battlefields of life, social and personal, material and spiritual. When faith delivers us from idols and idolatry, this liberation is not only a spiritual, personal one, it is a profound dimension of a historical, social, and political liberation.

III. THE MEDIATIONS OF THEOLOGY

1. The God of History: History and Theology

There is only one history, and God is present, revealed, and saving in this single history. To have faith is to believe that God intervenes in history; thus, we confess the God of history. To have faith is to believe that history is ever more than itself, and that in history there is always a novel presence and a word of God that catches us by surprise—that history has an absolute, transcendent dimension. History is the basic mediation of the encounter with God. All of these propositions constitute the basic tradition common to all liberation theology.

However, history is not an abstract reality. Concrete history is always the history of domination or liberation—history marked by the contrariety of death and life. Here we are interested above all in the perspective of the history of the liberation and salvation of the poor and oppressed. Only from the outlook of the liberation of the poor does history become concrete. The poor constitute a total, conflictive reality. The poor are discovered in terms of their economic, political, cultural, ethnic, and religious totality. The liberation of the poor is historical and concrete when it accepts conflict: after all, the history of the poor is always the history of the struggle of the poor for their liberation.

Concrete history is also a dynamic reality. It is not the sum of a number of phenomena and events, but a historical process, with its laws, structures, conjunctures, and strategies, with its entire organic, theoretical, and political density.

History can also be either opaque or transparent. The history of domination is always opaque; it is permeated with the dominant ideology, which conceals conflicts and justifies domination. On the other hand, the history of the liberation of the oppressed is always transparent, since it reveals conflicts and impels us toward their resolution. Revolutionary processes, then, are history's most special moments, when history is at its most dense and most transparent, when history reveals to us its totality, its conflictual nature, its dynamism and density. It is the history of liberation, the concrete liberation of the poor and oppressed, that is the fundamental mediation of the encounter with God: the discovery of the divine presence, revelation, and salvation.

A key concept for an understanding of history as mediation of God's presence, revelation, and salvation is the concept of *transcendence*. Etymologically, the word denotes a reality that subsists *beyond* some limit (more exactly, one that *climbs beyond* a limit). What is beyond the limit is *transcendent*, and what is short of the limit is *immanent*. It is important, then, to define the limit in question. In the case at hand, there are two kinds of limits, different but interrelated. *The first limit is oppression.* The oppressed are *limited* by the structures of oppression, oppressions of all kind: economic, political, cultural, ethnic, sexist, ideological, ethical, and religious. If we take this first limit as our point of reference, God is transcendent in the sense that God delivers us from oppression. God breaks our chains, liberates us from all of the limits oppression imposes on us, and grants us life in fullness beyond those limits. Thus, God is transcendent because God is liberator, and God is liberator because God is transcendent. God the transcendent liberator tolerates no oppression, and grants to the oppressed to live beyond those limits. For the poor, then, transcendence is critically important because the transcendent God is the God who delivers from all oppression.

The second limit is more universal and radical: death. Every creature experiences this limit. This time God is transcendent in the sense of surpassing this limit and guaranteeing life beyond death. Immanent life is the life that ends with death, and transcendent life is the life that definitively overcomes death. We call it eternal life—a life that does not die. It is the same life as before, only this time it is without death. God is transcendent as the God who delivers from oppression, and also as the God who delivers from death. The transcendent God is the God of life, since this is the God who guarantees a fully liberated life, a life without oppression and without death.

This liberated life is a life *in this history.* God does not transcend history, God transcends oppression and death within our history. God delivers us from oppression and death in our history. We often conceptualize transcendency as if it were something beyond the visible, beyond the material, beyond history. We think of the transcendent as invisible, immaterial, a-historical or transhistorical. This is a false conceptualization of transcendency—or at least it is not the biblical, liberative conception of transcendency. In the Bible, transcendence is full life—material, bodily, historical life, become reality beyond all oppression and beyond death. God is transcendent because God delivers us not from the body or from matter but from oppression and from death. Full life is the bodily life that never dies. This is the justification of our faith in the resurrection, in the transformation of our mortal body, in the transfiguration of our matter, in the glorification of our historical existence. Faith in the bodily, historical resurrection of the flesh has always been a central element in the theology of liberation. This concept of transcendency as the defeat of death is a datum of faith alone. It is our faith in God as transcendent that enables us to hope for resurrection, the transformation of our mortal body in immortal life – a life that never dies. But we must insist that this full life is present in history – in an immortal, transfigured, glorified, but historical form. We do not know exactly how this full, immortal bodily life shall be. But we hope in it, as a new creation of the liberating, transcendent God within our own, single history.

Biblical language is better adapted to an understanding of this intrahistorical transcendency – not because it corresponds to a determinate culture, but because it better expresses the experience of the transcendent God who causes the poor and oppressed to be believers within history. By way of an example, let us examine two biblical texts, which stand in clear continuity with each another: Isaiah 65:17-25 and Revelation 21:1 – 22:5. Each text combines a cosmic language with an historical one. The cosmic language is not a-historical, but serves solely to radicalize the historical experience of the prophet. Let us cite certain parts of these passages.

> Lo, I am about to create new heavens
>   and a new earth. . . .
> For I create Jerusalem to be a joy
>   and its people to be a delight;
> I will rejoice in Jerusalem
>   and exult in my people.
> No longer shall the sound of weeping be heard there,
>   or the sound of crying;
> No longer shall there be in it
>   an infant who lives but a few days,
>   or an old man who does not round out his full lifetime;
> He dies a mere youth who reaches but a hundred years. . . .
> They shall live in the houses they build,
>   and eat the fruit of the vineyards they plant;
> They shall not build houses for others to live in,
>   or plant for others to eat. . . .
> My chosen shall long enjoy
>   the produce of their hands. . . .
> The wolf and the lamb shall graze alike. (Isa. 65:17-25)

In this passage, what is defeated, clearly, is *oppression*. The new creation of cosmos, city, and people is the creation of a world without oppression. God proclaims a full life, without children dying, without exploitation, without theft or robbery, without suffering, without wars, but with death still in the offing. Premature death is a thing of the past, having been the fruit of oppression, but when all is said and done, death abides.

> Then I saw new heavens and a new earth. . . . I also saw a new Jerusalem, the holy city. " . . . And there shall be no more death or mourning, crying out or pain, for the former world has passed away."
> [Jerusalem] gleamed with the splendor of God. . . .

On either side of the river grew the trees of life. . . . [His servants] shall see him face to face. . . . The lord God shall give them light, and they shall reign forever. (Rev. 21:1–22:5)

This time the portrayal is clearly of the defeat of death itself. Here heaven and earth represent the cosmos, and the city represents social organization. The cosmos and the city are new, for death is no longer in them. It is a transformed world; its light is God's glory, and all see God directly. A new creation is here: a new cosmos and a new social organization. History goes on, then, but this time without death and in the visible presence of the glory of God. Material, bodily continuity of history, and discontinuity with death — both elements are essential to the text. Other biblical texts express this continuity of history and defeat of death in the image of the new man and the new woman, the new creature, the spiritual body. Even Jesus' resurrection is paradigmatic of this transformation. Jesus raised is the same Jesus, bodily present (and not a phantasm — he takes nourishment with his disciples), but at the same time there is a transformation, a glorification (they recognize him only in his word and in the breaking of the bread).

2. The God of Life: Economics and Theology

The contradiction between death and life is a basic historical contrariety in Latin America. The economic, the social, the political, the cultural, the anthropological, the ethical, and the spiritual dimensions are all at stake in an essential way in this contrariety. *Life* means concrete human life: work, land, housing, food, health, education, family, participation, cultural ambient, festival. All of these basic needs are essential bodily realities, and in each of them all of the above-mentioned dimensions are at stake. No life reality is solely economic or soley spiritual. For a native campesino, for example, *land* denotes at one and the same time an economic and political reality, but also a cultural and spiritual one. In Latin America, when we speak of basic needs, or essential bodily needs, we are not as yet making a distinction between infra- or superstructural realities. All are total realities of life or death. In the Third World, when you are out of work, you are out of life. For the natives, culture is agriculture, and in it the life of their nation is at stake. The life of the marginalized is also at stake in any question of education or participation. The poor also assert their option for life and their hope of more life in community festival and shared joy.

Ethics and spirituality find an essential mediation in this concrete human life. Work, land, housing, health, and other aspects, are economic, political, and so on, imperatives, but they are also ethical imperatives. There is an ethics of life, where the defense of concrete human life is the fundamentally ethical imperative. The ethical good is for all to have life. Death is immoral. Unemployment, hunger, illiteracy, and so forth, are a political, social, or cultural problem, but they are also an ethically perverse reality. Concrete life becomes the criterion of discernment between what is ethically good and what is ethically evil. Similarly, concrete human life also becomes the basic mediation of spirituality. Life, work, land, housing, culture, and so on, are economic, political, and social realities, but they are also spiritual realities. To be sure, spirituality is not exhausted in the life or death of the human being. But the basic needs to which we have referred are the criterion of discernment between an authentic and a false spirituality—or rather, between a spirituality of life and a spirituality of death.

In Latin America one hears a great deal about the "logic of life," or the "logic of the masses." Concrete human life is taken as the essential criterion of logic or rationality. For all to have life is the most logical, the most rational thing. Unemployment, disease, hunger, illiteracy, are illogical and irrational. This logic of life is the opposite of the logic of the dominant system, where the rational is always maximum profit. Life for all, especially for the very poorest, can become irrational for the logic of maximum profit. Unemployment, concentration of land, social and economic marginality—and even the death of the poor—can be rational in the dominant system.

To speak of the satisfaction of basic needs, or of life for all, is not yet to speak of objectives, or a program, or an ideology, or a model of development. We are dealing with something anterior and more basic here. We are dealing with criteria that assist us in a discernment of our objectives, in a discernment of one ideology or development model from others. It is a matter of choosing a criterion that will enable us to discern what is more rational, more logical, better, most beautiful. This criterion is life for all, especially for those in whom life is more threatened than not: the poor and oppressed.

All that we have said concerning life as a basic mediation of the economic, political, ethical, and spiritual, we can also apply to our reflection on God. The expression, *God of life*, sums it all up perfectly—but on condition we understand *life* as concrete human life and as fundamental logic or rationality. Otherwise the expression evaporates into an abstract, spiritualistic theology. God is the God of life because the basic actual divine will is that all men and women have life and life in abundance (cf. John 10:10). The poor believe and hope in the God of life because this is the God who ensures concrete human life for all, especially for them. God is the God of life because God takes on human life as absolute truth, goodness, and beauty. The best summary expression of all of this is St. Irenaeus's celebrated declaration, "The glory of God is the living human being." The glory of God, that is, the divine essence—what God is and what defines God—is manifested in concrete human life. The glory of God is at stake in the life or death of the historical human being. Concrete human life, which is an economic, political, social, ethical, and so on, reality, now attains to its maximal spiritual reality. Work, land, housing, health, food, and education become the very expression of the glory of God. Likewise, the glory of God is trampled under foot in any person who suffers hunger, destitution, and oppression. The relation between life and theology thus comes to be an intrinsic relation. The theology of life is the theology in which concrete human life is the basic mediation of the presence and levelation of God. Others express the same thing in the intrinsic relation between economics and theology. The option for life thus becomes the basic content of theology—the logic of God in our history.

3. The God of the Bible: Bible and Theology

The taproot of our theology is the experience of God in the world of the poor. God becomes present and is revealed in history and life as the God who liberates the oppressed, and as the God who guarantees life for all, especially for the poor. This experience of God must be discerned and expressed. The Bible is the criterion or canon of the performance of this work of discernment. "God wrote two books: the book of life, and the Bible" (St. Augustine). In the history of the liberation of the cosmos and humanity alike, God has engaged in a self-communication with us. But on account of sin, and especially on account of idolatry, which has filled the world with so much "religious chatter," with so much "spirituality of death," with so much "theological idolology," a second book became necessary, which would help us to read the first. This second book was the Bible. St. Augustine says:

> The Bible, the second book, was written to help us decipher the world — to restore to us the gaze of faith and contemplation, and to transform all reality into a grand revelation of God.

Thus, the Bible is our fundamental criterion for discerning the living word of God in our life and our history. We say that God becomes present in a most special way in the world of the poor since, after all, the Bible is the basic tool for discerning this presence and for articulating it, uttering it, communicating it, and crying it to the whole world.

It is classic doctrine to distinguish three meanings in the Bible: the textual sense, the historical sense, and the spiritual sense. The *textual sense* is the meaning of the text as text — as independent, organized literary structure. The *historical sense* is the meaning the text acquires in light of the history in which it arose and in which the text became history. The *spiritual sense* is the meaning the text acquires when it is read in order to discern and communicate the word of God in our current reality. In other words, the Bible has meaning when we interpret the text in itself, when we interpret the past history in which it arose, and when it interprets our reality, transforming it into a "grand revelation of God." We read the Bible, history reads the Bible, and the Bible reads our reality. In all three cases, there is a *production of meaning* that affects the very text of the Bible. When we discover the textual, historical, and spiritual senses of the Bible, then the Bible becomes the mediation of the word of God in history. It is then no longer a dead text. It rises again, as a living mediation of God's word. This discovery and resurrection of the Bible, by way of the recovery of its textual, historical, and spiritual meaning is assisted by *biblical scholarship* in the life of the *Christian community*, which is in turn inserted into the *people's liberation process.* The textual and historical sense usually require the help of biblical scholarship, but the spiritual sense has a very special need of the Holy Spirit, whose activity becomes living and effective in the faith of the church community in its insertion in history. The exegetes basically contribute their *science*, while the community contributes its *faith* in the Spirit of truth as well as its *human and political knowledge of the history of liberation*, into which it is inserted. When the exegete participates in the community's political and spiritual experience, and when the latter in turn also makes use of biblical scholarship, then the Bible multiples still further its capacity to mediate the word of God.

When the Bible, with all of its textual, historical, and spiritual wealth, is interpreted by biblical scholarship, by the Christian community, in the context of the history of the people's liberation, then it is the living, effective mediation of the word of God. This is the living Bible, which discerns God's presence and revelation in the world of the poor. But there is a problem. The Bible as it has reached us is a book *without a text* — a dismembered book, shattered into a thousand pieces, without structure, without internal cohesion. Further, it is a book *without history* — cut off from the history in which it was born and in which its text became history. Finally, it is a text *without spirit* — without the capacity to discern and express the living word of God in our current reality. This "textless, historyless, and spiritless" Bible is a dead Bible — dismembered, abstract, alien, cut off from the community and from history. Thus destroyed, the Bible can now be reconstructed in *another* text, in *another* history, and with *another* spirit. Sprung from the memory and historical consciousness of the poor in a context of liberation, the Bible is now interpreted in terms of a history of domination and in a dominant ideological consciousness. Accordingly, a "hermeneutic breach" (a break in interpretation) is needed, one that will permit us to recover the spiritual, critical, living, and effective force of the text for the discernment of the word of God today in the world of the poor. The people, poor and believing, organized in the church community, with all the support of their committed Bible teachers, must succeed in recovering the Bible, in order that holy scripture may once more come to be a living mediation of the word of God in our liberation history.

4. The God of the People of God: Church and Theology

The fundamental mediation of the experience of God in salvation history has always been the people of God, and in a very special way the people of the poor and oppressed. In Exodus itself God appears as the one who sees the humiliation of the people and hears their cry. God strikes a covenant with the people, and it is the people who liberate the promised land and take possession of it. It is the people who maintain the oral tradition, the historical memory of the poor, from which the Bible will take its rise. When the beasts who oppress the people of God are destroyed, it is the holy people who will receive power (Dan. 7). Jesus is born identified with his people, and as his ministry begins he organizes the community of the twelve apostles. Jesus sheds his blood, the blood of the New Covenant spilled for the multitude. The Holy Spirit descends on the people of the New Covenant. At the end of the ages, God renews the divine covenant with all humanity, which is symbolized by the New Jerusalem. "This is God's dwelling among men. He shall dwell with them and they shall be his people and he shall be their God who is always with them" (Rev. 21:3). The experience of God is basically given in the historical experience of being God's people. Nothing runs more counter to the divine pedagogy than religious individualism or spiritualism. The experience of God is always "popular"—that is, it always has the people of God as its interlocutor.

The base ecclesial community is the most immediate, most concrete experience of the people of God in Latin America. The community is not a rigid, uniform model, nor does it correspond to a specific movement in the church. We have a base community when we have, simply and generally, at the grassroots or *base*, a *community experience of ecclesial plenitude.* The base ecclesial community, as such, is the fundamental, the most dense, most explicit, and most popular, mediation of the experience of God in Latin America today, especially among the poor and oppressed. When believers organize in communities, they begin to live, to think, to communicate, and to celebrate their experience of God in a radically different way. Only in the small community do those who have been marginalized by secular society begin to share as creative agents in the reconstruction of the church. Out of their historical experience and their own culture the oppressed begin to create a new spirituality, new symbols, new prayers, and a new way of celebrating the faith, of reading the Bible, and of reflecting on faith. If God becomes present and is revealed in a special way in the world of the poor and oppressed, then it is surely the base ecclesial community that can best render this experience of God visible, inasmuch as that community is the most immediate and direct ecclesial expression born of this world of the poor. All of this is especially visible and meaningful in the liberation spirituality of the base communities, and even more in the thousands upon thousands of martyrs who, by giving up their lives, are revealing to us where and how God is present and acting today in the history of Latin America.

A new model of church is appearing from the base communities of Latin America today: the church of the poor. This church is not a new church, but a new way of conceptualizing and organizing the church. The basic mission of this new model of church is to make God credible in this world of the poor and oppressed third-world masses. The base ecclesial communities are the primary force in the construction of this new model of church. They are its most visible and extensive part. To be sure, they do not exhaust the reality of the church of the poor. The church of the poor also exists, less visibly and with less concentration, in popular religiousness, popular spirituality, and popular theology. After all, this entire popular Christian world is touched and transformed by a liberative evangelization and finds its identification and identity in the most visible expression of the church of the poor. The church of the poor is a universal church, then—by reason of its profound insertion into the world of the poor, surely, but also as a movement of conversion and renovation whose call goes forth to the whole church. This is the model of church that, in Latin America today, constitutes the fundamental mediation of the presence and revelation of God.

In all of this new ecclesial experience, born and thriving in Latin America today, theology, the magisterium, and the hierarchy all hold the positions in the people of God assigned to them by tradition. Theology, the magisterium, and the hierarchy all express the sense of faith of the people of God. Thus, they are all concrete mediations of the experience of God. The theology of liberation, in dialogue and communion with the magisterium and the hierarchy, has been performing this function of mediating the experience of God in Latin America today altogether creditably. Liberation theology accomplishes this function on three levels: as liberative spirituality in the very depths of the popular religious awareness, as popular theology in the base communities, and as critical, systematic theology in the professional centers of theological production.   — *Translated by Robert R. Barr*

8

Christology in the Theology of Liberation

JULIO LOIS

The purpose of this article is, very simply, to present a summary of the christology of Latin American liberation theology, with special attention to its specific emphases and its most significant written works.

As Jon Sobrino indicates, the new Latin American christological reflection originated at Medellín in 1968.

Medellín did not produce a document on Christ or sketch a christology. But it did make a number of statements with profound implications for the understanding of Christ and for the subsequent development of Christologies in Latin America. . . .

These statements concerning Christ, while obviously "remaining ever faithful to the revealed word" (Medellín Religious Education, no. 15), have had a powerful influence on the fashioning of a new image of Christ in pastoral ministry as well as on the appearance of what has come to be called Latin American christology or the christology of liberation.[1]

Since Medellín, liberation christology has been filling in this new image of Christ with more precision. An uninterrupted series of christological studies, still in progress, has begun to appear.[2] Rather than developing any systematic christology, these investigations merely center on certain basic aspects of the Jesus event. Their overriding concern is to underscore the salvific-liberative dimension of that event for the Latin American peoples who live today in poverty and oppression.[3]

It is precisely the reflection on these basic aspects that I shall attempt to summarize in the present chapter. First, however, I should like to tarry a moment over certain antecedent methodological considerations, since it is here—it seems to me—that we shall find the greatest originality of our christology, as well as its finest, most profound, and most universal contribution.

I. METHODOLOGICAL CONSIDERATIONS

Liberation christology emphasizes the great relevancy of the social and ecclesial locus of a theological reflection—the "place from which" theological subjects do their reflecting, as well as select their hermeneutics. We may call this the subjective aspect of the point of departure of liberation christology, or its "real" point of departure.[4]

It likewise emphasizes the importance of determining "that aspect of the total and totalizing reality of Christ that will better enable us to find access to the total Christ."[5] We might call this the objective aspect of the point of departure of liberation christology, or its "methodological" point of departure.

Finally, liberation christology holds that, between the social, ecclesial locus, as well as the subjective aspect considered as a whole, and the objective aspect of the point of departure, a relation of dialectical circularity obtains, in the sense that we shall presently specify.

Let us now develop these questions, bearing on the point of departure, with a view to specifying the necessary conditions for the creation of an authentic christology of liberation.

1. Social Locus in Liberation Christology

Current epistemology seems to agree that there are no raw data, free-floating facts, or pure experiences, independent of the interpretative processes of the cognitive. More concretely, the sociology of knowledge demonstrates that all human reflection is *situated activity*: it has a social locus, which can and must be detected in its origin (the "social conditions of the production" of cognition) and in its finalities (the "social functionality" of any cognition). Thus, all knowledge, consciously or not, has a praxic and ethical dimension—a certain "historical operationality," of whatever cast or hue.

If we accept these considerations and apply them to the matter at hand, we shall have to surrender the dream of a pure, or neutral, christology. Such a christology would be impossible. As Leonardo Boff so clearly says:

Theologians do not live in the clouds. They are social actors with a particular place in society. They produce knowledge, data, and meanings by using instruments offered and permitted them by their situation. Their findings are also addressed to a particular audience. Thus, they find themselves situated somewhere within the comprehensive social fabric. The themes and emphases of a given Christology flow from what seems relevant to the theologian on the basis of his or her social standpoint. Thus, we must admit that there is no such thing as a neutral christology, nor can there be. Every christology is partisan and committed. Willingly or unwillingly christological discourse is voiced in a given social setting with all the conflicting interests that pervade it. . . . so let us set down this basic affirmation: Christology . . . takes shape within the context of a particular moment in history; it is produced under certain specific modes of material, ideal, cultural, and ecclesial production, and it is articulated in terms of certain concrete interests that are not always consciously adverted to.[6]

The social location is an important point of reference for an explanation of the existence of so many, different images of Christ, with their various functionalities and distinct christologies.[7]

It will be in order, then, to ask ourselves what social location permits the development of the christology of liberation. "From where" must one reflect in order that the interpretation of the Jesus event may have an authentically liberative meaning?

Before answering this question, it seems necessary to explain that, in the current situation of domination in which the peoples of Latin America live, the liberative meaning of liberation christology will depend most of all on its ability to show forth the truth of Christ in connection with the praxis of transformation of reality that includes a structural change in society, even at its socioeconomic level.[8]

In this light, the question formulated above can be answered as follows: The social location permitting and enabling the development of a liberation christology is that of the option for the poor and their cause. That is, it will be the location of commitment in solidarity with the oppressed and with their struggle for liberation. This is the new hermeneutic locus—the "place from where" that makes it possible to sketch a new image of Jesus Christ the liberator. It is a place that presupposes an insertion in the historical reality of oppression, in order to *take it on*. That is to say, first, to *take up* this reality for purposes of examination, and then to *take it upon oneself*—to commit oneself to the praxis of its transformation.[9] This is what Leonardo Boff says when he points out that liberation christology "presupposes and depends on a specific social practice, one with the intent of breaking with the prevailing context of domination." He goes on:

> The social setting of this christology is the setting of those social groups for whom a qualitative change of the social structure would represent an opportunity to liberate themselves from existing forms of domination.[10]

2. Ecclesial Locus in Liberation Christology

Theology arises from a faith that seeks to understand. Without faith lived in the church community, no theology whatever is possible. All christological reflection, then, must be carried out within the church—a church identified by faith in Christ, whom it professes, experiences, and celebrates.

But there have always been, and there are today, different implemented models of church. These give rise to church communities of various stamps, because the situations in which believers live are very different and because the totality of their faith in Christ is not undifferentiated. It so happens that there is always a hierarchy of values in which greater emphasis is placed on particular elements of that totality. Thus, there have always been, and are today, distinct ecclesial settings, which obviously influence any possible christological reflection carried on within.

What is the ecclesial setting that makes it possible to develop the christology of liberation? *From where* must the theologian reflect in order that the liberative potential of the Jesus event may unfold?

The response of the theology of liberation is that this setting is the church of the poor. Here the encounter with the living Jesus, who is present today in history, occurs in a privileged manner in the encounter with the poor (cf. Matt. 25:31-46), and an essential moment of faith in him is his discipleship, made concrete in the option for the poor and a commitment to liberation. The church of the poor, then, is the communitarian milieu that makes possible and lays claim to the experience of faith in Christ the liberator, present and alive in history today.

> [The] realization of faith has two characteristic traits: the practice of liberation and the presence of Christ in the poor. . . . The former [refers] to the discipleship of Jesus, as demanded by Jesus himself, the latter to Jesus' incarnation in poverty and the world of the poor. The two traits taken together specify the theologian's ecclesial locus, ineluctably, as the church of the poor.
>
>   . . . Christology's ecclesial placement, accordingly, means one thing in Latin America and something different elsewhere.[11]

It is important to note that, between the social and the ecclesial loci a relation of a kind of dialectical circularity, or reciprocal implication, obtains, such that each locus demands the other. Believers who live their faith in Christ from the locus provided them by the church of the poor will feel the urgency of being in the social locus from which an active participation is possible in the liberation processes that realistically take up the cause of the poor of the earth. In turn, the social locus of the liberative commitment will urge believers to seek their ecclesial situation in the church of the poor.

It does not appear crucial to determine whether one of the two settings has priority over the other, and in case of an affirmative determination, to specify the nature of that priority. It is more important to verify their mutual interrelationship, their reciprocal implication and fruitful fertilization, and to acknowledge that, in any case, the presence of both settings is the fruit of the free gift of God, who grants quest and goal alike.

3. The "Epistemological Breach" Required by the Theology of Liberation

Both settings together — the social and the ecclesial, interrelated in the way that we have indicated — constitute the basic nucleus *from which* christological reflection can be authentically liberative. That is, they constitute the basic subjective aspect or point of departure for a liberative christology. They are a necessary, although not sufficient, condition for the creation of a christology of liberation.

These considerations bring us directly to the furthest-reaching and most specific element of the Latin American theology of liberation. The methodological novelty of that theology is rooted precisely in its demand that the theologian who would do a Christian theology with a liberative meaning must first be converted to the Lord Jesus, present today in a privileged manner in the poor. To this purpose the theologian must follow Jesus, making the same option for the poor and their cause that he made, and translating this option, in current circumstances, into a commitment to a liberative transformation of reality. This "discipleship / option for the poor / praxis of liberation" constitutes what liberation theologians call a *first act*. They distinguish this from the reflection, carried out in the light of faith, in which theological elaboration properly consists—which in turn they call the *second act*. At stake here is not an abstract question of theological methodology, but something that directly affects the objectively theological life or spirituality of the subject/agent of theology. In calling for conversion (or first act) as a previous condition of liberation theology (or second act), this methodology is identified with spirituality.

The first act of which we speak implies, at the experiential level, the breach/conversion required by the following of Jesus made concrete in the option-and-praxis of the entry of solidarity into the world of the *others*, who are the poor. At the cognitive level, it implies the *epistemological breach* that is indispensable if theology is to cease to be liberal (laissez-faire capitalistic) or idolatrous, cease to be a discourse that complacently legitimates the given or that is submissive to the dictatorship of the established order, and be transformed into a discourse of a critically prophetic and salvific-liberative cast—good news, a proclamation of concrete beatitude for the poor of the earth.[12]

In more specifically christological terms, only in the following of Jesus—with all of the implications of that following—can it be understood who Jesus is and what his salvific-liberative meaning is. Discipleship becomes a noetic category, or basic hermeneutic principle, that enters as an internal moment into the very process of christological reflection, a *conditio sine qua non* of the very epistemology of the christology of liberation. Jon Sobrino puts it pithily: "To know Jesus is to follow Jesus."[13]

4. Toward a Hermeneutics That Is Historical Praxis, Not Mere Interpretation

From the vantage point of the social and ecclesial loci, as we have explained them above, we readily perceive that theological reflection must have a praxic dimension, a historically liberative functionality. Accordingly, liberation theology understands itself as being at the service of a faith that is historically fertile in terms of its capacity to contribute to the liberation of the poor of the earth. Thus the temptation is overcome of attributing a liberative meaning to theological knowledge when the latter is limited to explaining reality without contributing to its transformation, or if it is content with elucidating the coherence of its truth before the bar of theoretical reason. From a point of departure in the experience of oppression, the theologian doggedly seeks to arrive at truth precisely through the capacity of that truth to transform intolerable reality. Consequently, no merely interpretative models are selected—models that merely explain, and at least indirectly justify, reality in its current configuration. Rather, we choose operational hermeneutic models, models with a capacity for influencing the liberative transformation of reality itself.[14]

From the outset the encounter with Christ the liberator demands a historico-praxic christological hermeneutics, a hermeneutics operatively connected with history and its liberative transformation, a hermeneutics that will permit the discovery of the salvific meaningfulness of Christ through its capacity to arouse liberation praxis in believers. Jiménez Limón is right, then, when he says that the christology of liberation is a "christology for conversion to the struggle for justice," and that therefore one of its basic intentions or "what is at stake is that the mystery of Jesus not be used in order to maintain injustice."[15] This intention is clearly and concisely expressed by Jon Sobrino in *Christology at the Crossroads*, when he states in his introduction that the "direct aim" of his christology "is to give Latin Americans a better understanding of Christ and to point up his historical relevancy for our continent."

This is the final point in what we have called the subjective aspect of the starting point of liberation christology, or its "real" point of departure. The basic nucleus of this aspect of the starting point is the living faith of the social and ecclesial loci discussed above, which secure the indispensable "epistemological breach" for the appearance of a christology of liberation. A further product of these loci is the demand for a historically relevant hermeneutics, a hermeneutics capable of bringing out the potential of the Jesus event for the praxis of liberation.

5. The Historical Figure of Jesus of Nazareth

For the christology of liberation, the aspect of the comprehensive reality of Christ that provides the best route of access to the total Christ is the historical Jesus. "The christology of liberation elaborated from the standpoint of Latin America stresses the historical Jesus over the Christ of faith," says Leonardo Boff.[16] In Sobrino's terminology, as we have seen, the Jesus of history is the "objective" aspect of liberation christology's point of departure, or its methodological starting point.[17]

The current christological panorama, as we well know, is governed by the conviction that it is possible, and theologically necessary, to return to the Jesus of history. As González Faus points out:

After a total absence of the historical Jesus, both in Bultmann who ignores him . . . and Thomas Aquinas who limits himself to justifying the episodes of his life with a priori considerations, today we witness a return to the Jesus of history, that is, to what history can tell us of the real life and concrete person of the human being whose name was Jesus of Nazareth.[18]

But in Latin American liberation christology, this return to the Jesus of history has certain specific characteristics, which confer on that christology an identity of its own:

> In Europe, the historical Jesus is an object of investigation, while in Latin America he is a criterion of discipleship. In Europe the historical Jesus is studied for the purpose of establishing the possibilities and rationality of the phenomenon of believing or not believing. In Latin America the appeal to the historical Jesus is for the purpose of facing the dilemma of whether to be converted or not.[19]

Liberation christology does not deny the propriety of an investigation of Jesus in terms of historical criticism. We know that this is necessary in order to overcome a mythologized presentation of Christ and to be able to develop a basic christology capable of demonstrating the element of rationality in faith in Christ as God's eschatological salvation. However, this is not the intent that governs its own return to the Jesus of history. The primary purpose of the christology of liberation in seeking to recover the history of Jesus is in the prosecution and furtherance of this same history in the current situation of oppression in Latin America. It is not primarily the rationality of faith in Christ, but the historical relevance of that faith in terms of liberation, that must be set forth in the situation of the Latin America peoples with their believing, oppressed majorities. Therefore—and still more concretely—what liberation christology seeks to recover is Jesus' concrete manner of creating history by way of a salvific-liberative practice in the service of the Reign of God; and the manner in which he "became Jesus" through this same practice, in order that all of this may be known, re-created, and furthered today by believers in the context of Latin America, that thus the image of Christ may be prevented from being presented in connivance with the idols of oppression and death.

> Latin American christology understands the historical Jesus as the totality of Jesus' history, and its finality in beginning with the historical Jesus is to serve the continuation of his history in the present. . . .
> The most historical element in the historical Jesus is his practice, that is, his activity brought to bear upon the reality around him in order to transform it in . . . the direction of the kingdom of God. . . .
> For us, then, the historical element in the historical Jesus is first and foremost an invitation (and a demand) to continue his practice—or, in Jesus' language, an invitation to his discipleship for a mission.
> . . . What must be safeguarded in speaking of the historical Jesus is, before all else, the continuation of his practice.[20]

In terms of the importance assigned to the historical Jesus, in the sense that we have indicated, once more we encounter the new hermeneutic model characterizing liberation christology and demanded by the social and ecclesial locus from which this christology is developed. That locus assigns priority to *doing* as opposed to mere *explaining* and basically seeks to guarantee that Jesus' way of making history, and becoming in history, in obedience and fidelity to the Father, is continued today by those who believe in him.

Between what we have called the fundamental nucleus or basic subjective aspect of the starting point of liberation christology (the *whence*, or the social and ecclesial settings), and this priority assigned to the historical Jesus, or the objective aspect of that same starting point, the same relation of reciprocal involvement or dialectical circularity, and mutual fertile enrichment, obtains as that prevailing between the social and ecclesial settings themselves. Neither in this case is it of any crucial importance to decide which aspect is to be assigned chronological or logical priority; rather, the essential thing is their mutual implication and requirement.

> Latin American christology ... believes that the theologian's prioritarian placement must be the world of the poor and the church of the poor. ... This placement refers theologians more obviously to the historical Jesus when they address the theme of christology.[21]

On the other hand, in the figure of the historical Jesus, and more concretely in his liberative practice or way of making history, we are invited to encounter him in preferential form in the face of the poor of the earth (cf. Matt. 25:31-46); to follow him leaving everything else behind (cf. Matt. 6:24, 10:37-38, 16:24; Luke 9:57-62, 18:22; John 12:24); and to proclaim and render present the Reign of God as good news of liberation for these same poor (cf. Matt. 5:3-12, 11:4-6; Luke 4:16-21, 6:20-23, 7:22-23). That is to say, we are invited to assume a place in the social and ecclesial setting where the poor exist and where their liberation is at stake.

Given this relation of circularity, it is not strange to observe that both aspects — the subjective and the objective — converge in the demand for the same hermeneutic model, one primarily concerned with the historical relevancy of theological cognition.

II. BASIC CONTENT OF LIBERATION CHRISTOLOGY

Still keeping in mind the methodological premises that we have now established, let us turn our attention to the questions that are the prime concern of the christology of liberation. Without any pretension whatever to completeness, let us simply present, in very hasty synthesis, some of liberation christology's basic content — the content we believe constitutes its most specific and meaningful contribution.

1. The Return to the Historical Jesus

The return to the historical Jesus, as understood in liberation theology, discovers Jesus' constitutive relationship with the Reign of God and the God of the Reign.

It is a commonplace in christology today that the historical life of Jesus of Nazareth as presented in the gospel accounts has its center and ultimate, decisive meaning in two key realities: God, whom Jesus calls *Abba*, and the Reign of God. But these two realities are inseparably interrelated; they cannot be understood in separation. For Jesus, God is always the God of the Reign, and the Reign is always the Reign of God. As a result, rather than speaking of two realities it would perhaps be more appropriate to speak of a "dual totality" (Sobrino), that is, of the Reign of God in its reference to the God of the Reign.

One of the basic tasks of christological reflection is to determine the meaning content of the Reign of God, in order to be able to explain who Jesus, the herald and servant of this Reign, is, and who the God of Jesus is as God of the Reign.

Jesus and the Reign of God

As Leonardo Boff reminds us, "Systematically speaking, we can say that the historical Jesus did not preach about himself or the church or God but about the Reign of God."[22] Neither himself, nor even God purely and simply, was for Jesus the absolute, decisively ultimate reality. That functionality was performed, in his preaching, as in his life, by the Kingdom or Reign of God. Thus, "it is his constitutive relationship to this dual totality, the 'Reign of God,' that in principle provides the key to access to Jesus and to a consistent organization of his life and mission."[23]

What is the Reign of God for Jesus? In the response to this question, or more concretely, in the methodology selected in order to make a response, we find one of the most specific and meaningful contributions of the christology of liberation. Let us see what it is.[24]

According to the gospel accounts, Jesus never directly explained what he meant by the Reign of God. He announced it, and its proximity, and even its presence (cf. Mark 1:15, Luke 17:21), referred to it constantly in many of his parables—the term occurs 104 times in the gospels—and called for conversion in order to enter it, but never expressly said what it consisted in. For this reason, it is necessary to identify its meaning through the use of a methodology of indirect approach. Concretely, there are two routes open to christological reflection today to a biblical specification of what Jesus meant by the Reign of God. These avenues of approach are not mutually exclusive, but complementary. Still, depending on which of the two is assigned priority over the other, we shall arrive at a different notion of the Reign of God.

The first avenue of approach is *notional*. This means, as Sobrino indicates, "ascertaining what the Reign was for Jesus in terms of the notion that Jesus himself must have had of it," and therefore analyzing "the various notions of the Reign in the Old Testament and among Jesus' contemporaries, and searching out what Jesus took from these notions and in what way he differed."[25] The conclusion we reach by this route—using mainly certain important contemporary christologies like those of Kasper or Pannenberg—is valid but insufficient. The Reign is presented as a utopia, the full salvation to which all have access as a free gift of God. A further concretion is required in order to avoid abstract formalism.

The second route is that of Jesus' *praxis*. This approach seeks to identify the meaning of the Reign by assigning methodological priority to a consideration of what Jesus did, his "signs" (*erga, sémeia*), and all of his liberative activity of denunciation and exposé, designed to motivate a personal conversion and a social transformation that would occasion the beatitude of the poor of the earth.

The christology of liberation elects this second route. However, the originality and specific contribution of that christology does not reside purely and simply in this option.[26] More concretely, it resides in the special emphasis laid on the foremost addressees of this liberative praxis of Jesus, who are likewise the addressees or subjects of the Reign: the poor of the earth.[27] Let us briefly list the principal conclusions at which liberation christology arrives when it follows its chosen route.

1. Jesus did not restrict himself to announcing the Reign and passively awaiting its coming; he placed at its service his activity, his transforming "doing" (cf. Mark 1:39; Matt. 4:23, 9:35, 11:5-6; Luke 4:16-21; Acts 10:38; etc).

2. With unequal intensity, to be sure, at the various stages of his life Jesus performed a series of actions calculated to signify the partial presence of the Reign of God among us: miracles, exorcisms, welcome of sinners with forgiveness of their sins, and so on.

3. Jesus' miracles, as "cries of the Reign," or "signs" that the Reign of God is becoming present among us as saving power, wrought under the impulse of Jesus' compassion and mercy toward the weak and oppressed (cf. Mark 1:41, 6:34, 8:2; Matt. 9:36, 14:14, 15:21-28 and par., 15:32, 17:14-29 and par., 20:29-34 and par.; Luke 7:13-14, 17:11-19; etc.), show us that the Reign of God is salvation understood in the sense of the defeat of concrete evils (hunger, diseases, the despair of the scorned sinner, and so on) and deliverance from historical oppressions (caused, as was believed, by the power of the Evil One and by unjust ostracism).

4. The gospel accounts tell us of a constant activity on Jesus' part calculated to expose, denounce, and dethrone the false gods or idols of oppression who maintain the structures (civil and religious, socioeconomic, juridical, and cultural) that oppress the poor and sinners and assert themselves at the cost of these persons' dignity, freedom, and very life.[28] This more comprehensive activity, correlative to the totality of the Reign, inasmuch as it is intended to combat the historical causes of the anti-Reign and to shape society in a radically different way, shows us that the Reign, without ceasing to be an eschatological, "theological" (objectively theological, or divine) reality, also has a historico-social, and therefore political, dimension.[29]

5. This entire praxis of Jesus, performed in the service of the Reign, is *in process, situated, partisan*, and *conflictive* praxis, always having a clear signification in terms of salvation-liberation and constituting for every believer an urgent invitation to continue it in his or her own historical present.

6. As a complete human being, Jesus makes history in the compass of his own becoming in history. Liberation christology insists on the gradual development of the believing relationship of Jesus to God the Father and the change experienced by the former in his way of understanding the Reign and how to place himself at its service.[30]

7. Liberation christology also insists that Jesus' practice in the service of the Reign is a situated practice; that is, a practice realized in a determinate geographical and historical context. Hence the importance it assigns to the study of the socioeconomic, political, and religious world of the time of Jesus, inasmuch as only in relation to that world can we grasp the scope of his activity in general (controversies, position-taking, denunciations, and so on) and consequently, the meaning content of the Reign and all its implications.[31]

8. Furthermore, Jesus' practice is partisan. That is, its addressees are the poor, as it is precisely they to whom the Reign of God is addressed or consigned. Liberation christology establishes an essential bond between Jesus and the poor:

> An essential element of the life and mission of Jesus is his reference to and membership in the world of the poor. And by "essential" element, we mean that in the absence of this reference Jesus himself is either misunderstood or cancelled as savior of humankind.[32]

This essential bonding is expressed in Jesus' poverty, as well as — and this is what is most important — in his option for the poor and their cause; he places his life at their service, proclaiming to them and from among them the Reign of God and sharing their lot to its ultimate consequences.[33]

9. Latin American liberation theology regards the determination of the poor as consignees of the Reign of God to be a datum of exegesis, and even a presupposition of the same.[34] What this theology has contributed is in terms of the actual notion of the poor as collective, conflictive subject, a socioeconomic reality of dialectical history with a frank political significance.[35]

10. If the poor are the addressees of the Reign — that is, if the Reign comes in order that the poor may be blessed, in terms of Jesus' beatitude (Matt. 5:3, Luke 6:20) — then it must be understood as a utopia that defeats unjust poverty. In Jon Sobrino's frank expression: "It might be said simply that the Reign of God is a world, a society, in which the poor can have life and dignity."[36]

11. Being historically situated in a world of poverty and oppression, and being partisan in the sense that we have indicated, Jesus' practice in the service of the Reign could only be steeped in conflict. Liberation christology regards the dimension of partisan conflict as surely the most specific characteristic of Jesus' practice. By emphasizing this aspect of Jesus' practice, liberation christology seeks to recover the whole "abysmal" and "subversive" dimension of the Jesus event, and thus to call attention to the shattering, disconcerting transcendency of the God of Jesus and the radical divine displeasure with this bourgeois world that ostracizes or oppresses the poor.

12. In terms of all that we have said, we can now state something about the Reign of God, and in consequence, about Jesus as herald and, with his praxis, mediator, of that Reign. In the signs performed by Jesus, the Reign is presented to us as a salvific-liberative reality that rescues women and men from concrete necessities (bestowing bread on the hungry, health on the sick, hope on the despairing, and so on), and delivers them from historical oppressions (slaveries and ostracisms of various concrete kinds). In the totality of Jesus' unfolding,

situated, partisan, and conflictual practice, the Reign is presented to us as God's alternative to the overall existing situation, which is historically dominated by the values of the anti-Reign, as the ideal of a new society. This society is destined to implant in history the definitive realization of justice, the utopia of the poor, the terminus of their unjust ostracism, liberation from their slaveries, and the opportunity for them to live with dignity.[37]

In this perspective, Jesus is presented to us, with his signs and his whole practice, as the herald and servant of that Reign of God. His cause, which he served with utter fidelity, and for which he laid down his life, was the cause of the Reign. Indeed, he is likewise presented to us as the one who invites us to conversion and to his following in order that that Reign may continue to be known, proclaimed, and served (cf. Luke 9:1-6 and par., 10:1-12), and that thus his cause may be furthered.

In selecting the avenue of praxis as the more adequate route to a determination of what the Reign of God is and who Jesus is, the christology of liberation proceeds in a manner that is consistent with the basic epistemological presupposition to which we have already referred; namely, that in order to know and have access to Christ the liberator, decisive importance must be assigned to the historical Jesus, and more concretely, to his practice, which is the "most historical thing about the Jesus of history." We then added that the fundamental finality envisaged by the christology of liberation in considering Jesus' practice is not that of merely knowing and explaining it, but of actually prosecuting it.

After all, this is what Jesus called his disciples to—to follow him and to further his cause, as we have seen—and it is to this that he invites us again today when we approach him as Servant of the Reign by the route of practice. And thus we find ourselves once more within the hermeneutic circularity so dear to the heart of the christology of liberation. That is to say, it is our practice of service to the Reign—a practice today, as well, that is in process, situated, partisan, and conflictive—that enables us to know Jesus. To put the same thing in another way, it is following Jesus that makes it possible to know him. That cognition and knowing, in turn, translate into a demand of a more faithful practice and discipleship. And the circular movement goes on.

The God of Jesus as God of the Reign

We have already observed that the determination of the meaning of the Reign of God also leads us to a surmise of the nature of the God of Jesus, since Jesus' practice in the service of the Reign is his response to the will of his God. From his constitutive relationship with the Reign springs the revelation of God as the God of the Reign.

We know that the God of Jesus is God the Father, whom Jesus called *Abba*, an Aramaic term expressing an altogether unique relationship of filiation, experienced with special connotations of intimate, trusting familiarity, the kind of nearness experienced in a family.[38] But this Father God is the very God of the Reign, so that a dialectical bond is established between the two terms *Abba* and *Reign*, in the sense that the meaning of either requires the other in complementarity. Thus, to speak of God the Father of Jesus is actually to speak of the God of the Reign, and vice versa. Precisely because God is merciful Father, radical and original Love, the Reign comes to history, and therefore access to the Father is by way of acceptance of that Reign, by way of the commitment that places us in its service. The category of the Reign makes concrete the signification that calling on God the Father has for human beings.[39]

Faithful to its methodology, liberation christology places a great deal of emphasis on the strictly theological revelatory force attaching to the Jesus event considered historically—and more concretely, to his practice (in process, situated, partisan, and conflictive) in the service of the cause of the Reign of God. Surely, as we shall see, the revelatory force of the historical Jesus is fulfilled on the cross—the ultimate fate to which his praxis led—and very especially in the resurrection. But it is equally certain that "the Resurrection does not dispense us from a consideration of history. It inculcates precisely a more attentive concern for history, as the gospels themselves show."[40]

What traits does the God of Jesus acquire from a consideration of Jesus' praxis in the service of the Reign? Liberation christology singles out the following:

1. A first, general characteristic, embracing the others and specifying the God of the Reign according to the christology of liberation, is the abysmal, scandalous dimension of God. For Latin American theologians, Jesus' practice evinces the fact that his Father God of the Reign-at-hand is a different, "reverse," "dissident" God. In a world with a cheap, middle-class image of God, a complacent paraphrase or sacral legitimation of the given, liberation christology insists that accepting Jesus as God's revelation implies accepting the scandal of a "different God."

2. God's scandalous dimension is made concrete first and foremost in the fact that the God of the Reign is the God of the poor, and therefore "different from the god of the lords" (Gutiérrez).

If the Reign of God presented to us through Jesus' practice is, as we have seen, good news of liberative salvation for the poor, then the God of the Reign is the God of the poor, a God in solidarity with the poor and their cause. And the poor are a *locus theologicus*, in being God's ultimate mediation, or the mediation of God's ultimacy, the special sacrament of God's presence and the preferential space of access to and encounter with God.

Suffering in their unjust poverty, it is the poor who prolong among us the revelation and presence of a God helpless and weak, absent and suffering, rejected and crucified. They are the scandalous sign of God's failure in history, the unmistakable sign that the Reign of God, as beatitude for the poor, has not yet come.

But the poor not only suffer. They also struggle and hope—many of them, at least, along with those who identify with them. They denounce their unjust situation and struggle in hope to overcome that situation. If their poverty is a sign that the Reign of God is not yet reality among us, their hope-charged struggle is a sign that it is indeed present. God is in the poor, not only mysteriously suffering with them, but also actively rejecting their painful present—proclaiming, demanding, stirring up a new future to transcend this time of oppression. Thus, for the poor, the God of Jesus is the God who is courage, the God who is fantasy, the God who is hope, the God who is utopia, the God who is liberator, who intervenes salvifically in history as the One who wishes to establish justice and the rights of the poor.[41]

3. The liberator God who seeks to establish justice and right for the poor — in a world such as Latin America, where poverty puts persons to death, a death "untimely and unjust" — must have the profile of a God of life.

This characteristic of the God of the Reign — that of a God of life — also comes in for special emphasis at the hands of the christology of liberation, which thus recovers a fundamental biblical category (cf. Deut. 30:15, 9-20; Matt. 22:32; Mark 12:27; Luke 20:38; John 10:10, 14:6). In the situation of oppression as it is experienced in Latin America, the following consequences derive from this characteristic.

— Theology should not be developed in abstraction from the radical contrariety of death and life. Archbishop Romero, making concrete the ancient formula of Irenaeus, declared: "The glory of God is the poor person who lives."

— The true God is the guarantor of human life and accords that life an ultimate, not a provisional, value, thus making all other values relative. The latter are nonvalues when they oppose human life.

— What is most properly opposed to the God of life is not atheism, but idolatry, or the worship of gods who deal death or who require victims in order to subsist.

— Faith in the God of Jesus is expressed — not solely, but inescapably — in the commitment to the poor.[42]

4. Liberation christology reformulates the transcendence of God — the quality of the divine as "ever greater," as unattainable, nonmanipulable mystery — from the premise of God's condition as God of the poor. Sobrino expresses it precisely:

The "novelty" and "unthinkability" that the poor are destined to possess the Reign becomes a historical mediation of the novelty and "unthinkability" of God, of the mystery of God, of God's transcendence vis-à-vis human images of God. To accept that the consignees of the Reign are the poor is an efficacious way of letting God be God, of allowing God to engage in the self-manifestation selected by the divine will itself. The transcendent reality of God can be analyzed from other perspectives. But ... it can also be analyzed from the self-showing of God *thus* and in no other manner. Paul basically did nothing else when proposing the cross as the wisdom of God: this was obviously insanity and scandal, and yet through it occurred God's self-manifestation as God. Something of the kind occurs when we assert that the Reign of God is that of the poor *qua* poor and only *qua* poor. Thereby God is shown as God, as nonmanipulable mystery.[43]

5. But liberation christology, faithful once more to its basic hermeneutic orientation, is primarily concerned to stress that the God of the poor cannot be professed without opting for the cause of that God, nor the God of life

professed without a battle against the idols that legitimate the injustice that causes the untimely death of so many, and so on. When all is said and done, the dissident God revealed to us in Jesus' practice cannot be truthfully professed in a society such as ours without our adopting this dissidence in practice. Access to the God of Jesus by the route selected by liberation christology evinces that to profess God is to "practice God" (Gutiérrez). Accordingly, the battle with the idols of death, with the injustice that crucifies the poor, is the assertion of God; and the practice of injustice or resigned passivity in the face of such idols and such injustice is the rejection of God.

2. The Historical Dimension of the Cross

Liberation christology ascribes a central importance to Jesus' cross, or Jesus crucified. First of all, as we have seen, it is a christology realized from the cross, or from the following of the Crucified One who became option for the poor— that is, from the locus of real solidarity with the crucified of the earth. But what is more, in considering Jesus crucified as the explicit, central object of its reflection, liberation christology has subjected certain aspects of the classic theological consideration of the cross to a renewal. Let us see some of its more significant contributions in this area.

1. The historical recovery of the cross, that basic concern and outstanding acquisition of the christology of liberation, has decisively contributed to the liberation of the cross from the condition of a mere symbol of the onerous character of our reconciliation with God.[44]

2. Historically considered, Jesus' cross, that ignominious torment specially reserved for slaves and political subversives or tamperers with the established order, was the outgrowth of his entire life—of his proclamation and of his situated, partisan, and conflictive praxis. "Jesus did not seek death. It was imposed on him from outside. He did not simply accept it with resignation. Instead he shouldered it as an expression of his freedom and his fidelity to the cause of God and human beings."[45] Those directly and principally responsible for it were those who wielded religious and political power, who sentenced him for blasphemy and subversion.

3. Liberation christology vigorously denounces the insufficiencies of the so-called expiatory theories and their principal models—expiatory sacrifice, substitutive satisfaction, "ransom"—as attempts to explain the redemptive meaning of Jesus Christ as a "punctualistic" or decontextualized consideration of Jesus' cross, the shedding of his blood, his suffering and passion.[46] The violent elimination or removal of the real historical context of the cross implicit in such theories has led to a distortion of the image of the Christian God, a positive evaluation of human pain considered in itself, and the loss of the dimension of the cross as prophetic criticism and of its consequent meaning in terms of political liberation.[47]

4. Any reading by which we hope to extract the salvific and redemptive meaning of Jesus' cross must begin with the historical recovery of that cross. The cross is bound up with the totality of Jesus' life and message; with concrete,

identifiable individuals who were responsible for it; and with Jesus' own consciousness as servant of the Reign, a consciousness he faithfully maintained to his final moment.

5. To be sure, the salvific meaning of the cross can only be discovered in its fullness in the light shed on it and on Jesus' whole life by the eschatological event of his resurrection. Thus, it is important to recall that neither can a believing reflection on the cross be separated from that resurrection — the final lot of the Crucified One and the ultimate sense of his historical life and its culmination on the cross. But Jesus' resurrection, while it refers "beyond" history and opens it to the definitive encounter with God, likewise refers to history itself, as we have said, and is confirmation of Jesus' life with its culmination on the cross. As we shall see, one of the major points of emphasis in the christology of liberation is that the One who was raised is the One who was crucified.

6. Divorced from its historical context and directly linked to the will of the Father, the cross can readily become a sacral legitimation of all unjust suffering. In the light of history, however, as one contemplates Jesus on trial, sentenced, and crucified by the mighty of his time, the perverse mechanisms of the civil and religious powers are exposed, and a prophetic denunciation is lodged against all who, in any circumstances, in order to defend the interests of the status quo or out of an obdurate political prudence, occasion the death of an innocent.[48] Thus, in liberation christology the cross recovers all of its critical and liberative force, as a judgment against sin, and against the mighty who crucify the just, and becomes an urgent invitation to the struggle against the perversion of the mighty who put their victims to death. This is how José Porfirio Miranda's expression is to be understood: "Christ died in order that it be known that not everything is permitted."

7. With this historical recovery, liberation christology generates a spirituality of the cross that cannot be dissociated, conceptually or factually, from the following and discipleship of the Crucified One, which today means embracing the cause of those crucified by the sin of the world. Thus, the believer's subjective, personal cross is linked to the objective cross of those who suffer by being unjustly oppressed. Only in terms of this linkage is the theology of the cross open to resurrection, legitimately transformed into a theology of hope, as we shall see.

Consequently, we embrace Jesus' cross today (cf. Mark 8:34-35 and par.) when, following in his footsteps, we take up his loving solidarity with the poor and make it our own. In a participation in the historical processes of liberation of the crucified poor of the earth, the cross of Jesus Christ is present.

> Identification with the crucified must take place on the way of the cross. If it strays off that path, then the spirituality of the cross will turn into something else: e.g., stoicism, masochism, or, worst of all, an excuse for not taking the way of the cross on the assumption that one is already doing so. . . . The cross is the *end* of a process [and therefore of a real following of Jesus, not a merely intentional one]. If we do not go through that process, then the cross to which we offer our acceptance may not be the Christian cross.[49]

8. A great part of current christology sees in the cross the scandalous hermeneutic principle or gnoseological key to knowledge of the God of Jesus. An in-depth reconsideration of the truth of the Christian God from the viewpoint of the cross of Jesus—which means Jesus' incorporation into the being of God by his free and loving decision, suffering, weakness, absence, and respect for human freedom and the autonomy of history—is also frequently met with in the christology of liberation.[50] But we find in this christology some emphases that bestow on it a certain originality. Let us underscore two of these.

—Today, to reflect on God from the standpoint of the cross means to reflect on God from the standpoint of the crucified poor of history. Only those who choose to be poor, and who make an option for the cause of the poor, can assume the scandal implied in the revelation of a God who saves by accepting the fate of one crucified.

—God crucified and suffering, impotent and weak, whose self-manifestation is on the cross of the reconciliation of God and human beings (cf. 2 Cor. 5:19-21), is the same God that saves and liberates. From the perspective of liberation christology, the dialectical consideration of the cross and resurrection, with their respective significations, is basic: the God who suffers with Jesus the death of the cross is the same God as raises him, opening the most negative thing in history to a future of hope.

This last reflection leads us to a consideration of the central event of the Resurrection.

3. The Resurrection

1. Liberation christology, with all christological reflection, discerns in the eschatological event of the resurrection an activity of God that anticipates definitive liberation and breaks continuity with the present world. It does so by correcting the negativity inherent in the death of the suffering Just One and bringing Jesus' life to a fulfillment that is not definable or deducible from history, a fulfillment no longer subject to the limitations of space and time. It likewise sees in Jesus' resurrection the proclamation of his glorious coming, and the great Amen to all of God's promises (cf. 2 Cor. 1:20), generating, on the level of humanity, the world, and history, a tension of universal eschatological hope, whose final goal is the resurrection of the dead and the consummating re-creation of all things, the gathering of all things together again in Christ under the absolute sovereignty of God (cf. 1 Cor. 15:12-20, Rom. 8:18-23, Eph. 1:9-10, Col. 1:15-20).

2. But in liberation christology, the emphasis placed on the resurrection is owing to the character of that event as confirmation of the truth of the life, cause, and person of Jesus. That is to say, the christology of liberation insists on reading the resurrection from a position of solidarity with the crucified of the world: the One who is raised is the One who was crucified, and what occurred in the Easter event finds its Christian identity in what had been manifested in the historical life of Jesus. In sum, for the christology of liberation it is impossible to cling to the Risen Lord "and ignore or blot from memory the

ostracized, disturbing preacher who appeared in Galilee" (Echegaray).
   As Sobrino points out:

> The importance of this identification [consists] in understanding, through
> this identification, through the narrative and interpretation of the life of the
> crucified one, what Jesus' resurrection is all about.
>   One who lived thus, and therefore was crucified, has been raised from the
> dead by God. Jesus' resurrection is not only a symbol of God's omnipotence,
> then—as if God had decided arbitrarily and without any connection with
> Jesus' life and lot to show how powerful he was. Rather Jesus' resurrection
> is presented as God's response to the unjust, criminal action of human
> beings. Hence God's action in response is understood in connection with the
> human activity that provokes this response: the murder of the Just One.
> Pictured in this way, the resurrection of Jesus shows *in directo* the triumph
> of justice over injustice. It is the triumph not simply of God's omnipotence,
> but also of God's justice. ... Jesus' resurrection is thus transformed into
> good news, whose central content is that once and for all justice has tri-
> umphed over injustice, the victim over the executioner.[51]

Accordingly, the crucified of history can have hope: God has raised one who
was crucified.[52]
   3. What characterizes the paschal vision of liberation christology's view of
Easter is the intimate relationship it establishes between cross and resurrection,
or between resurrection and cross: that the Crucified One is the Risen One, or
that the Risen One is the Crucified One.
   A non-dialectical consideration of the cross and resurrection of Jesus can
serve a reactionary purpose. A consideration of the cross in dissociation from
the dialectical relationship of cross to resurrection can lead to a presentation
of suffering as something pertaining essentially to the being of God and therefore as something invincible. Suffering is sacralized, and hope is out of the
question. The only sane attitude will then be to identify with suffering, not to
pretend that it can be overcome. A consideration of resurrection without the
cross can sacralize the ideology of an outcome or future of reconciliation that
has not passed through the crucible of present injustice and oppression, thus
generating an enthusiastic, ahistorical conception that projects us beyond the
stars and alienates us from reality and its current tensions. Without the resurrection, the cross can be an instrument in the service of a theology that
endorses the suffering of the poor of this earth. Without the cross, the hope
generated by the resurrection is not credible, at least for those who suffer
injustice.[53]
   4. Consistent with what has been said, and in function of its specific methodology, liberation christology posits as the hermeneutic background for an
understanding of the resurrection the experience of a hope springing from the
cross, a hope against hope. The truth of the resurrection can only be believed
in, resurrection can only be hoped in, from the cross, from the following of the
Crucified One of Galilee, and therefore only in solidarity with the crucified of

today, who seem bereft of any historical future. For us, as for Jesus, resurrection is not a promise that can be fulfilled apart from an acceptance of history's real conflictivity—that is, apart from the task of liberation implied in this same conflictivity. Only from here, inescapably, without passing, as the poet accused some, with a rose in our hand through this earth's fields of corpses, experiencing our life as already won when we can lose it in the battle for justice, can we lift our hopeful gaze and profess with truth that Jesus is coming. Only then can we say that he will finally come at the end of time, and that, with his coming, the ultimate enemy, death, will be destroyed and the executioners will not emerge triumphant:

> Thus, we face a new formulation of the hermeneutic circle of resurrection. The God revealed in the resurrection of the Crucified one is most specially mediated in the oppressed: in order to find the face of this revealed God, one must make an option for the oppressed. In soteriological terms: in the intent of liberation of the poor from their oppression, the liberator God of the poor becomes understandable, manifested in the crucified face of the Risen one.[54]

And we find ourselves once more with our oft-repeated thesis: Discipleship is the locus from which the revelation occurring in Jesus becomes known in greater depth, and faith in Jesus comes to be professed with greater truth and radicalism. "The decisive locus of the experience of the Risen one is neither theology, nor profession, nor liturgy, but following."[55]

5. Jesus' resurrection has a frank pneumatological meaning. That is, it is the root of the full sending of the Spirit. Inasmuch as the conversion-breach demanded by the following of Jesus is possible only in the desire and power granted by his Spirit, liberation christology asserts that solely in the newness of a life lived according to the Spirit can the ultimate truth of the life and person of Jesus as revelation of the Father and way to the Father be captured. Thus, we must say with Jon Sobrino that the christology of liberation seeks to be a trinitarian christology because "liberation theology poses the hermeneutic circle in trinitarian terms. . . . Reflection on Jesus can only be carried out in trinitarian terms."[56]

III. SOME BASIC OBJECTIONS LODGED AGAINST LIBERATION CHRISTOLOGY

We must not bring this presentation of the christology of liberation to a close without making some reference to certain basic objections that have been raised, and that continue to be raised.

The fundamental objection, which implies all or most of the others, is lodged directly with its methodology. This objection might be formulated as follows. The methodological priority assigned to the historical Jesus inevitably leads to the denial, or at least the obscuring, of Jesus' divinity. The same objection could be formulated in another way: In taking insufficient account of the church's faith in Christ, expressed in the conciliar dogmatic formulas that recapitulate the fullness of the New Testament christologies, liberation christology is reduced to a "jesuology," and thus the central mystery of Jesus Christ as Son of God and universal Savior is evacuated.

In technical terms, the objection is that liberation christology is carried out "from below," by way of an "ascending" methodology, and therefore abandons faith in Jesus as the incarnate Son of God, whose profession calls for the use of a "descending" route, or a christology carried out "from above" — a "high christology."

At the same time, turning our attention to what we have called the subjective aspect of its point of departure, we find liberation christology criticized for the partiality of its selection of social and ecclesial loci, which is said to vitiate its entire reflection and effectively lead to a denial of the eschatological and universally salvific meaning of the Jesus event.[57]

We must keep in mind that these objections are lodged against liberation christology in its totality, and not the brief summary presented here, which has centered almost exclusively on its most specific and significant aspects, its special emphases. I say this because if liberation christology were to be reduced to our summary, and if we admitted the perverse interpretative principle that whatever is not *expressly* asserted is thereby denied, such objections could have their validity. Indeed we have not taken up the question of the divinity of Jesus explicitly, nor have we made express, systematic reference to titles in the Christian scriptures that profess Jesus' transcendence or to the dogmatic formulae of the great christological councils. But we are surely not thereby denying Jesus' divinity or suggesting that we regard these titles or dogmatic formulas as unimportant. Actually, if our presentation of Jesus' divinity and transcendence is considered in depth, it will be found to be utterly unobjectionable.

Across the board, the christology of liberation certainly *has* given explicit attention to Jesus' scriptural titles and to the conciliar dogmatic formulas, and has thereupon immediately and unhesitatingly asserted Jesus' eschatological transcendence and divinity.[58] It has even responded to the objections to which we have referred above. By way of a conclusion, I shall attempt to summarize these responses.

1. The Return to the Historical Jesus

In his preface to Hugo Echegaray's *The Practice of Jesus*, Gustavo Gutiérrez observes that Echegaray is "warning his readers against a simplistic interpretation which might be given of the statement that Latin American theology is interested primarily in the historical Jesus." Precisely therefore, he adds, Echegaray "thought it necessary to emphasize from the beginning the full complexity of the relationship between the Jesus of history and the Christ of faith, the glorified Kyrios and the carpenter's son from Nazareth."

This concern on the part of the late Peruvian theologian is shared as well by the rest of the theologians of liberation. Thus, their return to the historical Jesus must by no means be understood in the sense of a reductionism, such as would entrap their christological reflection in a sheer "jesuology."

The christology of liberation forthrightly and explicitly accepts the scriptural and conciliar propositions on the divinity of Christ. It has not, however, regarded it as its specific task to enter upon an in-depth investigation of these propositions, nor has it erected them into the methodological starting point of its reflection. We already know the reason:

The profession of Christ's divinity will only be "Christianly real" and will transcend a mere knowledge *about* Christ—although this knowledge about his divinity is important and indispensable—will only become genuinely "comprehensible"—while ever remaining mystery—will only show itself to be efficacious for salvation—in the humble, unconditional discipleship of Jesus, where one learns "from within" *that* God has come unconditionally near in Jesus and *that* God has promised the divine self to us unconditionally in Jesus: that Jesus is true God and that the true God has been made manifest in Jesus.[59]

Indeed, liberation christology has actually made the divinity of Christ an explicit theme, from its most specific viewpoint—the presentation of the figure of Jesus.[60]

2. A Christology "from Below"

While understanding itself as a christology "from below," which sets its priorities an "ascending" methodology, liberation christology knows the following perfectly well:

The mystery of Christ has been formulated in orthodoxy in descending fashion, both in the gospel statement that "the Word became flesh" (John 1:14), and in the dogmatic statement of the hypostatic union, according to which the union of natures in Christ obtains in the person of the Logos. Whatever its difficulties, this descending facet of christology is indispensable, as it posits the mystery of Christ formally as mystery. . . . In order to understand Christ as mystery, then, one must understand him from a point of departure in God—although it is precisely this point of departure that renders him ultimately incomprehensible.[61]

Nevertheless, it remains true that "the very descent of God cannot be grasped, even as a gift, in its pure, abstract formality, but only when it is observed in its concrete content, Jesus." This is why liberation christology, "from a systematic and pastoral viewpoint," attempts to approach "Jesus Christ from Jesus,"[62] in such wise that it is the human condition of the Nazarene itself, and especially his practice, that fills with concrete content the titles and formulations expressing the transcendence and divinity of Jesus.[63] Thus, we might speak of a theological priority of the Christ of faith and a logical and methodological priority of the historical Jesus.[64]

3. The Option for the Poor as Locus

For liberation christology, the social and ecclesial locus of the option for the poor stipulates a necessary "partiality" as a condition for an evangelical understanding of Jesus' true universality. Precisely, and paradoxically, Jesus is sacrament of the universal salvific will of God in his constitutive, forthright partiality for the poor:

> For Jesus becoming incarnate did not mean setting himself in the totality of history so as to correspond to the totality of God from there; it meant rather choosing that particular spot in history that was capable of leading him to the totality of God. This spot is none other than the poor and the oppressed. Conscious of this partiality, which reached him as an alternative to other partialities based on power, or to an innocuous universalism that always means collaboration with power, Jesus from the beginning understood his mission as addressed to the poor; he unfolded his incarnation historically in solidarity with the poor and in the parable of the final judgment — declared the poor and the oppressed to be the setting from which the praxis of love can be discerned.[65]

— Translated by Robert R. Barr

NOTES

1. Jon Sobrino, *Jesus in Latin America* (Maryknoll, N.Y.: Orbis Books, 1987), pp. 4-6.

2. Following are some of the works I regard as most important: Leonardo Boff, *Jesus Christ Liberator: A Critical Christology for Our Time*, trans. Patrick Hughes (Maryknoll, N.Y.: Orbis Books, 1978); Gustavo Gutiérrez, *A Theology of Liberation: History, Politics and Salvation*, trans. and ed. Caridad Inda and John Eagleson (Maryknoll, N.Y.: Orbis Books, 1973), pp. 168-88 ("Christ and Complete Liberation"), pp. 225-31 ("Jesus and the Political World"); José Porfirio Miranda, *Being and the Messiah: The Message of St. John*, trans. John Eagleson (Maryknoll, N.Y.: Orbis Books, 1977); Raúl Vidales, "¿Como hablar de Cristo hoy?" *Spes* 1 (1974):7ff.; Segundo Galilea and Raúl Vidales, *Cristología y pastoral popular* (Bogotá, 1974); José Míguez Bonino, Pablo Richard, Hugo Assmann, G. Casalis, Severino Croatto, et al., *Faces of Jesus: Latin American Christologies*, ed. José Míguez Bonino (Maryknoll, N.Y.: Orbis Books, 1984); Raúl Vidales, "La prática histórica de Jesús," *Christus* (Mexico City) 12 (1975):43-54; Jon Sobrino, *Christology at the Crossroads: A Latin American Approach*, trans. John Drury (Maryknoll, N.Y.: Orbis Books, 1978); Leonardo Boff, "Christ's Liberation via Oppression: An Attempt at Theological Construction from the Standpoint of Latin America," in *Frontiers of Theology in Latin America*, ed. Rosino Gibellini (Maryknoll, N.Y.: Orbis Books, 1979) pp. 100-132; idem, *Passion of Christ — Passion of the World*, trans. Robert R. Barr (Maryknoll, N.Y.: Orbis Books; José Comblin, *Jesus of Nazareth: Meditations on His Humanity*, trans. Carl Kabat (Maryknoll, N.Y.: Orbis Books, 1976); "Cristología en discusión: Panel sobre la Cristología desde América Latina ["Christology at the Crossroads"] de Jon Sobrino," *Christus*, no. 511 (1978), pp. 25-54; Hugo

Echegaray, *The Practice of Jesus*, trans. Matthew J. O'Connell (Maryknoll, N.Y.: Orbis Books, 1984); Jon Sobrino, *Jesus in Latin America*; Juan Luis Segundo, *Jesus of Nazareth, Yesterday and Today*, 5 vols. (Maryknoll, N.Y.: Orbis Books, 1984-88); Jon Sobrino, "Jesús de Nazaret," and "Seguimiento," in *Conceptos fundamentales de pastoral*, ed. C. Floristán and J. J. Tamayo (Madrid, 1983), pp. 480-513, 936-43; C. Bravo Gallardo, *Jesús, hombre en conflicto* (Santander, 1986).

3. I think that this basic concern orientates, informs, and confers a certain identity on all of the studies mentioned in note 2. Nevertheless, it must be acknowledged that the differences among these works are considerable. One need only compare, for example, Segundo's *Hombre de hoy* with the Boff or Sobrino material, to cite some of the more important works on our list, in order to verify these differences. While we acknowledge the importance of Segundo's contribution, its depth and its originality, we shall be following Boff and Sobrino more closely in this chapter, as we regard them as more representative of liberation christology.

4. Sobrino, *Christology at the Crossroads*, p. 351; idem, *Jesus in Latin America*, pp. 59-73.

5. Sobrino, *Christology at the Crossroads*, p. 351.

6. Leonardo Boff, "Epilogue: A Christological view from the Periphery," *Jesus Christ Liberator*, pp. 265-66 (this Epilogue was added to the English translation [1978]). For the relationship between social locus and theological reflection, see Clodovis Boff, *Theology and Praxis: Epistemological Foundations*, trans. Robert R. Barr (Maryknoll, N.Y.: Orbis Books, 1987), pp. 159-74. It is precisely the impossibility of a pure christological science with pretensions to universal validity that leads Segundo to renounce christology and postulate his anti-christology, understood as a situated reading of Jesus from the always relative perspective provided by the concrete historical coordinates in which one lives. Cf. Segundo, *Jesus of Nazareth*, vol. 2, pp. 13-21.

7. Cf. Julio Lois, "Condiciones mínimas de posibilidad para el encuentro con un Cristo liberador," in *Jesucristo en la historia y en la fe*, pp. 239-41.

8. What we have been saying is in no way intended to reduce the scope of meaning that the term *liberation* has for Latin America theology (cf. Julio Lois, *Teología de la liberación: opción por los pobres* [Madrid, 1986], pp. 204-205), or to deny the importance that surely attaches to other liberative aspects of the truth of Christ. We only wish to emphasize that, typically, "christological reflection in Latin America seeks to respond to the second phase of the Enlightenment [represented especially by Marx]. ... It seeks to show how the truth of Christ is capable of transforming a sinful world into the kingdom of God" (Sobrino, *Christology at the Crossroads*, p. 349; cf. pp. 34-37).

9. Cf. Ignacio Ellacuría, "Hacia una fundamentación filosófico del método teológico latinoamericano," *ECA* 322-23 (1975), p. 419.

10. Leonardo Boff, "Epilogue," *Jesus Christ Liberator*, p. 267. We must keep in mind, of course, that this social setting merely *permits* or *makes possible* the emergence of a genuinely liberative christology. It does not of itself guarantee that emergence. Cf. ibid.

11. Sobrino, *Jesus in Latin America*, p. 61. On the church of the poor, see Lois, *Teología de la liberación*, pp. 170-74, with the bibliography included there.

12. On this methodological innovation, see Lois, *Teología de la liberación*, pp. 223-31, esp. nn. 167-69.

13. Sobrino, *Christology at the Crossroads*, p. 305.

14. On the cognitional, ethical, and praxic character of the theological enterprise, see Sobrino, "Theological Understanding in European and Latin American Theology," in *The True Church and the Poor*, trans. Matthew J. O'Connell (Maryknoll, N.Y.: Orbis Books, 1984), pp. 7-38.

15. Javier Jiménez Limón, "Una cristología para la conversión en la lucha por la justicia," *Christus* (Mexico City) 511 (1978), p. 47.

16. Leonardo Boff, "Epilogue," *Jesus Christ Liberator*, p. 279.

17. Sobrino, *Christology at the Crossroads*, pp. 1-16. Sobrino shows that liberation theologians concur in assigning priority to the historical Jesus.

18. José Ignacio González Faus, *El acceso a Jesús* (Salamanca, 1979), p. 20.

19. José Ignacio González Faus, "Hacer teología y hacerse teología," in *Vida y reflexión: Aportes de la teología de la liberación al pensamiento teológico actual* (Lima, 1983), p. 79.

20. Sobrino, *Jesus in Latin America*, pp. 65-66 (cf. pp. 55-59). The priority of the relevancy for salvation, in terms of liberation, of the return to the historical Jesus, always in connection with the continuation of his practice, is a christological constant: Leonardo Boff, "Christ's Liberation via Oppression," pp. 100-103; Lois, "Condiciones mínimas," pp. 245-47.

21. Cf. Sobrino, *Jesus in Latin America*, p. 64.

22. Cf. Leonardo Boff, "Epilogue," *Jesus Christ Liberator*, p. 280.

23. Sobrino, "Jesús de Nazaret," in Floristan and Tamayo, eds., *Conceptos Fundamentales*, p. 485. The central position of the Reign of God in Jesus' preaching and life is acknowledged, in principle, throughout current christology. See, for example, Hans Küng, *On Being a Christian* (New York: Doubleday, 1976), p. 214.

24. I shall follow very closely Sobrino's "La centralidad del 'reino de Dios' en la teología de la liberación," *Revista Latinoamericana de Teología* 3 (1986):247-81, reproduced in this volume. The question of the relationship between Jesus and the Reign of God has been subjected to extensive study in liberation christology. See, for example, Leonardo Boff, *Jesucristo y la liberación del hombre* (Madrid, 1981), pp. 26-28, 83-109; Segundo, *Jesus of Nazareth* vol. 2; Sobrino, *Christology at the Crossroads*, pp. 41-78; idem, *Jesus in Latin America*, pp. 81-97; idem, "Jesús de Nazaret," pp. 484-91.

25. Cf. Sobrino, "La centralidad del 'reino de Dios,' " pp. 254-55.

26. Edward Schillebeeckx, too, for example, asserts that "the concrete content of the Reign arises from his ministry and activity regarded as a whole" (*Jesus: An Experiment in Christology* [New York, 1979], p. 143). See also Christian Duquoc, "El Dios de Jesús y la crisis de Dios en nuestro tiempo," in *Jesucristo en la historia y en la fe*, pp. 47-50.

27. Sobrino says this very clearly when he observes that a preferential consideration of the addressees "appears to be the most specific methodological contribution of the theology of liberation," having its starting point in the basic presupposition that the "content and addressees of the Reign shed light on each other." Sobrino regards this point as of the utmost importance: indeed, he holds that, along with the first, notional *via*, and the second *via*, that of praxis, a third *via*, that of the addressees, should be stipulated in order to "insist on the limitation and risk of regarding only the first *via* and in order to emphasize the need for the second and especially the third" (Sobrino, "Centralidad del 'reino de Dios,' " pp. 262-64). To my understanding, the two latter *vias* can be fused into one, that of praxis, as long as in regard to praxis we keep account of its addressees as being of

decisive importance. Sobrino himself states that "it is only for methodological reasons that we separate this *via* [the second, that of praxis] from the third, the *via* of the addressee" (ibid., p. 257).

28. We cannot develop this point more extensively here. Cf. Lois, "Jesucristo liberador," *Estudios Trinitarios* 20 (1986), pp. 45-60.

29. "When Jesus says, in his preaching, that the Reign of God is already at hand, what he really means is that the situation longed for by all the discontent of the earth is at last about to materialize — the situation in which [there is] justice, that is, protection and help for everyone who cannot cope alone, for all of the disinherited of the earth, for the poor, the oppressed, the weak, the outcast, and the defenseless. . . . The Reign of God, then, as Jesus presents it, represents the most radical transformation of values that it would have been possible to proclaim: the negation and change of the established social system from its foundations up" (J. M. Castillo, *El proyecto de Jesús* [Salamanca, 1985], pp. 36-37). The unquestionably political dimension of the Reign is extensively and magnificently developed in Segundo, *Jesus of Nazareth*, vol. 2.

30. Cf. Sobrino, *Christology at the Crossroads*, pp. 67-75; Bravo Gallardo, *Jesús, hombre en conflicto*, p. 255.

31. See, for example Echegaray, *The Practice of Jesus*, pp. 74-109; Vidales, "La prática histórica de Jesus"; Bravo Gallardo, *Jesús, hombre en conflicto*, pp. 257-65.

32. Ignacio Ellacuría, "Pobres," in *Conceptos fundamentales de pastoral*, ed. Floristan and Tamayo, p. 792.

33. For Jesus' option for the poor, see Lois, *Teología de la liberación*, pp. 157-61.

34. Cf. Sobrino, "La centralidad del 'reino de Dios,' " p. 263.

35. Cf. Lois, *Teología de la liberación*, pp. 95-192.

36. Sobrino, "La centralidad del 'reino de Dios,' " p. 264.

37. Let us observe that, in the orbit of liberation christology itself, in which we are moving, we are restricting ourselves to a clarification of the notion of the Reign of God with a view to identifying who Jesus is as herald and mediator of that Reign. We intend no systematic development of the category "Reign of God," which would oblige us to pose other important questions explicitly, for example, its eschatological dimension of present and of future, its historical and trans-historical dimension, its gratuity and the possibility and necessity of cooperating in its realization, and so on.

38. Cf. Joachim Jeremias, *The Central Message of the New Testament* (Philadelphia: Fortress Press, 1981) and idem, *New Testament Theology* (New York: Scribner, 1971).

39. Cf. Xavier Pikaza, *Los orígenes de Jesús* (Salamanca, 1976), p. 110; Echegaray, *Practice of Jesus*, p. 88; González Faus, *El acceso a Jesús*, pp. 46-49.

40. Leonardo Boff, "Christ's Liberation via Oppression," p. 124.

41. For a more extensive development of this point, see Lois, *Teología de la liberación*, pp. 149-57, with the bibliography included there.

42. Cf. Gustavo Gutiérrez, "El Dios de la vida," *Christus* (Mexico City) 47 (1982), pp. 28-57, elaborated in *The God of Life* (Maryknoll, N.Y.: Orbis Books, 1991); Sobrino, "The Epiphany of the God of Life in Jesus of Nazareth," in Pablo Richard, et al., *The Idols of Death and the God of Life*, trans. Barbara E. Campbell and Bonnie Shepard (Maryknoll, N.Y.: Orbis Books, 1983), pp. 66-102.

43. Sobrino, "La centralidad del 'reino de Dios,' " p. 265.

44. Cf. Christian Duquoc, "Actualidad teológica de la cruz" in *Teología de la cruz*, (Salamanca, 1979), p. 26.

45. Leonardo Boff, "Epilogue," *Jesus Christ Liberator*, p. 288.

46. Cf., for example, Leonardo Boff, *Passion of Christ — Passion of the World*, trans. Robert R. Barr (Maryknoll, N.Y.: Orbis Books, 1987), pp. 86-101.

47. Cf. Lois, "Recuperación histórica de la cruz," *Pastoral Misionera* 152 (1987), pp. 90-94, an attempt to explain the sense in which the death of Jesus can be integrated into the will of the Father and his salvific design, in accord with the Christian scriptures, without the evisceration of the image of the God of Jesus.

48. "If the Christ of God was executed in the name of the politico-religious authorities of his time, then, for the believer the higher justification of these and similar authorities is removed. In that case, political rule can only be justified 'from below' " (Jürgen Moltmann, *The Crucified God* [New York: Harper & Row, 1974] p. 328).

49. Sobrino, *Christology at the Crossroads*, p. 217, cf. pp. 215-17; Leonardo Boff, *Passion of Christ*, pp. 129-33.

50. Cf. esp. Leonardo Boff, *Passion of Christ*.

51. Sobrino, *Jesus in Latin America*, p. 149. "The input of total liberation to be found in the resurrection appears only when we tie it in with Jesus' struggle to establish God's Reign in the world. Apart from this link it could degenerate into pious cynicism vis-à-vis injustices in this world, and an idealism unconnected with history. Thanks to his resurrection, Jesus continues to exist among human beings, giving impetus to their struggle for liberation" (Leonardo Boff, "Epilogue," *Jesus Christ Liberator*, p. 291).

52. Cf. Sobrino, *Jesus in Latin America*, pp. 151-52.

53. Sobrino, *Jesus in Latin America*, pp. 152-54; Jon Sobrino, "La esperanza de los pobres en América latina," *Misión Abierta* 75 (1982), p. 602.

54. F. J. Vitoria, *¿Todavía la salvación cristiana?*, vol. 1 (Vitoria, 1986), p. 352. For the hermeneutics of the resurrection in liberation christology, see Sobrino, *Christology at the Crossroads*, pp. 236-58.

55. Bravo Gallardo, *Jesús, hombre en conflicto*, p. 284.

56. Sobrino, *Christology at the Crossroads*, p. xxiii.

57. These objections, while not the only ones to be raised, are those that underlie the criticism lodged against liberation christology by the "Instruction on Certain Aspects of the Theology of Liberation." In this case, however, the criticism looms so very surprisingly large that it becomes quite difficult to see what christology is being referred to. See also, on this point, the interesting observations of the International Theological Commission (1979 session, I A and B), which are very different from those of the "Instruction," vis-à-vis the potential risks of a christology understood "from below" and the importance of understanding the historical Jesus and the Christ of faith as one and the same being.

58. See, for example, Leonardo Boff, *Jesus Christ Liberator*, pp. 178-205; Segundo, *Jesus of Nazareth* vol. 5; Sobrino, *Jesus in Latin America*, pp. 19-54, 148-65; idem, *Christology at the Crossroads*, pp. 273-99.

59. Sobrino, *Jesus in Latin America*, p. 29.

60. Ibid., pp. 19-29.

61. Ibid., pp. 40-41.

62. Sobrino, "Jesús de Nazaret," p. 481.

63. On this point see Bravo Gallardo, *Jesús, hombre en conflicto*, pp. 80-92;

Gonzalez Faus, "Hacer teología y hacerse teología," pp. 80-81; Sobrino, *Jesus in Latin America*, pp. 50-54.

64. Cf. Vitoria, *¿Todavía la salvación cristiana?* 2:394ff.

65. Sobrino, *Jesus in Latin America*, p. 135. Cf. Leonardo Boff, *Teologia de cativeiro e da libertação* (Lisbon, 1976), p. 216; Gutiérrez, *The Power of the Poor in History: Selected Writings*, trans. Robert R. Barr (Maryknoll, N.Y.: Orbis Books, 1983), pp. 212-14. For a more extensive consideration of the dialectical relation between the universality and particularity of Christian love according to Latin American liberation theology, see Lois, *Teología de la liberación*, pp. 277-82.

9

Ecclesiology in the Theology of Liberation

ALVARO QUIROZ MAGAÑA

Augustine's observation to the effect that theology has meaning primarily because it contributes to the fortification, purification, and invigoration of the faith, becomes particularly applicable today in the case of ecclesiology. No one today harbors the slightest doubt of the need for a serene, discerning, rigorous, and committed reflection, solidly based and pastorally oriented, on the church; that is, on what is and should be the church of Jesus today. What ought to be the manner of realization of the essence and mission of the church is not obvious and cannot simply be taken for granted in the present historical circumstances.

I. AN INESCAPABLE THEOLOGICAL TASK

This need for a reflection on the church has been very vividly experienced by the Christian consciousness of Latin America. We see it in the sheer number of ecclesiological works produced in recent decades. Many of these have been written with an eye to a particular pastoral situation which, in turn, supplies the raw material for the development of more complete and comprehensive syntheses.

There is nothing strange in this abundant ecclesiological production; for Latin America the current epoch has been one of great ecclesial vitality. We have the impulse of Vatican Council II. We have the challenge, confronted by Medellín, of effecting an ecclesial *aggiornamento* in lands of pillage and inequality, lands of misery, oppression, and injustice. We have the exodus of priests, laity, and religious to the periphery, out to where the poor live. We have the surprising resurgence of the church amid and from among these same poor, who burst upon the historical scene denouncing their unjust suffering and demanding justice and emancipation. We have the conflicts and tensions that arise within a society that resists change, and in a church the majority of whose members are more accustomed to preserving of the status quo than to proposing in social transformation. We have the dogged determination of Puebla not to give up, not to forget the poor, not to shut itself off from the grace of making its option for them. We have so much vitality in the church. All of this—truly the gift and power of the Spirit—lived in the midst of the humble and joyful, persevering and sanctified, crucified and suffering effort of men and women, groups and communities, has been the foundation, and is the substance, of this ecclesiological reflection.

This emerging, progressive ecclesial vitality stimulated the need as early as the 1970s, and with a growing urgency, to rethink the church. The classic ecclesiologies, which tended to be deductive, ahistorical, clerical, and hierarchical, were deemed insufficient for giving an account of faith and ecclesial life in this situation, amid the waxing, developing Christian praxis. It became essential to narrate the believing life anew, to allow the light of the gospel to shine upon it, to impel it toward a further pledge and commitment.

II. A NEW ECCLESIOLOGY FOR A NEW HISTORICAL SITUATION

In this context, an ecclesiological reflection of a liberative tenor has been taking shape within the vigorous current of Christian thought that is the theology of liberation. It is an ecclesiological reflection that presents itself first and foremost as "second word" (the first word is praxis), as critical reflection in the light of the gospel on life and on ecclesial Christian practice. It is a theological reflection that faces the question of the meaning of the church from the starting point of believers' growing commitment to the liberation of our peoples, from the liberative practices emerging in the midst of the poor.

1. A "New Praxis"

When we speak of a "new praxis," one demanding new kinds of theological reflection, we find it necessary to say something about the new and the old in the church of the Lord. There has been a great deal of reflection these last decades on the possibility and reality of change in the church. On the one hand, there has been a sense of the need to assert the indefectibility of this church, which is the Lord's, and which receives from him in ongoing fashion nourishment, origin, and life. On the other hand, it has been considered urgent to emphasize the fact that this very life, this very nourishment require that the church, at once holy and in need of purification (*Lumen Gentium*, no. 8), be constantly renewed, reshaped in every age in conformity with the demands of its being and mission. In this sense, new praxis is the same as renewal in fidelity. New praxis is response to a word that constantly summons us to emerge, to take the road, to go on a pilgrimage to a new land, to take up the cross and follow Jesus.

But a mere acceptance in principle that ecclesial change may be legitimate does not make it easy to identify and characterize that change. At any given moment the "new element" to be introduced is seen to be novel. Then it is gradually seen to be something belonging to all ages, a substantial datum of the church's fidelity. However, this does not cancel the novelty. The One who makes all things new is present and alive in the church, and communicates within it that novelty which, when all is said and done, is fidelity to what is most authentic, profound, and proper to that church. Thus, it is part and parcel of ecclesial commitment and responsibility to welcome, drive forward, and direct the element of the new that is being stirred up by the Spirit in the church of Latin America.

Latin American liberation ecclesiology does not pretend, then, that this is the first time the church has been renewed, or even the first time that the church has approached the poor. Indeed, this very ecclesiology has taken on the responsibility of demonstrating that, deep down, the church has always been faithful to the option for the poor (Eduardo Hoornaert, Clodovis Boff). Rather, what is meant is rather that for the first time in history, since this is what our epoch requires, the church has addressed the challenge of identifying with the poor and of walking with them along the road to liberation, to sociohistorical transformation. And this is seen as a privileged way of bringing into history the liberation of the gospel of Jesus.

On what does the novelty of this praxis rest? What is the basis and justification of this nascent ecclesiology? We are confronted here with a praxis that has come to be shaped by an emerging awareness that the current social situation is unjust and inhumane, that it cannot be willed by God — and likewise by an awareness that liberation is attainable, indeed part and parcel of God's salvific plan. It is a committed praxis, which seeks to overcome, with lucidity, all forms (so often dissimulated and concealed) of slavery, exploitation, institutionalized violence, and socioeconomic marginalization. It is a praxis that consists and can be summed up in the ecclesial option for the poor and their liberation.

In the same fashion this new praxis consists in the poor themselves bursting upon the historical and ecclesial scene. Our eyes have been opened; we cannot continue to overlook the suffering and unjust oppression of the poor who surround us. We went to them to bring them the gospel of liberation, and we discovered that we were being evangelized by them. We came to understand that we could not evangelize without a concrete involvement in the liberation of the poor, and we realized that the poor were the most important agent of this evangelizing liberation — these poor who, with their awareness, their words, and their actions, were proclaiming the gospel in a new way in our lands.

2. New Ecclesial Praxis, New Understanding of Reality

The theses of developmentalism have failed. Instead of diminishing, "underdevelopment" or socioeconomic marginalization has grown tragically and enormously, compounded by political oppression and repression. This has obliged Latin Americans to formulate new conceptualizations of the reality of our peoples. Thus it has come to be understood that the situation in question is largely to be explained in terms of dependency; structural inequality; systematic exploitation; and the economic, political, and military interests of the mighty. Likewise, it has come to be seen that no change truly worthy of the name is possible without profound economic, political, and social transformation—a change in the social system itself. This, now formulated in terms of social theory, had previously become living reality in the concrete political practice of those who had already involved themselves in the process of transformation for justice.

Christians were not the pioneers here. Often others assumed the first, most difficult commitments. Providentially, however, Christians were soon incorporated into this dynamic, this practice of historical liberation. They committed themselves to it and gradually began to reflect on the situation of the church and the demands of the mission of that church in today's Latin America. Does the church have a concrete responsibility regarding the oppression of the poor in Latin America? Is part of the mission of the church to undertake a serious evangelical involvement in the historical liberation of our peoples? Does it pertain to the vital reality of the church to make a contribution to the formation of a historical agent capable of carrying forward this project of liberation?

All of these questions entered Latin American Christian consciousness, amidst a great ecclesial vitality. The church in Latin America had rediscovered the prophetic dimensions of the proclamation of the gospel, which remembered that persecution and martyrdom can result from following Jesus, and which found in communities of the poor, gathered around the word of God and living in a new way the kernel of the evangelical message, the very birth of the church by the power of the Spirit. Thus began one of the most important chapters in the history of the church of Latin America, and consequently of the history of the ecclesiology of liberation.

III. STAGES OF LIBERATION ECCLESIOLOGY

The history of liberation ecclesiology lies in the future, in two senses. First, there is a road to be taken. There must be growth, development, and advancement in commitment, reflection, and discernment. There are discoveries to be exploited, a pilgrimage in need of direction. One must persevere. Second, there must continue to be reflection on this life in the light of the gospel. Better theological syntheses must be constructed of what is most worthwhile in this reflection—a reflection to be carried out especially by the people of the poor and by those who are near them in a very special way. These must employ the charism they have received in gathering and restoring to the people the wealth aroused by the Spirit of God by way of that same charism.

Nevertheless, it is already possible to identify certain stages in liberation ecclesiology—stages that by no means constitute discrete, static, disconnected compartments adequately functioning on their own. In each of these stages, obviously, we shall encounter, however differently, the main components shaping the present historical and ecclesial era in Latin America. In each of them we shall observe the entry of the church into the world of the poor, and the irruption of the poor into the church and history. In each stage, we shall also observe an escalation in the quality of questioning — always in dependence upon the advance of life — a particular pace and tone in each step of this ecclesiology.

Pastoral Concerns: Approach to Life, to Reality

In a first stage, we might cite the ecclesiological reflections that have occurred as challenges to forms of pastoral ministry and church life that were no longer felt to correspond either to the reality of the times or to the requirements of change that were making themselves felt in our lands. Ecclesiological reflections were uncovering a certain "ecclesial malaise" in various groups of Christians, expressed in letters, communiqués, requests, proposals, and pastoral letters. Ecclesiology was registering the emergence of a "new awareness of the church of Latin America" (Ronaldo Muñoz). More critical and analytical reflections, undertaken by theologians involved in this pilgrimage, were yielding the first elements of the theology of liberation. This first stage in Latin American ecclesiology is remarkable for the beginnings of a fertile interaction between church life, theological reflection, and episcopal magisterium. Conflicts between the magisterium of certain bishops and the propositions of certain theologians had not yet appeared. Later there would be talk of a "parallel magisterium."

Such reflections called attention to the inadequacy of a pastoral praxis that failed to take account of historical realities understood in the light of more critical analyses. A need was recognized for an understanding of the church in theological forms and models that would permit evolution, change, and adaptation (Juan Luis Segundo, Gustavo Gutiérrez, and others). It came to be seen that the battle for social justice, social commitment, and the transformation of the inhumane conditions of the concrete life of the majority of the inhabitants of Latin America ought to occupy the center of Christian life and the proclamation of the gospel.

Beginnings of Liberation Theology: Place of Reflection on the Church

The first extensive presentations of the theology of liberation (Gustavo Gutiérrez, Hugo Assmann, Juan Luis Segundo, Leonardo Boff, and so on) assigned a central place to ecclesiological reflection. These presentations reached the widest audiences, those of decisive importance in the shaping of this vigorous theological current in the contemporary church. They were not ecclesiologies themselves; far from it. They were works whose central reference, in the course of their advocacy of a new way of doing theology, was the central content of the evangelical proclamation. Their fundamental questions went back to basics. What is salvation? What does it mean to proclaim God as Father in a world of injustice and inhumanity? In what do the authentic life and message of Jesus of Nazareth consist? And so on. Of course, as they raised such radical questions, these works could scarcely avoid touching on their ecclesiological implications. Accordingly, they spoke, with prophetic vigor and unusual pastoral repercussions, of a decentralized church, a church in the service of the world and in solidarity with the poor and their cause, a church with a prophetic vocation, a church no longer able to use its much-vaunted uniformity as a palliative for historical division and antagonism among human beings, or its worship as a pretext for evasion or for the legitimation or dissimulation of reality.

Even the christological works that followed (Leonardo Boff, Jon Sobrino, and others) had decisive repercussions when the moment arrived for a reflection on a church that claims to be, seeks to be, and must be, a church that follows Jesus, a servant of the Reign of God, a sacrament of salvation in concrete history.

Reflection on "Models" of the Church

Liberation ecclesiology pointed out the insufficiency of the earlier models — christendom and neo-christendom — to respond to the new situation. The dual-level theologies, and the others that fail to account for the unity of history as authentic salvation history, must give place to theologies that speak more realistically of salvation in history and demonstrate the unity of the human and Christian calling (Gutiérrez, Ignacio Ellacuría, Leonardo Boff). Of course, this had repercussions on a view of the church; on the understanding of its fundamental being; on the way in which its biblical images ought to be understood, especially that of the people of God so dear to the heart of Vatican II; on the way in which the "notes" of the church, and the services and structures of that church, ought to be understood and projected. This was ecclesiology's "incarnational" way of accepting the invitation of Vatican II to make the church a church of communion.

All this made it necessary to examine at greater depth the various models of church. The clerical models had to be identified for what they were; more participatory models, which would enflesh an ecclesiology of communion already proclaimed at Vatican II were proposed. Thus it was useful to characterize the various models, the various ways of being church, that had prevailed in history. These models represented concrete manners of incarnating the ecclesial calling, but not the only such manners. As models, they had their good points, but their limitations as well, and none could pretend to an exclusive validity for our own age.

On one hand, the models in question referred to the internal structure of the church (vertical model, participatory model). On the other, they had to do with its relationship with its broader surroundings, with its place in society as a whole, with its interconnections with the various sectors and classes of society (christendom, neo-christendom, *mysterium salutis*, church of the poor, and so on). This reflection on and discussion of ecclesial models rendered Christian consciousness more flexible, thus permitting the quest for a new model, a model shaped from the starting point of the poor, in the option for them, in the life rising up among them. This new model would respond to concrete situations of oppression and to the steps already beginning to be taken in the direction of liberation. The important thing, it was emphasized, was to find a model of church that would imply an interconnection, adequate for today, of the key categories of church, Reign of God, and world (Leonardo Boff), a model that would incarnate for present history the response of fidelity to the call of the gospel.

A Reflection at Once Convergent and Differentiated

It might be objected that, in the ecclesiological reflection of Latin American liberation theology, various necessarily united aspects of one and the same reality have come in for uneven emphasis. While sharing the same perspective, some ecclesiological works have attended more to the life of the church as community of faith and life, while others have emphasized the life of the church in its quality of concrete signification in and to the world.

Thus, some have set themselves the task of showing the Christian legitimacy of a new emerging model. They have sought to reinforce the thrust of a church reborn among the poor and making itself a charismatic community of faith and service—becoming a space for participation on the part of the poor, and remodeling its services and forms of authority. Others have insisted especially on the phenomenon of a people of the poor bursting upon the scene of a history built until now behind their backs and on their backs—an irruption that is a denunciation of death and proclamation of life, the presence of the God of life in a new experience of church and evangelization. Here it is that they have located the rebirth of the church.

Both tendencies or focuses have emphasized the potential for renewal with which this ecclesial rebirth is endowed. In these communities, poor and believing, weak and committed, praying and caught in the most unfavorable material conditions, the Father of Jesus, by the divine Spirit, is renewing the church of God.

Let us repeat: it is a matter of different emphases, not of mutually exclusive approaches. Indeed, if we examine the overall work of the various theologians respectively, we find what they regard as the two aspects of church: the ecclesial *ad intra* and *ad extra*. But this difference of emphasis is enriching for theology and for the life of the community. It calls attention to the reciprocity of a way of being church that, the more churchly it is, the more capable it becomes of plunging evangelically into the history of the poor and thus being a leaven of renewal for the church at large.

Finally, let us observe that these emphases also have their explanation in the various concrete ecclesial contexts in which liberation ecclesiology is produced—the various paths taken by a people whose constant suffering and trust in the Father of Jesus is reminiscent of the figure of Job, a people who, time and again over the course of their pilgrimage, drink from the well of their own spirituality (Gustavo Gutiérrez).

The Critical Accompaniment of the Church among the People

Beyond a doubt, in gathering up the experiences of the Christian community and handing it back as critical enlightenment and new impulse, this ecclesiological reflection has meant something precious to the pilgrimage of a church reborn with and among the poor—the church of a people, nevertheless, who pursue their course to liberation amidst an ever more evident and prolonged captivity.

Now, it is precisely in this last sense that liberation ecclesiology cannot be a finished whole, a closed system. It is an ongoing task, challenged at every moment by the novelty of history. What does it mean to be church in the midst of the emergence of the people? What is it to be church amidst repression and this obvious historical backsliding? What is it to be church amidst revolutionary struggles? What is it to be church amidst historical transformation, with the powerful seeking to apply a brake to the advance of the poor? And so on. All of these questions, which are anything but theoretical, constitute anguishing problems posed by reality itself. They must be addressed by ecclesiology on this continent of hope, as it has been called. It is indeed the continent where a believing community feels called to resist and to hope, even when there would no longer appear to be room to do so, a continent where successes are only seeds of future hope. In this sense, then, we must continue to speak of current liberation ecclesiology as an ongoing critical accompaniment of the pilgrimage of a people answering the call of the gospel of liberation.

IV. FUNDAMENTAL THEMES OF THE ECCLESIOLOGY OF LIBERATION

It is not easy to order the fundamental thematics of liberation ecclesiology. On the one hand, that theology has reformulated the central themes of classic ecclesiology and of the ecclesiology that stems from Vatican II. On the other, it has taken new paths in its search for a way to express, rather tentatively as yet, the effervescence of life engendered by the Spirit of God in the midst of the poor. Numerous ecclesiological compositions identify the notes of this new church. It will be useful, however, to present the main contributions of these various works.

1. The Church: Sacrament of Historical Liberation

Characteristic of Latin American life and ecclesial consciousness, and of Latin American critical reflection on the church, is the emphasis on the "mission of the church" in the face of the urgent need of salvation represented by, first, our all but universal misery and oppression, and second, by our longings and struggles for liberation. What we have, then, is an eminently practical consciousness, which keeps before its eyes the question of how to be and how to create church in the face of concrete challenges of this kind. Accordingly, when that consciousness reflects on the church as sacrament of salvation, it underscores the decentralization that this requires. The church is for the world. It exists because there is and must be salvation, and so it asks itself of what salvation it is the sacrament. It is the sacrament not of an individualistic salvation concerned with afterlife and existing outside of history, but rather of a salvation for the individual and for the collectivity. Such a salvation, while greater than history, is nevertheless realized in history itself. It is a salvation that, in today's Latin America, must be realized in the form of liberation — must be mediated in the economic, political, and social realities of human existence. Finally, it is a salvation that will be the rising up of the massacred and the eradication of institutionalized violence; a salvation consisting in real, concrete change, in a real community of sisters and brothers, reflected in the very structures of our social life. This is where eschatological salvation will have its starting point.

This is where the church of Latin America is coming to experience its mystery. Here, in the presence of the God of Jesus, this church is coming to discover that it will be a sacrament of salvation to the extent that it becomes a church of the poor and oppressed. This is meant not only in the sense that it makes an option for them, lives for them, and is persecuted for their sake (which would be no small matter), but mainly in the sense that it arises from them, from their believing response, and that thus they come to be the authentic and first subject of ecclesial life and structure.

2. The Church: Sign and Servant of the Reign of God

This understanding that the church is a sacrament of salvation has been deepened, in Latin American ecclesiological awareness, by a reflection on the church as sign and servant of the Reign of God. Appealing to Jesus' preaching and history as the foundation of the church, the church discovers itself to be the seed of the Reign, an entity in the service of the Reign. This service will necessarily be performed in the following and discipleship of Jesus—in the adoption of his Messianic practice and his cause. This is its response to the gift of the Reign of God, which it approaches in all awareness of its gratuity—a gift received, as well, where there is no actual church, but where there is an option for the human being, service rendered to the poor, a pilgrimage to a new, more just society of brothers and sisters. Shoulder to shoulder with those who, without professing the Lord, nevertheless do his will, the Latin American church understands that it must also labor in the construction of the anticipation of the Reign of God, the construction of its mediations.

Jesus centered his life on the proclamation of the Reign of God as gratuitous and salvific proximity. It was to be a Reign that, in conformity with the traditions of his people, would come as justice for the poor, eradication of sin, and actual transformation. Jesus himself was concretely at the side of the poor and oppressed, and he proclaimed them the special addressees of the Reign of God—not because they were better, surely, but because this is God's way of exercising sovereignty. He also preached the Reign as something future, while nevertheless corresponding to its approach by positing effective liberative acts even in the present. For the sake of the Reign—which necessarily comes in conflict with the selfishness and unjust power that oppresses the weak and thereby contradicts the spirit of God's family—he was sentenced and crucified. For his faithful obedience to death, he received in his resurrection not only the endorsement of his path and mission, but the definitive irruption, however inchoate, of the Reign he had proclaimed.

There can be no other authentic route for the church, then, than the following of Jesus in the service of the Reign. The ongoing conversion of the church, its words and its deeds, its internal structuring and its manner of presence in society, must be good news—an evangelization opposed to sin and effectively presenting the imminence of the Reign of God. In a historical reality like that of Latin America, then, the church must unequivocally embrace the service to the Reign that is to be performed by the church of the poor. After all, the latter are not only the priority addressees, but the actual vessels, as well, of evangelization, in their liberative practice as well as in their believing proclamation of its salvific, gratuitous meaning.

3. The Church: People of God

One of the biblical categories dearest to the heart of Latin American liberation ecclesiology is that of the people of God. In the wealth of this key biblical image, the theology that reflects from the underside of history, at the side of an oppressed, believing people, has found enlightenment and prophetic strength, a demanding calling and an attitude of thanksgiving, the opportunity to live in the following of Jesus amidst persistent captivity, and an implacable thrust toward liberation.

The expressions, "church among the people," "church of the poor," and "church of the people," are attempts to express the wealth of revelation in terms of a renewed ecclesial experience. They are expressions that have been and must continue to be submitted again and again to analysis and critique, so they may be consistent with the intention that has generated them; that is, the intent to give an account of an ecclesial renewal, arising from and transpiring among the poor. We speak of an ecclesial renewal that is calling, hope, and gladness for the entire church.

In keeping with Vatican II, liberation ecclesiology has underlined the fact that the church, the people of God, is not only structure and organization, but also, and principally, event. The church is the convocation of the people by God, and it is the people's response to God. Liberation ecclesiology has insisted on the primacy of Christian existence in the community over organization and functional differentiation within the same. It has understood and formulated with unusual clarity that the church that "recognizes in the poor and suffering the image of its poor and suffering founder" (*Lumen Gentium*, no. 8) must, in Latin America, be shaped as a church of the poor and oppressed, as a church of the people, if it is actually to be the people of God. Along these same lines, the ecclesiology of liberation has adopted the formula that the building of a church of communion must overcome the vertical, authoritarian, and closed structuring of a pyramidal, hierarchical model of church that fails to adapt to the basic content of the biblical category of people of God.

In order to begin to elucidate this theological category—people of God—liberation ecclesiology has developed a reflection along three intimately related lines. First, it seeks to explain what is meant by *people* in Latin America. This will be a necessary reference for a more concrete understanding of the church as people of God. It has identified the people as a people especially of the poor—those who answer the call of faith from out of their poverty—as well as of those who make an option for the poor, entering into solidarity with their suffering and their pathways of emancipation.

Second, liberation ecclesiology seeks in the biblical revelation concerning the old and new people of God elements that might shed light on the meaning of the church in its concrete configuration in Latin America today. Here it deals with a people summoned by the gospel of liberation and called in ongoing fashion to emerge from captivity and oppression to a life in the freedom and justice of the Reign of God, a people called to fidelity and ongoing conversion in the spirit of the Beatitudes: an authentic, persevering following of Jesus in this concrete history of ours.

Finally, on the basis of what has gone before, ecclesiological reflection plumbs the depths of the intense, concrete experience in Latin American lands of the birth of the church of a people poor and oppressed from out of their faith and their response to the Lord, from out of the experience of his mercy and his salvific tenderness. There the reflection discovers aspects of meaning and ecclesial vocation that have significance for the entire church. Thus, it finds that in a special way the base church communities are the locus of the gospel call to the poor and lowly. They, as communities of a crucified people, are the servant of Yahweh, called to establish justice and right, to uproot sin from the world precisely by taking it upon themselves.

In the privileged experience that the base church communities have begun to have is the vital root of this theological construction. It is here that the believing community experiences and formulates itself as people of God met together, as people of God called to emerge from oppression, as pilgrim people who, in conversion and faithfulness, are to become in truth a people. It is here that an oppressed, believing people has begun to take shape as agent of its own history—church history and overall history, sociopolitical history and spiritual history. It is here that an oppressed, believing people feels and knows that it is a people on the way to eschatological realization.

Particularly revealing, in this experience, has been the fact that the communities in question live in a renewed manner the communitarian dimension that typifies the people of God. This same experience is decisive in the accomplishment of the vocation of a scattered people to become a people assembled. The masses, which are not yet a people, find in these communities the indispensable impulse to raise their consciousness, "have their say," hear the word, respond to that word, and gradually become truly people of God.

When we speak of a church of the poor, then, we mean to testify to the rebirth of the people of God that is taking place on the outskirts of our cities, in rural areas, in native regions, in the places of socioeconomic marginalization and helplessness. The expression *church of the poor* connotes a church in which laity and religious, priests and bishops, have experienced a new call and have sought to respond with fidelity in service and solidarity with the poor; a church in which the gospel is announced in solidarity with the exploited classes; a church gathered by the proclamation of the gospel of liberation at the heart of the actual struggles for liberation; a church that is a congregation of all who, accepting Christ, receive the proclamation of his Reign and so serve to make that Reign a living reality.

A very special aspect of this acceptance and this service is solidarity with the poor. The solidarity in question is a concrete charity. It is solidarity with the individual and collective neighbor, solidarity with those near and far, solidarity with the compatriot and with the refugee, solidarity with the peoples who journey toward concrete, historical liberation.

The reason Puebla rejects the expression *popular church* is that it seems to indicate an alternative church to another, nonpopular, alienated church (Puebla Final Document, no. 263). Thus, with an insistence overlooked in certain ecclesiastical sectors, liberation ecclesiology emphasizes that, in Latin America, becoming the church of the poor is experienced not as the construction of an alternative church, but as the realization of a vocation. A church born of the people as church of the poor is the church of Jesus itself, a church of fidelity, of humble conversion and response to the call of the Lord who becomes living word in the oppressed, believing neighbor. It must be emphasized that this vocation of the church is the same vocation it has always had. After all, in all ages the purpose of the church has been to serve the Reign of God in the following of Jesus by the power of his Spirit. The new element today is that this purpose must be made concrete in the particular historical conditions of Latin America.

In this journey of a people of God, of the communities that in their lowliness are an authentic grace for the church of Latin America, liberation ecclesiology has also had a new experience and understanding of Mary—Mother of God and Mother of the poor—and of her role in Jesus' deed of liberation, of her place in the life of the believing community. It sees Mary as prototype of the church. She becomes once more the simple woman, the woman of the people, the mother of Jesus the carpenter's son, in solidarity with her folk and with the hopes of her people, handmaid of that Lord who topples the mighty from their thrones and exalts the humble, who fills the poor with good things and sends the rich empty away.

In this woman, who is blessed because she accepts and performs the will of God and maintains her fidelity to the last, her son's cross, in this nurturing mother of the nascent church gathered in the faith of the Risen One, liberation ecclesiology has found strength for the endorsement of Latin American women—doubly oppressed, as poor and as women. It has found the thrust to acknowledge and foster their participation in the management of the church, their role in the journey of a poor people who now burst upon history. In Mary, ecclesiology finds the creativity it needs to pursue the needed evangelization of popular religion.

4. Unity and Conflict in the Church

Inevitably and from the outset liberation ecclesiology has had to be concerned with the key theme of the unity of the church. In addressing this concern it has emphasized that the most serious breaches of this unity are those that reflect the objective division of society into counterpoised social classes. Here, our ecclesiology insists that the question of church unity cannot be dealt with apart from the sacramental reality of the church and its essential reference to the world. After all, the most profound truth of the unity of the church consists in the communion of believers with God and with one another, in the sharing of the trinitarian love that constitutes the concrete basis of all Christian relationships. The church, then, in our historical conditions, receives the gift of its unity and makes that gift real to the extent that it serves the process of the unification of the world. And in a world radically divided, the unifying function of the church community will be actualized in the struggle with injustice as the cause of division, and in the upbuilding of justice as the incarnation of concrete community.

By way of consequence — although on occasion it has been rather a point of departure — this approach to church unity seriously criticizes any ideological manipulation of church unity that promoting genuine unity, conceals and even legitimizes the historical divisions under which the poor of this continent are suffering.

Hand in hand with this reflection on unity, another is in progress: one concerning conflict in the church. The great ecclesial vitality to which we have been referring has been accompanied by significant tension in our church. Not all accept change in the same fashion, especially a sociohistorical change orientated toward a genuine participation and communion of our peoples. Not all accept the way in which the church must be committed here. This produces tension and conflict in the church.

The key to managing these tensions has been subordination to the Reign of God. Structures, norms, and institutional realities must be submitted to the norm of the Reign, and not vice versa. One must acknowledge one's own sin in this conflict-ridden situation; one must understand that it is not easy for the church to adopt this novel, liberative will of God, in the consciousness of which the new ecclesiology has been constructed. A spirituality of conflict, which is not plunged into panic by it but, which is capable of discerning the will of God within it, which honestly seeks to transcend conflict in the direction of the Reign of God, and which is capable of undogged perseverance and deathless hope — all of this is the gift of the Spirit. It is a reproduction of the equally conflict-ridden experience of the first Christian communities, that is, their gradual discovery of God's will for the church in circumstances altogether novel and unforeseeable.

In this same area, the church of Latin America, and consequently the ecclesiology of liberation, inquires into the problem of ecclesial pluralism. How is the church to be *one*, faithful to the call of the Lord in the poor and oppressed, and at the same time a pluralistic church, marching to different drummers and expressing its response and its fidelity in different ways?

This whole theology of church unity is an actual experience, in hope, in the poor communities, the base church communities, which are like a "blessing from the Father who fills his church with new life" (Puebla Final Document, no. 96). These communities of true communion gradually are built up in a workaday reality. They are communities that make an effort to do honor to the name of God; communities in which the various charisms come to bear concretely on the building of a single church; communities that are not always heard within the church itself; communities that see their prophetic vigor and concrete commitment rejected by fear and power. Yet these communities not only maintain communion with the church universal but strive to promote it. Tirelessly they announce that the one gospel we must live in the church is that of Jesus Christ, the gospel of him who was crucified by the mighty of his time and raised up by the Father as savior for all women and men. They know and experience their weakness in complete surrender to the Father's mercy, and they know that their life and their opportunity to be seeds of the future in the church and in history rest in God.

5. New Services, Structures, and Ministries in the Church

Protesting concrete oppression and socioeconomic marginalization, and promoting actual participation on the part of Christians in the struggles and strivings of liberation, the Latin American church has felt the need for authority and ministry to be exercised in a different way. In the pastoral practice of the church of Latin America, and in the promising experience of the base church communities, a lively impulse of renewal has been at work. Initial successes have been realized in charismatic forms of ministry, service, and participation that are more in accord with the demands of the church's vocation today.

First, we see a growing, theologically sound participation on the part of laity—laity who are poor—in church administration. Everywhere we behold the appearance of new lay ministries. We witness greater autonomy of the laity as they participate as Christians in concrete struggles for liberation. There is an awareness that the praxis of liberation in actual ecclesial experience is a radical response to the Christian calling, and not the implementation of a charge received from the hierarchy. Nonetheless, this still calls for greater reflection and more practice before we arrive at a further clarification of the status of the laity in the church, a status that, on the other hand, must be on guard against an undue "clericalization" of the new lay ministries.

Second, there are new ways of exercising the priestly and episcopal ministry—more participatory ways, more democratic ways, ways that are more in the spirit of service and solidarity, ways more prophetic and more committed. Many pastors have carried their love to the limit, giving their lives for their brothers and sisters. This has not failed to have a clear impact on Christian awareness, which postulates that the service of Peter in the church universal be performed as that of a pope of the poor.

Before concluding this part of our reflection, we must cite the authentic transformation that is transpiring in the forms of religious life, as well—a life that has taken to the desert, to the outskirts, to the places of poverty whither none goes willingly or marches in triumph, to the frontier where the Spirit of God calls for the liberation of the people of God. There can be no doubt that the theological formulations that have inspired so many religious of both sexes in our time have to a large extent drawn upon the theology being developed from these new manners of practicing the following of Jesus and the service of the Reign of God.

V. ASPECTS OF CONFLICT AND POINTS OF DISPUTE

Discussion at the early stages, not only in the Latin American church but throughout the church, focused on the Christian legitimacy of liberation theology. An effort was made to show that the best liberation theology is a genuine contribution to the rediscovery of the Christian face of the church. It is a way of taking Vatican II seriously (Segundo). In this discussion, and in the indications of the pope and the bishops, a stimulus was found to avoid the dangerous extremes to which any theological reflection might be exposed. The same sources, however, provided a confirmation of the vocation of the church to become the faithful church of Jesus in the world of today.

Another important discussion, this time in the area of ecclesiology, centers on whether the church described in the ecclesiology of liberation is the authentic church of Jesus or an alternative church, a different church at the base or grassroots. As we have repeatedly stated throughout this chapter, the answer of the liberation church is that in Latin America becoming the church of the poor and being committed to the cause of their liberation is experienced not as an alternative, but as a calling of the entire church. Nor is this statement merely a piece of argumentation. Rather, it is witness borne in thanksgiving to the deed of the Spirit of God amid the people of God. It is also recognition of the church one and universal as both the source and the increasingly hearty welcomer of this same impulse.

Both discussions have a great deal more to do with the development of current events than with theoretical speculations—a great deal more to do with concrete solidarity with the cause of the poor and oppressed and their struggles for liberation than with dogmatic texts and definitions.

Precisely here is where a discussion has had to be sustained by the ecclesiology of liberation with other ecclesial sectors on the topic of the meaning of the option for the poor. Christian love cannot be divested of its radicality with adjectives that ignore God's partiality for the poor. Surely God wills that all persons attain salvation and come to the knowledge of the truth. But it is high time for an acknowledgment of the route that this universal salvific will has taken in the normative history of Jesus.

Once more in the area of liberation ecclesiology, an important investigation pursues the lines of an authentic integration of the political dimension into Christian and ecclesial life. What can be done so that we Christians, individually and in our communities, may responsibly assume the ineluctable political dimension of our faith? What aspects of this political dimension have a bearing especially on individuals? Which aspects concern Christian communities as such? What is the legitimate role, the role demanded by the gospel, of bishops, priests, and religious in their accompaniment of the poor? Here once more, the proposals that arise are in relation to the various concrete situations of our continent. Liberation ecclesiologists insist that concrete liberation is an intrinsic component of faith. Faith is more than an extrinsic motive for political praxis— as can be seen so clearly in the praxis of Jesus himself. Liberation ecclesiologists endorse a political participation on the part of the poor, a participation ever better, ever more lucid. We seek criteria for an adequate participation in this area on the part of priests and religious. We ascribe to politics a broader connotation than that of simple partisan militancy, especially in those countries in which any demand, any quest is considered in and of itself a confrontation with the power of the state.

What we are after, then, is a more adequate system of interconnection between the church reborn among the poor and the people's pilgrimage of liberation. What we promote is the creation of a subject characterized by solidarity and capable of seeing to it that history moves in the direction of the justice and communion of the Reign of God. In the face of such a challenge there are many different responses, but they all recognize the fact that praxis — experience subjected to reflection — will be able to contribute something more solid and reliable in this area.

VI. THE OUTLOOK FOR LIBERATION ECCLESIOLOGY

As we have indicated, one of the tasks that liberation ecclesiology has taken up is that of a committed, critical accompaniment of a people "on the way." In the execution of this task ecclesiology finds that the source of its progress is on the underside of history. It is not a matter of writing thicker and thicker books, with longer and longer indices. What is important is that the people live, that they have life in abundance, as the God of the Good News would have it. It is important that the pilgrimage of the people of God, the church reborn among the poor, is narrated with fidelity, criticized with authenticity, and thrust forward with vigor. Here, then, is a challenge to militant holiness, to full-time devotion to the people of the poor and to reflection with them. Here too is a challenge to theological dialogue and to teamwork — those characteristics so proper to the Latin American production of the theology of liberation.

Another of the tasks of the ecclesiology of liberation is to continue to demonstrate to the greater church the legitimacy of this way of being church. At issue, then, is not so much the legitimacy of a theoretical system as the legitimacy of a life that flows in novel, hope-filled channels, channels charged with pain and suffering, channels of conflict and cross, but channels, after all, of the precious grace that our divine Father has willed to give us in his beloved Child, Jesus. A greater openness on the part of the church in the difficult times of this winter of faith may be decisive if the people are to have life. The ecclesiology of liberation, with its solid, serious, and believing toil, its radical testimony rendered in communion (albeit at times in conflict as well), can be an important contribution to the maintenance, recovery, and enablement of that openness.

All of this takes place in the following and discipleship of the Crucified One, whom God has raised from the dead. God has given us in Jesus the true life that we ask for every day in the Our Father — that perpetual supplication Jesus bequeathed to us — when we ask for the Reign, for bread, for pardon, and for deliverance from every evil.

— Translated by Robert R. Barr

10

Fundamental Moral Theory in the Theology of Liberation

FRANCISCO MORENO REJÓN

Ever since Vatican II, we in the field of moral theology have witnessed a process of in-depth renewal that has had vast consequences. This change has perhaps been more spectacular and more widely known in matters of particular, more polemical questions of concrete moral theory. The root of these changes, however, is found in the area of ethical foundations. Here is the origin of the propositions of this renewed moral theology, propositions articulated around the current of the "ethics of autonomy," with its principal expression in the intent to provide theological ethics with a critical basis.[1]

In turn, in these same years in which moral theological reflection was facing the challenge of systematizing its critical foundation and giving a new shape to the expression of fundamental moral theory, an original theological thought had crystallized in Latin America. The current of liberation theology was bursting upon the theological scene with two basic contributions on the methodological level: the incorporation of social analysis into theological reflection and the perspective of the poor as the theological locus—the "place from which" the focus of theology ought to be determined.[2]

While certain basic theological themes monopolized attention in the initial years and achieved considerable development (God, Christ, church, pastoral theology, spirituality), specific moral themes and fundamental moral theory underwent comparatively minor development, walking in the shadow of and in dependency on the other theological areas. After a logical period of growth and consolidation, we have been able to say for some years now, without exaggeration, that moral theological reflection in Latin America has attained its majority; it has attained a level of expression that merits attention.[3]

The intent of the present chapter is to lay out, in synthetic fashion, the genesis, development, content, and principal contributions of the current of thought known as the theology of liberation in the area of fundamental moral theory.

I. HISTORICAL APPROACH

1. General Considerations

Many regard theology as a kind of mannikin in the concert of the sciences. It rarely has the floor and is relegated to the limbo of "metaphysics" by those who have regard only for empirically verifiable data. To them, theology is an imposter among the sciences, whose advance has been mistrusted for centuries.

What has occurred in Latin America over approximately the last three decades shows that reality is not as simple as this generalization would have it. Theology, theologians, and their work are no strangers to reality; rather, through Christian communities of men and women profoundly committed to their peoples, theology has come to be one of the most important factors contributing to the historical process of transformation of that same reality throughout Latin America.

At the same time, this mutual bond between theology and historical context has brought out the pertinency of theology as a comprehensive field of knowledge. In the ensemble of the disciplines that scientifically study and analyze particular sectors of reality, the presence of comprehensive approaches is also needed to help in a synthesis of the world, the human being, and history. Hence the ever more urgent appeal to the ethical universe emerging from cultural, social, popular, and political frameworks. Although in theory ethics enjoys a frank autonomy in regard to theology, the ethical motivations of flesh-and-blood Christians are incomprehensible without a reference, often only implicit, to their theological world view.

This aspect has been set in bold relief by the theology of liberation. It is no exaggeration to state that both in its execution and in its methodology it is the "most moral" of all the theologies. After all, on one hand it requires the theologians to make a commitment to do their reflecting from the locus of their actual Christian life; at the same time, its methodology posits praxis as the point of departure and arrival of the hermeneutic circle.

Consequently, we are dealing with a theology whose ethical connotations are substantive, not merely peripheral derivatives.

2. Genesis and Development of Liberation Ethics

What we have said above evinces the close connection between the theology of liberation and ethics. As we know very well, in scripture and in classic theology, from the Fathers of the Church to scholasticism, theological questions always have their ethical dimension. The theological question and answer (who God is) is inseparable from the moral question (what to do).

Here the pioneer work, and the most important in Latin American theology, is Gustavo Gutiérrez's classic *A Theology of Liberation*.[4] Its way of conceiving and articulating theology and the theologian's task is basically identical not only with that of authors like Bartolomé de las Casas, but also with the works of more academic authors, such as Vitoria or Soto. In all of these writers we find a fluid integration of the questions emerging from daily life with the Bible, the contributions of the human sciences and disciplines, spirituality, morality, and so on.

This fact, which obliges us to regard the classic theologians as representatives of both dogmatic and moral theology, was variously evaluated in the case of liberation theology. Some saw in the latter a certain amount of good will, surely, but an undue confusion between theology and morality.[5] Others preferred to interpret it as a simple ethical reductionism: liberation theology was only a point to be made in a chapter on social morality.[6]

At issue, however, in those early attempts at a systematization of Latin American liberation theology was the reassertion of the intimate bond between theology and morality. The second step was the task of filling the holes in systematic presentations of fundamental moral theory.

The first intuitions sketched in this area by Juan Luis Segundo and H. C. de Lima Vaz had few repercussions. Then came Medellín, with its sudden, powerful impulse for a period of fertile creativity and a dynamism both pastoral and theological. Obviously Medellín offered no systematic treatment of ethics, let alone of fundamental moral theory, any more than did Vatican II. Nevertheless, its methodology and content constitute an ethical reading of Latin American reality from the perspective of an integral liberation and from a point of departure in a preference for the poor.[7] The dominant tone of its texts, however, is eminently in the line of a pastoral theology.

Specific reflection in the area of moral theology begins to appear in the early works of certain authors like Bernardino Leers and J. Snoek, who stand out as maintaining a dedication to moral theology in their later work as well. They devoted most of their attention to teaching, but also did research and publishing.[8] In the area of moral philosophy, the work of Argentineans Enrique Dussell and Juan Carlos Scannone is the most important.

The following years saw the appearance of the work of Brazilian moralists Antonio Moser and M. F. dos Anjos, and Colombian A. Múnera. In moral philosophy, again in Colombia, the important name is L. J. González. What most consolidated and reinforced the work of Latin American moralists, however, were the Meetings of Professors of Moral Theology of Brazil, which culminated in 1987 in the First Latin American Congress of Moral Theology. The congress saw the presentation of the first two volumes of the collection *Teología Moral en América Latina*, and the official inauguration of the Alfonsianum Institute of Moral Theology, with its academic activity from 1988 onward.

The publication of the Acts of the congress[9] contains the most important contributions and names in moral theology in Latin America. The new authors who have been publishing significant works in recent years are T. Mifsud in Chile, Francisco Moreno Rejón in Peru, and E. Bonnín in Mexico.

Despite differences and nuances, it may be asserted that the great majority of the moral theologians of Latin America share the intuitions, methodology, and basic postulates of the theology of liberation. Furthermore, there is a spirit of ecclesial communion and teamwork among them; an explicit consciousness of being part of a confluence of converging currents.

To synthesize: We find ourselves with data evincing not only a constant growth in Latin American moral theology, but a consolidation and a maturity in the development and expression of its propositions. These data include:

1. In the area of publications there are numerous articles and books in moral theory. Salient among these are the above-mentioned collection, *Teología Moral en América Latina*, along with *Moral de discernimiento,* the first manual of moral theology composed by a Latin American moralist.[10]

2. In the field of research and instruction, the Institute of Moral Theology of São Paulo and the Association of Professors of Moral Theology of Brazil are the principal vehicles of the work of our moralists, through their annual meetings and their congresses at the subcontinental level.

These elements, the most readily quantifiable ones, only serve to show that moral theology in Latin America has come of age. They are evidence, on the one hand, of the magnitude and urgency of the ethical problems posed by Latin American reality, and on the other, of the sensitivity of certain Christian communities, which demand of their theologians a formulated, systematic response to the challenges of that reality.

II. FEATURES OF FUNDAMENTAL MORAL THEORY IN LIBERATION ETHICS

In terms of the necessary bonding and mutual reference between theology and ethics, which, as we have indicated above, liberation theology especially emphasizes, it is only logical that the central aspects of liberation theology should be reflected in the questions and answers proposed by its ethics. In making explicit its theological component, moral theology is only taking on and developing in a specific area the common basic traits it shares with the other theological disciplines. Hence the first step of this part of theology is to focus attention on these general features, and then to move on to a treatment of the particular characteristics of liberation ethics.

1. Liberation Theology and Ethics: Basic Elements

Despite its familiarity, it is proper to recall Gutiérrez's formulation of the essential notes of the theology of liberation: "In the theology of liberation, two central intuitions, besides being chronologically first, have always been its vertebrae: its theological method, and the perspective of the poor.[11]

Here we have, altogether neatly and authoritatively formulated, what has been from the outset the spinal column, as it were, the articulating axis, upon which all theological reflection along the lines of liberation necessarily turn. According to the same author, these two primary intuitions are inseparable; together they constitute the principal contribution and commanding feature of this theological current. Hence the necessity of referring to the method proposed and developed by liberation theology as a demand of scientific rigor, and to the perspective of the poor as governing outlook of the sense of a theological proposition.[12] The two aspects are mutually conditioning and reinforcing.

The Method of Moral Theology

To assert that theology, or utterance upon God, is a "second moment" implies that there is a "first moment," antecedent to all theological formulation, consisting in the silent language of prayer and Christian commitment. When all is said and done, methodology, as understood by the theology of liberation, sinks its roots in the soil of spirituality. This implies no neglect of the requirements of methodological rigor. It only sets in relief certain prerequisites, which it is necessary to render explicit.[13]

The first demand of the methodology of moral theology, then, is that substantive part of the theological undertaking that is the militant, believing, and ecclesial character of the theologian.[14] Despite the necessity of these requirements, they are insufficient to guarantee the validity of a theological method. Also required, logically enough, is an articulation of the various mediations shaping a particular way of doing theology.

In the concrete case of liberation ethics, an appropriate integration of the contributions of the socioanalytic mediation, the philosophico-metaphysical mediation, and the hermeneutico-theological mediation is required.

Recourse to the social sciences provides a better, more critical knowledge not only of social phenomena themselves, but of the structures of these phenomena, and thereby a more precise perception of the challenges posed by reality to the reflection of moral theology. There is no question, of course, of reducing theology or moral theory to the data of social analysis. It is only a matter of recognizing that the social sciences provide theology with some of its *raw material*—certain data that must be subjected to theological processing.

Philosophical rationality offers theology a comprehensive view of reality, the human being, history, and the world that has always been regarded as an integral part of the theological universe. Hence the insistence of liberation theologians on a recourse to philosophy. This insistence came later, however, and is less emphatic.[15]

In turn, the *hermeneutico-theological mediation* is the defining element of the theological status of any reflection. Here the primacy belongs to scripture, as font of theology and continuous challenge to Christianity and the theologian. Once again we find ourselves dealing with the connection between theological language (theory) and Christian practice (praxis). In moral theology, these converge in a special way; it is not that orthopraxis is the criterion of orthodoxy, but the former does function as a touchstone of the latter.

We are dealing, then, with a methodology that integrates various rationalities in order thereby to arrive at moral *ratio* or reason. Reality, and praxis as a part of that reality, having been read by the social sciences (socioanalytic mediation), are interpreted by philosophical rationality (philosophico-metaphysical mediation) and reflected upon in the light of faith (hermeneutico-theological mediation) until they finally propose certain moral criteria and exigencies that shape the ethics of liberation.

Perspective of the Poor

The other vertebral characteristic of liberation theology and ethics is that it adopts the viewpoint of the poor in order to mold its content. All theology, intentionally or not, explicitly or not, is a historically, socially, and geographically situated cognition. Its expressions are formulated in a precise context and have an interlocutor to whose demands they attempt to respond.[16]

Liberation ethics expressly identifies the locus from which it is developed, that is, its point of view, its situation, and even its interlocutor. In other words, it takes its contextual position explicitly. This is what is meant by the expression *perspective of the poor.* Reality is explicitly observed from the locus of the poor, and with the eyes of the poor. The concrete interests of the immense majority of poor are adopted, and an attempt is made to respond to the demands of a God who has revealed a preferential love for the poor.

We are not, of course, advocating moral relativism. We are merely adopting the datum that all thought is a matter of thinking in a situation. As Bernard Häring wrote in his pioneer work of renewal in moral theology, theology "proclaims *eternal truth*, but for *its* time. It must therefore *x-ray the problems and topics of its time* under the light of eternity."[17]

Summing up: From the concrete situation of Latin America a formulation of an ethics in a liberation key implies that it will be formulated:

1. *From the underside of history* and the world: from among the losers of history, from within the invaded cultures, from dependent countries without genuine autonomy and suffering the manifold limitations that all of this implies.

2. *From the outskirts of society*, where the victims of all manner of oppression live, the ones who "don't count" — the ones whose faces reflect "the suffering features of Christ the Lord" (Puebla Final Document, no. 31).

3. *From among the masses of an oppressed, believing people*: it cannot be a matter of indifference to moral theology that the majority of Christians and humanity live in conditions of inhuman poverty.

These, then, are the coordinates that determine what has been called the perspective of the poor. Now, the explicit adoption of this perspective entails as a primary consequence an incorporation of the option for the poor (an existential, not a theoretical option, but one having inescapable ethical repercussions) into the orbit of systematic formulation. It means positing the poor as the *preferential interlocutor* of reflection in moral theology and redefining the content of that theology's propositions.

Surely we have here the roots of a basic difference from what is called a new moral theory, one whose interlocutor is the person sprung from modernity, the person whose challenges are those of a cultural universe marked by secularization and who attempts to respond plausibly to the problems posed by a society of affluence.

For this open, progressive moral theory, the basic categories are the *person* and personal autonomy, in function of the current increase of the predominance of subjectivism in the various manifestations of thought, politics, and behavior in the societies of the highly developed countries.

For its part, liberation ethics posits as the category of reference of its questions and propositions the *nonperson* — persons as they really exist: the poor. The condition of "poor" is not an adjectival one, but a manner of being person.

Ultimately, the concern of the former current of moral theology is to develop an "ethics at the service of the human being," which will seek to respond to the question of *how to be good in this society*, a society that of course might be improved. Liberation ethics, on the other hand, attempts to build a response, as provisional as the question is complex, to the question of *how to be good by making this society good*, that is, by transforming it, with a view to a full, integral liberation.[18]

2. Characteristics of Liberation Ethics

We have seen the basic features of liberation ethics: the use of a particular method in moral theology, the adoption of a perspective that will shape this meaning, and the option for the poor and their world as interlocutors, which gives a particular slant to its questions and propositions. But the fundamental moral theory developed by liberation ethics presents other notes that characterize it, as well. For purposes of a synthesized presentation, we shall group them under three rubrics: (1) their articulation as a *moral model* centering on the key concept of *liberation*; (2) the systematization of an ethics of a clearly Christian stamp that binds it closely to *spirituality*; and (3) their *pastoral accent*, the property of a reflection cut to the pattern of the evangelizing task of the moralist rather than to that of the world of academe.[19]

Liberation Ethics as Moral Model

As may be gathered from the name itself, liberation ethics, in continuity and harmony with the postulates of liberation theology, erects this category, liberation, precisely into the key concept of its structure as moral model. The consistency of the epistemological status of this reflection proceeds from an adequate comprehension of the term *liberation* and its various meanings.

An ethical reading of our situation, from a starting point in the dialectical tension between oppression and liberation, the twin poles of the reality of that situation, presents three levels of meaning or signification:

1. On the *economic, social, and political plane*, an ethical reading of our situation refers to the peoples and social sectors that aspire to be liberated from oppressive structures and systems.

2. On the level of *concrete utopian signification*, it refers to the human being as sovereign of history, struggling to control his and her own destiny and in search of the utopia of the new person in a new world.

3. In the *theological* dimension of *redemption and salvation*, it points to Christ the Savior, who redeems and delivers the human being from sin, the radical alienation that is the origin of all oppression and injustice.

These three planes or levels of meaning are to be understood not as juxtaposed or chronologically successive, but as corresponding to three constitutive, interdependent dimensions of a single, complex process.[20]

To each of these levels corresponds an epistemologically distinct rationality. The social sciences permit a critical knowledge of reality, and enable the ethician to perceive the structural dimension of macro-moral questions.

Philosophical rationality finds in the metaphysics of otherness the foundation of a normative ethical *ratio*; and theological reflection, as a discourse in the light of faith, resituates moral problems. In a Christian perspective, ethical matters are not merely human; God is at stake in them.

This affords a clearer understanding of the correspondence obtaining between the conception of the category of liberation as key concept of an ethical model, and the proposition of a moral methodology whose socioanalytic, philosophical, and theological mediations enable the moralist to approach the various dimensions of an object of study consisting of a complex, multifaceted reality.

Another consequence of the inseparability of the three levels just cited is the inescapable reference of the category of liberation, understood in a Christian key, to God and Christ. This sets in relief the markedly *theo*-logical and *christo*-logical components of moral thinking as basic ones for liberation ethics. Accordingly, *sin*, with all of its personal, social, and structural consequences and manifestations, is a permanent object of attention on the part of the theology of liberation—not because the goal is a moral theory centered on sin, but because liberation theology's moral thinking is centered on Christ as savior and liberator, and there is no way to refer to his salvific deed without emphasizing that from which he delivers us.[21]

Another aspect that emerges from the model of liberation ethics is its *utopian dimension*. The utopian, by virtue of its projection into the future, bears a criticism of the currently established order along with the proposal to construct an alternative order. The utopian and the ethical converge in a twofold function: criticism and dynamization. On the one hand, they call into question the inadmissible aspects of reality; on the other, they push and pull reality in the direction of its ideal. Ethics has a utopian potential, and the utopia of full liberation poses inescapable moral demands.

Spirituality

An ethics that would be something more than a code of good behavior must accentuate its theological condition, and here we encounter the close ties that obtain among the various theological disciplines. Furthermore, a methodological presupposition of the theology of liberation is the theologian's commitment and Christian praxis. After all, the preferential option for the poor is not a mere theoretical category of theological reflection; before all else it is a spiritual experience of encounter with the Lord in service to the poor. Consequently, a liberation ethics posed from the perspective of the poor implies a spiritual motivation as a prerequisite to its systematic elaboration.

The experience of the following of Christ, of living "according to the Spirit," gives rise to an ethics of discipleship that calls for an organic, critical formulation. Moral theology in a liberation key comes forward at once as a lived spirituality and as a theological discipline, that is, as a *spiritual wisdom* and as a *rational knowledge*.[22]

Pastoral Accent

A salient note in liberation theology and ethics is rooted in their effort to reconcile the requirements of a theoretical, academic order with a pastoral projection. Thus, we are dealing with a moral theology that, far from repeating timeless, ahistorical principles, presents itself as a reflection vigorously involved with the people's daily experience.

When all is said and done, theology is only a ministry, an ecclesial service to the unfolding of the task of evangelization. To proclaim the need for conversion and to announce the Good News to the poor are the core both of the systematization of theological ethics and of pastoral praxis.[23] We find a clear reflection of this in the attention devoted to the study of the *popular ethos*, and more concretely, to the relationships between Christian ethics and popular piety.

Hence too the frequent appearance—an outcome of the concert of several of the traits indicated—of the use of a rather *narrative ethical language*, one more concerned with transmitting an experience than in casting it in academic molds.[24]

In synthesis, it may be said that the fundamental moral theory posited by the ethics of liberation combines the following traits:

1. It adopts the core intuitions and categories of the theology of liberation in order to shape an ethical model.

2. Its theological method has its point of departure in reality, in order that its reflection may be pertinent first and foremost to this reality.

3. It integrates into its method the rationality of the social and human sciences, philosophy, and theology.

4. It conceives moral theory within the unity of theological science, which reinforces its identity as moral theology.

5. It proposes an ethics of praxis that brings out the bond of moral theory with spirituality and pastoral theology.

6. It outlines a utopian, prophetical ethics, which, sinking its roots deep in its biblical inspiration, maintains the hope that a better world is concretely possible, and that consequently the realization of that world is a task to be taken up not only by believers, but by all persons of good will.

7. It insists on the ethical primacy of charity, which holds as its priority an effective love for the poor and their cause as the criterion of morality.

—Translated by Robert R. Barr

NOTES

1. For a comparative study of the positions taken with respect to fundamental moral theory in the most important manuals see R. Gallagher, "Fundamental Moral Theology 1975-1979: A Bulletin-Analysis of Some Significant Writings Examined from a Methodological Stance," *Studia Moralia* 18 (1980): 147-92.

2. See Roberto Oliveros, *Liberación y teología: Génesis y crecimiento de una reflexión (1966-1976)* (Lima, 1977); and Juan Ramos Regidor, *Jesús y el despertar de los oprimidos* (Salamanca, 1984).

3. For a study of the emergence, evaluation, and propositions of fundamental moral theory in Latin American theology, see Francisco Moreno Rejón, *Teología moral desde los pobres: La moral en la reflexión teológica desde América latina* (Madrid, 1986); English trans., *Moral Theology from the Poor: Moral Challenges of the Theology of Liberation* (Quezon City, Philippines: Claretian Publications, 1988).

4. Gustavo Gutiérrez, *A Theology of Liberation: History, Politics and Salvation*, trans. and ed. Caridad Inda and John Eagleson (Maryknoll, N.Y.: Orbis Books, 1973; revised edition, 1988).

5. M. Vidal, agreeing with A. Fierro's position, spoke of the "confused epistemological status of theological ethics." For Vidal, "the peculiar function of theological ethics has been usurped by liberation theology as a whole." See M. Vidal,

"La autonomía como fundamento de la moral y la ética de la liberación," *Concilium* 192 (1984), p. 291.

6. Many critics of liberation theology, holding Daniélou's well-known position, think to invalidate liberation theology on the grounds that it is simply the "social question" all over again, being raised this time by theologians of the underdeveloped countries.

7. The documents of Medellín continue to be rather broadly studied and analyzed. For that synod's contributions in the area of moral theory, see Francisco Moreno Rejón, "La teología moral en América Latina a partir de Medellín," in José Dammert, et al., *Irrupción y caminar de la Iglesia de los pobres: Presencia de Medellín* (Lima, 1989), pp. 247-69.

8. To the names of Snoek and Leers must be added those of Hugo Assmann, Pinto de Oliveira, J. B. Libânio, G. Giménez, J. Aldunate, José Porfirio Miranda, Rubem Alves. Julio de Santa Ana, and José Míguez Bonino. For a reasonably complete bibliography of their various works see Francisco Moreno Rejón, "Información bibliográfica sobre la moral fundamental desde América latina," *Moralia* 7 (1985): 213-31.

9. Cf. M. Fabri dos Anjos, ed., *Temas latinoamericanos de ética* (São Paulo, 1988). For a chronicle of the congress, together with a review of the papers presented, see Francisco Moreno Rejón, "Notas a propósito de un Congreso y un libro," *Páginas* 94 (1989), pp. 103-11.

10. See T. Mifsud, *Moral de discernimiento* (Santiago de Chile, 1983-87). For the publications in question, besides the lists published in the *Moralia* in 1985 and 1987, see Francisco Moreno Rejón, *Bibliografía latinoamericana sobre moral* (Lima, 1989). Nevertheless, there are those who, through ignorance, or in a superficial spirit of division (which, incidentally, ill conceals its disdain for the people, the church, and Latin American theologians), are willing to grant the status of theologian only to three or four better-known figures. Their refusal to include any moral theologian serves to demonstrate their contempt for any of the work being done in Latin America in the area of moral theology.

11. Gustavo Gutiérrez, *Teología desde el reverso de la historia* (Lima, 1977), p. 42.

12. Both of these central questions in liberation theology, that of method and that of the poor, will be developed in their appropriate places in this work. The present chapter approaches them only from the specific angle of their impact on the formulation of fundamental moral theory.

13. Gutiérrez, once more, is the author who has formulated the synthesis most trenchantly: "Our methodology is our spirituality." See Gustavo Gutiérrez *The Power of the Poor in History: Selected Writings*, trans. Robert R. Barr (Maryknoll, N.Y.: Orbis Books, 1983).

In turn, another author, cautious lest theology be transformed into a system of knowledge that could easily escape the discipline of a critical rigor, recognizes that theological practice presupposes a "pistic experience" and an "agapic practice"— "something which, on the other hand, belongs to the very tradition of theology" (Clodovis Boff, *Theology and Praxis: Epistemological Foundations*, trans. Robert R. Barr [Maryknoll, N.Y.: Orbis Books, 1987], p. 100).

14. Cf. Johann Baptist Metz, "Un nuevo modo de hacer teología: tres breves tesis," in Gregory Baum, et al., *Vida y reflexión* (Lima, 1983), and his excellent considerations on the subject of theology. For a more extensive development of this

point, see Francisco Moreno Rejón, "Aportes metodológicos de la reflexión latinoamericana a la teología moral," *Moralia* 7 (1985): 167-68, with bibliography.

15. Two authors whose influence is more evident on the postulates of liberation
ethics are Xavier Zubiri, with his efforts to link metaphysics and reality, and E.
Lévinas, with his insistence on regarding the "other," or more precisely the "face"
of the other, as the origin of all ethics and all philosophy.

16. This is what V. Jankélevitch was referring to when he wrote: "One must
constantly stipulate and specify the irrational clause of the viewpoint" (V. Jankélevitch, *La paradoja de la moral* [Barcelona, 1983], p. 226). This "clause" may appear
to be a circumstantial, and thereby negligible, detail; yet it "inverts all value judgments, and is morally decisive" (ibid.).

17. See Bernard Häring, *The Law of Christ* (Westminster, Md.: Newman Press,
1961-63).

18. Although this is not the place to develop this in more detail, it is in order
to observe that these respective basic stances when it comes to fundamental moral
theory have profound repercussions in the area of concrete morality, both at the
moment of the assignment of priority to certain problems rather than others, and
in the actual treatment of these problems once selected. The basic stance of a
Christian ethics that makes the life of the poor its criterion of morality impinges
upon the normative guidelines of that ethics. See Francisco Moreno Rejón, *Salvar
la vida de los pobres: Aportes a la teología moral* (Lima, 1986), pp. 14-25.

An open confrontation occurred between the two tendencies indicated in our
text at the Congress of Redemptorist Moralists held at Aylmer, in Canada, in June
1989. The papers presented there appear in the periodicals *Studia Moralia* and
Moralia. For the moment, we need only notice the titles of the presentations by
Spanish moralist M. Vidal, "Moral Theology as Service to the Cause of the Human
Being," and Brazilian M. Fabri dos Anjos, "Option for the Poor and Doing Moral
Theology." As the titles are sufficiently illustrative for our purposes, we shall dis-
pense with any commentary.

19. A more extensive exposition of the characteristics of fundamental moral
theory in liberation ethics can be found in Moreno Rejón, *Teología moral desde los
pobres*, pp. 73-158.

20. The Medellín document correctly and perspicaciously discerned that "we are
on the threshold of a new era in the history of our continent," an era characterized
by "aspirations for total emancipation, for liberation from every servitude, for personal maturation and collective integration," which lead to an "encounter with Him
who ratifies, purifies, and deepens the values achieved by human effort."

In turn, the Puebla Document synthesizes the same notion when it speaks of
liberation in terms of "three inseparable planes: our relationship to the world as
its master, to other persons as brothers or sisters, and to God as God's children"
(Puebla Final Document, no. 322).

21. The subjects of sin and utopia are important enough to warrant their respective specific treatments in the present collection. The reader may also profitably
consult Antonio Moser, "O pecado social en clave latinoamericana," in *Temas
latinoamericanos de ética*, ed. Fabri dos Anjos, pp. 63-91. For two brilliant examples
of utopias formulated in our times, see Martin Luther King, Jr., *The Trumpet of
Conscience* (London, 1962); and Gabriel García Márquez, "La soledad de América
Latina," *Páginas* 51 (1983), pp. 26-28.

22. In the matter of the relationship between moral theory and spirituality, see

Pablo Richard, "La ética como espiritualidad liberadora en la realidad eclesial de América Latina," *Moralia* 4 (1982): 101-14.

23. Actually, the markedly pastoral character of liberation ethics is not inconsistent with the fact that the majority of moralists of this current are not "professional" theologians, but individuals who join in their own lives a dedication to pastoral practice and theology.

24. A good example of this can be seen in Bernardino Leers, *Jeito Brasileiro e norma absoluta* (Petrópolis, Brazil, 1982).

11

Women and the Theology of Liberation

ANA MARÍA TEPEDINO
MARGARIDA L. RIBEIRO BRANDÃO

In order to approach the subject of woman in the light of faith, from a starting point in women's concrete experience, and in women's own language, we must keep in mind the context in which women find themselves today in society and in the church.

The Christian women of Latin America are beginning to perceive the extraordinary power for transformation of which they are the vessels. In founding mothers' clubs, child care centers, and community centers, in participating actively in base communities and mutual aid associations, in forming feminist movements, in demanding their civil rights, in valiantly searching for their children and grandchildren who have been "disappeared" in the political repression, in struggling for the conquest of the land, the Christian women of Latin America are discovering their own identity and the strength that vibrates in their seeming fragility. They discover this strength in practice—moved by an experience of God, who infuses them with the courage and hope they need to face life's challenges. The God on whom Jesus called, a God who is a community of love, summons these women to the practice of justice—that concrete love that leads them to feel in their very flesh the structures of injustice which must be transformed (cf. John 1:4, 4:8, 13:34; Luke 10:25-37, Lev. 19:18). From within the reality of their lives, they reread the Bible from their own viewpoint as woman, as they go in quest of a hermeneutics that will enable them to join their praxis and their theory in the perspective of the Reign of God. Women's power of transformation still encounters obstacles when it comes to the manifestation of all its potential, but it is beginning to gain its own space.

"Woman" is not an abstract entity. Women do not live in isolation from others, but do have a special way of relating to others. The discovery of women's relational dimension—a deep bonding with life—confers a special capacity for solidarity in the struggle for transformation, justice, and peace. Women see with different eyes the groups and communities to which they belong, and they open themselves to the world when they emerge from the private sphere in which they have been restricted in time and space—the sphere that encloses the roles of wife and mother in family life, the place customarily reserved to her by a patriarchal culture.

In recent years the topic of woman has gained currency in the social sciences, politics, religion, society, and the church. This phenomenon began to emerge in the 1960s. This is not to say that women had always been entirely confined to the domestic sphere. There have always been women—a few—who marched in the vanguard, especially beginning in the past century. And their voices were heard. But they were isolated voices.

I. BROKEN SILENCE

The number of outstanding women has increased noticeably in the last decades as women strive to break with the conditions of unjust structures, which reduce them to a "culture of silence." It is precisely their raised consciousness, their enhanced awareness of this injustice, that leads them to burst through the barriers imposed upon them and bravely confront all difficulties in order to have "voice and vote"—to make actual use of the strength for transformation that they carry within them. This strength gives them the courage to discover themselves—in their characteristic openness to others and in the struggle for peace, justice, and liberation. In their faith experience Latin American women situate the liberation of women within the process of the concrete economic, political, and social liberation of Latin America. They learn that the liberation of the marginalized is a daily victory, and a dynamic, creative process initiated by themselves. This means that liberation must necessarily pass by way of the intimacy of the daily affective life. The oppression that weighs most heavily on women is the oppression that occurs in their most intimate bond, that of their relationship with men. Thus, woman's liberation means a crisis for the feminine image inculcated in them by a patriarchal culture. Woman's liberation initiates a progressive quest for a new personhood, which cannot be lacking in the dimension of gratuity and affectivity. The biblical texts most forcefully expressing female oppression show woman silenced or silent before the violence done them (cf. 2 Sam. 13:13, Judg. 19:1-30). The purpose of our meditation on these texts from women's perspective is to find in the Bible a memory of the past that will help women transform the present and build the future.[1]

What is new in these outstanding women of today is that behind each of them there is a group or community that means to be heard. Women speak for themselves individually, of course, but each of them also speaks in the name of their community. This elevation of their self-awareness is an indispensable initial step if they are to put their relational character to work in search of a new future marked by justice and love. By way of support, they have the base communities, the neighborhood associations, the mothers' clubs, working women, prostitutes, black women, feminist groups, and the emergence of a feminist theology that finds in the theology of liberation its nearest interlocutor. Women's struggle to make themselves heard is not detached from their dedication to the battle for civil rights; their efforts are not for themselves alone, but for all who are deprived of their most basic rights, all who struggle to realize themselves as free human beings created in the image and likeness of God.

Bridging the gap between silence and women's new found visibility has been an object of reflection on the part of many female theologians of the Christian churches, as well as of many other female pastoral ministers. While their numbers are still insignificant, women do hold some positions of leadership in ecclesial and ecumenical entities. But they find difficulty in being heard, and in developing a distinct manner of acting.[2] Women want to be heard, want to articulate their discourse themselves. Uttering words is not the point — speaking for the sake of speaking. Women are moved by the desire to assert themselves as women, as subjects and not as objects, and above all as persons in relationship with others, women and men, in reciprocity and equality of rights. Women's word springs from life and returns enriched by the dialogue of mutual apprenticeship.

The testimony of Raimunda Gomes da Silva (of the Bico do Papagaio region of Brazil), a woman of the rain forest who learned to read by reading the Bible, serves as an example of the life experiences that women exchange with one another. She states, "Women have made up their minds to take the lead." She says this by way of explaining her attitude among working women and her commitment to bear witness to what she has seen and continues to see in the struggle for the land, which means martyrdom for so many of its activists. "Go out and get heard," she says, explaining her decision to testify to all that she has seen. She battles to be heard because she has something to say, and she says it in the frank, direct manner of the woman of the hinterland: "I haven't talked to anybody yet who wouldn't pay attention to me!"[3]

Countless testimonials could be adduced of poor women who have spoken up before others with the feeling of being persons, experiencing their dignity as human persons — persons who have discovered their female identity in the common struggle for the liberation of all of the oppressed.

II. WOMAN AS PERSON

It is the dialectic of listening and being listened to that governs the reflection developed by women concerning the female condition. The dialectic in question is that of an ability to listen to the voice of the other, the outcast, the one who asks for justice. Breaking silence, women become visible. Nor is this visibility a passive one — the visibility of a mere object. It is a creative, active visibility. In this kind of visibility, women come forward as subjects — as responsible, capable, and participating persons. In the biblical and Christian perspective, attention to the word is the necessary condition for persons being seen and held in account with all of their dignity (cf. Deut. 26:7). The heart, the sensitivity of a person, the whole person in her integrity, is summoned to be present in her entirety in the practical realization of what Jesus indicates when he asks, "Are your minds completely blinded? Have you eyes but no sight? Ears but no hearing?" (Mark 8:17-18; cf. Jer. 5:21, Isa. 6:10).

Christian women, when they are listened to in their reflections on their own condition, make no attempt to burden men with the whole weight of responsibility for the injustices committed against women. Nor do women regard men as an insuperable obstacle to their liberation. Instead, women are bent on a courageous examination of the preconceptions and stereotypes inculcated through social and cultural structures that place women in a position of inferiority through the assimilation of a masculinity marked by domination, *machismo* and violence, sexual aggressiveness and self-indulgence.[4] Women's liberation involves a reciprocal redefinition of what it means to be female and male.

In rediscovering themselves as persons, women are redefining the sense of the alternatives customarily presented to them in the Christian perspective. To be a person means to be open to self-realization, which is never wrought in isolation or disconnection from human history. Women and men as persons have been made in order to live in a reciprocal relationship, open to one another in their common equality before God, called to a life of communion and solidarity in the world that God has given them to tend and preserve (cf. Gen. 1:27-28, Gal. 3:28).

III. FROM PERSON TO COMMUNITY

Women are rediscovering that motherhood is more than procreation. It is creation, as well—in the sense of a creativity marked by resistance, and by gradual adaptation to new situations. Motherhood involves body, reception, space, service to another, solidarity, participation. It requires a unique nearness to the child the woman is about to deliver to the world. This openness to her offspring establishes her in solidarity with other mothers and readies her to be present in all places in which shared life is born. From the needs of their offspring, from their experience as mothers, women, especially poor women, move to the experience of community, burst the confining limits of their domestic tasks, and discover themselves as creators of history. The service to the community in which they find themselves represents both continuity with and breach with their condition as mothers. It is a service which, as work performed by women on behalf of the offspring to whom they tenderly offer the first experience of human nearness, represents women's deep commitment to the mystery of life. It is a service that arouses them to toil, in solidarity with the community to which they naturally belong or in which they share, not as mothers but as human persons, open to others in virtue of their love for God.

Women feel God's presence in a particular way. From the inmost depths of their being, body, and life experience—which may be or have been chaos, blind numbness, and confusion—springs the certitude that they are loved by God just as they are. This certitude floods women with the grace to comprehend the ultimate meaning of love for God and neighbor. Women joyfully proclaim this presence of God in songs and poetry, after the example of the prophetesses of the Old Testament—Miriam, Deborah, Judith, Anna, and Mary. Like Mary Magdalen and the other women (cf. Mark 16:1, Luke 24:9, John 20:18, Matt. 28:10), they hasten to testify to their experience of the resurrection. The poetry of the prophetess lives yet today, on the lips of the women of the communities:

One day the woman cried,
"I am a warrior!"

And the echo of her voice resounded
beyond the borders.

"I am woman: mother and warrior!
My confines are no longer hearth and home.
I am called Queen of the Hearth:
yet I am greater than ocean and sea.
I emerged—not yet had the dawn ascended to the sky—
and I went to the sepulcher of my people—
like Magdalen one day—
and I saw: Here was a life to proclaim!
And my confines were hearth and home no more.

"I am a mother: I am life.
I am a wife: I am understanding.
I am a woman: I am suffering.
I am a people, I am love: annunciation.
Where someone lies fallen, that one I raise up.
Where someone lies dead, someone sick,
someone weeping—I am a warrior!

"I am a bird: I sing!

"I lift my people's head, and lead them out of slavery.
My name is: Liberation.
I am peace, I am hope.
I am a rainbow in this world of injustice.
I am equality . . .
My name is Sister and Brother.

"I am called: The People.
I am humanity.

"Ever so easily shall you find me:
For I am no longer only in the home!
I am in the fray now: I am a warrior,

I am black, I am poor,
I am old, I am widowed,
and all but illiterate.
But you can find me, ever so easily:
in the battle,
in the people's movement.

"Everyone knows me —
I am gladness and love overflowing.
I am all that is good, all that we dream of, all that is heaven.

"Me?
I am only
María Miguel."[5]

Women grasp by their own experience that the offspring they engender belong to themselves, their father, society, the world, and God. Motherhood has more than biological or procreative characteristics; its traits are essentially creative of new life, which confers on it a social dimension transcending the narrow confines of the woman-female relation. This calls for a rediscovery of the meaning of woman's body not as object of sin or cause of sin, but in its capacity to redeem the human body in its totality — man and woman — by fighting for its resurrection, its life. In the perspective of the Reign, then, this redemption of the body, of the "flesh" from which we have been formed, converges with a unitary anthropology of equality that can re-create man and woman in the image of God and God in the image of man and woman (cf. John 1:14, Gen. 1:27).[6] There is a whole theology implicit in the exchange of experience that takes place among women; it waits to be made explicit by the women who make of their professional theological task a service to the Reign.

IV. A DIFFERENT MUSIC FOR SINGING OF GOD

As for women's theological enterprise in particular, we women theologians do our thinking from a starting point in our personal experience as theologians. Nor is this experience ours alone. It has been the experience of women doing theology in Brazil since 1985, in a process of dialogue and mutual apprenticeship with other female theologians — with those of the First World, but especially with our Latin American colleagues.

Thus, the theology being developed by women has its roots in concrete experience, especially in the popular sectors; we share "our being and our toiling, our looking and our feeling, our utterance and our silence."[7]

This theology is rooted as well in our experience of God in a life on the "other side" — the side opposite power and domination. The God we experience in daily life is the one ever at the side of the weakest, sustaining them and giving them courage and hope.

A new perception is arising: the liberating fertility of a rereading of the Bible in terms of the female experience of oppression, poverty, resistance, and hope.

We are beginning to hear the echo and resonance of the texts of sacred scripture in the heart of women. Women know the fragility of life, and the need to protect it and care for it. They also have an original viewpoint, which is beginning to express itself in terms of the very viewpoint of God, who, through the Bible, speaks of fullness of life for all human persons.

From these twin starting points, the experience of life and the experience of God, women reread revelation and reality with a view not only to a personal liberation but to a liberation for all the people—a common liberation. A theological reflection that springs from women means to make its voice heard as a service to all the outcast. Therefore it is necessary for women to develop a "militant and combative theology, that is, one which gives them theological and biblical tools to tear out by the roots the sources of their marginalization."[8]

Another point of departure, in close articulation with the other two, might be called the "praxis of tenderness," that is, the quest for new relations between women and men, with youth and the elderly—in a word, among all persons.

In their distinctive way of doing theology, women adopt an integration between scientific rigor and sensitivity, between the experiential datum and scholarly seriousness, which helps overcome the partiality of any theology reduced to speculation with insufficient attention to the Spirit. Women are able to do this because they have never learned to see themselves as compartmentalized. They are too integrated. In the Meeting on Theology in Woman's Perspective held at Buenos Aires in 1985, which was a milestone along the pilgrimage of women theologians in Latin America, it was striking how women strove to join the experience of the home with pastoral commitment and theological reflection.

As theology of liberation from the viewpoint of women, the feminist theological undertaking begins with our concrete experience, seeks to know it through the human and social sciences, and then interprets it in the light of the Bible. We begin with certain basic observations. The Bible is not a neutral book. This is true in two senses.

1. The texts of the Bible, written in various ages and contexts, reflect the socioeconomic, political, and cultural conditions through which the people of Israel passed. Generally speaking, the culture of this people was strongly patriarchal. Theirs was a society guided and governed by men; women were caught in a position inferior to that of males. Further, the biblical texts were written by men. Accordingly, the view of things that these writings offer us is a male view.

2. When the Bible is read a whole, the great axes that underpin it reveal an awareness of a God who takes sides with the poor, the oppressed, and the despised, among whom are multitudes of women. God is a God who hears the cry of the people (cf. Exod. 3:7-10), and who comes to heal not the healthy and perfect, but the weak and sinful (cf. Matt. 9:10-13).

Now, if the Bible is not neutral, then neither may our reading of it be neutral. We must attempt to pierce through the cultural and literary envelope of the texts and read them from the viewpoint of God-with-us (*Em-manu-el*: cf. Isa. 7:14) and the concrete practice of Jesus. Especially, Jesus' behavior toward the women around him becomes a reading key for the interpretation of the texts of the entire Bible. Thus, we men and women, but especially we women, will be able to hear the word of God uttered in women's behalf, even when the text or the readings that have been made of it obscure the Good News of the Lord.[9]

Elsa Tamez, a pioneer in Latin American feminist theology, proposes two methodological steps toward a biblical hermeneutics in the perspective of woman: withdrawal and approach. One "takes one's distance" from the text, hearing it as if for the first time, and concentrating on every word. This procedure allows questions to arise, in function of the presence or absence of particular elements in the text. But this withdrawal must be "impregnated" with the experience of the one executing it—which converts the initial withdrawal into approach, an indispensable condition if the word of scripture is to come to life. In approach, the sorrow and gladness, oppression and struggle, hope and festival contained in the texts help us to discover attitudes for the present. They become a living experience.[10] These two interconnected steps— withdrawal and approach—enable us to find liberative reading keys that transcend a discrimination of women.

The presence of women in the professional exercise of theology, as spiritual advisers to the communities, as theology teachers publishing theological works, moved Paul VI to say, "Theology is another matter when it passes through the heart of a woman."[11]

In their pastoral and Christian experience, the female theologians of Latin America are learning that the option for the poor becomes concrete in the option for poor women—and women today are the poorest of the poor. Women's power for transformation achieves a certain synthesis in these theologians, in their particular way of demonstrating women's resistance for survival, in their creativity in the discovery of a new place for women in society, and in their freedom, which, in the religious sense of the word, means living by and speaking of God.[12]

The expression *feminization of poverty* was coined to describe the composite image of poverty prevailing in North America. That image reflects far more serious situations, surely, throughout the rest of the world. But even in the affluent society of the United States, the composite image of a poor person is female, black, without a high school diploma, unmarried, and with at least two children, one of them under six.[13]

The picture is a true one for Brazil and Latin America, as well. In fact, it is worse: the annual per capita income for poor mothers in the "destitution zone" is less than twenty-five dollars a year (in 15 percent of Brazilian families), and quite a high percentage of women are illiterate or semi-literate. In Brazil, a fatherless household means poverty. Thus, a disproportionate number of poor families, especially at the lowest poverty levels, are single-mother families.[14]

V. PASSION AND COMPASSION

Poverty is a reality of women's very constitution. They are physically overextended. Their bodies are always with others, in their openness to others and to the experience of community.

Women's sensitivity to the pain of others—women's capacity to suffer with, feel with, enter into a solidarity of compassion with others—renders them receptive to the problems of others, to the values of shared generosity, and to the struggle for better living conditions, as well as to the handing on of the faith in the struggle for justice.

Women, who together with men constitute the image of God (cf. Gen. 1:26), express God's quality of tenderness (*ḥeṣed*), the motherly breast (*raḥamim*) of God, God's concern for the children of God who have the most to suffer.[15]

Women do theology with passion. They give themselves completely, passionately, intent on charging abstract concepts with living, existential reality.[16]

The women who followed Jesus as his disciples did the same in the total gift of their lives, in dedication to him and to the mission of furthering the Good News, in a way that the scent of their perfume filled all the earth (cf. John 12:1-8; cf. Matt. 26:13).

VI. WOMEN'S MISSION OF DISCIPLESHIP

Luke's gospel shows us that women's eschatological vocation is that of being disciples. To the woman who cried out, "Blest is the womb that bore you and the breasts that nursed you!" Jesus responded, "Rather . . . blest are they who hear the word of God and keep it" (Luke 11:27-28)—revealing that women's eschatological vocation is discipleship.

Mark, at the close of his gospel (15:40-41), introduces us to various women who had come from Galilee with Jesus, and so had been with him from the outset of his mission, and who had remained faithful to the end, when the male disciples had fled. The women's attitude was to "follow" and to "serve"—theological words for discipleship. Thus Mark presents them as disciples, mentioning by name Mary Magdalen, Mary the mother of James the younger and Joses, and Salome, as if these constituted the closest group, although without forgetting the "many others" who had also come from Galilee to Jerusalem to the cross.

It is interesting to observe that, both in the Bible and in the recent history of our countries, women come forward when the situation becomes most dangerous: Tamar (Gen. 38), Ruth in her widowhood, Judith the warrior, Mary the mother of Jesus (Mark 15:40-41), and the women of the 1970s in Latin America.

John's gospel (4:2-42, 11:4-28, 12:1-8, 20:10-18) shows us four women as disciples: the Samaritan, Martha and Mary of Bethany, and Mary Magdalen. Both the Samaritan and Mary Magdalen are sent forth (another characteristic of discipleship) with the same words with which Jesus sends men in his priestly prayer (cf. John 17:17). Martha of Bethany is presented by John as the spokesperson of her community. To her Jesus confides the greatest revelation of his mission. He has revealed himself to the Samaritan woman as the Messiah; now he explains to Martha what sort of Messiah he is speaking of. "I am the resurrection and the life. . . . Do you believe this?" (John 11:25-26). And Martha's faith response makes her the first Christian theologian: "Yes, Lord, . . . I have come to believe that you are the Messiah, the Son of God: he who is to come into the world" (John 11:27). Just so, joining the christology of the Synoptics to the mission christology proper to John's community, Mary of Bethany demonstrates the praxis of the true disciple: she hears the word of the Master and then places herself in its service, anointing Jesus' feet and thus symbolizing the attitude of *agape*, which must be the attitude of the disciple (cf. John 13:14-15). All of these women followed Jesus, and in his company and community felt themselves well again—recovered, human persons who see their dignity respected, with its whole potential. And in the following of Jesus women have arrived at this experience all through the centuries. This is why they fight to posit tokens of the Reign, to establish signs of community, signs of life.

Women also demonstrate their faith, love, and hope through celebration, through festival. The Bible shows us Miriam (cf. Exod. 15:21), Deborah (cf. Judg. 5:1-31), Judith (Jth. 16:1-6), Anna (cf. 1 Sam. 21:10), and Mary (cf. Luke 1:46-55). Women celebrate their particular experience of God, so intimate and so fulfilling that it cannot but be contagious (cf. John 20:1-10, Luke 24:22, etc.). Often they burst forth in song, as in the citations above.

It is especially difficult to speak of the experience of God when we have only begun to speak. But it is something that fills us with gladness, love, hope, and the confidence we need to keep forging ahead, even when the challenges are immense.

We women, today's Mary Magdalens, want to carry the "message of new life." We are driven by the power for transformation that maintains us. We want to shout to the world that Love is stronger than death, and that with Love we too shall defeat the idols of death that hold sway in society. We cry out in company with our brother theologians in order to bring a new theology to the light of day, thus working shoulder to shoulder with them, "bending our efforts in the Lord" to the building of the new society of which we all dream.

Ivone Gebara concludes her essay "Woman Doing Theology in Latin America" with the following words:

The day will come when all people, lifting their eyes will see the earth shining with brotherhood and sisterhood, mutual appreciation, true complementarity. Men and women will dwell in their houses; men and women will eat the same bread, drink the same wine, and dance together in the brightly lit square, celebrating the bonds uniting humankind.[17]

The Lord, your God, is in your midst,
   a mighty savior;
He will rejoice over you with gladness,
   and renew you in his love,
He will sing joyfully because of you (Zeph. 3:17).

—*Translated by Robert R. Barr*

NOTES

1. Cf. Phyllis Trible, *Texts of Terror* (Philadelphia: Fortress Press, 1984); Elsa Tamez, *Bible of the Oppressed* (Maryknoll, N.Y.: Orbis Books, 1982).

2. Elizabeth Schüssler Fiorenza, Editorial, *Concilium* 182 (1985), pp. ix-xiii. See also M. B. Assad, "When I Was Called: Women in a Changing World," *WCC* (1986), p. 22.

3. Testimonial given at the National Meeting on Theology in Woman's Perspective, Rio de Janeiro, 1986.

4. Cf. the draft pastoral letter of the U.S. Catholic Bishops, "On the Participation of Women in the Mission of the Church" (March 1988); Cora Ferro, "Jesus God, A Path for Latin American Women: Women in a Changing World," *WCC* 22 (1986), pp. 12-13.

5. María Miguel (Comunidad de San José, Itaim, São Paulo), in *Tempo e Presença* (1985), p. 204.

6. Cf. Ivone Gebara, "A mulher: Contribução à teologia moral na América latina," in *Temas latino-americanos de ética* (Santuário Aparecida, 1988), pp. 195-209.

7. Cf. "Final Statement," Latin American Conference on Theology in Woman's Perspective (Buenos Aires, 1985), in Elsa Tamez, ed., *Through Her Eyes* (Maryknoll, N.Y.: Orbis Books, 1989), pp. 150-53.

8. Elsa Tamez, "The Power of the Naked," in *Through Her Eyes,* p. 6.

9. Tereza M. Cavalcanti, *Uma leitura de Bíblia na perspectiva feminista* (São Paulo, 1988).

10. Cf. D. Brunelli, "Libertação da mulher," *CRB* (1988), p. 46.

11. Paul VI, cited by C. Militello, *Teologia al feminile. Donne: Studio, recerca, insegnamento della teologia* (1985), p. 5.

12. Cf. Ivone Gebara, "Option for the Poor as an Option for the Poor Woman," *Concilium* 194 (1987), pp. 110-17.

13. Cf. [North] American Bishops' Conference, draft of pastoral letter, "On the Participation of Women in the Mission of the Church" (1988).

14. Cf. various authors, "Brasil: reforma ou caos," *Paz e Terra* (1989), p. 75.

15. Cf. Maria Clara Bingemer, "Reflection on the Trinity," in *Through Her Eyes,* pp. 56-81.

16. Cf. Virginia Fabella and Mercy Oduyoye, eds., *With Passion and Compassion: Women Doing Theology* (Maryknoll, N.Y.: Orbis Books, 1988). The book includes certain presentations from the Intercontinental Meeting on Theology from Woman's Perspective held at Oaxtepec, Mexico, in which woman theologians from Latin America, Asia, and Africa participated.

17. Ivone Gebara, in *Through Her Eyes,* p. 48.

PART II

SYSTEMATIC CONTENTS OF THE THEOLOGY OF LIBERATION

TRANSCENDENCE AND HISTORICAL LIBERATION

12

Option for the Poor

GUSTAVO GUTIÉRREZ

The poor occupy a central position in the reflection that we call the theology of liberation theology. Only theological method and a concern for evangelization need be added in order to have the original—and still valid—core of this effort in understanding of the faith. From the outset, liberation theology has posited a distinction—adopted by Medellín in its "Document on Poverty"—among three notions of poverty: real poverty, as an *evil* (that is, as not desired by God); spiritual poverty, as *availability* to the will of the Lord; and *solidarity* with the poor, as well as with the situation they suffer.

The importance of this point is proclaimed by biblical revelation itself. A preferential commitment to the poor is at the very heart of Jesus' preaching of the Reign of God (and we shall take up this matter in part II). The Reign of God is a free gift, which makes demands on those who receive it in the spirit of children and in community (as we shall see in part III). Real poverty has therefore been a challenge to the church throughout history, but due to certain contemporary factors it has acquired fresh currency among us (the subject of part I).

I. A NEW PRESENCE

Our days bear the mark of a vast historical event: the *irruption of the poor*. We refer to the new presence of those who had actually been absent in our society and in the church. By *absent* we mean of little or no significance, as well as being without the opportunity to manifest their sufferings, solidarities, projects, and hopes.

As the result of a long historical process, this situation has begun to change in recent decades in Latin America. Of course the same change has been occurring in Africa, with the new nations; in Asia, with the independence of old nations; among the racial minorities of wealthy nations as well as poor ones. Another important movement, taking many forms, has also gotten under way: the new presence of woman, regarded by Puebla as "doubly oppressed and marginalized" (Puebla Final Document, no. 1135, n.) among the poor of Latin America.

The poor, then, have gradually become active agents of their own destiny, initiating the solid process that is altering the condition of this world's poor and despoiled. The theology of liberation—an expression of the right of the poor to "think their faith"—is not the automatic result of this situation and its incarnations. It is an attempt to read these signs of the times—in response to the invitation issued by John XXIII and Vatican Council II—by engaging in a critical reflection in the light of the word of God. That word should lead us to make a serious effort to discern the values and limitations of this event, which read from the standpoint of faith, also represents an irruption of God into our lives.

1. The World of the Poor

Expressions like, "dominated peoples," "exploited social classes," "despised races," and "marginalized cultures"—along with the reference to that constant, coextensive phenomenon, "discrimination against women"—have become common formulations in a framework of the theology of liberation for the unjust situation of the poor. The purpose of these formulations is to call attention to the fact that the poor—who constitute a de facto social collectivity—live in a situation of "inhuman misery" (Medellín, "Document on Poverty," no. 1) and "anti-evangelical poverty" (Puebla Final Document, no. 1159).

Furthermore, a great and constantly growing commitment to the poor has afforded us a better perception of the enormous complexity of their world. We are dealing with a veritable universe, in which the socioeconomic aspect of poverty, while fundamental, is not the only aspect. Ultimately, poverty means *death*. Food shortages, housing shortages, the impossibility of attending adequately to health and educational needs, the exploitation of labor, chronic unemployment, disrespect for human worth and dignity, unjust restrictions on freedom of expression (in politics and religion alike) are the daily plight of the poor. The lot of the poor, in a word, is suffering. Theirs is a situation that destroys peoples, families, and individuals; Medellín and Puebla call it "institutionalized violence." Equally unacceptable is the terrorism and repressive violence with which they are surrounded.

At the same time—and it is important to remember this—to be poor is a way of life. It is a way of thinking, of loving, of praying, of believing and hoping, of spending free time, of struggling for a livelihood. Being poor today also means being involved in the battle for justice and peace, defending one's life and liberty, seeking a greater democratic participation in the decisions of society, "organizing to live one's faith in an integral way" (Puebla Final Document, no. 1137), and committing oneself to the liberation of every human person.

Again — by way of a convergent phenomenon — we have seen during this same period the emergence of a more acute awareness of the racial problem among us. One of our social lies is that there is no racism in Latin America. There may be no racist laws, such as prevail in other lands, but we do have racist customs — a phenomenon no less grave for being hidden away. Marginalization of and contempt for the Amerindian and black populations are things we cannot accept, neither as human beings, nor still less as Christians. Today these populations are coming to a more acute awareness of their situation and consequently are voicing an ever more powerful demand for their most elementary human rights. This raised consciousness is pregnant with implications for the future.

We must also mention the unacceptable, inhumane position of women. One of the most subtle obstacles to its perception is its almost hidden character in habitual, daily life in our cultural tradition — to the point that when we denounce it, we seem a little strange to people, as if we were simply looking for trouble.

This state of affairs among us is a challenge to pastoral work, a challenge to the commitment of the Christian churches. Consequently, it is also a challenge to theological reflection. We still have a long way to go in this area. Matters of culture, race, and gender will be (and have already begun to be) extremely important to liberation theology. Doubtless the most important part of this task will fall to persons who actually belong to these respective human groups, despite the difficulties lying in the way today. No sudden burst of resistance is in the offing, but the voice of these downtrodden has begun to be heard, and this augurs well for the future. Here we surely have one of the richest theological veins for the coming years.

The cargo of inhuman, cruel death with which all of this misery and oppression is laden is contrary to the will of the God of Christian revelation, who is a God of life. But this does not blind us to the positive elements that we have indicated. These things manifest an ever-promising human depth and strength in terms of life. All of this constitutes the complex world of the poor. But our overall judgment remains: real poverty, a lack of the necessities of life (of a life worthy of a human being); social injustice, which plunders the masses and feeds the wealth of the few; the denial of the most elementary of human rights, are evils that believers in the God of Jesus can only reject.

2. Going to the Causes

In this complicated, narrow universe of the poor, the predominant notes are, first, its insignificance in the eyes of the great powers that rule the world of today, and second, its enormous human, cultural, and religious wealth, especially in terms of a capacity for the creation of new forms of solidarity in these areas.

This is how the poor are presented to us in scripture. The various books of the Bible paint a powerful picture of the cruel situation of spoliation and abuse in which the poor abide. One of the most energetic denunciations of this state of affairs is in the shatteringly beautiful — despite the painfulness of the topic under consideration — description we find in chapter 24 of the Book of Job. But it is not a matter of a mere neutral presentation of this reality. No, the biblical writers — the prophets, especially — point the finger of blame at those responsible for the situation. The texts are many. These passages denounce the social injustice that creates poverty as contrary to the will of God and to the meaning of the liberative deed of God manifested in the exodus from Egypt.

Medellín, Puebla, and John Paul II have all adopted this outlook in recent times. Today, pointing out causes implies structural analysis. This has always been an important point in the framework of liberation theology. The approach has been a costly one. True, the privileged of this world accept with a certain amount of equanimity the fact of massive world poverty. Such a fact is scarcely to be concealed in our day. But when causes are indicated, problems arise. Pointing out the causes inevitably means speaking of social injustice and socioeconomic structures that oppress the weak. When this happens, there is resistance — especially if the structural analysis reveals the concrete, historical responsibility of specific persons. But the strongest resistance and greatest fear are aroused by the threat of a raised consciousness and resulting organization on the part of the poor.

The tools used in an analysis of social reality vary with time and with the particular effectiveness they have demonstrated when it comes to understanding this reality and proposing approaches to the solution of problems. It is a hallmark of the scientific method to be critical of the researcher's own premises and conclusions. Thereby science constantly advances to new hypotheses of interpretation. For example, the theory of dependency, so frequently employed during the first years of our encounter with Latin American reality, has obviously turned out to be an inadequate tool. It is still an important one; but it has taken insufficient account of the internal dynamics and complexity of each country, and of the sheer magnitude of the world of the poor. Furthermore, Latin American social scientists are becoming more and more attentive to factors, not in evidence until more recent years, that express an evolution in progress in the world economy.

All of this calls for a refinement of our various means of cognition and even for the application of other, new means of the same. The social dimension is very important, but we must go deeper. There has been a great deal of insistence, in recent years, altogether correctly, on the contrast between a developed, wealthy northern world (whether capitalist or socialist), and an underdeveloped, poor, southern one (cf. John Paul II, *Sollicitudo Rei Socialis*.) This affords a different view of the world panorama, which cannot be reduced to confrontations of an ideological order or to a limited approach to confrontations between social classes. It also indicates the basic opposition implied in the confrontation between East and West. Indeed, the diversity of the factors that we have cited makes us aware of various types of social oppositions and conflicts prevailing in today's world.

The important transformation surely occurring in the field of social analysis today is needed in the theology of liberation. This circumstance has led liberation theology to incorporate into its examination of the intricate, fluid reality of poverty certain valuable new perspectives being adopted by the human sciences (psychology, ethnology, anthropology). Incorporation does not mean simply adding, without organic splicing. Attention to cultural factors makes it possible for us to penetrate basic mentalities and attitudes that explain important aspects of reality. Economic reality is no longer the same when evaluated from a cultural viewpoint. And surely the reverse is true as well.

It is not a matter of choosing among instruments. As a complex human condition, poverty can only have complex causes. We must not be simplistic. We must doggedly plunge to the root, to the underlying causes of the situation. We must be, in this sense, truly radical. Sensitivity to the new challenges will dictate changes of focus in the process of our selection of the routes to be taken to an authentic victory over the social conflicts that we have cited, and to the construction of a just world, the community of sisters and brothers for which the Christian message calls.

II. THE REASON FOR A PREFERENCE

While it is important and urgent to have a scholarly knowledge of the poverty in which the great masses of our peoples live, along with the causes that lie at the origin of this poverty, theological work properly so called begins when we undertake to read this reality in the light of Christian revelation.

The biblical meaning of poverty, then, will be one of the cornerstones of liberation theology. True, this is a classic question of Christian thinking. But the new, active presence of the poor vigorously re-posits that question. A keystone of the understanding of poverty along these theological lines is the distinction among the three notions of poverty, as we have stated. That is the context of a central theme of this theology, one broadly accepted today in the universal church: *the preferential option for the poor*. We are dealing with an outlook whose biblical roots are deep.

1. A Theocentric Option

Medellín had already encouraged giving "preference to the poorest and neediest, and to those who are segregated for any reason" ("Document on Poverty," no. 9). The very term *preference* obviously precludes any exclusivity; it simply points to who ought to be the first — not the only — objects of our solidarity. From the very first the theology of liberation has insisted on the importance of maintaining both the universality of God's love and the divine predilection for "history's last." To opt for either of these extremes to the exclusion of the other would be to mutilate the Christian message. The great challenge is to maintain a response to both demands, as Archbishop Romero used to say with reference to the church, "From among the poor, the church can be for everyone."

In the harsh, hard years of the late 1960s and early 1970s, this perspective occasioned numerous experiments in the Latin American church, along with a theological reflection bearing on these experiments. Here was a process of the refinement of expressions translating the commitment to the poor and oppressed. This became plain at Puebla, which adopted the formula "the preferential option for the poor" (cf. the chapter of the Puebla Final Document bearing that name). The expression had already begun to be used in the theological reflection of that time in Latin America. Thus, the Puebla Conference bestowed a powerful endorsement. Now the formula and the concept belong to everyone.

The word *option* has not always been well interpreted. Like any slogan, it has its limits. What it seeks to emphasize is the free commitment of a decision. This option for the poor is not optional in the sense that a Christian need not necessarily make it, any more than the love we owe every human being, without exception, is optional. It is a matter of a deep, ongoing solidarity, a voluntary daily involvement with the world of the poor. At the same time, the word *option* does not necessarily mean that those who make it do not already belong to the world of the poor. In many cases they do. But even here it is an option; the poor themselves must make this decision, as well. Some important recent documents issuing from the ecclesiastical magisterium at the universal level, echoing the outlook of the Latin American church, explicitly employ the expression *preferential option for the poor.*

Some have claimed that the magisterium would be happy to see the expression *preferential option* replaced with *preferential love* which, we are told, would change the meaning. It seems to us that the matter has been settled by the latest encyclical of John Paul II. Listing certain points and emphases enjoying priority among the considerations of the magisterium today, the pope asserts: "Among these themes, I should like to mention, here, the *preferential option or love* for the poor. This is an option or *special form* of primacy in the exercise of Christian charity" (*Sollicitudo Rei Socialis,* no. 42).

When all is said and done, the option for the poor means an option for the God of the Reign as proclaimed to us by Jesus. The whole Bible, from the story of Cain and Abel onward, is marked by God's love and predilection for the weak and abused of human history. This preference manifests precisely God's gratuitous love. This is what the evangelical Beatitudes reveal to us. The Beatitudes tell us in extremely simple fashion that a predilection for the poor, the hungry, and the suffering has its basis in the Lord's own bounty and liberality.

The ultimate reason for a commitment to the poor and oppressed does not lie in the social analysis that we employ, or in our human compassion, or in the direct experience we may have of poverty. All of these are valid reasons and surely play an important role in our commitment. But as Christians, we base that commitment fundamentally on the God of our faith. It is a theocentric, prophetic option we make, one which strikes its roots deep in the gratuity of God's love and is demanded by that love. Bartolomé de las Casas, immersed in the terrible poverty and destruction of the Indians of this continent, gave this as the reason for his option for them: "Because the least one, the most forgotten one, is altogether fresh and vivid in the memory of God." It is of this "memory" that the Bible speaks to us.

This perception was asserted in the experience of the Latin American Christian communities, and thus it came down to Puebla. Puebla maintains that for the sole reason of the love of God manifested in Christ, "the poor merit preferential attention, whatever may be the moral or personal situation in which they find themselves" (Puebla Final Document, no. 1142). In other words, the poor are preferred not because they are necessarily better than others from a moral or religious standpoint, but because God is God. No one lays conditions on God (cf. Jth. 8:11-18), for whom the last are first. This shocks our ordinary, narrow understanding of justice; it reminds us that God's ways are not our ways (cf. Isa. 55:8).

There has been no shortage of misunderstanding, then, or undue reduction on the part of self-styled champions of this preferential option as well as its overt adversaries. Still, we can safely assert that we are dealing with an indefectible part of the understanding maintained by the church as a whole today of its task in the world. We are dealing with a focus that is fraught with consequences—one which is actually only taking its first steps, and which constitutes the core of a new spirituality.

2. The Last Shall Be First

In a parable that we know from the first gospel alone, Matthew sets in relief—in the contrast between the first and the last—the gratuity of God's love by comparison with a narrow notion of justice (Matt. 20:1-16). "I intend to give this man who was hired last the same pay as you," says the Lord. Then he assails the envious with a pair of incisive questions: "I am free to do as I please with my money, am I not? Or are you envious because I am generous?" Here is the heart of the matter. The literal expression "bad eye" (for "envious") is revealing. In the Semitic mentality it denotes a fierce, jealous look—a look that petrifies reality, that leaves no room for anything new, leaves no room for generosity, and especially, here, undertakes to fix limits to the divine bounty. The parable transmits a clear lesson concerning the core of the biblical message: the gratuity of God's love. Only that gratuity can explain God's preference for the weakest and most oppressed.

"Thus the last shall be first and the first shall be last" (v. 16). Frequently we cite only the first half of the verse: "The last shall be first," forgetting that, by the same token, the first shall be last. But what we have here is an antithesis. The two statements shed light on each other, and therefore should not be separated. The antithesis is a constant in the gospels when the reference is to the addressees of the Reign of God. The gospels tell us of those who shall enter the Reign heralded by Jesus, and at the same time they tell us who shall be unable to do so. This antithetical presentation is highly instructive concerning the God of the Reign. Let us approach this matter by way of certain examples.

1. In Luke (6:20-26), the Beatitudes are followed by the Woes. The Greek word for *poor* here is *ptochoi*. Its meaning is beyond any doubt: etymologically the word means the "stooped," the "dismayed." It is actually used to speak of

the needy, those who must beg in order to live—those whose existence, then, depends on others. In other words, it means the helpless. This connotation of social and economic inferiority was already present in the Hebrew words that *ptochos* translates in the version known as the Septuagint. Scholars agree that this is the basic meaning of the word *ptochos* in its thirty-four occurrences in the New Testament (twenty-four of them being in the gospels). Very different is the situation of the rich, who have already received their consolation. Here again the sense is clear: the rich (*plousioi*) are those who possess a great deal of material wealth. Luke frequently contrasts them with the poor: the parable of the rich man and the poor Lazarus, in which, it is worth mentioning, it is not the rich man, but the representative of the anonymous of history, who is designated by a name (16:19-31); the vanity of the highly placed and the oppression of the poor (20:46-47); the widow's mite, accentuating the contrast presented in the parallel text in Matthew 21:1-3, its possible source.

We also have a contrast between the hungry and the satiated. The Greek word used by Luke for the hungering, *peinontes*, like the Hebrew words it translates in the Septuagint, indicates that this is not simple hunger but a deprivation resulting from evil acts of violence perpetrated over an extended period of time. The reference is to an endemic food shortage. "Starving," then, or "famished" would be better words for *peinontes* than simply "hungry." The satiated, by contrast, are the fully satisfied. Thus, the song placed by Luke on the lips of Mary strikes a definitive contrast between the rich and the hungry (Luke 1:53). Indeed, in Luke we often find poverty and hunger associated, as we find wealth and abundance of nourishment associated.

Those who weep—now we are in the third Beatitude—are those who experience a pain so acute, a sorrow so intense, that they cannot but express it. Weeping is a manifestation of feelings to which Luke is sensitive; he uses the verb *klaiein*, "to weep," eleven times. The pain expressed by this word is not momentary. This suffering is profound and springs from permanent marginalization. Rarely, on the other hand, do the Christian scriptures mention anyone laughing (*gela-*). Laughing can be a legitimate expression of joy (Luke 6:21), but it can also be the manifestation of a merriment that is oblivious of the sufferings of others, one based on privileges (6:25).

These are real situations—even social and economic situations—of poverty and wealth, hunger and satiety, suffering and self-satisfaction. The Reign of God will belong to those who live in conditions of weakness and oppression. For the wealthy to enter the Reign will be more difficult than "for a camel to go through a needle's eye" (Luke 18:25).

2. The gospels let us know, in various ways, that it is the despised, and not persons of importance, who have access to the Reign of God and to knowledge of the word of God. When the Lord cries, "Let the children come to me. Do not hinder them. The kingdom of God belongs to such as these" (Matt. 19:14), we immediately think of childlike docility and trust. We miss the radicality of Jesus' message. In the cultural world of Jesus' time, children were regarded as defectives. Together with the poor, the sick, and women, they were relegated to the status of the inconsequential. This shocks our modern sensibility. But

testimonials to this abound. To be "such as these," therefore, to be as children, means being insignificant, someone of no value in the eyes of society. Children are in the same category as the ignorant, on whom God our Father has willed to bestow a self-revelation (Matt. 11:25), or the "least ones," in whom we encounter Christ himself (Matt. 25:31-46).

Opposite these small, ignorant persons stand "the learned and the clever" (Matt. 11:25), who have seized control of the "key of knowledge" (Luke 11:52), and who despise the lowly, the people — *'am ha-'arets*, the people of the earth, of the land — whom they regard as ignorant and immoral. ("This lot, that knows nothing about the law" [John 7:49]). The gospel calls them the simple folk, "merest children" (Matt. 11:25) — using the Greek word *nepioi*, with its strong connotation of ignorance and simplicity.

Here again we find ourselves confronted with concrete, contrasting social situations based on unequal degrees of religious knowledge. Ignorance is not a virtue, nor is wisdom a vice. The biblical preference for simple folk springs not from a regard for their supposed moral and spiritual dispositions, but from their human frailty and from the contempt to which they are subjected.

3. We should actually do better to call the parable of those invited to the wedding banquet, as recorded in Matthew (22:2-10) and Luke (14:14-24), the parable of the *un*invited, since it is really they who constitute the core of its lesson. Exegetes are gradually abandoning the common interpretation of this text as a parable of an Israel called by God, but rejected for its faults, and thereupon a non-Israel called in place of Israel. Today the tendency is rather to understand those who were invited first as the "upper crust" of the time — persons who enjoyed both a high social rank and a knowledge of the Law; and the second group as those to whom Jesus preferentially addressed his message, the poor and the dispossessed — those regarded as sinners by the religious leaders of the people. Matthew goes so far as to say: "The servants then went out into the byroads and rounded up everyone they met, bad as well as good. This filled the wedding hall with banqueters" (Matt. 22:10). "Bad" and "good," we read, in that order. Once more we are dealing not with a question of moral deserts, but with an objective situation of the "poor and the crippled, the blind and the lame" (Luke 14:21).

4. Jesus is emphatic. He has come not for the sake of the righteous, but for sinners; not for the sake of the healthy, but for the sick (cf. Mark 2:17). Once again we have an antithetical presentation of the addressees of Jesus' message. On this occasion the tone is ironic: Are there perhaps righteous, healthy people who have no need of Jesus' salvific love? No, the "righteous," here are the self-righteous, those who pretend to be sinless, while the "healthy" are those who think they do not need God. These, despite the tokens of respect that they receive in society, are the greatest sinners, sick with pride and self-sufficiency. Then who are the sinners and the unhealthy, for whom the Lord has come? In terms of what we have just observed concerning the righteous and the healthy, we must be dealing here with those who are not well regarded by the "upper crust" of the social and religious world.

Those afflicted with serious illnesses or physical handicaps were regarded as sinners (cf. John 9). Hence, for example, lepers were segregated from social life; Jesus returns them to society by restoring them to physical health. Similarly public sinners, like tax collectors and prostitutes, were the dregs of society. It is that condition, and not their moral or religious quality, that makes them first in the love and tenderness of Jesus. Therefore he apostrophizes the great ones of his people: "Tax collectors and prostitutes are entering the kingdom of God before you" (Matt. 21:31). The gratuity of God's love never ceases to amaze us.

III. CHURCH OF THE POOR

One month before the opening of the Council, John XXIII called into being a church of the poor. His words have become familiar ones: "As for the underdeveloped countries, the church is, and wishes to be, the church of all, and especially the church of the poor" (Discourse of September 11, 1962). This intuition had strong repercussions on Medellín, as well as on the life of the Latin American church, especially by way of the base church communities. An examination of the meaning of the notion of spiritual poverty will help us to understand why the disciple, the person who belongs to the people of God, must express an acceptance of the Reign of God in a commitment of solidarity and loving community with all, especially with the actual poor and dispossessed of this world.

1. Discipleship

The Beatitudes are recorded in two versions in the gospels, one in Luke and the other in Matthew. The contrast between the two versions is frequently attributed to an attempt on the part of Matthew to "spiritualize" the Beatitudes, that is, to convert to a recital of purely interior, disincarnate dispositions what in Luke had been a concrete, historical expression of the coming of the Messiah. We disagree with this interpretation. Among other things, it is scarcely to be denied that Matthew's gospel is particularly insistent on the importance of performing concrete, material deeds in behalf of others, especially the poor (cf. Matt. 25:31-46). What Matthew does is view the Beatitudes through the lens of the central theme of his gospel: discipleship. The spiritual poor are followers of Jesus. The Matthean Beatitudes (Matt. 5:3-17) indicate the basic attitudes of the disciple who receives the Reign of God in solidarity with others. Matthew's text can be divided into two parts.

1. The *first block* of Beatitudes closely resembles Luke's version. Luke, as we hear so frequently, speaks of materially poor persons. To whom is Matthew directing our attention, then, when he says "in spirit" in the first Beatitude? In the biblical mentality, spirit connotes dynamism. Spirit is breath, life force — something manifested through cognition, intelligence, virtue, or decision. Thus, "of spirit" transforms a reference to an economic and social situation into a disposition required in order to receive the word of God (cf. Zeph. 2:3). We are confronted with a central theme of the biblical message: the importance of *childlikeness*. We are being exhorted to live in full availability to the will of the

Lord—to make that will our sustenance, as Jesus would have us do in the gospel of John. It is the attitude of those who know themselves to be the sons and daughters of God, and the sisters and brothers of the others. To be poor in spirit is to be a *disciple* of Christ.

The *second Beatitude* (the third, in some versions) is sometimes seen as implied in the first. Be this as it may, the fact is that the Hebrew words *'anaw* and *'ani* ("poor"), too, are translated by the Greek *praeis* (used later in this same block) meaning "lowly," or meek. Thus, we must be dealing with a nuance of the expression "poor in spirit." The meek, the lowly, are the unpretentious. They are open, affable, and hospitable. The quality is specifically a human one. (The Bible never ascribes "lowliness" to God. It does ascribe it to Jesus: cf. Matt. 11:28-29, where Jesus is "gentle and humble of heart"). To be meek is to be as the Teacher. To the meek is promised the earth, the land. The earth, the land, the soil is the first specification of the Reign of God in the Beatitudes, and in the Bible it carries the clear connotation of life.

In the *third Beatitude* Matthew uses a different verb from Luke's, but the meaning is similar: "sorrowing," *penthountes*. The word suggests the sorrow of mourning, catastrophe, or oppression (cf. 1 Macc. 1:25-27). Blessed, then, are those who refuse to resign themselves to injustice and oppression in the world. "They shall be consoled." The verb *parakalein*, "to console, to comfort," is an echo of Second Isaiah: "The Lord comforts his people and shows mercy to the afflicted" (Isa. 49:13). The consolation in question sounds a note of liberation. Luke presents us with a Jesus who fulfills the promise of the consolation of Israel (cf. Luke 2:25). Blessed are those who have known how to share the sorrow of others to the point of tears. For the Lord will console them: he will wipe away their tears, and "the reproach of his people he will remove from the whole earth" (Isa. 25:8; cf. Rev. 21:4).

In the *fourth Beatitude* a central theme for Matthew's gospel appears: the towering importance of *justice*. The use of the verbs "to hunger" and "to thirst" adds a note of special urgency and a religious overtone. The object of this burning desire is justice, or righteousness, as a gift of God and a human task; it determines a manner of conduct on the part of those who wish to be faithful to God. To be righteous or just means to acknowledge the rights of others, especially in the case of the defenseless; thereby it supposes a relationship with God that can appropriately be styled "holiness." The establishment of "justice and right" is the mission entrusted by the God of the Bible to the chosen people; it is the task in which God is revealed as the God of life. To hunger and thirst for justice is to hope for it from God, but it is likewise to will to put it in practice. This desire—similar to the "seeking of holiness" of Matthew 6:33— will be slaked, and its satisfaction will be an expression of the joy of the coming of the Reign of love and justice.

2. With the *fifth Beatitude*, the *second block* of Matthew's text begins. This block is constituted for the most part of Beatitudes proper to his gospel. The mercy of God is a favorite theme of Matthew. The parable he recounts in 18:23-35 is an illustration of the fifth Beatitude. The behavior required of the follower of Jesus is characterized by mercy. Matthew dovetails this outlook with that of

the Hebrew scriptures when he cites Hosea 6:6: "It is love [i.e., mercy] that I desire, not sacrifice" (cf. Matt. 9:13, 12:7). These are basic attitudes, not formalities. It is practice, and not formality, upon which judgment will be rendered. The text of Matthew 25:31-46 speaks to us precisely of works of mercy. Those who refuse to practice solidarity with others will be rejected. Those who put mercy into practice are declared blessed; they shall receive God's love, which is always a gift. This grace, in turn, demands of them that they be merciful to others.

Who are the "single-hearted"? The common tendency to relegate the religious to the domain of interior attitudes and "recollection" can make the *sixth Beatitude* difficult to understand—or rather, too easy to misunderstand. Single-heartedness implies sincerity, wisdom, and determination. It is not a matter of ritual or appearances. It is a matter of profound personal attitude. This is the reason for Jesus' disputes with the Pharisees, which Matthew presents to us in such energetic terms. Every Christian runs the risk of being a hypocrite: professing one thing and doing another, separating theory from practice. The letter of James—who is like Matthew in so many ways—employs a particularly suggestive term. On two occasions, James rejects "devious" persons—literally, "double-souled" persons, *dipsychoi* (James 1:8, 4:8). The God of the Bible requires a total commitment: "No man can serve two masters. He will either hate one and love the other or be attentive to one and despise the other" (Matt. 6:24). To draw near to God means "cleansing the heart," unifying our lives, having a single soul. Being a disciple of the Lord means having the "same mind" as the Teacher. Thus, a person of pure heart, an integral person, will see God— and "face to face," as Paul says (1 Cor. 13:12). This promise is the cause of the joy of Jesus' followers.

The building of peace is a key task for the Christian. But in order to perceive the scope of this task, we must be rid of a narrow conception of peace as the absence of war or conflict. This is not the peace to which we are invited by the *seventh Beatitude*. The Hebrew word *shalom* is a familiar one and exceedingly rich in connotation. It indicates an overall, integral situation, a condition of life in harmony with God, neighbor, and nature. *Shalom* is the opposite of everything that runs contrary to the welfare and rights of persons and nations. It is not surprising, then, that there should be an intimate biblical link between justice and peace: "Justice and peace (*shalom*) shall kiss" (Ps. 85:10). The poor are denied both justice and *shalom*. This is why both are promised particularly to those deprived of life and well-being. Peace must be actively sought; the Beatitude is speaking of artisans of peace, not those who are commonly termed pacifists or peaceable individuals. Those who construct this peace, which implies harmony with God and with the divine will in history as well as an integrity of personal life (health) and social life (justice), "shall be called sons of God"— that is, will actually *be* children of God. Acceptance of the gift of filiation implies precisely the forging of community in history.

The *eighth Beatitude* joins two key terms: "reign," and "holiness," or justice. To have life and to establish justice (to hunger and to thirst for justice) is to call down upon one's head the wrath of the mighty. Of this the prophets, and Jesus' own life, are abundant testimonial. Those who have decided to be dis-

ciples cannot be above their Teacher (cf. Matt. 10:24). The fourth Lukan Beatitude had already enjoined this outlook on the disciple: "Blessed shall you be
when men hate you, when they ostracize you and insult you and proscribe your
name as evil because of the Son of Man" (Luke 6:22). A focus on discipleship
is not directly present in the first three Lukan Beatitudes; Matthew, however,
adopts it in all of his own. Furthermore, Matthew reinforces his statement
concerning persecution "for holiness' sake" with a promise, in the following
verse, of felicity for those who are abused "because of me." Matthew 5:11, then,
comes very close to Luke 6:22, which speaks of persecution "because of the
Son of Man," along with establishing an equivalency between justice and Jesus
as the occasions of the hostility of which the blessed are the object. In this way,
Matthew proclaims the surprising identity, which he will also maintain in chapter 25, between a deed of love in behalf of the poor and a deed done in behalf
of the Son of Man come to judge the nations. To give one's life for justice is
to give it for Christ himself.

To those who suffer for *justice*, or "holiness' sake," is promised the *Reign of
God*. By repeating this term, "Reign of God," which he has already used in the
first Beatitude, Matthew closes his text with an impact, through the use of the
literary device known as inclusion. The promises of the six Beatitudes enclosed
between the first and the last are but specifications of the promise with which
the Beatitudes as a unit open and close: the promise of the Reign. The land,
consolation, satiety, mercy, the vision of God, the divine filiation are but details
of the life, love, and justice of the Reign of God.

These promises are gifts of the Lord. As the fruit of the free divine love,
they call for a response in terms of a particular behavior. The Beatitudes of
the third evangelist underscore the *gratuity of the love of God*, who "preferentially" loves the concrete poor. Those of Matthew flesh out this picture by
indicating the *ethical requirement in order to be a follower of Jesus*, which flows
from that loving initiative of God. It is a matter of accent. Both aspects are
present in each of our two versions of the Beatitudes. And the focuses are
complementary. The followers of Jesus are those who translate the grace
received—which invests them as witnesses of the Reign of life—into works in
behalf of their neighbor, especially the poor. The disciple is the one who strikes
a solidarity—including "material" solidarity—with those for whom the Lord
has a preferential love. Behold the sum and substance of the reason why a
person is declared blessed and fit to "inherit the kingdom prepared for you
from the creation of the world" (Matt. 25:34). Blessed are disciples—those who
make the "preferential option for the poor." Gratuity and demand, investiture
and dispatch to a mission, constitute the twin poles of the life of discipleship.
Only a church in solidarity with the actual poor, a church that denounces
poverty as an evil, is in any position to proclaim God's freely bestowed love—
the gift that must be received in spiritual poverty (cf. Medellín "Document on
Poverty," no. 4).

2. The Poor Evangelize

The "church of the poor" is a very ancient concept of church. It is as old as
Paul, and Paul's description is matchless. To the church living in the splendid,
wealthy city of Corinth, the Apostle writes:

Brothers, you are among those called. Consider your situation. Not many of you are wise, as men account wisdom; not many are influential; and surely not many are well-born. God chose those whom the world considers absurd to shame the wise; he singled out the weak of this world to shame the strong. He chose the world's lowborn and despised, those who count for nothing, to reduce to nothing those who were something; so that mankind can do no boasting before God. (1 Cor. 1:26-29)

In order to perceive God's predilection for the poor, the Corinthians need only look among themselves in the Christian community. It is a question of historical experience. (2 Corinthians 8:2 will speak of the "deep poverty" of the communities of Macedonia.) But Paul's text does a theological reading of this experience and expresses a comprehension of the church from the true, most demanding focus: the viewpoint of God. The mercy of God and the divine will for life are revealed in this preference for what the world regards as foolish and weak: for the plebeian, for the condemned, for the "nonexistent." The gratuity of God's love is manifested in the confusion and humiliation of the wise, the strong, the "existing."

Thus, the church is a sign of the Reign of God. Luke gives us the content of the proclamation of the Reign in his presentation of the Messiah's program (Luke 4:18-19). The various human situations enunciated in the text (poverty, captivity, blindness, oppression) are set forth as expressions of death. With Jesus' proclamation, death will beat a retreat; Jesus injects into history a principle of life, and a principle that will lead history to its fulfillment. We find ourselves, then, before the disjunction, central to biblical revelation, between death and life. It is a disjunction that calls upon us to make a radical option.

The central fact of the Messiah's proclamation is that the proclamation itself is Good News for the poor. This Good News is then made concrete in the other actions it proclaims: liberating captives, restoring sight to the blind, and bringing freedom to the oppressed. In all of these actions freedom is the dominant notion—even in the case of sight for the blind, if we keep in mind the Hebrew text of Isaiah 61:1-2, which alludes to the deliverance of those chained in the darkness of prisons. Thus, the core of the Good News announced by the Messiah is liberation. The Reign of God, which is a Reign of life, is not only the ultimate meaning of human history. Its presence is already initiated in the attention bestowed by Jesus—and by his followers—on the poor and oppressed.

In response to the cry of the poor for liberation, Medellín proposes a church in solidarity with that aspiration for life, freedom, and grace. A beautiful, synthetic text tells us that the conference seeks to present "the face of an authentically *poor, missionary, and Paschal* church, without ties to any temporal power and boldly committed to the liberation of the whole human being and of all human beings" (Medellín, "Document on Youth," no. 15, emphasis added).

At Medellín, as in the pastoral practice and theological reflection that had preceded that conference, thereupon to be enshrined in its texts, the concept of a church of the poor has a frank christological focus. That is, there is more at stake here than a sensitivity to the vast majority of the people of our continent, the poor. The basic demand in our pastoral practice, in our theological reflection, and in the Conference of Medellín itself—the element that confers the deepest meaning on the entire matter—comes from faith in Christ. The "Document on Poverty" makes this altogether clear. There are many passages to this effect, of which we shall cite only one: "The poverty of countless people calls for justice, solidarity, witness, commitment, and extra effort to carry out fully the salvific mission entrusted to [the church] by Christ" (Medellín, "Document on Poverty," no. 7). Complete liberation in Christ, of which the church is a sacrament in history, constitutes the ultimate foundation of the church of the poor.

This christological option is inspired as well in another declaration, this time from Vatican II. In *Lumen Gentium* we read that the church "recognizes in the poor and suffering the image of its poor and patient founder . . . and seeks to serve Christ in them" (*LG,* no. 8). This identification of Christ with the poor (cf. Matt. 25:31-46) is a central theme in our reflection on the church of the poor. Puebla expresses it beautifully in one of its most important texts, speaking of the traits of Christ present in the "very concrete faces" of the poor (Puebla Final Document, nos. 31-39; here, no. 31).

In other words, in addressing the subject of the church of the poor, the Latin American church (in the magisterium, in pastoral practice, and in theology) adopts a "theo-logical" perspective. To speak of such a church is not only to accentuate the social aspects of its mission; it is to refer first and foremost to the very being of that church as a sign of the Reign of God. This is the heart and soul of John XXIII's intuition ("The church is, and wishes to be . . ."), which was developed in depth by Cardinal Lercaro in his interventions at the Council. It is important to underscore this. There is a tendency to view these matters only from the angle of "social problems" and to consider that the church has attended to the question of its poverty by setting up a secretariat for social affairs. The challenge goes deeper than that. What John XXIII had in mind was an in-depth church renewal.

The deep, demanding evangelical theme of the proclamation of the gospel to the poor was broached at Vatican II but did not become its central question, as Cardinal Lercaro had requested at the close of the first session. At Medellín, however, it did become the main question; it was the context of the preferential option for the poor that inspired the major texts of the conference. We have recalled the biblical bases of the proclamation of the gospel to the poor. What we wish to do here is emphasize that this outlook has marked the life of the Latin American church throughout all these years. A great many experiments and commitments have made of this notion—a proclamation of the gospel to the disinherited—their central intuition and have sought to make it a reality. It is by embarking on this course that the church has found its deeper inspiration in its efforts for the liberation of the poor and oppressed of our continent.

All of this has made for a very profound renewal of the activity of the church. The missionary requirement is always to break out of one's own narrow circle and enter a different world. This is what large sectors of the Latin American church have experienced as they have set out along the pathways of an evangelization of the despoiled and insignificant. They have begun to discover the world of the poor, and to encounter the difficulties and misunderstandings that their option provokes on the part of the great ones of this world.

At the same time, years of commitment to a "defense of the rights of the poor, according to the gospel mandate" (cf. Medellín, "Document on Peace," no. 22) and the creation of Christian base communities as the "prime, fundamental, basic nucleus of the church, which should make itself responsible for the wealth and expansion of the faith" (Medellín, "Document on Joint Pastoral Ministry," no. 10) have opened up new perspectives. These experiments with church "have helped the Church to discover the evangelizing potential of the poor" (Medellín, "Document on Poverty," no. 1147). This is one of Puebla's basic declarations. It has its roots in the experience of the church in Latin America. It also demonstrates Puebla's continuity with Medellín.

Not only are the poor the privileged addressees of the message of the Reign of God; they are its vessels, as well. One expression of this potential is to be seen in the base ecclesial communities, which are surely among the most promising phenomena of the church of Latin America today. These communities sail in the broad channel opened up by the Council when the latter spoke of the people of God in the world of poverty. They constitute an ecclesial presence of history's insignificant ones — or, to use the words of the Council, of a "Messianic people" (*LG*, no. 9). That is to say, here is a people who walk the roads of history in the hope of the Reign that ever realizes the Messianic paradox: "The last shall be first."

The option for the poor, with all of the pastoral and theological consequences of that option, is one of the most important contributions to the life of the church universal to have emerged from the theology of liberation and the church on our continent. As we have observed, that option has its roots in biblical revelation and the history of the church. Still, today it presents particular, novel characteristics. This is due to our better understanding of the depth and complexity of the poverty and oppression experienced by most of humanity; it is due to our perception of the economic, social, and cultural mechanisms that produce that poverty; and before all else, it is due to the new light which the word of the Lord sheds on that poverty. This outlook thereby becomes the core of the "new evangelization," which got under way in Latin America two decades ago, but which it is so important to keep fresh and up to date. The novelty we cite was acknowledged, in a certain way, by the synod held on the occasion of the twentieth anniversary of the close of Vatican II. Among the synod's conclusions: "Since the Second Vatican Council, the Church has become more aware of its mission to serve the poor, the oppressed, and the outcast."

This service is a perilous one today, in the lands we live in. The vested interests at stake are powerful, and many are the victims of imprisonment, abuse, slander, exile, and death who have met their fate as a result of a wish to enter into solidarity with the poor. This is the reality of martyrdom, a reality at once tragic and fruitful. And it is a fact of life in a church that is learning day by day that it cannot be greater than its Master.

—Translated by Robert R. Barr

13

The Historicity of Christian Salvation

IGNACIO ELLACURÍA

I. THE PROBLEM

The historicity of Christian salvation is still one of the most serious problems for the understanding and practice of faith. It is a problem in the North Atlantic countries, in the oppressed countries, and finally, in the magisterium and discipline of the institutional church.

There are different interpretations of the historicity of Christian salvation. A first distinction might be made between questions about the historical character of the salvific acts and questions about the salvific character of historical acts. Those in the first group are mainly concerned with historically grounding and objectively proving fundamental acts of faith, from the resurrection of Jesus as the most important act to the miracles or the series of salvific events in the Hebrew scriptures; those in the second group are especially concerned with which historical acts bring salvation and which bring condemnation, which acts make God more present, and how that presence is actualized and made effective in them. These are not mutually exclusive perspectives; rather, the second presupposes the first and accepts without serious reservations that the great salvific, revealing, and communicating acts of God have taken place in history, even though their critical justification cannot achieve or be reduced to proofs from historical science.

The present essay is mostly within the second of these perspectives. It seeks to rethink the now classical problem of the relationship between Christian salvation, which would seem to be the formally definitive aspect of the mission of the church and of Christians as Christians, and on the other hand, historical liberation, which would seem to be the formally definitive aspect of states, social classes, citizens, people as people. The objective of rethinking this problem is not the purely intellectual one of resolving an uncomfortable theoretical paradox. The objective is, first, to clarify a fundamental point for the understanding of the faith and for the effectiveness of Christian praxis, especially in the context of the Third World and Latin America in particular; and second, to respond to critics of the liberation theologians' efforts to rethink the whole revelation and the life of the church in the search for the salvation-liberation of the poor, but also in the search for a profound renewal of the thinking, the spirituality, the pastoral practice, and even the institutionality of the universal church.

The theologians of liberation are increasingly accepted as representing a new way of doing theology, which has great importance for the life of the church and for the understanding and explanation of the Christian faith. After a first stage in which their importance was discounted on the grounds that their work was more sociological than theological, and that at best they were dealing with issues of social ethics, it was later recognized that their issues are fundamental to theology, and moreover, that it is a total theology, capable of displacing other forms of theology that were considered uniquely classical and universal. Thus the International Theological Commission, meeting in 1976, assumed that the principal object of the theology of liberation was the connection between Christian salvation and human promotion, and that "this unity of connection, as well as the difference indicated by the relationship between human promotion and Christian salvation, in its concrete form, should be sought for and re-analyzed; that is, without any doubt, one of the principal tasks of present theology."[1] At that same meeting, Hans Urs von Balthasar concluded his critical observations with these words:

> The theology of liberation has its specific place in a theology of the kingdom of God; it is one aspect of theology among others, and it demands practical action from the church to shape the world around Christ.[2]

But more recently Cardinal Ratzinger has given special emphasis to the universal character of the theology of liberation by recognizing (a) that it seeks to be "a new hermeneutic of the Christian faith," that is, a new way of understanding and realizing Christianity in its totality; (b) that it brings together several currents of thought, and in turn it influences regions far beyond the geography and culture of Latin America; (c) that it acquires an ecumenical character: "a new universality for which the classical separation of the churches should lose importance."[3]

This question of the historicity of Christian salvation, as we have said, is not exclusive to the theology of liberation, but the theology of liberation gives it singular importance and special characteristics.

Its singular importance is not due to the supposed nature of the theology of liberation as a formal political theology. The book of Clodovis Boff, so many chapters of which are excellent, might cause a distorted image of the theology of liberation or might lead it into theological regionalizations that are neither necessary nor desirable.[4] The theology of liberation should not be understood as a political theology, but as a theology of the Kingdom of God, so that the material distinction between a T 1 that deals with the classical themes of God, Christ, the church, and a T 2 that deals with more specifically human and/or political themes,[5] is not acceptable in itself, although secondary considerations may occasionally suggest methodical separations. Indeed, the theology of liberation deals primarily with everything that has to do with the Kingdom of God; but it focuses on every theme, even the most elevated and apparently suprahistorical, in the context of and often with special attention to its liberating dimension.

Neither are the special characteristics of the theology of liberation due to its supposed primary emphasis on the political, or even on integral liberation. They are due rather to the Christian and epistemological locus in which the theologian is situated, to the theologian's preferential option for the poor, and to the desire to place the "inbreaking" of the Kingdom of God at the service of the historical salvation of humanity, keeping this historical salvation in the closest possible relationship with the Christian salvation of humanity and the world.

The permanent problem of the relationship between the divine and the human thus takes on new importance, and more important, is seen in a new perspective. What do human efforts toward historical, even sociopolitical liberation have to do with the establishment of the Kingdom of God that Jesus preached? What do the proclamation and realization of the Kingdom of God have to do with the historical liberation of the oppressed majorities? Such questions represent a fundamental problem for the praxis of the church of the poor, as well as an essential problem for the present history of Latin America. It is not primarily a conceptual issue, but a real issue; it requires the use of concepts to resolve it in theory, but it is not primarily or ultimately a purely theoretical question. It is not primarily a problem of bringing two abstract concepts together in theory, one referring to the work of God and the other to human work. It causes unnecessary difficulties to start with concepts, and with the more or less explicit assumption that clearly different concepts represent different realities. The assumption is that there are two clearly different concepts, to which are attributed two clearly different realities as correlates. In other words, a long, intellectual elaboration, carried out over centuries, has led to the conceptual separation between what appears in biographical and historical experience to be one thing. That conceptual separation is increasingly taken for granted; it has become the point of departure from which to return to a reality no longer seen as it actually happened, but through the "truth" attributed to the concept. The problem not only is not resolved, but is concealed, by separating the concept from real historical praxis and placing it ideologically and uncritically at the service of institutionalized interests. The problem is concealed, not mainly because the concept is abstract, but rather because it is not historical. There is an ahistorical conceptual universality and there is an historical, or historicized, conceptual universality. The former may seem more theoretical and more universal; that is not so much because it conceals a historicity that by its concealment operates perversely, as because it ignores the universal dimension of historical reality. If theology does not reflect critically on what specific historical praxis the conceptualizations come from and what praxis they lead to, it places itself at the service of a history that the concept may be trying to negate.

This epistemological suspicion, repeatedly confirmed in the historical praxis of the church in Latin America, leads us to the position of the theology of liberation on the problem of the relationship between the different moments of a single praxis of salvation. It is not primarily a problem of conceptualization or a theoretical problem that must be resolved in order to protect orthodoxy.

It is, at least primarily, a problem of praxis, the praxis of certain Christians who have sought to participate in a Christian way in the struggles that the people have undertaken for their own liberation. These Christians, compelled by their faith and as an objective realization of that faith, seek to make human action correspond as much as possible to God's will. They have heard the cries of the people — of my people, as the bishops of northeastern Brazil have written[6] — an exploited people, who deserve something better, who often know that they are children of God. These believers have seen that those who call themselves Christians are responsible for many of the evils that befall the poorest people, while those who call themselves nonbelievers have committed themselves truly and sacrificially to the liberation of the poorest and most oppressed. Faced with this terrible paradox they wonder how it can be this way, and what they should do with their faith and their works to put an end to this scandal, which can kill the faith that today remains so vigorous among the popular majorities.

To approach this problem, which is so fundamental to ecclesial praxis and to the confession and understanding of the faith, we shall make use of a traditional concept: transcendence. Without getting into preliminary arguments on the concept of transcendence, we can see in it something that calls attention to a contextual structural difference without implying a duality; something that enables us to speak of an intrinsic unity without implying a strict identity. Although in the last part of this essay we shall offer some reflections on this unity without separation and without confusion, to begin with we shall assume that there are not two histories, a history of God and a human history, a sacred and a profane history. Rather there is a single historical reality in which both God and human beings intervene, so that God's intervention does not occur without some form of human participation, and human intervention does not occur without God's presence in some form. What we need to discern is the different ways in which God and human beings intervene, and the different types of relationship between those interventions. God's intervention and God's presence in human intervention are of different types when the human intervention occurs in the context of sin and when it occurs in the context of anti-sin, or grace. God's omnipresence in history is always divine, by definition, although that presence takes different forms not easily classified in the simplistic division between natural and supernatural.

Christian thinking on this point suffers from pernicious philosophical influences, which do not respond to the problem as it is presented in the history of revelation. Transcendence is identified with separateness, and it is thus assumed that historical transcendence is separate from history; the transcendent must be outside or beyond what is immediately apprehended as real, so that the transcendent must always be other, different, and separated, whether in time, in space, or in its essence. But there is a radically different way of understanding transcendence, more in line with the way reality and God's action are presented in biblical thinking. This is to see transcendence as something that transcends *in* and not as something that transcends *away from*; as something that physically impels to *more* but not by taking *out of*; as something that pushes *forward*, but at the same time *retains*. In this conception, when one reaches God historically—which is the same as reaching God personally—one does not abandon the human, does not abandon real history, but rather deepens one's roots, making more present and effective what was already effectively present. God can be separated from history, but history cannot be separated from God. And in history, transcendence must be seen more in the relationship between necessity and freedom than between absence and presence. God is transcendent, among other reasons, not by being absent, but by being freely present—sometimes in one way and sometimes in another, choosing the ways freely as the Lord, with different levels of intensity, in God's own self-giving will. As we shall see later, even in the case of sin we are fully in the history of salvation; sin does not make God disappear, but rather crucifies God, which seems like the same thing but in fact is profoundly different. It may be possible to divide history into a history of sin and another of grace; but that division presupposes the real unity of history, and the real and indissoluble unity of God and of the human being in history. It also presupposes a very close relationship between sin and grace, so that sin is defined by grace and grace by sin.[7]

Here we do not propose a philosophical discussion on the problem of transcendence, although we shall use the concept in order to fill it with precise meaning through some examples from the Old and New Testament. Rather, what we propose here is to show the fundamental unity of the divine and the human in history, a unity so fundamental that only by long reflection has humanity been able to make separations and distinctions, some of them justified and some not. The transcendence of which we speak is seen historically, and history in turn is seen as transcendent, despite the great difficulty of finding adequate concepts to maintain that indivisible unity without confusion.

Several essential points of the Christian faith could be taken as examples; above all, the transcendent mystery of the humanity of Jesus. It is in Jesus—true man and true God, as the Christian faith maintains—that the unity is best realized and can best be studied. We shall not do that here, because the limited scope of this essay could not even begin to outline that study. The same problem could also be studied in the church, with its evident and palpable history on the one hand, and on the other its character as a mystery to be confessed by faith; such a study could offer important theoretical clues, since the historicization of the mystery of the church, subjected to the appropriate criticism, would undermine many of the arguments used to attack the historicization of the faith proposed by the theology of liberation. We could also study the singular case of the sacred books, in which on the one hand human action is so evident as a vehicle of revelation, and on the other, God's authorship has to be acknowledged by faith.

For practical reasons we shall take two more modest cases as the object of study, in order to show what historical transcendence might be in the Old and New Testament. We do not assume that we are dealing with two different forms of divine transcendence in history, with the second surpassing or invalidating the first. When von Balthasar affirms with respect to the theology of liberation that "in Israel the religious is always political, and the political religious, down to the very core of the people's eschatological hope," and adds that "this monism of religion and politics, which constitutes the essence of Israel, has been and remains entirely detrimental for the church, always and in all its forms (caesaropapism, *cuius regio*)"[8] his affirmation distorts the problem. The theology of liberation has often been accused of being more like the Hebrew scriptures than the Christian in its fundamental historico-political concern. Appearances have been cited to that effect. We shall not overcome that objection by abandoning the inspiration of the historico-salvific events of the Hebrew scriptures, but by shedding on them the light of the Christian scriptures, without putting the problem in terms of the age of grace that leaves behind the age of the law. It would be a mutilation of the Hebrew scriptures to try to take from them only their religious spirit without their historical flesh; and to try to keep the spirit of the Christian scriptures without their historicity, or to use their sense of historicity only to support their spirit. In both testaments spirit and flesh, God and history, are so inseparably united that the disappearance of one would disfigure, or even destroy, the other.

Clearly we are not going to study historical transcendence in depth in either the Old or the New Testament, or the relationship between them, in this essay. It is enough to point out some of their significant aspects, in order to reach a greater clarity on the problem at hand; Christian historical transcendence includes both perspectives, but it also includes what the Spirit has been creating and making manifest, which must be discerned as "signs of the times".[9]

II. HISTORICAL TRANSCENDENCE IN THE OLD TESTAMENT

The point chosen for this serious problem can be formulated as follows: Who brought the people out of Egypt, Yahweh or Moses? This question contains the following presuppositions: (1) The departure of the people of Israel from Egypt is an historical event or is presented as an historical event; (2) the departure from Egypt is a salvific event of transcendental importance for the fulfillment of Yahweh's plan for the chosen people; (3) Moses is a man who uses human and political means to carry out that historico-salvific event; and (4) Israel does not hesitate to believe, despite the demonstrable presence of human beings in the action, that it is Yahweh who is liberating them.

1. The Historicity of the Old Testament Events

It does not matter for our purposes if the scientific and critical historicity of the events narrated in Exodus is denied, because the question remains valid, from a theological viewpoint, why the revelatory tradition saw a need to give historical flesh to the supposedly nonhistorical content: God's revelation and self-giving. We do accept that what happened in that history or in that historification, as the inspired author expresses so explicitly, is something that must be faithfully accepted as the salvific presence and action of God. The rationalist and nonbelieving assumption, in which the Exodus story is mere mythology or mere ideologization dressed up as history, would require a different treatment. Here we assume in faith that God's intervention is possible, that this intervention is always free, and that this intervention occurred, or at least the sacred author interpreted it as having occurred. But we repeat: whether or not it happened as narrated, the narration itself, in what we might call its revelatory internal logic, is sufficient to demonstrate what we mean here. To acknowledge only a purely extrinsic relationship between the medium and the message does not do justice either to the text or to the intention and purpose of the writer.

Even believers debate among themselves what is the historical character of the history of salvation or of the salvific events, and what gives them historicity.[10] De Vaux accepts the interpretation of von Rad, who affirms that there is a great difference between the history of Israel, as it has been reconstructed by modern historical science, and the history of salvation, as it has been written in the sacred books. But acknowledging this difference, de Vaux holds that salvation history depends on events that the historian can prove to be real. Wright would also acknowledge that the central events on which faith is based can be scientifically corroborated, but he says that God's actions are not pure history but history interpreted by faith, a projection of faith on the events, a projection which is considered as the real meaning of those events. Von Rad holds that the biblical narratives cannot be taken as a certain source of historical information, because despite their factual basis, their degree of historicity is debatable; nevertheless, he holds what should clearly be called salvation *history* as a fundamental category of his theology.

Throughout this debate, history is seen more as historical science than as historical reality; more attention is paid to the historical character of the corroboration than of what is corroborated. For example, the apparently historical narratives of the Old Testament are accepted as a literary body, which is better described as story than as history (scientifically corroborated historical events); they might be called history-like narratives. Thus what they seek to transmit, more than information, is a message, a meaning, using the fictional genre for that purpose, so that their effectiveness is independent of whether what they relate actually happened or not. They might be paradigmatic stories or myths, which seek to express something profound, permanent, and very meaningful for humanity; it is not hard to accept that poetic creations can capture the real character of an event more effectively than a purely factual description. Thus what is described in the Exodus as an act of God seeks to show the deep meaning of the event for the community; it gives the community a revelation of God, not so much about a particular event, but about permanent values and meanings. Thus it is not the event that inspires the community, but its own experience transmitted in the story. The acts of God, transmitted in the Exodus, are problematic from a strictly historical viewpoint, but not as paradigmatic myths or stories, which are meaningful for the light they shed on essential aspects of the human condition.

Nevertheless, the biblical text, as Mircea Eliade acknowledges, does not present Yahweh as an oriental divinity, the creator of archetypal deeds, but as a personality who ceaselessly intervenes in history and who reveals his will through events. Historical novelty is regularly introduced in the Exodus story, not by natural necessity, but by a free intervention of God, who is experienced as such by a specific people in specific times and places. This opens the way for the revelation of Yahweh's transcendent power. The unpredictability of historical experience is celebrated as a revelation of Yahweh's transcendent power, a power which changes history and which shows both human contingency and human hope in historical change. Yahweh is greater than what might be expected of any historical conditionality. Thus human history is held up as the privileged arena in which to show the transcendent irruption of God as an unforeseeable novelty that opens human contingency to divine hope. Human experience does not close in on itself, but is opened to the hope of divine intervention.

2. *History as Corroboration and Demonstration of God*

But we must return to the question of why human history, or the historical genre, is used to show the revealing presence of God. Is it because the historical arena facilitates apologetic proofs of the rationality of faith, or because the marvelous historical acts lead more compellingly to religious confession? This rationalistic or psycho-social explanation does not take into account either the sacred text or the people's experience. It is true that they use palpable and amazing events, signs and portents, to show that Moses' call to the people to leave the oppression of Egypt was inspired and supported by the will and power of Yahweh. But they are not used to confirm the rationality of our belief in what happened there or its transcendent meaning. They are used to confirm the historical action of the people themselves, who were invited to leave oppression and go to the promised land, and to show in that action who their God was and how God acted. History thus becomes a proof of God because history is itself a demonstration of God; only in history is God understood in relation to humanity, and humanity in relation to God. (Here we include biographical and personal human experience by extension; that experience itself is not historical, but it has characteristics of historicity, which permit this extension.) If God is not understood in history as the Lord of history, that is, as God who intervenes in history, then God is not understood as the whole, rich, and free, mysterious and accessible, scandalous and hope-giving God. Rather, God would be understood as the mover of natural cycles, as a paradigm of eternal sameness; there might be an after, but not an open future, so God remains as the mover and perhaps the end or goal of a necessary evolution. But Moses invokes Yahweh and the acts of Yahweh not to repeat the sameness but to break the process, and that break in the process is where something more than history becomes present in history. In this sense it is important that this happens in a specific situation rather than through a formal miracle, because the situation offers the possibility of becoming a novelty that breaks into the normality of the experience.

It is not at all obvious why history was chosen as the theophanic locus, as the privileged place for God's self-manifestation and self-giving. Other peoples have chosen to approach God through nature with all its majesty, its mystery, its unappealable finality from a human viewpoint; or at the other extreme, through subjective or intersubjective inner experience. One might say that history encompasses and surpasses both the natural and the subjective, personal arenas; far from excluding them, it frames and empowers them. But without history the arena of God's revelation and self-giving would be drastically reduced. History opens up, first, what humanity and the whole of reality can give of themselves, and therefore also the effective possibility of showing what God is to humanity and what humanity is to God. In history God's self-giving is not once and for all, as it would be in nature, even if we accept the possibility of a creative evolution (Bergson) or an evolving creation (Zubiri). In history we have the possibility of a permanent revelation and self-giving, not only for those who receive it but—and this is more radical—for the one who gives it. We are increasingly able to scrutinize nature, both in its distant origins and in the depth of its elements, but that nature is given, and even its evolution is basically predetermined. History is the arena of novelty, of creativity; God's self-revelation comes by making "more" history, that is, a greater and better history than existed in the past. Two things filled Kant's spirit with admiration and respect, which grew every time he reflected on them: the starry heaven above and the moral law within.[11] Hegel saw history theoretically as an object of great admiration; even before Hegel, scriptural revelation established history as the place to find, not only the fullness of being and reality, but the truth and gift of God, which in the New Testament conception led to the divinization of a man, and of all humanity through him.

Moreover history, as it is lived and understood in the Hebrew scriptures, is *open to the future*. Moses speaks of a past within a present toward the future. It is the God of the fathers who is seeing the present oppression of God's children in Egypt, and who launches them toward a future that will come through Yahweh's covenanted promise to his people. This is more than a God of the fathers, received in a past experience, even if that God continues to live in the people; there is also a present, the present of an oppressed and exploited people, in which the past experience of the fathers is taken up and renewed by historical experience, an experience so negative that the God of life, liberty, and social unity is obliged to return. And finally there is a future of promise and hope, which invalidates that negativity and recovers the old experience in a new way; it is a future in which God and humanity collaborate, and which will depend, although in a different way, on God's faithfulness and human response. In an experience of oppression and liberation, from God's viewpoint, the oppression is seen as sin and the liberation as grace; God is revealed as a God who not only forgives, but also effectively liberates. This strictly future character—which is not only in the beyond, but activates itself by projection in the interplay of promise and hope, of God's action and human response—is what permits the historical revelation of God and obliges human beings to open themselves, not to close in on a past experience or a preset limit. The *Deus semper novus* is one of the ways we encounter the *Deus semper maior*. Thus history is the fullest place of transcendence, of a transcendence that does not appear mechanically, but only appears when history is made, and which irrupts in novel ways in the constant disestablishment of the determining process.

History is also the *place of the people*. Moses' experience on the holy mountain is not the experience of a solitary man who has an inward encounter with divinity and later transmits that experience so that everyone can reproduce it inwardly and individually. On the contrary, Moses begins from a historical experience, which is the experience of his people. He lives at first by that which he has received, by that which has been given him by tradition (Zubiri). As an adult he lives the day-by-day experience of his people and even participates violently in it. Only later does he withdraw to reflect on what he can do, from the viewpoint of the God of the fathers. His primary intention is not to do something for God, but to do something for the people, although this doing of the people is seen from the perspective of God. He begins with the doing of the people, he reflects on it before God, and he returns to the people to work together with and for that chosen people and for the God who has chosen them. His point of departure is not only the people, but the sociopolitical experience of the people; his point of arrival is the sociopolitical action of the people. All this is not leverage to help him reach an experience of God; rather, the experience of God is subordinated to the saving action of the people and goes on to raise the people to grateful actualization of their election — and to the recognition that Yahweh alone is their God. In this immersion of the divine action and reality in the problems of history, experience breaks in on itself and becomes open to something that surpasses all its brokenness. Only a God who has come down into history can raise it to God. But this happens in the history of a people. As M. Noth has pointed out, the first book of the Pentateuch speaks of singular figures, while in the second book the subject is Israel as a collective entity.[12] Only the whole people, which does not exclude the singular richness of a personage like Moses, can manifest the true God, who is not enclosed in the solitary subjectivity of the great heroes, but becomes present in the sorrows, struggles, and hopes of the popular majorities. For good reason the fundamental article of Israel's faith is the liberation of a whole oppressed people, a people who had to leave the house of slavery, because God ordered them to do so although the order was mediated by Moses.[13] Thus this fundamental article of faith does not refer to God alone, to a God apart from human history, nor even to a God who gives meaning to individual life and whose fullness is projected beyond history. On the contrary, it is from and in history itself that God becomes present as the fundamental and foundational religious event, not only not separated from the sociopolitical process but established and re-lived in that process. The takeoff point is the oppression of a specific people, an oppression with precise characteristics that God and God's people cannot tolerate. The ancestors of the Israelites had entered Egypt in freedom and had been assimilated with the Apiru, prisoners of war, and were forced with them into the works undertaken by Ramses II in the delta. The Egyptians did not want to lose this free labor; they saw the Israelite protest as a slave rebellion, and their flight as a prisoner escape.[14]

It is in and by this historical experience that *the name of Yahweh is revealed*. The theophany arises from a theopraxy and leads to a new theopraxy: the God who acts in history, in a very specific history, can be discovered and named in a more explicit, and even a more transcendent, way. Without getting into an etymological debate over the exact meaning of the name revealed in the theophany of the burning bush, there seems to be no doubt about the meaning of the historical origin of the divine name, of its historical revelation. And this is what remains as a gift and eternal possession of the people: not just the separate name of Yahweh, but the name of Yahweh associated with an historical act: "I am Yahweh, your God, who have brought you out of the land of Egypt" (Exod. 20:2, 39:46; Deut. 5:6; Lev. 19:36, 25:38). This historical experience formulates the fundamental covenant, "I will be your God and you shall be my people." The God of Israel is defined by that divine presence, which brings the people out of the oppression of Egypt; the people of Israel reach God *more*, and in a different way than their fathers, because Israel has experienced in its new history something new of God. The act of leaving Egypt, leaving the place of material oppression—the evidence does not show so clearly that in Egypt the people were unable to worship their God—is not a profane act, but the originating place of a new revelatory experience of God, the experience that provides the most explicit revelation of humanity and of the true God. Transcendence here does not mean leaving the people and their struggles, but empowering the people for their struggles, their passage from the land of Egypt to the land of Canaan. The revelation of the name and the entire theophany are intended to cause the people to shake off their yoke and begin the search for a new land. The experience and the memory of the departure and the journey would keep alive their experience of God in the generations to come. Even when the re-living became fundamentally cultic, they would seek to nourish the re-living by recalling and invoking that history.

3. The Salvific Acts of Moses

From this perspective, the question whether Yahweh or Moses brought the people out of Egypt cannot be answered simplistically—either that it was Moses (the rationalistic or naturalistic interpretation) or that it was Yahweh (the supranaturalistic interpretation). Yahweh did not bring out the people without Moses, nor Moses without Yahweh. This "without" is absolutely positive and essential. Undoubtedly the Exodus presents decisive actions that were taken exclusively by Yahweh (plagues, the Red Sea, the manna, and so forth), and Moses would not take any action except by the order or inspiration of Yahweh. But if we examine this separation more closely, it tends to disappear. Thus it is variously reported that Pharaoh hardened his heart and that Yahweh hardened Pharaoh's heart. The same is true of his obstinacy. (Exod. 7:13, 22; 8:15; 9:12, 35; 10:20, 27; 7:14; 9:34; 10:1) The significance of the plagues pales in comparison with the miracle of the passover night when Israel was miraculously liberated from Egypt, a miracle in which the human participation is much more evident.[15] And even with respect to the "miraculous" character of the plagues, they do not appear as something separate (a kind of sign in the heavens); rather, they have historical finality (the departure of the people from Egypt), which affects important realities in Egyptian social and economic life. The plagues do not happen outside the activity of human agents. Yahweh appears as the transcendent moment of a single praxis of salvation, the moment which breaks the limits of human action and/or redirects the deepest meaning of that action. This does not mean reducing God to history; on the contrary, it means elevating history to God, an elevation that becomes possible only because Yahweh has previously descended to it through Moses. Yahweh intervenes because he has heard the cry of the oppressed people.

Thus it is historically evident (in the framework of the historicity that is critically attributed to the Exodus story) that Moses and his historical actions play a relevant role in the salvific action implied in the people's departure from Egypt, and in the transcendent interpretation of that action which is given to the people through Moses. To speak here of instrumentality, elevation, and so on, is to invoke explanations and rationalizations, which may be appropriate as long as they do not obscure the fundamental event: the decisive historical action of Moses and the innateness of that historical action to the formally divine action, both of which are presented as an indissoluble unity. The believing authors of the Exodus accept it as evident that God is the principal author of these deeds, but they also report it as evident that Moses is the arm of Yahweh and that his historical action is simply a salvific action. What looks to unbelievers like the action of a religious chieftain appears to believing eyes as God's action; the believers simply discover the entirely gratuitous transcendence that becomes freely present in the historical action. This does not mean that every historical action can be seen in that way, because it must have a specific content (not all contents are the same for the self-revelation that God seeks to make), and God must be present in that content in a special way. We cannot pursue the question here of what criteria distinguish some historical events from others, although it is an essential point for both a theology of revelation and a theology of the signs of the times.

Therefore, it is meaningless to ask what is sacred and what is profane in the Exodus narrative. A rationalist historian might have given a profane description of that action, but from the believer's viewpoint, that would have been a mutilation achieved by abstracting one of the essential elements of the historical unity. At the other extreme, the sacred description of the history of Israel would be an enumeration of supposedly transcendent or supernatural elements, which would be only incidentally and parabolically related to the historical events; that also would be a mutilation by separation and abstraction. Neither of these occurs in the Exodus or in the other historical and prophetic books. What we see, rather, is that in the one history there are actions in favor of God and the people, and there are actions against the people and God. There is an historical praxis of salvation and an historical praxis of perdition; an historical praxis of liberation and an historical praxis of oppression. The salvation and liberation are material, sociopolitical, fully real, and demonstrable in the first place; only in a second moment do they appear as the privileged locus of the revelation and presence of God. Certainly this second moment is not a purely mechanical reflection of the first; it required God's special but intraworldly intervention in order to go beyond the historical action. God has become freely present in history, in a way that is peculiar to a people and their state of prostration;

whoever makes contact with that people and their state of prostration makes contact with the God who acts in history. They are in contact with grace and justification if they are in the line of justice and liberation; in contact with sin if they are in the line of oppression and limitation. Theopraxy is the starting point of the process of salvation, just as the rule of sin and evil is the starting point of the process of condemnation. Moses enters fully into God's theopraxy, while Pharaoh enters fully into the denial of the God of life and freedom, perhaps in the name of the god who upholds his form of domination. Just as their starting points in the history of salvation are different, so is the corresponding theophany: for Moses and his people it is the theophany of a liberating God; for Pharaoh and his people it is the theophany of a God of punishment. But the liberation and the punishment come through historical events. Only by reaching this theophany is the theopraxis completed and the fullness of history demonstrated, the fullness of God in history. And this constantly renewed theophany is the measure by which to regulate what should be the historical praxis of salvation.

Thus historical transcendence in the Hebrew scriptures does not come from the fact that stories are used to make paradigmatically present God's will for humanity in history. It comes rather from God becoming present in history, even if the story that expresses this presence is not historical in a critical sense. The paradigmatic element is in the historical repetition of what scripture expresses as theopraxy, so that a theophany can be seen in that historical praxis. This is what happens in situations of historical liberation, when sin and the negation of God are made manifest, and when all the power of the Christian God must therefore be used to overcome that sin. If the forgiveness of sins only comes through grace, the annulment of objectified sin only comes through the objectified presence of the power of grace.

4. The Praxis of Salvation

This praxis of salvation, however, should not be understood in purely ethical terms, especially if ethical acts are seen apart from the faith that puts the believer in contact with the God of salvation. Much less should the praxis of salvation be seen as a merely political praxis. The so-called politicization of the faith, which should rather be called the historicization of the faith, does not consist of reducing salvific action to the transformation of the sociopolitical structures, or even sublimating the historical structures (which are broader than sociopolitical ones). It consists of saying that salvation does not reach its fulfillment if it does not attain that historical dimension, and when appropriate, that political dimension. Neither do politicization and historicization consist of ethical consequences which should be drawn from faith but which are no longer directly related to faith, to salvation, or (as we shall see in the Christian scriptures) to the Kingdom of God. The total unity of a single history, of God in humanity and of humanity in God, does not permit the evasion of focusing on either extreme: only God or only humanity. But neither does it leave us with the duality of God and humanity; rather it affirms the dual unity of God *in* humanity and humanity *in* God. This *in* has different functions and has different levels of meaning depending on whether it is God acting in humanity or humanity acting in God, but it is always the same *in*. Therefore it is not a merely political, or merely historical, or merely ethical praxis, but a transcendent historical praxis, which makes manifest the God who becomes present in the acts of history.

This moment can occur in two ways. One is virtual, for although a person may follow very closely what amounts to a praxis of salvation, he or she may not know or explicitly name the God who is present in this praxis and who ultimately makes it possible. The other is more formal and explicit, when within that same praxis one meets and recognizes God, so that the recognition illuminates, criticizes, and inspires the action itself. The example of Moses is important here. His character as leader of the people does not conflict with his character as an individual person, and his character as a political actor does not conflict with — rather it requires — his recourse to God, so that in him theopraxy becomes theophany, and the theophany leads him to a new theopraxy.

But this affirmation does not mean that the liberation of the exodus has a salvific character only because it is based on the cult of the covenant celebrated at Sinai. We can say, with Urs von Balthasar, that "the first liberation immediately points to a more than political salvation in the covenant of Sinai and in the cult established there by the law."[16] Indeed, the first liberation is followed by successive liberations, the basis of which is more explicitly religious and cultic. But whatever the origin of these stories,[17] their real basis is very precise: the cult (the covenant itself is a different question) does not give meaning to the liberation from Egypt, but rather the liberation gives its specific meaning to the cult, which celebrates and draws the explicit consequences of that historical experience, that historical praxis. The cult of Sinai is true worship because the worshiping people have really met the liberating God in a praxis of liberation; it is not in any way true and sufficient by itself. So it is not easy to agree with what the International Theological Commission says on this point:

> The objective of felt needs in specific cases is a less important element; what is important is the experience which leads the people to hope for salvation and solutions only in God. Therefore one cannot speak of this type of salvation, as it affects human rights and well-being, without at the same time referring to all the theological reflection in which it is God, not humanity, who changes the situations.[18]

It is entirely possible that the Old Testament society did not see things that way. For them, as for today's oppressed people in Latin America, the object of their felt needs is fundamental, because God would not have appeared as the liberator of the people — an article of faith for the Jewish people — if they had not had that historical experience of salvation; to say otherwise is to deny the historical character of both history and revelation. Furthermore, one cannot say that the people hoped for salvation and solutions only in God, when Moses and the people played such an important role in their liberation. To affirm on that basis that it is God and not humanity who changes situations is a false statement, distorting Christian praxis and favoring the people who do in fact propose to change situations from a perspective of domination and of sin. As we shall see later, it is closed human actions that bring perversion and condemnation in history, and it is open human actions that bring grace and salvation. Open and closed here are in relation to God, but the relationship does not at all exclude the formally salvific and transforming power of human action, not only in itself but in history.

Historical transcendence in the Hebrew scriptures can and should be studied in other places besides the liberating action of Moses, and it can and should include other aspects besides those mentioned here. But those discussed here with respect to the original Jewish passover demonstrate some essential points for an understanding of historical transcendence. History is a special arena of divine action. Although in their mental exercises theologians do not discount the possibility that God's self-giving could have occurred "supernaturally" in a purely material nature, a nature neither historicized nor personalized, it is more plausible to think that God's personal communication — personal for God and for those who receive it — could only have occurred in the biographical and historical realm. This would lead us to consider a communication and presence of God in nature as over against a communication and presence of God in history; nature would be the most appropriate place for what is called the natural presence of God, and history would be the most appropriate place for what is called the supernatural presence of God. We shall return later to this mistaken way of speaking. What is important here is that the history of Israel has not only revealed the real importance of the historical element, but it has made the historical the richest place of God's presence and self-giving.

One might say that historical transcendence in the Hebrew scriptures is not the definitive form of historical transcendence, as it has evolved in the course of revelation and historical development. That is evident. But this does not detract from certain essential points: a) It is that historical transcendence which has given way to other forms of historical transcendence; b) that historical transcendence touches essential elements of humanity and society which cannot be left out, and which in certain historical circumstances may attain a higher level of actuality; c) that historical transcendence shows God's will not only in the past but in the present, without leading to fundamentalist interpretations; d) that historical transcendence is opening itself from within to subsequent forms of transcendence, and remains in them, in a transformed way, giving them a dynamic of their own; and e) to neglect or discount the historical dimension of the Hebrew scriptures mutilates God's revelation and detracts from the content of the historical transcendence of the Christian scriptures.

III. HISTORICAL TRANSCENDENCE IN THE NEW TESTAMENT

The New Testament clearly and specifically demonstrates the problem of historical transcendence by showing the what and the how of the relationship between God and humanity, between Christian salvation and human fulfillment.

The specificity of the New Testament is not primarily logical and conceptual, but consists of a qualitatively new step in the same historical process of salvation. This qualitative leap is not a break; rather, it surpasses what has gone before by giving new concreteness and fulfillment to what before was somewhat indeterminate in both aspects, the historical and the transcendent. This indeterminateness is surpassed with new terms; it is also made more definitive by the appearance of Jesus as the supreme form of historical transcendence, although that definitiveness still leaves many things open. The resurrected Christ gave us the Spirit to help us discover, discern and fulfill those things.

1. Jesus, the New Moses

To approach this *surpassing novelty* in a way that parallels our study of historical transcendence in the Hebrew scriptures, let us look at the figure of Jesus from a limited but fundamental perspective: Jesus is the "new" Moses. If it is Moses who historically and theologically established the people of Israel in the exodus story, it is Jesus who historically and theologically establishes the new people of Israel. Jesus as the new Moses is one of the fundamental themes of the New Testament, to which we cannot do justice in a few pages, but on which there is an abundant bibliography.[19] Here we shall discuss a few signs, which are sufficient to present the problem and outline the solution. We must also recognize that historical transcendence in the New Testament is not expressed only in terms of Jesus as the new Moses, which means this essay is even more limited. But this focus is sufficiently correct, because in itself it sheds important light, and because this light is not diminished by what can be said in other contexts.

Let us examine some of the fundamental aspects presented on this point in the Fourth Gospel. We might also focus on it from the perspective of the sermon on the mount, where the new Law is given to the new people. But perhaps there are prior and more essential things to say on the basis of the Gospel of John.

It is well known that the juxtaposition of Jesus with Moses appears in the prologue to the gospel, in a text that certainly was not in the first level of the writing;[20] therefore, it cannot be taken as the point of departure but as the point of arrival, which can serve as horizon. The text reads as follows:

> Indeed, from his fullness
>   we have, all of us, received—
> one gift replacing another,
> for the Law was given through Moses,
> grace and truth have come
>   through Jesus Christ.
> No one has ever seen God;
> it is the only Son,
>   who is close to the Father's heart,
> who has made him known. (John 1:16-18, *NJB*)

This is a highly theologized juxtaposition of Moses and Jesus. It is centered on two principal points: (1) Moses gave the Law, while "faithful love"[21] has been given us by Jesus, the Messiah; and (2) Moses could not see the divinity, but the Logos, who is more than a visual contemplator of the divinity, can explain what God is like. The juxtaposition is made in strictly religious terms; neither in the case of Moses nor in that of Jesus are their respective concrete realities affirmed in totality, but only some of their essential aspects. Of course a historical context, or rather, a historical destination, is recognized indirectly, because the Law is addressed to the people and has a very explicit combination of sociopolitical contents, and because what the Logos assures us of the Father is love par excellence, a love which cannot fail and which is a new and renewing gift with respect to the Law. This was to become the basis of the essential juxtaposition of the new and the old Moses, and thus of the new and the old Israel. History has almost completely disappeared, becoming a purely theologal, and at most religious, reality. But not because history is negated. History is to be lived with a different spirit in the new eon; the law prevailed in the old eon, and love is to predominate in the new. And in love one sees an even greater demand for commitment to others and historical commitment, because God's love is a love of total self-giving unto death.

If we move from this juxtaposition in the prologue to what was probably the first editorial level of the Gospel of John, which suggests greater interaction with the Samaritan context,[22] we see a much more nuanced vision of the relationship between Jesus and Moses. The basic text is Philip's words to Nathanael: "We have found him about whom Moses in the law and also the prophets wrote, Jesus son of Joseph from Nazareth" (John 1:45, *NRSV*). The affirmation responds to a clearly defined problem. Both the Jews and the Samaritans were waiting for the Prophet who would culminate the action of Moses according to the old promise, "Then the Lord replied to me: 'They are right in what they have said. I will raise up for them a prophet like you from among their own people; I will put my words in the mouth of the prophet, who shall speak to them everything that I command' " (Deut. 18:17-18). The Samaritans expected that the prophet would really be like Moses, and would therefore achieve the definitive liberation of the people of God, of the Samaritan people, in a new exodus.

This early christology in the basic narrative of John begins, therefore, with the same classical experience of the unity between salvation and history: it is God who saves, but God saves through an historical envoy and historical actions; in the expectation of the Samaritans, formally sociopolitical actions. Thus it makes sense that Nathanael should recognize that the Prophet of whom the Law speaks is truly the king of Israel (Samaria). Precisely because Nathanael has somehow seen characteristics of the Prophet in Jesus, he confesses Jesus as the king of Israel (John 1:49). The function of John the Baptist and the baptism of Jesus are clear in this context: John's mission is analogous to that of the prophet Samuel, both of them charged with designating and manifesting the king that God has chosen for Israel.[23] It is precisely this character of kingship that in a second moment would be interpreted as the Messiah: Jesus' Messianic character in the first stratum of the Johannine presentation refers clearly to historical and political realities, even though the failure of the historical and political realization leads gradually to an interpretation of this realization in terms of a different — less political and more religious — transcendence. But the basic principle is always there, loaded with historical tradition, that the Baptist is not Christ or the awaited prophet (John 1:49), Jesus is the Messiah and the Prophet proclaimed by Moses (John 1:45).

God gave Moses the power to carry out three successive miracles in order to show that his mission was authentic and so that people would believe in that mission. Moses carried out three miracles, three signs (*athoth*, *semeia*), which are enumerated so that he would be recognized as an envoy of God. The disposition of Jesus' first three miracles, in Boismard's interpretation, shows Jesus as the new Moses who would definitively fulfill what was prefigured in Moses. The wedding at Cana (John 2:1-12), the healing of the son of the royal official (John 4:46-54], and the miracle of the fishing boat (John 21:1-8) all follow the same pattern as the Exodus (4:1). Thanks to Jesus' signs he is recognized as God's envoy and, at this first level of John's writing, as the new Moses, whose coming was promised in Deuteronomy (Deut. 18:18). This connection between the Gospel of John and the Exodus narratives is the more notable because in the synoptic tradition the miracles are ordinarily conceived as a consequence of faith in Christ, not as a sign that should lead human beings to faith.[24]

But this connection between Jesus and Moses, specifically Moses the liberator and not Moses the lawgiver, makes it clear that with Jesus too, one must be careful about separating his historical acts from his salvific acts. The three signs of Moses were intended to corroborate his divine mission and the divine character of the action he was undertaking; that mission and that action were of a markedly sociopolitical character. In this sense, John's reference to the Exodus is significant. There are also differences. Although the miracles of Jesus have a clear worldly sense (the wedding at Cana, the healing of a sick child, the abundance of fish), they are not formally sociopolitical but more familial in character. This is because those were the signs needed in that concrete situation of the proclamation of the faith, and there would be other signs in different situations: the Messianic entrance into Jerusalem (John 12:12-19), the expulsion of the merchants from the temple (John 2:13ff), the healing of the blind man (John 9:1ff). In each case there is a need for signs and admirable works that show God's presence and will. Whether these signs are a consequence of faith in Christ, or a prologue to faith in Christ, varies from case to case, but in both interpretations we see an intrinsic connection between the sign and what is signified; moreover, the sign can be understood as the unity of the signifier (the historical event as it refers to the salvific content) and what is signified (the salvific content made present in the historical event). The unity of the transcendent and the historical remains fully valid, even when the historical circumstances and the arena in which the revelation develops lead to different manifestations distinguishable both by what they show and give, and by the situation of those to whom the manifestation and the gift are addressed.

Thus O. Cullmann takes it as corroborated that "the gospel of John has linked the central event of the life of Jesus with the other historico-salvific periods."[25] Certainly the raising of the serpent and the manna are understood differently in the Mosaic and in the Johannine traditions. But on the other hand, the replacement of the temple as the place of worship by the figure of Jesus himself forbids a naive spiritualization of the transition from the Old Testament to the New Testament tradition.

We cannot continue this overview of the presence of the new Moses in the earliest stratum of John's gospel. In speaking of historical transcendence in the New Testament, we cannot overlook the dehistoricization of the Mosaic character of Jesus, the archetypal realization of what was only a prototype in Moses, in other strata. But the fact that the historical has been transcendentalized does not detract from the need to emphasize that the first level is historical and refers to historical events and corroborations in the past, present, and future; without them that transcendentalization would be unfounded and even to a certain extent meaningless. The clear historicization to which the Gospel of John subjects all Jesus' polemics with the Jewish religious and political authorities — the "Jews" — and especially his trial, crucifixion, and death clearly proves that the transcendentalization is not an escape from historical realities but another way of confronting them, a way no less effective and polemical than that of a confrontation in terms of political power. As so many authors have emphasized so often, the reference to a mixture of religious and political accusations in the passion narratives, while it shows the interpretive tendency of his accusers to see the religious factor as indissolubly united with the political factor, which led them to an erroneous understanding of what Jesus was doing, also shows that the presence, the words, and the actions of Jesus did not represent a sufficient break with the religious-political tradition to keep them from seeing him as a dangerous rival. To interpret that break as if Jesus intended to make a radical separation between the salvific and the historical, and the Jews saw this as a negation of their fundamental tradition and a threat to powers maintained for religious reasons, would go beyond what the sacred texts were trying to communicate, or at least beyond the way they communicated it.

Because of the above, perhaps it is not an exaggeration to draw some *consequences* for our problem, which could be formulated in the following theses: (1) The gospel of John, which reaches the highest formulations of the transcendence of Jesus and his divinity, begins by seeing Jesus as a new Moses who would carry out a liberating function with his people. (2) Jesus would first be presented to his people, in this case the people of Samaria, as someone who would respond to their need for both religious and historical liberation. (3) This liberation and historical presence of salvation would lead in other directions in a praxis different from that of Moses, but would not abandon the historically constituted element in either its fundamental purpose or its original form; one of its fundamental distinctions is that the liberating presence of God no longer takes the form of a theocracy, but becomes a force without political power — which would transform historical reality from the viewpoint of the people, precisely against the powers that presented themselves as theocratic, and consequently as idolatrous, insofar as they claim dominion in God's name. (4) This new liberating praxis of Jesus sets him against the powers of this world insofar as they dominate and lead it toward death, so that he cannot enter the promised land with his people, which would lead to a rethinking of historical salvation in terms of an eschatology that is both individual and collective. (5) Jesus' historical praxis reveals in him a new and definitive presence of God, which would give new perspectives and new dimensions to transcendence in its specifically, fully Christian sense.

2. The New People

It is clear, therefore, that this new Moses would also make way for a new people, a new Israel. While the memory and presence of Moses and the people he accompanied speak to us of historical continuity, the novel character with which the "new" Moses, the "new" people, the "new" passover, the "new" command, the "new" law, and so on are presented, speak to us of a qualitative difference, which perhaps should not be described as a break; without calling it a discontinuity, we have to speak of something different. Indeed, already in the Old Testament the "new" people of Israel was being established in its ceaseless novelty, as the remnant to which the promise was addressed, but at the same time as a seed of the promise that was to be fulfilled. And it was established or was being established by the historical experience of a political failure, which put God's promise in a different perspective: the historical failures — both Israel's failure to achieve political power and triumph through it, and the failure to establish new relationships among human beings and between humanity and God — were leading to a new reading of the divine promise. This experience of failure was even clearer in the days of the New Testament, not only because of Jesus' scandalous end as the Messiah, but because of the destruction of the people of Israel and the subsequent establishment of a new type of religious relationship among human beings and between humanity and God. The change would come in two directions. First, the ethnic particularity of Israel would be opened to universality, which the prophets also pointed to, but which possessed great novelty because now Israel alone was not seen as the object of salvation and as the savior. Rather, the whole world was to be saved and a new figure of the savior was taking shape, which in the first historical instance was Jesus, but which would later need to be prolonged in a diversity of places and times. Second, the historical plan of salvation in the Old Testament, which certainly brought together faithfulness to Yahweh and fullness of life, but which also functioned theocratically and on the basis of political power, would be opened to a new historical plan in which the *relationship* between holiness and the good of the world would be perfected and made concrete. In this plan salvation would no longer be imposed from above by the means which the lords of this world possess.

This is where the church appears as the new locus of salvation: the church as the new people of God, which the new Moses has brought to life, and which is enabled to carry forward the history of salvation, inspired by the Spirit that was promised by the dead and resurrected Christ. But for our purposes it is not enough to affirm that the church is the new historical locus of salvation. Even granting that the visible and historical church still maintains that exceptional character as the place of salvation, by the will of Jesus Christ and with the help of the Spirit, we must ask what in that historical church is able to play that role and what in that historical church is working against it. The problem is to find what is truly church in the true church. And this question of what is truly church, which may not be historically separable from what is false in the church — just as the wheat cannot be separated from the tares until the end of time, because to do so would ruin the whole harvest — cannot be answered without first asking about Christian historical transcendence in and within the church, that is, without leaving it. This means seeking out the tangible realities which, in themselves and by Christ's will, make the church the place that *most* reveals the Christian God, who takes no pleasure in either the wisdom sought by the Greeks or the signs sought by the Jews. A new wisdom and new signs will be needed for the definitive fulfillment of the promise that God is with us, that we are God's people, and that the true God is really our God.

IV. THE SEARCH FOR CHRISTIAN HISTORICAL TRANSCENDENCE

Keeping in mind the perspectives of historical transcendence in the Old and New Testaments, we can now return to the question of what Christian historical transcendence should be. The problem has two currents: first, what is the relationship between what is called profane history and salvation history; second, what is the specifically Christian contribution to that moment of historical transcendence in which the transcendent somehow becomes historical and the historical somehow becomes transcendent.

To present the problem in a general theoretical way before entering into a more concentrated analysis of the perspective of liberation theology, let us briefly outline two European viewpoints, one Catholic and the other evangelical, in which the problem is meaningfully expressed.

In a brief essay titled "History of the World and Salvation History,"[26] Karl Rahner has formulated certain theses which, although they come from a time when he was less interested in the political projection of religion, together express viewpoints that are fundamental to his thinking: (1) The history of salvation occurs in and is interwoven with the history of the world, for salvation occurs now, it is freely accepted by the human being, and it remains hidden within profane history in its dual possibilities of salvation and condemnation. (2) Salvation history is different from profane history, since profane history does not permit a single interpretation of salvation and condemnation; however, we do speak of a constant interaction and coexistence between profane history and the history of salvation and revelation, although God through his Word, which is a fundamental element of salvation history, has set apart one part of history to establish it expressly, officially, and in itself as the history of salvation. (3) Salvation history explains profane history by demythologizing and dehuminizing it, by viewing it as conflictive and shrouded in darkness, by interpreting it as existentially powerless, and by explaining it christocentrically. In the final analysis, profane history is the necessary condition for the history of Christ, which is also the history of God, just as natural history in its materiality and vitality is the necessary condition for the emergence of the finite spirit.

W. Pannenberg, in our second example, has also formulated his thesis around the relationship between revelation and history: (1) God's self-revelation has not been carried out directly, as a kind of theophany, but indirectly, through God's works in history. (2) The revelation does not occur at the beginning, but at the end of the revelatory history. (3) Historical revelation is open for all who have eyes to see; it has a universal character. (4) The universal revelation of God's divinity was not yet realized in the history of Israel, but only in the fate of Jesus of Nazareth, inasmuch as that fate anticipates the end of all that happens. (5) The Christ event does not reveal the divinity of the God of Israel as an isolated event, and it is only comprehensible from the viewpoint of the history of God with Israel. (6) The formation of non-Jewish concepts of revelation in the Christian churches of pagan origin expresses the universality of eschatological self-revelation in the fate of Jesus. (7) The word of God relates to revelation as preaching, as precept, and as story.[27]

Now let us compare this with the way the theology of liberation approaches the double problem defined above with regard to Christian historical transcendence. We shall take it step by step, beginning with the experience of Latin American believers—of course it is not only their experience—especially that of the poorest and most oppressed sectors, and of Latin American believers who are compelled by their faith to political commitment with the conquest of freedom through a process of liberation.

1. History as a Whole

Granting that there may be a difference between salvation history and real history as it is lived empirically, we can say that at bottom believers see these two histories as one, that is, united in what might be called the great history of God. This perception presupposes that history is presented as a whole, with two parts. The first is what can be called salvation history, which certainly is not limited to sacramental or cultic or strictly religious life. The second, which has a more profane appearance, is also part of the great history of God with humanity. If we are asked whether profane history takes its meaning from salvation history and is subordinate to it, we respond by presenting the problem in deeper terms. Salvation history and the so-called profane history both belong to a single history, which includes God's history; what God has done with all of nature; what God does in human history; and what God wants to come from God's constant self-giving, which can be imagined as going from eternity to eternity. In this sense the salvation history that culminates in the person of Christ is subordinate to that greater history of God. We could say that this concept gives living expression to Paul's experience when he saw God's mysterious plan "for the fullness of time, to gather up all things in Christ, things in heaven and things on earth" (Eph. 1:9-10, *NRSV*).

For all things are yours, whether Paul or Apollos or Cephas or the world or life or death or the present or the future — all belong to you, and you belong to Christ, and Christ belongs to God (1 Cor. 3:21-23).

When all things are subjected to him, then the Son himself will also be subjected to the one who put all things in subjection under him, so that God may be all in all (1 Cor. 15:28).

This affirmation of God's history as the true history embracing everything that happens in history, which does not identify salvation history with the autonomy of the profane, comes to us through popular religion and also through pre-Christian religious traditions, which take it for granted that God has made and continues to make human beings along with everything else that exists. Christian preaching was grafted onto an earlier religious tradition, which in some places is still very active, which sees God's action among human beings as a part of nature. The gods of the *Popol Vuh*[28] and the still prevalent cosmovisions of peoples like the K'ekchi'[29] serve as background to this acceptance of a single God, who begins by making earth and heaven, who is still behind natural events, and who is in some degree also behind historical events.

In this history of God, Christian faith gives absolute primacy to the salvific event of Christ, but this does not imply a caesaropapist and/or religionist subjection of profane history to the specificity of Christ as head of the church, and therefore to the church as continuation of the work of Christ. It does, however, imply a subordination to what can be called the historical-cosmic Christ, called to make history as a whole effectively God's history, which on earth means building the Kingdom of God. The historical Jesus of Nazareth, as presented and interpreted throughout the New Testament from his historical origins and life to his resurrection and lordship over the universe and history, is the key to this historical-cosmic Christ. Therefore the Kingdom of Heaven is, in a first moment, a seed sown in the fields of the world and in history, to make it a history of God, of a God who is definitively all in all. In this first moment the field is not subjected to the seed, but the seed to the field; or, as the other evangelical parable puts it, the leavening of the Kingdom is modestly and effectively mixed into the dough of the world to make it ferment and rise.

All this is expressed with absolute naturalness in the relationship of the believing people of Latin America to nature and to one another. To be committed only to the religious aspect of the Kingdom, without concern for its essential reference to the world and history, would be a clear betrayal of God's history; it would leave the field of history to God's enemies. This is not reductionism, either reducing God's history to the history of Christian salvation in its restricted sense or reducing God's history to the history of political, social, economic, or cultural events. Rather, it is an attempt through Christian faith and action in the midst of the world—which has its own autonomy just as Christian faith and action have—to build God's history, in which Christ's action and human actions, the dictates of faith and of reason, come together in their different forms and different levels of reality.

This way of expressing the problem of Christian historical transcendence may seem rather abstract. In reality it is not. In the conceptual formulation, which may miss the mark, we must not forget that the experience belongs to the believers, who see everything as a unity in which they are directly involved and which must be respected. This unity is based on the profound conviction that there is only one God and Father, only one creation, only one Savior, only one Kingdom of God, only one eschatology, only one world, and only one humanity. The things of God and the things of humanity, therefore, must not and cannot be separated; that would mean confusing God with humanity. Jesus himself, who as Christ will bring all things together in himself, enters history as the one who has come to serve human beings and to give his life for them. The church, in turn, must also fulfill its mission by placing itself at the service of human beings and giving its life and institutionality for them, knowing that this is the fulfillment of God's great history. The example of Jesus' life remains the fundamental criterion showing how God enters the service of humanity.

To structure salvation history and the history of the world into what we have been calling God's history does not imply accepting a separation and duality between the first two, subsumed in the higher unity of the third; God's history is nothing but the structural unity of salvation history and the history of the world. The history of the world determines salvation history in many ways; salvation history determines the history of the world in many ways; and God's history is involved in both. Thus the history of the world, rightly analyzed and discerned—herein lies the importance that Clodovis Boff attributes to socioanalytical mediation[30]—presents salvation history with its specific task for each moment, which is partly shaped, without diminishing its specificity in each case, by this fundamental mission. But at the same time, the history of revelation, rightly interpreted—herein lies the importance that Boff attributes to hermeneutical mediation[31]—tries to orient the history of the world to the demands of God's history, which is also manifested in different ways in the information conveyed by revelation, in the signs of the times, and even in the most basic conditioners of material nature. Thus God's self-giving to humanity continues, not only in the limited arena of a salvation history in its restricted sense, but in the total arena of history. Salvation history takes axiological priority in this total arena, because it is the preeminent way in which God's self-giving becomes present, especially in the figure of Jesus and in the revealed word; however, as we shall insist later, Jesus becomes present and intervenes in a special salvific way as the fundamental mediator of God's history in seemingly profane places, such as that of the poor in this world.

2. Grace and Sin

Closely related to the first point is the problem of what is natural and what is supernatural in this whole history of God.

This formulation of the problem is itself somewhat disconcerting. Is the diversity of God's different forms of self-giving greater than the unity that comes from the fact that it is one God, self-giving in different ways? This question is even more valid if we ask it not about the sanctification and divinization of persons, but about God's presence and intervention in history. Are Moses' action in bringing the oppressed people out of Egypt and God's presence in that action different from their respective action and presence in giving the law or celebrating religious rites? Are Jesus' action in the feeding of the hungry multitude and God's presence in that action different from their respective action and presence in expelling the merchants from the temple or proclaiming the Kingdom of God and institutionalizing the eucharistic supper? Are we right to describe the more "profane" cases as God's natural intervention and the more "religious" cases as supernatural intervention?

The believing people of Latin America do not see, let alone reflexively affirm, one type of natural intervention and another type of supernatural intervention; at most they may distinguish between them in terms of miracles, but not in terms of a supernatural communication over against a natural communication by God. They may see some things as more or less distant from God, or God as less present in them, but they do not clearly separate the work of grace and the work of nature; that is, they do not separate the natural from the supernatural. They accept, for example, that God becomes present in the sacraments in what we might call a more religious way, but they know that the same God of the sacraments is present in their life and destiny and in the course of historical events. Everything is included in the category of God's will. Sometimes they may think fatalistically that something happened because it was God's will; other times they may see clearly that an action is against God's will — not only or mainly in the arena of personal actions but in the course of historical events.

For this reason they raise the question in different terms. The fundamental difference is not between nature and the supernatural; since they are part of the whole history of God, who in creating human beings raises them to personal participation in God's own divine life, the difference is between grace and sin. Some actions kill (divine) life, and some actions give (divine) life; some belong to the kingdom of sin, others to the kingdom of grace. Some social and historical structures objectify the power of sin and serve as vehicles for that power against humanity, against human life; some social and historical structures objectify grace and serve as vehicles for that power in favor of human life. The former constitute structural sin; the latter constitute structural grace. Hans Urs von Balthasar rightly sees that "the New Testament is a confrontation between two types of existence: that which is subjected to sin (*hamartia*) and that which is liberated from sin through Christ."[32] But he judges Medellín unfairly for speaking of unjust and oppressive structures as constituting a situation of sin when he says that "situations can be unjust, but they are not in themselves sinful.[33] Some situations may not be sinful, but they can be an objectification of sin, and they can themselves be sin when they are a positive negation of an essential aspect of the God of life. To think that sin exists only when and insofar as there is personal responsibility is a mistaken and dangerous devaluation of the dominion of sin. The theology of liberation encourages people to change specific structures and to seek new ones, because it sees sin in some and grace in others.

In the former it sees the negation of God's will and self-giving, while in the latter it sees the affirmation and fulfillment of God's will and self-giving.[34]

This does not mean that the classical question about the natural and the supernatural is an idle question, only that it is not the first question. The first question is what there is of grace and of sin in humanity and in history, and this with grace and sin seen not primarily from a moral viewpoint, let alone from the fulfillment of laws and obligations, but from that which makes God's life present among human beings. God's presence is what makes possible the fulfillment of laws and obligations, not the other way around. It is not the law that saves, but faith and grace, a faith and grace that operate and are sometimes objectified in history.

No special discernment is needed to identify objective sin in the situation that the people of Latin America are living. It is all around us. It has been recognized by Medellín and Puebla, it has been denounced a thousand times by the bishops, and it is clearly recognized by what can be called the *sensus fidei* of the poor. For the oppressed believers in Latin America, injustice and whatever brings death and denies dignity to the children of God are not merely historical effects, nor even a legal failing; they are sin in a formal sense, something that formally has to do with God. The death of the poor is the death of God, the ongoing crucifixion of the Son of God. Sin is the negation of God; the negation of sin moves, sometimes in unknown ways, toward the affirmation of God, toward the presence of God as the giver of life. The perception of a world submerged in ambition, hatred, and domination is nourished by faith and by the Christian sense of those who live their faith simply. It is a way of seeing the sin of the world, sin Christ came to redeem and Christians must work to make disappear from the world. Sin cannot be studied abstractly; it is concretely present in subtle forms that require more careful theological analysis.

3. Creation, the Presence of the Trinitarian Life

In order to go more deeply into this whole history of God, which is fundamentally a history of sin and grace, we can offer some reflections that may seem theoretical, but which shed light on what we have been saying; they can also serve as a practical orientation.

Everything depends on how we understand creation. If by *creation* we mean an effective act of God in which the creature is a separate effect, having at most a remote resemblance to God, then it is very hard to see the unity of the creature with the creator and to understand God's single history. But creation can be conceived in a different way, as X. Zubiri so often pointed out in his classes. Creation can be seen as the grafting *ad extra* of the trinitarian life itself, a freely desired grafting. It would not be an abstract causality, but an act of communication and self-giving by the divine life itself. This grafting and self-communication has degrees and limits; each thing, within its own limits, is a limited way of being God. This limited way is precisely the nature of each thing. God's communication, the grafting *ad extra* of the divine life, has gone through a long process toward the grafting of that divine life in the human nature of

Jesus and ultimately toward the "return" of all creation to its original source. In that long process we find the purely material form of creation, the different stages of life, and finally the form of humanity and human history. Humanity as a formally open essence, and history in its essential openness, are the realities in which that grafting of the triune life are more and more present, although always in a limited way—open but limited, limited but open.

This would be the "theologal" character of all things, and especially the theologal character of humanity and history. It would not be simply that God is in all things, as essence, presence, and potential depending on the character of those things; it would be that all things, each in its own way, have been grafted with the triune life and refer essentially to that life. The *theologal* dimension of the created world, which should not be confused with the *theological* dimension, would reside in that presence of the trinitarian life, which is intrinsic to all things, but which in human beings can be apprehended as reality and as the principle of personality. There is a strict experience of this theologal dimension, and through it there is a strict personal, social, and historical experience of God.[35] This experience has different degrees and forms; but when it is a true experience of the real theologal dimension of human beings, of society, of history, and in a different measure, of purely material things, it is an experience and physical probing of the triune life itself, however mediated, incarnated, and historicized.

From this perspective we see more clearly not only the unity of God's history, but the fundamental dimension in which to reflect on the problem of grace and sin. All created things are a limited way of being God, and the human being in particular is a small God because the human being is a relative absolute, an acquired absolute. What happens is that this limited way of being God is in principle open. This openness must be seen dynamically, but that dynamic openness is precisely the growing presence of the divine reality in the creature. When this dynamism remains merely limited, because at a certain level of creaturehood the self-giving is held back, it is not yet sin but only a deficient presence of the divine, although that deficiency can only be measured in comparison with more elevated and less deficient forms of presence. But when the dynamism is limited, not only in natural evolution but in the historical process— whether personal or social—by deliberate negation, which by absolutizing the limit impedes and even explicitly negates the dynamism of the trinitarian life (although it cannot destroy it), then we have a case of sin in its formal sense.

Making absolute this personal and social limit has two aspects. First, it impedes the renewed presence of God's "more," which deprives but does not formally deny the God who wants to become more present. Second, it makes absolute and divine a created limit, and in this sense positively denies God and enters the realm of idolatry. In this sin, although it may appear paradoxical, there is an affirmation of God insofar as the sinner is oriented to a good which is the presence of God; but there is an even stronger negation of that affirmation, because it presents something that is only a partial and transitory presence of God as a full and definitive presence, thus denying a "more" which is the historical presence of the transcendent. To put it differently, idolatry, by making absolute what is limited, closes and denies the divine presence that is in all historical things. This closing in on a limit is precisely what negates the presence of that "more" and that "new" through which transcendence becomes present in the form of personal revelation. Thus a divine character is attributed to what is not divine but rather limited, because a limit is made absolute. But that attribution and that absolutization are only possible through the presence of the divine, from the theologal dimension. Therefore we must speak not of atheism but of idolatry, of making absolute that which is only relatively absolute. That is how grace becomes sin.

This, which may seem so abstract, is easy to exemplify in real and pastoral life. Monseñor Romero, in his pastoral letter "The Church's Mission amid the National Crisis,"[36] seeks to unmask the idolatries of our society. He exposes from this perspective the idolatry implied in making absolute wealth and private property, national security, and organization. In wealth and power it is easy to see aspects that have to do with the presence of God, but the historical absolutization of wealth and power converts them into idols to which all other human possibilities are sacrificed. In the individual self and its freedom something is also present which has to do very directly with the God who becomes present and operates in history, but the absolutization of the self and its freedom converts them into idols, makes grace present as sin. In institutional mechanisms and objective realizations, too, one sees God's potential to achieve a more humane and open history by means of structures, institutions, and social bodies that open human beings more and more to themselves and to others, but their idolatrous absolutization converts the limit into a positive obstacle and a negation of something that is always greater than any objective realization or any subjective intention.

If we look at things this way, it is possible to conceive God's history at once as a history of grace and a history of sin. There is a greater or lesser presence of the divine life, of grace; and there is sometimes privation, sometimes negation, of grace.

4. Unjust Poverty

The problem, then, is to discern what there is of sin and of grace in a specific historical situation. We must ask in all seriousness what the sin of the world is today, or in what forms the sin of the world appears today; this sin is different from personal sins but is often conditioned by them and continues or prolongs them. Here is where the theology of liberation, situated at the heart of the passive and active praxis of the poor, has spoken its word and has shaken the conscience of the church, and in some ways also the conscience of the world.

If we look at the reality of the world as a whole from the perspective of faith, we see that the sin of the world is sharply expressed today in what must be called unjust poverty. Poverty and injustice appear today as the great negation of God's will and as the annihilation of the desired presence of God among human beings. Both poverty and injustice are empirical phenomena whose universality the First World, the source of traditional theologies, has been reluctant to see. Without losing their empirical character, which must be analyzed with the aid of scientific mediations, precisely the same phenomena appear in the light of faith as a fundamental event in the history of God with humanity. The scriptural perspective of historical transcendence takes very seriously the realities of the poor and their unjustly inflicted poverty; the social, economic, and political structures on which their reality is based; and their complex ramifications of hunger, illness, imprisonment, torture, murder, and so on. Their empirical character is never lost from view, but they are interpreted in the light of God, as revealed in scripture, in tradition, and in the continuing inspiration of the Spirit. They are all negations of the Kingdom of God; one cannot sincerely proclaim the Kingdom of God with one's back turned to these realities, or while throwing a cloak over their shame. It is not necessary to pursue this point, which has already been sufficiently emphasized by the experience of the believers, by the magisterium of the church, and finally by the theological elaboration of the experts.

At the same time we must ask what there is of grace in this historical moment. The answer from the perspective of historical transcendence, especially in the New Testament, is that the poor themselves, impoverished and oppressed by injustice, have become the preferred locus of benevolence and grace, of God's faithful love. To look at things first and foremost from the viewpoint of the poor is one of the essential characteristics of Christian historical transcendence: the crushing-down that leads to exaltation, the death on the cross that leads to resurrection, the suffering that leads to glory, the least of these who are the greatest in the kingdom, the poor who are promised blessings. These are the historical ways in which the God of Jesus becomes present among human beings and in the march of history. These are specific signs that the New Testament offers in abundance as the typical forms of Christian transcendence. For good reason the theology of liberation has repeated as one of its fundamental texts of inspiration, the Old Testament words—promising good news to the poor, liberty to the captives, sight to the blind, release to the oppressed (Isa. 61:1-2)—that the evangelist attributes to Jesus to show the accomplishment of the Old Testament in the New: "Today this scripture has been fulfilled in your hearing" (Luke 4:21).

Therefore we are not only speaking of the existence of the poor and their growing awareness of salvation history, which the church has neglected throughout the centuries; we are speaking first of their desire that the church follow the will of Jesus, and second, of their active participation in gradually turning the proclamation of the Kingdom into an historically palpable fact. The poor have been evangelized; they have been conscientized and have decided to use their Christian power for their liberation. This sometimes leads them to political commitments, just as European Christians were once supposedly led by Christian inspiration to intervene in politics, in that case without scandal and with the clear support of the ecclesiastical authorities. The political commitment in this case is quite naturally with the revolutionary sectors, which puts them in contact with ideologies that can affect them, just as the earlier European and Latin American Christians were affected by capitalist ideologies. But that does not mean they have exchanged the inspiration of their faith for the interpretation of ideologies, as if one were equivalent to the other; on the contrary, they have made the ideologies themselves more open, both in practical application and in relation to the Christian faith.

Thus the theology of liberation is accused of converting the evangelical poor into a social class, and the struggle for liberation into a class struggle. That is said to favor Marxism and anti-capitalist tendencies, a point which seems particularly important to the institutionalized church. The theology of liberation is said to be not only influenced by Marxism, but at bottom subordinated to it. The accusation is entirely mistaken, from both the methodological and the pastoral viewpoint.

It is wrong from the *methodological viewpoint*, because it mistakes the part for the whole, the subordinate for the principal. For example, to speak of the theology of liberation as Marxist-inspired and to take one of the works of Jon Sobrino as the prime example, as Cardinal Ratzinger has done,[37] is a striking methodological error. Marxism may be present to different degrees in other theologians, but in Sobrino's theology its presence is absolutely marginal. The presence of Marxism in the whole of the theology of liberation is derivative and subordinate, in the first place, and in the second, it has diminished over the years. Moreover, to insist on the viewpoint of the poor, although that may sometimes favor the revolutionary struggle, does not make of them a social class; in a stricter sense this calls for a break with the model of social classes, which is based on ownership of the means of production, and presents a theological interpretation that overflows the narrow model of the proletariat, as such. From this viewpoint, the theology of liberation sometimes represents a strong internal critique of what would otherwise be a sociological theory historically untested by differences in reality.

From the *pastoral viewpoint*, we need to distinguish between the clear preferential option for the poor and the subsequent political options that specific social groups may choose once they have understood their obligation to the oppressed majorities. Here there is a very clear progression, from being moved by faith to work on behalf of the poor, to choosing the best way of doing so. The first is a purely Christian choice, which requires little mediating effort and in which Christian historical transcendence becomes clearer. The second leads to two subsequent options: to work on behalf of the oppressed majorities from a methodologically more religious viewpoint (feeding them with discernment, conversion, and so on) or from a more political viewpoint (support or affiliation with groups that try to promote the cause of the poorest in diverse ways). The church has something to say on this option, but clearly it must speak with respect for the autonomy of strictly political positions, without assuming that the political options most in line with the preferences and needs of the institutionalized church are necessarily the options most favorable to the Kingdom of God and to the popular majorities. Let us remember, just in passing, how often the church has interpreted actions that went against its temporal political or social power as going against the will of God, when in reality they were inherently good actions that eventually brought great benefit to the church.

5. Power

Christian historical transcendence, as it incorporates both Old Testament and New Testament historical transcendence, relates to power in a unique way. The Old Testament tradition would seem inclined to use God's power in the form of state or quasi-state power; the New Testament tradition, following lines clearly marked out in the Old Testament, would seem to abandon that power and focus more on power over individuals. In the latter tradition religious power would seem more personal and internal, while in the former it was more structural and public. It was not entirely that way, as we see by the church's secular determination to affirm itself as an institutional power, drawing even on state power, seeking to be a perfect society just as state societies are. Nevertheless, Christian historical transcendence does not repeat either the personalistic or the institutional model.

There are in fact three historical models, each of which contains several variations.

There was a first attempt to save Israel by means of power, but *power conceived theocratically*. The hope was that God would save the people and save history as the kings and lords of this world do, but with a purification of their entirely secular way of doing it. This model was followed by Moses, the judges, the kings, the Maccabees, and others. The attempt was based on an essential element of truth: God's will is a historical salvation, an integral salvation embracing the whole condition of humanity and of peoples, so that salvation is not reduced to something spiritual or trans-temporal. But it also contained an element that would later be seen as invalid and even anti-salvific; that element was hidden behind the belief that salvation must come through power – military, economic, political, religious, even miraculous power – that is, power shaped by the powers of this world, although they acquired a sacred character that established them as theocratic power.

With the repeated failure of this attempt, an opposite model appeared in history: the way of power not only leads to historical failure and the triumph of evil, but *it makes the way of salvation impossible*. Therefore it was necessary to abandon the world to the powers of evil and seek salvation and holiness through separation from this world. Thus it should and would happen some day, at the end of "these times," that God would break into history to crush God's enemies, definitively uprooting sin and making a new world for God's children. The fundamental element of truth in this attempt was the affirmation that God's salvation surpasses and transcends the structure and the possibilities of the strictly political, and the affirmation that the political, however necessary, can never bring the integral salvation that humanity needs. But it had another element which invalidated that solution; salvation was not seen as something historically operative and present in real human situations, gradually transforming the situations and bringing them closer to a real, though not definitive, presence of the Kingdom of God. Certainly even the Essenes seem to have seen the need for historical salvation, for they awaited and in different ways even anticipated a new presence of God, a triumphant irruption of God over the sin of this world; however, they did not make that hope and anticipation historical, but left for later the salvific presence of God among human beings and human things. They failed to see the positive sense of both the "not yet" and the "already," although they emphasized the truth of the "not yet" and the historical limitation of the "already." The same is true of those who hope for salvation only in the next world, reducing it in this world to purely internal or moral dimensions. They attribute such autonomy to the world that they separate it from God's history and leave it at the mercy of those who dominate it, except when those who dominate it limit the wealth and power of those who claim to be seeking God.

The third model is the one most marked by Christian historical transcendence; it seeks *to save history by making God's power present in it,* but the power of God that is revealed in Jesus, and in the ways it is revealed in him. This is a truly historical presence, which really operates in history and seeks to transform it, but in a unique way that neither spiritualistically retreats from history nor takes on the forms of theocratic power that easily become idolatrous power. It makes the classical figures of Moses, the Messiah, the king of the Jews, and more historically real in the figure of the historical servant of Yahweh, not to reduce that figure to a cultic expiation of sins and a plea for grace, but to give it historical embodiment in words and action. Thus it goes beyond the first two models, incorporating what is true and fundamental in them, but leaving out and negating their ambiguous and false points. It is clear from the New Testament that Jesus did not seek theocratic power; it is also clear that he did not withdraw from the sociohistorical arena, if we look at both his life and his death. His unique way of intervening in history, of making God historically present among human beings, is of course by proclaiming the Kingdom of God, making it present in himself and setting it in motion. One of the essential elements of this proclamation and this setting in motion of the Kingdom is the commitment of God's cause to the human cause, and more concretely, the commitment of God's cause to the cause of the poor. It is God in the poor who will save history, but in real poor people who really operate in history when, within their material condition of poverty, they recover their total blessedness as the gift of God.

This is where we should look for the uniqueness of Christian historical transcendence. The novelty of this transcendence is its break with what the world has understood as God's "glory," as God's true presence. People have seen that glory, which is also partly visible as the power of the divine majesty in the greatness of material nature, in such historical factors as human wisdom, the theocratic miracle, the religious law, and the wealth and power of the ecclesiastical institution. But these ways have shown that they do not lead the transcendence revealed to us in Jesus, but immediately become absolutized limits, which are sin and an obstacle to grace and therefore a negation of God. On the contrary, Jesus has discarded what humanity sees as great and has taken as sacrament of God what is despised by the powers of this world. This admirable greatness and this contemptible smallness can take different historical forms, but they represent a historical constant: the privileged status of the rich and powerful, and the domination and exploitation of those who have nothing but poverty and weakness. We must respond to the false paths of Christian historical transcendence by opening the path of negation, that is, the negation of the false paths to God, of the false gods, and of the false messianisms. We must also positively open the true paths of God. These are, in contrast to the others, Christian faith confronting the wisdom of the world, the power of the Crucified One confronting the theocratic miracle, grace and love confronting the religious law, poverty and service confronting wealth and power. All of this is reduced to the commandment of love, but of love understood in Christian terms and appropriately historicized.

All this happens in history. Therefore both the negation and the affirmation must take flesh in history. The proof that this is happening is persecution. What is foolishness to the Greeks and a stumbling block to the Jews, is seen as a threat and met with persecution by those who live by sin. Persecution for the sake of the Kingdom is credible proof of two fundamental things in the historical praxis of salvation: that the salvation that is proclaimed is becoming present in history, or it would not lead to historical persecution; and that the salvation that is proclaimed is real and truly Christian, or it would not be denied and persecuted by those who represent and objectify anti-Christian values.

Thus the problem is not that God's power, mediated by human beings, should not be used to improve historical realities; the problem is how to use it according to God's will. Once we have analyzed the concrete situation in which we must act, we know God's will primarily in Jesus. Jesus makes his message present in different ways but remains the fundamental criterion by which to test any action taken in his name.

6. Spirituality

We have been emphasizing some objective aspects of Christian historical transcendence; when these aspects are present, there is transcendence. But we have not sufficiently stressed a personal encounter with that Christian historical transcendence. That is the problem of spirituality in the theology of liberation, which is becoming increasingly important to Latin American theologians, who are unjustly accused of being too secular and too political.[38] Gustavo Gutiérrez has begun focusing on this subject with the well-known Ignatian concept of contemplation in action. The action represents the objective element and contemplation the subjective; only when contemplation is achieved in action are we truly on the way to realizing and assuming Christian historical transcendence.

The problem is to determine what action, or fundamental plan of action, most fully represents Christian historical transcendence. From a Latin American viewpoint, and that of the Third World in general, such action is fundamentally an action of liberation from all that keeps the Kingdom of God from becoming present among human beings, from all that keeps God from being made manifest as a power of life and not a power of death. This implies that the greatest problem of the world and the greatest sin of the world are seen as the universal and structural situation which forces most of humanity to live in conditions that St. Thomas himself saw as making it practically impossible to live a human life ruled by moral principles. This is the situation caused by the objective culpability—whether it is a sin of commission or of omission—of the dominant minorities which have made domination, exploitation, and consumerism the gods of their institutional existence. This fundamental plan of action is the place with the greatest possibility today of objectively manifesting the will and presence of the God of Jesus. This is not the only sin that is in the world, but it is the fundamental source of many other sins, which must be measured in terms of this one. Taken on a global scale, combatting this historical sin, which is objectified in easily visible ways, overcoming it, and opening the way to a new situation present the fundamental challenge to Christian mission in proclaiming and fulfilling the Kingdom. This sin is the negation of the fatherhood of God, of the human kinship revealed in the Son, and of the love that the Spirit has spread throughout the world; this sin is the negation of humanity in its most fundamental rights; this sin is the source of violence, conflict, and division; this sin blocks the ways between God and humanity.

In another sense, we are speaking of a universal liberation. It is an integral liberation expressed not only in terms of economic or political problems, but also a universal liberation. The poor must be liberated from their poverty, but the rich must also be liberated from their wealth; the oppressed must be liberated from their condition of domination, and the oppressors from their dominant condition. And so on. The preferential Christian option is clear in this contrast, without denying its universality: it is an option for the poor, for the oppressed.

But if we want this liberation to be real, that is, not only forgiving sin but taking it away, we must use not only analytical but also practical mediations. Here and only here is where the theology of liberation finds it necessary to use Marxist analysis and, sometimes, forms of praxis that can be considered Marxist. We shall not enter into discussion of this point. Everything said so far shows that the problem of historical transcendence can be presented without reference to Marxism and without subjecting Christian ideas to Marxist ideologies. But it is worth noting that when the theology of liberation seeks the conceptual assistance of Marxism, it does not subject its discourse to Marxist discourse, but the other way around. It tries in this way, more or less successfully, to do what every other theology has done with other ideologies—sometimes scandalizing the magisterium and sometimes with tacit hierarchical approval, at least after a period of caution—that is, to strengthen its theological discourse with elements that do not close off transcendence but make it possible.

If this is the fundamental action in which we must be contemplative, then we must ask briefly what the Christian characteristics of this contemplation are. The fundamental point is given in action, because it would be an error of subjectivism to try to contemplate God where God does not want to be contemplated or where God cannot be found. The parable of the Samaritan (Luke 10:25-37) is clear on this point: the true neighbor is not the priest or the Levite, who pass by the suffering of the marginalized and wounded, but the Samaritan, who takes responsibility for him and offers him material care, thus resolving the situation in which he is unjustly involved. This apparently profane, apparently natural act, apparently taken without awareness of its meaning, is much more transcendent and Christian than all the prayers and sacrifices that the priests could make with their backs turned to the suffering and anguish around them. Moreover, contemplation can and must be scrutinized to see whether it is of God or something idolatrous. There are dangers in action, but there is no less danger in contemplation. In Jesus' saying, "Not everyone who says Lord, but those who do the will of the Father"; in many scriptural warnings, especially those of John who identifies (contemplative) light with acts of love and (God-concealing) darkness with hateful or unloving acts (1 John 1:5ff); and finally, by the masters of contemplation, we have repeatedly been warned against the types of contemplation that divert our gaze and our purpose from the action in which God seeks to become really present.

Once we have identified the needed action, both in the general plan of Christian life and in its particular diversifications, we must try to see some of the specific characteristics of contemplation itself. The contemplative in action must be truly contemplative, must try to find God subjectively in what he or she is doing objectively. There may be anonymous Christians, there may be unthematic experiences of God, but that is not the ideal; ideally the richest objectivity becomes the fullest subjectivity.

This contemplation should be undertaken from the most appropriate place. The "where" from which one seeks to see decisively determines what one is able to see; the horizon and the light one chooses are also fundamental to what one sees and how one sees it. The where, the light, and the horizon in which one seeks God are of course precisely God, but God mediated in that place chosen by God, which is the poor of the earth. This mediation of the poor does not limit, but rather strengthens the power of God as it is presented in scripture, in tradition, in the magisterium, in the signs of the times, in nature itself, in the march of history, and so on. Contemplation depends on a spirituality of poverty; that is one way of interpreting what it means to be poor in spirit, knowing how to live with a spirit of poverty and identifying with the cause of the poor, understood as God's cause. From this perspective of the poor one sees new meanings and new inspiration in the classical heritage of the faith. Since this is a task rarely undertaken in the course of history, at least at the level of theological reflection, new things appear here that have been unnoticed by those who sat on the high mountaintops, the better to scan God's horizon. The ones who see God most and best are those who have received God's self-revelation.

I thank you, Father, Lord of heaven and earth, because you have hidden these things from the wise and the intelligent and have revealed them to infants; yes, Father, for such was your gracious will. All things have been handed over to me by my Father; and no one knows who the Son is except the Father, or who the Father is except the Son and anyone to whom the Son chooses to reveal him (Luke 10:21-22).

This text can be read in several ways,[39] but one is applicable to what would be a necessary condition for Christian contemplation of God's historical transcendence, for an understanding of what there is of God in history.

It is prejudicial to judge the degree of contemplation by whether the object of contemplation appears more or less sacred, more or less internal, more or less spiritual. That would mean assuming that God is more present, more readily heard or contemplated in the internal silence of idleness than in committed action. This may not be so, and there is no reason why it should be so. On the road to Emmaus one may find the person one was looking for in the past, in the memory of sacred actions, or on the road to Damascus a false and Pharisaic religiosity may be broken in favor of a contemplation and conversion qualitatively incomparable with any prior experience. It is not certain that Christian transcendence can better be found in the temple than in the city, in concern for oneself than in concern for others. A really Christian praxis—which takes the people in greatest need as the starting point of the search for the way to remove the great sin of the world and to implant divine life in the human heart and in the nucleus of human structures—brings with it great richness because of the urgency and depth of its demands, the shared experience, the understanding that these are the very cleavages by which one can most rapidly and profoundly reach the Spirit of Christ that inspires his people.

All this does not diminish the importance of contemplation—and of the necessary conditions for contemplation, without which there is little possibility of discovering what is the true action. Some of these conditions are explicitly revelatory. It is not only erroneous but heretical to try to learn from praxis what God is saying, because although God speaks and has spoken "in many and various ways" (Heb. 1:1), God has spoken definitively through the Son; all revelation and tradition must be placed in this context. Conditions of personal life are also important, because although God is made manifest even to the greatest sinner, that manifestation usually begins with conversion and purification; it is the pure in heart who see God best (Luke 5:8). And psychological and methodological conditions are important; immersion in action is a rich source of reality, but contemplation requires special moments in which to gather up and consciously deepen the confrontation between the word of God heard in revelation and the urgent problems that come from reality through the mediation of centered reflection.

Contemplation in action can only mean the contemplation that becomes possible and necessary when one is acting. This does not only mean contemplating the actions one has taken, but making one's past or intended actions themselves into contemplation, an encounter with what there is of God in things, and an encounter with God in the things. This does not permit an activism without spiritual withdrawal, especially without liturgical celebration. On the contrary, it seeks to make explicit in word, in communication, in living, what one has found less explicitly in action. We know that it was found in action, first because Jesus promised that it would be so in Christian commitment with the people in greatest need; and second because the discernment of contemplation enables us to contrast that which is of God with that which is against

God. Thus, for example, it is when the celebration of the word, penitential gatherings, or eucharists are invested with all the personal and community needs that arise from the work of the participants (*opus operantis*) that the gratuitous efficacy of those celebrations (*opus operatum*) is fully given and received. Thus contemplation represents an effort to actualize what is already present; that which is already present is the fundamental principle of its actualization, but it requires a prepared subjectivity for its full actualization.

That completes the framework of what should be a full discussion of Christian historical transcendence. Other subjects should also be discussed, especially the church as a privileged place for showing Christian historical transcendence;[40] and the subjects outlined here should be more rigorously analyzed. Here we have tried to show the importance of the problem and some elements for its solution or, at least, for later discussion. Pannenberg has written: "History is the most elusive horizon of Christian theology."[41] One sees from the article in which that sentence appears that for Pannenberg history is the most globalizing horizon, not only for theology but for revelation itself. That is very true. A history that embraces both the historicity of real people and the real history of empirical events; a history whose empirical character is itself transcendent, that is, open to God, because God has first become present within it.

Thus historical transcendence is not exclusively a subject for the theology of liberation, but this theology has a unique way of understanding the formal meaning of Christian historical transcendence. In these pages I have tried to suggest some expressions of that unique understanding. By that means I have tried to point out the uniqueness and the universality of the theology of liberation, and at the same time, its novelty and traditionalism. The purpose was not to expound what the theologians of liberation have thought on this point, but only to show a possible way of conceptualizing the problem. Much more remains to be done through biblical, hermeneutical, dogmatic, and pastoral studies. The continuing vitality of the theology of liberation is so great that we can expect those studies to be done.

— Translated by Margaret D. Wilde

NOTES

1. Hans Urs von Balthasar, in International Theological Commission, *Teología de la liberación* (Madrid, 1978), p. 181.

2. Ibid.

3. J. Ratzinger, "Vi spiego la teologia," *30 Giorni* (March, 1984), p. 49.

4. Clodovis Boff, *Teología de lo Político* (Salamanca, 1980).

5. Ibid., pp. 27-29.

6. *Eu ouvi os clamores de meu povo* (Salvador, 1973).

7. Cf. the works of X. Zubiri, *Sobre la esencia* (Madrid, 1962); *Inteligencia sentiente* (Madrid, 1980); *Inteligencia y logos* (Madrid, 1982); *Inteligencia y razón*, (Madrid, 1983).

8. Urs von Balthasar, in *Teología de la liberacion*, p. 170.

9. M.-D. Chenu, "Les signes des temps," *NRT* 1 (1965); M. McGrath, "Los signos de los tiempos en America Latina hoy," in *Los textos de Medellín* (San Salvador, 1977), pp. 137-58.

10. J. J. Collins, "The 'Historical' Character of the Old Testament in Recent Biblical Theology," *The Catholic Biblical Quarterly* (April, 1979): 185-204.

11. I. Kant, *Critique of Practical Reason*, 3rd ed. (New York: MacMillan, 1993).

12. M. Noth, *Exodus* (Philadelphia: Westminster, 1982).

13. R. de Vaux, *Histoire ancienne d'Israel* (Paris, 1971), pp. 305 ff.

14. Ibid., p. 310.

15. Cf. M. Noth, *Exodus*.

16. Urs von Balthasar, in *Teología de la liberación*, p. 167.

17. De Vaux, *Histoire ancienne d'Israel*, pp. 306 ff.

18. International Theological Commission, *Teología de la liberación*, p. 192.

19. Cf. the biblical commentaries on the sermon on the mount, on the new Law, and more specifically on Hebrews 3:1-6.

20. M. E. Boismard and A. Lamouille, *L'évangile de Jean* (Paris, 1977), pp. 9-70.

21. *Jaris* and *aletheia*, more than "grace and truth," mean "love" and "faithfulness," with "faithfulness" as an adjectival term, so that in this case we should speak of a "faithful love." Cf. J. Mateos and J. Barreto, *El evangelio de Juan* (Madrid, 1979), pp. 45-46. Brown also translates it as "constant love": cf. R. F. Brown, *The Gospel According to John* (Garden City, N.Y.: Doubleday, 1970).

22. Even if Boismard's interpretation is not chronologically exact, his logical stratification permits an appreciation of the movement from the historical to the theological, of the upward movement from the "lesser" to the "greater" in Jesus himself. Cf. Boismard and Lamouille, *L'évangile de Jean*.

23. Ibid., p. 95.

24. Ibid., p. 104.

25. O. Cullmann, *La historia de la salvación* (Barcelona, 1967), p. 320.

26. K. Rahner, in *Theological Investigations* V (London: Darton, Longman & Todd, 1966), pp. 97-114.

27. W. Pannenberg et al., *La revelacion como historia* (Salamanca, 1977), pp. 117-46.

28. *Popol Vuh: Las antiguas tradiciones históricas del quiché* (San Salvador, 1980).

29. C. R. Cavarrús, *La cosmovisión k'ekchi' en proceso de cambio* (San Salvador, 1979).

30. Boff, in *Teología de lo Político*, pp. 31-144.

31. Ibid., pp. 135-285.

32. Urs von Balthasar, *in Teología de la liberacion*, p. 179.

33. Ibid.

34. X. Zubiri sees a need to speak of historical sin as well as personal sin and original sin. Cf. X. Zubiri, *Naturaleza, historia, Dios* (Madrid, 1963), p. 394.

35. On these points, cf. Zubiri's posthumous book, *El hombre y Dios* (Salamanca, 1981).

36. Cf. Oscar Romero, *Voice of the Voiceless* (Maryknoll, N.Y.: Orbis Books, 1985), pp. 114-61; on idolatries, pp. 133-36.

37. J. Ratzinger, "Vi Spiego la teologia."

38. Cf. G. Gutíerrez, *We Drink from Our Own Wells* (Maryknoll, N.Y.: Orbis Books, 1984); J. Sobrino, "Espiritualidad y liberacion": *Diakonia* (June 1984), pp. 133-57; I. Ellacuría, "Espiritualidad," in C. Floristan and J. J. Tamayo, eds., *Conceptos fundamentales de pastoral* (Madrid, 1983), pp. 301-9, which gives a bibliography.

39. Boismard and Lamouille, pp. 169-70.

40. The problem of the popular organizations in El Salvador, as reflected in *Iglesia de los pobres y organizaciones populares* (San Salvador, 1979), is one place to observe this problem in a practical way. The publication analyzes a pastoral letter from Monseñor Romero and Monseñor Rivera on this issue. More generally, all the bibliography on the church of the poor is relevant here.

41. W. Pannenberg, *Basic Questions in Theology*, trans. George Kehm (Philadelphia, 1970-71).

14

Utopia and Prophecy in Latin America

IGNACIO ELLACURÍA

Utopia and prophecy, if presented separately, tend to lose their historical effectiveness and become idealistic escapism; and so, instead of becoming forces for renewal and for liberation, they are at best reduced to functioning as a subjective solace for individual persons or for whole peoples.

That is not the case in the classic manifestations of prophecy and of the great utopian concerns. It is not so in the Bible, of course, but neither is it so in other significant events of the history of salvation. However, a real danger must be acknowledged. It repeatedly happens that utopia and prophecy are separated and both prophecy and utopia are disincarnated, whether by subjectivist reductionism or transcendentalist reductionism. They are read in a timeless cipher of eternity. However, Christian eternity is inexorably linked to temporality ever since the Word became history.

To achieve an adequate conjunction of utopia and prophecy, however, it is necessary to situate oneself in the proper historical place. Every conjunction of these two human and historical dimensions, if it is to be realistic and fruitful, must be situated in precise geo-socio-temporal coordinates. Otherwise the unavoidable thrust of the principle of reality disappears, and without it both utopia and prophecy are mental games, more formal than real. But some historical places are more favorable to the emergence of prophetic utopians and of utopian prophets. It is said that in cultures that have grown old there is no longer a place for prophecy and utopia, but only for pragmatism and selfishness, for the countable verification of results, for the scientific calculation of input and output—or, at best, for institutionalizing, legalizing, and ritualizing the spirit that renews all things. Whether this situation is inevitable or not, there are nonetheless still places where hope is not simply the cynical adding up of infinitesimal calculations; they are places to hope and to give hope against all the dogmatic verdicts that shut the door on the future of utopia and prophecy and the struggle.

One of these places is Latin America. At least, this is a preliminary supposition that I shall return to. For the moment, I can point to facts such as revolutionary movements and liberation theology. In the case of Latin America not only can the theoretical relationship between utopia and prophecy be better historicized, but the general outlines of a utopian future of universal extent can also be marked out through a concrete exercise of historical prophecy.

To think that utopia in its own intrinsic formality is something outside of every historical place and time supposes an emphasis on a single characteristic of utopia to the neglect of its real nature as it is found in the thought of those who have been true utopians in one form or another. There is no escape from the historicity of place and time, although neither is it inevitable to remain locked into the limits of a certain place and a certain time. Neither can it be said that the best way to universalize prophecy and utopianism is to try and abolish or escape every limiting conditioning. In themselves, prophecy and utopia are dialectic. Prophecy is past, present, and future, although above all it is the present facing the future and the future facing the present. Utopia is history and metahistory, but above all it is metahistory, although springing from history and inexorably referring to history, whether by way of escape or by way of realization. Hence our need to place our feet firmly on a fixed earth in order not to lose strength as Antaeus did when he was lifted off the ground.

That is what I propose to do here, by setting forth prophecy as method and utopia as horizon in the historical context of Latin America, from an explicitly Christian perspective in regard to both.

I. CHRISTIAN UTOPIA

The historical concretion of Christian utopia is not settled in advance and even less a priori, and only a concrete Christian utopia is operative for historicizing the Kingdom of God. This global affirmation includes a whole set of affirmations, which I am not going to anticipate here, since my development will explain their meaning and justification. Such affirmations are: (a) that there is a general and undefined Christian utopia; (b) that this general utopia must be made concrete in historico-social terms; (c) that this utopia is in relationship with the Kingdom of God; (d) that the Kingdom of God must be historicized; (e) that the Kingdom of God is made operative by actually working toward a concrete utopia.

1. The Kingdom of God as Utopia

Certainly Christian utopia, arising from Christian revelation, from tradition, and even from the magisterium, has certain characteristics without which it cannot be called Christian. For example, a utopia that means to be Christian cannot set aside the prophecy of the Hebrew scriptures (prophets and nonprophets), the Sermon on the Mount, the Last Supper discourse, the Book of Revelation, the primitive community, the Fathers of the Church, the great saints, or certain conciliar and papal documents. But the importance of these or other characteristics, their joining together to form a whole, their historical realization in each time and place, is not only an evolving problem but an open-ended one. Solutions to the problem must be attained by means of an option which, when all is said and done, is an option by God's people, whose organic character has priority over the hierarchical (Rom. 12:4-8; 1 Cor. 12:4-31), and in whom there is room for many charisms, functions, and activities, some more pertinent than others in defining the observable historical characteristics of Christian utopia.

This utopia can be called general and universal, because it possesses certain minimums that cannot be absent, at least in the intention, and because it points toward a universal future with an eschatological outcome. This utopia must be made concrete precisely to bring the Kingdom of God closer. Up to a certain point, Christian utopia and the Kingdom of God can be considered the same, although when one speaks of Christian utopia one accents the utopian character of the Kingdom of God and not its other characteristics. But the concretion of utopia is what historicizes the Kingdom of God, both in the hearts of human beings and in the structures without which that heart cannot live. This is not the time or place to develop the idea, much treated by liberation theology, that a historicizing of the Kingdom of God must be achieved in the personal, in the societal, and in the political. Although liberation theology has historicized the Kingdom in its own way, all of the church's tradition has always tried to do this. If one reads, for example, *Gaudium et Spes* or the various papal encyclicals on the church's social teaching, one sees there the need to historicize, if not the Kingdom, at least the faith and the Christian message. Whether this be done with greater or lesser prophetic and utopian vigor, the need to do it is still recognized.

The question, then, is how better to achieve that concretion, accepting the fundamental proposition that the general and universal utopia is already proclaimed and promised, so that its concretion not only cannot negate it or supersede it but must live by it, although creatively, because the same Spirit that animated it in its earlier and foundational dynamisms keeps on making new dynamisms possible. The reply points toward Christian prophecy. Prophecy, rightly understood in its complexity, is at the origin of the universal and general utopia. That same prophecy is needed for the concretion of utopia, a prophecy that will need the help of other instances—for example, that of the magisterium—but cannot be replaced by them. Without prophecy there is no possibility of making a Christian concretion of utopia and, consequently, a historical realization of the Kingdom of God. Without an intense and genuine exercise of Christian prophecy, the concretion of Christian utopia cannot be arrived at theoretically, much less practically. Here too the law cannot replace grace, the institution cannot replace life, established tradition cannot replace radical newness of the Spirit.

2. Prophecy: Contrasting the Kingdom of God with a Particular Historical Reality

Prophecy is understood here to be the critical contrasting of the proclamation of the fullness of the Kingdom of God with a definite historical situation. Is this contrasting possible? Are not the Kingdom of God and historical realities with their worldly projects two radically distinct things moving on different planes? The reply to this objection or question, although complex, is still clear. The fullness of the Kingdom is not identified with any personal or structural project or any determined process, but it is in necessary relationship with them. One need only see how the scriptures approach the matter. There can be, according to the case, greater importance given to the transcendent than to the incidental, to the inner than to the outer, to the intentional than to realizations. But one of the two aspects must always be there. The Kingdom of God is, after all, a transcendent history or a historical transcendence in strict parallel with what the life and person of Jesus is, but in such manner that it is the history that leads to the transcendence, because indeed God's transcendence has become history ever since the beginning of creation.

The fullness of the Kingdom of God, which implies that all of the Kingdom of God and all of the projection of the Kingdom of God be taken into account, must be placed in contrast with a definite historical situation. For example, if the Kingdom proclaims the fullness of life and the rejection of death, and if the historical situation of human beings and of structures is the kingdom of death and the negation of life, the contrast is evident. The contrasting of a historicized kingdom makes manifest the limitations (lack of divinization or of grace) and above all the evils (personal, social, and structural sins) of a definite historical situation. Thus, prophecy, which initiates this contrasting, is able to predict the future and to go toward it—assuming indeed that there is the general vision of the Kingdom previously alluded to, which God's revelation has been making known to humanity in various ways. In this manner, which could be called dialectical, the desired future is sketched as a way of reaching beyond the present, reaching beyond the limits and the evils of the present, which are historical limits—as a future more and more in accord with the demands and dynamisms of the Kingdom.

In turn, the present, reaching beyond the announced and hoped-for future, helps to surpass those limits and those evils.

3. Historical Commitment

When prophecy is conceived thus, it is seen how necessary it is so that utopia not become an abstract evasion of historical commitment. "Religious misery is, on the one hand, the *expression* of real misery and, on the other, the *protest* against real misery. Religion is the sigh of the oppressed creature, the heart of a heartless world, just as it is the spirit of a situation without spirit" (Marx, 1844). But, if this is so, it does not have to become the opium of the people, as the same text of Marx goes on to call it. If it is more a protest than a mere expression, if it is more a struggle than a mere comfort, if it does not remain a mere sigh, if the protest and contrast become historical utopia which negates the present and impels into the future; if, in short, prophetic action is initiated, then history is made by way of repudiating and surpassing and not by way of evading. Thanks to prophecy, utopia does not fail to be efficacious in history, even though it is not fully realizable in history, as is the case with Christian utopia. If it were not realizable at all, it would run the almost insuperable risk of becoming an evasive opium; but if it must achieve a high degree of realization and is put into close relation to prophetic contradiction, it can be what animates correct action. A utopia that is not in some way what animates and even effects historical realizations is not a Christian utopia. It is not even an ideal vision of the Kingdom; instead, it is an idealistic and ideologized vision of itself. For example, if nothing is done toward turning swords into plowshares, but it is only dreamed about evasively, utopia fades away. Instead of fighting against the arms race, it becomes a bucolic expenditure of leisure time. This is not the intention or the reality of utopia and of Christian prophecy.

But if utopia cannot really be Christian utopia without prophecy to inspire it, neither will prophecy be really Christian without the animation of utopia. Christian prophecy lives by Christian utopia, which, as utopia, lives more and is nourished by the intercession that the Spirit makes throughout history. But, as Christian, utopia lives more by the proclamation and the promise that are explicitly and implicitly expressed in the revelation already given. A prophecy that did not take into account the proclamation and the promise already given would be ill-prepared to contradict evil. And especially such prophecy would be wholly unprepared to put together a historical design of something that would try to respond to the concrete demands of the Kingdom of God, such as it has been proclaimed from of old, but especially by the historical Jesus.

Priority in the fullness of Christian action is to be attributed to the revelation and the promise of Jesus, even in the destructive phase of prophecy. This is still more valid when what is sought is to realize God's will or designs, for whose discernment both the Spirit of Christ and the historical outlines of Jesus of Nazareth's march through history are indispensable. It almost seems tautological and unnecessary to say that the Christian character of utopia cannot be given in fullness except from Christian faith explicitly accepted and lived, although without ignoring either that the Spirit can make use of Christians who are not formally such and even of anti-Christians, like Caiphas, to announce and realize some fundamental features of Christian utopia.

It happens, however, that what is given must be actualized, in Xavier Zubiri's meaning of the term. For him, *actualizar* does not primarily mean to update or make conform to current style, as it generally means in Spanish. To *actualize* means to give present reality to what is formally a historical possibility and, as such, what can be taken or left, what can be read in one way or another. What must be actualized, then, is what is given, but the reading and interpretation of what is given, the option for one part or other of what is given, depend on a historical present and on historical subjects. The historical actualization of the already given utopia arises especially from the intercession (signs of the times) that is being given through the Spirit in history. But these signs of intercession are historical, even though what is signified by them transcends the merely historical. The Spirit once again has priority for that transcendence, but in inseparable relationship with historical concretions. This is valid for the interpretation and even more so for the realization.

Indeed, utopia has a certain idealistic character that is ultimately unrealizable, but at the same time it has the character of something asymptotically realizable in a permanent process of approximation and, therefore, it implies theoretical and practical mediations taken more from the categorical dimension of history. It is, of course, a Christian utopia that is under discussion, and thus it maintains very explicitly the transcendent dimension of the Kingdom. But even this dimension cannot be formulated apart from what is categorical, even in the most strictly evangelical formulations. It is not only or primarily a language problem—the Kingdom as a banquet, as a field of labor, and so forth—but of something deeper, of the unavoidable need to make the Kingdom's transcendence historical. This is easy to see in the moral recommendations related to daily life, but it also refers to political and social objectifications—cases about soldiers, about authorities, about laws, about social customs, and so on. Such cases occur not only in all of the Old Testament but also in the New.

And so, it must be unitarily sustained that the Spirit's intercession in history is needed in order to hit upon the transcendent character of the categorical and to categorize the transcendent interpretively and practically. It is by means of the true and the false, the good and the bad, the just and the unjust, and so forth, unitarily valued from what is faith as gift received and as daily practice, that the transcendence of the historical is grasped and, in turn, something that is unitarily historical and suprahistorical is projected and realized transcendently. What prophecy gathers and expresses is the historico-transcendent intercession of the Spirit, which makes present the utopia already offered and contrasts it with the signs of the times. Thus prophecy and utopia, history and transcendence, nourish each other. Both are historical and both are transcendent, but neither becomes what it is meant to become except in relation to the other.

II. LATIN AMERICA TODAY: PROPHECY AND UTOPIA

It is not a willful or arbitrary affirmation to designate Latin America at the present time as a privileged place of utopia and prophecy. Its own reality and some of its achievements prove it.

As a reality, it is a continent with particular characteristics like those attributed to the Servant of Yahweh. This condition makes it like other regions of the world, almost the greater part of the world's regions. It is a region ill-treated ever since the armed conquest made four centuries ago by Spanish Christendom. Without losing its human heart, it nonetheless has its face disfigured, almost unrecognizable as human except in its pain and tragedy (Isa. 52:2-12); it has, besides, almost lost its own identity as a people (Hos. 1:6-9;1 Pet. 2:10). But that identity, which in great part shapes it as an objective reality, contains a very active protest awareness and, more specifically, a very live, Christian liberation awareness. All this places it in an excellent position to exercise a strong theoretical and practical prophecy. This is confirmed by its great and significant achievement in this regard with its recent martyrs and prophets, who have arisen everywhere in every stratum of the people and of the church. Latin America is a region whose great potentiality and wealth of resources contrast with the state of destitution, injustice, oppression, and exploitation imposed upon a great part of the people. This provides an objective basis for the contrast of utopia, found in its rich potentiality, with prophecy, already present in the negation of utopia by the everyday reality. The ceaseless revolutionary movements in the political area and the Christian movements in the religious area are distinct ways that a powerful collective utopian and prophetic awareness has reflected and apprehended the objective reality.

Consequently, Latin America struggles both outside and inside the church in a powerful attempt to break its chains and build a different sort of future, not only for itself but for all humanity. The conditions suffered in its own flesh, along with its effective protest, constitute trustworthy evidence that convicts the historical world order, and not only the international economic-political order. By negation these are a proclamation of a different order. The actual truth of the present-day historical arrangement is cruelly reflected, not only or principally in the fringes of destitution and, especially, of degradation in the wealthy countries, but in the reality of the Third World, consciously expressed in Latin America's many-sided protest.

That truth demonstrates the impossibility of reproducing and, especially, of enlarging the present historical order significantly. It demonstrates, even more radically, its undesirability, since this present order cannot be universalized. It brings with it the perpetuation of an unjust and predatory distribution of the world's resources, and even of each nation's resources, for the benefit of a few nations. The result is that prophetic and utopian Latin America does not seek to imitate those who today are in the forefront and position themselves on top. Rather, it seeks a different order in the objective and in the subjective, an order that will allow a humane life not only for a few but for the greater part of humanity. The developed world is not at all the desired utopia, even as a way to overcome poverty, much less to overcome injustice. Instead, it is the sign of what should not be and of what should not be done.

This historical movement is reflected inside the church as something qualitatively new. The preferential option for the poor, understood in a radical and effective way in which the poor are those who take the initiative dynamically, can, first of all, transform the church radically, and it can thus become the key to and the energizer for what a Christian utopia must be as a historical liberation project. Such a movement is reflected already in the different theoretical and practical forms of liberation theology, which in itself is an effective kind of prophecy for animating a new historical Christian utopia. That is why it is feared both inside and outside the church.

But the privileged place that Latin America is for prophecy and utopia must not lead to the illusion that all of it or all of the Latin American church is presently exercising the prophetic-utopian mission. Latin America in its entirety is shaped by the same "sin of the world" that affects the rest of humanity. The "structures of sin" prevail there, and Latin America is not only the passive subject that endures them but the active subject that produces them. The modes of realizing the capitalist pseudo-utopia and, in far lesser degree, the socialist pseudo-utopia prevail in the makeup of the society and peoples of Latin America. The economic as well as the social, political, and cultural modes of capitalism are reproduced and aggravated in Latin America, because it consists of dependent societies, the kind that have to leave the waste products from their operations within their own boundaries instead of sending them elsewhere, as more powerful nations try to do. There are no reforms of capitalism in Latin America, although some attempts at reforms of socialism have begun. Nowhere is the preferential option for the poor in force, or anything beyond the dynamism of capital and the demands of the international order. A way has not even been found for the primary subject of the processes to be the dominated and oppressed people. But it is not right to lay all the blame for all the ills of Latin America on others, because such an exoneration either legitimates or covers up behaviors and actions that are totally blameworthy. The systems, the processes, the leaders, even though dependent, still assume and even take advantage of the wrongs of their dependence.

Neither is the whole church in Latin America, nor even a large part of it, fulfilling its vocation of utopian prophecy. Scandalous as this is in a situation like Latin America's, a continent where injustice and faith live side by side, a great many Christians, including religious, priests, bishops, cardinals, and nuncios, not only lack the prophetic charism but contradict it and even set themselves up as adversaries and persecutors of prophecy and as favorers of the structures and forces of domination, so long as these structures and forces do not put their institutional advantages and privileges in jeopardy. Although the part of the church that performs an anti-prophetic and anti-utopian task is not a majority in the institutional church, nonprophecy and even distrust of any form of prophecy do prevail. Prophecy tends to be confused with the misnamed parallel magisterium. If the preferential option for the poor is taken as the touchstone, a certain nominal respect for it can be seen after long struggles, but the hierarchy has done little to put it into practice. If the criterion is the stance taken toward the liberation theology movement, there has been some formal improvement, but distrust continues, if not more subtle forms of attack.

However, even though there are these negative aspects, it cannot be ignored that, as was said earlier, there has been a flowering of utopia and of prophecy in Latin America, situating its people and in some way its church in a vanguard position for defining what is to be its mission in the present-day world. This cannot be seen from an abstract place, still less from a place incarnated in the structures of the dominant world.

III. A NEW FREEDOM AND HUMANITY

1. Radical Prophetic Critique

The very reality of Latin America, especially when seen from the vantage point of Christian faith, constitutes a radical prophetic protest against the international order, both in its North-South confrontation and in its East-West confrontation. It is also a protest against the attitude, behavior, and expectations promoted by those in the cultural vanguards and the models previously proposed as ideals of freedom and humanity.

Dependency

The clash of interests in the North-South and East-West conflicts makes most countries in the world more and more dependent and systematically impoverished. In particular, it gets them into a loss-of-identity process through the pull toward imitation, which reinforces their dependency and even slavery. This is not to deny that there are in the advanced capitalist and socialist countries valuable theoretical and practical principles that can and should be assumed critically and creatively by other countries. Simply going back to a supposed primitive state is impossible and can lead to multiple forms of dependency. Furthermore, it is impossible to escape the only real history, that of interdependence, in which all peoples must necessarily play a part. But the imperialistic form in which North-South, East-West relations exist must be rejected for the good of the countries that suffer it and for the good of the countries that impose it.

This is an indictment made very clearly by dependency theory and then by liberation theology. It has been understood and expressed prophetically by John Paul II in *Sollicitudo Rei Socialis,* following Paul VI's *Populorum Progressio* and Vatican II's *Gaudium et Spes*: "Each of the two blocs harbors in its own way a tendency towards imperialism, as it is usually called, or towards forms of neocolonialism: an easy temptation to which they frequently succumb, as history, including recent history, teaches" (no. 22).

A phenomenon as dramatic as Latin America's external debt is one of the clearest symptoms, both in its origin and in the way its payment is demanded, of how unjust is the relationship and how deadly is the harm done to peoples, when supposedly the desire is to help them. In general, it can be said that the present type of relationship between the powerful and those who are not as strong is making a few countries or social groups richer, while the majority are made poorer and the breach between them widens and becomes more serious. In the case of the foreign debt, it can be seen concretely how the originating loans were often made one-sidedly and with the complicity of governments and the upper social classes yet without any benefit whatever for the mass of the people. But the demand for payment of these debts weighs especially heavily on the common people, whom it deprives of the possibility of escape from their poverty through harmonious development. It favors the interests of capital much more than the priority of work over capital, and a basic principle of the Christian faith, the priority of the many poor over the few rich. The world thus comes to be ruled by the lack of solidarity, mercy, and concern for others, and hence shaped and formed by injustice and opposition to the gospel. It shows itself as the patent and verifiable negation of the Kingdom of God proclaimed by Jesus.

The Capitalist System

In particular, Latin America's actual situation points out prophetically the capitalist system's intrinsic malice and the ideological falsehood of the semblance of democracy that accompanies, legitimates, and cloaks it.

It is customary to ask why the voices of Latin American prophecy do not denounce the socialist politico-economic forms of the socialists and tend instead to design utopias of an anti-capitalist type. The factual reason is that prophecy currently devotes itself to present evils and these, for the most part, are due to capitalist forms of domination. The evils of the socialist systems, both in the economic and the political arenas, appear in situations like those in Cuba, Nicaragua, and some revolutionary movements. But, excluding extreme cases like that of Shining Path in Peru, the evils of the socialist systems cannot begin to compare with the dimensions and degrees of the evils of the capitalist system in Latin America. Hence, historical prophecy is directed mainly to rejecting capitalism rather than socialism.

The church, previously more inclined to condemn socialism than capitalism and readier to see in the latter correctable defects and in the former intrinsic evils springing from its very historical essence, today tends to place both systems on an equal footing at least. "As we know, the tension between East and West is not in itself an opposition between two different levels of development but rather between two concepts of the development of individuals and peoples, both concepts being imperfect and in need of radical correction. ... The church's social doctrine adopts a critical attitude towards both liberal capitalism and Marxist collectivism" (*Sollicitudo Rei Socialis*, no. 21). But local prophecy should be centered, by its very nature, on the negation of what is in fact the cause of the evils that affect a determined reality.

In regard to capitalism especially, once it passed through its stage of pitiless exploitation in the Western countries, permitting the first accumulation of wealth, its intrinsic malice has been observed in all its magnitude only beyond the boundaries of the rich countries, which in numerous ways export the evils of capitalism to the exploited periphery. The problem is not just that of the foreign debt or the exploitation of raw materials or the search for third world sites to dispose of the wastes of all sorts that the more developed countries produce. More than that, it is an almost irresistible pull toward a profound dehumanization as an intrinsic part of the real dynamics of the capitalist system: abusive and/or superficial and alienating ways of seeking one's own security and happiness by means of private accumulation, of consumption, and of entertainment; submission to the laws of the consumer market promoted by advertising in every kind of activity, including the cultural; and a manifest lack of solidarity in the individual, the family, and the state with other individuals, families, or states.

The fundamental dynamic of selling one's own goods to another at the highest price possible and buying the other's at the lowest price possible, along with the dynamic of imposing one's own cultural norms so as to make others dependent, clearly shows the inhumanity of the system, constructed more on the principle of *homo homini lupus* than on the principle of a possible and desirable universal solidarity. Predatory ferocity becomes the fundamental dynamic, and generous solidarity remains reduced to curing incidentally and superficially the wounds of the poor caused by the depredation.

The fact is that 170 million of the approximately 400 million inhabitants of Latin America now live in poverty. Poverty levels in the Third World are not the same as those in the First World; those in the latter would be levels of affluence in the former. (A family of four with an annual income below $10,000 is classified at the poverty level in the United States.) Of the 170 million in poverty, 61 million live in extreme poverty. To overcome this situation, $280 billion would be needed, equivalent to 40 percent of the gross domestic product of Latin America. But this is so difficult as to be almost impossible, because debt service produces a net export of capital, without counting capital flight, which is estimated to be much greater than all the investment and foreign aid received by the whole region. This reality, fomented both by international capitalism and by the capitalism of each nation, and due not to the will of persons but to the structure and dynamics of the system, is an overwhelming historical proof of the evils that capitalism has brought about or has been unable to avoid in Latin America.

On the other hand, the ideologized propaganda about capitalist democracy, as the only and absolute form of political organization, becomes an instrument of cover-up and, at times, an instrument of oppression. Certainly in the democratic package come values and rights that are very much worth taking into account, especially if they are carried out to their final consequences and real conditions are created for enjoying them. But the ideologized operation of the democratic model seeks, not to let the people determine their own political and economic model, but to cover up the imposition of the capitalist system and, especially in the case of Central America, the imposition of United States interests. Democracy is supported only insofar as those interests are presumed to be furthered.

Hence, more regard is paid to national security by the United States than to the self-determination of peoples, or to international law, or even to respect for fundamental human rights, which are defended derivatively so long as they do not endanger the military and police structures. It is in these military and police structures rather than in any democratic structure that confidence is placed for the defense of United States interests. Thus it becomes a point of honor to have elections involving awful decisions affecting millions of people and to assure the enjoyment of certain civil rights that can only be actively exercised by the economically privileged who have sufficient resources, while much less vigor is shown in demanding an end to murders, disappearances, tortures, and such. Undercover actions by the CIA are even undertaken, involving not only illegal actions but outright terrorist practices.

Most serious is that the offer of humanization and freedom that the rich countries make to the poor countries is not universalizable and consequently is not human, even for those who make it. Kant's keen way of putting it could be applied to this problem. Act in such a manner that the maxim of your will can always serve, at the same time, as the principle of a universal law (*Critique of Practical Reason*). If the behavior and even the ideal of a few cannot become the behavior and the reality of the greater part of humanity, that behavior and that ideal cannot be said to be moral or even human, all the more so if the enjoyment of a few is at the cost of depriving the rest. In our world, the practical ideal of Western civilization is not universalizable, not even materially, since there are not enough material resources on earth today to let all countries achieve the same level of production and consumption as that of the countries called wealthy, whose total population is less than 25 percent of humanity.

That universalization is not possible, and neither is it desirable. The lifestyle proposed in and by the mechanics of development does not humanize, it does not fulfill or make happy; this is shown, among other indices, by the growing drug consumption which has become one of the principal problems of the developed world. That lifestyle is motivated by fear and insecurity, by inner emptiness, by the need to dominate so as not to be dominated, by the urge to exhibit what one has since one cannot communicate what one is. It all supposes only a minimum degree of freedom, and it supports that minimum freedom more in externals than internals. It likewise implies a maximum degree of separation from the greater part of human beings and of peoples of the world, especially the neediest.

If this type of historical law, which proposes to go on shaping our times, has scarcely anything of what is human, and is fundamentally inhuman, it must even more clearly be said to be anti-Christian. The Christian ideal of finding happiness more in giving than in receiving—and still more than in seizing (Acts 20:35)—more in solidarity and community than in confrontation and individualism, more in personal development than in accumulating things, more in the viewpoint of the poor than in that of the rich and powerful, is contradicted and hindered by what is in practice, beyond the enunciated ideal that commits to nothing, the real dynamism of the present-day models.

The Institutional Church

From the reality of Latin America there also comes a prophetic protest against the way the institutional church is structured and behaves. The Latin American church has been too tolerant of the conditions of structural injustice and institutionalized violence that prevail in the region. Above all, until recently the universal church itself has been blind and mute before the responsibility of the developed countries relating to that injustice.

Certainly since the time of the conquest examples can be found of prophecy both in the church's rank-and-file and in its hierarchy. But at the same time those willing to overlook wrongdoing have been preponderant, showing greater concern for personal and institutional interests than for the oppressed mass of the people and for the Kingdom of God. In our own days, Medellín and Puebla, despite their great merit and value, have had little real effect on church structures and behavior. The behavior of martyrs like the bishops Romero, Valencia, Angelelli, and others, although it is not completely rare and exceptional and has been accompanied by that of dozens and even hundreds of men and women—lay people, religious, and priests—is very significant and encouraging. But it is far from being the norm, and it is still seen as "dangerous" and not quite normal.

The universal church, always prompt to condemn Marxism, has been more tolerant of the evils of capitalism, even in its most damaging imperialist forms. There are clear advances by Vatican II and by the recent popes in this respect; very estimable also are some positions taken by the bishops of the United States in regard to their government's stance toward the Latin American peoples. But it was practically necessary for *Sollicitudo Rei Socialis* to appear in order to make things finally clear after the grand impulse given in this respect by the promulgation of *Gaudium et Spes.* However, what has been achieved on the doctrinal plane has scarcely progressed to that of pastoral orientation and to producing a more decidedly prophetic attitude. The church that lives in the wealthy countries does not denounce with sufficient vigor the exploitative conduct of these countries toward the rest of the world. It preaches mercy rather than justice, thus leaving aside one of the central themes of historical prophecy.

Neither has the church made a minimally sufficient effort in Latin America to inculturate itself in a situation very different from that of the North Atlantic countries. It is still thought that there is a historical continuum between the rich countries and the poor countries, and more attention is paid to the unity of language or learning than to the profound gap between the state of economic development and to the position occupied in the international economic order. There is a question here of two distinct inculturations, or two sources of profound diversification which inculturation ought to take into account. On one side is the tremendous difference of cultures, of fundamental modes of being, originated by a complex series of factors (racial, psycho-social, linguistic, educational, and of every sort). On the other side is the likewise fundamental difference in the gross national product and in per capita income, which makes impossible for Latin America many of the cultural modes of the wealthy countries. It is not just a question of the indigenous or colored populations but of something that affects the whole continent, if we interpret the continent by looking at the mass of the people. Institutionally, the mentality is still that when it comes to theological thought, forms of religious practice, the world of rituals, and so forth, Latin America is considered an appendage to Europe and a prolongation of Rome's Catholicism, whereas it is a new reality and, what is more, the majority reality of the Catholic church.

This very reality is one that itself becomes a prophetic denunciation. It summons to a profound transformation of the way the church sees itself and understands its mission. To ignore this summons, having recourse to the presumed unalterability and universality of the faith and of Christian institutions, is to ignore the Spirit's voice of renewal, which always appears along with some degree of prophecy. This prophecy points out the limitations and evils that the institutional church has picked up as dead weight on its way through history. History has been fundamentally the history of the rich, dominant, and conquering peoples, not the history of the poor peoples, which should have been the fundamental matrix of the church but was lost from the times of Constantine. Although an important remnant of the gospel did not fall into the trap of riches or power and always remained alive, and in the most vivid forms, it has always been poorly tolerated.

2. Prophecy: Denunciation and Utopia

The prophecy of denunciation, on the horizon of the Kingdom of God, marks out the ways that lead to utopia. Prophecy's *no*, prophecy's negation pointing beyond, in itself generates utopia's *yes* by virtue of the promise that is the Kingdom of God already present among human beings, especially ever since the life, death, and resurrection of Jesus, who has sent his Spirit across death to renew all people and all things.

The negation of reductive particularism leads to the affirmation that only a new global project that is universalizable can be acceptable for humanity. Independently of all ethical or theological consideration, the basic principle remains valid that any world order or conception that generates a constantly greater number of people in poverty, that can only be maintained by force and by the threat of humanity's total destruction through increasing ecological destruction and nuclear annihilation, that generates no ideals of qualitative growth, and that gets entangled with constraints of every kind is not acceptable. Out of purely selfish considerations, where the self is all of humanity and likewise the self of each individual, such a world order is nonviable in the long run without the viability of humanity's self. Substantial changes in the conception and in the dynamism of such so-called progress are necessary.

But beyond all selfish realism and realistic selfishness, it is clear that a world order favorable for a few and unfavorable for most is something that dehumanizes and dechristianizes each person and humanity. From a human viewpoint, actions and projects must be measured by the classic "I am human and nothing that is human is foreign to me," meaning that whatever alienation, action, or omission makes another human being a "foreigner" breaks down the humanity of the one who so behaves. From a Christian viewpoint, one is not to pass by the wounded person on the roadside, for then one refuses one's neighbor—the opposite of the "foreigner"—and that is the denial of both the second and the first of the commandments that the Father has renewed in the Son.

The principle of universalization certainly is not a principle of conformity and, still less, of conformity imposed from a powerful center on an amorphous and subordinated periphery. That, however, is the way to universalization proposed by those who wish to impose the model of existence that at the moment is more favorable to them. This conformity is today ruled above all by the laws of the economic marketplace and is a most forceful statement that materialism, not historical but economic materialism, is what determines all else in the last analysis. Contrary to this a universalism must be generated that does not reduce but enriches, so that the entire wealth of peoples may be respected and developed, and their differences seen as the completion of the whole and not as the clashing of the parts. In this way, all the members will complement one another, and in this complementing the whole will be enriched and the parts strengthened.

Preferential Option for the Poor

Universalization must result from the preferential option for the poor, for the universalization resulting so far from the preferential option for the rich and powerful has brought more ill than good to humanity. Until now, the historical world order and the church's institutions have been universalized from a preferential option for the rich and the powerful. In the secular order it has been made by the strong for the strong, and this has brought some advantages in scientific, technological, and cultural advances. But these rest upon great evils for the majority, who are sometimes forgotten and at other times exploited. Also, the church has become worldly. That is, it has followed this fundamental behavior of the "world" and has shaped its message and even its institutions more from the standpoint of a power that dominates and controls than from that of a ministry that serves. Both the secular order and the church have lived by the principle so contrary to the gospel, that devoting oneself to the rich and behaving so as to favor the more powerful is how the mass of the people, how humanity, is better served and how the gospel is better spread. Ecclesiastical pomp in imitation of royal pomp, the establishment of a state political power, submission to the laws of the marketplace, and so forth on the church's part show how it has submitted to the worldly principle that the option for power and for the powerful is what best secures institutions.

Now, this is not the Christian viewpoint. From the Christian viewpoint it has to be affirmed that the poor are to be not only the preferential passive subject of those who have power, but the preferential active subject of history, especially of the church's history. The Christian faith affirms — and this is a dogma of faith that cannot be contradicted under penalty of gravely mutilating that faith — that it is in the poor that the greatest real presence of the historical Jesus is found and therefore the greatest capacity for salvation (or liberation). The fundamental texts of the Beatitudes and of the Last Judgment, among others, leave this point settled with total clarity; many other things are affirmed as dogma with much less biblical support. How this historical subjectuality should be made concrete and how it should be exercised are questions open to theoretical discussion and historical experimentation. But it does not for that reason cease to be an operative principle of discernment to ask oneself always what is most needed by the mass of the people so that they can really achieve what is due to them as human beings and as members of God's people.

In Latin America, prophecy puts more emphasis on the active and organized poor, on the poor-with-spirit, than on the passive poor — that is, the poor who suffer their destitution with resignation and hardly notice the injustice they suffer. It does not deny the importance, even the prophetic importance, that belongs to the poor by the simple fact of their being the poor, for there is no doubt that as such they enjoy Jesus' special predilection and his very particular presence. But when those poor spiritually incorporate their poverty, when they become aware of the injustice of their condition and of the possibilities and even of the real obligation they have in the face of destitution and structural injustice, they are changed from passive to active subjects, and with that they multiply and strengthen the salvific-historical value that is theirs.

There is a further argument for searching for the new universal ideal of human being and of Christian, for the new ideal of world and of humanity coming out of the mass of the people (secular version) and out of the poor

(Christian version). In reality, they represent the greater part of humanity. This means, again, from the negative-prophetical viewpoint, that many of the various past civilizations have not been really human but rather class and/or nationalist civilizations. From the prophetic-utopian viewpoint it means that the goal unavoidably must be the development-liberation of every human and of all humans—but understanding that "all" humans are those who in some way condition the "all" of each human and that those "all" humans are mostly the poor. Until now, development-liberation has not been that of all human beings nor is it going in that direction, as is shown in the fact that, far from leading to the development-liberation of all humans, it has led to the underdevelopment-oppression of most of them. This is a long historical process, certainly, but the question is whether we are going in the right direction or instead are going toward humanity's dehumanization and dechristianization.

In Latin America this prophetic march toward utopia is driven by a great hope. Beyond all rhetoric and in spite of all the difficulties, there are rivers of hope on the continent. Christian hope thus becomes one of the most efficacious dynamisms for going out of the land of oppression and toward the land of promise.

Hope

This march from oppression to promise is sustained on hope. It is received as grace (there would not seem to be many motives for hope, in view of the enormous problems and difficulties in taking hope as something natural), but it goes on being nourished historically and growing in the praxis of liberation. It is a verifiable fact that hope, which animates the poor-with-spirit, inspires them in long and hard processes that to others seem useless and futureless. It is a hope that appears, therefore, with the characteristics of hope against all hope—a very Christian characteristic—although once it appears it is nourished by the results already achieved. It is not the secure reckoning that leads to making an investment with the calculated expectation of desirable fixed-term results; it is not an idealistic dream that removes from reality. Rather, it is the accepting of God's promise of liberation, a fundamental promise that propels to an exodus in which historical goals and objectives unite with transhistorical certainties.

In contrast to the emptiness of nonmeaning found in a life that tries to fill itself with activities and purposes without deep meaning, Latin America's poor-with-spirit are a real and effective sign that in the present-day world there are tasks full of meaning. Thus, in a real criticism—that is, criticism from hope-filled reality—of hopeless reality, of the confusion between being entertained or amused and being happy, between being occupied and being fulfilled, space opens for another form of life completely different from the one imposed today as ideal in a consumer society, a society for which improvements are proposed without consistency and without greater meaning. That space is traveled by the poor-with-spirit in a new Christian disposition, which leads to giving their life for others, so that in giving it they find it and they find themselves. It leads to being able to despise all the world, whose conquest means nothing if it means the loss of oneself, of the spirit of oneself (Mark 8:34-38 and parallels). It leads to emptying oneself to find oneself again after the emptying in the fullness of what one is and of what one can be (Phil. 2:1-11).

The hope of the poor-with-spirit in Latin America — probably in other places also — is something qualitatively new. It is not a question of absolute despair that leads to a type of active desperation in persons who can go ahead and lose everything because they have nothing to lose but the all-nothing of their own lives — which have become unlivable. This is not despair, but hope. Hence, the attitude and the actions are not desperate actions, but attitudes and actions that arise from life and that seek a greater life. This is a verifiable fact in thousands of men and women in refugee camps, in marginal communities, among the thousands of displaced persons, people for whom often it is not "political spirit" moving them but "Christian spirit" animating them. That spirit will have to be historicized and politicized in order for it not to evaporate in fruitless subjectivisms, but politicization is neither first nor fundamental.

This hope that arises from life, that arises together with the promise and with the negation of death, is celebrated festively. The sense of fiesta, as it exists in these poor-with-hope, indicates for now that they have not fallen into the fanaticism of desperation and of struggle for the sake of struggle. But neither do they fall therefore into the error of the fiesta purely for amusement that characterizes the Western world — fiesta lacking in meaning and lacking in hope. Fiesta is not a substitute for missing hope; it is the jubilant celebration of a hope on the march. The more or less explicit search for happiness is done in other ways, which do not simply mistake for it the forgetfulness drugged by consumerism or the mere consumption of entertainment. It is not simply in leisure where fulfillment is sought but in the gratuitous and gratifying labor of distinct liberating tasks.

Beginning Anew

In the search for a historically universalizable utopia, in which the poor, or the mass of the people, will have a determining role, and from the hope that urges them toward utopia, one glimpses a new revolution with the prophetic motto, *Begin anew*. To begin anew a historic order that will transform radically the present one, based on the promotion and liberation of human life, is the prophetic call that can open the way to a new utopia of Christian inspiration.

To begin anew does not mean the rejection of all of the past, which is neither possible nor desirable, but it does mean something more than just setting out to make things new in linear development with the previous. It means a real "beginning anew," since the old, as a totality, is not acceptable; nor is the principal dynamism that drives it acceptable

Even in the most radical of revolutions, total rejection of the past is not possible and is not desirable, because it deprives humanity of possibilities without which it would find itself obliged to begin from zero, which is impossible. In addition, not all that has been achieved is bad; nor is it intrinsically infected with evil. There are elements of every type — scientific, cultural, technological, and so forth — whose malignity comes not from their essence but from the totality in which they are enlisted and from the finality to which they are subordinated. There are certainly unacceptable elements, but this is not sufficient to advocate an impossible and sterile nihilism. In this sense, to begin anew supposes neither previous annihilation nor creation of a new world from nothing.

But neither is it just a matter of making new things; rather, it is a matter of making all things new, given that the old is not acceptable. This belongs to the essence of utopian prophecy. The "if you are not born anew" (John 3:3), the incorporation in the death that gives life (Rom. 6:3-5), the seed that needs to die to bear fruit (John 12:24), the disappearance and destruction of the old city so that the new one can arise in a different world (Rev. 18:1 ff.; 21:1 ff.), and so many other scriptural proclamations offer and demand a radical transformation. For in the Christian interpretation of the new life, death always intercedes as mediation. Certainly, the Good News is a message of life, but a message of life that assumes not only the reality of death but the positive validity of the negation of death. To die to the old human being, to the world that is past, to the former age, and so on, is a fundamental part of the biblical message. Christian prophecy can go against one or other concrete fact, but in addition and above all it goes against the totality of any historical order where sin prevails over grace. As negation and as affirmation, Christian utopian prophecy proposes to make a radically new human being and a radically different world.

The fundamental principle on which to base the new order remains "that all might have life and have it more abundantly" (John 10:10). This is the utopian cry coming from historical prophecy. The historical experience of death, and not merely of pain, but of death by hunger and destitution or death by repression and by various forms of violence, which is so living and massive in Latin America, reveals the enormous necessity and the irreplaceable value, first of all, of material life — as the primary and fundamental gift in which must be rooted all other aspects of life, which in the final analysis constitute development of that primary gift. That life must be expanded and completed by internal growth and in relation to the life of others, always in search of more life and better life.

Not that it is evident what the fullness of life consists of, still less how fullness of life is to be achieved. But it is not so hard to see what it does *not* consist of and how it will *not* be achieved. And this not only by logical deductions from universal principles, but by historical verification from the experience of the mass of the people. To seek life by taking it away from others or without concern for how others are losing it, is certainly the negation of the Spirit as giver of life. From this perspective, the basic Christian message of loving others as oneself, and not just that of not wanting for oneself what is wanted for others (pragmatically formulated by the Declaration of the Rights of Man and of the Citizen of 1793 in its sixth article), of preferring to give rather than receive, and of resolving to give all one's property to those who are poorer, are utopian ideals. The prophetic historicizing of these ideals can begin to generate that radical newness in persons and in institutions. With it, not only is there a drive to seek something radically new, but some lines are drawn for the attempts to begin anew, since what has been realized up to now is not the right way to benefit the greater part of humanity, which is made up of masses with scarcely even access to life.

Prophecy and Liberation

Latin American historical prophecy presents itself in our day as liberation. The utopia of freedom is to be attained by means of liberation prophecy. The utopian ideal of a complete freedom for all human beings is not possible except through a liberation process; hence it is not primarily freedom that engenders liberation but liberation that engenders freedom, even though between the two there is a process of mutual reinforcement and enrichment.

Thus it has been historically. The well-known English liberties of the Magna Carta or of the Bill of Rights are concrete achievements—fewer taxes, just judgments, protection against the arbitrary domination of kings, and so on—obtained by a process of liberating struggle through which definite rights are acknowledged and then formalized in agreements, laws, or constitutions. Basically, it is a process of liberation from injustice, from domination, from institutionalized and falsely justified abuse. Only later was the process of liberalism turned into the model of freedom and the way to preserve rather than obtain this freedom. But real freedom is obtained fundamentally through a liberation process. This is so in the personal realm, in the communitarian, in the social, and in the political as well. On the other hand, liberalism, as it is contradicted by historical prophecy in Latin America, is today the juridical and formal cover-up for those who have already been liberated from certain oppressions and dominations and who in turn see to it that others do not achieve the same through succeeding and more complex liberation processes.

Both personal freedom and social and political freedom are effectively such only when one *can* be and do what one desires to be and do. Freedom without those very real conditions that make it really possible can be an ideal, but it is not a reality since without due and sufficient conditions one cannot be or do what one wants. But, if besides the absence of real conditions for exercising freedom, liberties, and formal rights, there is positive oppression and domination that hinder that exercise even more, it is not only unreal but positively ideological and hypocritical to talk of freedom. There is no personal freedom when, for example, there is internal domination by very powerful internal pre-conditioning or external advertising and propaganda that is not duly counteracted. For example, there is no personal freedom in a child who does not have the intellectual development and the minimum knowledge to be able to discern and balance the weight of internal and external motivations. If parents or educators impose in all sorts of ways their own ideas, attitudes, or patterns of conduct besides, it is practically a mockery to talk of the child's freedom.

The same should be said about economic and social freedoms. They can be enjoyed only by those who have effective access to them and for whom that access is not positively hindered by all sorts of means, at times covertly and other times openly. What freedom of movement is possessed by someone who has no roads, no means of transport, or even the ability to walk? What freedom is there to choose a job or type of studies when there are jobs or places for students for only 50 percent of the population? What freedom of expression is there when there is active access to the media for only 1 percent and only passive access—for lack of literacy, lack of receiver sets, lack of means, and so forth for over 60 percent? What economic freedom is there when access to credit is for the very few? What political freedom is there when one lacks the resources to create a political party and when the apparatus of the state and of associations maintains a climate of terror—or at least of generalized fear? It will be said that liberalism ideally desires nothing of this, that it seeks to offer equality of opportunity for all individuals and all inclinations. But in fact this is not so, and the least exercise of historicizing shows that freedom and conditions of freedom are not given to but are won by people in a historical liberation process.

Liberalization is one thing, but liberation is something very different. Liberalization processes are only possible if liberation processes have gone before. Liberalization is a problem of and for the elite, whereas liberation is a process of and for the mass of the people; it begins with liberation for basic needs and then builds positive conditions for the increasingly adult exercise of freedom and for the reasonable enjoyment of liberties. The fact that certain liberation processes tend to become new processes of domination of the many by the few is something to think about very much. But it does not invalidate the axiological priority of liberation over liberalization in attaining freedom.

To want to pose the question of freedom outside of liberation is to want to evade the real question of freedom for all. In the realm of the personal, freedom is not actualized fully except by laborious liberation processes confronting all sorts of more or less determinant necessities. There is an internal basis and an ideal of freedom that up to a certain point and in a generic way are given "naturally" to a person. But fundamentally this personal ideal is about capacities and freedoms that need to be actualized to be changed into full realities, for whose actualization quite precise conditions are required. With due distinctions, something similar must be said about social and political freedom. Such freedoms suppose a liberation from oppressive structures, which the classic liberals struggled against on the supposition that only the state limited or oppressed the individual, without realizing that there were social groups that oppressed and exploited other social groups. They suppose, besides, the creation of conditions where the capacity and the ideal of political and social freedom can be shared equitably.

Liberation, therefore, is understood as "liberation from" every form of oppression and as "liberation for" a shared freedom that does not make possible or permit forms of domination. It makes little sense to talk of freedom when opportunity for its actualization is reduced because of unsatisfied basic needs, drastic limitations on real possibilities to choose among, and impositions of every sort, especially those depending on force and terror. But a mere "liberation from" is not enough since a "liberation for" or a "liberation toward" freedom is required; freedom can be full freedom only when it is the freedom of all. The freedom of a few resting on the slavery of the rest is not acceptable, nor is a freedom resting on the non-freedom of the majority acceptable. Hence, freedom here too must be seen from its historicizing in the mass of the people within each country and within the oppressed peoples in the world as a whole. It is humanity that must be free, and not a few privileged members of humanity, whether individuals, social classes, or nations.

From this perspective the question of the priority of justice over freedom or of freedom over justice is resolved by the unity of both in liberation. There can be no justice without freedom and no freedom without justice, even though in the social and political order there is a priority of justice over freedom, since one cannot be free unjustly. Justice, in giving to each what is due to each, not only makes freedom possible but also makes possible what is moral and just. Liberation from every form of oppression whatever is a real process of *"justi-fication."* This justification is the real means of promoting freedom and the conditions that make it possible. Thus, liberation is a process of *"adjust*ment" with oneself, in that it seeks to break one's internal and external chains. It is a *"just"* process in that it tries to overcome manifest injustice; and it is a *"justi-*fying" process in that it seeks to create adequate conditions for the full development of all and for an equitable use of the conditions.

In more explicitly Christian terms, liberation is a march toward the utopia of freedom through a real, prophetic liberation process, which implies liberation from sin, from the law, and from death (Rom. 6-8). Its goal is to reveal truly what it is to be God's children, what the freedom and the glory of God's children actually mean—a goal only possible through a permanent conversion and liberation process (Rom. 8:18-26), which follows Jesus by means of the personal reproduction of the "features of his Son, so that he may be the eldest of many brothers" (Rom. 8:29). A complete development of what is liberation from sin, from the law, and from death would give greater theological and historical clarity to how freedom is the result of liberation and how it is dangerous to pose the problem of freedom without regard to precise liberation tasks. This would demand a more extensive treatment of this question, but its mere suggestion points to the pressing need for processes of prophetic liberation so that the utopia of freedom can be really historicized.

IV. A NEW HEAVEN AND NEW EARTH

1. The New Human Being

The new human being is delineated from the Christian ideal, but from a historicized ideal which proposes to take the place of the old human being that has been the worldly and even Christian-worldly ideal, proposed as such or at least as a practically irresistible focus of attraction. This is done starting from the conviction, nourished both from faith and from historical experience, that the ideal and/or the dominant *focus* of the human person maintained in Latin America is anti-Christian and does not respond to the challenges of reality. Not everything in that ideal is imported to the extent that one can speak of an inculturation of that ideal transmitting its own features to its historicizing. Prescinding for now from which ones are imported features and which are native, a sort of catalog of its traits can be made.

In regard to the ideal of the dominant old human being in the so-called North Atlantic and Western Christian civilization, certain features have to be rejected. These include its radical insecurity, which leads it to take wild and irrational self-defense measures; its unsolidarity with what is happening to the rest of humanity; its ethnocentrism, along with its absolutizing and idolatrizing of the nation-state as fatherland; its exploitation and direct or indirect domination of other peoples and of their resources; the trivial superficiality of its existence and of the criteria by which types of work are chosen; its immaturity in the search for happiness through pleasure, random entertainment, and amusement; the smug pretension of setting itself up as the elite vanguard of humanity; its permanent aggression against the environment shared by the rest of humanity.

To feel the multitudinous effects of this Northern-Western human being on the Latin American human being, effects that are oppressive and destructive, causes us prophetically to reject its false idealism and to delineate a different kind of human being on the basis of that negation. But before this, we must reject the proposition that Latin America simply belongs to the Western world and to the Westernized Christian world. This is because Christ has been falsified by means of this ideologizing and used as a lure by a civilization that is not humanely universalizable. The attempt is to export it as the ideal model of humanity and of Christianity. When Hobbes wrote in *Leviathan* in 1651 that the causes of struggles among humans are three and that the three are written in human nature — insecurity, competition, and desire for glory — he was describing the experience of the emergent Western human being rather than anything necessarily innate to human nature. When official Christianity makes optional and intentional virtues out of what ought to be the outright negation of anti-Christian attitudes and deeds, then it is giving a biased reading of the faith that annuls its real truth and effectiveness.

The return to the historical realism of the gospel proclamation, a historical realism that is by no means fundamentalist precisely because it is historical, obliges a return to the fundamental gospel theme of wealth-poverty. The biased reading of the faith has made it possible to reconcile material wealth with spiritual poverty, when the authentic reading, attested to by the church's greatest saints, is the opposite reconciliation of material poverty with spiritual wealth. Now, the historical verification of the dialectical relation of wealth-poverty reclaims the depth of the gospel message, making poverty not a purely optional counsel but a historical necessity. Correlatively, this makes wealth not something indifferent, easily reconcilable with following Jesus, but one of the fundamental hindrances to setting up the Kingdom. Poverty and wealth are not here spoken of apart from each other, but in their dialectical relationship: poverty as a correlate of wealth and wealth as a correlate of poverty.

Not only from the viewpoint of faith but also from the viewpoint of history, one sees in wealth and in greed, or desire for wealth, the fundamental energizer of a heartless and inhuman culture and the greatest resistance to the historical construction of the Kingdom of God. The path of rapid and unequal enrichment has led to a Cainite rupture of humanity and to the formation of an exploitative, repressive, and violent human being. The relationship of human beings with wealth, a question so essential in the gospel, again becomes a central point in defining the new human being, who will not come into existence until there is an entirely new relationship to deal with the phenomenon of wealth and the problem of unequal accumulation. Asceticism and individual and group spirituality have tried to resolve this problem, but it must be taken up again because it has become a historical necessity to curb the dehumanization of both rich and poor in their dialectical confrontation.

Enticed by the allure of wealth, of wealthy persons and peoples, one loses the marks of one's own identity. To seek one's own identity in the imperfect appropriation of these foreign models leads to dependencies and mimicries that impede one's own self-creation. The culture of wealth proposes models and establishes means to attain them, and it does so in a way that outdazzles the possibility of seeking other models of fulfillment and happiness. It subjects to alienating dynamisms all those who devote themselves to adoring the golden calf, which becomes the central idol of a new culture that in turn reinforces the central role that this golden idol plays in it. Where your treasure is, there is your heart, which comes to be shaped with the features of your treasure. Hence the importance of the choice of one's treasure. When one takes one's treasure to be the accumulation of wealth, the type of heart and of human being that results is subjected to a double alienation. This human being's own freedom is subjected to money's dynamisms which create needs and focus on things. And its own identity as a human being is subjected to a model created not for liberation but for submission. Certainly, wealth does have some possibilities for liberation, but at the cost of other possibilities of slavery for oneself and others.

All these evils, in great part induced from outside, are accompanied and rejected by others arising from within. Tendencies to machismo and violence are examples of these evils that degrade both men and women and are reflected in profound deviations in sexual and family life, or in a whole interdependent combination of submission, fatalism, and inertia. How much of this is ancestral or even natural and how much is a reflection of external stimuli is a matter to be investigated in each case. But to place the origin of all evils in outside agents would not be the right way to recover one's own identity, because this would make harder the task of constructing the new human being from within.

The ideologizing that corresponds to this set of real tendencies and deeds reveals itself as negative and nullifying of one's own individual and collective consciousness. This ideologizing presents itself as religious, economic, and political, and what it does basically is reinforce fundamental interests, latent or explicit. Religious fatalism, the economic competition of free enterprise and the urge for profit, the democratic system offered as a controlled and mapped-out participation of the mass of the people all are examples of this ideologizing, which, although based on certain goods and values, transmits greater evils.

In its negativity, the foregoing points to what should be positively the features of utopia. In the light of Christian inspiration that negativity indicates what the new human being is to be, in contrast to the old one. Since it is not primordially an intentional exercise but a praxis already underway, some of those features can already be appreciated in what is in existence.

The central point concerns the preferential option for the poor as a fundamental way to combat the priority of wealth in the shaping of human beings. There is a movement toward a greater solidarity with the cause of the oppressed, toward a growing incorporation into their world as the privileged place of humanization and Christian divinization. Such incorporation is not done in order to take perverse pleasure in miserable poverty, but in order to accompany the poor in their desire for liberation. Liberation cannot consist of passing from poverty to wealth by making oneself rich by means of the poverty of others. It consists rather of surmounting poverty through solidarity. We are, of course, talking about the poor-with-spirit, the poor who accept their situation as the foundation for constructing the new human being. Out of the materiality of poverty, this construction of the new human being arises actively from the poor-with-spirit, impelling them toward a process of liberation in solidarity that leaves out no human being. In other words, these are active poor, whom necessity spurs to escape from an unjust situation.

Hence, this new human being is defined in part by active protest and permanent struggle. This new human being seeks to overcome the dominant structural injustice, which is considered an evil and a sin because it keeps most of the human population in conditions of inhumane living. This unjust situation is negative, but its negativity propels escape from it as from a catapult. The positive aspect is the dynamic of overcoming. In that overcoming the Spirit breathes in multiple ways, of which the supreme way of all is readiness to give one's life for the rest, whether in tireless daily commitment or in sacrifice unto death violently suffered.

Typically, however, the motive of this new human being who is moved by the Spirit is not hatred but mercy and love, for all are seen as children of God and not as enemies to be destroyed. Hatred can be lucid and effective in the short range, but it is not capable of constructing a really new human being. Christian love is not softhearted exactly, but it does propose very decidedly not to let itself be entrapped and hardened in selfishness or hatred, and it has a very clear vocation to service. The lords of this world set out to dominate and to be served, while the Son of Man, the new human being, has not come to be served but to serve and to give his life for the rest, for the many (Matt. 20:25-28).

Along with love comes hope. To be really new, the new human beings must be persons of hope and of joy in the building of a more just world. They are not moved by despair but by hope, because despair tends toward suicide and death, and hope tends to life and to giving. It may at times be hope against all hope, but therein can be seen joy and the security of one who is above humans and their thoughts, the impulse of a vocation to build the Kingdom, which fundamentally is the Kingdom of God, because God is its final goal and its constant motive. Latin America, which has so often been called the continent of hope, is exactly that in its multitudes of people full of hope, and not merely just as a pure natural potentiality not yet developed.

It is an open and untiring hope. The new human being is an open human being who does not absolutize any achievement in the illusion of making something finite into something infinite. The horizon is necessary as a limit that gives orientation, but it is more necessary as a permanent opening for the one who moves forward. To absolutize wealth, power, the organization, the institution, and such is to make idols of them, and it makes the idolater a dull and subjugated person. Such a one is the opposite of the person who is open to a God who is ever greater and to a Kingdom that is to be historicized in an ever greater proximity to reality that, for various reasons, surpasses each partial achievement and surpasses it qualitatively through the interpretation of new developments that are logically and conceptually unforeseeable.

Thus one arrives at not only a new relationship among human beings but also a new relationship with nature. When the first inhabitants of Latin America maintained that no one can own the earth, that it cannot be the property of anyone in particular, because it is a mother goddess that gives life to so many people, they maintained a respectful and worshipful relationship with nature. Nature cannot be seen merely as raw material or a place to invest; it is a manifestation and gift of God that is to be enjoyed with veneration and not ill-treated with contempt and exploitation.

To make all this possible, liberation theology outlines a new human being, at once contemplative and active, one who transcends both leisure and business. Activity is not sufficient and contemplation is not enough. Against the temptation of sloth hidden in the leisure of contemplation, the urgency of the task impels to efficacious action, for the seriousness of the problems admits no delay. Against the temptation of activism concealed as the constant creation of new opportunities, the emptiness and destructiveness of its promises demand the wealth of contemplation. Action without contemplation is empty and destructive, while contemplation without action is paralyzing and concealing. The new human beings are hearers and doers of the word, discerners of the signs of the times, and accomplishers of what is offered them as promise.

Other historical features of Jesus' life ought to be projected also on this new human being who dawns on Latin America's horizon already in the poor and in those who have cast their lot with them. But those features pointed out here, especially when they make explicit reference to a God ever present, in whom to confide and to whom to confide the ultimate meaning of the seed sown, are those which unify and nuance those other features of Jesus' life that are taken on with distinct nuances, and especially with different concretions, according to the particular vocation of each person.

Between the negative superseding of the old human being and the affirmative realization of the new one, between the prophecy that denies by affirming and the utopia that affirms by denying, the Latin American praxis of Christian faith begins to open up new ways, right ways for all human beings, right ways to build a new earth and a new world.

2. The New Earth

The creation of the new earth implies the utopia of a new economic order, a new social order, a new political order, and a new cultural order. The so-called New World, far from being really new, became, especially in Latin America, an impoverished imitation of the old. Only now that the earlier model has failed is there a disposition to raise a really new world upon its negation.

This is not to remain on the level of voluntaristic idealisms. Historical inertia, quasi-necessary laws, and a weight of tradition cannot be abolished, but they must be countered and, as far as possible, transformed by the force of the utopian ideal that arises from an objective and not merely intentional need to overcome the grave and universal evils of the present. The existence of historical evolution's own dynamisms, never completely dominated by any historical subject whatever, cannot be ignored. But that is no reason to accept an absolute historical determinism that leads to fatalism or that, at best, merely permits an attempt to improve the structural whole by the improvement of each individual or of some of the social groups. The alternative proposal of "every man for himself" in this world disorder may be the momentary solution for a few, but it is the ruin of the majority. Hence utopia, the recourse to the utopian ideal as the effective force assimilated by many, is necessary to counteract and even to direct what otherwise becomes the blind and mechanical course of history. It is not correct that the freedom of each will lead to the freedom of all, when the inverse is much more real: general freedom is what will make possible the freedom of each one. And that ideal of realizing utopia can become the principle of freedom and of spirituality incorporated through the subjectivity of persons into the determinism and the materiality of the historical processes. From this perspective Marx's passage in *Towards a Critique of Hegel's Philosophy of Right* (1844) could be read in a radically new form: "It is true that the weapon of criticism cannot substitute for the criticism of weapons, that material force must be overcome by material force; but theory also becomes material force as soon as it takes possession of the masses." The utopian ideal, when it is presented historically as gradually realizable and is assumed by the mass of the people, comes to be a stronger force than the force of arms; it is at once a material and a spiritual force, present and future, hence able to overcome the material-spiritual complexity with which the course of history presents itself.

A New Economic Order

In the economic order, Christian utopia, seen from Latin America, arising from real historicized prophecy in a determined situation, proposes a civilization of poverty to take the place of the present civilization of wealth. From a more sociological than humanistic perspective, this same utopia can be expressed by proposing a civilization of work to take the place of the dominant civilization of capital.

If the world as a totality has come to be shaped above all as a civilization of capital and of wealth in which the former more objectively and the latter more subjectively have been the principal moving, shaping, and directing elements of present-day civilization, and if this of itself has already contributed all that it had that is positive and is now causing constantly greater and graver ills, what must be favored is not its correction but its replacement by something better, by its contrary—that is, by a civilization of poverty. From the times of

Jesus, whenever poverty is preferred to riches in order to enter the Kingdom, a great rejection arises on the part of those who are already rich or have placed in riches the essential foundation of their lives. But what Jesus proposed as personal ideal can and must be expanded to socio-historical reality, with suitable adaptation.

The civilization of wealth and of capital is the one that, in the final analysis, proposes the private accumulation of the greatest possible capital on the part of individuals, groups, multinationals, states, or groups of states as the fundamental basis of development, and individuals' or families' possessive accumulation of the most possible wealth as the fundamental basis for their own security and for the possibility of ever growing consumption as the basis of their own happiness. It is not denied that such a type of civilization, prevailing in the East as well as in the West and called capitalist civilization deservedly — whether state capitalism or private capitalism — has brought benefits to humanity that as such should be preserved and furthered (scientific and technical development, new modes of collective consciousness, and so forth). But these civilizations have brought greater evils, and their self-correction processes do not prove sufficient for reversing their destructive course.

In consequence, seeing the problem in its worldwide totality from the perspective of real needs and of the expectations of the greater part of the world's population, that civilization of wealth and capital must be radically superseded. On this point the church's social doctrine, especially in its new formulation by John Paul II in *Laborem Exercens*, is to be added in a very significant way to the established demands of liberation theology. Materialist economism, which shapes the civilization of wealth, is not ethically acceptable in its own internal dynamism, and much less so in its real effects. Instead of materialist economism, a materialist humanism should be proposed, which acknowledging and therefore relying on the complexly material condition of human beings, would avoid every type of idealistic solution to the real problems of people. This materialist humanism aims to go beyond materialist economism, since it would no longer be economic matter that finally determines everything else, as is the case in any type of civilization of capital and wealth, but human material, complex and open, which conceives human beings as the limited but real subjects of their own history.

The civilization of poverty, on the other hand, founded on a materialist humanism transformed by Christian light and inspiration, rejects the accumulation of capital as the energizer of history and the possession-enjoyment of wealth as principle of humanization. It makes the universal satisfying of basic needs the principle of development, and the growth of shared solidarity the foundation of humanization.

The civilization of poverty is so denominated in contrast to the civilization of wealth, and not because it proposes universal pauperization as an ideal of life. Certainly, strictly evangelical Christian tradition has an enormous distrust of wealth, following in this the teaching of Jesus, a teaching much clearer and more forceful than others might be that are presented as such. Likewise, the great saints of the church's history, often in open struggles for reform against church authorities, have incessantly preached the Christian and human advantages of material poverty. These are two aspects that cannot be ignored, because in the case of the great religious founders—for example, in the case of St. Ignatius Loyola in his deliberations on poverty—explicit reference is made not only to the personal, but also to the institutional. But, even admitting and taking account of such considerations, which call into question wealth in itself, what is here meant to be emphasized is the dialectical wealth-poverty relationship and not poverty in itself. In a world sinfully shaped by the capital-wealth dynamism it is necessary to stir up a different dynamism that will salvifically surpass it.

This is achieved, for the moment, through an economic arrangement relying on and directly and immediately addressed to satisfying the basic needs of all humans. Only this orientation responds to a fundamental right of human beings, without the observance of which their dignity is disdained, their reality is violated, and world peace is endangered.

In regard to identifying basic needs, even accounting for cultural and individual differences that give rise to distinct subjectifications of those needs, not much discussion is needed if one looks at the conditions of extreme poverty or destitution of more than half of the human race. Such needs include, first of all, proper nourishment, minimal housing, basic health care, primary education, sufficient employment, and so forth. It is not proposed that this exhausts the horizon of economic development; it is simply a point of departure and of fundamental reference, a sine qua non of any sort of development. The great task remaining is for all people to be able to gain access to the satisfaction of those needs, not as crumbs fallen from the tables of the rich but as the principal portion from humanity's table. With the satisfying of basic needs institutionally assured as the primary phase of a liberation process, people would be free to be what they want to be, provided that what is wanted not become a new mechanism of domination. Rather than capital accumulation, the civilization of poverty proposes as dynamizing principle the dignifying of work, of work that will have as its principal object not the production of capital but the perfecting of the human being. Work, viewed at once as the personal and collective means to assure the satisfaction of basic needs and as a form of self-realization, would supersede different forms of self- and hetero-exploitation and would likewise supersede inequalities that are both an affront and the cause of domination and antagonism.

It is not merely a matter of the new human beings ceasing to make wealth their basic idol to which they offer all they have—their ability to work, their moral principles, health, leisure, family relationships, and so on. It is, above all, a matter of making a society that, negatively, does not oblige one to make wealth the supreme value because without it one is lost. (What does it profit a man to save his soul, which is not seen and not esteemed, if he loses the world, which is seen and is most esteemed?) Positively, such a society is structured so that one is not required to keep looking for wealth in order to have all that is needed for human liberation and fulfillment. It is clear that a society not structured by the laws of capital, but one giving primacy to the dynamism of humanizing work, would be shaped in a way very different from the present one, because the shaping principle is totally different. The humanistic and moral failure of present society, of the present earth, shaped according to capital's dictates, has begun in various ways to move those in the more or less marginal vanguards to shape a different society, even though for the moment, that is, by escaping from the structures and dynamics of the society that presently dominates. The definitive solution, however, cannot be in escaping from this world and confronting it with a sign of prophetic protest, but in entering into it to renew it and transform it in the direction of the utopia of the new earth.

In part, this will be gradually achieved if a fundamental characteristic of the civilization of poverty, shared solidarity, grows positively stronger in contrast to the closed and competitive individualism of the society of wealth. To see others not as part of oneself, yet to see oneself in unity and communion with others, combines well with what is deepest in Christian inspiration and goes along with one of the best tendencies of Latin America's popular sectors, which unfolds in contrast to individualistic, separating tendencies. This solidarity is facilitated in the common enjoyment of common property.

The private appropriation of common property is not needed in order to care for it and enjoy it. When the church's social doctrine, following St. Thomas, holds that private appropriation of goods is the best practical manner for their primordial common destiny to be fulfilled in an orderly way, it is making a concession to "the hardness of their hearts," but "in the beginning it was not so." Only because of greed and selfishness, connatural to original sin, can it be said that private ownership of property is the best guarantee of productive advancement and social order. But if "where sin abounded, grace abounded more" is to have historical verification, it is necessary to proclaim utopianly that a new earth with new human beings must be shaped with principles of greater altruism and solidarity. The great benefits of nature — the air, the seas and beaches, the mountains and forests, the rivers and lakes, in general all the natural resources for production, use, and enjoyment — need not be privately appropriated by any individual person, group, or nation, and in fact they are the grand medium of communication and common living.

If a social order were achieved in which basic needs were satisfied in a stable manner and were guaranteed, and the common sources of personal development were made possible, so that the security and the possibilities of personalization were guaranteed, the present order based on the accumulation of private capital and material wealth could be considered as a prehistoric and prehuman stage. The utopian ideal is not that all are to have much by means of private and exclusive appropriation, but that all are to have what is necessary and that the nonacquisitive and nonexclusive use and enjoyment of what is primarily common be open to all. The indispensable dynamism of personal initiative cannot be confused with the natural-original dynamism of private and privatizing initiative. Nor is excluding others as competitors to one's selfhood the only way to work for oneself or to be oneself.

The new, utopian arrangement of an economy at the service of human beings and certainly leading to a new earth must be the economic arrangement oriented by the above principles and favoring the development of the new human being. At present it is a shared complaint that human beings are subordinated to the economy and the economy is not subordinated to human beings. Although this phenomenon indicates, among other things, the predominance of what is common and structural over what is individual and integral, the way in which the phenomenon appears—dominance of the economic over the human—is not acceptable as utopian ideal, much less is it compatible with the Christian ideal.

Which of the two great economic arrangements available today, capitalist or socialist, is more fitting for the attainment of that utopian ideal?

In Latin America the failure of capitalist models, which have been clearly dominant here for decades, is quite clear. It will be said that they have not been sufficiently capitalist; but, if that is so, it has not been because of opposition to capitalism, but because of the objective inadequacy of imposing a capitalist system in a situation like Latin America's. Capitalist systems in Latin America have been unable to satisfy the basic needs of the greater part of the population, they have created bitter inequalities between the few who have much and the many who have little, they have led to a gigantic foreign debt imposed on human beings who in no way enjoyed or received benefit from the loans, they have often produced deep economic crises, and they have promoted an immoral culture of consumption and of easy profit. Sadly, all this has been done by persons and classes that consider themselves Catholic and who see no contradiction between their economic praxis and their Christian praxis. From this reality, the least that can be said is that only a radical transformation of the capitalist economic arrangement is minimally reconcilable with what the Christian utopia is. Marxism, insofar as it is the great contradictor of that arrangement, insofar as it profoundly attacks the spirit of capitalism and analyzes the mechanisms that sustain it, and insofar as it utopianly proclaims the liberation of human beings through the liberation of labor, plays a long-reaching prophetic and utopian role in Latin America and offers a scientific method for unraveling the profound dynamisms of the capitalist system.

On the other hand, the economic results—later we will turn to the political ones—of the socialist arrangements are not satisfactory either, at least for entering world competition. The recent attempts by the larger socialist nations to correct their economic systems with procedures more proper to the opposing system, without meaning the abandonment of what is principal in their own system, point to certain limitations that well deserve to be considered. On the other hand, it would be premature to condemn beforehand the failure of the reformed socialist models because of what is presently happening in Nicaragua, although it would be a mistake to ignore the real difficulties which that system has in the concrete way it exists, considering the places and the times. Even the Cuban model, although it has achieved the best satisfaction of basic needs in all of Latin America in a relatively short time, still has intrinsic difficulties that can be overcome only with a massive external support. Hence, there are also serious problems in the realization of the socialist model as the most effective instrument to historicize Christian utopia.

Nevertheless, it can be defended that in economic matters the socialist ideal is closer than the capitalist to the utopian demands of the Kingdom. The socialist economic ideal rests on profound values of the human being, but it does not prosper economically precisely because of its moral idealism, which does not take into account the empirical state of human nature. The capitalist economic ideal rests, at least in part, on the selfish vices of human nature, and it is, in this manner, not more realistic, but more pragmatic than its opponent, and for that reason it has superior economic successes. It could be said, therefore, that if the new human being were to be attained, the socialist arrangement would function better, whereas under the dominion of the old human being, structures that are fundamentally unjust for the greater part of the world's population work better. For this reason, although one cannot be naive in recommending one or other mediation of the Kingdom, the Christian utopia, which strives for a new human being on a new earth, cannot help inclining in economic matters toward formulations that are closer to socialism than to capitalism as far as Latin America and, more generally, the Third World are concerned. It is not too much to recall that the church's social teaching has been drawing closer to this way of seeing things.

The objection can be made that the satisfaction of basic needs is better assured in the capitalist countries than in the socialist countries. But the objection is not so solid if one considers, first, that the capitalist countries take care of a much smaller part of the world population and, second, that this satisfaction is achieved at very high cost to a great part of that capitalist population and, third, that the system is not universalizable, given the limited world resources and the private appropriation of those same resources by a few privileged countries.

In both cases, although not equally because of differing situations, prophecy and Christian utopia need to be critical of the theory and the practice of the dominant economic systems. At times the church's social teaching has been too naive and tolerant toward the theory and, especially, toward the practice of capitalism for fear of losing perquisites and out of fear of the Marxist regimes. But liberation theology has also on occasions been naive and tolerant toward the theory and practice of Marxism because of a certain inferiority complex before the commitment of the revolutionaries. Without ignoring prophecy's and utopia's difficult relationship with the historical mediations, which should not be anathematized from an unreal purism, what finally is important to underline is that, whatever the case, the civilization of work and of poverty must take the place of the civilization of capital and of wealth. And it would seem — and this is a most serious problem — that the civilization of capital and wealth is imposing itself worldwide, both where there is private capitalism and where there is state capitalism. Hence, Christian prophecy and utopia have a permanent task of leavening to do.

A New Social Order

Corresponding to that new economic order, a new vigorous and multi-polar social order must arise in which it will be possible for the people to be more and more the agents of their own destiny and to have greater possibilities for creative freedom and for participation. Just as it is the people of God who should have priority in the Kingdom of God, and not a set of institutional superstructures that takes its place, likewise in this world's history it should be the social groups that carry the weight of history, and they should do so on their own. In other words, the social should be given more weight than the political, without individualism thereby becoming the highest form of humanization. The social dimension should prevail over the political dimension, but not take its place.

Between individualism and statism a strong type of society should be built to overcome the licentiousness of the former and the dominating interference of the latter. It is not a question of compromising between two existing extremes, but of finding new forms to supersede both existing models by negating them. Of course, deemphasizing statism must not be understood as a neo-liberal demand for a lesser weight of the state before the demands of so-called private initiative and before the laws of the marketplace. Deemphasizing the state implies, rather, a socialization that promotes a communitarian and social initiative that is not delegated either to the state or to parties or to vanguards or to bosses. It is a question of overcoming social apathy in the management of historical processes without for this reason lapsing into either gremialisms or corporativisms. Basically what is proposed is, positively, to give more life and decision to social enterprises and, negatively, to overcome the unruly dynamisms of political power That is, the principal characteristic of this socialization would be the seeking of the community good from community pressure and through community means without delegating this force to political enterprises, which become autonomous and can never adequately represent the social.

There is no reason to confuse the public enterprise with the political enterprise, or to accept reservation of the whole public sector to the state and to political parties, to the detriment of social enterprises. The social represents not a mean but a mediation between the individual and the political, so that the individual's essential communal dimension is primarily realized not in the political dimension of the state but in the public dimension of the social. At distinct moments in the Latin American political struggle there has been a certain disdain for parties in the interest of the popular organizations. But this tendency has not contributed all it could when it has proposed that the organizations take on state political power. And these organizations have again fallen into the advised use of politics to further their real interests. Likewise, the church has often abdicated its role in social enterprise to become an appendage of political power, thus impairing its mission and weakening thereby its historic potential for the service of the mass of the people.

In regard to the permanent problem of freedom and equality-justice, the question does not reside in giving primacy to the individual over the state or vice versa. The union of liberty-justice-equality is better achieved in the mediation of the social, which is neither of the state nor of the individual. The mediation of the social permits individual-personal freedom that is not individualistic. At the same time that it permits political freedom—that is, freedom of individuals and of groups vis-à-vis the power of the state. What generates real conditions for personal freedom is, first of all, social freedom. In turn, it is not only the individual but the community that becomes the best real and effective guarantee against the domination and oppression of politico-state structures.

This implies that excessive and conflict-producing inequalities are to disappear in the real area of the social without thereby giving rise to mechanical equalities that do not respond to different preferences in values and to the diversity of contributions by individuals and groups to social well-being. An obligatory equality does not respond to reality and is not demanded by ethical or religious considerations. What must be excluded, for the time being, is the present outrageous difference between those who squander and those who lack enough to subsist — this, even though there be no causal or functional relation between the poverty and the wealth. What is indeed a pressing obligation is that all be assured satisfaction of basic needs. But beyond that minimal level particular choices and greater labor or performance are to be respected, so long as equality of opportunity is respected and the processes leading to attention-getting and conflict-provoking inequalities are avoided.

These positions would be normal and reasonable ones for making possible an adequate freedom-justice-equality. But the utopian ideal of Jesus goes much further. Paradoxically, the follower of Jesus seeks to take the last place as the surest way to reach the first. In this first place one is not dominant but a servant, one seeks not one's own honor but that of the rest. In general, what Jesus' message propounds is to exchange the real dynamisms of this old world, of this old earth, for the dynamisms of the Kingdom as utopian ideal of the new earth and as negation — death and resurrection — of the old one. Christian scriptures' tremendous reservations about wealth, power, and worldly honor and emphatic proclamation of poverty, service, and the humiliation of the cross can and should be translated to the visible and the social. They represent not only a possible ideal for the individual, but a model for society. That the realizations of this have not been totally satisfactory — for example, in the case of religious orders which are social groups which bring individuals together without leaving them at the mercy of more globalizing institutions — does not keep these from raising the question of the need to give social, historical flesh to the invitation from Jesus to follow him. Social institutions, unlike political ones, can be impregnated with that spirit, which would seem to be reserved for individuals, and so the great founders of the religious orders have intended.

A New Political Order

The new political order, prophetically outlined on the utopian horizon, is based on the attempt to go beyond the political models that are the result and at the same time the support of both liberal capitalism and Marxist collectivism.

What is being proposed is not a third way between liberalism and collectivism in the economic area or between liberal democracy and social democracy in the political. Such a third way does not exist in the latest documents of the church, not even as an ideal solution (*Sollicitudo Rei Socialis*, no. 41). In this historical phase, there can be different forms of one or other way, both in the economic and in the political sphere, some better than others in their applicability to a determined reality. It would not be hard to prove that some socialist political forms are much better than some capitalist political forms and, vice versa, that some capitalist forms are better than some socialist forms. This appraisal is indeed interesting. It is usually presented as an opening of one system to the other, which in practice brings them nearer to each other in spite of their fundamental differences. Of particular interest are recent rather widespread efforts to democratize socialism, but there is hardly any equivalent effort toward a much-needed socialization of the democracies, perhaps because the more advanced ones have already done so in some way.

This two-way opening up of each of the systems could be evidence not only of the insufficiency of each but also of a possible leap forward to a now scarcely recognizable new political system. It is one of the few instances where one might appreciate a positive dynamism of history that goes against the blind dynamism of the demands of capital—subject to constant corrections by what might be called the dynamism of humanization-divinization. Signs like the increasingly connatural appreciation of human rights, of a larger democratic opening, of a more effective world solidarity, are, among other things, manifestations of the struggle between good and evil, between the closure of the systems and the openness of humanity. They are positive and hopeful signs that can scarcely hide the heaviness and inertia of their opposites, but they nevertheless point toward possibilities of change through reform.

In Latin America, however, the search has been and continues to be for revolutionary change rather than for reformist change. Hence, on occasion the effort has been made to take advantage of the subversive dynamism of the Christian faith, just as the dominant systems have tried to take advantage of the conservative dynamisms of the same faith. The reason is obvious. On the one hand, there is such a degree of structural injustice affecting the very structure of society, that it appears indispensable to demand a quick and profound change of structures—that is, a revolution. On the other hand, the prevailing dynamism does not in fact lead to a reform that might build a revolutionary change, but instead to a deepening and spread of the structural injustice, and this under the guise of reform whose path is development.

From this viewpoint, it can be affirmed both from theory and from verification of historical reality and, of course, from utopian prophecy, that a revolution in the present dynamisms and structures is needed, an anti-capitalist revolution—"anti" to the capitalism found in the underdeveloped and oppressed countries—and an anti-imperialist revolution—"anti" to every type of external empire that tries to impose its own interests. The question is not, then, if a revolution is needed or not, but *what* revolution is needed and how to bring it about.

The revolution that is needed, the necessary revolution, will be the one that intends freedom deriving from and leading to justice and justice deriving and leading to freedom. This freedom must come out of liberation and not merely out of liberalization—whether economic or political liberalization—in order to overcome in this way the dominant "common evil" and build a "common good," a common good understood in contrast to the common evil and sought from a preferential option for the mass of the people.

The imposition of the dogma that liberal democracy is the best path for combining freedom and justice in any time and circumstance is simply presumptuous, and it often conceals accompanying advantages for an elite. Likewise, the dogmatic imposition of the so-called social or popular democracies as the best and only way adequately to join freedom and justice does not square with some of the forms in which they have actually appeared. It would be better to stick to the more radical principle that it is reality as experienced by the mass of the people, and not dogmatic principles or even historical models, that is to be imposed as selection criterion leading to genuine self-determination. The real measure of a duly ordered and quantified system of human rights takes precedence over the formal criteria of one or other type of democracy.

From this perspective, social liberation appears more necessary and urgent than political liberation in the Central American countries and in the greater part of the Third World, something that is perhaps not the case in other situations in the First World and the Second World. Of course, they are not mutually exclusive and, even less, contradictory. But social liberation, which rests on satisfying the basic needs of the masses and supports the autonomous exercise of social life, is above political freedom, which intends equality of opportunity for attaining political power, and above what are called strictly political freedoms, as distinct from fundamental freedoms. This is because, in order to be enjoyed by most people, political freedoms require liberation from basic needs; they also require social freedom, even though these in turn demand areas of political freedom.

For all that, in the present stage of the Kingdom's realization, with the greater part of the population living in extreme poverty and oppression, the socialist ideal appears more connatural to the profound inspiration of the Christian message than the capitalist ideal, although neither of them is identified with the Christian utopian ideal. Another matter altogether is the possibility of actually realizing each of these two ideals.

Many trials and attempts to formulate a Christian correction of capitalism have been made, and the results have not been good even for satisfying basic needs, not to mention the area of ethics — of forming a new human being and a new earth better conformed to the utopian ideals of the Kingdom. Although in the church's social teaching useful corrections of capitalism have been formulated, frequently the mistake has been made of thinking that capitalism is fundamentally good and is the system more conformed to Christian values. On the other hand, while the influence of the Christian faith and even of the historical forms of Christendom in correcting capitalism (as it has existed in Latin America, where the official faith has been Christian since the time of the conquest) has not been completely ineffective, it shows notable weaknesses. These in turn have made the church worldly and capitalist more than they have made the structures and behavior of the world Christian and evangelical.

The attempt to make the Christian faith the yeast and leaven of Marxist positions has been put to the test much less. Something has been done in this regard, as Latin American revolutionaries from Fidel Castro to the Sandinista leaders and those of the Salvadoran FMLN have acknowledged. Liberation theology in different forms has sought to contribute important corrections to Marxism, as the church's social teaching had sought to do until recently with capitalism. Not that liberation theology proposes that the church relinquish its social and political function to movements, parties, or vanguards who will represent it. On the contrary, liberation theology demands a direct and independent commitment of the church to the defense of human rights and to the promotion of greater justice and freedom, especially for those most in need. But it does propose that the Marxist forms of revolution, and not only the human beings who bring them about, be profoundly transformed, because in their theory, and especially, in their practice, Marxists tend toward reductionisms and effectivisms little in accord with the Christian utopian ideal. In turn, the experience of the best of Marxism has served to spur the church and has obliged it to turn — to be converted — toward radical points in the Christian message that the passage of years and inculturation into capitalist forms had left merely ritualized and ideologized without historical value for individuals and peoples.

A New Cultural Order

The new cultural order ought to free itself from the models of Western culture, for these leave much to desire when it comes to achieving the perfecting and the happiness of human beings. Only by removing and freeing oneself at least from the deception found in Western culture can one begin to seek another type of culture as a way to true human progress.

The consumer cultural order is a product of the consumer economic order. Hence it is not adequate for mobilizing a civilization of poverty, which must also have its corresponding cultural development. The cultural tradition will not be enlarged through constant entertainment changes. To confuse being entertained with being happy favors and promotes the consumption of products by inducing needs in the marketplace, but at the same time it reveals and induces the greatest inner emptiness. The civilization of poverty, far from provoking consumption and activity in the cultural sphere, tends to further what is natural and to facilitate attitudes of contemplation and communication more than attitudes of activity-consumption in some and of pure passivity-receptivity in others.

The huge cultural wealth amassed through thousands of years of human life diversified in multiple forms and in various times and places. It must not be allowed to remain overwhelmed by cultural modes that seek in what is new the affirmation and consolidation of human beings that are not new and that only endeavor to sell newness. It is necessary to reclaim those age-old riches, not so as to rest in them conservatively but to open up possibilities of new developments to surpass but not replace them. Many of the technological and consumer models are losing sight of and losing the use of — if not destroying altogether — the reality and the deep meaning of the great cultural achievements that have proceeded from a true cultural identity. It is through one's own identity that one can assimilate the values of other cultures without becoming lost in them. For example, the case of the inculturated assimilation of the Christian faith made by the liberation theology movement is a good demonstration of how a universalizable reality can be historicized and particularized, and at the same time be enriched.

Culture, first of all, must be liberating. It must liberate from ignorance, from fear, from inner and outer pressure, in search of a fuller and fuller truth and more and more fulfilling reality. In this liberation process culture will become the generator of real freedom; it will not be reduced to selecting from among — rather than electing among — distinct conditioned and conditioning offers. But this culture will be oriented toward persons, communities, peoples, and nations who are constructing their own self-being in an effort of creation and not only of acceptance. Everywhere in the world there is a tremendous cultural imposition from powerful centers that universalize the world's vision and values with the most varied communications media. In various ways this cultural imposition keeps the huge masses of Latin America and of other lands alienated from understanding themselves and from understanding and valuing the world. Something that ought to favor a plural unity becomes an impoverishing uniformity. At the same time, the facility of the communications media leads to another kind of alienation. These media promote the leap from a primitive state of culture, which is at times a very valuable and healthy state, into sophisticated and decadent phases of a culture imposed more by its milieu and by its attendant baggage than by its own basic content.

Here too the question is one of seeking a culture for the majority and not a culture for the elite with much form and little life. That all, if possible, and not just a few, have life and have it in abundance should be the motto of the new culture on the new earth. This is a really utopian task, but one to which real prophecy stimulates — and the stimulus is seen in many places. This real prophecy repudiates and overcomes the blemishes of an alienating and, at bottom, dehumanizing culture.

3. A New Heaven

The creation of a new heaven supposes achieving a new presence of God among humans that will let the old Babylon be transformed into the new Jerusalem.

Certainly the foregoing, expressed under the headings of new human being and new earth, is a very special presence of the Spirit of Christ in the world as sent by the Crucified and Risen One. But it needs to be made more explicit and more visible, which is what is expressed in the new heaven — not as something superimposed on human beings and on the earth, but as something integrated and structured with them.

A Christological Heaven

So, by *new heaven* must be understood that presence of God on the new earth that permits and encourages that God be all in all and in everything (1

Cor. 15:28), because Christ is that for all (Col. 3:11). It is, therefore, a new christological heaven and not simply the heaven of an abstract God, univocal in his abstraction. Neither does it mean heaven as the final place of the risen in grace, but the heaven present in history, the historical and increasingly operative and visible presence of God among human beings and public human structures. The historical Jesus must be constituted not only the Christ of faith but also the Christ of history.

The Church of Christ

In this view the new heaven exceeds what is habitually understood as church, although not what should be understood as the city of God, and of course as Kingdom of God. Nevertheless, the reference to the church is indispensable for adequately describing the new heaven, under and in which to live historically, while God's history continues its journey, or God continues to journey through history as historical Christ. Indeed, one of the principal forms in which this new heaven ought to be historicized is the church of Christ as historical body of Jesus crucified and risen.

It is not enough to affirm that the church makes the divine life present to us, transmitted sacramentally. This is important, but it is not enough. For the present, that sacramental presence of the church as a whole and of the distinct sacraments in which that fundamental sacramentality is actualized (Rahner) ought both to be revitalized beyond the ritual and formal until the effectiveness of the Word and the active correspondence of the one who receives the grace of the sacrament are recovered. To confuse the mystery, which is the sacrament, with a process given in the interiority of the person is to devalue the mysteriousness of the sacrament's efficacy through an unverifiable and ineffective pure affirmation. Even from this viewpoint, a profound renewal, without which revitalizing sacramental life is unthinkable, is indispensable, prophetically and utopianly.

But the church must go beyond the sacramental ambit or, at least, its sacramentality must be understood more widely. For this it needs permanently to be open and attentive to the newness and the universality of the Spirit, which breaks the fossilized routine of the past and the limits of a restricted self-conception. Only a church that lets itself be invaded by the Spirit renewer of all things and that is attentive to the signs of the times can become the new heaven that the new human being and the new earth need.

The church as institution tends to be more conserving of the past than renewing of the present and creative of the future. Certainly, there are things to preserve, but nothing vital and human, nothing historical, is preserved if it is not maintained in constant renewal. Fear of what is new, of what is not controllable by already established institutional means, has been and still is one of the church's permanent characteristics. When one reviews the positions of the different ecclesiastical authorities previous to the religious renewal movements that have afterward proved to be fundamental for the church's advance (for example, the founding of the great religious orders, new forms of thought, new methods and even data of biblical research, and so on), not to mention positions taken in the face of scientific and political advances, it is hard to maintain that church authority and its institutional organs have been open to the newness of history and to the creative breath of the Spirit.

This opening to the Spirit of Christ from earthliness, which implies the following of the historical Jesus, is, however, absolutely indispensable. There is no ecclesiastical enterprise that can replace this need, for the Spirit of Christ has not delegated the totality of its presence and of its efficacy to any institution, although their historical corporeity is also a demand of the Spirit. What often happens is that the church's institutions are configured more from the law than from grace, as if church institutions ought to be configured more according to totalitarian-like sociological and political laws — disguised as God's will and proper obedience to God's will — rather than according to the dictates and power of the Spirit. On the contrary, this is not just about an ordinary spirit concocted by some charismatic, but it is the Spirit of Jesus, which animated his conception, was manifest at his baptism, and was evident in his person and in his living, and which he finally promised to send to us when he should no longer be with us.

It is in this context that the signs of the times become present, some in one epoch and some in another, some in certain regions of the world and others in another. It is precisely the signs of the times that add the element of the future and without which an essential element is lacking for the interpretation of the word of God and of one of the greatest forces of renewal. But these are signs of the times framed here and now in the utopia-prophecy dialectic, without which one would fall back into ineffective idealism.

From the present situation of Latin America, the church's renewal and its projection toward the future must be as the church of the poor if it is to become the new heaven. On the one hand, to be a church that has made indeed a preferential option for the poor will be proof and manifestation of the renewing Spirit present in it; on the other, it will be a guarantee that it can become the new heaven of the new earth and of the new human being. The church has been shaped in great part by the dynamisms of Western capitalism as a church of the rich and of the powerful, which at best directs toward the poorest the crumbs falling from the table of abundance. But the utopian exercise of prophecy can lead it to become — in a genuine conversion — a church of the poor that really can be the heaven of a new earth where a civilization of poverty becomes dominant and where humans are not only intentionally and spiritually poor, but really and materially so; that is, detached from what is superfluous and from the constraining dynamisms of individual monopolizing and collective accumulation. Money can be an incentive for material development for human beings and for states, but it has always been, and it remains more and more, a deadly poison for a genuine humanism and, of course, for a genuine Christianity. That this arouses a powerful rejection from the world, that this is a scandal and even an affront to the civilization of wealth, is one more proof of the continuity of these ideas and of this practice with the fullest way of the gospel, always attacked with the same reproaches.

It is in this sense that the church of the poor becomes the new heaven, which as such is needed to supersede the civilization of wealth and build the civilization of poverty, the new earth where the new human being will live in a friendly and not in a degraded home. Here there will be a great encounter between the Christian message without disfiguring glosses and the present degraded situation in the greater part of the world—certainly in Latin America, still for the most part a depository of the Christian faith. That faith has nevertheless little served to make this region a new earth so far, in spite of its having originally been presented as the new world. The signs of the times and the soteriological dynamic of the Christian faith historicized in new human beings insistently demand the prophetic negation of a church as the old heaven of a civilization of wealth and of empire and the utopian affirmation of a church as the new heaven of a civilization of poverty. Although always in the dark, these new human beings continue firmly to proclaim an ever greater future, because beyond the successive historical futures is discerned the God who saves, the God who liberates.

— Translated by James R. Brockman

15

Revelation, Faith, Signs of the Times

JUAN LUIS SEGUNDO

The reader could think at first sight that the terms in the title of this article are three vaguely related items grouped together for an economical use of space. The very arrangement of the three items could suggest the arrangement of elements, in descending order, found in the customary theoretical treatment of the fundamental concepts of theology in any theological dictionary. Indeed, it would be strange if *revelation* were not one of these concepts. How could there be a theology that did not treat of what God has revealed? Or still more basically, of what is meant by God's "revealing" something? And one might likewise suppose that, if a particular theology has some specific characteristic, it will have to reflect on the manner in which divine revelation is approached, studied, and used; and therefore that, after having treated of *revelation,* it should have to treat of the *faith* with which human beings must respond to this revelatory message when they discover that it actually comes from God, from infinite Truth. Finally, a theology like liberation theology, which as we know is characterized by, among other things, an attachment (even in its initial moment) to the practice of faith, cannot, in its work of "understanding" that faith, prescind from the signs that the history of that practice and its crisis throw up to it as so many interrogations: "the signs of the times," as Jesus calls them in Matthew's gospel (Matt. 16:3).

This amounts to detecting an order—all but necessary, apparently—proceeding from the word of God to faith to the most significant concrete problems presented by history, that these problems may be "illuminated, guided . . . and interpreted in the light of the Gospel,"[1] that is, submitted to the criterion of the revealed word of God.

This order, while doubtless logical, is not, I think, the order in which the three elements are presented in the human being's existence and concrete history. It surely represents a "theological" order. Nor does this mean that its use is restricted to scholarship. Reflection on the most ordinary pastoral activity shows that Christians routinely follow this path. It is not, however, the only possible order. What would happen, for example, if the order of these three concepts were reversed? Unless we are mistaken, this second order would be an "anthropological" or "existential" one. That is to say, we should now have the order in which the three factors appear (although in a different way, and at least as a problem) to believers and nonbelievers alike.

Let it not be thought that this hypothesis—which we shall examine here—indicates the need for an option for either of the two orders as being the "correct" order. Each, in its own domain, has its explanation and raison d'être. They are not mutually exclusive, then, and it would be imprudent and naive to regard one of them as constituting the only correct way of relating the three terms in the list.

Nevertheless, we hold that the second orientation or sequence, in that it represents a more general process transpiring among human beings, has pedagogical advantages. We propose, then, to devote the three parts of this chapter to showing how each of the three items in our title conditions God's communication to human beings, and how, in this respect, the one last on the list is actually the first of these conditions.

I. REVELATION

When we proclaim that God has determined to reveal to human beings truths that they could by no means, or only with excessive difficulty, find by themselves (Denziger 1785-86), we correctly indicate the bountiful, gratuitous origin in the divine plan of that intervention of God in human history. God has determined to communicate certain truths concerning (1) God and (2) the human being. And always *both at once*.

Anyone claiming this "communication" to be possible is constrained to admit from the outset that the message communicated must fall into the category of what is understandable and important for the human being. It would be vain to pretend to conceive a word of God addressed to human beings but not expressed in the language of human beings, or one failing to call their attention to some value to be derived from knowing it.

Here, then, are two logical conditions, converging on the same activity: that of communicating. In terms of the simplest definition, one who communicates conveys to the interlocutor "a difference that makes a difference."[2] If there is no understanding of the message, the (presumed) *difference* is not verified. Something whose identity is unknown is not added to what is already known. But secondly, if this transmitted difference does not *make a difference* in the existence of the one receiving the message, neither is anything communicated. And since knowledge, despite the old saw, really does "take up space" in the mind, our psychology rapidly strives (by forgetting) to regain the space taken up by supposed differences which, while transmitted, change the receiver in no way.

Of these two preconditions for God's being *able* to reveal something to us (since any revelation is either accommodated to our human manner of communication or it simply does not exist), theology has by and large accepted the first, although not without certain strings attached out of respect for the divine initiative and the divine object of that special communication.

Obviously the Infinite Being cannot speak to us in a language of its own, which would have the characteristics of that limitless being. For example, it cannot speak in an atemporal manner to a being whose (transcendent) imagination is structured by time. To put it another way, the human being cannot understand an "eternal" language, because the one destined to be and permitted to be the receiver of the transmitter's self-communication varies with time and circumstances.

Even before becoming personally incarnate in the Son, God, having willed to become revealer, had to speak to human beings by "enfleshing" the divine word in a human language, which uses signs limited in their being and their power of signifying. Hence in that act of communication, what is understood is only an infinitesimal particle, as it were, of a truth which always reaches us only "to the extent that we can understand it" (Denziger 1796; cf. Mark 4:33).[3]

The greatest risk of deviation, however, lies in neglect of the second precondition: The difference must also *make* a difference. Otherwise the message, however well received and, so to speak, well deposited in the receiver, will not signify anything, and the receiver will forget it. The difference transmitted commences to signify when the receiver perceives what it should affect or change in his or her actual existence or behavior; that is, when the perceived difference is related to another, correlative difference, which ought to take place in the existence of the receiver. Let us have an analogy from the material order. When the air temperature becomes different from the limits established on the thermostat, it does not yet strictly communicate anything until the thermostat "understands" that what has been transmitted regarding the different temperature ought to "differentiate" its current state, so that it will now turn on the furnace. Only then is there a true communication: there is a difference that makes or produces a difference.

This is a law of all communication. It is therefore valid for any self-revelation that God might wish to make to human beings. St. Augustine explains it in less scientific, but very expressive language. Commenting on a passage from the Gospel of John (5:25), where Jesus is presented as promising a kind of resurrection of the spirit or mind to take place *before* the universal resurrection of the flesh, Augustine declares that this resurrection must be understood realistically, but spiritually. Is it not the (spiritual) recovery of life, he asks, to pass "from unjust to just, from impious to pious, from foolish to wise?" Augustine indicates that the promise of these "resurrections" is a common thing. Every founder of a religion or sect has claimed to have a divine revelation regarding those transformations that may well be called resurrections or radical changes of life.

This is precisely what we mean here. "For, no one has denied this spiritual resurrection, lest he be told: If the spirit does not resurrect, then *why are you speaking to me?* ... If you are not making me better than I was, then *why are you speaking to me?*"[4] Augustine's repetition of the question, "Why are you speaking to me?," is intended to emphasize that, for the structure of the human mind, a communication, even a divine communication, that indicates (or signifies) no "difference" (direct or indirect, for the short or long term) has no meaning or raison d'être. It signifies nothing.

On this precise point, Vatican II complemented and in a certain sense corrected a potential misunderstanding of the texts of Vatican I, which suggested and asserted that in order to speak to human beings, God could only "enflesh" the divine word in the limited language of human beings. It must follow that, if God wished to speak to us of the divine mystery itself, this could be done only in a limited, obscure way that our finite capacity for understanding would, as it were, place at the divine disposal. Thus, that God is at once one and three remains "mysterious" even after being "revealed," or communicated by God (cf. Denziger 1796). It seems as if God has communicated something for the sole purpose of our knowing it, or better, has repeated it without its meaning any difference in our way of existing. Its relevance for us might seem to proceed not from our understanding our life more and living it better, but from a kind of power intrinsic to that message, which would be salvific before the judgment seat of God, although having in no way modified the existence of the human being – like a magical safe conduct, an "Open, Sesame!"

Vatican Council II, speaking of divine revelation, agrees with Vatican I that "God spoke by means of human beings *in a human manner*" (*Dei Verbum*, no. 12). But at Vatican II the accent was no longer on the limitation that this "human manner" imposed on divine revelation, and thus on the mystery that that revelation allows to subsist. At Vatican II the emphasis was on the fact that all of God's messages to us are authentic, integral communication: a difference in the conception of God intended to become a difference in the way in which we understand and live our creative, communitarian destiny.

Indeed, the most complete, total, and personal revelation of God is, indivisibly, also a revelation of ourselves and our destiny: "The *same* revelation of the Father and of his love [in Christ] *fully* manifests the human being to the human being himself, and discovers to him the sublimity of his destiny" (*Gaudium et Spes*, no. 22). Vatican Council II, then, does not regard revelation as something that, without transforming our historical life – without "making us better," to use Augustine's expression – constitutes a "truth"; that is, something that can be possessed, be deposited, and have value in God's sight (cf. Matt. 25:24, and parallels) by performing its salvific activity in a magical manner (cf. *Gaudium et Spes*, nos. 7, 43).

Thus, according to the Council, the intent of God's revelation is not that we know something that otherwise would be impossible or difficult for us to know, but rather that we *be* different, and act better.

When this conception of divine revelation is analyzed in more depth, it becomes possible to understand the dogmatic reorientation that a Council that meant to be pastoral saw itself obliged to undertake in order that the difference entailed in its most novel orientations might be understood. Indeed, the Council is teaching that faith in God's self-revelation, far from turning the mind from the temporal and ephemeral toward the necessary and eternal, "directs the mind toward fully human solutions" of historical problems (*Gaudium et Spes,* no. 11). Thus, Christians do not possess, not even by understanding it, the truth that God communicates to them until they succeed in transforming it into a humanizing difference within history. Until orthopraxis[5] becomes reality, no matter how ephemeral and contingent that reality, Christians *do not yet know the truth*. On the contrary, in virtue of an imperative of their moral conscience, they must "join the rest of human beings [Christians and others] in the *quest* for the truth" (*Gaudium et Spes,* no. 16).

II. FAITH

But this places us precisely before the problem of the priority of revelation to faith or vice versa. We had thought that faith came second, as a response to God's revelation of divine truth. Now we perceive that, in order for us to receive this truth, it must find us somehow engaged in a common quest of human liberation. This of itself implies a kind of faith—and what is more, a kind of Abrahamic faith, that is, a faith occurring before any religious classification. Indeed, this is how Paul presents Abraham (Rom. 4), as someone who, before being "religiously classifiable" in a particular category, already believes in a kind of promise that the history of human liberation and humanization seems to address to those who struggle for it. Abraham believed in "the God who gives life to the dead and calls to being what is not" (Rom. 4:17; cf. 4:21; 2:6-7).

What is this faith that precedes revelation, and which, as we have seen, makes revelation possible as the necessary precondition for the revealed "difference" to effect the essential praxic "difference" without which there could be no authentic communication between God and ourselves?

One of our essential dimensions as human beings is what we might call the quest for the meaning of our existence. Absorbed as we may be in the urgencies of day-to-day survival, and little as we may perceive that we have a freedom that opens to us a certain spectrum of opportunities or routes to various values or satisfactions, all the same we realize that our free existence is a kind of wager. Why a wager? Because we have only one existence and cannot "test out" in advance what we are going to choose. We are not granted to traverse a course to the end, observe whether it has been a satisfactory one, and then, in all assurance and (empirical) cognizance of cause, return to our starting point and *then* make our option, knowing beforehand what awaits us at the end of the road. When we fall in love, we have no way of knowing what our beloved will be like fifty years from now. When we choose an ideal, and spend long years in preparation for it (for example, a professional career), we can as yet have no experience of what awaits us at the end of the road of our professional practice. When we start a revolution, we do not know what historical price it will demand of us, or what will remain of our project even after we have paid the price. And so on.

History is exciting. It is like an open promise. But there is no antecedent verification of anything, at least no direct one. This does not mean that the wager of our entire freedom, and oftentimes our life (in one way or another), is blind and irrational. Human society provides each of its members with a kind of collective memory, within which the option under consideration becomes a reasonable one. But it is still a wager. The human species with its different cultures—the nation, the clan, the family—provides each individual with "witnesses" or "testimonials" of meaningful lives. The option of freedom is based on that memory, makes it its own, hefts it, tests it, uses it, modifies it, and makes an option among the opportunies it offers. But at bottom, when all is said and done, it places its faith in one or more of the testimonials that that memory presents.

This faith—which we shall call an anthropological faith because it is a human dimension, and both religious and nonreligious persons possess it—is different in each human being. The proof of this is that there is no one who, in the course of his or her life, does not pay a high price for things that he or she has not experienced in advance, even when they are feasible or satisfying, regardless of whether they lead to felicity or frustration. Indeed, meaning is so important for human beings that they are able to give all of the being that they have at their disposal, including their very lives, that these lives may have meaning and thus redeem their value. In Latin America we know only too well that this is not the privilege or peculiarity of Christians. But the gospel does not mean to proclaim something meaningless when Jesus says: "Who seeks to save his life will lose it; but who loses his life for me and the gospel will find it" (Mark 8:35, Matt. 16:25, and par.).

In summary, every human being, as a free being, structures the world out of what for him or her bids fair to have meaning and value, relying on other existences that are testimonials to how a satisfying human existence can be lived. Everyone makes one or more of the choices that present themselves within this collective testimonial. And everyone does this who, after the fact, is destined to be called virtuous or vicious, mediocre or heroic. This structuring option, while arising in connection with one or more testimonials, is complex— as complex as an existence that must confront ever different situations and select, in each of them, the most consistent option available in view of the value held highest and always present and active in the mind (usually translated in terms of images rather than of abstractions). Thus we have a value, or constellation of values, dominated by one that faith has enthroned as *absolute*. Indeed, independent of whether an Absolute "Being" exists or not, and previous to that question, all human beings establish—by their anthropological faith—their *own* absolute; what each one seeks not as a means to something else, but for its own sake. Persons true to themselves will not negotiate it. They will not sell it for any price, even that of their lives. Its loss would be the death of meaning.

What does this have to do with our subject, which is God's revelation? A great deal. Why? Because the usual order in which the problem is presented is a theological order—and rightly so, in scholarly theology. But in the process of a human existence, the order is different—reversed, in fact. We are tempted to think that God reveals, and we, faced with this revelation (perceived and accepted as such), make an option to accept it or reject it (in unbelief or idolatry). But what we have just seen obliges us to modify this routine conceptualization. We are forced back on Augustine's radical question: If you don't make me better than I was, why are you talking to me at all? Augustine is not being impertinent. Human beings *understand only what affects them*, only what makes them better or worse. Now, this means that in God's revealing, faith does not come after something has been revealed. Faith is an *active*, indispensable part of revelation itself.

But there is more. True, the quest for the meaning needed to establish communication between God and human beings is not the same in everyone. But it is always faith. God addresses the divine word to an (anthropological) faith that is always there, and that in each human being is the fruit of an option (antecedent to hearing).

To put it another way, the role of freedom is more active or decisive than has seemed. It is part of the very process of revelation. Orthopraxis is not an ultimate application of revelation to practice; it is a necessary condition of the sheer possibility that revelation actually reveal something.[6]

But so far we have only taken the first step. We have shown that, in its very definition, there is no such thing as divine revelation (although there is such a thing as the word of God in the Bible) unless there is a human quest that converges with this word, a quest for which the word of God signifies a liberation of human potential and human values: the making of a human being better than he or she was. This is the game God agrees to play in the divine self-communication to the human being.[7]

And yet, there is a great deal more. What God communicates to this human being is not a pure, simple, ready-made answer, valid once and for all and for all questions, regardless of context or the problem before which we find ourselves. And this despite the fact that the church sometimes seems to utilize the Bible—the deposit of God's revelation—as a repertory of stock, universally valid answers.

In the first place, if we examine this deposit of revelation, constituted, for us Christians, by the Hebrew and Christian scriptures, it is possible and even fitting that we should be struck and overwhelmed by the multitude of images, words, testimonials, and episodes that we find there. God has supposedly made use of these to reveal something. Indeed, it is very possible that we should be equally surprised that such a process of communication between God and human beings is supposed to have terminated on a certain vaguely specified date, as if that revelation had exhausted its content, or as if we now needed no more of God's words in order to be delivered from all that prevents us from being collectively and individually human.

There are certain questions that Christians must ask themselves, regardless of their particular degree of perspicacity. One, perhaps the most obvious one, is the following. Now that God has revealed both God and the human being in the only-begotten Son, and now that in that Son (and in the witnesses of his life and message) the deposit of revelation has been closed for good and all — why should we continue to regard the previous words, images, and personages as a revelation that continues to call for our faith (cf. Denziger 783, 1787)?

Another question, a related one, arises from the fact that, as we have said, very frequently in all of this deposit of revealed truth, stock answers are sought to the questions of the human being of today. For example, what about marriage? To this question the church generally responds with the words that Jesus is regarded as having said about marriage (see Matt. 19:1-9), forbidding the separation of the spouses ("what God has joined together"), the repudiation of the female partner ("except in case of fornication," which no one is quite sure how to interpret), and the contracting of another marriage on the part of the husband (or the wife — see Mark 10:12).

Now, if faith obliges us to accept, on faith, this response for all cases today, then is that polygamy licit today that the patriarchs once practiced with God's approval, as well as the repudiation of the wife approved by the law of Moses (Deut. 24:1ff.)? If the answer to this question, which is only one in a thousand that we might ask, is yes, then it is in direct contradiction with what Jesus says. And if we answer no, then what meaning can there be in the claim that the entire Old Testament is the word of God, just as the New Testament is? Thus, there would not seem to be any logical response to this question the disciples put to Jesus, as long as we keep thinking of the revelation or word of God as a repertory of questions and answers valid in some atemporal fashion, after the manner of information, ever true, since it proceeds from Truth itself.

The solution is not that this occurs only with regard to moral usages and questions. Almost up until the end of Old Testament times, we find that the authors and personages of that collection of writings do not believe in a life after death. In what sense, then, can Christians say they believe in God's revelation in the Hebrew scriptures in the same fashion and for the same reason that they believe in it in the Christian scriptures?

In fact, even with regard to God there are important variations among the various Old Testament authors. The most eloquent case is that of the Book of Job, where, on the basis of the misfortunes afflicting this legendary personage, the book presents a dispute between two theologies. According to the one, represented by Job's friends and by Elihu — as also by most of the books of the Hebrew scriptures — the evils that befall a person are in strict proportion to that person's sinful actions. Job, examining his own experience, and even taking his admitted sinfulness into consideration, denies such an equation, and thus opposes traditional theology. God decides the question in favor of Job's position, despite Job's imprudence in demanding of God an account of his misfortunes. The "suffering just," who can even die without Yahweh's accommodating their fate to their moral behavior, thus become a theological crisis (cf. Ps. 73:44, Eccl. 3:16-22, among others), to which Israel will give different solutions. After all, how indeed can the faithfulness of Yahweh—an essential divine quality—be reconciled with an entire human life in which justice does not have the last word?

Vatican Council II, precisely in its constitution *Dei Verbum*, that is, the document that treats of the word of God and the divine revelation, indicates the most deep-reaching and complete solution to these comprehensive problems. There we read that, although the Hebrew scriptures "contain certain imperfect and transitory things, they nevertheless demonstrate the *true divine pedagogy*" (DV, 15).

This declaration is worthy of consideration on a number of counts. The *first* is that "imperfect and transitory things" are said to be part of "true" divine revelation. Obviously, in speaking of "transitory things," the allusion is to things that have ceased to be true (or at least completely and perfectly true), although they have been true in times past. It would appear that the concept of truth is made relative. Jesus indicated the same thing in referring to the validity or truth of his conception of marriage (cf. Matt. 19:8), or, to recall only one celebrated instance, in the matter of knowing what obligations God has imposed with regard to human activities on the sabbath day (cf. Mark 2:27). Once again, God seems concerned not that the divine revelation be true in itself—be eternal truth, unchangeable truth—but that it "become" true in the humanization of the human being. In other words, God speaks only to those who seek, and gives them no recipes, but rather guides them in their searching.

This brings us to the *second* thing we must consider in the passage we have cited from *Dei Verbum*. Divine revelation is not a deposit of true information, but a *true pedagogy*. The divine revelation of God and the human being does not consist in amassing correct information in their regard. That revelation is a process, and in that process we do not learn "things." We learn to learn— just as in any pedagogy in which children are guided (the etymology of *pedagogue*) to learn to seek after truth through trial and error. In any process of education, then—even in the most *true*, indeed infallible, educational process of all—there are imperfect and transitory things. Thus, it is enormously important to know where the "truth" is located in these kinds of educational processes. It is not irrelevant that the Council uses the adjective *true* to characterize not the first level, but the second. Pedagogy is a process of *apprenticeship in the second degree*. Its truth lies not in some timeless truth on the first level, where information is accumulated, but on the second level, that of an apprenticeship, where the factors for seeking and finding truth are multiple.

Thus, to return to the example already given, if an author or reader of most of the books of the Old Testament is asked whether there is a life after death or not, we should have, on the first level, an erroneous (negative) response. To be sure, only rarely was this response explicit, since the question of life after death was not a problem that usually arose in an Old Testament context. But there is not the slightest doubt what answer we should have received had we actually asked about life after death (cf. Pss. 30:10, 88:11, 115:17; Eccl. 3:19-21). The answer would have been: There is no such thing. However, a pedagogy as correct and true as the God who conducts it is faithful and true, will one day lead to a resolution of the equation between a God who is justice, and the fact that a good, just person must live and die in pain. Thus, the day will come when human beings, guided in this fashion, will think that the justice practiced during life must survive death (cf. Wisd. of Sol. 1:15). That moment, that of the *true* state of the question, will swell the liberative courage of the solution found, and a new, eschatological dimension will be added to the historical (limited to the earth and this life), factoring its meaning.

But — to continue with the same example — would "truth" have been gained if this same information about life after death had been imparted much earlier, for example in the age of the Exile or of the great prophets? We realize, of course, that it is rarely either easy or useful to manage hypotheses not actually verified in history. Nevertheless, we think we can say that the educational processes that we know lead to the conclusion that "leaking" information — giving it without waiting for the proper moment in the pedagogical process — would have obliterated a series of important truths whereby Yahweh was bestowing a self-revelation in Israel in the many critical experiences of fully historical quests. Premature information as to the reality of an afterlife would have plunged Israel into a misguided search for Yahweh outside of history. And thus, while materially true — orthodox — this information would have generated deeper errors, difficult to correct in the future. This is the problem facing the pastoral ministry today.

Hence the necessity of conceiving revelation not as a mere providing of correct information about God and human beings, but as a true pedagogy, a divine pedagogy. We must seriously modify our conception of the relationship between revelation and truth. However — and here we come to a *third* observation — *Dei Verbum* speaks of the imperfect and transitory only with regard to the Hebrew scriptures, it says nothing like this with regard to the Christian scriptures. This is food for thought. Will God have changed methods of "revealing" since the coming of Christ? Will God have begun to provide us with perfect and invariable, or perhaps merely explanatory, information? Indeed, in the presence of divine, eternal Truth itself, now revealed, will God perhaps have terminated this process of search, demonstrated in the Hebrew scriptures?

Vatican II's attribution of the imperfect and transitory specifically to the Hebrew scriptures, as well as certain explicit declarations of the ordinary church magisterium (e.g., Denziger 2012), might seem to suggest this. But there are serious reasons for thinking that, even after God's revelation in Jesus Christ, the only-begotten divine Son, the revelatory function of the Spirit of Jesus continues to accompany the process of the humanization of all human beings.

For one thing, the New Testament itself states this. According to the Johannine theology, the very physical disappearance of Jesus Christ, his transitus from this earth to his glorious invisibility, is "fitting." St. Augustine expressed it very simply, and with peerless eloquence: "The Lord himself, as he deigned to be our Way, did not seek to detain us, but rather moved on."[8] Jesus himself says this, in different words, in his farewell discourse, according to the Fourth Gospel (which, while not synonymous with historical fidelity, does belong to God's revelation or word). And he explains the reason for this strange fittingness: "If I do not go away, the Paraclete will not come to you. I should be able to tell you many other things, as well, but you could not manage them now. When the Spirit of Truth comes, he will guide you to the whole truth" (John 16:7, 12-13).

At once we find the concern of every process of apprenticeship in the second degree — the concern in any process of teaching a person to think — with not "leaking" information on the pretext of its being true. The "truth" at issue in this process is situated on another level, and that level demands that one problem lead to others, and that information be framed within the problematic of the real. But furthermore we find, as in any pedagogy, that the need for (mere) information diminishes with increasing maturity. At some point, learning to learn postulates the absence of a teacher — or better, the replacement of the physical teacher to whom one can go in case of doubt, by the "spirit" of the teacher, which, through what has already been learned and new historical challenges, will continue to carry the process forward.

Paul makes this maturity the very core of the Christian message. The "pedagogue" — in this case a revelation "deposited in writing" — has fulfilled its function. It must now make way for the Spirit, who will lead the community of Jesus to learn by creating in history, daughters and sons that we are of our creative Parent (cf. Gal. 3-5; 1 Cor. 1:10-16, 3:1-9, 21-23; Rom. 8:14-21). God's progressive, gradual, "pedagogical" communication to us of the divine truth, which is our truth as well, the truth that sets us free in the history in which we become brothers and sisters to one another (cf. 1 Cor. 3:9; 10:23-24), cannot cease with Jesus. The Teacher who speaks to us from the midst of a "scripture" is no longer with us, but something more important, effective, and mature is: the Spirit of Jesus, who suggests to us that which Jesus, were he present, would have wished to say to us regarding the problems of today.[9] A question to which Vatican II points, although it seems to have been forgotten today, is whether the church believes, really and truly believes, in that Spirit that leads the community to all truth.

With what we have said up to this point, we have taken a second step in our consideration of the relationship among revelation, faith, and the signs of the times. At first it appeared to us that the divine revelation was already complete from God's side, and that all that remained, from our side, was to receive it in faith, hold it in reverence, and apply it in praxis. With this second step, we see that revelation presupposes not only a search and an antecedent faith, but also the constitution of a people that will *hand on* a wisdom from generation to generation.[10] Through things ever imperfect and transitory, handed down by the very existence of the community, that *people* becomes *tradition.*[11] This means that memory and collective pedagogy have a decisive function in the very process of revelation; thanks to these, each new generation is exempt from starting its (second degree) apprenticeship "from scratch." Through a process of remembering and readopting, in a vital fashion peculiar to its own identity, the past experiences of another process in which the search, solutions, and challenges of history converge, each generation is thrust toward a more perfect maturity, and toward a new, deeper, and richer truth.

In order to be part of this community-in-process-toward-the-Truth, under the guidance of God, we must have faith in it. It is not in God directly that we place this faith, because it is not God directly who speaks to us. God speaks through witnesses, and these divine witnesses are not isolated individuals; they constitute a community, a people, whom God, with a true pedagogy, ever dispatches toward the liberative truth of all the creative potential of the human being.[12] The Israelite people, the Christian people, perform a function of interpretation and transmission without which we could not recognize where and how the word of God sounds today. Without Israel, or the church, in the world we know, and in Christian tradition, there is no revelation of God.

Thus, this second step that we have taken, from revelation to faith, shows us that the very fact of God's revealing something with meaning supposes not only an individual in search of truth, but a community, a people committed to this intent to "learn to learn," as it searches for the truth. Only then does God communicate something. Faith is not the mere consequence of a passive, individual acceptance in faith of a word addressed to us by God. Thus, the faith community does not follow the *fait accompli* of a revelation wrought by God. It is an integral part of it.

But we must now take a further step, and discover to what extent, and in what way, the faith community is part of that revelation *in a creative manner*.

III. SIGNS OF THE TIMES

Indeed, from what has now been said, an important question still remains to be resolved. How may we distinguish God's word from other, "merely human" words? The language used is the same, and the options posed by that language are ranged along a spectrum of more or less equivalent possibilities. We have also seen that it is not required that divine revelation even deal with or explicitly cite the divinity. We must not forget that, even in Israel, not to mention other religions, two prophets, for example Jeremiah and Hananiah, can appeal to the same God to justify contrary orientations on the part of the same "divine pedagogy" (cf. Jer. 28). What entitles us to include in the collection of words of God the prophecies of Jeremiah, and not those of Hananiah (especially since neither of the two prophetic messages was confirmed by subsequent events)? The Bible itself informs us that, for centuries, contradictory opinions — and actual biblical ones, espoused by different sacred authors — prevailed in Israel as to whether the institution of the monarchy represented the will of God or Israel's sinful rejection of Yahweh as king (cf. 1 Sam. 8-10).

What is more, there is no radical change in this state of affairs when we come to the Christian Scriptures. It is not as easy to perceive this in the New

Testament, since all of the works it contains were redacted over the course of a period lasting surely no longer than half a century, while the redaction of the Old Testament extends over a millennium. But even in this reduced time span we notice serious unresolved divergencies between Paul and the author of the Letter of James (cf. Rom. 3:21-30 and James 2:14-26), or again between Paul and James the "brother of the Lord" (or at least his followers—Gal. 2:12). Here and there the question seems to have been resolved by the simple recourse of including only one of these opinions in the New Testament. In other instances, it is left to the Christian community of the future to solve the problem.

Although it constitutes an important datum for this particular question, we shall not treat here of the options the church will have to make regarding the "interpretation" of what had been consigned in that deposit of revelation that is the Bible. Our sole interest here is in this mystery constituted by the very existence of the Bible: How is the word of God recognized and distinguished from what seems to be that word but is not?

At the level of theoretical theology, the answer is simple, and almost tautological:

> When God reveals, we are obliged to offer him full obedience in faith. . . . This faith . . . is a supernatural virtue by which . . . we believe to be true what has been revealed by Him not by the intrinsic truth of things, . . . but on the authority of God himself revealing. (Vatican Council I—Denziger 1789)

The whole difficulty for the ordinary person is in distinguishing when God reveals from very similar occasions that might wrongly be taken as God's revelation. To be sure, the ordinary person identifies this special "when" that is deserving of our faith with the redaction of the Bible that we hold in our hands today. But then it will doubtless occur to us to ask: How did the church make this collection that separates what God has revealed from what God has not revealed? Here again, the theological solution is easy, and once more is furnished by Vatican I:

> The church holds [the books of the Bible] as sacred and canonical not because they were composed by human industry alone and then approved by her; nor only because [they] contain revelation without error; but because, written under the *inspiration* of the Holy Spirit, they have God as their author. (Denziger 1788)

As we have said, this answer is almost a redundancy. Obviously, if we claim that God has used something of human language to communicate to us, and if such writings nevertheless have a human author, then this author must be inspired by God in order for what is written to be regarded as divine revelation. But we speak of redundancy because *historically speaking* the problem of a criterion is still unresolved. Now, however, instead of claiming to know when

God reveals (in order to be able to have faith in what is revealed), we must ask how we know when God *inspires* an author's writing.

The theology of liberation is especially sensitive to this question — a perfectly logical one, but one that is absent from the concerns of most current theology — because the recognition today of what would be for our reality the word that God would speak, is a task that we must undertake a thousand-and-one times in the communities that form the base of the church and inquire into the enriching, liberative content of their faith. If God continues the work of divine revelation by the Spirit, how to recognize the divine word today becomes a crucial ecclesial criterion.

Actually, there are two answers to the question. One is Jesus' (paradigmatic and) absolute refusal to help his hearers identify the presence of God in his deeds and messages by means of signs from heaven. The other is constituted by the data furnished by the formation of the canon (or list of the books regarded as inspired by God) of the Old as well as of the New Testament. This history, while not completely known, is sufficiently well understood to support a judgment.

According to Luke, Jesus' refusal to call down signs from heaven as a criterion of whether or not his hearers were in the presence of God and a divine revelation has a very precise context. Jesus has just restored the faculty of speech to a person who had somehow lost it. The bystanders now wonder whether they are in the presence of an event evincing the power and hence the presence of God, or whether there could be some other explanation — even, for example, the power of Satan (who was supposed to have deprived the victim of his speech in the first place), transferred to Jesus.

According to Mark, Jesus' refusal is absolute. This generation will be given no sign from heaven. But there is something else. As to the possibility that Jesus has delivered the victim of Satan's affliction by the power of Satan, Mark now indicates the argument that all three Synoptics will use: even hypothetically, the objection has no meaning. After all, whether it is God or Satan who humanizes a person, that humanization, in and of itself, is a sign that "Satan's reign has come to an end" (Mark 3:26). Then the Reign of God must be beginning, Luke explicitly concludes (Luke 11:20).

God's self-communication to us is bestowed by way of actions or ideas. In both cases this communication will be understood only by one who is attuned to the priorities of the heart of this God. For such a one, the historical sign of the liberation of a person is the sign of the presence and revelation of God. By the same token, one cannot understand what God wishes of the sabbath just by reading a book, however divine the book, and regardless of how many thunderclaps or bolts of lightning may have accompanied its publication. Knowledge of God as "revealing" something to us occurs when we are discovered to have a historical sensitivity that converges with God's own intentions.

Hence, in Matthew and Luke (in dependence upon Q), Jesus gives two examples of persons who, without knowing "biblical revelation," have understood what God wishes to communicate to them and have perceived God's revelatory presence in history: the inhabitants of Nineveh, and the "queen of the South" (cf. Matt. 12:38-42). According to Luke, these pagans "have themselves judged what is just" (Luke 12:57); that is, they have recognized a sign that is in history, or as Matthew says, a "sign of the times" (Matt. 16:3).

In other words, the identification of God's presence or revelation, first in the history of Israel, and then in the deeds and words of Jesus, does not fall from heaven packaged and labeled. God has entrusted us with the responsibility of searching it out, of verifying it in the best way possible, with the eyes and priorities of God, which are also those of the Reign of God. Only from a point of departure in this commitment, which is the fruit of a certain sensitivity, has it been defined "when" God has revealed what today comprises the Bible. Thus, it is true today, as well, that in the task of interpreting when we are in the presence of God, the documents of Medellín define the task of a liberative theology:

> Just as another Israel, the first people, experienced the salvific presence of God when God delivered them from the oppression of Egypt, ... so also we, the new people of God, cannot escape the experience of the divine passage that saves whenever there is ... a passage, for each and all, from less humane conditions of life to more humane conditions. (Medellín Final Document, Introduction, no. 6)

These "signs" are already sufficiently clear and experiential for us to believe that "all growth in humanity moves us closer to reproducing the image of the Son, that he may be the firstborn of many siblings" (Medellín Document on "Education," no. 9).

We have said that, besides the evangelical paradigm concerning the basic importance of the signs of the times, we have sufficient historical data to construct what we might call a paradigm of the "theological fact" of the formation of the canon. With these data in mind, let us construct an example of how that paradigm functions. Let us take the case of Moses in the Exodus. For simplicity's sake, let us say that we are not interested in the establishment of this paradigm, in knowing who wrote the actual account. Tradition attributes it to Moses himself, but we think that its redaction is actually that of one or more chroniclers writing in the time of David or Solomon. As we have said, the fact is that the account was written. Neither, for the purposes of this study, are we interested in the "historiographical" status of the account at the moment of its redaction—whether it was taken as actual history or as a mythical event. In either case—and this is what interests us—it came to form part of the Yahwist faith.

Now, one of the theologians who, to our knowledge, has taken most seriously the *theology* implied in the construction of a canon, or list of writings containing "divine revelation," is A. Torres Queiruga, in his *La revelación de Dios en la realización del hombre*.[13] Here is how this author summarizes the interaction of God and human beings in the creation of the word of God concerning the exodus—or, if you will, how divine revelation is recognized *in* the liberation of the Jewish people from their oppression in Egypt.

From his religious experience, Moses *discovered* the living presence of God in the longing of the Jews to be delivered from their oppression. The "experience of contrast" between the actual situation of his people and what he felt to be the salvific will of God, who seeks the human being's liberation, gave him the intuition that the Lord was present in that longing, and supported the people. As he gradually succeeded in instilling this certitude of his in others, helping them, as well, to *discover* this presence, he awakened history, promoted the religious sense, and ultimately created Yahwism.[14]

Let us begin with this text and make a series of observations on what it tells us explicitly, and especially implicitly.

1. The Action of the Author

Torres speaks of a personage who has what he calls an "experience of contrast." It is unimportant for the moment what the name of this personage is. The biblical account calls him Moses and presents him as the protagonist of the exodus narrative. But it is evident that, whatever the historical value of his account, the author must have had this actual, historical experience; indeed, the author judges it relevant to recount it and set it in relief as basic for Israel's faith in its God. It is this author who "discovers" in the facts of the past that others transmit a revelatory presence of God, and separates these facts from the rest. Now, the first thing we observe about this author is that this "experience of contrast," as it is designated here, *presupposes* an already existing (anthropological) faith—that is, a determinate structure of values that sensitizes the author to this situation of oppression and instills the notion that God cannot wish it, when others think that this is the normal situation or the lesser evil (cf. Exod. 4:1-9, 6:12, Num. 11:5). Here is the source of the author's interest, which makes of a mere event or situation a "sign" of something to be done. And it is this that converts the action of the author, the narrative, into a transforming enthusiasm that then infects others.

2. The Author's "Faith"

Why do we say that this faith of Moses (whether of Moses, the Yahwist, or the author of Deuteronomy) was "anthropological"—that is, something seemingly contradistinguished from "religious" faith in Yahweh? By this we mean that this Moses has no Bible. He cannot have recourse, as we customarily do, to the word of God in order to know what values to strive for and in what order to strive for them. Nor, therefore, did he have access, among the manifold voices of historical reality, to an unequivocal "sign" that would enable him to make a divinely guaranteed discovery of the revelatory presence of God. To this purpose, he had to do what, according to the gospel, the Ninevites, or the queen of the South did, who worshiped gods who were not Yahweh. True, in the account, narrated when Moses had already been accepted as Yahweh's witness, it is recounted that Yahweh gave Moses "signs from heaven," that is, magical signs that his mission, his duty, actually came from God. But let us notice, first of all, that other persons in the account claim, on the basis of similar magical arguments, that this is not the will of God (cf. Exod. 11:22). Furthermore, other books of what today is the Bible have been acknowledged as the word of God without the mediation of any divine apparition to their author, indeed without so much as a single mention of God by that author (as the Song of Songs), in a work that could have been written, for example, by an atheist. "Moses," here, by definition, is—under pain of having to appeal to an infinite chain—the person without a Bible, without a deposited word of God. Moses must place a wager on what God "must" wish. And those who follow Moses must believe in the same way.[15]

3. Meaning in History

Our text speaks of an "experience of contrast"—an experience of something that becomes a "sign" of what God does *not* wish, and therefore a sign of the divine will to liberate human beings from it, in this case the Israelites. However, there are other signs of the times that appeal to the same faith (to the same structure of value or of being), from other experiences than those of contrast; for example, the experience of the celebration of value attained (as in many of the psalms), the experience of the covenant in the search for some of these same values (as in the preaching of various prophets), or the experience of the promise of a future or impending realization of such values (as in the Beatitudes). Common to all of these experiences is the presence in history of events or qualities in which the very meaning of existence is at stake. Whether or not these events or qualities will be noticed as signs—which is what happens in the case of Moses—rather than their being allowed to slip by as irrelevant, will depend on the strength with which this faith, which is antecedent to revelation (of which these peak moments are the vehicle), becomes sensitive to the vicissitudes of these values rather than others on our human earth.

4. The Readers

But now let us move from the *facts* of the Book of Exodus to the *readers* of that book. And once more, we are not concerned with the difference between those who were with Moses in his deed and those who now, centuries later, excitedly read of this same deed. In both, this accompaniment indicates the contagion of an enthusiasm and commitment. In consequence of the preceding, Moses' Israelite contemporaries regard him as "inspired by God"—exactly as those who now read, with reverence, and as addressed to their lives, the Book of Exodus hold the writer as inspired. (We too, for simplicity's sake, shall call him Moses here, but he was the Yahwist, the Elohist, the Deuteronomist, and so on.) Moses' contemporaries made an option between following him and following leaders who proposed other alternatives as the will of God. Later readers make an option among *books*, among various possible or real accounts of these events. There were works in which these same events either are not narrated, or are narrated in a different light, or finally, are not regarded as "signs" of the active presence of God. And all of this occurred also before a

Bible existed. In fact, it is the Bible that arises from this selection among books (guided by the same witnesses and criteria as the events recounted there).

5. Historical Process

The passage from Torres upon which we are commenting tells us that, by contagion of the enthusiasm aroused by the discovery of signs of a divine liberating presence, Moses—and hence the author or authors who recount his deed—"aroused history." This means that they gave rise to a historical process. They did so by creating a community, a people, whose fundamental identity lay in the tradition (in the original sense of "transmission") that opted for the same values and for the same historical signs. We say that it is a "process" that is created in this way, because that discovery of the presence of God is not static. For example, that discovery is different in Exodus (with its Yahwist and/or Elohist background) and in Deuteronomy. There are various "Moses." But their plurality lies along a growth line, in the face of various historical challenges. Moses does not teach a package of truth. He teaches how to learn to learn— how to discover more signs in the history of the same revelatory, liberative presence of God.

6. The Experience of Foundational Liberation

Torres has the colossal audacity to say that this Moses—multiple and progressive—who awakened history, "created Yahwism." But was it not divine revelation that inspired Moses, that created it? Of course. But the data we have on how what we today call the Old Testament was compiled in Israel—that is, the written deposit of revelation—tell of the crucial participation in this historical creation, beginning with the Exile, of the people of Israel themselves. The restriction of divine worship to the one temple of Jerusalem under Josiah, the impossibility of that divine worship during the captivity, and its later limitations, along with a swelling diaspora, had the result that the doubly "lay" institution of the *synagogue*, centered on "reading" and interpretation, gradually displaced worship. This became, "more than any other factor, responsible for the survival of Judaism [Yahwism] as a religion and of the Jews as a distinct people."[16] God speaks a human language, surely; but the divine revelatory word becomes such only when it is recognized, among so many other words, in the experience of the foundational liberation (in "Moses") and in the continuity of that liberation, which sustains Israel.

7. Learning to Learn

Finally, there is no reason to suppose that what is said here, with complete historical foundation, of the creation of Yahwism would not hold as well for that of Christianity. We are not speaking of some parallel that imitates a previous event. From the historical viewpoint, it is the continuation of the process of that "Moses" whose discovery founded a people, a tradition, an apprenticeship in the second degree. The initial "being attuned" that is required for one word out of a thousand to be recognized as a sign that God is speaking is later criticized by this same word in the face of new challenges. The hermeneutics is circular, or, as some would have it, a spiral. Jesus and Paul have a new liberative experience: that of leaving the servitude of a situation of privilege and trying to be on the watch for signs of the times that come from where human beings suffer, are poor, oppressed, limited in their human opportunities. Thus, as Paul sees it, new branches are grafted onto the old tree. The old people learns, or better, keeps on learning to learn. It does not cease to seek the truth, because truth is only truth when it is transformed into real humanization.

Thus, too briefly and with too little development, we have attempted to show that the relationship of these three terms—revelation, faith, and signs of the times—can, like christology, be read in two directions, and that this is what must be done in order to seize their wealth.

The theological order is not erroneous; it draws from the dogma of revelation the logical consequence that, if God uses human beings and human language for that revelation, then the authors who by divine inspiration have consigned this word to writing are witnesses worthy of faith in the strictest and most theological sense of the word.

This is the sense in which St. Thomas asserts: "In faith, the *ratio formalis* is the first truth, that is, that we adhere to the truths of faith *only because they have been revealed by God*, and in the measure that they have been revealed by God."[17]

In the same manner we may conclude that this first truth must perform its function of interpretation and discernment of all human aspirations, which, like the aspiration for liberation, arise in history as signs of the times.[18]

Nevertheless, just as with christologies "from above," from God to us, we may be in danger of forgetting the order in which, in the process of our cognitive and praxic history, truth proceeds from the less perfect to the more perfect— and that, following this route, which the gospel records and the history of redaction and of the canon of the Bible shows, the opposite order, as well, has its truth, and its great liberative meaning. It is the signs of the times, read with an open, sensitive heart, that prevent the "letter" by which the whole of revelation is bound to human language from becoming lethal (2 Cor. 3:6)—even the letter of the gospel—and leading us astray instead of leading us to an encounter with the heart of God. These signs show us a path that in being shared fashions a people, and history. They are indications of the fact that history has meaning, and that it is reasonable to wager on that meaning. From the wealth of this liberative experience, shared in community, springs a reasonable faith, not a fideism or a magical instrument. When that faith becomes tradition, leads us to the truth that humanizes our sisters and brothers and commits us definitively, then we know that God is present in it, guiding us, revealing to us the truth of the human being that should be.

—*Translated by Robert R. Barr*

NOTES

1. Congregation for the Doctrine of the Faith, "Instruction on Certain Aspects of the Theology of Liberation" (Vatican City, August 1984), part 2, no. 4.

2. See Gregory Bateson, *Mind and Nature: A Necessary Unity* (New York: Dutton, 1979), pp. 487ff.

3. It cannot be said that this first condition for a *revelation* — a communication between God and the human being — has been generally understood. Accepted, yes. But a current originating outside of Christianity and biblical thought (and introduced into them with neo-Platonism) has, throughout the centuries, placed its deepest hopes of approaching God in a certain "emptying" of the mind — as if it were by way of a denial or suspension of the limits of the linguistic, conceptual, and historical signs that one could arrive at a deeper, surer understanding of these signs. The mystics themselves, perhaps under the influence of this philosophy, in transmitting their experiences conceptually, have spoken of experiences of God showing alienation from or contempt of the created; experiences bearing almost no resemblance to those of the Bible.

4. Augustine of Hippo, *In Ioannis Evangelium Tractatus* XIX, 14.

5. Correct praxis is the final *truth*. Hence, for the Johannine theology, truth is not "had," but "done" (cf. John 3:21; 1 John 1:6). Truth is not something that can be "put down" in a book or a formula, or in the perfection of some knowledge. Truth is *done* — put into operation.

6. Readers wishing to see an example of this, propounded by the magisterium of the church itself — although the term *anthropological faith* does not occur — can find the equivalent of that term in the explanation proposed by *Gaudium et Spes* of the process leading the person of good will to atheism while others, on the contrary, despite their repetition of the words of divine revelation, may practice and lead others to practice a "faith" that is actually idolatry. The values with which they confuse the word of God do not correspond to the true God:

> Atheism results not rarely from . . . the absolute character with which certain human values are unduly invested, and which thereby already accords them the stature of God. . . .
> . . . Believers can have more than a little to do with the birth of atheism. . . . To the extent that they . . . are deficient in their religious, moral, or social life, they must be said to conceal rather than reveal the authentic face of God (*Gaudium et Spes*, no. 19).

7. "Behold, I stand at the gate and knock" (Rev. 3:20). Of course, this does not mean that God recognizes any obligation to "say" precisely what we are ready to hear. Along with confirming our most authentic expectations, the word of God also "judges" us. As we shall presently see more clearly, there is a circularity in this hermeneutic process. Hence the word invites us to conversion, or to the betterment of something existing. But even in this case, in order to be understood in its human element the word of God must be addressed at least to a kind of search or aspiration that we may have relegated to a second level, to a hypothesis that would be valid if reality were better, to something that could be, and that therefore we favor even though it means the overturning and upsetting precisely of values (or anti-values) that we are applying.

8. St. Augustine, *PL* 34:33. Cited by Henri de Lubac, *Catholicism* (New York: Sheed and Ward, 1950).

9. Indeed, in the first centuries the writings of the Fathers and dogmatic declarations of the first ecumenical councils were assimilated to the inspired "word of

God," worthy of belief to the "last jot and tittle," even though they were not "deposited" in the Bible (cf. Denziger 164-65, 270). The fact that Jesus does not detain us, but *moves on*, as Augustine wrote, is the ultimate foundation of the great theological principle adopted by Vatican II in the matter of ecumenism. But it goes much farther still; from the Bible on down, there is "an order or 'hierarchy' in the truths of Catholic teaching, in view of the diversity of connections between such truths and the foundation of Christian faith" (*Unitatis Redintegratio*, no. 11). This is tantamout to saying that final truth is the aim of a pedagogy, not a piece of information.

10. What von Rad wrote of the "wisdom" whose most specific quest characterizes especially the last period of the Old Testament, is true here of the *entire* biblical process and tradition:

> One might almost say that knowledge of the good is acquired only in the common life, person to person and from situation to situation; however, an absolute beginning is not made each time, because there is always the base of an ancient knowledge, of a very rich experience (Gerhard von Rad, *Israel et la Sagesse* [Geneva: Labor et Fides, 1970], p. 98; English trans., *Wisdom in Israel* [New York: Abingdon, 1973]).

He explains how this "base" of collective wisdom is laid:

> No one would live a single day had he or she not succeeded in being guided by a vast empirical cognition. This knowledge, drawn from experience, teaches one to understand what is occurring round about one, to foresee the reactions of one's neighbor, to employ one's strength at the opportune moment, to distinguish the exceptional from the ordinary event, and a great deal else. We are not particularly conscious of being guided in this way, as neither of having ourselves developed more than a small part of this experiential knowledge. This knowledge is imposed on us, we are steeped in it from our most tender age, and [we are aware of it] only if we ourselves somehow modify it. . . . This experimental knowledge acquires its importance and character of obligation only when it comes to represent the common good of an entire people, or a great part of the population (pp. 9-10).

11. This is what was called, and should continue to be called today, tradition— not the dubious and unverifiable notion that Jesus personally "revealed" to one or more of his apostles or disciples things that were not consigned to the Christian scriptures, and thus remained lost until they reappeared years or centuries later. This is how the existence of a font of revelation other than the biblical is understood. While Vatican II did not wish to settle the question of the single or double font, everything in *Dei Verbum*, as well as the best post–Vatican II theology, tends to understand by *tradition* not a separate, "other," font, but the fact that the process of transmission consists not in a book or a formula, but in a knowledge transmitted in the experience (institutional, to be sure) of a living community, the church.

12. While this faith is in continuity with what we have called anthopological faith, it has special characteristics that make it "religious." Indeed, it is the adherence of a community that possesses a "truth" about God and about what this God means for all humanity.

13. The rigorously dogmatic problem posed by the formation of the canon (list) of the books containing "revelation"—the Bible—is conspicuously absent from works otherwise as perspicacious and profound as Karl Rahner's *Foundations of*

Christian Faith (New York: Crossroad, 1978). One of the most recent theological works to have attempted to remedy this lack, and to have gone most to the heart of the matter, is that of A. Torres Queiruga, *La revelación de Dios en la realización del hombre* (Madrid: Cristiandad, 1987). Note, in this work, the similarity between the application the author makes to the Bible of the Socratic "maieutic," and what we have here called "second-degree apprenticeship," or "learning to learn." Both methods presuppose that truth, even the truth of the mysteries of God, is not received from "without," as if it were mere information.

14. Torres, *Revelación de Dios*, p. 63. We do not mean to make this author responsible for the conclusions and extensions that we add to the passage cited. We do permit ourselves, in the spirit of friendship, to *use* this passage from his work for our intent. However, we understand that this excerpt has not been penned hastily, but is presented by way of conclusion of a lengthy discourse. The author repeats this summary, in the same or similar terms, in other places in the same book (cf. pp. 122, 125-26).

15. What we say of Moses here is paradigmatic, as we have indicated. Did Jesus not find himself in a similar situation? It will be said that Jesus did have the Bible, and thus could base his claims on the word of God, and that he never hesitated to use it. But would this be strictly the case? Hans Küng is correct (although he draws a conclusion different from ours): "Jesus' whole preaching and behavior are nothing but an interpretation of *God*. . . . Anyone accepting Jesus with firm trust necessarily observed at the same time an unexpected, liberative transformation of what he had thus far understood by 'God' " (Hans Küng, *On Being a Christian* [New York: Doubleday, 1976]). Thus, Jesus could not rely on the Bible alone, without indicating an attitude that would cause a different hermeneutics of that Bible. Hence his allusions to the signs of the times, and to this antecedent, hazardous criterion: "Why do you not judge *for yourselves* what is just?" (Luke 12:57) – and this in the presence of God and of the word of God present in the Bible.

16. John L. McKenzie, "Synagogue," in *Dictionary of the Bible* (New York: Bruce-Macmillan, 1965), p. 855. We call the synagogue doubly lay in the sense that not only was it an institution where the people (*laos*) assembled to feel themselves to be and maintain themselves as a people, with their own identity (among those who surrounded, governed, and oppressed them), but it was directed by laity (nonordained persons, elders). And the ordained, priests or scribes, when they visited the synagogue, were not essentially distinguished from the others, although they were treated with special courtesy (cf. ibid.).

17. Cited by A. Liégé, in the collective work, *Initiation Théologique* (Paris: Cerf, 1952), 3:518.

18. Congregation for the Doctrine of the Faith, "Instruction on Certain Aspects of the Theology of Liberation," part 1, nos. 1-2; part 2, nos. 1-4.

16

Central Position of the Reign of God in Liberation Theology

JON SOBRINO

I. LIBERATION THEOLOGY AS A THEOLOGY OF THE REIGN OF GOD

All authentic theological renewal is the fruit of an attempt to answer the question: What is "ultimate" in Christian faith? The question implies that Christian faith is made up of divers elements that can be organized and arranged in a hierarchy. That the truths of faith are hierarchically ordered became obvious at Vatican II, but their actual organization and ordering in respect to an ultimate principle is the task of theology. It is up to theology to seek out that ultimate element that will give the best account of the totality of the faith, and the element selected will determine the character of the theology that selects it.

In our opinion, this is what has been occurring in theology for a century now, with the rediscovery that Jesus' message was eschatological. Those who made the discovery proposed a concrete content for this eschatological message: the Reign of God. But the importance of the discovery went far beyond a determination of content. For theology, it meant the end of a mere theological, dogmatic, or biblical positivism and the inauguration of the eschatological theologies — those theologies that attempted to name the ultimate element in faith and to develop from there. Unfortunately, these theologies fell into the error of identifying eschatology with the Four Last Things. Actually, to name the ultimate means to determine an *eschaton* from the specificity of the faith and the *primacy of reality*. The *eschaton* might be the proclamation or kerygma of Jesus Christ crucified and raised again (Bultmann), the communication to history of the mystery of the Holy (Rahner), the Omega Point (Teilhard de Chardin), or the universal resurrection (Pannenberg). Correlatively, then, a metaphysical and anthropological primacy would be accorded respectively to existence and decision, the future, promise and hope, evolution, unconditional openness to mystery, and so on.

1. *Liberation Theology's Answer to the Question of the* Eschaton

The theology of liberation is formally and organically integrated into this method and concept of theology. It names an ultimate, which then functions as an organizing and ordering principal for everything else. That to which this theology assigns the primacy is indicated in its very name: liberation, which is understood essentially as liberation of the poor. In this sense, liberation theology is also an eschatological theology, since it assigns liberation more than a mere place (however important a place) in the content of theology; it assigns it an ultimate and ordering content. Thus, it is neither a regional theology (a part of theology, or of a particular theology—the part bearing upon liberation). Still less is it a reductionistic theology (a theology whose sole object would be liberation). In assigning a primacy to the liberation of the poor, the theology of liberation is positing the liberation of the poor as that part of the content of theology around which all of theology can be organized—all questions of who God and Christ are, what grace and sin are, what the church and society are, what love and hope are, and so on. We call the theology of liberation eschatological not because by adding the adjective "integral" to the noun "liberation" we can quantitatively augment the content of liberation so that it will extend to the whole of theology, but rather because from the *viewpoint* of the liberation of the poor we deem it possible—indeed, in Latin America it is appropriate and necessary—to impose a qualitative, ordered organization on the entire content of theology.

The analyses conducted in the present chapter constitute an attempt to answer the question, What faith reality, what *eschaton*, most adequately corresponds to a theology that assigns historical primacy to the liberation of the poor? In other words, how might one formulate the ultimate in such a way as to do justice to both the revelation of God and the concrete, historical liberation of the poor? In the choice of this *eschaton* for theology—obviously there is no question of selecting it for faith—two possibilities stand out, of which much account is taken by creative theologies today and which, in principle, would also be capable of incorporating the essential liberative interest of the theology of liberation. Those two possibilities are the resurrection of Christ (understood as the initiation of the "universal" resurrection) and the Reign of God. Both realities are eschatological, in a biblical understanding as in a systematic one, and both intrinsically express liberation. Thus, they are both used in various modern theologies, although some of these incline toward the one, and some toward the other.

To recall some important examples: Bultmann inclines exclusively toward the resurrection—or more precisely, toward the preaching of the kerygma of Jesus Christ crucified and raised again, as the genuine eschatological event, with the triple connotation that, with Christ, judgment, salvation, and the presence of the ultimate have become historical. The Reign of God is not regarded, any more than anything else about the historical Jesus, as belonging to the presuppositions or the theology of the New Testament. Pannenberg places more eschatological value on the Reign of God, since the proclamation of its coming—imminent, but not realized—furnishes the possibility and the demand that one live in history in radical openness, and that thus the ultimate be realized. The definitive eschatological event, however, even for theology, is the resurrection of Jesus, since it is there that, however provisionally, the object of the openness of the human being and the revelation of God has been fulfilled. The younger Moltmann was more favorable to the resurrection and its correlative hope, but he has gradually come to formulate the *eschaton* in terms of the historical, as well, that is, in terms of the poor and their liberation, and thus, in terms of the Reign of God.

We recall these various positions on the selection of a theological *eschaton* only for the purpose of erecting a framework for a better understanding of liberation theology's solution to the same problem. For liberation theology, the ultimate is the Reign of God. This does not mean, of course, that it ignores the resurrection, or that it does not see the clearly eschatological dimension of the resurrection. It is only that, for purposes of a theology that assigns primacy to the liberation of the poor, it sees the *eschaton* better expressed in terms of the Reign of God.

This primacy of the Reign of God is deduced not from this or that explicit assertion in the Christian scriptures (although there are such assertions), but from liberation theology's concrete task—from that in which it shows more interest and which it analyzes more in detail, from that which more frequently stands in a relationship with the object of this theology's priorities: the liberation of the poor. In the very beginning, in Gustavo Gutiérrez's classic *A Theology of Liberation*, the eschatological focus of theology underwent a frank recasting, but at the service of the key problem of that book: historical liberation and salvation. The work concludes that the Reign of God is the most adequate reality for expressing liberation, although for the moment the Reign is treated not from the biblical standpoint, but from that of the ecclesiastical magisterium.[1] From the publication of *A Theology of Liberation* onward, it has been impossible to deny that the christologies[2] and ecclesiologies[3] of the theology of liberation have attributed great importance to the Reign of God and have made of it their central and ultimate element, or at least more central and ultimate an element than others. Ignacio Ellacuría has made the central character of the Reign of God in the theology of liberation explicit, stating that the latter "is the very object of Christian dogmatic, moral, and pastoral theology: the greatest possible realization of the Reign of God in history is what the authentic followers of Jesus are to pursue."[4]

2. Primacy of the Reign of God

The fact is clear, then. The theology of liberation prefers the Reign of God as the *eschaton*. But it is very important to understand why. There are various reasons. Let us attempt to summarize the most important of them.

1. In its very enterprise, liberation theology has a particular leaning that it cannot deny, whatever the advantages and disadvantages of that leaning or attitude. In this it is not altogether unlike other theologies, but it does emphasize certain dimensions of the theological undertaking that are more specific to itself than to other theologies.

Liberation theology is clearly an *historical* theology. It seeks to locate historically, to verify in history, the entire content of the faith, including strictly transcendent content. Its very name is no more than the historicization of the core of Christian faith: salvation. Liberation theology is the theology of salvation as liberation. Liberation theology is also a *prophetical* theology, which takes account of sin—and historical sin—as central to its concern, something that must be exposed and denounced. It is a *praxic* theology, which understands itself as an ideological moment of an ecclesial, historical praxis. That is, it is interested before all else in transforming reality, although it defends its *theological status* and believes itself to be a theology that can help in the transformation of history. Finally, it is a *popular* theology—although there are various understandings of this concept—a theology that sees in the people, in the twin connotation of "people" as poverty and as collectivity, the addressee, and in some theologians, however analogically, the very subject of theology.

This being the case, it is scarcely surprising that liberation theology spontaneously finds in the Reign of God a more suitable reality than others for the development of its particular tendency and the guidance of its particular endeavor. Let us see, then—since the question cannot be avoided—why liberation theology does not make of the other great symbol of the *eschaton*, the resurrection, the center and focus of its organization of the whole of theology.

Jesus' resurrection, understood as the firstfruits of the universal resurrection, would surely be an apt candidate for the function of the ultimate symbol. It is absolute fulfillment and salvation, and thereby absolute liberation—liberation from death. It is the object and pledge of a radical hope, a death-transcending, death-defeating hope; it is the ultimacy and universality of the revelation of God. The resurrection can also be interpreted—and not necessarily arbitrarily, but with a basis in the biblical texts—in such a way as to recapitulate and illuminate elements that will be of great interest for the theology of liberation. Thus, we can say that the resurrection of Christ is not only a revelation of the power of God over nothingness, but the triumph of justice; that the resurrection offers not a universal hope, but a "partial," partisan hope—although one that can thereupon be universalized—for the victims of this world, the crucified (like Jesus) of history; that the resurrection can fire an absolutely radical hope for history, since if God is shown to have the power of deliverance from death, God will have all the more power to deliver from oppression; that the resurrection is a symbol not only of personal, individual hope, but of a collective hope, as well, since Jesus' resurrection is presented in its most intimate and direct meaning as the resurrection of the firstborn One, to be followed—as demanded by the internal logic of the very concept—by the resurrection of many others; that (unlike other expressions of the hope of survival, as for example in Greek thought) the resurrection implies and communicates the due importance of the corporeal and the material, since it is the whole human being who is raised, and raised to complete fulfillment; even that the resurrection can be lived in history itself, by causing its specific power to be felt in a particular manner of living the following of Jesus in joy and freedom—two realities that reflect in limited history the fullness of the resurrection.

All of this is developed in various theologies and is valued by the theology of liberation.[5] Still, it is evident that, in order for the resurrection to function as the ultimate for a theology with the disposition and attitude that we have described, an immense effort of interpretation will be necessary. To put it another way, the resurrection can be interpreted in such a way that it will function as the ultimate for liberation theology; but this interpretation has less obvious underpinnings in a first glance at a presentation of historical reality. With all its power to express the ultimate meaning of history, with all of its radical hope, the resurrection does not have the same capacity to show how one should live in history. It has great power to show us the final utopia, but it has less to show us how we are to live here and now, to show us which pathways to walk in our journey toward that utopia.

Furthermore, like any other symbol of plenitude that might be selected, including that of the Reign of God, the resurrection—not in its concept, since that can be corrected, but for real life—comports a particular danger. These words should not dismay us, since everything we human beings touch, however good and holy it may be—prayer, the struggle for justice, or what have you— is a potential victim of our limitations and concupiscence. It cannot be denied that, as history constantly teaches us, the resurrection can and does feed an individualism without a people, a hope without a praxis, an enthusiasm without a following of Jesus—in sum, a transcendence without history. From the enthusiasm of the community at Corinth to those of Catholics, Protestants, and sectarians today, history demonstrates this abundantly. Liberation theology is especially sensitive to this danger in virtue of its attitude and inclination, as described.

All that we have said concerning the resurrection must be correctly understood. We are not denying, of course, that the resurrection of Christ, the firstfruits of the universal resurrection, is a reality, and a central reality, for faith and theology. It is not that liberation theology fails to ascribe to the resurrection its due importance; it is duly treated in our christologies and is kept in account in our formulation of the Christian utopia. We are not ignorant of the fact that in the resurrection certain aspects of our faith are better and more radically expressed than elsewhere, even better than in the Reign of God: the radical character of our utopia, the definitive manifestation of God, ultimate gratuity. We do not deny that the resurrection can function as an antidote for a purely doloristic, resigned conception of the cross, that tendency of traditional popular piety; nor, on the other hand, do we deny its utility for purposes of a criticism of utopias that fail in a consistent radicality.[6] We only wish to say that for liberation theology the resurrection is not regarded as being as suitable as the Reign of God for organizing and ordering the entire content of faith. We take great account of the resurrection, but we situate it within something more comprehensive: the Reign of God.

2. Besides corresponding better to liberation theology's posture and scope, the Reign of God evinces a greater potential for systematically organizing the whole of theology, as theology ought to be practiced in a reality like that of the Third World. Ignacio Ellacuría, who places a great deal of emphasis on the Reign of God as the object of theology, exemplifies this. While the passage we are about to cite is a lengthy one, it will spare us an extensive commentary.

What this conception of faith from a point of departure in the Reign of God does is posit an indissoluble conjunction between God and history. . . . The Reign of God is immune to a whole series of perilous distortions. It is impervious to a dualism of (earthly) Reign and (heavenly) God, such that those who cultivate the world and history would be doing something merely positivistic, while those who devote themselves to God would be doing something transcendent, spiritual, and supernatural. It rejects an identification of the Reign of God with the church, especially with the institutional church, which would imply both an escape from the world into the church, and an impoverishment of the Christian message and mission that would culminate in a worldly church — a secularization of the church by way of a conformation of its institutional aspect to secularistic values of domination and wealth, and by subordinating to it something greater than it by far, the Reign of God. It rejects a manipulation of God, a taking of the name of God in vain in support of injustice, by insisting that that name and reality are properly invoked in the historical signs of justice, fraternity, freedom, a preferential option for the poor, love, mercy, and so on, and that without these it is vain to speak of a salvific presence of God in history.

The Reign of God in history as a Reign of God among human beings exposes the historical wickedness of the world, and thereby the reign of sin, that negation of the Reign of God. Over and above a certain natural sin (original sin) and a personal sin (individual sin), the proclamation of the Reign and the difficulty of seeing it implanted evinces the presence of a "sin of the world," which is fundamentally historical and structural, communitarian and objective, at once the fruit and the cause of many other personal and collective sins, and its propagation and consolidation as the ongoing negation of the Reign of God. Not that structures commit sin, as liberation theologians are sometimes accused of saying; but structures manifest and actualize the power of sin, thereby causing sin, by making it exceedingly difficult for men and women to lead the life that is rightfully theirs as the daughters and sons of God.

This sinful power is utterly real. It is intrinsically sin, and the fruit of sin, and here we may recall the traditional explanations of original sin; but further, it causes sin by presenting obstacles to the dynamism of the Reign of God among human beings, to the presence of the lifegiving Spirit amidst the principalities and powers of death. Thus, without being deprived of its essential immanence, the evil of the world acquires a transcendent dimension. . . . The destruction of human life, or its impoverishment, is anything but a purely moral problem: it is also, absolutely and unqualifiedly, a theological problem — the problem of sin in action, and the problem of life denied in human existence.[7]

We see very clearly, in this lengthy citation, that the primacy accorded to the Reign of God resides in the capacity of the latter to unify, without either separation or confusion, transcendence and history. It is from this point of departure that essential content such as Christ and the church can and ought to be understood, without hint of idealistic abstractions or spurious substitutions of what the Reign of God is not. Furthermore, although this terminology is not used in our citation, it is the Reign of God that enables us to rediscover the anti-Reign, the world of sin, that is—both historical and transcendent. Reality's ultimate duality, its irreconcilable duality, is properly identified not in the binomial "transcendence and history"—which can and should be reconciled—but in the irreconcilable binomial of Reign and anti-Reign, the history of grace and of sin.

Thus understood in its radical character, the Reign of God furnishes the theology of liberation with two things it cannot renounce. The first is a totality— needed if liberation theology is to be simply *theology*. The second is a particular historicization of that totality—needed in order for liberation theology to be a theology of *liberation*. The various tensions that crop up in any theology seeking to keep faith with the totality of its message are seen to have their place in the reality of the Reign of God, but in the theology of liberation these tensions are resolved in such a way as to maintain and even enhance the primary specificity of the theology of liberation. The Reign of God comports transcendence and history, salvation and liberation, hope and practice, the individual and the communitarian-and-popular. The elements appearing in the latter member of each of these tensions are more specific—in virtue of their novelty, not because they militate against a recognition of the importance of the former element in each case—to the theology of liberation. Thus, the Reign of God supplies the necessary conditions for taking the more novel aspects of liberation theology seriously and developing them within the totality of the faith. Thereby both the specificity of the theology of liberation and its Christian identity are maintained. A view of liberation in terms of the Reign of God does justice to liberation theology's original intuition and frames that theology within a totality that cannot but incline it to liberation in its plenitude—"integral liberation," as an orthodox, if not very expressive, language would have it—without which the original intuition would be deprived of its radicality.

3. One of the reasons for the primacy of the Reign of God in the theology of liberation is the thrust and intent of that theology to systematization. But there is an even more basic reason. Theology is always a second act, within and in the presence of a reality, and liberation theology lays explicit emphasis on this point. But it is the reality of Latin America and of the Third World in general that calls for a Reign of God, of whatever conceptual formulation. The major fact in Latin America is the massive, unjust poverty that threatens whole populations with death. At the same time, the most novel fact is the hope of a just life, of liberation. It is this twin reality that calls for reflection and a primary reaction—logically antecedent to any theological reflection and even any specific, determinate faith. It is reality itself that demands to be seen as a reality of life or death, that poses the question of hope or despair, that calls for an option for life or death. A grasp of the primary reality as being unjust poverty and the hope of a just life, requiring one to throw in one's lot with the alternative of life, can then be reformulated in theological reflection as the pre-

understanding necessary for an adequate understanding of revelation, and theologized as a sign of the times and a manifestation of the will of God. All of this is true, and liberation theology includes all of it. But in itself this grasp is of something more primordial: it is the grasp of a reality that raises its own, autonomous cry.

After all, when theology sees Latin America's reality in this first, pre-theological moment, it finds, without falling into naiveté or anachronisms, a social situation remarkably akin to that in which the notion of the Reign of God was first formulated, biblically in so many words, or extrabiblically in other terms. It is true today, as well, that entire peoples are unjustly oppressed and that they have a hope of life. It is true today, as well, that this is the most important fact for a grasp of the totality, as well as the various ethical, praxic, and semantic dimensions that emerge from that totality. If this is the case, and if this is historically akin to the reality in which the formulation of utopia in terms of the Reign of God was originally crystallized, then it is fairly obvious why a theologization of third-world reality might be undertaken in terms of the theology of the Reign of God. It is current historical reality that ultimately renders the concept of the Reign of God more useful today than other concepts for a theological elaboration of reality. It is the kinship between both realities, that of the Third World today and that of the peoples who forged the notion of the Reign of God, that makes it possible to have a better understanding of what the Reign of God meant when it was first conceived. The fusion of horizons required by hermeneutics is accomplished first and foremost in reality itself.

What has occurred then in liberation theology is that, in a pre-theological moment, reality has been grasped as an irruption of the poor with a hope of liberation. This grasp comports a prejudgment, if you will, but therein is the origin of the theology of liberation. When that theology is formally constituted a theology in terms of the primacy of the poor, or more precisely, of the liberation of the poor, then a course is set similar to that theologized so many centuries ago in the Hebrew scriptures and with Jesus: the Reign of God. It is the historical situation that ultimately forces this election. Elsewhere, where theology has been unable to discover the irruption of the poor — either because the latter has been less perceptible or because of a lack of interest in discovering it — the course taken has been in the direction not of the Reign of God, but of the resurrection. In Latin America, however, as in the Third World generally, the current, historical situation continues to force theology to strike a course toward the Reign of God. An ultimate hope in a universal resurrection can be maintained, but the more urgent cry is for the coming of the Reign of God as such. And this — above and beyond the urgency of calling attention to the theoretical and practical disregard that seems to prevail in the church — is the reason and finality of our return to this theme in this chapter. The Third World continues to stand in urgent need of liberation, and the best theological way to deal with liberation continues to be to do so in terms of the Reign of God.

II. DETERMINATION OF THE REIGN OF GOD IN THE GOSPEL

The fact that the Reign of God is central to the theology of liberation says nothing as yet about the quality and character of that Reign. Such a determination for the present time, which we shall attempt in part III, is no easy matter. But neither is an evangelical determination of the nature of the Reign of God, and this for an obvious reason: while using the expression countless times, and eager as he is to explain it in his parables, Jesus never says exactly *what* this Reign is. "Jesus nowhere tells us in so many words *what* the Reign of God is. He only says that it is near," Walter Kasper rightly says.[8]

This is not to suggest that nothing can be known of what the Reign of God meant for Jesus. What it does suggest is the need for a method, or to speak more modestly, a way of ascertaining this. To our view, the approaches used by systematic christologies are three. They might be called: (1) the notional way, (2) the way of the practice of Jesus, and (3) the way of the addressee of the Reign. These ways or paths are not mutually exclusive, but complementary. Still, depending on which is used or most emphasized, theologians' conclusions will vary. Liberation theology's contribution to a determination of the Reign of God consists not so much in exegetical discoveries, but in an insistence on the limitations and dangers of taking only the first way, and in its emphasis on the need for the second way, and especially the third. Liberation theology shows this in its own procedure when it analyzes Jesus' proclamation of the Reign of God. What we shall do in the following paragraphs is analyze each of the three ways separately, calling attention to those aspects on which the theology of liberation especially insists. The most specific contribution of our theology, then, is in its method for arriving at a determination of what the Reign of God is.

1. The Notional Way

The notional way attempts to ascertain what the Reign of God was for Jesus from a starting point in the notion Jesus himself might have had of it. This way analyzes the various notions of the Reign in the Hebrew scriptures and among Jesus' contemporaries (John the Baptist, the Zealots, the Pharisees, the apocalyptic groups, and so on). So, the researcher attempts to ferret out what Jesus thought about the Reign. The substance of these investigations—expressed in formal terms—is usually the following. Jesus proclaimed a utopia, something good and salvific, that was at hand.

All of this is true, of course, and liberation theology embraces it. Leonardo Boff, for example, has a beautiful statement: In proclaiming the coming of the Reign, "Jesus makes a radical statement about human existence, its principle of hope and its utopian dimension. He promises that it will no longer be *utopia*—the object of anxious expectancy (cf. Luke 3:14)—but *topia*, the object of happiness for all the people (cf. Luke 2:9)."[9] The problem is how this notion of the Reign of God can become rather more concrete; it is here that we note the importance, or unimportance, attributed to the other two "ways." When the latter are not actively present in the investigation—we say "actively" because they are always present in some way—the notion of the Reign tends to abide in supreme vagueness and abstraction. This does not militate against the fact that what is said of the Reign is something true, good, and holy— something, so to speak, with which Jesus himself would agree. But the vagueness and abstraction are of no help to anyone desirous of learning what, in the concrete, the Reign was for Jesus. Indeed, they can be dangerous if they relegate to a secondary level, or even simply ignore, important things that Jesus meant by the Reign of God. Let us look at a pair of examples.

In his christology[10] Kasper analyzes the Reign of God as Jesus' central message, and its eschatological and theological character. But when he wishes to tell us *what*, when all is said and done, this Reign is, he merely pauses very briefly to say a word about its addressee according to the gospels and in some of Jesus' deeds, concluding — formally — that the Reign of God is salvation. Naturally, we expect to find something concrete as to what salvation is. Kasper responds to our expectations with the following:

> We can summarize as follows: The salvation of the Reign of God means the coming to power in and through human beings of self-communicating love of God. Love reveals itself as the meaning of life. The world and the human being find fulfilment only in love. (p. 86)

Here the answer to the question of what the Reign is, is systematic, of course. But one supposes that it is intended as a conclusion from the analysis of the gospels just made. This, then, is the objective reality of the Reign: love. In that case, what the proclamation of its imminence adds is the following:

> Everyone can now know that love is the ultimate, that it is stronger than death, stronger than hatred and injustice. The news of the coming of the Reign of God, is therefore a promise about everything that is done in the world out of love. It says that, against what is done for love will endure forever; that it is the only thing which lasts forever. (Ibid., p. 87)

Love, hope, and promise — these are supremely important, central realities in the gospels and throughout the Christian scriptures. They are also things that have to do with the Reign of God preached by Jesus. It is disconcerting and disappointing that they are presented — in this degree of abstraction — as the result of an investigation into the Reign of God and its proximity in the gospels. What the Reign of God is said to be here could as well have been said of Jesus' resurrection, or the First Letter of John, or the hymn to charity in 1 Corinthians 13, or the hymn of hope in Romans 8:31-39. Not that it is false in itself, but how does it explain the concrete content of the Reign of God as preached by Jesus? Instead, one has the impression that it hides something very important about this Reign. Thus, the Reign of God loses not only concreteness, but centrality; it becomes practically interchangeable with other New Testament realities.

Our second example is from Pannenberg's christology.[11] This author emphasizes the importance of the Reign of God preached by Jesus. Its imminence is salvation, as implied in the title Father, by which Jesus addresses the God who now draws near. This calls for, and makes possible, a life lived in love. But if we ask what the salvation of the Reign is and how the proximity of the Reign can be salvation, Pannenberg replies with the following solution. In itself, it seems to us, the solution is an altogether original one—indeed, a stroke of genius—but when all is said and done, not very enlightening. In Jesus' proclamation of the imminent coming of the Reign, human beings see themselves obliged to "emerge from their everyday securities," to "transcend any currently real or possible fulfillment of existence or security." Inasmuch as the God who comes is still in the future, the proclamation of God's coming calls for, and makes possible, an "openness to God's existence." In a word, faced with the imminence of the Reign of God, human beings discover themselves for what they truly are—beings essentially and radically open to God. But it is precisely this unconditional openness which makes possible, indeed demands, the proclamation of the coming of the Reign, which is the human being's salvation.

> Because salvation, the fulfilled destiny of man, consists in the fulfillment of openness for God, it is already present for those who long for the nearness of God proclaimed by Jesus. (p. 228)

Pannenberg's argument here is formal. On the basis of his own anthropology,[12] there can be salvation in the fact that the Reign, near but not realized, demands and makes possible the human being's radical openness in the form of a life rooted in trust: "Expressed in a more modern way, Jesus brings man into the radical openness that constitutes the specific fundamental element of human nature" (p. 231).

But this formal argumentation is asserted to be required and justified by Jesus' activity: "The healing he performed demonstrated concretely that where the message of God's nearness is grasped completely and in full trust, salvation itself is already effective" (pp. 228-29).

The Reign of God is salvation, then, because, in its approach, without ever arriving in fullness, it enables us to live as genuine human beings. Pannenberg concludes that once human beings have arrived at their proper essence, they come under the obligation of acting in the manner of the divinity itself, the way that God acts: in love (pp. 232-33).

Pannenberg's solution takes account of hope, love, and salvation. More than this, it is an electrifying interpretation of Cullmann's classic "already, but not yet." But once more, the notion of the Reign of God remains general; it is universalized, and ignores extremely important elements of the Reign of God.

These two examples demonstrate the use of what we have termed the notional way of approaching the question of the content ascribed by Jesus to the Reign of God—practically in isolation from the other two "ways." As we see, there are serious limitations and dangers involved in such a procedure. The theologian attempts to fit the Reign of God into a basically preconceived notion of what, in the mind of this theologian, the Reign of God ought to be. This danger is always in part inevitable and cannot be entirely overcome. But the necessary means of making the concept of the Reign of God concrete, and thereby of avoiding its precipitous universalization simply in terms of the investigator's own interest, are available in the application of the other two ways that we have listed above.

2. The Way of the Praxis of Jesus

The premise of the way of the praxis of Jesus is that what Jesus did will shed light on what the Reign of God is. This is Schillebeeckx's position. "The concrete content of the Kingdom arises from [Jesus'] ministry and activity considered as a whole."[13] This methodological option is clearly justified in the case of those actions which Jesus himself referred to the Reign of God, whether explicitly (as with the expulsion of demons, or preaching in parables) or implicitly (for example, in his meals). But the option is reasonable for the rest of Jesus' activity, as well—certainly for the first great part of his public life, since in that period the proclamation of the Reign was precisely the central element in his work.

In order to clarify the importance of this point, the first thing we must emphasize is the very fact of Jesus' practice, which, in strict logic, needn't have existed at all. Let us ask the following logical, hypothetical questions. If Jesus thought that the Reign of God was imminent and gratuitous, then why might he not have restricted himself to its proclamation? Why not await that coming in passivity and confidence? Why not accept the situation of his world, if it was soon to change? These purely logical questions have only a historical response. Jesus *did* many things. In pure logic, once more, one could ask whether he did them because the Reign was already present, or in order that it might become present. Were Jesus' deeds purely sacramental, the expression of a Reign that drew near in all gratuity, or were they also service to the Reign, deeds performed in order that it might draw near? Whatever the answer to these questions, the important thing is to emphasize that Jesus did many things; he did not passively await the coming of the Reign (or ask this attitude of his hearers). Not even for the short period of hope in the imminence of the end could Jesus tolerate the situation of his world, as Cullmann says.[14]

Jesus' activity in the service of the Reign is understandable, since even in Isaiah (and in Luke's conception) the proclamation of the Good News, the content of the Reign, is essentially accompanied by activity: "This news will only be *good* to the extent that the liberation of the oppressed becomes reality."[15] But such an a priori approach is not the only way to understand Jesus' activity. Besides the programmatic summary of the proclamation of the Reign in Luke, we have other, earlier summaries of Jesus' activity: Jesus "went into their synagogues preaching the Good News and expelling demons throughout the whole of Galilee" (Mark 1:39). Jesus healed many persons, suffering from various illnesses, and drove out many demons (Mark 1:34 and par.). In the summary that we find in Acts 10:38, Jesus "went about doing good works and healing all who were in the grip of the devil."

The fact of Jesus' activity is clear. To place it in relationship with the Reign of God is often exegetically justifiable and is systematically reasonable. The important thing, then, is to see what his activity contributes to a determination of the nature of the Reign by making concrete the vagueness of the formulation of the latter. Let us briefly analyze three stages in Jesus' activity, while stating from the outset that it is only for methodological reasons that we separate this second way, the way of Jesus' praxis, from the third, the way of the addressee.

1. Jesus' Miracles

Jesus performed a series of activities that he understood as signs of the Reign. As signs, they are not the totality of the Reign. But if they render it present, then surely they must tell us something about it. Among the signs of the Reign are Jesus' miracles, his expulsion of demons, and his welcoming of sinners. His meals are signs of the celebration of the Reign. We will concentrate on the miracles.

Taken formally, the miracles are signs that the Reign of God is approaching "with power." They have been called "cries of the Kingdom." Thus, they are not the Reign in its totality, nor do they offer a comprehensive solution for the evils for which the Reign will provide the remedy. As signs of the Reign, the miracles are before all else salvation — beneficent realities, liberative realities in the presence of oppression. Hence, the miracles occasion joy by their beneficent aspect and generate hope by their liberative aspect.

How do the miracles help us understand the Reign of God if they are only signs? Basically, in affirming that the Reign of God is salvation, they make two important qualifications. The first is that salvation is concrete, and also plural. In the miracles we see that God fulfills real, immediate needs, without prejudice to what other needs the Reign will satisfy. This is important, because after the resurrection — as with other elements of the historical Jesus, his miracles are not mentioned a great deal in the Testament apart from the gospels — salvation becomes a technical, comprehensive term, and is used in the singular: Christ brings salvation. But in the Synoptics, salvation is presented in the plural. There is no such thing as salvation — only salvations, only the defeat of concrete evils. "To save, then, is to heal, to exorcize, to forgive, by way of actions that affect the body and one's life."[16] Thus it was that, precisely by reason of their concreteness, their "littleness" in comparison with the grandeur of expectations of the coming of the Reign, the miracles were not understood by all. They were not understood by the apocalyptic groups, who awaited portentous prodigies as signs of the coming of the Reign. But they were understood by those who needed salvations in their daily life. Schillebeeckx says it beautifully:

> In the miracle, we are confronted with a memory of Jesus of Nazareth as he came across more especially to the ordinary country folk of Galilee, neglected as they were by all religious movements and sectional interests.[17]

The second qualification that the miracles bring to the concept of the Reign of God as salvation is that they are not only salvation, they are liberation, and this in the strict sense. The concrete needs from which they deliver their recipients are the product of some kind of oppression. Illnesses — and this appears far more radically in the case of the demonic possessions — were understood as a product of the oppressive power of the Evil One, consistent with the demonological conceptions that permeated the mentality of the age. "An intense terror of demons reigned," says Joachim Jeremias.[18] In the case of Jesus' welcome of sinners, it was a matter not merely of benevolently accepting their company, but of receiving those whom religious society rejected, those oppressed by the prevailing piety. Jesus' miracles, and his signs generally, occur not merely in the form of the satisfaction of needs, such as could occur in a neutral context; Jesus satisfies the needs of people caught in a situation of oppression, in a situation of the anti-Reign. Therefore they are not signs of salvation alone, but of liberation, as well. They are not only salvations from concrete needs, they are concrete liberations from oppressions.

Jesus' miracles (and acceptance of sinners) also explain something very important that will become more explicit when we speak of the addressee. They explain the reason why the Reign is drawing near, and this will tell us something about what the Reign is. The basic reason for which Jesus is described as working miracles is mercy; he felt compassion for the weak and oppressed. We hear this repeatedly. "When . . . he saw the vast throng, his heart was moved with pity, and he cured their sick" (Matt. 14:14). We read that he felt compassion for a leper (Mark 1:41), for two blind persons (Matt. 20:34), for persons who had nothing to eat (Mark 8:2, Matt. 15:32), for those who were as sheep without a shepherd (Mark 6:34, Matt. 9:36), for a widow who had just lost her son (Luke 7:13). It is this mercy that also appears in the miracle accounts. On at least four occasions Jesus performs a cure upon hearing, "Have pity on me/ us!" (Matt. 20:29-34 and par., 15:21-28 and par., 17:14-29; Luke 17:11-19).

It is this mercy that explains Jesus' miracles. Jesus is presented as deeply moved by the pain of others, the pain of the weak. He reacts to this pain, and more important, reacts with ultimacy. There is something ultimate in the need of the weak—something to which one *must* react. It is important to notice that the verb with which Jesus' attitude is described in the passages cited is *splagchnizomai*, which comes from the noun *splagchnon*, meaning "belly, entrails, heart." The mercy expressed in Jesus' miracles is not a simple attitude of performing something prescribed or enjoined, then—not a reaction motivated by something apart from the pain itself. It is a reaction—therefore an action—to a reality that has been internalized, and which refuses to leave one in peace. It is a primary reaction, therefore—one which, when all is said and done, has no other explanation than the reality of the suffering of the weak, although it can be correctly denominated virtuous, or a compliance with the will of God, *afterwards*. With mercy we touch on something ultimate, something not arguable any further. So true is this that, when Jesus wishes to define the complete human being, he does so in terms of the Samaritan of the parable, who was "moved to pity" (Luke 10:33); when he defines God, in the figure of the parent of the prodigal child, he speaks again of someone who has been "deeply moved" (Luke 15:20). (Jesus himself is described in the Letter to the Hebrews as the faithful one, the person of mercy.) That the signs of the Reign are signs of mercy means that the reason—if one can speak of a reason in a free initiative of God—for the imminence of the Reign of God lies in the mercy of God, and precisely as we have explained that mercy: the gripping of God's entrails at the sight of the suffering of the weak. God will draw near for this reason, and for this reason alone.

Thus, Jesus' miracles and other signs already make somewhat concrete what the Reign of God is for Jesus, and thus we have already come a little way beyond general definitions of salvation as love, or as living in complete openness to God. Although they are only signs, the miracles express the character of the Reign of God as salvation from urgent concrete needs. This means liberation, since the needs from which one is saved are those produced by elements of oppression; the reason for the Reign is nothing other than, nothing apart from, these needs themselves.

2. Jesus' Denunciations

We have referred to the signs wrought by Jesus as actions in the service of the Reign. But we may ask whether Jesus performed some more comprehensive activity, some activity correlative to the totality of the Reign of God — something from which we might deduce what that Reign meant in its totality. Granted, Jesus formulated no theory of society as such. However, neither can it be said that Jesus has nothing to transmit to us in terms of the Reign's dimension of totality. That dimension appears in his view of the anti-Reign as a totality; from that view we can deduce something of what the Reign itself signified as a totality. After all, the anti-Reign is not only different from the Reign, it is formally its contrary. In this sense, perhaps we might denominate certain activities of Jesus as praxis, since they were intended as a denunciation of society in its totality. The purpose was to expose the causes of the anti-Reign and transform it into the Reign, although on this point Jesus offers no technical means but only calls for conversion.

That Jesus is convinced of the existence of the anti-Reign is clear. The world and the society in which he lived were not totalities in conformity with the will of his Father, God. But more than this, they were strictly the contrary. This is what we are taught by the controversies in which Jesus was caught up. These are never simple exercises in casuistry, or in the resolution of secondary *quaestiones disputatae*. They always deal with the central question of all: who God is. In the religious society of Jesus' time and place, this automatically led to the next question: what would a world according to God be like? In the controversy over the ears of grain plucked on the sabbath day in a stranger's field, for example, what is in question is the priority of life over worship (the religious dimension of the controversy) and over ownership (the social dimension). Jesus declares that, for God, life has priority over all else; he holds that, in today's language, God is a God of life, and that therefore society ought to be organized in service of life. What underlies the controversies is the exclusive alternative between the God of life and other gods, between Reign and anti-Reign. What is directly clear in the controversies is Jesus' rejection of the anti-Reign. But indirectly they also explain this minimum: in the name of God, there should exist a society organized in service of life.

Jesus' denunciations demonstrate his forthright condemnation of those responsible for the anti-Reign. Certain anathemas may be directed against individuals, but in general the addresses of the denunciations and anathemas are formulated in the plural. Not that Jesus had a theory of social classes, but he does assume the existence of social groups responsible for the anti-Reign. The wealthy, Pharisees, scribes or doctors of the Law, priests, and civil rulers are denounced and anathematized. Various things are thrown up to them: that they are hypocrites, that their existence is vain and empty, that they will have to give an accounting on the day of judgment, and so on. But in (almost) all of the denunciations there is a fundamental element: the addressees are the cause of the anti-Reign, they are oppressors, they produce victims. In the abundant denunciations of those responsible we discern a denunciation of the society that they mold as an oppressive society, rotten to the core. Here is a society in which power, at its various levels, oppresses the masses. This is the anti-Reign.

Jesus exposes the anti-Reign and its roots. He exposes the mechanisms by which the anti-Reign can masquerade as the Reign. He exposes the religious traditions human beings have created for the purpose of canceling the actual will of God and maintaining oppression in the name of God. Therefore he declares that oppression exists, why it exists, and how such and such a situation of oppression can be justified ideologically.[19]

In sum, we can say that Jesus rejects these particular social groups and the society that they shape. By way of his denunciations of the groups responsible for it, he denounces the configuration of society that they create. A society that produces this many victims is the anti-Reign; it must change in order to be in conformity with the will of God. From this it is possible to deduce only a minimum, but it is an important minimum for what the Reign of God is: it will be the contrary of the anti-Reign. There will be no oppression of some by others. In today's language, as in the language of the Hebrew scriptures, the Reign of God will be a reign of justice, a world organized in service of the life of those who had been victims, a world that will tear up death and oppression by the roots. Love as a possible formulation of the substance of the Reign will have to be made concrete in terms of justice. Otherwise Jesus' denunciations and exposés will not make much sense.

3. Jesus' Lot

Jesus' denunciations and exposés, seen as a whole, function as praxis, independently of his explicit consciousness of it; that is, they are pronounced with the purpose of transforming social reality. This is verified in Jesus' lot, which in turn will explain what the Reign of God is. Almost no one today continues to accept Bultmann's thesis that Jesus' death at the hands of the political authority as a punishment for a political misdemeanor was simply an absurd, tragic mistake. Both trials or processes, the religious more so than the political, make it abundantly clear that Jesus' adversaries knew very well what they were doing and why they were doing it. In the religious process, Jesus stands accused of blasphemy, an accusation whose formulation is religious. But alongside this indictment, which would appear to be redactional, appears the basic accusation: Jesus wants to destroy the temple. In this religious formulation, Jesus is implicitly but unambiguously accused of seeking the radical subversion of society. The temple was the symbol of the totality of society, in the religious, economic, financial, and political areas. In his political trial he is charged with acts of concrete subversion. These charges are dismissed, as they are seen to be unfounded. But he is also accused (and this is the charge of which he is found guilty and sentenced to death) of offering a distinct — and in the formulation of the gospels, exclusive — alternative to the Empire. From a historical viewpoint, the accusation leveled against him in the religious trial is far more solidly founded than his indictment in the political. But the conclusion is the same: Jesus objectively represents a menace to established society, and for that he must die. In situations very much like those in which Jesus lived and acted, Archbishop Romero used to explain, with consummate simplicity and clarity, that anyone who gets in the way is killed. The ultimate agent of Jesus' murder is not to be sought among individuals. The ultimate agent of Jesus' murder is that which Jesus disturbs: his society. In systematic language, the mediator of God is murdered by the mediators of other gods, because God's mediation, the Reign, is an objective threat to the mediations of other gods (the temple theocracy, the Empire). The attempt to do away with Jesus was a historical, structural necessity. Thus, the fact that he was killed is altogether understandable historically. The mystery lies in why God should have permitted it, which is something we cannot investigate here.[20]

But what does Jesus' murder tell us about the Reign of God? Once more, we learn something minimal, but basic. Persons who preach an exclusively transcendent Reign of God do not get themselves murdered. People who preach a Reign that is only a new relationship with God, or only "love," or only "reconciliation," or only "trust in God," are not murdered. All these things may be legitimately regarded as elements accompanying the message of the Reign of God, but they alone do not explain Jesus' death, and therefore they alone cannot be the central element of the Reign. The Reign of God must have had some bearing on the historico-social, not only on the transcendent. Jesus proclaimed it for religious reasons, surely: because the Reign of God represents the will of God, as does Jesus' proclamation of that Reign. But the content of the Reign was not religious in the sense of being nonhistorical or asocial. To bring out this point, Juan Luis Segundo asserts that the Reign of God proclaimed by Jesus was a political reality — not by contrast with the religious element, but by contrast with the purely transcendent or purely individual.[21] Segundo goes on to say that the purely religious element of the Reign of God only reinforces its political dimension, since concepts like *Reign* (and *poor*) are "all the more crucially political insofor as their underlying motivations are religious."[22] Whether the Reign of God be called a political reality or a historico-social one, the important thing to bring out is the historical, concrete dimension it had in the mind of Jesus. For Jesus, the Reign is the Reign *of God*. It is what happens in history when *God* reigns. But when God reigns, something happens *in history* that transforms that history and shapes it in a particular manner, in contrast with the anti-Reign.

It will not be superfluous to recall that, for Jesus, the Reign of God was a historical reality, which does not militate against its being an eschatological and theological reality. Rudolf Schnackenburg, in his well-known work on the subject,[23] is at pains to be altogether clear: "The salvation proclaimed and promised in the Reign of God is a purely religious dimension." Further, he draws a conclusion that will concern us below: "By reason of its purely religious character, Jesus' message concerning the Reign of God follows a universal trajectory." How can one commit such an oversimplification — or, at least, make such an undialectical assertion? In defense of his thesis, Schnackenburg rightly recalls that Jesus took his distance from exalted theocratic, apocalyptic expectancies and marvelous popular messianisms. But one may not conclude from this that the Reign of God was purely religious. It seems to us that it is possible to draw such a conclusion only by ignoring Jesus' ministry, his activity, his praxis, and his fate as things he does in the service of the Reign.

When, on the other hand, these things are taken seriously, they tell us something important about the Reign of God. The Reign is plural salvation from concrete needs (illness, hunger, demonic possession, the worthlessness and despair of the outcast sinner). It is liberation, since these needs are seen as the product of historical causes. But furthermore, in its totality the Reign stands in strict contrariety to the historical anti-Reign. As opposition, it is not an extrapolation from present possibilities; and as opposition to the historical anti-Reign, it is something occurring in history. It is a historico-social reality — a political one, if you will. None of this militates against the character of the Reign as that *of God*. On the contrary, Jesus sees it as such precisely because this is the way he understands *his* God, and he serves that God — to the point of being put to death — because he believes that the Reign is the will of God for this world.

3. The Way of the Addressee of the Reign

The third way, or approach to a determination of what the Reign of God is, is that of the addressee, which we have already sketched out to some extent in our consideration of the second way. An emphasis on the third way, it seems to us, is liberation theology's most specific contribution to theological methodology. The basic premise of this third approach is that the content and addressees of the Reign are mutually explanatory; all the more so when the addressee is considered not in a vague and undifferentiated manner, but concretely; and especially, when it becomes possible to know the reason why this is the addressee of the Reign. The effect of an analysis of the addressee is a concrete identification of the utopia and salvation of the Reign — and surely a concrete identification of the anti-Reign — such that salvation can no longer be universalized or be found in all manner of interchangeable conceptions, precisely because the addressee is concrete.

An exegetical determination of the addressee of the Reign of God had already been achieved by the time liberation theology arrived on the scene, although other theologies had not drawn the necessary consequences. Joachim Jeremias, for example, as early as 1971, had clearly identified the addressees of the Reign.[24] After an analysis of Jesus' proclamation and the imminence of the Reign, Jeremias says: "We have not yet completely described [Jesus'] preaching of the *basileia*. Indeed, we have not yet cited its essential trait." That trait consists in its addressees, who are the poor. Jeremias makes the radical assertion: "The Reign belongs *solely to the poor*. . . The first Beatitude: salvation is intended *solely* for beggars and sinners." It could scarcely be put more clearly. The same author determines the identity of these poor, who are thus proclaimed the addressees of the Reign. They are those cited in the first Beatitude (Luke 6:20), and those to whom the Good News is preached (Matt. 11:5, Luke 7:23). Jeremias tries to systematize the identity of the poor along two lines: the poor are those who are crushed under the burden of life (the absolute character of material — or, as we should say, socioeconomic — poverty), and the despised and outcast of society (the relational character of poverty: sociological marginalization).[25] While it is no easy matter to gather both lines into a univocal concept, it is obvious that poor, here, denotes a concrete, historical reality: it means those for whom life is a harsh burden for historical — economic and social — reasons. At all events, the poor are addressees of the Reign not by reason of anything in their interiority, and certainly not because they are human beings and therefore subject to limitations.

The theology of liberation takes this exegetical determination of the addressee very seriously and systematizes the reality of the poor on the basis of the data of the gospel.[26] The poor are an economic and social reality. They are those for whom to live is to bear a heavy burden, by reason of the difficulty of their lives and by reason of their marginalization. The poor are a collective reality; they are poor peoples, or poor as a people. The poor are a historical reality; they are poor not mainly for natural reasons, but historical ones — poor because of injustice. The poor are a dialectical reality; there are poor because there are rich, and vice versa. The poor are a political reality; in their very reality, they have at least a potential for conflict and the transformation of society. This systematization of the reality of the poor is not deduced, especially on the last point, immediately from evangelical data. But it does systematize fundamental traits, and we offer it in order that the reality of the poor not disappear into thin air, as so often happens. In any case, what is of interest to the theology of liberation, and what that theology proposes methodologically, is that it be taken seriously that *these* poor, the poor of the gospel, are the addressees of the Reign of God, and that it is in terms of *these* poor that the nature of the Reign of God can be made concrete. These propositions, which seem so utterly obvious and logical, are nevertheless not usually accepted, or at least not consistently. This is understandable, because they ascribe a "partiality," a partisanship, to God. God is taking sides — being partial to one group rather than to another, and this, today as in Jesus' time, is scandalous. Indeed, the preaching of the Good News to the poor, simply as such, produces scandal (cf. Matt. 11:6, Luke 7:23). After a long analysis in the work previously cited, Segundo emphasizes this partiality:

> The Reign of God is not announced to everyone. It is not "proclaimed" to all. . . . The Reign is destined for certain groups. It is theirs. It belongs to them. Only for them will it be a cause of joy. And, according to Jesus' *mind*, the dividing line between joy and woe produced by the Reign runs between *the poor* and the rich. (p. 90)

He gives the reason for this partiality, which usually causes still greater scandal:

The Reign comes to change the *situation* of the poor, to put an end to it. As the first Beatitude tells us the poor possess the Reign of God. That is not due to any merit of theirs, much less to any value that poverty might have. On the contrary, the Reign is theirs because of the inhuman nature of their situation as poor people. ... If the poor were still subject to (moral and religious) conditions in order to enjoy the coming Reign of God, that would mean the collapse of the original Beatitudes and their revelation of God. They could not say of the poor that the Reign is theirs, precisely *because* of what they suffer from their inhuman situation. (pp. 107, 140)

On the basis of the proposition that the poor are the addressees of the Reign of God, and that they are that simply in their quality as poor, two supremely important consequences follow. The first, an obvious one, bears on the content of the Reign. The poor define the Reign of God by what they are. They make concrete a utopia customarily formulated in the abstract—partly out of logical necessity, but for the most part because of a reluctance to make it real—in order that its addressees be not the poor alone, but others as well, and ultimately all. It is not easy to select a single term in which to formulate this reality, since, as we have said, needs—those of the poor, as we can now specify—are plural. But for the purpose of formulating the termination of the misfortunes of the poor, words like *life, justice,* and *liberation* continue to be meaningful. What the best formulation of the Reign of God would be is, at bottom, something only the poor themselves can answer, since theirs is the Reign, and it is they who know that from which the Reign delivers them. But the important thing is that, whatever the formulation, the poor make concrete the content of the Reign as the defeat of poverty. Perhaps we might simply say that the Reign of God is a world, a society, that makes life and dignity possible for the poor.

The second important thing that makes concrete the addressee of the Reign of God is precisely the element denoted by the prepositional phrase, *of God* in the name for that Reign; in other words, the transcendent dimension of the Reign. This thesis may sound strange at this point. A determination that the poor, as described, are the addressees of the Reign of God is frequently invoked in support of an indictment of liberation theology for reductionism, "economicism," "sociologism," or the like. Our proposition may sound strange for another reason, as well. In citing the transcendent, we could seem to be automatically transporting ourselves to some timeless, immaterial world. There is still the tendency, in addressing the question of transcendence and history, not only to distinguish them, but to set them in mutual opposition. Nevertheless, the transcendency of the Reign of God ought to be analyzed, at least in a first moment, in terms of the character of that Reign as being "of God," whatever the manifestation of this being "of God."

To our view, the fact that the Reign is of the poor, that it belongs to the poor, is a very effective way of expressing its being "of God," both with respect to the formality of God as mystery and with respect to the ultimate content of that mystery. As for the former, the poor are addressees of the Reign not in virtue of any moral or religious quality they may happen to possess, not because poverty makes it possible (as it in fact does make it possible) to live in greater openness to God. The reason the Reign is addressed to the poor is simply the way God is. God's being thus, and not otherwise, is neither conceptualized nor conceptualizable (in addition to being, for the adversaries of the poor, neither desired nor desirable). It is a manifestation of the divine reality, which, at least from a historical viewpoint, outstrips, transcends, the expectancies of natural reason, and certainly of sinful reason. Jesus' entire life shows the extent to which "the way God is" transcends conventional notions. The Reign's partiality to the poor occasions scandal and conflict. And having proclaimed to the poor in the Beatitudes that the Reign of God is theirs, in his parables Jesus must constantly defend this partiality of God's, in controversy with his adversaries. It is as if Jesus constantly had to say, "God is *not* the way you think God is, but just the opposite." Jesus cannot actually argue *why* God is this way; he can only assert the fact in the hope that his adversaries will accept a new God, the God who embraces the sinner, who pays the same wage to those who arrive at the eleventh hour as to those who come at the first, who is distraught and anxious over a single sheep that has gone astray.

The novelty and unthinkability that it should be the poor who are the addressees of the Reign thus becomes a historical mediation of the novelty and unthinkability of God, of the mystery of God, of the transcendency of God as regards human images. To be willing that the addressees of the Reign be the poor is tantamount to letting God be God—allowing God a self-revelation in terms of the way God actually is and in the terms in which God may elect to make that self-manifestation.

The transcendent reality of God can be analyzed from other perspectives; for example, in its suprahistorical function "in the beginning" and in the future, in creation and in final fulfillment. But the transcendence of God can also be analyzed in terms of the divine self-manifestation *thus* and not otherwise. Basically, Paul does nothing else when he proposes the cross as the wisdom of God. It is obviously insanity and scandal, but that through which God is being manifested as God. Something of the kind occurs when we assert that the Reign of God is of the poor in their quality as poor and only in that quality. It is through this that God engages in a self-manifestation *as God*, as unmanipulable mystery.

But the addressee also helps us make concrete the content of the mystery of God. The Christian scriptures make the radical statement that God is love; but the addressee of the Reign makes that love concrete in terms of love for the weak, in terms of affection for the weak, and in terms of the defense of the weak. From a point of departure in the flagrant inhumanity to which the poor are subjected, the humanity of God is manifested, in terms of tenderness, loving self-abasement, and joy when the poor and sinful accept the divine welcome. In terms of the addressees of the Reign, it is possible to know not merely that God is "this way," but that God is *this good*.

The poor as addressees of the Reign, then, have the potential to make concrete the historical content of that Reign, but they also have the potential to make the God of the Reign better known. With the poor as our starting point, we must let God show God, without attempting to determine beforehand what the divine self-revelation ought to be or what a plausible revelation would be. We must allow God the freedom to make a self-revelation as God wishes, not as desired by those who regard themselves as just and upright. We must let God be Good News as God wishes, as well as—to the consternation of many—bad news. We must let God be partial, as God showed partiality throughout the Hebrew scriptures as well as in Jesus. We must "let God be God," and let God manifest the divine love as God has decided—in a salvific approach to those who are not loved, but oppressed and despised in this world. Surely there are other ways, as well, of approaching the reality of God in fidelity to the scriptures. But it is of no small help to consider the poor as addressees of the Reign of God. At least they ensure the surprise we need to feel in order to be sure that we are actually dealing with God's revelation. And they demand a pre-understanding, which is also conversion, on the part of those who would be open and who would succeed in grasping this God whose self-manifestation proves to be thus.

In terms of Jesus' service to the Reign, as well as in terms of its addressees, then, we think it possible to say what the Reign of God was for Jesus. The Reign of God continues to be utopia, and thereby indefinable. But with what we have seen, we can safely assert that it is the utopia of the poor, the termination of their misfortunes, liberation from their slaveries, and the opportunity to live and to live with dignity. And again, from this point of departure, we can better understand the meaning of the Reign as a Reign *of God*, the God of the Reign is a God who desires life for the poor and who delivers them from the anti-Reign.

III. SYSTEMATIC CONCEPT OF THE REIGN OF GOD

An evangelical determination of the Reign of God is surely of the highest importance for our faith. But in itself it does not furnish a systematic concept of the Reign for today. Liberation theology, which unlike other theologies maintains the central character of the Reign, considers that the systematic concept of the Reign should be based on and should synthesize what is essential to the evangelical concept. But, while necessary, this is insufficient.

> The gospel invites us to creative fantasy, and to the elaboration of ideologies sprung not from some aprioristic quantity, but from an analysis of, and the challenges of, a situation, with a view to a project of liberation. This being the case, the Christian, in faith, should not be afraid to take a concrete decision—with the risks of failure that that decision will involve—a decision that can be the historically mediated coming of the Reign. Therefore he or she can ask, ardently, day after day: "Thy kingdom come to us." Neither faith nor the church know in advance what the concrete shape of such a decision will be.[27]

This citation from Leonardo Boff forbids an absolute formulation of the Reign. It emphasizes the need (and the risks) of its historicization today. But it demands some notion of what the Reign may mean today—some horizon against which a response to present challenges can be understood as a realization, however provisional, of the Reign.

1. Current Reassertion of the Reign of God

Before all else, it must be observed that the theology of liberation, with all its risks and all its provisional character, reaffirms the need to maintain the Reign of God as a central concept today. We have already seen the specific reasons for this assertion. What remains to be explained is in what sense liberation theology continues to maintain this when other theologies abandon it as their central concept. To make it more understandable, we may recall the celebrated question of *when* the Reign is to come. That answer depends basically on what we mean by the Reign. As we know, the exegetical solutions to the question of the moment of the coming of the Reign are varied. In terms of a consequent eschatology, the Reign will be reality only at the end of time (Albert Schweitzer); in terms of a realized eschatology, the Reign has already become reality, in the person and activity of Jesus (C. H. Dodd). According to Cullmann's familiar thesis, the coming of Jesus signals the commencement of the end of the ages, since the Evil One and sin have now been defeated in principle, although only at the close will the fullness of Christ be revealed; thus we have the thesis of the "already, but not yet." In systematic theology, it is said that the coming of the Reign can be regarded as "something provisionally fulfilled with the resurrection of Jesus itself," since "the universal resurrection of the dead" must be understood as "entry into the Reign of God" (Pannenberg).[28] Bultmann abandons all reference to the Reign and asserts that the ultimate occurs in history whenever the kerygma is received.[29]

The question of the *when* is ultimately answered in terms of what one understands the Reign to be, and it is this comprehension of the Reign that determines whether it will be maintained or abandoned as the central element in theology. In order to understand in what sense liberation theology continues to assign the Reign central position, let us make two antecedent clarifications.

The first clarification consists in distinguishing between a *mediator* and a *mediation* of the will of God. In the concrete economy of salvation, God always operates through a mediator, an envoy, someone who announces, and initiates by way of signs, what the will of God is for this world, and what direction the world should take in order to arrive at a condition in conformity with the divine will. In this sense, it must be said that the eschatological mediator has *already* appeared, that the mediator already is reality. And in this sense again, but only in this sense, Origen's beautiful profession is true: Christ is the *autobasileia* of God, the Reign of God in person. Of course, this is nothing but a reformulation, in the language of the Reign of God, of the nucleus of christologic faith: Christ is the definitive mediator. But at the same time, the will of God is not simply that a mediator appear in history, but also that the divine will for the world be realized in history. We call the realization of that will *mediation*—or in the language of the gospels, the Reign of God. Mediator and mediation are therefore intrinsically related but are not the same.

The second clarification will be in the form of a distinction between the *signs* and the *reality* of the Reign. The presence of signs is of the first importance for the symbolical explicitation of the reality of the Reign and for generating a hope that that reality is possible, that it is near at hand. But once more, such signs are not adequately the reality of the Reign. Acts of healing do not eradicate disease, nor the multiplication of loaves hunger, nor the expulsion of demons the omnipresent power of the Evil One, nor a welcoming of sinners marginalization and social contempt.

In what sense, then, can we say that the Reign of God is or is not reality? On what antecedent criteria will the reality of the Reign be verified and measured? The theology of liberation asserts that the Reign of God is reality in the sense of already having its mediator, no other eschatological mediator need be awaited. It asserts that the Reign is reality as far as signs are concerned, whenever they do occur in history. But it insists that the Reign is not a reality on the level of mediation, as St. Paul, using other words, insists: God is not yet "all in all" (1 Cor. 15:28). Cullmann's "already, but not yet" can be a valid response, provided it is correctly understood. The "already" is definitive as far as the *mediator* (the definitive, eschatological mediator) is concerned—although temporal mediators can and must continue to arise, now measured by the stature of Jesus himself. The Reign is "already" in history as long as signs of the Reign occur. But that Reign is "not yet"—in the reality of the Third World we should have to say "certainly not yet"—as far as *mediation* is concerned, the realization of the will of God for this world.

What the theology of liberation states, then, is the following. In the first place, this theology insists that the Reign of God has not come at the level of mediation, and that, nevertheless, the will of God continues to come to this world. From the non-arrival of the Reign, liberation theology does not adopt the conclusion leapt to by other ideologies, which, being ignorant of mediation, concentrate exclusively on the mediator, who indeed has come. That the mediation has not come raises an intrinsic difficulty for its determination, this is true; but liberation theology asserts that that determination must continue to be sought today. In the second place, liberation theology insists that there is at once a continuity and a discontinuity between the systematic and evangelical concepts of the Reign of God. The discontinuity is obvious, since it is unclear what the will of God is today for the current real world. From this liberation theologians come to their well-known demand for analytical mediations in order to arrive at a determination of the content of the Reign. The continuity is obvious, too—*for faith*. Liberation theology completely agrees that the mediator has indeed come, and that, accordingly, in its view of the Reign, in its activity in behalf of the Reign, there is something essential and permanent. This essential and permanent factor stands in need of becoming concrete but will never have to be canceled. It will always be needed in order to guide any future determination of the Reign of God. Simple as it may appear to say it, liberation theology accepts the fact that, throughout the historical life of Jesus, not only in the Jesus of the resurrection, the will of God for this world has appeared, with ultimacy, and that this has never been revoked in subsequent history.

2. *Premises for a Determination of the Reign of God*

What we have said up to this point shows that the theology of liberation makes a theological option for the Reign of God. It is a justified, or at least justifiable option, and therefore reasonable in terms of revelation. In terms of the situation of the Third World, it is also necessary and urgent. And it is an option that can appeal to many current church documents. But at bottom it is an option — a concrete, ultimate manner of grasping and formulating Christian faith.

In the background of this option in the formulation of the faith, however, are concrete, historical, existential premises, which are necessary for an understanding of why a basic theological option for the Reign of God is meaningful, and why this option is made concrete in the way that we are about to see. First, then, let us suggest what these premises might be.

The Basic Premise

The basic premise is the primacy of the reality of the poor. In modern language, we should say that the basic premise is the option for the poor. From this primacy flows the expectation — a logical enough premise even in itself, but reinforced by its actual realization, that the very reality and revelation of God will become more attainable and transparent.

This premise in itself is an option. When all is said and done, one cannot argue for or against it. Juan Luis Segundo has expressed this altogether radically in order to explain his own theology on the concrete point of the necessary premise for the reading of the gospel. The option for the poor, he states, "is not a theme of liberation theology, but the epistemological premise for interpreting the word of God."[30] This author insists that this premise must actually be posited before a reading of the biblical text is undertaken, that not even the text forces this presupposition on the reader (although it does require some presupposition, some pre-understanding). Thus, when all is said and done, the premise is a wager.

It will be open to discussion, as Segundo concedes,[31] whether, in the concrete case of an approach to the text of the gospels, the option for the poor is really only a pure option — a simple premise — or whether the text itself inclines in its favor and calls for it. But regardless of the answer to this question, it remains clear that, in liberation theology and in all its varieties, the option for the poor — however one comes to it — is necessary for a reading of the gospel, and furthermore, for an adequate reading of reality. Let us remember that the option for the poor is the heritage, not of Christians and believers alone, but of many other human beings as well.

The important thing is that the option for the poor is not pure evangelical or sociohistorical content, is not merely an ethical demand, and is not, of course, something that must be carried out because church documents say that it must, so that, if these documents had not said so, Christians would be under no obligation to make such an option. The option for the poor is something more primordial than this. It is an ultimate way of regarding the reality of the poor and of seeing in the liberation of the poor the necessary mode of correspondence to reality.

The internal structure of this option is open to theoretical discussion. The position of liberation theology is that it has the structure of conversion, since it is made in distinction from, and historically in opposition to, other options. This option may therefore have an ethical component. But the level on which it is taken is more primary. As St. Paul asserts, human beings tend to—indeed, according to the universalizing language of Paul, they not only tend to, but inescapably do—imprison the truth. Primary conversion, then, means letting truth be truth, seeing the world as it is, without oppressing it beforehand by dictating how it is to appear. In this sense, the option for the poor in Pauline language is necessary for a release from prison of the truth of the world, the world of the oppressed and the world of oppressors.

It is open to discussion, once more, how one manages existentially to make the option for the poor. Liberation theology insists that that option is made possible (or is strengthened) *from a point of departure* in the poor. How one manages to make an option from a point of departure in the poor is open to theoretical discussion. But in any case one must allow oneself to be affected radically by the reality of the poor—allow the poor to penetrate oneself with ultimacy and without conditions. Thus, the option for the poor is an option that one believes necessary for historical reality and the gospel, for responding and corresponding better to both, for entering into harmony and kinship with what they both say and with what they both demand. Once the option has been taken, one can grow in the conviction that all this is the case, and on the basis of this conviction come to a better and more adequate grasp of history and the gospel. Thereupon, the option can be theorized as the necessary hermeneutic premise for an understanding both of reality and of the gospel. Then the poor can be theologized, posited as a *locus theologicus*, recognized as constituting a world in which the signs of the times occur. Now one can even accept Isaiah's scandalous thesis: in the poor, in the crucified Servant, there is salvation and there is light. There is a mutual historical and theological reinforcement between an option for the poor that sheds light on reality, and the reality of the poor that convinces one that this option is right on target. But when all is said and done, what liberation theology emphasizes is simply the making of the option with (logical) anteriority to the development of a theology of liberation.

This means, concretely, that it is the poor who will guide the fleshing out of what the Reign of God is today. Theoretically and historically, the concept of the Reign of God can be worked out in terms of other primacies than the poor. It can be developed from universal human needs, from the longing for freedom, from the desire for survival after death, from the utopia of continuous progress. This has actually been the point of departure for other theologies, and the differences among them in terms of their systematic concepts of the Reign of God are ultimately to be explained by the premises on which they read the gospel text and current historical reality. In terms of the option for the poor, the systematic concept of the Reign of God plies a precise course: the Reign of God is the Reign of the poor.

Hermeneutic Premises

From the premise of the option for the poor, two important hermeneutic propositions flow. These propositions are necessary for an understanding of the Reign of God, and the option for the poor bestows on them novel formulations. The first is the question of hope. Modern theology has the great merit of having rediscovered the dimension of the future on the metaphysical level, hope on the anthropological level, and promise on the level of revelation. But it has also declared that the Reign is a reality that of its very nature demands hope in order for its meaning to be grasped. To put it another way, the reality of the Reign of God is such that, if, *by an impossiblity,* human beings had no hope, its content would be a logical contradiction. Hope, then, is essentially necessary for an understanding of what the Reign of God is. But once more, we must ask ourselves what manner of hope is in question here. Liberation theology insists that we are dealing with the hope of the poor. It does not deny, of course, that the human being is the being of hope and can therefore succeed in forging utopian concepts. However, it insists that hope as an anthropological dimension is only a necessary condition, not a sufficient one, for an understanding of the Reign of God.

By analogy with what we say of faith, we may say that there is *an object of hope* and *an act of hoping*—and that both must be made concrete in service of the poor in order to provide access to an understanding of the Reign. The object of hope is the object of the hope of the poor of this world—an end to their misfortunes, an opportunity for life, a just configuration of this world that oppresses them. The signs the poor hope for are those that already offer them a little life and enable them to hope that life is possible.

As for the act of hoping, the poor exercise their hope within a dialectic of realized signs, the foundation of hope, and a massive, cruel, structural reality that actively militates against their hope. The dimension of counter-hope is inherent in hope itself, and this has always been recognized, from Paul to modern theology: radical hope in resurrection is maintained in the face of death. But again, the poor make concrete the inherent opposite of hope: the current situation of oppression, the anti-Reign. The hope of the Reign is actively realized as hope in spite of, and in opposition to, the anti-Reign. Hope always has the structure of victorious action against what opposes it. Therefore it is important to see what it is that opposes it. For those who have no reason to see life as an object of hope because they already have life—although they may question its meaning—the obstacle to hope will be final death. But for those for whom living is still an object of hope, the obstacle to hope will be the anti-Reign. Not that the poor (at least in Latin America) have no transcendent hope in a resurrection; they surely do. But for them, to live right now would be as much of a miracle as to live after death. They see the opposite of hope not only in death, but in the impossibility of life here and now. This is why their hope, when they have it, is so radical.

The theology of liberation, then, asserts that in order to grasp what the Reign of God is, not just any hope will suffice. Only the hope of the poor will do. The hope of the poor must, in some manner, be adopted as one's own. But once this has been accomplished, one also has a better systematic understanding of what the Reign of God ought to be: a promise of life in the face of the anti-Reign.

Praxis

The second question is that of praxis. Modern theology is at one with the whole of the New Testament in insisting on the need for a praxis. The problem, then, lies not in the need for a praxis in the Christian life, but in relating this praxis to the Reign of God. The latter, we are reminded, is a gift of God and cannot be forced by human activity. As for hermeneutics, it is claimed, the Reign of God is a reality that requires hope in order to be understood, but no praxis in order to be realized.

Far from denying the gratuity of the Reign, liberation theology emphasizes it. But the same theology demands a practice, as well, even in terms of the Reign. The evangelical reason for this lies in the fact that Jesus himself did a great many things in the service of the Reign of God; he made some kind of demand on his hearers as a matter of principle. In terms of the primacy of the poor, the need for a praxis in behalf of the Reign is evident. A need for praxis, then, is not under discussion in the theology of liberation. What must be analyzed is the hermeneutic value of praxis—praxis as a means of grasping the nature of the Reign of God, in such wise that, conversely, without praxis an understanding of the Reign of God would be crippled and diminished. Indeed, praxis assists in an understanding of the very gratutity of the Reign.

A practice in the service of the Reign leads to a better concretization of the object of hope. In Ignacio Ellacuría's language,[32] taking up and adopting a reality (the praxic dimension of the intelligence) enhances one's grasp of the reality to be taken up and adopted. Let us begin with a negative consideration. In the doing of justice appears all the depth of injustice. The positing of signs of denunciation arouses a mighty reaction in those who experience the coming of the Reign as bad news. In other words, it is in praxis, and not in the pure concept, that the existence and reality of the anti-Reign appears with greater radicality. It comes to light not only that our present reality is not the Reign, not only that the Reign has not yet come, but that the anti-Reign is actively militating against the Reign. The numberless persecutions, murders, and martyrdoms of the poor who seek liberation, and of those who accompany them, demonstrate this clearly. Practice, then, helps us comprehend, with a radicality not otherwise attainable, that the anti-Reign really exists—as well as what it is in the concrete, since the anti-Reign reveals itself in its opposition to, not just any activity, but specific activities. Once again, by looking at its contrary, we find what the Reign of God is today.

Positively, it is in practice that we learn what generates hope in the poor. Many good deeds can be done in behalf of the poor. These good deeds alleviate their needs. But not all good deeds, however welcome, generate hope. It is in practice that one decides which signs, which proclamation of the Good News, which denunciation, which seedlings of a new society generate hope and therefore point in the direction of the Reign. It is in practice that one decides which things the poor celebrate as signs of the Reign. And it is also in practice, therefore, that one decides which paths lead to the Reign, paths that walk the tightrope between feasibility and the utopian "reserve" that moves one to search out new paths.

Practice, then, is not only an obvious ethical demand, but also a hermeneutic principle of comprehension. Before doing something in behalf of the Reign of God, less is known about that Reign than after doing something for it. In terms of practice, the signs of today are made concrete and thereby grasped. New signs are discovered. The roads to be traversed are identified. This sort of argumentation admittedly corresponds to a specific theory of knowledge. But it is based especially on liberation theology's reflection upon what occurs in reality when one toils for the Reign. Practice reveals what the Reign is. One might even ask whether Jesus himself may not have shaped his initial proclamation in service of his concrete activities and practices, and of reaction to them on the part of various social groups.

But further, for liberation theology, practice is not opposed to the gratuity of the Reign. Rather it presupposes it; it even helps to explain it. Liberation theology accepts and values the gratuity of the Reign, and this from two standpoints. In the first place, it confesses that the consummation of the Reign of God is the transcendent deed of God, as is its creation. Hope in the ultimate consummation is placed in God. The same gratuity that appears in the radical coming of God appears as well in the definitive attainment of God. In no way does the theology of liberation seek to place at risk the gratuity of the definitive Reign of God, and only the most backward interests would accuse it of uttering such nonsense. No, human beings will never build the perfect utopia! In the second place, liberation theology accepts and validates the notion that the reason God wishes to draw near in the Reign is in the divine initiative alone, which neither can nor need be forced by any human action. This occurs simply (as we have stated so emphatically) because this is the way *God is*.

These reminders ought to be unnecessary. They ought to be obvious, since liberation theology is authentically Christian and orthodox. But they are not obvious, since they are questioned. What may perhaps be behind these obtuse questions and accusations is an interest in ignoring or softening something on which the theology of liberation *does* insist: that gratuity is in no way opposed to practice; that, from a Christian viewpoint, it rather calls for it. What stands in need of analysis is not the need for both gratuity and practice, but a Christian understanding of their mutual relationship. From a historical viewpoint, we need only recall that Jesus proclaimed the gratuity of the Reign, and at the same time he himself exercised a practice and required one of others. From a systematic viewpoint, in scriptural language, let us remember that God has loved us "first," and draw the ineluctable conclusion in terms of the practice of a historical, concrete love, a love among brothers and sisters. Gratuity in no way exempts from practice. What Christian faith does is proclaim where the initiative is, and what it means for practice that the initiative should be with God. It means that practice must be performed not with *hubris* but with gratitude; that God's first practice, the antecedent unconditional divine love, shows how historical practice is to be carried out and how one is enabled to perform it. The mystery of God is that God "has created us creators" (Bergson). In the most gratuitous of all the divine acts, God has stamped us with this analogy with the divinity, that we may be with others what God has been with us, that we may do for others what God has done for us, and that we may deal with others as God has dealt with us.

We must hear, and proclaim, that the coming of the Reign of God is ultimately a gracious gift of God. But from this should flow not passivity, but the urgency of historical proclamations, an obsession with positing signs of its advent, with proposing ways in which human beings may live in conformity with that ultimate gift that will be reality only at the last. That the Reign is proclaimed to us and given to us ought to move us to carry out our practice with a particular attitude—that of response to gratuity. We are "free to love," as Gutiérrez says, and "liberated to liberate."[33] That the Reign is ultimately the Reign of God ought to move us to a practice without *hubris*—indeed, to a practice in a consciousness of our limitation and even sin ("to wage revolution as one forgiven," as José Ignacio Gonzalez Faus recommends). But an attitude of thankfulness and humility shapes practice; it does not suppress it.

In practice itself, furthermore, one can have the experience of gratuity. This can only be observed when it happens, but it happens. There is no reason why gratuity—the overarching fact that everything has its origin in God—should have to be expressed only with new eyes to see what without God could not be seen or with new ears to hear what without God could not be heard. It can also be expressed with new hands to do what without God could not be done. Many involved in the building of the Reign formulate gratuity in the following way. Something has been given us, and what has been given us is precisely that we can build the Reign of God, can posit signs that have not been posited before, can proclaim what has not been proclaimed before, can run risks that have not been run before, can accept a persecution that has previously been fled. *Before*, here, means what is normal, what is consonant with human potential. Now what appeared impossible has become possible; that is, to work with wholehearted determination and decision for the Reign. And this is experienced as a gift.

The theology of liberation, then, proposes the practice of the Reign not only as an obvious ethical exigency, but as a hermeneutic principle for a knowledge of the Reign of God and even for the knowledge of it as a gift. That practice, and the adoption of the hope of the poor, are concrete manifestations of the option for the poor that today bestow the ability to understand the Reign of God.

3. Systematic Concept of the Reign of God

After these reflections we can answer the question of what liberation theology understands systematically by the Reign of God. Formally speaking, by the Reign of God the theology of liberation understands a historical reality that has in itself the potential of openness to and indication of a "more." Materially speaking, it ascribes to the concept of the Reign of God the basic element of the evangelical concept as that concept is historicized in terms of the hermeneutic principles set forth above. Thus, the Reign of God is a reign of life; it is a historical reality (a just life for the poor) and a reality with an intrinsic tendency to be "more" (ultimately, utopia).

It should be clear, in this definition, by virtue of the primacy accorded them in the gospel and in the option, that the poor are the primary addressees of the Reign. A definition of the content of the Reign as *life* must be explained. What is at stake, of course, is not the term in itself; other, equivalent expressions could be found. *Life* is selected, we believe, because it is a better expression of both the historical and the utopian elements of the Reign. *Just* is added to indicate both the route to the the attainment of life in the presence of the anti-Reign and to express the condition in which life subsists.

The theology of liberation insists on life as the historical content of the Reign because, in the Third World, poverty means proximity to death. The poor are those "who die before their time" (Gustavo Gutiérrez). *Life* means that, with the advent of the Reign, the poor cease to be poor. Liberation theology insists on the primary sense of life, without being over-hasty to analyze the element of the "more" that is inherent in all life. Paradoxically, it focuses more on (an idealized) protology than on eschatology: more on creation than on fulfillment. Life is not simply a leaven which, kneaded into the dough of reality, gives rise to the truly human, so that at last the Reign of God is here. In the Third World, life is not the premise; it is always the proposition itself. It is a finality in itself. In negative terms, the primary sin of the anti-Reign is not against eschatology, but against creation.

Today it is the concept of a just life that bridges the gap between the systematic and the evangelical concept of the Reign. The words, "a just life," ring as Good News in the ears of millions of human beings. It is they that move people to posit signs whose inner thrust is an overwhelming sense of mercy at the sight of the faces of the poor; and it is they that move people to denounce the pervasive presence of the anti-Reign. Efforts in behalf of life today also constitute a continuing occasion of scandal, conflict, persecution, and death. The upshot of all of this is that the Good News of the Reign can have a meaningful Christian formulation today as the life of the poor.

But life is also a reality which, of its very nature, is always open to the "more." Its concept is dynamic and directional; it points to an unfolding of itself in multilevel realization, a realization charged in turn with new opportunities and exigencies. Life points to the perpetual element of the "more" in the concept of the Reign of God.

In the Reign of God there must be bread—the prime symbol of the Good News today. But this same reality, bread, raises the question of how to obtain it, thereby demanding some kind of activity and toil. Then once there is bread, the question arises how to share it (the ethical element and the communitarian element), the temptation arises not to share it (sin), and the need arises to celebrate it, for the gladness that the bread produces. Bread obtained by some is intrinsically a question of bread for other groups, other communities, for an entire people—and the question of liberation arises. But then the attainment of bread by a whole people means practice, reflection, functional ideologies, risks, perils. And the need can arise to risk one's very life in order that bread be transformed into a symbol not of selfishness but of love.

And now bread is more than bread. It has something of the sacramental about it, and so the festival of maize is celebrated, and those who come together not only eat bread, but sing and recite poems, and bread opens out upon art and culture. And none of this happens mechanically. At each stage of the reality of bread, the need for spirit appears—a spirit of community for sharing and celebrating, a spirit of valor to fight for bread, a spirit of strength to persevere in the struggle, a spirit of love to accept the fact that to toil for the bread of others is the greatest thing a human being can do.

The Good News of bread can lead to an expression of gratitude to God for what God has done, or the question of why God does not see to it that there is plenty of bread for all. It can lead to the question of who that one is who multiplied loaves to satisfy hunger and then was killed for it. It can lead to the question of whether the church takes bread seriously as Good News, and how it relates it to its mission. It can lead to the question of whether there is anything more than bread, whether there is a bread of word, needed and Good News, even when there is no material bread; whether, if it is true that at the close of history there will be bread for all, it is worth the trouble to seek and toil in this history for the same thing, though at times darkness is everywhere; whether the hope of bread for all is really wiser than resignation; and so much more. Life is always more, and in bread there is always more than bread. But it must be emphasized that the reality of bread develops in this direction when the bread in question is not just any bread—the bread of luxury, or the bread that produces wealth—but the bread of the poor.

This brief phenomenology of the "more" that is in bread—whatever a description of that "more" may happen to be—is only intended to show how life itself always unfolds into "more." Thus, the theology of liberation emphasizes the historical character of the Reign—life—which intrinsically leads toward the "more." As it places no limits on this "more," the life of the Reign leads to the utopian. This is the ultimate reason why liberation theology has to speak of an "integral" liberation—not in order to add something that will balance "material" liberation with other, more spiritual, liberations, but because in that primary material that we call the life of the poor is always the germ of a "more" of life. It is in this sense that we can say that the Reign of God is life, abundant life, and a plenitude of life.

Thus, liberation theology emphasizes the historical and utopian aspect of the Reign. This is nothing especially new; what is new is the relationship it posits between the two, by contrast with what other theologies do in this regard.

In the first place, liberation theology insists on and defends the historical element inherent in the Reign of God, both by reason of obvious ethical exigencies, and because it believes that this is the way to come to a better grasp of the utopian element of the Reign without the usual risks of alienation. Its purpose is to prevent the final fulfillment of the Reign from becoming a pretext for ignoring or relegating to a secondary level the realization of the will of God for the poor. As Archbishop Romero said repeatedly: "One must defend the minimum, which is the maximum gift of God: life."

In the second place, the utopian element of the Reign is understood in the theology of liberation as a guide along the pathways to be traversed in history, and not merely as a relativization of the paths already traversed. Unlike other theologies, liberation theology does not emphasize, although of course it accepts, the relativizing character of the utopian Reign where anything historical is concerned. It knows the "eschatological reserve." It would be very surprising if it did not; the reality of the poor makes it abundantly clear that current history is not the Reign of God! A warning of the danger of equating history with the utopia of the Reign would, in Latin America, sound like sarcasm. The theology of liberation does not reject the function of the eschatological reserve, but it interprets it in another way. Eschatology not only posits "reservations" with regard to the historical, but it condemns the historical. In positive terms, eschatology does not relativize historical configurations on an equal basis; it ranks them. A fallacy lurks in an insistence simply that "nothing is the Reign of God" — as if the distance between that Reign and any historical configuration whatsoever is equal to any other because it is infinite. The theology of liberation knows very well that utopia is that which by definition is never realized in history (*ou topos*). But it also knows that there are *topoi* in history, and that the will of God is better realized in some than in others.

Finally, liberation theology understands the utopian element of the Reign of God not only as an element of the final event of history, but as a force of attraction that becomes present in history by way of a real anticipation of the end. This force does not reside, as Pannenberg would have it, in the unreality of the utopia, which enables us and requires us to live in a particular way and thus to live as persons saved. With all respect for the provisional nature of all historical achievements, there are formulations of the utopia that draw history onward, that make history to be more than itself: justice, a communion of sisters and brothers, liberation, or, in the great words of Rutilio Grande: "A common board, with a broad tablecloth, and set for everyone, as at this Eucharist. No one left out. Napkins and place settings for everyone." The utopia is like a powerful magnet. It mobilizes. It moves human beings time and again to give their best to make the Reign come true. The theology of liberation believes that the final utopia, while beyond history, moves history here and now.

4. Comprehensive Nature of the Reign of God

Thus understood, the Reign of God is central for liberation theology. The last question we must ask is whether and how the Reign of God, as central theological object, has the capacity to organize the whole content of theology. Let us suggest, in hasty summary, how the Reign of God can be integrated with the most important themes of theology in such a way as to organize and enrich them, with the observation that, although this organization is effected conceptually, we believe that it is based on the experience of many who believe, toil, and suffer for the Reign of God.

In the area of *theo-logia*, the concept of the Reign of God includes, by definition, God, and does so with the ultimacy proper to God. The concept of the Reign of God evinces the ultimacy of the will of God, the design of God, the transcendence of God — as well as the content of the concept of God as the supreme good: love and tenderness. Liberation theology calls this God the God of life. By virtue of the very nature of the Reign, God does not appear as a God jealous of the good of human beings; on the contrary, the glory of God consists in the life of the poor. But God is jealous of other idols — the idols with which God is in strict contrariety. Therefore the love of God can be denominated justice — love in opposition to the death procured by other gods. God becomes the God of the victims of this world, and this divine solidarity goes as far as the very cross, and so authentically that it becomes meaningful to speak of a crucified God. But that God continues to be asserted as the one who — gratuitously and definitively — is capable of extracting life where there is none, is capable of causing a definitive Reign to arise amid the anti-Reign of history.

We may wonder about the relationship between the God of the Reign and that other great symbol of the reality of God, *Abba*, Father. This title, this sacred appellation bestowed by Jesus, is also an essential of faith, and so we must ask ourselves how it can be related to the concept of the God of the Reign. The fact that God is Father for Jesus, as for today's believer, is shown in the trust Jesus placed in God, on the strength of his conviction that this Father is good. Hence the aspect of faith that is trust in and reliance on God. But this goodness of God, which enables Jesus and us to call God our Father, is what Jesus describes in his parables precisely when he speaks of a love of God not in general terms, but as a love for the addressees of the Reign. Systematically, this can be expressed as follows. The goodness of God by which God is named *Abba*, Father, is expressed precisely in the fact that God is the God of the weak, and thereby unequivocally the God who is good. Conversely, the reason, the logical reason, why Jesus can proclaim the coming of the Reign to the poor is his conviction that God indeed is, once again, a God who is good, a Father. Accordingly, the Reign of God does not militate against, but precisely endorses, the reality of God as cited by Jesus — that of Father.

In *christo-logia*, the assertion that Jesus is the proclaimer and eschatological mediator of the Reign of God is itself an affirmation of christological faith, and in the strict sense. Faith in the divinity of Jesus comes into existence only after the resurrection; nevertheless, Jesus' essential relationship with the Reign of God can shed a certain light on the logic by which this profession of his divinity is reached. One should not neglect the sheer fact that Jesus, in the midst of history, dared proclaim the ultimate secret of history and its close. The ultimate element of history is salvation, and furthermore, this salvation is at hand. Jesus' resurrection can also be interpreted as God's confirmation of the truth of this Jesus as the eschatological herald of the Reign. A believer's argumentation in favor of the divinity of Christ — as the profound reflections of the Fathers of the Church reveal — to the effect that if Christ were not God there would be no definitive salvation, can be reformulated in the language of the Reign: If Christ is not God, vain is the hope of salvation promised by the Reign.

As for the true humanity of Jesus, the relevancy of Jesus' relationship with the Reign is evident. The element of historical practice and historicity in the subjectivity of Jesus, in this constitutive relationality, shows him to be a true human being, subject to whatever is universal in the human, but also demonstrating what true humanity is. His sharing in humanity's current of hopefulness, which expects a Reign, his pro-existence or existence for others and their cause, his mercy, his love to the very end, his strength and perseverance in trials external and internal (temptations, the Galilean crisis, ignorance), his hope against hope, show him as a human being, and—according to the christological profession—as the true human being.

The Reign of God, therefore, is also a reality from which the logic of the christological profession can be explained—once it is accepted in faith—with the advantage over other formulas that it emphasizes the reality of this particular person who reveals God, and the reality of that God who is shown in the human. The dangers of a degeneration of the christological faith into abstractions lessens, and the invitation and exigency of following in the historical footsteps of Jesus as a way of coming to know him and professing him as the Christ is more obvious from a point of departure in the Reign of God.

In *ecclesio-logia*, the Reign of God furnishes the ultimate horizon of understanding of the identity and mission of the church. It reminds the church that it is not the Reign of God but of its very essence the servant of that Reign—and that its internal realizations ought to be a sign of the Reign in history. The Reign of God requires of the church that its mission, like that of Jesus, be Good News to the poor, evangelization and denunciation, proclamation of the word and historical realization of liberation. In this manner the church today can be a "sacrament of salvation."

The primary addressees of the Reign of God, the poor, require of the church a real incarnation in the history of the passion of the world, with which incarnation the church solves in principle the difficult problem of being in the world without becoming worldly, without being ruled by the worldly values with which the poor are oppressed. The poor make concrete the internal reality of the church as people of God in terms of the fundamental equality of the human, but also in terms of the partiality of that human element for which God entertains a predilection, and which of its very nature can produce a more evangelical faith and hope. The church must adopt an internal organization having its center in the materiality of the poverty of this world, with the spirit that can arise more spontaneously from that poverty. In the language of Puebla, this means in terms of the evangelization practiced by the poor themselves; and in systematic language, in terms of "the poor with spirit," as Ellacuría indicates.[34]

It is this church of the poor that is in real history and that grows in history—the church that rejoices when the signs of the Reign appear, the church that begs forgiveness when it effaces those signs itself, the church that celebrates the sacraments and the word.

Let us conclude with a few words on the *spirituality*[35] of the Reign of God, since this is something that liberation theology develops explicitly, and something that should be mentioned in view of certain accusations to the effect that this theology neglects spirituality. The spirituality of the Reign of God is before all else objectively theological, since it must come in confrontation with the ultimate. It demands that we make the inescapable choice between serving God and serving the idols. It is a spirituality that calls us to traverse the pathways of life that give life, rather than the pathways of death that deal death. It takes very seriously, then, the election between grace and sin in the concrete. In terms of the Reign of God, we gain a powerful understanding of what sin is, and its prime analogate — putting a person to death — as well as of what grace is — giving someone life. We understand the historical, social, and structural dimension of both, but we grasp their personal dimension as well. This is so because, whether by action or omission, all of one's humanity, all of one's power of decision, is engaged in the choice of one of these alternatives.

A spirituality of the Reign of God is a christologic spirituality, since it sees in the following of Jesus the paradigm of all spirituality — a following that is practice, mission, and a building of the Reign. This following, however, this discipleship, must be practiced not mechanically but "with spirit" — with the very spirit that became present in Jesus' life and Jesus' exigencies, precisely when he served the Reign and when he spoke of the Reign: a spirit of mercy, of single-heartedness, of courage, of impoverishment, and all the rest.

The spirituality of the Reign of God is a spirituality, finally, that believes in the activity of the Spirit of God in history today. This is the Spirit who animates every search for and discovery of new historical pathways to the building of the Reign, the Spirit who animates the hope that the Reign really is at hand despite appearances, the Spirit who animates the maintenance, actualization, and deepening of faith in God. The possibility and necessity today of prayer, of placing ourselves before God, of allowing God to speak to us and ourselves to speak to God, is no routine affair; it is something which of its very nature confronts one who labors for the Reign, and something that is made possible by the Spirit of God.

Liberation theology insists on the need for spirituality. Liberation, the practice of justice, the construction of the Reign is not optional. It is a basic decision in behalf of the life of the poor. But this basic decision must be filled with spirit. Both — practice and spirit — are necessary and mutually reinforcing. The epistemological primacy of liberation practice calls for spirit, but it renders possible a particular spirit, one that is not drawn from other wellsprings. The spirit with which the practice of liberation is to be filled does not incline the "spiritual" person to renounce that liberation, but it does heal the inevitable dangers and one-sidedness of liberation — and even endows it with greater force. This mutual relationship has been expressed in the concept of a "contemplative in liberation" (Leonardo Boff), or a "contemplative in action for justice" (Ignacio Ellacuría). One can speak of "political health and wholeness" — of a unification of faith and justice, of knowing God by doing justice, and the like. The formulas are varied, but they all imply the same basic element; that is, that the building of the Reign of God requires a particular spirit, but that it makes that spirit possible, as well. And this is why the theology of liberation has a spirituality.

This sole purpose of this rapid overview has been to illustrate what liberation theology does as a whole. But it may be sufficient to show not only that the Reign of God is the central material object of theology, but that it can be the formal object, as well: the organizing principle—in the Third World better than elsewhere—of the whole of theology. In selecting the Reign of God as its material object, liberation theology intends neither to diminish nor reduce the totality of theology, nor has it actually done so. Indeed, the contrary is the case. In the concrete reality of the Third World it thinks it has found the best way to enhance the power of the whole of theology.[36]

In the last analysis, what liberation theology says is that the Reign of God is to be built in history—together with other human beings, hence the radical ecumenism of the concept of the Reign of God—and that, in the light of faith, we see ourselves to be on the road, as we accomplish this partial construction, to the definitive Reign of God. Like the prophet Micah, the theology of liberation knows very well what is to be done: "To do right and to love goodness" (Micah 6:8), to foster the life of the poor in history. And like that prophet, the theology of liberation has faith in what in the last analysis this practice means: "To walk humbly with your God" (ibid.) in history. The former calls for a constant positing of signs that shape the Reign, denouncing the anti-Reign, and proposing forms of more abundant life for the poor. The latter calls for faith in the ultimate meaning of history, faith in the fulfilling design of God—simply faith in God as God has been manifested in Jesus. This faith is the hope that history will be saved by God. Thereupon—but not before—the Reign of God becomes theologically interchangeable with the resurrection of the dead or with the Pauline "God . . . all in all."

—Translated by Robert R. Barr

NOTES

1. Gustavo Gutiérrez, *A Theology of Liberation: History, Politics and Salvation*, trans. Caridad Inda and John Eagleson (Maryknoll, N.Y.: Orbis Books, 1973), pp. 153-68.

2. Leonardo Boff, *Jesucristo y la liberación del hombre* (Madrid, 1981); Juan Luis Segundo, *Jesus of Nazareth*, trans. John Drury (Maryknoll, N.Y.: Orbis Books, 1984-88); Hugo Echegaray, *The Practice of Jesus*, trans. Matthew J. O'Connell (Maryknoll, N.Y.: Orbis Books, 1984); Jon Sobrino, *Christology at the Crossroads: A Latin American Approach*, trans. John Drury (Maryknoll, N.Y.: Orbis Books, 1978); idem, *Jesus in Latin America* (Maryknoll, N.Y.: Orbis Books, 1987); idem, "Jesús de Nazaret," in *Conceptos fundamentales de pastoral*, ed. C. Floristán and J. J. Tamayo (Madrid, 1983), pp. 480-513.

3. Leonardo Boff, *Ecclesiogenesis: The Base Communities Reinvent the Church*, trans. Robert R. Barr (Maryknoll, N.Y.: Orbis Books, 1986); idem, *Church: Charism and Power* (New York: Crossroad, 1985); Ignacio Ellacuría, *Conversión de la Iglesia al reino de Dios* (Santander, Spain, 1984); R. Munõz, *La Iglesia en el pueblo* (Lima, 1983); A. Quiroz, *Eclesiología en la teología de la liberación* (Salamanca, 1983); Sobrino, *The True Church and the Poor*, trans. Matthew J. O'Connell (Maryknoll, N.Y.: Orbis Books, 1984).

4. Ignacio Ellacuría, "Aporte de la teología de la liberación a las religiones

abrahámicas en la superación del individualismo y del positivismo," manuscript of an address to the Congress of Abrahamic Religions held at Córdoba, Spain, in February 1987.

5. We have developed various aspects of this interpretation of the resurrection in *Jesus in Latin America*.

6. José Porfirio Miranda goes so far to say that Marx lacked the dialectic to arrive at a conception of a transformation of the world that would include the "resurrection of the dead" (José Porfirio Miranda, *Marx and the Bible: A Critique of the Philosophy of Oppression*, trans. John Eagleson [Maryknoll, N.Y.: Orbis Books, 1974], p. 277).

7. Ellacuría, "Aporte de la teología de la liberación," pp. 10-12.

8. Walter Kasper, *Jesus the Christ* (London: Burns of Oates, 1976), p. 72.

9. Leonardo Boff, "Salvation in Jesus Christ and the Process of Liberation," *Concilium* 96 (1974), p. 81. A consideration of the other two "ways" also plays a very important role in Boff's reflection.

10. Kasper, *Jesus the Christ*, pp. 72-88.

11. Cf. Wolfhart Pannenberg, *Jesus—God and Man* (Philadelphia: Westminster Press, 1968). In a later book, *Theology and the Kingdom of God* (Philadelphia: Westminster Press, 1969), Pannenberg approaches the subject of the Reign of God with a bit more attention to its social and historical repercussions.

12. Wolfhart Pannenberg, *Was ist der Mensch?* (Göttingen, 1962).

13. Edward Schillebeeckx, *Jesus: An Experiment in Christology* (New York: Seaburg Press, 1979), p. 143.

14. Oscar Cullmann, *Jesus and the Revolutionaries* (New York: Harper & Row, 1970).

15. C. Escudero Freire, *Devolver el evangelio a los pobres* (Salamanca, 1978), p. 270.

16. G. Baena, "El sacerdocio de Cristo," *Diakonía* (1983), p. 26.

17. Edward Schillebeeckx, *Jesus*, p. 184.

18. Joachim Jeremias, *New Testament Theology* (New York: Scribner, 1971), p. 115.

19. See Segundo's suggestive interpretation (*Jesus of Nazareth*, vol. II, pp. 119-30) of Jesus' parables as exposing and shattering ideologies.

20. Cf. Sobrino, "Jesús de Nazaret"; Ignacio Ellacuría, "Por qué muere Jesús y por qué to matan," *Diakonía* (1978), pp. 65-75.

21. Cf. Segundo, *Jesus of Nazareth*, pp. 87-103.

22. Ibid., p. 88.

23. Rudolf Schnackenburg, *God's Rule and Kingdom* (New York: Herder and Herder, 1963).

24. Jeremias, *New Testament Theology*.

25. In his interpretation of Luke 6:20, Jeremias refers to the material poverty of Jesus' followers, which he distinguishes from that of Matthew 5:3. But he enlarges the concept of real poverty in a systematization consistent with the line of the prophets.

26. Cf. Ignacio Ellacuría, "Pobres," in Floristán and Tamayo, *Conceptos fundamentales de pastoral*, pp. 786-802.

27. Boff, *Jesucristo y la liberación del hombre*, p. 388.

28. Pannenberg, *Jesus—God and Man*.

29. According to "the New Testament, *Jesus Christ is the eschatological event—*

the action of God by which God has set an end to the old world. In the preaching of the Christian Church the eschatological event will ever again become present and does become present ever and again in faith. The old world has reached its end for the believer, he is a 'new creature in Christ.' For the old world has reached its end with the fact that he himself as the 'old man' has reached his end and is now 'a new man,' a free man." Rudolf Bultmann, *The Presence of Eternity* (New York: Harper & Bros., 1957), p. 151.

30. Juan Luis Segundo, "La opción por los pobres, clave hermenéutica para leer el evangelio," *Sal Terrae* (June 1986), p. 476.

31. "I am not very sure where this circle has begun. I do not know to what extent, by the very reading of the Bible, I have come to realize that the gospel says something. ... Once we have entered into the hermeneutic circle with the pre-understanding of which we have spoken, of course we convince ourselves that the gospel says this" (ibid., p. 482).

32. Ignacio Ellacuría, "Hacia una fundamentación filosófica del método teológico latinoamericano," *ECA* 322-23 (1975), pp. 418ff.

33. Cf. his basic work on spirituality, *We Drink from Our Own Wells*, trans. Matthew J. O'Connell (Maryknoll, N.Y.: Orbis Books, 1984).

34. Ellacuría, *Conversión de la Iglesia*, pp. 129-51.

35. See the work mentioned above by Gutiérrez as well as Jon Sobrino, *Spirituality of Liberation: Toward Political Holiness*, trans. Robert R. Barr (Maryknoll, N.Y.: Orbis Books, 1988).

36. This does not mean that liberation theology has developed all of the topics of theology with the same creativity. The ones we have mentioned are the ones that seem to be the most important. But as liberation theology itself is well aware, many tasks remain to be completed, among others, the problem of inculturation, the theology of women, the personal and family aspects of daily life, and so on.

THE LIBERATING DESIGN OF GOD

17

Trinity

LEONARDO BOFF

John Paul II, in his opening address to the Latin American bishops assembled at Puebla, made a statement of fundamental importance for our trinitarian understanding of God:

> Our God, in his most intimate mystery, is not a solitude, but a family. For he intrinsically contains paternity, filiation, and the essence of the family that is love: this love in the divine family is the Holy Spirit. (Puebla, January 28, 1979)

Christianity's most transcendent assertion may well be this: In the beginning is not the solitude of One, but the communion of Three eternal Persons: Father, Son, and Holy Spirit. In the remotest beginning, communion prevails. This communion constitutes both the essence of God and at the same time the concrete dynamic of every being of the whole creation. Nothing exists only in itself and for itself. Everything is situated in an interplay of relationships through which all beings live in a coexistence with one another, by one another, and in one another. The Trinity, which is the coexistence and co-life of the Father with the Son and the Holy Spirit, constitutes the root and prototype of this universal communion. Unfortunately, this trinitarian truth and this reality of communion have largely fallen into oblivion. It is of the first importance to carry out a critique of the causes that produce this amnesia so deleterious to society and to our local and regional churches.

I. POLITICO-RELIGIOUS DIFFICULTIES FOR THE LIVING EXPERIENCE OF A TRINITARIAN FAITH

The difficulties besetting an authentic, profound experience of our trinitarian faith are many. We should like to emphasize two of these—one of a political and the other of a religious nature.

In the area of the *political*, we are heir to an age-old political authoritarianism, a concrete historical concentration of power. In the family, the father holds sway; a centuries-old patriarchy has forged relations of inequality in family and parental bonds. In civil government, monarchs have created a monopoly of power in their own hands. The chiefs of tribes or nations have almost always exercised power autocratically. The ideology created by these political phenomena has taught that, just as there is but one God, so there is but one king and one law. Genghis Khan's dictum, which could have come from the lips of any Christian ruler, has become paradigmatic: "In heaven is one God alone, and on earth but one lord: Genghis Khan, the son of God." A similar mentality prevails in religious discourse. Just as there is one God, so also there is but one Christ, one church, and one representative of Christ; for the whole world the pope, for the diocese the bishop, and for the local community the pastor. The organization of social coexistence on the basis of the concentration of power in the hands of one or few persons does not create favorable conditions for the experience of God as communion.

In the *religious* sphere, we witness a phenomenon similar to that of the political. We know of the centralized exercise of sacred power in the figure of the High Priest or *Pontifex Maximus*. Indeed, it is not rare to see the accumulation of royal and priestly power in one and the same figure. The hierarchical conception of the Roman Catholic Church has favored a unitarian view of God. A certain understanding of theological monotheism, inasmuch as it conceives God as the vertex of a pyramid of all beings, is the upshot of political and religious experiences characterized by authoritarianism and despotism. A twin phenomenon is the result. Socioreligious reality serves as a basis for the construction of a non-trinitarian, pre-trinitarian monotheism; and monotheism serves as the sacred legitimation for centralized forms of the exercise of political and religious power. It is the merit of Erik Peterson (*Monoteísmo como problema político*, 1931) to have demonstrated that, behind a certain rigid monotheism, a political problem lurks, in antiquity as in our own time. A trinitarian amnesia in the Christian experience of God is in large part owing to these phenomena. The faithful have few concrete experiences of communion, participation, and inclusive relationships that furnish them with any concrete, created reflections of a God who, in their faith, is a Trinity of persons. Dogma may teach that the true God is a communion of three divine persons until it is blue in the face; our common experience, expressed in language, is that of an exclusively monotheistic conception of God. This is not to deny, of course, the legitimacy of emphasizing the true sense of monotheism within a trinitarian understanding of God; after all, the union among the three divine persons is due to the oneness of the essence or nature of God, which is life, love, and communion.

This ascendency of monotheism occasions in many Christians a disintegrated experience of the Trinitarian mystery. Each divine person is adored as a kind of separate God, to the exclusion of the other two persons. Thus, we have a kind of modern tritheism (the doctrine that there are three gods).

Thus, there is a religion of God the Father, found in social groups of an agrarian cultural mentality. In patriarchal societies God is represented primordially as the almighty, all-knowing Father, the Judge who is Lord of life and death. There is no room beside him for a Son; created persons, instead of being God's daughters and sons, are only servants who must conform to the sovereign will of the Father in heaven. The Son and the Holy Spirit are regarded as somehow dependent on the Father (subordinationism).

There is also a religion of God the Son in certain modern circles where horizontal relations predominate and leaders and committed activists rise up in the interests of a great cause, with charismatic figures leading groups and moving the masses. In this context the figure of Christ emerges and is honored as our Teacher, our Brother, our Chief and Leader. But this "christocentrism" becomes a christomonism, in which Christ seems all, as if he had not been sent by his Father or did not have a Spirit who would see to it that his message and person would be relevant for each successive stage in history.

Finally, there is a religion of God the Holy Spirit, found particularly among charismatic groups, whether in popular milieus or among the social elite. Its hallmarks are enthusiasm, spiritual creativity, and respect for the intimate meaning found by each individual in an inner quest. In this experience, valid as it is in itself, interiority prevails to the detriment of the historical dimension and to the neglect of a crucial concern for the impoverished and their concrete, integral liberation.

The disintegration of the trinitarian experience is due to a neglect of the principal, essential perspective of the mystery of the triune God, which is communion among the divine persons. Actually, God is a coexistence of upward (the Father), lateral (the Son), and depth (the Holy Spirit) dimensions, all of which ought to be integrally present in the living experience of the believer. In trinitarian language; the Father is ever with the Son in the Spirit. The Son is interiorized in the Father by the Spirit. The Spirit joins the Father to the Son and is itself united in them. Finally, the Trinity permeates creation in its proper divine reality. Communion is the first and last word of the mystery of God and the mystery of the world.

II. LATIN AMERICAN PERSPECTIVE ON THE TRINITARIAN MYSTERY

Any theology must evince its evangelical dimension. It must be a piece of good news for persons in the situation in which they live. In Latin America the crucial challenge comes from the side of the poor, who constitute the vast majority of our population. What does it mean for the poor to believe in the Trinity? It is more than a matter of professing a dogmatic truth and managing to understand its terms. It is also a matter of an existential actualization of the mystery of communion, so that people may be concretely helped to live their humanity in a fuller and freer way.

For the believing Christian, then, two lines of reflection are available. The first begins with the trinitarian faith and meditates the insights that derive from that faith for personal and social life. The second begins with personal and social reality and asks to what extent this reality is an image and likeness of the Trinity; to what extent it contradicts, in its concrete organization, a communion among differences; and finally, whether concrete reality permits an experience of the essence of the Trinitarian mystery: the egalitarian interrelationship among the three divine persons in a communion of life and love. In the case of Latin America, we perceive how great a change in individual and social reality will be required if that reality is to become a sacrament of the holy Trinity. Here are the trinitarian roots of a Christian commitment to the transformation of society; we seek to change society because we see, in faith, that the supreme reality is the prototype of all other things, and that this supreme reality is the absolute communion of three distinct Realities, each of equal dignity, with equal love and full reciprocal communion of love and life. Furthermore, we wish our society, our visible reality, to be able to speak to us of the Trinity through our egalitarian and communitarian organization, and thus to afford us an experience of the three divine persons. Ours is the motto of the late nineteenth-century Orthodox socialist reformers of Russia: "The holy Trinity is our social program."

Having concluded our introduction, let us now address the normative data of the trinitarian faith.

III. THE FATHER'S TWO HANDS: SON AND HOLY SPIRIT

How has the holy Trinity been revealed? The holy Trinity has been revealed along two routes, and both routes must be kept in mind: the route of history, and the route of the word. Both are expressions of revelation. First, the Trinity was revealed in the lives of persons, in religions, and in the common history of human beings. Subsequently, it has been revealed in the life, passion, death, and resurrection of Jesus Christ. And finally, it has been revealed in the manifestation of the Spirit in the Christian communities. Despite the fact that men and women knew nothing of the Trinity, nevertheless the Father, the Son, and the Holy Spirit have always dwelt in the lives of all of these persons and were present in all historical processes. St. Irenaeus proclaimed, in phraseology pregnant with theological meaning: "The Son and the Holy Spirit are the two hands of the Father, by which he touches us, embraces us, and molds us to his image and likeness." These two divine persons have been sent to humanity that humanity may be inserted into the trinitarian communion. An explicit revelation of this mystery occurred only with Jesus and with manifestations of the Spirit, particularly in the primitive church. Until then, the presence of the Trinity had been conveyed only through indirect intimations. The phenomenon of Jesus made it possible for us to have a clear awareness that God is a Father who sends a Son in order to bring about, in and through the Spirit, an integral liberation of human history. We find, therefore, that the Trinity was revealed not as a doctrine but as a practice—in the attitudes and words of Christ, and in the action of the Spirit in history and in people's lives.

The most important text commonly cited to establish the revelation of the trinitarian mystery is that of Matthew 28:19: "Go, therefore, and make disciples of all the nations. Baptize them in the name of the Father, and of the Son, and of the Holy Spirit." Exegetes are of the opinion that the formula reported in this verse came into being considerably later than other sayings attributed to Jesus, alluding as it does to the baptismal experience of the primitive community at the time when the Gospel of Matthew was written, around the year 85. By then, the community had meditated a great deal on the life and words of Jesus. They understood that Jesus had actually revealed who God is: the three divine persons, in whose name all who had come to believe were to be baptized. In this sense, Jesus is indeed the source of this ecclesial formula.

It is in Jesus that we find the revelation of the trinitarian mystery.

Let us begin with the revelation of the *Father*. We know from the gospels that Jesus expressed his experience of God by constantly referring to God as a Father. He uses an expression taken from baby talk—*Abba*—especially in his personal prayer (cf. Luke 3:21-22, 5:16, 6:12, 11:1-5; Mark 14:32-42). This Father is of an infinite goodness and mercy, one who "is good to the ungrateful and the wicked" (Luke 6:35). This experience is more than a doctrine. It is at the origin of a practice of liberation in favor of the poor and outcast, the straying and the sinful. Jesus' relationship with his Father reveals a certain distance and distinction, along with a deep intimacy. Distinction is revealed in the fact that Jesus prays and prostrates himself in God's presence. Intimacy is evinced in his name for God: Papa. Someone who calls God "Father" does so because of a sense of actually being God's child (cf. Matt. 11:25-27; Mark 12:1-9, 13:32).

In Jesus is also revealed the *Son*—not so much because he referred to himself in this way (cf. Matt. 11:25-27; Mark 12:1-9, 13:32), but because he acted as the Son of God. His actual, living practice bespeaks an authority that can only be situated in the sphere of the divine. He represents the Father in the world, and he makes that Father visible in his goodness and mercy. As his fellow Jews said so well, Jesus "made himself God's equal" (cf. John 5:18). Peter grasps the mystery of Jesus and professes, "You are the Messiah, the Son of the living God!" (Matt. 16:16). The text that most directly speaks of the Trinity is that reported by Matthew (11:25-27), especially in its Lucan version:

At that moment Jesus rejoiced in the Holy Spirit and said: "I offer you praise, O Father, Lord of heaven and earth, because what you have hidden from the learned and the clever you have revealed to the merest children.

"Yes, Father, you have graciously willed it so. Everything has been given over to me by my Father. No one knows the Son except the Father and no one knows the Father except the Son—and anyone to whom the Son wishes to reveal him." (Luke 10:21-22)

Here we have an explicit reference to the three persons, and in their reciprocal relationship.

As for the revelation of the *Son*, the testimony from heaven on the occasion of Jesus' baptism is also important. We do not know whether the account refers to an actual event, or whether it is simply an attempt to express Jesus' intimate experience in a literary form. In any case, in his baptism, just as in his transfiguration on Tabor, the divine testimony is explicit: "This is my beloved Son. My favor rests on him" (Matt. 3:17; cf. 17:5).

Another text of basic importance is the one formulated by the theology of John: "The Father and I are one" (John 10:30); "That all may be one as you, Father, are in me, and I in you; I pray that they may be [one] in us, that the world may believe that you sent me" (John 17:21). The text does not say that Jesus and the Father are "one" in the sense of being one *person* (for which the Greek would have used the masculine gender, *heis*, "one [person]"); it says that they are one *thing* (using the neuter *hen*, "one [thing]") — that is, a reality of participation or sharing, and of reciprocal communion. Finally, the moment of the great revelation of the Son is surely the moment of the Paschal mystery, in which we have the essence of the Trinity as communion, with the Son delivering himself up out of love and in loyalty to the Father, and the Father, once more out of love, responding to the Son by raising him from the dead. The fullness of Jesus' new life shows the presence of the Spirit, an expression of the new life of communion prevailing among the divine persons.

Theological reflection has sought to express this mutual implication by developing the doctrine of the Trinity, from the first centuries of Christianity until our very day.

Finally, we have the revelation of the *Holy Spirit*. This occurs in Jesus' own life. He is the permanent vehicle of the Spirit. The Spirit is that power (*dynamis*) and that authority (*exousia*) by which he performs wonders and deeds of liberation (Mark 3:20-30). Jesus says explicitly: "If it is by the Spirit of God that I expel demons, then the reign of God has overtaken you" (Matt. 12:28). The Spirit is the power dwelling in Jesus and taking everyone by surprise, as in the case of the woman with a hemorrhage: "Jesus was conscious at once that healing power had gone out from him" (Mark 5:30). This power is in Jesus, and at the same time it is distinct from Jesus. A trinitarian understanding will later say: the Spirit and the Son have the same nature of life, communion, and love, but are distinct divine persons.

There are other texts in the Christian scriptures that speak of God in trinitarian fashion. They present not a developed doctrine, but an awareness that Jesus Christ, the Holy Spirit, and the Father are equally God. For example, the text from Second Corinthians that we use in our eucharistic celebrations reads, "The grace of the Lord Jesus Christ, and the love of God, and the fellowship of the Holy Spirit be with you all!" (2 Cor. 13:13). Another very meaningful text is that of Second Thessalonians: "We are bound to thank God for you always, beloved brothers in the Lord, because you are the first fruits of those whom God has chosen for salvation, in holiness of spirit and fidelity to truth. He called you through our preaching of the good news so that you might achieve the glory of our Lord Jesus Christ" (2 Thess. 2:13). Here a thought is formulated that is organized in trinitarian style; it will culminate later in the theological reflection of the second to the fifth centuries. See also this other text, from Galatians: "The proof that you are sons is the fact that God has sent forth into our hearts the spirit of his Son which cries out 'Abba!' ('Father!')" (Gal. 4:6). Many other texts reveal the conviction of the first Christians that, with the Jesus event, there had been communicated to them the true understanding of God as a communion of persons (see 1 Cor. 12:4-5; 2 Cor. 1:21-22, 3:3; Rom. 15:16, 15:4; Phil. 3:3; Gal. 3:11-14; Eph. 2:18,20-22, 3:14-16; Rev. 1:4-5; among others). The sense of all of these texts is that, in God's approach to us for our salvation, there was revealed the communion of the divine three who always act together and who insert persons into their life and their love.

We Christians take a trinitarian point of departure in reading the Hebrew scriptures, as well. There we discover signs of the trinitarian mystery in the personification of the word of God (Pss. 119:89, 147:15ff.; Wisd. 16:12) and wisdom (cf. Prov. 1:20-23, 8, 9:1-6; Job 28; Sir. 24; Wisd. 16:12), and the hypostatization of the Holy Spirit. Basically, the Spirit is God in the divine strength. The Spirit is the divine presence in creation and history. This strength and presence gradually come to be seen as autonomous, while always "relational," realities, such that they appear as the Spirit of the Son, the Spirit that has us say *Abba*, Father, the Spirit who dwells in us as in its own temple.

IV. HUMAN REASON AND TRINITARIAN MYSTERY

Reflexive thought never has the first word. First comes life, celebration of life, and work. Only then do reflection and doctrines appear. This is what occurred with the trinitarian faith of the first Christians. They began by expressing their trinitarian faith in doxologies (prayers of praise), sacraments (baptism and the eucharist), and the first professions of faith. Afterward, they began to reflect on what they celebrated and believed. It was then that the trinitarian doctrine came into being.

The first question to arise was: How is faith in one God, to which the whole of the Hebrew scriptures attest, to be reconciled with faith in the Trinity, as professed in the Christian scriptures? In an attempt to answer this question, the first heresies arose — erroneous ways of understanding the mystery. What generally occurs in theology is what happens in the other sciences: it is in combating errors that we arrive at truth. The Christian community rejected three forms of representation of the trinitarian mystery: modalism, subordinationism, and tritheism.

Modalism declares that there can only be one God, who dwells in inaccessible light. But, the modalists teach, when that God undertakes a self-revelation to human beings, God appears under three distinct "modes," which are a kind of mask with which one and the same God is presented now as Father, now as Son, now as Holy Spirit. This interpretation, which was never accepted by the church, rejects Christianity's original understanding of the communion of three really distinct divine persons. Modalism leaves us with an unqualified monotheism.

Subordinationism says that only the Father is fully God. The Son and Holy

Spirit are subordinate to the Father. Surely they are the most exalted of creatures, nearest to the Father, but they do not have the same nature as the Father.
Some subordinationists went so far as to say that the Son is adopted by the
Father (adoptionism) and therefore is elevated above the station of any other
creature, but is not God as the Father is God. This formulation rejects the
equality of the divine persons, who are all equally God by virtue of the same
nature of life and love. The Council of Nicea (325) condemned this doctrine
in particular.

Tritheism asserts that the three divine persons are indeed distinct, in fact,
completely autonomous and independent of one another. Thus, there are three
Gods. But how can there be three infinite things, three absolutes? This doctrine,
too, was rejected by the church, because it neglects the communion obtaining
among the three divine persons, an interrelationship so profound and so absolute that the three persons are but one God.

After a hundred and fifty years of reflection, discussion, and ecumenical
councils (the principal ones, bearing directly on our subject, are Nicea in 325,
Constantinople in 381, Chalcedon in 451, as well as the Fourth Lateran in 1215,
and Florence in 1431-47), a technical language was created, a language of
theological reflection that could obviate mistaken understandings of the trinitarian faith. But the language coined paid a high price in terms of faith experience in exchange for its great theoretical rigor. It is formalistic. Let us consider
its key words.

1. *Nature* or *essence* or *substance*. These words each denote the unitive factor
in God, which is absolutely identical in each of the divine persons. The divine
nature (essence, substance) is numerically one, and unique.

2. *Person* or *hypostasis* is the distinguishing element in God. It denotes each
of the respective persons of Father, Son, and Holy Spirit. By *person* we mean
concrete, intellectual individuality, existing in itself, but always in openness to
other persons. Thus, the Father is distinct from the Son (each person exists *in*
itself), but the entire existence of the First Person consists in its "facing" the
Son and the Holy Spirit (each exists *for* the others). The same is true in turn
for the Son and the Holy Spirit.

3. The term *procession* designates the manner and order in which one person
"proceeds" from another. The word *procession* is not to be understood in a
causal sense, as if the Son and Holy Spirit were less eternal, infinite, or almighty
than the Father. It is a technical expression denoting communion in a certain
logical, but real, order of understanding. There are two processions in the
Trinity: the generation of the Son and the "spiration" of the Holy Spirit. The
explanation that has prevailed is that the Father knows himself so perfectly
that he generates an absolute image of himself, which is the Son. The Father
and the Son contemplate each other and love each other so radically that the
expression of this relation emerges concretely: the Holy Spirit, as bond between
Father and Son, as their love for each other.

4. *Relations*: These are the connections among the divine persons. The
Father, in relation to the Son, has parenthood; the Son, in relation to the
Father, has filiation; Father and Son, in relation to the Holy Spirit, have active

spiration; the Holy Spirit, in relation to the Father and the Son, has passive spiration. The relations distinguish the persons from one another.

5. *Perichoresis* or *circuminsession*: As the etymology of the words suggests, these expressions denote the radical coexistence, cohabitation, and interpenetration of the three divine persons with one another in virtue of the relations among them. It is a total circulation of life and love, in perfect coequality, without any anteriority or superiority. This is the model on which we Christians develop our social utopia, which is also a community of equality in respect for differences: a full, living communion of the most diverse relationships.

6. A *mission* is the presence of one or more of the divine persons in the concrete history of creation. It denotes the self-communication of a divine person to someone distinct from it. We know of two missions: that of the Son, who became incarnate in order to divinize us, and that of the Holy Spirit, who dwells in us in order to unify all things and to lead all creation to the Reign of the Trinity.

With these theoretical instruments, we can construct an orthodox reading of our faith in the Trinity of persons and unity of the single nature consisting of one communion and love. The history of trinitarian reflection is the history of three great tendencies to systematization. These tendencies do not materialize in a vacuum. We find them in social and ideological conditions that explain precisely why one of them surfaced in a given case rather than either of the others.

The Christians of the Roman Empire lived in an atmosphere of social dissolution, in which the prevailing religion was polytheistic. It was natural, then, for them to underscore the oneness of God, and to de-emphasize the distinction among the divine persons. To preach the Trinity was to run the risk of misinterpretation on the part of their pagan audiences; the Christian discourse could sound to them like a confirmation of their own polytheism. Thus, the social and ideological context of the time and place encouraged Christians to focus their reflection first and foremost on the oneness of God, and only then, on this basis, on the distinction of persons in God.

In another atmosphere, that of the Greeks, an insistence on monotheism and the absolute monarchy of God might have made it impossible to profess a faith in Jesus Christ as the divine Son. Here, reflection shifted from the distinction among the divine persons to their unity.

In a situation in which individualism and a lack of communion predominate, as in the modern world, especially in Latin America, reflection will appropriately direct its examination not so much to monotheism or trinitarianism, but to the manner of relationship that prevails among the divine persons. Consequently, insistence is on communion as the essence of the Trinity and the foundation of all human solidarity.

Throughout, we discern the presence of the history that permits an appropriation of the mystery conformed to prevailing human questions. Detailing the various kinds of systematization, we have:

1. The *Greeks* begin with the person of the Father. Here is the source and origin of all divinity. The Creed suggests this: "We believe in one God, the

Father, the Almighty." In the act of self-expression, the person of the almighty Father generates the Son as its Word, at the same time as it spirates the Spirit as its Breath. To both it communicates its nature. Thus, the persons are "consubstantial"; they possess the same nature as the Father. Therefore there is no multiplicity in God; that is, the persons are but one God. The principal significance of this systematization resides in its constant personalization of God. God is thought of as Father, and not merely as an infinite, eternal substance that is God. There is still the risk of subordinationism. All is concentrated in the Father. The Son and the Spirit are expressions of the single principle contained in the Father.

2. The *Latins* begin with the single divine nature. In the Creed, they underscore the first part of the initial verse: "We believe in one God." This God is an absolute, and absolutely perfect, Spirit. But it is the property of spirit to be *reflexivus sui*: to think and to will. Now, in thinking itself absolutely, the person of the Father generates an absolute expression of itself: the Word, or Son. In generating the Son, God is revealed as Father. Father and Son love one another so completely that they spirate the Holy Spirit as the expression of their reciprocal love, thus consummating the trinitarian circle. This approach safeguards the trinitarian oneness from the outset. But it runs the risk of modalism—the doctrine that the persons are only distinct presentations of the one divine substance, rather than being really distinct persons.

3. Many *modern theologians* begin with the relations among the divine persons. The primary datum of the revelation in the Christian scriptures is that God is Father, Son, and Holy Spirit. But that revelation also insists upon a perichoresis among the persons: an "intimate, perfect indwelling of each person in the others," such that among the persons prevails the unity of one God. The persons are three infinite subjects of a single communion, or three lovers in the same love. It is this third approach that we adopt, as it responds to the deepest needs of the poor, who seek participation, communion, and a more egalitarian coexistence, maintained in respect for differences. The poor find inspiration in the holy Trinity.

V. A LIBERATIVE CONCEPTION OF THE TRINITY

As we have already indicated, the harsh contradictions of Latin American reality invite us to experience and reflect on the trinitarian mystery as a mystery of communion among distinct persons. This perspective offers Christians the ultimate foundation of their commitment to the liberation of the oppressed— a liberation undertaken with a view to social justice, equity, and the construction of a society of sisters and brothers that will be viable in our conditions.

We shall have to begin with the major theo-logical datum of the Christian scriptures: that God is the Father, the Son, and the Holy Spirit, in communion. The only God who exists is the Trinity of persons. The divine oneness is communitarian; each person subsists in total, absolute communion with the other two.

What does it mean to say that God is communion, and therefore is Trinity?

Let us observe that only persons can be in communion. To be in communion implies that one person is present to another in radical reciprocity. It implies that one person "opens" to the other in a self-bestowal without reserve. To say that God is communion means that the Father, the Son, and the Holy Spirit are ever together, emerging together and constantly face to face. The scriptures proclaim this reciprocal communication among the divine persons in these terms: God is one God of life and of all life. Jesus himself, the eternal Son incarnate, presented himself as a vessel of life, and of life in abundance (John 10:10). Let us briefly analyze what *life* implies, with a view to a better grasp of the communion obtaining among the three divine persons. Life is a mystery of spontaneity, in an inexhaustible process of giving and receiving, of assimilating and of surrendering one's own life for the life of another. All life has presence. To be present is not simply to be "here." Presence is an intensification of existence. A living being "speaks for itself"; it has no need of words in order to communicate itself. It is already communication—so much so that its very being forces others to take a position in its regard, a position either of acceptance or of rejection. All life expands and enters into communion with its surroundings, establishing relations with those surroundings. Every living being is "for" another living being, and this relation guarantees its own life. Something of the kind occurs in the case of the holy Trinity. Each of the divine persons is for the others, with the others, and in the others. Accordingly, we understand that the only category capable of expressing this reality is *communion*, and that this concrete communion will generate the divine community. There will be no simple Father-Son duality here—an independent relationship of two and only two distinct persons face to face. This is a Trinity, and thus it will include a third member, the Holy Spirit, thus establishing a richer manner of living coexistence than that of the mutual contemplation of two divine persons alone.

Life is the essence of God. And life is communion given and received. This kind of communion is love. Communion and love are the essence of God the Trinity.

In order to express this interpenetration of the divine persons, theology has coined a special word. The term achieved its currency with St. John Damascene: *perichōrēsis*. *Perichoresis* denotes, first of all, the action of involvement of each person with the other two. Each of the divine persons penetrates each of the others and allows itself to be penetrated by it. This phenomenon is the property of love, and it is natural in the process of communion. Thus, the divine three are locked from all eternity in an infinite encounter of love and life, each in the direction of each of the others. The second meaning of the divine perichoresis is that, as an effect of this interpenetration, each person lives and dwells in each of the others. As the Council of Florence (1441) taught: "The Father is wholly in the Son and wholly in the Holy Spirit. The Son is wholly in the Father and in the Holy Spirit. The Holy Spirit is wholly in the Father and in the Son. None precedes another in eternity, exceeds it in greatness, or surpasses it in power." The holy Trinity, then, is a mystery of inclusion. The Son and the Spirit have been sent to us that all creation may "participate" or share in them.

By reason of the perichoresis obtaining among the divine persons, the relations among them are always triple. Thus, the Father is revealed by the Son in the Holy Spirit. The Son, in turn, reveals the Father in the power of the Spirit. Finally, the Holy Spirit "proceeds" from the Father and rests upon the Son. In this wise, the Spirit is from the Father through the Son ("*ex Patre Filioque*"), as the person of the Son recognizes itself in the Father by the love of the Spirit ("*a Patre Spirituque*," we might say). The divine perichoresis precludes any superimposition upon or subordination of one person to another. All are equally eternal and infinite. The perichoresis permits us to say: There are not first the three persons, and thereupon their relation; the three are intertwined, and live their relation of eternal communion from the outset. Therefore there is one God: God-Trinity.

The trinitarian dynamic enables us to construct a social and ecclesial critique and to discover in the perichoresis of the divine persons inspiration for our human relationships. Undeniably, human beings have a basic aspiration for participation, equality, respect for differences, and communion with God. In our peripheral societies these values are by and large denied. Hence the longings for liberation there, and the age-old struggles of the oppressed for their life and freedom.

In the capitalist system, under which we all suffer, everything is centered upon the individual and individual development. There is no essential regard for others or for society. Goods are privately appropriated, to the exclusion of ownership on the part of the vast majority of persons. Individual differences are valued to the detriment of communion. The socialist system, for its part, emphasizes universal participation, which, as far as the ideal is concerned, more nearly resembles the trinitarian dynamic. But personal differences mean little here. Socialist society tends to constitute a mass rather than a people, because a people is the fruit of a whole network of communities and associations in which persons count. The trinitarian mystery invites us to adopt social forms that value *all* relations among persons and institutions and foster an egalitarian, familial community in which differences will be positively welcomed. As the Christians of the base church communities have formulated it: The holy Trinity is the best community.

A contemplation of the mystery of the Trinity helps local and regional churches improve their internal organization. The Roman Catholic Church, especially, tends to live a societal model rather than a communitarian one. Power is centralized in the clerical corps, and the faithful are guided in a manner that tends to be authoritarian, with very little differentiated participation on the part of all. A monarchical conception of power was imposed on the church historically. Here it was not a trinitarian reflection, a mindset governed by the notion of communion, that prevailed; instead, the dominant view was pre-trinitarian, even a-trinitarian. If we accept, in faith, that the holy Trinity is the best community, and that it is by communion that the divine persons are joined together in one God, we can then postulate a model of church more adequate to its source, from which its life and oneness spring (cf. *Lumen Gentium*, no. 4). The church, theologically, is the *communitas fidelium* — the community of believers. Each member has his or her gifts, and these gifts ought to be experienced in such a way that they are turned to the benefit of all. What builds community is precisely the living experience of communion, which involves everyone's acceptance of and respect for everyone else.

To the extent that anyone creates communion, that person becomes a sacrament of the holy Trinity. In the church community a consideration of the trinitarian communion ought to prevent the concentration of power and open the way for a broad, egalitarian participation on the part of all. Not everyone can do everything. Each person performs his or her own task, but in communion with everyone else. In this fashion the whole church is transformed into a sign of the Trinity; after all, now it lives the essence of the holy Trinity itself, which is communion.

VI. DISTINCT PERSONS

Having set forth the principal considerations of the trinitarian mystery, let us now consider—still in the perichoretic dialectic—the distinct persons.

1. The Father: Unfathomable Mystery

The person of the Father is bottomless mystery, and therefore invisible. "No one has ever seen God. It is God the only Son, ever at the Father's side, who has revealed him" (John 1:18; cf. 6:46; 1 Tim. 6:16; 1 John 4:12). The Son has revealed the Father precisely as a Father who has a Son and who lives in an eternal coexistence with the Holy Spirit. Jesus' intimacy with his Father is such that he was able to say: "Whoever has seen me has seen the Father" (John 14:9). The Father is the one who eternally is, even if no creature had ever existed. This person is the Father, not because the Father has created anything, but because the Father has "generated" the Son in the Holy Spirit. In the Son, the Father has projected all created or creatable daughters and sons. Thus the Father is the root of all parenthood, as well as of all brotherhood and sisterhood.

When we refer to the Father, we indicate the ultimate horizon of all, the One at the origin of all and containing all. Only from a point of departure in the Father is it possible to understand anything of the Son or of the Holy Spirit. True, the three divine persons are ever "simultaneous," eternally together. But in order to grasp anything of the mystery of God, we must begin with the Father. Here is the person who is "first" among the simultaneous three, if we wish to set down a certain order among the divine persons. But this is our manner of speaking, in our human faith. It is always important to remember that in the trinitarian communion no person is before, after, higher, or lower than either of the others. The divine three are coequal, coeternal, and co-loving. But it is in the person of the Father that the entire divine mystery demonstrates its bottomlessness.

2. The Son: Mystery of Communication and Integral Liberation

God's self-revelation is the revelation of God as God actually is: as a Trinity of persons. In revealing themselves in the world, the divine persons reveal their essential condition as members of a Trinity. The Son is the absolute expression of the Father. All that is communicable of the mystery achieves concrete form in the person of the Son. The Son is the visible image of the unfathomable Father (cf. Col. 1:15). Thus, this person is supreme communication. Now, this eternal Son has been sent by the Father and has become incarnate by the power of the Holy Spirit. His life, his liberative practice, his struggles with those who hold power, his tenderness with the abandoned, his passion, death, and resurrection have revealed God in a definitive way. Not only has he communicated to us the truth of God as Father of all and advocate of the poor, but he has acted as the Son sent by that Father. He adopts the same attitudes of mercy as his Father. He builds the Reign of the Father: "My Father is at work until now, and I am at work as well" (John 5:17). But the Son's grandest communication has been that of making us, as well, sons and daughters of God. The meaning of his incarnation is not exhausted in the process of redemption, although the latter is a necessary step for a fallen creation. The most radical element in his incarnation consists in giving all creatures a share in his filiation. By its incarnation, the word [*Verbo*] has "verbified" the entire universe, and thus has led it into the very heart of the trinitarian mystery.

3. The Holy Spirit: Mover of Creation toward the Reign of the Trinity

The Holy Spirit transcends the face-to-face relation of the Father and the Son to introduce a new element: the "we" of the divine persons. Thus, the Holy Spirit is, par excellence, the unity of the divine persons. All of the persons face one another, but it is in the person of the Holy Spirit that we best see this characteristic of the whole divine perichoresis. What the Spirit is in the "immanent" Trinity, thereupon appears in the "economic" Trinity—the Trinity in the history of creation. The Holy Spirit is the power of union within all beings. By the power of the Spirit, radical novelty bursts into history and thus anticipates the substance of the Reign of the Holy Trinity. In particular, it is the Holy Spirit who bestirs our memory of Jesus. The Spirit does not allow the words of Christ to remain a dead letter, but brings it about that they ever be reread, gain new meanings, and inspire liberative practices. The Spirit is also the principle of liberation from all that diminishes existence "in the flesh," to use the scriptural term. Where the Spirit is, there is freedom (cf. 1 Cor. 3:17). And where there is freedom, differences emerge, along with the most varied gifts. It is the Spirit who prevents differences from degenerating into inequalities and discrimination, maintaining all things in communion.

The Spirit, too, has been sent to the world, along with the Son. Luke suggests that it was the Virgin Mary who first received the Holy Spirit substantially: "The angel answered her: 'The Holy Spirit will come upon you and the power of the Most High will overshadow you; hence, the holy offspring to be born will be called Son of God" (Luke 1:35). *Overshadow* is the expression the Bible uses when God enters a tent to dwell there (cf. Exod. 40:34-35). Thus, in our text from Luke, the Holy Spirit is said to be not only about to enter Mary, but to dwell within her permanently. Well does tradition call Mary the "sacrarium of the Holy Spirit" (cf. *Lumen Gentium*, no. 53). A unique relationship obtains between Mary and the Spirit, inasmuch as it is through the presence of the Spirit within her that the Son takes flesh and human form. The humanity of the eternal Word is the humanity of Mary, who, by the action of the Holy Spirit, brings it about that her offspring is a being both divine and human.

Finally, it is the deed of the Spirit to "lead back" to its eschatological plenitude the whole of creation. The new creation, redeemed and spiritualized, will finally be introduced into the Reign of the Holy Trinity. Only then will God-Trinity be "all in all" — everything in everything.

VII. SACRAMENTS OF THE TRINITY IN HISTORY

Faith is not expressed only by the intellect that delves into mysteries, nor indeed only by the heart that loves and trustingly surrenders itself to the divine persons. We think that it is expressed by the imagination, as well — that measureless capacity of the human being ever to add something to reality, ever to identify the potentialities concealed in every being. Imagination sees connections to which reason is often blind. And so, for the sake of a nearer approach to the trinitarian mystery, many analogies have been used. Let us briefly refer to three of them.

First, the human person is seen as a great parable of the trinitarian mystery. Every person is an unfathomable mystery. But this mystery is communicated through the light of the intelligence and opens to others in love and commitment through the will. Now, these three dimensions are not merely juxtaposed realities; they interpenetrate to constitute the single dynamics of the person in his or her existential oneness. The Father appears in the dimension of the human person that is mystery, the Son in the intelligence that communicates this mystery, and the Spirit in the love that unites it with all other beings.

Another symbol of the Trinity is the human family. The psychological unity of the person is structured as a triad. Man opens to woman and vice versa. This relation does not turn in upon itself but bears fruit in the generation of a child. If this openness is missing, the human relationship falls short of its fullness. In the family we have all three relational terms: father, mother, and child. Each of the three is distinct from each of the others, but all are intertwined by bonds of love. They are three, but they are one communion of life. The case is somewhat the same with the divine family: here too are three distinct persons, bound together in a single dynamic of life, love, and complete communion.

Finally, human society itself can be seen as a symbolic reference to the mystery of the holy Trinity. Any society will be constructed on the basis of an articulation of three forces, which always operate in simultaneity: the economic, the political, and the cultural. Through the economic force we ensure the production and reproduction of life. This is the most fundamental force, as it is the necessary condition for each of the others. By the political force we organize socially, distributing power and common responsibilities. Politics, or the political force, is a function of the human relationships through which we build the kind of society that is possible in a given segment of history. By culture, we project values—existential meanings, including transcendent meanings, through which we express the nature of the human being as that being that can view its existence as a problem and endow its task with a meaning.

Every society is constructed, consolidated, and developed by the coexistence and interpenetration of these three forces. They always act together in such wise that the economic is in the political and the cultural, and so on in turn. There is a certain similarity here with the holy Trinity; the three divine persons, while distinct, are everlastingly together, and they act together within and without the trinitarian circle.

In conclusion, we acknowledge the insufficiency of our human concepts and expressions to signify the mystery of the Father, the Son, and the Holy Spirit in their reciprocal communion. Our words conceal more than they reveal. The end of our quest, then, must be not in the intelligence that examines, but in the heart that praises—the heart that opens itself to an acceptance of the divine mystery within the human mystery. All of the great theologians—St. Augustine, St. Bonaventure, St. Thomas Aquinas, and the rest—concluded their treatises on the holy Trinity with hymns of adoration to such an august mystery. We honor the Trinity with our silence, in the awareness that all that we can say is no more than stammering concerning a mystery ever to be lauded and praised: Glory to the Father, and to the Son, and to the Holy Spirit. Amen.

—Translated by Robert R. Barr

18

God the Father

RONALDO MUÑOZ

I. CURRENCY OF THE TOPIC OF GOD

A renewed *experience* of God has been the core of the new Christian consciousness in Latin America ever since this reawakening began.[1] Reflection on the *topic* of God, however, has acquired its importance in Latin American theology only more gradually. Indeed, only recently have our theologians begun to address that topic in systematic fashion.[2]

From the earliest years of this renewal, the biblical image of a God of liberation and justice for the oppressed of the earth has been an ongoing, joyful discovery for us. Precisely this God is the heart and soul of our movement. The God of our discovery contrasts sharply with the God of punishment and passive resignation — whom we now begin to recognize as having been imposed by dominant groups and by agents of the church having ties to the same.[3]

In a first stage (the late 1960s and early 1970s), the experience to which we refer was primarily that of small groups of educated persons concerned with "becoming more political." In those years the principal biblical referents were the God of the Exodus and of the prophets, together with certain psalms, and the historical Jesus seen as the inspiration for an urgent social and cultural revolution.

Further down the road (in the late 1970s and in the 1980s) our experience broadened to include the people of the poor themselves, in and through the base communities and with the support of a considerable number of priests and pastoral ministers of the various local churches. Here the effort was not only to inspire social struggles, but to rescue popular life in all its facets. Now the central biblical referent for the renewed experience of God was Jesus Christ himself, the Messiah of the poor and the preacher of the Reign,[4] the one crucified by the mighty and raised again by the God of life, the Son of the Father.

This shift, this process of Christian maturation, has not meant a blurring of the profile of our new experience of the biblical God, or any tempering of the conflict that experience implies with received religious forms and the beliefs of the dominant groups. On the contrary, while we had originally spoken of a diversity of *images* of God, now our tendency was to adopt the realism of the radical confrontation posited by the Bible itself between the one God, living and true (revealed to the poor, and standing in solidarity with their cause) and the *idols* of death and the lie (revealed in the discourse and practices of the dominant groups and in the "structures of sin" imposed by these latter).[5]

II. THE GOD OF JESUS AMONG US

The Latin American recovery of the experience of a God of liberation, who has always acted in the history of the poor, is profoundly marked by a rediscovery of the *human Jesus*, who lived and made commitments in a public ministry and concrete history.[6] The question here is not that of any possible distinction between a "Jesus of history" and a "Christ of faith." The latter is a question posed by the academic theology of Europe. On the contrary, what is important to us on our continent, what gives us rebirth and liberation, is precisely the rediscovery of the full humanity of Jesus Christ, the Lord who was raised and the Son of the Father — that very one who walks with us now, the one in communion with whom we live by faith. We make this rediscovery in those two, inseparable loci of our Christian faith: the people of the poor, with the beliefs and practices of their popular Christianity and with their liberative solidarity; and the church community among these same poor, with its concrete brotherhood and sisterhood, its proclamation and celebration of the word, and its ministries and services. Here is the twin font of our engagement in an ongoing reencounter with the Jesus of the gospels — our rediscovery of the one who has shown us the love, presence, and project of his divine Father in a historical situation that offers so many profound analogies with our own, and who has done so through human attitudes and deeds, through concrete social options and liberative practices that are our norm and our hope precisely because they are the testimony and call of the living God in our midst.

In this sense the rediscovery of the historical Jesus is becoming more and more a characteristic of our very experience of God. Little by little, along this route, we are transcending the schema of the customary Catholic catechesis, which has only been a simplified summary of the scholastic theology taught in seminaries. That theology had started with God *in se*, whom it attempted to "explain" in a speculative philosophical language; it then went on with the Trinity, approaching the latter as a kind of divine secret revealed to Christians, and then showed that Jesus Christ is one of this Trinity, the Son, who became incarnate, founded the church, and then returned to the Father. In this schema it seemed taken for granted that God as such was a more or less evident reality for us, and the Trinity a kind of enigmatic code for the divine transcendence.

But we cannot actually be sure of knowing the true God, nor can the Trinity have any meaning for us before we meet that singular human being called Jesus of Nazareth. Failing this encounter with the historical Jesus, then, frequently the God conjured up for us resembled more the supreme principle and change-less perfection of the philosophy of an intellectual elite than the merciful Father who is revealed to the simple. God seemed more the almighty one invoked by the ideology of the dominant classes than the liberator of the oppressed and avenger of the lowly. We even projected this celestial personage upon our image of Christ, whom we therefore frequently confounded with the figure of this almighty, impassible "God."

Today we apply something of a reverse schema. More and more in the foreground is Jesus of Nazareth, in his Messianic history as narrated in the gospels. Then this Jesus the Christ shows us the Reign of God as a dynamism of liberation and life, a dynamism among the poor. Next, here is a Jesus who personally experiences, and restores to us, a communion with our divine Father, a communion we share with all his brothers and sisters, who thus become *our* brothers and sisters. But Jesus is rejected by those who feel secure and who hold power; indeed, he is executed by the authorities on the gallows of the cross. This same Jesus—raised from the dead—now walks with us, calls to us, and encourages us.

"God as such," then, appears before us only in an indirect manner. God *in se* is not the central "theme" of Jesus' preaching, nor therefore is it the direct "object" of Christian experience. What we properly experience and practice, what we suffer and build, is our human history. But in this history of liberative solidarity and shared joy—the history of Jesus, and our own history "in his name"—the living God becomes present in God's liberating love and God's joy. This God of the Reign, the Father of Jesus Christ, is the one who raises the Crucified One from the dead, and who bestows on us the gift of the Spirit of the one raised, that we too may embrace his cause and follow his way, and thus "ver-ify" and "know" the one true God.[7]

This is why the first Christian preaching, like the whole of Christian scriptures, calls upon its hearers with such urgency to "follow Jesus Christ," to "believe in the Son," to "accept the word" and to respond to that word with their whole lives, insisting that Jesus alone "has the words of eternal life," and is "the way, the truth, and the life." Hence the decisive importance ascribed by ancient Christian theology and by the church's Creed to the assertion of the full divinity of Christ and his equality with the Father. For it is this Jesus, and he alone—Mary's son, crucified under Pontius Pilate, as human and historical a person as ourselves—who is "the only Son of God, eternally begotten of the Father, God [proceeding] from God, Light from Light, true God from true God, . . . one in Being [consubstantial] with the Father."[8]

Indeed, that Jesus, in exercising his public ministry and in sending forth his disciples, as recounted in the Christian scriptures, comes not to purify the concepts of the dominant religions, or to salvage the intuitions of a "natural knowledge of God," or merely to restore the religious traditions of his chosen people. That same Jesus—as God's witness—in the conflict-ridden, religiously ambiguous world of his time, made very precise options, and took very clear, concrete positions, battling upstream against so many oppressive religious and social practices. He struggled to reverse the deformations in the conception of God that these practices betrayed, and—when it was all over—he was sentenced and executed for acting in consistency with his testimony to a God in contradiction with the "God" of the established sociopolitical and religious order.

Accordingly, in the testimony of this Jesus concerning God, a testimony which God has personally confirmed by raising him from the dead, we have been given the definitive key to the recognition—at any time, in any social or ecclesiastical situation—of the true image of the living God, which we can now distinguish from its caricatures and falsifications.

III. GOD IN THE LIBERATION OF THE OPPRESSED

We have "known" the God of the Bible—we have had the experience of the living reality of this God, we have been caught up and involved in communion with this God—because God has personally sought to intervene *in collective history*. That is, God has executed "judgments" upon this history, in order to liberate oppressed, exploited, and disintegrated human groups and make of them a people of free human beings living in solidarity. These groups have lived their condition of oppression and servitude as a condition "sacralized" in the cult of the false gods of the despotic power and the privatized wealth of the dominators: of Pharaoh and the magnates of Egypt, of the haughty monarchs and monopolistic groups of Israel itself, of the heads and privileged groups of the great empires. Their new condition as an organized, free people, a people of brothers and sisters, is the product of their encounter with the true God, a product of the covenant that this God bestows upon us. Here is a covenant of humble service, and of the sharing of goods among the poor of the earth. Liberation and access to the Reign of God mean abandoning the idols of domination and massacre, and converting and belonging to the living and true God, the God of solidarity and a fully human life for all. In our reading of the Bible today—Old and New Testaments—in the faith-filled pilgrimage of our people, we do not "confuse" our Christian faith with the tasks of collective liberation that we may share with nonbelievers, we do not "reduce" that faith to these tasks. But neither do we separate, in our Christian faith and practice, the spiritual, religious dimension from the more temporal, social one. We do not sever our experience of the living God, and fidelity to that God, from our commitment to the liberation of the oppressed and our struggle for a just society of brothers and sisters.[9]

Thus the one true God personally reveals an active presence and call not in the great ones of the earth, not in the "sacred power" of human hierarchies, not in an elitist culture and the prestige of the "governing classes," but *in our neighbor in need*, recognized and served as our brother or sister, and *in the multitude of poor and outcast*, with their privations, their misery, and their hope. God's dynamic presence and summons is not in the simulated order and cliquish security of a classist, repressive society, but in a longing and an effort for a more just and more human life and coexistence, along the path of love, solidarity, and the surrender of our very life. The God of liberation is not in competitive, monopolistic economic success, not in the technological progress and finicky welfare of a privileged minority, but in the experience of solidarity we behold in a lowly people, in communities of brothers and sisters, in which we acknowledge ourselves to be responsible for one another, and where we learn to share goods and services. The God of our deliverance comes to us in the inspiring utopia of a universal relationship of love, a utopia that mobilizes us for action.

As we read the Bible and discover its living tradition from the outlook of the poor, we find that if there is a "sacred" dimension and "religious" experience when it comes to the power of the great, repressive order, and the individualistic accumulation of wealth, it is the experience of the negative or perverse sacred: an idolatry of wealth and "structures of sin," the gods of oppression, the "Prince of this world." These are lying, lethal gods. They are this for the outcast, oppressed multitudes, of course; this goes without saying. But they are deadly, mendacious gods for the dominating minorities as well (cf. Matt. 6:19-24; Luke 4:5-8, 12:13-34, 16:1-15, 20:20-26, 22:39-53; John 12:31-32, 14:30; Rev. 13:1-18). The true God is the God of the Beatitudes and the Magnificat, the God of the Reign bestowed on the poor and those who hunger and thirst for justice, the God who raises him who has been crucified by the powers and sacred hierarchies of this world, the "all in all" God of universal reconciliation and kinship; in brief, the God of life, the God of a full life, shared by all.

From the locus of the impoverished and repressed of the earth, that true God communicates the wisdom and power of the divine Spirit, distributes gifts and talents, *with an appeal to human responsibility* to reverse the social dynamics of greed and domination and build a coexistence of justice, solidarity, and love. This God appeals to the generous, intelligent responsibility of individuals, groups, and organizations, and a whole people. This God is determined to have a response on the part of the individual or the people to a divine, summoning, and challenging word — to the divine initiative of the first deliverance and founding covenant, and then of radical deliverance and a new covenant of Jesus Christ. This God will have a response that will mean *conversion* — a turning away from idols to the service of the one God living and true, a renunciation of endless apostasies of sin in favor of perseverance in fidelity to the God of the covenant. Or conversely, this God will have radical liberation from sin — a conversion and fidelity to the living God verified in a love marked by solidarity with the needy and a commitment to justice in behalf of the oppressed.

The revelation of God in the history of the oppressed — a revelation bestowed in behalf of their liberation, committing the responsibility of human beings — has been documented, as we have suggested, all through the Bible.[10] This revelation stretches from the founding event of the Exodus from Egypt and the covenant of Sinai, to the gospel of the Reign and the Paschal event of Jesus Christ, to the sure hope of new heavens and a new earth where justice shall dwell and God will actually be "all in all." This is the content of the historical traditions of Israel, and of the laws intended to guarantee the people's coexistence in the land of promise. This is the burden of the preaching of the prophets, the prayer of the psalms, and the hope of the apocalypses. This is the proclamation, when all is said and done, of the gospel of Jesus, the message of the apostles, and the practice of the primitive Christian communities. The God of the Bible is always — and ever more clearly and more radically — the God who liberates the oppressed, the God who is revealed to us and challenges us from the midst of the poor of the earth, the God who expects of us, as the substance of authentic religious worship, that we show mercy to the needy and make a commitment to justice and peace in our world.

IV. GOD IN UNJUST SUFFERING AND VIOLENT DEATH

We notice, however, in the step-by-step faith pilgrimage of which we speak, and in the theology that accompanies it, a certain shift of focus, roughly corresponding to the two periods referred to above. No mere academic research is at stake here. What is at stake is a response to the historical process experienced by our peoples, whose poverty, cruel repression, and frustrations have generally worsened. In the first period, then, the crucial task was the arousal of a social awareness and of practices of political liberation. Currently, in wide regions of Latin America, fortitude in suffering and the hope of future liberation are more evident. In the former circumstances, the focus of reflection was on the "oppression/liberation" antithesis; now it appears to be rather on "death/life."

This shift of focus is reflected in the very titles of the more important theological works published in these respective periods. For the first period, we might cite *A Theology of Liberation*[11] and *The Power of the Poor in History*[12] by Gustavo Gutiérrez, as well as *Theology for a Nomad Church* by Hugo Assmann.[13] Here, God as such appears especially as the *God who delivers* from oppression. For the second period, we may mention *La misión del pueblo que sufre* (Carlos Mesters),[14] *Desde el lugar del pobre* (Leonardo Boff),[15] "Dios de vida, urgencia de solidaridad" (Jon Sobrino),[16] and *On Job: God-Talk and the Suffering of the Innocent* (Gutiérrez).[17] And here God appears especially as the *God of life* amid so many forces of death.

In the first period—as we have indicated—the principal biblical referents are the Exodus, the pre-Exilic prophets, and Jesus' ministry in Galilee. In the second, they are rather the prophets of the Exile, the psalms and the apocalypses, and Jesus' final journey to Jerusalem. In the former circumstances Jesus appears as the new Moses, the Messiah "Son of David," and God as the *God of the Reign*, who takes the side of the poor and marginalized to lead them to the new land of justice. In the latter circumstances Jesus appears also as the "servant of Yahweh" and the new Job, and God more emphatically as the *Father of Jesus*, who allows his dearly beloved Son to die in the extreme impotence of the cross, and who then raises the Crucified One from the dead.

But what we find reflected in this shift is not only an objective process in the history of our peoples. We also find the subjective change experienced by personnel of the church, who have shifted the focus of their activity from the dominant sociocultural centers or small, more politicized minorities to the "peripheral" majorities of the poor and marginalized. Here they not only proclaim anew the Paschal message and summon the people to read the gospel in community, but also learn things from the age-old suffering and traditional Christianity of the poor themselves.[18]

Jesus Christ, the Messiah of God who reveals to us God's true face and committed love for us, is the one who was persecuted and crucified, who continues his passion in the oppressed of our land and in all of the crucified of history. At the same time he is the one who was raised—the conqueror of unjust suffering and violent death, the liberator of human beings from the root of all their oppressions. He is the "Author of life" (Acts 3:15; cf. Heb. 2:10, 12:2), authentically human life and community, the "firstborn of many brothers" and sisters (Rom. 8:29; cf. Col. 1:18) in the full joy of the Father and the Reign of God.

The first dimension of Jesus, that of the *Crucified One,* has always had deep roots in the religious faith of our humble people, ever since the first evangelization of the continent and the first prophetic testimonials of the "scourged Christs of the Indies" (Las Casas). This dimension is the identification the oppressed themselves recognize in the images—so abundant and expressive throughout Latin America—of Christ humiliated and covered with wounds. The crucifix and Good Friday are the core of the traditional piety of the people. It is always accompanied by the Christian recollection, so important and expressive among the poor, of the beloved departed, especially when they have been victims of a violent death.

The second dimension, that of the one who was *raised*, has become more and more salient with the new evangelization of the religious faith and life expressions of our people, in and around the base communities. In fact, this new evangelical awareness has entailed a new outlook on the other dimension, that of Jesus Crucified, the more historical perspective of the conflict that prevails in society. Jesus suffers persecution and dies on the gibbet of the cross not only because "thus it had been written," and surely not by the direct "will of God." He suffers all of this because he is faithful to his mission to the end, in a society dominated by the power of sin. In a society ruled by an idolatry of money, by the arrogance of the great, and by a formalistic, corrupt "piety" and "religious observance," it is logical to expect that Jesus' proclamation of the Reign to the poor, his program of the Beatitudes, and his practice of the liberation of the oppressed, should enter into a conflict to the death with the dominant "values" and power groups. It is these groups who slander and persecute, sentence and execute, Jesus the Christ of God.

In contrast with the religious ideology of sacrifice, or the theological theory of penal expiation for sin, the Crucified One is not seen as having taken on sin, supposedly replacing sinners and making reparation "for" them.[19] On the contrary—in a theological perspective that we see to be more Johannine than Pauline—sin, with all of its lying, murderous might, is seen in the crucifiers. These persons—far from being instruments of God!—are instruments of sin, oppression of the humble, and deicide.

In this explanation, God—the God of the Reign, the Father of Jesus—is regarded as present and active not so much in the passion and cross as in the resurrection. On the cross, God is seen as absent—rejected, routed. God as mighty God is absent, present as a suffering God, suffering with the Crucified One. God is held to be revealed, paradoxically, as a God marginalized, outcast, repressed, tortured to death. Where God is seen acting with grandeur and power, on the other hand, is in the God who raises Jesus, the Christ and the dearly beloved Son. As in the first apostolic preaching,[20] God appears as the one who wondrously vindicates the one unjustly condemned—the God who raises and bestows glorious, astonishingly fecund life on the one the oppressors have executed so cruelly in their attempt to erase his countenance from the face of the earth.

Thus, our sisters and brothers, this oppressed people, can say: God is with us always, especially at the most difficult times. It is then that we experience the God who inspires and encourages, who unites us in service and commitment. Thus, the church communities more directly affected by the repression of the church have been empowered, through the Spirit of the one who was raised, to live, in our own day, the rich Christian tradition of persecution and martyrdom.[21] Here is an authentic evangelical tradition, and one that has been of enormous enlightenment and support to us in these years. Shepherds like Romero and Angelelli have known how to interpret it with prophetic lucidity—and deepen it with the witness of their martyrdom.

And so it comes about that, *beyond the death* of those persecuted and murdered "for the sake of the justice" of the Reign of God, words like these keep echoing in our ears: "If they kill me, I shall rise again in the Salvadoran people." "May my blood be the seed of freedom." "You shall rise again in the struggle of the people." Today, men and women like these are our confessors and our martyrs. It is they who, along the course of the pilgrimage of our oppressed people, are the great witnesses of Jesus raised, and of the God of life.

V. MERCIFUL FATHER

The invocation of the divinity as Father is not exclusive with biblical religion. On the contrary, the occurrence of this invocation in the Hebrew scriptures is rather discreet by comparison with its frequency among the peoples who precede or surround Israel in the ancient East.[22] For the Bible, in contrast with the other religions, God is the creator of human beings, their maker, on the basis of a free divine initiative. They are different from God. It is not as if God had generated them by some natural process; nor have they emanated from the divine being itself in the form of a more or less deficient expression of the same. Rather, the God of Israel is the God *of* the poor, *of* the patriarch Abraham. In no wise does God appear as the actual patriarch or mythic ancestor of the people. In this sense, Yahweh, for Israel, is first of all a God of gratuitous encounter and concrete pilgrimage, rather than of origins and of universal, necessary destiny. Yahweh is the God of history and historical hope, rather than the God of cosmic nature and an absolute future. Therefore when God is called Father in the Bible, and human beings (or the people) are called God's children, the reference is to an option, or "ad-option," on the part of God, and not to an intrinsic property of the human condition.

In the Bible expressions like "merciful Father" or "rich in mercy" do not refer to a necessary essence of God from which the nature of human beings would derive. Instead, they speak — symbolically — of an attitude freely adopted by a transcendent, intensely personal God. This attitude is understood as that of a father who is attentive to the call of his children, a parent ever disposed to pardon from the heart those who have withdrawn but who turn back once more, ever ready to lift the fallen, ever desirous of giving them good things and leading his children along the road of liberty and life. Indeed, more than an attitude of the "heart" of a father, this attitude is rather that of the "bowels" of a mother, which wrench at the sight of the suffering of her innocent creatures, or thrill with inexpressible delight at the return of a lost child. Nothing could be further from the philosophic conception of impassible perfection and immutable principle, essentially beyond the reach of human contingency.[23] The living God of the Bible, whom our people are rediscovering today, and continuing to seek along their route, is the holy, transcendent God, the fullness of life and power. But the people discover this God because this God has wished to become involved in our history in order to enter into communion with us. This God has done so from the free and gratuitous movement of a visceral love for us — for a suffering, sinful people.[24]

It is against this background that we must understand the God of Jesus' gospel message, the God of the Beatitudes.

The material of the Sermon on the Mount, which Matthew presents as Jesus' inaugural discourse (Matt. 5 – 7), is not the transcendent world of God as such, nor even — directly — the "supernatural" activity of God in our own world. The material of the Sermon on the Mount is precisely this world of ours itself, the most ordinary elements of human existence: wailing and rejoicing, work performed for food and clothing, poverty and wealth, domestic relations, injustice toward or solidarity with neighbors and companions, condemnation or pardon of enemies, and everything of the sort. The proclamation of the Sermon on the Mount focuses on all of these things in order to announce to us the unbelievable novelty that what is at stake in these affairs of ours is actually God, who seeks to intervene in them as our solicitous, infinitely able Parent.

But Jesus knows that this same God can allow us to be hungry, to suffer hatred and persecution, and to die. In fact, Jesus proclaims blessed those who suffer, the persecuted, and so on. How can this be reconciled with his call to concrete, unlimited filial trust?

The answer is simple. Jesus is telling us that the hour has come for rejoicing, because the Father has become attentive to the misery and exploitation that weigh upon the children of God. He summons us to make an effort to eradicate poverty and oppression from our midst. After all, God wishes to do away with them!

Thus, in his discourse, as in his entire messianic practice ("Go back and report to John what you hear and see" [Matt. 11:4; cf. Luke 4:16-22, 7:18-23]), Jesus reveals to us the tender, efficacious attention of God to the life of each of us, and especially to the multitude of the poor and forsaken. But Jesus' "revealing" this to us does not mean drawing back the curtain hiding "another world." He is only affording us the intuition that, at the center of our own lives, at the heart of this world, and among the poor and outcast of the earth, is the mysterious, salvific presence of God—of a God who takes our life and world just as they are—with their noblest expressions and aspirations, as well as all their weight of selfishness, cruelty and death—and has determined to set his creation free.

This message of a merciful Father appears with the greatest force in Jesus' confrontation with the God of the temple and the priests, and especially of the scribes and Pharisees (cf. Mark 2:1-3, 12, 12:38-40; Matt. 5:23-24, 7:21-23, 21:28-31, 23:1-36; Luke 8:1-3, 13:22-30, 15:1-32; John 7:11—11:54). In the power and authority of this particular elite—which was closest to the daily life of the simple people and possibly their worst oppressor—the gospels find the antagonist of Jesus' most frequently recurring, and most profound, confrontations. The scribes and Pharisees were the educated, and they were the teachers. Here were the fraternities of the pious—"clergy" and "religious"—who were closest to the people and who taught them. In their practice, and even more in the moral and religious discipline that they sought to impose on the people, Jesus discovers a formalistic degradation of biblical faith. The God of the covenant, who chooses persons out of pure love, gathers them together, and delivers them, has become a "god of law," the enjoiner of myriad "observances," and the appointer of stern retribution. Jesus' God has becomes the marginalizer and oppressor of the lowly, the people. Here is a harsh god, obsessed with a long series of prohibitions and commandments, taboos or religious practices, missteps to be avoided or good works to be multiplied, all of which he draws up on his balance sheet, his "book," and all of which deserve the reward or punishment sure to come, in just measure, in this life or the next. Along this route, a relationship with the living God, freely loving and acting in human history, forgiving and radically liberating, and awaiting from men and women a response from the heart, is degraded into a cold moralism of intrinsic justice, a prideful pretension to an accumulation of merit before God and in competition with one's fellows, in a ritualism of religious practices motivated by fear or niggardly interests. Here Jesus' criticism of temple ritualism converges with a criticism that had already seen a long history in the prophetic tradition of Israel: "It is love that I desire, not sacrifice, and knowledge of God rather than holocausts" (Hos. 6:6; cf. Matt. 9:13, 12:7). Here is Jesus' criticism of a sacral god, the god of a "religious world" apart, a god cut off from daily life, with his castes of consecrated holiness specialists. Here is Jesus' criticism of a hierarchic god, one accessible to the people only through the mediation precisely of these castes with their supposed monopoly on religious knowledge and sacred power.

In this sociocultural and religious context — so strongly marked by Pharisaism and the formalistic worship to which we have just referred — Jesus is born and lives. He is a member of the laity. He is interested in the lives and concerns of the common folk, and in those lives and concerns reveals to the people directly — and not by way of "religious" words or symbols — the Father's love and human beings' responsibility for the coming Reign. The signs wrought by Jesus are not liturgical rites, but human deeds calculated to heal and save men and women suffering from misery, marginalization, and demonic possession. Jesus "relativizes" any practice or religious "performance" with a concrete appeal to the well-being and worthy life of concrete persons. He teaches his disciples to recognize his risen presence and the Father's love, not in the temple and its rites, not in solitary contemplation, but in their neighbor suffering or sharing, and in the living experience of a community of sisters and brothers.

Jesus' God, then, appears, most strikingly, as the God of the lowly and simple, not of the learned and prudent (Matt. 11:25-27). Here is the God who is most radically revealed as a God of grace and pardon, as the Father who is gladdest when forgiving and giving life and who awaits our wholehearted response, in the divine presence, in behalf of our neighbors. In the condensed and mighty formulas of John's gospel, Jesus' God is a God of life and truth, a God in stark contrast with the god of the religious and cultural establishment, which shows by its practice that its god has been a murderer and a liar "from the beginning" (John 8:44; cf. 1 John 3:8-15). Here is the God of daily, "profane" life, with all of its so material joys and miseries, the God of the common folk, of the simple, of "this lot, that knows nothing about the law," the God of these sinners (John 7:49).

VI. FATHER OF JESUS AND OUR FATHER

The content of the entire biblical tradition reaches its plenitude and is synthesized in the gospel proclaimed by Jesus of Nazareth to the poor and outcast of his people, the message that the witnesses of the one who was raised began to spread throughout the underworld of the Roman Empire. The Good News is that God is at hand, preparing to exercise a royal and divine authority in a

Reign that has already begun with the humble practice of Jesus as he tore sin up by its very roots, and just as radically subverted the dominations of this world. Behold, that God has raised up the Servant of God Jesus, whom the tribunals of his nation had condemned, vindicating his divine sonship and universal Messianism, and our own universal kinship. Now God has vindicated the Holy Spirit, with its signs of interior activity, as the witness and invisible agent of this profound transformation of human life and coexistence, making all human beings children of God and setting them free, establishing them as co-heirs of the divine Reign and collaborators, in a communion of sisters and brothers, in the arrival of the fullness of this same Reign of justice and knowledge of the Father.

The actual power of the message of Jesus of Nazareth concerning the merciful Father lies neither in its internal logic or appearance of likelihood, nor in its consoling effect as religious discourse, but in the fact that it transmits Jesus' own experience — an authentically human experience of our life and our world, and at the heart of that human experience, an intimate experience of God as his Parent.

The Sermon on the Mount — like all of Jesus' preaching, dialogues, and polemical confrontations — transmits to us the words of a person who practices what he preaches and preaches what he practices. Jesus himself experiences the hard indifference of the rich. He knows the hatred and persecution of enemies. He meets the hungry and the weeping every day along his life journey, and he has made them his companions. He sees through hypocrites and superficial people at a glance. He knows the loving gaze of his divine Parent upon all of this misery and reacts to it just as that Parent does.

Jesus lives in the sight of women and men the life he describes in his parables and offers to his followers: a life staked entirely on the grand cause of the human being, which is God's cause; a poor life, threatened and assaulted, in the unwavering, serene certitude of being in the Father's hands. Jesus' entire life — all the way to his "*Abba*, . . . take this cup away from me" (Mark 14:36) — shows us his intimate secure conviction that nothing would be able to separate him from the love of his Parent. And he invites us to share this bedrock security by trusting in his personal experience as dearly beloved Son of God.

Indeed, for the gospel tradition, Jesus' life is governed by his awareness of living it in a unique relationship with God — with God his *Abba*. According to Luke, for example, the first and last words of his earthly life refer to his Father (Luke 2:49, 23:46). According to Matthew and Luke, "No one knows the Son but the Father, and no one knows the Father but the Son — and anyone to whom the Son wishes to reveal him" (Matt. 11:27, Luke 10:22; cf. Matt. 21:37, 24:36; John 1:18, 10:15, 17:1-8, 20-26). The knowledge here is one of intimate transparency, unlimited trust, and total commitment, a knowledge revealed precisely to "the merest children," to those "who are weary and find life burdensome" (Matt. 11:25-28). And Jesus' prayer, usually reported by the gospels in some particularly difficult or tragic situation in his life, expresses his limitless trust in his Father's love for him, and his own unreserved determination, in all things, with no ifs, ands, or buts, to try to see to it that that Father's "will be done."[25] Thus, on the eve of his passion, Mark tells us, Jesus addresses God with the Aramaic term *Abba* (Mark 14:36), the word children used in addressing their fathers in the intimacy of the family. It was unheard of, in Jesus' time and culture, that God would be addressed with this word.[26] Christians took the liberty of employing this same word—in the Spirit of Jesus—when they called "Our Father" (cf. Rom. 8:15, Gal. 4:6; cf. also Matt. 6:9, Luke 11:2, John 20:17). They were expressing this same shared experience that "neither death nor life, ... neither the present nor the future, nor powers, neither height nor depth nor any other creature, will be able to separate us from the love of God that comes to us in Christ Jesus, our Lord" (Rom. 8:38-39).

It is the very bones and blood of the gospel, then, that the *God of the Reign* is identical with the *Father of Jesus Christ*, his *Abba*. *Reign* is a political term; *Abba* connotes family intimacy.[27] In concrete terms, the Reign Jesus shows us in his practice as Messiah of the poor and the filial experience he reveals to his "least brothers" and sisters do not bring to the world a new hierarchy, a new religious dependency that would leave a people in the status of religious minors. Quite the contrary! This Reign and filial experience bring to the world a profound dynamism of equality, communion, and service among equals. Jesus the servant, the Messiah as persecuted prophet, who brings the world this kind of Reign of God, is God's only Son, now seated at the right hand of the Father. Jesus calls his disciples, whom he sends forth, not as servants, but as friends, his sisters and brothers. For them, the fact of having one Father and one Teacher does not authorize them to force themselves on one another as parents or teachers, but just the opposite; this fact is the strength of their companionship, deep friendship, and humble service among equals (cf. Mark 12:38-40, Matt. 20:20-28, 23:1-12; Luke 22:24-30; John 13:1-17).

After all, in the last analysis the root content of the message of Jesus Christ—and of the mystery of God—is love. And the love that is truly worthy of the name, the love in which God consists and which has been revealed to us in Jesus Christ, is not, in its profoundest mystery, a cascade of benefits in a relationship of monarchy and subordination, but rather communion among equals: the Father, the Son, and the Holy Spirit. The Spirit is in us and with us in the Son, facing the Father.[28]

Granted—and this, too, is part of the mystery of love and life—this communion among equals does not suppress difference in origin, or gratitude for the gift that founds that communion. The Father is still the Father, even, and especially, of the only Son. The Lord is still the Lord, even, and most of all, for his disciples and friends, among whom he is as one who serves. God is still God, even, and especially, of creatures whom God has personally chosen and sanctified and whom God loves "in the Son." But the very difference is assumed and transformed in the dynamism of communion among equals—to their inexhaustible surprise and greater joy in love.

On the limited level of our experience we may experience this when it falls to us to be teachers, with a certain degree of commitment. The youth of our popular world may experience this when they themselves come to be parents. In either case our concern will not be to assert our own authority, to maintain distance or possession, but quite the contrary; now our urgent desire will be to give the best we have to offer, in order that our child or disciple may grow, may become open to receive from others rather than merely disposed to bestow, may be free. Now our impatient longing and hope will be that this "minor" of ours may come to be equal to ourselves as soon as possible, and be — if he or she so desires, freely — our friend and companion.

In this perspective there appears in our cultural situation, even for the youth of our people with their so frequently traumatic family history, a new access route to the understanding that God is our Father.[29] We can understand God as Parent from a point of departure in our experience of *having* earthly parents, of course; but we can understand the same thing (and this is often the only way for our youth, as far as having a father is concerned) from our experience of *being* a parent. This seems to be the route Jesus himself suggests in the gospel: "Would one of you hand his son a stone when he asks for a loaf . . . ? If you, with all your sins, know how to give your children what is good, how much more will your heavenly Father!" (Matt. 7:9-11). In the same Sermon on the Mount we are taught to ask the Father to give us "our daily bread," and to "forgive us the wrong we have done as we forgive those [our children?] who wrong us" (Matt. 6:11-12). God our Father is like the parent in the parable in Luke (15:11-32), who so tenderly welcomes and forgives, who will not even think of leaving his prodigal child in this servile condition, but forgives and forgets and spreads a feast — and hopes that his other child ("You are with me always, and everything I have is yours") — will act in the same way with his returning brother.

VII. FIRST PERSON OF THE TRINITY

In conclusion, I should like to observe that (except in the passage in which we speak expressly of the divine mystery of the communion of Father, Son, and Spirit) whenever we speak of God here we are referring concretely to the God of Abraham, Isaac, and Jacob — the intensely personal God of a self-revelation to our ancestors as liberator and God of life, the very God whom Jesus of Nazareth acknowledged as his own God and with whom, as his *Abba*, he maintained a unique relationship, the very God who raised the Crucified One and whom we, moved by the Spirit, can invoke in truth as our Father. We are not referring to a "God" of the universe and of life in the sense of the religions of the earth, or to a supreme Being or absolute Future discerned by philosophy. Neither are we referring, in terms of Christian theology beginning in the fourth century, to that "one God who is the Most Holy Trinity" (St. Augustine).[30] We are not calling these perspectives into question, but here we have preferred to follow the obvious usage of the Christian scriptures itself, as we have rediscovered how to read it today in our communities among the poor.

In the Christian scriptures the terms *one God*, or simply *God* (*ho Theos*), does not mean — as it does for later theology — the unity (of substance) of the three divine Persons. In the Christian scriptures, these terms are more direct and concrete. They designate the "God of our fathers," who has been revealed to believers today as the "God and Father of Jesus Christ."³¹ This is always the case, first of all, when we find these expression on the lips of Jesus. But it is also the case, for example, in the trinitarian formulas of Christian faith that we find so frequently in the Pauline letters: "Lord Jesus ... Spirit ... God" (Rom. 15:30; cf. 1 Cor. 12:4-6, 2 Cor. 1:21-22, 13:13; Eph. 4:4-6; 1 Pet. 1:2). In other words, these terms denote (in later theological language) the person of God the Father. This is the denotation these terms still have in the ancient Christian "symbols" (which we still use today as the "creed" of our common faith). Through these "symbols," with their tripartite structure, we profess the trinitarian faith of the church. But when, in the first article of the Creed, we state our faith in "one God," we are speaking not of the "one God in three persons," but of the person of the Father. This is concretely "the God" (*ho theos*), one and personal, of whom the "one Lord" Jesus Christ is the "only Son," and who (with that Son) pours forth in our hearts "the Holy Spirit."

— Translated by Robert R. Barr

NOTES

1. Cf. Juan Luis Segundo, *Our Idea of God*, trans. John Drury (Maryknoll, N.Y.: Orbis Books, 1973); Ronaldo Muñoz, *Nueva conciencia de la Iglesia en América latina* (Santiago de Chile, 1973); CLAR, *La vida según el Espíritu en las comunidades religiosas de América latina* (Bogota, 1973); Frei Betto, et al., *Experimentar Deus hoje* (Petrópolis, Brazil, 1974).

2. Cf. Victorio Araya, *God of the Poor: The Mystery of God in Latin American Liberation Theology*, trans. Robert R. Barr (Maryknoll, N.Y.: Orbis Books, 1987), with its extensive bibliography.

3. Cf. Rubem Alves, *Religión: ¿opio o instrumento de liberación?* (Montevideo, 1970); Gustavo Gutiérrez, *A Theology of Liberation: History, Politics and Salvation*, trans. Caridad Inda and John Eagleson (Maryknoll, N.Y.: Orbis Books, 1973); Hugo Assmann, *Opresión-liberación: desafío a los cristianos* (Montevideo, 1971).

4. Cf. Jon Sobrino, "La centralidad del 'reino de Dios' en la teología de la liberación," *RLT* (San Salvador) 9 (1986), pp. 247-81; reprinted as chapter 15 in this volume.

5. Cf. J. L. Sicre, *Los dioses olvidados: poder y riqueza en los profetas preexilicos* (Madrid, 1979); Pablo Richard, et al., *The Idols of Death and the God of Life: A Theology*, trans. Barbara E. Campbell and Bonnie Shepard (Maryknoll, N.Y.: Orbis Books, 1983); Sobrino, "Reflexiones sobre el significado del ateísmo y la idolatría para la teología," *RLT* (San Salvador) 7 (1986), pp. 45-81.

6. Cf. Leonardo Boff, *Jesus Christ Liberator: A Critical Christology for Our Time*, trans. Patrick Hughes (Maryknoll, N.Y.: Orbis Books, 1978); Jon Sobrino, *Christology at the Crossroads: A Latin American Approach*, trans. John Drury (Maryknoll, N.Y.: Orbis Books, 1978); José Comblin, *Jesus of Nazareth*, trans. Carl Kabat (Maryknoll, N.Y.: Orbis Books, 1976); Hugo Echegaray, *The Practice of Jesus*, trans. Matthew J. O'Connell (Maryknoll, N.Y.: Orbis Books, 1984).

7. Cf. K. Schäfer, "The Testimony of Jesus about God," *Concilium* vol. 6, no. 8 (1972); Edward Schillebeeckx, "The 'God of Jesus' and the 'Jesus of God,' " *Concilium* vol. 3, no. 10 (1974). Sobrino, *Christology at the Crossroads*.

8. These are the words of the *Symbolum* of the First Council of Constantinople, A.D. 381 (Denziger, no. 150).

9. Cf. Vatican Council II, *Gaudium et Spes*, nos. 34, 38-39.

10. Cf. J. Severino Croatto, *Liberación y libertad: pautas hermenéuticas* (Buenos Aires, 1973); Carlos Mesters, *El misterioso mundo de la Biblia* (Buenos Aires, 1977); idem, *Defenseless Flower: A New Reading of the Bible*, trans. Francis McDonagh (Maryknoll, N.Y.: Orbis Books, 1989), pp. 55-155; Elsa Tamez, *Bible of the Oppressed*, trans. Matthew J. O'Connell (Maryknoll, N.Y.: Orbis Books, 1982); Carlos Mesters et al., "A Biblia como memoria dos pobres," *Revista Eclesiástica Brasileira* (Petrópolis, Brazil) 173 (1984); Ana Flora Anderson, et al., "Caminho da libertaçaõ," *Revista Eclesiástica Brasileira* (Petrópolis, Brazil) (1984).

11. As cited in note 3.

12. *The Power of the Poor in History: Selected Writings*, trans. Robert R. Barr (Maryknoll, N.Y.: Orbis Books, 1983), a collection of earlier writings.

13. Hugo Assmann, *Theology for a Nomad Church*, trans. Paul Burns (Maryknoll, N.Y.: Orbis Books, 1975; originally published in Spanish in 1973).

14. Carlos Mesters, *La misíon del pueblo que sufre* (Madrid, 1983).

15. Leonardo Boff, *Desde el lugar del pobre* (Bogota, 1984). Cf. idem, *Faith on the Edge: Religion and Marginalized Existence*, trans. Robert R. Barr (New York: Harper & Row, 1989).

16. *Diakonía* (Managua), no. 35 (1985). Cf. idem, *The True Church and the Poor*, trans. Matthew J. O'Connell (Maryknoll, N.Y.: Orbis Books, 1984), pp. 125-59.

17. Gustavo Gutiérrez, *On Job: God-Talk and the Suffering of the Innocent*, trans. Matthew J. O'Connell (Maryknoll, N.Y.: Orbis Books, 1987).

18. Cf. Ronaldo Muñoz, *The God of Christians*, trans. Paul Burns (Maryknoll, N.Y.: Orbis Books, 1990), chap. 2: "God on Our Journey in Faith."

19. We are not questioning the biblical theology of expiatory sacrifice, applied to the death of Christ by the New Testament with reference—especially—to the Servant of Yahweh in Isaiah 53. Our communities' faith perception does contrast with the "theological theory" (of medieval origin) and the "ideology" that we have mentioned and that are so used and abused in the pulpit today. See Boff, *Teología del cautiverio y de la liberación*, 3d ed. (Madrid, 1985), pp. 179-204; idem, "How to Preach the Cross of Jesus Christ Today?" in *Passion of Christ—Passion of the World* (Maryknoll, N.Y.: Orbis Books, 1987), pp. 129-133.

20. Cf. J. Schmitt, *Jésus ressuscité dans la prédication apostolique* (Paris, 1949).

21. Cf. Ivo Lesbaupin, *Blessed are the Persecuted: Christian Life in the Roman Empire, A.D. 64-313*, trans. Robert R. Barr (Maryknoll, N.Y.: Orbis Books, 1987); Boff, *Passion of Christ—Passion of the World*; idem, "Systematic Reflection on Martyrdom," *Concilium* 163 (1983). J. Hernández, "Martyrdom Today in Latin America," *Concilium* 163 (1983); "Espiritualidad del martirio," *Diakonía* (Managua) 27 (1983).

22. Cf. W. Marchel, *Abba, Vater!* (Düsseldorf, 1963); C. Orrieux, "La paternité de Dieu dans l'Ancien Testament," *Lumière et Vie* (Lyon) 104 (1971):59-74.

23. Cf. Abraham Heschel, *The Prophets* vol. 2 (New York: Harper & Row, 1962), chap. 6; Wolfhart Pannenberg, "La asimilación del concepto filosófico de Dios como problema dogmático de la antigua teología cristiana," in Pannenberg et al., *Cuestiones fundamentales de la teología sistemática* (Salamanca, 1976), pp. 93-149; Jürgen Moltmann, *The Trinity and the Kingdom: The Doctrine of God*, trans. Margaret Kohl (San Francisco: Harper & Row, 1981).

24. Cf. Albert Gélin, *The Key Concepts of the Old Testament*, trans. George Lamb (New York: Sheed and Ward, 1955); T. C. Vriezen, *An Outline of Old Testament*

Theology (Oxford, 1958); Yves Congar, "Mercy, Sovereign Attribute of God," in Congar, *The Revelation of God*, trans. A. Manson and L.C. Sheppard (New York: Herder and Herder, 1968); W. Eichrodt, *Theology of the Old Testament* vol. 1 (Philadelphia: Westminster, 1961); G. Von Rad, *Old Testament Theology*, vols. 1-2 (New York: Harper, 1962-65); Heschel, *The Prophets* vol. 2; A. Deissler, "La revelación personal de Dios en el Antiguo Testamento," in *Mysterium Salutis*, ed. vol. 2/1 (Madrid, 1969), pp. 262-311; H. Cazelles, "Le Dieu du Yahviste et de l'Elohiste . . .," in *La notion biblique de Dieu* (Gembloux, 1976), pp. 77-89; B. Andrade, *Encuentro con Dios en la historia: estudio de la concepción de Dios en el Pentateuco* (Salamanca, 1985).

25. Cf. José Comblin, *La oración de Jesús* (Santiago de Chile, n.d.); Sobrino, *Christology at the Crossroads*, pp. 146-78.

26. Cf. T. W. Manson, *The Teaching of Jesus* (Cambridge, 1959), pp. 89-115.

27. Cf. Moltmann, *The Trinity and the Kingdom*; Leonardo Boff, *Trinity and Society*, trans. Paul Burns (Maryknoll, N.Y.: Orbis Books, 1988), pp. 28-30.

28. S. Vergés, *Dios es amor: el amor de Dios revelado en Cristo según Juan* (Salamanca, 1982); Boff, *Trinity and Society*.

29. Cf. A. Vergote, *The Religious Man*, trans. Marie-Bernard Said (Dayton, Ohio: Pflaum Press, 1969); Paul Ricoeur, et al., *The Conflict of Interpretations*, ed. Don Ihde (Evanston: Northwestern University Press, 1974); A. Manaranche, *Creo en Jesucristo hoy* (Salamanca, 1973), pp. 149-57: "La simbólica del Padre."

30. Augustine, *De Trinitate*, Book I, chap. 6, no. 9.

31. See Karl Rahner, "*Theos* in the New Testament," in Rahner, *Theological Investigations*, vol. 1 (Baltimore: Helicon Press, 1961); Bernard Lonergan, *De Verbo Incarnato*: "Thesis Prima (ad Usum Auditorum Editio Altera" (Rome, 1961); J.N.D. Kelly, *Early Christian Creeds* (London: Longmans, 1950; New York: Green, 1950).

19

Jesus of Nazareth, Christ the Liberator

CARLOS BRAVO

I. STARTING POINT

1. The Faith of an Oppressed and Believing People

Christian faith refers to three histories: (1) present history; (2) its founding history, of Jesus; (3) which is mediated by the history of the church community, and is an experience of life rather than a reflection on life.

In Latin America this is the faith of an oppressed and believing people, in whose five-hundred-year history faith has been interrelated with both oppression and liberation. When we speak of oppression we are speaking about a conquest that manipulated God's name in favor of its economic and political interests, institutionalized violence, infant deaths, violation of human rights, illiteracy, hunger, unpayable foreign debt. And when we speak of living faith we are talking about love in practice, solidarity, the search for justice, organization, a sense of festival, and the experience of freely receiving in the presence of God, while struggling for life and freedom.

In an unjust and unequal society the person of the risen Jesus acquires a new dimension as the inspirer of liberating utopias. We who have been found by him see oppression and injustice in a different manner, not just as a social phenomenon, but as that which makes the Kingdom impossible and betrays the Father's name. Once this encounter has taken place we cannot behave as if it had not happened.

So faith begins to develop new formulations to speak about him. Our experience of Jesus as Messiah is mediated by the experience of life-threatening evils. This requires us to make a political and social commitment—to stand against the situation that prevents the Father's reign. In Jesus' life we do not find the explanation for why history is as it is. But we do find the impulse driving it to cease being a history of death and become a history of life. This is very important both to overcome the christology of resignation (of a suffering Christ with no resurrection) and the christology of domination (the imperial or conquering Christ who manipulates the memory of Jesus in favor of imperialist projects).

So we start by assuming that in Latin America we believe in Jesus as the Son of God, Lord of history, liberating Messiah. But we have to explain the content of these titles. They mean different things from the viewpoint of the conqueror's world and the world in which Indians die, from the viewpoint of the White House and that of Nicaragua.

2. The Truth of Confessions of Faith

This does not mean that the titles given to Jesus are neutral. They are formulas which in their time faithfully expressed in symbols of their own culture Jesus' saving significance for believers. Their validity comes from their continuity with the founding reality of Jesus as their *norm*, and the cultural reality of believers as their *cultural conditioning*.

Every expression of faith has to pass the double truth test: truth to Jesus in whom Emmanuel (the Son of God with us) was given and revealed to us, and truth to the particular people whose faith it expresses and bears. Hence the need for many different formulations of the inexhaustible mystery of Jesus. The Christian scriptures model this with many functional christologies, corresponding to different communities.[1]

First and foremost the Christian community must submit its formulations and practices to the critique made of them by Jesus' own practice. Otherwise they are subject to fashion and their language merely trendy (academic, neo-liberal, guerrilla, even extraterrestrial). This fails to convey the fundamental novelty of the fact of Jesus; that is, that God, while remaining transcendent and unattainable ("no one has ever seen God" [1 John 4:12]), entered history, moved within our reach in Jesus.

This raises a series of questions: why did Jesus come? To confirm history as it is, leaving it untouched? To condemn it? To save it? But how? By spiritu-alizing it? Ritualizing it? Telling it about God? Or by subverting it? In the unequal and oppressive society in which Jesus lived, which side was he on and what kind of life did he lead? The answers to these questions cannot be deduced from an idea of God prior to what was revealed about God in the new and unrepeatable life of Jesus of Nazareth. This is what gives meaning to the titles we give him, not the other way around with the titles showing the meaning of his life and behavior.

Second, in order to be faithful to Jesus the formulations reached by the Christian community must be mediated by a knowledge of the actual oppression from which history needs to be liberated in order to be faithful to Jesus. A Christian cannot just stand contemplating Jesus, or gasp in moral indignation against injustice. We must move on to make the connnection, that is, to "the effective pity" which liberates (cf. Exod. 3:7 ff.).

This leads to further questions: Is the christology elaborated faithful to this Jesus and to what continues to be his cause: liberation? To whom is it com-mitted: the oppressors or the oppressed? Is it in solidarity with the actual project for which Jesus gave his life? Does it realize that all theology, in fact, regardless of its intentions, takes sides and is involved, even when it claims to be neutral?

We realize that discipleship is the indispensable way to reach the mystery of Jesus, and that without it no theology enables us to "see" Jesus. In this chapter we shall try to express what we believe about Jesus from the standpoint of the poor.

The two aspects of theology, the narrative and the systematic, intermingle. The gospel narrative justifies us in not doing our theological thinking from above, but from below, not deductively but inductively. Finally, by way of con-clusion, we shall briefly sum up the fundamental statements of faith in Jesus.

II. CHRISTOLOGICAL NARRATIVE

1. Methodological Base: The Jesus Who Makes History

A fundamental task of biblical studies has been to determine the minimal structure of Jesus' practice. This is very important to ensure we do not end up with a fundamentalist reading, out of context, which manipulates Jesus' work to suit us. (We might turn him into a moral teacher or an ahistorical figure whose death would have nothing to do with his choices and his practice.) But this minimal structure is not enough for discipleship. In Latin America the search for the historical minimum regarding Jesus does not *formally* require the objective determination of what Jesus *did*, but rather what he *would do today*, if he were driven by the Spirit in this different situation. This task also requires a knowledge of the present situation. Both faith in Jesus and commitment to the situation today are fundamental for discipleship.[2]

In "Jesus who makes history" there are three dialectical terms which make up the fact of Jesus: (1) Jesus of Nazareth as the originating fact; (2) the Risen Jesus confirmed by the Father; (3) the movement of his followers in which his Spirit continues to inspire the promotion of his cause. This is what appears in Mark's final narrative (16:6ff.) (see Figure 1 below).

The first term, the thesis, is the life of Jesus of Nazareth, which is denied in the antithesis, the crucifixion. This in turn is overcome (but not ignored) by the resurrection, which is the synthesis, a "negation of the negation." It is not a return to life but a leap forward, which assumes the life denied by death and the death itself, whose marks are kept by the Risen Christ on his hands and side. But in its turn this resurrection becomes a thesis, which is denied as "verifiable here" in the tomb (antithesis). His new presence is in Galilee, by way of "going before them." He only precedes those who follow him. So following is the final synthesis; it is the epistemological condition for the experience of Jesus. Galilee, the place where Jesus worked, now becomes the place to follow him to, the only place where he can be "seen."

So, to "see" Jesus it is not enough to have access to the historical Jesus, who could become entombed. This would be like the women who sought him in the memory of one who died, to find and leave embalmed and inactive for the rest of history. We have to have the Paschal experience and to bear witness, which is what gives him permanent presence in history. We could show the terms again in a dialectical diagram (see Figure 2, p. 424).

In this task of following it is important to take seriously the humanity of

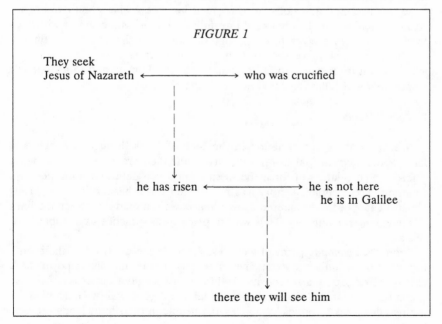

FIGURE 1

They seek
Jesus of Nazareth ⟷ who was crucified

he has risen ⟷ he is not here
he is in Galilee

there they will see him

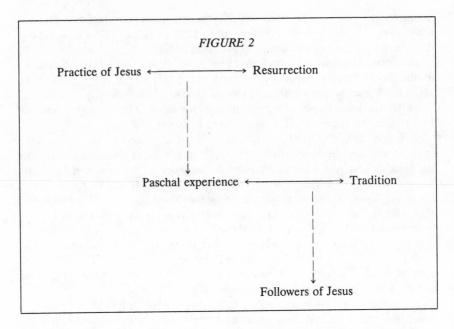

FIGURE 2

Practice of Jesus ⟷ Resurrection

Paschal experience ⟷ Tradition

Followers of Jesus

Jesus' consciousness. Not out of psychological curiosity. The important thing is his human reality and the very possibility of our being able to follow him. If Jesus was just an ordinary man, if he had not been confirmed by the Father as his Son in the resurrection, we *would not have* the Christian duty to follow him. If he was just God and not man (that is, if he were a kind of superman) we *could not* follow him. Neither could we follow him unless a chain of witnesses to his life had come down to us through the church, a chain which continues.

Therefore, it is important not only to know *what he did* but also *how and why* he did it; to respect God's decision to become human; and to assume the responsibility of following Jesus in promoting his cause.

2. Jesus' Roots

We know about the situation in the time of Jesus through research. We know about the principal groups that existed and their practices and ideologies. There is a correlation of forces between them which determines the people's situation. This people's history was not written down because no one writes about the fate of the conquered. Nevertheless, we can read it between the lines of the conqueror's history. Thus we can place Jesus' practice as a response to this situation.

From the *economic* point of view Jesus' people are deprived of their land, exploited by an unjust system. They must pay tribute and are impoverished; they lack living space and security. And this has a religious dimension, because it empties of content the promise of the land and goes against God's plan for the people. Jesus responds by helping the people in their basic living requirements: health and food. He breaks the exclusive circle of property and prophetically criticizes the rich. He turns human values upside down—the central thing is not to accumulate and to have, but to share. Therefore it will be the poor who possess the Kingdom and also the land. From this conviction he outlines the egalitarian utopia of the Kingdom: abundance for all based on the free gift of the Father to all God's children.

Politically this is a subject people, sometimes with bloody repression. No one responds to their just aspirations; they have no power to decide their own destiny. The people resist and agitate with Messianic hopes of liberation. But they are caught up in passivity and fatalism born of historical frustrations and the present foreign rule. This also has a religious dimension, because it is an affront to the reality of God's dominion over the people. In the face of this, Jesus announces the Father's sovereignty in favor of the poor. He prophetically denounces the ruling power through a lucid critical analysis and breaks the vicious circle of power and violence by denouncing its inability to build a newworld. He subverts the idea of authority by saying it can only be exercised in service. He outlines the egalitarian utopia of the Kingdom: peace born of justice, in which all God's children share.

In the *religious* sphere they are an expectant people but disorientated in their expectations. Excluded by their religious leaders as impure and as "the accursed people" without rights before God, they are marginalised from the promise of the Kingdom. This is where Jesus points to the principal contradiction: the establishment has derpived the people of hope. Jesus responds by offering them an alternative in God's preference for the poor and the marginalised. Thus he generates new hope. He corrects the Messianic idea of God's vengeance against sinners. He breaks the exclusive circle of the law of purity. He reincorporates the marginalised into the people of God. He strips the Jewish establishment of its authority and its interpretation of the the law, by teaching with authority. He changes the center of value for the law, which becomes a matter of loving—mercy and justice—rather than a matter of knowing or being pure. He prophetically criticizes the cult and its ritual observances. Thus he outlines the egalitarian utopia of the Kingdom. It is brotherhood and sisterhood deriving from a common Father and requires truth and freedom in this relationship.

3. Becoming Incarnate: Being a People

As he was a Jew, Jesus' image of God would be on the following lines: Yahweh is the God of the promise made to a people who do not possess the land; Yahweh is the God of the covenant, the people's only Lord, who has been supplanted by a foreign idolatrous power. Yahweh is the God of resistance to injustice, who hears the cry of the people and acts upon it. And now the time has come for Yahweh God to intervene.

Like the lay people to whom he belongs, and to whom he never ceases to belong, Jesus is offered many religious options: Apocalyptic thinking speaks of a world governed by evil, in which God has decided to intervene finally to inaugurate the kingdom. The Saducees reject this, secure in their own well-being, because the prophetic proclamations seem to them to be "liberationist novelties." The Pharisees commandeer the Kingdom, excluding the "accursed people who do not know the law" (John 7:39); they believe they can hasten its coming by strict observance of the law of purity and exclusion of the impure. There is an incipient armed resistance movement. John the Baptist speaks of another way of saving oneself from the "wrath to come," through baptism and conversion.

4. A Different God

This movement of John's is a challenge to the Jewish leaders: forgiveness is being offered in an outsider context, not just in Jerusalem. It is offered through conversion and baptism, and not through sacrifices and ritual purifications. Further, the mediator is a lay prophet, not a priest. News of the hopes being raised by John reach Jesus in Nazareth. The decision to leave home and go to find John is a vital one, which changes the direction of Jesus' life forever.

Jesus has an experience of a different God. This God is the people's *Abba* (Daddy). Poor people's lives matter to *Abba* (Matt. 6:9-13). They manifest the reality of God's fatherhood in history. God has decided to reign *now*, changing the situation of those who are outcast, not by magic, not through a power like that of the powerful, but through *kenosis* and hiddenness, because what is being offered is love.

Jesus experiences himself as absolutely and unconditionally committed to the task of announcing this Reign and making it accepted. It is in this that "being the Son of God in history" consists—being responsible for his life-project in a world of death, answering in the Father's name, doing it justice. We can speak of a conversion in Jesus: a change of life that leads him inward and drives him to communicate this new experience of God, to regenerate hope.

But how to go about it? What he has experienced clashes with the ideas of those in authority, even with what John is preaching. Jesus is tempted about the means. Should he continue along the same lines as John? Should he throw himself into a spectacular campaign of public Messianism? Should he ally himself with any of the already existing groups? What should he do about the foreseeable antagonistic reactions of the Jewish establishment? What is at stake is his faith in God—a God concerned with life, the *Father*, who cannot be subjected to a magic test doing violence to history, because God is offering *a free gift*, one which does not enter into alliance with other powers or do deals with any system. God's gift is free and not negotiable.

Mark and Matthew refer to the event that offered Jesus the occasion to avoid this situation of temptation: the arrest of John (Mark 1:14ff.; Matt. 4:12 ff.). Jesus will not continue John's work; he leaves the Jordan and decides to go off to Galilee to preach the Good News of the *Abba, who is coming to reign.*

5. The Reign of Life in a World of Death

Henceforth this will be his only cause. The life of the poor is where the Father's name is proved holy. The Kingdom cannot come until the lot of the poor has changed; it will not come while there is still injustice and inequality. Jesus' project is the reordering of two relationships (1) between human beings and God; whom they must treat as a Father; and (2) among human beings themselves, who should treat one another as brothers and sisters, God's family. The earth is the common heritage given by God for the life of all. Thus human beings can live together in the right way, dependent upon God and upon each other. Jesus says he has been sent to announce this Good News to the poor; it is the year of grace for the blind, the oppressed, the prisoners (Luke 4:18 ff.). His experience of the Father does not remain in heaven, because he knows his Reign is also an earthly and historical matter. It has to do with food for all people, forgiveness of sins, the overcoming of the actual evil that threatens us, the recognition of God's fatherhood, which makes us all equally children of God. For this to be possible Jesus makes three things clear: there is an irreducible opposition between the Kingdom and money, the Kingdom and prestige, and the Kingdom and power.

The Kingdom and Money

The kingdom belongs to the poor (Luke 6:20), and the rich as such have no part in it (Luke 6:24ff.; 16:19-31; Mark 10:23-25). Because money is an idol that seeks to be an absolute, it is not possible to serve God and money (Matt. 6: 24). Jesus does not idealize poverty; it is the result of sin, of exclusive possession. His ideal is abundance for all (expressed in the symbol of the banquet of the Kingdom). But for this to become possible he teaches detachment and giving up the goods of this world (Matt. 6: 25-33). He invites people to share in the life of the poor (Luke 14:13ff.), so that we can have a common family life on earth, neither rich nor poor. Meanwhile he stands firmly on the side of the poor, through effective pity for them and at the same time through love for the rich, whose complicity with the kingdom of Satan places them in danger. Money creates a divided society of haves and have-nots. It makes God's fatherhood in history impossible.

The Kingdom and Prestige

In a society which gave enormous importance to social status, Jesus stands on the wrong side, with those no one wants to be with; he realizes that prestige is also a divisive principle, opposed to equality. He declares that God is on the side of the little people, those who have no value for society (cf. Matt. 18:10). He says that welcoming them is welcoming him and the Father (Mark 9:37). He attacks the scribes and pharisees (Matt. 6:2, 5, 16; 23:5-7; Luke 11:45-52), and he is glad that the Father's self-revelation has been to the simple, not the wise (Matt. 11:25ff.). This is why Jesus makes himself the last of all and the servant of all, when in an act of "madness" to the world he kneels down before his disciples (John 13: 2-5). In the end he will die disgraced before all (Mark 15:29-32), outside the walls of the city, between two rebels (Mark 15:27ff.)[3]

The Kingdom and Power

The final divisive principle is what decides who has power over whom. This power tends to be murderous because it stays on top only by suppressing the rights of those it dominates. Against this power Jesus places service as the constructive force in the new society. He unmasks political power when he says "those who claim to govern nations behave despotically and the powerful oppress the people" (Mark 10:42). Speaking in code language—because of the danger he runs—he denies that Caesar has any right to collect an idolatrous tax. He demands that what belongs to God should be given back to God; that is, the government of the people, which Caesar unjustly holds (Luke 11:39-52; Matt. 23:1-36; Mark 7:1-23; 11:15-17; 12:1-12, 35-40). Because he stands on the side of the oppressed, Jesus will die "under the power of Pontius Pilate" as an accursed criminal (Gal 3:13) in total powerlessness and abandon.

6. The Galilean Spring

There was a real blooming of life around Jesus. Many hopes found an echo in his message and his behavior. To enlarge his sphere of action Jesus gathered a group of disciples, as new shepherds for the forsaken and ill-treated people (Matt. 9:36). At one point this call seems to have had an eschatological character; they will be the twelve foundations of the people of the promise. This is provocative to the establishment. The real Israel is being set up now in Galilee by common people. In this initial heterogeneous group some probably secretly hoped: that Jesus was the Messiah, one who would put an end to Roman rule, by military means, of course.[4]

Jesus' popularity becomes a temptation to Peter and other comrades, who see the opportunity for a popular triumph for their imagined Messiah. Jesus overcomes this temptation to regionalize the Kingdom in the illusion of a facile territorial triumph and decides to enlarge his field of action (Mark 1:35-38).

By his cures Jesus is not claiming to prove anything about himself, but to give signs of the liberating presence of the Father who reigns. Their importance does not lie in being anything exceptional, but rather in pointing people to God: "If by the finger of God I cast out demons, this is a sign that the kingdom of God has come upon you" (Luke 11:20). Identifying in a "scandalous" way with sinners, he also restores them to the promise, rescuing their dignity and freeing them from shame and guilt. By his solidarity he shows people that God accepts them.

The effects do not take long to show. The change taking place in the world of the poor through Jesus' actions makes people compare teaching with teaching, practice with practice, that of Jesus and that of the scribes, and to conclude that Jesus indeed teaches with authority. He speaks and changes the situation for the outcast. With the scribes it is the opposite; they talk and talk and nothing new ever happens. But this comparison is a warning to Jesus. The establishment will not easily tolerate such parallel authority (Mark 3:6), which is moreover beginning to make the people criticize their leaders (Mark 1:22, 23).

The connection between the miracles and the Kingdom was not plain. Jesus did not respond to the apocalyptic type of expectations and those aroused by John. He does not present himself as the bringer of God's judgment. To the question whether he is the one or should they wait for another, Jesus replies by quoting Isaiah. The culminating point of this text is not the miracles but the final phrase: "The poor have the good news preached to them" (Luke 7:22). The miracles are the sign that the alternative God is offering is true. They do not put an end to all misfortune and evil, but they clearly signal the direction faith in him should follow; his most important task is the struggle against all human misery, disease, hunger, ignorance, slavery, all kinds of inhumanity. And blessed are they who are not scandalized that this is what the Kingdom of God is like (Luke 7:23).

The first cloud appears when Jesus begins to increase activities that transgress the law of purity: he heals on the sabbath (Mark 1:21-23; 3:1-6; Luke 13:14ff.; Matt. 12:9-13); he becomes impure by touching the impure (Mark 1:3-31; 5:27,41; 6:5; Luke 13:12ff.), especially a leper (Mark 1:41-45), to make them feel God's nearness, which the establishment has deprived them of, declaring them to be accursed by God (John 7:39); he calls a tax-collector to follow him and eats with him and his friends (Matt. 9:9 ff.); he is not afraid of dealing with prostitutes (Luke 7: 36-50), to whom he also opens a door of hope in the Kingdom (Matt. 21:31). A number of women work with him. They too have been barred from any activity for the Kingdom by the Jewish laws of purity (Luke 8:1-3; Mark 15:40 ff.).

Arguments with the scribes and pharisees seem to have been frequent (Mark 2:1-3,6; 7:1-23; 11:15 – 12:48; Luke 11:37-53; Matt. 23; John 2:13-22; 5:16-47; 7:14-39; 8:12-59; 10:22-39). What is in question is not something peripheral to his faith but the very core of the reality of the God in whom he believes. The consequence is that very early on we hear of plans to bring about Jesus' death (Mark 3:6; Luke 4:22ff.; Matt. 12:14; John 5:16; 7:30, 44; 8:20, 59; 10:31; 11:8, 49-53, 56).

Jesus tries to protect himself against these threats. He never acts with foolish imprudence (cf. John 6:1, 15; 7:1-10; 8:1, 59b; 10:39ff.; 11:54; Luke 4:30; Matt. 12:15; Mark 3:7). In Mark, one of the objects of the parables appears to be to give the message in cryptic form to protect Jesus, who was accused of blasphemy (punishable by death 2:7), breaking the sabbath (also punishable by death, 3:2,6), being possessed by the devil (3:22) and mad (3:20). Perhaps he is expressing his own experience in his advice to his disciples to be "cunning as serpents and simple as doves" (Matt. 10:16b).

7. The Beginning of the Crisis

But what happens to the Kingdom? In the beginning Jesus expected the triumph of his religious mission, but later he began to realize that his mission would lead to a fatal conflict with his politicoreligious society. His disciples have false hopes and cannot understand (Mark 4:13, 35-41). He himself realizes he is at risk from his own work and the people (Mark 3:9ff.; 5:30-32). His compatriots are shocked by the works he does, seeing he is one of them (Mark 6:2ff.). Jesus understands the mortal logic of all this: no prophet is accepted by his own people (Matt. 13:57); prophets are murdered. But why does his work not arouse faith? (Mark 6:6a).

It is painful not to be able to make himself understood by his people. They did not understand John, and they do not understand him (Matt. 11:18 ff.). They do not realize that now the final era has arrived, that Elijah has already come. The cities in which he has done the most miracles are the ones most closed against him. His people have stubborn hearts; they do not want to think of anything beyond their own health and food for the day.

In this context Jesus intensifies his activity in the service of life and sends out the Twelve to widen his sphere of action. There was one event which must have had particular resonance among the oppressed people: what Mark enigmatically calls "that of the loaves" (6:52). A large crowd, which had been following Jesus for several days, was hungry. The people's situation does not bother their shepherds at all. So Jesus takes care of them (Mark 6:34). He not only gives them the word of God but also gives them food in abundance. In this way he shows that God feeds his people and that physical needs, hunger, and sickness, are a matter for the Kingdom.

The people go in another direction. They want him to lead them as their king (John 6:15). Jesus sends his disciples away, so that they do not encourage this kind of uprising (Mark 6:45); he takes leave of the people and goes into hiding (John 6:15). He faces this moment of temptation in prayer to his Father (Mark 6:46). Why do the people not see the signs of the Kingdom? Why are they only concerned with the material side of his activities?

The growing conflict with the establishment reaches its height, according to Mark's narrative, because his disciples eat without bothering about purification rites (7:1ff.). The Pharisees' criticism becomes the occasion for Jesus to unmask the deep unfaithfulness they hide beneath their apparent piety. They fuss about trivialities but violate the fundamental tenets of the law—mercy and justice—which are truly a matter of life and death for the people, whereas fulfilling ritual prescriptions is not.

Now Jesus is a danger to the Jewish establishment. So he has to get out of their reach. He does not go into Syrian territory on a missionary journey but to take refuge (Mark 7: 24). And there the Galilee crisis brews.

8. Crisis and Confirmation

Rahner speaks of "extreme crises of self-identification"[5] in Jesus. There are sufficient indications of the people's dismay as their interest in Jesus declines. They are disappointed by this Kingdom he proclaims. John the Baptist himself expresses this disappointment: "Are you the one who was to come or should we look for another?" (Matt. 11:2-6). Some of his disciples desert (John 6:67). Jesus stakes everything. "Who do people say that I am ... And you, who do you say that I am?" This is not an educational question laying the ground for teaching. The disciples' reply stays at a merely human level: "You are the Messiah" (Mark 8:29), with whose triumph they hope to be associated (Mark 9:34; 10:35-45). They misinterpret his Messiahship.

Such a proclamation does not fit the truth about Jesus, and under Roman rule it places him in obvious danger. This is why he corrects the reply and enjoins silence (Mark 8:30), but he takes on the struggle to the end: "I am going to die at the hands of men" (cf. Luke 9:44). It is quite clear what is important to Jesus and for what he has risked his life. Now he has to accept the consequences of having adopted the Father's cause and the cause of the poor. He does this convinced that the Kingdom is greater than the failure of his strategy. Violent death, perhaps by stoning (cf. John 8:59; 10:31-33), is now a real threat to him.

There must have been a serious problem with Peter in this matter; the community would not have just invented this confrontation between them. We are told that Peter rebuked Jesus (Mark 8:33). Orthodox in its formulation, his confession remained at the purely human level, and there was no room in it for such a radical commitment to the death. Jesus remonstrates with him in the harshest words he ever uses against anyone: "Get behind me, Satan." Peter's proposal is a temptation for him.

Jesus risks remaining alone (John 6:68). But he has to state honestly the change that has taken place in his mission. Because of it, anyone who goes on following him has to be ready for death (Mark 8:34-38). He proposes a new radical mode of discipleship. During the first stage the Kingdom was mediated by the preaching of conversion and by miracles. Now it is not just a matter of words and deeds. What is required is total commitment (Luke 12:49f.) to unmask the power that makes the Kingdom impossible: the religious power which has kidnapped the freely-giving God of the covenant and put in God's place a deity of laws, merits and purifications. Only with a total commitment can a free space for the Kingdom be created; the only way of saving one's life is to risk it with Jesus for the Kingdom (Luke 9:24-26).

In his prayer Jesus has a deep experience of confirmation by the Father (Luke 9:28). He has not preached himself or focused the people on his person; in everything he has behaved as the Son. Disaster strikes him because of the inevitable confrontation between his declaration for the Father and the poor, the outcast, in a world which speaks of a "God" who favors the select few. "This is my beloved Son in who I am well pleased. Listen to him" (Matt. 17:5). The voice confirms Jesus as the only way for the disciples. Now there will be neither Moses (Law) nor Elijah (Prophets) (Matt. 17:8); Jesus alone is enough, the Son who has done what pleases the Father and who is the one to follow.

9. Training of the Disciples

Unmasking the religious power is a challenge to the Jewish establishment, which will very probably end in death. But the disciples are not yet well enough trained to take on the cause of the Kingdom. In view of the certainty of approaching death, Jesus leaves off working with the people and decides to train his disciples (Mark 9:30-31a), in order to consolidate more organically the community which will make his mission possible. One by one he starts correcting their judgments and values. They have to understand that these are new times now; the coming of Elijah (John the Baptist, cf. Matt. 17:13) is the signal. In these times the conditions for fighting against evil are faith and prayer

(Mark 9:14-29). They must welcome the little ones (Mark 9:36ff.) because they are the ones God prefers (Mark 10:13-16); they have to understand that riches are a fundamental obstacle to the Kingdom (Mark 10:17-27), and as the ideal of the Kingdom is abundance for all, the way to it is poverty in order to share with those who have nothing (Mark 10:28-31); in the Kingdom the original equality between man and woman is fundamental (Mark 10:2-12). But above all, their hearts must be preparing for the style of the Kingdom. Instead of the disciples' ambitions for power, Jesus offers them service as the norm (Mark 9:33-35; 10:35-45); then they will be able to discern what alliances to make and which to reject (Mark 9:38ff.).

10. The Final Confrontation with the Jewish Establishment

Jesus' death only has meaning when it is seen from *after* the resurrection. But it is not enough to look at it from a Paschal perspective. We must also look at it as it was *before* the resurrection. And to do this first we must ask these questions: Why did Jesus go to Jerusalem and for what? Let us reply to these questions from the gospel texts themselves.

We will not go into the controversy about the number of times Jesus went up to Jerusalem and when. We start, rather from the obvious fact that there was a *last* journey to Jerusalem, in which the whole history of Jesus' difficult relationship with the establishment culminated. Jesus made this journey aware that "every prophet dies in Jerusalem."

Rather than formulating hypotheses on his intentions, let us look at what he in fact *does*. Three large blocks appear. In the first two Jesus is the principal character, and his actions unmask and condemn the establishment. In the third, Jesus hardly acts at all, he is the passive object of the whole drama and is condemned and assassinated by the establishment.

Jesus Unmasks the Establishment at Its Center

John and the Synoptics show the confrontation over the temple differently. We shall follow the Synoptic account because, whatever happened, this fact was decisive in Jesus' last confrontation with the Jewish establishment: the fundamental accusation is that he intends to destroy it.

The moment comes when Jesus decides to confront the establishment at its center. What he said in outlying Galilee is not enough. He chooses the moment of the passover celebration, the festival of Jewish liberation. It is a careful, thought-out decision, and he knows his life is at stake. He is aware of the Messianic hopes that have arisen around him. The corrections he has made to these expectations have not been enough. Therefore his first action is symbolic; he enters Jerusalem on a donkey. This means hopes of his leadership cannot be maintained.

The scope of the temple episode has been much discussed. We think it should be interpreted not as a purification, after which it could go on being the symbolic center of the people of the promise. We see it as a taking over of the temple, whose sterility it unmasks. Jesus preaches its destruction and the need to abandon it, because God's presence is no longer to be found there (cf. Matt. 27:51ff.).

But why does Jesus go against the religious establishment and not against the Roman political establishment? We must seek for what light we can find on this question. It is evident that Jesus rejects Roman rule, which goes against the exclusive Reign of Yahweh. The burden of the tribute is not only unjust, but it is also intolerable because it appertains to the cult of the emperor. Because of the danger of the situation he says in coded language: "Render to Caesar this idolatrous coin which is a blot upon Israel and give to God what belongs to him, which is the government of the people, unjustly held in Caesar's power." He analyzes Rome's political domination and judges it unjust (cf. Mark 5:9,13; 10:42; 12:16,17; 13:14; Luke 13:32ff.)[6] But the travesty the religious leaders make of God and his project is the principal obstacle to the people's hope.

So two elements are fundamental to Jesus' condemnation: the way in which he unmasks the temple, revealing its sterility and injustice ("not one stone will be left upon another"), and the opposition to the payment of tribute, for this is how his enemies interpret his words. The people, or at least some of them, support him and acclaim him. We may suppose these are the ones who have come with him from Galilee, not the people of Jerusalem, who are keener to maintain their status than to support change. But this only sharpens the conflict with the authorities, who cannot find a way to kill him. The opportunity is offered by the treachery of one of the Twelve, Judas.

The Meaning of Meaninglessness

The circle closes round Jesus. What is he to do? In the context of the memorial of the passover, a liberation frustrated by the domination under which they are living in their own country, and facing betrayal, Jesus understands that this is not the moment to flee or to resist violence.

Now the word *denounce* is not enough. The moment has come to *renounce*, so that his death will openly show the murderous nature of that power which is so seductive, especially when it is exercised in God's name, but which continues to cause the death of every prophet, because it continues to cause the death of the poor, God's children.

In a prophetic action with deep symbolic meaning, and with the eschatological certainty that the Kingdom will triumph, Jesus expresses the meaning of his life. He gathers together with his friends for the last time and sums up in a gesture what he has always done: he is departing and he shares himself for the life of the people, so that they may have a part in him; he pours out his life so that the crowd can become an organized *people*, the people *of God*. This is how he wants us always to remember him—in the shared bread and his blood poured out for the life of the people. He orders us to do likewise, to break apart and share the bread, and to depart, to set out and share ourselves so that his subversive memory may go on generating this same way of being-in-the-world. This will be his new form of presence in history: giving himself for the life of the people. This subversive memory of Jesus is betrayed again every time it is ritualized and held up for worship so that it need not be disturbing and transforming.

This taking on of renunciation is not done openly in broad daylight. He experiences the deepest threat that a human life and work can suffer—the meaninglessness of an unjust and violent death. A natural death would not threaten the future of his work in the same way, even though it would also be a final point. But to die (perhaps by stoning) as a false prophet? Who will believe in his proclamation of the Kingdom? Won't his death mean the death of his Father's cause?

This is the next to last moment of temptation. How is Jesus to react to the unjust violence of the Jewish establishment? To flee would leave the field open to the lie that the establishment operated with regard to God. It would be equivalent to saying that the cause he had lived for was not important enough to risk his life for. Neither can he defend himself by violence. But there is no reply to his questions. The Son has to trust in his *Abba*, even in his silence. God is different from how he imagined. "Everything is possible," God says, but Jesus discovers that God cannot go against human decisions. God does not leap into history and spare him any of the human condition. As it says in Romans, "He did not spare his own Son" anything (8:32); he did not spare himself the pain of giving up thus unconditionally his Son. Jesus discovers that God's way of being in history is not in power but in *kenosis*, in hiddenness, respecting human freedom even when it is used against God's plan.

Jesus goes down into an abyss of loneliness. The disciples do not seem to understand what is about to happen. Jesus decides not to assume his own defense but to leave himself in his *Abba's* hands, with a faith greater even than the catastrophe. The Son's trust is answered by the Father's faithfulness. The Father "cannot" reassure his Son that God is near and give him the certainty that his cry is heard (cf. Heb. 5:7-10). The Father also shows trust in Jesus; the Father keeps quiet and does not intervene. This tells us that it is not God we need to call to account for silence in the face of human violence. We have to question the murderers themselves. God did not manipulate history either in the face of the Son's death or in answer to his cries.

The Establishment against Jesus

Jesus is not so much judged as condemned. However, the accusations sound truthful. From the religious point of view the leaders understood very well what this was about: the Yahweh of their cult against Jesus' *Abba*. Jesus' behavior was an attack on the Temple. He himself understood it to be so: "I give you my word that anyone who says *to that mountain*: 'Move and throw yourself into the sea' will get what he asks for" (Mark 11:23). He is confident that his faith will obtain the overthrow of the religious establishment of Israel.

From the political point of view, an effective love, which confronts an unjust situation, can be misinterpreted as an ambition for power. Jesus ran this risk rather than run the greater risk of letting it be thought that his love was neutral—a matter of feelings and wishes but inactive.

What finally brings Jesus to judgment is his fight for the outcast masses, so that they are not banished from the Kingdom. Jesus is condemned for the God in whom he believes, the *Abba* whose fatherhood is a public matter. And he is condemned for the way he says this Father can be reached: through grace and his preference for the poor rather than through sacrifices; by the practice of love, not in the Temple but in suffering human beings.

Whether there are two religious trials or just one, whether the Jewish authorities could really pass sentence of death, whether Pilate tried to save Jesus or not, are all things which do not qualitatively change the reality: we human beings killed the Son whom God sent to save us. We cannot minimize this great injustice by calling it a superhuman drama in which God "settles accounts" with humanity at the price of the Son's blood. We killed him, and we go on killing God's children whenever they disturb the plans of the powerful. We condemned God's own Son as a blasphemer; he sought total and complete liberation for humanity, and we condemned him as subversive of the established order.

This explanation of the historical background to Jesus' death (reasons of state and national security, orthodoxy) does not give an adequate account of the total meaning of this event, which from faith's point of view is the chief milestone in history. God integrated this injustice into the plan of salvation. God did not annihilate the murderers, but showed the final salvation of Jesus and his cause through his resurrection and followers. Without the resurrection our faith in him cannot be justified; without followers faith in him would be impossible.

In the search for this explanation many formulations of faith developed: "he died for our sins;" "it was necessary for Christ to suffer and thus enter into his glory;" thus the Father's love is shown (Rom. 8:31; John 3:16).

There are three basic soteriological schemes that try to explain the meaning of Jesus' death: it is a sacrifice offered to God for sinners; it is a worthy satisfaction to God for human offenses; it is the redemption (release) payment to free us from the power of the devil. These were formulated in cultural contexts very different from our own and need to be reformulated to determine what they contain of normative revelation and what is cultural accretion, which today covers up rather than *dis*-covers the meaning.

Does speaking of salvation mean we are talking about overcoming a previous situation of perdition? What does *perdition* mean today in Latin America? Is it something that refers only to another life? Does it only concern our relations with God, or has it got anything to do with interhuman relations? And what is salvation? Is it a change in the situation regarding a broken relationship in the past? Does this future have anything to do with present history, or does it merely have an eschatological dimension? Is it only of an intimately subjective order, or has it got anything to do with transforming the external world?

Both the sacrificial schema and the satisfaction schema see sin as an offense directly against God. The redemption schema sees it also as slavery in the power of the devil. The first of these schemes sees the passion as placating God and purifying humanity. The satisfaction schema sees it as the way to restore God's blemished honor; the redemption formula sees it as the price to be paid to release a slave. There are three principal objections to these schemes: they are fundamentally sin-centered; they reduce the work of salvation to the suffering of the passion; and they are not talking about the God revealed by Jesus, the Father who appears in the gospels. Moreover, they turn human salvation into a suprahistorical drama in which humanity has no part; everything is arranged between Jesus and God. Further, reducing the saving dimension merely to the cross runs the risk of canonizing suffering, inducing passivity, and hiding the saving dimension of Jesus' life, including his resurrection, and therefore also that of discipleship.

Nevertheless, we cannot ignore the fact that these schemes speak in the language used by revelation. This is because they contain a fundamental nucleus which must not be lost.

1. The sacrificial schema contains the popular insight that we have to sacrifice our life for others. *Sacrifice* means "make sacred, dedicate, consecrate." This was Jesus' life, a life consecrated to others; he offers us an alternative to the inhuman. In this life consecrated to the Kingdom we see revealed what it means to be children of God and how we should live as brothers and sisters.

2. The schema of substitute satisfaction contains the Hebrew insight of human solidarity. Properly speaking, nobody substitutes or stands in for anybody; rather, we are all involved with one another. It is not a matter of Jesus taking our place "before" God, but that he takes his proper place, which is to head (be the head) of this "great I" of salvation, in which each one of us has our own place and responsibility. He heads us, but not instead of us. He lives as the Son so that those of us who believe in him can also live as God's children and as brothers and sisters with our fellow human beings (cf. John 1:10-13). The letter to the Hebrews speaks of Jesus as the "first in line," the first of those who believe (6:20; 12:1ff). Brought to life with him, we will be his body in history so that "by his stripes we are healed" (Isa. 53:5). Through his wounds we learn the damage done by power to God's children and by money, lies, exploitation, injustice, and the law. On the other hand, we have to be clear that it is not precisely God whom we have to "satisfy" or make up to, because God lacks nothing. It is the Creator's project for humanity and history that we have to "satisfy" (= fulfill sufficiently), because this is what is not "satisfied" in history.

3. Finally, the fundamental core of the redemption-release schema coincides with the Latin American intuition that one has to pay a price for freedom and for life; and this price can be life itself. This is what Jesus offered to release us, in pure blood, from slavery to the anti-values in which we were caught and the fear that engulfed us. The Letter to the Hebrews formulates this dimension in an interpretative synthesis which embraces both the theological and the historical: "That through death he might destroy him who has the power of death, that is, the devil, and deliver all those who through fear of death were subject to lifelong bondage" (Heb. 2:14f).

11. Resurrection and God's Protest

God was absolutely dissatisfied with the death of his Son. In the last resort death resolves nothing, only life does. Hence God's absolute and radical protest, which did not involve the death of the murderer but confirming and bringing to life his murdered Son. True protest consists in confirming life. Only this response does justice to God's fatherhood.

The Father confirms Jesus by exalting him and placing him at the Father's right hand; thus God confirms Jesus' whole life (as a road to go along) and his doings (as a cause to pursue). The faith of the disciples is confirmed through the Paschal experience. Thanks to this we have witnesses, a reconstructed community, and the possibility of following Jesus. The essence of the resurrection is for it to be proclaimed. Both things require one another dialectically, and one cannot exist without the other. Without its proclamation the resurrection would only be the suprahistorical denouncement of the drama, but history with its injustice and death would remain untouched and have no exit. Without a real resurrection, its proclamation would be mere ideology.

So it is not death (suffering) that brings salvation, but the loving whole of the mystery of the Lord's passage through our history: his life, whose consequence is death, and the resurrection, which is its fulfillment. Once again we can express this in a dialectical schema (see Figure 3 below).

Life (thesis, God's gift to humanity is denied by death (antithesis, humanity's response). Life is not ignored or annulled by death, but death is the consequence of a life lived *in this way*. This resurrection (new synthesis, God's gift to Jesus and humanity) is the "negation of the negation." But again this negation does not delete life and death; it confirms both. Once again we have Mark's synthesis: Jesus of Nazareth (life), who was crucified (death), has risen (new life) to make possible his return to "Galilee" and new experience (there they will see him). The resurrection does not save Jesus from death and life; he passes through them and is saved with them. That is why the risen Christ still

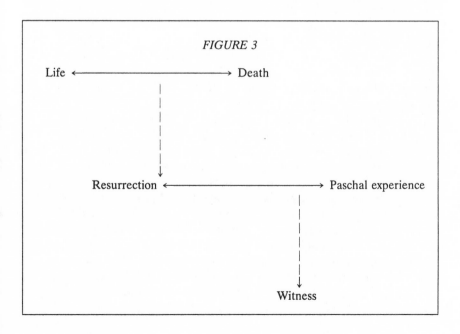

FIGURE 3

Life ⟷ Death

Resurrection ⟷ Paschal experience

Witness

bears the marks of this life-and-death: the wounds of his hands and side.

But the truth about all this will only be known by those who return to Galilee to follow him.

III. FUNDAMENTAL STATEMENTS ABOUT JESUS

Beneath narrative christology, which puts us formally in touch with what Jesus *did*, there are underlying statements that tell us formally who Jesus of Nazareth, the Liberator, is. By way of conclusion, we list them in the form of theses, or if you like, a creed.

• The final and absolute reality, which conditions all Jesus' practice, the ultimate criterion of discernment, what is not negotiable for him, is the Kingdom of God, the Father. This absolute reference to the Father's reign is the fount of his freedom in the face of every human mediation and proposal.

• Jesus is the Son of God in human history. It is his life and work that gives historical density to the title; he lives unconditionally referred to the Father and the Father's project. He who is "from the beginning" in eternity, the Son, had to learn how to be this in a human manner in history (cf. Heb. 5:7ff.). What makes him the Son in history is that he makes himself responsible for the Father's name, the Father's cause.

• Jesus is truly man; he is not man in the generic sense, but rather this particular man. This is the pole of the mystery of the incarnation that is immediately accessible to us. Precisely *in this* particular human life he is truly God. He is not a superman (like the mythological heroes), but "tempted in every respect as we are, yet without sinning" (Heb. 4:15). In this way he fully becomes the new man, the new human being.

• The titles we give him gain their reality from his life and practice. They do not say any *more* than this. Formulated in particular cultural circumstances, they contain a normative nucleus and a conceptual apparatus, which is in dialectical relationship with the cultural changes taking place during the course of history. Therefore these titles must be reformulated so that they go on faithfully expressing the deep reality of what Jesus *continues to be for us today*.

• Jesus' whole life is a work of salvation. This characteristic is sealed definitively by his death and resurrection. It is the totality of the mystery of his passage through our history which makes total liberation possible for us, both historically and eschatologically, as a task and a gift, for "now and not yet." We are saved not because he reveals to us a new, more demanding law than the first, but because he gives us a new capacity, a Spirit to enable us to live as children of the Father, as brothers and sisters of our fellow human beings. This is how we pursue Jesus' cause. And this is how Jesus is fully the Liberator.

• Through his resurrection Jesus becomes "a vivifying Spirit" (1 Cor. 15:45). We are integrated into him and form his body in history. The horizon of our understanding of the resurrection and incorporation into him is the hope we have for history. Only those who hope for better possibilities in history realize the definitive reality of Jesus. And the final horizon of our experience of the risen Jesus is following him by promoting his cause.

— Translated by Dinah Livingstone

NOTES

1. "The New Testament feels free to speak of the experience of salvation with Jesus in a variety of ways, though in fact these differing interpretations simply articulate what has really come into being with Jesus. This also gives us the freedom to express in a new form the experience of salvation in Jesus that we may have described in terms taken from our modern culture with its own particular problems, expectations and needs, though these in turn must also be subjected to the criticism of Israel's expectation and to what has found fulfillment in Jesus. Moreover, we should do this *in order* to remain faithful to what the New Testament Christians felt to be an experience of salvation in Jesus" (E. Schillebeeckx, *Interim Report on the Books Jesus and Christ* (New York: Crossroad, 1982), p. 16.

2. This is how Jon Sobrino formulates it: "By historical we formally mean here the practice of Jesus as that place of greater metaphysical density of his person. This practice is all activity, in deeds and words, by which it transforms the surrounding reality towards the kingdom of God and through which he creates and expresses his own person. This practice of Jesus is what gives us the best access to his person. But it has also unleashed a history which has reached *us* in order to be continued. Thus our present-day practice is a requirement of Jesus, but it is also the hermeneutic place for understanding Jesus" (Jon Sobrino, "Jesus de Nazaret," in C. Floristán and J. J. Tamayo, eds., *Conceptos fundamentales de pastoral* [Madrid, 1983], pp. 483ff.).

3. The word *lestes* in Greek does not mean an ordinary thief, but a rioter, a rebel, a violent person. Cf. Fl. Jos., *Bell. Jud.* 2.254-7.

4. It is not clear whether we can speak of any of them belonging to the Zealot movement, which came later (66 C.E.). But it is very probable that some of them were sympathetic to armed resistance against the Romans and the temptation was increased at this period of apocalyptic expectations.

5. See Karl Rahner and W. Thüsing, *A New Christology*, trans. David Smith and Verdant Green (New York: Seabury Press, 1980).

6. Only by regarding Jesus as the guardian of Caesar's interests (then and henceforth) can we interpret his response to the trap about paying tribute to Caesar (Mark 12:13-18) as representing approval.

20

Systematic Christology: Jesus Christ, the Absolute Mediator of the Reign of God

JON SOBRINO

The preceding article has presented a christological account of Jesus of Nazareth as Liberator. The present chapter will develop, in the form of a sketch, the core of a systematic christology that presupposes the content of the foregoing account, as well as the specific premises of liberation theology,[1] that is: (1) that the central object of the theology of liberation is the *Reign of God*,[2] (2) that the goal of this theology is *liberation*, and therefore that it understands itself as the theory of a praxis,[3] and (3) that liberation theology is developed from a determinate locus, that of *the poor of this world*.[4]

I. THEORETICAL CHRISTOLOGY: JESUS AS THE MEDIATOR OF THE REIGN OF GOD

All christology must assert the ultimacy and transcendence of Christ, and the christology of liberation must do so from what it regards as actually ultimate: the Reign of God. To this end, methodologically, liberation christology begins its reflection with the person of Jesus of Nazareth himself, since it is here that the relationship between Jesus and the Reign of God appears with all clarity.

Let us state from the outset that our attention to Jesus is not a reduction of christology to a pure "Jesuology," but only the selection of a determinate methodology. Whether our approach will be a fruitful one will be seen after the execution of our analysis. But let us observe that it is at least possible for it to be fruitful, as other systematic christologies today have established. Karl Rahner, for example, concludes that a christology could be developed from something central to the historical Jesus and wonders "whether a human being who is the vessel of an absolute, pure love, free of any kind of selfishness, must not be something more than merely human."[5] For our purposes, the important thing in this citation does not reside so much in its specific understanding of Jesus ("an absolute, pure love"), but in the proposition of the possibility of constructing christology on the historical Jesus. For our part, we shall attempt to do so in terms of the relationship of the historical Jesus with the Reign of God.

1. Ultimacy of Jesus in Terms of the Reign of God

In the Synoptics, Jesus' relationship with the Reign of God, which we here define formally as the ultimate will of God for this world, is central. That Reign and its proximity are presented by Jesus as the *actual ultimate*. This shapes his person, in the exteriority of his mission (with respect to "making history") and in the interiority of his subjectivity (his own historicity). It is also this that precipitates his historical destiny, that of the cross. His very resurrection is God's response to one who, for serving the Reign, has been put to death by the anti-Reign. In other words, in order to come to know the specifically Christian element of the Reign of God, one must turn to Jesus. But just so, conversely, in order to know Jesus one must turn to the Reign of God.

Jesus himself asserts this relationship between the Reign of God and his person. At times his assertion is explicit: "If it is by the Spirit of God that I expel demons, then the reign of God has overtaken you" (Matt. 12:28 and par.). At other times he posits this relationship in an implicit but real way: in various of the actions of his praxis which can and should be interpreted as signs of the coming of the Reign in behalf of the poor (his miracles, his exorcisms, the welcome he extends to the weak and oppressed); in his struggle with the anti-Reign (controversies, denunciations, exposé of oppressors); or in his celebration of the presence of the Reign (meals).

Thus, Jesus appears in an essential and constitutive relationship with the Reign of God, with the ultimate will of God—with that which we call systematically the *mediation* of God. And systematically we call this Jesus, in his relationship with the mediation, the *mediator* of the will of God; that is, the person who proclaims the Reign, who posits signs of its reality and points to its totality.

For systematic christology, the question is how to move from the reality of Jesus as mediator to his reality as *definitive mediator* of the Reign of God. All christologies must face this question, since all of them must take the step—the leap, really—from Jesus' historical reality to a profession of his ultimacy. (We could make an exception for those obsolete christologies in which certain of Jesus' deeds—his miracles, or his prophecies—or his resurrection automatically provide the step, the leap, to the ultimacy of Christ. But almost no one today accepts the miracles and prophecies as automatically forcing this transition, and the leap justified by the resurrection ultimately requires faith in the Resurrection.)

In an analysis of the qualitative bound from Jesus as mediator to Jesus as the definitive mediator of the Reign, it must be taken into account whether and where there is some kind of *discontinuity* that would make that transition reasonable—although to accept it as radical discontinuity will in the last analysis always be a matter of faith. Along these lines we might recall Jesus' daring proclamation of the imminence of this Reign and the indefectible victory of God, his daring in declaring the symmetry broken forever in which God could possibly come as a savior or possibly as a condemning judge—to all of which would correspond the discontinuity in his hearers: "At last salvation has come for the poor." This daring on Jesus' part in announcing the coming of God in the Reign, and in proclaiming the gratuitous, salvific, and liberative reality of God that draws near with the proximity of God, would offer some kind of discontinuity regarding the historical viewpoint, in terms of which theology could now reflect upon the special relationship of Jesus with the transcendent.

At the same time, Jesus appears in *continuity* with other, earlier mediators — Moses, the prophets, the Servant, and so on. In other words, Jesus appears as a human being immersed in this same current of a historical course traversed with honesty before the truth, mercy before the suffering of another, justice before the oppression of the masses, a loving dedication to his mission, total fidelity to God, indestructible hope, the sacrifice of his life. (This last element — although disdained by christologies that seek only the specific, peculiar element in Jesus — offers a very considerable systematic advantage when it comes to establishing the later dogmatic tenet of the true humanity of Jesus as a participation in the best that the human being has ever been or done.)

The assertion of Jesus' absolute discontinuity is a matter of faith, as we have said. We cannot, therefore, propose a reality of Jesus that would mechanically force the qualitative leap to his status as *the* mediator (as Rahner cannot move mechanically from Jesus' love presented historically to a total love in total discontinuity). What we can propose is a reality of Jesus in terms of which we can also gain a meaningful formulation — in our opinion, a more meaningful formulation than we gain from a point of departure in other realities — of this leap to *the* mediator. What we have called Jesus' daring can function as an index, a pointer, an indicator, of the transcendent ultimacy of his person. And a grasp of what is human in Jesus — which is in no way novel in its formal characterization — can point to his human ultimacy, not as differentiation, but as fullness of the human.

Christians actually made this qualitative leap after the resurrection. From our perspective we add that the resurrection can also be presented as confirmation of the truth of Jesus as the mediator of the Reign, and not only as an arbitrary act posited by God for the purpose of revealing the reality of that God — which could have just as well occurred in the resuscitation of any other corpse. If this had been the only "reason" for the resurrection, the resurrection would be something extrinsic to Jesus' life and would say nothing of his being as mediator. But if the one to whom "life has been restored" is one who proclaimed the commencement of life for the poor and therefore was deprived of life himself, if the one who has been raised is one who ended as a victim of the anti-Reign, then the resurrection can very well be understood systematically as the confirmation of the mediator, the confirmation of his (objectively) theological daring, and the confirmation of the fullness of the human occurring in his person. Then the qualitative leap of faith can be made, and the christological concept formulated of Jesus of Nazareth as *the* mediator of the Reign of God.

In terms of the Reign of God, then, the reality of Jesus can be formulated, and in terms of the ultimacy of the Reign the ultimacy of Jesus can be formulated. What must be analyzed — due to the fact that it has been consecrated in the dogmatic formulations — is whether this formulation, in terms of the

Reign of God, is compatible with the more usual focus on the divine ultimacy of Jesus in relation to the person of God the Father, as well as with a focus on his human ultimacy (the former, surely, usually being held much more in account in a theological analysis of the historical Jesus than the latter).

Jesus' Divinity

With respect to establishing the divinity of Jesus, it is clear that the gospels place Jesus in a relationship with the person of God in which he calls God his Father. However, the content of this concept of God as Father is not incompatible with that of the God of the Reign — although each of these expressions of ultimacy has its own specificity. They are not interchangeable as concepts, nor can either be adequately deduced from the other by way of pure conceptual reflection. But at least it must be admitted that they are related, and that to a large extent they converge. To this same extent, Jesus' relationship with the divine ultimate — on which his own divine ultimacy will be based — can be developed in terms of the God of the Reign and in terms of God as Father. And then, also in terms of the ultimacy of the Reign of God, the divine element in Jesus can be approached. Let us briefly examine the convergence of the God of the Reign with the Father of Jesus.

In both perspectives Jesus appears in a relationship with a God who has a specific content — a positive one for human beings, with the qualities of mercy, justice, partiality toward the poor, the weak, and the little ones, and a God who generates, and elicits, honesty, trust, hope, freedom, joy, and the like. This fundamental convergence can be observed in the texts in which Jesus appears in his personal relationship with God the Father, as well as in the many parables of the Reign that show this kind of God, a God who makes possible and who demands such a relationship.

At the same time, once more in both perspectives, Jesus appears in a relationship with a God who is mystery — who must be allowed to be God, and with whom one must strike a relationship of absolute openness and availability. Thus, in darkness before this Father, Jesus asks that the divine will be done; and in the darkness of the coming of the Reign, he exclaims that only the Father knows the hour of that coming.

Jesus' personal relationship with the divinity, then, can be analyzed in terms of his relationship with his Father, surely; but it can also be analyzed in terms of his relationship with the God of the Reign. In this sense the *mediator* of the Reign of God can also be understood as the *Son* of God without doing violence to either term.

Jesus' Humanity

When it comes to establishing the humanity of Jesus, Jesus' relationship with the Reign of God offers greater advantages than any other biblical or dogmatic focus (such as a general profession of his human nature, an analysis of his attitudes, or the like). The fundamental reason for this is that, in confrontation with the Reign of God, the totality of the person of Jesus in action comes into view. Guided by Kant's three questions — to which we shall add a fourth — in the answer to which is expressed the totality of the human, we readily observe that Jesus' relationship with the Reign of God evinces (1) the *knowledge* Jesus has and communicates concerning the Reign of God and the anti-Reign, (2) the *hope* that he stirs in others and that supports him as well (hope in the coming of the Reign), (3) the *praxis* he performs in the service of that Reign, and his historical *celebration* of the fact that the Reign has "already" come.

Should someone wish to argue that this comprehensive actualization of the human element of Jesus can also be deduced from his relationship with the Father, we answer that, quantitatively, there are far fewer texts bearing on Jesus' relationship with the Father than with the Reign of God; systematically, Jesus' human interiority is better known from the exteriority of his relationship with the Reign. It is this exteriority that shows us concretely a Jesus who is honest with the truth, merciful and just, a denouncer and exposer, available and faithful. It is this exteriority, required by the building of the Reign of God, that shapes his personal interiority with reference to God.

Finally, his relationship with the Reign sets in deeper relief the specific characteristics of the authentically human: honesty with reality, mercy as a primary reaction, justice demanded in the face of the oppression of the masses, fidelity in trial and persecution, and the "greatest love" of the laying down of one's life.

In synthesis, Jesus' human element, when seen in relationship with the Reign of God and in its service, appears with certain particular characteristics. Furthermore—something that is not usually emphasized in systematic christologies—this human element appears as *partiality*, in Jesus' placement and incarnation, in the addressees of his mission, and in his very fate. It appears as a human element in *solidarity*—as a specific realization of the human in regard to other persons, as their brother, as a human being who is for others and who wills to be with others.

2. Comparison of the Christology of "the Mediator of the Reign of God" with Other Theoretical Christologies of the New Testament

The ultimacy of Jesus can be established from a point of departure in the Reign of God, then. Now let us compare this way of proceeding with the christologies of the New Testament. We make this comparison for the sake of a better understanding of the specificity, and novelty, of the focus that we have presented, as well as in order to discover a possible biblical justification for our focus.[6]

The Titles

Generally speaking, as the New Testament proceeds, the Reign of God tends to disappear as an expression of the ultimate, and more specifically, as an explanation of the ultimacy of Jesus. Not that there is no longer an expectation of the arrival of the ultimate—now joined to the parousia of Christ—or that the notion of the Reign has no theological equivalent, such as the "new creation," or "new covenant," which are also set in an essential relationship with Jesus. But while there are surely these analogies with the Reign of God, the latter—as Jesus proclaimed it—gradually dwindles away, along with an attempt to identify Jesus' ultimacy in terms of his relationship with that Reign.

Indeed, the christologies of Jesus' titles and destiny show that some titles by their nature bear more directly on the Reign of God (the Prophet who announces it, the Son of Man who proclaims it at the end of the ages, the High Priest who strikes a new covenant, the Servant who burdens himself with the anti-Reign), but these titles never become central in the New Testament discourse itself and have practically disappeared in later history. The title of Messiah (the Anointed One, the Christ) constitutes a case apart: it does bespeak a primordial relation to a people's hopes of liberation (in various ways, as we know). It is akin, then, to our systematic title Mediator, but in coming to be transformed into the proper name Jesus *Christ*, paradoxically it lost its essential reference to the Reign of God.

In its place, New Testament christology explicitly developed the ultimacy of Christ in titles that express his direct relation to the person of God: Son of God, Lord, Word, Son. At the same time, although there are titles that express the concrete manifestation of Jesus' humanity, these never attain the importance enjoyed by the others. Expressions like Revelation's "lamb that was slain" or Hebrews' "brother," for example, do not come to be regarded as titles of Jesus' humanity.

The reason why theoretical reflection took this direction could seem to be that Jesus' humanity was too obvious to need this sort of penetration. But the fact is that we have a concentration on the titles that point to Jesus' relationship with the divinity, and the divinity understood rather as the person of God the Father of Jesus than as the God of the Reign.

The Gospel Narratives

Surprisingly, along with these theoretical "title" christologies, and after certain of them have been developed, the Christian scriptures show us another way of doing theoretical christology: that of the gospel narratives. The latter have, on the one hand, assimilated Jesus' special relationship with the Father and so profess Jesus as Son of God (in John, simply as Son). But the Synoptics react to this previously established christology by showing Jesus' ultimacy in his relationship with the Reign of God, and showing the reality of his humanity as history. They do not doubt that Christ is the Son of God; but they emphasize, and from the very outset, that—in our terminology—the mediator of the Reign of God has a concrete, specific history.

In the first place, the gospels turn to Jesus of Nazareth in a very precise manner: by narrating his history. True, the gospels find themselves unable to historicize Jesus without theologizing him. The gospels are theological narratives, then. But the converse is also true: they are unable to theologize Jesus without historicizing him. This is supremely important for systematic christology, at least as a possibility, and it is this possibility that the narrative christology of the preceding chapter reduces to reality.

In the second place—and more decisively for our topic—in the gospel narratives what for Jesus is the ultimate is presented, it is true, in two expressions:

Reign of God and *Abba*. But quantitatively, the former appears more than the latter, and the latter can well—indeed, better, to our view—be understood in terms of the former rather than vice versa. Thus we have an undeniable attempt on the part of the gospels to express the ultimacy of Jesus in terms of the Reign of God.

In the third place, the gospel narratives present the ultimacy of the Reign in the presence of what we may call an anti-Reign. The Reign, then, is a dialectical reality, subsisting in conflict with its antithesis. This point—which is not frequently made in the systematic christologies—is essential for an understanding of the mediator, as well. The mediator's mission in behalf of the ultimacy of the Reign is carried out in the presence of and in opposition to other ultimacies. Thus, the mediator proclaims and serves the Reign, but he does so precisely by denouncing and exposing the anti-Reign. He is presented in a relationship of ultimacy with a God who is his Father, but he maintains this relationship by renouncing and combating the idols (all manner of oppressive power) that hold themselves out as God. He strikes a solidarity with everything human, but he does so by taking upon himself that which is dehumanizing: sin.

To be sure, this dialectical, conflictive dimension of reality is present in other New Testament writings; but the concrete form in which it appears in the gospel is more adequate—by reason of being historical and narrative—to the purpose of making it understood. We might say that Jesus does not appear as mediator, as Son and as human being, on a *tabula rasa*, but amid a reality with which he struggles. He must *come to be* mediator, Son, and human.

Finally, the gospel narratives show forth the partiality of God, the mediation, and the mediator. This celebrated central point of the Hebrew scriptures—the partiality or partisanship of God's revelation in favor of the poor, the weak, and the oppressed—could understandably have lost its central place in the New Testament. After the resurrection, undeniably, the universality of salvation is proclaimed. That is, in order to belong to the new people of God one need no longer belong to any particular people or religion. It is enough simply to be a human being. In this sense Jesus' vision of a primary mission to the sheep of Israel is transcended. But this real universalism—in which the very existence and self-understanding of the church is at stake—implies no reason why the partiality of the mediation and the mediator for the poor should be eliminated. This is the meaning of the gospel narratives: the Reign of God is of the poor. The resurrection of Christ cancels one kind of partiality, that based on religion or ethnic origin. But there is no reason why it should cancel the partiality of the Reign and its mediator based on poverty and oppression. On the contrary, the gospels emphasize this partiality.

Choosing an Approach

We have entertained this brief reflection on two distinct theoretical ways of doing christology in the New Testament, not in order to deny the validity of one of them, that of the titles, which is the more consecrated approach in the history of christology, but in order to come to a realization that, throughout history, christology has de facto developed more along the lines of only one of these possibilities, and that it happens to have been that of an expression of the ultimacy of Jesus in terms of his relation to the person of God. The gospel narratives show that there is another possibility. Theoretical christology can also be done in terms of historico-theological narratives. As Albert Schweitzer remarked, the most important thing about the gospel of Mark is that it should have been written at all. When we proceed in this manner, the ultimacy of Jesus can be expressed in terms of his relationship with the Reign of God.

These two ways of doing christology are not mutually exclusive; indeed, they actually require one another. In this brief systematic sketch, we have expressed Jesus' ultimacy precisely with a theoretical title, that of the mediator of the Reign of God; but we have done so after, and on the basis of, the previous chapter, which concerns itself with a narrative christology. We have no intention, then, of excluding a christology of titles. However, we do wish to analyze where systematic reflection ought to assign logical priority: whether to narrative or to conceptual titles. Narrative offers the obvious advantage of history itself: Jesus' real life preceded his theorization at the hands of faith. Furthermore, a narrative approach in christology enables us to avoid the grave dangers that beset a christology of titles divorced from christological narrative. Thus, the gospel narratives not only function as expositive christology, but they also perform a critical and corrective operation vis-à-vis a christology of titles alone.

The most serious danger, in terms of the perspective adopted in this chapter, has already been cited: the titles can incline us to prescind from the central thing about Jesus, the Reign of God, and ignore a christology consistently based on the Reign. Furthermore, the titles, in their concrete, historical development, can lead us to ignore the human element in Jesus (a problem of content for christology), and to the serious error of imagining that we know the content of his titles—his being lord, being Son, being high priest, and so on—before knowing Jesus himself (a methodological problem).

In summary, we may say that Latin American systematic christology sees within the Christian scriptures the theoretical possibility of beginning christology with the evangelical narratives, and of finding in them the ultimacy from which the ultimacy of Jesus will be better understood. Thus, it sees a "New Testament justification" of its particular approach. Finally, it finds in those same scriptures the importance of assigning priority to the narrative concerning Jesus over his pure titles, inasmuch as the dangers to which the former responds in the Christian scriptures continue to be present in current history: ignoring the Reign of God, and the poor as its correlate; neglecting Jesus' humanity; and manipulating the concrete reality of Christ.

II. PRAXIC CHRISTOLOGY: THE FOLLOWING OF JESUS

The believer's faith does not create its object (*fides quae*). It is of the essence of the Christian comprehension of the faith that God has made a self-bestowal on us by grace. At the same time, however, no object would have come to be recognized as an object of faith had it not occasioned an act of faith (*fides qua*).

Now if, as Rahner explains, nothing created can be an object of faith, then, if there is such a thing as faith, it must be a faith in something actually transcendent. A *fides qua*, accordingly, testifies to a reality believed in and is an existential help to understanding what the concrete content of this reality is. For christology, this means that, besides being theoretical and analyzing a *fides quae*, it must also analyze the corresponding *fides qua* — for existential and pastoral reasons, as well as because to do so will help in an understanding of the object of faith, in this case, Jesus Christ.

1. The Following of Jesus as an Existential Expression of Faith in Christ

The *fides qua* can become real in the act of accepting the transcendence of Christ, which can be proclaimed liturgically and doxologically. But this *fides qua* can be expressed in another way, and it seems to us a more radical way, by explicitly confronting the historical Jesus. To cite Rahner once more:

> If the moral personality of Jesus in word and life, really makes such a compelling impression on a person that they find the courage to commit themselves unconditionally to this Jesus in life and death and therefore to believe in the God of Jesus, that person has gone far beyond a merely horizontal humanistic Jesuolatry, and is living (perhaps not completely spontaneously, but really) an orthodox Christology.[7]

An Existential, Praxic Expression of Faith

This, we think, is what has actually occurred in the Christian scriptures. Faith in Jesus was originally expressed in an existential, praxic form, before Christians ever undertook to supply themselves with a theoretical formulation of Jesus' reality. Thus, they professed Jesus, liturgically and doxologically, as the One raised, the One exalted, the Lord. But while this is an expression of the *fides qua*, it is not its maximal expression. Jesus' ultimacy is expressed before all else — and in very principle — in the ultimacy of one's own life. This means a kind of life that, generally speaking, is nothing other than a reproduction of the life of Jesus. One must have the same sentiments as Christ (Paul), one must keep one's eyes fixed on Jesus and, as Jesus did, remain steadfast in suffering (Hebrews), and so on. Comprehensively, one must follow Jesus. Thus, the Christian scriptures testify that existential faith has priority over formulations of faith, and that the former is expressed more radically as praxis of faith, as following or discipleship.

A following of Jesus is the maximal expression of faith in Christ, since the formal reason for it (although it may be accompanied by ancillary motivations, such as the hope of a reward) is the sheer fact of the call of Jesus; its content flows simply from the fact that this is the way Jesus was. We see this relationship in the Christian scriptures between the act of faith and following; it is all the more significant when we take account of the opinion of some exegetes to the effect that the historical Jesus did not call everyone to his discipleship, but only those who wished to be his active followers. After the resurrection, however, when genuine faith in Christ begins, "following and discipleship began to be the absolute expression of Christian existence."[8]

We must conclude that, whatever the explicit consciousness that the first Christians were acquiring of Jesus, as indicated in their ascribing titles to him, they were expressing in their very lives and death the ultimacy they attributed to him. It is this existential ultimacy that is consecrated in the word "following" of Jesus. This is how the historical Jesus is recovered in faith. When one attempts to reproduce the following of Jesus, then the Reign of God reappears once more in a central place. Let us recall that, in the first stage of Jesus' public life, discipleship or following meant proclaiming and positing signs of the Reign, while in the second stage it meant steadfastness in the face of the mighty reaction of the anti-Reign. Without the Reign of God, the following of Jesus would have neither its central motivation nor its central content.

Historicization of the Following of Jesus

The following of Jesus throughout history must be historicized and transformed into the continuation of his deed and his intent (as actually occurred in the Christian scriptures), but the most important thing for systematic christology is that there actually be this following in history. This is what is happening in Latin America; the magnitude and quality of the phenomenon are such that christology must take it seriously into account. It cannot be doubted that the act of faith in Christ exists in Latin America, and that this is shown in the following of Jesus and martyrdom. Nor can it be doubted that the continuation of Jesus' deed and intent in Latin America recovers the fundamental structure of the historical Jesus. Therefore, following stands in an essential relationship with the building of the Reign of God and the destruction of the anti-Reign. This is occurring—in historical factuality, without passing a judgment upon subjectivities—in a clearer fashion, and in a more similar fashion to that of Jesus, than in other forms of following throughout history. Nor can it be doubted that the actual martyrdoms are historically very similar to that of Jesus and inflicted for the same reasons as that of Jesus: the proclamation to the poor of the Reign of God and the defense of the poor in combat with the anti-Reign.

2. Meaning of Following for Theoretical Christology

If this is the case, then we may say that the act of faith in Jesus, the *fides qua*, still exists today in its maximal expression, following. What we must ask ourselves is whether that following has a meaning for christology, and if so, what meaning.

Witnesses of Faith Shed Light on the Fides Quae

The follower is a witness, someone who reproduces—in historicized fashion—the life of Jesus. To what extent, and in what degree, this occurs is open to discussion, of course, and should be analyzed; but it ought to occur in principle, since otherwise the design of God that human beings be sons and daughters in the Son would be in vain. And if *per impossibile* there were no such thing as following, we should have the utter failure of God, and Christ would not be the Son. Then, of course, there would be no christology.

But if there actually is following, there can be christology, and account will have to be taken of its content. Human beings may be faulty or defective ways of being Christ, as Rahner says, but this implies positively that there is something of Christ in them. To formulate the same thing in traditional theological terms, and once more positively: if we are by grace what Christ is by nature, then something of the reality of Christ must be knowable even by looking at us, graced ones that we are.

Within this circularity, obviously the criterion of an analysis and verification of the extent to which current witnesses express what is Christian will be Jesus. But it is also clear that these current witnesses can say something about Jesus. This is the familiar hermeneutic problem, only here its circularity is demanded by the very essence of revelation. If Jesus is true God and true human being, then anyone transparent to the divine and the human will say something of Christ.

Our theoretical assertion seems to us to be an undeniable reality in Latin America. Although the argument has to stand on its own, since one can only point to the fact, it happens that many who saw Archbishop Romero — to cite a single example of a faith witness — assert that he made Jesus better known to them. It is also a fact that the Latin American witnesses have at least opened the eyes of us who are exegetes, supplying us with new hermeneutic horizons. It is a fact that peasants who hear the reading of the passion of Jesus state very simply: "Exactly what happened to Archbishop Romero." Conversely, in terms of their knowledge of Archbishop Romero they better understand the passion of Jesus. It is also a fact that the witnesses have led persons to a more in-depth understanding of how the authentically human becomes a sacrament of the authentically divine. In the words of Ignacio Ellacuría, "With Archbishop Romero, God has visited El Salvador."

Theoretical christology can and should incorporate this argumentation. It should argue in part from the reality of current witnesses. That this argumentation ought to be cautious is supremely evident; but it would be even more incomprehensible if no argumentation were ever based on witnesses in order to know the antonomastic Witness, the witness *par excellence*. It would be vain to ask the witnesses to keep their eyes fixed on the Witness, if thereupon no reflection of him could ever be found in them.

Following Makes Possible the Limit Assertion of the Reality of Christ

Besides supplying content, the following of Jesus expresses the fact that the object of faith is regarded as something ultimate. But like any ultimate reality — which will be a mystery in the strict sense — this object not only is unapproachable, it cannot be directly intuited. It can be meaningfully conceptualized and verbalized after a "journey" — a transition from what is already in some manner subject to experience and verifiable, to the limit assertion in question.

The need to make this journey in order to be able to formulate limit assertions has already been acknowledged by various christologies. For example, it has been emphasized that the limit assertions of Chalcedon can have meaning only after the completion of the theoretical pilgrimage of the New Testament and the tradition of the first centuries. That is, knowing who Jesus was and how he was theorized in the scriptures and church tradition has logical and chronological priority if the limit assertions of Chalcedon are to have any meaning.[9] Without this journey, this pilgrimage, the Chalcedonian formula would be not only mysterious and incomprehensible, in the sense of being ultimately unfathomable, but simply unintelligible, which is not the same thing.

What we wish to emphasize here is that this journey must also — and more radically — be praxic. That is, one must traverse the route of real following in order for the formulation of ultimacy to have any meaning. This need abides throughout history, and it would be naive of theoretical christology to think that the task of traversing the route of actual following, in order to be able to make limit formulations, could be delegated to the first Christians alone, while afterward it would suffice to analyze these formulations, as formulations, and to rest content with a theoretical development of their virtualities throughout the rest of history.

This ultimate task is necessary and good, but — if it is a matter of asserting the ultimacy of Christ — one cannot prescind from the *fides qua*. Thus, one cannot prescind from realized following. Only in the following of Jesus do we become like unto the reality of Jesus, and only on the basis of this realized affinity does the internal knowledge of Christ become possible. That Jesus is thereupon professed as the ultimate is the fruit of the leap of faith, but it is supremely important to determine with the greatest possible precision the locus of this leap. According to what we have said, that locus is following, since apart from following one could not actually know what is being spoken of when Christ is mentioned. After all, following means doing, in terms of the present, what Jesus did, and doing it in the way that he did it. It means the mission of building the Reign with the attitude and spirit of Jesus. In this praxis a kinship is acquired — greater or lesser, obviously — with Jesus, and this praxis (like all praxis) explains one's antecedent concept of Jesus, his mission, and his spirit.

On the other hand, our praxis, like that of Jesus, is also subject to the vagaries of history. That is, although its horizon is the ultimate, its concretions are not, and depending on how these come to be, the same praxis can be verification of or temptation for faith itself. As a logical consequence, even following could be the locus of not making the leap of faith, since it could happen that, in following Jesus, one would come to the conclusion that this route does not offer ultimacy.

Within following, then, one can make the act of faith and the limit assertion concerning Christ (just as one can omit it). But then this act of faith is transformed into victory, as well, as John's theology teaches. We can only conclude that a following realized in terms of the present is the reality in which limit assertions concerning Christ can have meaning, or cease to have it.[10]

In summary, christology must take serious account of a realized following, for two important reasons of christological epistemology. A contemplation of the witnesses of the faith can help us know the Witness better; and in actual following, a conviction of the ultimacy of Christ can be deepened (or abandoned).

III. CHRISTOPRAXIS OF LIBERATION

The ultimate finality of theology, as of all Christian activity, is — according to the theology of liberation — the maximal building of the Reign of God. But in our current situation of oppression, this building must be liberation. Therefore liberation theology understands itself as a theory of a praxis, as an *intellectus amoris*, which must be historicized as *intellectus justitiae*. This being the case, christology in the concrete must develop and supply a knowledge concerning Christ that by its nature will further the building of the Reign of God. Because that Reign is effected in opposition to the oppression of the anti-Reign, this knowledge of Christ must be a knowledge of liberation, *intellectus liberationis*.

1. Specific Christological Moment of Praxis

Christology must propose a knowledge concerning Christ such that, of his very nature, this Christ will move a person — the person who knows him, in order that this person may know him — to a salvific activity. This means introducing into the very reality of Christ the dynamism of the dispatch to that salvific activity. It is not, then, a matter of first knowing who Christ is and then adding the knowledge that one of the elements of his reality is to be someone who confers a mission. To be sure, a hermeneutic circularity obtains between an understanding of the being of Christ and a grasp of his conferral of a mission. But at least the moment of dispatch as essential to the being of Christ must be maintained as central.

In the Christian scriptures, it is a matter of conjecture whether the dispatch to a salvific activity is essential to the very being of Christ, in such wise that — systematically speaking — without the availability to be so dispatched one would be unable to know Christ adequately. That at least there is in Jesus this unified duality of being and sending appears in programmatic terms in the evangelical "being with Jesus and being sent by Jesus." In certain gospel scenes the dispatch even seems to have priority over knowledge of Jesus. And in the scenes of the apparitions, Jesus appears not to "seers," but to "witnesses"; that is, he is at the same time one appearing and one sending, and correlatively, availability for an activity — bearing witness — is essential, according to the interpretation of certain exegetes, in order to grasp the being of Jesus in the apparitions.

No unequivocal thesis can be deduced from these fragmentary reflections, but at least we have an indication of what interests us here. Both in life and after his resurrection, Christ appears not simply as a someone-in-himself who can simply be known, or even a someone-for-us of whom salvation can be hoped, but also as a someone-who-sends, whose mission must be prosecuted. Thus, the praxis inspired by Christ is essential to Christ himself (and to christology). Here we have the context in which we must speak of the christopraxis of liberation.

In this understanding of Christ as one who sends we confront a theoretical novelty. It is not a novelty that Christ is presented salvifically — and let us remember that a salvific concern is what moved the development of christology in the scriptures, in patristics, and in the conciliar dogmas. This is accepted by liberation christology, which formally prosecutes this line and radically transcends the dissociation that began to appear in the Middle Ages between christology and soteriology. The novel element is in (1) the determination of salvation as liberation, and (2) the manner in which a concern for liberation has an influence on theoretical christology, that is, not only for having to *think* the reality of Christ in such a fashion that he can be savior (the interest of the New Testament and of patristic speculation), but in thinking him in such a fashion that he may already *produce* historical salvation.

In the context of this chapter, this means that it is not enough to assert that Jesus is the mediator of the Reign of God; it must also be asserted that he is the one who of his very nature dispatches to the building of the Reign. He is a mediator by essence *sent* (the dimension of gratuity with respect to us); and he is a mediator by essence *sending* (his fundamental demand on us). Besides the sheer fact of the essential dispatch to praxis, a starting point in Christ can determine the content and utopian horizon of that praxis (the Reign of God), the spirit with which to perform it (that of the mediator), and the hope to be maintained amid the praxis (the possibility of defeating the anti-Reign).

2. Christopraxis

Inasmuch as this Reign to be constructed comes into being in the presence of and in opposition to the anti-Reign, the Reign is a good entity, of course. Specifically, it is a liberative entity. This explains why it is called Good News; it is the apparition of the good that is hoped for in the presence of evil, oppressive realities. Consequently, the praxis of building the Reign will be good, but it will also be liberative. In order to show what it is that is good and liberative in the praxis to which Christ sends, let us analyze the various levels of the reality of Jesus in which he appears as Liberator.

Liberative Aspect of Jesus' Mission

The most specific mission of the historical Jesus is the proclamation and inauguration of the Reign of God in behalf of the poor and outcast. This is how the Markan-Matthean gospel begins, and even more explicitly, in the language of the Good News, that of Luke. This does not militate against the need for salvation from sin or transcendent salvation. Indeed, part of the responsibility of current christology will be to show how all of the plural salvations converge in the Reign of God. But it is with Jesus' proclamation and inauguration of the Reign for the poor and outcast that one must begin if one would understand liberation. In other words, liberation is the coming of the Reign of God for the poor. In terms of the reality of the poor, the content of liberation will have certain basic minimal content: a just life worthy of a human being. We might call it an economic and sociological opportunity, since what is at stake is an *oikos*, house and home, the basic element of life; and a *socius*, or social relationships of authentic kinship. This Reign is formally liberation, and not simply the good that is hoped for, since it will come in contravention of the anti-Reign.

This is what is directly meant—although it is not the only thing meant—when Jesus is called Liberator, and this is why we have called him the mediator of the Reign of God. Without a central inclusion of this meaning of liberation, there can be no christology of liberation. And let us note in passing that it is in this manner, after twenty centuries, that Latin American christology recovers the nucleus of Jesus' most primitive title, that of Messiah (*christos*), which had become his proper name, but had been deprived of any reference to a popular hope of liberation.

Someone might object that this conception of liberation neglects a key element of the later New Testament: liberation from sin. Here it must be granted that one of the essentials of the historical Jesus' liberative mission in behalf of the Reign of God is his salvific attitude toward sinners. But this assertion must be understood precisely and correctly. Those we might call sinful out of weakness, or more precisely, those regarded as sinful by their oppressors, Jesus cordially and affectionately welcomes, with an attitude that includes, but goes further than, simple forgiveness of sins. To the sinners in the sense of oppressors, Jesus announces the Good News, it is true, but in the form of a demand for radical conversion, as in the case of Zacchaeus.

Liberation from sin, even the universality of such liberation, is present in Jesus' mission, then, although it is present there in historicized fashion and without the elements introduced by later speculation based on explanatory theoretical models (sacrifice, expiation, and so forth, in the New Testament; assumption of the totality of the human, in patristics; satisfaction *de congruo*, in the Middle Ages). The historical Jesus surely appears as the liberator from sin, but what we must emphasize is that sin, sinner, and forgiveness are all understood in reference to the Reign of God.

Liberative Aspect of Jesus' Person

Another assertion implied in the denomination of Jesus as Liberator is that the very person of the mediator is liberative. It is liberative because Jesus was as he was. In pure theory, the liberation of the Reign of God could have been proclaimed and furthered by another kind of mediator (acting with power, at a distance from the poor but acting in their behalf, with more rigidity and less tenderness, with more calculation and fewer risks, and so on), who thus could have delivered the victims of oppressive structures, but whose spirit or interior attitude would have been different from that of Jesus.

The liberative element in the person of the mediator is the spirit with which he executes the proclamation and inauguration of the Reign of God. His personal fidelity to God and his mercy to human beings—to summarize systematically, as Hebrews does—his way of being before God and human beings as related in the gospels, the spirit of the Beatitudes as expressed in himself, a life lived in gratuity, his empowerment by truth—all of this is something good, as well as human, and humanizing for others.

We call this spirit of Jesus liberative, not only good, because Jesus came to be thus in the presence of the temptation to be otherwise, as appears in the scene of the temptations. The mediator is shown to be liberated himself, then. This is also liberative for others; yes, one can live this way, delivered from self, delivered from selfishness and dehumanization (a problem that also occurs in historical liberation processes), one can walk humbly with God in history, at once in absolute confidence in a God who is Parent and in total availability to a Parent who is still God.

In Latin America christology has focused from the very beginning on the Jesus who is Liberator of the poor and marginalized, but it is coming to emphasize more and more as well the Jesus who is himself liberated, and who thereby delivers us from ourselves if we keep our eyes fixed on him. But Latin American christology insists on relating the two elements; without this interrelationship, the historical liberation of the poor goes one way and the personal spirit of Jesus another. It observes — not only by virtue of its acceptance in principle of the gospel narratives, but through actual historical experience — that the practice of historical liberation with the spirit of Jesus is efficacious for liberation itself, as Archbishop Romero exemplifies so very well.

To put it simply, many rejoice that Jesus proclaimed and initiated the liberation of the poor of this world (the Reign of God), and rejoice as well that the mediator (Jesus of Nazareth) was as he was. The mediation, and the mediator, are Good News.

Liberative Aspect of Jesus' Resurrection

In the Christian scriptures it is evident that the Reign of God is not the only symbol of utopia — a new earth and a new heaven. Jesus' resurrection, as well, is a symbol of this utopia. It is likewise evident that the specific element in the latter symbol is liberation from death. Liberation christology accepts all of this. Nevertheless, the theology of liberation also regards it as essential to determine what elements of historical liberation are generated here and now by Jesus' resurrection.

In the first place, Jesus' resurrection generates a specific *hope* — indirectly, perhaps, for all, but directly for this world's victims, the addressees of the Reign of God. Indeed, Jesus' resurrection is presented in Peter's first discourses as God's reaction to the injustice that human beings have committed against the just, innocent Jesus. In this sense the resurrection is hope especially for this world's victims, and it is a liberative hope, because it occurs in the presence of the despairing fear that, in history, the executioners may triumph over their victims. It occurs in the presence of the temptation to resignation or cynicism.

A further liberative aspect of Jesus' resurrection is that it indicates the present sovereignty of Christ over history by generating human beings who are not history's slaves but its sovereigns. But sovereignty over history does not consist in living immune and detached from history; still less does it mean attempting — intentionally and idealistically — to "imitate" the immaterial conditions of the state of resurrection (as ancient theologies of the religious life recommended). It consists in triumphing over the slaveries to which human beings are subjected by reason of the fact that they live in history.

The fulfilling element in Jesus' resurrection is shown forth here and now, in history, in the *freedom* with which the following of Jesus is lived. Liberty is not license here; nor is it some mere type of esthetic or existential freedom. On the contrary, the freedom of the following of Jesus is a freedom to become *more* incarnate in historical reality, to dedicate oneself *more* to the liberation of others, to practice the love that can become the *greatest* love. Here is a freedom, then, realized not in fleeing the historical and material, but in incarnating oneself in it *more*, for love. Here, when all is said and done, is Jesus' own freedom, the freedom to lay down his life without anyone's taking it from him; the freedom of a Paul, voluntarily enslaved to all to save all.

The fulfilling dimension of the resurrection is also shown forth in the ability to live with *joy* in the midst of history. It appears in finding in the following of Jesus the pearl of great price, the hidden treasure for which one will sell everything one owns, for the sake of the joy it produces. It is living for others and receiving from others (grace). It is being able to be with others, being able to celebrate life "right now," being able to call God Parent, and to call that God, in relationship with all others, *our* Parent.

This fulfilling dimension of the resurrection is also liberative because it is a victory. The freedom made flesh in history, which does not flee that history, is destined to conquer the slaveries generated by history: fears, failures, persecutions, the cross. Joy transpires in the midst of suffering, and especially in the face of the understandable temptation to sadness, the temptation of meaninglessness. Thus, Jesus' resurrection is recognized as a liberative element introduced into history itself.

In synthesis, Jesus' resurrection is liberative because it enables and inspires people to live in history itself as risen ones, as persons raised; because it enables and inspires people to live the following of Jesus, too, as a reflection of the fulfilling, triumphal note of the resurrection with indestructible hope, freedom, and joy. Let us remark in passing that, when this occurs, then the One who has been raised is shown to be Sovereign of history. In this sense, it could be said — and it comes as a shock — that he has left it in our hands to make him the true Sovereign of history.

Liberative Aspect of the (Metaphysical) Reality of Christ

Let us observe, finally, that liberation christology must show that the element of Good News, of liberation, also resides in dogmatic truth concerning Christ, a truth that liberation christology unequivocally accepts.

The assertion that dogma is not only truth but Good News is an assertion of faith, and of an intrinsically gladsome faith. Thus, it is not available to further analysis; although the *vere Deus* and *vere homo* can surely be interpreted and received not only as truth, but as the Good News of the bounty, indeed the tenderness, of a God who has deigned to descend to that which is human and the Good News that the human can be a sacrament of God.

Nevertheless, christological dogma can be specifically one of liberation if we reformulate it in the following words: Jesus Christ is *verus Deus et verus homo*. Then Jesus Christ is strict revelation of that which is supremely basic for the human being—what it is to be God and what it is to be a human being—and is victorious revelation over the innate tendency of human beings to decide beforehand, on their own authority and in their own interest, the truth of both basic realities. Christological dogma appears as liberative if it is accepted not only as an unveiling of what until now has not been known, but as the victorious revelation of repressed truth. That is, it is seen to be liberative if one accepts that the proposition that Christ is *vere Deus* and *vere homo* is true not because it fulfills the conditions that we human beings impose on the truth of both realities, but because this truth has the power to transcend—and radically—our self-interested comprehension of the divine and the human.

To say it in simple words, it is great Good News of liberation that at last, despite the innate propensity of human beings to evade and oppress the truth, the truth has appeared of what God is and of what we human beings are. What it is to be God and what it is to be a human being have been seen in Jesus, have been revealed in Jesus, triumphing over the concupiscent inclination of human reason to decide both realities in terms of its own interests.

The fact that the dogma presents the subsistence in Christ of both realities, divine and human, without division yet without confusion, is Good News, liberative news. The manner by which the divine and the human subsist in Christ is a strict mystery and hence not subject to analysis. But if we observe the reverberation of this mystery in historical reality, we can assert that it is indeed Good News.

It is good that the divine and the human be "without division," especially if their unity be understood as transcendence in history, such that history renders God present historically, and God, being transcendent, causes history to transcend itself and give more of itself. Also good is the "without confusion," the nonmixing of the two realities, let alone their mutual reduction to each other. History shows that a reduction of the divine to the human necessarily deprives the divine of its mystery, while an elevation of the human to the divine absolutizes the human and transforms it into a troop of monsters: those idolatries that go by the name of despotism and triumphalism. We might say simply that it is good to let God be God and human be human.

History shows how deleterious it is for human beings to violate, on the religious level, this elementary truth of christological dogma. But the violation is just as pernicious in its historical, secular equivalents. For example, utopia (corresponding to the divine) is sometimes divorced from concrete realities in such a way as to be relegated to the trans-historical exclusively, and thus deprived of any influence on the attempt to render it real in concrete realities; thus these realities lose their value as signs of utopia. This is the temptation of the right. Or again, all of the concrete (corresponding to the human) can be subordinated to utopia, as if the concrete had no entity of its own. This is the temptation of the left, even in liberation processes, which can be tempted to replace the whole of the concrete (personal, family, social, artistic) with what is deemed to be the correct route to take to utopia—the political or the military route, depending on the case.

These attempts either to separate the two constitutive elements of dogmatic christology or to reduce one to the other have dehumanizing effects. Hence, the dogmatic formulation of the reality of Jesus Christ is both good and liberative. Despite the dehumanization occasioned by both the separation and the reduction, we human beings undertake to commit these errors because we think that we already know the ultimate structure of reality. The dogma reminds us that the structure of reality is that of transcendence in history, and this is good and liberating news.

Integral, Transcendent Liberation

On the strength of what Jesus does, of the fate that overtakes him, and of what he is, both in his historical reality and in his ultimate transcendent reality, he can and must be called the Liberator. Each of these liberative aspects enjoys its own entity and autonomy, so that none of the three can be deduced from another by pure conceptualization. But if they all be taken together and seen as a whole, then we have the christological basis for the possibility and necessity of the *integral liberation* so earnestly recalled and demanded by the magisterium.

From a point of departure in Christ, that integral liberation is possible and necessary. But in view of what has been said, we think that there are three things to be insisted upon. First, liberation is transformed into integral liberation not by the mere accumulation of disconnected liberative moments, but by the complementarity of all liberative moments in the dynamics of the following of Jesus. Second, in dealing with the christologic liberative dimension, it is necessary (or, in our view, at least very useful) to invoke a logical reproduction of the route that we have proposed chronologically: to begin with and center on the liberation of the poor, thereupon, in virtue of the very dynamics of that liberation, to integrate the other liberative aspects of Christ. Third, an analysis of the integral liberation of which Christ is the vehicle is carried out ultimately in order to foster a liberative christopraxis.

Finally, let us say that, in terms of the adoption of all of the liberative moments cited, objectively theological, transcendent liberation can be formulated. Those who implement Christ's mandate to liberate are thereby realizing the demand voiced by God in the Book of Micah: to act with justice and to love with tenderness. In so doing, these persons can walk humbly with God in history. Now they can really interpret theoretically, and live existentially, their own lives as a life with God. And they can, theoretically and existentially, interpret that life as a journeying toward the definitive encounter with God, when God will be all in all—the Pauline formulation of the transcendent fullness of the Reign of God.

IV. THE POOR AS LOCUS THEOLOGICUS OF CHRISTOLOGY

Let us say a brief concluding word on the locus of christology, as we have developed it in these pages. As we know, liberation theology has developed the topic of the *locus theologicus* in a new manner, and this by way of its own existential experience. In doing theology from a determinate place or locus, with the poor as the point of departure, it has rediscovered content of extreme importance, content central for the faith. This content has not been rediscovered from a starting point in other loci; hence the extreme importance of an analysis of the theological locus. Theology knows that it must respect a methodological distinction between theological locus and font of theological cognition. "The distinction," however, as Ellacuría says, "is not a strict one, let alone an exclusive one. The locus itself, in a sense, is a font, in that it is the locus that determines whether the font yields this or that. The upshot is that, thanks to the locus, and in virtue of the same, a certain determinate content is actually rendered present."[11]

The sketch that we have attempted to present here has been constructed from the theological locus that in Latin American theology, admittedly, is constituted by the poor. We should only wish to add that, in the case of christology, there is an additional, specific reason why theology must be done from the locus of the poor. The poor are not only a reality from which one can reread the whole of theology. They are a reality with which christology must eventually come into confrontation as its object. Thus, with christology, the reason why theology must be done from a theological locus among the poor is more than one of methodological exigency or convenience. It proceeds from revelation itself: the Son of Man is present in the poor of this world.

This presence of Christ in the history of today can be accepted or rejected. But if it is accepted, it would be supremely irresponsible on the part of christology not to take it into central account. This is what is transpiring in Latin America. In simple, nontechnical words Medellín asserts that, where sin is committed against the poor, "there we have a rejection of the Lord's gift of peace and of the Lord himself" (Medellín, "Document on Peace," no. 14, citing Matt. 25). Puebla makes the very carefully considered statement that "with particular tenderness [Jesus Christ] chose to identify himself with those who are poorest and weakest" (Puebla Final Document, no. 196, citing Matt. 25). Archbishop Romero said, in his homilies to a persecuted community, "You are the image of the divine, transfixed with pain," and he compared the Salvadoran people to the Servant of Yahweh. Ellacuría, in a strictly theological reflection, declared that the great sign of the times—the current presence of God among us—is always the crucified people, the historical continuation of the Servant of Yahweh, of Christ crucified.

These statements are not casual ones, nor do their authors intend them as merely pious reflections. They are to be taken seriously. The poor function as the locus of christology in virtue of the concrete content with which they supply that discipline. They tell it something important about Christ. They tell it of his self-abasement, his *kenosis*, his concealment, his cross. And especially, they function as the locus of christology (and of course of faith and following) because, as locus of the current presence of Christ, they are a light illumining all things, and specifically illumining the truth of Christ.

This argumentation is helpless in the face of questions that can be lodged from other theological loci (and these loci always exist, acknowledged or not). Therefore, it can only invite other christologies to place themselves, as well, in the locus of the poor. But as a counterargument, Latin American christology points to the undeniable fact that, from among the poor as its *locus theologicus*, it has rediscovered basic christological realities—realities central to the gospel message, as the Vatican Instruction on the theology of liberation observes—which, lo, these many centuries, have slept the sleep of the just.

From the locus of the poor, christology has made the theoretical rediscovery of Christ as Messiah, as Liberator, and as definitive mediator of the Reign of God. But the situation of the poor and the crucified peoples is intolerable. Therefore these poor and these peoples have set christology its fundamental task. It is a praiseworthy endeavor to demythologize Christ in order to present a reasonable Christ, so that the "name" of Christ may be acceptable by the modern, enlightened human being. But it is a more urgent endeavor to "depacify" Christ, lest reality continue to be abandoned to its misery "in his name"—and in extreme cases, to replace an idolatry of Christ, that the poor may come to see in Christ someone for them rather than against them, and no longer think they have to resign themselves to being oppressed "in his name."

Understood as a substantial *quid* rather than as an accidental *ubi*, the theological locus has always been decisive for christology. It has given it its profoundly pastoral character. If Luther developed a christology of the "Christ for me," Bonhoeffer a christology of the "person for others," Teilhard de Chardin a christology of the "Omega Point of evolution," and Karl Rahner a christology of the "absolute vehicle of salvation," it is because reality demanded it, albeit in various ways. Reality itself had posed the questions: How may one encounter a benevolent God, how may one present an authentic Christ, in a world come of age, a world in evolution, a secularized, antidogmatist world? This pre-christological (but pastorally determinative for christology) reality has always been present in creative christologies. It is present today once more in the theology of liberation: the reality of a dehumanizing poverty and of the hope of its eradication.

Gustavo Gutiérrez declares that the decisive question for Latin American theology is "how to tell the poor that God loves them." Christology responds with Jesus Christ the Liberator, the absolute mediator of the Reign of God to the poor. The reality of poverty both motivates this "theorization of Christ" and renders it possible. The agreeable surprise is that, thus theorized, Christ is a bit more like—it seems to us—Jesus of Nazareth.

—Translated by Robert R. Barr

NOTES

1. Many of the methodological presuppositions of the theology of liberation are analyzed in this volume. For christology specifically, see Chapter 8, "Christology in the Theology of Liberation."

2. See, in this volume, Chapter 16, "Central Position of the Reign of God in Liberation Theology."

3. See Ignacio Ellacuría, "La teología como momento ideológico de la praxis eclesial," *Estudios Eclesiásticos* 53 (1978):457-76; Sobrino, "Teología en un mundo sufriente: La teología de la liberación como *intellectus amoris*," *Revista Latinoamericana de Teología* 15 (1988):243-66.

4. See Ignacio Ellacuría, "Los pobres, 'lugar teológico' en América latina," in

Ignacio Ellacuría, *Conversión de la Iglesia al reino de Dios* (San Salvador, 1985), pp. 153-78.

5. Karl Rahner and K. H. Weger, *Our Christian Faith* (London: Burns & Oates, 1980), p. 93.

6. An analogous comparison ought to be made with patristic theology, especially in regard to the destiny of the Reign of God, although we cannot address this here.

7. Rahner and Weger, *Our Christian Faith,* p. 93.

8. M. Hengel, *Seguimiento y carisma* (Santander, Spain, 1981), p. 105.

9. See D. Wiederkehr, in *Mysterium Salutis*, vol. 3/1 (Madrid, 1969), p. 558.

10. An analysis of the systematic concept of following or discipleship must invoke an analogy of discipleship precisely in view of the reality of the poor. In his own age — and with his expectancy of the imminence of the Reign — Jesus made different basic demands on, respectively, his disciples and the poor. Of the poor he seems to demand not discipleship, but an active hope in the coming of the Reign. Today a theological treatment of the discipleship of the poor must take into consideration the non-imminence of the Reign. Meanwhile, the material condition of the poverty of our times seems to render the following of disciples impossible, which would lead to the paradox that the poor, to whom the Good News is directly addressed, and whom Christ seeks to liberate, could not acquire a similarity to Christ precisely as disciples. Therefore one must speak of an analogy of discipleship or following. That is, while the poor participate more radically (generally speaking) in the destiny of the cross, and at times, in the hope of resurrection, than disciples do — still, the active aspect of mission can be more absent in the case of the poor, by reason of their material conditions. Thus, Ignacio Ellacuría proposes an analogy of the systematic theological concept of the poor. The poor are: (1) the material, impoverished poor, (2) the poor who have become aware of the causes of their poverty, (3) the poor organized in a struggle to be liberated, and (4) the poor who wage this struggle *with* the spirit of the Beatitudes. See Ellacuría, "Los pobres, 'lugar teológico,'" pp. 81-163.

11. Ibid., p. 168.

21

The Holy Spirit

JOSÉ COMBLIN

The Latin American experience of the Holy Spirit is the one described by the Bishops' Conference at Medellín:

Latin America is obviously under the sign of transformation and development. . . . This indicates that we are on the threshold of a new historical era of our continent, an era that will be charged with aspirations for total emancipation, for liberation from all servitude, for personal maturation and collective integration. Here we perceive the omens of the painful gestation of a new civilization. We can only interpret this gigantic effort at a rapid transformation and development as an evident sign of the Spirit who leads the history of individuals and peoples toward its vocation. (Medellín Final Document, no. 4)

In the current context of suffering and of hope for present transformation, Medellín (no. 5) applies the passage from Paul on the groanings and firstfruits of the Spirit (Rom. 8:22-23).

The Puebla Document reasserts this confidence in the activity of the Spirit in history, and specifically, in the current history of Latin America:

The renovation of human beings, and subsequently of society, will depend first of all on the action of the Holy Spirit. Laws and structures will have to be animated by the Spirit, who gives life to human beings and enables the Gospel to be fleshed out in history. . . .

The Spirit, who filled the whole earth, was also present in all that was good in pre-Colombian cultures. That very Spirit helped them to accept the Gospel. And today the Spirit continues to arouse yearnings for liberative salvation in our peoples. Hence we must discover the Spirit's authentic presence in the history of Latin America. (Puebla Final Document, nos. 199-201)

Neither Medellín nor Puebla developed an explicit theology of the Holy Spirit on the foundation of these basic assertions. Neither has Latin American theology, we must acknowledge, developed a specific theology of the Holy Spirit. Until now, theology on our continent has been in the debt of the theology of the Latin church, which, instead of developing a theology of the Holy Spirit, has only repeated what it has received from the patristic era. So far, Latin American theology—like all Latin-tradition theology, both Protestant and Catholic—operates under the sign of a "christomonism."

Instead, a theology of the Holy Spirit is something we can discern in outline, but do not yet have in hand. From a point of departure in the basics of Latin American theology, we can project where such a theology would go.

The Pentecostal movement in Latin America is growing by leaps and bounds and has seen a momentous expansion in its Protestant as well as in its Catholic form. The Protestant Pentecostal churches are by far the most vigorous of all of the Protestant denominations among us. They do a great deal of proselytizing and are winning adherents by the millions. Their triumph is precisely in the popular world, especially among the miserable populations of the outskirts of our cities, but also in rural areas. The message they carry is not specific, but implants in Latin America just what we have seen in the United States. Nearly all of the Pentecostal churches, however, have Latin American pastors and their own resources. They are, in a way, the churches the least dependent economically on the outside. By reason of their origins, the Pentecostals are fundamentalist in their teachings and indifferent to the political. Still, when members of their communities are directly attacked, ministers and communities react. Thus, Pentecostals have a very effective collaboration to offer the popular movements in behalf of labor unionization, broader political efforts, and even the revolutionary struggle.

The Catholic charismatic movement has penetrated the middle classes, and there it has remained. Class segregation is so radical in Latin America that a movement implanted in one class is incapable of passing to another. An obstacle or "block" in the mentality of the middle classes prevents them from developing any sensitivity to social problems. These same middle classes carry this "block" to any religious movement they adopt. In Europe or North America the Catholic charismatic movement may be capable of opening up to social problems. In Latin America doing so is all but impossible.

I. EXPERIENCE OF THE HOLY SPIRIT

Very frequently the experience of the Holy Spirit is anonymous. In theology, just as among the Christian people, we hear simply of the experience of a *Dios liberador*—a God who delivers. Admittedly, the impact of the Hebrew scriptures, especially the texts of the Exodus, have been very powerful. The language of our experience takes its inspiration there. While the content of the experience has been enriched by the Christian scriptures, the formulation often remains faithful to its Hebrew sources.

Theology, like the popular Christian religious experience itself, knows very well that the *Dios liberador* will not deliver the people of God by means of physical miracles, as in Egypt or the wilderness. God will not deliver from without by sheer blows of the divine will. God delivers the people by means of the forces and energies that God places within the people, by means of the enlightenment and prophetic charisma of mighty leaders, by means of the union and solidarity of living communities, and by means of the enthusiasm of the multitudes that these communities and prophets succeed in arousing. Latin American Christians recognize the God of liberation and feel the presence of such a God in their very midst, acting in their own actions and commitments. This *Dios liberador* is the Holy Spirit—whether known by name or not.

In the heat of political action, Christians may feel that they are operating in terms only of social or political forces and factors. They may not recall the sources of their action. However, when the poor rise up to a collective action in this world, sheer social forces are surely not at work. After all, what we have here is a resurrection of the human being, a new birth of whole peoples, an utter transformation of persons.

Whence do such movements proceed? From the presence of the Holy Spirit. At the level of this divine presence, the (objectively) theological life and the political life constitute a single action. Faith, hope, charity, and political action are one reality in the human person who is really and concretely born to a new life. It is not a matter of mere pragmatic options. It is a matter of the very existence of the people: the Holy Spirit is involved here. At the heart of these experiences of historical actions, the liberative power of the Spirit is present.

1. Experience of Action

Ever since the Iberian invasion and importation of African slaves, the Latin American multitudes have been subjected to an absolute passivity. The majority of the population, until the past century, was made up of slaves. Few peoples have been reduced to such passivity for so many centuries by such a small number of dominators. Even today a great proportion of the Latin American people live in inaction—a passive object struggling to survive amid societies manipulated by the mighty. Latin Americans are but masses of isolated individuals. The native or African peoples to which they belong have been destroyed. Systematically, all efforts to reestablish community ties have been prevented. These peoples are permitted neither continuity nor solidarity. On the one hand, they have been deprived of their memory of the past; on the other, they are forbidden to imagine a future.

When communities are formed, a genuine resurrection occurs. The passive masses learn to act. The miracle accounts of the gospel that have had the strongest attraction for Latin American ears are those in which the lame walk, the deaf hear, the blind see, and the dead rise; in other words, the accounts in which those who have not acted begin to act. In the beginning the kinds of action undertaken are the most humble: simple cooperation among neighbors, meeting for particular actions like petitioning the authorities, or simpler still, celebrations of the events of the community. The mere fact of taking the initiative and assuming collective responsibility constitutes a new life. When favorable circumstances appear, these same communities, formed in such humble activities, show themselves capable of assuming concrete responsibilities decisive for the future of the peoples. This is what has occurred recently in Central America, especially in Guatemala, Nicaragua, and El Salvador. Christian communities no longer act as objects manipulated by more powerful forces. Now they act on the basis of their own initiative, their renewed consciousness, the energies that they themselves have mobilized.

The Christian communities interpret the birth of this new action of theirs in the light of the Bible. Beginning in the Hebrew scriptures, the Spirit inaugurated its liberative action by raising up the judges (Judg. 13:25, 14:6) and kings (1 Sam. 10:10, 11:6, 16:13; 2 Sam. 23:2). Later this Spirit acts by way of the prophets in the promise of a more plenteous coming of the same Spirit upon the future Messiah, that he may act with greater strength (Isa. 42:6-7, 61:1-2). This last text has been applied to Jesus by Luke in one of the most frequently cited pericopes in the theology of liberation:

> "The spirit of the Lord is upon me;
>   therefore, he has anointed me.
> He has sent me to bring glad tidings to the poor,
>   to proclaim liberty to captives,
> Recovery of sight to the blind
>   and release to prisoners,
> To announce a year of favor from the Lord." (Luke 4:18-19)

Paul had to deal with the enthusiasm of a community that had received the gift of tongues. That gift produces no outward fruit, but only affords inward satisfaction. So Paul calls his addressees' attention to the gifts that "build" community (see 1 Cor. 14:4, 14:12). This tireless activity on the part of the Apostle Paul is itself an extraordinary manifestation of the Holy Spirit (1 Cor. 2:4-5, 10-16).

Latin American communities are beginning to experience the fulfillment of Jesus' promise to his disciples: The one "who has faith in me will do the works I do, and greater far than these" (John 14:12).

The activities of the Spirit are different from the actions produced without the Spirit. Latin America has always been famous for its pharaonic works— mighty human deeds built on the dead bodies and superhuman sufferings of millions of slaves or quasi-slaves. Such were the conquest itself, the gold and silver mines, the plantations. Today we see similar works throughout Latin America, especially in Brazil. These works have always been celebrations of the pride of their promoters, and they have revealed the utter contempt of the latter for the dignity of the millions of persons sacrificed to the glory of a few. They stand as testimony to the implacable will of a few, and to their total domination of the multitudes.

2. Experience of Freedom

From the outset the experience of the Latin American peoples has been an experience of the frustration of freedom. Promises of freedom have never been wanting, yet slavery always came. The economic, cultural, and political distance between the great and the small is such that freedom is the exclusive perquisite of the powerful. The mighty have always made the slavery of the multitudes the condition of their own freedom. Freedom is the privilege of the mighty. The Latin American peoples have expressed their longings for liberty by flight. They have fled to the rain forests: natives expelled from their lands or pursued by the slave-traders, blacks who rebelled on the plantations, rural poor whose lands were seized by the large landholders. In Latin America freedom has always meant flight and exile. And this is what it means today. It does not mean participation and responsibility.

The experience of freedom is something the poor have when they begin to gather together in order to think together to form associations, leagues, unions, and communities. They have the experience of freedom when they begin to elect representatives, seek common objectives, and struggle for their autonomy, rights, and dignity. They experience their freedom precisely in the battle for liberation. Theirs is never a complete, established freedom. It is always the freedom to fight for freedom. There is freedom when horizontal relationships appear among equals—when large numbers acknowledge one another as brothers and sisters and cooperate with one another, without any of them arrogating to themselves special privileges over the others. This freedom is the opportunity to be and to exist for oneself, to grow for oneself, not to be robbed of all one's progress by a superior power that monopolizes all production. In Latin America freedom is inchoate. It has always been the perquisite of the elite; not even national independence has ever been anything but the independence of the great.

Today, the small are beginning to learn what freedom means. They understand this freedom in the light of the Bible. True, it is the reading of the Book of Exodus that has especially fed the experience of Christian freedom. But this reading is more than a simple absorption of that scriptural text. Most meaningful of all for us has been the rereading of this book as done by Jesus and the gospels.

It is true that there has not been a great deal of insistence on the relationship between freedom and the Holy Spirit. But the teaching of Paul and John on the Spirit is first and foremost a message of freedom. This message is one of liberation for Latin America, since it sets one free from any religion of slavery. In Latin America official religion has insisted on obedience. It has erected obedience into the very foundation and core of Christianity. Official religion has been a reflection of the spirituality developed in Europe under the sign of Trent. But it has also been a reflection of a society based on the total subordination of the masses.

Paul delivers religion from any spirit of slavery, even where he must make practical concessions to the customs of Judaism or the social structures of his time. The proclamation of the Holy Spirit is the inauguration, the radical inauguration, of a new time, the time of freedom: "Where the Spirit of the Lord is, there is freedom" (2 Cor. 3:17). "Remember that you have been called to live in freedom" (Gal. 5:13). "It was for liberty that Christ freed us" (Gal. 5:1).

The message of John, as well, is the freedom of the Spirit:

Flesh begets flesh. Spirit begets spirit. The wind blows where it will. You hear the sound it makes but you do not know where it comes from or where it goes. So it is with everyone begotten of the Spirit. (John 3:6-8)

An hour is coming, and is already here, when authentic worshipers will worship the Father in Spirit and truth. Indeed, it is just such worshipers the Father seeks. God is Spirit, and those who worship him must worship in Spirit and truth. (John 4:23-24)

Thus Christian religion begins with the liberation of human beings from religious slavery, or slavery for religious "reasons." This is the foundation of all other kinds of emancipation.

The Second Vatican Council launched a process of emancipation of Christians in its *Declaration on Religious Freedom*, although it does not cite the dependence of this freedom on the proclamation of the Holy Spirit. The teaching of Vatican II is over twenty-five years old, and weak. Yet it has always been either attacked or ignored in practice. Vatican II had no doctrine of the Holy Spirit, and therefore was unable to develop a message of freedom that would be clearly Christian. The same shortcoming crops up in the 1984 and 1986 Instructions of the Congregation of the Faith on freedom and liberation. Nor does Cardinal Ratzinger have a theology of the Holy Spirit. Such a theology can emerge only from a genuinely and concretely free Christian people. That people can only be the people of the poor. A church that is not a church of the poor will always be afraid of freedom. A theology of the Holy Spirit can emerge only from the praxis of a free Christian people.

3. Experience of the Word

Only oppressed peoples know the value of the word. Dominators talk, and talk a great deal, but they talk mainly in order not to say anything—to prevent certain words from being pronounced. Dominators know that freedom begins with the word, and this is why they censor words. They all know that society is based on injustice, but no one says this, because with them, fear is stronger than truth. Latin America has become accustomed to the silence of the masses. In the presence of their white landlords, the natives seem mute. They make themselves seem as stupid as possible. They know that, if they happen to be right, they will be more severely punished for speaking the truth than for a lie. They lie because those who have disposition over them expect them to lie and will punish them unless they do. Thus it is with black workers, whether on the countryside or in the city. Thus it is with all of the poor; they are constrained to be ignorant and to confess their ignorance. They must confess that only the "boss" knows, and that only the "boss" has the right to know and to speak.

Hence the extraordinary impression of liberation had by the poor when they begin to speak, when they begin to tell the truth, to say what is really happening, to recount actual, factual history. The word is the first expression of rebellion against domination. The word has no magical powers, but it has the virtue of expressing personhood, and it helps personhood to exist. The word is self-assertion. What matters is not so much the content of the word as the very fact of speaking.

The word of the poor in Latin America is not a scientific word. It is not pure explanation. It is not science offering solutions by mighty means. It is not philosophy, system, or developed reflection. It may seek words or expressions in various philosophies, but it is not philosophy. It may use Marxist words or schemas, but the word itself is not identical with the Marxist system. The word of the poor communities is the self-assertion of those communities, their will to exist, an expression of their dignity.

A word of this kind denounces the silence in which the peoples have been kept under the thumb of the oppressor. It denounces the structures of domination. It announces a new life, a different society. It calls together and unites the poor. It stimulates, it animates, it strengthens the communities, it enunciates projects, it points to horizons and goals. The word of the poor is far simpler than an ideology would be. It is the arrival in society of those who have managed to exist, incapable though they may have been of forging ideologies. Subsequently, intellectuals may add ideologies, if in this way they can reinforce the word of the poor. But that word is antecedent to all ideologies, and of more worth than all of them. It would stand on its own even if all ideologies were mere illusions. It stands because it is the manifestation of actual persons who have been unable to exist and who wish to exist.

This is the word in the biblical sense. It is a basic concept in the message of the Bible. The word—at least the word in its strong, specific sense—is inspired by the Spirit.

As inspired by the Spirit, the most basic word is the outcry of the oppressed. The cry of the oppressed arises in Egypt and resounds all through the history of Israel. It is the cry of the oppressed people in Egypt, the cry of the oppressed of Israel in the land of Canaan, the cry of the people in exile, the cry that belongs to the poor by right. Jesus, too, cried out on the cross, recapitulating all the cries of the oppressed of all centuries.

The Christian people, a people poor and oppressed from birth, also have the right to cry out to the Father, and to rely on that Parent's attention and response. The Holy Spirit is at the root of the cry of the Christian people groaning in the hope of resurrection (Rom. 8:14-27):

All who are led by the Spirit of God are sons of God. You did not receive a spirit of slavery leading you back into fear, but a spirit of adoption through which we cry out, "Abba!" (that is, "Father"). (Rom. 8:14-15)

The proof that you are sons is the fact that God has sent forth into our hearts the spirit of his Son which cries out "Abba!" ("Father!"). (Gal. 4:6)

The cry does not die out with the resurrection. The struggles and the anguish abide. But the light of the resurrection endows the cry with a greater sureness. In the light of the resurrection, the cry wins a gospel, a proclamation of liberation. The Spirit gives strength to the gospel of the poor. It was the Spirit who inspired the prophets, as the Nicaeo-Constantinopolitan Creed declares. Since Pentecost, the number of the prophets has been multiplied many times over, for the Spirit is sent to all men and women who serve that Spirit. The elders and leaders of the people are dumbfounded, for they are ignorant of the fact that the Spirit is present: "Observing the self-assurance of Peter and John, and realizing that the speakers were uneducated men of no standing, the questioners were amazed" (Acts 4:13).

The Holy Spirit produces words. The Book of Acts is a clear exposition of this production of words by the Spirit. According to Luke's gospel, the same Spirit had already made Jesus a herald of the Reign of God. According to Paul's theology, it is the same Spirit. once more, who now makes the apostles persons of the word. Paul himself is obvious proof of the strength of the Spirit: "My message and my preaching had none of the persuasive force of 'wise' argumentation, but the convincing power of the Spirit" (1 Cor. 2:4).

In Johannine circles, as well, the Spirit is bound up with the word: "This is how you can recognize God's Spirit: every spirit that acknowledges Jesus Christ come in the flesh belongs to God" (1 John 4:2).

4. Experience of Community

Inasmuch as Christian communities acknowledge that they are word (both in the words of the Bible and in the ministries of the word that have been instituted by the Bible), they also acknowledge that they are Christian communities precisely in the light of the Bible. Here, as well, the Bible sheds light on Christian practice.

The popular Christian communities are not the simple upshot of spontaneous social factors. They are not the natural product of misery—a means the popular cultures invent in order to survive.

We shall not deny the sociological factors. Without them the phenomenon of the communities would be very difficult. True, the Latin American masses have been reduced to the state of masses by the successive conquests. Colonial and neo-colonial domination have provoked immense migrations, and local solidarity, on the part of destroyed peoples and families. It crams into the mines, the plantations, the outskirts of the teeming cities, the slum ghettos and rural slums, whole populations—millions of separated, isolated, rootless persons. In a situation like this, the poor survive because they help one another. They make an effort to form new ties and new solidarities. However, the very society that has dissolved the old ties is opposed to the formation of new ones. The triumph of community over the forces of dissociation that prevail in society requires something more than purely natural forces. It is perfectly possible for a population to become simply asocial, anarchical. There are human masses that live under the permanent threat of a world without law or order.

Of themselves alone, then, sociological factors do not explain everything. There is something new in the Christian communities, and it comes on the scene as a miracle of God. There is a force at work within them that arouses generosity, dedication, and sacrifice — something akin to Christianity in its first origins. Within the spaces described by sociology — spaces open to new kinds of association — extraordinary forces are appearing in persons willing and able to devote their lives to the birth of a genuine community life. This community never arises of itself. It springs into being only by virtue of the help, inspiration, and prophetic word of persons devoted to it.

The Christian community is comprehensible only in the light of biblical revelation. In it is something of the Reign of God. It proceeds from the power of the Spirit of Jesus Christ. Christians understand what is happening among them as a renewal of what occurred in the first age of the church, when the activity of the Spirit became overt and perceptible. In a certain way, this renewal is also a sensible sign of the Spirit in the world. Furthermore, the small community does not close in upon itself; it opens up to become the seed of a new people founded on relationships of kinship rather than domination.

The community sees itself in the light of the first community of Jerusalem, and of the Pauline communities in which the Spirit was manifested in such a visible way. The communities of the primitive church clearly exhibited the model of a community church, whose life comes from the Spirit through the mediation of the apostles, but comes as the life of an autonomous, locally present entity. Today, as well, the communities are the church alive in a small number of laity. It is served by ministers, but it has its own self-consistency, and does not depend upon the clergy. The Spirit enables the poor to maintain their community by themselves, and yet to create bonds of communion with other communities.

The community is communion, and communion proceeds from charity (in Greek *agape*, for which "solidarity" is a better translation). Charity is the firstfruit of the Spirit, the most excellent charism of all (1 Cor. 12:30 — 13:13, Gal. 5:22-25). From the union of the communities springs the greater church — the communion engendered of all nations by the Spirit (Eph. 2:11-22, 4:2-4).

The Spirit creates not only a communitarian church, but a humanity-in-communion. Latin American communities seek to renew not only the shape of the church, but rather, first of all, the structure of society. Community life as lived on the basis of groups of families of the people constitutes the fabric of a new social life — a promise of renewal for all of society. Such renewal cannot be created by political decrees alone. It must emerge from the will of living, breathing persons.

5. Experience of Life

Latin America has the experience of the God of life in a world that is so often the reign of death. When existence is experienced in a situation of dangers, threats, and ongoing fear, the great miracle is life. Life is seen as victory over the forces of death.

The daily struggle is often a pure struggle for survival, for daily bread. The majority of people do not even have the opportunity to think of great liberation projects. Liberation is experienced as the gaining of their daily nourishment — a triumph that must be renewed each day, since insecurity is all-pervasive and absolute.

The life of the poor is a diminished life: stunted, emaciated bodies, prematurely shriveled up, diseased, deprived of effective remedies, without adequate means of subsistence, undernourished,undereducated, culturally deficient. The longing of the poor is that their children may know a better life than theirs. Many times, however, they wonder whether their children's life will be even worse.

Hence such a strong will to live. There are no suicides among the poor. The poor want to live. With all its limitations, they appreciate life. For the poor, life is neither wealth, nor power, nor glory, nor grandeur. Life has an intrinsic value, simply as life, even without the ingredients the rich regard as indispensable. But life is also shared; life worth living is life lived with others, in community.

The God of the Bible is the God of life. And the God of life is the Holy Spirit. In their quest for life, Latin Americans thirst for the Holy Spirit.

From Old Testament times (see Ezek. 37), the Spirit has always been the power of life. The Spirit can actually raise the dead. The gift of the Spirit bestowed by the Risen Christ is a promise of resurrection and eternal life, to follow this earthly existence (see Rom. 8:11). But Christians believe that the resurrection of Christ produces its firstfruits on this very earth:

"If anyone thirsts, let him come to me; let him drink who believes in me. Scripture has it: 'From within him rivers of living water shall flow.'" (Here [Jesus] was referring to the Spirit, whom those that came to believe in him were to receive. . . .) (John 7:37-39)

Faith does not instantly transform enfeebled bodies, but it does confer new life on them. The frail frames of the poor become vessels of the energies of the Spirit, and their fecundity is astounding. The Spirit produces new vitality in this people shattered by so many physical and moral miseries. The Spirit is seen to be present. In the activity of the Spirit is hope of liberation for the oppressed. Thus, we profess in the Nicaeo-Constantinopolitan Creed: "We believe in the Holy Spirit . . . the giver of life."

II. THE HOLY SPIRIT IN WORLD HISTORY

In the old christendom, Christians aspired to no marvelous transformations. Official theologies were content with saying what Thomas Aquinas had said; that is, in the church God had already bestowed every divine gift that human beings would ever receive in this world. There is nothing to hope for outside the church as such. Today's Christians refuse to resign themselves to this reductionistic hope. For believers today, the biblical themes suggest something more. Christians hope for a transformation of the world. They understand that the biblical themes proclaim a new age of creation—a genuine renewal of all creation, and not only of the individual life of some saints by way of the practice of heroic virtue. Among the oppressed poor a hope is alive which the established churches seem to wish to stifle. Clergy invoke the disillusioned wisdom of Ecclesiastes: "nothing new under the sun." In Latin America the poor want more. Nor can their hope be interpreted in purely political terms. They want more than a political revolution. They want a complete conversion of the world. And this, only the Spirit of God can accomplish.

1. The Spirit and the Renewal of the World

The Holy Spirit is the source and principle of the resurrection of the body (Rom. 1:4, 8:11; 1 Cor. 14:44). If the very Spirit that will raise up our bodies is already present, will that Spirit not be able to produce effects of initial resurrection even now, right in this world?

The Holy Spirit is the presence, in our own time, of the Reign of God. The Spirit is the first stage of that Reign—the beginning of the Reign of God on this earth (2 Cor. 1:22, Gal. 5:5, Eph. 1:13-14). The substitution of the Holy Spirit for the Reign of God in the successive writings of the Christian scriptures is frequently interpreted to mean that the utopian Reign of God had now come to be replaced with a more "realistic" concept, that of the Holy Spirit. The Holy Spirit becomes the sign of a purely interior transformation of the human being. Thus, anything the expression *Reign of God* might suggest in terms of a social meaning, a concrete, palpable meaning, is eliminated. Little by little, we are told, Christianity had lost the utopian sense of the oldest gospel tradition. Will this interpretation be correct? Will the Holy Spirit produce only "interior" fruits, and nothing in the world, nothing in concrete history?

A mighty protest wells up among an oppressed people of the poor. The oppressed reject such interpretation. Nor is this the first time in history that they have done so. To reduce the Holy Spirit to the sphere of interiority is to project upon the Christian scriptures a restriction of meaning that will later appear in the established church. But let us observe that there has always been an element in the church that has refused to resign itself to this elimination of the Spirit from the world and from history. To be sure, in the era of christendom these believers were under a cloud of suspicion and were usually rebuffed and rejected. They were driven into "heresy" (a concept currently under thoroughgoing historical reexamination).

The Holy Spirit is the principle of creation and of the new creation. Christian tradition has understood that the "wind" that "swept over the waters" (Gen. 1:2) at the beginning of creation was the Holy Spirit. The medieval hymn "Veni, Sancte Spiritus" ("Come, Holy Ghost") is still sung today. The Canticle of Judith celebrates the creative Spirit: "Let every creature serve you; for you spoke, and they were made, you sent forth your spirit, and they were created" (Jth. 16:14). The Psalms, too, have it: "When you send forth your spirit, they are created, and you renew the face of the earth" (Ps. 104:30). If there is a new creation—a renewal of the face of the earth—how could it be limited to a purely interior renewal? Will there be nothing in this renewal for the present life of the world and human society?

The Spirit actually generates a new human being. It creates a new birth (John 3:5, 6, 8). Vatican II interprets the biblical texts that bear on the new creation as meaning that we are "redeemed by Christ and made a new creature in the Holy Spirit" (*Gaudium et Spes*, no. 37).

Similar texts, relating the Holy Spirit to creation and the new creation, occur throughout the Council documents. Here are some further examples.

The People of God believes that it is led by the Spirit of the Lord, who fills the earth. Motivated by this faith, it labors to decipher authentic signs of God's presence and purpose in the happenings, needs, and desires in which this people has a part. (*Gaudium et Spes*, no. 11)

The Lord's Spirit . . . who fills the whole earth . . . (*Presbyterorum Ordinis*, no. 22).

Christ is now at work in the hearts of men through the energy of His Spirit. He arouses not only a desire for the age to come, but, by that very fact, He animates, purifies, and strengthens those noble longings too by which the human family strives to make its life more human and to render the whole earth submissive to this goal. (*Gaudium et Spes*, no. 38)

These texts show the Spirit at work in the renewal of the entire earth, and not only of the interior life.

In today's liberation movements among the peoples, the Spirit of God is at work. There is something of the Spirit in these movements that Christians have the task of discerning and claiming. Christians will have to follow the signs, the "tracks" left by the Spirit in these liberation movements. In other times movements for social change were rejected as inspired by the rebellion of the devil. There are Christians of this same mind in Latin America today. But these persons are no longer the whole voice of the church. Another awareness has sprung into being—a consciousness endowed with the capacity to discover the Holy Spirit active in the movements of the world itself, and not just in ecclesiastical space.

2. The Holy Spirit and the Poor

The Holy Spirit acts in the world by means of the poor. This principle has been unambiguously established by Paul (1 Cor. 1:26–2:16). Nor is it a particular, isolated statement in the Bible; on the contrary, it is the core of the biblical view of history. From the outset Israel was chosen to be the vehicle of the divine designs because it was the weakest and poorest of the peoples. Then, within Israel itself, God once more selects the very weakest to represent the authentic remnant of the people of that election. The Messiah foretold by Isaiah, Zechariah, and all the prophets was to be a king who is poor, and a king of the poor. Jesus is the fulfillment of the Messianic prophecy contained in the Isaian Servant of God, whom the great ones of the earth humiliated and despised. In his prophetic mission in the land of Israel, Jesus acts in the midst of the poor, addresses his message to the poor of Israel, selects his disciples from their number. His church begins amid the poor.

It is not to be wondered at, then, that reforms throughout church history commence with movements that set poverty as a priority. From Anthony the desert monk, to the medieval reformers, to the champions of twentieth-century renewal, the power of the Spirit has impelled the reformers to a life of poverty in an encounter with the poor and oppressed masses of the earth. Spirituality is something having to do with poverty.

Thus, the Spirit acts on the underside of history. It does not reject the mediation of concrete, historical forces—neither scientific and technological development, nor economic development, nor political power, nor even, in extreme cases, military mediations. But it subordinates them all to the power of the poor. The Spirit acts by means of patience, perseverance, protest, petition. Only as a last resort do the poor have recourse to violence. While it may be true that violence has been the womb of history, it is not the way of the poor. The poor have ever been the *victims* of violence, not its protagonists. The action of the Spirit runs counter to violence and the exploitation of labor. The weapons of the Spirit are the weapons wielded by the poor. The tension between the violent means of the mighty and the peaceful means of the poor is a constant in the history of the Spirit.

As a result, the Holy Spirit is the source of a radical conflict in history, an ongoing conflict fueled by that Spirit's active presence, the conflict between the forces of domination, which use the resources placed at their disposal by history itself, and the prophetic forces of resistance, which are unarmed, deprived of means of action. The poor build their means of action with their own toil.

The peace of the Spirit is built up only on the foundation of restitution to the poor of the fruits of their labor and the stripping away of the privileges unjustly accumulated by the powerful.

3. The Holy Spirit and a Temporal Messianism

The Messianic prophecies of the Hebrew scriptures proclaim the coming of an age characterized by an abundance of temporal goods. Jesus endorses these prophecies, for example in Luke 4:18-19. He focuses his own activity on the material condition of his people: he heals the sick, feeds the hungry, and alleviates bodily suffering. For centuries, especially during the christendom centuries, a dominant interpretation had it that these Messianic boons were mere images, literary figures, of the spiritual goods now at hand and available in the church: interior conversion, faith, the virtues. Christians, however, especially the poor, have tended to remain unconvinced. They have been unwilling to accept the proposition that everything Jesus promised was only a literary figure of purely interior blessings.

In medieval times these tendencies came to their most powerful literary expression in the works of a thirteenth-century monk known as Joachim of Fiore, whose writings had a great influence on the so-called spiritual Franciscans. According to Joachim, Jesus proclaimed the coming of an age of the Holy Spirit. Under the christendom of Constantine, Christianity had realized only a transitory, imperfect phase of the message of Jesus. Some kind of domination survived. But an age of the Holy Spirit was in the offing—the age of the poor and of nonviolence.

The ideal proclaimed by Joachim of Fiore coincides almost perfectly with the modern revolutionary utopias. The official church condemned Joachim's predictions, insisting that the Holy Spirit had already been completely bestowed in the church. Beyond the church was nothing. In the world, nothing could be expected from the Holy Spirit. From that moment on, Messianic and spiritualistic aspirations were constrained to keep their distance from the official church. In the fourteenth century revolutionary movements appeared, and they continued in succeeding centuries. At first the revolutionaries believed themselves to be inspired by the Holy Spirit. But as time went on they gradually shifted to a purely secular interpretation of the content and dynamism of their revolutions, as if these movements had sprung from the human being alone—from matter without the intervention of a Holy Spirit. Finally they evolved into the altogether atheistic, antireligious revolutions of the twentieth century.

The theological meaning of the revolutionary movements, like the meaning of the Christian poor, is currently under reexamination. Can the forces at work in the transformation of the world be purely natural ones? Can the Holy Spirit be aloof from such movements? The theology of liberation insists on the opposite. It seeks neither purely secular revolutions, nor a purely interior, "privatized" Christianity. It believes that there is some truth in the Messianic prophecies of the prophets and Jesus, as well as in the Messianic interpretations of Christians of all times. A transformation is possible in this world, even though it will never be definitively achieved or perfectly realized.

Above all, liberation theology now holds that modern revolutions have not been useless or devoid of human and spiritual content. It recognizes signs of the Spirit in them, in spite of all the suffering and all the violence they have occasioned. The anti-colonial revolutions, with the American Revolution of 1776 in the forefront, have not been in vain. The French Revolution of 1789, and all its offspring of the nineteenth century, have not been in vain. The socialist revolutions of the twentieth century have not been in vain or without content. None of these revolutions has been totally ineffective for the creation of a better world. The world has never been the same.

The Latin American people believe that their future revolutions, too, will find another way to live—a better life, a Reign of God. They look for no paradise on earth, but they do expect the future Reign of God to come nearer. They believe that Spirit will be efficacious in history, promoting a concrete and temporal Reign, however incomplete. They do not believe that all of the activity of the Holy Spirit can be shut up in the confines of the church, or that there is nothing to be expected of the church but precisely the church. So they adopt the perspectives of old Joachim of Fiore, the spiritual Franciscans, and a whole Christian tradition that was sometimes an underground one. They glean from the Book of Revelation its outlook of partial realizations on this earth. No book is read with more passion than that "Apocalypse of John"—the book that sets down in black and white the current condition of the oppressed and expresses their hopes. This is also the book of the prophecies of the Spirit.

4. Dialectic of Church and World

The Christian church sprang from a reconciliation between Judaism and paganism by the power of the Holy Spirit (Eph. 2:14-22). The Spirit created a new society by kneading the leaven of Judaism into the legacy of all the nations of the earth. What was created then was neither a mixture nor a mere synthesis, but a genuinely new phenomenon—something in which Judaism and pagan civilizations could find themselves anew, elevated and perfected. Both poles shook off their limitations and all that divided them from each other, while losing nothing of the positive within them.

Some have understood the text of Ephesians as if the task of this reconciliation were already completed. Even in the Letter to the Romans, however, Paul proclaimed that the people of Israel would abide in separation until the end of the ages, in testimony to the incompletion of the work. The encounter between Judaism and paganism will always be a task to be performed anew, until the end of time—not only because Judaism abides, but because the other civilizations of the world, as well, represent ever more difficult challenges.

The church is the mediator of this work of reconciliation. It is the tool of the Holy Spirit, and the primary sign of the concrete efficacy of that Spirit. However, the church itself lives in concrete history and suffers history's impacts and influences. Despite its assignment to the work of reconciliation, the church allows itself to be reduced to the status of an "instrument of the already." It is simply like Judaism. And then like paganism. And then like Judaism again. And so on. By calling, it ought to transcend both. But historically, it vacillates between both poles of corruption. In the second and third centuries the church reassumed many of the elements of Judaism, and seemed another synagogue. From Constantine onward, the church allowed itself to be integrated into the Roman Empire and tended toward paganism. Up until the end of the Middle Ages the tendency toward paganism prevailed; hence the calls to reform that resound throughout the christendom centuries. Since the great Protestant schism and the gradual secularization of Western society, the church has inclined once more toward Judaism, defending itself by taking the shape of a synagogue. It defends itself through its law, its separation from the pagans, its intransigence, its fidelity to the letter and to its traditions. Today, the problem of reconciliation is posed once again. Vatican II took cognizance of the reality of a new pagan world to evangelize. Once again, then, the church is challenged to emerge from the protective walls of the synagogue. The Holy Spirit encourages this dialectic, showing Christians the signs of the times. Nowadays the prime challenge is the pagan world and evangelization. The stronger voice will have to be that of Paul, not James, of Corinth, not Jerusalem.

III. THE SPIRIT AND THE CHURCH

1. The Church Is Born of the Holy Spirit

A constant thesis of Latin American ecclesiology has been that the church is "born of the poor" (Leonardo Boff, Gustavo Gutiérrez, Jon Sobrino, Ronaldo

Muñoz, and so on). This thesis is an expression of the doctrine of the creation of the church by the Holy Spirit. The church was not born directly of the human obedience of the disciples to the instructions of Christ. Jesus did not found the church in the way that individuals found human institutions. He left everything very indeterminate. Although the church is the "continuator of Christ," the concrete, practical manner of its imitation of Christ does not proceed from a simple meditation of the teachings of Jesus. The role of the Spirit is far more radical than that of simply offering help. The sheer distance, in the books of the Christian scriptures, between Jesus and the church of Corinth testifies to the radical role of the Holy Spirit. It would be impossible to have "deduced" the church of Corinth directly from the teachings of Jesus. Indeed, a number of thinkers have called Paul, rather than Jesus, the creator of Christianity. Actually, it was the Holy Spirit who created the church, making use of Paul's services and creating a new expression of the will of Jesus. This creation of Christianity by the Spirit occurs in each succeeding age of church history. Vatican II acknowledged that we were on the threshold of a new era. Thus, the Holy Spirit is engaged in a new creation of the church.

The Holy Spirit causes the church to spring up in communities scattered throughout the world. The church is born not of a center, through a process of decentralization from that center, but is born of the periphery. It springs up in various places in the world simultaneously, or at least without apparent order. Subsequently, the various groups that have thus come into being seek out an appropriate manner of establishing contact with one another. While preaching is surely necessary in order to call forth a new community, that preaching is done discreetly and humbly by believers who undertake journeys from already established Christian communities to communities that have not as yet heard the Good News. This is church today, as well. Communities have arisen, in no predictable order, in various places in Latin America. They continue to spring up, without planning. These communities do not seek isolation. On the contrary, they seek closeness to all other Christian communities. They place themselves under the legitimate authority of the bishops and the pope. But they are born neither by the will of the bishop nor by the initiative of the pope.

The mystery of the church is bound up with its birth of the Spirit. The birth of the church is not the spontaneous effect of sociological forces, although these forces do have an influence on its concrete history. The church is born, in mysterious ways, of the Spirit, who finds created persons to be instruments of this birth.

The work of the Spirit is communion, within the communities and among the communities. Ecclesial communion must be more than a mere interior disposition. In the Christian scriptures, it necessarily includes material relations of an exchange of goods according to each one's needs. Where are these material relations to be found? They are present in the concrete reality of the communities of the poor, as well as in the service of those who, born rich, have stripped themselves of their wealth and become like the poor. Medellín's call for a poor church is a precondition of church communion.

The presence of the Spirit at the root of the church takes on an ethical orientation in communion and an esthetic orientation in prayer and festival. The Spirit is the source of the churches' joy. In prayer, the products of the Spirit are joy, gratitude, and praise of the divine Parent. Although the creation of a new liturgy in Latin America is still lacking a great deal, it is an ongoing concern. In the meantime, the old forms of popular prayer are acquiring a new vitality.

2. The Spirit and the Marks of the Church

The Spirit is the driving force of unity in the church (1 Cor. 12:13, Eph. 4:5). In Latin America oneness among the communities is sought spontaneously. Unity with the bishops and the pope is taken for granted. No one calls it into question, despite the great diffidence manifested so often by bishops or the Roman Curia when it comes to the base communities. Many observers have the impression that the hierarchy is still obsessed with heresy and schism. For such a hierarchy, all laity are suspected of wishing to destroy the church and its unity. Therefore the hierarchy redoubles its application of human means in order to impose unity through uniformity: theological, liturgical, and canonical uniformity. In Latin America this approach to unity is interpreted as a lack of faith in the Holy Spirit. Will the Spirit be so feeble as to have need of so many purely human resources, after the fashion of political societies, indeed of the dictatorships of this world?

Will it not be an insult to the Holy Spirit that certain bishops, contrary to the will of their national episcopates, contrary to the desires of their clergy and their people, currently withdraw from their fellow Christians, simply because certain persons are more faithful executors of all the desires of the Holy See? Will it not be an insult to the Holy Spirit to engage in a general practice of informing against others as the predominant means of communication between the Holy See and the local churches? Will it not be an insult to the Holy Spirit to regard certain church matters as "classified information," with the result that the Christian people can know nothing of financial management in the church, nominations to higher offices and their motivation, or the reasons for the promulgation of certain local canons? Will it not be an insult to the Holy Spirit to engage in a practice of censorship that employs methods so reminiscent of the dictatorships that stink in the nostrils of Latin America? Will it not be an insult to the Holy Spirit to dispense with an authentic judicial system, in which the judge and the accuser are not the same person?

For the church born of the people, neither heresies nor schisms are problems of great urgency at the present. What is urgent is the evangelization of the poor, who have been abandoned by the clerical church for so many centuries. The poor place their trust in the power of the Spirit to maintain unity through dialogue, patience, and perseverance.

Ever since the first Pentecost the Spirit has seen to a church willing to be open to its neighbors. From the beginning Catholicism in Latin America has been crippled by the will of the Conquistadores and their successors. Officially, the colonization has sought moral legitimation through an appeal to the conversion of the Indians as its motive. The slavery of the Africans has been defended on the grounds of the boons of evangelization. In both cases, however, Christianity has been imposed by force. To our very day, a genuine evangelization of natives and blacks, apart from exceptional cases in widely scattered localities, has never left the drawing boards. The Christianity proposed to them is a Western culture that they are helpless to resist. A gospel in Western trappings is imposed upon them, and it is very difficult for them to distinguish between what is Christian and what is Western. The Holy Spirit is without a doubt on the point of raising up a native church and a black church, with all the necessary autonomy, in communion with the white church.

The church of the poor is inventing a new model of holiness. On a continent scarred by gigantic social and personal sins, where life counts for nothing, where murder always goes unpunished when it is committed by the powerful, where injustices reach incredible levels of oppression, where corruption is the very principle of public life, the emergence of such peaceable, such patient communities of solidarity constitutes an ongoing miracle. The word of the gospel stirs up miracles of holiness. This holiness culminates in thousands upon thousands of martyrs giving up their lives with calm and dignity: community advisers, leaders of popular associations, humble collaborators of the communities. Tens of thousands have earned the name of martyr. Here are witnesses of the Spirit indeed.

The apostolicity that proceeds from the Spirit is irreducible to the formal and juridical elements so frequently proclaimed in an apologetical ecclesiology coming down to us from the end of the Middle Ages. Authentic apostolicity consists in fidelity to the witness of the apostles as we find it in the Christian scriptures. The essential element of apostolicity is a return to the message of the apostles, delivered in a time when the church was poor, politically powerless, and without cultural prestige. Apostolicity is a spiritual phenomenon, then, and not merely a sociological one.

3. The Spirit and the Offices of the Church

The church is spiritual in its evangelization. By the Spirit, the church becomes a servant of the word of God. It submits to the written word of the Bible. By the enlightenment of the Spirit, the church discovers the current meaning and application of the written words of the Bible. The office of evangelization is not reserved to a few ministers. It belongs to the whole community and all of its members, within the common mission of the community. The Spirit awakens and feeds the "evangelizing potential of the poor," as Puebla calls it. The Spirit bursts the barriers of culture, and the wall of separation between the intellectual and the laborer. The Spirit enables the poor to discover the concrete scope of the biblical word.

In the Spirit, the church celebrates the event of liberation. "Christ our Pasch" is experienced in millions of particular Easters. Christ's Easter becomes today's Easter in the phenomena of the death and resurrection of the peoples. Christ relives his Easter amid the practice of liberation. The poor celebrate their sufferings and victories in the sufferings and victories of Christ. Thus they rescue the liturgy from the formalism that has infected it for so many centuries, or from the magical distortions so common among the poor (and the less poor). The sacraments are authentically spiritual when they produce a bonding between Christ and the lives of actual persons. The poor live their lives as an ongoing Easter. They are willing to recognize Christ in those lives.

The church also has the office of service through the various charisms. The rebirth of community life produces an abundance of services. The charisms are reappearing. The church is opening itself to the needs of the whole people. The service of human rights, of human dignity, of justice to workers, of the protection of life, is acquiring new meanings. In the church of the poor, service is no longer an expression of the paternalism of the privileged toward their victims. It is an expression of the solidarity of the poor.

4. The Holy Spirit and the Ministries of Authority

For centuries, indeed since Constantine, the ministries in the church have largely been understood by the analogy of the rungs in the ladder of civil authority. The office of bishop has been conceptualized as analogous to that of the governor of a province or city of the Roman Empire. Since Vatican II Latin America has begun to see departures from this model. Spiritual authority cannot run parallel to civil or military authority. There is a spiritual manner of exercising authority: "Since Vatican II and the Medellín Conference, a great change can be noted in Latin America in the way that authority is exercised within the Church. Greater emphasis has been put on its character as service and sacrament and on the dimension of collegial concern" (Puebla Final Document, no. 260).

Puebla insists that Paul's recommendation be applied to the bishops: "not to 'stifle the Spirit' or 'despise prophecy' (1 Thess. 5:19-20)" (Puebla Final Document, no. 249).

Indeed, a new model of episcopal action has appeared on the Latin American scene. The "Medellín generation" launched a phenomenon that is, at least in some degree and in particular countries, irreversible. The model to which we refer has found its ideal expression in the bishop-martyrs: Geraldo Valencia Cano of Buenaventura in Colombia, Enrique Angelelli of La Rioja in Argentina, and Oscar Romero of San Salvador. Together with them, the framers of Medellín make up a group deserving of the title the Holy Fathers of Latin America.

In the base church communities, many laity exercise genuine authority. Spontaneous and charismatic at first, this authority has gradually come to be recognized by the hierarchy itself, although it has not yet been authenticated by the universal laws of the Latin Church.

Many religious women and men have seen themselves challenged by the changes in the church. Frequently, these missioners had introduced in Latin America, mechanically, the same institutions they maintained in their native lands. In the light of the new church of the poor, they have been led to review their whole pastoral or spiritual involvement. They too have discovered the world of the poor. In the light of the poverty of the poor, they have questioned their vow of poverty. In the light of the slavery of the poor they have questioned the meaning of their vow of obedience. In the light of the misery and abandonment of the poor they have questioned themselves on the meaning of their vow of chastity.

The Spirit transforms all structures. It even manages to prick the tranquility of centuries-old customs and formalisms sacralized by time. The Spirit renews all forms of authority.

IV. THE NEW SPIRITUALITY IN LATIN AMERICA

1. A Spirituality of Liberation

The basic trait of the new spirituality of liberation is its spirituality *of* the laity *for* the laity. This spirituality is not the watered-down spirituality of a religious order or congregation. It springs not from the special experience of a specially gifted founder, but from the simultaneous practice of thousands of committed Christians, living in widely separated regions of our continent but in similar concrete conditions.

These Christians' basic spiritual experience is that of an integral liberation. They have felt in their own flesh domination and alienation in all its dimensions: political oppression, threats, prison, torture (sometimes to the death), the exploitation of their labor, subjection to official lies and to the brain-washing perpetrated by the media in the service of the dominators. They had assimilated the domination and made it their own, like the vast majority of the poor of Latin America. They had been convinced of the justice of injustice. But in the renewal of the church, their personhood has been gradually delivered from all of the bonds of slavery: political, economic, cultural, and all others. They have experienced this liberation as an action of the Holy Spirit within them. They know that the road is narrow and dangerous. Liberation costs a terrible price, but they are ready to pay that price.

Liberation engenders no pride, selfishness, individualism, or spirit of libertinage, as modernity has. To serve one another Latin American Christians have renounced any individual advantages that may be available to them in a consumer society. They seek to share in the common lot of their poor brothers and sisters. Their gradual liberation engenders service to the community and solidarity.

The spirituality of liberation is not taken from books, nor does it bring a great deal of literary expression itself. The poor live their spirituality; they do not write about it. Some day, perhaps, someone may be able to write about it as well. But it is living it that counts.

2. The Prayer of the Poor

By contrast, any spirituality is expressed in the language of prayer. The poor in Latin America have not lost contact with their traditional religion or the old popular expressions of Christianity. Often enough, these traditional expressions of popular piety have been deflected by the dominators and placed in the service of domination. But often enough as well, it is possible to restore to the poor the riches of their past. Traditional formulas can take on liberative meanings. Popular piety can be delivered from its distortions.

Further, in the popular communities the poor are learning to express themselves "on their own." They acquire freedom of speech even in their religious celebrations. In other times they were silenced, and silence was their sole participation. Now they learn to pray spontaneously—to transform their life and their death into prayer. As Paul recommends, they live in thanksgiving. Joy is their dominant theme. In the midst of their torments and misery, their fears and the threats made against them, they attain to gladness in a fashion altogether unfamiliar to the high and mighty. They live in joy because they live in deep, sincere friendship with one another. As one *campesino* put it, the wealth of the poor is friendship.

The basic theme of the new spirituality is the oldest Christian theme of all. It is the theme of the gospels themselves: the following of Jesus in his humanity—the imitation of the works of Jesus over the course of his earthly mission. There is no attempt to copy these works literally. The grace of the Spirit enables Latin American Christians to discover today's equivalents of the actions of Jesus. The Spirit shows them the hidden correspondences. And, lo, the life of Jesus revives, in the hidden, heroic life of the church of the poor.

—Translated by Robert R. Barr

22

Mary

IVONE GEBARA
MARÍA CLARA BINGEMER

I. ASSUMPTIONS

When we think about the mystery of Mary and mariology from the viewpoint of liberation theology, we make certain anthropological and hermeneutic assumptions. We base our new thinking about traditional mariology on them and use them as guidelines.

1. Anthropological Assumptions

Liberation theology sees and thinks about Mary within a *human-centered anthropology*. It does not consider only men to be the history-makers, image of the divinity and mediator of the relationship between God and humanity. All humanity, men and women, are regarded as the center of history and revealers of the divine. This anthropology takes into account women's historical activity for the Kingdom, and thus does justice to Mary, to women, in fact, to humanity created in the image and likeness of God.

It is also a *single anthropology*, not dualist, which affirms the existence of a single human history. It does not set up two competing histories, one divine and one human. Its starting point is human history, the scene of conflicts, joys, and sorrows of generations of different peoples. A Marian theology with a single anthropology returns to the realism of human experience marked by historical differences and shares profoundly in the mystery of the incarnation. The Word becomes flesh in human flesh, flesh of men and women, historical flesh marked by space and time, life and death, joy and sorrow, building and destroying, in short, by all the conflict inherent in being human in history.

Moreover, it is a *realist anthropology*, which combines objectivity and subjectivity. It does not claim to be purely objective and idealist, but takes on board the multiplicity of interpretations, hypotheses, and theories about different events. A realist anthropology sustains mariology in its attempt to respond to the changeable reality of human existence. The eternal is always historical. This viewpoint enables us to see the figure of Mary in a constantly new way. We cannot make her into an eternal model, or way of being; this historical figure of Mary must always enter into dialogue with the time, space, culture, problems, and actual people who relate to her. It is life today that gives life to Mary's life yesterday.

It is also a *multidimensional anthropology*, no longer one-dimensional. It looks at different human aspects in terms of their development, which is affected by countless different factors. A human being is not primarily a definition or essence, but a history marked by space and time. A human being is not initially good and then depraved, or initially perverse and saved later; the human is this complex reality, full of division and conflict, whose nature is both limited and unlimited. Its multidimensional anthropology gives Marian theology a human-divine foundation, which enables it to observe with justice and profound respect the human phenomenon — maker of history, created, loved and saved by God. It also allows these different aspects to appear in relation to Mary without one necessarily excluding the other. Each aspect is a profile, an expression, a word about human aspiration toward the divine, which dwells in human nature and structures it. Mary is the divine in the feminine expression of the human, a key expression of what we call wholly human.

Finally, it is a *feminist anthropology*, whose meaning is linked to the historical moment in which we are living, a time when women have become conscious of their oppression for millennia and their conniving submission over the centuries to these oppressive social structures. In general terms, a feminist anthropology means humanity's other side, the female side, recalling vital realities from which women have been alienated. A mariology with a liberation perspective does not try to bring out Mary's qualities as a woman, qualities which have been idealized and projected by different needs and cultures. It tries to take a fresh look at

Mary from the viewpoint of our own time and its needs, and in particular, this special moment for humanity of the awakening of women's historical consciousness.

2. Hermeneutic Assumptions

For the hermeneutic used by liberation theology to speak about Mary we need to distinguish certain points:

1. After having been someone who lived in history, Mary has become someone who lives in God. Those who live in God have projected onto them the situation of those who live in history, a situation of limitation and at the same time unlimited desire. Everything in the life of those who live in history that mars the harmony, perfection, health, integrity, security, fulfillment, happiness, love, and values belonging to this desire for the unlimited, is what is sought and asked for in those who live in God. In Latin America the relationship of those who live in history with those who live in God helps them to overcome the deep sense of abandonment and dismay felt by the continent's poor and oppressed majorities. The cry for God and for those who live in God—Mary preeminently among the poor and believing people of Latin America—is a cry for help, whatever form this may take. This is what Latin American spirituality and, in particular, its Marian spirituality are made of. Mary is the hope, the mother, the protector, the one who does not forsake her children. So for a Latin American Marian theology, analysis of biblical texts and tradition is not enough. It is fundamentally important to grasp the type of human experience to which devotion to Mary corresponds. In the Latin American continent this experience is essentially the experience of the poor discovering themselves as subjects of history—history makers—and organizing for liberation.

2. A Marian theology from the viewpoint of Latin America today must also have a different and special way of reading the biblical texts. The written text must always make the reader wonder and ask about what was not written, what was lost, and what was left out on purpose. A written text is always selective. The scriptural texts that speak about Mary are very few, but from these texts and different popular traditions, each historical epoch constructs an image of Mary and her past and present historical activity. Hence we cannot say that the only truth about Mary's life is in the little that we are told by the Christian scriptural texts. What is not said is also important.

3. The idea of the Kingdom of God is essential for the hermeneutics of a Marian theology concerned with liberation To understand this idea we must go beyond the person of Jesus. It affects his whole movement, in which men and women actively share. So we read the facts about Mary in terms of the different images which the Kingdom of God assumes in scripture, tradition, and traditions. The facts about Mary make present the signs of God's Kingdom; they are particular actions that manifest the presence of salvation in human history. Mary speaks of God and the Kingdom, of divinity in a woman's life; she speaks of God's Son, who is born of the people and of a woman; she speaks of the many children engendered by the Spirit of God who are not born of the

flesh or man's desire, but of God. A Marian theology from the viewpoint of the Kingdom will also enable us to see Mary's passion for the poor, her passion for God's justice. This theology enables us to recover through her the force of the Spirit acting on women in all eras. It is the recovery of the "dangerous memory" or "subversive memory," capable of changing things, because it not only keeps alive the hopes and struggles of women in the past, but gives birth and growth to a universal solidarity among the women of past, present, and future. In this light Mary is not only the sweet and charming mother of Jesus; she is a working woman, working for the harvest of the Kingdom, an active member of the movement of the poor, just as Jesus of Nazareth was. So this is the end for the old limited view of Mary as subject to her Son, as women were subject to men. It opens up a broader horizon in which Mary becomes one of those who see a new light shining from Nazareth, the symbol of the edge of the world.

II. MARY IN SCRIPTURE

A scriptural narrative may center upon a particular character, but it is really referring to a collective, a people. Thus the Hebrew scriptures' female figures who appear before Mary—Miriam, Anna, Ruth, Judith, Esther, and others— are at the same time images of women and images of a people. Through their actions God's power is revealed saving God's people. These female figures also represent this people's resistance. We do not deny that each individual has a mission, especially some with special gifts. But in our time we need to rediscover the collective dimension of human actions in the web of history past and present, the collective making of history.

This is how we read scripture in Latin America for our understanding of Mary's place and role today. We are not dealing only with the individual person Miriam of Nazareth, but with a woman who is the image of a faithful people, God's particular dwelling place. The statement "God became flesh in Jesus" must be completed by another with the same theological status: "God is born of a woman." The Christian scriptures try to show that with Mary and with Jesus a new time begins in the history of humanity. There is a sort of qualitative leap, the awareness of the presence of God in human flesh. God dwells on human earth and is discovered and loved in human flesh.

Although Mary is born into a patriarchal context, in which a woman is a thing, man's property at all levels, she is a figure standing between the two Testaments. She shares in and savors the new liberating experience of her Son's movement, which offers equal discipleship to men and women. Together with the other women at the church's beginnings, she is the bearer of a new hope and a new way of being a woman. She is the legitimate representative of the people of Israel, the symbol of faithful Sion. Equally she is the bearer of the new Israel, the new people, the new covenant God makes with humanity. In this women are no longer passive and subject to men, no longer inferior beings, but active subjects. They stand side by side with men and assume with them, shoulder to shoulder, many of the tasks inherent in the proclamation of the Good News.

In its few texts relating to Mary the Christian scriptures illustrate these perspectives.

Paul: In Galatians 4:1-7 Paul says that "in the fullness of time God sent his Son born of a woman." Here the figure of the woman who gives birth to the Son of God in the fullness to time means the convergence between eschatology and history, anthropology and theology. Henceforth there is no room for andro- centrism or dualism of any kind. Any anthropological or theological reduction- ism gives way to the confession of faith that the Word became flesh in human flesh, flesh of men and women. It also says that the Kingdom has come, the fullness of time is now, the new creation has become reality because God has sent the Son, born of a woman. In the light of this mystery the kingdom happens in the community of men and women, whose struggles and sufferings, sorrows and joys, constantly blossom with the inexhaustible freshness of love.

Matthew: This gospel looks at the story of Jesus as the fulfillment of Yahweh's promises to his chosen people. Upon the woman comes the Spirit of God as in the creation text (Gen 1:2). So Mary gives birth "without Joseph knowing her." Joseph is the synthesis of the ancient people, the primitive Jewish tradition which recognizes the Messiah in spite of doubts and difficulties. The woman is the symbol of the faithful people from whom the Messiah is born, and Joseph the ancient people called to a new wedding to begin love anew. Matthew's Mary is the symbol of virgin hope, a woman pregnant with life, the light-filled face of the people, God's faithfulness constantly reemerging from the ruins of destruction.

Mark: Mary's motherhood is a historical reference, a fact identifying the carpenter miracle-worker, who knows the Law and the prophets and defends the people, who is accepted by some and rejected by others. Mary, Jesus' mother, shares in this environment which opens and closes horizons, welcomes and rejects Jesus. Mary stands with the humanity that "almost" rejects him; she is involved in the group of those who think "he is mad." But she is also pointed out as the one who has overcome the biological level of her relationship with Jesus and is among those who do God's will (cf. Mark 3:35).

Luke: This is the gospel with the most references to Mary. The annunciation to Mary (Luke 1:26-38) is in line with the many manifestations of God's faith- fulness to his people (Sara, Abraham, Samson's mother). Mary (representing the people) is the new ark of the covenant, God's dwelling place, the place where God lives, the place where God can be met and loved. Luke uses the experiences and theological expressions of the Jews and gives them new mean- ing in terms of the great novelty experienced by Jesus' followers. Mary's visit to Elizabeth (Luke 1:40-45) is the encounter of the old with the new. Mary is now "blessed among women." The one who recognises and proclaims this is Elizabeth, an old Jewish woman from whom the last of the prophets of the old Law is to be born. Mary's song, the *Magnificat* (Luke 1:46-55), is a war song, a song of God's combat in human history, God's struggle to bring about a world of equal relationships, respect for every person, in whom the divinity dwells. The image of the pregnant woman who can give birth to the new is the image of God, who through the power of the Spirit brings about the birth of men and women dedicated to justice, living out their relationship with God in a loving relationship with their fellow human beings. Mary's song is the program for God's Kingdom, and also Jesus' program proclaimed in the synagogue at Nazareth (Luke 4: 16-21). Mary's delivery (Luke 2:7) has a collective meaning. All men and women are involved in it as it goes beyond the limits of human biology and physiology. It is God's birth into humanity. In the two final texts that mention Mary (Luke 2:34-35 and Luke 2:48-49) Simeon's prophecy extends Mary's scope to all time. Those who struggle for God's Kingdom suffer hostility in this world. A sword continually pierces the heart of the poor and those who struggle for God's justice, those who put God's matters first and are possessed by a passion for liberation of their fellows.

Acts of the Apostles: This book shows us Mary present at the roots of the primitive Christian community, persevering in prayer and united with her Son's disciples. Present as the mother, the sister, the friend, the disciple, and teacher of a movement organized by her son Jesus, a movement whose historical roots lie in the proclamation of the presence of the Kingdom among the poor, those deprived of all recognition by the established powers.

John: The fourth gospel presents Mary on two occasions: the first is the wedding at Cana (John 2:1-11), when Jesus, at her intercession, works the first of his signs, changing water into wine. Mary's faith conceives and gives birth to the new Messianic community; it inaugurates the new people's time. This is the community of the Kingdom, where poor and despised Cana of Galilee becomes the place where God's glory is revealed. The second episode is at the foot of the cross, when Jesus is dying. Jesus entrusts his beloved disciple to her as her son. In the line of great female maternal figures of the Hebrew scriptures (Deborah, the mother of the Maccabees, and others) Mary stands as the mother of the new community of men and women who have become followers of Jesus because they believe in God's glory manifested in him. John's gospel sets Mary at the center of Jesus Christ's salvation event. She is the symbol of the people who welcome the message of the Kingdom and the fullness of Messianic times.

Revelation: In chapter 12 of Revelation a woman appears clothed with the sun and crowned with stars. She is in labor and fighting the dragon. Her vocation is victory, to be the bride of the lamb, the new Jerusalem where all who keep God's commandments and bear witness to Jesus will finally be united. The persecuted and martyred people of God bear the pledge of Jesus' victory. Mary is identified as this woman in Revelation 12, the figure of the people's humble and laborious faith, the suffering people who believe in the crucified savior without losing hope. She is the figure of a church persecuted by the world, by the forces of the anti-Kingdom and the powerful and oppressors of all kinds who, like the dragon in Revelation, want to "devour" the children and descendants of the woman, devour the project of the Kingdom, all that is life and liberty for the people, all that is the mature fruit of the woman's fertile womb. The new people of God, of whom Mary is the symbol and figure, is the "sign" that appears in heaven and on earth that to the woman Eve's descendants the grace and the power to triumph over the serpent has been given through the woman Mary's descendants. From her flesh the Spirit formed God's incarnation. She is the woman–people of God, from whose womb salvation has sprung, the community of those who "keep God's commandments and bear witness to Jesus."

III. RE-READING THE MARIAN DOGMAS

In Latin America today we need to rethink the church's dogmas — and in this case the Marian dogmas — in the light of the anthropological and hermeneutic assumptions we outlined above for liberation theology. We must rethink them in terms of the key theme guiding the Latin American church since the conferences at Medellín and Puebla: the option for the poor.

1. The Mystery of the Theotokos, Mother of God

Unlike other dogmas, whose biblical roots are questioned and which constitute genuine ecumenical problems, Mary's divine motherhood has deep and solid support in scripture. The Christian scriptures give Mary the title Mother more times than anything else (twenty-five times). For the gospel narratives, Mary is above all Jesus' mother. At the center of the mystery of the incarnation, a mystery which is salvation for the whole human race, the Christian scriptures set a man and a woman, Jesus and Mary. God takes on man's flesh through the flesh of a woman. The Council of Ephesus (431) expressly declares Mary to be *Theotokos*, Mother of God. Mary's divine motherhood is stated in the conciliar declaration as the key for interpreting the mystery of the incarnation. It explains the union of the two natures of God's Word and shows how it is possible. He who is begotten eternally by the Father is born of a woman according to the flesh, that is, he has united human nature to himself, hypostatically. After Ephesus the divine Mother becomes a unique title of honor and glory for her who is the mother of the incarnate word.

Recognizing Mary as Mother of God means professing that Jesus the carpenter of Nazareth, the Crucified, the son of Mary, according to human generation, is Son of God and himself God. The anthropological vision underlying this statement is a single whole. Every woman is the mother not only of the body but the whole person of her child. The mystery of Jesus, the Son of God's incarnation in Mary of Nazareth, teaches us that the human person is not split into an imperfect material body and a great transcendent spirit. On the contrary, only in the weakness, poverty, and limitations of human flesh can we experience and worship the Spirit's ineffable greatness. It also means proclaiming the Kingdom's arrival: "Now it is among us." God took on human history from within, himself living through its struggles and successes, defeats and victories, insecurities and joys. Mary is the figure and symbol of the people who believe in and experience this arrival of God, who now belong to the human race. She whose flesh formed the flesh of God's Son is also the symbol and prototype of the new community, where men and women love one another and celebrate the mystery of life, which has been revealed in its fullness. This also reveals all the greatness of the mystery of woman — a mystery of openness, source of protection and life. Mary is mother of all the living, the woman where the mystery of the source and origin of life reaches its maximum density. Thus she reveals a new and unexplored side of the mystery of God, who became incarnate in her womb; he himself is like a woman who gives birth, who suckles the child of his womb, and does not forget it (cf. Isa. 66:13; 42:14; 49:15). Finally, the *Theotokos* means we must recognize that this same woman, whom we call mother and our Lady, is the poor and obscure woman of Nazareth, mother of the subversive carpenter who was condemned to death, Jesus. We must look behind the glorious titles and the luxurious images with which traditional piety represents her to the no less real and theological title of Handmaid of Yahweh. This is an inspiration for the church, whose role in Latin America is to serve the poor, for whom Jesus' incarnation in Mary carries the Good News of liberation.

2. Virginity

Mary is a true daughter of Judaism, and Judaism does not think of virginity as having particular value. It is equivalent to sterility, to non-procreation; it attracts contempt and implies death because survival is in children. Mary's virginity cannot therefore be regarded as making a moralist or idealizing point. The biblical texts mean that the Son conceived in Mary is a divine being. The chain of human genealogy undergoes a radical break to give way to the Spirit, who invades history with a creative breath and makes life spring where it would be naturally impossible. Jesus, the new Israel who springs from Mary's womb, is the seed of the new people formed by the Spirit. Mary is also the figure and symbol of this people. The church's tradition has taken this indication to proclaim Mary's perpetual virginity throughout the history of the early centuries and finally at the Lateran Council (649).

Mary's virginity throws light on the anthropological question of what a human being is. The human creature is like unexplored virgin land, where anything can happen. And everything that happens should lead this human creature to the point Mary reached: forming God in her womb. Mary's virginity, fertilized by the Spirit, corresponds to the vocation of every human being to be an open and available temple and dwelling place. The importance of Mary's virgin body lies in being a metaphor for human inability to achieve its own salvation without God's grace. Mary's virginity is a sign of total surrender to the God of life. It totally abandons the death-dealing idols and is a sign to all men and women who want to tread the path Jesus trod and live the historico-eschatological reality of God's Kingdom. Mary's virginity also shows the specific vocation of women as bearers of fullness of life, unlimited open space, a latent potentiality which grows ever greater the deeper its self- surrender. The dogma of Mary's virginity declares women to be an affirmative space where the Spirit of the Most High can alight and make its home. It also shows God's omnipotent glory, which is manifest in that which is poor, powerless, and despised in the world's eyes. Virginity, despised in Israel, is the place of the *shekinah*, the dwelling place of Yahweh's glory. God's preference for the poor becomes clear and explicit when God becomes incarnate in the womb of a virgin. Like her motherhood, Mary's virginity belongs to the service of Yahweh's poor who say, "Behold the handmaid of the Lord, do to me according to your word" (Luke 1:38).

3. The Immaculate Conception

This dogma, proclaimed in 1854 by Pius IX, does not have such explicit biblical roots as the previous ones. Our reference is the text of Genesis 3:15 (also called the *proto-evangelium*), in which the woman and her descendants appear as mortal enemies of the serpent, whom she finally destroys by crushing its head. As well as other less important references to the Ark of the Covenant, the Holy City, and others, there is the angel's greeting in Luke's gospel, which declares Mary to be "full of grace" (Luke 1:28) and Elizabeth's greeting, which declares her to be "blessed among women" (Luke 1:42). So Mary appears as God's most excellent miracle, creation that has reached its fulfillment, the blessed one who is full of grace. Christians expressed this feeling in their devotion before the church's magisterium officially recognized it as a dogma of faith.

By her immaculate conception Mary is the personified synthesis of the ancient Zion-Jerusalem. She is the exemplary beginning of the process of renewal and purification of the whole people, so that they can live God's covenant more fully. Belonging wholly to God, Mary is already the prototype of that which the people is called to be. The immaculate conception is thus a utopia that gives strength to the project and sustains the people's hope in their God (cf. Puebla Final Document, no. 298). It is the pledge that Jesus' utopia— the Kingdom of God—can be realized on this poor earth. But it is not just Mary's soul which is preserved from sin. Her whole person is penetrated and animated by grace, by God's life. Her body is the dwelling place of the holy God. Her immaculate conception proclaims to the people, whose figure she is, that the Spirit has been poured out upon all flesh and the lost paradise has been regained. Woman's body, which Genesis denounces as the cause of original sin, laying upon the whole female sex a defect and a burden difficult to bear, is rehabilitated through the gospel and the magisterium of the church. This body, animated by the divine Spirit, is proclaimed blessed. In it God has worked the fullness of his wonders. Finally, we should not forget that the Immaculate Conception venerated on altars is the poor Mary of Nazareth, handmaid of the Lord, a woman of the people, insignificant in the social structure of her time.

The blessed Mary is the confirmation of God's preference for the most humble, little, and oppressed. Thus the so-called Marian privilege is really the privilege of the poor. The grace with which Mary is full is the inheritance of the whole people. Mary, the poor one of Israel, upon whom the gaze of the Most High rests with favor, is a model and a stimulus for the church to become increasingly the church of the poor.

4. The Assumption

The most recent of the Marian dogmas is the assumption, defined and solemnly proclaimed by Pius XII on November 1, 1950, in the Apostolic Consti-

MARY 491

tution *Munificentissimus Deus.* The dogma's foundations are biblical texts, but read by the eyes of the church's tradition. The road traveled to the proclamation of the dogma is a road of faith, which has had to deal with obscure and challenging elements, scarce and contradictory objective data, relying on the people's religious feeling and what this has to say about their beloved Mary's final destiny.

The dogma of the assumption proclaims Mary to have been assumed into heaven "body and soul." The subject of the assumption is Mary's whole person. Mary is not a soul provisionally wrapped in a body, but a person, a body animated by the divine breath, penetrated by God's grace in every nook and cranny. Her bodily nature is fully assumed by God and carried into glory. Her assumption is not the reanimation of a corpse or the exaltation of a soul separated from its body, but the total fulfillment in God's absoluteness of the whole woman Mary of Nazareth. It also tells us something about the final eschatological destiny to which we are called. We are not a soul imprisoned in a body, and our body for its part is not an impediment to our fulfillment as human beings united to God. What we believe and hope for is already the case with Mary. Mary, glorified in heaven in body and soul, is also the image and the beginning of the church of the future, an eschatological sign of hope and comfort for the people of God marching toward its final home. This people, already redeemed and full of hope, but still in pilgrimage along the road of history, sees in Mary the real possibility of the Lord's Day arriving. With the assumption of Mary as the figure and symbol of the new people of God, the church is already, even in the midst of ambiguity and sin, the community of salvation, the faithful people it is called to be.

Mary's assumption also restores and reintegrates women's bodies, humiliated by the Jewish and Christian patriarchal prejudices, into the very heart of the mystery of God. Through Mary, women have the dignity of their condition recognized and assured by the creator of these same bodies. The masculine and the feminine in Jesus and Mary respectively are raised and assumed into heaven, finally to share in the glory of the Trinity.

Mary's assumption is closely connected to the resurrection of Jesus. Both events are concerned with the same mystery: the triumph of God's justice over human injustice, the victory of grace over sin. Just as proclaiming Jesus' resurrection means continuing to announce his passion, which goes on happening in the crucified and those who receive no justice in this world, so, by analogy, believing in Mary's assumption means proclaiming that this woman, who gave birth in a stable among animals, whose heart was pierced by a sword of sorrow, who suffered poverty, humiliation, persecution and her Son's violent death, who stood beside him at the foot of the cross, the mother of the condemned man, was exalted. Just as the Crucified One is the Risen Christ, so the Sorrowful Mother is the Mother assumed into heaven, the Glorious Mother. The assumption is the glorious culmination of the mystery of God's preference for what is poor, small, and unprotected in this world; there God's presence and glory can shine. The Father's same word confirms Jesus in the resurrection and Mary in the assumption. By doing this he indicates the road to follow, with Mary's example. Mary's assumption is sign of eschatological hope for the church, the people of God. It confirms its place among the poor, the outcast, all who are on the margins of society.

IV. HISTORY OF DEVOTION TO MARY IN LATIN AMERICA

In the history of Latin America there has always been devotion to and a cult of Mary. The first generation of the conquest was marked by much religious violence and destruction of the indigenous culture in the name of Christian purity and truth. The Conquistadores believed that the indigenous gods were evil and would certainly lead them to hell. As heaven was more important than earth, everything was permissible so that people did not lose the happiness of heaven after this fleeting life. For the Conquistadores Mary was always at their side against the Indians, whom they regarded as infidels. Theirs was a holy war, and so the Virgin protected them in the hard task of bringing the Indians to the faith.

With the second generation after the conquest the cult of Mary began to be integrated into Spanish-American and Portuguese-American customs. After the elimination of millions of infidels and the victory of the Conquistadores over the natives, there began a process of accommodation by the Conquistadores of the newly dominant religious culture. The integration of the cult of Mary did not take place immediately and without incident. The gospel preachers of the time strove to replace the native mother goddess by Mary, to prevent, they said, the continuation of idolatry. Despite this, we later find a syncretistic integration of the great indigenous divinities – and later of the black divinities – with Christianity. One example of this integration is the sanctuary in Mount Tepeyac in Mexico, a place of pilgrimage to the goddess Tonantzin-Cihuacoatl and later to Our Lady of Guadalupe.

During the nineteenth-century wars of independence from Spain and Portugal Mary played just as important a part as in the colonization period. The leaders of independence struggles in the Latin American countries believed that their devotion to the Virgin was one of the most important weapons they had in their fight for autonomy. In Portuguese America this happened on a lesser scale, but devotion to the Virgin was very popular from the time of the founding of the colony, where hermitages, oratories, and chapels were built in her honor. Mary was also the protector of many liberation movements, like that of the slaves.

Devotions to Mary multiplied in the eighteenth, nineteenth, and beginning of the twentieth centuries, with the growing influx of European religious congregations, who brought with them their homegrown devotions to the Virgin. Mary was the great companion and mother of many popular struggles in Latin America. Many peasant movements in Brazil, Bolivia, and Peru were stimulated by the people's love of the Virgin fighting with them for liberation. Another significant example is the devotion to the Purisima in Nicaragua during the period of the Sandinista struggle against Somoza. In El Salvador this same love for Mary led Oscar Romero to say: "The true homage a Christian can pay the

Virgin is to strive with her to make God's life incarnate in the vicissitudes of our fleeting history."

Of all the devotions to the Virgin Mary in Latin America, the only one that can be said to result from an apparition held to be supernatural is the Virgin of Guadalupe. In other places on the continent devotion to the Virgin centers around an image, either found or sculpted by the natives or brought by the missionaries themselves. So Guadalupe has a special place in Latin American mariology. Fundamentally, its meaning is that the Virgin maternally adopts the "natives" of Mexico and with them the whole Latin American people. The apparition of the woman later called the Indita (little Indian woman) or Morenita (little dark woman) to the Indian Juan Diego has important historical implications. It demands absolute respect for the *other*; we must welcome this otherness and allow its right to be so. In this apparition the "divinity" of the white ones takes on the indigenous, or rather the indigenous takes this divinity as its own in order to assert its right to life in the face of white power. In her apparition the Virgin Mary speaks the same language as the Indian. She speaks his language, the language of his people, and not the colonists' language. The divinity appears to be taking sides with the weak, with the one to whom it is speaking and revealing itself. In order to raise the indigenous and give him power, the divinity speaks his language. The Indian understands her and feels absolutely certain of her protection. The apparition becomes an ally of the Indian, collectively, as the representative of an oppressed culture. The mission given to the Indian by the Virgin is to build her a temple. The initiative for this building comes from her, but the work of building it is done by the Indian. In this indigenous popular tradition it is the woman Mary who sends him out on a mission; in the Christian scriptures it is Jesus who sends. The Virgin does not have the same problems as the white oppressor. She loves the Indian and adopts him as her son. This gives him strength to fight for his own cause against the established church authorities. The carrying out of the Virgin's request means the affirmation of the identity of a people beginning a new moment in history. The apparition of the Virgin of Guadalupe and the growing devotion to her plays an important part in the restoring to an exploited people a religious identity that will help in the construction of a new national identity.

Our Lady of the Immaculate Conception, patron of Brazil, turned black in the waters of a river. She was welcomed by the poor and protected slave men and women and presided over black groups. When they "met" her in the waters of the River Paraiba, the fisherman Joo Alves and his two companions, who had not caught anything for a long while, suddenly caught an enormous haul of fish. The enslaved blacks of Brazil read the signs of Mary — among others she freed a slave chained to the door of her sanctuary — to indicate her disapproval of slavery in Brazil. Henceforth the black Virgin, who appears to the poor, has become a part of the inalienable heritage of the oppressed and marginalized black people of Brazil.

Many other faces and many other devotions signify the presence of Mary in the Latin American continent. However, we note these two because they relate to two sectors of the Latin American people who are particularly oppressed and discriminated against: the Indians and the blacks. For centuries both have been struggling and crying out for justice and for their place and their right to be acknowledged. The presence of Mary as an ally in their struggles is a significant factor for Marian liberation theology.

V. MARY AND THE ECCLESIAL BASE COMMUNITIES

It is not possible today in Latin America to speak of the church of the poor, of organization and the liberation struggle, without mentioning the ecclesial base communities. They are a new way of being a church, which has arisen among the people through God's Spirit. When we speak of the ecclesial base communities we turn to Mary again, this woman who carried in her womb and gave birth to the Liberator of the poor. She is the figure of the church and also of this church born among the poor.

The ecclesial base communities are a practical way of carrying out the church's mission. Their roots lie in God's word, in history, and in the new and original forms taking shape in their ordinary daily life. The base communities are made up of poor and suffering people who meet to reflect and celebrate their life and struggles in the light of God's word. This is why they are Good News. Mary was and is an actual person who carried out a project among the poor. With Jesus and Joseph she makes up a decent simple family struggling to live by the daily bread earned with difficulty. They are faithful followers of the line of Israelites who are "the poor of Yahweh." In her poverty and insignificance God plants in her the seed of liberation for a whole people.

The communities are a prophetic church happening in the midst of conflict. They worry the powerful, they are attacked and insulted by many, others want to manipulate them. Amid this web of conflicts the ecclesial base communities are trying to make their way and discover how to direct their faithfulness to the God of life. Conflict also underlay Mary's whole experience, through her "different" pregnancy up to her firm and faithful stance at the foot of the cross of her son, condemned as a subversive. At the heart of the dialectical tension between anguish and hope, love and sorrow, Mary and the people in the ecclesial base communities raise their prophetic cry of denunciation against injustices and proclaim the liberation that has already taken place for those who hope in God.

The ecclesial base communities have Mary very much in mind in their daily life and struggles. As well as a heavenly mother, holy and merciful, they see her as an earthly sister, a companion on the journey, mother of the oppressed, mother of the despised. She is the protagonist and the model for a new spirituality which has arisen from the well of life, the suffering and joys of the Latin American people. If Mary is — according to the Council — a figure of the church, we can surely say that in Latin America she is becoming more and more the figure of this church of the poor, happening in a special way in the base communities.

In her song the *Magnificat*, the people in the ecclesial base communities hear Mary's constant yes to God and God's plan, and at the same time her no to injustice and the state of affairs with which it is not possible to come to terms, no to the sin of indifference to the sufferings which make victims of others. Mary, the perfect figure and expression of the faithful people, the handmaid of the Lord, is also a prophetic woman who takes on God's word and the people's aspirations, who speaks and lives the denunciation of sin and the proclamation of the covenant.

So the church of the poor taking shape today in the ecclesial base communities needs to reflect more upon the person and mystery of Mary within the context of its oppression, struggle, resistance, and victory. Reflecting and working out a new theological discourse about Mary helps this church to take a look at itself, its identity and mission. It means confronting the person and figure of Mary, examining and discerning the truth of her yes and the timely daringness of her no. It means testing its witness and role as prophet, evangelist, and also martyr. It means evaluating itself in its commitment to announcing the Good News to the poor and outcast and denouncing everything that prevents this Good News becoming reality.

The document *Marialis cultus* vigorously asserts that Mary of Nazareth was "something quite other than a passively obedient woman to an alienating religiosity. She was the woman who had no doubt about proclaiming that God is the vindicator of the humble and oppressed and puts down the mighty from their seats" (no. 37). And Pope John Paul II states:

> The God of the covenant sung by the Virgin of Nazareth in the lifting up of her spirit is both the one who puts down the mighty from their seats and exalts the humble, he fills the hungry with good things and sends the rich empty away. . . . Therefore the Church is aware — and in our time this awareness is reinforced in a very particular way — that not only can these two elements of the message contained in the *Magnificat* not be separated, but we must also carefully safeguard the importance that "the poor" and the "option for the poor" have in the word of the living God. These are themes and problems organically related with the Christian meaning of freedom and liberation (*Redemptoris Mater* no. 37, par. 3, 4, and 5).

The church must look to her, mother and model, to understand in its wholeness the meaning of its mission. With her in mind the church must strive always to be converted every day to become a better servant of the Lord, the handmaid to whom he does great things.

— Translated by Dinah Livingstone

SECTION II.3

THE LIBERATION OF CREATION

23

Anthropology:
The Person and the Community

JOSÉ IGNACIO GONZÁLEZ FAUS

I. SHEDDING LIGHT ON THE GEOGRAPHY AND THE HISTORY OF THE PROBLEM

1. Europe and Latin America

A recent work of Latin American theological anthropology (J. Comblin's) bases its study on the experience of the *communities* of believers: "What Christians can offer (on human beings) is the life and practice of their communities." On the other hand, any one of the classical European treatises on the same topic (Flick-Alszeghy, Ladaria, Pannenberg . . . including my own recent *Proyecto de hermano*) always speaks of human beings as *individuals* (despite claiming to speak of human beings by studying them at a level of abstraction making their affirmations valid for all).

I am not trying to appraise this difference, but I do consider it a *symptomatic fact*. The West continues to be the heir (and at times the slave) of the individualism of Modernism, characterized by the "discovery of the subject," as it has been said repeatedly. The novelty of Latin American theology is the extent to which the faith experience and the spiritual personal experience are communitarian experiences in the way they are carried out, but often in their content as well.

It is true that on various occasions, European theology has been conscious of that limitation of its anthropological expositions: already in the 1960s, J. B. Metz launched the programmatic call "to deprivatize faith" and theology. However, we must also acknowledge that, for all intents and purposes, that program continues to be unfulfilled in Europe. This may not be due to a lack of awareness concerning the importance of the task, but because there is no established subject capable of accomplishing that task and because the cultural framework in which theology is done may be rejecting that program rather than demanding it.

2. The Instability of Human History

This environmental, geographical anecdote introduces us fully into the importance and the difficulty of the problem individuals-community. Europe is the heir of Greek philosophy that was amazed and tortured by the irreconcilable experience of "the one and the multiple." And the Greeks considered being to be an "entity," an inanimate thing. When, with the Enlightenment, being became considered primarily as a person, as an awareness of being (*Dasein*), as a subject (and "unique" in this sense), the problem of the one and the multiple became the problem of the multiplicity of subjects. And the problem of the relations individuals-community appears as the unsolvable enigma of a multiplicity of absolutes.

This may be the reason why Hegel seemed to think that human history is made up of a series of various figures of relations individuals-community, and that every period of balance in these relations is followed by another period of unbalance in favor of one of the two poles. Later, this was resolved by moving toward a new figure of balance, always unstable. In turn, S. Freud left deeply engraved in Western consciousness the notion that even though the established community (the "culture" in the terminology of Freud) is necessary for individuals, it is only possible at the cost of an important dose of "malaise" for them. That "malaise in culture" is *intrinsic* to culture itself and it differs from those other Western or supererogatory malaises which can come from the distortions or evils of a determined culture.

What we are saying is not only typical of a particular philosophical reflection. The political history of human beings gives witness to these two facts: on one hand, the efficacy and splendor of the social "wholes" in which individuals were oppressed, to the degree they were induced to put up with this oppression (let us think of ancient Egypt, the Greece of the slaves and the "Helots," or modern Japan); but, on the other hand, the tragic human greatness which the rebellion of the individual reaches in some cases (as in Sophocles' *Antigone*).

Yet, that undeniable and impressive human greatness also entails a danger of "anomie" and disintegration of the social "wholes." Hence the necessity to reacclimatize individuals, perhaps not through force this time, nor through the divinization of the powers of the "whole," (Antigone's greatness is found precisely in losing her fear of the coercive force of the whole) but rather through more subtle and more acceptable mechanisms. Let us mention some examples of those mechanisms: the falsification of patriotic feelings (characteristic of every form of fascism and of all the doctrines of "national security,") or the acclimatization of the individual through an insane and insatiable material consumerism (wherever this is possible); or both factors at the same time.

In fact, when the rebellion of the individual exceeds its limits and becomes individualism, an exclusive self-affirmation of the I, then community becomes impossible, violence looms in the environment like a storm about to unleash its force, and the old theoretical problem of "the one and the multiple" is converted into the practical lie through which individuals appropriate "the One," instead of situating themselves in its truth: in the multiple. Thus, individuals identify with Max Stirner's famous title (*The One and its Property*) claiming necessity and absoluteness for themselves. Human beings become "wolves" toward one another and human history will be defined (at best) as a "class struggle," or as "the war of everyone against everyone." No wonder M. Stirner's theses irritated K. Marx so much because, in addition, they cannot easily be scientifically refuted, and Marx only wanted to believe in this type of argument. But, and perhaps even better than Marx, we can refute them through this other thesis coming from the wisdom of the ancient East:

And if one sees something selfishly as if it were everything, independently of the One and the many, then one finds oneself in the darkness of ignorance (*Bhagavad Gita*, 15).

All these introductory references (both geographical and historical) may be helpful in presenting our topic in all its importance and breadth.

II. FACTS OF CHRISTIAN FAITH

1. The Christian God

In all the previous context, it is amazing to find the categorical Christian affirmation that God is not an individual and that God's "personality" consists in being a communion of persons. It is amazing that Christianity maintained this Trinitarian profession of God as its fundamental identity card, since countless times the Trinity has been assailed by "reasonable" voices which considered it "absolutely useless" (Kant's case), or by theological, political movements defending the "monarchy" of God as the supreme paradigm of the individual monarchy of the emperors (as was the case of Arianism).

The fact is that within Christian theology itself, the doctrine of the Trinity has always insurmountably fluctuated between explanations that stressed more the unity (in order to preserve the biblical monotheism that Christians could not renounce) and explanations that stressed more the plurality (in order to preserve the identity of the Christian God, threatened to be absorbed by the Platonic or Aristotelian One). In spite of this, these following facts always remain as a "sacred" remnant inaccessible to human reasoning and as a summary of the Christian doctrine of God: *a*) in God, the persons are at the same time different in their relationships among themselves and in their mission with human beings; and *b*) yet, they are also consubstantial and equal. Difference does not imply any type of "subordination," nor does consubstantiality imply any form of modality. Neither one of these statements takes priority with regard to the other.

In this sense, and without ceasing to be an Absolute Mystery, the forever inaccessible mystery of God becomes the guiding principle of the Christian understanding of human beings: "Tell me what is your image of God and I will tell you what is your human ideal." This is the way we should understand the seemingly arrogant remark which a patriarch of the Russian church made to a reporter's question concerning the church's political program: "The political program of the Russian church is the Trinity."

2. The Work of God in History

According to the Christian message, this way of being of God becomes transparent in human history. It becomes evident, though only in an emergent way, in its struggle against the opaqueness of history and against the contradiction of human sin. God is always calling a *people* and for them to become a people, or better yet, the people of *God*, which implies their being established in equality, fellowship and justice. God reveals himself as the One who creates a people out of what was "no people" (cf. Hos 2:1-25; 1 Pt 2:10). God's election of particular persons is an election "for others" rather than a particular privilege focusing on the chosen individual.

But, in turn, God's work in history is poisoned by "weeds" (cf. Mt 13:25ff). which can be graphically visualized in what the emergence of the monarchy against amphictyony signified for the history of Israel. In the beginning, the monarchy appeared to have made Israel greater, but at the expense of freedom for all, and with it, at the expense of equality and fellowship. Thus, in the long run, the monarchy will end up by destroying itself.

In a similar way, human history has not progressed at the same pace in terms of what creates fellowship and community as when it produces material well-being and ease. Things very effective for this second goal but harmful for the first one were accepted on a large scale and without any form of limitations or compensations. Thus, theologians justified slavery in sixteenth-century Latin America, in the same way as they justified the accumulation of capital in a few individual hands in the nineteenth century, because both things were "necessary for the economy," which means that they were effectively favoring the material well-being and the rapid enrichment of a few.

As a historical balance sheet, there arises the faith judgment that our world has wrongly progressed and that our progress is seriously impaired because it became established on slavery and the spoliation of some individuals by others (who justify it by their fast material profits) rather than being based on human community.

And, to come back to God's work in history, to compensate the above, we should add that the Old Testament was already marked by a dialectic which affirmed the communitarian virtuality of all that, in its individual aspect, is an authentic human quality according to God. I am referring to the famous biblical dialectic of "representation," or vicariousness, which Western theology has never been able to explain fully. In Sodom, one just person could redeem the whole nation; the "remnant" of Israel recreated the fidelity of the entire people; in his personal suffering the servant of the Lord endured all the suffering of the community, and as a result, he "justified many" (cf. Is 53:4-12). The insignificance of the chosen people is explained because they were not chosen for their particular greatness, but rather to be a light and a magnet for all the nations. On the other hand, the sin of the people will consist in preferring a particular, competitive greatness "as other nations have" (1 Sm 8:5) to their mission of being the light of all nations from their own insignificance. The attempts to recover a theological justification for their ambiguous option for the monarchy (in which, as the Lord said to Samuel: "It is not you they reject, they are rejecting me as their king," 1 Sm 8:7) are attempts invented by the concept of a "universal quality" of the king. For that very reason a king makes sense only to the extent that he is the vindicator of the poor, of the defenseless and voiceless, the have-nots and those who are marginalized from the community. What Israel is asking God for the king is for him "to defend the afflicted among the people, to save the children of the poor and to crush the oppressor ... to rescue the poor when they cry out and the afflicted who have no one to help them, to have pity for the lowly and the poor, to save the lives of the poor, because the lives of the poor are precious in his sight" (Ps 72:4, 12-14). All personal power which is neither defined nor justified by such a mission or, as it has been the case in almost all individual powers in human history, a power that serves to crush the poor and to support the exploiters will always be a rejection of God, "not wanting God as our king" (1 Sm 8:7). It will be an unjustified individual arrogance bound to crumble in the end just like the monarchy in Israel. That kind of power becomes what the Bible calls the "power of the bramble," that is to say the power of the worst, those who come into power because the quality of the good ones (the olive tree, the fig tree or the vine) consists in their capacity to renounce power precisely because they feel they "are not going to give up their fruits that delight gods and men to wave over the other trees" (cf. Jgs 9:7-15).

This way of God's working in history finds its culmination in Christ who proclaimed the fatherhood of God through the reign of human love and who would only become king "from the cross." All the Old Testament titles containing the dialectic between what is personal and what is communitarian apply to Christ: the servant of the Lord, the Son of Man, and so forth. The resurrection, as the exaltation of Jesus to the very dimension of God, implies the universalization of Jesus and, therefore, it includes the resurrection of all human beings, transforming Jesus into the first-born and the first fruits of those who have died (cf. Col 1:18 and 1 Cor 15:19).

3. The Communion of the Holy or the Imprint of the Transcendent in History

This theology of "representation" culminates in the Christian dogma of the communion of the holy. The *communio sanctorum* must be translated both as masculine and neuter. But it must begin by this second translation in order to include the first one: the saints are in communion, because the very holiness of God *is* communion. The "communion of the holy" simply expresses the communitarian aspect, the fruitfulness and the universality of love, which is God. By professing it, believers dare to hope that they can be justified by the gift of humanity *of others,* which belongs to them by virtue of the communitarian nature of the holy. They also dare to hope that if there is some supernatural faith, hope and love in them, it will serve to justify all those who do not believe and who do not love, because that faith, that hope and that love are not exclusively theirs, but they belong to everyone through the communion of the holy. As a result, that communion of the holy holds a specific place in the Creed and we must be even more specific: it appears next to the marks of the church and next to the forgiveness of sins.

It appears next to the forgiveness of sins in the Creed because, as Albertus Magnus, one of the great theologians of the *communio sanctorum* explained, "There can only be communion where what is one's own and exclusive disappears, and that is the sin of each one." In this way, human beings who are sinners "have in others what is lacking in them."[1]

It also comes after the marks of the church. Fundamentally, oneness, holiness, catholicity, and apostolicity all point to communion. This communion which characterizes the church is not only possible by way of the common faith experience, but also through the very content of that experience of faith, that is to say: the Holy is communion.

All of this will immediately bring about its practical consequences in the imperative given to the church to structure itself as a communion (*koinonia*), as we will see later in the fifth section of this chapter. For the time being, we will limit ourselves to pointing out how the communion "of saints" arises from the communion of the holy. At first, this communion of saints referred to all the believers; today it can provide an authentic reason for the Catholic veneration of the saints. It is a way to express that the saints *do not belong to themselves,* rather they belong to all the Christian people and to all human beings, as this was accurately stated in the canonization of Joan of Arc. However, for this to happen, the church must not feel tempted by canonizations that appear to bless a peculiarity of an excluding nature (even if it is the very peculiarity of the interests of the hierarchy). Instead, the church must maintain the schema of the Israelite monarchy and of Jesus in their being close to the marginalized, that is to say that something can only be universal on the basis of and through the preferential option for the most excluded. If the church really wants to be a sacrament of communion, today it must look for its saints among those who worked to "rescue the poor when they cried out and the afflicted who had no one to help them," and among those who fought to "help the poor and crush the oppressor" (cf. Ps 72). This is the fine theological intuition which so often pulsates in the hearts of the faithful when, in a spontaneous way, they want to canonize people like Archbishop Romero. If that canonization makes the ecclesiastical hierarchy uneasy, that will be a more serious call for a self-examination before God, asking if it is really a sacrament of communion, or if it has fallen back into the very sin of the Israelite monarchy. The attempt to silence people like Archbishop Romero constitutes a form of manipulation much more serious than the one in which the poor of this world may be involved with Romero, whom they claim as their own.

4. The Christian Concept of Faith

Finally, this uni-Trinitarian understanding of God culminates in the Christian theology of faith. For Christians, faith in God is only possible thanks to God's communitarian being, by virtue of which God cannot only be the inaccessible end of faith (*the Father*), but also the gift of that inaccessible end whereby God is, *at the same time,* the mediator from us to the absolutely transcendent Father (*the Son or the Word*) and the very driving force which conveys and interiorizes that mediation in us (*the Spirit*).

For this reason, at the same time, personal faith has an equally communitarian structure because, for the Word and the Spirit of God, the separation that characterizes what is created, a separation according to which what is most personal seems less communitarian and vice versa is no longer valid: the Son is the universal recapitulator and, being poured out into all flesh as the "soul" of the body of believers, the Spirit is the personifier of the many.

In Christian churches, occasional discussions have emerged about the way of reciting the profession of faith usually known as the Creed, about whether we should say "I believe" or "We believe." The risks involved in each option (a gregarious faith without personal risks or a solitary faith, in terms of personal merit) are understandable, and this is why Christians should know how to combine both formulas in their professions of faith. However, if the law of prayer is somewhat binding in terms of believing, we should remember that, when Jesus taught us how to pray, he proposed a prayer using terms like *we* and *our.* He never spoke of *my* or *I* (*our* Father, *our* bread, forgive *us* as *we* forgive, lead *us* not, deliver *us*). This deatil must be understood on the basis of Jesus' conviction that prayer is a person's most intimate action. Moreover, the same Spirit who cries out in us *Abba* (Father: cf. Gal 4:6) is the same Spirit who also cries out in us: "brother or sister," in the presence of every human being, and above all, before those who are treated the worst.

The above statements will enable us to follow what J. B. Metz calls "the totally simple idea which is not evident in ordinary theological circles, in spite of everything, the idea that according to biblical-Christian data, the subject of the act of faith is not the singular I in its characteristic of being an isolated subject, but rather it is the I in its initial intersubjective aspect, in its condition of brother, sister." For Metz, this is so much so that the impulse to isolation of faith will always be an impulse of concupiscence, whereas intersubjectivity "can be considered as an essential determination, if not *the* central determination of the *Christian* believing subject. For our author, this means that "we are not saved in consideration of our faith but only in consideration of our brothers and, through them, of God in whom are hidden the ultimate existential plurality and division of our believing existence (Col 3:3)."[2]

But if the plurality and division of our believing existence are hidden in God, as we said a short while ago, for the community of believers, this marks the most decisive task of its mission in the world: the task of being in fact the sacrament of communion among people, in a world marked by divisions, differences, and hostility. This is the last aspect that we still have to examine.

5. The Christian Concept of "Communion" (Koinonia)

The concept of *koinonia* is derived from the concept of God and of God's action that is received in faith. It is one of the concepts most present in all the works of the New Testament. It encompasses countless expressive variations that we cannot analyze here. One of the characteristic components of this concept is that of being communion *with diversity.* A complement of this diversity is the primacy of the weakest or the least visible, because it is only a diversity in terms of functions, not in terms of personal worth or values. In Christ Jesus, there is no longer male or female, slave or free, and so forth.

The image of the body extends to the allegory that we should treat with greater care and attention what seems the weakest and least worthy, and that when one member suffers, all the others suffer along with it. This image functions as the most elemental visual image of that Christian communion (cf. 1 Cor 12:12ff). As a result, *koinonia* is just as opposed to massification as it is opposed to uniformity. Koinonia admits of neither disintegration, nor authoritarianism because, drawing once again from the analogy of the body, it is the spirit that is creative, and not a superior member. The unity of the body is present not only at the heart of diversity, but at times, even in the midst of tensions.

In this context, orientation to service and a humble life becomes the object of recommendation for individual Christians. Precisely because in individuals, obstinacy (or self-love) is sin, it must be pressed to the other extreme (in a kind of Ignatian *agere contra*), attempting to transform it into service so that it might become communion, "considering others superior to ourselves" (Phil 2:3), "considering oneself the servant of all" (cf. 1 Cor 9:19) so that "no one should seek one's own interest but rather that of one's neighbor" (1 Cor 10:20), etc. Individuals who may often experience a sensation of death in the practice of service, will rise transformed when they come to the experience of communion through service.

Finally, for the early Christians, this *koinonia* will have two consequences that are already almost lost and which the theology of liberation is trying to recapture. They deserve to be emphasized now.

a) The first one involves an extension to the *material* aspect of life. Precisely because what is spiritual is intrinsically communitarian, as we saw a moment ago, it belongs to everyone, Christians feel called to what also involves the material, since the Spirit of God does not exclude, but rather it transforms what is material. "Hold everything in common with others and do not claim anything as your own, because if you have *koinonia* in terms of immortal goods, all the more so in terms of temporal goods." This advice is often echoed in various texts of early Christian preaching and it is reflected in the familiar descriptions of the book of Acts concerning the praxis of the early community. It is essential to underscore this "all the more so" used in the argumentation of the quoted texts: if the Spirit (that is the most personal that can exist) is intrinsically communitarian, "all the more so for what is material," totally devoid of personal qualities. According to this, more than a simple "social function" of ownership, or even more than a "social mortgage" (undoubtedly a stronger term), the early church speaks of a *social objective* and a *social truth* of ownership.

b) The second consequence in which *koinonia* is at work is the categorical command to change authority into service (and not merely by an invisible intention, but by the visible ways in which it is exercised). Precisely because personal power can become the utmost affirmation of the individual and the greatest denial of its communitarian pole, it is one of the greatest sins for the New Testament. Since, on the other hand, authority is indispensable in any human society (although it is also insufficient), and since the church is not exempt from the laws of history, the New Testament goes back to the advice of Jesus (Lk 22:24-27) and to the praxis of Jesus (whose *exousia* "was not like that of the scribes and the Pharisees": cf. Mk 1:22 and 10:45), by changing authority into service. By this we mean that power is not what embraces and represents everyone, because of the mere fact that it is power. It became that way ever since God emptied himself of his power before human beings and identified himself with slaves (cf. Phil 2:6ff). On the contrary, selfless love is what really embraces human beings as brothers and sisters because such love proceeds from God.

Hence, a final decisive element emerges for the Christian vision of human beings and of the question individuals-community. In the New Testament, the concept that is most opposed to the idea of *koinonia* may be that of *pleonexia* (greed, yearning for more, desires). The New Testament writings oppose this concept on countless occasions and it is even defined as utter idolatry (cf. Eph 5:5; Col 3:5). Thus, the New Testament is aware of the same suspicion as the great Eastern religions in terms of desire as the root of all evil. However, the New Testament response to this drama is never formulated as the mere death or annihilation of desires through some type of apathy or nirvana; instead it proposes an authentic transformation of desires into solidarity and non-possessive communion. As human beings, obviously we cannot attain such a transformation. Yet, the New Testament believes it is possible through the action of the Holy Spirit "poured out into our hearts" (cf., for example, Rom 5:5). This appears to be one of the most characteristic aspects of Christian faith on the theme of therelations between individuals and community.

III. HOW THESE ASPECTS OF FAITH RESONATE IN EUROPEAN THEOLOGY AND IN THE THEOLOGY OF LIBERATION

Liberation theology has shown a greater capacity for integrating all these elements of the Christian sources into its reflection than the theology of the First World has been able to do. This is probably one of the factors that explain its unexpected resonance throughout the world in spite of the paucity of its means of production or distribution and in spite of the interested resistances that are already known.

It is logical to think that this greater fidelity is due to the various sociocultural situations to which we alluded at the beginning of this essay. This is why now it becomes imperative to examine these situations more thoroughly, especially because their paths appear paradoxical when we look at them more closely. It would seem that they follow a way of affirming one's life which leads to losing it, and another opposite way whereby one's life is saved when it has been lost (cf. Mk 8:35).

1. The Vicious Circle of the First World

The paradox that we evoked is manifested in the fact that it is precisely in the individualistic West that individuals feel the most threatened and dissatisfied. It is as if the First World experienced the fulfillment of one of those divine biblical punishments which consist in "leaving human beings to follow their own desires." Today, the West is experiencing various things: its culture of unconditional affirmation of individuals has left them at the mercy of their own solitude; its people educated in the value of selfishness and self-preservation have come to know a lack of communication; their ideological recourse to disguising individual death has led to producing individuals who are secretly anguished by an authentic neurosis about health and a system designed to defend their individual privileges at any cost, above and beyond any communitarian necessities, has left people alone and dwarfed in the presence of a macrostructure which is crushing them and which seems to be taking them where they did not wish to go, namely to their own possible annihilation through nuclear destruction, ecological impoverishment, or the asphyxiation caused by the supercontrol of the computer age.

Individuals, Community, and Authority

We must, however, introduce some distinction in this "individualistic decadence" of the West, since not every aspect of it has been equally unilateral and equally false, especially if we consider the process from its beginning. In the origins of the modern West, the recovery of the individual and of individual reason gave rise to one of the greatest achievements in modern history. This conquest had its roots in the French Revolution and it entailed the slow historical birth of a desacralization of authority and the emergence of what we usually call democracy. We will understand the meaning of this entire process better if we compare it not only to the situation that immediately preceded it (the "divine right" of absolute monarchs), but also to other situations with more authoritarianism in the course of history.

For example, the Greco-Roman antiquity knew a spectacular sacralization of authority which may have been based on the experience of its absolute necessity and of its social benefits for the peace in the empire (an experience which, on the other hand was also unilateral since it tended to forget the victims of those benefits). In that situation, Pope Saint Leo the Great came to concede to the emperor (that is to say to political authority) the "Holy Spirit's inspiration" and a quasi infallibility with regard to his decisions. Saint Leo was leaning on his good experiences with the emperor as a result of the Council of Chalcedon. However, he may not have realized to what extent the emperor's interests were not merely religious, but instead eminently political: the unity and the peace of the empire.[3] The theophanic concept of ecclesiastical authority flows also from the same sacralized vision of the world, and within that vision, from the need of authority. If power is theophanic in and of itself, it follows that all power will be theophanic, whether it is civil or ecclesiastical.

Therefore, starting with the eighteenth century, a radical desacralization of authority took place in the West. Authority is necessary but that does not mean that it is sacred. Instead, what predominates is the idea that God would be more present wherever total "consubstantiality" or fellowship made authority unnecessary. Authority does not symbolize the presence of God as much as it does his absence.

Yet, in the church there was an attempt to maintain ecclesiastical authority as sacred, even while the secularization of civil authority was being accepted. Today the West feels that there is an important hidden inconsistency in that distinction to the degree that it could be stated that the schismatic Archbishop Lefèbvre was more consistent with his radical aversion to political democracy (as logical as it is anachronistic). In addition, this could be a biased inconsistency insofar as the sacralization of authority seems to free it from the morality of means: acting in God's name, one will always do the right thing. In this way, there is a tendency to identify much too hastily the victims with the guilty ones, without looking into the many nuances that the secularization of the notion of authority could bring to that identification.

In this way, it also happens that some debatable procedures from Antiquity — like the exile of heretics — which were perpetuated in the Middle Ages through the Inquisition, still subsist now, and although these methods have been reduced because of social pressure, they are not sufficiently criticized in their theological foundations. But those methods which used to form part of the moral conscience *of society* and of the world in earlier days, have already been superseded by that conscience and they seem outrageous and they make the church unbelievable. "Because the church shows such a lack of moral conscience in the solution of its own communitarian problems, it cannot really teach morality" — this is what can be heard in the West today.

Theology should understand that in this harsh criticism, it is not only the worst of the modern West expressing itself, but instead this strange human composite in which justice and sin are both involved. This presents the church with a series of important tasks if it really wants to evangelize this Western world that is starving for some "good news."

Individuals, Freedom, and Individualism

In this entire context, we must admit that the individualistic "preoccupation," shown in many theological works of the First World, is a legitimate one. But, we should also add that the described situation may lead some to look to faith or to the imprecise environment of "what is religious," for desperate individualistic ways out which, in fact, turn out to be mere flights or escapes into the future. This type of solution could possibly make people more credulous, but it will obviously never make believers out of them. And once again, J. B. Metz deserves undeniable credit for having opened our eyes to this form of "bourgeois religion," and for having indicated the urgent need to overcome this approach to the North Atlantic world. On the contrary, the experience of First World believers who have lived in the Southern Third World, becomes a decisive point of reference to show that the solution of "individuals' ills" in the North cannot come from a reinforcement of that vicious circle of individual claims, but instead it has to come from some painful rupture of that circle.

Because of this, the exposition of Third World problems in the First World and their consideration cannot be quickly ignored as if they only pertained to the Third World which is the last alibi that has recently started to be used in the West. Although the solutions cannot be uncritically transplanted, these problems constitute a plea to change a whole way of life which is not only coresponsible for the subhuman situation of the Third World (and which demands the conversion of the First World so that such a situation may be changed), but in addition, this way of life has become an insurmountable dehumanizing trap for the First World itself.

An Example Taken from the World of Religion

In citing this vicious circle of the North Atlantic world, that seems to go from individualism to deceiving individuals, it becomes unavoidable to say something about the most serious and the most powerful attempt to overcome this entropic circle, which is perhaps shown in the work of Marcel Légaut. The program of that endeavor might be formulated this way: to rescue individuals from their insignificance by teaching them to be themselves.[4] Even though it is not easy to evaluate Légaut's theological work in a short page, I would like to point out at least three things: it merit, its unilaterality, and its danger.

1) Let us consider its merit first. A genuine redemption of spirituality took place in Légaut. Since Rahner's death, he may be the only author who is opening the way, communicating truths, and instilling a breath of life. The only master who "speaks with authority and not like the scribes and Pharisees of the system," this author who does not quite anyone desperately, comes from the field of mathematical sciences. His writings do not pretend to reinstate theology in the forum of universality, but rather in the depth of the human heart. Légaut presents no other theological reasons than the following: the authenticity of human experience vis-à-vis the safely doctrinaire; the path to human authenticity vis-à-vis unfaithful gregariousness and the life of human interiority vis-à-vis religious superficiality. No one else, and perhaps unintentionally, has been able to restore such depth and seriousness to the category of "adoration" in a religious world where the name of God is so often trivially taken in vain. This explains why in people assailed or shaken by doubt, disappointment and abandonment, Légaut is leaving a deeper mark and he obtains a greater audience than any "official" ecclesiastical statement.

2) It was necessary to say all that precedes in order to be able to deal, in

the second place, with Légaut's unilaterality rooted in the markedly individual characteristic of his spirituality. In Jesus and in Christianity, Légaut only appears to find a call to each person, to fidelity to oneself, to the treasures, unknown to each one, of the "interior life." The categories of the "reign of God," the Good News for the poor, or Jesus' constant reference to "his own," "his people," (so many aspects emphasized in the theology of liberation) are totally absent from Légaut, not only in the configuration of his thought, but they are neither alluded to nor mentioned. Légaut's references to others occur almost always in terms of I to you relationships: love, parenthood, the figure of the teacher, or very small communities of spiritually similar people. The dimension of a people, of the community of different members is absent from the whole and it only appears (as a pole of reference inevitably implicit in the nature of the theme) when the author deals with authority, and when he rightfully criticizes many of the ways in which it is exercised. Frequently, Légaut, once again rightfully, insists upon the "ultimate solitude" of human beings, especially in the case of "spiritual" people. But, he seems totally oblivious of the fact that such a solitude can be accompanied (perhaps not at the level of experiential contents, but definitely at the level of the experiences of feelings) by the experience of the community, communion with the poor, the possibility to "give life," and to be evangelized by the poor. In contrast with Jesus' invitation "to give one's life for one's friends," here we only have the living of one's life in order to find oneself.

3) Finally, let us examine the dangers of that unilaterality. Putting it rather crudely, it is fitting to speak of the danger of its degenerating into an aristocratic type of Christianity which, in turn, will almost unavoidably lead to a certain gnosticism whereby "the spiritual being" may become an expression with more of a Gnostic sense than a Pauline meaning. That is to say that, even unintentionally, such a being appears to be a person above others rather than a person for others. Therefore, all that inevitably pertains to *structure* in faith (necessarily implying community) will become for such a person a *superstructure*, meaning that instead of being a bond of communion, it will be a useless armor that the interior life will invite the individual to castaside. Such a person will open up to a kind of faith which, however naked it may wish to be, it will always be under the threat of being clothed only by the self.

Obviously, because of their fineness and subtlety, M. Légaut's formulations never reach the point of expressing all the above. But, in my opinion, there is an almost lethal danger latent in them all unless, without absolutely rejecting them, the other pole is presented as a complement and with the same intensity. We mean the communitarian pole of faith and of the person which is what appears to be emerging in the theology of Latin America.

2. The "Great Work of God" Because "He Has Looked upon the Humiliation" of the Oppressed World

In the same paradoxical way, we have to say that what made liberation theology more sensitive to the previously presented aspects of the Christian message, was not precisely a situation of a "realized" community. Obviously, Latin America is neither living that situation nor the situation of a "forgotten" community as in the case of the North Atlantic culture. Instead, it is in the rather painful situation of a "trampled upon" and crushed community. The clamorous presence of great impoverished masses, of offensive differences of standards of living, as remote in terms of possibilities as they are close in terms of space, the existence of millions of refugees, of families with various "disappeared" members, all these are facts that cannot be concealed in Latin America because we are not dealing with small negligible minorities, but with the great masses of that continent. This reality gives a better understanding of what Medellín and Puebla called structural sin and which Puebla defined as follows:

> Sin, a force of disruption, is a permanent obstacle to the growth in love and communion, because it comes from the hearts of men and also from the various structures constructed by them and in which the sin of their authors left their destructive imprint (no. 281).

The text situates human growth in communality (love and communion). It considers sin to be something individualistic (like a "force of disruption" of that growth) and it not only situates that force in the interiority of individuals but also in the systems of coexistence that they have established. This perspective is more understandable in a community like the Latin American one which has experienced the falsification of all the communitarian mediations (nation, class, city, church) and the negation of all the forms of otherness upon which the community is built (cultural, racial, sexual). In the final analysis, that falsification and that negation were at the root of the subsequent masses in situations of extreme, or nearly extreme poverty. Yet, they can also give rise to a clear awareness of themselves and to a conversion for the recovery of the mediations and respect for otherness. Perhaps, this point deserves further development.

The "Humiliation" of Falsified Communitarian Mediations

Among falsified communitarian mediations, we cannot merely evoke the classical concept of the "social classes." In Latin America, they experience more intensely and in a more simplified manner the situation of class aggression, traditionally known as class "struggle." In addition to this, it is fitting to refer to the falsification of the national communities by the anti-Christian doctrine of "national security," which is only a disguised extension of another doctrine of "imperial" security.

This doctrine of national security shatters the national community itself when it presupposes that only a reduced percentage of the nation has the right to be considered as such, and moreover that it has the right to defend this appropriation even through violence. In this context, it is impossible to deal with the theme individuals-community in Latin America without mentioning an alarming word about the abominable reality of the Latin American armies placed in the service of that national security. If the very institution of the army seems necessary to some because of the need to concentrate and control the required forces for defense, while to others it appears questionable because it gives rise to insurmountable temptations of power, and because it indirectly reinforces the vicious circles (increasingly more threatening) of violence; in Latin America, it is no longer possible to hesitate in this ambiguity which has been fatally resolved in favor of the second hypothesis. It would be difficult to find Latin American armies that have not greatly betrayed *their own people* whom they were supposed to serve by placing themselves at the service of the interests of a privileged minority and of an outside empire which, in the name of those interests, became literally genocidal. If there is an image which incarnates the antithesis of all we considered above, concerning royal power in ancient Israel, that image is that of nearly all the Latin American armies: "To be merciless with the poor who cry out and the afflicted with no one to protect them; siding with the mighty and, on their behalf, crushing the lives of the poor which are worthless in their sight" (cf. Ps 72, previously quoted). The cry of anguish which cost Archbishop Romero his life ("They belong to our own people! You are killing your own brothers. Before the order of a man who tells someone to kill, God's word saying, 'You shall not kill,' must always prevail. And so, in the name of God, I ask you, I command and I order you: Stop the repression!") was not a casual or untimely cry, but instead the expression of a more than justified anguish before the consequences of that ideology called national security and which Puebla had considered anti-Christian, although later on, an unforeseen secret manipulation of the text voted by the bishops removed that condemnation. The murderous reaction that was unleashed was the best proof of it.

To proceed with our enumeration, we could also evoke the falsification of the urban communities which has taken place in Latin America by way of the sudden mushrooming of the most inhuman megalopolises (at the same time bigger and worse that the biggest European capitals, whose errors they have multiplied). These cities have surfaced too hastily, at the wrong time, without any possibilities of a healthy assimilation for a mostly agricultural society, which has not been able to produce the slow process of the formation of the middle classes, and the emergence of small and average-sized towns which characterized the Europe of the thirteenth and fourteenth centuries. This insane and irresponsible explosion of these huge megalopolises, almost exclusively due to foreign economic interests, appears to be another of the undeniable factors increasing wretchedness and powerlessness and making them more visible.

The "Humiliation" of Despised Otherness

Along this falsification of the communitarian mediations, we have also spoken of the contempt for otherness. The passive experience of this contempt marks first the birth, and then the history of the Latin American nations whose original native inhabitants and whose autochthonous cultures felt that their human identity and their human dignity were ignored by the conquerors in spite of the heroic and admirable defense of a whole generation of bishops and missionaries (or more accurately some of them who "were also abandoned by their fellow bishops and brothers at table," as Bishop Casaldáliga would write).

Peoples, individuals, and cultures were denied their human condition in order to be "legitimately" conquered and subjected to slavery, to *encomienda* or vassalage.

We should also enumerate other anti-communitarian experiences in which otherness was rejected. In addition to the otherness of the Indians, there is the otherness of women, structurally and personally trampled upon by the well-known Latin American machismo that is still powerful today. There is also the cultural otherness which is subjected to a tacit European or North American colonization and forced into futile mimicry. Europeans should feel ashamed when they see Latin American television commercials advertising what is European, more or less the same way as Europe appeals to sexual enticement in advertising.

In this way, the Latin American situation seems to break that classic Hegelian-Marxist schema speaking of a first phase (or "thesis") of "crude" communism, that is later contradicted by another phase of absolute individualism, both being later subsumed in the synthesis of a perfect communism or a realized community whose full realization coincides with the full realization of each of its members. Be that as it may, Latin America seems to have moved from "crude communism" to a shattered community. This is not the time to discuss whether the causes of that destruction are exclusively external, as stated in the languages of "economic imperialism," "the theory of dependency," and so forth, or if the causes are only internal, as alleged by those who deny these languages. As usual, we have to think that both elements are involved.

It is crucial, however, to observe that precisely in this situation of a shattered community, experiences of reconquering what is communitarian have been emerging and developing. Moreover, these experiences involve a seriousness and an intensity difficult to imagine from the developed world.

Although we must limit ourselves to the *theological* aspects of the theme, it will be good to bear in mind that the theology under consideration was prepared by genuine precursors, or by the "signs of the times" which Latin American theology has been able to read. To prevent his falling into oblivion, it might be good to mention the first of those signs, the gesture of the president of Costa Rica, Figueres Ferrer, who abolished the army in 1948, establishing this into a constitutional mandate. An isolated, utopian, "unviable" gesture about which someone wrote almost forty years later that it served to familiarize some people with the idea that having no armies was a blessing from the Lord. And, closer to us, we must mention how recent Latin American fiction has reconquered a privileged place in the world's literature practically at the same time as liberation theology was born. Many believers have been able to recognize these and other small "miracles," as signs of the Spirit announcing a coming of the Lord for Latin America. As a result, it is not by chance that the work that gave its name to all the current theology (G. Gutiérrez' *A Theology of Liberation*) begins with a long quotation from the novelist, J. M. Arguedas, or that Pedro Trigo dedicated a good part of his theological work to commentaries about recent Latin American novels. Thus, community with the poor opens the way for a re-encounter with Latin American identity and community.

Important communitarian experiences of faith have emerged in this context. They are usually polarized around the so-called "basic communities," which must not be mythified since they are still fragile and threatened like all incipient life. However, it is fitting to say that the Spirit of God has hovered much more authentically over them than over the First World spiritual renewal attempts. These have frequently turned into unreal forms of spiritualism or into communitarian forms of docetism, or they have appeared much more sensitive to the individual gift of tongues than to the communitarian gift of prophecy, to use the Pauline terminology ("Whoever speaks in a tongue builds up himself, but whoever prophesies builds up the church," 1 Cor 14:4). Here, it is fitting to apply Paul's criteria for discernment, namely that the greatest charism is the one most capable of building up the community, not merely internally (cf. *ibid.*, 14:5ff) but also for outsiders (*ibid.*, 14:24ff).

And so, we might suspect or even whisper that these experiences of the Latin American communities are the fulfillment of the words of Jesus' prayer when he thanked his Father for communicating the secrets of his reign to the childlike, and not to the wise and the powerful. All the liberation theologians may be in agreement not only about the fact that (as J. Comblin did as we mentioned at the beginning of this article) their theological reflection on humankind cannot ignore the experience of the communities, but above all about the fact that the very life and existence of these communities is really more important than liberation theology itself. It is in these communities that a first rebuilding of the falsified mediations took place on the basis of the faith experience. In addition, there has been another profound faith experience: the affirmation of otherness. Indeed, what is at stake there is the utmost otherness, the otherness of the poorest that we strive to respect and to affirm: "We will build up the community when the poor believe in the poor" (Salvadoran mass). Therefore, we should not be surprised by such references to these communities which speak of an authentic "ecclesiogenesis," a "re-inventing of the church" by the basic communities (L. Boff), or of a "resurrection of the true church" (J. Sobrino). We can already confirm the above in spite of the remaining problems in terms of the praxis and the theology.

Furthermore, all of the above can be affirmed even when, on the other hand, we recognize that this experience is not all-embracing, nor does it involve the majority in the churches or in the theology in Latin America. Nevertheless, it is Latin America's most characteristic and most powerful experience.

This may not affect the majority of believers because a great part of those churches, of their hierarchies and of their theological output is still resisting the transformation described as a rising from death and they prefer to maintain the "colonial" situation, for their theology and also for the life of the church. Moreover, this orientation enjoys the support and the great power of many institutions of the "Center," and in it the classical risks of all colonial situations are mirrored: copying all the faults of the metropolis and practically none of its virtues. This emerging, minority (or at least not complete) character is acknowledged by the representatives of liberation theology:

Not all the Latin American churches are in a position to question anyone. Many of them should be questioned because they leave much to be desired.

There is not a Latin American church that is a holy church capable of awakening the other churches from their religious or dogmatic dream.[5]

Yet, even though the majority is not yet involved, we can still attest that this conversion process previously described is both *the strongest and the most characteristic* process in Latin America. What has occurred is an undeniable feeling of a recovery of identity: it is no accident that, from its beginning, liberation theology has been called the *"Latin American* theology of liberation," despite three apparent reasons against this. In spite of the fact that those beginnings were still so hesitant and so dependent that they did not earn their identity until those reflections of the early days were immersed in the lives and the sufferings of Latin American men and women of faith. Also, in spite of the fact that the theological quality of the "liberation" category extends beyond the Latin American borders and is in fact universal (Catholic), Christian, and symptomatic of the New Testament. Lastly, in spite of the fact that, in Latin America, there are *other* theologies and other ways of living one's faith, although they lack the sufficient quality and identity to be able to abort what the Spirit was bringing to life in Latin America, in a discreet form of action, always in need of discernment, and always easily rejected because of working "between chaos and the waters" (cf. Gn 1:2). And I repeat, they failed because they lacked sufficient quality and identity, not because they did not try with the reasons of force and manipulation, more than with the reasons of truth and transparency. Once more in Latin America it has become true that "the deep waters could not quench love" (Sg 8:7). This explains why Gamaliel's prediction in the book of Acts did prevail: "Have nothing to do with these men, and let them go. For if this endeavor or this activity is of human origin, it will destroy itself. But if it comes from God, you will not be able to destroy them; you may even find yourselves fighting against God" (Acts 5:33-39).

From this, Latin American theology should learn in its still anguished and difficult moments that if it is in fact moved by the Spirit of God, its greatest enemy will never be found in the attacks from the outside, in the suffering caused from outside, nor in the contradictions that are unleashed by every passage of God through history. Its worst enemy will be its own temptation to infidelity which shakes and threatens God's elects.

IV. A FEW IMPLICATIONS

After this brief reflection of sections II and III on the sources of Christian faith and its resonance in the life of today's Christian churches, we can now return to the focal point of our theme and draw some more specific teachings. We are going to present them according to the direction indicated by the Puebla assembly in its search for the genuine balance between what is individual and communitarian, equally distancing itself from all liberalism and all collectivism, since they both failed in their attempt to produce a synthesis individuals-community because they are two forms of self-centered materialism unreceptive to the spiritual.

1. *Toward the Communitarian Overcoming of the North Atlantic Individualism*

The so-called First World has to destroy the myth on which it was founded, that is to say the myth of the *universality* of individual reason and of individual freedom. Reason and freedom may be legitimate, but they are not universal. On the other hand, according to the cultural unconscious of the First World, reason is probably universal because of its power to enter into the very nature of reality, and freedom is probably universal because the harmonious nature of the real acts as an "invisible hand" reconciling all the forms of individual egoism under the guise of service for the common good.

Today, both assumptions have come to a crisis in the developed world itself although the possibility of redemption is provided along with the crisis. The dreadful experiences of the irrationality of reason and of the enslaving possibilities of freedom (which manifest themselves in the increasingly more offensive inability for coexistence) have opened the path to the categories of "dialogue," not in the merely personal or political, but in the *philosophical* sense, or of "communicative reason," and so forth.

But if this dialogic reason is not to become the prisoner of a new "original sin" which would falsify it, as happened to the "universal reason" of the Enlightenment, we should not mention it without immediately emphasizing *the conditions* indicated by its promoters: dialogue will not be true dialogue, and it will self-destruct, unless there is an attempt to exercise it in the best possible conditions of communication and equality. But such a condition proves to be extremely difficult to fulfill in the developed world where equality is reduced to an abstract formality used to confirm a multitude of real inequalities.

If this is the case, then dialogic reason or the determination to create a consensus and coexistence in situations which structurally do not make it possible, will have to make an additional effort to incorporate the point of view of the excluded and of the victims of every social situation in its communication, and it will also have to provide this point of view with a privileged place in the dialogue. Victims must be the goal of communicative reason precisely because they are individuals who are crippled in their most basic individual rights.

This is the only possible way to correct the previous distortion characterizing reason entering into dialogue, as reason converts what should be "particularities that are added up" into "privileges that are subtracted." Otherwise, the new Western reason that seems to be in the making would not become *communitarian* reason, but instead and at best a majority reason which would use its majority power to establish itself on a remnant of people reduced to the condition of "voiceless," and therefore without reason. Such a form of "reason" would have replaced the power of communion (which reason itself claims to seek) by the power of numbers.

And, in this context, the fact that in the First World some have recently started to speak of a society which they call "of the two-thirds" is no accident but a rather serious warning. One-third made up of privileged people, and another made up of people well established, tacitly agree to despoil the other third made up of the "submerged," namely the victims whom they silence and over whom they establish themselves. The minority character of this group of victims (made possible both by the world's technological revolution and by the interdependence of the world allowing a "sweeping out" of many other victims) radically upsets all the Marxist expositions of the past century which presupposed the majority power of an ever-increasing number of victims. But this does not redeem the lie of Western individualism, instead it disguises it more and makes it more difficult to overcome.

On the contrary, if communicative reason allows that feeling of "responsibility in solidarity" (to use Adela Cortina's terms) to question it, the developed world could also realize the other and absolutely necessary criticism of its own concept of progress and of the "instrumental reason" which produced it. This is where the First World could come to understand that not all the already *factibile* is therefore *faciendum*: not all that *can* already be done *must* be done. In other words not every material step forward represents real progress in an authentic human direction. Instead, and in view of the irreversible unity and interdependence that has already been attained worldwide, all progress that fails to be universal, in solidarity and attentive to the plight of the victims of our planet, necessarily becomes a kind of unilateral and monstrous development which distorts the human organism and breaks the harmony of the body of humanity.

All these considerations are forcing the First World into a major revision of the sacrosanct slogan of "human rights." Until now, in most of the history of the First World, "human rights" have meant no more than "individual privileges." The slogan has to recapture its value according to the essence of Augusto César Sandino's basic truth: "The rights of the poor are *more sacred* than the rights of the powerful." The First World could easily relate the previous phrase with N. Berdiaeff's expression: "Bread for me is a material problem, whereas bread for my brother is a *spiritual* problem." This approach would allow us to understand the term "sacred" in Sandino's phrase, and enable us to see that in this phrase, we are in the presence of a truth which is religious in itself because, as with the reality of God, it can only be *recognized*. It cannot be imposed by itself, since the weak are supposed to be those who lack the power to impose even their most basic rights, while the powerful have the power and means at their disposal to impose their secondary, or tertiary rights or even false or unhealthy rights.

Establishing that concrete hierarchization of human rights is not something that has to be done here; it pertains to the area of ethics. However, theology must emphasize that today the possible openness to this communitarian principle so necessary to the individualism of the First World could be found only in ethics. This openness may also bring about openness to the reality of God. I am personally convinced that without this far-reaching revolution or "conversion," the West will become more and more unable to find a path to God although, in its most desperate moments, it may look for him in pseudo-religious evasions. Thus, the classical Pauline judgment will be fulfilled in the First World: "They became vain in their reasoning, and their senseless minds were darkened" (Rom 1:21). These words are developed much more specifically in this other New Testament passage which seems to be a brief summary of the "enlightened" world's history: "Knowing that we brought nothing into the world, just as we will not be able to take anything out of it, we have to learn to be content if we have food and clothing. Those who want to be rich are falling into temptation and into a trap and into many foolish and harmful desires, which plunge them into ruin and destruction. For the love of money is the root of all evils, and some people in their desire for it have strayed from the faith and have pierced themselves with many pains" (1 Tm 6:7-10).

Love of money is what was left over from the reason and freedom of the Enlightenment. According to the text quoted, this yearning seems to have three consequences: *a*) the adulteration of human reason (that can even lead to incapacitation for faith); *b*) the oppression of others (causing their ruin and death); and *c*) thousands of unnecessary torments for oneself.

After making these observations, we must admit in all honesty that for the time being, the dangers of the degeneration of the new Western reason seem greater than the hopes for its redemption. It is extremely difficult for executioners to incorporate the perspective of their victims. And liberation theology must know that it can find its strong support and its real faith brothers and sisters in these outbursts of hope in the First World. In this manner, the redemption of the First World would really coincide with the liberation of the Third World.

2. Toward the Spiritual Overcoming of Marxist Collectivism

If the situation of what we call the Western world deserves the attribute of *individualism which is the degeneration of the person*, the situation of communist countries, generally referred to as Eastern bloc countries, deserves the attribute of *collectivism which is the degeneration of the community*. Or, to put it in the words of Marx himself, the situation in the East is still that of a "crude communism," although its imperfection does not come from the lack of development of the means of production, where Marx situated this "crude" form of communism.

The fact remains that for Marx himself, the realization of the human being consisted in identifying "individual being and generic being." In the way Marx viewed the planning of the economy, this identification would not only cover all the real needs of all the members of the social collectivity, but in addition it would enable concrete individuals "to be anglers in the morning and hunters in the afternoon," according to their wishes.

In the communist countries, not a trace is left of this dream of Marx, although an honest Westerner would have to admit that they are ahead of us in the achievement of economic justice, of equality among people, and also in terms of overcoming the most pressing hunger and poverty. But, this important communist failure must be analyzed at the level of the intrahistorical causes and motives, just as the West analyzes the reasons why the Enlightenment project failed. Yet, in addition to these causes and without interfering with them, it is time to raise the question of the role to be ascribed to Marx' *concrete form of atheism* in such a failure. To put it graphically: Marx' project pretended to attain the divine by denying God. For Christians, the simultaneousness of the personal being and the communitarian being (which, as we pointed out, was the realization of the human being for Marx) is the definition of God and the realization of the "divine image" in human beings.

The failure of that pretension to attain the divine by denying God when people tried to concretize it in history should not come as a surprise. Marx may have believed that it was possible because, without any scientific reason and in a merely dogmatic way, he attributed divine qualities to matter, considered dialectically and in process. Presenting such an attribution as the ultimate word of science and of philosophy, no longer merits to be called atheism, but rather superstition. This is why when Marxist atheism was concretized in history, it always tended to be militant, confessional, and persecuting. In his critique of that superstitious form of the Hegelian left, Max Stirner was absolutely right to state that rather than being atheistic, these people were in fact "bigots." They were bigots of a myth, which is the most superstitious form of bigotry. As we already mentioned, this epithet really irritated K. Marx and his irritation, reflected in his attacks on Stirner in *The German Ideology*, is undoubtedly the greatest proof of the truth of the epithet.

These affirmations must be maintained even if, on the other hand, we recognize the genius of the Marxian project of human realization, the genius of his economic analyses concerning the lies and the injustices of capitalism, and even the possibility of a rupture in Marx' personal itinerary which would have led him to give up the philosophical questions of his early years, to limit himself to the economic analysis of his adult years. (A *chronological* reading of the Marxian texts on religion, which are decreasing both in number and in size to move on to a critique of the *nature* of religion and a critique of its *social functions* at that particular historical point, would support the possibility of such a rupture.) However this possible rupture in the person of Marx, was not reflected in *the systems* appealing to his authority.

Therefore, if the criticism of the individualism of the West was previously encapsulated in the already quoted words of N. Berdiaeff ("Bread for me is a material problem; bread for my brother is a spiritual problem"), now we should add that the criticism of Marxist collectivism can be encapsulated in the words from the gospel that the West usually addresses to the Eastern bloc: "One does not live by bread alone." For the moment, we are disregarding whether or not this is the precise meaning of the phrase in the gospels, and also disregarding whether or not the West is using this truth for its own interest and ideology, forgetting that one does not live by bread *alone*, but one *necessarily* has to have bread to live. Just the same, the phrase is true and it continues to be true although some may claim that the bread in question is "dialectic, in process." And so, the communist regimes have discovered that once the most basic human needs such as food, housing, health and education are fulfilled, demands of another type begin to surface. They are more spiritual and equally powerful but the communist systems are totally unprepared to meet them.[6]

This brings us back again to the necessary classification and hierarchization of "human rights" from the perspective of the rights of the poor. I already stated that it was not the task of this chapter to proceed to this classification. However, I would like to draw attention to one of these rights which is practically never listed or even mentioned. I am referring to the right to be respected, to be acknowledged as a person, as a subject of dignity, and deserving affection. To what measure is this need basic, almost a priority, so that it is inserted in the core of every individual, however poor he or she may be (or perhaps even more because of a greater poverty) appears to be a detail that has been unnoticed by the materialism of Western individualism and by the collectivism of Eastern materialism.

This may be the precise place where liberation theology can have a role, in terms of rising above both systems, which is the program that Puebla left us. For the theology of liberation, coming back to the poor has meant, first of all, *acknowledging* the poor as subjects, which leads to the project of their transformation into authentic subjects of the society, of the church, and of theology. This project may appear unviable but, in fact, it has been discussed by some liberation theologians themselves, in the name of the present subhuman situation of the poor which would demand, as a priority, that they be *objects* of the attention and total dedication on the part of Christians and of the church. Without entering into this debate, it is fitting to say that the project of liberation theology must be maintained at all costs, at least in the sense in which the New Testament speaks of anticipating the eschatological goal already in the midst of history, because "our resurrection with Christ" has already taken place in a certain sense.

Here, once again, we see the importance of the basic communities for Latin American theology as the primary places where it becomes possible for the poor to recapture their quality as subjects. In this way, we also see to what extent these communities are not a "pastoral addition," or an accidental complement of Latin American theology, but instead they are the very heart of its theological reflection.

In this way too, the plan of the theology of liberation to turn upside down the individualistic concept of the First World transforming the poor into *objects of exploitation,* also turns upside down the collectivist Leninist concept of the Second World denying the poor the quality of subjects "for themselves" by forcing them to go through the conscience of the Party and transforming them into *objects of direction.*

V. CONCLUSIONS

We can summarize all these reflections about the theological question of the relations individuals-community in five conclusions presented in the form of a thesis.

1. Persons must be defined by their *openness* to communion and to transcendence. The unlimited character of the first characteristic opens up to the second one whereas the absolute claim of the second characteristic serves as

the foundation of the first one. And so, men and women are ontologically the image of God and they are ontologically a reference to God. Closing oneself intentionally to this double openness would be sin or the destruction of the person.

From this first affirmation, we can infer two complementary theses.

2. Community must be defined as a *communion of freedoms,* in other words, only what is freely given creates community. In their ultimate truth, individuals and community do not grow in opposite but in direct proportion. This is why we have said that, to the extent that they falsify the person, all forms of individualism will fail to realize the community, and, to the extent that they falsify the community, all forms of collectivism will fail to realize persons. Human existence on earth can only be a slow and endless journey toward the overcoming of both stumbling blocks.

3. The two previous theses presuppose, as a limit at least, the *similarity between the concepts of freedom and love.* The antithesis of both is self-centeredness, that is to say, the falsification of freedom and the destruction of love. If love can only be achieved with freedom, we should also add that freedom can only be achieved in solidarity. This explains the warning of Galatians 5:13.

4. The last two propositions unavoidably lead us to the theological doctrine of *grace.* Without "the love of God poured into our hearts through the Holy Spirit who has been given to us" (cf. Rom 5:5), a human being would appear as a passion, useless because it is impossible. If, in spite of everything, faith in the Spirit inspires human beings, to proclaim the possibility of this human passion, then such a proclamation points to God as the condition for a possible harmony between "individual being and generic being." From this perspective, we may understand these famous words by H. de Lubac: "It is not true that man cannot organize the earth without God. However, it is true that without God he will inevitably organize it against man."[7] Because, without God the relation individuals-community is bound to degenerate either into authoritarianism (perhaps with good intentions) leading to collectivism, or into liberalism (I am not convinced of the goodness of its intentions) leading to the most clamorous situations of injustice and death.

5. Lastly, all that precedes also leads us to say a few words about the *church.* The decisive dilemma of the church in the world is whether it gives the witness of *believing* in God (in an attempt to make him transparent) or it gives the impression of *using* God for its own defense. This is the reason why it is by no accident that the theology of liberation (although at the beginning it did not think about this at all) has been viewed as "the opportunity of a second reform for the church."[8]

In fact, if the church wants to be the sacrament of that unity between what is individual and communitarian that we have been seeking throughout this work, it will have to let go most of its present societal organization in order to learn to build itself as a "community of communities." This is undoubtedly an inexhaustible task which constitutes the journey of the church in history. As a result, Christians must be profoundly and wisely patient with the church's shortcomings in the accomplishment of this task. However, it does not suppress the evangelical insight according to which ecclesiastical authoritarianism (with its subsequent and convenient confusion between unity and uniformity) can no longer be justified not even by appealing to the need to preserve the "deposit of faith." This authoritarianism already means the greatest falsification of that deposit since Christian truth "is built on love" (Eph 4:15). In this regard, we should recall K. Rahner's serious admonition when he warned the church not to fall into a "collectivism of hearts." If the church does not take this criticism seriously, it will deprive itself of its credibility, all its references to God will be impossible to hear and so will all the exhortations to democracy that it occasionally addressed to the West and all the criticism of collectivism that it occasionally addresses to the Eastern bloc.

But this transformation toward its truth will only be possible on the day when more "masters of the Spirit" and many less mere "cogs in the administrative wheels" are present in the hierarchy of the church.

— Translated by Colette Joly Dees

NOTES

1. *In III Sent.,* section 24 B, article 6.

2. J. B. Metz, "Unbelief as a Theological Problem," *Concilium* vol. 6, no. 1 (1965), pp. 32-42. Emphasis from the author.

3. This aspect has been dealt with in A. Grillmeier's great work: *Jesus der Christus im Glauben der Kirche,* II, Freiburg i.B., 1986, pp. 160-170.

4. Cf. *El hombre en búsqueda de su humanidad; Creer en la Iglesia del futuro; Devenir soi.*

5. I. Ellacuría, "Las iglesias latinoamericanas interpelan a la iglesia de España," *Sal Terrae* 806 (1982), p. 219.

6. These pages were written in April of 1988. Their objective was to reflect the most accepted opinion about the Eastern bloc nations among people with some degree of social concerns. For many people, the subsequent fall of the socialist nations questioned that vision. At the moment, I do not have the time to rewrite this article according to the latest events, nor do I think it is absolutely indispensable since the references of the text are presented more as archetypes than as mere descriptions or social analyses. And, in that sense, the role of incentive (or threat if you prefer) that the image of these Eastern countries played in many social conquests of the West, seems undeniable to me. It is, therefore my opinion that as Westerners, we should not merely look at the collapse of communism as if it were the confirmation (or quasi "canonization") of our system. It would be wiser to look at this collapse according to the analysis proposed by Saint Augustine in *The City of God:* the fall of Rome started precisely on the day the Carthaginians were finished. Because then, Rome no longer had an *external* reason to live. And without that reason, authoritarianism, corruption, internal struggles, the empire . . . began to appear. This is why, even though they were weaker militarily, it was only a matter of *time* before the "barbarians" put an end to that formidable empire.

7. H. de Lubac, *El drama del humanismo ateo* (Madrid, 1949), p. 11.

8. J. B. Metz, *art. cit.*

24

Grace

JOSÉ COMBLIN

For purely practical reasons we shall divide this chapter into two parts: the grace of God from the point of view of being and the grace of God from the point of view of acting. Thus for purely didactic reasons we shall adopt the scholastic distinction between habitual and actual grace.

I. GRACE FROM THE POINT OF VIEW OF BEING

1. Visible or Invisible Grace? Material or Immaterial Grace?

Old scholastic theology firmly stressed that grace was invisible and could not be felt because of its "supernatural" character. Some scholastics defended the thesis that between a person gifted with supernatural grace and another deprived of this grace there would be no perceptible difference. According to this conception grace only affects the soul and would not penetrate into the human body; it is purely a modification of the soul. From our point of view grace is naturally nonmaterial and invisible in its origin: if God is invisible his gift of grace, his love for humanity, is also invisible; or rather, it is invisible in God, its source. However, if God's gift is received by a material bodily human being, it must in some way also be bodily and material. If grace does not produce material and bodily modifications, it does not exist for the human being, it does not penetrate human life, it remains alien to humanity. Therefore grace is material and bodily in the sense that it brings about modifications in the material and bodily human being. A human being does not have a pure spirit, which could remain separate from the body. It is not possible to imagine that something could penetrate a human soul without also penetrating the body. This bodily effect can be looked at from three points of view.

1. The human being is his or her relation to the material world, the cosmos. Human beings relate to the material world primarily through work. Therefore God's grace brings about a change in that work, the work regime, relationships, and experience. Communion with God is inscribed into the work regime; because God relates to human beings through matter, God's grace enters into conflict with slavery, with forms of servitude, with capitalism, and with all

regimes of alienation and exploitation at work. The sign of God's presence is the actual conflict itself with such work regimes.

2. The human being is also his or her relationship with fellow human beings. This means the relationship between man and woman and the relationship between brothers and sisters, community, primary or secondary groups, tribe, nation, race, the whole of humanity. These relationships are inscribed in customs, institutions, commitments, alliances, different forms of communion, conflicts, reconciliation. God's grace is thus a new relationship in all these dimensions, from the relationship between the sexes to the relationship between races and nations.

Relationships among human beings are also bodily ones—family relations of course, but other relationships are all conditioned by geography and set within the different situations of bodies on earth. They are set in villages and towns, houses and roads, natural regions and frontiers, continents and seas, mountains and rivers, climates and in the process of material production. God's grace is set geographically. We may think it was more present in ancient villages than in our present megalopolises with their shanty towns and cardboard cities. It was more present in the Paraguayan "reductions"—Indian settlements set up by Christian missionaries—than on the Conquistadores' great estates. It was more present in the indigenous villages themselves than in the Potosi mines.

3. God's grace has effects on the actual individual human body. Jesus' presence was a source of health for the sick, the blind, the deaf, and the dumb. There is a continuity throughout Christian tradition: grace restores health. It is true that in recent centuries the bourgeois churches have discredited the healing of the sick as a pastoral practice, but it has always carried on in the popular churches. It has always belonged to popular Christianity. It is not healing by magic, the automatic application of a formula of words, signs, or remedies. But it does have beneficial effects upon the body's health.

A grace of God that only affected the human soul would not have any value for ordinary people. Grace must have visible and palpable effects, evident in the human body. This bodily effect is not something alien to the natural body. On the contrary, it is the body's health, a healthy way of living together for human beings, and health at work. The effect of grace is not something "over and above" the human body but within the natural mortal body. God has approached the human body and made it worthy of his intervention. Grace does not create another body but gives health to the body we have.

It is quite certain that what always constituted Christianity's great attraction for ordinary people was God's compassion for the human bodily state. Christianity was not a religion of notions and ideas, a religion for philosophers or intellectuals. It offered remedies for human ills, sufferings caused by sickness, social battles and disagreements, exploitation and alienation at work. God entered into the life of the human body.

Grace does not confer actual immortality; it does not eliminate all physical and moral evils, either individual or social. It does not eliminate them but it does alleviate them and make living in this world more tolerable, more human.

2. *Grace as the Presence of the Future*

The Christian message is Good News, that is, openness to a future, an open history. It offers humanity a future. This is not just a promise of a future life, especially not just a future life in another world after death. Ordinary people abandoned Christianity when they were given to understand that all the church had to offer them was heaven after death. This message is of no interest. It is of interest only to the privileged in this life, because it enables them to reject the just demands of those who are unjustly oppressed in order to preserve their privileges.

In Christianity the future becomes present. The life of heaven is of interest in so far as it offers a goal and a content for this life here on earth. Eternal life is of interest if it sets up a norm and a pointer to a better life here on earth. Jesus never separated his proclamation of the Good News from the present. What he proclaims, he demonstrates and creates in the present. In fact, in the Christian scriptures promises for the future mean the coming of a present reality. Grace is the presence now of humanity's future, of creation's final success. Jesus does not offer a present emptiness for the sake of future fulfillment. The future fulfillment is already a present fulfillment, limited only by the limitations of the present human condition.

A New World

The Christian scriptures announce the coming of a new creation. This has already begun. The Word of God, which was present at the creation, is acting again. It is remaking creation, restoring it. This means that human beings cannot be separated from the earth and the material world; their transformation is part of a transformation of the world, even though human beings are the culmination and heart of this new creation. Grace is the beginning of the new creation, as it can be experienced at the present stage of evolution. The Spirit is renewing the face of the earth. Grace is this renewal, necessarily linked to the renewal of humanity.

A New Humanity

Paul proclaims the coming of a new human being. The new human being is virtually the whole of humanity. It is Christ and it is humanity restored in the Risen Christ. It is the new humanity of the Risen Jesus, which penetrates human beings, and also groups, bodies of people, and human relationships at all levels.

The new humanity is the Kingdom of God spoken about in the synoptic gospels. God conquers the Kingdom, God battles to restore the Kingdom in creation. God reigns to the extent that justice and true peace are restored.

God's Kingdom is the reconquest of humanity. It is a struggle against alienation, corruption, and death. It is the resurrection of humanity in its perfection. The Kingdom of God is humanity restored to its dignity and true worth.

The Kingdom of God is among the poor and oppressed. It is the struggle for the release of the oppressed and the exaltation of the poor. God's Kingdom has been proclaimed by the Beatitudes, which are the heralds of the Kingdom. There, amid the poor and oppressed, God begins to reign once more.

The new humanity is also called the new people of God. Among the poor and oppressed a new people of God is arising. Among the poor and oppressed a new people is arising with all the attributes of the people of God. From a scattered multitude God creates a people. From the weakness of the poor God creates a power that challenges the powerful of the earth.

In this people of God there is a new covenant between God and humanity. In the festival of eating and drinking the eucharist, the new people celebrates its new covenant with God. Grace is the experience of this covenant in the life of the new people, in their common struggles, hopes, sufferings, and victories. Through the covenant God is committed to the poor and oppressed. God's faithfulness is the grace which lays the foundation of all rights and the dignity of the new people.

The Community

The new people is embodied in particular communities, in which particular people live their lives in their multiple day-to-day relationships. The community makes present all God's gifts and is the particular way in which grace becomes actual among the poor and oppressed. In the community the risen body of Jesus becomes present. Christ's body is experienced in the small communities. In the eucharistic communion the bodies of those present form a continuity: they all share the same bread and are united in the same loaf of bread and the same cup of wine. The Holy Spirit is in the community. The community is the time of the Spirit. In the multiplicity of its interwoven activities the diversity of the gifts of the Spirit are manifest. These gifts are the grace of God.

Christian life is lived, nourished, educated, expressed, and created communally. There is no individual grace isolated from other graces. God's graces in individuals are connected and form one single grace. God does not open to one person alone but to each person with his or her community and to each community within the community of communities that forms the people of God.

The Person

The communitarian character of grace does not take away its personal value, because the community is an exchange and communion of persons. The grace of God is the restoration of personality, the firmest guarantee of the human person, what permits it to exist in the fullness of personality, because the person is the correlative of the community, rather than being in contradiction with it. God's grace is directed toward every person within his or her community, which is precisely what enables a person to become a person. The human being is not a person to the extent that he or she shuns others, but to the extent that he or she communicates with them. The measure of personality is also the measure of community. It is true that grace is a dialogue between God and the human person, but this dialogue is not a closed dialogue—"God and my soul"—but a dialogue in which many other persons are present, with whom each person communicates, and who give him or her the actual content of their personality.

In the Bible grace is called life or eternal life. This life becomes present now. It is both the life of the person and the life of the community. It is the life of the people in the life of all the communities.

Grace is also justice and holiness. It is the moral perfection of the human being. It is the human being restored to fullness, although within the limits of the development of the individual, community, and culture to which the community belongs.

Finally, grace is freedom. Freedom is both a gift and a vocation. It is the supreme gift because it is the gift, that makes a human being the image of God. God's grace is very far from absorbing the human being into God. Far from making the human being disappear into a divine pseudo-totality, grace restores freedom; it establishes the human being as a personal subject distinct from God, independent of God, autonomous, capable of taking up a position, even against God who has given him or her this freedom.

Freedom exists in a conditional and limited way in this world. However, it is not just an illusion. It can be born and grow. It does not have to exist. It requires work and conquest, a struggle against many obstacles and adversaries. Nevertheless, it can exist, and it is what constitutes both the person and the community.

Freedom does not remain on a purely metaphysical level. It is experienced at many levels in daily life. Freedom is experienced in the formation of individual autonomy within the bosom of the family and the community. It is experienced in the formation of the couple and the procreation of children. It is experienced at work, in the relationship between classes, and in struggles for human rights, both for individuals and the community. Freedom is not just given; freedom must be conquered or it does not exist.

3. The Traditional Attributes of Grace

The Gratuitousness of Grace

The traditonal authors liked to stress the fact that grace was extrinsic. Within a mystique of obedience which was almost servile, appropriate to the mentality of the sixteenth and seventeenth centuries, centuries of despotism and absolute monarchies, they liked to stress human beings' total dependence and what amounted to God's arbitrariness. They insisted, as if it were a virtue, upon total passivity in the hands of an absolute despot — God. In this context grace was an almost arbitrary gift, like the gifts kings gave at whim to their favorites. These pure gifts were received with the highest gratitude and the most exaggerated expressions of servility. Can grace be this gratification of an absolute monarch, whose pleasure is everything?

People today dislike begging and groveling. They would not want to receive alms from God, particularly alms called grace. They see this as against human dignity. Even more, people today dislike a gift which constitutes an obligation. Because then it would be a gift that all are obliged to receive. What does a compulsory grace mean? Is there any point in keeping the vocabulary of "grace" if we then add that those who do not accept the gift will be severely punished?

This is why it is important to stress that God's grace comes to us through the work of the Holy Spirit, as an energy, a force, an internal movement which, far from doing violence to individuals, awakens them and sets them in motion.

God takes the initiative, just as in creation. But this is not a gift which cancels human freedom, which pushes human beings along a road contrary to their own value judgment. The gratuitousness of grace cannot be the foundation of a spirituality which annuls the human, as happened in the past, particularly in the sixteenth and seventeenth centuries. This was a phenomenon of the times related to a culture which is now clearly superannuated and has almost disappeared. In the religious works of that period there is a language we find intolerable today. Of course God is God and the creature is creature. But God did not create human beings in order to humiliate them by reminding them continually that they are only creatures and God alone is God. This would be attributing to God those absolute kings' mentality—kings who felt the need to be told over and over again that they were the absolute sovereigns, who lacked personal security. We may suppose that God does not suffer from an insecurity complex! Through creation and through grace, God intends human beings to exist and to be able to share in the divine freedom and autonomy.

Divinization

Greek theology made the concept of divinization the center of its soteriology. Historians can show the connection between this theology and the religious and philosophical context of the Byzantine Empire. There is an immense cultural heritage in this concept. Peoples who have not inherited this idea do not find it easy to understand what divinization means.

At any rate, one thing that divinization cannot mean is the raising of the human being above the human condition to a different level, imagined as a higher condition than the human one. Divinization cannot mean that human beings leave the human condition behind, and in particular, it cannot mean that they leave their bodily condition in order to enter a purely spiritual or nonmaterial pseudo-condition. So it is not a question of minimizing the bodily condition or bodily activities. The divinization of humanity can only mean access to human fulfillment. It can only be justified as greater humanization.

At present there is the fear that through divinization human beings might lose their identity, dissolve into a pseudo-divinity, as if they were taking on a divine pseudo-condition. People today suspect that this soteriology of divinization expressed a certain contempt for the body, which did in fact exist in a particular oriental monastic tradition. For the poor, a spirituality that rejects the body and exalts the purely spiritual is a constant trial, it is a legitimization of the condition imposed on them by the oppressors.

Divinization can be understood only in the sense that humanity has been introduced into the dialogue of the divine person. Their actions make them one with Christ. Their actions are inspired by the Holy Spirit and are therefore acts of dialogue with the Father. Human beings have been admitted to the consortium of divine persons. However human, bodily, and material their actions are, they are worthy of God and constitute valid responses to the Father's word.

Forgiveness of Sins

The West has lived with guilt for centuries. Preachers and priests have made denunciation of sins the core of their message. Sin was seen as essentially the product of human malice. For the preacher this was an opportunity to denounce human malice, make people feel guilty, and humiliate them. Human sin was the church's joy; it provided it with its public and kept human beings tied hand and foot to the good will of their pastors. Sin enabled the church to blame people.

Today we are more aware that some of the blame for human actions comes from human poverty. Sin is often the consequence of this state of wretchedness. Some human beings are more deserving of compassion than blame. Although sin is committed by human beings, it is committed collectively and anonymously; it comes from established structures rather than the personal malice of individuals. This does not exclude the possibility of individual malice, but what is due to it bears no comparison with the enormous mass of evils proceeding from structures of domination and exploitation, in which human beings are more often manipulated than manipulators. Sin is the expression of an immense human passivity, a lack of freedom.

Consequently, sin does not so much need forgiveness that cancels it or removes the punishment, but rather liberation. If human beings are victims of a sin that is stronger than their individual will, they need to be liberated from their sin. In this sense grace is not an absolution, which cancels the sin and all the penalties laid down for the sin. Grace and forgiveness are instead the actual liberation movement through which people liberate themselves from the structures that crush them and take away their freedom. Grace, then, is liberation from sin and the achievement of freedom.

Sin oppresses a human being, first internally by fears or anguish that paralyze action. Individuals can know they are sinning, want not to sin, yet lack the strength to do what they want to do. Liberation conquers sin within the person themselves, making them capable of making decisions personally and acting freely.

Sin also oppresses human beings from the outside, through external pressures. The strongest of these come from education, the family, the immediate environment, the school environment, the group, and the closed world of everyday life.

Sin also comes from the pressures of economic and political forces, domination by wealth or weapons. Human beings can enter into complicity with the sin that comes from outside. They both commit the sin and suffer from it. Grace frees from sin; it is liberation. This liberation is both emancipation from the force that comes from sinful structures and the capacity to resist the temptation to sin, which is personal.

This aspect of sin's domination over human beings does not mean that it is not also an offense against God and that forgiveness for the offense is not also part of the remission of sins. Nevertheless, we cannot separate this aspect from the other.

II. GRACE FROM THE POINT OF VIEW OF ACTING

Grace renews the human being and human action. Action cannot be separated from being. In fact, we have no words to name a "being" that is not also an "acting." God's grace enters into human being-acting. Human beings exist in their action and inseparably are their action, as is the case with all living things. Nevertheless, the limits of our language oblige us to separate conceptually and verbally what is in reality united.

1. God's Action and Human Action

God's action and human action are inseparable. God's action is expressed through human action. God's action — grace — does not destroy or suppress or diminish or replace anything in human action. A human action directed by God's action has no less initiative, no less spontaneity, no less creativity, no less autonomy than human action in general. On the contrary, the presence of God's grace makes human action more fully human, with more initiative, more spontaneity, more autonomy, than if grace were not present.

We cannot see human action animated by grace as an experienced passivity. Just as there was monophysitism in certain deformations of ancient christology, there was also a certain anthropological monophysitism of grace, which persisted through Christian history. In a certain monastic or mystical tradition God's grace takes the place of human will and makes the human being a mere instrument that lets itself be used. Passivity, if this is the adequate word, usually refers to a purely abstract and metaphysical level, without any contact with human psychology and behavior. But grace acts like creation. Just as creation makes human beings the doers of their own actions, so too, and even more so, does grace make human beings the doers of their own actions, more autonomous, freer, more fully human than without grace.

The Father acts by means of the Holy Spirit and according to the way of the Spirit. The Spirit gently penetrates human beings and accompanies them. There is no question of forcing. The Spirit gives energy and dynamism, restores human beings to the fullness of their powers. The Spirit sets up a long restoration process for human action, following all the stages marked by obstacles, slowness, and human rhythms. An individual life is a history analogous to the history of communities and peoples. The Spirit adapts to the slowness of history. The Spirit does not make great leaps; there are strong moments and weak moments. There are eras which appear to be dead and other times when history speeds up. God does not do violence to history. The way in which God accompanies the development of history means that the presence of grace cannot be precisely pinpointed. There are no phenomena of which it can be said: here is the pure grace of God. The Spirit acts in the continuum of human action.

2. Individual and Social Grace

If sin is both personal and social, never purely personal, never purely social, so is grace. The human being acts socially. Even prophets who anticipate and appear to cry in the wilderness need at least a small audience to listen to them. Without an audience they would not be prophets. There is an initial nucleus, the beginning of the people the prophet wishes to enlighten. The grace animating the prophet acts at the same time in the nucleus of the audience. The prophet's grace would be ineffective if it were not linked to the grace of the group that receives the prophecy. In reality, both constitute a single action.

The same thing happens in all manifestations of divine grace. A single grace envelops the family, the community, the group of believers, the Christian people, the whole church. Its effects are correlative. There is a single action, which acts at a multiplicity of application points, all connected. The same grace can act with varying intensity at its different application points. The important thing is to be aware of the solidarity of actions by human beings. A purely solitary act would have no meaning and would be impossible. Nobody invents anything. All share in inspirations, suggestions, examples, invitations from others. Even the most solitary monks are within a monastic tradition of hermits and act together with the tradition in which they live.

This solidarity and continuity of God's grace is symbolized by the sacraments, which are community acts in which the community shows in communal signs that it is receiving the grace of the Holy Spirit.

3. Grace and the History of the Poor

God's grace enters human history. But it does not identify with the history of empires or civilizations. The dominant history is made by the great, the strongest, the conquerors in the competition among peoples and human groups. Grace does not intervene in the conquests of the great or in their efforts to hold on to their empires. In former times, even in the Hebrew scriptures, it was held that God gave victory in battle, that God was with the conqueror. We know this is a lie.

It was explained to the inhabitants of the Americas that God had granted victory to the invaders and had delivered their kingdom in this world to the king of Spain or Portugal. The indigenous people believed them and accepted their conquerors' religion through fear. Nevertheless, we believe they were wrong. It is not true that God is the author of conquests and empires. If a deity of the conquerors, God would not have allowed the Son to be crucified and conquered by his enemies. The cross shows us that God enters human history, but not on the side he is usually believed to. The Father enters history on the side of the oppressed and the poor. He is the God of the liberation of the poor. Thus God's grace is the force that awakens, animates, and maintains the struggle of the oppressed, who are victims of injustice and evil.

Grace is the liberation movement itself, or rather, the soul of this movement. It is not identified with everything that happens in such movements, of course. Nevertheless, it is present according to the way of the Holy Spirit at the root of the liberation of the poor.

Grace produces a history, not the one that is written, but the one that is experienced in the hidden part of the world. It produces a parallel history of those who suffer in the midst of the triumphs of the conquerors and the persecuted. Grace is present in the hidden history of the poor. It produces resistance, faith, hope. It produces in all peoples something similar to the history of the poor of Israel, as it is recorded in the Bible.

This liberation history of the poor also has its victories and is not pure patience. It has its moments of glory. It keeps the memory of its past glories. These victories are the winning of poor people's rights, the overthrow of systems of domination. Although the poor never get total justice in this world, neither can we say that they are always suffering in the same way. Some systems are more intolerable than others. It is not true that because complete justice is never achieved, it is not worth struggling for justice, as if all struggles were ineffectual. God's grace is not ineffectual. It does not remain on the purely spiritual level, remote from this earthly history. Its effects are perceptible even if they do not bring about in this world what is reserved for the end of time. Grace does not destroy determinisms, inertia, the weight of the past and of structures. Nevertheless, it introduces a new element, a force which revives the hope of the oppressed. If there were no perceptible effects, grace would be nothing but a stimulus to resignation. People today are very much aware of everything that might become a paralyzing force in human life. A grace that produced only resignation could not be from the God of life.

God's grace accompanies the development of history. The needs of the oppressed change with the times. There are times of adversity and pure patience; there are times of organization and protest; there are times of insurrection and initiative. There are times when the dominators are at the height of their power; at other times they are divided and then there is scope for the weaker to break in. Grace will have different effects according to the situation. Things that give opportunities to the poor are mistakes, rivalries, and the irrational behavior of the great. By and large, empires and all forms of domination destroy themselves. Action by the poor depends upon the signs of the times. God's grace also follows the signs of the times. The Spirit sends the signs and the power to act in accordance with what they are indicating. The Hebrew scriptures show how God withdraws grace from the powerful, and how their empires destroy themselves by their own lack of vitality or by rivalry among themselves. Amid the battles of the giants, the little people seek their way. This is why the books of the Bible are still relevant today. If the Bible is the history of the poor, it is also the history of God's grace. To read the Hebrew scriptures is to read the history of God's grace in paradigmatic form. What is written there is relevant to all periods.

4. God's Grace and the Challenges of History

By and large human beings make their own circumstances. God's grace also consists in setting human beings in situations which oblige them to go beyond themselves, to overcome their limitations and increase their forces. An external circumstance is the beginning of a conversion, a new road. Human beings who live in a state of protection or overprotection cannot produce miraculous results. God's grace consists in taking their protection away from them, along with their security and peace of mind and body. God's grace may consist in taking away one person's wealth, another person's power, another person's health, another person's family. In such a situation the human being is called to accomplish much more than the usual, to produce more vigorous effects.

God's grace can set before a human being the challenge of persecution and martyrdom. Then we see that the important thing is not how long that person has lived but the density and value of these years. Jesus only lived for thirty-three years, but his years are worth more than others' who lived for seventy or eighty. For many, God's grace has meant prison, concentration camp, exile, giving up their wealth, work, career, social position, even though God's grace is not always recognized in these challenges.

— Translated by Dinah Livingstone

25

SIN

JOSÉ IGNACIO GONZÁLEZ FAUS

I. THE RICH WORLD AND THE LATIN AMERICAN WORLD

On the theme of sin the European and Latin American cultural situations look very different. So we need first to glance at these two situations.

In Europe there is endless talk about the "sin crisis"; sometimes there is even a denial that sin exists. There is no lack of data or cultural analyses of human experiences which seem to adopt such postures. Even though in Latin America there is the insistence that sin "brings death," in Europe the victims of this death may be ignored as not belonging to this world or are reduced — within it — to an easily hidden minority, or a minority unworthy of "democratic" consideration just because it is a minority.

However, in Latin America the vast majority are victims. Massive daily atrocities, oppression of human beings by others — or structural oppression — exist on such a huge scale that they are one of the most obvious factors in any assessment of the Latin American situation. This factor is so disproportionately great that when we perceive it we cannot help realizing that such atrocities cannot in any way be regarded as being caused by the limitations of a finite reality. They are gratuitous, unnecessary sufferings, caused by human responsibility and wrong-doing. They are not caused by the "unbearable lightness of being" so fashionable in Europe.

Hence, the danger in Latin America might perhaps be the overlocalizing of sin, thus *localizing it too partially*. The European danger lies in *blindness to responsibility* in the face of the shocking reality and the frightening depth of human guilt.

1. Human Beings Don't Just Sin — They Are Sinners

We must add that these cultural differences are not only to do with (economic and other) infrastructures. They are also linked to traditional superstructures, which in our case are theological ones.

To give an example, European theological tradition was very marked by the polemical insistence on works (resulting from arguments with Protestants), and also by the statement that humans are not radically corrupted beings (a statement also made in a polemical context against the so-called extreme Augustinians). So part of what is happening in the Catholic churches in the rich world can be explained by the fact that there is a price to pay for the onesidedness of those polemics.

The price of this one-sidedness has been that, although the two above-mentioned statements were valid in themselves, they left the theological unconscious with the image of the human being as neutral in the face of good and evil, equidistant from both, not conditioned to decide for one or the other. (We might also inquire to what extent this latent image relates to the "sin crisis" characteristic of the First World. But for now we must leave aside questions of this sort.) In Europe the topic of sin is often tackled with this unconscious presupposition or image.

It was a Latin American (Uruguayan J. L. Segundo) who most clearly uncovered this latent image and brought it to consciousness. Instead of this "neutral" image (neither one thing nor the other), the Latin American trend has been to think of human beings in a more dialectical way (both the one and the other). Humans are beings infected by evil, almost identified with it; *at the same time* they are also beings enveloped in goodness and grace, called by it, and its seeds are sown in the deepest depths of their humanity. Both aspects belong to Latin American spirituality's most vivid experience.

2. Sin Is Not a Matter of Weakness, But of Lying and Blindness

This theological difference has repercussions on a second point that is fundamental to the Latin American treatment of the theme of sin. We can illustrate this by another historical allusion.

In European ecclesiastical practice before the Council there was the impression that the fundamental example (the "first analogy") for speaking about sin was Paul's celebrated lament in Romans 7:14ff ("I do not do the good that I want but the evil that I do not want"). That is, the stress was on human experience of weakness and dividedness. Pre-conciliar preaching directed all the harshness of Paul's judgments toward this. Sermons harping on God's anger and human inexcusability amounted to a "pastoral tactic of fear." This probably also had something to do with the First World "sin crisis" we mentioned earlier.

To our surprise, the celebrated lament for human weakness in Romans 7 is situated in the chapters of the letter dealing with the justified person, who has "died to sin" and "lives in Christ Jesus" (cf., for example, Rom. 6:11). In these verses in Romans Paul does not mention God's anger at all. Indeed, he concludes with a surprising exclamation: "Thanks be to God through Jesus Christ!

... There is now no condemnation for those who are in Christ Jesus" (Rom. 7:25-8:1).

On the other hand, Paul's judgment upon human sin and threat of God's anger are found, as we know, in the two first chapters of the letter. So it is here we must look if we want to find the fundamental analogy to speak about the theme of sin.

3. The Definition of Sin: Oppressing the Truth through Injustice

To sum up these two chapters, we can say that in them Paul vigorously unmasks the sin of pagans and Jews. Toward the end of chapter 3 he concludes that all are sinners and that in this respect the believer has no advantage over the Gentile.

It is important to note here that "Jews" and "pagans" do not simply designate two ancient peoples who no longer exist today. They refer to two ways of being human, or two components of every human being, personified in these peoples, but not confined to them. The proof of this lies in the fact that Romans 2: 14ff. calmly recognizes that there are good and honorable pagans, in spite of what has been said in chapter 1. This shows that chapter 1 was not talking about individuals—or groups of people—but about ways of being human. Likewise at the beginning of chapter 2, which speaks about the sin of the Jews, Paul is not speaking about the Jews as such but about "any man who sets himself up as judge," which shows that here too he is not talking about particular individuals but about ways of being human.

Of these two ways of being human, Paul says that God's anger is revealed toward the one (1:18) and that the others are inexcusable (2:1). Both these strictures affect each of the ways, because God's anger only threatens those who are inexcusable. Likewise, the definition of sin is the same in both cases, in spite of the difference that might occur in particular instances. So let us look at this latter fact a bit more closely.

The evil of the "pagan" way of being human lies in "oppressing truth through injustice" (1:18ff). The evil in the "Jewish" (or religious) way of being human lies in "judging the other while being the same as him" (2:1ff.). That is, the religious persons destroy the truth of their own equality with others through the injustice of one person condemning another. That is why Paul repeats throughout this chapter that only God is competent to condemn human beings. Pagans destroy the truth of their being as God's creatures and as the brothers and sisters of other human beings through the injustice of thinking of themselves as unique and like God and regarding their own wishes as the only moral norm.

The processes described by Paul are the following. "Pagans" commit "egolatry" of their own freedom; they oppress in this unjust "egolatry" the truth about the dignity and freedom of others. God's anger is revealed against them because they find they have become idolaters of things and, therefore, slaves to all the objects of their desire. The excuse mechanism generated by "pagans" to justify the divinization of their desires makes them become victim to them.

On the other hand, "Jews" make egoistical statements about their own morality and their own belief in God, thus using the good and even God as an excuse for setting themselves above others through the injustice of their pride in being superior. They too becomes inexcusable because by judging others they end up thinking of themselves as gods (like the pagans) and by raising themselves above others, they become subject to the same "dictatorship of desire" as the "pagans."

4. The Masking of Sin

"Jews" and "pagans" behave like this "without realizing." But they themselves are responsible for this unawareness, which makes it sinful, because it is the result of an impressive mechanism of excuses to blind and deceive themselves. For "pagans" the excuse is that God does not exist or is not concerned with what becomes of humans, or that the supreme norm of action is a presumed "rationality," which is not used as a means of criticizing the self and its desires but in the service of egoism. For "Jews" the excuse is that God is on their side because they say they are on God's side, or that God cannot fail to condemn the "pagans," and so on.

From this analysis of Pauline texts it follows that the first analogy for speaking about sin is not actions that we recognize as transgressions (*paraptomata*) for which we are sorry, suffer, or feel a sense of guilt. The sense of guilt acts a bit like a temperature in the sick organism; it is difficult to bear, but it implies a reaction against the disease by the healthy part of the organism. Real sin (Paul's *hamartia*) involves an *identification* with the sin by the one who commits it, which makes him or her become a liar (cf. John 8:44: Satan who is a liar and father of lies) or blinds his or her heart (cf. Mark 3:5). In this way sin is masked from human beings (or rather it is human beings who mask it from themselves) to the point where the sense of guilt becomes anesthetized. This, for example, is the sin of the Pharisees throughout the whole of the Fourth Gospel. Jesus comes to unmask this sin; if they recognized that they were blind they would no longer be guilty, but because they say they can see, their sin remains (cf. John 9:41).

Through this view of sin perhaps liberation theology, without realizing it, has acted in the same way as the Jesus of the Fourth Gospel did in confronting the religious power (or like Nathan the prophet before David); it has unmasked the sinful arrogance of the First World, which was camouflaging the truth with injustice to the point where "they became futile in their thinking and their senseless minds were darkened" (Rom. 1:21). In this context, as a very clear example, it is worth noting how often — in writings on spirituality! — Jon Sobrino has spoken about "keeping faith with the real" and paying attention to "the obvious" as surprising elements in any radical following of Jesus.

What we have to show now is that from this conception of sin as the masking of the truth by unjust egoism, derive the two other characteristics we must comment on as typical of liberation theology: the structural aspect of sin and the content of sin as damaging the human being.

II. STRUCTURAL SIN

One of the most characteristic contributions of Latin American theology to the theme of sin has been the notion of structural sin or structures of sin. One feels tempted to compare this notion with the traditional legend of the ancient Guarani people, about the search for a "land without evils." But here we must confine ourselves to the theological aspects of the subject.

For Cartesian individualism born together with the modern era in Europe, it has not been easy to understand this idea which, nevertheless, enables us to explain how personal evil is both active and masked at the same time. One person alone could not construct this whole system of excuses, which we saw in the previous section. Neither could a single individual reason place itself so effectively at the service of "pagan" covetousness if it were only acting individually and instantly. But where people live together they are never merely contiguous like a simple juxtaposition of stones. They are inserted into a world of mediations and institutions: family, marriage, profession, city, economy, culture, state, and so on. Therefore the human community is always more than the sum of single human beings.

This is why the community and the structures governing life together in it can create, more easily than the individual, a series of situations making necessary (and therefore apparently reasonable) ways of behaving which favor individual greed, even though these harm the life and dignity of many others. Therefore evil, like the human being, is never just personal, although it is also personal. And therefore any personally sinful human being is both responsible and a victim.

In the space we have here we can only try to justify this notion of structural sin and show some of the consequences it entails.

1. Discussion and Justification of Structural Sin

By this insight Latin American theology has recovered another fundamental scriptural idea—the Johannine notion of the sin of the world. This notion is so central to the evangelist that sometimes he calls the sin of the world simply "the world," giving the world a negative significance it does not always have in his gospel. In these cases "the world" means a socioreligious order hostile to God or an oppressive system based on money or power for the few. This sin makes the world unable to grasp the truth: the truth that God is a Father and Just (cf. John 17:25) and human beings are therefore God's children and brothers and sisters of one another. For this evangelist the sin of the world is the decisive antagonist of Jesus, who both unmasks it and dies as its victim. But then the evangelist sees this murderous death as the most radical demonstration of the sin of the world.

Liberation theology has recovered this Johannine notion, even though it may be said that it has formulated it almost exclusively in terms of economic structures (a logical procedure given the enormous cry for the most basic human necessities lacked by the great majority of Latin Americans). The recovery of this concept has met both with radical condemnation from some European theologians and the decisive support of Medellín and Puebla, as well as that of Pope John Paul II.

In fact, even in the introduction to its documents, Medellín spoke about oppressive structures which are the fruit of exploitation and injustice. It spoke of unjust situations in which the sins of unsolidarity are crystallized. Puebla teaches that sin, which it defines as a "rupturing force," prevents human growth in fellowship. Sin is not just something done by each individual but is also committed in these sinful structures, which are created by human beings (Puebla Final Document, no. 281). The teaching of both assemblies can be summarized in this simple circular phrase: *When human beings sin, they create structures of sin, which, in their turn, make human beings sin.*

But perhaps the best definition of structural sin, together with an intuitive perception of its novelty and profoundly Christian roots, is found in the following words of Oscar Romero's Second Pastoral Letter, written in 1977:

> The Church has denounced sin for centuries. It has certainly denounced the sin of the individual, and it has also denounced the sin which perverts relationships between human beings, particularly at the family level. But now it has again reminded us of what has been fundamental from its beginning: of social sin, that is to say, the crystallization of individual egoisms in permanent structures which maintain this sin and exert its power over the great majorities.

This language was adopted by John Paul II when he visited the Puebla Assembly in Zapopán and spoke of "multiple structures of sin." More recently, in his encyclical on the social question, this language appears to have intensified. The pope asserts the legitimacy of the notion of structural sin. He also uses it to talk about the "theological reading of modern problems." Finally, in the conclusion he sums up by saying that liberation should overcome "sin and the structures of sin that produce it" (*Sollicitudo Rei Socialis*, nos. 36, 37, 46).

These teachings allow us at least to question the severe strictures by certain great theologians (Urs von Balthasar and J. Ratzinger, among others) against the language of structural sin. They accuse this language of denaturing what is most profound in sin—that it is the fruit of a personal and responsible freedom. These words cannot be applied to a structure. Therefore, according to these theologians, the concept of structural sin goes against Christian teaching on sin.

But it would not be theologically correct to limit ourselves to criticizing these attacks through an appeal to external authorities, even the authority of the church's magisterium. We must also point out in what way they are wrong. They forget the analogy of the Christian notion of sin. According to their argument, it would also not be Christian to speak of original sin, given that this cannot be defined as the fruit of a free and responsible decision by each person (or can only be explained thus in a completely mythological manner by supposing that the freedom of all human beings was already present in Adam's free will, as some post-Tridentine theologians say). If it is theologically legitimate to speak of original sin, it is also legitimate to speak of structural sin.

In the Christian notion of sin there are other features besides the fact that sin is the fruit of a personal and responsible freedom. Sin also means that which God rejects and cannot accept in any way. Therefore denying the notion of structural sin is equivalent to saying that the present situation of the world (and in particular the third-world countries) is not a situation that arouses God's rejection and anger. Accepting the notion of structural sin means we are saying that the relationship of all humanity with God has been degraded, precisely because of the degradation in the relationships of human beings to one another.

2. Consequences and Examples

It is necessary to stress that structural sin is the sin of the world and not only of a particular situation. Puebla speaks of it as a "permanent process" (Puebla Final Document, no. 281). It is structured in different circles according to the different cultural situations or economic relations. The center of each of these circles is always falsification or the oppression of some human beings by others.

Let us give some examples. The two ruling systems in our world are based upon a lie that is never stated but transmitted through the injustice of their socioeconomic relations. The false truth of capitalism is that a human being *is not worth anything.* The false truth of the communism existing at the moment is that a human being is *always an enemy.*

From these structural attitudes, personal forms of behavior necessarily follow, which are justified by the reasons inherent in the system. It is a well-known fact that during the great earthquake in Mexico City the owners of some firms were first concerned to get their machines out of the ruins, before the—still living—bodies of many of the buried women operators. This anecdote is not exclusive to a single country, especially not a "backward" country. The German journalist Günter Wallraff disguised himself as a Turkish immigrant and spent two years working in Germany in this disguise. The incredible stories he relates are far more inhuman than the Mexico story.

Facts like this seem incredible when we hear them as isolated anecdotes out of context. But they are completely rational within the logic of competition and profit maximization; the machine cannot be replaced without a considerable investment, whereas it is quite easy to replace the worker.

On the other hand, current socialist systems do not deny the value of human beings, but they do deny that human beings can be trusted. Because any human being may belong to another class, or may not have a correct consciousness of his or her own class (and so if left free will be an obstacle to the true interests of his or her class, which are only properly represented by the minority of Party members), Party members feel not just authorized but obliged to reserve to themselves all power of taking initiatives and making decisions—and denying this power to everyone else. This gives rise to a system as oppressive as the previous one.

One more smaller example, which is nevertheless worth quoting because it is very topical, is this. In my opinion the present culture of the North American masses (especially the culture "for export") is a system which exudes justifications and exaltations of violence—a violence which is indeed always masked as the defense of justice or freedom, even the defense of God (and sometimes simply boldfaced defense of one's own interests). It is impossible that a world which subliminally inhales these values, as a form of entertainment or relaxation, should not in the long term become inhumanly aggressive and violent.

All these examples show how difficult the struggle against structural sin is, because structural sin is not the sin of one single human system but of the whole human system. Fighting it and unmasking it can mean dying at its hands as Jesus did. Victory over it only happens gradually and slowly, and the human forms it takes are frequently forms of crucifixion.

III. SIN AS HUMAN DAMAGE

By the route outlined above and—above all—through the shocking experience of the suffering of so many innocent people, liberation theology has been able to identify the true meaning of the Christian notion of sin: human damage.

Perhaps this definition scandalizes scholastic theology, which has become accustomed to repeating mechanically that sin is only an "offense against God," managing by its routine traditionalism to confuse an offense against love with a mere offense "against the master." Therefore it is useful to remind ourselves that even in scripture the father of sin (Satan) is, even etymologically, the "enemy of man." This has an even stronger reading in the Fourth Gospel: Satan, "a liar and father of lies," is therefore "a murderer from the beginning" (John 8:44). Masking the truth is, as we have said, the way to kill or damage other human beings.

We cannot deny that here liberation theology appears also to be reacting to another theological tradition that immediately preceded it. This was an excessive stress on sin as a pure transgression of a law. This notion can have some legitimacy, but when it becomes exclusive it is enormously dangerous.

1. Sin and Transgression of the Law

Its legitimacy is rooted in the fact that if lying belongs, as we have said, to the essence of sin, human beings will always tend to deceive themselves with respect to what constitutes their true fulfillment and what damages it (as we saw happened to the "pagans" and "Jews" in our first section). In this sense Paul—in spite of his harsh attacks on the law—does not flinch when he then goes on to speak provocatively of the "law of Christ." But the conception of sin as a mere legal transgression is also subject to the following dangers:

1. The notion of law *through its very nature* never manages to overcome the impression of a certain arbitrariness. Here we may recall the blind alley that certain hoary old scholastic discussions got themselves into: Is something evil because God forbids it, or does God forbid it because it is evil? If we answer the second, then God is not free to be the ultimate lawmaker, because God is also subject to an external law and dependent on it. But if we answer the former,

then God cannot help being an arbitrary God, because whether things are evil or no, the content of sin is often reduced to the unjustifiable pure whim of the lawmaker.

This sense of arbitrariness is reinforced by the abusive practice of the ecclesiastical power, which declared as mortal sins (that is, causes of a human beings *ultimate* failure!) certain practices connected with Sunday Mass, annual confession, and church tithes. This teaching contributed to the encouragement of the image of sin as an arbitrary or voluntary imposition rather than as real damage to the human being. This image is also the basis of the Western sin crisis.

The shocking experience of suffering and deprivation of the most basic conditions for humanity, affecting so many Latin Americans, has redeemed liberation theology from this one-sidedness into which first-world theology had fallen. If the capitalist who grows rich by paying miserable wages offends God by missing Mass on Sunday but not by letting his employees die of hunger, God becomes a sort of arbitrary little king, more like Herod than the Father of Jesus.

2. Law *in human experience* never manages to be free of all imperfection and injustice, especially toward those who are the most oppressed in any situation and have the least voice in it. Here we may quote the vigorous verses of Bishop Casaldáliga:

> ... I want to subvert the law
> that turns the people into sheep
> and the Government a slaughterhouse.

He does not appear to be referring to a single law, because he also writes:

> Cursed be all laws
> drawn up by the few
> to defend fences and cattle
> and make the earth a slave
> and slaves of human beings.

Putting it more prosaically, with less lyrical imprecision, laws are bound to be *made* by the powerful, and therefore formulated to defend their *own* interests against the interests of the poor. The law is also *applied* by the powerful, and therefore even if it were perfect its application would always be (at least partially) unjust. The sabbath in Israel or the laws of the Indias in Latin America can be cited as typical examples of the enormous distance between their day-to-day application and what Jesus—in his polemic against the sabbath—calls "doing good to human beings" (cf. Matt. 3:4). Damage to human beings as the true compass point for any notion of sin is the only one that can overcome this degeneration and with it the degeneration of the consciousness of sin.

2. Sin and Offense against God

Finally, it is only through this fundamental compass point of human damage that we can recover the notion of sin as an offense against God. The church's magisterium has defended with clear insight that sin must also be defined in this way, in spite of apparent philosophical reasons against it. But the notion of an offense against God would have no meaning if we did not add something that was fundamental in primitive Christian theology (up to Thomas and his commentators): an offense against God is *human damage.*

Unfortunately, quite often both church practice and Western scholastic theology have been marked by an idea of sin as an immediate offense "against the gods," without any human intermediary. This is actually a pagan idea and comes from Greek mythology: Ixion, Prometheus, Sisyphus, and others. The first of these raped Juno. The second stole fire from the gods to give it to human beings. The third revealed to Aesop the place where Zeus was holding his kidnapped daughter. Their punishments are well-known in the corresponding myths. The important point to note here is that both Prometheus and Sisyphus offended the gods *for the sake of human beings.* The offense against the god was, in their case, good for human beings. Even when it rejected and demystified this conception of sin, Christian theology sometimes remained more imbued with it than it should have been. In my personal opinion (which I want to stress is not part of liberation theology) the claim of the past that the pope had power to impose things under the threat of a "grave offense against God" — even though this power is not used today — has been one of the greatest sins committed by the papal power and sometimes an offense against human beings, who were brothers and sisters of those popes and liberated by Jesus Christ from the curse of the law.

IV. CONCLUSION

Having said this we must recover the other element and add that this human damage lies precisely in the theologal dimension of sin. Let us describe this dimension in Jon Sobrino's words. He presents it as a *trinitarian* dimension. In every sin, precisely because there is an attack upon human beings — God's image recapitulated in Christ — there is a falsification of the trinitarian truth of God: God as God is and God who is the salvation of humanity. It so happens that human (historical, personal, and social) fulfillment comes about in a trinitarian form. Sobrino continues:

> Put negatively there is a sin against the Father when the mystery of being-referred-to-the-other in a saving way disappears in favor of one person's self affirmation. But sin also occurs when the Father is made exclusive and absolute. Then political monarchies appear and ecclesiastical paternalism, which confuse the Father's free plan with the imposition of an arbitrary will, the Father's absoluteness with despotism. They ignore the fact that God's mystery is expressed in Jesus and produces the liberty of the Spirit.
>
> There is sin against the Son when the scandalous actual historical reality of Jesus disappears in favor of pure transcendence or sentiment, as if Jesus were provisional and not God's definitive approach to human beings and of human beings to God. But there is also sin when the Son is made exclusive

or absolute. Then we get voluntarist imitation, law without spirit, the closed sect instead of open fraternity. This ignores the joy of the Father's free giving and the Spirit's inventive imagination.

There is sin against the Spirit when openness to historical novelty disappears as a manifestation of God. Acceptance of this openness brings life to history, instead of simply judging it from the outside from the standpoint of a truth that has become a deposit. This suffocates the ecstatic movement, which not only liberates us but makes us come out of ourselves. But there is also sin when the Spirit is made exclusive or absolute. Then we get anarchy, that disregards the actual reality of Jesus and rejects what is dangerous in his memory (Sobrino, "God," in *Concepos fundamentales de pastoral*, pp. 257-58).

Or in other words:

It is true that God is the term of "relegation" for human beings. But the power God has over human beings is none other than the human truth of the Word and the humanizing force of the Spirit—not a coercion alien or external to the human being. Thus the nature of humanity and the nature of an offense against God coincide.

It is also true that God has definitively approached human beings. But this approach does not cancel human history, making it merely a stage for a "test" of each human being or authorizing humans to escape it. God offers history to human beings as scope for their human creativity, so that they can transform it into the Kingdom of God: a space of freedom and justice, for giving and fellowship. Therefore an offense against God is through damage to human beings.

It is also true that God is inexhaustible newness for humanity; God is always greater than everything human and an affirmation of a supreme and unassailable freedom. But this newness has certain well-defined features in the new humanity of Jesus and the struggle for a new humanity for us. Therefore, lack of respect for the human or falsifying it is always an offense against God.

— *Translated by Dinah Livingstone*

CHURCH OF THE POOR, SACRAMENT OF LIBERATION

26

The Church of the Poor, Historical Sacrament of Liberation

IGNACIO ELLACURÍA

The theology of liberation[1] understands itself as a reflection from faith on the historical reality and action of the people of God, who follow the work of Jesus in announcing and fulfilling the Kingdom. It understands itself as an action by the people of God in following the work of Jesus and, as Jesus did, it tries to establish a living connection between the world of God and the human world. Its reflective character does not keep it from being an action, and an action by the people of God, even though at times it is forced to make use of theoretical tools that seem to remove it both from immediate action and from the theoretical discourse that is popular elsewhere. It is, thus, a theology that begins with historical acts and seeks to lead to historical acts, and therefore it is not satisfied with being a purely interpretive reflection; it is nourished by faithful belief in the presence of God within history, an operative presence that, although it must be grasped in grateful faith, remains an historical action. There is no room here for faith without works; rather, that faith draws the believers into the very force of God that operates in history, so that we are converted into new historical forms of that operative and salvific presence of God in humanity.

From this perspective the church presents itself, first, as that people of God who pursue in history what Jesus clearly marked as the presence of God in humanity. In this chapter we shall examine what the church must be today, historically, in the situation of the Third World and, especially, of Latin America. To what degree that presence in the Latin American situation also represents historical universality will become clearer in the following analysis.

The result of this examination can be formulated as follows: *The church is a sacrament of liberation and must act as a sacrament of liberation.* This formulation, which derives from the feelings and lives of the believing majority and is an essential element of the faith of the people sojourning in history, is the fundamental premise of these lines. Its purpose is simply to reflect on the living action of the people of God, a reflection which begins from that action and seeks to return to it for enablement.

I. THE CHURCH, HISTORICAL SACRAMENT OF SALVATION

There is nothing new about understanding the church as a sacrament, even less as a sacrament of salvation. Jesus is the primary and fundamental sacrament of salvation, and the church, in continuing and fulfilling Jesus' ministry, shares that nature at least indirectly. The relative newness appears when we speak of the church as *historical* sacrament of salvation. What is the contribution of this historicity to its sacramentality and to salvation, to the salvific sacramentality of the church? To pose the problem in these terms may sound excessively sacral: both the idea of sacrament and the idea of salvation have lost value and seem to refer to a sacral sphere that has little to do with palpable, everyday reality. Nevertheless, we cannot discard the meaning that lies behind the terms *sacrament* and *salvation*; it is necessary, however, to purge them of self-interested sacralization in order to recover their full meaning. That is best done by "historicizing" them, which does not mean reciting their history but establishing their relationship to history.

An historical understanding of salvation cannot theorize abstractly on the essence of salvation. Not only is that abstract theorizing more historical than it appears, and as abstraction it can deny the real meaning of salvation, but it is also impossible to speak of salvation except in terms of concrete situations. Salvation is always the salvation *of someone*, and *of something* in that person. This is so much so that the characteristics of the savior must be understood in terms of the characteristics of that which needs saving. This would seem to diminish the meaning of salvation as the gift of God, who anticipates the needs of humanity, but it does not. It does not, because the needs, understood in their broadest sense, are the historical path by which we move toward the recognition of that gift, which will appear as a "negation" of the needs, because from the perspective of that gift the needs appear as a "negation" of the gift of God, of God's self-giving to humanity. But beyond that, the needs can be seen as the outcry of God made flesh in human suffering, as the unmistakable voice of God, who moans in pain in God's own creatures, or more exactly, in God's children.

One might say that biblically, salvation is salvation from sin. But this does not deny what we have just said; rather it confirms it, at least if we appropriately historicize the concept of sin, which is supported by a vigorous and lasting biblical tradition. The concept of sin, in fact, emphasizes the nature of evil that is revealed in human needs, and its relationship with God; thus it is a historical theologizing on need, understood in all its breadth as we have done here. It is perhaps this perception of evil as sin that has made the history of God among humanity a history of salvation; but for that very reason, salvation, as the presence of God among humanity, is not yet fully effective except in the struggle to overcome the power of evil and sin.

Let us set aside, for the moment, what salvation should be. It is clear, and has been said many times, that salvation in spiritualistic, personalistic, or merely trans-historical terms is not only not self-evident, but also implies a false and self-interested ideologization of salvation. Moreover, an exclusive concern for otherworldly and extrahistorical salvation would deserve the reproach of John: those who say they are concerned for the salvation that is not seen, but do not value the salvation that is seen, are liars, for if we do not care about what stands before us, how shall we care about what we do not see? Let us therefore consider what the church must be with respect to salvation, before going on in turn to the historical essence of salvation and what the church's action should be with respect to that salvation. This is the theme of historical sacramentality.

The sacramentality of the church is based on a prior reality: the corporeality of the church. It was ingenious of the early church, especially of Paul, to conceive of the church in bodily terms. We shall not go into the rich biblical and dogmatic bibliography on this concept of the church as a body, and as the body of Christ. We shall only point out what this truth of the corporeality of the church, and its bodily nature with respect to Christ, means for the historicization of salvation. Briefly, the historical corporeality of the church implies that the reality and the action of Jesus Christ are embodied in the church, so that the church will incorporate Jesus Christ in the reality of history. A few words on each of these two aspects.[2]

To *be embodied* entails a series of interrelated aspects. First, it means that something becomes corporeally present and thus present in reality for a person to whom only a corporeal presence is real. It also means that something becomes more real simply by being embodied, it becomes real by becoming something else without ceasing to be what it was. It also means that something is actualized in the same way that we say the body actualizes a person. It means, finally, that something that could not act before is now able to act. Seen theologically, *being embodied* corresponds to the Word, which "took flesh" so that it could be seen and touched, so that it could intervene in a fully historical way in the action of humanity. As St. Irenaeus said, if Christ is Savior by his divine condition, he is salvation by his flesh, by his historical incarnation, by being embodied among humanity.

Incorporation is the activation of being embodied; it is becoming a body with that global and unified body that is the material history of humanity. Incorporation is an indispensable condition for effectiveness in history, and thus for the full realization of that which is incorporated. Incorporation thus presupposes being embodied, but it also means adhering to the single body of history. It is only possible to speak of incorporation when that which is not historical is historically embodied; but on the other hand, only an effective incorporation can demonstrate the degree to which something is embodied.

It is clear that Jesus was embodied in history, which means that he took mortal flesh, but he overcame the fact of having taken flesh; it is also clear that he was incorporated in human history. Once his historical visibility disappears, it is the task of the church, that is, of everything that represents his historical continuation, to continue being embodied and incorporated. One can say that the true historical body of Christ, and therefore the preeminent locus of his embodiment and his incorporation is not only the church, but the poor and the oppressed of the world, so that the church alone is not the historical body of Christ, and it is possible to speak of a true body of Christ outside the church. This is true, as we shall see, and it leads us to consider that the church by its very nature is the church of the poor and that, as church of the poor, it is the historical body of Christ. Its very embodiment and incorporation demand and entail an obligatory individualizing concreteness; to be embodied and incorporated is to be engaged concretely in the complexity of the social structure.

We shall analyze this subtheme later on, but let us return now to the church as historical body of Christ:

> The foundation of the church should not be understood in a legal and jurid-ical sense, as if Christ had delivered to a few men a doctrine and a foun-dational Magna Carta, and kept himself separate from that organization. That is not so. The origin of the Church is something much deeper. Christ establishes his church in order to maintain his own presence in human his-tory, precisely through that group of Christians who form his church. The church is, thus, the flesh in which Christ, through the centuries, makes his own life and his personal mission concrete.[3]

Jesus was the historical body of God, the full actualization of God among humanity, and the church must be the historical body of Christ, just as Christ was of God the Father. The continuation of the life and mission of Jesus in history, which is the task of the church, animated and unified by the Spirit of Christ, makes the church his body, his visible and operative presence.

This expression, *historical body* should not be seen as over against the more classical *mystical body*. The church is the mystical body of Christ insofar as it tries to make present something that is not immediately and totally palpable; even more, and this is something impossible to grasp and express, it is the historical body of Christ insofar as that presence must continue throughout history and must be made effective within it. Just like the historical Jesus, the church is more than meets the eye, but that "more" is and must be present in what is seen; here we have the unity of its mystical and its historical nature. The church's mysticism does not derive from something mysterious and occult, but from something that surpasses history within history, from something that surpasses humanity within humanity, from something that forces us to say, "Truly, the finger of God is hidden here." The supernatural should not be conceived as something intangible, but as something that surpasses nature in the same way that the historical life of Jesus surpassed what one might "naturally" expect of a man. If the life of Jesus—and what could be seen in that life by being embodied in it—is not supernatural, then the supernatural has no Christian meaning.

One example will clarify the importance of this distinction. There is an apparent divergence between the historical salvation proposed in the Old Testament and the mystical salvation proposed in the New. "They were liberated or led out of Egypt" seems a very different point of departure from "they were baptized in Christ"; those who began with a historical experience and a historical-political concreteness like that of a people who find themselves liberated from the oppression of another people and who receive the promise of a new earth in which to live freely, would seem to be a world away from those who begin with a sacramental experience like that of baptism, with regard to the "mystical" event of the death, burial, and resurrection of the Lord. In the first case, the praxis of faith seems to lead in a direction that could not possibly coincide with the praxis of those who receive the salvific gift of God mysteriously and freely by faith. One of these directions would lead to the mystical body, and the other would lead to the historical body. Since the New Testament would lead to the mystical body, we would take it that mystical salvation is the Christian way.

There is a very real danger in this interpretation, and the early church or some communities of the early church took it as real. That is why they felt obliged to round out the more mystical interpretation of Paul by referring to the historical Jesus as transmitted through the synoptic gospels and John. This shows that the salvific or soteriological nature of the death of Jesus is inseparable from his historical nature; the "why did Jesus die" is inseparable from the "why did they kill him."[4] Moreover, the "why did they kill him" has a certain priority over the "why did he die". But, from the perspective of the historical Jesus, we understand that dying with Jesus and being resurrected with him in baptism, according to Paul, are not primarily mystical but primarily historical; they are the most faithful reenactment and continuation of the life of Jesus, and they bring consequences like those that Jesus suffered, as long as the world remains like the world in which Jesus lived. Its "mysticism" derives merely from the fact that the grace of Jesus and his personal call make it possible, for those who live as Christians, to follow the road of death that leads to life, instead of following the road of life that leads to death. Thus it is not right to set "they were baptized" over against "they were led out of Egypt," because the former is not a purely mystical event, nor the latter a purely political one.

Now then, it is from this historical corporeality, which does not exclude but demands mystical corporeality, that we should understand the historical sacramentality of the church. From the outset we must repeat that the primary sacramentality of the church does not derive from the effectiveness of what we call sacraments, but that on the contrary, the sacraments are effective insofar as they participate in the sacramentality of the church. Of course that sacramentality derives from the radical and fundamental sacrament that is Christ, and this is true, as we have just noted, not only because Christ is the head of the church—the head-body relationship is not the one we assume in speaking of the corporeality of Christ and the subsequent corporeality of the church—nor only because the Spirit of Christ gives life to the body of the church, but also because the church carries on the life of Jesus, in and by the same Spirit. Sacramentality has been presented with the double mark of mediational visibility and effectiveness. Therefore when we refer to the sacramentality of the church, we are expecting the church to give visibility and effectiveness to the salvation it announces.[5]

This fundamental sacramentality of the church, because it is historical, requires the church to be present through particular actions, which must be a visible presence and effective realization of what the church is historically and mystically. Certainly the seven sacraments are among those actions and must be historicized, not reduced to cultural mimicry; those actions, which touch human life at such fundamental points as birth and incorporation into a new community, the struggle with sin, love, death, and so on, show how deeply Christian salvation seeks to be incorporated in history. But these actions, despite their fundamental and often irreplaceable nature, are not the only loci of the sacramentality of the church.

Classical theology, which saw the sacraments as privileged "channels" of grace, acknowledged that they were not the only channels; it acknowledged that the grace of Christ is also made present, visible, and effective through other channels. In other words, the sacramentality of the church can and must be made historically present in other ways. And those other ways, although they may not have all the exclusive marks of the seven sacraments, are no less and may be even more fundamental with respect to the sacramentality of the church. They cannot be considered profane actions of the church, if they are actions that put its salvific mission in practice. We cannot go more deeply into this theme, because what concerns us here is the fundamental sacramentality of the church and not the particularity of its sacramental actions.

The church makes real its historic, salvific sacramentality by announcing and fulfilling the Kingdom of God in history. Its fundamental praxis consists in the fulfillment of the Kingdom of God in history, in action that leads to the fulfillment of the Kingdom of God in history.

We do not need to insist, although it must be kept very much in mind, that the church is not an end in itself, but that the whole church, in following the historical Jesus, is at the service of the Kingdom of God. The church must understand itself from two points outside itself, Jesus Christ and the world, as they become one in the Kingdom of God; all its action must have that same, non-self-centered orientation. The church faces few temptations more serious than that of considering itself an end in itself, and of evaluating each of its actions in terms of whether they are convenient or inconvenient for its survival or its grandeur. It has often fallen into this temptation, as nonbelievers have often pointed out. A self-centered church—and one need only skim through ecclesiastical documents to observe just how self-centered it is—is not a sacrament of salvation; it is, rather, just another power in history, which follows the dynamics of other historical powers. It doesn't even help to say that the center of the church is the Risen Jesus, if that Risen Jesus is deprived of all historicity; it is true that the guiding center of the life of Jesus was in the experience of God, but a God who was historically embodied in the Kingdom of God. If the church does not incarnate its central concern for the Risen Jesus in the fulfillment of the Kingdom of God in history, it loses its touchstone and, thereby, its assurance that it is effectively serving the Lord and not itself. Only by emptying itself, in self-giving to the neediest people, unto death and death on the cross, can the church claim to be an historical sacrament of the salvation of Christ.

It is beyond debate that Jesus centered his action and his proclamation not on himself, nor even on God, but on the Kingdom of God. The essence of the complexity of the Kingdom of God, with all its wealth of nuances is not beyond debate, but in general it is clear that the Kingdom of God implies a specific historical world, that is, that the Kingdom of God cannot be identified with any type of human relationship. The Kingdom of God, as the presence of God among humanity, goes against everything that instead of making the God of Jesus Christ present, conceals and even negates that God, who is not only the God of religions or the God of the powerful in this world. The Kingdom of God, rather, upholds everything that makes all people children of the one Father who is in heaven. Few theological expressions are as corporeal and historical as this one of the Kingdom of God, which refers to God on the one hand, but also and inseparably alludes to God's salvific presence among humanity. It is the church's task to go on historicizing the demands of this Kingdom of God in each situation and each moment, because the church itself must take shape as a historical sacrament of salvation, a salvation which consists of implanting the Kingdom of God in history.

Generally speaking, the fulfillment of the Kingdom of God in history implies "taking away the sin" of the world and making the incarnate life of God present in humanity and human relationships. It is not just a matter of taking away sin where it is (in the world), but of taking away the sin-of-the-world. What that worldly sin is, the sin which condemns the world, must be determined in each case. The other sins must be interpreted in terms of that sin-of-the-world — without forgetting that all sin leads to the destruction of the sinner and is objectified in one way or another in structures that destroy humanity. It is clear that the annunciation of the Kingdom entails a very special attention to the nature of humanity in its own human freedom and intimacy, both to defend and to promote it; it is clear that the sin-of-the-world moves in the individual consciousness and will, but that should not cause us to forget the presence of worldly and historical sin. Against this sin-of-the-world, incorporated in individuals and social groups, the annunciation of the Kingdom proposes a very clear alternative: the life of the historical Jesus.

This sin-of-the-world has a unique importance in the shaping of history and, thereby, in the shaping of personal lives; that is why the presence of God among humanity takes shape in what we call salvation. But then, it is clear that that salvation, which generically means salvation from sin, takes a different historical shape according to the specific sin in question and according to the historical situation in which it occurs. That is why there is a history of salvation, because salvation takes different shapes in different historical moments, and that is why this history of salvation must be embodied and incorporated in history by assuming the nature of a salvation that is also historical. Now we can better understand why anyone is a liar who claims to be concerned for trans-historical salvation without first being concerned for historical salvation. The latter is the way to the former; historical salvation is the truth and the life of trans-historical salvation. This is another way of saying that the love of God moves in human love and cannot exist without it.

II. LIBERATION AS THE HISTORICAL FORM OF SALVATION

In 1977 the International Theological Commission published a *Declaration on Human Promotion and Christian Salvation.*[6] This amounted to a confrontation with the theology of liberation and grew out of the annual session that was dedicated to the subject in October 1976. The document, although it had some merit and gave a certain academic and professional respect to the theology of liberation, shows a lack of understanding of the epistemological and methodological groundwork of that theology and seems positively to ignore the best efforts of what might be called the second wave of liberation theology. Its value therefore does not lie in that almost shadow-boxing confrontation, but in having given theological legitimacy to what has been the fundamental theme of Latin American theological efforts, although that theme is formulated in the aseptic and historically disengaged terms of human promotion.

Not only does the title of the declaration speak of human promotion "and" Christian salvation, but the document affirms:

This unity of connection, as well as the difference that marks the relationship between human promotion and Christian salvation, in its concrete form, must certainly become the object of new investigation and analysis; that is without a doubt one of the principal tasks of theology today.[7]

So now the radical concern of Latin American theology, which was formerly viewed by the theologians of reaction as a digression and a sociologizing deformation, is recognized as one of the principal tasks of theology today, a task scandalously neglected until now by the dominant theologies. How could they have failed to advance theological principles to resolve a subject that is not only central to any historical situation, but essential to the history of salvation and to the Christian message? How could such an essential theme in the history of revelation as that of liberation have had so very little importance in biblical analyses and theological reflections until it was moved forward by the theologians of liberation? Even if they had succeeded only in obliging the "international" theologians to pay attention to this fundamental theme, by providing them with the basic elements of its formulation, that would have been a Christian and theological task of the first magnitude.

But clearly they have done much more than that. We cannot go into a systematization of what they have accomplished here, or even summarize my own modest contribution to a solution for this problem, which has been the fundamental vantage point of all my theological work.[8] What we will do here is to pick up some central points, not to discuss the problem in all its breadth, but to hint at ways in which liberation is the historical shape of salvation and not a generic "human promotion" which, in its abstract generality, has little to do with the historicity of salvation but a lot to do with a positive historical disengagement.

To recognize that salvation is related to human promotion does not represent a great advance from the customary praxis of the church or from its own ecclesial self-understanding. Although it may often have misunderstood the meaning of authentic human promotion, we cannot deny that the church has always recognized the need to carry it out in one way or another; nor can we deny that many of its best efforts have been focused on human promotion. A real advance would mean, first, defining what kind of human promotion the church should undertake, and only then what concrete kind of human promotion is related to Christian salvation and what the relationship is. That is a problem that cannot be posed at the margin of history as if it were a concrete expression of other general themes such as the relation between the natural and the supernatural, between reason and faith, and so forth. Rather, it must be posed historically, that is, looking at what humanity needs to be saved from and looking at how that salvation is inseparable, although it can be differentiated, from Christian salvation. Those people are right, therefore, who pose the problem in terms of faith and justice or, more generally, in terms of salvation and liberation, although sometimes when it is posed in a subtly dualistic way, it leads to contradictions in speaking of justice or liberation as a component, an integral part, an inescapable demand, and so on. They are right because they are using concrete historical terms, but they encounter serious problems insofar as they do not adequately conceptualize unity and do not open the way for a unitary praxis.

This problem can only be resolved with reference to the life of the historical Jesus, as it is apprehended in the tradition and in the experience of the early communities. Those who accuse Latin American theological and pastoral efforts of excessive historicity—which has nothing to do with historicism—must take into account (as the International Theological Commission does not adequately recognize) the radical importance the second wave of the theology of liberation attributes to the historical Jesus as cornerstone of the understanding of history and of action on it. This turn toward the historical Jesus—where, again, historicity should not be understood in an academic sense, but in the sense of his embodiment in history—might not have occurred if there had not been a believing praxis in the specific situation of Latin America; just as the rediscovery of biblical liberation might not have occurred if that same believing praxis had not demanded it, which only confirms the theological virtualities of the Latin American theological method. But this does not prevent us from giving primacy to that which is most fundamental in the historical Jesus, or from taking this historical Jesus, and the obligation to follow him, as the criterion and norm of historical ecclesial praxis. The inspiration and the achievements of the theology of liberation do not derive directly from other mediations, although these mediations may have drawn attention to the reality from which, in faith, people have sought and found an irreducible newness in the Christian message.[9]

Fundamental aspects of the life of Jesus, like the subordination of the sabbath to humanity, the unity of the second commandment with the first, the unity of "why did he die" with "why did they kill him," show how we should look for the unity between Christian salvation and historical salvation.

From this viewpoint we must affirm, once again, that there are not two levels of problems (the profane level on one hand, the sacred level on the other), neither are there two histories (a profane history and a sacred history), but only one level and one history. This does not mean that in that one history and that one level there are not subsystems which have an autonomy of their own, without breaking the unity but drawing their full reality from that unity. The unity between the two worlds is structural; we might say that structural unity, far from imposing uniformity on all its structural moments, is nourished by its plural diversity. There is not a single moment, nor is there a mere plurality of equal moments; rather there is a single unity, which shapes the particularity of the moments and which is shaped by that same particularity. When unity is seen structurally, when we see the structural unity of history, we need not fear that one autonomous moment will nullify another autonomous moment, although the autonomy of each is subordinate to the unity of the structure. Only a structural model is capable of giving shape to an action which, although it is single, is also diverse; only a structural model can safeguard the relative autonomy of the parts without breaking the structural unity of the whole.

But if there is not a sacred history and a profane history, if what the historical Jesus, gathering together all the revelational richness of the Hebrew scriptures, came to show us is that there are not two worlds incommunicado (a world of God and a human world), what there is instead — and what the same historical Jesus shows us — is the fundamental distinction between grace and sin, between the history of salvation and the history of perdition. Yes, both in the same history. This is shown by the contrast between two apparently contradictory readings in the Christian scriptures ("he who is not with me is against me" and "he who is not against me is with me"). The fundamental division of the single history resides in being with Jesus or not being with him, in being with him or against him. There are historical fields in which one of these formulations seems more appropriate: everyone who is not against Jesus is for him; there are other fields in which the field of choice, so to speak, is narrower, and in that case whoever is not positively with Jesus is against him. One of those fields is found, without doubt, in the relationship between oppressors and oppressed; only those who are positively with the oppressed are with Jesus, because those who are not with the oppressed are, by commission or by omission, with the oppressors, at least wherever the positive interests of the two groups are in conflict, either directly and immediately or indirectly and apparently remotely. This not being with Jesus or being against him, which can occur in very different forms, is what divides history and divides personal lives in two, without leaving neutral space; there may seem to be neutral space insofar as it possesses a specific technical autonomy, but there is not insofar as everything human is linked together, forming a single historical unity with one meaning. From this viewpoint we have even gone beyond the classic discussion of morally indifferent acts; the acts are not indifferent, although they may seem so, because each one in its concrete reality prepares, slows, or impedes the coming of the Kingdom.

The apparent impossibility of transforming history, or even the subtle interest in improving history so it would not be transformed, is what has led to the spiritualization, individualization, and trans-temporalization of historical salvation. By definition, history is so complex, so long and structural, so earthly, that it seems as if Christian faith, the continued life of a man like the historical Jesus, can do little about it; if he ended up as a failure on the cross, as far as his historical life is concerned, it seems the best thing is to renounce historical salvation and to take refuge in the faith of the resurrection, in the spiritual and individual salvation by grace and sacrament that leads to a final resurrection, for only at the end will there be a salvation or a condemnation of history. But this attitude ignores the real meaning of the resurrection and misunderstands the mission of the church with respect to history.

The resurrection, in effect, is not the transplanting of the historical Jesus to a world beyond history. For good reason the resurrection is expressed in the scripture less as Jesus' reassumption of his mortal body than as his resumption of his transformed historical life; the Risen Jesus extends his transformed life beyond death and beyond the powers of this world to become the Lord of history, precisely because of his incarnation and his death within history. He will never again abandon his flesh and, therefore, he will never abandon his historical body, but rather he continues to live in it so that, when the rest of his passion is fulfilled, the rest of his resurrection will also be fulfilled. Historical death and resurrection will continue until the Lord returns. The Spirit of Christ continues to live and animate his historical body, just as it animated his mortal and risen body.

Only when the church is confused about what it can and should do as church will it be vulnerable to discouragement or, at the other extreme, to the ambition for earthly power. Like the mission of Jesus, the mission of the church is not the immediate fulfillment of a political order, but the fulfillment of the Kingdom of God, and, as a part of that fulfillment, the salvation of any existing political order. By political order we mean here the global institutionalization of social relations, the institutional objectification of human actions, which comprises the public venue of their personal and interpersonal actions. The church does not have sufficient corporeality or materiality to bring about the immediate fulfillment of this political order, which extends to everything from collective knowledge to social organization, from the structures of power to social forces; other entities exist for that purpose.

But the church does have the function of leavening, that is, the ferment that transforms the dough to make of it the bread of life, human bread that gives life to humanity; the dough of the world and its organization is a necessary condition for the church, while the church's appropriate role is to become salt which inhibits corruption and leavening which transforms the dough from within. It is equipped for that task just as Jesus was; and it is not equipped, as Jesus was not, to become a power in this world, which takes pleasure in having the power to subdue its subjects. So the church cannot close in upon itself as if its principal objective were the conservation of its institutional structure and its comfortable place in society; rather, it must open itself to the world, put itself at the world's service in the march of history. The church knows that what is involved in the problem of humanity is not the problem of God as God, but the problem of God in history; it also knows that what is involved in the problem of God in history is the problem of humanity. If each individual, as a member of the church, must fulfill his or her salvation in relationship with others, the church as a body must fulfill its own salvation in itself, but in relationship with historical structures.

Thus, what the church contributes to the salvation of history is the fundamental sign of the history of salvation. The church belongs intrinsically to this history of salvation and carries within it the visible part that reveals and makes effective the whole of salvation in us. It makes no sense directly or by insinuation to accuse the theology of liberation of proposing only a sociopolitical salvation; even Marxism does not make such a reduction of salvation. What the theology of liberation affirms is that the history of salvation is meaningless if it does not include the sociopolitical dimension, which is an essential part but not the whole of it. If we include in that dimension everything that has to do with justice and with doing justice, everything that is sin and a cause of sin, there is no way to avoid saying that it pertains fundamentally to the history of salvation. Obviously, that is not the full extent of God's action with humanity, which the church must announce and fulfill, but without it that action is gravely mutilated.

Now then, this historical salvation must be as responsive as possible to the situation that is to be saved, and in which human beings are immersed, since salvation is fundamentally addressed to them. In the situation of the peoples of the Third World, the fulfillment of the history of salvation is presented primarily in terms of liberation, because their situation is defined in terms of domination and oppression. That oppression can be analyzed by means of different theoretical instruments, but as a fact, and a definitive fact, it is independent of all such instruments. Neither is it a valid objection against the theology of liberation to say that Marxism, for example, also defines that situation in terms of oppression and exploitation and that, therefore, the theologians of liberation are only repeating what others have said rather than speaking from Christian inspiration. This is not valid for two reasons: in the first place, the fact under analysis is not altered by the fact that it has already been recognized; and second, the Christian faith lends specificity to the fact and our response to it. Thus, the same historical facts the oppressed perceive as unjust oppression, and which Marxism interprets as the exploitation of human labor and as the consequences of that exploitation, are interpreted by faith and theology as the reality of sin and as an injustice that cries out to heaven.

We must bear in mind that what goes down in history, as Zubiri has pointed out, is not the intentionality of human acts, what is called the *opus operans*, but the objective result of those acts, the *opus operatum*. History does not judge or condemn intentions; it does not accuse people of personal sins. What is judged and condemned by history is what matters because it is the only thing that is objectified in history. Whatever in history is a source of salvation or of oppression is, therefore, what is being objectified in history, and it is in the realm of those objectifications that liberating action must take place. As we shall immediately see, this historical liberation is not the full extent of the liberating process, but it is an essential part of it, because without liberation, sin prevails in the place of grace. Only by measuring and experiencing what this situation of permanent and structural oppression means to human beings can we see how central the Christian struggle against oppression is to the essence of the history of salvation. It matters little at first that that structural oppression is maintained with the trademark and mechanisms of "national security" and such; what matters, for Christian reflection and ecclesial praxis, is the fact of structural oppression itself. When one lives as the majority of the people do (those for whom Jesus, for profound theological and human reasons, felt an undeniable preference), subjected to inhuman situations, it is not hard for the believer to see that what is happening is a new death of God in that person, a renewed crucifixion of Jesus Christ, who is present in the oppressed. Consequently, the insistence of the theology of liberation on undertaking its reflection from this fundamental *locus theologicus* should not be seen in pietistic terms, but in purely Christian and strictly theological terms; if theology as an intellectual act entails a particular set of technical requirements, as an intellectual Christian act it also entails certain Christian requirements that are more than a matter of accepting certain items of faith. This is what some groups of academic theologians seem not to understand.

It is through incarnation in that situation of oppression (it is very hard to live in a situation of oppression in the First World) that one understands the realities of the duality between oppression and liberation, as seen by faith and by theological reflection. Oppression which is not merely natural, that is, which does not follow from the physical laws of nature, thus a strictly historical oppression is always a sin, that is, something positively unacceptable to God. In other situations finding "meaning" in the Christian message can be a hard task; in situations of oppression, the whole of the Christian message offers such an immediate "meaning" that there is nothing to do but pick it up and run with it. In these situations of oppression one sees the love of God and human love at issue in the negation of the very existence of children of God and brothers and sisters in Jesus Christ. The experience of the proclaimers of liberation, when they read the Good News to the simple and believing peoples, proves the tremendous force of the liberating word of God; they feel the radical truth of the words of Isaiah and Jesus of Nazareth. The proclaimers and the receivers of the proclamation, in a single shared word, feel the depth of meaning of the whole Christian message for the poor, the persecuted, the oppressed, and those in need. It is not only that the Christian message is preferentially addressed to the poor; it is that only the poor are capable of drawing the full meaning from that message. This is the affirmation of the theology of liberation, and this is what shapes its method of doing theology.

Reading the word of God from this situation of structural sin and violence, we are forced to see Christian love in terms of struggle for the justice which liberates and saves the crucified and oppressed human being. The justice asserted by the Christian faith should not be set apart from Christian love in a situation defined by an injustice that makes human life impossible. The struggle for justice, without making justice itself unjust by the methods used, is very simply the historical form of active love; although not all love can be reduced to doing good to the neighbor, this doing good, if it is generous, if it does not recognize boundaries, if it is humble and kind, is a historical form of love. Not all struggles for justice are the incarnation of Christian love, but there is no Christian love without a struggle for justice when the historical situation is defined in terms of injustice and oppression; therefore, the church, as a sacrament of liberation, has the double task of awakening and increasing the struggle for justice among those who are not committed to it, and of making those who are committed to it carry out the struggle in Christian love. Here too the example of the historical Jesus is decisive. In his society, divided and antagonistic, Jesus loved everyone, but he placed himself on the side of the oppressed and from there he struggled energetically but lovingly against the oppressors.

Finally, if we consider the universality in our time of the historical cry of the peoples, social classes, and individuals for liberation from oppression, it is not hard to see that the church, as a universal sacrament of salvation, must become a sacrament of liberation. This cry of the oppressed peoples, when we look at their real characteristics from the viewpoint of revelation, is divinity crucified in humanity, the servant of Yahweh. This is what it means to be a prophet; it is the great sign of the times. The historical shape of the church, as a salvific and liberating response to this universal cry, presupposes first its permanent conversion to the truth and the life of the historical Jesus; and second, its historical participation in the salvation of a world that can only be saved by following the way of Jesus. The cry of the immense majority of humanity, oppressed by an arrogant minority, is the cry of Jesus himself historically embodied in the flesh, in the need, and in the pain of oppressed humanity.

Certainly there are other forms of oppression besides the sociopolitical and economic, and not all forms of oppression derive exclusively and immediately from that one. Christians would be wrong, therefore, to seek only one type of social liberation. Liberation must extend to everyone who is oppressed by sin and by the roots of sin; it must accomplish liberation both from the objectification of sin and from the internal principle of sin; it must extend to both unjust structures and the people who do injustice; it must extend both to the inner life of people and to the things they do. The goal of liberation is full freedom, in which full and right relationships are possible, among people and between them and God. The way to liberation can only be the way that Jesus followed, the way which the church must follow historically, the way in which it must believe and hope as an essential element of human salvation.

III. THE CHURCH OF THE POOR, HISTORICAL SACRAMENT OF LIBERATION

We have just said that the church must be a sacrament of liberation in the same way Jesus was; adjustments are possible and necessary in the way it carries out its task of salvation, but only when they are a continuation of the ways Jesus used. The institutional nature of the church, necessarily derived from its social corporeality, entails clear requirements that only an anarchizing idealism can fail to see. But that institutionality does not have to be shaped, as has often happened, in accordance with the institutionality required by the powerful of this world to maintain their power. That institutionality must be subordinated to the deeper nature of the church as a continuation of the work of Jesus. The church must continue to believe in the specificity of the way of Jesus and must not fall into the trap of generic and rational salvations.

Jesus had a unique way of struggling for the salvation and liberation of humanity. It is unique not only for the content of that salvation and liberation, a point we cannot go into here—that is the question of the Christian praxis Jesus asks for—but it is unique because of the way it addresses the salvation and liberation of humanity. Jesus does not view them in a generic and abstract way that leads to human promotion, the defense of human rights, and so forth, but in a unique way. Facing the situation of a divided society, Jesus' way seeks human promotion or human rights from the side of the oppressed, on their behalf, and in struggle against the side of the oppressors. In other words, his action is historical and concrete and goes to the roots of the oppression. The church must follow the same pattern and confront the same alternative, and this is what should correct both its false institutionality and an institutionality placed on the side of the oppressive structures. In our time, base communities are advanced as a way of countering the exaggerated institutionalization of the church. In a brief talk to a German group of base communities, Rahner has said: "The church today needs base communities. The churches of the future will be built up from below through base communities of free initiative and membership."[10] Supposedly, the force of the Spirit will be more active and alive in these communities, so that their initiatives will flow up freely from the base to the head, thus avoiding the excess weight of the ecclesial structures, which can suffocate both personal initiative and Christian inspiration. This leads to opposition between base communities (small groups meeting freely to live their faith and undertake action accordingly) and the institutional structures, which are needed, but which are not the proper initiators of any ecclesial activity.

The theology of liberation would pose the problem in different terms. The base communities can serve as a basis of the church of the future because they are *of the base*. This language may sound Marxist, because of the word *base*, but the term is used by communities that not only have nothing to do with Marxism, but interpret the word *base* exclusively in the sense that they are the basic elements or original cells of the ecclesial organism. From the viewpoint of the theology of liberation, the evangelical *base* of the Kingdom of God is made up of the poor, and only the poor in community can induce the church to avoid both excessive institutionalization and attachment to the world. The ultimate reason why the institutional church can oppress its own children is not so much its institutional nature, but its lack of dedication to the people of greatest need, in following what Jesus was and did. Consequently, it can only resist worldliness by placing itself at the service of the poorest and those of greatest need; and having resisted worldliness, it will no longer fall into all the defects that come naturally to an organization and power closed in on itself.

The base of the church is the church of the poor, which takes diverse forms in accordance with historical conditions. What does it mean to say that the base of the church is the church of the poor?

It is not easy to conceptualize the poor, especially when some parts of the Christian scriptures have softened and spiritualized their condition, and even more, after so much exegetical effort to reconcile the Kingdom of God with the kingdom of this world.[11] But no matter how much we reinterpret scripture to focus on the poor in spirit, on detachment from the things of this world, and so on, we cannot forget that those "spiritual ones" must be poor in substance, which is not impossible for God, but extremely improbable and difficult from the viewpoint of evangelical preaching. The need to be poor, to be one with the poor, is an ineluctable mandate for anyone who wants to follow Jesus.

But even with these corrections, the fact remains that their purpose is not to exclude any person—all are called to salvation, based on proper and real conversion—but this in no way negates the real preference shown by Jesus. The massive weight of Jesus' dedication to the poor, his frequent attacks on the rich and the dominant, his choice of apostles, the condition of his followers, the orientation of his message, leave little doubt about the preferential meaning and will of Jesus. That is so true that one must become poor like him, with all the historical attributes of poverty, in order to enter the Kingdom. From the historical reality of Jesus it is clear, with no possibility of evasion, what he meant by the Kingdom of God among humanity.

The question of who are the poor, in the real situation of the Third World, is not a problem that has to be resolved with elaborate scriptural exegesis or sociological analysis or historical theories. Certainly it is dangerous to speak of "the poor" in front of other, more politicized groups. But as a primary fact, as the real situation of the majority of humankind, there is no room for self-interested equivocations. What makes it worse is that, to a large extent, those poor and their poverty are the result of a sin that the church must struggle to take away from the world. This is the only possible polestar of the historically constituted mission of the church, its primordial purpose. This is not only because the poor represent the majority of humanity and, in this sense, are the necessary condition of universality, but above all because the presence of Jesus is especially in them, a hidden presence, but no less real for being hidden. It follows that the poor are the historical body of Christ, the historical locus of his presence and the base of the ecclesial community. In other words, the church is the historical body of Christ insofar as it is the church of the poor; and it is a sacrament of liberation insofar as it is the church of the poor. The reason for that is found both in the celebrated passage of the Last Judgment, and in the missionary essence of the church. If the church is truly shaped as church of the poor, it will cease to be a church installed in and attached to the world and become again a predominantly missionary church, that is, open to a reality that will force it to draw on its best spiritual reserves; that will also force it to become Jesus Christ truly present in a special way in the prisoners, in the suffering, in the persecuted, and so on.

The church of the poor, therefore, refers to a basic problem of the history of salvation. Because *poor*, in this context, is not an absolute and ahistorical concept, nor is it a profane or neutral concept. In the first place, when we speak here of the poor, we are speaking of a relationship between poor and rich (more generally, between dominated and oppressor), in which there are rich people because there are poor, and the rich make the poor poor, or at least deprive them of a part of what belongs to them. Certainly there is another valid sense of the word *poor*: one who feels or is marginalized by "natural," not historical causes; but the first meaning is the fundamental one in both its dialectical and its historical nature. In the second place, this relationship is not purely profane, not only because we have already rejected the sacred-profane duality in general, but more particularly, because its special dialectic is deeply rooted in what is essential to Christianity: loving God by loving humanity, justice as the locus of love fulfilled in a world of sin. Thus the singular Christian and historical importance of a church of the poor, whose mission is to break that dialectic for the sake of love, in order to achieve the salvation of both sides together, which are now bound together by sin and not by grace. The very evasion of those who keep saying "you will always have the poor with you" is turned against them, because what it would mean is that, when the visible Jesus disappears, then the poor take his place, making him present in a way that is invisible to the eyes of the world, but visible to the eyes of faith.

This conception of the church as church of the poor has great practical consequences. Only a few are mentioned here, as synthetic types.

1. The Christian faith must mean something real and palpable in the life of the poor. This may seem obvious, something the church has always attempted but not always achieved. But it is not. It is not, in the first place, because "the poor" has not been understood as we are interpreting it here, that is, as a dialectical and historical concept. And it is not, in the second place, because that real and palpable meaning does not refer only to a problem of individual behavior, but also—and just as essentially—to real life in the real structures that form a part of human life as a whole; it refers, therefore, to the sociopolitical aspect of their life and to those structural sociopolitical realities which decisively shape personal lives. In more general and more theological terms, let us repeat that the "history of salvation" must also be a historical salvation. It must also save historically, and it must also be a principle of integral salvation here and now. To understand this, it is sufficient to look at the fundamental criterion of Christian theory and praxis: the historical Jesus. The preference of Jesus for the poor is not a purely affective preference; it is also a real dedication to their achievement of a salvation that is not only a promise of a life beyond earth, but is eternal life already present; it is impossible to ignore all the real and historical work that Jesus did for the poor of his time. And it is clear that this historicization of salvation, referring to a people and an oppressed people, has and must have unique characteristics in accordance with the nature of the oppression.

This does not necessarily mean that the poor should be treated as a "class," or otherwise categorized, which diminishes their personal nature. The effective and pressing existence of social realities does not negate the irreducible existence of personal realities. One should not be confused with the other, and it cannot be assumed that a solution at one level will be valid at the other. On the other hand, although to some extent this focus enables us to separate individuals from the category they represent—and in this sense it overcomes, or can overcome prejudice—it does not nullify the fundamental option, which is still the liberation of the oppressed, with all the sociopolitical meaning that concept implies.

2. *For that reason the Christian faith, far from becoming an opiate—and not only a social opiate—should establish itself as what it is: a principle of liberation.* This liberation must include everything as a single whole. There is no liberation if the heart of the person is not liberated; but the heart cannot be liberated when the whole person, which is more than inner being, remains oppressed by collective structures and realities that invade the whole being. The church should avoid letting its more structural concerns turn it into an opiate with respect to personal problems; it should also make sure its more individualistic and spiritualistic concerns do not turn it into an opiate with respect to structural problems.

This places the Latin American church in a difficult position. On the one hand, it brings persecution on the church, as it brought persecution unto death to Jesus himself. The Latin American church, more precisely the church of the poor, must be convinced that if it is not persecuted by the powerful in a historical world, it is not authentically and completely preaching the Christian faith. While not all persecution is a sign and miracle proving the authenticity of faith, the absence of persecution by those who hold power in a situation of injustice is a sign, irrefutable in the long range, that the proclamation of its message lacks evangelical courage. But on the other hand, the fact that the church cannot and should not be reduced to a pure sociopolitical force, working exclusively from an ideological locus against unjust structures or giving absolute priority to that work, brings on it incomprehension and attack from those who have embraced personal and political partiality as if it were the whole of humanity. These people do not know the damage they are causing not only to a profound and long-term work of the church, but more importantly, to themselves; they consider themselves servants, when at times they are serving themselves in order to carry out an impossible political project that does not even take into account the whole range of material conditions in which they find themselves.

3. *Thus the church of the poor does not permit us to make a sharp separation between faith and religion, at least in specific social contexts and in the early stages of a conscientizing process.* The distinction between faith and religion, which has a lot of validity in both the general theoretical order and the practical order of specific social environments, must be used carefully in situations like those of Latin America. This distinction, which is theologically well founded, is needed to recover the uniqueness of what is Christian, but it can be manipulated and does not always fit the reality of a church of the poor. It can lead us to underestimate the authentic needs of a cultural situation and can also disembody the

faith, dehistoricize it, on the one hand by turning it into something purely individual and purely parochial and not structural, or on the other by bypassing the need to embody the faith "also" in religious form, as the "corporeal" nature of the social reality requires. It is true that the Central European emphasis on faith vis-à-vis religion brings in a recovery of fundamental dimensions, but it also entails the danger of individualistic subjectivity and idealization, and also the danger of becoming an option for the elites. An authentic church of the poor must respond to these dangers by understanding and practicing the faith as a historical following of the person and work of Jesus, and also as a historical celebration; both the following and the celebration must respond to the problems and the situation of the oppressed majorities that are struggling for justice.

That is one way of approaching the problem of popular "religiosity," the problem of the "religious" ways of cultivating and celebrating the faith. With all their weaknesses, these ways are needed as a way of responding historically to the historicity of faith itself, and they can be the corrective needed to ensure the continued historical mediation of the historical faith. For example, it is wrong when priests collectively abandon or undervalue the proclamation and living practice of the sources of faith in order to engage in political struggle; to claim that this is "faith" over against "religion" involves a secularization of the faith that goes beyond the need to historicize and politicize it. Evangelization should indeed come before sacramentalization in the proclamation and living practice of the Christian faith, precisely because evangelization is an essential part of sacramentalization. Evangelization can and must be political and historical, but above all it is the proclamation of the salvation that is offered and given to us in Jesus.

4. Therefore, this church of the poor must not become another form of elitism. The very concept of church of the poor goes beyond the elitism of those who see Christianity as a way to refinement that only the perfect can enjoy or practice. The church of the poor closes its doors to no one, nor does it diminish the fullness and universality of its mission. It must always conserve the fullness of its force, although this means foolishness to some and a stumbling-block to others.

But it also must not leave room for another form of elitism: that which is appropriated from the whole people by the most conscientized, and from the conscientized ones by those who consider themselves the most committed vanguard, and from this committed vanguard by the vertical leaders, who lead from above with preestablished plans, dogmatically monopolize the needs of the people, and set the direction and pace of their resolution. That leads to a preference for the dramatic and quick success of political action rather than the slow growth of the evangelical seed, planted and carefully tended in its own soil.

In the face of these different forms of elitism, the alternative of the church of the poor does not constitute either a stupefying opiate or a stimulant. The Christian faith should be neither an eternal opiate nor an apocalyptic and millenarian stimulant; it is a small seed that little by little can become a great tree sheltering all people. Revolutionary haste and desperate eschatology do not respect the reality of either the people or the church. And it is neither just nor evangelical to confuse the select, elitist pace of individuals with the pace of the real people. Lack of faith and confidence in the salvific potential of the preaching of Jesus easily leads away from following Jesus in history to purely political action. That action may be fully justified, and must be shaped by rigorous technical considerations, but it alone does not constitute the Christian faith and cannot substitute for it, although it can sometimes be an incarnating sign of faith in a given situation.

We still need to analyze the possibility of a certain elitism in the gospel itself: people, followers, disciples, apostles, the three, Peter, and more. But however this knotty problem is resolved, we can suppose that the gospel never fails to give ultimate respect to the potential self-giving of a particular social group at any particular time. If the church of the poor is to be shaped by the fullness and energy of the Christian faith, each of the human groups within it and, above all, each person, must receive the infinite respect that Jesus showed in his ministry of evangelization, except in cases of clear exploitation of one person by another.

I do not want to end these reflections on the church of the poor as sacrament of liberation without bringing in the feelings of the peasants evangelized by a prophet of the church of the poor, Father Rutilio Grande, a martyr of that church in El Salvador, who for giving active witness to the Christian faith was riddled by the bullets of the oppressors. Here are some of the peasants' testimonies.

I think Rutilio has fulfilled his priestly mission. . . . He understood the Christian commitment that God wants all people to carry out. He made this commitment by serving others; he related to the humble people in the countryside and in the city, teaching them the true way of Christianity that we must show to others.

He began to develop a line, putting it in practice with the delegates of the word, and later he began opening a Christian way, committing himself to the people, until one day we saw him killed by the murderous bullets of the enemy, who did not want him to go on working with his people . . . taking them on the way that Christ wanted to show us.

He related to the humble people to show them that the gospel must be lived in struggle, not to leave it in the air, but to be able to overcome injustice, exploitation, and misery. That is why the enemies of the people decided to kill him along with his people.

Because the work of Father Rutilio Grande and the other missionary fathers were the first to lift up this community, that is why the communities feel their spirit evangelically uplifted, because they received very deeply when Father Rutilio came to say mass. That is why the communities have grown in number. When he formed those communities, he left eight delegates there. Now there are eighteen delegates in the community, but delegates who have really understood what it means to follow Christ and why they should not stop for anything that people invent in this oppressed world.

Father Grande and his missionaries also enlightened us that it was good to celebrate the festival of the products that we harvest, like corn. . . . In that festival it didn't matter if people had a suitcoat, good shoes, or if they went barefoot, or with sandals made of rubber tires; we were all the same there, there were no class differences.

The challenge to us of Father Rutilio's death is to go forward, not to faint — to see clearly the position of this man, a martyr and prophet of the church. We have to maintain the position that this prophet maintained and, if possible, give our lives in service to others, because the grain has to die before we see the fruit.

Meditating on these words of living faith would inspire many reflections. They show very well what a church of the poor can be as a sacrament of universal liberation, which only leaves out the same people who stayed out when Jesus died for all people — the ones Rutilio Grande forgave at his death, as Jesus did, because they did not know what they were doing.

— Translated by Margaret D. Wilde

NOTES

1. Although this term denotes a diversity of currents — it would have to, given its own definition as an historical task — I prefer to keep the term for the sake of differentiation.

2. Cf. X. Zubiri, "El hombre y su cuerpo," *Salesianum* 3 (1974), pp. 479-86.

3. Oscar A. Romero, *Voice of the Voiceless*, trans. Michael J. Walsh (Maryknoll, N.Y.: Orbis Books, 1985); see the Second Pastoral Letter.

4. Cf. I. Ellacuría, "Por qué muere Jesús y por qué le matan?" *Misión Abierta* (March 1977), pp. 17-26; on the bibliography cited there, cf. H. Schürmann, *Comment Jesus a-t-il vecu sa mort?* (Paris, 1977).

5. This point was developed in I. Ellacuría, "Iglesia y realidad histórica," ECA 331 (1976), pp. 213-20.

6. I refer here to the French translation, which appeared in *La Documentation Catholique* 1726 (1977), pp. 761-68. (For an English translation, see *Liberation Theology*, J. Schall, ed. [San Francisco: Ignatius Press, 1982], pp. 363-83.)

7. Ibid., p. 766.

8. Cf. "Historia de la salvación y salvación en la historia," in *Teología política* (San Salvador, 1973), pp. 1-10; "El anuncio del evangelio a la misión de la Iglesia," ibid., pp. 44-69; "Liberación: misión y carisma de la Iglesia latinoamericana," ibid., pp. 70-90; "Tesis sobre posibilidad, necesidad y sentido de una teología latinoamericana," in *Teología y mundo contemporáneo* (Madrid, 1975), pp. 325-50; "Hacia una fundamentación del método teológico latinoamericano," ECA (August-September 1975), pp. 409-25; "En busca de la cuestión fundamental de la pastoral latinoamericana," *Sal Terrae* 759/760 (1976), pp. 563-72; "Teorías económicas y relación entre cristianismo y socialismo," *Concilium* (May 1977), pp. 282-90; "Fe y justicia," *Christus* (August and September 1977).

9. J. Sobrino, in his *Christology at the Crossroads* (Maryknoll, N.Y.: Orbis Books, 1978) and in many of his writings, has shown *in actu exercito* how the primacy of the historical Jesus can and should be maintained from and for an historical incorporation.

10. K. Rahner, "Oekumenische Basisgemeinden," in *Aktion* 365 (Frankfurt a.M., 1975).

11. From here on I am following some reflections that I have already published in "Notas teológicas sobre religiosidad popular," *Fomento Social* (July-September 1977), pp. 253-60; therefore, the following pages may contribute some ideas on the important subject of popular religiosity.

27

Evangelization

JUAN RAMÓN MORENO

I. INTRODUCTION

Evangelization is a complex term. On the basis of the word itself, we could define it as the communication of good news. But it is the convergence of a number of diverse things that make good news both news and good: its source, content, bearer, recipient, what it is about this news that makes it good for this recipient, and so forth.

Moreover, what I want to clarify here is to some degree not evangelization in general, but *Christian* evangelization. Not just any "good news" proclaimed is Christian, nor is just any way of proclaiming it Christian.

1. Importance of the Issue

This issue is crucially important. That is why it is so insistently raised in living communities within the church, whether directly or in the form of questions on the mission of the church, religious life, base communities, or the parish. The official magisterium of the church has also devoted special attention to this issue: the 1974 synod, *Evangelii Nuntiandi*, the Puebla conference, the focus of the celebration of the five hundredth anniversary of the European discovery of Latin America, in which the emphasis falls on "new evangelization," are but expressions of a deep concern.

It could not be otherwise, if, as was stated at the 1974 synod and repeated in *Evangelii Nuntiandi*, "the task of the evangelization of all human beings constitutes the essential mission of the church," and if, as Paul VI insists, "to evangelize is the joy and particular calling of the church, its deepest identity. It exists in order to evangelize" (EN, 14). Thus it is clear that in evangelization the church's very raison d'être is at stake and, accordingly, that of religious life and of all movements of Christian life. Consequently, evangelization is not one issue among the various issues that can and must be considered, but is itself the central issue. When we inquire about what it means to evangelize, we are inquiring about the very essence of the church.

I think this is now quite clear in the awareness of the church and in our own awareness as men and women seeking to live out our Christian and ecclesial vocation in religious life. Perhaps, however, we should clarify more what this demands of the church and of the various ecclesial institutions.

2. Difficulties and Demands

Today we encounter particular diffculties in evangelizing the modern world, but if we intend to be honest we have to ask ourselves: Are these difficulties simply the product of the resistance and particular obstacles raised by the world today, such as atheism, secularism, consumerism, hedonism, and all the other "isms" that could be added on? Or might they also be the product of a church that has not proved itself capable of shaping itself and structuring its pastoral work in a way that might invigorate its ability to transmit credibly to today's men and women the Good News of Jesus?

No one denies that a changed world requires new ways of evangelizing, but does it not also demand a new way of being church, and for us within the church, a new style of religious life? How are we to be good news for today's world? The church is not something that is first built in itself and then receives the gospel to transmit after it is already set up. Not at all. In its very constitution the church is mission and its mission is to evangelize. The church of Jesus is set apart and established in the very act of evangelizing. The Holy Spirit, bringing the church to birth, is given as a power for carrying out this mission. "As the Father has sent me, so I send you" (John 20:21). "You will receive power when the Holy Spirit comes down on you; then you are to be my witnesses in Jerusalem, throughout Judea and Samaria, yes, even to the ends of the earth" (Acts 1:8).

The aim is to give witness to Jesus, God's definitive gospel. The oldest gospel we know bears this title: "Beginning of the good news of Jesus, the Christ" (Mark 1:1). But we should not forget that before being the Christ who is proclaimed, he is the Jesus who proclaims, the Jesus who evangelizes. One of the merits of *Evangelii Nuntiandi* is that it sheds light on the topic of evangelization through Jesus, "the first and greatest evangelizer" (EN, 6). This leads to an understanding of evangelization not in the abstract, but out of the historic embodiment that is Jesus of Nazareth. It is by looking at Jesus that the church learns to be evangelizing.

II. JESUS AND EVANGELIZATION

1. The Principle and Foundation of Evangelization

The first thing we must learn is what comes *first* in evangelization. First not simply in the chronological sense, but in a radical sense: what is most at the source, the root from which the whole evangelization process springs and at the same time sustains and nourishes it; its principle and foundation—that is, that which grounds and gives origin to evangelization by being the principle of a way of being and acting, which, precisely because it has such a foundation, becomes good news.

When Jesus, answering the scribe who asks which commandment is most basic, offers the parable of the Samaritan, he gives us important clues for understanding what it means to evangelize, to become good news. For that man, attacked by bandits on the way to Jericho and left half-dead, the priest who saw him, and took a wide detour around him and kept going, was not good news, nor was the Levite who passed by later. The one who was good news was the Samaritan, who was able to understand his situation of need, be moved by it, and take effective action to save the man and provide for his needs.

I am going to take the liberty of pausing over this parable to analyze what is essential about it. Lying on the roadway is this wounded man on the verge of losing his life. Suddenly the Samaritan comes on the scene and the gospel text says he was "moved with pity at the sight. He approached him and dressed his wounds, pouring on oil and wine. He then hoisted him on his own beast and brought him to an inn, where he cared for him." It all begins with his being moved with pity "at the sight," the act of looking, becoming aware of a presence there. But that becoming aware of a suffering and needy presence does not in itself lead to hope and joy; it is not automatically good news. The priest and the Levite passing by also "saw," but their way of looking, and what fell within their glance, could not inspire the subsequent steps leading to good news: they "saw him, but continued on." Looking is not enough; what is behind the gaze is crucial, and consequently the Samaritan and the two servants of the temple have different ways of looking, different eyes. The latter two look without solidarity, from a distance, and do not let themselves be affected by the situation of the other, who simply does not arouse enough interest in them to make them go through the trouble of changing their travel plans and coming forward. They do not have compassionate love, the ability to become concerned over the situation of other persons, and in view of their precarious situation, to become involved. The Samaritan's gaze is very different—the gaze of one who is open to the situation of others, because he has a heart of solidarity, because he is capable of committed love. Consequently what his gaze captures in suffering, in excruciating reality, affects him to the point where he is "moved to pity."

Luke here uses the Greek verb *splanchnizomai*, which the gospels repeatedly apply to Jesus. Literally it means that one's guts are stirred. And one's guts are affected when there is something foreign irritating them, something that must be expelled and gotten rid of, if one is to be at rest. This is *compassion* in the strong sense of the word. Solidarity with others leads to being identified with them so that their pain, their passion, become one's own (com-passion), and they pain one to the point of being unbearable: they have to be relieved, something must be done to change the situation of suffering. That leads to action, to doing something that relieves the suffering of the other, which is also one's own suffering.

Consequently, the parable here tells us that the Samaritan "approached him." Being identified with the other in solidarity leads him to move and come foward, to make himself neighbor to the other, to enter into his world in order to be able to familiarize himself with his need and deal with it. But this demands leaving one's own world, one's own interests and concerns, to change one's own plans, in order to adjust to what serving the other's life demands. The Samaritan puts aside his travel plans in order to enter into the situation of suffering of the wounded man, to become involved with him and take him toward curing, toward life. He has proved capable of becoming good news for the man assaulted by robbers. The only grammar in which the Christian Good News can be expressed is the grammar of merciful love, the grammar of solidarity with the other. And at the root, at the originating source of this Good News, are the innermost recesses of mercy.

It is significant that this way of acting, which Jesus presents as a model ("go and do the same"), simply reflects Jesus' own way of acting. It is striking how often the gospel describes for us Jesus' activity through a set of three gestures inseparably interconnected: "Jesus looked at him with love and told him . . ." (Mark 10:21), "he saw the vast throng, his heart was moved with pity, and he cured their sick" (Matt. 14:14). Before speaking or acting comes the gesture of looking, expressing a heart of mercy, a concern to penetrate reality, as crude as it is, without evading anything. When this situation of the other person is a situation of suffering, the heart allows itself to be affected by this suffering and looking becomes compassion.

This gaze falls most frequently on what the gospels call *ocholos*, crowd, mass. In Matthew chapter 4, at the outset of Jesus' public life, when the evangelist presents one of those summaries, which are subsequently repeated and pull together what is most basic in Jesus' Messianic activity, we read:

> His reputation traveled the length of Syria. They carried to him all those afflicted with various diseases and racked with pain: the possessed, the lunatics, the paralyzed. He cured them all. The great crowds that followed him came from Galilee, the ten cities, Jerusalem and Judea, and from across the Jordan (4:24–25).

Mark chapter 3 further describes this multitude as pressing in on Jesus so much so that he asks them to ready a boat lest he be overwhelmed. "Because he had cured many, all who had afflictions kept pushing toward him to touch him" (3:10). This is no doubt a suffering multitude, a multitude of the ragged, the needy and the sick, who discover in Jesus something that awakens hope within them: there is something in Jesus that tells them that their situation of suffering can be changed, that things are going to change. In their anguish they seek out Jesus to the point where they are pressing in on him and not even leaving him room to eat, as the evangelist notes later on. In fact, when Jesus at one point, seeking a moment of relief, asks them to take him across the lake in a boat, the crowd is already there waiting for him. "When he disembarked and saw the vast throng, his heart was moved with pity, and he cured their sick" (Matt. 14:14).

This is the world to which Jesus draws near, the one he enters, and over whose situation he allows himself to be moved, and which he commits himself to change. When John's disciples ask him if he is the one who is to come, his answer is, "Look and give witness to what you have seen and heard." What have they seen and heard? That things are changing, "the lame walk, the blind see, the dead rise, and the poor hear the good news" (Cf. Matt. 11:3–6). There is a change in the situation that engenders life and hence engenders hope. It is compassion seeking to effectively change what is preventing the other person from living.

2. The Good News of the Incarnation

In trying to understand what the Good News means from the perspective of the overall mystery of the incarnation, we encounter the same root from which springs the possibility of the Good News: mercy. When St. Ignatius Loyola in his *Spiritual Exercises* presents contemplation on the incarnation, a key passage for understanding Ignatian and Jesuit spirituality, he sets up, as it were, an opposition between the world affected by sin and the trinitarian God looking at this world. It is a world without solidarity, a lost world, a world without hope. And God looks at this world in the only way God knows how to look: with the Father's gaze, with a look that arises out of loving concern over what happens in the world. And despite what this gaze sees, and just because of what it sees, there wells up in God's heart—so to speak—compassionate tenderness; God's merciful heart is stirred. "God so loved the world that he gave his only Son" (John 3:16). St. Paul will say: "It is precisely in this that God proves his love for us: that while we were still sinners, Christ died for us" (Rom. 8:5). God's response to this world stretched out on the roadside, this world in the throes of a despairing death, is, as in the parable of the Samaritan, to come close to the world, to enter into the world: "the Word became flesh and made his dwelling among us" (John 1:14). Love is what brings together whatever can be brought together in our history of nonsolidarity, suffering, and frustration, but not in order to leave that history as it is, but to transform it, to make it be what it should be. It will no longer be possible to find God outside human history and outside the struggle to make that history shot through with God, a history of salvation.

Thus the Good News exists simply because God is a God with a heart of mercy, a God who seeks our good not because we are God but because God is good, who loves us not because we are lovable but because God is love. And this mercy acts by coming close, by taking on solidarity, by being identified with the one who is loved and who thus receives the Good News that something basic is going to change in his or her situation.

St. Paul uses the expression of self-emptying to describe this movement. It means entering into the other's little world, taking on the limitation of human flesh. The uncreated Word, which was together with God, which was God, now becomes human Word, expresses itself in Aramaic, becomes incarnate in a specific culture, enters into one people's history. This movement also supposes a moment of passivity: to become flesh is to allow oneself to be given flesh. In every drawing near, there is a moment of receiving, of allowing oneself to be taught by the other who offers his or her reality. In Mary's virginal womb, the Word accepts being given a body, a historic and human body. And this human flesh will be born small and limited, as is true of all human flesh. The newborn child, who, wrapped in swaddling clothes as a symbol of his weakness, has to be raised and taught, has to be aided to "grow in wisdom, grace, and age," expresses with amazing adaptability what it means to become incarnate.

Both Matthew and Luke, the two evangelists of infancy narratives, attach a great deal of importance to the genealogy of Jesus, although in different perspectives. The genealogies, which may be tedious and rather meaningless for a modern reader, are for the evangelists the way to express that the incarnation demands being inserted into the life of a lineage, a specific people, in this case the Jewish people, from which one receives one's history and culture, and whose fate one takes on. To take on a real body is to become incorporated into the struggles and hopes of a people on the march. The author of the Letter to the Hebrews powerfully describes this movement in solidarity with the incarnation by stating that Jesus "was tempted in every way that we are, yet never sinned" (Heb. 4:15).

The importance of this moment of passivity for Jesus — allowing himself to be given a body, a culture, a human identity — comes out sharply in the more than thirty years of silence and obscurity he spends in Nazareth. All Jesus' activity is simply that of one more person within his people. Only after he has allowed himself to be given speech, when he has been thoroughly imbued with his people's way of being, does he go out, moved by the Spirit, to openly carry out his Messianic activity. Indeed his first public act will be that of standing in solidarity with the sinful people, and as one more among them, receiving the baptism of penance from John's hands.

3. Being Good News in a Divided World: Partiality toward the Poor

Going on now to focus on Jesus' public activity, it seems quite clear that the fundamental horizon within which that whole activity unfolds is what Jesus calls the Reign of God. As the synoptic gospels indicate, what Jesus proclaims is the Reign of God as a something approaching, which, when it breaks into history, will change it at the root. It is especially important that the center of Jesus' preaching is not simply God but God's Reign. The God of Jesus is not disinterested in what goes on in the world, but on the contrary is concerned over what takes place in history and is affected by the situation of humankind even to the point of becoming part of that history through the incarnation, as we have just noted.

But this is a divided world, and in a divided world the Good News must inevitably be partial. It does not ring the same in everybody's ears. Already in the Jewish context in which Jesus carries out his mission, the proclamation of the approaching Reign evokes the presence of a God who comes to do justice, to make things be as they should be. In every society there are strong and weak, powerful and impotent. As a result of the nonsolidarity of the human heart, most often the powerful use force to take advantage of the weak, violating their dignity and crushing their rights. The weak have no way to defend their rights; they can only die or be resigned to bearing the oppression and abuse imposed on them by the selfishness of the powerful. This unleashes a logic within history in which the powerful become ever more powerful by making the weak ever weaker and ever more subject to the whim of the strong. The idea of a just king who comes to exercise effectively his sovereignty entails his coming to establish justice by defending the rights of the poor and weak, who have no way of making that right effective.

That is precisely what the Hebrew expression *malkuth Yahweh*, Reign of Yahweh, evokes in the minds of the Israelites listening to Jesus. When they were liberated from slavery in Egypt, the people of God experienced God's justice-bearing action. But when oppressive abuses, and the scandalous division into poor and rich, appear amid the people of Israel, Yahweh again comes to the defense of the weak — orphans, widows, emigrants, day laborers, the poor — to make their right respected. So much is God seen to be taking sides with the poor — not only in the prophetic books — that there are even texts in the Hebrew scriptures that describe Yahweh to us not so much as a judge pronouncing sentence, but as one of the parties in court, taking on the defense of the poor and the oppressed, and accusing the rich oppressor. A quick reading of Psalm 72, a psalm of royal enthronement, is enough to grasp its understanding of a just king:

> He shall defend the afflicted among the people,
> save the children of the poor,
> and crush the oppressor. . . .
> For he shall rescue the poor man when he cries out,
> and the afflicted when he has no one to help him.
> He shall have pity for the lowly and the poor;
> the lives of the poor he shall save.

Hence, when Jesus proclaims that the Reign of God is coming, what he is announcing is the exercise of God's sovereign mercy, which in an unjust world takes the form of implanting justice and effectively recognizing the rights of the impoverished. This will entail a radical change in the situation of the poor, who until now have been condemned to inhuman living conditions, to die before their time and see their loved ones die before their time, clearly as a result of the arrogance and exploitation of the powerful. Naturally the change cannot but resound as good news, as great news, in the ears of the poor. Here is the meaning of the saying "Blessed are you who are poor, for yours is the reign of God." It means the proclamation of the end of their unjust oppression, the source of so much suffering and death. Things are going to change, for the better.

That the situation of the poor really changes, that the tears of those who weep will be dried, that the poor will leap for joy over the Good News Jesus brings, thus constitute Jesus' programatic presentation of his mission and the fundamental criterion for recognizing him as Messiah:

> The spirit of the Lord is upon me:
> therefore he has anointed me.
> He has sent me to bring glad tidings to the poor (Luke 4:18).

> Go back and report to John what you hear and see (Matt. 11:4).

If what is proclaimed is not good news for the poor, it is not the gospel of Jesus. Hence the initial response the proclamation of the Reign produces within the poor is one of joy and happiness. Later there will be a call to live up to the values of the coming Reign, by allowing God's merciful love to fill and transform them, but first they must feel the consolation of this presence that ends the causes of their affliction. The first word that the oppressed adulterous woman hears from Jesus is "No one has condemned you; you may go." But to receive God's mercy is a call to become merciful; the next line is "from now on, sin no more" (John 8:11).

4. The Dilemma of the Rich

But this change in the situation of the poor has to take place in a context where there is a causal, dialectical relationship between poverty and wealth. Basically the poor are *impoverished* due to hoarding and exploitation by the rich; and the rich are *enriched* at the cost of the impoverishment and misery of the masses. To free the poor by giving them access to living conditions consonant with their dignity as human beings and children of God entails sacrificing the privileges of wealthy oppressors. Hence when faced with the news that the Reign of God is coming, the rich feel challenged and called to accept God's justice and kindness, by allowing themselves to be re-created and changed by that justice into brothers and sisters, and persons in solidarity. "Be converted and believe the good news" (Mark 1:15). Only conversion, *metanoia*, change of mentality, new eyes in order to see reality with love in solidarity with which God views it, can enable the approach of the Reign to ring out as Good News in the ears of the rich—conversion to the God who comes in gratuity and kindness to remake things, to the God of the Reign.

But to be converted to this God is to be converted to the poor and their cause: "What you do to one of these, you do to me." And this conversion is hard, it is a frightfully radical change that demands that one be decentered, abandon the viewpoint of one's own interests and privileges, whether individual or of class or nation, in order to take a stand in favor of the interests of the poor. "I give half my belongings, Lord, to the poor. If I have defrauded anyone in the least, I pay him back fourfold" (Luke 19:8). At that point the Reign of God becomes Good News for Zacchaeus and salvation enters his house.

But what happens when the privileged, who monopolize wealth, knowledge, and power, take advantage of their strength to stubbornly defend their privileges and refuse to be converted to this God who is in solidarity with the poor? Jesus bluntly describes the inescapable choice: "You cannot serve God and money." After hearing Jesus' loving request, to "Go, sell what you have, and give to the poor," the rich young man's "face fell. He went away sad, for he had many possessions" (Mark 10:21–22). For him Jesus' word becomes bad news that makes him sad.

But even worse, the approach of the Reign that is coming to change the state of things in favor of the poor is seen as a threat to the interests of the rich. It interferes with the law of dog-eat-dog, with the law of selfishness. And the rich, clinging to their privileges, are not going to allow that: these dangerous edges of the gospel will have to be blunted and it will have to be reduced to spiritualistic discourse that has no impact on reality, or it will have to be silenced permanently. Jesus' life is marked by conflict with the socioreligious and religious powers of his age, because he stubbornly insists on not announcing a God without the Reign, but a God committed to the life of the poor. Religious challenge likewise becomes social challenge, and hence subversion, seeking to restructure society as God wants it. The powers of the world undertake a war to the death against this way of conceiving God, against this Good News to the poor. Jesus ends up being crucified.

How is it possible that God's goodness, acting humanly in Jesus, should provoke this rejection and aggression to the point of death, and death on a cross? The parable of the Good Shepherd sheds light on this question. A good shepherd is one who is concerned for the life of the sheep, and precisely out of that concern, is devoted to providing effective protection for their weakness. But what makes the good shepherd *good* is that he "gives his life for his sheep." Being concerned for the life of the sheep and giving one's life for them are inseparable; they are the essential traits of the good shepherd. Why? Because there are wolves who feed off the death of the sheep. When the good shepherd steps in to defend the sheep, the destructive power of the wolf falls on him, not because the wolf is concerned with the shepherd himself, but rather because the shepherd prevents him from getting at his prey. If the good shepherd could be bought off or intimidated, there would be no need to do away with him. But the good shepherd is the one who, as Archbishop Romero said — and he made it real with his own blood — "does not want security as long as it does not provide security for his flock."

III. WORD AND DEED: THE CONTEXT OF EVANGELIZATION

Having considered at least briefly the fundamental content of evangelization and how this content affects its bearer and its addressees, let me now say a word about how evangelization should be carried out in the concrete.

I have repeatedly emphasized that what comes first is mercy, the love that lets itself be affected by the other's situation. After Jesus sees and lets himself be moved by what he sees, his impulse of solidarity seeks to remedy the pressing situation of the other, and to communicate life to those who are prevented from living. But how to carry out this task?

The Synoptics summarize Jesus' evangelizing activity with this basic description: "he went about . . . proclaiming the good news of the reign, curing every kind of illness and disease." Proclaiming the Good News in words has been the usual, and until recently practically the only way of understanding evangelization. No doubt transmitting the gospel message through preaching, catechesis, liturgical celebration, and so forth is an essential element in the task of evangelization. It is the word that illuminates the meaning of events; it is the word that makes the Good News heard and issues the invitation to accept it through conversion; it is the word that explicitates and celebrates the hidden presence of God in the course of history: it is the word that unmasks and denounces the anti-Reign powers of resisting its transforming power.

But in order to be evangelizing, to be Good News, the word must be effective; a word that in some manner effects what it announces, an existential word that, like the uncreated Word, becomes incarnate in history and transforms it from within. In Jesus the word is accompanied by concrete deeds that make it real by transforming reality and effectively communicating life: "the lame walk, the blind see, the dead rise." It is these deeds that give the word its credibility, as anticipations *already* communicating life, although they are not the fullness of life: deeds that liberate from oppression, although they are not the final and complete liberation from all slavery; deeds that are an active presence of the reign, although they are not the eschatological and definitive incursion of the reign.

But word and deeds are the existential dimensions through which the primary reality of all evangelization, compassionate and merciful love, becomes embodied in history. It is this love that sometimes becomes word and at other times becomes deed, or both at once, in accordance with the concrete situation of those to whom it is addressed. Again it is enlightening to see how often the evangelists connect the gesture of *seeing* with all Jesus' activity, including preaching or issuing a personal challenge: "seeing the crowd . . . he taught them saying . . ."; "Looking at him, he loved him and he said to him . . ." Evangelizing is not repeating or having others memorize set formulas, as polished as they might seem. Evangelizing is saying the word needed, the word that is indeed Good News in the existential situation in which addressees find themselves. Evangelizing means changing the situation so that others can live the life that is theirs as human persons and children of God.

Whether the accent is to fall more on word or deeds will depend on the situation in which we are trying to make God's goodness present. When the Samaritan is lying unconscious on the road, what is useful right away is not a word, but action to save his life and heal his wounds. The moment will come, however, when the words can be heard and can help shed light on the deep meaning of some events in which God's loving mercy acting salvifically through the one who was capable of becoming a brother or sister has become present, even though no attention has hitherto been paid to that presence.

Word and deeds are both the concrete expression in history of what Jesus is: the clear visibility in human flesh of God's mercy; a concerned love that comes to liberate and communicate life. Of Jesus it is said that he "went about" places; his love does not remain still but is an impatient love from which there flows a way of being and acting that is in itself Good News. That Jesus is this way, that he speaks as he speaks, that he accepts the poor and sinners as he accepts them, that he stands up to the powers that be as he does, that he strives and wearies himself going about the roads of Palestine, that he forgives as he forgives the sinful woman and those who crucify him, that he dies as he does and rises as he does—in a word, that Jesus is as he is, is Good News. In his humanity, in what he is, there appears the very being, the very goodness and tenderness, of God: "Whoever sees me, sees the Father" (John 14:9). The God seen in Jesus is not the arbitrary God who imposes fear and punishes those who violate the established order, but the God who is close at hand and accepting, who more than anything else wants human beings to live, especially those whom the sinful structures of the world do not let live: the poor and the humble. The whole Jesus event is Good News.

Although I believe that what I have been saying up to this point sheds considerable light on the path we should follow as evangelizers today, I am going to try to spell out some aspects that may be more relevant in our present context.

1. Characteristics of Today's World

Without the slightest intention of being exhaustive, I am going to go over in summary fashion some of the characteristic traits of this contemporary world of ours in which we must carry out our vocation to evangelize.

To begin with, there is the phenomenon of the globalization of history. The enormous advance of communications has so shortened distances that for the first time we can speak correctly of *one* humankind, *one* history, and of social, economic, and political problems that are *common* to all humankind. A decision is made in the First World, and there is a great deal of suffering in Afghanistan, Central America, Angola, or the Middle East. The president sneezes in Washington and the great stock exchanges in Europe, Asia, or the Americas tremble. The International Monetary Fund stubbornly maintains an economic policy, and hundreds of miners and workers in Bolivia, Brazil, or Argentina are thrown into unemployment and hunger. The spread of international organizations, headed by the United Nations, clearly expresses the extent and importance of this phenomenon.

Paralleling such phenomena we find the rapid advance of science and technology, which is leading to the spectacular domination over nature that humankind is acquiring. The resulting spread of technology is unquestionably improving the quality of life of many men and women, and is arousing new hope in others. However, this is a technology monopolized and jealously guarded—at least in its most advanced levels—by the most powerful societies. The consequence is an increasing distance separating the strong from the weak and the appearance of new instruments and forms of oppression and exploitation.

Ours is an overdeveloped world with an impressive supply of consumer goods and services, but one in which there are more poor than ever. John Paul II states:

> Without going into an analysis of figures and statistics, it is sufficient to face squarely the reality of an *innumerable multitude of people*—children, adults and the elderly—in other words, real and unique human persons, who are suffering under the intolerable burden of poverty. There are many millions who are deprived of hope due to the fact that, in many parts of the world, their situation has noticeably worsened. (*Sollicitudo Rei Socialis*, no. 13)

Despite providing the technical possibility to do so, this development without solidarity has not been able to eradicate the dire poverty that condemns so many millions of human beings to early deaths.

Our world is marked by the lack of solidarity and the mistrust of people toward each other. A world is divided into blocs or groups whose interests are in conflict: East-West, North-South, capital-labor, rich-poor, Jews-Arabs, oppressive races-oppressed races. . . . They are different worlds within the one world. Today we speak of a First World, a Second World, a Third World, and even a Fourth World—worlds with quite different situations and conditions. A study made in 1983 sponsored by the Rockefeller Foundation and other respected institutions estimated that since the last world war there have been some 125 major armed conflicts, 95 of them in the Third World, resulting in many millions of deaths. Just in Central America more than two hundred thousand persons have been murdered since 1978, many of them horribly mutilated. The 1985 arms production reached $663 billion, almost $2 billion a day, which is itself triple the average annual budget of a country like El Salvador, while in the world every day fifty thousand children die of sheer malnutrition.

It is true that dozens of nations previously subject to the whim of empires have moved into political independence in recent years, but it is also true that instead of becoming autonomous and intent on moving toward participating justly in the goods and services destined for all, they become cogs in a huge machine. A new form of imperialism has arisen.

A plague typifying and revealing the imbalances and conflicts of the contemporary world are the millions of refugees whose "tragedy . . . is reflected in the hopeless faces of men, women, and children who can no longer find a home in a divided and inhospitable world" (*Sollicitudo Rei Socialis*, no. 24). To these are to be added the illegal immigrants subject to the greatest dangers and humiliations, rejected by a society that is afraid of seeing its own living standards lowered if it has to share its goods and resources with others.

I could certainly go on listing further characteristics: terrorism, foreign debt,

illiteracy, discrimination, unemployment, drugs. All of them contribute to reinforcing the image of a world that as a whole is inhospitable and inhumane, a
devastating world that has nothing in common with the project of a Father who
wants us all to be brothers and sisters. It is a world where, if in personal matters
there can be and is human sensitivity and solidarity, on structural levels, both
national and international, the law of the jungle still prevails. "Our vital interests," "the security of the nation," and so forth, are the high-sounding words
that conceal the idols of death. The real enemy of the God of Jesus is not the
atheism that denies God's existence, but far more this idolatry that sacrifices
millions of human victims before the altar of power and money.

Alongside all this there is a new awareness of the dignity and rights of the
poor—starting with the right to life, this minimum that is the maximum in
Archbishop Romero's phrase, and with it the right to participate in their own
history and destiny. God does not want things to go on as they are:

> From the depths of the countries that make up Latin America a cry is rising
> to heaven, growing louder and more alarming all the time. It is the cry of a
> suffering people who demand justice, freedom, and respect for the basic
> rights of human beings and peoples. (Puebla, 87)

2. Challenges to Evangelization

I now raise the key question: How to evangelize this kind of world? How to
respond to the "muted cry that wells up from millions of human beings, pleading
with their pastors for a liberation that is nowhere to be found?" (Puebla, 88).
How are we to make ourselves Good News for them? To begin with, by what
we are. It is the whole of our existence that has to be evangelizing. It is our
way of being church, it is the way we live as a religious institution, as Christians,
our way of relating to the situation of others, which primarily must be Good
News today, as in the time of Jesus, for the wretched of the earth, for the poor
and oppressed of this world. What we are, our charism and our manner of living
it out, must resound today in this world as a cry that proclaims God's mercy
and makes those who encounter and nourish their hope through us leap with
joy.

The Latin American bishops tell us that "the church must look to Christ
when it wants to find out what its evangelizing activity should be like" (Puebla,
1141). Let us recall rapidly what I noted about "the first and greatest evangelizer," applying it to ourselves.

Today the first thing we must do is let ourselves be evangelized, accept the
Good News of the merciful goodness of God and let ourselves be shaped by it
to the point of making our own mercy its manifestation and channel. This
means, as we were reminded earlier, conversion to the poor and oppressed,
conversion to our brothers and sisters in whose suffering faces we recognize
"the suffering features of Christ the Lord, who questions and challenges us"
(Puebla, 31). This conversion should apply to the whole church and to ourselves
along with it, for—I continue to quote the bishops at Puebla—"not all of us

... have committed ourselves sufficiently to the poor" (see nos. 1134 and 1140). Conversion and reconversion go forward where merciful love continually grows within us, leading us to an ever greater commitment and identification with the poor and their cause.

In a second moment, not so much chronological as dialectical, mercy takes on eyes to see the situation of the poor more profoundly. In our complex, unified, technological world, in which we are conscious that the shocking poverty and suffering of so many are not due to purely natural causes, but are the product of economic, social, and political situations and structures, we must especially look with merciful eyes, but also utilizing any tool that the human and social sciences can offer for interpreting these data coming from reality, so that our looking will not be naive but critical. An example of this new awareness is the Puebla Document "Evangelization in the Present and in the Future of Latin America." Part one bears the title "Pastoral Overview of the Reality that is Latin America." No "scientific" approach can replace the "pastoral" in this overview. Mercy remains the basic moving force of evangelization; but in the complexity of our world no uncritical and unenlightened mercy will be able to replace a mercy that in seeking effective response to real needs does not hesitate to also look through the lens of the human and social sciences in order to grasp better the drama of today's world and to be able to discern what is the appropriate word or action.

We should take this pastoral look, however, not from a far-off and protected tower, but from the committed closeness of incarnation. We must approach the situation of those for whom we must become Good News. And to approach is to enter into their painful reality, to let ourselves be moved by the brutality of their wounds. It means entering into this culture of poverty; it means suffering the impotence and outcast condition of indigenous people, the despair of drug addicts, the bitterness of mothers who weep for the children who have been snatched away from them. Today we have become aware of this characteristic of true evangelization, and we talk a lot about incarnation, inculturation, insertion, perhaps sometimes without grasping all that this demands of being humbled, of self-emptying. It is a matter of letting the situation and experience of the other speak to us and teach us, patiently, without rushing. In Latin America the initial evangelization took place under the sword; deities and cultures were overturned by force, and the faith was imposed, along with alien religious expressions and symbols. Today the hierarchy is speaking to us of a new evangelization, one made from within, from the very heart of outcast cultures, with absolute respect for the identity and freedom of peoples.

Looking and drawing near in this manner will lead to *compassion*. The other's passion becomes my passion as well, his or her suffering that hurts in my own flesh — and hence the urgency to do something to relieve the pain, to eliminate its causes. It will be a word that consoles, whether announcing or denouncing; it will be a concrete action that helps break chains, opening horizons of hope.

There are different ways of drawing near to the situation of the poor in a Christian manner. We do not have to think that the approach that enables us to grasp the situation of the other person and take action must necessarily entail coming close geographically. In this globalized world with modern means of communication, information flies. Solidarity between communities enables us to be very well informed and very close to the needs of the poor and take action about them by strengthening the evangelizing activity of those who are in fact physically in the midst of those needs. Today more than ever before, the image of the body acting through various organs illustrates the possibilities of the church's missionary action. It is organic solidarity that unleashes the capability of the whole for service.

I can attest firsthand how those Christians, including priests and religious, who challenge the laws that unjustly prohibit sheltering poor displaced foreigners are Good News in El Salvador; I have in mind the sanctuary movement. Or how those men and women who on the capitol steps struggle for the cause of peace in Central America or on behalf of Mexican immigrants enhance the credibility of our preaching of the gospel. No one can be everywhere or exhaust all the possibilities of evangelizing activity—not even Jesus, who precisely in becoming human flesh emptied himself and limited himself to one tiny point among the space-time coordinates of history. It is we who must embody him concretely and historically in our space and time. But the church as a whole is sent to "all nations," "to the ends of the earth," in order to be sacrament of salvation and to announce and realize the Good News of the Reign.

Let me continue to illustrate this presentation from the concrete situation of my own Salvadoran church. In order to contribute to the evangelization of El Salvador, there must be an incarnate presence of Christians, priests, men and women religious, missionaries who enter into the reality, history, and culture of this people and right there take up the crucial struggle for life and liberation, volunteers who are ready to carry their witness to the point of martyrdom. Ita, Dorothy, Maura, and Jean, along with Archbishop Romero and so many other martyrs today, continue to be Good News for the poor of El Salvador. "As long as there are persons like them who leave everything in order to come to share our life, to suffer and struggle with us, and to die like us and for us, we will have hope, since we know that the God of life has not abandoned us," said an old Salvadoran woman not long ago when the memory of the North American martyrs was being celebrated in a refugee camp.

Solidarity is giving and receiving. The evangelizer is evangelized. Faith, hope, grateful acceptance, the joy with which these persons celebrate life and the courage with which they take on death, the fact that they are as they are—all this in a thousand ways becomes Good News that provides the evangelist with meaning, joy, and affection. In them Christ becomes present, more crucified than glorious of course, but he is there and recognizable for those who have eyes to see him. Archbishop Romero used to say, "With this people it is not hard to be a good shepherd." This is the experience of the power that the Lord gives through the ones who, as in the time of Jesus, crowd together in hope around the good news and find there the strength to carry on with their liberating struggle.

Finally, we should not forget that a *good* shepherd is one who gives up his or her life. "Blessed are you when they insult you and persecute you and utter every kind of slander against you because of me. . . . They persecuted the prophets before you in the very same way" (Matt. 5:11). The world continues to resist being transformed by the Reign of God. The forces of the anti-Reign are frighteningly powerful and skillful. They know how to hide evil, distort truth, divide, and when they find it necessary, crush brutally. Archbishop Romero, and the thousands of martyrs who mark the recent history of Latin America, are a convincing proof of that.

In this world we have to pay a price for taking on the cause of the poor, a price that is not a matter of funds but of sharing the same lot and fate, by way of contempt, oppression, and repression. But what is important for our church and for our religious institutes: that the powerful of this world look on us approvingly and support us, or that we be a cry of hope, Good News for the despised of the earth? Jesus' words — "Whoever would save his life will lose it, but whoever loses his life for my sake will find it" — are applicable institutionally to the church and to ourselves.

IV. CONCLUSION

At the end of this survey at least three things seem to be clearly established: genuine evangelization can spring only from the root of a mercy that is translated into active solidarity. Whatever form evangelization may take, an inescapable criterion of whether or not it is Christian will always be its ability to be truly Good News for those crucified within our history. There is a price to pay, the "ransom for the many" (Mark 10:45), for fidelity to the evangelizing mission within a divided and sinful world.

From whatever may be our specific charism within the church, we must let ourselves be questioned and affected by the sufferings of our world and continually, under the guidance of the Spirit, strive to approach that world so we may really be the Good News of Christ. An exemplary model of this evangelizing attitude is Mary, type of the evangelizing church. She is the servant of the Lord, who places herself unconditionally at the liberating service of the God who approaches in goodness and mercy. She gives the Word its human flesh. She hands the Word over to humankind. In her are integrated, without reductionism of any sort, the two essential dimensions of evangelization, that which unites us with the one sending: the Father, from whom all salvation comes, and that which unites us to those to whom our mission directs us: the humble of the earth. Mary is "wholly Christ's and with him . . . wholly the servant of human beings" (Puebla, 294).

The mystery of the visitation is a beautiful compendium of what the church should be. With Christ made flesh in her womb, Mary undergoes the risks of the road to come near to her whose situation has been revealed as a sign. By her being and acting, which out of simplicity radiates the saving kindness she bears in her womb, she becomes Good News for Elizabeth, for the Baptist, for these poor persons to whom she in the Magnificat proclaims the joy of a God who does wonders in those who are humble like her, while casting the powerful down from their thrones.

May Mary's example help us to discern the signs of the times, faithful both to the Christ who sends us and to the poor to whom we are sent, and to find the path of evangelization that the modern world needs.

— Translated by Phillip Berryman

28

THE CRUCIFIED PEOPLE

IGNACIO ELLACURÍA

If we are to understand what the people of God is, it is very important that we open our eyes to the reality around us, the reality of the world in which the church has existed for almost two thousand years, since Jesus announced the approach of the Reign of God. This reality is simply the existence of a vast portion of humankind, which is literally and actually crucified by natural oppressions and especially by historical and personal oppressions. This reality prompts in the Christian spirit inescapable questions: What does the fact that most of humankind is oppressed mean for salvation history and in salvation history? Can we regard suffering humankind as saved in history when it continues to bear the sins of the world? Can we regard it as savior of the world precisely because it bears the sins of the world? What is its relationship with the church as sacrament of salvation? Is this suffering humankind something essential when it comes time to reflect on what the people of God is and what the church is?

Posing these questions indicates the historic gravity and theological relevance of the issue. Many christological and ecclesiological topics are wrapped up in this question; in fact, we could say that we find here the whole of christology and ecclesiology in their character as historic soteriology. How is the salvation of humankind achieved starting from Jesus? Who continues in history this essential function, this saving mission that the Father entrusted to the Son? The answer to these questions can give historic flesh to the people of God, and thus avoid dehistoricizing this basic concept, and also avoid spiritualizing or ideologizing it falsely. Historic soteriology provides an essential perspective in this regard.

Historic soteriology here means something referring to salvation, as it is presented in revelation. But the accent falls on its historic character and that in a double sense: as the achievement of salvation in the one and only human history and as humankind's active participation in that salvation, and specifically the participation of oppressed humankind. Which historically oppressed humankind it is that preeminently continues the saving work of Jesus, and the extent to which it does so, is something to be uncovered throughout this chapter. That task is one of the things required of historic soteriology and clarifies what such a soteriology must be. To begin with, it must be a soteriology whose essential reference point is the saving work of Jesus, but it must likewise be a soteriology that actualizes in history this saving work and does so as the continuation and following of Jesus and his work.

The analysis will be carried out from only one angle: the passion and death which unify the figure of Jesus with that of oppressed humankind. There are other angles but this one is essential and merits study by itself. At this point all life flows together and from it the future of history opens outward.

I. THE PASSION OF JESUS AS SEEN FROM THE CRUCIFIED PEOPLE; THE CRUCIFIXION OF THE PEOPLE AS SEEN FROM THE DEATH OF JESUS

Here we have something required by theological method as understood in Latin American theology: any situation in history should be considered from the angle of its corresponding key in revelation, but the focus on revelation should derive from the history to which it is addressed — although not any moment in history is equally valid for providing a proper focus. The first aspect seems obvious from the angle of Christian faith, even though it conceals a problem: that of finding the proper key in order not to take as the key for one situation one proper to another. The second aspect, which has a circular relationship with the previous one, is not so obvious, especially if we mean that the situation enriches and makes present the fullness of revelation, and if we mean that revelation cannot bear its fullness and its authenticity in any situation whatsoever.

In this instance we confront two crucial poles with regard to both revelation and situation. Treating them together clarifies a basic problem: the historicity of the passion of Jesus and the saving character of the crucifixion of the people. In other words, both the saving character of the salvation of Jesus and the saving character of the history of crucified humankind are clarified, once it is accepted that salvation is present in Jesus and this salvation must be worked out within humankind. Both the passion of Jesus and the crucifixion of the people are thereby enriched, and that means an enrichment of Jesus and of the people. However, that approach faces a very serious problem: making sense of the seeming failure involved in the crucifixion of a people after the definitive proclamation of salvation. Involved here is not only the failure of history, but also the direction and meaning in history for the vast majority of humankind, and even more important, the historic task of saving it.

Hence, the focus here is primarily soteriological. The accent will fall not on what Jesus and the people are, but on what they represent for the salvation of humankind. Of course we cannot separate what are called the ontological from the soteriological aspects, but we can accent one side or the other. Here the accent will be on the soteriological aspects, keeping in mind that the aim is not to reduce the being and mission of Jesus nor the being and mission of the people to the dimension of soteriology in history, although neither being nor mission in either case is properly illuminated if soteriological reflection is left aside.

If this warning is important for avoiding one-sided reflections on Jesus, which are so only if they are absolutized, it is also important for avoiding confusion about the historic task that falls to the oppressed people in their struggles in history. This task does not come down to simply that which shines out when it is likened to the passion and death of Jesus. Neither Jesus nor the crucified people, as they will be considered here, are the only salvation of history, although the salvation of history cannot reach fulfillment without both of them, even with respect to salvation in history. The former is clear and acknowledged, as long as the structural complexity of human history is taken into account; the latter is clear for believers, at least with regard to the first term, but it must be proven to nonbelievers. This should be done in such a way that their contribution to salvation is the historic verification of Christian salvation; at the same time, it should not be turned into a sweetening and mystification that would hinder the political organization of the people and their effective contribution to liberation in history.

To propose salvation on the basis of the crucifixion of Jesus and the people assumes the same scandal and madness, especially if we wish to give to salvation a content that can be verified in the reality of history, where *verifiable* does not mean *exhaustible*.

Today from a Christian standpoint it is not scandalous to say that life comes from the death of Jesus in history, even though it was indeed a scandal for those who witnessed that death and had to proclaim it. Nevertheless, we must recover that scandal and madness if we do not want to vitiate the history-making truth of the passion of Jesus. We must do that in three dimensions: with regard to Jesus himself, who only gradually was able to comprehend the true path toward proclaiming and bringing about the Reign of God; with regard to those who persecuted him to death, because they could not accept that salvation involved particular positions in history; and finally, with regard to scandal in the church, which leads the church to avoid passing through the passion when it proclaims the resurrection.

It is indeed scandalous to hold the needy and the oppressed as the salvation of the world in history. It is scandalous for many believers who no longer think they see anything striking in the proclamation that the death of Jesus brought life to the world, but who cannot accept in theory, and much less in practice, that today this life-giving death goes by way of the oppressed part of humankind. It is likewise scandalous to those who seek the liberation of humankind in history. It is easy to regard the oppressed and needy as those who are to be saved and liberated, but it is not easy to see them as saviors and liberators.

It is only fair to acknowledge that there are movements in history that regard the oppressed as the radical subject of salvation, and especially the subject of the liberation of peoples in history. We have, for example, this well-known text of Marx's from "Toward the Critique of Hegel's Philosophy of Law":

Where, then, is the *positive* possibility of German emancipation?
Answer: In the formation of a class with *radical chains*, a class in civil

society that is not of civil society, a class that is the dissolution of all classes, a sphere of society having a universal character because of its universal suffering and claiming no *particular* right because no *particular wrong* but *unqualified wrong* is perpetrated on it; a sphere that can invoke no *traditional* title but only a *human* title, which does not partially oppose the consequences but totally opposes the premises of the German political system; a sphere, finally, that cannot emancipate itself without emancipating itself from all the other spheres of society, thereby emancipating them; a sphere, in short, that is the *complete loss* of humanity and can only redeem itself through the *total redemption of humanity*. This dissolution of society as a particular class is the *proletariat*.

The proletariat is only beginning to appear in Germany as a result of the rising *industrial* movement. For it is not poverty from *natural circumstances* but *artificially produced* poverty, not the human masses mechanically oppressed by the weight of society but the masses resulting from the *acute disintegration* of society.

Heralding the *dissolution of the existing order of things*, the proletariat merely announces the *secret of its own existence* because it *is* the *real* dissolution of this order.

This text is clear proof that the oppressed have been regarded as an element of salvation when it comes to revolution. We must say that there is a deep religious inspiration in this text, which shows through the terminology. It does not, however, represent the whole of Marxist thought—much less its historic praxis—on the question. Marxist attacks on the lumpenproletariat as hindering the revolution, moreover, signal a viewpoint that if read not very vigorously could leave a vast sector of crucified humankind outside the course of history. We cannot enter into this point now, but we should not forget it. If it has been Marxist theory's genius that for historic reasons it attributes to the dispossessed a primordial role in the overall rescue of humankind, and in the building of the new person and the new earth, this does not mean that it has posed in all its universality and intensity, that is in its overarching scope, the contribution of the dispossessed to the integral salvation of human history.

Whether or not it is a scandal to hold that the passion and crucifixion of Jesus and of the people are central for human salvation, it is clear that precisely because of its implausibility as salvation, the passion of Jesus casts light on the implausibility of the people's crucifixion as salvation, while this latter hinders a naive or ideologized reading of the former.

On the one hand, the resurrection of Jesus and its effects in history are hope and future for those who remain in the time of passion. Certainly Jesus maintained hope in the definitive victory of God's Reign, to which he devoted his life and for which he died. Behind Luke 22:16-18 (and its parallel, Mark 14:25), despite the touching up done by the early community, we can reconstruct a double prophecy of the death of Jesus: after his death, Jesus will again celebrate the passover and will organize a banquet in the Reign of God, which of necessity must arrive. His death will not prevent the salvation to come and he himself will not remain imprisoned by death forever. Hence, as Schürmann says, the inbreaking of the Reign and Jesus' sudden death are not to be separated. Jesus' death is inseparately connected to the eschatological and historic coming of the Reign, and for that purpose the resurrection means not only a verification or consolation, but the assurance that this work must continue and that He remains alive to continue it.

This hope of Jesus was not of such a nature that the passion ceased being so, even to his anguished cry of abandonment on the cross. His struggle for the Reign, and his certainty that the Reign of God would triumph definitively, did not prevent him from "seeing" the connection between his personal days of tears, between the momentary failure of the coming of the Kingdom, and the glory of final victory. That is why he is an example for those who look more like the wretched of the earth than like its saviors. In being condemned personally, Jesus had to learn the road to definitive salvation—a salvation, let us repeat once more, that was essentially a matter of the coming of God's Reign and not a personal resurrection separate from what had been his earthly preaching of the Reign.

On the other hand, the ongoing passion of the people and paralleling it the historic reign of sin—as opposing the Reign of God—do not permit a reading of the death and resurrection of Jesus removed from history. The fundamental flaw in such a reading would lie in uprooting the history of the Reign of God so as to relegate it to a stage beyond history, so that it would no longer make sense to continue within history the life and mission of Jesus, who announced the Reign. That would be a betrayal of Jesus' life and death, which was entirely devoted not to himself but to the Reign. Moreover, identifying the Reign with the resurrection of Jesus would leave unfulfilled Jesus' message which predicted persecutions and death for those who were to continue his work. When Paul speaks of what is still wanting in the passion of Christ, he is rejecting a resurrection that ignores what is happening on earth. It is precisely the reign of sin that continues to crucify most of humankind and that obliges us to make real in history the death of Jesus as the actualized passover of the Reign of God.

II. THEOLOGICAL IMPORTANCE OF THE CROSS IN SALVATION HISTORY

An ascetic and moralizing focus on the Christian cross has nullified the importance of the cross in history and led to a rejection of everything that has to do with it. Such a rejection is fully justified if it is not simply a matter of the immature outburst of people being liberated from their emotional fantasies . The renewal of the mystery of the cross has little to do with gratuitous repression, which places the cross where one wants it and not in its real site, as though what Jesus had sought for himself was death on the cross and not the proclamation of the Reign.

Even more dangerous is the effort to evade the history of the cross in those theologies of creation and resurrection that at most make of the cross an incident or an isolated mystery that mystically projects its efficacy over human relationships with God.

A "naturalistic" view of creation, as faith inspired as it might regard itself, is ignorant of the novelty of the Christian God revealed in salvation history. It even ignores the fact that Israel did not come to the idea of the creator God through rational reflection on the course of nature, but through theological reflection on what had happened to the chosen people. Von Rad has shown clearly that it is in the political struggles of the Exodus that Israel becomes aware that Yahweh is its savior and redeemer, that this salvation has been conceived as the creation and launching of a people, and that faith in God who creates the world is a subsequent discovery that occurs when the historic experience of the people of Israel in the failure of the Exile gradually points it toward a universalizing consciousness, which demands a universal God, creator of all humans. Hence a faith apart from history, a faith apart from historic events, whether in the life of Jesus or in the life of humankind, is not a Christian faith. It would be at best a somewhat corrected version of theism.

Neither is a position that takes its support exclusively from the faith experience of the Risen One and ignores the historic roots of the resurrection. That temptation is an ancient one, and most probably came up even in the early communities, forcing them to emphasize very soon the continuity of the Risen One with the Crucified One. Otherwise, people live with the false assumption that the struggle against sin and death is over with the triumph of the resurrection. The Reign of God again would be reduced to something in the future, which either does not require human effort (because it is imminent), or reduces the Reign to the resurrection of the dead (because it is a long way off). If the life of the Risen One victorious over death is the future of salvation for Christians and for a new humankind, as Pannenberg points out, the life of the Risen One is the same life as that of Jesus of Nazareth, who was crucified for us, so that the immortal life of the Risen One is the future of salvation only insofar as we abandon ourselves to obedience to the Crucified One, who can overcome sin.

Hence, to connect creation and resurrection is false from a Christian viewpoint, whatever the understanding of the original "image and likeness," the historic process of death and resurrection. Every process in history is a creation of the future and not merely a renewal of the past. The fallen human is not restored, but rather the new human is built up; that new human is built up in the resurrection of one who has struggled from death against sin. To put it another way, eschatological hope is expressed equally as Reign of God and as resurrection of the dead, which for Pannenberg—who is not exactly a liberation theologian—means that the Reign of God is not possible as a community of human beings in perfect peace and total justice, without a radical change of the natural conditions that are present in human life, a change that is called the resurrection of the dead. He also says that the individual destiny and the political destiny of human beings go hand in hand.

Thus, the resurrection points back toward the crucifixion: the Crucified One rises, and rises because he was crucified; since his life was taken away for proclaiming the Reign, he receives a new life as fulfillment of the Reign of God. Thus, the resurrection points back toward the passion, and the passion points toward Jesus' life as proclaimer of the Reign. As is well-known, that is the sequence followed in putting the gospels together. The need to historicize the experience of the Risen One leads to a reflection on the passion story, which occupies a disproportionately large space in the gospel accounts, and which, in turn, requires historical justification in the narration of the life of Jesus. In any case, the gospels as a whole seek to give theological weight to two facts that are part of a single reality: the fact of Jesus' failure in the scandal of his death, and the fact of the persecution that the early communities soon undergo.

Hence, this is not an expiatory masochism of a spiritualizing sort, but the discovery of something real in history. It is not a matter of grief and mortification, but of making a break and a commitment. Jesus' death makes it clear why really proclaiming salvation runs up against the resistance of the world, and why the Reign of God does combat with the reign of sin. That is made manifest both in the death of the prophet, the one sent by God, and in the ravaging and death of humankind at the hands of those who make themselves gods, lording it over humankind. If a spiritualizing approach to the passion leads to an evasion of that commitment to history that leads to persecution and death, a historic commitment to the crucified people makes it necessary to examine the theological meaning of this death, and thus, to go back to the redeeming passion of Jesus. Reflecting historically on the death of Jesus helps us to reflect theologically on the death of the oppressed people, and the latter points back toward the former.

III. THE DEATH OF JESUS AND THE CRUCIFIXION OF THE PEOPLE ARE REALITIES OF HISTORY AND THE RESULT OF ACTIONS IN HISTORY

1. Historic Necessity of Jesus' Death

We may admit that the death of Jesus and the crucifixion of the people are necessary, but only if we speak of a necessity in history and not a merely natural necessity. It is precisely their nature as historic necessity that clarifies the deep reality of what happens in history, at the same time as it opens the way toward transforming history. That would not be the case if we were dealing with a merely natural necessity.

The scriptures themselves point out this necessity when they try to justify the passion of Jesus, and they even formulate it as a kind of principle: "Did not the Messiah have to undergo all this so as to enter into his glory?" (Luke 24:36). But this "having to" undergo "so as to" reach fulfillment is a historical "having to." It is historic not because the prophets had announced it, but because the prophets prefigured the events in what happened to them. Through what happened to the prophets, this necessity is grounded in the opposition between the proclamation of the Reign and the fact that sin is obviously a reality in history. The resistance of the oppressive powers and the struggle for liberation in history brought them persecution and death, but this resistance and struggle were simply the consequence in history of a life in response to God's word. That long experience, explicitly recalled by Jesus, leads to the conclusion that in our historic world arriving at the glory of God requires passing through persecution and death. The reason could not be clearer: If the Reign of God and the reign of sin are two opposed realities, and human beings of flesh and blood are the standard bearers of both, then those who wield the power of oppressive domination cannot but exercise it against those who have only the power of their word and their life, offered for the salvation of many.

Hence, this is not the biological image of a seed dying in order to bear fruit, nor of a dialectical law that demands undergoing death in order to reach new life. Of course, there are scripture texts that speak of the need for the seed to die; these texts point toward the necessity and the dialectical movement of this necessity, but they do not make it "natural." Making it natural would entail both eliminating the responsibility of those who kill prophets and those who crucify humankind, thereby veiling the aspect of sin in historic evil; it would also imply that the new life could emerge without the activity of human beings, who would not need to be converted internally or to rebel against what is outside. It is true that biological images of the Reign sometimes emphasize how the growth is God's affair, but we cannot, thereby, conclude that human beings should cease caring for the field of history.

Necessity in history, on the other hand forces us to emphasize the determining causes of what happens. Theologically speaking, the fundamental cause is expressed countless times to scripture: passing from death to glory is necessary only given the fact of sin, a sin that takes possession of the human heart, but especially a sin in history that collectively rules over the world and over peoples. There is, in Moingt's phrase, a "theological and collective sin," and it is to that sin that the proclamation of the death of Christ for our sins refers, not directly to our individual and ethical sins; it is a "collective reality," grounding and making possible individual sins. It is this theological and collective sin that destroys history and hinders the future that God wanted for history; this collective sin is what causes death to reign over the world, and hence, we must be freed from our collective work of death in order to form once more the people of God. It is Moingt himself who goes so far as to say that redemption is simultaneously "the political liberation of the people and their conversion to God."

This historic necessity differs in its relationship to death and to glory: it is necessary to go through death to reach glory, but glory need not follow death. There is one attitude for struggling against death and another for receiving life. In both cases, there is something external to the individual human being. The evil of the world, the sin of the world, is not simply the sum of particular individual actions, nor are these foreign to this sin that dominates them; likewise, the forgiveness and transformation of the world are things that human beings initially receive so as to then offer their own contribution. The external aspect is different in the case of evil and of good, of sin and grace; sin is the work of human beings, and grace is God's work, although it is something that operates within and through human beings, and thus, there is no question of passivity. Although God gives the growth, the effort of human beings is not excluded but in fact is required, especially for destroying the objective embodiment of sin, and then for building up the objective embodiment of grace. Otherwise, necessity would not have any historic character but would be purely natural, and the human being would be either the absolute negation of God or a mere executor of presumably divine designs.

The "necessary" character of Jesus' death is seen only after the fact. Neither his disciples nor he himself saw in the beginning and not through reflection on scripture, that the proclamation and victory of the Reign had to go by way of death. When it happened, the surprised minds of the believers found in God's designs, manifested in the words and deeds of the scriptures – Moses and the prophets – the signs of the divine will that made death "necessary."

This "necessity" is not based on notions of expiation and sacrifice. In fact, when the Servant of Yahweh in Deutero-Isaiah is used to explain the meaning of the death of Jesus, the thread of discourse is not "sin – offense-victim-expiation-forgiveness." This framework, which may have some validity for particular mindsets and which expresses some valid points, may turn into an evasion of what must be done in history in order to eliminate the sin of the world. In times when consciences were oppressed or felt oppressed by a Christianity centered on the idea of sin, of guilt, and of eternal condemnation, it was utterly necessary that there be a framework of forgiveness, in which a God offended forgave sin and wiped out condemnation. But even with its valid points this framework does not emphasize either the collective embodiment of sin or human activity – destroying injustice and building love – which are "necessary" in history. A new theology of sin must move beyond the expiatorial frameworks but should not permit the existence of sin itself to be forgotten. To forget it would, among other things, leave the field open to the forces of oppression, which are overwhelmingly dominant in our world, and it would also neglect the area of personal conversion.

2. Implications

Emphasizing the historic character of the death of Jesus is fundamental for Christology and for a history-engaged soteriology, which as such would take on a new meaning.

The historic character of the death of Jesus entails, to begin with, that his death took place for historic reasons. New christologies are increasingly emphasizing this point. Jesus dies – is killed as both the four gospels and Acts so insist – because of the historic life he led, a life of deeds and words that those who represented and held the reins of the religious, socioeconomic and political situation could not tolerate. That he was regarded as a blasphemer, one who was destroying the traditional religious order, one who upset the social structure, a political agitator, and so forth, is simply to recognize from quite distinct angles that the activity, word, and very person of Jesus in the proclamation of the Reign were so assertive and so against the established order and basic institutions that they had to be punished by death. Dehistoricizing this radical reality leads to mystical approaches to the problem, not by way of deepening but by way of escape. We cannot simply settle the matter of the "died for our sins" by means of the expiatory victim, thereby leaving the direction of history untouched.

It likewise implies that Jesus followed a particular direction in history not because it would lead to death or because he was seeking a redemptive death, but rather because that was what truly proclaiming the Reign of God demanded. Whether the emphasis be on the soteriological character of Jesus' death, as in Paul, or on the soteriological character of the resurrection, as in Luke, it cannot be forgotten that the historic Jesus sought for himself neither death nor resurrection but the proclamation of the Reign of God to the point of death, and that brought resurrection. Jesus saw that his action was leading to a mortal showdown with those who could take his life, and it is utterly inconceivable that he did not realize that he was probably going to die, and even soon, and realize why this was so. Indeed, he was aware earlier and better of the saving value—in a broad sense—of his person and his life than of the saving value of his death. He does not begin by focusing his activity on waiting for death but on the proclamation of the Reign; even when he sees death as a real possibility, he does not hesitate in that proclamation or shrink back from his conflict with power. Putting all the saving value on his death cannot be reconciled with his life and his demands of his disciples; it cannot be said that there is in him a gradual shift from life to death as the center of his message, since ever in the many texts about following him being difficult and contradictory, the accent is on the continuity of life with death and not on the break of death with regard to the way of salvation that his life represents.

Salvation, therefore, cannot be made exclusively a matter of the mystical fruits of the death of Jesus, separating it from his real and verifiable behavior. It is not merely a passive and obedient acceptance of a natural fate, let alone a fate imposed by the Father. It is, at least in a first level, an action that leads to life by way of death, in such a way that in the case of Jesus what is salvific cannot be separated from what is historic. Consequently, Jesus' death is not the end of the meaning of his life, but the end of that pattern that must be repeated and followed in new lives with the hope of resurrection and thereby the seal of exaltation. Jesus' death is the final meaning of his life only because the death toward which his life led him shows what was likewise the historic meaning and the theological meaning of his life. It is, thus, his life that provides the ultimate meaning of his death, and only as a consequence does his death, which has received its initial meaning from his life, give meaning to his life. Therefore, his followers should not focus primarily on death as sacrifice, but on the life of Jesus, which will only really be his life if it leads to the same consequences as his life did.

Historic soteriology is a matter of seeking where and how the saving action of Jesus was carried out in order to pursue it in history. Of course, in one sense, the life and death of Jesus is over and done, since what took place in them is not simply a mere fact whose value is the same as that of any other death that might take place in the same circumstances, but was, indeed, the definitive presence of God among human beings. But his life and this death continue on earth, and not just in heaven; the uniqueness of Jesus is not in his standing apart from humankind, but in the definitive character of his person and in the saving all-presence that is his. All the insistence on his role as head to a body, and on the sending of his Spirit, through whom his work is to be continued, point toward this historic current of his earthly life. The continuity is not purely mystical and sacramental, just as his activity on earth was not purely mystical and sacramental. In other words, worship, including the celebration of the eucharist, is not the whole of the presence and continuity of Jesus; there must be a continuation in history that carries out what he carried out in his life and as he carried it out. We should acknowledge a trans-historic dimension in Jesus' activity, as we should acknowledge it in his personal biography, but this trans-historic dimension will only be real if it is indeed trans-historic, that is, if it goes through history. Hence, we must ask who continues to carry out in history what his life and death was about.

3. The Crucified People, Principle of Universal Salvation

We can approach the question by taking into account that there is a crucified people, whose crucifixion is the product of actions in history. Establishing that may not be enough to prove that this crucified people is the continuation in history of the life and death of Jesus. But before delving into other aspects which prove that such is the case, it is well to take the same starting point as that of the saving value of the death and life of Jesus.

What is meant by crucified people here is that collective body, which as the majority of humankind owes its situation of crucifixion to the way society is organized and maintained by a minority that exercises its dominion through a series of factors, which taken together and given their concrete impact within history, must be regarded as sin. This is not a purely individual way of looking at every person who suffers even due to unjust actions by others or because such a person is immolated in the struggle against the prevailing injustice. Although looking collectively at the crucified people does not exclude an individual perspective, the latter is subsumed in the former, since that is its historic context. Nor is the viewpoint here one of looking at purely natural misfortunes, although natural evils play a role, albeit derivatively, insofar as they take place in a particular order within history.

Not only is it not foreign to scripture to regard a collective body as subject of salvation, but that is in fact its primordial thrust. For example, as J. Jeremias points out, an individual can only become a servant of Yahweh insofar as he or she is a member of the people of Israel, since salvation is offered primarily to the people and within the people. The communal experience that the root of individual sins is in a presence of a supra-individual sin and that each one's life is shaped by the life of the people in which he or she lives, makes it connatural to experience that both salvation and perdition are played out primarily in this collective dimension. The modern concern to highlight the individual side of human existence will be faithful to reality only if it does not ignore its social dimension. That is not the case in the individualistic and idealistic frenzied individualism and idealism that is so characteristic of Western culture, or at least of its elites. All the selfishness and social irresponsibility borne by this notion is but the reverse proof of how false this exaggeration is. There is no need to deny the collective and structural dimension in order to give scope to the full development of the person.

From a theological standpoint, this assertion is not arbitrary, and it is even less so in terms of the real situation. It is something obvious in historical experience now viewed from the standpoint of soteriology. One who is concerned as a believer for the sin and salvation of the world cannot but realize that in history humanity is crucified in this concrete form of the crucified people; by the same token one who reflects as a believer on the mangled reality of this crucified people must inquire what there is of sin and need for salvation here. In view of this situation, which is so extensive and so serious, considering the particular cases of those who do not belong to the crucified people becomes quite a secondary matter, although we should here repeat that the universalist and structural approach by no means has to do away with the individualistic and psychological approach, but simply provides it with a framework rooted in reality. What Christian faith adds after it is really clear that there is a crucified people is the suspicion that, besides being the main object of the effort of salvation, it might also in its very crucified situation be the principle of salvation for the whole world.

This is not the place to determine the extent and the nature of the ongoing oppression of the bulk of humankind today or to carry out a detailed study of its causes. Although it is one of the fundamental realities that should serve as a starting point for theological reflection, and although it has been scandalously ignored by those who theorize from the geographical world of the oppressors, it is so obvious and widespread that it needs no explanation. What it does need is to be lived experientially.

Now although there are undeniably "natural" elements in the present situation of injustice that defines our world, there is also undeniably a side that derives from actions in history. Just as in the case of Jesus, we cannot speak of a purely natural necessity, so the oppression of the crucified people derives from a necessity in history: the necessity that many suffer so a few may enjoy, that many be dispossessed so that a few may possess. Moreover, the repression of the people's vanguards follows the same pattern as the case of Jesus, although with different meanings.

This general formulation should be made in historic terms. It does not happen everywhere in the same way or for the same reasons, since the general pattern of the oppression of humans by humans takes on very different forms both collectively and individually. In our universal situation today, oppression has some overall characteristics in history that cannot be ignored, and those who do not take a stand on the side of liberation are culpable, whether actively or passively.

Thus, within this collective and overall framework more specific analysis must be carried out. While maintaining the universal pattern of people crucifying others in order to live themselves, the subsystems of crucifixion that exist in both groups, oppressors and oppressed, should also be examined. As has often been pointed out, in a number of ways among the oppressed themselves, some put themselves at the service of the oppressors or give free rein to their impulses to dominate. This serious problem forces us to get beyond simplistic formulas with regard to both the causes of oppression and to its forms, so as not to fall into a Manichean division of the world, which would situate all good in the world on one side and all evil on the other. It is precisely a structural way of looking at the problem that enables us to avoid the error of seeing as good all the individuals on one side and as evil those on the other side, thus leaving aside the problem of personal transformation. Flight from one's own death in a continual looking out for oneself and not acknowledging that we gain life when we surrender it to others, is no doubt a temptation that is permanent and inherent in the human being, one that structures and history modulate but do not abolish.

The focus on the death of Jesus and the crucifixion of the people, the fact that they refer back and forth to each other, makes both take on a new light. The crucifixion of the people avoids the danger of mystifying the death of Jesus, and the death of Jesus avoids the danger of extolling salvifically the mere fact of the crucifixion of the people, as though the brute fact of being crucified of itself were to bring about resurrection and life. We must shed light on this crucifixion out of what Jesus was in order to see the salvific scope and the Christian nature of this salvation. To that end we must examine the principles of life that are intermingled with the principles of death; although the presence of sin and death is overwhelming in human history, the presence of grace and of life is also very prominent and palpable. We must not lose sight of either aspect. Indeed, salvation can only be understood as a victory of life over death, a victory already announced in the resurrection of Jesus, but one that must be won in a process of following his steps.

IV. JESUS' DEATH AND THE PEOPLE'S CRUCIFIXION IN TERMS OF THE SERVANT OF YAHWEH

One of the approaches on which the primitive Christian community fastened in order to understand Jesus' death, and give it its adequate value, was the figure of the Servant of Yahweh as described in Second Isaiah. This entitles us to appeal once more to the Suffering Servant in order to see what, in one of its aspects, the death of Jesus was, and especially what, in one of its aspects, the crucifixion of the people is.

Thus, this section will have three parts. In the first, we shall list some of the characteristics of the Servant as proposed in Second Isaiah. In the second part, we shall align these characteristics with the concrete reality of Jesus' life and death. Finally, in the third part of this section, we shall draw up a corresponding list of what are or ought to be the characteristics of the oppressed people if they are to be the extension of Jesus' redemptive work. The first two parts will be orientated toward the third: thus, even if we do not manage to show that the oppressed people are the historical extension of the crucifixion, and of the Crucified one, at all events we shall have indicated the route to be followed if that people is to conform its death with that of Christ—keeping account, meanwhile, of the distinction between the two realities, and of the different functions incumbent upon each.

1. Characteristics of the Servant of Yahweh

We shall make our analysis of the afflicted servant of Yahweh from the outlook of the crucified people. Any reading is done from a situation—more than from a pre-understanding, which is in some sort determined by the situation. Those who claim to be able to do a neutral reading of a text of scripture commit a twofold error. First, they commit an epistemological error: they attempt to do a nonconditioned reading, which is impossible. And they commit a theological error: they neglect the richest locus of any reading, which will always be the principal addressee of the text in question. This addressee is different at each historical moment, and the hypothesis with which we are working is that at this particular moment of ours the addressee of the Songs of the Servant is the crucified people—a hypothesis that will be confirmed if indeed the text sheds light on what the crucified people are, and if, conversely, the text is enriched, and endowed with currency, by the reality that is this historical addressee. This is not the place for a discussion of the epistemological and theological justification of this methodological procedure—which does not exclude the most careful utilization of exegetical analyses, but only subordinates them. Suffice it to have enunciated this procedure in order not to go astray in our analysis of the text at hand.

Our analysis will prescind from whether the "servant" is a collective or individual personage, a king or a prophet, and so on. None of this is relevant for our purpose, since what we formally intend here is to see what the text says to the oppressed people—what the text declares to this historical addressee. What we propose, of course, is not an exhaustive treatment, but an indication of the basic lines of the text in question.

The theology of the Servant proposes that the encounter with Yahweh occurs in history, and that that encounter thus becomes the locus both of Yahweh's intimate presence with the people, and of the people's response and responsibility (Joachim Jeremias). The unity prevailing between what occurs in history and what God seeks to manifest and communicate to human beings is, in the text of Second Isaiah, indissoluble. We need only recall the references we find in that text to the humiliation of Babylon, or to the triumph of Cyrus, in order to have overwhelming proof of this. This is the context in which the four Songs of the Suffering Servant must be read.

The First Song (Isa. 42:1-7) speaks of the election of the Servant. He is a chosen one, a favorite of Yahweh: upon him God has placed his spirit. The finality of this election is explicitly proclaimed: "He shall bring forth justice to the nations." Indeed, not content with this quite explicit formulation, the sacred writer emphasizes and amplifies it:

A bruised reed he shall not break,
and a smoldering wick he shall not quench,

> Until he establishes justice on the earth;
>   the coastlands will wait for his teaching.

In question, accordingly, is an objective implantation of right—especially, of justice in the real, concrete sense of justice to be done to an oppressed people. It is a matter of creating laws in which justice, rather than the interests of the mighty, has the preeminence (although account is also kept of the need for an interiorization of the love of justice). That is, what is at stake is the appearance on the scene of a new human being, who would actually live, and experience, right and justice. Likewise, there is a universal gaze upon the nations and the "coastland"—that is, a purely Judaic ambit is transcended. Finally, all of this will be God's response to that which peoples deprived of justice and right await, what they hope for—a response to be implanted by the Servant, who will never waver or be shaken in his mission.

The election, the choice, is God's. Political as the Servant's mission may appear in its first stage (there is no talk of restoring worship, converting sinners, or the like, but only of the implantation of right), this is what is wanted by that God who "created the heavens and stretched them out," by the God who consolidated the earth. After all, it is that God who has chosen the Servant in order to cause justice to be, in order to do justice:

> I, the Lord, have called you for the victory of justice,
>   I have grasped you by the hand;
> I formed you, and set you
>   as a covenant of the people,
>   a light for the nations. (NAB 2:6)

And the Song repeats, with explanation, what it is to do justice:

> To open the eyes of the blind,
>   to bring out prisoners from confinement,
>   and from the dungeon, those who live in darkness. (42:7)

And thus says the Lord, for "Lord" is his name: that is, this is how his being for created persons is expressed, in this is his proclamation of a future in contrast to what has been occurring.

The Second Song underscores the nature of this election by God. God has chosen someone whom the mighty despise, who seemingly lacks the strength to have justice reign over the world, and who, nevertheless, has God's backing and support:

> Yet my reward is with the Lord,
>   my recompense is with my God . . .
> Thus says the Lord,
>   the redeemer and the Holy One of Israel,

To the one despised, whom the nations abhor,
    the slave of rulers;
When kings see you, they shall stand up,
    and princes shall prostrate themselves
Because of the Lord who is faithful,
    the Holy One of Israel who has chosen you. (49:4, 7)

The purpose of the election is the building of a new land and a new people: "To restore the land and allot the desolate heritages" (49:8). The people will emerge from their state of poverty, oppression, and darkness into a new state of abundance, liberty, and light. And the reason for God's intervention through his servant is clear:

For the Lord comforts his people
    and shows mercy to his afflicted. (49:13)

This notion, that God is on the side of the oppressed, and against the oppressor, is fundamental in the text, and refers to an entire people, and not merely to particular individuals:

I will make your oppressors eat their own flesh,
    and they shall be drunk with their own blood
    as with the juice of the grape.
All humankind shall know
    that I, the Lord, am your savior,
    your redeemer, the Mighty One of Jacob. (49:26)

The Third Song takes a new step, setting in relief the potential importance of suffering in the people's march toward liberation. The long experience of being crushed can lead to a shattered confidence, of course, but the Lord means to support that suffering, and put an end to it, giving victory to someone seemingly confounded and routed:

The Lord God is my help,
    therefore I am not disgraced [*do not feel the outrages];
I have set my face like flint,
    knowing that I shall not be put to shame. (50:7)

A great hope arises, a hope bearing on the future of the afflicted and persecuted. The suffering of these is not in vain. God stands behind them. And this is a hope which they shall touch with their hands, and which will transform their lives altogether:

Those whom the Lord has ransomed will return
    and enter Zion singing,
    crowned with everlasting joy;

> They will meet with joy and gladness,
>   sorrow and mourning will flee. (51:11)

But it is the Fourth Song that most explicitly and extensively develops the theme of the Servant's passion and glory. Here the rhetorical figure of contraposition is employed, strikingly, in order to focus the Servant's real situation, and concrete capacity for salvation:

> See, my servant shall prosper,
>   he shall be raised high and greatly exalted.
> Even as many were amazed at him—
>   so marred was his look beyond that of man,
>   and his appearance beyond that of mortals—
> So shall he startle many nations,
>   because of him kings shall stand speechless;
> For those who have not been told shall see,
>   those who have not heard shall ponder it. (52:13-15)

It is here that the description of the persecution of the Servant in his mission of "implanting right" acquires characteristics very similar to those that the oppressed people suffer today:

> He grew up like a sapling before him,
>   like a shoot from the parched earth;
> There was in him no stately bearing to make us look at him,
>   nor appearance that would attract us to him.
> He was spurned and avoided by men,
>   a man of suffering, accustomed to infirmity,
> One of those from whom men hide their faces,
>   spurned, and we held him in no esteem.
>
> Yet it was our infirmities that he bore,
>   our sufferings that he endured,
> While we thought of him as stricken,
>   as one smitten by God and afflicted.
>
> But he was pierced for our offenses,
>   crushed for our sins;
> Upon him was the chastisement that makes us whole,
>   by his stripes we were healed.
> We had all gone astray like sheep,
>   each following his own way;
> But the Lord laid upon him
>   the guilt of us all.
>
> Though he was harshly treated, he submitted
>   and opened not his mouth . . .

Oppressed and condemned, he was taken away,
    and who would have thought any more of his destiny?

When he was cut off from the land of the living,
    and smitten for the sin of his people,
A grave was assigned him among the wicked
    and a burial place with evildoers,
Though he had done no wrong
    nor spoken any falsehood.

If he gives his life as an offering for sin,
    he shall see his descendants in a long life,
    and the will of the Lord shall be accomplished through him.
Because of his affliction
    he shall see the light in fullness of days.
Through his suffering my servant shall justify many
    and their guilt he shall bear.
Therefore I will give him his portion among the great,
    and he shall divide the spoils with the mighty,
Because he surrendered himself to death
    and was counted among the wicked;
And he shall take away the sins of many,
    and win pardon for their offenses. (53:2-12)

This text, which is fundamental for any salvation theology, any soteriology, admits of various readings, since it can elucidate different problems. In the problem at hand, it is impossible to ignore the applicability of the description in the text to what is occurring today among the crucified people. A reading that has become traditional sees a prefiguration of Jesus' passion here. But this is no reason why we should shut our eyes to the element of concrete description — all "scriptural accommodation" notwithstanding — of what is today a vast majority of humanity. From this outlook, we may underscore certain historico-theological moments in this impressive Song.

In the first place, the personage we contemplate is a figure shattered by the concrete, historical intervention of human beings. We have a person of sorrows here, someone accustomed to suffering, who is carried off to death in helplessness and injustice. Scorned and contemned by all, he is someone in whom there is no visible merit.

In the second place, not only is this figure not regarded as a potential savior of the world, but, quite the contrary, he is regarded as someone who might have leprosy, someone sentenced to death, someone wounded by God, someone brought low, and humiliated.

In the third place, he appears as a sinner — as the fruit of sin and as filled with sins. Accordingly, he was given burial with the wicked, and with evildoers. He has been reckoned among sinners, because he took upon himself the burden of the sin of so many.

In the fourth place, the believer's view of things is a different view. The Servant's state is not due to his own sins. He suffers sin without having committed it. He has been pierced for our rebellions and crushed for our crimes — wounded for the sins of the people. He has taken on sins that he has not committed: thus, he is in his desperate situation because of the sins of others. Antecedently to his dying for sins, it is sins who have carried him off to death. It is sins that kill him.

In the fifth place, the Servant accepts this lot, this destiny. He accepts the fact that it is the weight of sins that is bearing him off to death, although he has not committed them. By reason of the sins of others, for the sins of others, he accepts his own death. The Servant will justify so many, because he has taken their crimes on himself. Our punishment has fallen on him, and his scars have healed us. His death, far from being meaningless and ineffective, removes, provisionally, the sins that had been afflicting the world. His death is expiation, and intercession for sins.

In the sixth place, the Servant himself, crushed in his sacrificed life and in the failure of death, triumphs. Not only will others see themselves justified, but he will see his offspring and will live long years. He will see light, and be satiated with knowledge.

In the seventh place, it is the Lord himself who adopts this condition. God takes our crimes on himself. Indeed, we read that the Lord actually wished to crush the Servant with suffering, and deliver his life over in expiation for sin, although afterwards he will reward him, and give him complete recompense. This is very strong language. But it admits of the interpretation that God accepts as having been wished by himself, as salutary, the sacrifice of someone who has concretely died for reason of the sins of human beings. Only in a difficult act of faith is the sacred writer able to discover, in the Songs of the Servant, that which seems to the eyes of history to be the complete opposite. Precisely because he sees someone burdened with sins that he has not committed, and crushed by their consequences, the singer of these songs makes bold, by virtue of the very injustice of the situation, to ascribe all of this to God: God must necessarily attribute a fully salvific value to this act of absolute concrete injustice. And the attribution can be made because the Servant himself accepts his destiny to save, by his own suffering, those who are actually the causes of it.

Finally, the comprehensive orientation of this Fourth Song, together with that of the three that have preceded — their prophetic sense of a proclamation of the future, and their ambit of universality — prevent a univocal determination of the Servant's historical concretion. The Suffering Servant of Yahweh will be anyone who discharges the mission described in the Songs — and, par excellence, will be the one discharging it in more comprehensive fashion. Or better, the Suffering Servant of Yahweh will be anyone unjustly crucified for the sins of human beings, because all of the crucified form a single unit, one sole reality, even though this reality has a head and members with different functions in the unity of expiation.

For all the accentuation of the traits of suffering and seeming failure, the hope of triumph emerges paramount. And it is a hope, let us not forget, that must have a public, concrete character, and a relationship with the implantation of right and justice. No "substitutive" elements it may have militate against its historical reality and effectiveness.

2. Life and Death of Jesus, and the Servant of Yahweh

Before any Christian interpretation of the Suffering Servant had come to be, this figure had already been set in relationship with that of the Messiah. One line of theological reflection saw that the triumph of the Messiah would come only after a passage through pain and suffering, and this precisely because of the existence of sin. It is impossible to ignore the fact that Second Isaiah itself, which so strongly emphasizes Yahweh's love for the people, places harsh reproaches in the mouth of God when it comes to that people's wicked behavior. The mystery of sin and evil continues to make its way toward integration into a more complete interpretation of God's activity in history.

The New Testament does not teem with explicit references to the Servant of Yahweh. The title, *pais Theou*, appears only once in Matthew (12:15) and four times in Acts (3:13-26, 4:27-30). However, the theology of the Suffering Servant of Yahweh, along lines of suffering and oblation for sins, is of prime importance in the New Testament for the attempt undertaken there to present a theological explanation of the historical fact of Jesus' death. The almost complete disappearance of the term may be attributed to the fact that the Hellenistic communities very soon began to prefer the title, "Son of God," to that of "servant of God," which they less readily assimilated. For Joachim Jeremias, the christological interpretation of the Servant of Yahweh of Second Isaiah belongs to the earliest Christian communities, and corresponds to the Palestinian, pre-Hellenistic stage. Cullmann maintains that the christology of the Servant is probably the oldest christology of all.

However, it is not the common opinion of exegetes that Jesus himself was aware of being the Servant of Yahweh spoken of in Second Isaiah. We need not enter into this discussion here, since our concern is to emphasize that the primitive community justifiably saw the theological background of the Suffering Servant in the historical events of the life of Jesus, so that, without being explicitly aware of it, Jesus will have carried out the Servant's mission. It might be objected that the concrete events narrated in the gospels are only the historical flesh placed by the primitive communities on the framework of their theological thought concerning the Servant, in order to historicize that thought. But even in that case—which does not seem, across the board, to represent an acceptable explanation—we would be satisfied with this acknowledgment of the need for a historicization of salvation and of the manner of salvation. If, on the other hand, Jesus himself was aware that he was the full realization of the Suffering Servant of Yahweh, obviously he did not have this consciousness from the beginning of his life, or even from the commencement of his public life; from which we must again conclude that only his real, concrete life of proclamation of the Reign and of opposition to the enemies of the Reign led him to an acceptance, in faith and hope, of the salvific destiny of the Servant: in both

Jesus and the Servant, the struggle with sin came before death for and by sin.

On the face of it, it is difficult to admit that Jesus publicly and solemnly manifested the notion that his death was to have a salvific scope (Schürmann). Jesus' preaching and behavior are not orientated toward his future death, and do not depend upon it (Marxsen). A more difficult question is whether he did communicate the salvific meaning of his death to his closest disciples, at least on the eve of his passion, if not indeed when they were sent on the mission of announcing the Reign. In order to answer this question, we should of course have had to be present at the Last Supper. We cannot enter in depth into this question here, but we can rely on exegetes' intermediate positions, between Jeremias' literal positivism and Bultmann's historical skepticism. Schürmann, after a lengthy exegetical analysis, concludes as follows. The deeds of offering of someone who is going to die and who proclaims eschatological salvation are best explained in a soteriological perspective. In these deeds of the Servant performed by Jesus, eschatological salvation becomes comprehensible in the symbolic activity of someone willing to give the gift of self to the very hilt, to very death as a culmination of all of that person's life, which in turn has ever been a pro-existence — that is, it has always been a life defined by its total commitment to others. An acknowledgement, after the Resurrection, of the salvific value of Jesus' death was possible only on the basis of Jesus' pro-existent attitude, as solemnly expressed in the actions of the Last Supper and as reconsidered in the light of the scriptures, especially in the light of the Suffering Servant. It came to be seen that Jesus' death was necessary, that it was conformable to the scriptures, that it had a salvific value for those who had followed him and that that value could be extended to the sins of the many.

Running counter to a full self-understanding, in terms of his death, on the part of Jesus himself, however, is his cry on the cross as reported by Matthew (27:26) and Mark 15:35), which seems to indicate an absolute abandonment by God, and consequently a failing in Jesus' faith and hope. The difficulty presented by this text is so grave that the other evangelists substitute words of trust (Luke 23:46-47) or consummation (John 19:30). Indeed, since it is possible to see, in Jesus' words of abandonment, the first words of Psalm 22, which ends with words of hope similar to those of the Song of the Servant, we cannot be certain that the tenor and sense of the words placed on Jesus' lips by Matthew and Mark is one of dereliction by God. For Xavier Léon-Dufour, Jesus intended to express his state of dereliction, his condition of abandonment, that is death, a death which in and of itself is separation from the living God. However, the experience of abandonment is simultaneously proclaimed and denied in a dialogue expressing the presence of the one who seems absent — a dialogue that abides uninterrupted, even though God seems to have disappeared. Jesus calls Yahweh not "Father," but — the only time he does so in the Synoptics — "God." All of this arouses the suspicion that the "Why have you forsaken me" remains without immediate response, which will only appear after his death, and which the evangelists posit in the voice of the centurion: "Clearly this man was the Son of God!" (Mark 15:39).

Consequently, although Jesus would not have had an explicit awareness of the complete meaning of his death, he would have had the firm hope that his life and death were the immediate announcement of the Reign — in other words, that the definitive coming of the Reign was through his life and his death, between which a continuity must be accepted, so that his death was but the culmination of his life, the definitive moment of his total surrender and commitment to the proclamation and the realization of the Reign. And all of this to the point that the sacrificial and expiatory meaning of the sufferings of the Suffering Servant would be more clear than that of Jesus' death. Only later would that death come to be understood as that of the universal victim of the sins of the world.

Obviously, the crucified people is not explicitly conscious of being the Suffering Servant of Yahweh, but as in the case of Jesus, that is not a reason to deny that it is.

Nor would the fact that Jesus is the Suffering Servant be such a reason, since the crucified people would be his continuation in history, and thus, we would not be talking of "another" servant. Hence, it would be sufficient to show that the crucified people combines some essential conditions of the Suffering Servant to show that the people constitute the most adequate site for the embodiment of the Servant, even if that is not true in all its fullness.

If it is acknowledged that Jesus' passion is to be continued in history, it should also be acknowledged that in order to be historical that continuity can take on different shapes. Leaving aside individual figures, that is, the need for Jesus to continue in each of his followers, the continuation in history by the people should also take on different shapes. In other words, we cannot say once and for all who constitutes the collective subject that most fully carries forward Jesus' redeeming work. It can be said that it will always be the crucified people of God, but as corrected as it is, that statement leaves undefined who that people of God is, and it cannot be understood simply as the official church even as the persecuted church. Not everything called church is simply the crucified people or the Suffering Servant of Yahweh, although correctly understood this crucified people may be regarded as the most vital part of the church, precisely because it continues the passion and death of Jesus.

This historicity does not mean that we cannot come to an approximation of the present-day figure of the Servant. It might vary in different historic situations, and it might represent the Servant's fundamental traits under different aspects, but it would not thereby cease to have certain basic characteristics. The most basic is that it be accepted as the Servant by God; that acceptance, however, cannot be established except through its "likeness" to what happened to the Jesus who was crucified in history. Therefore, it will have to be crucified for the sins of the world, it will have to have become what the worldly have cast out, and its appearance will not be human precisely because it has been dehumanized; it will have to have a high degree of universality, since it will have to be a figure that redeems the whole world; it will have to suffer this utter dehumanization, not for its sins but because it bears the sins of others; it will have to be cast out and despised precisely as savior of the world, in such a way that this world does not accept it as its savior, but on the contrary judges it as the most complete expression of what must be avoided and even condemned; and finally, there must be a connection between its passion and the working out of the Reign of God.

On the other hand, this historic figure of the Servant is not to be identified with any particular organization of the crucified people whose express purpose is to achieve political power. Of course, the salvation promised to the historic mission of the Servant of Yahweh must be embodied in history, and such historic embodiment must be achieved through an organizing process that if it is to be fully liberating, must be intimately connected with the crucified people. But the aspect through which the crucified people—and not a purely undifferentiated people—brings salvation to the world, continuing the work of Jesus, is not the same as that by which it effects this salvation in historic and political terms. In other words, the crucified people transcends any embodiment in history that may take place for the sake of its salvation in history, and this transcending is due to the fact that it is the continuation in history of a Jesus who did not carry out his struggle for the Reign through political power. The fact that it transcends, however, does not mean that it can be isolated from any embodiment in history, for the Reign of God entails the achievement of a political order, wherein human beings live in covenant in response to God's covenant.

The crucified people thus remains somewhat imprecise insofar as it is not identified, at least formally, with a specific group in history—at least in all the specific features of a group in history. Nevertheless, it is precise enough so as *not to be confused* with what cannot represent the historic role of the Suffering Servant of Yahweh. To mention some examples with two sides: the First World is not in this line and the Third World is; the rich and oppressive classes are not and the oppressed classes are; those who serve oppression are not, no matter what they undergo in that service, and those who struggle for justice and liberation are. The Third World, the oppressed classes, and those who struggle for justice, *insofar as* they are Third World, oppressed class and people who struggle for justice, are in the line of the Suffering Servant, even though not everything they do is necessarily done in the line of the Servant. Indeed, as was noted at the beginning of this chapter, these three levels must by necessity develop—although we cannot here go into studying the ways this takes place—into some embodiments that are strictly political and others that are not formally political, though they are engaged in history.

This likening of the crucified people to the Servant of Yahweh is anything but gratuitous. If we can see common basic features in both, there is moreover the fact that Jesus identified himself with those who suffer—or that was the view of the early Christian community. That is, of course, true of those who suffer for his name or for the Reign, but it is also true of those who suffer unaware that their suffering is connected to the name of Jesus and the proclamation of his Reign. This identification is expressed most precisely in Matthew 25:31-46, and indeed, that passage appears just before a new announcement of his passion (Matthew 26:1-2).

The passage has a "pact structure," says Pikaza, in its two-part statement (I am your God, who is in the little ones, and you will be my people if you love the little ones); the pact takes place through justice among human beings. It is the judgment of the Reign, the universal and definitive judgment, that brings to light God's truth among human beings; this truth is in the identification of the Son of Man, become King, with the hungry, the thirsty, wayfarers, the naked, the sick, and prisoners. The Son of Man is he who suffers with the little ones; and it is this Son of Man, precisely as incarnate in the crucified people, who will become judge. In its very existence the crucified people is already judge, although it does not formulate any theological judgment, and this judgment is salvation, insofar as it unveils the sin of the world by standing up to it; insofar as it makes possible redoing what has been done badly; insofar as it proposes a new demand as the unavoidable route for reaching salvation. This is, lest we forget, a universal judgment in which sentence is passed on the whole course of history. Pikaza notes that Matthew 25:36-41 entails a dialectical vision of the Jesus of history; he has been poor and yet it is he who helps the poor. Seen from the Pasch, Jesus appears as the Son of Man, who suffers in the wretched of the earth, yet is likewise also the Lord, who comes to their aid.

Thus the crucified people has a twofold thrust: it is the victim of the sin of the world, and it is also bearer of the world's salvation. But this second aspect is not what we are developing here in terms of the Pauline "died for our sins and rose for our justification." This present chapter, halting at the crucifixion, presents only the first stage. A stage focused on the resurrection of the people should indicate how the one crucified for the sins of the world can by rising contribute to the world's salvation. Salvation does not come through the mere fact of crucifixion and death; only a people that lives because it has risen from the Death inflicted on it can save the world.

The world of oppression is not willing to tolerate this. As happened with Jesus, it is determined to reject the cornerstone for the building of history; it is determined to build history out of power and domination, that is, out of the continual denial of the vast majority of oppressed humankind. The stone that the builders rejected became the cornerstone, stumbling-block, and rock of scandal. That rock was Jesus, but it is also the people that is his people, because it suffers the same fate in history. Those who once "were not people" are now "people of God"; those who were "viewed without pity" are not "viewed with mercy." In this people are the living stones that will be built into the new house, where the new priesthood will dwell and will offer the new victims to God through the mediation of Jesus Christ (cf. 1 Pet. 2:4-10).

—Translated by Phillip Berryman
and Robert R. Barr

29

People of God

JUAN ANTONIO ESTRADA

To know a people is to know its history. A people without historical memory is deprived of a collective personality. Therefore one of the most efficient methods of cultural colonization is to exterminate the collective roots of its identity and to rewrite its history from the perspective of the conquerors. That permits a conquest much more radical than military conquest. A people's memory of the past, its own traditions, its folklore, its religious and sociocultural roots is always the last defense of its threatened identity and the original traits of collective awareness.

I. THE HISTORICAL ROOTS OF THE PEOPLE OF GOD

This is also true of the biblical people. Israel's fascination and contradictions reside in its durability as a people and as a clearly defined collective entity, even after it had lost its political, economic, and cultural independence over many centuries. It is left with only its history and the religious traditions that make up its identity. The Bible is the written testimony of an experience in which a people progressively discovers God as the one who reigns in human history and intervenes in it from within, through prophets and envoys, who becomes the Lord of a people and thus establishes a universal covenant with all humanity (Gen. 8:21-22; 9:8-18), and who is Father of all and Creator of the world. The formation of the people and its awareness of its personality go hand in hand with its discovery of God and the progressive experience of God's salvation. Yahweh formed the people through the patriarchs (Gen. 12:1-2; 17:4-8; 35:11), liberated them from oppression and made them the chosen people (Exod. 19:3-8; Deut. 7:6), and finally formed a covenant of grace (Exod. 19-24; Deut. 5). Thus the people received the gift and the imperative of a holy people (Exod. 19:6; Num. 16:3).

It is God's people and derives its identity from God. For Israel, its profane history is also salvific history. Its God is not someone far off and unconcerned with the fate of humanity; on the contrary, the source of life and the Lord of history intervenes by saving and showing the way of salvation. Its experience of the mystery of God, the progressive spiritualization and purification of its religious experience, and its awareness that God is a God of salvation are the impelling moments of its religious development and its evolution as a people. Its divine commandments and sacred worship refer to human life, which is protected by God, and are therefore incompatible with injustice, oppression, and exploitation.

At the same time, the denial of God leads to the disqualification of Israel; it becomes a non-people, and the divine promises and blessings become a curse and a condemnation (Jer. 7:16-28). In Israel, the denial of God is not that of atheism but of idolatry, as expressed in the divinization of the great powers in which Israel seeks refuge and security, and the divinization of money and worldly goods, which lead to human exploitation ("the poor, widows, orphans, and foreigners"). Being the people of God is incompatible with injustice and oppression, and the prophets who defend the poor are thus intervening on behalf of the very people of God (Amos 2:7; Isa. 3:13-15; Mic. 2:8-11, 3:1-4).

This is the history of Israel, which has permitted its survival as a people. It has overcome disasters, persecutions, and dispersion by hope in the God of the promise, in the arrival of a Messiah who will impose peace, justice, and reunification of the dispersion (Isa. 11). Religious life and human hope converge around a promise of life for each and every one of the people.

II. THE CHURCH AS PEOPLE OF GOD

This is also the history that the church takes as its own, and which has led the church to assume the title and meaning of people of God. The church knows that its origins are in the history of Israel, it assumes the heritage of the Hebrew scriptures, and it evolves from being the "sect of the Nazarenes" (Acts 24:5, 14; 28:22) to becoming the "people of God" (Rom. 9:25-26; 2 Cor. 6:16), the true "Israel of God" (Gal. 3:29). A collective emerges, bringing together Jews and Gentiles (Acts 28:27-28), into which the "remnant of Israel" is integrated. Between the church and Israel there is a long process of developing awareness and of ecclesial constitution (of "ecclesiogenesis"), which simultaneously marks the continuity and discontinuity between the two. The renewed idea of people of God expresses the permanence of tradition as well as change, the historical roots of the church as well as the irruptive novelty of the Christian event.

There is continuity: the Christians take as their own the historical memory of Israel, its vision of God, and its understanding of the people. They take that heritage and radicalize it: God is the Lord of history, intervening in it and taking a position on behalf of the poor, the oppressed, and sinners. They see the figure of Jesus in the context of Abraham, Moses, and the prophets. He is the Messiah, who brings the Messianic hopes to culmination, who leads a new Exodus, and who intervenes decisively on behalf of his people. With Jesus, the Reign of God begins to take effect on the people: the chains of oppression are broken, liberation is announced to the poor, the powerful and the rich are denounced, the day of Yahweh is proclaimed (Luke 2:47-55; 4:17-21). What was a promised future is now presented as a future beginning to become present, as anticipation and actualization of the ultimate fullness. God intervenes in human history, but in a more radical and perfect way. God comes to realize the human kinship that was dreamed of for Messianic times; to put an end to dependency on power, prestige, and money; to establish a community, that of the Messianic times, which becomes a sign and instrument of the Kingdom of God. Thus the allusions to Jesus as the new Adam, as higher than Abraham and Moses, as a descendant of David who is greater than he.

The Hebrew scriptures are at once fulfilled and surpassed. The Exodus serves as a model to explain Christian ecclesiogenesis, but at the same time the coming of Jesus serves as a key to reinterpret the promises and the idea of the Messiah, to separate it from its nationalistic and political accretions, from its desires for greatness and power, one of which is the dream of Israel's triumph over other peoples. It is the creation of a new people, not identified with any nation, without oppression or dependencies; a family of God without fathers, or teachers, or rich and poor; a people of equals, in which authority is a service, the most wealthy are the ones who share the most, the greatest are those who lower themselves, the first are the ones who become last. This type of relationship culminates and surpasses the promise, it assumes the heritage and reinterprets it, it emphasizes the Jewish root of Jesus and his character as the new Adam.

This character of equality, community, and kinship also leads the Christians to assume the title of church, a term applied in the Hebrew scriptures to the people of God assembled, emphasizing its character as a congregation "convoked" by God (*ekklesia* comes from the verb *kaleo*, which means "to call" or "to convoke"). The church is a community determined by its relationship with God, a congregation of people convoked (whom the Christian scriptures call "the elect," "saints," "the anointed," "the consecrated," and so forth). Thus the idea of the people of God takes on new nuances as "church of God." As an assembly of the people of God, it emphasizes the participation of all; the equality of all, beyond the differences of functions and charisma; the common sense of belonging and the dignity of a wholly holy, consecrated, and priestly people (1 Pet. 2:7-10). Its fundamental novelty lies in accepting members of all peoples and in surpassing the national particularism of Israel. Its universal vocation as chosen people now leads to the assimilation "of those who once were not a people" (1 Pet. 2:10) into the church of God, which is a people. The old congregated assembly now takes on a truly universal dimension, and a new communion emerges which assumes and surpasses that of the Jews. While the concept of people of God is inalienable in the sense that it places the Christian people in the covenant and in sacred history, new titles are added to specify the novelty that is introduced. "Body of Christ" and "temple of the Holy Spirit" are two of the most frequently used.

This new vision of what it means to be people of God also corresponds to a renewed understanding of who God is, what God is like.

That understanding moves from undifferentiated monotheism to the triune God. The fatherhood of Yahweh takes on new dimensions in light of the resurrection which is a new creation; God's option for the poor and sinners is expressed in a reaffirmation that we are all God's children, that mercy is higher than the law, that holiness includes human justice, and that the quintessence of worship and religion is the love of the children for God and of brothers and sisters for one another. It reveals the very God who shows us in Jesus the human form of divine sonship, and who comes to us in Spirit to divinize us and make us children in the Son. The communion of triune life is generated in the church, which has to express itself universally, making one people of Jews and Gentiles, and creating in the midst of history a sign of the kinship of the Reign of God. From monotheistic Israel emerges the people of the triune God, and thus the aspects of communion are underlined.

God's walking with God's people in history takes on new meaning from the incarnation of the Word and the inhabitation of the Spirit: the promise keeps its dynamic of faith and hope, but leads to thanksgiving and to commitment in the present, in which salvation is palpable and the Good News of liberation is evident. The not yet of salvation enters into the here and now of history, and liberates not only souls but also bodies; it is the whole person, corporeal and spiritual, who must experience in the Messianic community the answer to whose side God is on and what God demands of humanity. Thus the simultaneously immanent and transcendent content of the Beatitudes and of the sermon on the mount, which are the magna carta of the proclamation of the Kingdom of God and of the project of church.

III. THE PEOPLE OF GOD IN CHRISTIAN HISTORY

The history of the church, which has the conscious role of continuing and renewing the covenant between God and humanity, is marked by faithfulness and by sin, by the commitment to become the renewed people of God and the tendency toward re-Judaization. On the one side, the church maintains its traditional root and its specific originality. Its awareness of being the people of God is abundantly expressed in the great Fathers of the Church. In assuming the Old Testament (against the attempts of Marcion), it defends its Jewish heritage, which is Christianized by combining it with and reading it from the viewpoint of the Christian scriptures. The church accepts the Old Testament traditions without doubt as the roots of its own identity, and structures itself under the influence of Old Testament institutions, which leave their traces in Christian worship, ministries, discipline, and symbolism.

The very historical existence of the church permanently refers to Israel, whose durability as an entity (although in the form of a dispersed people who have lost their land, their worship, and their sociopolitical and economic independence) constitutes a question and a challenge for the Christian community. Israel is an unfinished task for the church (Rom. 11), the sign of Jesus' own historical failure (only a "remnant" followed him) and that of the apostolic community. From the beginning the early church attempted to convert the Jewish people. That was also the mission policy of Paul and the apostles in the dispersed communities of the Roman Empire, and the intent of the Apostolic Fathers, the Apologists and the Fathers of the Church: to convince the Jews that Jesus is the hoped-for Messiah, and that the Messianic times have already begun in the church.

The mission of the Jews is essential to the very existence of the church and is not just one among others. That mission must be based on witness, on demonstrating the Messianic fruits, on the sign of a community, in reference to God, which proclaims mercy toward sinners, solidarity with the poor, the liberation of the oppressed, and the establishment of fraternal relationships which are not those of earthly power, money, or prestige. Mission and witness as a Messianic community are the two complements of the relationship between Jews and Christians.

1. The Holiness and Sin of the People of God

Nevertheless, both complements are progressively deteriorating. Mission gave way to persecution: first the Jews against the Christians, whom they harassed and denounced before the Roman authorities. Then the reverse, from the fourth century on: the Christians persecuted the Jews, who were blamed for Jesus' death, as an ethnic and not only religious collectivity, forgetting that the church itself and not only the Jewish collectivity came out of ancient Israel. What should have been a history of reconciliation bringing liberation to Jews and pagans became a confrontation that unleashed both anti-Christian persecutions and later anti-Semitism. The church, which did not achieve the conversion of the descendants of the old Israel, fell into the temptation of annihilating them as a historical-religious entity and even favoring their physical persecution. The cross of Jesus, who died for his people and to make a people of all humanity, became a threatening symbol, generating hatred and fear. The salvation that God offered was transformed by sin into the very opposite of liberating Good News.

At the same time the church itself was becoming re-Judaized and taking on the behaviors and structures that Jesus came to overcome. The Fathers of the Church spoke of it as the "chaste prostitute." As a community it prostitutes itself to power, to the search for money and worldly prestige when it uses its salvific meaning and its linkage with God to constitute itself as the Kingdom of God on earth with the power and greatness of the kingdoms of this world; when it allies itself with the State and moves to legitimate and consolidate the injustices of society, forgetting the posture of denunciation and prophetic criticism that Jesus assumed. It forgets its Lord on the cross and falls into a triumphalistic vision, into the old temptations that Jesus rejected: to use religion as power for its own benefit and that of its members, and to attack Jews and non-Christians as enemies. But it is still chaste because it conserves the heritage of Jesus: the gospel and the force of his Spirit, which awakens in it the renewal and evangelical reformation (*ecclesia semper reformanda*) and guarantees its survival beyond its sins. The people of God are on a pilgrimage as a church, at once holy and sinful.

This re-Judaization also affected the church internally. The Hebrew scriptures increasingly served as an exemplary model for the organization of the church, which together with the influence of the civil and religious institutions of the society determined the institutional face of the church and the very forms of Christian life. Through a long historical process of osmosis, it took on categories that cast a shadow on the Christian uniqueness of the people of God. The fundamental kinship of all, beyond their differences of charisma and functions, gave way to a hierarchization that produced a hypertrophy of authority, a progressive separation and autonomy of the ministers from the community, and an individualization of the ministers in correlation with their loss of ecclesial sense and the reduction of the faithful to a passive mass.

The old title of "brothers," which expresses the equality of all, gradually became used by the ministers among themselves and later among the members of the religious life. In contrast, the category *people* was increasingly used as equivalent to the "plebe" as opposed to the "clergy," who took on the role of church dignitaries and whose lifestyle was similar to that of functionaries in the Roman administration. The priesthood of the people of God was moved to a secondary level below that of ministers, who assumed Old Testament categories and elements that, according to the New Testament, Jesus had overcome. The category of "consecrated ones," used to distinguish between the baptized and non-Christians, became the preferred term for those who had received the sacrament of holy orders and for those in monastic life, who tended to monopolize the ideal of the state of holiness that belongs to all Christians.

Thus the church was clericalized; people in secular life lost participation and influence; the communities transferred their functions to the ministers; the sacraments began to lose correspondence with daily life; and in the context of a globally Christian society, the spiritual level of Christians and their ability to be a transforming ferment in the society deteriorated. The Christian uniqueness as people of God subsisted as an ideal and as a goal, but entered into historical rivalry with the sinful tendency to build the church as one people among others, taking on worldly values and structures.

2. The Mission of the People of God

The missionary content of the theology of the people of God was also changing. At first the Christians often spoke of the church as the "third people," taking in all peoples and permitting the inculturation of Christianity in all cultures and nations. This was a theological and geographical basis for speaking of catholicity as a note of the church. Diverse churches emerged in this context: Syrian, Alexandrian, Greek, Latin, and others. As a people of peoples there was an awareness of ecclesial unity that was expressed in a single Bible, sacraments, and ministerial structure. To this was added a communion of faith and life, which brought together orthodoxy with the demands of orthopraxis. Beyond that there was freedom and plurality, which permitted people to use their own language, elect their own ministers with autonomy, and develop a discipline, canons, customs, and traditions according to their idiosyncracies. The church grew from within each people, and Christianity was implanted in each culture.

This was later lost. First came an identification between church and society in the Roman Empire, then between the church and the Byzantine and western sector of the old Empire. This changed the idea of the catholicity of the people of God; now it was less a matter of implanting Christianity in new peoples and enabling new churches to emerge, than of incorporating other peoples into the church itself, obliging them to accept the liturgy, discipline, language and traditions of the evangelizing church. This produced an "ecclesiastical colonization," which was definitive in colonial expansion from the sixteenth century on, and which hindered the birth of autochthonous churches and other forms of Christianity besides the Latin and Greek. The old equivalence between nation and people of God, which prevailed in ancient Israel, now reemerged throughout Europe; the conflict with the Malabar and Chinese rites confirms this tendency. The very idea of catholicity changed, and adding the adjective *Roman Catholic* to the church determined not only the primacy of the Roman church in the context of an ecclesiology of communion, but also the Romanization of Western Christianity and the later Europeanization of the Christianized peoples.

This is also seen with respect to the poor and oppressed. At first Christian witness in the Roman society was based on an effective solidarity with the poor and on a sense of kinship, which attracted the pagans. The church itself found acceptance among the popular sectors of Roman society. The maxim of St. Irenaeus of Lyon prevailed: "The glory of God is that man should grow and live, the glory of man is to meet God." God's salvation and the promotion and liberation of humanity are the two dynamics of the single Christian message. There is no opposition, nor even a separation, between the worship of God and commitment to humanity. This permitted Christians to present themselves as true citizens who sought the good of Roman society, with their prayers to God and their commitment to their neighbor.

This attitude of solidarity is one of the keys to the success of Christianity, as its critics acknowledged (Celsius, Julian the Apostate). The properties and goods of the church were justified as "the treasury of the poor," worship led to expressions of solidarity with them (for example, the eucharistic offertory), and catechesis emphasized the correlation between faith and social justice as a denunciation of the rich and an option for the poor. This tradition was never completely lost in the church, but in the course of history some of its elements were gradually lost or marginalized. On the one hand, the eschatological dynamic that led people to await the consummation of the Kingdom of God as a Messianic and pilgrim people in history, gave way to a church installed in society and losing its capacity to maintain critical distance. Eschatology tended gradually to become a "theology of the beyond," a theology beyond the grave from a spiritualistic and individual perspective, and the salvation "of souls" permitted unconcern for global humanity from a dualistic, platonic viewpoint. Thus the injustices of the society were legitimized, by pointing out that we live in the "regime of sin" and that God permits the injustices. The loss of Messianic and eschatological consciousness impoverished the life of the people of God. On the other hand, it was the monastic estate and the various evangelical and prophetic currents that best maintained the evangelical ideal, preserving a Messianic and historic eschatology.

IV. THE PEOPLE OF GOD IN THE SECOND VATICAN COUNCIL

Vatican II, which began with the resurgence of patristic studies, liturgical renewal, ecumenical contacts, and greater theological attention to scripture and historical evolution, has made the connection with the ecclesiological roots of the early church. This has crystallized in the first two chapters of the constitution *Lumen gentium*, which are the fundamental ecclesiological framework from which all the rest should be read.

It has returned to the mystery of the church as the point of departure for all ecclesiological reflection, reacting against an institutional, juridicial, and sociological idea of the church that has prevailed at least since the time of the counter-reformation. The mystery of Christ leads us to that of the church, which expresses its divine and human dimensions, its visible and invisible conditions, as institutional reality and charismatic event. The Council requires an analysis of ecclesial reality from a perspective of faith. The mystery of the church is that in a limited and sinful community like ours, the salvation of Christ is present in the Spirit. Therefore, to speak of the church entails beginning with the activity of the Holy Spirit, since the church is mentioned in the symbol of faith as a work of the Spirit, which continues the work begun by Christ. Christology and pneumatology, incarnation and inhabitation, are the points of departure for reflection on the church. The scandal of incarnation takes on an ecclesial dimension when we contemplate a community of sinful humanity in which the heritage of Jesus is conserved and actualized. The relation of God to the church permits us to believe in it as a work of God, as the locus of our faith, as the context of our commitment and witness, as the "we" that marks our personal faith.

1. From the Mystery of the Church to the People of God

This is the perspective chosen by the Council to speak of the church. From there it uses different images, concepts, and titles to define and clarify that ecclesial mystery. To affirm that the church is a mystery of faith is not to define it, since that mysterious character must impregnate all ecclesiology and each of its ecclesiological definitions. Therefore the mystery of the church cannot be used as a title over against the other concepts. Just as the christological titles seek to unveil the mystery of Christ, so it is with ecclesiological titles. This is what the Council has tried to do in the first two chapters of *Lumen gentium*. It offers various definitions, giving preference to the central concept of people of God, as chapter 2 of the constitution is entitled. The Council enters into the long biblical-historical-dogmatic tradition on which ecclesiogenesis is based. Naturally, this preference for the title people of God, with its broad ecumenical backing, is not exclusive or monopolistic; it requires the complement of other images, such as that of the church as sacrament of salvation (which it uses for the first time in the official magisterium of the church), the body of Christ, and others.

2. The Meaning of the People of God

In speaking of the people of God the Council has sought to emphasize what is common to all Christians rather than the ministerial or charismatic differences. It underlines the importance of baptismal consecration (LG, 10), which is the basis for understanding not only lay participation in the church, but also the sacrament of orders, which presupposes and is based on baptism as a consecration for a function or ministry in the church, and the same consecration for religious life (which is not a second baptism and cannot take its place with the religious profession). Thus it restores the common root of all dignity, function, and charisma in the church and lays the basis for an ecclesiology in which all who are baptized are active in both the internal life and the mission of the church (LG, 9). The community and the plurality of ministries and charismas together determine ecclesiology.

This theology of the people of God lays the basis for a revitalization of the theology of the laity. Strictly speaking, we are all members of the people of God, which includes ministers and lay people, but by approaching ecclesiology from a common and egalitarian viewpoint, it lays the basis for an ecclesiology of communion, which leads to the participation, co-responsibility, and initiative of all. This does not happen when ecclesiology is approached from the viewpoint of differences, or from the ecclesial institution represented by the ministers, or from a hierarchical conception in which the apostolic succession is seen as a lineal transmission outside or above the ecclesial community. That leads to ecclesiological deism: "God created the hierarchy and was not concerned with the rest" (J. Möhler). On the contrary, the ecclesiology of the people of God emphasizes that the hierarchy is only a part of the church, that the Spirit is given to the whole community, it is not a hierarchical monopoly (LG, 12), and that in the church we are all at once a teaching church and a disciple church (by virtue of our common vocation and spiritual experience), although we do not all have a hierarchical teaching function.

V. ACCEPTANCE SINCE THE COUNCIL

The ecclesiology of the people of God was not only crucial in the Council, but has had even greater acceptance since then; it is the one that has contributed most to the renewal of the church.

The theology of liberation, like other theological currents, has made that concept its point of departure for ecclesiology, attempting to clarify the mystery of the church from a communitarian and popular perspective. It seeks to recover the vitalistic, pneumatic, and soteriological elements that have been so neglected by objectivistic and juridical Western ecclesiologies. It is the mission of the Spirit that permits the configuration and evolution of the people of God, from a martyrial and prophetic ecclesiology which attempts to continue and actualize the story of Jesus. Thus the martyrology of the third-world churches has become a christological and pneumatological witness to the vitality of these churches in following Jesus. That is the source of a prophetic appeal to the churches in the developed countries regarding the need for an ecclesial ortho-praxis that responds to doctrinal orthodoxy and leads to interecclesial solidarity with the poor countries of the Third World.

At the same time the pilgrim dimension of the people of God is connected with the discernment of the signs of the times (*Gaudium et spes*, no. 11), reaf-firming the convergence between action for the liberation of humanity and the salvific offering of God, and giving precedence to the latter. Not all human liberation is convergent with the salvation of God, but neither can the two be separated in the life of the churches. The redeemer God is the Creator who defends human life. The history of the formation and internal development of the people of God takes place within (not outside or over against) profane history. Thus the Christian communities reflect on their meaning and function in the world, not in an isolated and abstract way, but in the historic and con-flictive context in which they live, which was the intention at Medellín and Puebla. This discernment belongs to the whole community, and all must share in promoting a mature awareness among all the faithful, enabling them to take on the role of evangelizing the world and building the Kingdom of God.

VI. MOVING TOWARD AN ECCLESIOLOGY OF COMMUNION WITH THE POOR

One of the greatest challenges of the theology of the people of God is the need to structure a communitarian church and to develop an ecclesiology of communion. The problem is not only theological but also practical: How do we move from "massified" and highly individualistic churches to communities that share the faith and Christian commitment? How do we promote awareness of ecclesial belonging in today's geographically and numerically large parishes? For that purpose the church has chosen the base ecclesial communities, which are very widespread in Latin America. In the base communities there is greater participation and ecclesial awareness by all the members, greater participation in social and ecclesial life, and a greater initiative by lay people and by people with diverse charismas. This entails a restructuring of the hierarchical ministries along amore communitarian line, better suited to channeling the energies and activities of the people (more pedagogical and inspirational than directive), the need for a more fraternal (not paternalistic) style, and an exercise of authority more attentive to the abilities and needs of the faithful.

The church is not a democracy, insofar as it is nourished by the life of Jesus and the experience of his Spirit. This must be promoted and witnessed to by the ministers and the faithful. But the exercise of authority can indeed be more democratic, that is, more respectful of initiatives and of all people, more flexible with regard to different charismas, more open to the principle of subsidiarity, and so on. If the church adopted a lordly style of ministry in the feudal period, and a monarchical hierarchical structure in the time of absolute monarchies, it is hard to see how it can ignore the democratic sensitivity of the present.

The concept of *people*, which by its interpretation as "plebe" in Roman society led to polarization of clergy and laity, can serve today in the same way for the promotion of a sociological people and of the laity in the church. Even the Council sometimes speaks of the people of God in a restrictive sense, separating the pastors from the others (LG, 23:1; 24:1; 26:3; 28:2; 45:1). In this sense one really can speak of a "popular church" and of a "church of the people," not as a non-hierarchical church or with pastors subordinate to the delegation of the people, since the people of God is always hierarchically structured in apostolic succession (Puebla, 263), but as an effort toward a church in which the simple people, whom we sometimes call the base, see themselves as active, listened-to, and co-responsible. It would require developing an ecclesiological model different from that of a clerical church in which the clergy exercise a kind of enlightened despotism: "Everything for the people but without the people." This popular church, rightly understood, would have great roots in tradition, as for example in the Cyprianic ecclesiology, which urged against doing anything without the support of the Christian people, or in early practices like that of popular participation in the designation of ministers.

Thus a great challenge of the ecclesiology of the people of God is that of promoting the poor within the church. It is true that we all make up the church, but it is also true that the poor and sinners are central to Jesus' evangelizing concerns and should also be to the church. In reality there is a theological harmony between the conception of the church and the preferential option for the poor; the church is the community of those who know they are poor before God and other people, of those who always begin worship by confessing their sins and their spiritual poverty, of those who have no gold or silver to give but only their witness and the life of Jesus of Nazareth. Thus the church as people of God has an affinity with the people of the poor. It must serve them as witness and hope, open them to the God who saves, and commit itself to their searches and their struggles as part of following Jesus. The people of God give themselves in the community, which evangelizes the poor and which nourishes them with the word and with deeds (James 2:1-10). The theology of liberation seeks a greater incardination of the church among the poor masses of the Third World, separating the church from the bourgeoisie and from the upper classes of society. The proclamation of the gospel is universal and interclass. It is addressed to all, but it must be done from the historical and social locus that Christ himself chose, with a call to solidarity and sharing with those who are weakest. This requires a reconversion of mentalities and a restructuring of institutions. Only thus can the church move from being an amorphous mass to becoming a structured people in which the people feel listened-to, defended, and evangelized. This is the great challenge of the people of God, since more than half its members belong to the poor peoples of the Third World. The fruitfulness of the Second Vatican Council and the very future of the Catholic church depend in large part on its response to this challenge.

—Translated by Margaret D. Wilde

30

Communion, Conflict, and Ecclesial Solidarity

JON SOBRINO

Communion is a central theme in the church and ecclesiology for several reasons. Positively, communion expresses the ideal of the church and an eternal aspiration of humanity; the communion of brothers and sisters is at the heart of scripture and tradition; and it is an increasingly urgent question in a pluralistic and antagonistic church and world. But it is also a theme that needs clarification, because until we determine what that communion is, and what generates it, we shall have advanced very little in our understanding of ecclesial communion. That communion can be beneficial, but it can also become harmful for the church, if it degenerates into submission or if it is used to shift more fundamental realities of the church into the background (it should be remembered that "communion and participation" were used in Puebla to soften the "option for the poor").

In this chapter we shall discuss ecclesial communion from the viewpoint of the church of the poor. We do this not only because we believe that this way of being church is the most appropriate for humanity at present, but also because we believe that this way of being church is the one that generates a more real and more Christian ecclesial communion.

I. THE CHURCH OF THE POOR AS CHURCH OF JESUS

To speak meaningfully of ecclesial communion one must begin by speaking of the ecclesial nature of that communion; in other words, of the church of Jesus and of what should be its true face in today's world. This problem is prior to that of communion, but it is a fundamental and perennial problem, whose solution should never be taken for granted. Here we shall not raise the problem of the true church in a dogmatic, but rather an historical form, according to the concrete face it presents in different churches. Neither shall we raise it, in the first place, in the usual polemical and apologetic way—positing a specific church in relation to and among other churches—but rather in a theological way—positing the church and all the historical ways of being church in relation to God. In simple words, which may even seem tautological but are not, we want to affirm that the true church of Jesus is the church that God wants today.

This, which is so obvious, is important to keep in mind because depending on the concrete present form we give to the true way of being church, ecclesial communion will develop in different ways and will produce different consequences. To say it from the beginning, a church of Jesus, centered in the poor, inspired by them and placed at the service of the Kingdom of God, will generate one type of evangelical and Christian communion, beneficial to the church itself and, above all, to the kingdom of God and the poor of this world. A church that is definitely not Jesus' church, which today does not historically resemble or remember Jesus — or even worse, hides or distorts him — will not generate real Christian communion, although it may generate uniformity, tactical alliances among churches, and an impression of monolithic unity with some distinguishing details, that is, superficial communion. Worse yet, and we must accept the possibility as scandalous as it sounds, it could even generate a communion harmful to the Kingdom of God and to the poor of this world. In other words, not every communion is Christian and desirable, but only that which arises around the crucified of this world.

Thus it is a decisive task, but not an easy one, to determine what the church of Jesus is today, historically. We possess a tradition, which is partly normative, but twenty centuries of history have given us a variety of ecclesial realities and a great — sometimes even contradictory — variety of ecclesiologies. In the church of Jesus throughout history there has been a lot of grace and sin. The church of Jesus has had many faces — many of them not at all like that of Jesus of Nazareth. Similarly, there have been different ecclesiologies, some of which have clearly shown the face of Jesus, while others have hidden or even distorted it.

This diversity itself is a serious problem, and — without falling into anachronisms — we should not try to wish it away by appealing to the "historicity" of the church and ecclesiology; that is true, but we must remember that in reality, historicization has arisen both from grace and from sin. Therefore we must look for the church of Jesus within this history of a varied ecclesial reality and varied ecclesiologies, with its contributions and its normative declarations. But above all, we must go on looking for it in our own time and times to come.

In this chapter we shall do so from the viewpoint of recent Salvadoran and Latin American experience. My answer, as I have already said — and what I learned from Ignacio Ellacuría — is that the true church of Jesus today is the church of the poor. That is supported by the rereading of scripture that is being done today in various magisterial affirmations of Vatican II, Medellín, and Puebla, and various theologies. But the most decisive argument is the experience of Latin American ecclesial reality itself in these years, and the conviction that God is moving within that reality with a power not seen in other ecclesial realities. Thus the argument is unproved, in the last analysis, but it is offered here with honor and sincerity.

For the sake of concise analysis, I shall begin by proposing two formal and methodological considerations for the historical analysis of what the true church is today — considerations which, in my opinion, are not usually kept in mind and may therefore be polemical — and then very briefly discuss what the church of the poor is. The purpose is to see what way of being church today generates true ecclesial communion.

1. The Church in Relation to God's "Today"

Throughout history there have been innumerable churches and ecclesial communities; there have also been innumerable ecclesiologies and a variety of magisterial declarations to shed light on what the true church is and to settle disputed issues.

The first of these gives us an historical perspective on the difficulty of the problem. Were the communities of Jerusalem, of Antioch, and of Corinth the same? Are the churches of Madrid or New York, and the communities of Chalatenango in El Salvador, the same? The second shows a long and multi-colored history of the church's theological and magisterial self-understanding. Which ecclesiology is more Christian, that of the body of Christ, or the *communio sanctorum*, or Boniface VIII, or the *societas perfecta*, or Vatican I, or Vatican II, or the Extraordinary Synod held in Rome in 1985?

These questions are not anachronistic, but are raised only to reach a simple conclusion: in the present too, even with the baggage and the normativity of the history that has gone before, the church must ask itself what it is. What I want to stress is that the church must ask this question not only in relation to itself and its tradition, but in relation to God. It must look for itself in relation to God, because God has a "today," not only a "yesterday" already known and interpreted; God has a will for the present of creation, not only for the past. In other words, the church must be very conscious of God's "today"; one of the gravest risks for the church is to ignore it, to fall into some type of deism, if we may use that language, as if God had been present in the past, but has nothing to say today to and about the church which has not already been decided once and for all.

Thus it is a fundamental task of the church, not only of the individual believer, to put itself in relation to God today, to be hearers of the word, in the beautiful words of scripture and of Karl Rahner. But we must be aware of what that means, and of its practical and even theoretical difficulty. To put itself in relation to God means above all that the church accepts that God can continue speaking today and saying something new, not only something that can be deduced or extrapolated from what we already know about God. This means that the church must strip itself of many things, even if it thinks it already has a handle on God. It means accepting that it does not know, in order to really know God and God's will today.

That is, I believe, the first step the church must take today, as hard as it is, if the church is to know itself. In other words, the church should not look first for its identity in the horizontal relationship with other created realities in order to approach them or distinguish itself from them, to dialogue or struggle with them as if that were the way to discover its identity. It discovers its identity by putting itself before God, allowing the irreducible otherness of God to animate and judge it, to illuminate and attract it, to give it present reality. I have said several times, although it seems shocking, that the church does not fear Marx-ism—why should it, after all, when Marxism is a created thing with which the church can speak as an equal?—but it fears God. Before God the church con-fronts an irreducible otherness that questions it, but also before God it recovers its identity today, if it listens to—and puts into practice—God's word.

All this means that the church, in order to know itself, must take the present in absolute seriousness. It is doing so in some ways, by trying to scrutinize the signs of the times (GS, 4), in order to know the world in which it must live and which, ideally, it should serve. But as important as this is, as much as it is already becoming a reality in the church, it is not the most important part of knowing what the church is today. To know the signs of the times is necessary and ultimately has theological-pastoral meaning; by scrutinizing them the church comes to know our present world and history, and that should facilitate its mission. But we must keep clear that this is not the only or the most specific task of the church. In its desire to know the present world it is no different from other human institutions—governments, armed forces, political parties, universities, multinationals, companies—that carry out similar discernments in order to achieve their purposes, whether these are legitimate or spurious.

What sets apart the church and its present is to know and respond to God's "today," to scrutinize the signs of the times in their theological sense, "the presence of God and his will," as we read in *Gaudium et spes* (no. 11). To accept that God has or may have a word for history and the church today, and may be speaking it in a new, clear, and open way, is the fundamental condition for the identity and mission of the church. And if God has a word today, it is not enough to affirm it routinely; we must energetically seek it out and put it to work with everything that the church is and has. That "today" of God makes present and real what the church has thought about itself in its past moments of truth, but it also goes or can go beyond those moments.

To put it graphically, if we recall the definition of church as "convocation of God," we must ask whom God is convoking today and for what. If we call it "mystery," we must ask what ineffable reality God is expressing in that mys-tery today. If we call it "body of Christ," we must ask what Christ wants to make present in it today, what responsibility he has entrusted to his body so that it will exercise—not only talk about—his lordship in history today. If we call it "sacrament of salvation," we must ask of what salvation it is to be a sign, by what means, with what credibility.

God's "today"—if that today is accepted—is what makes concrete the reality of the church. And if for some reason one thinks, explicitly or implicitly, that God no longer has a today, that God's word is no longer heard (which seems to be happening in various places in the First World), then it would be better for the church to hold silence for a long time about God and about itself, and to ask God to begin showing God's present face again.

The radical question for the church, therefore, is what is God's "today." From the viewpoint of El Salvador, of all the Third World, the most universal world, the world most beloved by God throughout revelation, God's "today" is a word of life, justice, hope, and liberation for the innumerable victims of this world. At the same time it is a word of radical denunciation against the idols that produce victims, unmasking the lie with which the idols try to hide themselves, and demanding conversion of the oppressors who worship them.

We all know that, and there is no need to pursue it further. In Latin America the church believes above all that God has a "today." It has rediscovered God, as one who hears the cry and lamentations of God's children and who intends to come and liberate them. It has also seen God hidden in the poor and crucified, in the millions of victims of this world. It has seen God in the hope of the oppressed for life and dignity, and as one who advances and encourages them. This is God's today in our world, and the new way of being church in Latin America is emerging from that. Let us say in passing that God's rediscovered today is what has effectively led to the rediscovery—within the hermeneutic circle—of God's yesterday in scripture, as is seen in the exegesis done by the theology of liberation and in the intuitive reading of scripture that is done by the communities of the poor. Not everything in God's today is new, of course; we can speak of a renewed past, but the important thing is that new or renewed, it is God's today that the church is hearing and putting into practice.

Certainly this is said in very general terms. We also accept that there are many other realities in today's world through which God speaks or which can speak God's word; we know that different churches and theologies focus the fundamental problems—and God's today—on other things; and that, in the end, is also why the theology of liberation is controversial. We also know in Latin America that liberation is more than the survival of the poor with a minimum of life and dignity, and for that reason we speak of "integral" liberation or of "utopian" liberation, in the words of Ignacio Ellacuría. But having said all that, the words of Oscar Romero in Puebla to Leonardo Boff are still true in Latin America: "In my country people are being killed horribly. It is necessary to defend the minimum which is the maximum gift of God: life." The words of Irenaeus, paraphrased for God's today by Archbishop Romero in Louvain, are still true: "The glory of God is the poor person who lives."

There is no doubt in Latin America that this is God's today: life against the death of the poor, oppressed, and hope-filled majorities. But even if this were challenged, the truth of what I have tried to say in this section would remain: it is fundamental for the church to look for God's today, and not to run off looking first for the today of the church, its institution and administration, its ecclesial or worldly policy, doctrine, pastoral practice or theology or religious life—all of which are certainly in grave danger of degeneration.

Perhaps all this will seem obvious, at least in theory. I have tried simply to emphasize that the church is above all a theological question, and without going into that question, we cannot properly go into the regional and categoric realities of the church. Let this be the first conclusion, therefore: to speak of ecclesial communion we must speak of the church, but to speak of the church we must speak of God, and to speak of God we must speak of God's "today"—what God wills today and what, by willing it, God is saying.

If we do not start there, we shall go round and round on communion mechanisms, which of course are necessary but categoric; I am also afraid that such communion will not be truly ecclesial, that is, the communion that God wills today, and it may even be less than evangelical. I still think a beautiful description of the church is the one that calls it the "convocation of God." What we must historicize for today is an answer to the question: By what present word is God "convoking" us?

2. The "Real" Response of the Church

A second consideration, still formal and methodological, and related to the first, is that the church can only generate ecclesial communion insofar as it responds and corresponds "in reality" to God's today. What I want to emphasize—this again is evident—is that this response must be "real" in the sense that it gives shape to the deepest part of the church, to what I shall call real ecclesial substance. And this real ecclesial substance, in general and traditional terms, is the exercise *in actu* of the community's faith, hope, and charity. In my opinion, this more than anything else is what will generate or fail to generate ecclesial communion.

Theology, liturgical celebrations, the proclamation and handing down of doctrines, canon law, administrative decisions, Christian culture—as we often say today—are all necessary in the church, and they can be good, although they sometimes are not. The important thing is that, good or not, they are not the primary real ecclesial substance. This must be emphasized because those things can lead to coincidences (or differences) among the various churches and be mistaken for ecclesial communion; but in my opinion, ecclesial communion cannot be accomplished through this type of coincidence alone, but only when the coincidence is expressed in real ecclesial substance.

What is this real ecclesial substance today? It is making real *in actu* the church's response and correspondence to God's today, in faith, hope, and charity, as a community of believers.

In the language of the Christian scriptures, real ecclesial substance is the realization (making real) of the true *people of God*, within which communal equality is realized, in grateful acceptance that all receive the word of God and faith; that all are open to speaking with one another and serving one another, from the pope to the last sacristan, because God is in them all; that all support one another on the long journey of history, bearing one another's burdens, forgiving and encouraging one another; that all walk humbly with God in history. That church is the real people of God in history.

Real ecclesial substance is the realization of the true *body of Christ* in history, which makes it present—without ambiguity, but with its limitations—so that whoever sees the church sees Christ (a little or a lot of Christ). This church is incarnated in the weakness of this world, which is worldly because it is in the world, but not worldlike by being based on or trusting in the values of this sinful world. It carries out the mission of Jesus of Nazareth, the Good News to the poor, the defense of the oppressed from their oppressors, the unmasking of the idols, especially wealth and power, which produce victims in order to survive. Thus it is a church focused not on itself but on the Kingdom of God, therefore converted, so as not to seek its own life and the life of the institution, but that of the suffering world, a church which is incarnated in the world of sin, which bears the burden of sin, suffers the consequences of bearing it, is attacked, persecuted and martyred, and ends up with Jesus on the cross. It is a resurrected church, able to communicate the triumph that comes in Jesus' resurrection: indestructible hope, freedom to serve — not itself, but the poorest — freedom to become a slave, as Paul says, and freedom to give its life, as Jesus says in the gospel of John. That church is the real body of Christ in history.

Real ecclesial substance is the realization of the *temple of the Spirit*, that is, of believers with spirit, of believers who in the reality of their life show the spirit of mercy, which means justice for the popular majorities; the spirit of a clean heart, of truth, of seeing, analyzing, denouncing and unmasking reality as it is; the spirit of peace, active peace for which one must struggle and not only pray or hope with arms crossed; the spirit of strength to withstand the many risks, threats, and attacks that come from the struggle for justice; the spirit of joy, because under persecution they are a little more like Jesus; the spirit of the highest love to give up their life for their brothers and sisters; the spirit of generosity, of having received from God — often from the God hidden in the poor — new ears to hear God's word, new eyes to travel new ways, and new hands to transform it; the spirit of prayer, of calling God "Father"; and the spirit of celebration in calling God "our" Father, as Jesus did.

This is what we mean by real ecclesial substance: the realization in the community of faith in the God of life and in the God of the victims; the communal following of Jesus, remaking the structure of the life of Jesus in history; the life of a community in the Spirit, with a tangible — not only by intention and internally — and verifiable spirit, when we look more like Jesus and make our destiny more like his. This is real ecclesial substance, and it is the present historicization of faith, hope, and charity that comprise the identity of the church when they are lived in and as a community, in and as a people.

We all know that this description is an ideal, that this reality exists in the church, but its opposite also exists, that the grace described here exists together with sin. But this focus, the ideal, is still enormously important in speaking of ecclesial communion, because real communion is made possible by the reality of the church that looks like Jesus. It is the church, insofar as it is the real church of Jesus, that generates communion. Therefore — let this be the second conclusion — in speaking of communion we must ask what exists in this world of real church, how much real ecclesial substance exists. Of course we must also keep in mind the church in its factual reality, in its ambiguity of holiness and sin, but communion is not generated around factual reality but around Christian reality, although factual reality is always there, we must bear its burden, and must even find categoric mechanisms so that it will not be an obstacle to real communion.

This also does not preclude the existence of structures, functions, and mechanisms which are *subsequent* to real ecclesial substance and have as a task precisely to advance and guarantee ecclesial communion. But to achieve ecclesial communion it would be a mistake to begin with these mechanisms, as noble as they are; doing so can lead to institutional communion, but not necessarily to ecclesial communion, and it may even lead to a false communion, which is really uniformity and may also mean the subjection of some Christians to others, of some churches to others. Put simply, it is Jesus who generates ecclesial communion, and that way of being church will generate communion that resembles Jesus a little more, in which real ecclesial substance is lived a little more than in other kinds of communion. Let us remember that resembling Jesus is verifiable, and the poor of this world have learned to do it very well.

3. The Church of the Poor: Church of God's "Today" and "Real Church"

What church or churches are responding to God's "today" from the reality of ecclesial substance? I think it is happening in several places, in different ways. It is happening in good measure in Latin America in what we call the church of the poor. It is not happening in most of the churches of the First World, although there are praiseworthy people and groups in solidarity with that way of being church. This church of the poor takes God's today and God's word in absolute seriousness, it tries to respond to God's cry in relation to the victims, and it tries to correspond to the reality of God with a serious commitment to the liberation of the oppressed.

That this church is a true church, at least the one that most resembles Jesus today, the one that best derives from what Jesus was and did, might be deduced a priori from God's revelation itself and from the life, activity, and death of Jesus, because the poor and poverty are essential mediations of that revelation. God has turned toward our world, entered our history and become part of our humanity as someone weak and small, poor and oppressed. Our God is an incarnate God, lowered to more than one level: lowered to humanity, lowered to the lowest of humanity, the poor and weak. This lowering is not accidental or passing, but rather God has taken the lowest place in history. The suffering of those who are lowest in history, without life, without dignity, without elementary rights or freedom, is what has moved God to self-revelation as the God in the Exodus, in the prophets, and in God's Son, Jesus of Nazareth. The bottom of history, the real poverty that takes away life, the injustice that takes away community, the world of tormentors that produces victims, that is the place of God in this world. It is not the only place, but unless we find God in that place, to look anywhere else is dangerous and suspect.

If this is true throughout the revelation of God, we see it still today in the Third World. That Third World, impoverished, plundered, oppressed, and devalued, is God's world today. Thus it is the necessary and appropriate place for the church, although not absolutely sufficient. A church that lives in the Third World can see God today, can speak of Jesus of Nazareth as Emmanuel, "God with us," can call Jesus "elder brother," without shame, as Jesus is not ashamed to call us "brothers and sisters." But it must also become church in the same way that God turned toward the poor of this world. It is obliged to do so by God's revelation and by the force of the historical reality of the Third World, where the majority of humankind and increasingly the majority of Christian churches are found.

Put simply, from the viewpoint of revelation and our present history, I don't know what church besides the church of the poor can maintain its Christian identity today and can be directly relevant for our Third World — and by extension for the whole world — with its overabundance of lies, oppression, poverty, indignity, and death. I don't know what other way of being church can take seriously the fact that its mission — like God's own mission and that of God's Christ, Jesus — is to put truth where there are lies; freedom where there is oppression; justice where there is inhuman poverty; community where there is indignity; mercy, love, justice, life where there is suffering, torture, murder, disappeared persons, in a word, death.

For me there is no doubt that the church of Jesus in today's world can only be a church of the poor, truly and directly in the Third World, but also by extension in the other worlds. This means being a church that has taken a radical option for the poor, understanding and practicing that option in an all-encompassing way, not reducing it to something purely categoric-pastoral, and not allowing it to be paralyzed by the sterile casuistry of debating whether or not that option is preferential.

That option for the poor is or should be existential, supernatural, and historical, embracing the whole being and doing of the church. That option determines its *vision* of God and of the world, its doctrine and theology, opting to see the whole, yes, but from the viewpoint of poverty and crucifixion. Thus it recovers the scandalous affirmation of Isaiah that the Servant of Yahweh has been set as "a light to the nations" and the scandalous affirmation of Paul that Christ crucified is "the wisdom of God." It determines the church's *place* in the world — not only geographically or even only culturally, but theologically — by bringing it back to the foot of the cross, as Bonhoeffer so beautifully said, and in the even more simple and intuitive words of the song of the oppressed blacks in the United States: "Were you there when they crucified my Lord?" It determines the church's fundamental *mission*, which begins with compassion and mercy — that of the good Samaritan, of Jesus, and of the heavenly Father — as its first and last reaction to the suffering of the man injured by the roadside — in the Third World, billions of human beings, whole peoples crucified, and for that reason mercy is justice. It determines that mission by proclaiming Good News to the poor of this world — Good News also, *sub specie contrarii*, for the oppressors, if they are converted — and by transforming it into good reality, into all kinds of miracles and exorcisms, by taking in all those who are deprived of dignity in this world. It determines this mission by denouncing and unmasking the structures of sin, the idols of this world — the accumulation of wealth, the security of States — and by anathematizing the ancient and modern wielders of all kinds of power: scribes, Levites, Pharisees, especially the rich and grasping, rulers, and so on. It determines the church's *destiny* of suffering false accusations, threats, persecution, imprisonment, and death on the cross; the destiny of the Servant of Yahweh, who carries our sins on his shoulders, the sin of the world that disfigures him. It determines the church's *hope*, that life is possible, that the tormenter will not triumph over the victims, that God will restore life to God's suffering people, and it joins it to that hope-filled current of history that is lived by the poor, who have everything working against them but God on their side. It determines the church's *celebration*, its ability to celebrate and even to rejoice when the Good News is heard by the poor of this world and they put it to work, when they celebrate events of resurrection, large or small. Finally, it determines the church's *faith* in God, in the mystery that God's goodness brings everything to God and gives people rest, and in the good God who is still a mystery with whom one must walk humbly — as the prophet Micah says — in history.

For the church, this is what it means to take an option for the poor. It goes beyond attitudes, methodologies, and pastoral decisions on the question of to whom mission is addressed. Certainly the church must address itself to everyone, but to everyone from the viewpoint of the poor. What is more important is that from the viewpoint of the poor the church reestablishes everything it knows, everything it must do, everything it can hope, and everything it can celebrate.

That option also determines — this is very hard — that the poor have an inalienable, privileged, and central place at the heart of the church, that they make it the church of Jesus, and they give direction to everything it must be. The option for the poor within the church is much more than the "democratization" or "community-building" — let us call it that — that Vatican II required of the church in proclaiming the fundamental equality and dignity of all the members of the people of God; it is a conscious "favoritism" and "popularization" of the church at its heart.

Moreover, the poor must be at the center of the church because — as Puebla says in impassioned words — they move it to conversion and evangelize it. The first of these is no small service by the poor to the church. They move it to conversion because in their own flesh — human table scraps in many cases — they are asking the church the great question of God: "What have you done to your brother?" And if those poor, inconcealable because they are at the very center of the church, do not move it to conversion, nothing will. But the second is even more scandalous. It is said that the poor do for the church what Jesus fundamentally did: they evangelize. Just so that will not be reduced to pure rhetoric, Puebla explains these words: they evangelize us by their evangelical values, by their openness to God, by their solidarity, by their sense of community. Thus the poor in the church are gospel for the church.

Does the church of the poor exist, or is it just a theological fiction? The answer is very important, because we have already said that what will generate ecclesial communion is a church as real church, insofar as it realizes the ecclesial substance. For me, there is no doubt that the church of the poor exists; we have seen, heard, and touched it. It had some shining moments in the decade after Medellín, but now people are trying to kill it with a thousand qualifications, disqualifying it at times by calling it a "popular church," "parallel church," with the corresponding "parallel magisterium." But it still exists. To prove it I shall mention just one criterion of verification, the most decisive one for the Christian gospel and tradition: love expressed in martyrdom, which is the maximum expression of love — to give one's life for one's brothers and sisters.

The church of the poor in Latin America has innumerable martyrs; it is the church that has produced the most martyrs since the Council. Most important, the martyrs of that church — I say this from an objective and historical viewpoint without prejudging the subjective holiness of other martyrs — more closely resemble the martyrdom of Jesus of Nazareth; the reasons for their death are more like those of Jesus, and the type of life that led to those martyrs' death is more like the life of Jesus of Nazareth.

These martyred lives began with true incarnation, with the *kenosis* of Jesus. As Archbishop Romero said in impassioned words:

> I rejoice, brothers and sisters, that they have murdered priests in this country. . . . For it would be very sad if in a country where so many Salvadorans are murdered, the church could not also count priests among the murdered ones. . . . It is a sign that the church has become incarnate in poverty. . . . A church that does not suffer persecution, that church should be fearful. It is not the true church of Jesus.

Thus the martyrs show true Christian incarnation, like that of Jesus. They are also the real symbol of so many other Latin American poor who die anonymously, slowly, or violently. They are a symbol because they publicly express a reality that goes far beyond them: the anonymous martyrdom of so many Latin American poor. They are a real symbol, because they participate in the reality of those poor and are finally impoverished in death.

Not just any church has been persecuted and martyred, but the one whose life most closely resembles the life of Jesus. Those Christians have been persecuted and killed for announcing the Kingdom of God to the poor of this world, for defending them from their oppressors, for working all kinds of "miracles" and "exorcisms" on their behalf, for gathering the poor to their breast and restoring their dignity, for struggling to transform and eradicate the structures of sin . . . and for doing all that in the presence of and against the anti-kingdom. This church announces the Kingdom and is thus an evangelizing church, but it also denounces the anti-Kingdom and is prophetic, bad news for the oppressors. What is unforgivable is to do both things at the same time. Thus the martyrs show that they are true evangelizers and true prophets, like Jesus.

Like Jesus, these martyrs have been devalued; they have been called crazy and blasphemous, communists and liberationists in the current language. As in the case of Jesus, Pharisees, Herodians, and high priests have quickly gathered to arrest them, and soon after Medellín the Rockefeller Report, the CIA reports found in Bolivia in the 1970s, and so many other machinations of the oligarchies, armed forces, and Latin American governments have declared them worthy of death.

Like Jesus, these martyrs have continued — even in the midst and fully aware of threats and persecutions — faithful to the end, all the way to Jerusalem. They have passed through their Galilean crises, they have stood before God with wailing and weeping, learning obedience, but they have followed the road to its end like the faithful high priest of the letter to the Hebrews, "merciful" to the poor and "faithful" to God. And thus, they have not only denounced the sin of the world, but like the Servant of Yahweh, they have borne not their own sins but those of their persecutors and tormenters.

But also as in the case of Jesus, "the grass has not grown on their graves." They are still alive and present among the poor, still producing hope, creativity, commitment, heroism, and life. They are still growing hope, freedom, and joy in this land. They are risen in the arms of the heavenly Father and in the hearts of the Latin American peoples.

These martyrs resemble Jesus in life and in death, and historically — again, quite apart from the subjective holiness of past martyrs — they are more like Jesus. To give a single example, before the assassination of Archbishop Romero in 1980, one would have to go back to the eleventh century to find an archbishop murdered at the altar, Thomas à Becket. But there was one difference between them. The Archbishop of Canterbury was killed for his — legitimate — defense of the freedom and rights of the church. Archbishop Romero was killed for defending the rights of the poor. And that is central in the church of the poor.

It is this church of the poor that God has always wanted, although it has rarely been successful on earth, and that is the church that God wants today. In Vatican II the expression "church of the poor" was not well accepted, although it was advocated by John XXIII and personalities like Cardinal Lercaro — the Third World was not very present at the Council — but the emerging light of the Council was picked up in Latin America, and the Latin American reality put it to work.

The church that the God of life wants in a world of victims, the church that God the defender of orphans and widows wants in a world of poor and oppressed people, is the church of the poor. The poor themselves also want it very much, and remember that before the church took the option for the poor, the poor had taken an option for the church, because they had always clearly intuited — consciously or unconsciously, in religiously appropriate ways and even in ways considered superstitious in the First World — that Jesus is on their side, that he is not ashamed to call them brothers and sisters, as the letter to the Hebrews so beautifully says. The theology of liberation has forcefully said this, as have Medellín and Puebla, as well — though sadly, in everyday life, the vigor of this real option has been waning, and it may yet degenerate into dead orthodoxy.

But this church does exist. It is a reality sometimes quantitatively greater and sometimes less in different times and places, with limitations and failures, of course, but it is a reality. It is a church that truly hears the word, that tries to listen to God's "today," and that humbly and decisively has tried to respond to God in its "real" life and death. Thus the church of the poor is God's great gift to today's world, the great reserve of ecclesial substance for the whole church and for all churches. If that church of the poor, with innumerable martyrs, is not the church of Jesus today, what church can be? Thus it is there that we must start to talk about ecclesial communion in a pluralistic world and church.

II. ECCLESIAL COMMUNION AROUND THE CRUCIFIED TO BRING THEM DOWN FROM THE CROSS

Let us now analyze ecclesial communion from the perspective of this church. First, we must say that ecclesial communion is something good and desirable, but it is also problematic and difficult for several reasons that we shall analyze briefly. The aging Simeon gave the fundamental reason: the problem of communion is raised by the very Jesus before whom one must stand. In the words of the letter to the Hebrews, the problem is the word of God, sharper than a two-edged sword. Thus the problem of communion is that it must be based on the truth of Jesus and on the truth of the word of God, as real things, not only as correctly formulated things. But both realities also generate the most radical conflict and division, not only between Christians and non-Christians, but within Christians themselves and within [among?] the churches.

Let us also recall that simultaneously and in parallel with the division that Jesus himself causes, we live in a world that is not only pluralistic and diversified, but divided and antagonistic. Medellín and Puebla said that very clearly in the customary language of Latin America: there are rich and there are poor; more exactly, there are rich because there are poor, and there are poor because there are rich, which is still a fundamental truth. We must keep this in mind in order to understand the fundamental pluralism that exists in today's world. The worst part is that the breach between rich and poor is growing, as the statistics show and the words of John Paul II declare. Thus we live in a world that is not a blank slate with symmetrical possibilities on one side or the other, but in an antagonistic, dueling world, in which some people, by necessity, work against others. To understand this it is not necessary to invoke class struggle, but to be faithful to scripture and true to the vision of our reality. The theological structure of reality is an antagonistic one. In real history there is the God of life and there are the idols of death, there is the Kingdom and the anti-Kingdom. The two are in conflict and an option for one is automatically an option against the other.

That antagonistic and dueling structure is also present in the church and among believers, whether they like it or not, whether they recognize it or not; the common formulation of doctrine and customs cannot make it disappear. In other words, the sin of the world, with its divisive and antagonizing power, is also present in the church. Therefore the antagonistic and dueling choice between faith and idolatry cannot be divided between believers and unbelievers, but cuts across all humanity, including believers and democrats, atheists, and Marxists.

Thus ecclesial communion must develop *around* the God of life and around Jesus, around the Kingdom, but also *against* the idols of death and the anti-Kingdom. This communion is then a victory, not only over division but over the antagonism of reality. So to reach communion we must overcome division, but above all we must overcome the idols and the anti-Kingdom. This makes communion more difficult, but it makes it Christian. For that reason, some approaches to ecclesial communion—although they may contribute something important—are limited by their very nature.

1. Inadequate Approaches to Ecclesial Communion

Uniformity

Above all, we must remember that the *uniformity* that preceded Vatican II, in the formulation of doctrine, customs, and theologies, is simply anachronistic today. For that simple reason, and not only because of the positive encouragement of the Council, it has been disappearing; it goes against history. In fact, it is not very Christian and is sometimes anti-Christian, because it has been a uniformity attempted on the basis of subjection, not of freedom or grace. We do not need to pursue this point, but we hope that it will not return, even in less offensive forms.

Pluralism

What has been proposed in its place is *pluralism*. Undoubtedly, the reality of our world is plural. We are all more aware of that today, and aware of the pluralism of ways of being church and of ecclesiologies throughout history. So, in theory at least, what has been suggested—sometimes fearfully—is a plurality of theologies and liturgies, a greater autonomy of local churches in their practices and customs. Even more, that plurality is seen as a possible complementarity and, therefore, as enriching to the church. It is hoped that the ecclesial institution, centered in the Vatican, will have sufficient creativity, understanding, and capacity for dialogue to maintain pluralism and make it enriching.

This pluralism has been moving forward in the church, but it creates two kinds of problems that must be kept very seriously in mind: one from the viewpoint of the conservative institution, and the other from the church of the poor. The conservative institution is not afraid of small, controllable, and ultimately manageable changes, but it is afraid of what is happening, in India for example, at the level of theology and liturgy. It is concerned about the reframing—even when it is done honorably and seriously—of Christian sexual morality in the First World, and it is afraid of the Latin American base communities, to give some important examples. And it is right to be afraid, because all of these raise problems that were effectively unknown in recent centuries, with ramifications that the institutional church cannot foresee. So then pluralism is reined in, and the church appeals to communion, not as a way for the local churches to participate with the church in Rome and Rome with the local churches, but as a way of subjecting the local churches and requiring them to accept what comes from Rome. Communion becomes a mechanism for coercion.

I do not want to minimize the real problems that derive from the examples given above, but I would like to call attention to the fact that the model of pluralism comes nowhere near solving the problem of ecclesial communion. What the model does do is help make the church aware of the theological assumption of pluralism: the real sincerity of all in relation to God's today, letting God be God, at least methodologically, and accepting the idea that communion is not a simple agreement on what we already know, but it is also walking new paths together and in dialogue. Thus pluralism presupposes what Irenaeus said so beautifully: "The Spirit slowly becoming accustomed to history." We should not be surprised that it is slow, but the important thing is that the church become accustomed to the new. In any case, there can be no doubt that in the present time pluralism is viewed more with distrust than with joy as a way of advancing communion.

On the other hand, from the viewpoint of the church of the poor, pluralism as a model of communion also involves risks and, certainly, it has its limits. Some things do not admit of differing interpretations; diversity on them is not enriching, but concealing. There are questions—"Were you there when they crucified my Lord?" There are demands—"What have you done to your brother?" There are primary realities—"A Samaritan found an injured man by the road." There are Beatitudes—"Blessed are you when you are persecuted for the sake of justice." And there are curses—"Woe to you, the rich." There are sentences—"I was hungry and you gave me to eat." There is "craziness"— "The wisdom of God is in the cross," "If they seek themselves, even if it is the church that seeks itself, they will not find salvation." These things cannot be ignored, or softened, or reinterpreted, or spiritualized in the name of any pluralism. It is very good that the liturgy is different in Rome and in Zimbabwe, that theology is different in Frankfurt and in Haiti, that the church is rethinking the issues of feminism, ecology, popular piety. It is urgently desirable that the functions of the bishops and the episcopal conferences are being reframed and resolved as well as possible. All that is very good. But we still hear the echoes of Micah's words about the minimum-maximum demand of God to all believers and all human beings, which puts a limit on pluralism and leads to true communion: "And what does the Lord require of you but to do justice, and to love kindness, and to walk humbly with your God?"

Thus pluralism is an important reality for enriching communion. But a pluralism that subtly or grossly obscures what is absolutely clear to Christian faith, that justifies that concealment in the name of a diversity of situations, cultures and theologies, will not achieve Christian ecclesial communion.

Communion and Disunity

The church also possesses mechanisms, functions, and charisms to *encourage communion and avoid disunity.* All this is well and good, and theologically and sociologically necessary. But we must avoid an important misunderstanding: these mechanisms can regulate, even encourage communion and limit division, but they do not and cannot generate the reality of ecclesial communion, because they were not made for the purpose of producing the primary ecclesial reality. Using the familiar spatial metaphor, communion is generated around a center, but that center, when it is a real center, when it is an effective source of communion, cannot be determined ahead of time. The center that attracts and generates communion is where it is, and nowhere else. In fact, according to the historians, when the church of Rome began to consider itself the center of the churches, it was on the basis of a primacy of charity, since it was there that Peter and Paul bore their witness to the greatest love. Quite apart from the obvious sociological reasons why Rome was the center of the Empire, it became the center of the emerging churches because it was the center of the ecclesial reality—of love and martyrdom.

This does not take away from the important function of Rome—and by extension the local episcopates—with respect to ecclesial communion, but we must not confuse the levels of communion. Rome may bring together what happens in the local churches, well or poorly—as history shows—but it does not generate the reality of the local churches or that which draws in other churches. It is the center of administration, of vigilance, of encouragement in the best of cases, but it is not necessarily the center of real ecclesial substance, nor need it be, although that would be good.

By all this we mean that the center or centers of ecclesial reality that generate communion change throughout history—as obviously happens with theology. Later on we shall see the positive role of Rome in communion, but here I have only tried to clarify a possible fundamental misunderstanding.

2. The Crucified People as Generator of Ecclesial Communion

What then is the real center of the universal church, which generates communion because it attracts or can attract the other local churches in a Christian way? We have already said it; that center is moveable. Today it is the church of the poor, churches almost always found in the Third World. That is true in fact and should also be so by right. But it is so—and this must be emphasized—precisely because the communion sought as a priority by that church of the poor is not communion between itself and the other churches, but with a world of crucified peoples.

It is the church of the poor that, before thinking about intra-ecclesial communion, empties itself in communion with the poor of this world, and that is also where the words of Jesus are fulfilled: "Those who seek to save their life will lose it, but those who lose it will save it." The church that is obsessed with its own communion will lose it, but the one that lives and dies for communion with the poor will gain it. Everything else will be added unto the church that effectively seeks the Kingdom of God for the crucified of this world. This communion with the crucified is what enables it to generate ecclesial communion, as well as the most specifically Christian division.

It has happened that way throughout history. It is a fact that today—to mention only the case I know best—the church in El Salvador attracts many Christians, solidarity groups, local churches (in fact, in the wave of persecution in November and December of 1989 many foreigners were threatened and expelled, and that was because they were there, not routinely as professional "missionaries," but attracted by the suffering and hope of the country). What started attracting attention and bringing others into the church was the incredible murder of priests, of an archbishop—remember that this happened in a Christian country, as the Western world likes to say. But that revealed to the world a church practically unknown until then, a church whose priests, catechists, and so-called "lay people"—in other words, the people of God—had emptied themselves to the poor and for doing so had suffered persecution and death. That in turn drew attention to the Salvadoran people, exposed to oppression and, more recently, repression. And finally, it revealed the great truth of the Salvadoran people: a crucified people, true suffering servant of Yahweh, as Ignacio Ellacuría used to say, a people in the throes of slow death from unjust poverty and of the fast and cruel death of repression. It is that crucified people that definitively attracts and produces ecclesial communion.

A church that is church of the poor because it has communed with the crucified people, that is the church that produces communion, which at a given moment becomes the center of the universal church. I have mentioned the case of El Salvador not out of triumphalism, but because it is a reality today. Today there are also other churches—ecclesial groups within them—that attract and convoke others—the church of Brazil, of South Africa, the church in some regions of India or Sri Lanka, and elsewhere. Tomorrow it may be other churches. But the important thing is that there are centers of ecclesial reality that generate communion. And, let us note clearly, they are the center not because they are higher in history, with all kinds of power, but because they are *below* in history, at the foot of the crucified peoples. They are the center not because they are at the center of worldly or ecclesiastical power, but rather because they are at the periphery of this world and of the constituted churches.

What we have shown in fact is also true by right. It is the suffering servant of Yahweh, the crucified peoples of this world, that have been set by God as "light of the nations." It is the Crucified One, because he is crucified, who "brings all things to him." This is not a philosophical truth or a mere theological conclusion, it is a central truth in the revelation of God that is repeated—in an historical and verifiable way—throughout history.

A church in communion with the crucified can generate communion among the different churches because it becomes a simply "real" church, Christianly and historically real. It is a real Christian church because it expresses ecclesial substance, as we have said before. And it is a real historical church because it becomes a "local" church, by which we mean locality not as a purely geographic concept or even as a purely cultural concept, but an historical one: it really participates in the history of the people. That church, doubly real, is credible; therefore it can proclaim the great truth that the church can be everywhere, if it becomes a historical church in each place. We have to thank Archbishop Romero, my martyred Jesuit brothers, and so many other murdered Salvadorans for having shown that faith and Salvadoran reality are not only not in opposition, but that they are mutually reinforcing, that in reality one can be both things, that the more Christian one is, the more one becomes engaged in the true Salvadoran reality, and the more intensely one lives that historical reality, the better Christian one can be. Many Christians have given their lives for the Salvadorans, and the Salvadorans can now be true Christians.

It is that real church that enlightens other churches, but it also questions and encourages them; it moves them to conversion, forgives them—why not say so?—and offers them grace. Precisely in this sense it is those churches that generate ecclesial communion. They may be small in size, they go through

difficult periods of survival because of the attacks of the powerful and, sometimes, of the institution itself, but qualitatively they are necessary and sufficient
to generate communion. This is what is happening, in a very new way, in the
universal church today.

3. Communion as Solidarity and Disunity as Conflict

A church of the poor generates communion in a specific way—not by imposing uniformity, certainly. Curiously, people from far away who have experienced
the reality of the Salvadoran church do not return to their people—with the
exception of some newly converted fanatics—with the idea of "imitating" that
church, but rather with the idea of reproducing its fundamental structure of
incarnation in objective reality, of looking at the world from below and of
defending the poor, although they do so in their own countries, in their own
way. Thus it is not a matter of imposing a new kind of uniformity.

Neither is communion generated by means of mere pluralism, as if the
church could now become a great orchestra with new instruments—among them
the church of the poor—playing a more wonderful melody. (Let us remember
that the Church Fathers used the metaphor of the zither, not so we would play
an ecclesial melody, but rather the melody that is Jesus Christ.)

Solidarity

The type of communion generated by the church of the poor is that of
solidarity, of "bearing one another." This is far more important than some
churches simply helping others at a time of need; it is the communion of giving
and receiving from one another the best that each has to give. The church of
the poor generates this process of bearing one another. The church itself is
borne by other churches when it receives all kinds of support: of material
assistance; of people who work for the crucified peoples at the pastoral, sup-
portive, human rights levels, together with them or in their own countries; also
the support of theologies that put their resources into shedding light on the
truth of the crucified peoples; and above all, when the members of other
churches are incarnated in that church of the poor and give of their best to it.
As an example, let us remember the four North American women murdered
in El Salvador in 1980—a martyrdom recently repeated by the North American
Sister Maureen on January 2, 1990—the most precious gift of the North American church and people to El Salvador. Thus, by the very act of coming together,
the church of the poor is borne by the local churches that come to them.

On the other hand, the church of the poor bears the other churches when
it offers them above all its very poverty, the ideal place for conversion and for
Christian faith, the place of life in community that overcomes endemic individualism, and the place of transcendence that overcomes blunt positivism; when
it offers them faith, hope, commitment, creativity, sacrificial love, the certainty
of meaning that they usually lack; when it embraces and forgives them—the
embrace is automatically forgiveness toward the First World and its churches,
even though the poor don't think of it that way; when it offers them grace, the
gift of God, unexpected, undeserved, and found in the least likely places—

among the poor; when it offers them the hidden treasure and the pearl of great price, because in unity with this church of the poor and in working for them, life and faith everywhere recover their deep meaning and one may joyfully sell all that one has to obtain it.

This solidarity is, definitively, solidarity in faith, but in a very precise sense. It is true that all churches, more exactly, all groups and Christians, come together in the substance of their common faith, but each of them contributes something specific of its own to faith in that God who is a mystery that the faith of a single person or a single church cannot comprehend. The faith of those who are below is different, by its nature, from that of those who are above. The faith of those who are below better expresses the disconsolate suffering of the creature before God and the sense of a hidden and crucified God. It better expresses radical hope in the life and higher holiness of subsistence or terrible death as a servant, even though the majority, in their situation of mere subsistence, may never possess the "paramount virtues" conventionally recognized by those who can take life for granted. It better expresses the need to live and struggle for justice, contagious hope, the "popular" nature of faith. It better expresses the grace that is found in history, the capacity for celebration and joy in the midst of countless tribulations.

The faith of those who are above, but who lower themselves, better expresses conversion, the radical exchange of oppressive life for life in community with the oppressed. It better expresses the conscious movement of *kenosis* and voluntary commitment—because they are not imposed by necessity, as in the case of the poor, but are voluntary and freely given. It better expresses the love that sacrifices and takes risks that they could have avoided. It better expresses how to put all one's skills at the service of the poor, skills that in this world only the elites can possess, and how to Christiánize every kind of power—as Jesus did—by putting it at the service of the oppressed. It better expresses faith as victory, because by its nature—in contrast to popular piety—that faith has been attacked by the prevailing secularism, agnosticism, and atheism of the First World.

Thus all of us, those who are below and those who lower themselves, can approach asymptotically the mystery of God, maintain an understanding of God as mystery, each of us bringing what we can in order to confess God as God among us all, rather than trying to explain God with a single formulation, conceptualization, or experience. What I want to emphasize is that the movement of solidarity, solidarity in faith, begins at the bottom of history, in the cross of the peoples. That is the source of the historical power that unleashes radical solidarity.

That is how I understand solidarity. I recall—from a slightly different context—the beautiful words of Karl Rahner, which I have often quoted, about the relation between the believer and the gospel. He says: "The gospel is a heavy light burden; the more one carries it on one's shoulders, the more one is carried by the gospel." That is how I see solidarity: a heavy light burden. The more we carry the church of the poor—a very heavy burden because the crosses of the peoples are in it—the more that church carries us.

Solidarity then means putting together two fundamental Christian dimensions: the willingness to give, transformative praxis in technical terms; and the willingness to receive, grace. That is how true and Christian ecclesial communion is created. This communion continually widens to become truly ecumenical communion, with other churches, and truly human communion with all men and women of good will. This is not at all relativizing, but simply a way of honoring those who generated the movement of solidarity: the crucified peoples.

The Problem of Disunity

It follows from this that what radically opposes communion is not only or primarily *division*, or even disunity. Neither of these is desirable in the universal church, of course, but they are not the greatest problem for communion. The problem of disunity must be framed above all as one of making a fundamental option for or against the crucified peoples. Division and disunity occur more or less analogously, of course, but with respect to division, one must emphasize that what mainly divides the church is the sin of the world, which surrounds and also enters the church. It is not only or primarily a matter of the obvious limitations and concupiscence of the church members, or even of the "categoric" sins that have never been lacking in the church, and in which we all participate.

It is a matter of fundamental sin. If a church or churches, for whatever reason, look more to themselves than to the crucified peoples, communion does not grow, despite their relations with, even assistance to, other churches. Worse yet, if churches—by what they do and especially by what they do not do—are against the crucified peoples, then communion in the church of Jesus is simply impossible. There is nothing left for them to do but go and be reconciled with their brothers and sisters before placing their offering at the altar.

The greatest intra-ecclesial conflict is expressed in the same terms as conflict in the world: it is the conflict between the God of life and the idols. The greatest challenge to ecclesial communion is whether the churches have taken their option for or against the victims. This is strong language, but it is so. And as tragic as it is to say it, there have been times when by action or omission the churches have supported idols more than the God of life; or to put it more gently, often the idols have not felt a serious protest from the church and have been able to act with impunity. At other times, fortunately, things have been different; the churches have opted for the God of life and have defended the victims. When this has happened, the intra-ecclesial conflict has been great, but solidarity has been greater, as happened paradigmatically in El Salvador during the three years of Archbishop Romero.

4. Ministerial Service to Ecclesial Communion

The considerations set out so far are central, and without them I do not believe true ecclesial communion can be generated. That is the fundamental lesson offered by the Salvadoran and Latin American ecclesial experience. But let us close with a brief reflection on ministerial, "categoric," service to ecclesial communion.

A universal church, which is both one and catholic, therefore pluralistic, needs a center; local churches, by analogy, also need it. This center must be established and analyzed dogmatically, theologically, and sociologically, and Catholic theology insists on that. The church of the poor cordially accepts that center of ecclesial communion, and—although with sporadic tensions and skirmishes between the bases and the hierarchy—it understands the need and benefits of that ministerial service to communion.

I have nothing new to add either to theological reflection on the center of communion or to the desire of the church of the poor for the true existence of such a center. I would only end with some brief historical reflections from the viewpoint of Latin American experience, in hopes of making the center of ecclesial communion a real and more fruitful service.

It is important above all that those who are at the ministerial center of the church, the Holy Father and his curia, the bishops and their curias, make an effort to know the church of the poor in its reality, in what I have called its real ecclesial substance. It is important that they make it known to everyone, without thinking of it only as a regional reality that must of course be kept in mind, and with which they must sometimes struggle. It is important that they encourage all the other churches to let themselves be touched by its suffering, by its hope, by its martyrdom. It is important that the ecclesial structures—new bishops, seminary formation—allow themselves to be penetrated by this church of the poor.

It is important above all for their service to ecclesial communion that they change the assumptions that now seem to prevail in the centers of the church. I shall enumerate them simply by giving their opposites. One does not see more clearly by being at the center, but on the contrary, one sees more clearly from the periphery. One must go from the center to the periphery, not only to teach but especially to learn. One is not more in communion by showing servility to the center—it is sad to see the prevailing fear in the church today, of not being able to speak freely, as brothers and sisters with simplicity and clarity—than by trying to dialogue, and by criticizing too, honorably and charitably. One does not love the church of Jesus more by silencing errors or mechanically applauding or defending its privileges, its worldly honors, than by trying to decenter it from itself, to lead it to real poverty, to bring it into conflict with the powerful of this world. One does not become more pastoral by warning and condemning than by proclaiming the gospel definitively as what it is: Good News to the poor of this world and to those who wish to accompany them.

And just one more thing, to close. Jesus said it very clearly: "No one has greater love than those who give their lives for their brothers and sisters." I can think of no better service to ecclesial communion than that of taking seriously so many martyred deaths, proposing the martyrs as present witnesses of faith—today, in Latin America, "a great cloud of witnesses" as the letter to the Hebrews calls them. It is not a matter of idealizing them all, but rather of presenting them as authentic Christians and followers of Jesus, Christians in whom we should all see ourselves, and by seeing ourselves in them we can be more united.

I believe that with these assumptions, when the ministerial center of communion accepts, learns, and gives thanks for them to the real centers of ecclesial substance, then it can offer an important and irreplaceable service to the ecclesial communion of all the churches.

"With this people it is not hard to be a good pastor," Archbishop Romero used to say. In the church of the poor it is not hard to be a good pastor; it is not hard to exercise the ministry of the Good News and of prophecy, and also that of service to ecclesial communion. Archbishop Romero began with a bitterly divided church in his archdiocese, and ended with a church in such communion as has never been seen before or since. It was his merit to have united it by his leadership, credibility, and commitment. But it was his wisdom to have united it with real ecclesial substance — faith, hope, love, and the martyrdom of the poor. There were tensions and conflicts, but there was ecclesial communion. Ecclesial communion is necessary, but above all it is possible because it happens. Gathered around the crucified peoples to bring them down from the cross, the church of the poor grows, and with it ecclesial communion.

— Translated by Margaret D. Wilde

31

Basic Ecclesial Communities

MARCELLO de C. AZEVEDO

Today in Latin America, basic ecclesial communities are an important ecclesiological element from the theological, pastoral, and institutional viewpoint. *Theologically* they express biblical elements, and aspects of the tradition and doctrine of the church, explicitly and in a new light. *Pastorally* they create and accelerate a process of evangelization and development of the faith and Christian life in a way that responds to the needs of the majority of the population. *Institutionally* they represent a paradigm of ecclesial organization different from earlier models, one which has an increasing influence on the broader institutionality of the church. Thus the basic ecclesial communities are a key element in Latin American ecclesial life and contribute to a clearer understanding of that life in the present historical moment.

There are at present a large number of publications on the basic ecclesial communities. Some of them are analytical and focusing on specific aspects. They offer documented examples of the reality of these communities. Other works study the issue with well-defined theological, ecclesiological, or pastoral dimensions. Some essays have come from the basic ecclesial communities themselves. Some investigations and documents have come from the hierarchical church. And there is a lot of mimeographed material, oriented to communication, motivation, or discussion in the communities themselves or in seminars and discussion groups about them.

With all their differences of tone and quality, this multiplicity of publications has a great hermeneutical value. It is like a tapestry that helps us understand the spontaneous weaving of the real, everyday journey of the basic ecclesial communities. One way to classify this vast material is to group it in three large categories: descriptive studies of the *phenomenology* of the basic ecclesial communities; works that reveal their *methodology*; and studies that reflect on the communities and develop their *theological* grounding or meaning in a variety of aspects.

From direct contact with the basic ecclesial communities, with the people who work in them, and from the analysis of their bibliography, one can identify a constant in the present ecclesial consciousness: the basic ecclesial communities are a new way to live the church, to *be* church and to *act* as church. This is not a new way, insofar as the basic ecclesial communities draw together and revitalize elements of the most authentic tradition of the church since its beginning. But it is a new way of being church if one compares it to the previously existing model of church, which has prevailed for the nearly five centuries of ecclesial presence in Latin America. This model, still the generally prevailing one, feeds into the evangelization, institutionalization, and pastoral action of the church that was consolidated in Latin America. It was the governing paradigm of the missionary expansion that coincided with the discoveries of the modern age, which remained throughout the colonial period and after independence, even through the period of "Romanization" in the second half of the nineteenth century. The origins and inspiration of this model are rooted in the context of the Council of Trent, with the organization of a body of doctrine, a homogeneous liturgical and disciplinary universe, and with a specific system of clergy formation and qualification designed to put them in practice and cultivate them. In terms of symbolic expression and structure, the model still involves typical elements of the earlier shape of Christianity in Spain and Portugal; these elements in turn come from a variety of influences.

In the aftermath of Vatican II and its contextualization in Medellín and Puebla, and in the complex framework of Latin American reality, the basic ecclesial communities introduce new fundamental options for the church. Rooted in tradition, the basic ecclesial communities offer something very creative. Thus it is not enough to look only at their past and present. One must also be open to their prospects for the future.

As can be seen in the reflection underlying the documents of the Second and Third General Assemblies of the Latin American bishops, in Medellín (1968) and Puebla (1979) respectively, theology in Latin America is directly related to the basic ecclesial communities. That theology offers a valid assortment of instruments for the analysis and interpretation of these communities. The same is true of the different theologies of liberation. Although one or another of the versions of the theology of liberation may not fully coincide with the theological boundaries, especially of Puebla, the theologies of liberation are a meaningful mediation for understanding the basic ecclesial communities.

I. WHAT ARE THE BASIC ECCLESIAL COMMUNITIES?

Some of the fundamental common characteristics of this ecclesial phenomenon are present in different parts of the world and are known as *base communities, Christian base communities*, or *basic ecclesial communities*. In the present state of ecclesiological consciousness and reflection it is hard to speak of the basic ecclesial communities in a single way. Despite their common origins they are, in fact, a diversified reality from which one can derive an analogous concept. Even in the more homogenous context of Latin America, there are notable differences among the ecclesial communities of Brazil, Peru, El Salvador, and Nicaragua, for example. This makes a rigorous analysis of them difficult, without specific qualifications. Thus we need a concrete reference point that permits the later verification of analogous cases. Here that reference point will be the basic ecclesial communities of Brazil, bearing in mind, however, that in this chapter I am also stressing what seems to apply to other Latin American countries.[1]

I do not presume to give a strict definition or even to describe the basic ecclesial communities. This would go against one of their fundamental characteristics, their flexibility and openness to change and transformation in tune with reality and the signs of the times, signs of God and humanity as expressed by the sensitivity of the communities. All this is part of the life of the communities and is difficult to conceptualize. But some characteristic elements are contained in their name itself: basic ecclesial communities.

They are *communities*. They are moving toward a Christian lifestyle that contrasts sharply with the individualistic and selfish, privatized, and competitive style that marks both the modern-contemporary Western culture and the ecclesiastical structure that until very recently was generally accepted in that context. Thus in their twenty-five or thirty years of evolution, before and since Puebla, the basic ecclesial communities have been emphasizing communion and participation. By emphasizing communion—the only viable basis of authentic community—the basic ecclesial communities seek to live the faith as a shared experience, mutually nourished and supported by their members. This dimension recovers the common inspiration of the scriptural traditions, in the sense that the faith is expressed in the covenant between God and humanity and is lived in the awareness of faith as the common inheritance of a whole people: the people of God. Faith is also expressed at the social and relational level, precisely because it is rooted in the individual and lived at the personal level. This underlying level of communion in faith must lead to a growing improvement in interpersonal relations within the community. This makes possible the dimension of participation, especially in shared responsibility for making and carrying out decisions. This characteristic overcomes passive or purely submissive attitudes toward the initiative and authority of the clergy, religious, and lay leaders in the community.

The basic ecclesial communities are *ecclesial*. This adjective has a truly substantive influence on the character of the communities. In the Brazilian community context, the catalyzers of this ecclesiality have been unity of faith and unity in the faith on the one hand, and on the other, their sense of belonging to the church as a visible institutional reality. Although they are open to ecumenical dialogue, the experience of the basic ecclesial communities has shown how important it is to begin with one faith for the conscious growth of the communities of faith. This is a fundamental characteristic because of the influence and importance of the word of God and biblical reading, reflection, and prayer in the basic ecclesial communities, as we shall see. Moreover, by emphasizing the link with the pastors and the visible reality of the church, as a mark of their ecclesiality, the communities seek to overturn the hostile, demanding, and confrontational model which characterized the basic communities in the 1970s, especially in countries like Italy, France, or the "underground church" in the United States. This does not mean that the basic ecclesial communities necessarily originate in the initiative of the clergy, although that sometimes happens. Therefore apart from the question of origin, what is certain is that the basic ecclesial communities have sought and found recognition and support from the bishops, while still enjoying broad autonomy.

The third characteristic of these communities is that they are *basic*. Because they are mainly an active community of lay people, they understand themselves as the "base," from an ecclesiastical perspective, with respect to the hierarchical structure of the church. But in Latin America, the basic ecclesial communities are also *of the base* from a social and sociological perspective. Their thousands or millions of members are poor people. This is not an exclusive posture but an understandable phenomenon. Poor people feel more strongly the need for mutual support and community. In their simplicity they are less demanding and sophisticated when it comes to establishing, modeling, and cultivating interpersonal relationships. Under the pressure of urgent common needs, they are also more open to participation. In short, the poor are more sensitive to the gift, because they are also more aware of what they lack, personally and socially, and of their need to receive. They rarely think of things and relationships as rights due them or deserved by them. They have a humility that comes true in simplicity. This opens their hearts to faith, a reality that belongs to the economy of the gift of salvation and liberation. The fact of being at the ecclesial and social base makes it easier for the members of the basic ecclesial communities to integrate faith and life, word and action. In the light of the gospel, this permits them to see their situation in the context of the oppression, violence, and injustice of a social organization that must be transformed. Being at the base leads them to a faith which is not only hearing or knowing the message, not only a liturgical expression of the word, but all that and much more, focused on concrete and conscious actions, on effectively transforming actions. Sensitive to the imperative of social change, being at the base allows them also to understand that they, so long and deeply marked by the unjust inspiration and structure of society, will be the principal authors of this irreversible transformation. Indeed, there is no hope that transformation will come from the beneficiaries of the status quo. The natural and immediate subjects of social change are the victims who actually suffer the consequences of the reality and who comprise the immense majority of the population. In this sense the basic ecclesial communities, by the intrinsic force of the historical incarnation of the Christian faith and by its inexorable ethical consequences, which must be expressed in Christian *praxis*, have a social and political dimension and influence. Living their faith entails the imperative of evangelical inspiration with respect to the structure and organization of society, the common good of their members, and the demand of active presence in the building of that project. From this intimate link between faith and life, between faith and action, between faith and its ethical projection, between the evangelical project and action to transform an oppressive and unjust society, comes the importance of a liberating *praxis* in the basic ecclesial communities in the context of a violent reality that oppresses them.[2]

II. HOW A BASIC ECCLESIAL COMMUNITY EMERGES

The formation of basic ecclesial communities is a process fed by three streams: renewal in the parish, biblical groups, and social and political awareness.

1. Renewal in the Parish

The earliest concern, even before Medellín, was to energize the parish. How could the church overcome the individualism and anonymity, the thinking and attitudes of a privatized or merely devotional and cultic religion so common in Latin American parishes with their vast territory and great numbers? In this mainly sociological perspective, of the internal energization of the parish, the basic ecclesial communities were seen as the primary ecclesial cell (Medellín). Today, the intention of multiplying small intra-parochial groups is still among the roots of the creation of basic ecclesial communities in many places.[3]

2. Biblical Groups

Beyond the jurisdictional boundaries of the parish, between Medellín and Puebla, everywhere to some degree there emerged groups of prayer and reflection in the light of the word of God. This was an intense, postconciliar phase of new Bible translations, wide distribution of the sacred text through the "month of the Bible," courses, introductions, and above all, the popularization of scripture. In some countries there was a notable effort to make explicit the implicit content of the Bible in the traditions of popular piety and the spirituality of the people. In Brazil the contribution of Carlos Mesters was invaluable in the development of a popular pedagogy of access to the Bible. From the 1960s to the present, biblical circles have been a first step in the development of basic ecclesial communities, and the hearing and reading of the word of God has been central to these communities. Thus the characteristic perspective of the basic ecclesial communities with respect to the Bible is to bring together what is read with what is lived. It is the linkage between word and reality, the identification in the Bible of situations that the people live and suffer today. Through this linkage the members of the basic ecclesial communities are initiated in a new vision of God, of the world and of themselves, which is decisive for the biblical grounding that animates the life of the communities.[4]

3. Social and Political Awareness

Similar concerns, problems, ideas, and aspirations related to everyday life develop in and among people an awareness of unity and a sense of solidarity. They discover one another in their common fate. The experience of fragmentation and impoverishment, of individual oppression and helplessness, gives way to perception of the possibilities when many people make an integrated effort. Many basic ecclesial communities have begun that way. The group forms around precise objectives: to build a bridge; to open or improve a road; to ensure the production of enough food for subsistence; to provide a school, water, or light for the community; to struggle for possession or ownership of the land. Little by little, as they become aware of their unity in faith, they come together in prayer and celebration, and especially, as they discover themselves in the biblical texts and passages, a basic ecclesial community emerges out of a group that was meeting occasionally for a specific purpose.

Whichever of these streams came first — parish renewal, biblical groups, or social and political awareness — experience has shown that the creation of basic ecclesial communities always entails interaction between the *religious* and the *social* streams. One may have dominated or preceded the other at the beginning, but the basic ecclesial community only emerges when the two are integrated. When only the social side lasts, the group is on the way to becoming a *popular movement*. When only the religious side lasts, there is a biblical or prayer association, movement, or group. The basic ecclesial community presupposes "people's faith and struggle, gospel and social reality"; it is an ecclesial reality based on a faith that embraces the totality of life.[5]

Two coordinates must cross, therefore, in the gestation of a basic ecclesial community. On one side, there is emphasis on the word of God, on the centrality of Jesus Christ, on the impact of his mission of salvation and liberation. There is awareness of communion in faith, a sense of being a people, and of assuming together the task of realizing the evangelical project. On the other side there is awareness of insertion in the world, of attentiveness to the signs of the times, of impetus toward social transformation, of commitment to building the future. There is a critical perception of the context of struggle, of the ideological forms involved, and of the inevitable conflicts. This double axis intersects in a personalized, adult faith, rooted in life and committed to overcoming oppression, violence, marginalization, and discrimination. The basic ecclesial communities seek to live this faith in hope, to sustain it in truth, and to animate it in love. This is the firm basis of a just society, an incipient form of the presence and the implantation of the Kingdom.

III. HISTORICAL CONTEXT OF THE EMERGENCE OF THE BASIC ECCLESIAL COMMUNITIES

Three factors were particularly decisive in the historical context of the appearance of the basic ecclesial communities in Latin America. The first was the Second Vatican Council. That was beyond all doubt a global ecclesial experience, but it was also the event that made the basic ecclesial communities possible. In contrast to a way of being church that had been crystallized since the Middle Ages and organized in a uniform way since the Council of Trent, Vatican II assumed and legitimated different tendencies that were being affirmed and were maturing since the first half of this century. The biblical and liturgical movements, the renewal of the church's ecclesiology and social doctrine, the growing participation of lay people, and sensitivity to the modern world were decisive elements in this early establishment of the very conditions of existence for the communities. Therein lie the roots of many aspects of this new way of being church, as represented by the basic ecclesial communities.

The second factor is also intra-ecclesial. With the Council's emphasis on episcopal collegiality, there was a resurgence of respect for and awareness of the local churches. The contextualized reading of the Council in Medellín and Puebla was attentive to our dramatic reality, marked by poverty and injustice. The new awareness of the underworld of the poor, the identification of that underworld as an inversion of history, and the consequent *preferential option for the poor*, which became the conducting wire of the new sensitivity, gradually transformed the ecclesiological shape and the pastoral praxis of many of our local churches. Made up mostly of poor people, who are the immense majority of our people, the basic ecclesial communities are a specific and living implementation of ecclesial preference for the poor. Seeing and thinking about reality from their viewpoint, being with them and serving them, the church today is returning to the form, inspiration, and identity of Christ's own mission. He came to evangelize the poor.

The third factor is found in the historical context lived today by several Latin American countries. The permanent situation of a stratified and discriminatory society, which comes from the colonial past, the consolidation of privileged national oligarchies that arose in the post-independence period, and the predatory and generalized invasion of international capital in our regions, were followed in the 1960s by the implantation of the political and economic models of National Security. All this led to the fusion of the national military and oligarchic powers with international economic power in a model of concentrated wealth, dependency, oppression, and repression. This model left the poor without a voice and without opportunity, without participation in the benefits of their labor, while the exploitation of their labor cemented the simultaneous movement toward modernization and material development in the production sectors. The economic factor, dominant and determinative, made this model unacceptable to the church because it perverted the Christian concept of humanity and the world. After a long history of tacit or open participation in power and alliance with it through the centuries, in several of our countries the church found itself on the other side this time, taking on a role as the voice of those who had lost theirs or who never had a voice. In this critical and challenging situation, in which the church paid a high price of persecution and martyrdom, the basic ecclesial communities emerged. They were nourished by this participation in the cross of Christ as they experienced it in the daily drama of their lives. In several countries the historical phase of repression acted as a profoundly pedagogical element, though a painful one, with a double dimension of conscientization: on the one hand, a maturation of a realistic church in solidarity with the least and poorest; on the other, evidence of a situation of social injustice that cries out to heaven, and an increasingly clear identification of the causes and processes that produce that injustice. One of the integrated results of this historical context was this way of being, living, and acting as church, which is precisely what the basic ecclesial communities represent. If the eventual democratization of our political regimes, social justice, and real participation in economic benefits, and the growing participation of all in the shape of their national destinies should ever become a concrete reality, the basic ecclesial communities, and the church that lives in them, would have at the same time the awareness of having played a meaningful part in building this new society and the challenge of finding ways to go on being church in the context of a more just and participatory, probably more egalitarian, and certainly more democratic society. We cannot foresee today, on the Latin American horizon, the possibility of realizing this ideal. But that the road is leading in that direction is undeniable.

IV. THE EVANGELIZING POTENTIAL OF THE COMMUNITIES

The relevance of the evangelizing potential of the basic ecclesial communities is evident in a structural confrontation between the paradigm of evangelization represented by the basic ecclesial communities, and the one that has determined the course of nearly five centuries of evangelization of the simple and poor people in the rural areas and urban peripheries of our countries. The earlier model was centered on the *priest*, on the *parish* and its dispersed chapels, on the *sacrament*, on the *individual person*, and on the salvation of the *soul*. In the vast rural areas, because of the chronic shortage of priests, the model was implemented mainly through pastoral missions and emphasis on fiestas. Missions were infrequent, short, and intensive visits by the priest, which allowed the faithful to receive the sacraments and express their awareness of belonging to the church. Fiestas, for the patron saint or other popular saints, simultaneously catalyzed the religious, social, playful and political dimensions of persons and groups. The regular repetition of this pattern and the people's faithfulness to it, although it did not clarify or enrich the rational content of the faith, and did not assign the faithful an active role in the ecclesial context, did contribute to the awareness and formal affirmation of the faith. The time between "father's" visits was covered by devotions (novenas, triduums, the month of May, religious practices related to the life cycle – birth, marriage, and death – or to nature—plants, animals, weather). Remote rural areas, almost in a state of hibernation and resigned to, but not shaken by the dispersion of modern life, permitted the transmittal of the faith over time with an impressive faithfulness to these patterns.

The basic ecclesial communities, as we have said, are located in this same environment. Their members come from the same population sector. The new paradigm of evangelization emerged slowly, not from the application of a theoretically conceived and predesigned alternative model, but from the reality lived by the communities and from their everyday experience, followed and even encouraged by the pastors. This model is centered on the *laity*, the *community*, the *Word*, and the *salvation* and *integral liberation* of the *whole human person* at the *individual* and *social* level. Instead of objects of the process, mainly passive spectators of the initiative and efforts of the clergy, the faithful became the active subjects of their own evangelization. This is nourished above all by constant reference to the word of God in scripture, read, reflected on, and prayed on in direct relation to the concrete life of the members of the community and people. Adherence to the postulates of the faith leads to the urgent necessity of individual conversion. It also leads, in the presence of the concrete reality lived by the people, to awareness of structural transformation as an imperative. Eucharist, reconciliation, and the anointing of the sick, in their direct relationship with the ordained minister, emphasize his importance for the communities. Lay people, nonetheless, become key elements in the preparation and accompaniment of sacramental life, in the initiation to baptism and confirmation, in preparation for first communion, confession, and marriage. Much of what used to be done by the priest, episodically and by improvisation, is done today by lay people in the context of a pedagogy that has matured in the communities. It is promoted by the bishops and by the pastoral agents (priests, religious brothers and sisters, lay catechists) and carried forward by the community itself. In this way new forms of service are emerging as an expression of new *ministries*.[6] They are not necessarily precarious substitutes for the scarce and absent ordained clergy. They are above all an active response to the rhythm of the group's life and faith, always confronted with new situations in a social context that does violence to its own way of being and living, and with growing awareness of the fragmentation of its cultural universe. This fragmentation is effected through the social communications media (transistor radios and television), through transportation which intensifies mobility, and through the growing presence in the rural areas of industrial, mining, agricultural, and other projects, with inexorable consequences.

A comparative approach to these two paradigms of evangelization explains why in Brazil, for example, the bishops give special attention to the basic ecclesial communities and make them a pastoral priority:

Today, in our country, the basic ecclesial communities constitute a reality which expresses one of the most dynamic characteristics of the life of the church and which, for diverse reasons, is awakening the interest of other sectors of society. We agree with the words of the bishops in Puebla: "The base communities, which were just an incipient experience in 1968 (Medellín), have matured and multiplied. In communion with their bishops, they have become centers of evangelization and engines of liberation and development" (Puebla 96). A strictly ecclesial phenomenon, the basic ecclesial communities in our country were born in the heart of the institutional church and have become a new way of being church. We can affirm that increasingly, in the future, the pastoral and evangelizing action of the church will be realized and developed around them.[7]

V. ECCLESIOLOGICAL DIMENSIONS

The development of a complete and coherent ecclesiology in the context of theology in Latin America is much broader than the *ecclesiological approach of the basic ecclesial communities*. But for the moment, in their own understanding and that of the bishops, the basic ecclesial communities are part of the corpus of an ecclesiology that has been developing in Latin America for the past twenty years.[8] The existence and development of the basic ecclesial communities are not a product of this theological elaboration. Historically the two phenomena have nourished each other, while each was defining itself. Chronologically the basic ecclesial communities were emerging even before the spread of a reflective expression of a theology of the church in the Latin American context. But the reality of the basic ecclesial communities and the experience of the theologians, bishops, and other pastoral agents, lived and assimilated during the evolution of theological and pastoral reflection and action, have themselves been an important factor in the process. The reality of the basic ecclesial communities effectively nourished, established, and confirmed the principles and development of this ecclesiology and defined its course. That reality gave the church an opportunity for field work. This theology and its ecclesiology, which are by now sufficiently elaborated, are revealed as one of the best keys for reading the meaning and impact of the basic ecclesial communities. Therefore, in order to understand and evaluate the ecclesiological impact of the basic ecclesial communities, it will help to recall briefly some aspects of the context in which that theological reflection arose in Latin America.

Theology in the church is generally fed by two principal streams: direct reference to the *sources* — the Bible, tradition, and the interpretation and teachings of the magisterium on them — for a better understanding of revelation and of the church as a part of the revelation; and *philosophical* support, mainly from Greek influence, through the dominant influence of Plato and Aristotle, and especially through St. Augustine and St. Thomas Aquinas. Up to the 1970s, theology in Latin America repeated or reflected European theological thought along these same lines. And until Vatican II it did so in the neoscholastic terms which prevailed in seminary formation. After the Council it was open to nonscholastic but always European influence, and above all it transposed into Latin America the conciliar focus on the relationship between church and world. *World* was understood here as the product of modern times, with respect to which, over time, the church had assumed an aggressive, defensive, or condemnatory posture. That world now became the interlocutor of the church, viewed optimistically, as is documented in *Gaudium et spes.*

This positive conciliar position left in the shadows a less ethnocentric and more rigorous analysis of modernity and its negative impact, not only at the level of ideas, but in its real and destructive effects on the structural organization of the world and most of the population, as expressed by the World Synod of Bishops on Justice in 1971. These effects are manifested in the problems of hunger, ecological imbalance, and institutionalized violence, of which the arms race and the nuclear threat are dramatic elements, but equally so are political dependency and the international commodity and financial market.

The sharp and fundamental experience of recent theological reflection in Latin America occurs in the context of *radical and structural poverty* in Latin America itself and in vast regions of the world. This has been produced, reproduced, and constantly aggravated by social, political, and economic organization on a global scale. The church's sensitivity to poverty is nothing new. In all its forms — material or spiritual poverty, sickness or ignorance, scarcity or rejection, loneliness or insecurity, discrimination or oppression — poverty and its different aspects, concretely perceived in human life, often have been a point of departure for great vocations, institutions, and movements in the church in every age. What is emerging now in Latin America, since the 1960s, is a *new* sensitivity to the poor and to poverty in the world. There is an internal dynamic in this experience that turns it into an impetus for the transformation of persons in the ecclesial context. And that is where theological reflection begins to take a new direction.[9]

Where does this new focus come from, and why is it new? It comes from a broader, more complete perception of causal relationships in the world in which we live. It objectifies the paradox of a world, which is approaching the historical culmination of scientific understanding, on the humanistic and technological level, but which is thoroughly marked by the dehumanization of humanity. And this translates into hunger, unemployment, and sickness, the violation of freedom, institutional violence, poverty on a macroscale lived by individuals or by whole societies. What is new about this phenomenon? We can answer that from three interdependent perspectives.

1. *The intuition that the world, in defiance of the convictions and present potential of humanity, has been organized in such a way as to produce and reproduce this poverty.* Given the premises on which many states operate, there is no hope of a way out, but certainty and evidence that the problem is becoming worse.

2. *The understanding that this poverty is not episodic or accidental.* It is recognized as systematic and structural. The result of a long evolutionary process, through the will of a few, today it is coming down inexorably anduncontrollably on a large part of humanity. One after another, calls and attempts to stop or redirect this process are being frustrated.

3. *The evidence that this poverty is the product of disrespect for the recognized rights of humanity.* It is the result of widespread oppression, less perhaps at the conscious level of individual action, but clearly seen in the ironclad unity and the internal dynamic of the economic and political systems that humanity has

created for itself. These systems work, penetrating everything, through the structural injustice that is both the condition and principle of their continued development.

Ironically, it is the global nature of today's world that makes this reading of it possible. The prophets of Israel or the holy Christians of the church in other ages could not feel or perceive the poverty of their time in the same way, at a global and interrelated level, even though they lived with the everyday poverty of the many poor that "you will always have with you," as Jesus said. The certainty of inevitable poverty is sad. But what is tragic is the organized production of poverty on a planetary scale, and the irreversible destruction of so many human beings on this planet.

Two increasingly evident characteristics of the church's recent position in many parts of the world—its conscious opening to humanity as a concrete whole, and its real communion with true human history—suggest convincingly that this poverty cannot be lived fatalistically. It is rather the result of selfishness, which translates into active and efficient injustice. For that reason it represents not only an imbalance in the equity that ought to exist, but an unequivocal negation of love and truth. In the Christian perspective such injustice perverts and subverts both God's plan and the dignity and destiny of humanity. The terminal reality that it creates, *the poverty that is the fruit of injustice*, carries the mark of sin. The acuteness and intensity of the church's perception in this regard is precisely what has given it this *new* sensitivity to the reality of poverty in the world and to the challenge it represents for a full and coherent living of the faith. This poverty, which the church everywhere is increasingly perceiving in this way, was and remains the daily, dominant experience practically everywhere in Latin America.

Living in this precarious world, the Latin American church did not find in the two streams of theological reflection mentioned above, adequate tools for its mission in history and for its reading of the meaning and historicity of humanity and the world. Two central problems had emerged that were not generally known in the theology of other times and places, and resolving them now became part of the theological process, reflected in evangelizing and pastoral action.

1. How should the church read and analyze, more deeply and conclusively, this empirically perceived reality? Certainly the earlier theologies also reflected the social and cultural context in which they were produced and gave it a diversity of interpretations. But in these theologies, *analysis of the reality* is not the main concern, let alone the point of departure for their reflection and their reference to the sources. The tools made available today by the social sciences, like those of philosophy in the past, have begun to be used to focus, analyze, and interpret reality, with reality now seen as the principal theological locus.[10]

2. How should the church read the history of salvation, the action of God, God's redemptive design for all humanity in and through Jesus Christ, the equality and fundamental dignity of persons, the universal fatherhood of God—how should it read all this in the context of our dramatic reality and growing awareness of that reality in our countries? How should it announce to the poor,

in their crushing situation, the word that speaks to their elemental humanity:
that God is a just Father? How can it presume to bring them to growth in faith
and hope, when their own existence and human condition are so profoundly
unlivable?[11]

The answer to this second problem—which is not so much tied to the analysis
and interpretation of reality as to a faithful *evangelization* of humanity within
that reality—was provided by the incorporation of another fundamental element in the process of theological reflection. Is it possible to approach the
Bible, not primarily from the starting point of the inherent mystery of God,
which people have already systematized and developed (by deductive reasoning), but from a direct grasp of God's constant action among human beings?
How can the church find in the Bible God's position toward human poverty,
toward the violence of some to others, toward the oppression that is woven
directly into human social organizations? Beginning from there, how can it
radically embrace the mystery of God and intuit within it other traits, previously
less noticed and theologically less scrutinized? Beginning from there, how can
it scrutinize the mystery of humanity, the meaning of human life in responding
to God and in freely building the people's own world?

This new approach is part of what has come to be called *a change of social
locus. Social locus* is the point from which people perceive, understand, and
interpret their reality or from which they act upon it. We all are situated in a
social locus. What is new here, in terms of theological reflection, is the step
toward a meaningful vision of the poor. By their very existence they witness to
the dynamic of *individual sin* and of *social sin*, and to the intimate *correlation
between them*. When we take the poor as a point of departure and as a central
reference point in the reading and understanding of humanity and history, and
also of God and God's action upon the world, they open a new perspective for
the evangelizing church. Only by a change of social locus, in our theological
perception of the mystery of salvation and in our salvation-based concept of
evangelization, can the church set humanity and the world on the road to the
needed conversion and transformation. Consequently, that is where the church
begins to understand what is perceived and suffered by those who do not benefit
from the present organization of this world and who have no decision-making
power within it. That is where the church discovers the dregs of sin that underlie
this reality. That is also where it discovers the radical meaning of human history,
which is the act of beginning, through the power of the total mystery of Jesus
Christ, in the truth and love that make justice real, to build the definitive
Kingdom that cannot be reached in this world. The transformation of the world,
like the conversion of the person, is a radical for full consistency with the
content and teleology of Christian faith.

VI. POLITICAL DIMENSION OF THE COMMUNITIES

An integral perception of humanity at the individual and social level and an
understanding of the historical and incarnational roots of the mystery of Jesus
Christ and thus of the Christian faith bring to the basic ecclesial communities

and the theologies of liberation an awareness of the importance of the political dimension, both for the human person and for the apostolic perspective of mission in the building of the Kingdom. On one side, the relational nature of the human person and the organization of human relations at the social level, oriented toward justice and toward the common good, shape the roots and direct the political expressions of the individual and of society. In this sense our actions or omissions, our word or our silence, will always have a political impact, especially in a society of conflicts and contradictions, of injustice and oppression. From the viewpoint of Christian faith, which establishes such a close relationship between the historical project and the eschatological destiny of human life, the *political* dimension must necessarily form part of the human effort to shape social reality itself, according to evangelical inspiration and values. The basic ecclesial communities have been increasingly aware of the political impact of their faith and of the political meaning of their presence and action in the world. On the other side, in a conflictive and pluralistic society the interplay of forces and interests, of ideologies and objectives, inevitably becomes present in the political dimension of human activity.

That contrasting interaction of persons and groups, of goals and mediations, related to the vision and building of a society, leads to *political practice*. This practice takes on a professional character through concrete instruments of association (parties) and representation (legislatures and governments), of political action and participation, and of trade unions or professional associations. In one way or another, the citizen will always be somehow involved in political practice, if only by exercising the right to vote or through the impact of the political consequences of actions by those who are directly active in politics.

In some countries the basic ecclesial communities have not expressed their participation at this second level of political participation. In other regions they have been active in that field. In a third group of countries the problem of political expression and participation of the members of the basic ecclesial communities as such has been intensely debated. This is the case of the basic ecclesial communities in Brazil.[12] The hierarchical church in this country, through documents at the national level or letters and guidance at the diocesan level, has made an explicit effort to awaken and critically educate the political consciousness of a people who for decades and centuries have been manipulated, subjected, repressed, or ignored in the political process. The more the members of the basic ecclesial communities, directly through the internal dynamic of their participation, become aware of their political contribution to the transformation of reality and see the emergence of active leadership, the more discernment and clarity the process will require. There is an open or latent tension, depending on the situation, between the *ecclesial* nature of the basic ecclesial communities (avoiding involvement as such in partisan politics) and a growing awareness of the urgency and importance of the political presence and participation of their members, as lay Christians, in political, labor, and professional struggles for the structural transformation of society. And it is not always easy in practice to draw a conceptually clear line between the basic ecclesial communities and popular movements of a different nature.

Although we cannot pursue that problem here, it is important to keep it in mind in the general context of the basic ecclesial communities, as a living reality and as a theological and ecclesiological subject.[13]

CONCLUSION

The basic ecclesial communities today, in Brazil and other Latin American countries, offer both an appropriate context and the necessary vitality for this ecclesiological approach, which characterizes the evangelization advocated by the Latin American Episcopal Assemblies of Medellín and Puebla, and fundamentally in the Second Vatican Council, as well as by a variety of pontifical documents in recent years, especially in the Apostolic Exhortation of Paul VI, *Evangelii nuntiandi*. The hierarchical church in Brazil and some other countries has praised them as pastorally decisive in the process of evangelization. Indeed, the basic ecclesial communities recapitulate in reality the intuitions that theology had already systematized on the basis of the same reality. The ecclesiological paradigm inherent in the basic ecclesial communities establishes important qualitative advances for evangelization. I will list the most suggestive of these here.[14]

• Moving from the ecclesiastical hegemony of the clergy to their specific and qualified insertion in the community, and to the importance and active ecclesial presence of lay people and religious sisters in the evangelizing and apostolic process of the church.

• Moving from a clearly spiritualizing and devotional approach to the total concept of the human person as subject of evangelization: as a material and spiritual whole, soul and body, individual and community, society and culture. All the dimensions of the human being and of humanity must be evangelized in depth, on a solid biblical and theological basis.

• Moving from the Christian believer, considered as the end object of the evangelizing effort, to the Christian believer as the subject who initiates and continues his or her own evangelization and radiates it to the world.

• Moving from a hierarchical and institutional church, oriented to instructing and maintaining, defending and conserving, to the model of a church that, in faithfulness to itself, is prepared to embrace and often to encourage and lead changes; a church open to self-transformation, at the personal and structural level, prepared to authenticate and legitimate in its own being the vitality of small communities, seeing them as a promise and recognizing their ecclesial fruitfulness.

• Moving from conceiving of transformation as a top-down process, or only at the juridical and organizational level, to valuing seriously the creativity that comes from below. New social relationships emerge here, at the level of communities within the church, based on participation and communion. This leads to the energizing not only of the evangelization process, but of the internal life of the ecclesial institution itself.

• Moving from the primacy of theoretical development, as an educational prerequisite for evangelization, to attentiveness to reality and lived experience as the point of departure for reflection or as a priority and permanent point of reference for the person's later experience and constant and always new assimilation of the theoretical elements to be acquired or previously established and offered by revelation, by tradition, by the magisterium, and by theology.

All this movement has occurred in concrete reality, by different paths, and flows into the ecclesial and ecclesiological reality of the basic ecclesial communities, a fruitful form of the church's presence in the present world, an extraordinary mediation for the evangelization of our peoples, a dynamic source of internal revitalization for the church itself.

— *Translated by Margaret D. Wilde*

NOTES

1. Regarding the choice of the Brazilian ecclesial base communities as a reference point, see M. Azevedo, *Basic Ecclesial Communities in Brazil* (Washington, D.C., 1987).

2. *Praxis* is not a synonym of practice, action, or behavior. It is not an antonym of theory. Praxis expresses the combination of action and reflection that manifests and attempts to realize the historicity of the human person. Praxis is a concrete form of historical realization. It results from a double insight: the awareness of history as something that is made in time; and the awareness that the history which is made is the result of human action, which results from concrete options. Praxis, therefore, is the conscious making of history. Christian praxis is the concrete expression in life of the historical impact of faith. See F. Taborda, "Fe crista e praxis historica": *REB* 41/162 (1981), pp. 250-278. For more extensive documentation of the language of the basic ecclesial communities, see chapter 2 of Azevedo, *Basic Ecclesial Communities in Brazil*.

3. For a perspective earlier than Medellín, see Caramuru de Barros, *Comunidade eclesial de base: uma opção pastoral decisiva* (Petropolis, 1967).

4. Direct contact with the word of God in the Bible, and its reading and assimilation in direct relationship to life, are fundamental traits of the basic ecclesial communities. They are also a qualitative leap in Latin American Catholic consciousness. Among the extensive works on this subject, I will only mention here the contribution of Carlos Mesters: *Defenseless Flower: A New Reading of the Bible,* trans. Francis McDonagh (Maryknoll, N.Y.: Orbis Books, 1989); "O uso da Biblia nas comunidades eclesiais de base," in S. Torres (ed.), *A Igreja que surge na base* (São Paulo, 1982); *Circulos Biblicos* (16 excellent pamphlets for the introduction of biblical reflection in the context of life), Petropolis, 1972-1978. For an appreciation of the use of Scriptures in the basic ecclesial communities from a Protestant viewpoint, see G. Cook, *The Expectation of the Poor. Latin American Basic Ecclesial Communities in Protestant Perspective*, Maryknoll, N.Y., 1985.

5. See J.B. Libanio, "Comunidade eclesial de base": *Convergencia* 21/191 (1986), pp. 175-184; L. Boff, *Eclesiogenesis,* trans. Robert R. Barr (Maryknoll, N.Y.: Orbis Books, 1986); "Notas teologicas da Igreja na base," in S. Torres (ed.), *A Igreja que surge na base*, São Paulo, 1982; Frei Betto, *O que e uma comunidade de base*, São Paulo, 1983.

6. See F. Pastor, "Ministerios laicales y comunidades de base: La renovación pastoral de la Iglesia en America latina," *Gregorianum* 68, 1-2 (1987), pp. 267-305,

with extensive bibliographical notes; C. Boff, "Em qué ponto estão hoje as comunidades eclesiais de base?," *REB* 46/183 (1986), pp. 527-38. This whole issue of *REB*, published after the VI Interecclesial Encounter of basic ecclesial communities in Trindade, Goias, Brazil (July 1986) provides abundant and timely material on the subject discussed here.

7. National Conference of Brazilian Bishops (CNBB), *Comunidades eclesiais de base na Igreja do Brasil*. Documents of the CNBB, number 25 (São Paulo, 1982), p. 5, note 39.

8. See A. Quiroz Magaña, *Eclesiología en la teología de la liberación* (Salamanca: Sigueme, 1983; L. Boff, "As eclesiologiás presentes nas comunidades eclesiais de base", in *Uma Igreja que nasce do povo* (Petrópolis, 1975); Boff, *Eclesiogenesis*. For a broader development of this theme, see M. Azevedo, *Basic Ecclesial Communities in Brazil*. The principal references to the Puebla Document, a meaningful point of arrival and departure in pastoral and theological reflection and action in Latin America, are found in this same book.

9. See M. Azevedo, *Los religiosos, vocación y misión*, Madrid, 1987, ch. 3.

10. *The analysis of reality* is a fundamental point not only for theological reflection, but also for the everyday life of the basic ecclesial communities. It is important to go beyond naive phenomenological observation. This requires a critical reading to reveal the underlying causes of the situations in which so many peoples are involved. The basic ecclesial communities, and indeed many other church groups in Latin America, have used the "see-judge-act" method transmitted by Catholic Action in recent years. But this method has been enriched by the basic ecclesial communities, either by their greater sensitivity to the *historical-diachronic* dimension of the real processes, or by a more technical development of the *critical* tools. See J.B. Libanio, *Formaçao da consciencia crítica*, 3 vol. (Petrópolis-Rio de Janeiro, 1977). G. Cook draws extensively on Libanio in his chapter 6, "Fundamental Orientations of Grassroots Communities in Brazil: A New Way of Seeing Reality," of *The Expectation of the Poor*, pp. 89-94. The widely debated issue of the use of *Marxist analysis* also emerges in this context. In that respect see C. Boff, *Theology and Praxis*, trans. Robert R. Barr (Maryknoll, N.Y.: Orbis Books, 1987); F. Taborda, "Puebla e as ideologias": *Sintese* 6/VI (1979), pp. 3-25; "Fé Crista e práxis histórica": *REB* 41/162 (1981), pp. 250-278; M. Azevedo, *Basic Ecclesial Communities in Brazil*.

11. See G. Gutiérrez, *A Theology of Liberation* (Maryknoll, N.Y.: Orbis Books, 1973); *Teología desde el reverso de la historia* (Lima: Centro de Estudios y Publicaciones, 1977); *The Power of the Poor in History*, trans. Robert R Barr (Maryknoll, N.Y.: Orbis Books, 1983).

12. See the debate, still in progress, in the review *Tempo e Presença* (published by the Ecumenical Center for Documentation and Information-CEDI in Rio de Janeiro), nos. 212 and 213, under the title: *Participaçac dos cristaos na política partidária*. There Clodovis Boff, Frei Betto, Pedro Assis Ribeiro de Oliveira, Luis Eduardo W. Wanderly, Luiz Alberto Gomes de Souza, and Herbert de Sousa discuss contrasting and/or complementary positions, which reveal a search more than a predefined position.

13. See also the Final Document of the Interecclesial Encounter of Basic Ecclesial Communities in Trindade, Goias, Brazil (July 25, 1986), and other works published in *REB* 46/183 (1986); Azevedo, *Basic Ecclesial Communities in Brazil;* J. B. Libanio, "Igreja e poder politico," *Vida Pastoral* 27/130 (1986), pp. 708-27; C. Boff

and L. Boff, "Comunidades cristãs e política partidária," *REB* 38/151 (1978), pp. 387-401.

14. In emphasizing so many positive aspects of the basic ecclesial communities, I am recognizing the present reality and the immense potential that they represent for the process of evangelization in Latin America. This does not mean that the basic ecclesial communities do not have difficulties, or that they do not present problems and risks. These can be synthesized, even today, in the words with which Paul VI affirmatively described the basic ecclesial communities in *Evangelii nuntiandi*, (no. 58). The basic ecclesial communities, said the pope, will be a hope for the universal church to the degree that:

— they are nourished by the word of God and do not let themselves be drawn into political polarization or into whatever ideologies are in vogue and prepared to exploit their immense human potential;

— they avoid the always threatening temptation of systematic contestation and of a hypercritical spirit, on the pretext of their authenticity and their spirit of collaboration;

— they remain firmly united with the local church through which they are inserted in the universal church, thus avoiding the danger, which is always real, of isolating themselves and believing themselves to be the only authentic church of Christ, and consequently falling into the danger of anathematizing other ecclesial communities;

— they never consider themselves the only subjects or the only agents of evangelization, nor as the only holders of the Gospel, but rather are aware that the church is incarnated in other forms and not only in them;

— they grow daily in awareness of their missionary duty and in their zeal, persistence and radiance in that duty;

— they remain always universalistic and never sectarian.

The historical process of ecclesial and political evolution in the present situation in Latin America requires of the basic ecclesial communities a critical awareness and an intense and constant discernment under the guidance of the Holy Spirit.

32

Sacraments

VICTOR CODINA

It has been rightly observed that the theology of liberation has not yet reflected very much on the sacraments. There is not much of a sacramentology of liberation to speak of.

It would be wrong to attribute this to a lack of sacramental interest among the theologians of liberation, as if their concern were only political, relegating liturgical matters to irrelevance. Indeed the authors who have written on this subject (I. Ellacuría, J. L. Segundo, R. Vidales, J. Sobrino, D. Irarrazaval, F. Taborda, and others) have emphasized the great importance of the sacraments for a liberating perspective. The liturgy is needed so that liberation will not be seen in merely political terms, so that it will not be forgotten that the ultimate root of all oppression is sin, and so the gratuitous and transcendent dimension of Christian liberation will not be lost. Moreover, if the people celebrate their liberating struggles, cannot Christians celebrate them sacramentally from their faith in Christ? Conversely, the church and especially theology are largely responsible for having contributed to the alienation of the people through a liturgy that is often evasive and separated from life, and for having presented such a unilateral vision of the effectiveness of the sacraments *ex opere operato,* which has often led to a mechanistic and magical understanding of them. Not even the recent liturgical renewal has succeeded in historicizing the liturgy or in breaking through the elitism that still keeps the liturgy out of reach of the great popular majorities.

Indeed there are understandable reasons for the scarcity of liturgical and sacramental material in the theology of liberation.

As the theology of liberation has emphasized, theology always presupposes a prior ecclesial and historical praxis. The theology of liberation cannot reflect on the sacraments until a new, liberating sacramental praxis has developed. The same was true in the history of theology: the treatise *De sacramentis in genere* dates from the twelfth century, long after the emergence of the theology of the Trinity, christology, and theological anthropology, but before ecclesiology (which would have serious consequences for medieval sacramentology).

The theology of liberation has begun by reflecting on God, christology, biblical hermeneutics, spirituality, anthropology, theological method, and so forth.

Now it can begin to focus its attention on other dogmatic sectors and, in particular, on the sacraments. It is moved to do so not only by zeal for the coherence and systematization of the theology of liberation, but by its conviction of the importance of the sacraments in the church and the need for a new reflection based on the new emerging reality in the Third World, especially in Latin America. The classical and even the modern sacramental patterns are no longer an adequate response to the new needs of the people of God.

I. A NEW REALITY

1. Social Reality

Latin America, like all the Third World, lives in conditions of poverty manifested in hunger, malnutrition, a high rate of infant mortality, subhuman housing conditions, illiteracy, unemployment, repression, and violence. It is a situation of premature death—slow or violent—that cries out to heaven. To these economic, social, and political problems we must add those that stem from racism, machismo, and cultural, ideological, religious, and military aggression from outside the region. Indians, blacks, and women are doubly oppressed. It is like an immense concentration camp, invisible to those who only visit the airports or the better neighborhoods of the great Latin American capitals.

Poverty in Latin America is a collective social and economic reality, due not to natural but historical reasons, dialectically coexisting with the wealthy classes and countries, and it contains great tension and potential for political explosions. Puebla speaks of the increasingly tumultuous and overwhelming cry that rises to heaven from the peoples of Latin America: "It is the cry of a people who suffer and demand justice, freedom, respect for the fundamental rights of humanity and peoples" (Puebla, 87).

2. Sacramental Reality

The world of the sacraments is affected by the complex reality of Latin America. We shall enumerate some facts and problems.

1. A great majority of the Latin American people live their faith through rites and ceremonies that guide the most decisive moments of their life, the new thresholds: birth, adolescence, marriage, death. One can speak of "the sacraments of the four seasons of life," although in some cases they are sacramentals rather than sacraments in the strict sense. Annual seasonal festivals are also celebrated from the perspective of popular religion. These popular sectors, especially in the countryside, usually receive the least pastoral attention because of the scarcity of clergy, long distances, poor planning, and so forth.

2. A wide range of middle and upper population sectors, especially in the urban areas, is characterized by a routinized sacramental practice, which often sacralizes the surrounding status quo and does not question the injustice for which these sectors are largely responsible and from which they benefit.

3. Christians committed to social change, who live their faith and the sacraments in the basic ecclesial communities, need a new formulation of the

sacraments in a liberating key, since the new praxis has overflowed the old sacramental patterns.

4. Other sectors have abandoned sacramental praxis because they consider it incompatible with secular modernity (the educated sectors), or simply alienating (some sectors committed to the political praxis of liberation).

This wide range of sacramental practices and positions calls for reflection. Is the sacramental practice of the popular majorities really alienating? Is the practice of the upper sectors acceptable and correct? How should the church respond to criticism based on educated reasoning or social practice? How should it bring the new sacramental practice of the base communities into a liberating sacramental theology? Do the liturgies of the base community meetings in Brazil, or the celebrations of the Andean Christian communities, or the eucharists of Archbishop Romero, including his last martyrial eucharist, have something to contribute to sacramental theology?

If there is a connection between lex orandi and lex credendi, and if the mysteries of the Kingdom of God have been revealed to the poor (Luke 10:21-22, Matt. 11:25-26), this emerging sacramental practice must have something to say to the sacramentology of the theology of liberation. For that reason the cry of the poor must make itself heard in the church's lex orandi. If one can speak of a church of the poor, one can also speak of sacraments of and for the poor.

II. A NEW HORIZON FOR UNDERSTANDING THE SACRAMENTS

The theology of liberation does not profess a sacramentology "parallel" to the magisterium of the church. It accepts the common sacramental doctrine and praxis of the church, but like any theology it tries to systematize them according to an ultimate principle, to set priorities and to organize all the information in a coherent way, and in the case of the theology of liberation, a way that responds to the cry of the poor and believing people.

What characterizes a new theology is not the new subjects it raises, but its new theological horizon; everything is seen differently because the mental paradigm or the cognitive framework is changed. The same is true of the theology of liberation, which is not a "genitive" theology of revolution or violence, but rather a reflection on the whole Christian mystery from the perspective of the liberation of the poor.

1. The Horizon of Traditional Sacramentology

During the first millennium the church celebrated the sacraments of faith without developing a systematic treatise on the sacraments, although it reflected unceasingly on Christian initiation, the eucharist, and penance. The church of the first millennium participated symbolically in the Christian mystery through its liturgy, without undue concern for defining or systematizing the different kinds of sacraments, or for structuring each one.

In the twelfth century the church began to elaborate the treatise De sacramentis in genere, which, enriched by the great scholastics, and fundamentally assumed by Trent and developed by the post-Tridentine and neoscholastic theologians, would remain prevalent until Vatican II.

Describing the outlines of traditional sacramentology, we might say that during these centuries what prevailed was not so much the symbolic dimension of the sacraments, typical of the patristic era, but its instrumental dimension: the sacraments are effective instruments of grace. Although the significative aspect of the sacraments did not disappear altogether ("effective signs of grace"), the accent was placed on their effectiveness, on their causality ex opere operato, which did not depend on the holiness of the minister but on the merits of the passion of Christ. For the validity of the sacrament it was necessary and sufficient that the minister have "the intention of doing what the church does." This objective effectiveness of the sacraments would be emphasized in the anti-Protestant polemic to make the point that the sacraments are not simple pedagogical aids for the faith of the subject. Although the condition of the subject who "receives" the sacrament (*opus operantis*) was always considered important, these conditions seemed to be reduced to "not putting an impediment" to the grace offered in the sacrament. The doctrine of the number of the seven sacraments, which had a markedly symbolic origin, was interpreted more and more arithmetically and less symbolically. The introduction of Aristotelianism into medieval theology offered very precise intellectual tools for the study of the sacraments (matter and form, substance and accidents, causality), but it led to the reification of sacramentality at the level of objective and impersonal realities. The sacraments always maintained their reference to Jesus, author of the sacraments, through his power of "excellency," and never ceased to be considered a "memorial of the passion." Some authors, like Thomas Aquinas, developed a sacramental anthropology, following the evolution of the great moments of personal and social life. Thomas himself related the sacraments to the liturgical worship of the church. But in reality, traditional sacramentology never developed the personal, let alone the ecclesial dimensions of the sacraments. The sacraments were seen as instruments of the humanity of Jesus, distributing to each person the grace that Christ obtained for us with his passion.

It was only a step from there to considering the sacraments as "channels of grace." The richness of early scholasticism was slowly lost, and the sacraments were increasingly turned into sacred objects that, regulated by ritual laws, produced sanctifying grace. The faith of the subject, the liturgical and ecclesial dimension, the very connection of the sacraments with the Paschal mystery, were slowly relegated to the shadows.

This sacramentology, typical of the church in medieval Christianity, incapable of reformulating itself in response to the criticism of the Reformation and later of the modern age, fell victim to the triumphalism, juridicism, and clericalism that characterized the church before Vatican II. Throughout these centuries the sacraments not only were instruments of grace, but also brought together and shaped "Christian society," and have served to sacralize unjust situations.

The cultural horizon of classical sacramentology is that of the objective, the natural, the static; the sacraments belong to the world of things, although they are "sacred things," in which the faithful participate when they receive the sacraments "administered" by the priests. The underlying theological horizon is that of juridicist positivism, in the framework of an Anselmian christology, without either ecclesiology or pneumatology.

All this should not be interpreted as unfaithfulness to its origins on the part of the church. The church, guided by the Spirit, continued to live and celebrate the sacraments of the faith and to defend their value. But through the centuries its reflective systematization of the sacraments, although full of insights and nuances, has lost much of the theological richness of the patristic and early scholastic periods. That is why Vatican II sought to renew sacramentology by invoking a "return to the origins."

2. The Sacramental Horizon of the Theology of Vatican II

The sacramental theology that emerged around Vatican II represented a change not only of content but of cultural and theological paradigm. Its horizon is that of *Modernity*: the predominance of the anthropological over the cosmic, of the subject over the object, of the evolutional over the static, of reason, consciousness and freedom over the individual, of the "I" over the "we." At a strictly theological level, we can say that it placed the sacraments in the ecclesial context, and specifically within a church that is wholly proto-sacrament, a universal sacrament of salvation. The seven sacraments are the essential moments of the ecclesial proto-sacrament, the clearest manifestations of the victorious and eschatological grace of Jesus in the church, expressions of the primordial sacrament. In each sacrament there is a personal encounter with the resurrected Kyrios. Ecumenical dialogue with the Reformation has helped to rediscover the dimensions of the word and of the faith, while conversation with the Eastern Church has led to new respect for the symbolic, iconic, and pneumatic dimensions.

This sacramental vision has recovered much of the early patristic and medieval tradition that was lost in the second millennium and has enabled the church to relate the sacramental world to the challenges of Modernity. The importance of the subject has been recognized and the individual's faith appears as an essential constitutive moment of the sacrament, which is "sacrament of the faith." The liturgy recovers its communal and celebrative character, in which the word occupies a decisive place. The epiclesis or invocation of the Spirit is recognized as a constitutive sacramental element, thus overcoming the unfortunate impression of cosmic automatism from the earlier period. The eucharist has returned to its central place in the church, and the other sacraments take their place around it. Once more "the church makes eucharist and the eucharist makes the church." The constitutions *Lumen gentium* and *Sacrosanctum concilium*, at the theoretical level, and at the practical level the reform of the sacramental rituals, have brought these rich ecclesial perspectives to the sacraments. The sacraments are once more becoming the essential symbolic and celebrative moments of the church as proto-sacrament.

Nevertheless, this sacramental horizon, with all its undeniable richness, still raises questions in the Third World and especially in Latin America.

The church's belated acceptance of the horizon of Modernity (the first Enlightenment) cannot conceal the ambiguous elements in which Modernity is rooted: its connection with the dominant sectors of the modern world (bourgeois, precapitalists, capitalists, neocapitalists), which are largely responsible for the dependency of the Third World; its enlightened rationalism, which not only leads to increased elitism but degenerates into privatistic individualism, into the technocracy of "instrumental reason," and into the idolatry of earthly goods; in short, a crass individualism that leads to materialistic consumerism and to the ecological destruction of the planet itself.

In the sacramental context the modern ecclesiological horizon entails the risk of degenerating into an elitist and ahistorical liturgy, into sacraments well prepared and well celebrated by the minority sector of society, into an encounter with the Resurrected One which neglects to follow the historical Jesus, into a progressivist and somewhat naive optimism which forgets about sin, suffering, and death in the world, into an aesthetic symbolism that does not include the poor person as privileged image of Jesus (Matt. 25), into celebrations that conceal the reality of cruel inequality with liturgical rites, into an excessive concern for the freedom of a few, without considering the lack of freedom of the great majorities, into drawing-room communitarianism rather than real solidarity with the people, into disrespect or at least ignorance toward popular religion and its sacramentals. This situation has led even first-world theologians to seek new and liberating ways for the sacraments.

When the theology of liberation seeks a new sacramental horizon, it does not do so out of intellectual zeal, but from a sincere desire to respond to unresolved questions which, thanks to Vatican II, can now be raised again. In this sense the new sacramental horizon of the theology of liberation — like the theology of liberation itself — is the fruit of Vatican II, although it goes beyond the Council. In the last analysis, was not John XXIII himself the first to speak of the church of the poor as the image of the conciliar church?

3. The New Sacramental Horizon of the Theology of Liberation: The Kingdom of God

The theology of liberation has made the Kingdom of God the central object of its reflection, the ultimate principle around which it articulates the content of the Christian faith and the paradigm which best responds to the reality of Latin America, to the cry of the mostly poor, mostly Christian people of this region.[1]

The key concept of the Kingdom of God permits the theology of liberation to unite transcendence with history, overcoming all dualism; it makes it possible to historicize historical salvation, and specifically as the liberation of the poor; it serves as a prophetic denunciation of the anti-Kingdom that is present in our history; thanks to this last principle it can respond to the hopes of the poor majorities and thus orient the praxis of historical transformation to God's plan: the Kingdom.

This structural principle of the theology of liberation corresponds to a new theological horizon, a change of trajectory, a new paradigm, a new matrix. For this reason the theology of liberation is not a "regional" theology but a new way of doing theology, though always provisionally, as anything historical must be done. There is an "epistemological break" from other ways of doing theology, and it is not simply a "postmodern" way. There is a change of social subject; it is done from below, from the viewpoint of the poor. This is one of the things that creates conflict in the church and in society, but also one of the things that arouse hope in the popular sectors.

This does not mean that the slate of earlier theologies is wiped clean, or that the basic elements of faith and theological tradition are not incorporated. But it is done within a new global horizon, from a new formal perspective: everything seems new.

Philosophically and culturally, this new paradigm moves in the dialectical relationship between the objective and the subjective, in the overlapping relationship between humanity and its world. It accentuates the social, the structural, the historical, and the liberative. Its dialogue is not only with the first Enlightenment, but with what has been called the second Enlightenment; not only with reason, but also with the praxis of social transformation.

This new horizon, which becomes specific in the Kingdom of God, has already served to structure different theological themes:

• God is the God of the Kingdom, the Abba of Jesus;

• Christ is the eschatological mediator of the Kingdom, but the Kingdom is still an unfinished task in history and requires successive historical mediations;

• the church is sacrament of the Kingdom and must continually undergo conversion to the Kingdom, if it seeks to be church of the poor and historical sacrament of liberation;

• spirituality is liberation with Spirit, following Jesus in the historical building of the Kingdom.

The affirmation that the Kingdom of God is the horizon of sacramentology in the theology of liberation is a logical step forward in this theological systematization, the practical corollary of which is to make the sacraments liberative, especially for the poor.

As we shall see, the horizon of the Kingdom of God, far from denying the valid aspects of the traditional and modern sacramentology, incorporates them in a new synthesis. The Kingdom of God incorporates both christological and ecclesiological affirmations, but it insists on certain presuppositions which are in fact new: the starting point is the cry of the poor. But there is something more: it is the new theological reflection on the mystery-sacrament that will intrinsically lead us to the sacramental horizon of the Kingdom of God.

4. The Kingdom of God as Primordial Mystery-Sacrament

All authors agree that both the etymological and the theological grounding of the sacraments must be oriented to the mystery, the biblical mysterion, which Tertulian translated as sacramentum in applying it to Christian worship.

In its biblical origins the mystery does not exclusively denote the cognitive dimension of a secret, and even less the cultic dimension of our sacraments. The essence of the mystery is the merciful plan of God, God's will for salvation, which is realized in this world.

Thus Daniel, in revealing to Nebuchadnezzar the mystery of his dream of that majestic statue with feet of clay, speaks of "a kingdom that shall never be destroyed, nor shall its kingdom be left to another people. It shall crush all these kingdoms and bring them to an end, and it shall stand forever" (Dan. 2:44-45, *NRSV;* cf. verses 18, 27-30, 45-47).

This mystery that Paul and the Pauline writings identified with Christ and saw specifically in the opening to the Gentiles (Rom. 16:25-27; 1 Cor. 2:6-10; 2 Thess. 2:7; Col. 1:27; Eph. 1:22, 2:11-22, 3:10-21; 1 Tim. 3:9, 16) would have its eschatological fulfillment at the end of time (Rev. 1:20, 10:7, 17:5).

This mystery is specifically the Kingdom of God, as it appears in the only passages of the Synoptics which refer to the mystery: Mark 4:11; Matthew 13:11; and Luke 8:10.

Thus it is necessary to unite the notion of mystery with that of the Kingdom of God; the primordial mystery is this salvific plan of God, revealed in successive stages, centered in Christ and consummated in the new earth and the new heaven. This Kingdom-Reign of God, announced by the prophets (of which Israel is an instrument), comes near to us in Christ (Mark 1:15). But the realization of it is extended and realized in the time of the church, so that God may be all in all (1 Cor. 15:28). This is the primordial mystery of the faith, the original sacrament.

To put it differently, placing sacramentality in the horizon of the Kingdom of God, as the theology of liberation tries to do, is not only a change from ecclesial tradition, but a return to the biblical and earliest historical origins of the mystery-sacrament. It reassumes the personalistic, christological, and ecclesiological horizon in the broader horizon of the Kingdom of God, of which Christ is the only eschatological mediator and the church is its visible ferment in history. This means that the seven sacraments must be interpreted in the light of the Kingdom of God, and therefore their meaning, their effectiveness, their validity, their very ecclesiality, must always be considered in reference to the Kingdom of God. If from the first millennium sacramentality referred only to the sacramental rites that seemed to be its only expression, and if since Vatican II it refers primarily to the church, the perspective of liberation theology places it in the Kingdom, which roots it in the earliest tradition of the patristic church.

Now let us draw a conclusion from this first affirmation. The Kingdom overflows the church. It is not merely intra-ecclesial; it is realized in history, in the world, in secularity, in the sociopolitical, economic, and cultural spheres, in the structures and conditions of life of the peoples. The sacraments must be oriented to this Kingdom. The cry of the poor comes into ecclesial sacramentality thanks to this horizon of the Kingdom. The cry of the oppressed can legitimately resonate in the liturgy without offending either esthetics or pastoral theology, because the mission of the sacraments is to dignify and prophetically celebrate this Kingdom, which as we shall see, has to do with the liberation of the poor. To ask the soldiers at a eucharist to stop the repression, as Archbishop Romero ordered "in the name of God" on the eve of his assassination (March 22, 1980), is not an injection of politics into the liturgy, but a clear prophetic orientation of sacramentality to the Kingdom of God. The Church Fathers did the same thing in the fourth century.

III. SOME CHARACTERISTICS OF THE KINGDOM OF GOD

The revealer of the Kingdom of God is Jesus (Heb. 1:1; John 1:18). We must look for the meaning of the Kingdom of God in his life, preaching, praxis, and Paschal mystery.

Of the many aspects of the Kingdom of God, we shall only point out those which are most relevant to the sacramental horizon.

1. The Theologal Character of the Kingdom of God

When we speak of *mystery,* the word itself seems to allude to its theologal and gratuitous dimension, which even after the revelation, transcends the limits of reason and the powers of human nature. In contrast, to speak of the Kingdom of God might give the impression that by implying historical, social, and political dimensions, it ceases to be strictly theologal. Nevertheless, the Bible affirms precisely that this salvific plan of God, which is called the Kingdom of God, is immeasurably deep and transcendent, because it is born of the trinitarian mystery of God. It is a plan that includes creation, the preparation of the Hebrew scriptures, the missions of the Son and the Spirit, the church as a communitarian, visible, and historical moment of this trinitarian history of God with the world, and the final eschatological consummation. The Kingdom of God is the gratuitous communication of God, ad extra, the "economy" in patristic terms, the "economic Trinity" in modern language, which reveals to us the deepest mystery of God, the Trinity ad intra, the "theology" of the Fathers, the immanent Trinity. This Kingdom of God is what moved Paul to cry out in amazement and reverent adoration (Rom. 11:33-36). That this mysterious Kingdom of God is realized in the diverse moments of history, according to the designs of the Father (Acts 1:8), and that its realization requires free human collaboration (for example, Mary's *fiat* in Luke 1:38), does not diminish but rather manifests its theologal character; it is the Kingdom of a God who creates history, enters into it, and submits to human freedom. The theologal element is not necessarily disincarnated and suprahistorical. The Kingdom of God is precisely the trinitarian life of God, who communicates with the world, with human life as the first symbolic mediation of that communication.

2. The Symbolic Dimension of the Kingdom of God

Precisely because the Kingdom of God is a mystery, it can only be revealed through symbolic gestures and actions, since symbols are the only way of inserting mystery into human history. The very word *kingdom* is a symbol of the sovereignty and salvific will of God.

In the Hebrew scriptures the great symbolic act of the Kingdom of God is the Exodus, with all its concomitant and subsequent events. The symbolic acts of the prophets (Isa. 20:3, Jer. 9:10-11, Ezek. 5:1-14) and the return from Exile are simply reenactments of the Exodus (Isa. 40:1-11, 41:17-20). The Exodus, in turn, is simply a symbolic anticipation of the eschatological fullness of the Kingdom in the midst of the nations (Isa. 2:1-5). All these symbols have a historical dimension; they are firstfruits of the definitive fullness of the Kingdom of God, types of the Kingdom, whose reality is insinuated beforehand in the symbol but which overflows it (1 Cor. 10:1-12).

In the Christian scriptures it is Jesus who gives the Kingdom this symbolic-historical character. He himself is the sign (Luke 2:12, 34, and 35; 11:29-32), and his preaching in parables as well as his symbolic miracles and acts (weeping over Jerusalem, condemning the fig tree, expelling the merchants from the temple, eating with sinners, submitting to anointment by the sinful woman, footwashing, the Last Supper) are historical symbols of the Kingdom of God, which is coming near in him (Mark 1:15). He exorcises demons to give a sign of the presence of the Kingdom of God (Luke 11:20). The catechetical narrations of the resurrection also have a profound symbolic character of announcing the new life of the Resurrected One and his victory over death.

The conciliar affirmation that the church is sacrament (LG, 1, 9, 48, and others) can be understood from this viewpoint: it is a symbol of the Kingdom of God in this world, a historical and communitarian symbol of the presence and nearness of the Kingdom, its seed (LG, 5).

What is the preferred symbol of the Kingdom of God? We can affirm that it is life, in all its manifestations: from the recovery of health to the forgiveness of sins, from the liberation from demons to the shared banquet, from salvation from a danger to the joy of a good wine in abundance. Life is the symbol and the first mediation of God. To say that Jesus came so that we might have life in abundance (John 10:10) is the same as saying that he came to bring the Kingdom of God.

3. To Whom Is the Kingdom Primarily Addressed?

Here again we see the theologal nature of the kingdom of God. God came to the world by the way of poverty (Luke 2:12; LG, 8). God is not primarily addressing the powerful and rich, but the poor and oppressed, those whose life is in danger. The act of the Exodus is the liberation of a people of slaves from the oppressive power of Pharaoh. The return from Exile is the liberation of those who were exiled from power by the great empires. The miracles of Jesus are acts of healing, forgiveness, exorcism and resurrection, addressed to the marginalized sectors of the society (Luke 7:20-23). God reveals the mysteries of the Kingdom to them (Luke 10:21-22, Matt. 11:25-26), and Jesus rejoices in that fact. The Kingdom appears as a concrete liberation from the evils that oppress the people, a true exorcism of the oppression of the devil (Acts 10:38).

This preferential treatment of the poor is an expression of God's benevolence, of the merciful heart of the Father (Luke 15:20), of the kindness of Jesus, who is moved by the suffering of the people (Matt. 14:4, 20:34, 15:32; Mark 6:34; Luke 7:13; Mark 1:41, 8:2). Theirs is the Kingdom of heaven (Matt. 5:1-12, Luke 6:20-23). The eschatological judgment and the definitive entrance to or exclusion from it are conditioned on acceptance of these "least ones," with whom Jesus identifies himself (Matt. 25:31-45). The gratuitousness and transcendence of the Kingdom of God appear in this way, not based on the metaphysical distance of the God who is in heaven, but on God's merciful nearness to the poor and rejected of the earth. The Kingdom is realized primarily as the liberation of the poor (Luke 4:16-21).

4. The Eschatological Character of the Kingdom of God

The Kingdom of God is the ultimate, the eschaton, the realization of God's project for this world, the loving triumph of his sovereignty, the fulfillment of the utopia that has been hidden for centuries.

This ultimate definitiveness of the Kingdom of God is a corollary of its theologal character; the Kingdom belongs to God, to the Abba, and is therefore a gratuitous work of God's mercy. It is God who invites to the banquet of the Kingdom, to the eternal wedding feast of the Lamb. It is God who communicates God's life to us through Jesus and in the Spirit. And the resurrection of Jesus is the beginning of this great utopia, the firstfruits of this definitive triumph over evil, sin, and death.

But this eschatology must be correctly understood. It is not only for the end of time, when God's judgment will bring about definitive justice, the resurrection of the dead, and everlasting life. Neither is it only the triumph of grace over personal sin in the intimacy of the conscience. It is also the incipient triumph of the Kingdom of God in present history, the conversion of the unjust structures into structures of communion and participation. The definitiveness of the Kingdom of God extends to the personal, the social-historical, and the metahistorical.

For that reason the symbols of the Kingdom must be prophetic, both in the Hebrew and Christian scriptures. In the important and intense moments of personal or community history, when words are not enough to express the increase of meaning, the prophets are moved by the Spirit to carry out symbolic acts, which they explain with the appropriate words. In these acts they announce the Kingdom of God as Good News for the present as well as the future, they denounce what is opposed to the Kingdom of God (the anti-Kingdom), and they anticipate the future Kingdom precisely by transforming present death into life. Thus forgiving sins, eating with sinners, or healing a sick person on the sabbath anticipates the fullness of the Kingdom of God by carrying out a historical transformation: the sin is forgiven, the marginalized are admitted to the table, the sick person is made whole. And these actions produce conflict with the socioreligious system prevailing in Israel.

Therein lies the effectiveness of these symbols of the Kingdom; eschatology begins to become a "yes, now" in the midst of the "not yet" (or the "no") of the historical opacity of the present. The ultimate becomes present, and the present, penultimate. The eschatology of the Kingdom becomes personal grace, social-historical life, and an anticipation of eternal life. Utopia becomes "topia," and the new heaven and the new earth (Rev. 21:1) are anticipated in the partial victories of history (Isa. 65:19-22). Struggle, evil, sin, and death continue, but hopeful new signs arise of the victorious grace of the Father and of the Spirit of the Resurrected One.

IV. THE SACRAMENTS AS PROPHETIC SYMBOLS OF THE KINGDOM

Let us now apply to the sacraments the new sacramental horizon of the Kingdom of God, which we have been proposing and discovering.

1. The Sacraments of the Kingdom in History: The Poor

In human history, inside and outside the church, we find situations of sin that produce victims. These victims of the anti-Kingdom are the poor. They are sacraments of the Kingdom sub contrario, precisely to the extent that the privation of life, the sin of the world, and the negation of the Kingdom are manifest in them. Their cry is a cry for the Kingdom; it is a protest against the whole society. Theologically, their cry is a sign of the times (GS, 4, 11, 44), the greatest sign of the times in today's world.

Paradoxically, in the light of a theology of the cross and of the Crucified One, Christ is made present in the poor. And responding to the cry of the poor becomes an ineluctable condition for entrance to the Kingdom (Matt. 25:31-45).

For this reason, by analogy but truly, the poor can be called sacraments of the Kingdom; they are a living prophecy of the Kingdom insofar as they denounce the anti-Kingdom, in anticipation of the eschatological judgment of God and proclamation of the mysterious presence of the Crucified One in them. Thus, C. Boff writes:

> The sacrament of the poor shows us the God they want and not God helping them; here God is challenge, not consolation; questioning, not justification. In effect, faced with the poor, human beings are called to love, service, solidarity, and justice. So receiving this sacrament is bitter to the taste. Yet it remains the *only "sacrament" absolutely necessary* for salvation. The ritual sacraments allow of exceptions, and many; this allows of none. It is also the *absolutely universal "sacrament"* of salvation. The way to God goes necessarily, for everyone without exception, through human beings—human beings in need, whether their need is of bread or the word.[2]

When we affirm that the church is sacrament of salvation or sacrament of the Kingdom, we mean that, among other things, in the church this analogical and anonymous sacrament of the poor becomes visible and explicit by reference to Jesus; and vice versa, that ecclesial sacramentality cannot be understood either in theological theory or in pastoral practice apart from the poor, who constitute the eschatological test of all sacramentality. This sacramentality must always be a response to the cry of the poor and must be oriented to their integral liberation. In the light of faith the acts, sometimes heroic acts, of many non-Christians who struggle and die for the liberation of their people, become profoundly meaningful because, without knowing it, they are anticipating the realization of the Kingdom of God. And the Spirit is with them.

Pedro Casaldáliga, the Brazilian bishop, poet, and prophet, has expressed it with his typical lucidity:

> The Spirit
> has decided
> to administer
> the eighth sacrament:
> the voice of the People![3]

2. The Sacraments of the Church: Prophetic Symbols of the Kingdom

The sacraments of the church are those prophetic symbols of the Kingdom that the church celebrates liturgically and that orient Christian existence not only to the church but to the Kingdom of God, of which the church itself is a sacrament. Let us make these affirmations explicit.

The Sacraments Are Prophetic Symbols of the Kingdom

The sacraments are those symbolic acts of the church that are oriented to the realization of the Kingdom of God, in continuity with the salvific actions of Yahweh in the Old Testament and of Jesus in the New. They are particularly intense and transparent moments of the Kingdom of God in the church, Paschal steps on the way from death to life, moments of pentecostal effusion in which the presence of the Kingdom of God is manifested as gift and as task. They are the privileged times (*kairos*) in the life of the individual and the community, in which the symbol is opened to its deepest meaning, transfigured into the eschatological grace of the Kingdom.

As prophetic symbols:

1. *They announce* the Good News of the Kingdom of God, especially for those who always receive bad news. It is a proclamation of life, forgiveness, hope, and communion, linked to Jesus and his word, and his life, death, and resurrection. In this sense the sacraments are a memorial of Jesus, *signum rememorativum* in the Thomist tradition (III q. 60 a. 3).

2. *They denounce* the sin of the world, the anti-Kingdom present in history and in persons, the root of death. In this sense a sacramental celebration can hardly be liberating if it does not in some way begin with the situation of personal and social sin. By demonstrating what the Kingdom is (signum demonstrativum), the sacraments denounce what is contrary to the Kingdom. For this reason the sacraments have a strong critical burden, for they question the prevailing system; they are a subversive memory of Jesus. The eucharistic symbol

of shared bread denounces the accumulation of goods by a few and the hunger of the world, as contrary to the Kingdom.

3. *They transform and demand the transformation* of personal and historical reality, and in this way they are an eschatological sign of the Kingdom of God, which is already present (*signum prognosticum*). The effectiveness of the sacraments springs from their very existence as *prophetic signs*; it is the effectiveness of prophecy in actu, of actions that realize what they symbolize prophetically. It is the effectiveness — feared by some, celebrated by others — of the prophetic acts of the prophets and of Jesus. In the sacraments the Kingdom is already present. Their effectiveness is not only *ecclesial* (establishing a link to the church) but *basileic* (on the order of the Kingdom or basileia). They are gift and task, opus operatum and opus operantis, they demand personal and social conversion; they move toward the transformation of the society in the direction of the Kingdom of God. For this reason the sacraments must be made effective in history; they impel the faithful to follow Jesus. This explains how the sacraments can be defined as "community celebrations of the following of Jesus in the important moments in the life of the person."[4] And the test of any sacramental celebration must always be the liberation of the poor, according to Matthew 25:31-45.

In terms of classical sacramentology, the sacramentum tantum is the prophetic symbol, the *res et sacramentum* is the ecclesial dimension, firstfruit of the sacrament, and the res tantum is the realization of the Kingdom.

But it is all grace and gift of the Spirit in the church, which itself is sacrament of the Kingdom.

Celebrated in the Church

The subject of the sacraments is the ecclesial community, itself a sacramental symbol of the Kingdom of God. The church not only teaches the gospel, not only exhorts the faithful to fulfill the gospel, but celebrates prayerfully, through symbols, the mystery of the Kingdom, which is embryonically [nuclearmente] realized in the death and resurrection of Jesus, but which must go on being realized in the history of persons and peoples.

The symbolic acts of the church are not empty, for the church itself is animated by the same Spirit who acted through the prophets and guided the work of Jesus. It is the community of Jesus and the Spirit that announces the Kingdom, denounces the anti-Kingdom and anticipates the Kingdom symbolically in its sacraments. The difference between these ecclesiological affirmations and the typical affirmations of postconciliar sacramentology is that in this perspective the sacraments not only accentuate their ecclesial linkage, but orient the church toward the Kingdom and invite it as a community to be converted to the Kingdom of God. In this way both the demand of commitment and the gratuitousness of the sacraments appear more clearly: it is God's Kingdom, and we must give thanks for its nearness in Christ, but it has not yet reached its fullness; we must go on building it, if only partially, because it always overflows and transcends our efforts. The epiclesis or invocation of the Spirit, typical of church tradition, especially in the oriental church, takes on a new meaning: the

Spirit transforms not only the symbolic gifts, not only the community, but the whole of reality, transfiguring it into the Kingdom. The invocation "thy Spirit come" is equivalent to "thy kingdom come," and in both cases it is an eschatological and also christological prayer of the church: it is the "come, Lord Jesus" of the early church (Rev. 22:20). In this supplication the church sums up not only its liturgical prayer but the cry of the people for the Kingdom and the liberation it brings. The sacraments as prophetic symbols are the church's liturgical prayer, the place where the cry of the people becomes the cry of Christ and his church to the Father, where the cry of the poor is condensed in the cry of the Crucified One and in the groaning of creation begging for liberation (Rom. 8:22ff.).

Finally, let us say that the festive dimension of these celebrations is increasingly emphasized by the praxis of the basic ecclesial communities and the popular sectors of the church. The people rejoice and celebrate, with a sense of gratuitousness. And through these celebrations they express their faith, as St. Thomas pointed out in discussing the faith of the least cultured sectors, who know and live the mysteries of faith in the liturgical celebrations of the church (*"de quibus ecclesia festa facit"*: *De Ver* q. 14, a. 11).

V. OUTLINE OF A LIBERATING SACRAMENTOLOGY

1. The Sacraments of the Poor: Sacramentals

Classical sacramentology distinguishes between the seven sacraments and the sacramentals. The sacramentology of liberation, in contrast, considers the sacramentals as sacraments of marginalization and of the poor; therefore, they should be considered in speaking of the sacraments. They comprise the sacramental practice that is most widespread and deeply rooted in the people, and they differ from one circumstance and place to another. Some are linked to the defining moments of life (birth, death, the passage from childhood to youth, from youth to maturity), to places (sanctuaries), to festive times (Christmas, Holy Week), to the agricultural cycle (planting, harvest), to special moments (inauguration of a house, a trip, illness, work). A whole range of symbols are mixed together: images, processions, candles, pilgrimages, blessings, flowers, meals, water rites. They are often led by lay people themselves; at other times they require a qualified presence of the ministers of the church. These sacramentals, typical of popular religion, can degenerate into magic, passivity, or excess. But in their basic form they are prophetic symbols of the Kingdom, which the poor and powerless long for. They are a symbolic expression of desire, of faith, of piety, of trust in the God of life. Through them is expressed the evangelizing potential of the poor. They must not be rejected. Nor should we fear to include them in the sacramental environment, since the early tradition of the church was not too disdainful to identify as sacraments such realities as footwashing, the consecration of virgins, the blessing of objects, funeral rites, and others.

A double theological task is required: to tie in these sacramentals with the sacraments of the church and with other sacramental moments of the Christian life.

2. The New Prophetic Symbols

Along with the classical sacraments, the theology of liberation is beginning to reflect on the new flowering of prophetic symbols in the Latin American church, brought about by a strong eruption of the Spirit. These are sacramental acts in Christian life, which enrich liturgical sacramentality and lead it to new configurations of Christian praxis. The new lay ministries of men and women, the emergence of the basic ecclesial communities, the new presence of women in the church and in theology, the new ways of living the episcopal and priestly ministry in service to the poor, the new forms of insertion of religious life, the transmission of the faith through families that are sometimes torn apart . . . these are prophetic and symbolic forms of the Kingdom and responses to the cry of the poor.

Certainly martyrdom is the clearest prophetic symbol of this new liberating sacramentality. The long list of martyrs in Latin America is a bloody testimony to the power of the Spirit, who inspires these living symbols of the Kingdom. They are a living prophecy of the God of life in a world of death, a denunciation of injustice, and an anticipation of the utopia of the Kingdom. All this is a way of following Jesus in defense of justice on the basis of the baptismal faith. The very fact that many have died at the hands of the governments and citizens who call themselves Christian shows the inadequacy of ecclesiality as a criterion for the evangelical discernment of sacramentality. One must look to the Kingdom, to following Jesus, for the evangelical discernment of sacramentality. Who can doubt that the life and death of Archbishop Romero are a prophetic symbol of the Kingdom? The simple people have understood it and visit his tomb to ask or thank him for favors.

The sacramentality of the church is not only ritual, but extends to the whole of Christian praxis. Medellín clearly affirms the Kingdom orientation of all Christian liturgy.

3. The Seven Sacraments

The seven sacraments of the church are the maximum symbolic expression of all these levels and types of sacramentality. They are the places and moments of clear ecclesial reference for human sacramentality, the sacramentals, and the new prophetic symbols. If classical theology tried to justify them by linking them to the institutional acts of the historical Jesus, and modern sacramentality has considered them as the constitutive moments of the church as proto-sacrament, the theology of liberation places them in the context of the Kingdom: they are privileged steps on the way from death to life, and they orient our life to the service of the Kingdom in the key moments of our existence. They are prophetic symbols of the Kingdom with respect to liberation from all that oppresses the person and society. Rather than drawing a priori deductions, the theology of liberation tries to show that the sacraments of the church are oriented to the Kingdom and reveal the great contents of the Kingdom: mercy, life, justice, liberation, gratuitousness, solidarity, hope, community. The number of the seven sacraments goes beyond arithmetic importance and enters into the symbolic, into the fullness of the Kingdom.

In an experimental way, let us dissect the aspects of liberation and of Kingdom orientation in each sacrament, respecting the traditional hierarchy among them: the principal sacraments (baptism and eucharist), and the secondary sacraments (all the rest).[5] It is not a matter of structuring a complete sacramentology, but only of specifying in the seven sacraments the sacramental horizon of the Kingdom of God, as it is emphasized in the theology of liberation.

The Principal Sacraments

i. Baptism. This sacrament, the most popular and widely celebrated even among the poorest people, has been considered for centuries almost exclusively in its individual dimension (erasing the original sin that impedes salvation). The general application of child baptism and the reduction of the symbolic meaning of water to that of washing contributed to this individualization, which is not false but diminishes the richness of the sacrament. The sacramentology of Vatican II has rediscovered the ecclesial dimension of baptism (LG, 9-10), and modern sacramental theology (for example, K. Rahner) has made incorporation into the church not merely one effect but the first effect of baptism, from which the others are derived. The theology of liberation considers baptism not only as incorporation into the church, but as eschatological orientation and initiation into the Kingdom of God, of which the church is a sacrament.

The biblical stories themselves reinforce this perspective. The baptism of John, a prophetic and popular rite especially for the marginal sectors of Judaism and of society, is oriented to the eschatological Kingdom of God, which is coming now (Matt. 3:2), and for which the people must prepare with radical conversion (Luke 3:1-20). John's baptism of Jesus implies the beginning of his evangelizing activities oriented to the Kingdom (Mark 1:15). But this baptism of Jesus in the Jordan would be existentially realized in his death (Luke 12:50, Mark 10:38-39), and in his descent into hell (Matt. 12:40, Luke 11:30), whence he would rise in triumph over death and sin (Rev. 1:18).

Water symbolizes the passage from death to life, from life marked by sin (personal, historical, and social) to life that begins to anticipate the utopia of the Kingdom. Thus the first baptisms of the Jerusalem community at Pentecost not only added new believers to the church (Acts 2:41) but led to a life of fellowship and solidarity (Acts 2:42-47) that anticipated the utopia of the Kingdom. The early history of this sacrament itself presupposes great seriousness in personal conversion and in orientation to the values of the Kingdom as they were incarnated in Jesus. The catechumenate, with its requirement not only of biblical formation but of conversion, expressed that baptism requires a clear orientation to the Kingdom. Baptismal grace is the gift of the Spirit that forgives sins and gives strength to follow in life the way of the Kingdom initiated by Jesus. It is the Spirit itself, sent by Jesus to announce the Good News to the poor and the liberation of captives (Luke 4:16-21), who impels the Christian to make the Kingdom of God present in history and to struggle against the structures of sin. This eschatological orientation to the Kingdom may have been lost over the years, giving way to an excessive ecclesiocentrism.

The [practice] of baptism in Latin America is not centered on the baptism of children but on the struggle against the structures of sin; in any case, the problem is the baptism of the rich. On the other hand, given the high rate of infant mortality today, it would be unconscionable to postpone baptism. The many popular rites centered on birth and baptism may be reinterpreted as sacramental forms, which in connection with baptism, orient the child to the Kingdom, to life, and to solidarity. The [practice] of baptism must interpret historically the generic concepts of sin and grace, death and life, and encourage the search for utopian alternatives to the prevailing structures of sin. All this is done in the church and with the church, but in openness to the Kingdom and liberation.[6]

ii. Eucharist. This sacrament has been studied since the Reformation from an apologetic, anti-Protestant perspective. The classical treatises on the eucharist have been about real presence, sacrifice, and sacramental communion. Vatican II has given the eucharist a communitarian orientation (*Sacrosanctum Concilium,* no. 10; *Presbyterorum Ordinis,* no. 6), rediscovering the ecclesiality of the eucharist as it was in the first millennium; as the aphorism describes it, "eucharist makes the church, the church makes eucharist" (H. de Lubac). The theology of liberation, far from denying this, deepens it. The primary eucharistic symbol is the fellowship of sharing one meal and cup. In the Bible it is the image of the banquet that best expresses the utopia of the Kingdom. In the gospels, meals and banquets symbolize the Kingdom in the parables (Matt. 8:11, 22:1-4, 25:1-13); in the miracles (the multiplication of the loaves for hungry people, Mark 6:34-44, Mark 8:1-10); and in the symbolic actions of Jesus when he ate with sinners and marginalized people (Mark 2:16, Luke 15:2, Matt. 11:19). The meals of the Resurrected One (Luke 24:13-35, Luke 24:41-43, John 21:12-13) also symbolize the newness of the Kingdom of life inaugurated by the resurrection. At the center of these meals is the Last Supper of Jesus, where in an atmosphere of farewell and in a clear reference to the table of the Kingdom (Matt. 26:29, Mark 14:25, Luke 22:15-18, 1 Cor. 11:26), the Lord gave us his body and his blood as the food of the Kingdom. In the eucharist we not only commune with Jesus, but with his Kingdom project; we not only edify the church but anticipate the banquet of the Kingdom. Thus the eucharist is inseparable from the fellowship of love and service, as John testifies in transmitting to us the symbolic act of footwashing (John 13). For this very reason a eucharist without real sharing, as occurred in Corinth, "is not the Lord's supper (1 Cor. 11:20-21). The patristic tradition corroborates this dimension of the eucharist, which is not only ecclesial but social: the offerings of the faithful for the poor; the presence of the slaves and the exhortation for their manumission; the preaching of the Fathers on justice and the defense of the poor; the liturgical excommunication of public sinners, who must be reconciled with the church in order to be readmitted to eucharistic communion.[7]

The eucharist cannot forget the Paschal context of the Lord's supper, the

Jewish passover, the feast of the liberation from Egypt, and especially the Paschal act of Jesus, murdered for preaching the Kingdom and for denouncing the anti-Kingdom. The gift of the Resurrected One must become the seed for a new earth and a new heaven, not only liturgically but historically (GS, 38-39). The eucharist is not simply a celebration of small historical victories, but a token of the final and full realization of the Kingdom of God. Thus it is not only a subversive memorial (J. B. Metz), but a source of hope and the beginning of transfiguration. The bread and wine are transformed into bread and wine of the Kingdom, the beginning of the final utopia. And Jesus, eschatological mediator of the Kingdom, is made present with his transforming power. The epiclesis is not limited to the transformation of the gifts or of the community, but of all history into the body of the Lord.

The theology of liberation has reflected on the eucharists of the first missionaries and bishops of Latin America, on the eucharists of the basic ecclesial communities, and on the eucharists of Archbishop Romero.[8] Once again, the *lex orandi* illuminates the *lex credendi*.

The Other Sacraments

The other sacraments, or secondary sacraments in the patristic formulation, are derived from or ordered by the first two. Let us reflect briefly on each of these, from the horizon of the Kingdom of God.

i. **Confirmation.** Originally a part of Christian initiation, it was separated from baptism for pastoral and historical reasons. Its theology was gradually unlinked from its baptismal roots and from the initiating perspective. Modern theology restored confirmation to its roots of initiation and emphasized its ecclesial and pneumatic dimensions (LG, 11). The theology of liberation emphasizes that the pentecostal and missionary aspect of this sacrament is oriented to the Kingdom. From the time of the Old Testament, anointment has symbolized the gift of the Spirit in the sense of righteousness and justice for the poor and weak (Ps. 72:1). What the kings of Israel could not bring about would be fulfilled by the Messiah, anointed by the Spirit, to establish righteousness and justice (Isa. 7, 9:6, 11:6, 61; Luke 4). Jesus, the Christ, was anointed by the Spirit in baptism for his Messianic mission; he passed through the world doing good and liberating those who were oppressed by the devil (Acts 10:38).

The gift of the Spirit, communicated by confirmation through the symbolism of anointment, possesses a prophetic and eschatological orientation to the Kingdom, to justice and liberation. It reminds the baptized one and the church that their mission is the world and the Kingdom. To reduce confirmation to a renewal of baptism or an affirmation of the Spirit, without referring to the historical Jesus and his commitment to the Kingdom, is to distort the meaning of this sacrament.

ii. **Penance.** This actualizes the power of baptism for sins committed after baptism. Its early ecclesial orientation, forgotten in the centuries when penance was privatized, and administered for a fee, has been renewed by the theology of Vatican II. The first effect of penance (*res et sacramentum*) is once again ecclesial reconciliation. What the theology of liberation emphasizes is that neither sin nor reconciliation is purely intra-ecclesial. Sin wounds the ecclesial body, but it possesses a dynamic of death that affects society and history: structures of sin. Sin kills the life of personal and ecclesial grace, and it also kills the brother or sister. Archbishop Romero's definition of sin is paradigmatic: "Sin is what killed the Son of God and what kills the children of God." It follows that conversion must be not only personal but also social, historical, and structural. Reconciliation with the church must be oriented to undoing the consequences of personal and social sin, to "taking away the sin of the world," following the way of Jesus (John 1:29). In penance the church prophetically announces God's mercy, denounces the sin of the world and initiates its transformation by communicating the Spirit of Jesus (John 20:19-23) for the forgiveness of sins. The dynamic of this Spirit leads to liberation from all slavery (Rom. 8:19-27). This sheds light on the many penitential rites of popular religion. It also shows the ambiguity of certain practices of communal penance, which soothe the economically powerful sectors with a collective absolution that requires no profound change of personal life. In contrast, this new horizon of the Kingdom must from time to time encourage the church as a community to seek the forgiveness of God and the world for its collective sins in the past (the colonial period) and in the present (its alliance with the powerful). As servant of Yahweh the church must bear the sin of the world, intercede for sinners, and anticipate liberation.

iii. Marriage. Few sacraments have suffered as much distortion as that of marriage. In the best of cases it is lived as a sacrament of the family or of an often very closed sort of personal love. Modern theology has struggled to transpose marriage into an ecclesial key, as symbol of the love of Christ for his church in line with Ephesians 5:32-33, "a domestic church" (LG, 11), but without great pastoral success.

Before the theology of liberation takes up this sacrament, we believe it must clarify a series of prior problems. The maturity (human, affective, sexual, Christian) of a couple requires minimal social, economic, and cultural conditions not present amid the prevalence of poverty, unemployment, the promiscuity of inhuman living quarters, and so on. Before reflecting on the sublimeness of Christian sacramental marriage we must reflect on the poor person's body as an object of continual exploitation, on sexuality, and on the condition of poor women, who are doubly exploited in Latin America by machismo and the culture of consumerism. We must also study the types of couples and marriage rites that prevail in Indian and Afro-American cultures. Only then can we elaborate a theology of marriage, which should be open not only to the ecclesial dimension, but to the eschatology of the Kingdom, symbolized in the union of Adam and Eve (Gen. 2:22), which prefigures not only the union of Christ with his church, but that of God with humanity. To the new Adam (1 Cor. 15:45) we must also unite the new humanity, the new Jerusalem, "prepared as a bride adorned for her husband" (Rev. 21:2). But meanwhile the bride is with child, crying out in her pangs of birth, in anguish for delivery (Rev. 12:2).

Christian marriage must proclaim the power of the generous love of God; it must denounce selfishness and begin to anticipate, not only in the family but also in society, the new humanity, new human and social relationships, which are described in symbolic and utopian terms in the paradise of Genesis. In this way marriage will be a sacrament of the church and of the definitive Kingdom of God, biblically expressed in the nuptial banquet and the wedding of the Lamb. Only the grace of the Lord is capable of carrying out this miracle, symbolized in the new wine at Cana (John 2:1-12). This eschatological dimension will also allow us to focus evangelically on a series of moral issues in marriage, for example, divorce.

iv. Ministry. For centuries the priestly order has been defined almost exclusively in relation to the sacraments: the priest is the man of the sacraments, the other Christ, who consecrates and who forgives sins. Modern theology transposes the ministry into an ecclesial key: the priest as man of the word and of the community, the one who presides over it "in the person of Christ and in the name of the church." The theology of liberation, by placing the priest in the horizon of the Kingdom, rediscovers other aspects.[9] As always, the theology of liberation does not begin with an a priori idea but with the situation of poverty and injustice in Latin America. What is the primary evangelizing service, the salvific approach of God to a poor people? What was the priesthood of Jesus? His whole life was a mediation, but this mediation was done through mercy (Mark 6:34, Matt. 9:36, Luke 7:13, Matt. 14:14, Mark 1:41, Matt. 20:34); in the letter to the Hebrews the high priesthood of Jesus consists in sympathizing with our weakness (Heb. 4:15), in being merciful (Heb. 2:17). Mercy is the constitutive element in the priesthood of Jesus, which led him to the cross and resurrection. This is the constitutive element of the Christian priesthood of the faithful and of the priestly ministry. The priest is not only the man of the sacraments, of the word and community, but above all the man of mercy to the poor and sinners. This does not devalue the liturgical element but orients the priesthood to the Kingdom, just as John did not devalue the eucharist by speaking of the fellowship of service, symbolized and recommended in the act of footwashing (John 13). In the sacrament of priestly orders this function of mercy takes on an ecclesial and official charge, and the grace of the Spirit for this pastoral function. Evangelization, sacraments, practice, and so on, should all be oriented to this horizon. The figures of the great bishops and missionaries of the first evangelization of Latin America and the figures of the modern bishops martyred for defending the rights of the poor people give this reflection a historical and theological grounding. That, in turn, sheds light on other subjects such as the new lay ministries, women and ministry, new priestly lifestyles, and more.

v. Anointing of the Sick. This is not only the sacrament of the dying but of the sick. That does not detract from its eschatological orientation to the Kingdom, still keeping in mind its ecclesial dimension (James 5:13-15). It is a prophetic way of announcing the salvation of Jesus, of denouncing the present sickness and death as consequences of sin, and of anticipating the wholeness of the Kingdom by the transformation of weakness into strength, of sin into grace, and even of sickness into health. It is the sacrament that speaks of eschatological wholeness and of the abundant life of the Kingdom of God.

This sacrament should not be limited to the liturgical anointing of the sick or to caring for the aged, but should include general concern for health and for removing the causes of so many curable diseases and so many premature deaths. Moreover, the ceremonial richness of popular religion with regard to sickness and death should not be unlinked from this sacrament, because anointing is a liturgical prayer for life in all its wholeness. It is an act of faith and hope in the God of life. In the last analysis the anointing of the sick is part of the early apostolic mission of announcing the Kingdom of God (Mark 6:12-13, Luke 9:3, Matt. 10:7-8).

VI. A FINAL POINT

Let us conclude with these brief observations:

1. Its approach to reality will always be the unalterable point of departure for liberating theological and sacramental reflection. We must walk "with one ear tuned to the gospel and the other to the people" (Bishop Enrique Angelelli). The cry of the people is still a privileged theological locus for sacramental theology and must be incorporated into ecclesial liturgy.

2. Sacramental theology will be strengthened to the degree that the church's option for the poor is made real, that the basic ecclesial communities grow in number and maturity, that popular religion is evangelically embraced, and that reflection on sacramental praxis is broadened (including theology done by women). But some of the traits that shape a new vision of sacramentality centered on the Kingdom, on liberation, and on the poor, are already appearing. The ultimate aspiration is not simply to possess a coherent theological synthesis that can compete with those elaborated in the First World, but principally, to make the sacraments liberating symbols for the people.

3. All systematization entails risks; the new sacramentology of the theology of liberation also does. If in its sacramentology the theology of liberation unlinks the Kingdom from the church, and the church from Jesus, the sacraments deteriorate into purely sociopolitical or humanistic symbols. If the sacraments are reduced to celebrating the historical liberations already achieved and pedagogically encouraging ethical commitment in the future, sacramentality loses its christological, ecclesial, and pneumatic identity and deteriorates into a simple method of conscientization. Sacramentality must always maintain its gratuitousness, its sense of feast and symbol. In order to avoid these risks we must continually return to ecclesial praxis, to scripture, to the gospel, to the historical Jesus, who in his symbolic acts, especially in baptism and the supper, prophetically united trust in the Father, solidarity with the people, and faithfulness to the Kingdom. The Kingdom of God is always a gift of the Spirit, and so too are its prophetic symbols. The sign of the coming of the Kingdom of God is the exorcism of all evils, and this is only done by the finger of God, that is, with the Spirit (Luke 11:20).

— Translated by Margaret D. Wilde

NOTES

1. See chapter 15 above.
2. C. Boff and J. Pixley, *The Bible, the Church, and the Poor,* trans. Paul Burns (Maryknoll, N.Y.: Orbis Books, 1989), p. 114.

3. P. Casaldáliga, *Cantares de la entera libertad* (Managua, 1984), p. 73.

4. J. Sobrino, *Introducción a los sacramentos* (Mexico, 1979), p. 29.

5. Y. Congar, "The Idea of Major or Principal Sacraments," *Concilium* 31 (1968), pp. 24-37.

6. V. Codina, "¿Es licito bautizar a los ricos?," *Selecciones de Teología* 57 (1975); "Dimensión social del bautismo," in *Fe y justicia* (Salamanca, 1981), pp. 99-133.

7. J. M. Castillo, "Donde no hay justicia no hay eucaristía," in *Fe y justicia*, pp. 135-71.

8. E. Dussel, "The Bread of Celebration, Communitarian Sign of Justice," *Concilium* 72 (1982), pp. 236-49.

9. J. Sobrino, "Hacia una determinación de la realidad sacerdotal," *Revista Latinoamericana de Teología* 1 (1984), pp. 47-81.

THE SPIRIT OF LIBERATION

33

Spirituality and the Following of Jesus

JON SOBRINO

The subject of spirituality has come in for unaccustomed interest in our times, and not only among those who devote themselves to "the things of the spirit," nor even only within the churches, but also, and especially—even when the word *spirituality* is not mentioned—in the world. Current history, with its crises and its questionings, its opportunities and its demands for the building of a human and humane future, challenges human beings and humanity as such. The challenge may go unheard; it may be manipulated or even perverted. But for perceptive persons, the questions mightily resound once more: What are you, and what ought you to be? What do you hope for, and what might you hope for? What are you doing, and what should you be doing? What are you celebrating, and what could you be celebrating? From out of the midst of history itself, the call has sounded: Answer for the truth of history truthfully. Shape that history; do not be dominated by it or merely slip and slide passively through it.

I. THE IMPORTANCE OF "LIVING WITH SPIRIT"

The task—the perennial, inescapable task—of responding to these questions, to this call, becomes all the more urgent in moments of crisis and "unhinging"—when the old hinges are no longer up to bearing the weight of the new edifice. The creation of new hinges for history to turn on, and turn well—a history in which men and women can live, or live again, as human beings—surely pre-supposes many elements, both of theory and of praxis. But integrating and living all of them adequately is a matter of spirit. It is this "being-human-with-

spirit"—which responds to the elements of crisis and promise residing in concrete reality, unifying the various elements of a response to that reality in such
a way that the latter may be definitively a reality more of promise than of crisis—
that we call spirituality.

In the churches, too, the emphatic question of spirituality arises. This is
primarily due to the fact that the churches participate—knowingly or not—in
the current history of humanity. More specifically, it is due to the fact that the
churches themselves have been the scene of an unhinging under the impact of
the novelty, the enormous element of the new, introduced by Vatican II and
Medellín. There is no use denying that new doctrinal, theological, pastoral, and
liturgical elements today accompany those bequeathed to us by tradition. Nor
can it be denied that the living experience of faith today occurs in a context in
which the world itself has irrupted into the life of the churches—the world with
its progress, surely, but also, and especially, with its concrete reality of terrifying
injustice, with the unconcealable cries of the suffering, hope-filled poor. Just
as undeniably, the urgent new synthesis of these and so many other things—in
theory, and far more so, in practice—presents its difficulties, and a variety of
attempts are under way to create it. In some persons and groups, a taste for
the new predominates, and they bend their efforts to integrate the old into the
new. In other persons and groups, a fear of the new provokes a longing for the
old.

The traditional mosaic of the church, with all its pieces and colors, has
shaken apart and now must be fitted back together again. In the face of such
an arduous and demanding task, with the dangers it might entail, one could of
course make an option for a simple reconstruction, with an appeal to doctrinal
security and calling on the hierarchy to take a firm stance administratively.
Surely doctrine and administration continue to be necessary and important. But
of themselves alone they will not be enough to rebuild the edifice. On the other
hand, absolutely necessary and urgent though Christian praxis surely is, neither
will it be enough, of itself alone, to re-create the whole edifice. Thus, Johannes
B. Metz speaks of a "mysticism and politics of discipleship"; and Ignacio Ellacuría called for "the contemplative in action for justice." Whatever terms we
may want to use to describe this new situation and challenge, the important
thing is the emphasis on something called spirit rather than only on theory and
praxis—or, of course, only on doctrine and administration.

Finally—for these and other, more specific, reasons—theology, too, has
taken a serious interest in spirituality. First, it was noticed that a doctrinal,
purely explanatory and deductive theology was no longer adequate to the twin
explosions of concrete reality and faith—since the first explosion was driving
believers back to something predoctrinal, something more comprehensive. This
is how the most alert theologians saw things. Hans Urs von Balthasar and Karl
Rahner had been urging for years that the wall between theology and spirituality
be torn down. A purely doctrinal theology, then, had become irrelevant. And
a distribution of the identity and relevance of theology among, on one hand,
the doctrinal dogmatic treatises or tractates, and on the other, those of Christian
praxis and spirituality, had not solved the problem either. After all, the problem

does not reside in the formal organization of the content of theology, but in theology's across-the-board attitude—the spirit with which theology is done, and the spirit communicated by the theology that is done.

In a like context, the in-depth renewal of theology has consisted primarily not so much in an emphasis on new or forgotten content, but in an effort to address and focus on content that by its nature engenders spirit, and that ought to be addressed and communicated with a particular spirit. For example, in my opinion the key discovery of modern theology is this: the objective reality of the Reign of God, and its corresponding subjective reality—hope and praxis— have become an increasingly important focus for many theologies, and indeed for liberation theology, the central content. But the reason why these become central in theology is not that we now know something important that Jesus proclaimed. The reason why this Reign and its corresponding hope and praxis suddenly belong to the core of Christian theology is precisely that the objective member of the pair launches a rocket of hope and calls for a practice. Without that, there is no grasping the meaning of the Reign of God. The hermeneutic problem is not reducible to the opportunity to understand a text. The hermeneutic problem is also a problem of spirituality—of what is the spirit that moves us to read a text, that enables us to interpret it, and that permits us to communicate its spirit for today. A theological treatment of the subject of the Reign of God, then, both requires and renders possible the doing of theology with a specific attitude. This hope-charged praxic attitude, this attitude of hoping and acting "with spirit," is what has set theology on the road to becoming spiritual through and through—to being shot through with spirituality—rather than relegating the latter to one of the tractates (usually, of course, regarded as secondary).

In Latin America the theology of liberation has been very attentive to spirituality, and the performance of its task has been steeped in a particular spirit from the very start. But it is not by some voluntary decision on the part of liberation theologians that this has been the case. Rather, it is because this theology wishes to take account of, and constitute a response to, concrete, historical church reality, with its real cries and real hopes. The very fact that liberation theology is an account of something concrete, formulated for the purpose of turning that concrete reality into something really new, demonstrates that a particular spirit has been present in the very execution of its task. And it is because the theological task has been executed with spirit, we think, that this theology has made spirituality something central. As Gustavo Gutiérrez said, with liberation theology still in its infancy: "A vital, comprehensive, and synthetic attitude is needed—one that will inform our life part and parcel. A spirituality." The important thing, again, is to remember the reason for this fact. The reason is that, from its first beginnings, the theology of liberation has sought to be a creative synthesis of what it means to be human and to be Christian in the real world of today, specifically in the world of the hoping, suffering poor, whose sudden appearance on the scene has been what has unhinged the old world and its theology, while at the same time giving the new synthesis its bearings and thrust.

From this outlook I should like in this chapter, to address spirituality as it is developing in Latin America. Rather than speaking of spirituality in the abstract, however, I should like to work from a point of departure in the concrete spirit that actually becomes present in human beings and animates their thoughts, feelings, and actions. After all, while it may be difficult to define spirituality, the presence of human beings is both evident and instructive. Let me begin, then, with the proposition that spiritual persons are persons who live with spirit—those who, in Christian terms, "are filled with the Spirit of Christ, and this in a living, observable manner because the strength and life of that Spirit invests their whole person and their whole action" (Ignacio Ellacuría).

It is not easy to discover a single methodological route to the treatment of the subject of spirituality. The various dimensions of "life with spirit" intermingle. We should now like to offer two kinds of reflections. The first turns on the basic spirituality of every human being, which we call the fundamental, objectively theological dimension. This reflection will be of a more comprehensive kind, then, but we think it necessary to entertain it if we hope to be able to restore spirituality to its original place, or to comprehend Christian spirituality not as something added to the human, but as a deepening of the human—such as occurred in the *homo verus*, Jesus. The second approach that we shall use will be an explicitation of the Christian element of spirituality, with its christologic and pneumatologic dimension, which we shall address simultaneously. Here, it will be a matter simply of answering these questions: What is the spirit required in order to live in a Christian manner? What is the spirit that produces the Christian life?

II. THE FUNDAMENTAL, OBJECTIVELY THEOLOGICAL DIMENSION OF SPIRITUALITY

Every human being has a spiritual life. Like it or not, know it or not, each of us is confronted with reality and endowed with the ability to react to that reality with ultimacy. The expression *spiritual life* is tautological, then. Every human being lives his or her life with spirit. It is another matter, of course, with what spirit a person lives. But at all events, he or she lives with spirit.

It seems to us important to recall this tautology, since, whatever spirituality may be, it does not directly intend a relationship with some manner of purely spiritual, invisible, immaterial realities, as if only in that case the spiritual life would begin to have meaning, and as if some human beings were spiritual and others were not. The spiritual life is not something "regional," and still less does it stand in opposition to another, "material" kind of life. Surely immaterial realities exist: first and foremost, we have the mystery of God. But this does not mean that the spiritual element of life consists in a direct relationship with the nonmaterial by way of nonmaterial or less material activities that would be, or would be intended to be, only spiritual. Indeed, this would actually prevent the revelation of God, by which God has actually become present in definitive attachment to the material element of Jesus' flesh, as well as to the material element of concrete history and of history's special offspring, the poor.

No, spirituality is the spirit with which we confront the real. It is the spirit with which we confront the concrete history in which we live, with all its complexity. Thus it will be possible to speak of what spirit is adequate and what is not; but each, the adequate spirit and the inadequate one, will have its reference to the real with a view to facing that real and deciding what to do with it. Let us now present what, in our opinion, is the adequate spirit with which that concrete reality ought to be confronted. It will be the basis of all spirituality, including the Christian, as well as the basis of the spiritualities (in the plural) that have been handed down to us by Christian tradition.

1. Honesty with the Real: Respecting the Truth of Concrete Reality

First of all, it is an act of spirit — and spirit is necessary in order to perform it — to be *honest with the real*. Intellectually, this means grasping the truth of concrete reality; practically, it means responding to the demand made by that reality. More precisely, it means — and this is why this honesty is not so very much in evidence — coming to a grasp of truth and actually making a response to reality. This is accomplished not only by way of overcoming ignorance and indifference, but in confrontation with our innate tendency to subordinate truth and to evade reality.

To grasp and accept truth is to allow reality to be, in the first place, that which it is, and not subject it to a violence calculated to adjust it to our own tastes and interests. To this purpose a spirit of honesty is required. In every human being the temptation is innate, and very often succumbed to, to imprison truth by means of injustice (see Rom. 1:18). The fact of the matter, however, is that the problem of truth is posed not only in terms of ignorance in the face of reality — when we start out with nothing to get to something, try to move from a not knowing to a knowing — but also in terms of our tendency to conceal of the truth by means of a lie. In John, let us remember, the Evil One is a liar (cf. John 8:44).

This mighty proclivity to the lie is an expression of human sinfulness. We should like to suppress the truth. To overcome this proclivity, we have need of spirit. Sin is that which puts persons to death, but precisely therefore, it simultaneously seeks to hide itself — to pass itself off as something it is not. And so every scandal comes clad in its own concealment.

Honesty with the real, then, is a matter of great activity and requires spirit. If this basic honesty with the real is not exercised, the consequences for the human being are catastrophic. As Paul says, the heart is darkened (subjectively) and concrete realities are no longer creatures, sacraments of God (as they are objectively), but manipulated things. Indeed, from the root of this basic dishonesty follow all the sinful fruits catalogued by Paul, and God's wrath, instead of God's grace, spills out over the heads of those who are not honest with the real.

What dialectical theology (especially in Karl Barth) has asserted of human cognition and the possibility (and actuality) that it be used against God in one's own behalf will of course apply to a cognition of concrete reality. There is a way of knowing the real whose purpose is to defend the knower from the real.

The right way to know is to know for the purpose of defending the real and its objective interests.

This is what we mean when we speak of honesty with the real. In polemical terms we mean overcoming the temptation to oppress truth. Positively speaking, we mean keeping our eyes open to the sight of reality—having the pure heart that enables one to see God, as the Beatitudes say.

2. *Honesty with the Real: The Reaction of Mercy*

Honesty with the real primarily means responding to the demand of concrete reality itself. To put it in still more general language, it means that, when the truth of reality is not imprisoned through injustice, that truth itself gives rise to an unconditional yes to life, and an unconditional no to death. Concrete reality cries no to its own negation—to the absence, lack, and annihilation of life. In biblical terminology this no is no to Cain the fratricide, no to the oppression in Egypt, and the prophets' no to those who sell the just for a pair of sandals. No theology or theodicy can subsequently silence or relativize this primary no uttered by reality.

To put it in a positive way, this ethical practice of honesty is mercy or pity in confrontation with reality. Mercy, here, or compassion, is not reducible to an affective movement of the emotions, although this may accompany it. Mercy denotes a reaction in the face of the suffering of another, which one has interiorized and which has become one and the same thing with oneself, with a view to saving that other. Mercy is the primary and ultimate, the first and the last, of human reactions. It is that in terms of which all dimensions of the human being acquire meaning and without which nothing else attains to human status. In this mercy, the human being is perfected, becomes whole, as Luke teaches in the parable of the Good Samaritan. The gospels use it to typify Jesus himself, who so often acts after being "moved with compassion." The Bible actually uses it to typify God, whose bowels grow so tender that the divine Father welcomes and embraces the prodigal. Mercy, then, is the correct manner of responding to concrete reality—as well as the ultimate and decisive manner thereof, as we learn from the parable of the Last Judgment. Everything—absolutely everything—turns on the exercise of mercy. On it depends not only transcendent salvation, but our living here and now, in concrete history, as saved human beings.

To be sure, this mercy will have to be exercised in a variety of ways, depending on the nature of the wound suffered by the victim lying in the ditch. Thus it must take various forms: emergency relief, assistance and support, reconciliation, and so on. In the presence of entire crucified peoples, as in Latin America, mercy must take the form of structural justice, which is having mercy on the masses.

What we are concerned to emphasize here, however, is the primary and ultimate nature of mercy as the primordial act of spirit. We have said that mercy is first and last; we mean that it is exercised for no other reason than that someone else is suffering, and that we have internalized that suffering.

This, indeed, is how mercy and pity are presented in the gospel. The Good Samaritan is presented as an example of someone who fulfills the greatest of the commandments; yet, in the parable, the Samaritan appears not as a person acting in order to fulfill a commandment, but as a person "moved to pity" (Luke 10:33). The father in the parable, like our heavenly Father, reconciles the prodigal with himself personally, but the reason he goes out every day to look for him and offer him the embrace of welcome is not that he is trying to find some tactic that will get the child to return the parent the honor that is the latter's due. It is because he is moved to pity. It is the same with God and us.

Here we notice that mercy is, as we said, first and last. All other things whatsoever—personal risks, doubt, the rights of the institution—must be subordinated to mercy. No other interests, not even legitimate ones, may be appealed to in order to ignore mercy or relegate it to secondary status.

This primordial mercy constantly makes its reappearance in concrete history at key moments to recall to us its quality as fundamental and ultimate—as that beyond which it is impossible to go. It is related of Jesus that, after having healed the person in the synagogue with the withered hand, he asked: "Is it permitted to do a good deed on the sabbath—or an evil one? To preserve life—or destroy it?" (Mark 3:4). Bartolomé de las Casas said: "A live Indian is better that a baptized corpse." Archbishop Romero said: "Nothing is more important for the church than life, especially the life of the poor, who are God's favorites . . . We must defend the minimum which is all the maximum gift of God: life." What all of these quotations have in common, in their different accents, is the primary and ultimate character of mercy. One cannot go beyond it, or argue with anyone in its favor, or avoid any risk it may require. In the solemn words of Micah, God says to each and every human being:

> You have been told, O man, what is good,
>   and what the Lord requires of you:
> Only to do right and to love goodness (Mic. 6:8).

Here is no anthropological argument, or even a religious one, in favor of mercy, as if mercy and compassion were being identified for the first time as a demand on the part of God. The great question, the invitation and demand for mercy, is concrete reality itself. When we respond with mercy, we are being honest with reality.

3. Fidelity to the Real

Honesty with the real must not only be exercised in our time, but it must be maintained all down through history, in whatever history proposes as a thing to be endured, or as something new, or as perilous or blessed surprise. Thus, honesty with the real becomes fidelity to the real. History has its span—an intuition that the Catholic tradition has always maintained—and the span of history ever introduces novelties, obscurities, and risks. History must needs be traversed — "walked with," as Micah puts it, "humbly," and not imagining that a first act of honesty, or the original direction of our route, will automatically carry us to our destination.

Historically, this is evident. To maintain that first honesty with the real is difficult and costly. We need spirit to maintain our honesty regardless of where it leads.

Concrete reality frequently clouds over, even after the first honest choice, and may become temptation. It is the cumulative experience of history, down to our very day, that when the truth about reality is maintained, when the lie that would imprison that truth is unmasked, when reactions of love, in all its forms — and certainly in the form of justice — are seen, they are not welcome; the one who seeks to foster life is expected to give of his or her own life, or even to give up that life. The honest denunciation of sin becomes having to take on the burden of sin, with all its consequences. In addition to attacks from without, one experiences the intrinsic difficulty of finding light — of changing course precisely in order to be honest with one's fundamental intuition in seeking to bestow life. This is when fidelity is demanded, amidst darkness, as with Abraham's fidelity; amidst petition and supplication, as with the high priest Jesus, of the Letter to the Hebrews. To be honest is to come to be honest by passing through the crucible of having failed to be so. One arrives at fullness through history, with all its vicissitudes, as did that high priest.

At the same time, however, it is also a fact that, rising up out of concrete reality itself is a hope that cannot be silenced, and that there exists a hope-charged current of humanity, which is endlessly fascinating. In Pauline language, it is as if creation were suffering birthpangs and crying to be delivered. In concrete reality itself, then, there is something of promise and of unsilenced hope. This is the experience of centuries. Reality itself, in spite of its long history of failure and misery, posits ever and again the hope of fullness. Always there arises a new Exodus, a new return from Exile, a deliverance from captivity — although none of these, surely, is ever definitive. And this hope, with which reality itself trembles, finds spokespersons all down through history. There was a Moses to proclaim a land of promise, then an Isaiah who once again announced a new heaven and a new earth, and then a Jesus of Nazareth who once again proclaimed the Reign of God, and then an Archbishop Romero who once again announced liberation. This recurrence of hope is part of concrete reality, too, and to it, as well, one must be faithful, especially when so many other concrete historical experiences counsel skepticism, cynicism, or resignation.

Fidelity to the real, then, includes hope — a hope made possible by reality itself. But this hope is an active one, and not only an expectant one. It helps concrete reality to come to be what it seeks to be. And that is love. Love and hope — in that order — are two sides of the same coin: the conviction, put in practice, that reality has possibilities. Love and hope mean helping to bring to light the better, the more humane, presently gestating in the womb of reality. Hope and love are each other's sustenance. That the world may have life can only be hoped for in the act of giving that world life; in the activity of giving life, hope grows that life is possible. This fidelity to the real, then, is not an exigency arbitrarily imposed, or even the observance of the most exalted of the commandments. It is the most finished and perfect harmony with reality.

4. Allowing Ourselves To Be Led by the Real

As we have said, hope is nourished by reality, and love is facilitated by reality. This means that concrete reality is an opportunity, not just a difficulty. It means that reality is also Good News, not merely demand. This reality is transformed into the "heavy burden become light," as Karl Rahner says of the gospel; the more you carry it, the more it carries you.

This means that concrete reality is also steeped in grace; reality itself offers us a direction and a strength to traverse, and make, history in that direction. This is the case because in concrete reality is an accumulated goodness, as well, which moves us. There is a hope-filled, honest, loving current there, which becomes a powerful invitation to us, and once we have entered it, we allow ourselves to be carried along by it. Just as there is an original sin that becomes a structural dimension of reality, so also there is an original grace, which becomes a gracious structure of reality. That structural grace is more original, surely, in the logic of Christian faith than original sin, although the fruits of the latter appear to be quantitatively greater than those of the former.

To accept that grace emerging from concrete reality, to allow ourselves to be permeated with this grace, to place our wager on it, is also an act of spirit. To accept that grace is to plunge headlong into reality and allow ourselves to be borne up on the "more" with which reality is pregnant and which is offered to us freely, again and again, despite all. To accept the grace emerging from reality is to allow ourselves to be borne forward by a future of goodness — a utopia — which, while it has never existed and never will, nevertheless gives us food for the future and supplies us with the strength to keep on searching for it and building it.

In more personal language, to allow ourselves to be supported and carried along by reality means allowing ourselves to be helped and supported by the "cloud of witnesses" (Heb. 12:1), those who have generated the best of human and Christian traditions, who invite us to graft ourselves onto these traditions and build on them. Tradition is that which has been handed over to us; in other words, what has been given us, and that too is grace. Reality, then, not only makes demands, but offers opportunities as well. This gracious structure of reality calls for a response with the spirit of gratuity and gratitude. And because concrete reality has this structure of grace, therefore it, too, is worthy of celebration.

5. Fundamental Theologal Spirituality

Honesty with the real, fidelity to the real, and allowing ourselves to be carried forward by the real, are acts of spirit that, in one form or another, by action or omission, every human being performs. Thus we have called them, all three taken together, fundamental spirituality, because they concern every human being, and every Christian is a human being. We also call them "theologal," because—although we have not yet mentioned God in connection with them, with the divine call and demands, with God's invitations and grace—the mystery of God does indeed become present *in* concrete reality. Transcendence becomes present *in* history. In this wise, in responding to reality, explicitly or implicitly we have the experience of God in history.

If we call it experience, it is because this contact with the transcendent in history is personal, as well. It is an individual experience (and analogously, a collective or group experience). The exigency and grace of reality are addressed to concrete persons, who have names, beings who are called—whether or not they interpret it in this way—by name to react to reality in this way. The believer will feel called by name by a God who also has a name. The nonbeliever will not attempt to give a name to reality's call, but will be unable to escape being called by name.

Indubitably, merely to have described—precisely as we have done, and not otherwise—a fundamental spirituality presupposes a particular view of God. The God in terms of which we have given our description is the God of Jesus. In the conclusion of this chapter, we shall make this explicit, and in Christian terms. What we have sought to emphasize thus far is only that the spirituality that we shall later call Christian, or the spiritualities that have proliferated throughout history, or the spirituality of liberation, are but concrete manners of realizing this fundamental human spirituality without which the others would be vain and empty.

III. CHRISTIAN SPIRITUALITY: THE FOLLOWING OF JESUS IN THE OPTION FOR THE POOR

What we have said so far will call for an option for or against a fundamental spirituality. But even if that fundamental spirituality is accepted as we have described it, it will become concrete in various forms. Christian spirituality is no more and no less than a living of the fundamental spirituality that we have described, precisely in the concrete manner of Jesus and according to the spirit of Jesus. This is the following of Jesus.

The following of Jesus has two dimensions, which are interrelated: the christological dimension, and the pneumatological dimension, that is, the concretion of Jesus as *norma normans*, and the Spirit that renders Jesus present in history.

The following *of Jesus* is what Jesus himself offered to and required of certain of his own, and what very quickly after the resurrection came to be understood by Christians as the essence of the Christian life. Paul raised it to an intrinsically theological category with the declaration that God's plan is for us to become daughters and sons in the Son. The christological dogmas of the church, if taken seriously and reread adequately, lead to the same conclusion. In Jesus, God has been revealed, and the human being has been revealed. Jesus was not merely *vere homo*, truly a human being; he was precisely *homo verus*—the true, authentic, genuine human being. What dogma is really saying here, then, is that to be truly a human being is to be what Jesus is. To live with spirit, to react correctly to concrete reality, is to re-create, throughout history, the fundamental structure of the life of Jesus.

This has been grasped very well by great Christians all through history, especially in ages of crisis, and of church and historical renewal. Francis of Assisi simply wished to be like Jesus. Ignatius Loyola constantly besought of Jesus an interior knowledge of Christ in order to love him and follow him. Dietrich Bonhoeffer pointed out that Jesus' first and last words to Peter were "Follow me." On the morning of the day he was assassinated (March 24, 1980), Archbishop Romero wrote to Bishop Pedro Casaldáliga that they could be "happy to be running the same risks as Jesus by identifying with the causes of the dispossessed."

The following of Jesus, then, is a constant in the history of the Christians who have lived with spirit. However, it adopts a particular guise in this or that particular era. This is what actually happens, and this is what ought to happen. Jesus should be followed, continued, updated in history—not imitated. The Spirit always adapts Jesus to a given time and place; at the same time, the Spirit can only refer a follower back to Jesus, can only actualize Jesus, and nothing else whatsoever. The dialectic is a familiar one: the Spirit, says Jesus, will introduce his disciples into all truth, all through history, and will even see to it that Jesus' followers do greater things than Jesus himself has done. And so Jesus says that it is a good thing that he is going away. On the other hand, the Spirit can only refer us to Jesus himself, who becomes present ever and again, throughout history.

This new actualization of Jesus in function of the context of a given time and place does actually occur. It focuses on a given new historical reality in which the activity of the Spirit is seen anew. For example, Medellín proclaimed the presence all around us of a longing for liberation from all servitude to be a sign of the Spirit. While not exhausted therein, the Spirit has its correlative in this emergence of Jesus' presence with each new, concrete, historical situation, as the latter comes along in its new focus. So it is that, in Latin America, the novelty of the Spirit is objectively manifested in the "irruption of the poor" on the social scene—their seeming sudden materialization as if from nowhere. From a point of departure in this novelty, the Christian "rereads" again, the *homo verus* who is Jesus—thereby rediscovering him once more as he really was, rediscovering him as the gospels present him. From the subjective standpoint, the fundamental act of the Spirit today, we believe, is the option for the poor.

While Christian spirituality today is as it always has been, the following of Jesus, it is not a "following of Jesus" by way of mechanically reproducing this or that aspect of his historical life. The authentic following of Jesus today occurs by reproducing the whole of that life in terms of the option for the poor. This can be real because that option is not only regional or pastoral, but comprehensive, all-embracing, as well. It is an option involving the totality of the human being in his or her confrontation with reality. In terms of what we are able to know, it means grasping and understanding the whole of reality, God and human beings alike, from a starting point in the poor. In terms of what we can hope for, that option means sharing and allowing ourselves to be led by the hope of the poor. In terms of what we have before us as a task, it means destroying the anti-Reign that victimizes the poor and building a Reign in which the world can be hearth and home to the poor. In terms of what is offered to us to celebrate, it means rejoicing with one another in the life, the hope, the creativity, and the love of the poor.

Jesus and the option for the poor can be set in a relationship. They *must* be set in relationship in our concrete history today as well as with our regard turned toward the past. An affinity between Jesus and poverty is abundantly evident throughout the Christian scriptures. In fact, that Jesus himself is the historical sacrament of God's option for the poor, and that he himself implements that option in his concrete life, appear altogether clearly. From the standpoint of the transcendent, we may say that Jesus is the maximal historicization or concretization of God's option for the poor. The gospels present his incarnation in a consciously slanted manner. They present it as a movement toward what is lowly, as an incarnation in the direction of the poor, the least, the oppressed. Indeed, the metaphor of impoverishment is used to express this abasement, this descent. And although we say metaphor, the question is why this particular form of incarnation was selected and no other. From a historical viewpoint, there can be no doubt that Jesus' life, mission, fate, and even resurrection would lack its internal logic without an essential relationship between Jesus and the poor of this world, or without his option for them.

What we mean by this is that the following of Jesus and the option for the poor, comprising the current formulation of Christian spirituality, have their own affinity. The new element manifested by the Spirit is the everlastingly old. According to this new-and-old element, and from this standpoint, let us now examine the structure of the life of Jesus that any Christian spirituality must reproduce as it acquires form and shape in our present age. We must see the successes and the problems of the currency enjoyed by this particular Christian spirituality. The structure to be reproduced can and must be examined in terms of the essential elements of Jesus' life. The actual reproduction of that structure today, when all is said and done, can only be recounted. It would be a contradiction in terms to speak of the Spirit without recounting what kind of life that Spirit produces — how that Spirit manifests itself in the spirit of human beings. In all consistency, then, we shall not speak only of a pneumatology of spirituality, but we shall narrate the acts of spirit that the Spirit requires and produces.

1. Incarnation: The Holiness of Poverty

The first element of the structure of the life of Jesus is the incarnation. Jesus was born a human being, of course, but not just any human being, any more than any of the rest of us. He came to the human state in a specific manner. He became flesh, in the weakness of flesh, of course, but not just any flesh. Altogether obviously, the gospels present him as a person of the poor, surrounded by the poor, and serving the poor. His initial, programmatic message has meaning only when seen within the scriptural tradition of God's option for the poor of this world, for the orphans and the widows, for the outcast and despised. Jesus' view of this world and his basic judgment of it is guided by how things are going with the poor. His hope is a hope of the poor and for the poor. Thus, Jesus comes before us as the human being united with the hopeful current of history, the current of so many who have come before him and who are to come after him, the current whose protagonist is the people of the poor.

Jesus' incarnation in poverty is basic for a spirituality of today. Systematically, that incarnation means making an option for the poor. Descriptively, it means that the poor are, as Puebla says, the locus of, or setting for, conversion and evangelization. They are the locus of conversion because their own situation is the clearest question about what we are and what we ought to be. Here, then, is the most universal setting for God's question: "What have you done with your brother?" (cf. Gen. 4:9), and thereby of the question of our fellow human beings precisely as our brothers and sisters.

The poor are the locus of evangelization by virtue of their positive values: their simplicity, their openness, their sense of community, their hope of life, and their love and commitment, to cite Puebla's list. Thus they become gospel, Good News, gift, and grace received unexpectedly and without desert.

The poor, then, are the locus of spiritual experience—encounter with God. They are an ethical demand, but they are more than that. Incarnation means descent and encounter, primordial decision to come to be within the authentic reality of this world; it also means allowing oneself to be found by the God who is hidden but present in that reality.

Hence it is that Gustavo Gutiérrez's words are more than rhetoric: the poor "drink from their own wells." The poor, and the world of poverty, are like some huge well filled with water—the symbol of life—for the poor have filled it with their life, their suffering, their tears, their hope, and their commitment. All of this water now becomes water for others. We can drink of it. It is a grace offered us. Indeed, we must drink from it. It is the basic option.

Incarnation, then, is costly descent, gladsome discovery, and decision ever to drink of that well of water in the lowlands of history. In this consists the holiness of poverty; it means a sharing in the history of that concrete reality in which the God who is holy, ever distant, and beyond us, becomes the God who is near, hidden but present, in the poor.

2. Mission: The Holiness of Love

The second element in the structure of Jesus' life is mission. Mission is an activity performed for the purpose of changing reality. The mission of Jesus' life materializes against a background of the Reign of God as God's will for the world, for history, and—within history—for each and every human being. Through his option for the poor, Jesus proclaims the Reign to the poor of this world and inaugurates it with signs (miracles, exorcisms, his welcome extended to sinners and to all who have been deprived of their dignity). Those signs are only signs; they do not change the structure of reality. But they point in the direction of the Reign, and they kindle a hope that the Reign is possible.

Besides working these signs, Jesus applies his teaching to society. He does so in a denunciation and unmasking of the negative, rather than in positive theoretical elaborations. He denounces and unmasks all structurally oppressive power — religious, economic, intellectual, and political. And, he proclaims a different society, one that will be delivered from those oppressive powers.

Words, signs, and praxis, then, are the concrete form that Jesus' mission takes. They all spring from the mercy of which we have spoken, and they find their adequate expression in any suffering whatever from which persons are to be freed. Thereby they enunciate, by making it concrete, the fundamental principle of the Christian life: love. Even had Jesus not declared this the greatest of the commandments, his life as mission would elevate it to the basic principle of the Christian life.

It is having a mission that gives meaning to Jesus' life. In fact, it is not Jesus who has the mission — although he begins with it in its broad traits; rather, it is Jesus' mission that constantly shapes his life — his outward life, of course, but also his interior life, his life in the presence of God.

Living with spirit, then, is action — a doing from love and with love. Doing is not everything, as we shall presently see. There is gift and grace, too. But without loving action, without at least a readiness to posit signs and foster a praxis, any spirituality is open to suspicion.

Mission continues to be central today, for any spirituality. It is mission that maintains the supremacy of love in the Christian life, and specifically, in Latin America, has concentrated the mission of the church in the liberation of the poor — understanding liberation in its most comprehensive expression. Upon this mission the theology of liberation has been erected.

Liberation, toil, and struggle for liberation, justice — this, before all else, is love, and great love. It means bringing Jesus' mission to the here and now on an oppressed continent out of love and with love. Without a practice of liberation, spirituality in Latin America today would have no meaning.

We shall delve no further here into this familiar concept, as it is addressed in other chapters in the present work. We should like, however, by way of an excursus, to examine two points that call for specific treatment: (1) the spirit needed in order to bring about liberation and to heal its negative by-products, and (2) the relationship between liberation and grace.

3. The Need for Spirit in the Practice of Liberation

The fact that there is a practice of and a struggle for liberation is itself a great testimonial to spirituality, as it is a great act of spirit. Indeed, that practice and struggle are the basic act, since it constitutes the introduction of Jesus' mission into the here and now, the actualization of a life lived with love and a struggle motivated by love. Generally speaking, this is what we discovered in Latin America in the 1970s: that there could be no spiritual life without real life. We came to see that faith and justice, God and this oppressed world, Jesus and the poor, must be brought together — that, with historical and Christian urgency, a practice of liberation was needed. This being said, however, we also observed and saw that the practice of liberation would need to be imbued with spirit, and with a specific spirit, and this was the lesson of the 1980s that so many Christians—theologians among them—accepted with all their heart. Combining the two insights, we came to know how good and necessary liberation is in order that there be spirit, and how good and necessary it is for there to be spirit in the practice of liberation.

The practice of liberation is right and necessary. It is good, and it is Christian. But, like any human practice, it is not only open to the finest opportunities, it is also threatened by limitations, temptations, even sinfulness. The practice of liberation does not mechanically solve all human and Christian problems. It helps prayer, for example, or the living of the religious life, or life in the base communities, or growth in faith and hope. But these things also need a specific cultivation of their own. Thus, while the practice of liberation furnishes a correct and necessary channel—the most correct and necessary channel in a situation of oppression—still the channel is not everything.

Furthermore, the most perceptive of those who have devoted themselves to the practice of liberation have grasped that, of its very nature, this practice, like any human thing—even prayer, for example, although that is often forgotten—also has a tendency to engender negative by-products, and that these side effects sometimes actually materialize. In the writings of Archbishop Romero—defender to the last of the practice of liberation—liberation generates the following temptations.

1. Diverse groups dedicated to the struggle for liberation may come into conflict with one another, to the detriment of unity and effectiveness.

2. The popular element may be gradually displaced: the popular masses may come to be replaced by organizations, the organizations by their officers or leaders, and the officers and leaders by the most outstanding among them, with the attendant danger of isolation from the concrete needs and sufferings of the people.

3. A dogmatism may crop up in the analysis (observation and interpretation) of the facts; now the facts will only seem to confirm set positions, which will no longer be subjected to verification by the yardstick of reality.

4. Some specific mechanism of liberation practice (social, political, or armed) may become absolutized, with the consequent reduction of reality to one of its parts, as if from the fullness of one of those parts the perfection of all of the others would automatically flow.

5. A false sense of ethical superiority may blind one individual or group to the contributions of other individuals or groups by the mere fact that the latter are not doing what the former are doing.

6. In some instances religion is manipulated—beyond its legitimate use in terms of the convergence of liberation and the gospel—and this may do violence to popular piety, the concrete religiousness of the peoples; furthermore, it may deprive these peoples of their important religious motivation for self-liberation.

7. Power is ambivalent. It has an innate tendency to be used for self-assertion instead of for service—especially in the case of armed power (where it might become legitimate, or at any rate historically inevitable), so that violence is transformed into a mystique.

8. Weariness or disenchantment may occasion the desertion of the practice of liberation because of the price to be paid and the risks to be run, and because liberation is so long in coming.

All of this shows us why liberation must be practiced with a particular spirit: in order to heal the negative by-products, maintain the correct direction, persevere in the practice of liberation, and enhance that practice exponentially. Therefore we speak of *liberation with spirit*. Whatever the spirit—besides the fundamental spirit of love—that will enhance the love of the practice of liberation and heal it of its most specific temptations, we present it here programmatically, from a starting point in those who exemplify the spirit of the Beatitudes.

The *single-hearted* (Matt. 5:8—literally, the pure of heart) are those who see God and therefore see human beings. They remain ever open to the truth, accepting that truth whatever it may be, without attempting to dominate or manipulate it, without deceiving themselves aboutthemselves or about the processes of liberation, and without falling into the temptation to transform the truth into propaganda. This purity of heart shows profound chastity of knowledge and will, whereby they refuse to impose their own ideas or to promote their own interests in liberation.

The *merciful* are those who take up the task because their hearts have been moved to compassion by the incredible suffering of the poor. This "original mercy" imbues their prophetical labors and makes their struggle a struggle waged for love. But it also requires of them that, in the practice of liberation, they continue to keep before their eyes, from first to last, the pain of the poor, which must never be reduced to the concept of a simple social price to be paid for progress. It requires of them that, in the strategies and tactics of liberation, in their alliances and divisions, they take very close account of what all of that is likely to produce in terms of an increase or lessening of the pain of the poor. Structurally, pity or mercy is the manner in which they express the presence, right from the start and all through the liberation process, of a great love for the people of the poor.

Peacemakers are those who have not made the battle itself their ultimate goal, "gotten used to" it, placed their whole trust in it, or transformed it into a mystique. Postively, they are those who, even in time of struggle and conflict—so inevitable in liberation—seek to humanize their conflicts, bringing all other means, as well, to bear on ending them, and through thick and thin, fostering the reconciliation to come with signs of reconciliation in the present.

Those who can *forgive* are unwilling to close off the future from their adversary or their enemy. They toil for reconciliation in its personal form and in structural forms—by dialogue, by negotiation—and they posit signs of the same, since without it no triumph is lasting and no society humane.

The *poor in spirit*, finally, believe that in weakness there is strength. They strive for the utopia of poverty or at least of a shared austerity. They live in and as community, overcoming any elitism—and isolation—of the personal or group ego. They are the wellspring of spirit.

What we are trying to say in all of this is that the practice of liberation is itself an act of spirit, and the most radical of all such acts, because it is an act of love. Thus, the practice of liberation is the indispensable channel of spirituality. It furnishes the material from which so many other acts of spirit can spring. But it needs spirit in its own turn, in order to maintain itself and not degenerate.

4. Practice of Liberation and Gratuity

Liberation is practice. It is a doing, a living, a desire to spend one's life for the life of the poor. This is what is required by concrete reality, and the gospel is supremely demanding when it comes to the practice of love, mercy, and justice. Just as emphatically, however, that gospel says that practice is not everything. Or rather, practice must be shot through with something else if it is to become Christian practice. That something else is gratuity and generosity: the willingness to give without receiving in return. In words of dire warning, we are told: "When you have done all you have been commanded to do, say, 'We are useless servants. We have done no more than our duty' " (Luke 17:10). In words of invitation, we hear: "God loved us first. Love one another" (cf. 1 John 4:19,7).

This generosity is perhaps the most difficult reality to conceptualize and put in words. But something can be said about it and its importance for liberation practice in the presence of a "graced" human being, who has had such a powerful experience of the divine gratuity. In terms of a need for healing on the part of the practice of liberation, while admitting that that practice calls for great enthusiasm, we must also say that generosity and gratuity forbid hubris — a feeling of ethical superiority — or anything like a personality cult. Generosity recalls that all have their limitation and sin. In the words of Ignacio González Faus, "One must fight a revolution as someone forgiven." Positively speaking, the experience of gratuity entails gratitude to something greater than oneself, and the response of the one who has been forgiven and "graced" multiplies spirit and practice exponentially. After all, from gratitude springs the generosity of commitment — although a convert's enthusiasm has its dangers — freedom of spirit, and the joy of having found the pearl of great price. The experience of gratuity engenders creativity.

The dimension of generosity in spirituality — the spirit of gratuity and its correlative of gratitude — is essential to Christian faith, and accordingly, to any Christian spirituality, including that of liberation. At the center of our faith is the fact that God has loved us first, and that a response to that love, a love for our brothers and sisters, has its life from, and is imbued with the power of, being loved by God. As Gustavo Gutiérrez says: we are "loved in order to love, set free in order to set free." Generosity is not only salvation for oneself, but liberation from oneself. And this enables the practice of liberation.

To give in grateful response to having received moves us to give anew and tremendously enhances our giving. This can only be observed. But to cite a single instance, the grace Archbishop Romero received not only converted him, it swelled his generosity to astonishing extremes; not only did he carry his people on his shoulders, but his people carried him as well. "With this people," he said, "it costs nothing to be a good shepherd."

To sum up what we have said in this section: the essential dimension of spirituality is mission — an activity that, today, has to be liberation, since this is the form that love for the masses will necessarily take. That love is healing if, as with Jesus' own mission, it is accompanied by the spirit of the Beatitudes and by grace. Then we see the holiness of love, and we see that, besides, this holiness is most fruitful for liberation. It bears concrete fruit, and we observe this in Latin America, where there are so many saints of liberation. Ignacio Ellacuría used to say: "Holiness is the ultimate weapon of the church of the poor."

5. The Cross: Political Holiness

Jesus was faithful to his incarnation and mission, and that led him to persecution and the cross. Neither of these was sought by Jesus; neither can supply spirituality with its foundation. But they are prerequisites. After all, spirituality presupposes utter fidelity to the real, and in the real world the Reign of God is not proclaimed and inaugurated on a clean slate. The Reign of God is proclaimed and inaugurated in the presence of, and in opposition to, the anti-Reign. The anti-Reign inevitably produces persecution and death, because the God of life — the God of Jesus — and the gods of death are locked in mortal combat. They do battle, just as do their intermediaries.

Christian spirituality, then, is not a spirituality of the cross or of suffering. It is a spirituality of honest, consistent, and faithful love — a wide-awake love that knows the necessary risks it is taking. Christian spirituality is the spirituality of a crucified love. This is not because of some secret design on the part of God, or because God requires or relishes human suffering. It is because incarnation occurs in a reality shot through with an anti-Reign that is determined to throw every possible obstacle in the way of the proclaimers and initiators of the Reign.

This is what we find exemplified in the cross of Jesus. There is an anti-Reign, and it has to be fought. This must be done from outside the anti-Reign, yes, but ultimately the anti-Reign can only be uprooted from within itself. From without, sin must be denounced and combated. But from within, one must take on the burden of sin and thus share in the annihilation exerted by sin upon the victims of this world.

If anything is clear in Latin America today, it is that we must take on the sin of the world. We must be open to the possibility of the cross. This possibility is very real. Since Vatican II Latin America has mounted many assaults on the anti-Reign; therefore there have been, overwhelmingly, more persecution and more martyrs on that continent.

A number of important things must be said of these martyrs. In the first place, today's Latin American martyrs appear concretely more like Jesus than did the martyrs of the past. We are not comparing the subjective holiness of the martyrs, all down through history. We only mean that, in our own times, a kind of martyrdom occurs for the same reasons as Jesus' martyrdom occurred. The Latin American martyrs are martyrs not for anything directly ecclesial.

They are martyrs for the cause of humanity. They are martyrs of the poor. While Thomas à Becket, for example, was murdered at the altar for defending the legitimate interests and freedom of the church, Archbishop Romero was murdered at the altar for defending the interests of the poor, not those of the church as such. The new martyrs, then, are martyrs of the Reign of God, martyrs of humanity.

In the second place, martyrdom in Latin America is the fullest, most integral expression of the incarnation that takes place in concrete Latin American reality. In the chilling words of Archbishop Romero: "I rejoice, my brothers, that priests have been murdered in our country. It would be a sad thing if, when so many Salvadorans are being murdered, no priests would be murdered. They show that the church has taken flesh in poverty." The martyrs, those active followers of Jesus, also become concrete, eloquent symbols of a far more secular, more massive, and more cruel martyrdom: the crucifixion of entire peoples.

In the third place, the martyrs show that it is possible—because it actually happens—to have a convergence between actual Latin American reality and actual Christian reality. They show that, the deeper you are immersed in the one, the deeper you are immersed in the other, and that is no small benefit that they bequeath to us.

Finally, martyrdom is the most integral form of a holiness today that we shall call political holiness. We call it political, because martyrdom here today is offered in the name of society, the city, the *polis*. Some, those who fight for the anti-Reign, kill others; they kill those who fight for the Reign. That Reign has a concrete social shape. Because they have proclaimed the Reign and attacked the anti-Reign—not only because they have exercised mercy toward individuals or small groups—the best of human beings and Christians are murdered. If anything shows that the martyrs' love has been political, it is—just as in the case of Jesus—their martyrdom. And if there is any doubt that Christian love needs to be political, the martyrs, those witnesses par excellence of faith, are there to remind us.

We call it holiness because martyrdom is the most remarkable exercise of faith, hope, and charity. Martyrdom makes concrete the specifically Christian. To put it somewhat scandalously (and Christianity is charged with the scandalous): Is it really more blessed to give than to receive? Do those who lose their lives really save their lives? Does salvation really come from a person who has been crucified? Is it true that we ought to leap for joy on the day we are persecuted? At stake in the answer to these scandalous questions is the essence of our faith. In faith, we accept the tragedy of history: that in order to give life, one must give of one's own life. But martyrdom also says, and says it straight out, with no beating about the bush, that the essence of Christianity is what it has always been said to be: love. There is no greater love than this, that one lay down one's life for one's friends.

The spirituality of martyrdom, then, is nothing other than love for a world of victims. This is the basic thing. Then comes the need for a spirit of courage to keep faithful to the end, and then the credibility that engenders martyrdom in others.

Actual martyrdom presupposes and generates aspecific spirituality in the survivors. First of all, the martyrs are not forgotten. "Woe to the peoples who forget their martyrs!" says Pedro Casaldáliga. Next is gratitude for their having shown the "greatest love." Finally comes the invitation to be grafted onto the tradition that the martyrs have created with their love and their blood. The martyrs — beginning with Jesus of Nazareth — engender a powerful, Paschal tradition. That is where we should be heading. We must build on that tradition if we are to keep moving forward in history.

6. Resurrection: The Holiness of Joy

It is said of Jesus that justice was done him, and that he was raised by the Father. For once, at least, the executioner has not triumphed over the victim. The action of human beings in putting the just and the innocent to death is answered by the action of God in restoring them to life in fullness. Jesus lives in fullness and pours that fullness out on the rest of human beings. He is the Lord of history.

Where spirituality is concerned — unless we have only been spouting words — this means that even here and now, in history itself, we can and should live as persons raised to life. Spirituality must take on the dimension of resurrection, too.

Resurrection has nothing in common with sterile attempts to live in concrete history the "immateriality" of Jesus' presence in history today, or with an effort to associate oneself with Jesus' presence today through some kind of act of "intention." The history of the church is a fine demonstration of all this. For a long time the religious life was presented as a state of perfection because the vows of religion were thought to place the members of religious orders and congregations, structurally, in a less material state. The dangers are obvious. In the name of immateriality, the flesh of this world is left to its misery.

If resurrection is life in its fullness, it can only be love in its fullness. How can one live in fullness in this life? The answer is simple: by repeating the following of Jesus in the spirit of Jesus on this earth. The one who lives in this way lives even now as someone raised to life amid the very conditions of history.

However, resurrection also has the dimension of triumph — the triumph of life over death — and the question becomes how that dimension can be reflected in the spirituality of Jesus' followers. The reflection, in history, of the triumphal element in resurrection consists, it seems to us, in hope that does not die, in freedom versus slavery, and in the joy that conquers sadness.

The hope that does not die is founded in the conviction that love does not die and that its fruits abide. It is founded in the conviction that the executioner will not triumph over the victim, that the deepest stratum of reality is good and positive, and that therefore we must keep calling, "*Abba* Father."

Freedom in the following of Jesus is not only, or even basically, the freedom of a laissez-faire liberalism jealous of its own rights (when they are its rights), or the freedom of an estheticism that urges human beings to "become themselves" freely (when there is indeed beauty in such an enterprise). Freedom in the following of Jesus is the liberty of love. It is the freedom of those who detach themselves from all things in order to do good, the freedom of those who give their life freely, without anyone taking it from them. It is the freedom of Paul to become a slave to all. It is the freedom of Jesus, whose life no one takes from him, but he lays it down himself.

Joy in the following of Jesus, finally, is having found the pearl of great price, the hidden pearl that banishes sorrow. As Gustavo Gutiérrez explains, in the words of a *campesino*: the opposite of joy is not suffering—and the poor have plenty of that—but sadness. And the *campesino* added: The poor suffer, yes; but they do not sorrow. To live with joy, to be glad to be alive, is to live with ultimate meaning—with the ability to be grateful and to celebrate, the ability to be for others and be with others. This is why we can pray with gladness, as Jesus did, when the "least ones," the outcast as well as his friends, sit around the same table.

In this fashion the element of resurrection in this very life, under the conditions of this temporal existence, becomes present. Resurrection is the presence of transcendence in the element of fullness and plenitude to be had under concrete historical conditions.

We do have to add that in Latin America, that continent of death, paradoxically, this life-in-fullness has been facilitated and offered to all precisely by the poor of this world. The crucified—who are precisely those on the point of resurrection—engender and enable that hope, that freedom, and that joy. They make them contagious.

IV. AN OBJECTIVELY THEOLOGICAL CHRISTIAN SPIRITUALITY

Having analyzed the spirituality of the following of Jesus in concrete history today, let us return, by way of conclusion, to the objectively theological dimension of spirituality—but this time, the objectively theological dimension of a specifically Christian spirituality. In other words, let us apply the foregoing analysis to our actual experience of God, the encounter with the God of Jesus.

Following implies moving along a path. Christologically, we are called to follow Jesus through history. Theologically, we are called to journey with the God of history—to walk with our God, as Micah says. On the basis of our faith, that walking with God, with all of the humility of which Micah speaks, leads to the ultimate, definitive encounter with God, that discovery of God that will occur when "God will be all in all" (cf. 1 Cor. 15:28). But what is there of encounter with God even now, in concrete history? Or more precisely, what is there even now, of allowing oneself to be found by God?

Concrete, mystical, contemplative, and ascetic spiritualities describe the experience of this encounter with God in various ways. In order to learn what is central in that encounter, however, we turn to Jesus. This is our methodology as Christians. We seek to conform all subsequent Christian spirituality, even the loftiest mysticism, to the norm that was Jesus' experience of God, and not the other way around.

When Jesus places himself before God, on the one hand he calls God his

Father and experiences God as such—as the One who is absolutely near, boun-
teous, and tenderly loving. In that Father Jesus' heart rests at last, and this fills
him with gladness. Jesus rejoices in his Father; he is glad that God is good, and
that it is good that there is a God. To find himself with God is for Jesus to
allow himself to be found by the God who is good, the God in whom he can
repose, and in whom he can ever place his trust.

On the other hand, when Jesus places himself before this Father of his, he
finds that Father to be God indeed—ultimate, ineffable, unmanipulable Mystery, whom one must in some sense leave alone, let be God. Hence Jesus' active,
total availability to God—his absolute obedience. Thus, Jesus reposes in the
Father, but the Father does not allow him repose. Once more in complete trust,
Jesus lets God be God.

This, we think, is how the encounter with God has occurred throughout
history: in a persevering openness to and acceptance of the dialectic of the
Father-God. In more systematic language, we might say that the encounter with
God is given in "affinity" and in "otherness." It is given in affinity inasmuch as
it kindles, in one's own self, time, and place, that trust in God that leads us to
become—in the concrete, historically—like God, who is good. Be good as your
heavenly Father is good (cf. Matt. 5:48, 19:17). It is given even in affinity with
the element of mystery in God, in our actualization of utopia, as we allow
ourselves to be borne up, borne along, by its attraction to a future that will be
more God's future, in peace, justice, reconciliation, and in our attempt to do
two things at once that resist being done together: peace and justice, truth and
forgiveness, and the like.

The encounter with God is also given in otherness. It occurs in our effort
ever to maintain our openness to the divine mystery, to the element of the new
and even of the scandalous in God, as we strive to grasp a crucified God. Yes,
God is surely mystery.

In the words of Gustavo Gutiérrez, "God is to be contemplated, and God
is to be practiced." We encounter God in bringing the divine goodness to a
concrete realization, which is a practice, and in letting God be God, which is
contemplation. We encounter God in responding to a God of complete otherness and in corresponding to God by rendering the divine reality itself real
in our history. To put it in still another way, I encounter God when I am a
"contemplative inaction," as St. Ignatius puts it. In activity, we correspond to
the God of goodness and bounty, and the objectively theological presupposition
of this activity is the goodness of God. In contemplation we seek the face of
God: we seek and find the divine will, as St. Ignatius so often urged us to do,
under the premise of that quality of the substance of God that God is mystery
and therefore is that which is to be sought and found.

This trust and obedience, brought to realization in the face of the mystery
of God, is what the Bible calls faith. Experience of God, encounter with God,
is nothing other than faith; conversely, faith is experience of God and encounter
with God. Hence it is that a synthesis of the theologal dimension of a theologal
spirituality is lived today in the form of mercy toward human beings (our correspondence to the Father who is good) and as fidelity (our constant response
to God's mystery).

Finding God, logically enough, always occurs in the human being whom God has found: "Before they call, I will answer" (Isa. 65:24), and God is the Father who goes forth upon the highway day after day, walking it as the father of the prodigal — in the hope that his child will come. This experience of gratuity — God's own supreme generosity — is central and specific to the Christian experience of God. That experience, by definition, can neither be programmed nor conceptualized before it occurs. But it occurs. Along with God's demand comes the divine self-offering and its acceptance: "You have seduced me, Yahweh, and I have allowed myself to be seduced" (Jer. 20:7). It is the dimension of Good News in the experience of God that permeates all things Christian, Good News in the form of the Good that is both unexpected and undeserved: God, who comes forth to meet us. Here is the God who "first loved us" (1 John 4:19).

The encounter with God, as trust, availability, and gratitude, occurs especially in the concrete life of the believer — in his or her actual faith, hope, and charity. But it must also be posited in word. The human constitution of the believer requires this, as does the content of the experience itself. Faith and availability must surely be put into words. But especially, gratitude must find such expression. Thankfulness cannot remain silent indefinitely.

The expression in words of a reality that has been personally experienced is what we may call prayer. Prayer is not distinct from real life, let alone divorced from it. Prayer and life overlap. Prayer is the meaning of a vital, living experience, issuing in condensed expression. To pray is to say, with Jesus, in utter availability and readiness: "Father, . . . not my will but yours be done" (Luke 22:42). To pray is to say, with Jesus, in trust and confidence: "Father, into your hands, I commend my spirit (Luke 23:46). To pray is to say, with Jesus, in gladness and gratitude: "Father, . . . to you I offer praise: for . . . you have revealed [this] to the merest children" (Matt. 11:25; par. Luke 10:21). For our own part, we shall have to add the prayer of the prodigal: "Father, I have sinned against heaven and against you" (cf. Luke 15:21).

The experience of God — the personal encounter with God in history and its verbalization in prayer — has a strictly individual dimension and a strictly communitarian dimension. The believer who follows Jesus, who lives in history, who makes history and suffers it, finds himself or herself confronted with truth, life, cross, and hope. All of this is placed by the individual in reference to the mystery of God. But this mystery comes forth to meet the individual, as well, giving him or her a concrete, nontransferable name. The God who is mystery calls Abraham by his name and asks him to leave his house and go to the place that God will show him. He calls Jeremiah by his name and sends him to prophesy. He calls Mary by her name and proclaims to her the Good News that, through her, God will be "God with us." In giving us names, God enters into a personal relationship with us. Therefore human beings, as well, have dared to give a name to God. Here is the personal element of the encounter with God. As something personal, a name connotes solitude and loneliness before God at some times, plenitude and fullness at others. But the important thing is that this personal encounter occur. Archbishop Romero loved to recall this eternal truth. Shortly before his assassination, in a famous homily in which he railed against atrocities and defended an oppressed people, he also spoke of the best he had to offer: "Oh, dear brothers and sisters, that someone would tell me that the fruit of this homily would be that every one of us should encounter God, and live the glory of God's majesty and our littleness! No human being knows himself or herself until that being encounters God."

But this experience is not an individualistic one. An essential element of the encounter with God is to have it within a people of God, a community. The personal experience of God must be open to the experience other human beings have of God. It must be open to giving of one's own experience of God and to receiving it from others. It may be said that God is the God of a people, and that the experience of God must be had by a whole people. In more systematic language it must be said that there is no concrete personal experience of God that would exhaust the mystery of God, and that amid the concrete personal experiences of God on the part of the whole people, one may approach asymptotically the encounter with God in plenitude. To the divine, or theologal dimension of spirituality then, belongs its "popularity," its openness to give to others and receive from others. No one ought to be so timorous as to think he or she has nothing to offer to others out of his or her own faith, and no one must be so presumptuous as to think he or she has nothing to receive for his or her own faith from that of others.

This is something that has become more and more evident in recent history. The old division—the language used until very recently—between the faith of an "enlightened" believer and the faith of the "man on the street," if presented as a hard and fast division, is scarcely a Christian one. To be sure, the faith of each of these persons, with their respective manners of encountering God, has its specificities. But the enlightened should offer the best of their faith to the more common person, and receive the best of the latter's faith in return—and vice versa. We see it constantly today: believers of all climes and milieus, with different personal histories and manners of faith, are coming to believe and to encounter God precisely in one another's company. *Campesinos* and intellectuals, Latin Americans and first-world groups, women and men, are leading each other in their respective faith experiences. This is the most splendid, most familiar, level of solidarity: the encounter with God as community, as a people internally differentiated, yes, but as a people from start to finish, within which each member, in his or her faith, leads and carries along, while being led and carried by, all of the others.

In conclusion, let us observe that the encounter with God has a place of its own. To determine that place is not, when all is said and done, something that can be done strictly beforehand, precisely because it is a matter of finding, or rather being found by, God. And no one can dictate to God where God must come forth to meet someone. But in terms of faith, two things can be said, if they are stated in dialectical unity: "It is not a philosophical truth, but it is indeed a Christian truth, that the one who seeks God has already found God" (Karl Rahner); and "It is a matter not of seeking God, but of finding God in the place where God has promised to be: in the poor of this world" (Porfirio Miranda).

The former proposition means something important, even if it is basically tautologically. God never abandons an honest person. (Indeed, God makes a self-bestowal even on the ungrateful.) And God is at work in this very honesty. The encounter with God employs manifold mediations, and history bears witness to the fact. But the second statement is no tautology. It is revelation. The locus par excellence, the privileged place of the encounter with God, and the most appropriate in the current concrete reality of this world, as well as in terms of the consciousness that this world has now generated, is the world of the poor. This is what Matthew 25 sanctions and declares. God is in the weak, in the poor, in the helpless. God is hidden there, but God is there. More radically, in the current Latin American situation God is present in crucified peoples, in countless women and men impoverished beyond imagining, in the imprisoned, in the tortured, in the "disappeared," in the murdered. In them, to borrow a phrase from St. Ignatius's contemplations on Jesus' passion, "the divinity hides itself." But, however hidden, God is there.

A contemplation of God in those crucified peoples is not what one might have expected to be invited to undertake. And yet, this is precisely where God is to be contemplated. Or at least, this is where one must begin to contemplate God. To practice God before these crucified peoples is to take them down from their crosses. Not every encounter with the poor of this world is mechanically and automatically an encounter with God, but there can be no encounter with the God of Jesus without an encounter with the poor and the crucified of this world. Thus, as we have heard so often in Latin America, the encounter with the poor is a spiritual experience, an experience of God. In these terms the proclamation of Micah acquires its historical logic. As we stand before the poor, as we stand before the crucified peoples, the demand becomes utterly clear: to practice justice and to love with tenderness. In this fashion one walks with God in history, humbly. What Jesus adds to this demand is that this humble walking is a genuine walking with God and toward God. To follow Jesus is to walk toward God, and to walk with God, in history. It is to that walk that God invites us. And that walk is spirituality.

— Translated by Robert R. Barr

34

Suffering, Death, Cross, and Martyrdom

JAVIER JIMÉNEZ LIMÓN

INTRODUCTION

Let us begin by stating three assumptions and setting out the parts of our chapter.

1. The Epistemological-Existential Assumption

The first epistemological-existential assumption states that all thinking and also all theology are silenced by the reality of suffering, death, cross and martyrdom. Only if there is a permanent basis of practical solidarity and believing prayer can we say anything meaningful. And what we do say must be very much aware of its function and limitations. Its function is to throw light on solidarity and make true prayer possible; its limitation is that it cannot be a rationalist word explaining the problem of suffering. It can only be a word that enables us to guard and even radicalize the negative mystery of evil as the ultimate mystery of solidarity, which shelters within it greater hope for the future.

If liberation theology has been bold enough to stammer a few credible words about these realities, this is due to the following factors: (1) it has taken seriously the terrible pain of the oppressed masses, and unmasked the dominant ideological explanations, including the pseudo-theological ones, given for these sufferings; (2) it expresses a real rebirth of effective solidarity; (3) it also expresses how many believers have found in the memory of Jesus Christ the demand and the possibility of living out their solidarity to the end, to the greatest love, even to the point of giving their lives. In a word, liberation theology can begin to articulate a liberating theology of the cross, because it tries to express and empower solidarity with the greatest suffering in our world and tries to do so by bearing witness to the greatest love—that shown in its central memory, the life and passion of Jesus and his martyrs, those whose solidarity has led them to give their lives in hope.

2. The Theoretical-Theological Assumption

The theoretical-theological assumption states that theological speech about suffering, death, cross, and martyrdom belongs within the soteriological christology of liberation, which is presented as historical soteriology. By soteriological christology we mean that which integrates the person of Jesus and his saving reality. And by historical soteriology we refer to that which announces salvation "transcending history in history and by means of history" (Ellacuría).

Let us distinguish two consequences of this assumption: (1) Everything we say here can only be understood as an essential part of a christology articulating the saving mystery of Jesus in liberating discipleship; and (2) the challenge to a liberating theology of the cross is to become a genuine historical soteriology. This includes confronting the great historical sufferings; confronting them historically, that is, with an authentic responsibility for historical transformation; and by this confrontation and responsibility, gaining experience of universal and definitive salvation and proclaiming it.

3. The Theological Assumption

The theological assumption consists of the various contributions made by liberation theologians to our subject. Here we simply note some of the most important:

1. Juan Luis Segundo has vigorously established that feeling for the suffering of others is an indispensable condition for any valid approach to revelation.

2. Leonardo Boff and Jon Sobrino have gone deeply into the relation between Jesus' death and liberation in history.

3. Leonardo Boff and José González Faus have criticized models of the redeeming value of Jesus' death that lean ideologically towards heterodoxy and have suggested those leading to a liberating orthodoxy.

4. Ignacio Ellacuría worked out a historical soteriology on the basis of the correlation between the crucified Jesus and the crucified people belonging to the oppressed masses. He was inspired by a rereading of the Servant of Yahweh.

5. Carlos Mesters and Gustavo Gutiérrez have contributed a profound theological narrative of the people's sufferings and hopes. The former, also inspired by Second Isaiah, describes "the mission of the suffering people." The latter gives a reading of Job's spiritual suffering for today in order "to speak of God from the viewpoint of the suffering innocent." This sets out the main lines of the liberating spiritual journey of the oppressed and believing people.

6. Leonardo Boff has returned again and again to the search for an adequate language and hermeneutics to "preach the cross in a society of crucified people."

7. Leonardo Boff, Jon Sobrino, Juan Hernández Pico, and Pedro Casaldáliga have given a theological account of the special nature of martyrdom in the context of the Latin American church.

Within the limits of this chapter we cannot summarize all these contributions. And, of course, a theology of the cross must be very modest and fundamentally narrative. Nevertheless, if it is true that in the response of solidarity to suffering and death, the Good News of the gospel becomes present — the cross and resurrection of Jesus Christ — it is worth trying to formulate in outline a liberation theology of the cross, even though the result can only be provisional and partial.

Within these limits we shall put forward six theses. The first two try to give a general description of liberation theology of the cross. What we state here is very simple, but we believe that it is radical and illuminating; that is, the theology of the cross must be, first and last, a theology of Christian solidarity with the oppressed. The first thesis, then, of a more polemical and epistemological nature, defines liberation theology of the cross through the attention it pays to history and action, as against all the individualist and idealist theologies of the cross. The second thesis, more concerned with content, defines this theology in terms of Christian solidarity. The last four theses say something, fundamental but not exhaustive about the four realities in our title: suffering, death, cross, and martyrdom. Their main aim is to show that in Christian solidarity with the victims, especially the poor, we can experience and proclaim the liberating and redemptive nature of Jesus Christ's cross and resurrection.

I. LIBERATION THEOLOGY OF THE CROSS: GENERAL DESCRIPTION

1. Thesis One

Liberation theology of the cross is a theology concerned with history and action, which can therefore actualize more effectively the memory of Jesus' passion, death, and resurrection. It evokes these eschatologically under the name of God. It is both a negative theology of sin and a positive theology of liberation and redemption.

First, liberation theology of the cross attempts to criticize and supersede the individualist, idealist, and fatalist theologies of the cross. In the various dominant contemporary cultures the theology of the cross has become insignificant. This is true both for the apathy of the capitalist ethos of possession and consumption, the progressive ethos, which is equally unimpressed by suffering, and for most postmodernist positions, whose rejection of reason and utopia merely sharpens and justifies individual selfishness with a whiff of neopaganism. Theological and pastoral insight is accurate here, as for example, in the 1984 synod, which demanded a vigorous theology and preaching of the cross. But it is insufficient, because the individualism and idealism of such teaching sets it firmly within the confines of the dominant systems. In fact, an individualist theology of the cross concentrates either on the individual valuing of the cross for necessary renunciations (ascetic theology of the cross) or in helping the individual find the meaning in his or her own suffering (existential theology of the cross). In addition, idealist theology tries to find the meaning of suffering through argument, interpretation, criticism, or historical reconstruction. But even when these theologies are successful, the values and projects propounded by individualism and idealism remain subject to the dominant systems. Thus ascetic or existentialist personalism have at most a psychological and therapeutic function for the individual. Even if unintentionally, this carries with it an ideological justification, at least in the sense of a new fatalism about the greater suffering of the poor and oppressed. So these theologies become incapable of announcing universal salvation and the call to solidarity proclaimed in the cross of Jesus. These theologies lead to pessimism about history, which is secretly allied to nostalgia for an institutionally powerful church with therefore, supposedly, the power to save. There is nothing mysterious about this paradox in a theology of the cross which does not point to death in solidarity with the abandoned and outcast, but, on the contrary, seeks more power for itself, power that is homogeneous with the power exercised at the centre of our present societies.

Second, liberation theology of the cross is concerned with history. It situates the various kinds of suffering, death, and cross in history. By setting them in an historical context it shows that suffering and death are not purely an individual matter, but collective and related to social structures. Suffering and death are seen at the point where the individual and social interrelate: in terms of responsible solidarity in history. This historical view is not taken primarily for sociological or political reasons, but for theological ones. Because the God in whom we believe is the one who calls all human beings to active responsibility and solidarity. In virtue of this responsible solidarity, although there is much that liberation theology of the cross still does not claim to know about suffering and death, nevertheless there are two things it does know, with a knowledge that is critical, existential, and has deep political repercussions: (1) the history of social (economic, political, racial) oppression is not a natural history. It is a human history, which is in many respects a guilty history, for which human beings have ethical and political responsibility; (2) individual histories of suffering and death — whether they are caused by social oppression, individual guilt, or finite human nature — only acquire Christian status (become liberated and liberating, redeemed and redeeming) if they are placed in the service of the suffering of others, especially, large-scale unjust, innocent suffering. "Only they who lose their lives for my sake and for the sake of the good news of the kingdom, will save it." Because of these convictions, liberation theology of the cross requires a serious sociohistorical analysis both of the structural causes of suffering, and of the ideologies and cultures which cover up these causes and promote injustice, apathy, and lack of solidarity

Third, liberation theology of the cross is concerned with action. This means that it does not work out what it wants to say only by theory but through action. In the face of suffering and death, it interrupts its arguments and reflections to struggle first against suffering and show solidarity with it. Through this action, which we will describe further under the next thesis, it gains knowledge. In particular, the practice of the option for the poor makes possible not only the criticism of structures of oppression, but also the search for the necessary historical utopia. It sharpens the sense of what is demanded by love. This unconditional giving appears in action as both an imperious requirement and a gratuitous possibility. It contains the urgency and hope of a future life for the victims, for the heroes and martyrs, for those who die and even for those who kill.

Fourth, because liberation theology of the cross is concerned with history and action, it can effectively evoke the passion, death and resurrection of Jesus. We do not say that this remembering becomes necessary but it does become natural with the affinity of compassion, commitment, struggle, self-denial, faithfulness, and hope. Moreover, there are in suffering and the struggle against suffering such abysses of inexpressible nonsense and sense that they create a space for expectation and rebellion, negatively open to the scandal and joy of the fact and word of the cross. These are evoked in God's name as a radical condemnation of sin and a radical redeeming liberation. On the other hand, a merely theoretical and individualist evocation of the Lord's passion tends to remain a prisoner to the values and social context of the one evoking it and thus becomes a religious adornment to an unredeemed life, resisting conversion and any real consolation.

Finally, it is important to stress that the liberating theology of the cross struggles historically against historical suffering and thus, with all human and Christian seriousness, is able to be both a negative and a positive theology. Negative because through its practical and existential closeness to unjust suffering it cannot gloss over and sweeten the non-sense of this suffering, but must keep with it and radicalize it theologically. A positive theology because in its experience of the gift and the practice of unconditional solidarity, including solidarity to the end, it can and must announce the Good News of liberating and redeeming hope.

2. Thesis Two

Liberating theology of the cross is defined materially by Christian solidarity. This solidarity is historical and practical, emotional and effective, partial and universal, transforming and kenotic, made possible by the liberating and redeeming event of Jesus Christ, which is its standard.

Here we cannot give a whole theology of solidarity but merely point out some of its particularly illuminating features for a liberating theology of the cross:

1. Christian solidarity makes explicit the historical and practical dimensions of what Christian scriptures call *agape* and *koinonia*. Therefore it must be emotional solidarity with our neighbor and the masses, and also effective solidarity to create real communion among human beings.

2. As historical and practical, emotional and effective love, Christian solidarity implies a rich and multiple relationship with suffering, death, and cross, the absolutely central historical-practical realities. It goes beyond being affected by the suffering of others—whether persons or groups—to take it on as one's own. It takes action against the socially or technically avoidable sufferings of others without becoming paralyzed through fear of its own suffering, even death, which such action may provoke. And it takes on the task of seeking (or proclaiming) hope for all sufferings, which are in themselves inevitable (like the suffering of finiteness and death) or in fact now inevitable (like suffering for those who have already died or for sins which have already been committed).

3. Christian solidarity is, above all, solidarity with the victims of human sociohistorical injustice: a) because this is what is proclaimed as the scandalous Good News in the words and deeds of Jesus of Nazareth, who announces and practices an essential correlation between God and his kingdom on the one hand, and the poor, oppressed, despised and their liberation on the other; b)

because if solidarity among human beings does not include the victims, it becomes perverted into a pact or an interested deal between the evildoers among themselves (who at the first opportunity will make new victims of their old associates); c) because even the search for or proclamation of hope for the more personal dimensions of suffering (finiteness, unavoidable disease, death, sins already committed) can become wrong and contradictory, if it accepts, through action or omission, the "death by killing," the untimely death of the great majority, which there is no doubt is the gravest and most mortal contemporary sin. Thus, because it must be first and foremost solidarity with the victims, its universalism becomes Christian and effectively redeeming through a liberating siding with the poor.

4. Even though there are different moments in its process, Christian solidarity must be a solidarity that is effectively transforming, incarnational, and kenotic. This is what makes it the key to the liberating theology of the cross. Therefore it has as much to do with the history of suffering due to social oppression as with sufferings due to finiteness and guilt. It relates the liberating aspects of both kinds of suffering (not adequately distinguished!) and notes the latter in the former according to the model of solidarity with God's Kingdom in the following of Jesus. Therefore it must strive always to make *agape* unconditional and engage in the responsible, risky, and creative search for *koinonia*. It must keep facing the urgent task of historical liberation and open spaces for the experience and proclamation of redemption, freely and hopefully because of the fact of Jesus. All this must done done in a spirit of unconditional love, transforming history by draining the cup to the end.

We shall return to this feature several times in our subsequent theses. Here we merely point out its basic meaning and foundation. Its most radical foundation is christological: Jesus struggled against sin and took on sin. Jesus struggled in solidarity for the sake of God's Kingdom against personal and sociohistorical sufferings and remained faithful to the end. He accepted the conflicts and death inflicted on him by sociohistorical powers. Even in mortal darkness he kept his trust in the God of love and the Kingdom as a radical prophetic judgment and the offer of universal forgiveness. He was killed for his solidarity and transforming prophetic action; he died for his radical redeeming solidarity. The practical expression of this solidarity is simply the following of Jesus: work for the Kingdom in liberating solidarity — on the side of the poor — and a passionate readiness to share his Messianic sufferings by identifying with those who suffer and by sharing the redeeming universality of his forgiveness for enemies and trust in the Father. To put it differently, it is a search for more liberating service of the poor; a search for more likeness to Jesus, precisely as the Servant of Yahweh, who takes on the sin of "many." The imperatives and ethical-theological dynamics sustaining this transforming and kenotic solidarity are: to be in solidarity principally with the poor and the lowest; effectively to confront the causes of oppression and marginalization; and not to fear the powers that will marginalize and oppress you, if those who confront the causes of oppression, but who cannot kill this unconditional solidarity which consists of God and indestructible life. Systematically, we should say that this kenotic transforming dynamic of solidarity cannot be systematized because within it lies both the negative mystery of sin, which must be unconditionally overcome because it kills the Son and God's children, and the even greater mystery of God's unconditional love, which kills sin and death by dying and letting itself be killed. So there is a tense unity, which can be described in the story of Jesus and which we can live in our following of him. We can only glimpse and savor this unity in the historical victories of God's Kingdom, for it will only fully be manifested in the definitive fulfillment of the Kingdom through the resurrection of the dead.

5. It remains to say a word about the cognitive dimension of our thesis. Through Christian solidarity—and only radically through it—we reach the redeeming word of the cross. The Hebrew prophets already had an intuition of this. Let us consider just one text: "Share your bread with the hungry and then your light will shine like the dawn" (Isa. 58:10). We could paraphrase this: "Show solidarity and then you will know the dawning of hope." The context of the passage shows clearly: a) that solidarity includes justice; b) that the enlightenment refers to a search for meaning and hope, which gives a general significance to the most various individual and social sufferings, both "earthly" and "religious"; and c) that the passage is arguing against the insufficiency and uselessness of other ways of searching for light (by mere cult or theory). As we realize, this thesis of Isaiah's reaches its major crisis—and its unexpected fulfillment!—in the cross of Jesus. Jesus' liberating solidarity provoked, as the language of John expresses it, the powers of darkness to overcome him. But because he kept up his solidarity to the end, the hour of darkness was transformed into the hour when the glory is revealed: "When I am raised on high, I will draw all to me" (John 12:32). "And we have seen his glory, glory like the only-begotten Son of the Father, full of faithful and gratuitous solidarity" (John 1:14). The cognitive power of suffering is unfolded in solidarity, and when this is both transforming and kenotic to the point of giving its life, it gives a glimpse, a "sight" of the cross's liberating shining redemption.

II. THEMATIC PERSPECTIVES

Although suffering, death, cross, and martyrdom are unfathomable realities, what we say about them will not perhaps be what is most important and deep—and therefore incapable of expression in systematic form—but that which we think can lead best to the practice of solidarity today. It is also what leads to hope and what can best guard the liberating word of the cross, which is experienced and proclaimed in this practice of solidarity and prayer. We are well aware that there are many other aspects of suffering and death that a liberating theology of the cross ought to deal with. We should also point out that our four theses are closely interrelated because the reality we are dealing with is a single one.

1. Thesis Three

Transforming solidarity with the suffering of victims of sociohistorical oppression—which must be considered as sin and as the central sin of our world—is the decisive place for the humanizing experience and practice of the redemption of all suffering and for its faithful and credible proclamation.

In this thesis we start with three presuppositions, which we may briefly state: (1) human suffering must be understood basically as a dimension of human beings' anthropological and sociohistorical practice. This means that suffering can be reified, as a fatal destiny, and can also reify human beings, so that they are unable to act in a properly human way; it can even kill them. But it is not properly speaking a thing; it is the negative of freedom and solidarity, which can either give impulse to or paralyze a liberating praxis of solidarity. (2) The fundamental theological question is: What is there in real suffering of non-sense and sin against which we must struggle unconditionally? What is there in suffering of sense and grace, which we should welcome and practice? What anthropological and social form should a liberating and redeeming practice of suffering take when it is illuminated, empowered, and consoled by the grace of Christ? (3) The final horizon is that of a full and reconciled life, in which every tear will be wiped away; but God's Kingdom is being brought about in history, with achievements of life and perfect abundance as well as with tribulations and persecutions.

On its negative side, our thesis says that the situation of poverty, marginalization, and death of the majority of humanity is not a natural fact—although it includes natural factors. It is a situation of sociohistorical oppression, which is due to "a social organization promoted and sustained by a minority dominating through a conjunction of factors, which, given their particular historic effect, must be considered to be sin" (Ellacuría). So we have a radical non-sense in three aspects: the practice of oppression by minorities lacks sense; the social objectivity of this practice is absurd, because it produces death in constant and recurrent form; the many sufferings of the crucified people—hunger, repression, torture—lack sense in themselves. Nothing can gloss over or sweeten either the practice or the structures of oppression, or the sufferings of the oppressed. A liberating theology of the cross does not gloss over or sweeten this non-sense, but absolutely radicalizes it; we are facing a situation of sin, including the central sin of our world, because it kills God's children and God's Son, and does so in a recurrent, massive, and covert manner (which corresponds to the dynamic of the sin of the world according to the Christian scriptures). A liberating theology of the cross must help unmask, express, and radicalize this non-sense. It must unmask its traditional fatalist naturalization, and its subtler forms of fatalism, which refer everything to mere structures with nobody responsible. It must maintain the non-sense in the face of all theological or secular attempts to recover its scandal. It must help to express its non-sense, accepting and helping to articulate the cry of the suffering people, which demands in "increasingly tumultuous and insistent form, justice, freedom, respect for the fundamental human rights of individuals and peoples" (Puebla, 87), by accepting and helping to articulate the innocent people's cry in God's presence. Like Job, these innocents refuse to explain their suffering as a punishment for their sins or simply their destiny. They seek God's face so that by maintaining the non-sense of the suffering inflicted on them they can give meaning to suffering assumed in the struggle against it. Finally, it must radicalize the non-sense by showing the real identification between the death of the crucified Son and the death of the crucified people.

Positively, we say that the central place for grace is transforming solidarity with the victims of oppression. From the many dimensions of this statement we select just two to explain: (1) the place of liberation and redemption of all suffering is solidarity with the victims of sociohistorical oppression; and (2) the people who suffer are not just the object of liberation and redemption, but they are called, christologically, to be the central subjects of redeeming liberation for all humanity.

1. To the radical non-sense of oppression the only fitting practical response is transforming solidarity. That should be obvious by now. But that this solidarity must be the central place of liberation and redemption of all suffering may appear to be saying too much. It appears to value the social but to have little respect for the weight of pain there is in an incurable disease, a heartbreaking disappointment in love, a neurosis that resists cure, and so on. It appears to promise too much, in a magic way, in the face of the irreducible diversity of suffering. Therefore we must offer a foundation for this statement that is both solid and precise. We are not talking about therapeutic techniques but about the deep structure of liberating redemption according to revelation. The nucleus of the person and the nucleus of peoples approach the radical redeeming liberation of their sufferings to the extent that they set solidarity with the victims of social oppression above their own pains. In this practice of solidarity—which is also personally painful and will provoke new sufferings through social persecution—we approach unconditional love, which in itself bears the unshakeable hope of love's victory. Without this solidarity we are in practice denying love's unconditionality and hope. Obviously with these reflections we have not exhausted the matter, but we have offered something that shows the liberating and redeeming scandal of the cross of Jesus Christ. We cannot do much more by argument. We can only invite people to the practice of transforming solidarity in God's presence, in the evocation of the Crucified, and in living fellowship with the people. Then the history of suffering will follow but within a redeemed and redeeming, liberated and liberating practice.

2. With respect to the liberating and redeeming mission of the suffering people, the crucified people, we must approach this mystery with caution. It is obvious, as against any cult of suffering justifying injustice with hindsight, that oppression and crucifixion in themselves neither liberate nor redeem They are a non-sense and sin at its greatest. But the crucified people are not merely objects; they are also active subjects. Suffering is not merely an imposition but also an action. So what must be said in the context of a historical soteriology is the following: the crucified people are called in Jesus Christ to be the liberating and redeeming servant of Yahweh for all history. They begin to be so when their own crucified life throws light on the sin of the world and denounces it, inviting to conversion, justice, and solidarity. Their mission grows when a) the oppressed resist oppression; b) they keep hope; c) they themselves struggle in solidarity to support right and justice; and d) they let God be God through

their own trustful surrender into the Father's hands and forgive their enemies.

Is there any practical verification of all these perspectives on suffering? Let us note just one: that of the Beatitudes. In the crucified people's painful solidarity there is joy:

> Because what is opposed to joy is sadness, not suffering. A joy that is not easy, but none the less real. It is not the superficial joy of unawareness or resignation, but that which is born of the conviction that ill treatment and unjust suffering will be overcome. It is a paschal joy corresponding to a time of martyrdom. (G. Gutiérrez)

2. Thesis Four

The "untimely death" of the oppressed masses is the fundamental visibility of sin. The "struggle to the death for life" in solidarity with the Kingdom and in hopeful surrender, without reservation or calculation, into the Father's hands, is the fundamental visibility of grace.

We wish to show that the modern theology of death, despite its admirable existential depth, falls short of denouncing and announcing the New Testament gospel of life. And we want to outline a liberating theology of death. Thus we shall indicate how, by confronting history in transforming and kenotic solidarity, the liberating theology of the cross stands with the gospel of life and can maintain, even deepen, the existential depth of death.

We can freely accept the first face death presents in modern theology,assuming with it that death is an abstraction concerned with the historicity of finite freedom. Thus death is the "natural end and free consummation of existence" (Rahner).

But in approaching the fact of death as it really exists, we ask about what there is in it of sin and of grace. Modern theology replies by keeping up the existential-personalist abstraction: as a consequence of sin death is experienced "as a violent dark cutting-off which puts an end to life"; and, as a possibility of grace, "death and dying in the Lord are the option of surrender and service, experienced both as agony and death and as an active consummation of life in God" (Greshake).

First, let us say that the negative face of death shows itself today and throughout history not primarily in existential anguish over the dark power that cuts short life, but in "death by killing," the "untimely death" (Las Casas) of the oppressed masses. Although it is not empirically universal, this way of dying is theologically important for various reasons: a) this was how Jesus died; b) it is the death died by the masses, or at least the victims, whose blood cries to heaven and reaches the heart of God; c) it shows the radical-transcendent and historical-temporal character (untimely dying) of death, and thus sets death in (present and future, historical and radical) opposition to the Kingdom of God; and d) it shows clearly the gravity of sin, its mortal character, its murderous face.

Second, untimely death manifests the mortal character of all sin and the sinful character of all death. The former is because all sin is a blow against God's Kingdom, both a closing off of the *agape* in which God consists and a destruction of the *koinonia* of his Kingdom. This is not always clearly visible. Because sin hides and justifies itself, it may appear as something merely private. But the prophetic happening uncovers it from its false appearances; for example, the pious religious legalism of the Pharisees really (and manifestly) kills the Son, as it was really (although covertly) killing the people with its contempt, its insupportable burdens, its plundering, its religious justification of the status quo, its lack of compassion. Sin always does this, and we see it clearly in the premature death by killing of the masses and the prophets. It may not at first sight be obvious that untimely death manifests the sinful dimension of all death. So let us try and put it more precisely: the sinful dimension of all death is its fear of love's unconditionality and the *koinonia* of the Kingdom. It is not simply fear of the unknown. For although this exists in all death, when it becomes an absolute in the consciousness of the person who resists dying, this is a result of hiding truth in injustice. Therefore anguish at death's violent cutting off is a by-product of an individual and collective life that has killed, that is inscribed in death-dealing dynamics, that has not practically opened up to recognize that the unknown invites us to *agape* and *koinonia*, but tends to shut itself off, to affirm itself, to rebel. The anguish of dying is the anguish of a hidden murder. "Because this is the message you have heard from the beginning: that we should love one another. Not like Cain, who was inspired by the evil one and killed his brother. And why did he kill him? Because his works were evil and his brother's works were just" (1 John 3:11-12). Abel's untimely death shows "Cain's anguish" at the "mortal" option of just and brotherly *koinonia*.

That grace's fundamental visibility should be "the struggle to the death for life in solidarity with the Kingdom" (Casaldáliga) can be shown better in our thesis on martyrdom. Here let us simply stress that this is the way in which grace can be understood and lived, "transcending history in history" in its Paschal character. Thus accepting grace is the most radical affirmation of life in solidarity now in history, and the most radical readiness for death in solidarity and for the sake of solidarity. The personal and the social, the historical and the trans-historical are thus shot through with Jesus' — mortally vital and vitaly mortal — Paschal grace.

Finally, let us answer a difficulty. Isn't this perspective too heroic, too elitist, too pelagian? Does it not do away with the good news of redemption for sinners and from all death, even "insignificant" and "private" death? In reply we may make two, apparently contradictory, points. First, it is not up to us to design the christological form of Paschal grace and liberating, redeemed and redeeming death. Second, the struggle to the death for life in solidarity with the Kingdom can only be lived, kept up, reassumed by real men and women — who are both justified and sinners — in deep theological solidarity, that is, gratefully, in humble prayer, in forgiveness of enemies and the experience of being forgiven, in surrender without reservation or calculation into the Father's hands, as strength in weakness, and so on. There is no insignificant and private death, because the impoverished and marginalized are the bearers of solidarity with

the kingdom of the One who was cast aside by the builders and whose ignominious death outside the city opened to us, through his flesh, a new public
history, which scandalously reaches from the poor to the heavens.

3. Thesis Five

Liberating solidarity with the Kingdom historically encounters and theologically situates the Christian cross as persecution, beyond any ahistorical cult of
pain or existentialism. It directs and inspires Christian self-denial beyond asceticism, which is more or less stoic or merely humanist.

In this thesis we point out schematically the historical and anthropological
dimensions of the Christian cross. We do so to some extent in dispute with
theoretical or practical currents linked to the theology of the cross.

First, the historical dimension — theological, transforming, and kenotic solidarity — is what leads us to the cross and enables us not to run away from it,
but to embrace it in hope, overcoming rationalization and the fear of dying.
This solidarity causes persecution by this world, which lacks solidarity and is
idolatrous. It wants to maintain its oppressive interests and rationalizations.
Because it is kenotic, this solidarity enables us not to run away from persecution,
condemnation, and the cross, and to show unconditional love crucified. We
keep hope by following the Lord. In this way, because in transforming solidarity
we "assume the cause of the poor as the cause of Christ himself" (Puebla), we
suffer, in kenotic solidarity the fate of the poor and persecuted as the cross of
Christ himself. And all this is possible in and through the presence of the Father
of Jesus. Certainly this is a theological mysticism of the cross. But it is bound
up with and made possible by a politics of the Kingdom, which is also theological. The politics of solidarity confronts this world in order to transform it,
unmask it, and thus liberate it and save it. Here we have no dolorist or merely
existential mysticism, standing on the margins of transforming solidarity with
the Kingdom.

Second is the anthropological dimension of the cross. As well as what we
have said above, it is certainly the case that in the gospels and in Christian
tradition the cross is spoken of in anthropological terms, as self-denial in the
face of allurements by this world and our own concupiscence. We think this is
derived and subordinate to the historical meaning of the cross, but important
and with its own relative autonomy in Christian life. Jesus, who knows what
there is in this world and in the human heart, foretells deprivations for his
followers when they welcome and live in solidarity with the Kingdom. But this
does not mean a stoic asceticism or a resentful Manicheism toward the bodily
and earthly, but the requirement and possibility of leaving everything for the
treasure of the Kingdom. Solidarity with the poor is the soul of evangelical
poverty: "Give it to the poor and follow me." Solidarity with the Kingdom is
the driving force and meaning of renunciation of power and prestige: "It shall
not be so among you because the Son of man has come to serve"; "Call no one
master, because you are all brothers." This is not just a question of acts of
renunciation. It also concerns structural options of renunciation, always set

within the perspective of solidarity with the Kingdom. All this does not exclude but includes self-control and discipline, but for the sake of solidarity.

This is a derived and subordinate aspect to the historical cross, because it is directed toward making effective kenotic solidarity possible. We said it was important and had its own relative autonomy because it implies structural daily options, governed by solidarity but not always immediately linked to it.

4. Thesis Six

Martyrdom for the sake of solidarity with the Kingdom is the supreme form of christological witness in a world which does not exclude faith but domesticates it and uses it idolatrously. Martyrdom integrates the active and passive dimensions, the confessional and practical, the historical and eschatological, the liberating and redeeming dimensions of Christian witness. It brings out faith's and the church's character of service in the world for the Kingdom.

There are many dimensions of martyrdom, as it is experienced and also spoken of theologically in Latin America. We merely point out three: (1) its historical setting; (2) its Christian integrity; and (3) its ecclesial dimension.

The first thing to stress is that martyrdom is an important reality—perhaps the most important reality—in the Latin American church of the poor during the last twenty years. We are not talking about a martyrist church, because what is being sought is not martyrdom but life and liberation for the poor. But we are talking about a church of martyrs because many have maintained their solidarity with the poor to the end.

Second, we note the initial strangeness of this martyrdom in the particular historical situation of Latin America. People are not being killed through hatred of the faith or by a militantly unbelieving or atheist world. They are being murdered in culturally Catholic countries belonging to Western civilization, apparently secular and tolerant. We think what is happening is the following: they are killed by a world that does not oppose the faith and ban it, but domesticates it idolatrously, perverting it so that it becomes an adornment and justification of oppression and injustice. This world does not kill through direct hatred of the confession of the faith; it kills those who try to make the faith genuine, by truly following Jesus Christ, in transforming solidarity with the poor, by prophetic unmasking of oppression and idolatry. These are martyrs for their solidarity with the Kingdom, but also and more profoundly, martyrs for genuine Christianity. We may also say that there is probably more likeness between the Latin American martyrs and the martyrdom of Jesus than in the martyrs of the Roman Empire of the wars of religion. Jesus too confronted the perversion of an authentic religion, rather than the banning of that religion. Furthermore, faithfulness to the death in Jesus consists of solidarity with the Kingdom, the *agape* and *koinonia* of the Kingdom, in trustful surrender to the Father. The Latin American martyrs are faithful till death for the sake of their transforming and kenotic solidarity with the victims of injustice.

So we are talking about the Christian integrity of martyrdom through solidarity with the Kingdom. Rather than offer more reflections, let us listen to the words of Archbishop Romero, which were sealed in his own blood:

Christ invites us not to be afraid of persecution because, believe me, brothers and sisters, anyone who commits themselves to the poor must suffer the same fate as the poor. And in El Salvador we know what the fate of the poor is: to be disappeared, tortured, arrested, to appear as corpses ... I am glad, brothers and sisters, that our church is persecuted, precisely because of its preferential option for the poor and because it tries to become incarnate in the interest of the poor. It would be sad if in a country where there are so many horrible murders, we did not also find priests among the victims. They are witnesses to a church incarnate in the problems of the poor. ... The only thing that consoles me is that Christ, who tried to convey this great truth, was also misunderstood, called a rebel, and sentenced to death, as they have threatened me today. ... I want to assure you, and I beg your prayers to remain faithful to this promise, that I will not abandon my people, but I will run with them all the risks demanded by my ministry. ... I have frequently been threatened with death. I must tell you that, as a Christian, I do not believe in death, but in resurrection. If they kill me I will rise again in the Salvadoran people. I tell you this without boasting, with the greatest humility. ... As a pastor I am obliged to give my life for those I love, who are all Salvadorans, even those who are going to murder me. If they fulfil their threats, as of now I offer God my blood for the redemption and resurrection of El Salvador. ... Martyrdom is a grace I do not think I deserve. But if God accepts the sacrifice of my life, let my blood be a seed of freedom and the sign that hope will soon become reality.

Finally, we must stress that a martyrdom like this is clearly a service to the Kingdom of God, and thus a service to the church and the Christian faith. Love to the end in solidarity with the poor serves the Kingdom of God because it encourages its historical liberation and because it makes people experience — first, the oppressed, but also all who do not shut themselves off from its witness — God's nearness as unconditional goodness, as *agape*. It is a service to the church and the faith, because it criticizes them and shows them the liberating and redeeming way to follow the Crucified. The martyrs show us how we can become incarnate in history and society without becoming worldly.

Thus they show how the liberating theology of the cross is an historical soteriology, because they struggle for God's Kingdom in history on the side of the poor, and how it is a redeeming and trans-historical soteriology, because they give their lives without reservation or calculation, in hope and unconditional love.

— Translated by Dinah Livingstone

35

Hope, Utopia, Resurrection

JOÃO BATISTA LIBÂNIO

I. TWO PARADOXICAL FACTS

Two paradoxical facts intrigue and challenge the theologian. One concerns the societies of abundance, both those within the geographical frontiers of the rich countries and those that exist within the poor countries. To some extent both share the same modern world, which is undergoing a profound change in its fundamental values. The other fact concerns the poor sectors that also exist in the rich countries and constitute the great majority of people in the Third World. We are concerned here in particular with the Christian areas of Latin America.

1. End of Utopia and Hope: There Is No Resurrection

The End of Utopia is not just the title of a work by Marcuse; it also expresses the modern spiritual climate. The death of utopia, the end of hope does not arise from a desperate situation, scepticism, darkening horizons. What it expresses is euphoria. There is no longer any room for utopia or hope, because the era has come to an end in which the objective conditions were lacking to make viable social and historical realities. "Any new way of life on earth, any transformation of the technical and natural context is a real possibility which has its own place in the historical world."[1] The only limits upon human enterprise are scientific laws of biology.

Research into the values held in nine rich European countries shows an anti-utopian mentality, precisely because Europeans "feel happy." Three-quarters of Europeans say they are happy, and one-fifth feel very happy. Only one in every hundred does not admit to being happy.[2] This happiness comes from family, profession, and financial satisfaction and is thought of on the strictly personal level.

Marxism has also declared the death of utopia, as it thinks of socialism as the definitive step from utopia to science. Now we no longer need to hope, as we can trace the future scientifically.[3]

The death of utopia and hope is the end of the long march of individualism in the West. From an individual born in-relation-with-God, the product of Christian teaching, and the value of the individual in opposition to the world belonging to the Hellenistic schools, we have progressed to the modern individual who turns this upside down and becomes the individual-in-the-world, without God.[4] Absolutely autonomous and self-sufficient, such individuals no longer need utopias or hope and can reach fulfillment within history with the resources they have acquired. In particular among these resources are unlimited planning powers with the help of computers and information science.

The death of utopia and hope shows a clear opposition in the West to the Christian resurrection as a victory over death. According to Ph. Murray's fascinating thesis, the nineteenth century, not simply as a chronological period but as a spirit, mentality, attitude, and style of knowledge, is characterized by implacable conflict with and obsessive rejection of the fundamental Christian dogma of the resurrection of the dead, in favor of history as the only eternity possible for humanity: a place in the final procession of the dead in the irreversible entropy of nature and humanity.[5]

2. Rise of Utopia and Hope: Faith in the Resurrection

In 1968 the Latin American bishops met at Medellín and proclaimed a "new historical epoch for our Continent, longing for total emancipation, liberation from all forms of slavery, personal growth, and collective integration" (Medellín, 4). *Liberation* became the word that galvanized the energies and longings of the whole Latin American continent. It is the great utopia. And given that it arose and grew in Christian Territory, it became closely linked with eschatological Christian hope. In the last analysis it implies faith in the resurrection, so that utopia, hope, and faith in the resurrection are an intimately connected trilogy.

Puebla takes up this utopia again with increased vigor. The theme of liberation permeates the whole document. It appears above all as the cry of the people. At Medellín it was a rumble, but now "it is clear, growing, impetuous and at times threatening"—a cry that is raised by millions of exploited people who are in a situation of "extreme poverty" (Puebla, 88-90). The origin of this utopia is a profoundly significant event in Latin America:

> Those who are absent from history are becoming present in it. The poor are passing to center stage in society and in the Latin American church. As they do so, they provoke fear and hostility among the oppressors and arouse hope among the dispossessed.[6]

This utopia and hope gives rise to the "birth of a new historical awareness" of liberation.[7] It is the "greater utopia" or "greatest utopia" of the people expressed as a general desire ("Oh, that all would gather, as God commands!") passing through historical hope ("The day when the people hold power in their hands") to end up with eschatological hope ("but this will only happen in heaven").[8]

The particular nurturing grounds for this utopia are the ecclesial base communities. They are not just "hope for the church" (EN, 58), but places that generate hope. In them people sing of utopia and hope, as we find graphically illustrated in this very common song in the communities:

I want to sing a new song, joyful
with my people celebrate the dawn.
My liberated people!
The struggle has not been in vain!
Pilgrim through a world unequal
Exploited by the greed of capital
By the plantation owner's power made landless
Not knowing where to go I'm homeless . . .
With hope I stick together with the rest
I know God never forgets the oppressed who cry
And Jesus sided with the poor and dispossessed.
The prophets keep on denouncing the evil-doers
because the earth belongs to us as family.
There should be share and share alike at table
Kindness makes the whole world lovable
and its bright stars light my way.
In rivers of justice, common labor,
Rice fields will flower . . .
And we will harvest liberty!

II. UTOPIA AND THE HOPE OF THE POOR IN LATIN AMERICA

The terms *utopia* and *hope* have a variety of meanings. So we need to define them in order to avoid misunderstanding. We start here by distinguishing between *utopia* and *hope* and giving precise definitions.

1. Preliminary Considerations

The term *utopia* was invented by the English Christian humanist Thomas More (1561), who used it as the title of his political novel. The term's possible twofold etymology gives us its basic semantic elements. *Utopia* comes from *ouk-topos*, "no place." It refers to a "place which does not exist anywhere." It is imaginary, ideal, unreal, not here, nowhere in this world. But the term can also have the etymology *eu-topos*, "good place." This expresses the dimension of happiness, joy, space, fulfillment. It reveals our human capacity to anticipate through imagination things which can become reality. In this sense *utopia* means "the place where we are really at home; the place where we can feel comfortable."[9] It exists somewhere, and so it can become a model to copy. The reality we desire (*eu-topos*) is the counterweight to the unreal dimension (*ouk-topos*). Thus the term has an intentional ambiguity between the real and unreal.

Utopia expresses a human aspiration toward a truly just order, a social world that is wholly human, which corresponds fully to the dreams, needs, and deepest aspirations of human life. It is the image of a perfect society, which acts as a horizon and guideline for a real historical project or for the desire for an alternative project to the present situation.

Utopia has two fundamental structural elements: it is a criticism of the present situation and a proposal for what should exist. As a criticism it shows its character of rejection, denunciation, "subversion" of the existing order. Through its property of "having no place" it accuses this world of not having permitted it to exist. It points toward what should exist, the right to want, seek, and aspire to another reality. In this case utopia is anticipatory. It offers alternative models, and it announces the plausibility of a different world, something completely new, different, other.

The term *hope* is considered here in its theological, eschatological dimension. Whereas the term *utopia* stresses the horizontal, intra-historical, immanent, worldly dimension, hope points to the absolute future, the divine mystery, toward fulfillment, God's self-communication.

Hope is theological because it is directed toward God. It is eschatological because it refers to our final end, which is already present in our historical reality in sacramental form, as sign and mediation, but will be unveiled and fulfilled beyond death.

Utopia says no to the present and points toward a future within history. Hope says yes to the absolute future, already present, which comes to meet every human being but is always future in the sense that it is never totally achieved and known. It always keeps its character of being something to come, an unforeseeable surprise, wholly new. Hope reveals the structure of the real as movement toward this absolute future and not toward emptiness or nothing.[10]

2. Historical Considerations

Utopias are born at moments of crisis and transition.[11] So in times of change, as with the passage from feudalism to the birth of capitalism, we get the Renaissance utopias (More, Campanella, Bacon). The struggle of the rising bourgeoisie against feudal lords generated the liberal utopias (Harrington, Rousseau, Locke). Protest against the oppression of the working masses gave birth to the social utopias (Saint-Simon, Fourier, Owen, Blanc). The dehumanizing effects of technology, progress, and the functionalization of human relationships gave rise to the commune utopias (hippies). Utopias arise when the present becomes unbearable. They point toward a possible change in human history, the creation of a new, different world.

Hope, however, grows in much more difficult and hostile ground. Its true origin is an impossible situation in human terms, one we cannot overcome by relying on our present potential and human strength, but only on God's promises and power. It is an experience of God within our own human courage, our own unbreakable hope. The biblical model is Abraham (Rom. 4:18-22), who hoped against all hope.

The current situation in Latin America is favorable to the rise of utopias and nourishes theological hope. Utopia's particular field is the economic and political crisis rocking the continent. Economically speaking, the most obvious sign of the crisis is the gigantic foreign debt, which in purely financial terms and within the orthodoxy of the ruling international economic order is absolutely insoluble. Politically, the crisis is manifest either through the continuing existence of illegitimate authoritarian regimes or the precarious nature of democratic institutions for those who enjoy at least an apparent legality. They are institutions whose instability does not allow for profound changes without the enormous risk of reverting to dictatorship. In a word, capitalism's savage power is strangling people's lives so that they are turning toward an alternative reality.

But the brutal reality sometimes seems to block even utopian imagination, only leaving space for hope in God. And as these oppressed people are Christians, their faith drives them to act. The bridge between faith and liberating action is hope in God. So it is not surprising that the most dominant tone in the people's songs and prayers is that of the psalmist crying: "Be pleased O Lord, to deliver me! O Lord, make haste to help me! . . . Thou art my help and my deliverer; do not tarry, O my God!" (Ps. 40:14, 18).

3. Anthropological Foundation

Humans are *utopian beings*. This fundamental condition derives from the insuperable tension between our openness to the world as a whole and our particular situation in limited time and space. On the one hand, we face boundless horizons, regions and lands without limit. We are self-transcending spirit. We are imagination, desire, creativity. Our questioning never ceases. Our will is not satisfied with any particular good. We want good in itself, unconditional good. We are directed toward the future. We are dynamic, in movement. "Every human being lives primarily to the extent that he or she aspires to the future."[12] We are beings-tending-to-be-more. We live with a permanent calling to the future. Our being is a project.

At the same time we are situated in very particular conditions. We live on the Latin American continent full of contradictions—a dark tunnel for our aspirations; a closed horizon to our possibilities; a territory with limited scope. The economic situation strangles the people and makes them become an oppressed mass, whose plans and projects are determined and defined by outside forces. The political situation offers no future to the poor. The cultural situation forces them continually to assimilate important elements that are alien to their tradition.

This violent tension between what they essentially are and how they exist in their concrete situation, between their aspirations and what they really experience, impels Latin Americans toward liberating utopias.

Their very being consists of theological hope. They want to transcend themselves not just within history, in relation to the present and their particular situation. They want transcendence that goes beyond history. This is being-for-the-absolute-future, not just for the more limited earthly future. The absolute future comes in the form of grace. Grace enters history as a real possibility. So in each free, historical human action human beings confront the ultimate, definitive, absolute future. With this theological hope as part of their being, Latin Americans do not consider the terrible oppression and exploitation they suffer as mere historical facts, but as "structural sin." Hoping means fighting against this sin, the work of evil, sin committed by human free will, which crystallizes into structures that end up leading to future sins. It is not just a utopia of liberation but hope of total liberation, which begins in history but goes beyond it, sustained by God's grace.

As utopian beings, Latin American people confront the oppression under which they live and where they experience their own limitation and weakness and the temptation to pessimism, bitterness, and fatalism. Creating utopias means staying alive in a situation which speaks of death on all sides. Utopia helps them to humanize the inhuman work processes to which they are subjected.

This utopian impulse is not exempt from risk and temptations. People committed to a utopia of liberation feel they are makers of history, creators of meaning for a reality they wish were different. The risk lies in believing they are able to give history its *whole* meaning. They believe they can create the perfect society within historical human space and time, the city of absolute humanity. They suppose human beings are capable of designing and building a radical definitive project that would be absolute perfection. They want to create the absolute Kingdom on earth with the fragile material of history.[13]

This danger is less in Latin America, because Latin Americans are believers and therefore imbued with theological hope. The horizon of the absolute future has a double function in the way they see themselves. On the one hand, they are more easily aware that no situation is nonviable, however closed and terrible it may be, because they hope in the absolute Lord of history and the universe. On the other hand, the claim to build the perfect city on earth gives way to the hope that only God can conquer all their adversaries, especially sin and death, by giving the gift of resurrection and glorifying history.

Thus for Latin Americans, *being-hope* corrects the arrogant pretension of *being-utopian*. But being-utopian offers particular ways of embodying hope in history. This leads us into politics.

4. Scope of Politics

Two fundamental political tensions underlie utopia. In fact, the political utopias of recent centuries turn in practice around two conflicting axes. On the one hand, they may try to create a utopia of unlimited spontaneous freedom, but at the expense of and in painful conflict with justice and equality; on the other hand, the utopia of justice and equality may be constructed at the expense of freedom.

A second fundamental tension lies in the political direction given to utopia. Utopia may become an apologia for what already exists, by assuming a clear conservative color and projecting a perfected (utopian) future as a prolongation of the present. We find this in its most expressive form in A. Huxley's *Brave New World*, where even death is thought of as continuing this pleasant world in which all suffering, fear, and anguish are overcome by the chemical means of drugs.

This utopia can be turned by the exploited and oppressed into a protest against the present situation, against kowtowing to the ruling system. It becomes a factor for change, in opposition to the real present and in favor of the desired future. It shifts the weight of the present onto a different future of novelty and creativity.

In the political field utopia has been attacked by Marxist socialism, which calls it alienation. Its ideal character is seen as demobilizing and a source of frustration, as idealism lacking in realism. Thus Marxism presents itself as a scientific reading of reality, which is incompatible with utopia in its vagueness and lack of scientific rigor. Utopia is seen as an evasion of the present, leading to historical irresponsibility and castle-building in the air, instead of taking on struggle and conflict with a view to setting up a new society.

Another political attack comes from historical experience. Utopias which begin from below, with the exploited, end up in the hands of those who are on top and become ideology. So utopia is degraded into ideology. Historically we know the case of the utopia of freedom — absolute, liberal, spontaneous — which ended up producing mechanisms of oppression and highjacking this freedom to serve the ruling classes. Thus the utopia of freedom destroyed the possibility of freedom for the masses.

We saw how utopia tempted people to turn finite human history into infinite perfection, inviting hubris. When this dynamic operates politically, the most violent forms of totalitarianism arise. For when people rely only on immanent historical forces to build a perfect society of justice overcoming human limitations, they brook no opposition and silence every enemy. Only by extreme violence can they employ the human demiurge in empirical time to construct the definitive future. They do not accept the possibility of any other freedom that is not embarked on the same revolutionary adventure. Thus they attribute the divine quality of perfection to their historical construct and cannot tolerate objections, opposition, or dissent. Their effectiveness is based on their capacity for fanaticism. So utopia becomes closer to violence than to dispassionate reason. It becomes a secularized religion leading to totalitarianism, as we saw with Nazism and Stalinism.[14]

However, these dangers accompanying utopia do not take away its fundamental role as a driving historical force. It does not cease to be so because it may succumb to human pride and lead by its internal logic to totalitarianism. There are many human realities which if taken to their logical extreme end up generating contradictions. This does not mean they cease to be necessary. Their logic can be halted at a certain point. Utopia belongs to this kind of thinking that must not be taken to extremes. What stops utopia on its road to pride and totalitarianism is hope.

Thus utopia is relevant to our situation without incurring the dangers pointed out by K. Popper and others. For a people left on the margin of history, or rather, living on the "underside of history,"[15] it is an historical force for liberation. It rejects the defeatism and fatalism generated and nourished by the

723 HOPE, UTOPIA, RESURRECTION

dominant ideology and is an anticipation of the future as a different, possible, longed for reality. It keeps alive the conviction that present reality can be changed, that it is not a natural order imposed by God but the result of interested human decisions. Utopia is a mysticism inspiring action for change. Utopia impels to action, opening new spaces, which previously appeared to be closed off.

When this utopia is animated and penetrated by Christian hope, its force becomes irresistible. At the same time this Christian hope offers it a critique which saves it from human pride with its absolute and totalitarian pretensions. The root of this hope lies in the revelation which entered history and reached its highest point in the mystery of the resurrection of Christ.

III. THE RESURRECTION, FOUNDATION OF THE THEOLOGICAL DIMENSION

1. Utopias in the Bible

Of course the term utopia, invented in the sixteenth century, cannot be biblical. Nevertheless, if by *utopia* we mean historical projects realized within this world, and by *hope* a theological attitude which maintains a direct relationship with God's presence acting in history and with the absolute future, we can say that the Bible contains utopias. Although its horizon is always one of hope, as it trusts in God for fulfillment, nevertheless at first this hope was thought of as preferably, if not exclusively, within history. So provisional models of how Israel should live, produced by prophets and constantly reinterpreted, should be interpreted as mediations of a final intervention by God at the end of time. Thus Israel's history knew a number of utopias. J. Pixley lists the utopia of a peasant society where "they shall sit every man under his vine and under his fig tree" (1 Kings 5:5, Mic. 4:4, Zech. 3:10) in a "land flowing with milk and honey" (Exod. 3:8,17; 13:5; 33:3, and elsewhere); the utopia of the beneficent king (Ps. 72:1-9, 12-14, 17; Ps. 101:1-8: Isa. 11:1-5); the utopia of a wise law and docile people (Jer. 31:31-34; Ezek. 36:24-32; Isa. 2:2-4); the priestly utopia of a land without blemish (Ezek. 40-48); the utopia of a communist society (Acts 4:32-35; 3:17-21); the utopia of holding spiritual goods in common until the Lord comes (1 Cor. 12:12-13; 7:21-24); the apocalyptic utopia of blessedness (Rev. 6:9-11; 22:1-5).[16]

2. Centrality of Hope in the Hebrew Scriptures

The biblical revelation that begins with Abraham is presented as a promise.[17] This experience of promise and hope is projected backward, so that the first pages of Genesis, with their account of the first sin also contain promise and hope: "Her descendant shall bruise your head" (Gen. 3:15). From the ruins of the flood, the symbol of the rainbow arises as the promise of God's covenant with future generations. It is God's promise that such a catastrophe will never happen again (Gen. 9).

Israel lives by hope, in hope: hope of its progeny (Gen. 13:16), the nation (Gen. 12:2), the land (Gen. 12:7), of liberation from slavery (Exod. 3:7ff.), of a perpetual covenant with God (Exod. 19), of the new covenant (Jer. 31:31ff.). In its pilgrimage Israel experienced reality in tension with this promise. God's self-revelation to the people is always related to promising land, a future, a covenant. And the promises are so great and so far removed from the present reality and foreseeable outcome that they always remain promises. So the people's spiritual food is hope. Hope becomes even sharper when Israel finds itself in exile, captivity, or suffers defeat and persecution. It is a hope which the people perceive as hope in history—until with the resurrection of Christ it is finally seen as being beyond earthly history.

The ultimate basis of this hope was Yahweh's faithfulness—faithfulness which the people celebrated in their great liturgical celebrations and the reciting of their short creeds. Yahweh's past deeds were set before the people's eyes to keep hope in God alive in the present and the future.

Israel's experience of hope was not easy. The people were required to leave the land, undergo trials and temptations, not despair over defeats and national catastrophes. Incomplete fulfillment and new adversities always brought the people back to this hope. This was the horizon for a nomadic people. But hope continued even after they took possession of the land. So Yahweh's name should be interpreted in accordance with the dynamic of hope rather than ontologically. Not "He who is" (an ontological reading) but "He who will always be with his people."[18]

Therefore Israel's decision to trust in God, who calls them, is directed toward the future and nourished by hope. Hoping means believing in love, and Israel experienced God's love as a promise. Thus hope is a constituitive experience of the people's awareness of God, and scripture's message-theology is hope. In this Israel was an exception, as the neighboring peoples lived under the religious-mythical threat of a return to the initial chaos. Their religions promised protection against this reversion, whereas Yahweh pointed Israel to the future through anticipatory signs of the divine presence among God's people. In the last resort this future was God, who became present while also announcing a future presence. Abraham's example is paradigmatic. When God grants him the child of the promise (fulfillment), God orders him to sacrifice the child in order to make him hope again. Every conquest by Israel is an Isaac, given to them and demanded from them, so that they may hope for it again as a new gift by Yahweh. As this promise is never completely fulfilled, it becomes a source of earthly utopias for Israel and also a critical standard for them, always driving the people toward the future true Isaac: Jesus Christ.

3. Jesus Christ, Source of Utopias and Reason for Hope

Israel of the flesh wanted the promises to be fulfilled on earth. Israel of the Spirit glimpsed—and therefore hoped (in the theological sense)—that the fulfillment of the promise would surpass the limits of this age. In Jesus' time the term in which this hope was expressed was the Kingdom of God. But the utopian expectations of this hope were different: kingdom of the law perfectly fulfilled (Pharisees), kingdom of the pure and spiritual living in a community of saints (Essenes), national kingdom free from Roman rule (Zealots), kingdom of the cult and temple (priests). In his proclamation of the Kingdom Jesus did not go against any of these utopias, but he criticized the arrogance and absolute claims made for them by human interests. This cost him his life.

Nevertheless, his preaching has given rise to countless earthly utopias throughout history. Millenarianism has caught the imagination of many Christians, who dreamed of an earthly kingdom of happiness before the last judgment. In particular, they were inspired by the famous passage in Revelation 20:4-10. Political thinking in the Middle Ages was subject to the paradox that, on the one hand, they hoped for a descent from heaven to bring judgment and redemption, and on the other, they had faith in the Holy Roman Empire as an earthly promise and expression of paradise.[19] The Holy Roman Empire was considered as an ideal, as the place for the desired reconstruction. Thus the biblical notion of the reign of David was translated into the Carolingian rule: David was the model for the Frankish king, who was also a new Moses—*rex et sacerdos*—through his anointing. Jerusalem was transferred to Gaul. Christian Europe in the Middle Ages lived with this tension between hope in the future possible rebuilding of Israel as a holy community, and eschatological hope in the form of individual salvation.[20]

Jesus Christ preached the kingdom of God as an "eschatological reality" in the future (Luke 11:2; Matt. 6:10; Luke 10:9; Matt. 10:7; Mark 1:15) and in the present (Luke 11:20; Matt. 12: 28).[21]

This Kingdom of God is God's power already acting in the present. It is the dynamic of God's sovereignty over humanity, history, and the cosmos. Its fulfillment will come only at the end of time, through definitive victory over its enemies—including death—and eternal dominion over all things and all people (1 Cor. 15:15, 24, 26, 28).

In this sense, God's Kingdom is not a utopia because its fulfillment will be the victory over sin and death. If historically it generated utopias with a purely earthly character, it nevertheless remains the critical standard for all utopias, including those of the church itself, which is its sacrament.

This reality is clarified theologically by the resurrection of Jesus. In this eschatological event Jesus' body, as a unique and personal center of decision as the representative of history and cosmos, achieves the definitive quality of life, which forever surpasses time and the confinement of space. With him, the cosmos and history become ripe for God's eternity.

The resurrection is not a terminus, it is not a *topia*, it is not to be found in any of the "utopias" which are simply the creations of human imagination, aspiration, and desire. The resurrection is the place, the *topia* of theological hope. Only through hope can we look toward the resurrection, since it is the work of God the Father's absolute freedom and love, by the power of the Spirit. The Son's humanity was snatched from the fragility of flesh to belong to the sphere of the "Spirit," as the "firstfruits of them that slept" (1 Cor. 15:20), "the firstborn of the dead" (Col. 1:18; Rev. 1:5), as the "precursor" (Acts 3:15; 5: 31) of all of us.[22]

Each of us shares doubly in Jesus' resurrection; sacramentally, in germ, in earthly history, through faith, baptism, the eucharist, charity, through every free act welcoming Christ's victorious grace. When we die we will share in Christ's resurrection fully. In God's final Kingdom, which during our lives was a spur, present as a sign, history reaches it final stage that began to be manifest in Jesus' resurrection. With the resurrection all human hope, which during history nourished the struggle of the poor—so many moments of victory and disaster—reaches its fulfillment. History, which it fertilized, comes to fruition. The truth of all utopias appears; in comparison with this fulfillment they are infinitely limited: "No eye has seen, nor ear heard, nor the human heart conceived, what God has prepared for those who love him" (1 Cor. 2:9). In their turn, the utopias appear as mediations directed toward this moment of fulfillment, a response to genuine human aspirations. Deep within human longing lies God's call to communion with the Holy Trinity in the fullness of the resurrection.

Thus human utopias reveal their true nature as anonymous Christian hope, and hope is the goal of every true utopia. This hope becomes clear in the resurrection, when human beings, laden with history and cosmos, finally break through the limits of time into God. God's finality, which is already present in history whenever human freedom confronts the divine freedom through human, cosmic, historical actions, now through the resurrection attains the whole of human life, giving it the dimension of incorruptibility, glory, power, spirit (1 Cor. 15:42-44).

Through the resurrection of the dead, which is God's fundamental act of love, the eschatological significance of God's preference for the poor appears more clearly. Those who suffered so greatly in earthly history, who were familiar with weakness, humiliation, now share in the victory, power, and glory of God, who raised Jesus and who will raise these poor of the earth.

IV. CONCLUSION

Utopias are human creations, that spring from human longing for a better life in the face of the hard sufferings of the present. It is above all the poor who dream of utopias, because the present is much harder for them. This human character of creating utopias as a spur to political activity, attempting to change things, would remain an enigma, lacking its true meaning, unless theological hope revealed its real origin and final destiny. Human beings were created by a Trinity that is community, the first and most perfect community. Therefore our whole lives are permeated by this deep aspiration toward living together in community.

Hope would also point toward a goal, a destiny which would remain a dark horizon. But Jesus' resurrection fully revealed humanity's utopian structure, its limits, and its anticipatory significance. The resurrection showed that hope in Yahweh does not lead to frustration but to life.

Jesus' resurrection is the prototype, precursor, and anticipation of all resurrections. In it the end of history has already happened. It also shows that only those who give their lives for their brothers and sisters rise again. Lastly, it is the ultimate key to all revelation.

The last word on history has already been said. No human power, no dictator, no ruling power will decide the final destiny of the poor. God's love raised Jesus and will raise all those he loves and who love him. And among these the poor have first place.

— Translated by Dinah Livingstone

NOTES

1. H. Marcuse, *El final de la utopía* (Barcelona, 1968), p. 10.

2. J. Stoetzel, *Les valeurs du temps présent: une enquête européenne* (Paris, 1983), p. 174.

3. L. Silbermann and H. Fries, "Utopie und Hoffnung," in *Christlicher Glaube in moderner Gesellschaft* (Freiburg, 1982), p. 69.

4. L. Dumont, *Essays on Individualism* (Chicago, 1986).

5. Ph. Murray, *Le 19e siècle à travers les âges* (Paris, 1984).

6. G. Gutiérrez, *The Power of the Poor in History* (Maryknoll, N.Y., 1983), p. 76.

7. L. Boff, *Teologia do cativeiro e da libertação* (Petropolis, 1980), p. 13.

8. G. Pixley and C. Boff, *The Bible, the Church, and the Poor* (Maryknoll, N.Y.: 1986), p. 213.

9. K. Kerenyi, *Ursinn und Sinnwandel des Utopischen* (Zurich, 1964), p. 12.

10. K. Rahner, "Marist Utopia and the Christian Future of Man," in *Theological Investigations* VI (New York: Crossroad), pp. 59-68.

11. J. A. Gimbernat, "Utopia," in C. Floristan and J.J. Tamayo, eds., *Conceptos fundamentales de pastoral* (Madrid 1983), p. 1016.

12. E. Bloch, *The Principle of Hope* (Cambridge, Mass., 1986).

13. H. Cl. Vaz, *Escritos de filosofía* (São Paulo, 1986), p. 296.

14. K. Popper, *The Open Society and its Enemies* (London, 1945).

15. Gutiérrez, *The Power of the Poor in History*, pp. 169-221.

16. J. Pixley, "Las utopias principales de la Biblia," in R. Vidales and L. Rivera, eds., *La esperanza en el presente de América latina* (San José, 1983), pp. 313-30.

17. E. Brunner, *Offenbarung und Vernunft* (Zurich, 1981), p. 98.

18. J. C. Murray, *Das Gottes-problem: Gestern und Heute* (Freiburg-Basel-Vienna, 1965), pp. 15ff.

19. L. Silbermann-H. Fries, "Utopie und Hoffnung" (1982), p. 59.

20. Ibid., pp. 66ff.

21. H. Merklein, *Jesu Botschaft von der Gottesherrschaft* (Stuttgart, 1983), p. 24.

22. M. Gourges, *A vida futura segundo o Novo Testamento* (São Paulo, 1986), pp. 62ff.

Bibliography

[Eds. note: This bibliography includes works on Latin American liberation theology available in English.]

I. DOCUMENTS OF THE MAGISTERIUM

Second General Conference of Latin American Bishops, convened at Medellín, Colombia (August 24-September 6, 1968), Final Documents, *The Church in the Present-Day Transformation of Latin America in Light of the Council*, vol. 2, *Conclusions* (Washington, D.C.: U.S. Catholic Conference, 1970). Documents on "Justice," "Peace," "Family and Demography," "Poverty of the Church," appear in *The Gospel of Peace and Justice*, ed. Joseph Gremillion (Maryknoll, N.Y.: Orbis Books, 1976).

Third General Conference of Latin American Bishops, convened at Puebla, Mexico, January 1979, *Final Documents*, in *Puebla and Beyond*, eds. John Eagleson and Philip Scharper (Maryknoll, N.Y.: Orbis Books, 1979).

Fourth General Conference of Latin American Bishops, convened at Santo Domingo, Dominican Republic, October 1992, Conclusions, in *Santo Domingo and Beyond*, ed. Alfred T. Hennelly (Maryknoll, N.Y.: Orbis Books, 1993).

"Instruction on Certain Aspects of the 'Theology of Liberation,' " Congregation for the Doctrine of the Faith (August 6, 1984), in *Liberation Theology: A Documentary History*, ed. Alfred T. Hennelly (Maryknoll, N.Y.: Orbis Books, 1990), 393-414.

"Instruction on Christian Freedom and Liberation," Congregation for the Doctrine of the Faith (March 22, 1986), in *Liberation Theology: A Documentary History*, 461-97.

John Paul II, "Letter to Brazilian Episcopal Conference" (April 9, 1986), in *Liberation Theology: A Documentary History*, 498-506.

II. HISTORY, METHODOLOGY, AND DISTINCTIVE FEATURES OF THE THEOLOGY OF LIBERATION

Antoncich, Ricardo, *Christians in the Face of Injustice: A Latin American Reading of Catholic Social Teaching* (Maryknoll, N.Y.: Orbis Books, 1987).

Aquino, María Pilar, *Our Cry for Life: Feminist Theology from Latin America*, trans. Dinah Livingstone (Maryknoll, N.Y.: Orbis Books, 1993).

Araya, Victorio, *God of the Poor*, trans. Robert R. Barr (Maryknoll, N.Y.: Orbis Books, 1987).

Assman, Hugo, *Theology for a Nomad Church*, trans. Paul Burns (Maryknoll, N.Y.: Orbis Books, 1976).

Berryman, Phillip, *Liberation Theology* (New York: Pantheon, 1987).

Boff, Clodovis, *Theology and Praxis: Epistemological Foundations*, trans. Robert R. Barr (Maryknoll, N.Y.: Orbis Books, 1987).

Boff, Leonardo and Clodovis Boff, *Introducing Liberation Theology*, trans. Paul Burns (Tunbridge Wells: Burns & Oates; Maryknoll, N.Y.: Orbis Books, 1987).

———. *Salvation and Liberation*, trans. Robert R. Barr (Maryknoll, N.Y.: Orbis Books, 1984).

———. *Faith on the Edge*, trans. Robert R. Barr (New York: Harper & Row, 1989; Maryknoll, N.Y.: Orbis Books, 1991).

———. *When Theology Listens to the Poor*, trans. Robert R. Barr (San Francisco: Harper & Row, 1988).

Brown, Robert McAfee, *Gustavo Gutiérrez: An Introduction to Liberation Theology* (Maryknoll, N.Y.: Orbis Books, 1990).

Croatto, J. Severino, *Biblical Hermeneutics*, trans. Robert R. Barr (Maryknoll, N.Y.: Orbis Books, 1987).

———. *Exodus: A Hermeneutics of Freedom* (Maryknoll, N.Y.: Orbis Books, 1981).

Dussel, Enrique, *Ethics and Community*, trans. Robert R. Barr (Maryknoll, N.Y.: Orbis Books; Tunbridge Wells: Burns & Oates, 1988).

———. *Ethics and the Theology of Liberation*, trans. Bernard F. McWilliams (Maryknoll, N.Y.: Orbis Books, 1978).

———. *A History of the Church in Latin America: Colonialism to Liberation* (Grand Rapids: Eerdmans, 1981).

———. *History and the Theology of Liberation*, trans. John Drury (Maryknoll, N.Y.: Orbis Books, 1976).

———. *Philosophy of Liberation*, trans. Aquilina Martinez and Christine Morkovsky (Maryknoll, N.Y.: Orbis Books, 1985).

———, ed. *The Church in Latin America: 1492-1992,* trans. Paul Burns (Tunbridge Wells: Burns & Oates; Maryknoll, N.Y.: Orbis Books, 1992).

Ellacuría, Ignacio, *Freedom Made Flesh: The Mission of Christ and His Church* (Maryknoll, N.Y.: Orbis Books, 1976).

Ellis, Marc and Otto Maduro, eds. *The Future of Liberation Theology: Essays in Honor of Gustavo Gutiérrez* (Maryknoll, N.Y.: Orbis Books, 1989).

Ezcurra, Ana Maria, *The Neoconservative Offensive: U.S. Churches and the Ideological Struggle for Latin America* (New York: Circus Publications, 1983).

Gibellini, Rosino, ed., *Frontiers of Theology in Latin America,* trans. John Drury (Maryknoll, N.Y.: Orbis Books, 1979).

Gutiérrez, Gustavo, *The Power of the Poor in History*, trans. Robert R. Barr (Maryknoll, N.Y.: Orbis Books, 1983).

———. *A Theology of Liberation*, trans. Sister Caridad Inda and John Eagleson (Maryknoll, N.Y.: Orbis Books 1973; revised edition, 1988).

———. *The Truth Shall Make You Free: Confrontations*, trans. Matthew J. O'Connell (Maryknoll, N.Y.: Orbis Books, 1990).

Hennelly, Alfred T., ed. *Liberation Theology: A Documentary History* (Maryknoll, N.Y.: Orbis Books, 1990).

Hinkelammert, Franz, *The Ideological Weapons of Death: A Theological Critique of Capitalism*, trans. Phillip Berryman (Maryknoll, N.Y.: Orbis Books, 1986).

Maduro, Otto, *Religion and Social Conflicts* (Maryknoll, N.Y.: Orbis Books, 1982).

Mesters, Carlos. *Defenseless Flower: A New Reading of the Bible,* trans. Francis McDonagh (Maryknoll, N.Y.: Orbis Books, 1989).

McGovern, Arthur, *Liberation Theology and Its Critics: Toward an Assessment* (Maryknoll, N.Y.: Orbis Books, 1989).

Míguez Bonino, José, *Doing Theology in a Revolutionary Situation* (Philadelphia: Fortress Press, 1975).

———. *Toward a Christian Political Ethic* (Philadelphia: Fortress Press, 1983).

Miranda, José Porfirio, *Marx and the Bible*, trans. John Eagleson (Maryknoll, N.Y.: Orbis Books, 1974).

Moreno, Fernando, *Moral Theology from the Poor* (Quezon City, Philippines: Claretian, 1985).

Moser, Antonio and Bernardino Leers, *Moral Theology: Dead Ends and Alternatives*, trans. Paul Burns (Tunbridge Wells: Burns & Oates; Maryknoll, N.Y.: Orbis Books, 1990).

Pixley, George, *On Exodus: A Liberation Perspective*, trans. Robert R. Barr (Maryknoll, N.Y.: Orbis Books, 1987).

———. *God's Kingdom* (Maryknoll, N.Y.: Orbis Books, 1981).

Santa Ana, José de, *Good News to the Poor: The Challenge of the Poor in the History of the Church* (Maryknoll, N.Y.: Orbis Books, 1977).

———. *Towards a Church of the Poor* (Maryknoll, N.Y.: Orbis Books, 1981).

Segundo, Juan Luis, *Faith and Ideologies*, trans. John Drury (Maryknoll, N.Y.: Orbis Books, 1984).

———. *The Liberation of Dogma*, trans. Phillip Berryman (Maryknoll, N.Y.: Orbis Books, 1992).

———. *The Liberation of Theology*, trans. John Drury (Maryknoll, N.Y.: Orbis Books, 1976).

———. *Signs of the Times: Theological Reflections*, trans. Robert R. Barr (Maryknoll, N.Y.: Orbis Books, 1993).

———. *Theology and the Church* (San Francisco: Harper & Row, 1985).

Tamez, Elsa, *Against Machismo* (Interviews), trans. John Eagleson (Oak Park: Meyer Stone, 1989).

———. *The Bible of the Oppressed*, trans. Matthew J. O'Connell (Maryknoll, N.Y.: Orbis Books, 1982).

———, ed. *Through Her Eyes: Latin American Women Doing Theology* (Maryknoll, N.Y.: Orbis Books, 1989).

III. SYSTEMATIC CONTENTS OF THE THEOLOGY OF LIBERATION

The Liberating Design of God

Boff, Leonardo, *Jesus Christ Liberator*, trans. Patrick Hughes (Maryknoll, N.Y.: Orbis Books, 1978).

———. *Trinity and Society*, trans. Paul Burns (Tunbridge Wells: Burns & Oates; Maryknoll, N.Y.: Orbis Books, 1988).

———. *The Lord's Prayer: The Prayer of Integral Liberation*, trans. Theodore Morrow (Maryknoll, N.Y.: Orbis Books, 1983).

———. *The Maternal Face of God* (San Francisco: Harper & Row, 1987).

Bussman, Claus. *Who Do You Say? Jesus Christ in Latin American Theology* (Maryknoll, N.Y.: Orbis Books, 1985).

Cardenas, José Pallares, *A Poor Man Called Jesus* (Maryknoll, N.Y.: Orbis Books, 1982).

Comblin, José, *Jesus of Nazareth*, trans. Carl Kabat (Maryknoll, N.Y.: Orbis Books, 1976).

———. *Sent from the Father: Meditations on the Fourth Gospel*, trans. Carl Kabat (Maryknoll, N.Y.: Orbis Books, 1979).

———. *The Holy Spirit and Liberation*, trans. Paul Burns (Tunbridge Wells: Burns & Oates; Maryknoll, N.Y.: Orbis Boooks, 1989).

Echegary, Hugo, *The Practice of Jesus*, trans. Matthew J. O'Connell (Maryknoll, N.Y.: Orbis Books, 1984).

Gebara, Ivone and María Clara Bingemer, *Mary: Mother of God, Mother of the Poor*, trans. Phillip Berryman (Maryknoll, N.Y.: Orbis Books; Tunbridge Wells: Burns & Oates, 1989).

Gutiérrez, Gustavo, *The God of Life*, trans. Matthew J. O'Connell (Maryknoll, N.Y.: Orbis Books, 1991).

Mesters, Carlos, *God, Where Are You?* (Maryknoll, N.Y.: Orbis Books, 1977).

Míguez Bonino, José, ed., *Faces of Jesus in Latin America*, trans. Robert R. Barr (Maryknoll, N.Y.: Orbis Books, 1984).

Miranda, José Porfirio, *Being and the Messiah: The Message of St. John* (Maryknoll, N.Y.: Orbis Books, 1977).

Muñoz, Ronaldo, *The God of Christians*, trans. Paul Burns (Tunbridge Wells: Burns & Oates; Maryknoll, N.Y.: Orbis Books, 1990).

Richard, Pablo, et al, *The Idols of Death and the God of Life* (Maryknoll, N.Y., 1983).

Segundo, Juan Luis, *The Christ of the Ignatian Exercises*, trans. John Drury (Maryknoll, N.Y.: Orbis Books, 1987).

———. *An Evolutionary Approach to Jesus of Nazareth*, trans. John Drury (Maryknoll, N.Y.: Orbis Books, 1985).

———. *The Historical Jesus of the Synoptics*, trans. John Drury (Maryknoll, N.Y.: Orbis Books, 1986).

———. *The Humanist Christology of Paul*, trans. John Drury (Maryknoll, N.Y.: Orbis Books, 1986).

———. *Our Idea of God*, trans. John Drury (Maryknoll, N.Y.: Orbis Books, 1973).

Sobrino, Jon, *Christology at the Crossroads*, trans. John Drury (Maryknoll, N.Y.: Orbis Books, 1978).

———. *Jesus in Latin America* (Maryknoll, N.Y.: Orbis Books, 1987).

———. *Jesus the Liberator*, trans. Paul Burns and Francis McDonagh (Maryknoll, N.Y.: Orbis Books; Tunbridge Wells: Burns & Oates, 1993).

The Liberation of Creation

Boff, Leonardo, *Liberating Grace*, trans. John Drury (Maryknoll, N.Y.: Orbis Books, 1979).

———. *Saint Francis* (New York: Crossroad, 1985).

Comblin, José, *Retrieving the Human*, trans. Robert R. Barr (Maryknoll, N.Y.: Orbis Books; Tunbridge Wells: Burns & Oates, 1990).

Segundo, Juan Luis, *Evolution and Sin*, trans. John Drury (Maryknoll, N.Y.: Orbis Books 1974).

———. *Grace and the Human Condition*, trans. John Drury (Maryknoll, N.Y.: Orbis Books, 1973).

Trigo, Pedro, *Creation and History*, trans. Robert R. Barr (Maryknoll, N.Y.: Orbis Books; Tunbridge Wells: Burns & Oates, 1991).

Church of the Poor, Sacrament of Liberation

Avila, Rafael, *Worship and Politics* (Maryknoll, N.Y.: Orbis Books, 1976).
Azevedo, Marcello, *Basic Ecclesial Communities in Brazil* (Washington, D.C.: Georgetown University Press, 1987).
Barreiro, Alvaro, *Basic Ecclesial Communities* (Maryknoll, N.Y.: Orbis Books, 1982).
Boff, Clodovis and Jorgé Pixley, *The Bible, the Church, and the Poor*, trans. Paul Burns (Tunbridge Wells: Burns & Oates; Maryknoll, N.Y.: Orbis Books, 1989).
Boff, Leonardo, *Church: Charism and Power* (New York: Crossroad, 1985).
————. *Ecclesiogenesis: The Base Communities Reinvent the Church*, trans. Robert R. Barr (Maryknoll, N.Y.: Orbis Books, 1986).
————. *New Evangelization: Good News to the Poor*, trans. Robert R. Barr (Maryknoll, N.Y.: Orbis Books; Tunbridge Wells: Burns & Oates, 1991).
————. *Sacraments of Life, Life of the Sacraments* (Washington, D.C.: Pastoral Press, 1987).
Comblin, José, *The Church and the National Security State* (Maryknoll, N.Y.: Orbis Books, 1979).
Fragoso, Antonio B., *Face of a Church*, trans. Robert R. Barr (Maryknoll, N.Y.: Orbis Books, 1987).
Gáldamez, Pablo, *Faith of a People*, trans. Robert R. Barr (Maryknoll, N.Y.: Orbis Books, 1986).
Hoornaert, Eduardo. *The Memory of the Christian People*, trans. Robert R. Barr (Maryknoll, N.Y.: Orbis Books; Tunbridge Wells: Burns & Oates, 1988).
López Vigil, Maria, *Don Lito of El Salvador* (Maryknoll, N.Y.: Orbis Books, 1990).
Pastoral Team of Bambamarca, *Vamos Caminando: A Peruvian Catechism* (Maryknoll, N.Y.: Orbis Books, 1985).
Richard, Pablo, *Death of Christendom, Birth of the Church*, trans. Phillip Berryman (Maryknoll, N.Y.: Orbis Books, 1987).
Segundo, Juan Luis, *The Hidden Motives of Pastoral Action*, trans. John Drury (Maryknoll, N.Y.: Orbis Books, 1978).
————. *The Sacraments Today*, trans. John Drury (Maryknoll, N.Y.: Orbis Books, 1974).
Sobrino, Jon, *The True Church and the Poor*, trans. Matthew J. O'Connell (Maryknoll, N.Y.: Orbis Books, 1984).
Torres, Sergio and John Eagleson, eds. *The Challenge of Basic Christian Communities* (Maryknoll, N.Y.: Orbis Books, 1981).

The Spirit of Liberation

Alves, Rubem, *I Believe in the Resurrection* (Philadelphia: Fortress Press, 1986).
————. *A Theology of Human Hope* (New York: Corpus, 1971).
————. *Tomorrow's Child* (New York: Harper & Row, 1971).
Barbé, Dominique, *Grace and Power: Base Communities and Nonviolence in Brazil*, trans. John Pairman Brown (Maryknoll, N.Y.: Orbis Books, 1987).
————. *A Theology of Conflict: And Other Writings on Nonviolence*, trans. Robert R. Barr (Maryknoll, N.Y.: Orbis Books, 1989).

Boff, Clodovis, *Feet-on-the-Ground Theology: A Brazilian Journey*, trans. Phillip Berryman (Maryknoll, N.Y.: Orbis Books, 1987).

Boff, Leonardo, *God's Witnesses in the Heart of the World* (Chicago: Claret House, 1981).

———. *Passion of Christ, Passion of the World*, trans. Robert R. Barr (Maryknoll, N.Y.: Orbis Books, 1987).

———. *The Path to Hope: Fragments from a Theologian's Journey*, trans. Phillip Berryman (Maryknoll, N.Y.: Orbis Books, 1993).

———. *Way of the Cross, Way of Justice*, trans. John Drury (Maryknoll, N.Y.: Orbis Books, 1980).

Cardenal, Ernesto, *The Gospel of Solentiname*, trans. Donald Walsh (Maryknoll, N.Y.: Orbis Books, 1986).

Casaldáliga, Pedro, *In Pursuit of the Kingdom: Writings 1968-1988*, trans. Phillip Berryman (Maryknoll, N.Y.: Orbis Books, 1990).

Comblin, José, *Cry of the Oppressed, Cry of Jesus*, trans. Robert R. Barr (Maryknoll, N.Y.: Orbis Books, 1988).

Cussianovich, Alejandro, *Religious Life and the Poor: Liberation Theology Perspectives* (Maryknoll, N.Y.: Orbis Books, 1979).

Galilea, Segundo, *The Beatitudes*, trans. Robert R. Barr (Maryknoll, N.Y.: Orbis Books, 1984).

———. *Following Jesus* (Maryknoll, N.Y.: Orbis Books, 1981).

———. *Spirituality of Hope*, trans. Terrence Cambias (Maryknoll, N.Y.: Orbis Books, 1989).

Gutiérrez, Gustavo, *On Job: God-Talk and the Suffering of the Innocent*, trans. Matthew J. O'Connell (Maryknoll, N.Y.: Orbis Books, 1987).

———. *Las Casas: In Search of the Poor of Jesus Christ*, trans. Robert R. Barr (Maryknoll, N.Y.: Orbis Books, 1993).

———. *We Drink from Our Own Wells*, trans. Matthew J. O'Connell (Maryknoll, N.Y.: Orbis Books, 1984).

Jaen, Nestor, *Toward a Spirituality of Liberation*, trans. Phillip Berryman (Chicago: Loyola University Press, 1991).

Libânio, J. B., *Spiritual Discernment and Politics: Guidelines for Religious Communities* (Maryknoll, N.Y.: Orbis Books, 1982).

Libanio Christo, Carlos Alberto, *Against Principalities and Powers: Letters from a Brazilian Jail* (Maryknoll, N.Y.: Orbis Books, 1977).

Paoli, Arturo, *Gather Together in My Name: Reflections on Christianity and Community* (Maryknoll, N.Y.: Orbis Books, 1987).

Romero, Oscar, *Voice of the Voiceless*, trans. Donald Walsh (Maryknoll, N.Y.: Orbis Books, 1985).

Sobrino, Jon, *Archbishop Romero: Memories and Reflections*, trans. Robert R. Barr (Maryknoll, N.Y.: Orbis Books, 1990).

———, ed. *Companions of Jesus: The Jesuit Martyrs of El Salvador* (Maryknoll, N.Y.: Orbis Books, 1987).

———. *Spirituality of Liberation*, trans. Robert R. Barr (Maryknoll, N.Y.: Orbis Books, 1988).

Sobrino, Jon and Juan Hernández Pico, *Theology of Christian Solidarity* (Maryknoll, N.Y.: Orbis Books, 1985).

Contributors

Ricardo Antoncich, a Jesuit priest, was born in Peru in 1931 and later studied philosophy and theology in Peru, Spain, and Germany. He was secretary of the Episcopal Commission for Social Action in Peru and coordinator of the National Commision for Justice and Peace in the Andean area. He has taught Catholic social teaching in various universities in Lima, Bogotá, and Rio Grande. He is the author of *Christians in the Face of Injustice.*

Marcello de C. Azevedo, a Jesuit, was born in Belo Horizonte (Brazil) in 1927. He has degrees in missiology, anthropology, and theology. He was national president of the Conference of Religious in Brazil, and currently teaches in the Pontifical Catholic University in Rio de Janeiro. He is the other of *Basic Ecclesial Communities.*

María Clara Bingemer is Professor of Systematic Theology at the Pontifical Catholic University of Rio de Janeiro. She is co-author of *Mary: Mother of God, Mother of the Poor.*

Clodovis Boff, a Servite priest, was born in Concordia Brazil in 1944. He received his doctorate in theology from the Catholic University of Louvain. He is professor at the Pontifical Catholic University of Rio de Janeiro, advisor to the Brazilian Conference of Religious, and a member of the National Pastoral Institute. His works include *Theology and Praxis* and *Feet-on-the-Ground Theology.*

Leonardo Boff was born in Concordia Brazil in 1938. He received his doctorate in theology from the University of Munich. His books include *Jesus Christ Liberator, Ecclesiogenesis, Church: Charism and Power,* and *Trinity and Society.*

Carlos Bravo, a Jesuit, was born in Guadalajara, Mexico in 1938. He is director of the journal *Christus* and professor of New Testament in the Jesuit Theological Institute in Mexico City. His books include *Jesús, hombre en conflicto.*

Victor Codina, a Jesuit, was born in Barcelona, Spain in 1931. Since 1982 he has lived in Bolivia, where he is professor of theology in the Catholic University. He has published many books, including *De la modernidad a la solidaridad.*

José Comblin was born in Brussels, Belgium in 1923. He has lived in Latin America since 1958, principally in Brazil, both teaching theology and doing pastoral work. His many books include *The Holy Spirit and Liberation, Retrieving the Human,* and *The Church and the National Security State.*

Enrique Dussel was born in Mendoza, Argentina in 1934. He received doctorates in philosophy (Madrid) and history (Paris), and his licentiate in theology in Paris. He is currently professor of ethics, the history of theology and of the Latin American church at the Institute of Superior Studies of Mexico. He also serves as president of the Commission on the History of the Church in Latin America (CEHILA). His books include *Ethics and Community, A Philosophy of Liberation,* and (as editor) *The Church in Latin America: 1492-1992.*

Ignacio Ellacuría, a Jesuit, was born in 1930 in Portugalate, Vizcaya in Spain. He was sent to El Salvador in 1949. He received his licentiates in the humanities and philosophy at the Catholic University of Quito (Ecuador), and his doctorate in philosophy from the University of Madrid. He was rector of the Central American University of San Salvador before his assassination by government troops in San Salvador on November 16, 1989. His publications include *Freedom Made Flesh.*

Juan Antonio Estrada, a Jesuit, was born in Madrid in 1945 and received doctorates in philosophy (Granada) and theology (Rome). He is currently professor of the philosophy of religion in the Faculty of Philosophy at the University of Granada. He has taught at a number of Latin American universities, and is the author of *La Iglesia: ¿institutión o carisma?* and *Del misterio de la Iglesia al pueblo de Dios.*

Ivone Gebara was born in São Paulo, Brazil in 1944. She received her doctorate in philosophy in Paris and a licentiate in theology from the Pontifical Catholic University in São Paulo. She is professor of theology at the Theological Institute in Recife. She is co-author of *Mary: Mother of God, Mother of the Poor.*

Gilberto da S. Gorgulho is a Dominican priest who was born in Cristina, Brazil. He received his licentiate in theology from the Catholic Institute of Toulouse (France) and in Sacred Scripture from Rome. He has taught in the faculty of theology in São Paulo and in various other institutes in Brazil. He is is editor of the Brazilian edition of the Jerusalem Bible and has published numerous commentaries on the New Testament.

Gustavo Gutiérrez was born in Lima in 1928. He studied medicine, psychology, and theology in the Universities of Lima, Louvain, and the Gregoriana of Rome. He received a doctorate in theology from the University of Lyons. He is founder and director of the Instituto Bartolomé de las Casas. His works include: *A Theology of Liberation*; *We Drink from Our Own Wells*; *The Truth Shall Make You Free*; *The God of Life*; *The Power of the Poor in History*; *On Job: God-Talk and the Suffering of the Innocent*; and *Las Casas: In Search of the Poor of Jesus Christ.*

Javier Jiménez Limón, a Jesuit, was born in Guadalajara, Mexico in 1944 and died in 1990. He received his doctorate in theology from the University of Barcelona. He served as professor in the Jesuit Theological Institute in Mexico City.

João Batista Libânio, a Jesuit, was born in Belo Horizonte, Brazil, and received his doctorate in theology from the Gregoriana in Rome. He is professor and director of the faculty of theology of the Society of Jesus in Brazil. His works include *Spiritual Discernment and Politics.*

Julio Lois, was born in Pontevedra Spain in 1935. He received his licentiate in law from Santiago de Compostela, a degree in sociology in Rome and a doctorate in theology in Rome. He is a professor at the Pontifical University of Salamanca. His books include *Teología de la liberación: opción por los pobres.*

Juan Ramon Moreno, a Jesuit, was born in Navarra, Spain in 1933. He was sent to El Salvador in 1951 and served as professor of theology at the Jesuit Central American University of San Salvador. He was assassinated there on November 16, 1989. He published numerous articles in the journal *Diakonía*, which he founded and edited.

Francisco Moreno Rejon was born in 1942. He studied theology in Salamanca, Madrid, and Rome, where he received his doctorate. He is professor of moral theology at the Institutos Superior of Lima, São Paulo and Madrid. From 1978 he has done pastoral work in a poor bario in Lima. He has published *Moral Theology from the Poor.*

Ronaldo Muñoz, a Sacred Heart priest, was born in 1933 in Santiago, Chile, and received his doctorate in theology at the University of Ratisbon in Germany. He is director of the journal *Pastoral Popular*. Since 1972 he has lived in a working-class barrio in Santiago. He is the author of *The God of Christians*.

Alvaro Quiroz Magaña, a Jesuit priest, was born in Guadalajara Mexico in 1942. He studied philosophy and theology in Mexico and received his doctorate in theology from the University of Barcelona. He is professor of ecclesiology at the Theological Institute in Mexico City.

Margarida L. Riberio Brandão is a Brazilian theologian.

Pablo Richard was born in Chile in 1939. He received his licentiate in theology from the Catholic University of Chile, in Sacred Scripture from the Pontifical Biblical Institute in Rome, his doctorate in sociology from the University of Paris. He is professor of theology in the National University of Costa Rica, and member of the Departamento Ecuménico de Investigaciones. He is the author of *Death of Christendom, Birth of the Church*.

Juan Luis Segundo, a Jesuit priest, was born in Montevideo Uruguay in 1925. He received a licentiate in theology from Louvain and a doctorate from the University of Paris. He is the author of *Theology for Artisans of a New Humanity* (5 vols.), *Jesus of Nazareth Yesterday and Today* (5 vols.), *The Liberation of Theology*, and *The Liberation of Dogma*.

Jon Sobrino is a Jesuit priest. He was born in Barcelona, Spain in 1938, and has lived in El Salvador since 1957. He received his licentiate in philosophy and master's in engineering mechanics at St. Louis University and his doctorate in theology from Frankfurt. He is director of the Centro Monseñor Romero and professor of theology at the University of Central America in San Salvador. His most important books include *Christology at the Crossroads*, *Jesus in Latin America*, *Spirituality of Liberation*, *Archbishop Romero: Memories and Reflections*, and *Jesus the Liberator*.

Juan José Tamayo was born in Spain and received his doctorate in theology from the Pontifical University in Salamanca as well as a licentiate in philosophy from the Autonomous University of Madrid. He is the author of *Cristianismo: profecía y utopía* and *Para comprender la teología de la liberación*.

Ana Maria Tepedino was born in Brazil and received her licentiate in theology from the Catholic Unviersity of Rio de Janeiro. She is currently professor of systematic theology at the Catholic University of Rio de Janeiro and Petropolis.

Index of Biblical Citations

Old Testament

All three indexes were compiled by William E. Jerman.

New Testament

Index of Authors and Titles

Index of Subjects